'One of the most important landmarks in Scottish publishing history . . . *The Biographical Dictionary of Scottish Women* is a unique contribution to the study of Scottish women's biography and an outstanding reference work which yields discoveries on every page . . . no home in Scotland should be without a copy.'
Textualities

'A landmark in the development of Scottish historical studies.'
Christopher A. Whatley, *History Scotland*

'A splendid book, with fascinating lives on every page.'
Ian Jack, *The Guardian*

'Reading this book is like opening a door and surveying a hidden and major part of our history – a host of intellectual, emancipated and adventurous women who were a force in shaping our country.
It is actually very moving.'
Kirsty Wark

'An extraordinarily moving book, not only because it gives us so wide-ranging a picture of female activity and achievement, but because these dictionary entries convey, remarkably, a real sense of flesh and blood, and of Scottish society, especially over the last 400 years.'
Jenni Calder, *The Scotsman*

This dictionary is dedicated to the memory of our co-editor and friend Sue Innes (1948–2005), who gave to it all the enthusiasm, dedication and flair she brought to everything in her life, and who was still working on it, and inspiring others, to the very end.

As an epigraph for the Dictionary, Sue chose these lines by Mary Brooksbank:

Politicians and rulers
Are richly rewarded,
But in one woman's life
Is our history recorded.

THE
BIOGRAPHICAL DICTIONARY
OF
SCOTTISH WOMEN

From the earliest times to 2004

Editors
Elizabeth Ewan, Sue Innes, Siân Reynolds

Co-ordinating editor
Rose Pipes

EDINBURGH UNIVERSITY PRESS

Edinburgh University Press Ltd
22 George Square, Edinburgh

Typeset in 9.5/11 Adobe Garamond
by Servis Filmsetting Ltd, Manchester, and
printed and bound in Great Britain by
Antony Rowe Ltd, Chippenham, Wilts

First published in hardback by
Edinburgh University Press in 2006.

A CIP record for this book is available from the British Library

ISBN 978 0 7486 3293 0 (paperback)

Contents

Acknowledgements   vi
Advisers to the project   viii
Contributors   ix
Abbreviations   xv
Readers' Guide   xxiii
Introduction   xxv

The Biographical Dictionary of Scottish Women   1

Thematic Index   386

The Plate sections are to be found between pages 126 and 127, and 286 and 287

Acknowledgements

This Dictionary is in every sense a collective work. It arose out of a joint initiative: from the steering committee of the Scottish Women's History Network (re-named Women's History Scotland in 2005) and from Edinburgh University Press. The editors thank all the members of the Network for their help, encouragement and many authorial contributions, and John Davey of EUP for commissioning the project and seeing it through to within a few months of completion. We also wish to express heartfelt gratitude to Moira Burgess and Jane Rendall, who acted as associate editors to the project during the final months. They wrote and edited a number of entries that were originally commissioned by or allocated to our late colleague Sue Innes, whose illness prevented her from completing the work. Our greatest debt is, of course, to our contributors. This is their book.

Thanks are due to those copyright holders who gave their permission for us to reproduce textual material and illustrations (see captions to the Plates). The *Oxford Dictionary of National Biography* (2004) was published before this work, and we are grateful to Robert Faber and Oxford University Press for their co-operation relating to modified entries written by authors who contributed to both publications.

A number of people were invited to act as editorial advisers to the initial project and throughout its gestation. We have greatly valued their expertise and advice on particular historical periods and fields of interest. Their names are listed on page viii. The editors also consulted other experts on various topics, several of whom deserve special mention: Christopher Dingwall (on gardeners), Lou Donovan (on science), John MacInnes (on Gaelic society), Lindy Moore (on education), Alison Robertson (on the churches).

Many archivists and librarians were of great help to us, in particular Gillian Whitley Roberts of the National Register of Archives for Scotland, Alison Fraser (Orkney), Brian Smith (Shetland), Lesley Richmond (University of Glasgow), Moira Stewart and David Catto (Aberdeenshire Libraries). The staff of the National Library of Scotland, as always, offered much help. Deborah Hunter, Julie Lawson and other colleagues on the staff of the National Galleries of Scotland provided valuable assistance with picture research, as did Dorothy Kidd of the National Museums of Scotland.

Central to the management of the project was the electronic database which was specially designed by Frances Allen. Her creative expertise, goodwill and considerable patience have been of inexpressible value. The professional skills of all the following people have also been central to the project: Kath Davies evaluated and copy-edited the entries, and went well beyond her brief in refining the text and eliminating inaccuracies; Mary Henderson researched large numbers of obituaries; Flora Johnston joined the team to research and write entries where no secondary sources existed; Anne Lynas Shah did much essential genealogical research, tracking down details from often incomplete information, as well as editing some entries. Of EUP staff, Carol Macdonald, Anna Somerville and Mareike Weber were of great help in dealing with author contracts, and James Dale with editorial issues. Roda Morrison took over from John Davey to lend support and assistance in the final months, and Jackie Jones backed the project throughout.

This publication would not have been possible without funding for research, management, administration and editorial assistance. We are extremely grateful to those listed below for their generous contributions. We are also indebted to: Margaret Ford, Ray Perman and Eileen Yeo for their help in seeking funding; Eileen Yeo (Director of the Centre in Gender Studies, University of Strathclyde) for administering the grants received from the Strathmartine Trust; and Ann Kettle, treasurer of Women's History Scotland, for keeping the project accounts.

Anonymous private donors
Centre for Scottish Studies, the University of Stirling
College of Arts, University of Guelph, Canada
Social Science and Humanities Research Council of Canada
University of Strathclyde Centre in Gender Studies

Acknowledgements

The Strathmartine Trust, St Andrews
Women's History Scotland
Women's Fund for Scotland (set up in 2002 to raise
the profile and obtain funds for work with
women. www.womensfundscotland.org)

The Scottish Executive Development Department,
Equality Unit

Women's History Network

The publishers are also grateful to the Scottish Arts
Council for awarding a grant towards the cost of
production.

Finally, we would like to acknowledge Allotment
No. 85, Inverleith Park, for providing much-needed
mental and physical nourishment to sustain all the
editors during the final stages of the project. The
same, and much more, was provided throughout by
John Clifford; Rebecca, Katie and Jean Innes; Peter
France; and Kris Inwood.

Advisers to the project

Helen Clark	Edinburgh City Museums and Galleries
Elizabeth Cumming	University of Glasgow
Helen Dingwall	University of Stirling
Sarah Dunnigan	University of Edinburgh
Julian Goodare	University of Edinburgh
Eleanor Gordon	University of Glasgow
Marjory Harper	University of Aberdeen
Grant Jarvie	University of Stirling
Jacqueline Jenkinson	University of Stirling
Jean Jones	Edinburgh
Jane McDermid	University of Southampton
Dorothy McMillan	University of Glasgow
Maureen M. Meikle	University of Sunderland
Stana Nenadic	University of Edinburgh
Lesley Orr	Formerly University of Glasgow
John W. Purser	Sabhal Mòr Ostaig, Isle of Skye
Jane Rendall	University of York
Adrienne Scullion	University of Glasgow

Contributors

LCA	Lynn Abrams	University of Glasgow
RPA	Rob Adams	Edinburgh
RA	Rosy Addison	Edinburgh
JA	Johanna Alberti	The Open University
CAA	Ceri Allen	University of Guelph, Canada
MA	Margaret Allen	University of Adelaide, Australia
CA	Carol Anderson	Falkirk
PDA	Peter Anderson	National Archives of Scotland, Edinburgh
SGA	Sheila G. Anderson	Bridge of Allan
LA	Liz Arthur	The Glasgow School of Art
BA	Bernard Aspinwall	University of Strathclyde
NCB	Nina Baker	University of Strathclyde
MB-J	Malcolm Bangor-Jones	Dundee
ICMB	Ishbel Barnes	Formerly Managing Director of the Scottish Archive Network
PB	Patricia Barton	University of Strathclyde
HEB	Helen Beale	University of Stirling
TB	Tom Begg	Formerly Queen Margaret University College, Edinburgh
MB	Maureen Bell	Ellon, Aberdeenshire
BB	Betty Bennett	Washington DC, USA
MgtB	Margaret Bennett	Royal Scottish Academy of Music and Drama, Glasgow
KBB	Kay Blackwell	Glasgow
SB	Steve Boardman	University of Edinburgh
VB	Valentina Bold	University of Glasgow, Crichton Campus, Dumfries
LB	Liz Bondi	University of Edinburgh
LAMB	Louise Boreham	Fife
KHB	Katherine Bradley	Formerly Oxford Brookes University
CGB	Callum Brown	University of Dundee
IB	Ian Brown	Pitlochry
YGB	Yvonne Galloway Brown	Glasgow Caledonian University
FB	Frank Bruce	Edinburgh
MTB	Mary Brück	Formerly University of Edinburgh
MARB	Moira Burgess	Glasgow
CB	Catriona Burness	Brussels
JB	James Burnett	Banchory, Aberdeenshire
PFB	Paul Burton	Milton of Campsie
ALRC	Angus Calder	Edinburgh
DC	Donald Campbell	Edinburgh
KMC	Katherine Campbell	University of Edinburgh
ACa	Audrey Canning	Gallacher Memorial Library, Glasgow Caledonian University
JJC	Jennifer Carter	Formerly University of Aberdeen
HC	Hugh Cheape	National Museums of Scotland, Edinburgh
JSC	Jane Cheape	Edinburgh
PAC	Patricia Adkins Chiti	Fondazione Adkins Chiti: Donna in Musica, Rome
ABC	Aileen Christianson	University of Edinburgh
AKC	Anna Clark	University of Minnesota, USA
HEC	Helen Clark	Edinburgh City Museums and Galleries

Contributors

JC	Jennifer Clement	Mexico City, Mexico
RC	Rob Close	Ayr
CC	Christine Collette	France
EJC	Edward J. Cowan	University of Glasgow
MC	Mairi Cowan	University of Toronto, Canada
KC	Krista Cowman	Leeds Metropolitan University
AC	Adriana Craciun	University of Nottingham
CEC	Carol Craig	Glasgow
MEC	Maggie Craig	Huntly, Aberdeenshire
BEC	Barbara Crawford	University of St Andrews
VEC	Viviene Cree	University of Edinburgh
JLC	Jenny Cronin	Glasgow
MAMC	Morag Cross	Kirkintilloch
VC	Victoria Crowe	West Linton
EC	Elizabeth Cumming	University of Glasgow
KMD	Kath Davies	Edinburgh
JEAD	Jane Dawson	University of Edinburgh
GD	Gordon DesBrisay	University of Saskatchewan, Canada
JD	Judith Devaliant	Auckland, New Zealand
BD	Beth Dickson	University of Glasgow
ED	Eric Dickson	National Library of Scotland, Edinburgh
SMD	Sheila Dillon	London
CHD	Christopher Dingwall	Blairgowrie
HMD	Helen Dingwall	University of Stirling
DD	Duncan Donald	National Trust for Scotland
RD	Rona Dougall	University of Glasgow
SMDoug	Sheila Douglas	Scone, Perthshire
FD	Fiona Downie	University of Melbourne, Australia
SD	Sarah Dunnigan	University of Edinburgh
BCD	Britta C. Dwyer	Cambridge
RE	Rosalind Elder	Courtenay, British Columbia, Canada
WE	Walter Elliot	Selkirk, Borders
ME	Margaret Elphinstone	University of Strathclyde
EJE	Elizabeth Evans	Gerrards Cross, Buckinghamshire
EE	Elizabeth Ewan	University of Guelph, Canada
†BF	Bill Findlay	Queen Margaret University College, Edinburgh
JAF	Joanne Findon	Trent University, Canada
DF	David Finkelstein	Queen Margaret University College, Edinburgh
JF	Janine Fitzpatrick	Glasgow
LF	Linda Fleming	Glasgow
TF	Tommy Fowler	Glasgow
JEF	James Fraser	University of Edinburgh
AF	Anne Frater	Lews Castle College, Stornoway, Lewis
AG	Alix Gaffney	Edinburgh
ESG	Ellen Galford	Edinburgh
JLG	Jane George	University of Stirling
PBG	Pamela Giles	Saskatoon, Canada
CG	Catherine Gillies	MacDougall Collection, Oban
JG	Julian Goodare	University of Edinburgh
EG	Eleanor Gordon	University of Glasgow
MJG	Mary Gordon	Edinburgh
LG	Laurence Gourievidis	University of Blaise Pascal, Clermont-Ferrand, France
EJG	Eric Graham	University of Edinburgh

RG	Ruth Grant	Lumsden, Aberdeenshire
CBMG	Chris Gregory	Edinburgh
SJG	Sarah Jane Gibbon	Orkney Library and Archive
PG	Patricia Grimshaw	University of Melbourne, Australia
LAH	Lesley A. Hall	Wellcome Library for the History and Understanding of Medicine, Glasgow
DJH	Douglas Hamilton	National Maritime Museum, Greenwich
MHH	Matthew Hammond	University of Glasgow
JBH	June Hannam	University of the West of England
MDH	Marjory Harper	University of Aberdeen
EMH	Elspeth Haston	Royal Botanic Garden, Edinburgh
EAH	Elspeth Haston	Milltimber, Aberdeenshire
JTH	Jim Healy	Perth
JVH	Janice Helland	Queen's University, Canada
MvH	Marij van Helmond	Dunoon
LFH	Lizanne Henderson	University of Glasgow, Crichton Campus
IMH	Mary Henderson	Dundee
JMH	Joy Hendry	Edinburgh
AH	Anne Hepburn	Edinburgh
LRH	Lorna Hepburn	National Trust for Scotland
SH	Sarah Hepworth	Glasgow University Library
LH	Leslie Hills	Edinburgh
ECH	Emily Holloway	University of Guelph, Canada
GH	Gwyneth Hoyle	Trent University, Peterborough, Canada
JH	Jean Hubbard	Kirkcaldy
SHH	Shannon Hunter Hurtado	Institute for Advanced Studies in the Humanities, University of Edinburgh
IH	Iain Hutchison	University of Stirling
†SI	Sue Innes	Edinburgh
NJI	Nicola Ireland	The Royal Scottish Academy
LJ	Laurie Jacklin	McMaster University, Canada
GJ	Grant Jarvie	University of Stirling
JLMJ	Jacqueline Jenkinson	University of Stirling
FJ	Flora Johnston	Edinburgh
AEJ	Ann Jones	Heriot-Watt University, Edinburgh
HEK	Helen Kay	Edinburgh
JK	Joyce Kay	University of Stirling
SKK	S. Karly Kehoe	University of Glasgow
AK	Alison Kerr	Glasgow
HK	Henny King	Dundee
LK	Lillian King	Kelty, Fife
AEK	Andrea Knox	University of Northumbria
WWJK	William Knox	University of St Andrews
NK	Natasha Kuran	Ottawa, Canada
EL	Evelyn Laidlaw	Edinburgh
CLEL	Cherry Lewis	University of Bristol
LLin	Lesley Lindsay	University of Dundee
MDL	Magnus Linklater	Edinburgh
LL	Leon Litvack	Queen's University, Belfast
CL	Christine Lodge	Ayrshire Archives
NL	Nancy Loucks	Independent Criminologist, Lanark
RL	Rhonda Lowe	Kirkwall, Orkney
ML	Maria Luddy	University of Warwick

Contributors

AML	Alison Lumsden	University of Aberdeen
EBL	Emily Lyle	University of Edinburgh
CJM	C. Joan McAlpine	Glasgow
ATM	Alison McCall	Kintore, Aberdeen
WBM	William Bernard McCarthy	Emeritus, Pennsylvania State University, USA
RMcC	Rosalind McClean	University of Waikato, New Zealand
MPM	Margery Palmer McCulloch	University of Glasgow
JMcD	Jane McDermid	University of Southampton
RAM	Andrew McDonald	Brock University, Canada
JBIM	Jan McDonald	University of Glasgow
MM	Murdo MacDonald	Argyll and Bute Council, Lochgilphead
IMacD	Ian MacDougall	Edinburgh
KAM	Katharine Macfarlane	University of Glasgow
IMcG	Ian McGowan	University of Stirling
JMacI	John MacInnes	Formerly School of Scottish Studies, University of Edinburgh
DGM	D. Gordon Macintyre	Edinburgh
AMcI	Arthur McIvor	University of Strathclyde
AM	Alison Mackinnon	University of South Australia
AMcK	Anne McKim	University of Waikato, New Zealand
HMcL	Hugh V. McLachlan	Glasgow Caledonian University
MMacL	Morag MacLeod	Isle of Scalpay, Harris
DAMcM	Dorothy McMillan	University of Glasgow
DLM	David Lee McMullen	University of South Florida, USA
JMcR	Jennifer McRobert	University of Lethbridge, Canada
PM	Paul Maloney	Glasgow
RKM	Rosalind K. Marshall	Edinburgh
LM	Lauren Martin	Folwell Centre for Urban Initiatives, Minneapolis, USA
IEM	Irene Maver	University of Glasgow
ABM	Alasdair B. Mearns	Sabhal Mòr Ostaig, Isle of Skye
MMM	Maureen M. Meikle	University of Sunderland
JHMM	Joyce Miller	Musselburgh
VM	Valerie Miner	University of Stanford, USA
BM	Bob Mitchell	Elie, Fife
SAM	Scott Moir	Cape Breton University, Canada
LRM	Lindy Moore	Rhyl Library, Museum and Arts Centre, North Wales
RJM	Bob Morris	University of Edinburgh
AM-L	Alison Morrison-Low	National Museums of Scotland, Edinburgh
BEM	Barbara Mortimer	Formerly Queen Margaret University College, Edinburgh
RM	Richard Mowe	Edinburgh
DM	David Mullan	Cape Breton University, Canada
CM	Candy Munro	Glasgow
IM	Isobel Murray	University of Aberdeen
SEM	Susan Murray	University of Guelph, Canada
JM	Jacqueline Muscott	Edinburgh
GMN	Gwyneth Nair	University of Paisley
SN	Stana Nenadic	University of Edinburgh
CJN	Cynthia Neville	Dalhousie University, Canada
BN	Brenda Niall	Monash University, Australia
JMN	Joan Morrison Noble	Victoria, British Columbia, Canada
GN	Glenda Norquay	Liverpool John Moores University
SO	Sybil Oldfield	Lewes, formerly University of Sussex
RO	Richard Oram	University of Stirling
LO	Lesley Orr	Edinburgh

CAO	Carol A. Osborne	St Martin's College, Lancaster
DP	Dorothy Page	University of Otago, Dunedin, New Zealand
GP	Geoffrey Palmer	Heriot-Watt University, Edinburgh
HP	Helen Payne	University of Adelaide, Australia
SP	Susan Pedersen	The Radcliffe Institute, USA
MP	Michael Penman	University of Stirling
KP	Kimm Perkins	University of Glasgow
RP	Ray Perman	Edinburgh
†CGP	Carolyn Proctor	Ballintoum, Perthshire
BP	Bob Purdie	Ruskin College, Oxford
JP	John W. Purser	Sabhal Mòr Ostaig, Isle of Skye
†NR	Neil Rafeek	Scottish Oral History Centre, University of Strathclyde
MSR	Mary Stenhouse Ramsay	Bothwell, Tasmania
IAR	Irene A. Reid	University of Stirling
LR	Lindsay Reid	North Lethans, Fife
NHR	Norman Reid	University of St Andrews
JRB	Jamie Reid Baxter	European Parliament, Brussels
JR	Jane Rendall	University of York
SR	Siân Reynolds	University of Stirling
MR	Margaret Ritchie	Edinburgh
PER	Pamela Ritchie	University of St Andrews
JRR	Julia Rayer Rolfe	Edinburgh
TSR	Tracey S. Rosenberg	University of Edinburgh
KBER	Ken Roxburgh	Samford University, USA
ECS	Elizabeth C. Sanderson	Linlithgow
MHBS	Margaret H. B. Sanderson	Linlithgow
JS	Jutta Schwarzkopf	University of Oldenburg, Germany
NRS	Nicki Scott	University of Stirling
AMcMS	Anne M. Scriven	Paisley
AS	Adrienne Scullion	University of Glasgow
MS	Mary Seenan	Skelmorlie, Ayrshire
MES	Megan Selva	University of Guelph, Canada
ALS	Anne Lynas Shah	Musselburgh
MBS	Maureen Sier	Scottish Interfaith Council, Glasgow
DLS	Deborah Simonton	University of Southern Denmark
BS	Brian Smith	Shetland Archives, Lerwick
EMS	Eunice Smith	Edinburgh
GRS	Graham Smith	University of Sheffield
LS	Lis Smith	University of St Andrews
MKS	Megan Smitley	London
JJS	Jim Smyth	University of Stirling
SS	Stephen Snobelen	University of King's College, Canada
JoS	Joanna Soden	The Royal Scottish Academy
HS	Hilary Stace	Wellington, New Zealand
DAS	David Steel	University of Lancaster
FS	Fiona Steinkamp	University of Edinburgh
LAMS	Laura Stewart	University of Edinburgh
DUS	Domhnall Uilleam Stiùbhart	University of Edinburgh
DS	Deborah A. Symonds	Drake University, USA
NEAT	Naomi Tarrant	Edinburgh
DAHBT	David A. H. B. Taylor	Independent art historian, Edinburgh
ST	Simon Taylor	University of St Andrews
MT	Margaret Tennant	Massey University, New Zealand

SLT	Suzanne Trill	University of Edinburgh
AT	Alison Twaddle	Church of Scotland
MV	Mary Verschuur	University of Nebraska at Omaha, USA
ARW	Anne Wade	Scottish Screen Archive, Glasgow
AW	Agnes Walker	Glasgow
DPW	David Pat Walker	Edinburgh
FEW	Fran Wasoff	University of Edinburgh
C-MW	Claire-Marie Watson	Dundee
FRW	Fiona Watson	Northern Health Services Archives, Aberdeen
JRW	Richard Watson	University of Durham
DMW	Diane Watters	Royal Commission on Ancient and Historical Monuments of Scotland
JW	James Weldon	Wilfred Laurier University, Canada
LW	Les Wheeler	Elphinstone Institute, University of Aberdeen
AWP	Annette White-Parks	University of Wisconsin, USA
MW	Morag Williams	Crichton Museum, Dumfries
KW	Karina Williamson	University of Edinburgh
JJW	Jason Wilson	University of Guelph, Canada
CW	Charles Withers	University of Edinburgh
EY	Eileen Janes Yeo	University of Strathclyde
FY	Fay Young	Edinburgh
GZ	Georgianna Ziegler	Folger Shakespeare Library, Washington DC

(† indicates deceased)

Abbreviations

Organisations, institutions, services etc. referred to in entries

AAS	Aberdeen Artists' Society
ACES	Arts and Crafts Exhibition Society
ACGB	Arts Council of Great Britain
AEU	Amalgamated Engineering Union
AHEW	Association for the Higher Education of Women
ALRA	Abortion Law Reform Association
AMSU	Association for Moral and Social Hygiene
ARA	Associate of the Royal Academy
ARP	Air Raid Protection
ARSA	Associate of the Royal Society of Artists
ASLS	Association for Scottish Literary Studies
ATS	Auxiliary Territorial Service
AWSS	Aberdeen Women's Suffrage Society
BCC	British Council of Churches
BD	Bachelor of Divinity
BFUW	British Federation of University Women
BGS	British Geological Survey
BL	British Library
BLEPS	British Library of Economic and Political Science
BM	British Museum
BMA	British Medical Association
BMWF	British Medical Women's Federation
BNA	British Nurses' Association
BSBI	Botanical Society of the British Isles
BSE	Botanical Society of Edinburgh
BWTA	British Women's Temperance Association
CAP	Common Agricultural Policy
CHE	Campaign for Homosexual Equality
CND	Campaign for Nuclear Disarmament
CPGB (CP)	Communist Party of Great Britain.
CPL	Central Public Library (Edinburgh)
CSWG	Church of Scotland Woman's Guild (in 1997 the name changed to The Church of Scotland Guild)
CTA	Class Teachers' Association
CUKT	Carnegie UK Trust
CUWFA	Conservative and Unionist Women's Franchise Association
CWG	Co-operative Women's Guild
CWS	Co-operative Wholesale Society
DBE	Dame of the British Empire
DCS	Deaconess of the Church of Scotland
DSU	Dundee Social Union
DWCA	Dundee Women Citizens' Association

ECA	Edinburgh College of Art
EFDSS	English Folk Dance and Song Society
EIFF	Edinburgh International Film Festival
EIS	Educational Institute of Scotland
ELEA	Edinburgh Ladies' Educational Association
EMS	Edinburgh Mathematical Society
ENSEC	Edinburgh National Society for Equal Citizenship
ENSWS	Edinburgh National Society for Women's Suffrage
ESU	Edinburgh Social Union
EWCA	Edinburgh Women Citizens' Association
EWLA	Edinburgh Women's Liberal Association
EWSS	Edinburgh Women's Suffrage Society
FANY	First Aid Nursing Yeomanry
FMA	Fellow of the Museums Association
FRMA	Fellow of the Royal Museums Association
FRCP	Fellow of the Royal College of Physicians
FRGS	Fellow of the Royal Geographical Society
FRHistS	Fellow of the Royal Historical Society
FRNS	Fellow of the Royal Numismatic Society
FRS	Fellow of the Royal Society
FRSE	Fellow of the Royal Society of Edinburgh
FSA	Fellow of the Society of Antiquaries (of London)
FSAgency	Food Standards Agency
FSAScot	Fellow of the Society of Antiquaries of Scotland
GAHEW	Glasgow Association for the Higher Education of Women
GBE	Dame or Knight Grand Cross of the British Empire
GCU	Glasgow Caledonian University
GLC	Greater London Council
GPO	General Post Office
GRPS	Glasgow Royal Philosophical Society
GSA	Glasgow School of Art
GSEC	Glasgow Society for Equal Citizenship
GSG	Geological Society of Glasgow
GSL	Geological Society of London
GSLA	Glasgow Society of Lady Artists
GSMD	Guildhall School of Music and Drama
GWCA	Glasgow Women Citizens' Association
GWHA	Glasgow Women's Housing Association
GWSAWS	Glasgow and West of Scotland Association for Women's Suffrage
ICE	Institution of Civil Engineers
ICN	International Council of Nurses
ICW	International Council of Women
IGS	Institute of Geological Sciences
ILP	Independent Labour Party
ISTA	International Seed Testing Association
IWM	Imperial War Museum
IWSA	International Women's Suffrage Alliance
LCC	London County Council
LDV	Local Defence Volunteers

LEDS	Ladies' Edinburgh Debating Society
LLA	Lady Literate in Arts
LRAM	Licentiate of the Royal Academy of Music
LSCC	Ladies' Scottish Climbing Club
LSE	London School of Economics
LWS	Ladies' Work Society
LWT	London Weekend Television
MA	Master of Arts
MA	Mathematics Association
MO	Medical Officer
MOH	Medical Officer of Health
MRC	Medical Research Council
MSA	Museum of Science and Art
NALGO	National Association of Local Government Officers
NAPSS	National Association for the Promotion of Social Science
NAS	National Archives of Scotland
NAWP	National Association of Women Pharmacists
NCW	National Council of Women
NEC	National Executive Committee
NFWW	National Federation of Women Workers
NGS	National Galleries of Scotland
NHM	Natural History Museum
NLS	National Library of Scotland
NMS	National Museums of Scotland
NPG	National Portrait Gallery
NRA	National Register of Archives
NRAS	National Register of Archives Scotland
NSA	Nursery Schools Association
NSEC	National Society for Equal Citizenship
NSWS	National Society of Women's Suffrage
NTS	National Trust for Scotland
NUHEW	National Union for the Higher Education of Women
NUSEC	National Union of Societies for Equal Citizenship
NUWM	National Unemployed Workers' Movement
NUWSS	National Union of Women's Suffrage Societies
NUWW	National Union of Women Workers
OBE	Officer of the British Empire
OUP	Oxford University Press
PEN	World association of writers (Poets, Playwrights, Editors, Essayists, Novelists).
POW	Prisoner of war
PRO	Public Record Office (now The National Archives)
RA	Royal Academy
RAC	Royal Automobile Club
RADA	Royal Academy of Dramatic Art
RAM	Royal Academy of Music
RAMC	Royal Army Medical Corps
RBGE	Royal Botanic Garden Edinburgh

RCAHMS	Royal Commission on Ancient and Historical Monuments of Scotland
RCHS	Royal Caledonian Horticultural Society
RCM	Royal College of Music
RCPE	Royal College of Physicians of Edinburgh
RCSE	Royal College of Surgeons of Edinburgh
RDS	Royal Dublin Society
RGI(FA)	Royal Glasgow Institute of Fine Arts
RGS	Royal Geographical Society
RHA	Royal Hibernian Academy
RHS	Royal Horticultural Society
RHSoc	Royal Humane Society
RIAS	Royal Incorporation of Architects in Scotland
RIBA	Royal Institute of British Architects
RMPA	Royal Medico-Psychological Association
RMS	Royal Museum of Scotland (formerly RSM)
RNLI	Royal National Lifeboat Institution
RSA	Royal Scottish Academy
RSAMD	Royal Scottish Academy of Music and Drama
RSBS	Royal Society of British Sculptors
RSCDS	Royal Scottish Country Dance Society
RSE	Royal Society of Edinburgh
RSGS	Royal Scottish Geographical Society
RSHS	Royal Scottish Horticultural Society
RSM	Royal Scottish Museum
RSL	Royal Society of London
RSPEE	Royal Society of Painter-Etchers and Engravers
RSSPWC	Royal Scottish Society of Painters in Watercolours
RSW	Royal Society of Watercolourists
SA	Society of Arts
SAC	Scottish Arts Council
SAMH	Scottish Association for Mental Health
SASA	Scottish Agricultural Science Agency
SAU	Shop Assistants' Union
SCC	Scottish Churches' Council
SCDA	Scottish Community Drama Association
SCLWS	Scottish Churches League for Woman Suffrage
SCM	Student Christian Movement
SCOW	Scottish Convention of Women
SCU	Scottish Christian Union
SCWG	Scottish Co-operative Women's Guild.
SCWS	Scottish Co-operative Wholesale Society
SCWT	Scottish Council for Women's Trades
SDF	Social Democratic Fellowship
SED	Scottish Education Department
SFC	Scottish Flying Club
SFSS	Scottish Federation of Suffrage Societies
SFWSS	Scottish Federation of Women's Suffrage Societies
SGH	Scottish Guild of Handicraft
SLA	Society of Lady Artists
SLF	Scottish Liberal Federation
SLGA	Scottish Ladies' Golf Association
SMBA	Scottish Marine Biological Association

SMIC	Scottish Music Information Centre
SMLA	Scottish Modern Languages Association
SNGMA	Scottish National Gallery of Modern Art
SNP	Scottish National Party
SNPG	Scottish National Portrait Gallery
SPCC	Society for the Prevention of Cruelty to Children
SPCK	Society for Promoting Christian Knowledge
SPRCD	Springthyme Records
SRGS	Scottish Royal Geographical Society
SSA	Society of Scottish Artists
SSWA	Scottish Society of Women Artists
SSWCP	Scottish Society of Water Colour Painters
STUC	Scottish Trades' Union Congress
SWH	Scottish Women's Hospitals
SWHA	Scottish Women's Hockey Association
SWLF	Scottish Women's Liberal Federation
SWMA	Scottish Women's Medical Association
SWRI	Scottish Women's Rural Institutes
TGWU	Tailor and Garment Workers' Union
T&G	Transport and General Workers' Union
TWU	Textile Workers' Union
UCL	University College, London
UFC	United Free Church
UNRRA	United Nations Relief and Rehabilitation Association
UPC	United Presbyterian Church
USDAW	Union of Shop, Distributive and Allied Workers
VAD	Voluntary Aid Detachment
WAAC	Women's Army Auxiliary Corps
WAAF	Women's Auxiliary Air Force
WASL	Women's Anti-Suffrage League
WCA	Women Citizens' Associations – as Edinburgh WCA, Falkirk WCA etc
WCC	World Council of Churches
WCTU	Women's Christian Temperance Union
WEA	Workers' Educational Association
WES	Women's Engineering Society
WFL	Women's Freedom League
WFS	Women's Friendly Society
WFTU	Women's Free Trade Union
WGE	Women's Guild of Empire
WIL	Women's International League
WILPF	Women's International League for Peace & Freedom
WLF	Women's Liberal Federation
WLL	Women's Labour League
WLUA	Women's Liberal Unionist Association
WMC	Women's Missionary College
WRAF	Women's Royal Air Force
WRI	Women's Rural Institutes
WRNS	Women's Royal Naval Service
WRVS	Women's Royal Voluntary Service
WSF	Workers' Suffrage Federation

WSL	Women's Suffrage League
WSPU	Women's Social and Political Union
WTUL	Women's Trade Union League
WVR	Women's Volunteer Reserve
WVS	Women's Voluntary Service (later WRVS, Women's Royal Voluntary Service)

YCL	Young Communist League
YWCA	Young Women's Christian Association

Publications referred to in entries

Journals

Amer. Jour. Physics	American Journal of Physics
Amer. Jour. Science	American Journal of Science
BMJ	British Medical Journal
Brit. Jour. Hist. Science	British Journal for the History of Science
BSS News	Botanical Society of Scotland News
Bull. Brit. Mycological Soc.	Bulletin of the British Mycological Society
Bull. Hist. Chem.	Bulletin for the History of Chemistry
Encycl. Brit.	Encyclopaedia Britannica
Geog. Jour.	Geographical Journal
Geol. Mag.	Geological Magazine
Geol. Soc. of London Q. J.	Geological Society of London Quarterly Journal
Hist. Edu. Rev.	History of Education Review
Int. Jour. Scot. Theatre	International Journal of Scottish Theatre
IBIS Jour.	Imaginative Book Illustration Society Journal
Jour. Ecc. Hist.	Journal of Ecclesiastical History
Jour. Hist. Astr.	Journal for the History of Astronomy
Jour. Hist. Soc. South Australia	Journal of the Historical Society of South Australia
Jour. Roy. Sanitary Institute	Journal of the Royal Sanitary Institute
Jour. Roy. Soc. Med.	Journal of the Royal Society of Medicine
Jour. Scot. Soc. Art Hist.	Journal of the Scottish Society for Art History
Kintyre Antiq. & Nat. Hist. Soc.	Kintyre Antiquarian and Natural History Society
LAC Jour.	Ladies' Alpine Club Journal
LSCC Jour.	Ladies' Scottish Climbing Club Journal
Nat. Geog. Mag.	National Geographic Magazine
NZ Jour. Hist.	New Zealand Journal of History
NZ Med. Jour.	New Zealand Medical Journal
Pharm. Jour.	Pharmaceutical Journal
Proc. Roy. Coll. Phys. Edin.	Proceedings of the Royal College of Physicians of Edinburgh
Proc. Geol. Soc. of London	Proceedings of the Geological Society of London
Proc. Roy. Music Assn.	Proceedings of the Royal Musical Association
Proc. Soc. Antiquaries Scot.	Proceedings of the Society of Antiquaries of Scotland
Proc. Soc. Psychical Research	Proceedings of the Society for Psychical Research
Rev. of Scot. Culture	Review of Scottish Culture
RIAS Newsletter	Royal Incorporation of Architects in Scotland Newsletter
SC	Scottish Co-operator
Scot. Art Rev.	Scottish Art Review
Scot. Econ. and Soc. Hist.	Scottish Economic and Social History
Scot. Educ. Jour.	Scottish Education Journal
Scot. Geog. Mag.	Scottish Geographical Magazine
Scot. Hist. Soc. Misc.	Scottish History Society Miscellany
Scot. Hist. Rev.	Scottish Historical Review

Scot. Jour. Agric.	*Scottish Journal of Agriculture*
Scot. Lab. Hist. Rev.	*Scottish Labour History Review*
Scot. Lab. Hist. Soc. Jour.	*Scottish Labour History Society Journal*
Scot. Lit. Jour.	*Scottish Literary Journal*
Scot. Marine Biol. Ass. Ann. Rept.	*Scottish Marine Biology Association Annual Report*
Soc. Arch. Historians of GB Newsletter	*Society of Architectural Historians of Great Britain Newsletter*
SSI	*Scottish Studies International*
Tas. Hist. Res. Ass. Papers	*Tasmanian Historical Research Association Paper*
Trans. Am. Phil. Soc.	*Transactions of the American Philosophical Society*
Trans. Bot. Soc. Edinburgh	*Transactions of the Botanical Society of Edinburgh*
Trans. Dumf. and Gal. Nat. Hist. and Antiqu. Soc.	*Transactions of the Dumfries and Galloway Natural History and Antiquarian Society*
Trans. Gael. Soc. Inverness	*Transactions of the Gaelic Society of Inverness*
Trans. Geol. Soc.	*Transactions of the Geological Society (of Glasgow/Edinburgh)*
Trans. RSE	*Transactions of the Royal Society of Edinburgh*
Trans. Roy. Soc. Lit.	*Transactions of the Royal Society of Literature*
Trans. SNHAS	*Transactions of the Stirling Natural History and Archaeological Society*
Trans. Unit. Hist. Soc.	*Transactions of the Unitarian Historical Society*
Univ. Sussex Jour. Contemp. Hist.	*University of Sussex Journal of Contemporary History*
Wom. Hist. Rev.	*Women's History Review*

Publications (other than journals)

AGC	*A Guid Cause. The Women's Suffrage Movement in Scotland.* Leneman, L. (1991, 1995 rev. edn)
BDBF(1)	*The Biographical Dictionary of British Feminists, Volume 1: 1800–1930.* Banks, O. (1985)
BDBF(2)	*The Biographical Dictionary of British Feminists, Volume 2: A Supplement, 1900–1945,* Banks, O. (1990)
BEHEP	*Bede's Ecclesiastical History of the English People.* Colgrave, B. and Mynors, R.A.B. (eds) 1991.
BP	*Burke's Peerage and Baronetage*
Crim. Trials	*Ancient Criminal Trials in Scotland,* 3 vols. Pitcairn, R. (ed.) (1883)
DBAWW	*A Dictionary of British and American Women Writers 1660-1800.* Todd, J. (ed.) (1985)
DLabB	*Dictionary of Labour Biography,* 12 vols (1972–2005)
DLB Gale	*Dictionary of Literary Biography.* Brothers, B. and Gergits, J. (eds) (1997)
DNB	*Dictionary of National Biography* (before 2004)
DNZB	*Dictionary of New Zealand Biography*
DSAA	*Dictionary of Scottish Art and Architecture.* McEwan, P. J. M. (ed.) (2004)
ER	*The Exchequer Rolls of Scotland,* 23 vols. Stuart, J. et al. (eds) (1878–1908)
HHGW	*The Hidden History of Glasgow's Women: the Thenew Factor.* King, E. (1993)
HRHS	*The Heads of Religious Houses in Scotland.* Watt, D. E. R. and Shead, N. (2001)
HSWW	*A History of Scottish Women's Writing.* Gifford, D. and McMillan, D. (eds) (1997)
MSWP	*Modern Scottish Women Poets.* McMillan D. and Byrne M. (eds) (2003)
ODNB	*Oxford Dictionary of National Biography* (2004)
RMS	*Register of the Great Seal of Scotland* (*Registrum Magni Sigilli*), 11 vols. Paul, J. B. et al. (eds) (1882–1914)
RPC	*Register of the Privy Council.* Burton, J. M. et al. (eds) (1877–1970)
RSS	*Register of the Privy Seal of Scotland* (*Registrum Secreti Sigilli*), 3 vols. Livingstone, M. et al. (eds) (1908–82)
SB	*Scottish Biographies* (1938)
Scotichron.	*Scotichronicon.* Bower, W. 9 vols, Watt, D. E. R. et al. (eds) (1987–99)
SHA	*The Scotswoman at Home and Abroad: non-fiction writing 1700-1900.* McMillan, D. (ed.) (1999)

Abbreviations

SLL	*Scottish Labour Leaders 1918-1939, A Biographical Dictionary.* Knox, W. (ed.) (1984)
SP	*Scots Peerage.* Paul, J. B. (ed.) (1904-1914)
SS	*The Scottish Suffragettes.* Leneman, L. (2000)
TA	*Accounts of the Lord High Treasurer of Scotland.* Dickson, T. et al. (eds) (1877–1913)
WSM	*The Women's Suffrage Movement: A Reference Guide, 1866-1928.* Crawford, E. (2001)
WWEE	*Women and Work in Eighteenth Century Edinburgh.* Sanderson, E.C. (1996)
WWW	*Who Was Who*

Readers' Guide

1. Organisation and nomenclature. The dictionary is organised alphabetically. For individuals from early periods, for royalty in all periods, and for most Gaelic names, this usually means by forename (e.g. AEBBE; MARGARET, Saint, Queen of Scotland; CATRIONA NIC FHEARGAIS). For later periods, and for the majority of subjects, this is by surname (e.g. KAY, Christina). For women who married, this may take the form HILL, Amelia, n. Paton, (n. = née, maiden name); or KING, Jessie, m. Taylor, (m. = married) indicating the name of the subject's husband, whether or not she adopted the name. Because Scottish women generally kept their own surname on marriage up to c. 1750, in entries for subjects living before this date, the husband's name is not listed in the heading. Details of any marriages are included in the body of the entry. For subjects dating from after c. 1750, who married more than once, m1, m2, etc. refer to first and subsequent marriages.

Square brackets indicate a pseudonym: e.g. DAVISON, Euphemia [May Moxon]. Round brackets indicate an alternative perhaps more familiar name, e.g. LEE, Janet (Jennie). Where a subject might be searchable under more than one name, a cross-reference is provided. Names beginning with Mac, Mc or M' are listed consecutively, as if they began with Mac.

2. Parents. The names of parents of subjects are given when known. Omission indicates lack of information. Unless otherwise indicated, the parents of the subject were married to one another.

3. Co-subjects. About 200 entries also include a co-subject (in bold type): sisters, colleagues, partners, or women in some way associated with the main subject. Co-subjects are all listed in the thematic index (see 6 below).

4. Group entries. There are three such: the 'Four Maries' – the attendants of Mary, Queen of Scots; the 'Glasgow Girls', women artists from the Glasgow School of Art; and the 'Scottish Women's Hospitals', an all-women initiative of the First World War. Some of the leading members of these groups have separate entries as well.

5. Cross-referencing between entries. An *asterisk before a name indicates that there is a separate entry on that individual. By following threads, readers will be able to trace pathways through the dictionary linking networks of women.

6. Thematic index. To follow up a field, such as medicine, media or women's suffrage, readers should use the thematic index (below, pp. 386–403), which contains 77 headings, and includes all subjects and co-subjects under their chief activities. A number of names appear under more than one heading.

7. Abbreviations within entries. Abbreviations have been used for institutions or organisations, ranging from the well known (STUC = Scottish Trades' Union Congress) to the less familiar (GAHEW = Glasgow Association for the Higher Education of Women). The reader is referred to the full list of abbreviations on pp. xv–xxii.

8. Further information and sources. Every entry contains a note about the sources of information and possible further reading, listed in the following order: archive sources; works by the subject; secondary sources. For reasons of space, here too a number of abbreviations have been used, e.g. NLS = National Library of Scotland. The full list is on pp. xv–xxii. A frequent reference is *ODNB* (2004), which refers to the *printed* version of the *Oxford Dictionary of National Biography*. One or two references are to the ongoing online update (www.oxforddnb.com). When prefixed with an asterisk thus *ODNB*, this indicates that the same contributor wrote the *ODNB* entry. The mention (Bibl.) indicates that a bibliography is provided by that source. For writers with a long list of publications, reference is made to bibliographies, or in some cases, where these do not exist, to the Women's History Scotland website. See 10 below. Generally, websites are only listed if they offer essential information.

Simply typing a subject's name into a search engine will often yield results.

9. Contributors: the initials at the end of each entry identify the contributor; for full list of contributors, see p. ix.

10. The backfile: Far more names were proposed to the editors than could be accommodated in a book this size, and we are acutely aware that because of lack of space, names with a good claim to be included have been omitted. The Biographical Dictionary of Scottish Women page on the Edinburgh University Press website contains both a list of all the entries in the Dictionary, and a list of names which could not be included. The latter has names, dates and occupations only. For some subjects, we have also provided on the website full lists of their published works, where these are not available elsewhere. From the website (www.eup.ed.ac.uk) search for the Biographical Dictionary of Scottish Women and download the lists.

The symbol ‡ next to a name indicates that there is an illustration of that subject in the Plates section.

Introduction

I

Why a biographical dictionary of Scottish women? It's a legitimate question, and it has several answers. The shortest one is that it aims to provide accurate, readable and stimulating information, not readily available anywhere else – despite the otherwise impressive amount of Scottish historical writing in recent years. But a dictionary with this title also makes larger claims. It should both contribute to 'a statement of national identity', and be 'a stay against oblivion', a memorial 'designed to stir thoughts on fame and obscurity, on mortality and immortality'.[1] It is the contention of the editors, shared we imagine by our contributors, that Scottish national identity has so far been largely construed in terms of the recorded achievements of men. Oblivion and obscurity was often the historical fate of women. There are various reasons why this was so in the past; at least part of the explanation was a lack of knowledge. But scholarship has moved on. Much more is now known about the women who have, in every thinkable way, contributed to the Scottish nation and its identity, and more than 1,000 of their names appear in the following pages.

The detailed thinking behind this dictionary is addressed at greater length in part II below. But readers consulting biographical dictionaries often prefer to skip the introduction and plunge straight in to the entries themselves. So we have started with an answer to the question every reader will probably want to ask (who's in, who's out?), by stating the criteria for inclusion and an explanation of nomenclature, before offering a more general essay, to which readers may return at leisure. See the Readers' Guide above for quick reference.

Criteria for inclusion

No living persons have been included. This was the only non-negotiable criterion for selection. We have, though, included a few quasi-historical figures whose claim to have been 'living' at all could be questioned (see for example Braidefute, Marion). Secondly, while virtually all the entries are indeed on women, one or two subjects are strictly speaking 'girls' (see Fleming, Marjory), and there is at least one case of disputed sexual identity (see Barry, James). Thirdly, the chronological range covered by the dictionary runs from the earliest records, taken to be Roman Britain, until a date of death before January 2005. Fourthly, geographically, while the great bulk of entries assume a Scotland within its present-day borders, some of those on early women relate to the area covered by the kingdoms of Northumbria/Bernicia, which included large parts of southern Scotland in the seventh and eighth centuries.

The criterion on which the editors have exercised most flexibility, but which has occasioned most discussion, is of course Scottishness. We have tried to be generous in our application of the term, within the limited scope of this single-volume dictionary. Broadly, to be included an individual should have been born in Scotland; or have lived in Scotland for an appreciable period; or have influenced some aspect of Scottish national life. Being born outside Scotland to Scottish parents was not regarded as qualification enough, unless the woman concerned met one of the other two criteria. (We should otherwise have had to include an impossibly huge number of persons who may certainly have thought of themselves as Scottish.) On the other hand, we have included a representative sample of women born in Scotland, but who made their mark as part of the 'Scottish diaspora' in Africa, Australasia, India, North America and other regions of the world – another potentially large group. We wanted to have a fairly open approach, in order to indicate that Scotland has not been a closed society: it has been alive to many influences from across the border and across the seas, and vice versa. At the same time, we felt that there was a strong case for the dictionary to confine itself to a defensible version of Scottishness, since existing dictionaries about 'British women' contained comparatively few Scottish names. As Sue Innes has put it, Scottish women have been doubly marginalised, in Scottish history because of their sex, in British history because of their nationality.[2]

But this is not a Women's Who's Who of Scottish History, in that 'fame' has not been a key criterion. If all the women listed here are in some sense Scottish, they are not necessarily celebrated. Some of the entries, especially from the early period, are on renowned historical figures; others are on women who will be reasonably well known to specialists within their fields of activity (art, literature, sport, science, suffrage, politics, for example). But many names will not be familiar to the average reader, or even to the specialist. They can all however claim to have made some impact – sometimes surprising and not necessarily positive – on national life, on Scottish society, economy, politics or culture, and in virtually all cases to have been known outside their immediate circle. For further discussion of the groups included, see Section II.

Nomenclature
The problem of nomenclature has been briefly outlined in the Readers' Guide. It is worth remarking on from the outset. The entries in this dictionary are listed alphabetically. But editors of books on women have to make decisions not usually faced by those dealing with men: under which name should they be listed? In Scotland, it was generally customary in the past for a woman to retain her family or 'maiden' name after marriage. This applied equally to the aristocracy, where a woman would take her husband's title (e.g. Duchess of Gordon) but might retain her own family name (see Maxwell, Jane). In the nineteenth and the twentieth centuries, however, it became more widespread to adopt the husband's surname, although writers and artists often kept their names professionally. And some women married more than once, being known by several surnames in turn. In the present day, practice is once more changing, but that has affected relatively few entries.

The approach taken by the editors to this question is as follows. Women living before about 1750 are listed under the family name they had at birth, unless there is a strong reason not to do so. Royalty, in whatever century, is generally listed by first name, e.g. 'Mary, Queen of Scots'. Most women whose surname was a patronymic, which applies to many Gaelic names, are listed under their first name, e.g. 'Catriona nic Fherghais'. For those who lived later, entries are normally listed under the name by which the subject was best known. For married women, this has usually meant providing an alternative surname, prefixed either by 'n.' = née; or 'm.' = married. (Examples: Greenlees, Allison, n.

Cargill; Rae, Jane, m. Coates.) The spouse's name, with dates, is provided, whenever this information is known – a practice we would like to see more widely used (that is to list the wives of male subjects in reference works). In a few cases, not specific to dictionaries of women, the best-known name may be a pseudonym (e.g. 'Wendy Wood'). We have made generous use of cross-references, both in the main text and in the index, to help resolve any ambiguities.

For further practical aids to reading this dictionary and following up the sources, see the Readers' Guide above.

II

Why is this dictionary needed? Its starting point was the renewal of the study of Scotland's history and culture in recent years, occasioned at least in part by the dynamic of devolution. Students of Scottish life and culture have reason to be grateful to those historians and publishers who have contributed to what can be called without exaggeration a renaissance in the study of this comparatively small nation.[3] But the very existence of these works has revealed gaps and silences in the record, and many of these concern the question of gender.

Not so very long ago, Clifford Hanley could describe the stereotypical portrait of the Scots as follows:

> The Scots are tall, rugged people who live in the mountain fastness of their native land, on a diet of oatmeal, porridge and whisky. They wear kilts of a tartan weave, play a deafening instrument called the bagpipes, are immediately hospitable but cautious with money…They are sparing with words, but when they speak they speak the truth. When they leave their native land they immediately rise to the top in other people's industries and professions.[4]

This passage has been much quoted as a parody or caricature, but its gendered assumptions are rarely remarked. In common with most national stereotypes, it is based on an unspoken male identity. In the past, and until very recently, the history of Scotland has been largely written by men and has chiefly concerned the doings of men, in what were often apparently all-male contexts: battles, churches, trade unions, formal politics, sport. The 'new histories', however, have often had the explicit aim of 'debunking many national myths and stereotypes',[5] and modern gender-conscious historians of Scotland have indubitably made strenuous efforts to include women in their histories. Consult the index of any recent general history and there will be a heading 'women': its references will be far more wide-ranging than was once the case, and a respectable number of pages, paragraphs, and indeed whole chapters will be devoted to 'women'.[6] This development is to be welcomed, as a start on what is really an immense programme of historical recovery: releasing the hidden past of women in Scotland.

It is clear though, after a closer look, that sections on women are obliged to rely on a comparatively small body of research, mostly published since the late 1980s, when T. C. Smout commented that 'the history of the family and of child upbringing and the place of the woman within and without the home, is so neglected in Scotland as to verge on becoming a historiographical disgrace'.[7] A later writer agreed with him about the neglect, but pointed out that mention of Scottish women's past 'has [indeed] tended to be in their capacity as wives and mothers, not as women in their own right'.[8] One could enlarge on that remark to say that despite the appearance of more evidence, even the most inclusive approaches have often been obliged to deal in generalities. 'Women' have frequently been treated in groups, rather than representing a broad range of human experience. Their history has a tendency to be told collectively, in terms of assumptions about motherhood and exclusions from most other spheres of life: from the churches, from military matters, from politics, from education, from property-owning, from employment, from proper wages. 'The introduction of female spinners to the Broomyard Mill in Glasgow in 1819–20 led to men burning it down'; 'public education was largely male-dominated and orientated'; 'as they were excluded from universities, girls normally did not learn Latin or mathematics'; 'job opportunities were limited for young women'; 'males had a vice-like grip on the learned professions'; 'women were once more subordinate: sexually, occupationally and socially'. Occasionally, again as an undifferentiated group, they are awarded merit points: 'women, now on the bench for the first time, managed a tough fight with credit'.[9]

Women are not ignored by the new Scottish history then, far from it: and present-day historians are often keen to demonstrate sympathy for women's rights, and where possible to find positive aspects of women's lives to comment on. Yet

women do not often emerge from recent historical writing as complex individuals. Very few *named* women figure in the indexes of general narratives, cultural surveys or monographs on Scottish history. We know quite a lot about named men, remarkably little about named women. This is, if anything, a phenomenon even more marked in popular histories or collections, let alone newspaper articles on 'Great Scots'.[10]

We can agree that there are plausible explanations for laying stress on what women did *not* do, rather than on what they did: history in Scotland, as in most other countries, is full of examples of discrimination and segregation, and the impact of feminist history over the last thirty years has meant that this is now widely recognised (for instance in the debate over 'the lad o' pairts'). But with a greater awareness of gender in historical studies, have come calls for more research. It has been an aim of the Scottish Women's History Network (renamed Women's History Scotland in 2005), from which the dictionary project emerged, to take a fresh look at the past of Scottish women, across all periods, regions, conditions and disciplines. One way of doing this is to re-people the Scottish landscape with more women than the few famous figures of whom everyone has heard. Another initiative from the same association is represented by a companion volume, the collection of essays on *Gender in Scottish History since 1700* (EUP, 2006), which takes a more analytical approach, considering how gender has helped shape the nation's history.[11]

For whatever reason, as Smout suggested, Scotland has rather lagged behind England, France, Canada and Australia – to take countries with which Scots have had historic links – in producing detailed and plentiful research into the past of its women. The record of publication, though now expanding out of all recognition compared with thirty years ago, is still somewhat patchy – dependent often on the initiative of individuals, who were in the past mostly outside mainstream university history departments.[12] The wealth of monographs published elsewhere is still only emerging in Scotland. Pioneering books in other disciplines – on Scottish women writers, or visual artists for example – have set out a promising agenda, and their findings are reflected in this dictionary.[13] But in historical studies, authors have sometimes had to make bricks without straw. The two chief publications on the women's suffrage movement in Scotland for example, were handicapped by a lack of biographical information about even the most important figures.[14] And the more work has been done, the more obvious it has become that most existing reference works are of little help in women's history. Biographical dictionaries in general, and certainly those devoted to Scotland, contain comparatively few women's names. This book therefore sets out to meet a perceived need for accurate, detailed biographical data.

If information about Scottish women is needed, why choose the form of a dictionary? The writing of biography, of an individual life story, has sometimes had a bad press with historians, although it has always attracted the general reader. Most academic historians in recent times have preferred to research broader social movements, longer timescales than a lifetime, or case studies of industries, towns or activities. There has, however, been some new-found respect for the perspective biographical studies can bring. The individual life-story can bring to light aspects of a period which broader surveys miss or neglect. Prosopography – the collective biography of an identified group, from teachers to folksingers to trade unionists – can enlarge this kind of insight on to a broader stage, in turn highlighting features not previously evident.[15] To take this one step further, to prepare a biographical dictionary, is to opt for a certain method of organising knowledge, not the only one, but a scheme which is readily accessible. In recent years, there has been a spate of such dictionaries, often of 'minority' interests or groups: sportsmen and women, politicians, musicians. Most impressive of all is the new *Oxford Dictionary of National Biography* (2004) for which many of our own contributors have written entries.

This is the place to say that our relation with the *ODNB* has been something of remarkable value. The editors of that huge work – 55,000 entries, 10,000 contributors, 62 million words, an investment of over £20 million – have made a special effort to include more entries on women. In the original *DNB*, edited by Leslie Stephen, women made up 5% of the entries. The percentage is still only 10% in the new *ODNB*, but that represents a large increase in absolute numbers. Two of the editors of *The Biographical Dictionary of Scottish Women* were themselves contributors to the new version, and some of our authors too have written entries for both reference works on the same individuals. On the other hand it was somewhat daunting to know that we were preparing our work in the shadow of such a mighty publication. In the

end, we have come to see it as a great bonus. Approximately 50% of the subjects in the present dictionary – mostly the better-known ones – also have entries in the *ODNB*, which are of course longer, and constitute a further source of information for readers, extending the reach of this work. Virtually all the entries in the present work were already written before the publication of the *ODNB*. We have routinely included it as a reference in such cases, and checked and cross-checked our information with it – not always finding this to be identical. One difference, for example, is that our contributors have often had more to say on Scottish affairs.

The comprehensive information available in the *ODNB* is greatly valued by scholars, as an hour sitting in any reference library will confirm. But a smaller biographical dictionary does something different, offering a form of reference to a wider public. This book provides a single-volume collection of findings about Scottish women, so that entries can be compared and followed through, creating a cumulative sense of women's participation in Scottish life. It can sit on a bookshelf and be quickly consulted. No specialist knowledge is needed to decipher a biographical entry.

It is, as well, a way of bringing together the scattered knowledge held by a large number of individuals, men and women. One attraction of the work has been that the editors could call on the interests, expertise and passions of people from all over Scotland and beyond, some within Women's History Scotland, many outside it. Some are specialists on a century or a field of interest; others are local historians, or have unearthed details of the life of a particular figure. The contributors – listed on p. ix – include members of staff and postgraduates from all the Scottish universities, from the four largest cities and all the regions of Scotland, but also from the rest of the UK, from Ireland, from across the Atlantic and the Pacific, and from a range of disciplines. Contributions have come from archivists and librarians, museum curators and art historians, and from experts on everything from architecture to zoology: a total of 277 women and men.

These authors had first to be found. The project has been a long time in the making. When Edinburgh University Press commissioned this work in 2001, the editorial team was composed of three academic editors, and the indispensable co-ordinating editor, Rose Pipes, who has had the huge responsibility of holding the project together. An advisory group, made up of experts on particular periods or fields in Scottish history and culture, was recruited (see acknowledgements). With their help, the draft head-list, based on existing reference works, was refined and expanded, and authors were approached. As time went by, more suggestions were considered, and the final volume contains entries on some 820 women, with another 200 or more cited as co-subjects. We wanted to balance the inclusion of as wide a range of lives as possible with the need to provide enough information about each to be meaningful. The longest entries are about 800 words long; many are between 300 and 400 words, and some are shorter still.

Length of an entry does not always equate with importance: in some cases, it means that little is known about the subject, in others it may reflect the discovery of data about a previously obscure figure. Some entries on well-known women are short, since the information is readily available elsewhere; and some on less-known women are longer, since they provide less accessible data. The editors had many animated discussions about coverage versus length of entry. As readers will know from the dedication and acknowledgements, our editorial colleague, Sue Innes, died in 2005, as the project was nearing completion. It was her strongly held desire that these biographies should tell not just of careers, but of lives. We have tried to be faithful to that guiding principle.

What then is the scope of this dictionary? It would be illusory to think that a book of this kind can achieve 'balance', be truly representative of every age and category of the inhabitants of even a country as small as Scotland. We found, predictably, that the amount of detailed knowledge about women is more plentiful for later than for earlier periods. We nevertheless set out consciously to include as many documented women from medieval and early modern Scotland as was readily possible, although they are fewer proportionately than their successors in later centuries. We have also tried to ensure that our geographical coverage is not concentrated in the Central Belt, despite the greater literacy and economic prosperity to be found in this largely urban region, and especially in modern Glasgow and Edinburgh. Urban women, for obvious reasons, may have had more visible lives, but we have made a deliberate effort to cover all the mainland regions and most of the islands of Scotland.

Given these preoccupations, who would be included? While we have tried to correct some potential imbalances (chronology and geography are only two examples) the selection in the end reflects the present state of research. It could have been far larger – the editors have a backfile of literally hundreds of names of women who could not be included in a book this size. Most of the entries in practice fall into one of several broad categories, briefly outlined here. (For a more detailed guide to categories of activity, see the Thematic Index, pp. 386–403.)

The first is of those women who are famous, eminent, celebrated, known about – a relatively small group of 'stars', whose inclusion would be expected by most readers, and who have been well studied by historians. Mary, Queen of Scots, probably heads anyone's list of famous Scotswomen, but this category also includes some well-known women whose Scottish identity is not so obvious, and may come as a surprise – Marie Stopes and Rebecca West (Cecily Fairfield) for example. And it includes one or two famous women whose 'Scottishness' may be controversial: the most obvious example is perhaps Queen Victoria, included for her passionate attachment to and frequent residence in the Highlands.

A similar group – but not necessarily household names – is composed of eminent and elite women, especially in the early period. Queens and aristocrats born into positions of power were the only women whose lives were noted in any detail in the contemporary records, which focused on politics and religion. Even then, such women might often be accorded only a single sentence in a chronicle. Surprisingly little is known even of queens: their birthplaces, places of death and sometimes even their parents are not recorded. The lack of personal documents from early centuries, such as diaries or letters, means we have little insight into their lives. Entries on these women are often short, not because they were unimportant, but because the record is lost.

Some of the best-known women in history, on the other hand, are famous more for what they were – in dynastic politics for instance, and/or as wives, lovers or relations of famous men – than for what they did (see for example Stewart, Margaret, of Ochiltree). Others are known about because of what was done to them: to call them victims may not be exactly right, but we have detailed records of a number of 'wise women' or 'witches' as they were variously known, who were the subjects of speculation or persecution, a key episode in Scottish history. The witchcraft episode was not unrelated to religious beliefs, and Scottish history has been marked by times of religious fervour and sectarian division. Recent research has uncovered far more knowledge about the experience, both active and passive, of named women in the religious sphere: the dictionary contains examples across a wide range of mostly Christian beliefs: Covenanting women, evangelical preachers, Presbyterians and Catholics, and, especially, expatriate missionaries.

One group of women, never entirely neglected, but receiving more attention in recent years, is what we have called the tradition-bearers: women who sang, or composed, or who passed on the traditional heritage of Scottish poems, ballads and songs. If Edwin Muir could write that while 'the greatest poetry of most countries has been written by the educated middle and upper classes; the greatest poetry of Scotland has come from the people',[16] this was what he meant. While most collectors of traditions have been men (not all, and we have some collectors here), their informants appear most often to have been women, who acted both as creators of and a repository for ancient music, folktales and poetry.

A further very large category is broadly covered by the term 'women of achievement': women whose names are known in some context – science or medicine for example – without their necessarily being household names. Mary Somerville, the nineteenth-century 'queen of science' is a good example. Here we have deliberately sought out fields of activity, from sport to opera, medicine to embroidery, gardening to cinema, and aimed to include women whose lives have contributed something within that field. Such women in some sense had 'careers' – and they are unsurprisingly concentrated in the later periods, especially the late nineteenth and early twentieth century, as opportunities opened up to them. But there are examples of women writers and artists from earlier times: such as the fifteenth-century poet, Iseabail ní Mheic Cailein, or the calligrapher Esther Inglis. Because the study of Scottish literature has been so enthusiastically renewed in recent years, the number of previously neglected or unknown women writers about whom details are now available has greatly increased. The same is true to a lesser extent of visual artists, and these two groups account for many entries, directly reflecting the present stage of research (see for example Traquair,

Phoebe). There are plenty of examples of male artists whose reputations have faded after their death, to be resurrected when, for one reason or another, their work touched something in later generations. This trajectory is often even more true of women.

But in case the term achievement should suggest that only 'good achievers' are included in the dictionary, it is worth pointing out that a nation's history is made up of all kinds of people, and that no purpose is served by hagiography. While there are several saints in these pages, there are not a few sinners, and in general, contributors have included references to criticisms, justified or otherwise, that could be made of individuals, both in their time and later. Women's transgressions may have tended to fall into different patterns from those of men, because of their circumstances, but some of those listed in these pages called down condemnation on their heads.

It is difficult to operate in the political arena without attracting criticism from some quarter, and a further broad category of entries is covered by the word 'political campaigner'. No one is in danger of forgetting the fight for the vote, which is studied today in schools, but the individuals who carried the women's suffrage campaign forward in Scotland are much less well known than the 'stars' of the British movement, such as the Pankhursts. Yet the Scottish suffrage supporters, from the militant Ethel Moorhead and the flamboyant 'General' Flora Drummond, to the suffragettes' doctor Grace Cadell, or the demurely-dressed but far from demure housemaid Jessie Stephen, were not the least important or controversial figures in the British movement as a whole. Some women, well known for other activities, were also firm supporters of the suffrage cause; Dr Elsie Inglis, the founder of the Scottish Women's Hospitals in the First World War, is one such case. That War itself gave rise to another episode of struggle, the Rent Strike on Clydeside, which made known to many the names of Helen Crawfurd, Agnes Dollan and Mary Barbour. The strength of the Independent Labour Party in Scotland – known for its support of women's rights – has yielded a number of women active in twentieth-century left-wing politics, as has the Scottish Co-operative Women's Guild, which had a membership of many thousands. But the dictionary covers all shades of opinion, including Unionist politics, and gives examples of women who vehemently opposed women's suffrage, as well as women who participated, less formally but sometimes to effect, in politics in earlier times; some women are known to have held local public office between the fourteenth and eighteenth centuries.

Lastly, mention should be made of two groups not usually included in such dictionaries. There is a (very small) group of entries on quasi-historical, mythical or fictional women. They are included because, after consultation with our advisers, the editors considered that they had a special place in the remembered Scottish past. Some of them are figures for whom exact identification seems to be lacking; such is the case of Jenny Geddes; others are quite mythical, such as Scota. One example of a woman for whom the only evidence is literary is Marion Braidfute (imaginatively credited with being the sweetheart of William Wallace); another, in a quite different vein, is Maw Broon, whose portrait has undoubtedly had some impact on the image of Scottish womanhood. On the other hand, one or two real women have been included because they inspired famous fictional portraits (see Helen Walker, a possible model for Jeanie Deans; and Christina Kay, the teacher who inspired the figure of Miss Jean Brodie).

There is one category which will not appear in most reference works of this kind. The editors particularly wanted to include some documented lives of women who were not remotely famous, but whose story in some way represented areas of Scottish life or economy, where women were generally present but rarely individually recorded. Entries were therefore commissioned on a range of occupations and professions in Scotland, across the ages, in which women are known to have played a significant part. Inevitably, these mostly date from close to our own time, since there are few detailed sources on ordinary women before about the eighteenth century. The proviso was that enough documentation was available to provide a real life story. These include, for example, a Borders bondager, an East Coast fishwife, a herring gutter, a coalminer, a shepherd, a jute weaver, a Shetland knitter, a prison warder, a prostitute, a printing compositor, as well as several types of teachers, nurses, midwives, engineers and farmers, and at least one example of 'all those small-town women who through their energy keep many a community running' (see Hastie, Annie). These subjects are listed in the index under their field of activity.

There are many individuals in the dictionary who do not fit easily into any of these categories, and one of the overall aims of the book, as noted above, was to provide a variety of examples of 'brief lives', rather than lists of achievements. How, after all, would one pigeonhole the Shetland woman who survived a lone sea-voyage, the first woman to accompany her fur-trapper husband to the north of Canada, the pioneer of girl guiding in Scotland, the aristocratic founder of the Soil Association, the spy, or the collector of fossils? We hope that readers will make discoveries all the time as they browse, following up cross-references or simply dipping in at random.

But it would be entirely illusory to think that the dictionary as a whole could, at a stroke, fill the void in the historical study of Scottish women left by so many years of inadvertent neglect or wilful avoidance. We are well aware of gaps and omissions, and hope that future research will take this work further (see Readers' Guide para. 10). With a view to this ongoing research, we have done as much as possible to help further enquiries. For example, we have provided full dates and places of birth and death and parents' names, wherever this information has been findable in the Scottish (and sometimes British or overseas) records. In so doing, we have made many discoveries about the inter-relatedness of subjects, and hope also to have provided useful genealogical material. In particular, we have tried to find the names of subjects' mothers, who are often buried under the patronymic dominance of fathers' names. Secondly, we have also where possible listed numbers of children. This serves two purposes – to indicate possible lineages, but also to record the life-cycle events of women, which are different from men's. Thirdly, it has been one of the priorities of the editors to ask that every entry be accompanied by a note of accessible source materials, which would enable readers to find out more. These sections list primary sources and archive collections, as well as recent secondary works. We have also relied in turn on a number of invaluable reference books, which are cited so often that we have adopted abbreviations for them (see above) and where readers will often find bibliographies. For further aids, see the Readers' Guide above.

In 1984, an article in the magazine *Cencrastus* called for 'a collective effort to uncover the social and cultural history of women in Scotland'.[17] This project aims to make a start in that direction, and to show how mistaken Hugh MacDiarmid was in his belief that 'Scottish women of any historical importance or interest are curiously rare'.[18] But it is more than that: by showing the detail of so many women's lives, across several centuries, it provides a new way of picturing Scottish life, and a rethinking of what is meant by Scottish national identity.

Notes

1. S. Collini, 'Our Island Story', *London Review of Books,* 20 Jan. 2005, review of the *Oxford Dictionary of National Biography* (2004).

2. See S. Innes, 'Reputations and remembering: work on the first biographical dictionary of Scottish women', *Études Écossaises,* no. 9, 2003–4, pp. 11–26, p. 15. Abridged versions of this article, which gives details of the genesis of this book, are published in *Scottish Economic and Social History* 23, 1, 2003, and *Scottish Studies Review,* 6, 1, Spring 2005, edited by M. Palmer McCulloch and M. G. H. Pittock. Older biographical dictionaries of Scotland contain very few women. Modern works have made more of an effort, while still concentrating on 'pre-eminent personalities': K. Roy (ed.) *Dictionary of Scottish Biography*, vol. I (1971–5) (Irvine Carrick Media, 1999), p. 5. See also R. Goring (ed.) *The Chambers Scottish Biographical Dictionary* (Chambers, 1992) which includes living persons; A. Crawford (ed.) *The Europa Dictionary of British Women,* 1983 (revised in 2003 as *A Historical Dictionary of British Women*), which covers all of Britain in 1,000 entries, so the place of Scottish women is necessarily reduced; and J. Uglow and M. Hendry (eds) *Macmillan Dictionary of Women's Biography* (Macmillan, 1998). Both the latter include only very well known Scottish women.

3. Examples of recent one-volume general works covering a long period include: T. M. Devine, *The Scottish Nation, 1700–2000* (Allen Lane The Penguin Press, 1999); R. A. Houston and W. W. J. Knox (eds) *The New Penguin History of Scotland: from the earliest times to the present day* (Allen Lane, 2001); M. Lynch (ed.) *The Oxford Companion to Scottish History* (OUP, 2001). The latter work contains a very full bibliography, indicating the increased number of publications of all kinds on Scottish history since about the mid-1980s.

4. C. Hanley, *The Scots* (1980), quoted here from Houston and Knox, *The New Penguin History of Scotland*, p. xv (see note 3 above).

5. Ibid., back cover.

6. A good example among several is the chapter 'Scottish Women: family, work and politics' in Devine, *The Scottish Nation* (see note 3 above).

7. T. C. Smout, *A Century of the Scottish People, 1830–1950* (Collins, 1986, p. 292).

8. Y. Brown, entry on 'Women' in Lynch, *Oxford Companion*, p. 647 (see note 3 above).

9. These examples are all taken from Houston and Knox, *New Penguin History of Scotland* (see note 3 above*),* pp.

300, 337, 394, 437, 515 – not in a spirit of criticism, since they clearly indicate an effort to integrate women into a mainstream narrative; but they also illustrate a tendency to see women as a more unified group than men.

10. It can be a dispiriting experience looking for the names of women in the indexes of most general works on Scotland, so no instance is singled out here. A good example of a popular 'Great Scots' book is Baxter's *Book of Famous Scots,* by B. Fletcher (Lang Syne Publishers, 1995, sponsored by W. A. Baxter & Sons). The author, who is aware of a gap in the story, suggests 'that there are no women in our lists' because Scottish education was 'entirely concentrated on male children', p. 15. We hope this book may help to dispel that impression (see also Baxter, Ethel). Cf. articles such as the 'Top 100 Scots', *Scotland on Sunday,* 25 August 2002, in which three women made the cut: St Margaret, Mary Slessor and Elsie Inglis.

11. Women's History Scotland, as it now is, brings together historians, both women and men, interested in furthering research into women's and gender history, in Scotland and other societies (www.swhn.org). *Gender in Scottish History since 1700*, edited by L. Abrams, E. Gordon, D. Simonton and E. Yeo, is published by EUP (2006).

12. For some early titles in the history of Scottish women, see Innes, 'Reputations and remembering' (see note 2 above); the new wave of historical writing can be said to have started with E. King's *The Scottish Women's Suffrage Movement* (Glasgow, The People's Palace, 1978); R. Marshall's *Virgins and Viragoes: a history of Scottish women from 1080 to 1980* (Collins, 1983); and Glasgow Women's Studies Group, *Uncharted Lives* (Pressgang, 1983). These were followed by several edited collections: E. Breitenbach and E. Gordon's two on the modern period: *The World is Ill-Divided* and *Out of Bounds*, both published by Edinburgh University Press (1990 and 1992), and E. Ewan and M. Meikle's collection *Women in Scotland c.1100–c.1750* on the earlier period (Tuckwell, 1999). It is notable that though most recent work has been done by women, these three collections also include chapters by male historians. Space prevents listing the many more monographic works which have appeared in the 1990s and since: see the bibliographical chapters by E. Ewan and J. McDermid in T. Brotherstone, D. Simonton and O. Walsh (eds) *Gendering Scottish History* (Cruithne, 1999), and see the website www.uoguelph.ca/wish

13. See for example D. Gifford and D. McMillan (eds) *A History of Women's Writing in Scotland* (EUP, 1997); J. Burkhauser (ed.) *Glasgow Girls: women in art and design 1880–1920* (Canongate, 1990); S. Dunnigan et al. (eds) *Woman and the Feminine in Medieval and Early Modern Scottish Writing* (Palgrave, 2004).

14. E. King, *The Scottish Women's Suffrage Movement* and L. Leneman, *A Guid Cause* (published in 1991, updated 1995, Mercat Press).

15. See for example J. Uglow, *The Lunar Men: the friends who made the future* (Faber, 2002); it could be argued that several books on the Scottish Enlightenment take this approach. An alternative is to select figures across historical periods, as W. W. J. Knox does in his book on 10 Scottish women, *The Lives of Scottish Women: women and Scottish society 1800–1970* (EUP, 2006).

16. Quoted in C. MacDougall, *Writing Scotland: how Scotland's writers shaped the nation* (Polygon, 2004), p. 156 (and many other places).

17. C. Anderson and G. Norquay, 'Superiorism', *Cencrastus*, 15 (1984), pp. 8–10.

18. Hugh MacDiarmid wrote this originally in 'Elspeth Buchan', *Scottish Eccentrics* (Routledge, 1936) and it is often quoted, cf. Innes, 'Reputations and remembering', p. 13, n. 3 (see note 2 above).

THE
BIOGRAPHICAL DICTIONARY
OF
SCOTTISH WOMEN

A

ABBOTT, Wilhelmina Hay (Elizabeth), n. **Lamond,** born Dundee 22 May 1884, died Dunmow, Essex, 17 Oct. 1957. Suffragist and equalitarian feminist. Daughter of Margaret Morrison, and Andrew Lamond, jute manufacturer.

Educated in London and Brussels, Wilhelmina Lamond trained as a secretary and accountant 1903–6. She later took the name Elizabeth, and married George F. Abbott, author, in 1911. She had at least one son. From 1909 she was organiser for ENSWS and in 1910 a member of the executive committee of the SFWSS, as well as of the Scottish Committee which produced a Minority Report on Poor Law Reform. From 1916 she was a successful international fundraiser for *Elsie Inglis's *Scottish Women's Hospitals, raising £60,000 from India, Australia and New Zealand. In 1920 she became secretary of the IWSA, and edited its paper *Ius Suffragii*. She represented NUSEC at the International Alliance of Women for Equal Suffrage and Citizenship in 1923. In spring 1927 she acted as spokeswoman for the 11 newly elected executive members who resigned from NUSEC, criticising 'new feminism' for turning towards social reform and away from 'the demand for the removal of every arbitrary impediment that hinders the progress, in any realm of life and work, of women' (Alberti 1989, p. 170). With *Chrystal Macmillan, in 1926 she founded the Open Door Council to press for the abolition of restrictions on women's right to work, and the Open Door International, after the IWSA refused to commit itself to opposition to all protective legislation in Paris in 1929. She was closely involved with the Association for Moral and Social Hygiene for 40 years; one tribute suggested that 'most of all she will be remembered for her work in the footsteps of Josephine Butler for the defence of prostitutes' (*The Times*, 1957). JR

• *AGC*; Alberti, J. (1989) *Beyond Suffrage. Feminists in War and Peace, 1914–1928*; Law, C. (2000) *Women. A Modern Political Dictionary* (Bibl.); Leneman, L. (1994) *In the Service of Life*; *The Times*, 31 Oct. 1957 (appreciation); *WSM*.

ABERDEEN AND TEMAIR, Ishbel Maria Gordon, Marchioness of, (Lady Aberdeen) [I. M. Gordon], n. **Marjoribanks,** DBE, born London 14 March 1857, died Aberdeen 18 April 1939. Philanthropist, campaigner for women's occupational, social and political rights. Daughter of Isabella Hogg, and Sir Dudley Coutts Marjoribanks, MP.

The youngest of five children, Ishbel Marjoribanks was raised in a strongly Liberal household, to which Gladstone was a frequent visitor. In 1877, following marriage to John Gordon, 7th Earl of Aberdeen (1847–1934), a Gladstonian convert, she moved to Haddo House, Aberdeenshire, where she immediately demonstrated the same zeal for charitable work among women that she had previously displayed among London prostitutes. The Haddo House Club, a local adult education society for the servants of estate tenants, evolved into the Onward and Upward Association, with more than 100 branches throughout Britain and the Empire and a fortnightly magazine, edited by Lady Aberdeen. In 1883, she founded the Aberdeen Ladies' Union, providing educational and recreational facilities for working girls, as well as a servants' registry and training home, while the Union's emigration committee arranged the removal of some 400 women overseas, mainly to domestic service in Canada, up to 1914.

In 1886 and from 1906 to 1915, Lady Aberdeen accompanied her husband to Ireland during his two vice-regal terms, and from 1893 to 1898 was resident in Canada during his Governor-Generalship there. Her own political and charitable endeavours took on an increasingly international dimension. During her first visit to Canada, in 1890, she launched the Winnipeg-based Aberdeen Association to promote the welfare of isolated prairie settlers, particularly women, and her establishment of the Victorian Order of Nurses in 1897 helped to initiate a Dominion-wide health service. In Ireland she launched a successful crusade against tuberculosis, supported village industries, and pioneered a mother-and-child welfare organisation, the Women's National Health Association of Ireland. A hyperactive philanthropist, she was not afraid to voice her political opinions. Her support for universal suffrage, as well as social and educational reform, was demonstrated through her lengthy presidency of the International Council of Women, created in the USA in 1888 to promote the social, economic and political welfare of women.

Lady Aberdeen had never heard of the ICW when she was asked to lead it in 1893, but she 'stuck to it with a vengeance', serving until 1936 with two breaks (1899–1904, 1920–2) (Rupp 1997, p. 15). Shortly after taking office, she dispatched her French- and German-speaking private secretary, Teresa Wilson, to Europe to build councils: 14 joined by 1904, 23 by 1914, and 36 by 1939. During the early years, Lady Aberdeen paid for all the organisation's expenses, 'finally closing the purse strings out of fear of setting a precedent for future officers' (ibid., p. 53). At the Paris peace conference (1919), she successfully lobbied for all posts in the League of Nations secretariat to be open to women, and in the 1920s tied the ICW to the League as part of her advocacy of world peace. She was also involved with the Red Cross, and in 1931 was instrumental in securing the ordination of women to the Church of Scotland ministry. The 1938 jubilee of the ICW in Edinburgh saw many tributes to her, and her honours included the freedom of the city (1928).

While Lady Aberdeen's domestic life was centred on Haddo House, the Aberdeens' public duties required them to take up official residence at Rideau Hall, Ottawa and at Dublin Castle. Buying two ranches in the Okanagan Valley, British Columbia, in the 1890s, they pioneered commercial fruit-farming. In 1920, with the family fortunes embarrassed and the Haddo estate reduced in size, they relinquished their Okanagan properties and retired to the House of Cromar in Aberdeenshire, where they wrote a joint autobiography, *We Twa*, recording a happy union. After her husband's death, continuing financial problems obliged Lady Aberdeen to move to Aberdeen. Her life was not without its sorrows: one daughter died in infancy and her youngest son died in 1909, aged 25, in a motor accident. The Aberdeens' daughter Marjorie married John Sinclair (as Lord Pentland, Scottish Secretary in the Liberal administration 1905–12). Marjorie's biography of her mother (Pentland 1952) is more discreet than that by French (1988). MDH
• NRA (Scotland): Survey No. 0055, Haddo House Papers; Provincial Archives of British Columbia, A-1277: Lord Aberdeen Papers pertaining to British Columbia; National Archives of Canada, MG 27, C-1352 1L, 1B5: The Journal of Lady Aberdeen (unpublished).
Aberdeen, Lady [Gordon, I. M.] (1893, 1994 intro. Harper, M.) *Through Canada with a Kodak*, (1896, R. M. Middleton, ed.) *The Journal of Lady Aberdeen: the Okanagan Valley in the Nineties*, (1936) *The Musings of a Scottish Granny*.

Aberdeen, Lord and Lady [Gordon, J. C. and Gordon, I. M.] (1925) *We Twa*, 2 vols., (1929) *More Cracks with 'We Twa'*; Aberdeen Assn. for the Distribution of Literature to Settlers of the North-West, *Annual Reports*, 1896–1902.
French, D. (1988*) Ishbel and the Empire*; Gibbon, J. M. (1947) *The Victorian Order of Nurses for Canada: 50th Anniversary, 1897–1947*; *ODNB* (2004) (Gordon, John); Pentland, M. (1952) *A Bonnie Fechter*; Rupp, L. J. (1997) *Worlds of Women*.

ADAM, Helen Douglas, born Glasgow 2 Dec. 1909, died Brooklyn, New York City, USA, 19 Sept. 1993. Poet, short story writer and dramatist. Daughter of Isabella Douglas Dunn, and William Adam, United Free Church minister.

After attending the University of Edinburgh for two years, Helen Adam worked as a journalist in London. She wrote ballads and later participated in the Beat Poetry movement, moving in 1939 to New York and San Francisco where she encountered poets Allen Ginsberg and Robert Duncan. Helen Adam published two collections before she was 16 – *The Elfin Pedlar and Tales Told by Pixy Pool* (1923) and *Charms and Dreams from the Elfin Pedlar's Pack* (1924) – followed later by several collections of poems, and one of short stories, *Ghosts and Grinning Shadows* (1977). She collaborated with her siblings Pat and Auste Adam on a play, *The City is Burning*, in 1963. By that time a cult figure, she also acted in the film *Our Corpses Speak* (1981) and her life was the subject of a documentary, *Death Magazine* (1979), directed by experimental film maker Rosa von Praunheim: both were filmed in Germany.

Her work is still not well known in the UK, although Edwin Morgan has spoken favourably about it. She is not in print in the UK and works are not easily available in the US. The American writer Kristin Prevallet continues to proselytise for her work. If we take Prevallet's description of Helen Adam, we can perhaps see why she has never had a secure literary place: 'Adam primarily wrote supernatural ballads which tell of fatal romances, darkly sadistic sexual affairs, jealous lovers, and vengeful demons'. In photographic collages by Helen Adam arising from these ballads, animating what she called her 'lethal women', 'the true desires of women are fulfilled not by mortal men, but by highly charged encounters with unhuman beings' (Prevallet, website). The first encounter with these dark poems is thrilling but the repetitiveness of the themes and Helen Adam's inflexible designs on the readers' nerves bring exhaustion.
DAMCM

• State Univ. of New York (SUNY) Buffalo: Helen Adam archive, Poetry/Rare Books Collection.

Adam, H., Works as above, and (1929) *Shadow of the Moon*, (1964) *Ballads* (1974) *Selected Poems and Ballads* www.eup.ed.ac.uk (Bibl.).

Christensen, P. (1991) 'Helen Adam', in *Contemporary Poets*; Knight, B. (1996) *Women of the Beat Generation*; Prevallet, K. 'Helen Adam's Sweet Company', *Riding the Meridian* vol. 2, 2, website: http://www.heelstone.com/meridian/adam4.html

ADAM (ADAMS), Jean, born Cartsdyke, Greenock, 28 April 1704, died Glasgow 3 April 1765. Poet and songwriter. Daughter of Jean Eddie, and John Adam, mariner.

Jean Adam had an elementary education in reading, writing, and sewing, before entering service at West Kirk manse, Greenock, where she was allowed the run of the library and absorbed English literary classics, Latin poetry in translation and religious works. Later she ran a village school in Cartsdyke. An ex-pupil recalled her as a popular, tender-hearted and unconventional schoolmistress. She read *Othello* to the class with such feeling that she fainted away at the end, and she sang songs. One song, given as her own composition, was 'There's nae luck about the house', described by Burns as 'one of the most beautiful songs in the Scots, or any other language' (Cromek 1810). Jean Adam's authorship was long contested but is now generally accepted. She was also one of the first Scottish women poets to have a volume of verse printed during her lifetime. *Miscellany Poems* was published in Glasgow by subscription in 1734, under the anglicised name of Jane Adams. These English poems were written after her enthusiastic discovery of Sidney's *Arcadia*. The combination of influences from romance fiction, Milton, Shakespeare and Calvinist theology produced an individual style, forceful and imaginative. The book failed to sell, however, and she sank into poverty. She gave up her school and struggled to survive independently as an itinerant domestic worker, but finally was admitted to a Glasgow workhouse, where she died. KW

• Adam, J. (1734) *Miscellany Poems. By Mrs. Jane Adams in Crawfordsdyke.*

Cromek, R. H. (ed.) (1810) *Select Scotish* [sic] *Songs, Ancient and Modern, with critical observations and biographical notices, by Robert Burns*, 2 vols; Overton, B. (2003) 'The poems of Jean Adam', *Women's Writing*, 10, 3, pp. 425–452; *ODNB (2004)*; Rodger, A. (1866) *Jean Adam of Cartsdyke*; Tytler, S. and Watson, J. L. (1871) *The Songstresses of Scotland*, 2 vols;

Williamson, G. (1886) *Old Greenock from the Earliest Times to the Early Part of the Nineteenth Century.*

ADAM, Mary, n. **Robertson,** 1699–1761. Correspondent. Daughter of Margaret Mitchell, and William Robertson of Gladney, manufacturer.

Mary Robertson married the architect William Adam (1689–1748), her father's business partner, in 1716 and became the mother of several architect sons, including the celebrated Robert Adam. William later named a colliers' village which he established on his Blair Adam estate Maryburgh in her honour. Through her own family (she was aunt to the noted historian William Robertson) and her marriage, Mary Adam was connected with some of the most brilliant figures of the Scottish Enlightenment. She led a largely domestic life, but in widowhood maintained an extensive correspondence with her son Robert during his travels abroad. She is the subject of a striking portrait by Allan Ramsay, painted in Edinburgh in 1754, now part of Yale University's Paul Mellon Collection. With her direct and unsentimental gaze, plain black dress and widow's cap, with spectacles and prayer-book in hand, she is an eloquent reminder of the serious piety of many 18th-century Scottish women. SN

• NAS: GD18/4754–88, Clerk of Penicuik muniments (Adam Family letters).

Gifford, J. (1989) *William Adam 1685–1748*; Smart, A. (1992) *Allan Ramsay, 1713–1784*, Plate 19.

ADAM SMITH, Janet *see* **SMITH, Janet** (1905–1999)

ADAMSON, Janet Laurel (Jennie), n. **Johnston,** born Kilmarnock 9 May 1882, died Bromley 25 April 1962. Labour activist, councillor, MP. Daughter of Elizabeth Denton, dressmaker, and Thomas Johnston, railway porter.

Jennie Johnston's father died young. Her mother Elizabeth supported her six young children by dressmaking, helped by her daughters. Life was hard. Jennie Johnston had some secondary education and worked as a dressmaker, in school teaching and in factory work. In 1902, she married William (Billy) Murdoch Adamson (1881–1945), a pattern maker and later a union official who became Labour MP for Cannock, Staffordshire, in 1922. They had four children. Early in their married life they moved around northern England and the Midlands in search of work, facing employment difficulties because of Billy's political activities. Jennie Adamson was involved in the suffrage movement in Manchester. A Labour Party member from 1908, she developed her political interests in socialism and the co-operative movement during a period in Lincoln where, as a member of the Board of Guardians, she focused on child and maternal welfare and led a campaign, 'Boots for Bairns'.

The family moved to London in 1922, where Jennie Adamson served on the Labour Party NEC (1927–47), chairing it from 1935 to 1936. She was prominent in Labour women's organisations and a member of LCC (1928–31). She was elected MP for Dartford, Kent (1938–45) and for Bexley, Kent, in 1945, resigning the following year. She also held government positions with the Ministry of Pensions. One of the few working-class women in Parliament, she 'saw herself as the special representative of such women' (*BDBF* (2), p. 5), pressing for higher status and better conditions for working-class wives and mothers at home and arguing that their work in bringing up children was undervalued but 'of the highest national importance' (8 March 1945, *DLabB* 1977, p. 3). She also argued for equal pay, for equal opportunities for women in industry and the civil service, and for equal compensation for war injuries. SI

• *BDBF* (2); *DLabB*, vol. IV p. 3; *ODNB* (2004); *Who's Who of British Members of Parliament*, vol. IV, 1981.

ADLER, Ruth Margaret, n. **Oppenheimer**, born London 1 Oct. 1944, died Edinburgh 18 Feb. 1994. Human rights and child welfare campaigner. Daughter of Charlotte Kissinger, lawyer, and Rudolf Oppenheimer, lawyer and importer and exporter of gloves.

The child of German Jewish immigrants to Britain in the 1930s, Ruth Oppenheimer grew up in London, one of two children. She was educated at North London Collegiate School and Somerville College, Oxford. She moved to Scotland in the late 1960s with her husband, Michael Adler, and taught philosophy part-time at the University of Edinburgh while their two sons were young. A feminist, she was a founding member of Scottish Women's Aid in 1974. Pursuing her interest in juvenile justice and welfare, she was a member for eight years of the Lothian Region Children's Panel. In 1983 she helped to establish the Scottish Child Law Centre and prepared the first comprehensive database of child law in Scotland. She completed a PhD in jurisprudence, published as *Taking Juvenile Justice Seriously* (1985). She spoke German as a native speaker and translated German legal theory into English in her spare time. From 1987 to 1991

she was assistant to the Lay Observer for Scotland, the legal ombudsman. Towards the end of her life, she became a magistrate and her final area of work allowed her to pursue her interest in human rights, as the first Scottish Development Officer for Amnesty International, from 1991 to 1994.

Ruth Adler's work in a number of areas in social welfare law grew out of her rare energy, a lifelong commitment to human rights and children's welfare and her conviction that the ethical principles of moral philosophy should be translated into practical action, particularly to support those who were vulnerable. She was the editor of the *Edinburgh Star*, the journal of the Edinburgh Jewish community, and a stalwart of the Edinburgh Graduate Theatre Group. FEW

• Adler, R. (1985) *Taking Juvenile Justice Seriously*. *The Scotsman*, 20 Feb. 1994 (obit.). Private information.

AEBBE, (Saint Abb) born Bernicia, died Coldingham c. 683. Abbess of Coldingham. Daughter of Aeðilfrith, King of Bernicia (584–616).

The daughter of pagans, Aebbe probably converted to Christianity while living in exile among Christian Gaels in the period 616–34. With the restoration of her brothers to the kingship of Bernicia, which included parts of southern Scotland and northern England, Aebbe returned to her home and founded Coludisburg, a 'double monastery' (monks and nuns) at St Abb's Head near Coldingham. Little is known about Aebbe's career as abbess. She admitted her nephew's retiring queen, *Aeðilthryð, to the monastery in 672, played host to various notables, and supported the controversial saint, Wilfrith. The burning of the monastery shortly after her death was attributed by some to God's displeasure at its sinfulness, but others were of the opinion that Aebbe had been relatively successful in combating the worst of these sins during her rule. She was commemorated as a saint, with her feast day on 25 August. JEF

• Bartlett, R. (ed.) (2003) *The Miracles of St Æbbe of Coldingham and St Margaret of Scotland*; BEHEP; Colgrave, B. (ed.) (1927) *The Life of Bishop Wilfrid*; *ODNB* (2004).

AEÐILTHRYÐ, (Saint Audrey), born East Anglia, died Ely, Cambridgeshire, 679. Queen of Bernicia, Abbess of Ely. Daughter of Anna, King of East Anglia.

Widowed around 660, Aeðilthryð was married to Ecgfrith (645/6–85), son of Oswy, King of Bernicia, whose kingdom included lands in northern England and southern Scotland. According to Bede, Aeðilthryð refused to consummate this marriage for twelve years. In 670, Ecgfrith became king; in 672, having donated land for Saint Wilfrith's foundation of the monastery of Hexham, Aeðilthryð, with Wilfrith's support, secured Ecgfrith's permission to retire to the monastery of Coldingham, founded by Ecgfrith's aunt *Aebbe. This story may have been invented to enable Ecgfrith to abandon a childless marriage. In 673, Aeðilthryð returned to East Anglia to found a monastery at Ely. She was abbess until her death from a tumour. Considered pious, wise and austere, she was commemorated as a saint (feast day 23 June). Her remains were translated into the church at Ely in 695. JEF

• *BEHEP*; Colgrave, B. (ed.) (1927) *The Life of Bishop Wilfrid*; *ODNB* (2004) (Æthelthryth).

AELFFLED, born Bernicia c. 654, died Whitby c. 713. Abbess of *Streanaeshalch*/Whitby. Daughter of *Eanfled and Oswy, Queen and King of Bernicia.

The infant Aelffled was promised to the church 'in perpetual virginity' by her father, who ruled over much of northern England and southern Scotland, in thanksgiving for victory over Mercia in 655. Placed in Hartlepool, where her kinswoman Hild was abbess, she moved in 657 with Hild to Whitby, where she became pupil and nun. Her mother Eanfled retired to Whitby in 670. In 680, mother and daughter became co-abbesses; Aelffled continued after Eanfled's death. Aelffled may have played key roles in resolving two succession crises. In 685, after her brother Ecgfrith's death (and after she was reminded of the fact), she apparently acknowledged that the potential successor, Aldfrith, whose paternity was disputed, was her brother. Aelffled seems to have helped Aldfrith's son secure the kingship, and brought the exiled bishop, Wilfrith, back to Northumbria. She was commemorated as a saint; her feast day was 8 February. JEF

• *BEHEP*; Colgrave, B. (ed.) (1927) *The Life of Bishop Wilfrid*; MacAirt, S. and MacNiocaill, G. (eds) (1984) *The Annals of Ulster* AU 713.3; *ODNB* (2004) (Ælffled).

AFFRICA (AUFRIKE) OF GALLOWAY, **Queen of Man,** fl. 1114–30. Daughter of Elizabeth, illegitimate daughter of Henry I of England, and Fergus of Galloway.

Affrica of Galloway is sometimes confused with her descendant, Affreca (fl. 1190), wife of John de Courcy of Ireland. Affrica is believed to have married Olaf, King of Man (r. c. 1114–53), at about the time his reign began. Only one child, Godred, King of Man (r. 1153–87), is known to have been born of the marriage, but Olaf had several other children by concubines, including Ragnhild-Rachel-Affrica (fl. 1140), who married Somerled of the Isles. Olaf's second marriage was to Ingibjorg Hakonsdatter, of Orkney. This suggests that Affrica may have died, perhaps as a result of Godred's birth or a subsequent pregnancy. The Irish Sea marriage market which includes the marriages of all these women from Galloway, Man, and the Western Isles, and eventually Ireland, illustrates the close political and economic connections of the Gaelic 'Irish Sea kingdom' and its separateness from the Scottish kingdom. SEM

• McDonald, R. A. (2000) 'Rebels without a cause? The relations of Fergus of Galloway and Somerled of Argyll with the Scottish kings 1153–1164', in E. J. Cowan and R. A. McDonald (eds) *Alba*; Munch, P. A. (ed.) (1874) *The Chronicle of Man and the Sudreys*, i pp. 60, 66; *SP*, iv, pp. 135–7.

AINSLIE, Charlotte Edith, OBE, born Edinburgh 15 Feb. 1863, died Edinburgh 24 August 1960. Headmistress. Daughter of Mary Ann Wood, and William Ainslie, pharmaceutical chemist.

Charlotte Ainslie attended George Watson's Ladies' College (1873–80) and taught and studied in France, Germany and Switzerland before being appointed head of Modern Languages, Dunheved College, Launceston, Cornwall (1889–92). Already LLA, St Andrews (1885), in 1892 she attended Bedford College (Reid Scholar, Gilchrist Scholar), graduating BA in 1895. Posts followed at Skinners' Company's School for Girls, London (1896–1901) and at Cambridge Training College (1901–2). In 1902 she was the first woman to be appointed head of an Edinburgh Merchant Company school, on becoming principal of her old school, George Watson's Ladies' College, with a roll of 930 pupils and an entirely male senior staff. She remained in post until 1926. Charlotte Ainslie held various committee and governing posts, and published articles on education. She was a member and president (1912–13) of the Secondary Education Association of Scotland, a member of the Scottish Education Reform Committee, and convener of the sub-committee on women's education. She was widely regarded as the Scottish expert on the secondary education of girls. A founding member, committee member and (1921) vice-president of the Edinburgh Women Citizens' Association, she received Hon LLD Edinburgh (1926) and OBE (1929). LRM

• George Watson's College Archives: George Watson's Ladies' College Collection.
Ainslie, C. E. (1911) 'Domestic science for girls in secondary schools', *The Secondary School Journal*, Feb. 1911, pp. 3–5, (1917) 'The education of girls and the position of women teachers in Scotland', *The School World*, 19, March, pp. 87–91. *ODNB* (2004); *SB*; *The Scotsman*, 11 July 1902 and 16 June 1938.

AITHBHREAC INGHEAN COIRCEADAIL, fl. 1470. Poet.

Wife of Niall Óg Mac Néill, Constable of Castle Sween in Knapdale, Aithbhreac inghean Coirceadail is remembered for her elegy composed to her husband around 1470. The elegy is remarkable on two counts. It is the earliest extant poem by a named female author in Scottish Gaelic, as well as being one of only four extant poems composed by a female author using a classical bardic metre, in this case *rannaigheacht mhór*. Her command of the language of classical bardic poetry, married to her strong personal feelings of loss, make this an outstanding example of 'bardic' poetry by someone who, because of her sex, was excluded from the formal training given to professional bards. AF

• Kerrigan, C. (1991) *An Anthology of Scottish Women Poets*, p. 339; Thomson, D. S. (1994) *The Companion to Gaelic Scotland*, p. 3; Watson, W. J. (1978) *Bàrdachd Albannach*, pp. 60–4.

AITKEN, Margaret, the 'great witch of Balwearie', died Fife c. August 1597.

Margaret Aitken was the single most important figure in the great Scottish witchcraft panic of 1597. Accused of witchcraft in about April of that year, when the panic was just beginning in Fife, she tried to save herself by claiming an ability to detect other witches by looking for a special mark in their eyes (there were folk beliefs about such marks). In May she claimed knowledge of a convention of 2,300 witches in Atholl. A special commission using special procedures was established to carry her around the country to detect witches: James VI himself took an approving interest. As well as her own testimony, the commission employed the swimming test (in which the water rejected the guilty) – almost the only occasion when this test is known to have been used in Scotland. The number of executions carried out by the commission is unknown but may have run into hundreds; it was active for three or four months. But early in August, a sceptical investigator took some of those whom she had declared guilty, re-presented them to her the next day in different guises, and obtained her statement that they were innocent. The trials ended abruptly. Margaret Aitken was returned to Fife, and executed after declaring that all she had affirmed was false, both about herself and about others. JG

• Goodare, J. (2002) 'The Scottish witchcraft panic of 1597', in J. Goodare (ed.) *The Scottish Witch-Hunt in Context*.

AITKEN, Sarah Ross (Sadie), MBE, born Belhaven 15 July 1905, died Edinburgh 5 Jan. 1985. Theatre activist, manager and producer. Daughter of Lily Birss, and William Aitken, master grocer.

By the time Sadie Aitken was seven, the family was living in Edinburgh, where she attended Stockbridge and Broughton schools. Having begun work in a lawyer's office, she joined the Church of Scotland social services in 1927. A fund-raising pageant at Craigmillar Castle brought her to the theatre. She was the first Edinburgh District secretary of the new Scottish Community Drama Association (SCDA), from 1928 until the 1970s, and she occasionally acted in amateur and professional roles. In the 1930s, at the Little Theatre in the Pleasance (then a slum area where her father was a church officer), she developed drama work with young boys, now recognised as pioneering community arts activity. In 1942 she helped found SCDA's St Andrews Summer School, which continued throughout her lifetime. When the Gateway Theatre in Edinburgh was presented to the Kirk in 1944 she became its manager. It put on films and amateur and professional productions and served as a youth club and multimedia centre. Sadie Aitken's dynamic management made the venture a success and in 1953 the Gateway Theatre Company was founded.

Her wider involvements included, according to Kathleen Gilmour's account (2004), drawing Robert Kemp's and Tyrone Guthrie's attention to the Assembly Hall's theatrical potential for the historic *The Thrie Estaitis* Festival production in 1948. With her encouragement, the Kirk Drama Federation flourished from 1950 until demitting its role in the 1980s to the Netherbow Arts Centre. When the Royal Lyceum Company was launched in 1965, the Gateway Company closed. Sadie Aitken retired but continued SCDA work, acting for television and film, frequently managing Edinburgh Festival venues, and working as a critic for the BBC. She was a Queen's Silver Jubilee Medalist. Her range and deep spiritual commitment justify the description 'the Caledonian Lilian Baylis', but solemn she was not. In perhaps ironic deference to the Kirk's prohibition on serving alcohol in the Gateway, she was said to keep her gin in the safe. IB

• Gilmour, K. (2000) 'Sarah (Sadie) Ross Aitken, MBE: a study of a career in theatre', *International Journal of Scottish Theatre*, vol. 1, No 2, Dec., pp. 1–23, website: www.arts.qmuc.ac.uk/ijost/Volume1_no2_gilmour_g.html, (2004) 'Sadie Aitken: the "Caledonian Lilian Baylis" ', in I. Brown (ed.) *Journey's Beginning: the Gateway Theatre building and company, 1884–1965*, pp. 37–52.
Interviews with Jean Benedetti; Clive Perry.
Private information.

ALCHFLED, fl. 653–6, born Bernicia. Queen, Middle Anglian kingdom. Daughter of *Raegnmaeld, daughter of Royth, and Oswy, King of Bernicia.

The daughter of the Christian rulers of Bernicia, which included parts of southern Scotland, Alchfled was married in 653 to Peada, King of the Middle Angles and son of the pagan Mercian over-king, Penda, on condition that her husband convert to Christianity. Her brother Alchfrith married Penda's daughter. Despite these marriages, war between Oswy and Penda followed in 655 and Penda was killed. Alchfled's husband's allegiances in this war are demonstrated by the fact that Oswy, in the wake of his triumph, extended Peada's authority, making him overlord of southern Mercia. Mere months later, around Easter 656, Peada was murdered. Bede reports that Alchfled was accused of betraying him. Nothing else is known of Alchfled, nor why and whether she became involved in the killing of her husband. JEF
• *BEHEP.*

ALCOCK, Nora Lilian Leppard, n. **Scott,** MBE, born Hampstead, London, 18 August 1874, died Berkshire March 1972. Plant pathologist. Daughter of Edgeworth Leonora Hill, and Sir John Scott, barrister and judicial adviser to the Khedive of Egypt.

After education mostly at home, but including time in Boston and Egypt, Lilian Scott married Nathaniel H. Alcock in 1905. In 1912, her husband was appointed professor of physiology at McGill University, Montreal, but he was working on radiation and died of leukaemia in 1913, leaving her with four children. Returning to London, she joined the recently formed Plant Pathology Laboratory of the Ministry of Agriculture, at Kew. There were more opportunities for women during wartime, and she acquired expertise in mycology studying with the Director, (later Sir) John Fryer, John Ramsbottom of the BM, and Professor Dame Helen Gwynne-Vaughan, the two latter becoming lifelong friends. Among British pioneers in plant pathology, Lilian Alcock was an early worker on seed pathology. A Fellow of the Linnaean Society (1922), in 1924 she moved to Edinburgh, both for her children's education and to take up the new post of plant pathologist with the Department of Agriculture and Fisheries in Scotland, at the RBGE. She was the first woman appointed to such a high-level job, one of the aims of which was to increase the level of food production through healthy seeds. Lilian Alcock built up a reputation for providing a quick and practical advisory service in plant pathology, training a succession of assistants who later made their mark in other countries. She herself researched fungal diseases, notably identifying the pathogen affecting strawberries in the Clyde Valley in the 1920s and 1930s. When she retired in 1937, her successor praised her gentle personality, firmness, integrity and wit. During the Second World War, she taught botany to POWs. Lilian Alcock is commemorated by a plaque on the Balfour Building, RBGE. AW

• Alcock, N. L. et al. (1930) 'Strawberry disease in Lanarkshire', *Scot. Jour. Agric.*, vol. 13, pp. 242–51; Alcock, N. L. and Foister, C. E. (1936) 'A fungus disease of stored potatoes', *Scot. Jour. Agric.*, vol. 29, pp. 252–57. *Botanical Society of Edinburgh News* (1973) 10, pp. 10–11; (1972) *Bull. Brit. Mycological Soc.*, p. 8; Desmond, R. (1977) *Dictionary of British and Irish Botanists and Horticulturists*; (1975) *Jour. Kew Guild*, 9, 79, p. 342; Smith, W. W. (1970) *The Royal Botanic Garden Edinburgh 1670–1970*.
Private information: Miranda Alcock (grand-daughter).

ALEXANDER, Helen, born West Linton 1653/4, buried Pentland 10 March 1729. Memoir-writer.

Married at 18 to Charles Umpherston (1646–81), tenant in Pentland, Helen Alexander bore three children before being widowed. She was attracted to radical field preachers in the area, including John Welsh and Donald Cargill. In 1679, she lost her land after refusing to attend her parish church where a curate preached, and fell into ever more perilous company. She employed Andrew Guillon, executed in 1683 for his presence at Archbishop Sharp's assassination. Helen Alexander was imprisoned and might have died for her loyalties but for the intervention of her lord,

Sir Alexander Gibson. According to family tradition, he entered for her a forged submission. She later sheltered the minister James Renwick, who in 1687 married her to James Currie (d. after 1729), another memoirist. She and Currie were associated with the Society Folk, radical conventiclers who refused to rejoin the main body of presbyterians in the Church of Scotland. She visited James Renwick in prison, and helped prepare his body for burial after his execution on 17 February 1688. She was distressed by the Treaty of Union. Helen Alexander's story, taken down near the end of her life, is her testimony to the cause and against contemporary corruption. DM
• ODNB (2004); 'Passages in the Lives of Helen Alexander and James Currie, of Pentland', in D. G. Mullan (ed.) (2003) *Women's Life Writing in Early Modern Scotland.*

ALLAN, Eliza MacNaughton (Dot), born Denny 13 May 1886, died Glasgow 3 Dec. 1964. Novelist. Daughter of Jean Luke, and Alexander Allan, iron merchant.

Dot Allan was the only child of a prosperous middle-class home in industrial central Scotland. She was educated privately and attended classes at the University of Glasgow. When still a young woman, she moved with her widowed mother to the West End of Glasgow, where she lived for the rest of her life. From there she pursued a successful freelance writing career. It was interrupted twice by nursing and charity work during the two world wars. A keen theatre-goer, she began by writing plays, interviewing Sarah Bernhardt when she visited Glasgow. From the early 1920s, her articles and short stories were published regularly in a wide range of newspapers and periodicals.

Dot Allan's first novel, *The Syrens* (1921), is set in Glasgow, as are several of her ten published novels. The last, *Charity Begins at Home*, appeared in 1958. Her later work, when she had turned more consistently to historical settings, is less notable, but two earlier novels show considerable originality and power in their critique of contemporary Glasgow society. *Makeshift* (1928) has as its central character a young woman determined that her life, unlike her mother's, will not be 'makeshift': she will not allow herself to be exploited practically or emotionally. *Hunger March* (1934) is a treatment of the Depression and the class struggle in Glasgow, predating better-known 'proletarian' novels. It strongly criticises the attitude of middle-class women towards waitresses, shop assistants and domestic servants. This recurrent theme in her fiction suggests a developed class and gender awareness. After inheriting money, she gave material help to other writers through Scottish PEN and supported an edition of *Marion Angus's poems. After the Second World War, although still writing, she gave time to charity work, particularly cancer relief. She died of breast cancer. MARB
• Allan, D., Works as above and see *HSWW* (Bibl.).
Burgess, M. (1998) 'Dot Allan: a Glasgow woman novelist', *ScotLit* 19, pp. 1–2; Cruickshank, H. B. (1976) *Octobiography*, p. 135; *HSWW* (Bibl.); Kyle, E. 'Modern women authors 3: Dot Allan', *Scots Observer*, 25 June 1931, p. 4; *ODNB* (2004).

ALLAN, Georgina Armour [Ella Logan], m1 (unknown), m2 **Finkelhoffe,** born Glasgow 6 March 1913, died Burlingame, California, USA, 1 May 1969. Singer and entertainer. Daughter of Annabella Macaulay, warehouse worker, and James Allan, spirit salesman.

Georgina Allan made her stage debut as a toddler, when she performed songs made famous by Sir Harry Lauder in music halls across Scotland. Briefly known as 'Daisy Mars' and, by her late teens, as 'Ella Logan', she was singing with London's top dance bands, broadcasting on the BBC, and starring in West End revues. In the early 1930s she toured Europe – once apparently singing for a Cologne audience, which included Hitler and several senior Nazis – before moving to the USA where she is believed to have married for the first time. There, she recorded with jazz greats including Benny Goodman. By the late 1930s, her exuberant swing recordings of traditional Scottish songs earned her the names 'The Swinging Scots Lassie' or 'The Loch Lomond Lass' when she topped the bill in nightclub revues.

From 1935, she was based in Hollywood. Just before she left New York, her sister **Mary Dalziel Short (May),** n. **Allan** (1901–69), and her family visited from Glasgow. May Allan and her husband Jack Short (1896–1982) had a music hall act, as The Logan Family, featuring their five children, including James Short (actor and comedian Jimmy Logan, 1928–2001) and Annabelle Short (the jazz singer Annie Ross, b. 1930). They believed that Annabelle could be the next Shirley Temple, and they left the five-year-old in her aunt's care in Hollywood, where Ella Logan was trying to forge a movie career. Between 1936 and 1938 she had minor roles in five films: *Flying Hostess* (1936), *Top of the Town* (1937), *Woman Chases Man* (1937), *52nd Street* (1937) and *The Goldwyn Follies* (1938), in which she introduced two of George Gershwin's last songs.

In 1941, Ella Logan married screenwriter and producer Fred Finkelhoffe, a marriage that raised her status in Hollywood society. After the Second World War, during which she entertained American forces in Italy and in Britain, she enjoyed her greatest triumph playing Sharon, a part written specially for her, in the original 1947 Broadway production of the musical *Finian's Rainbow*. Divorced in 1954, she was subsequently romantically linked to several well-known bachelors, including former New York City mayor William O'Dwyer. During the 1950s she worked occasionally on television. In 1955, she returned to Scotland for a high-profile run at the Glasgow Empire and, the following year, she visited Glasgow to perform in jazz legend Louis Armstrong's show. AK

• *Daily Record*, 7–14 Oct. 1955; Logan, J. (1998) *It's a Funny Life*; Sudhalter, R. M., sleeve notes for *Ella Logan – Swinging Scots Lassie 1932–1941* (Retrieval RTR 79021).

Private information: author interview with Annie Ross (2003).

ALLAN, Janie, born Glasgow 28 March 1868, died Spean Bridge 29 April 1968. Suffragette and socialist. Daughter of Jane Smith, and Alexander Allan, ship owner and merchant.

Janie Allan was one of eight children of a wealthy, philanthropic Glasgow shipping family. When her parents married in 1854 they united the Smith family of shipbuilders and the Allan Line and its Canadian sister company, founded by her grandfather and great-grandfather. Janie Allan was a member of the ILP, and from the First World War became active on the SCWT. In her public work, she combined her dedication to socialism and women's rights, and was editor of the women's suffrage column for the socialist paper, *Forward*. From 1902, she was on the executive committee of the GWSAWS. She was one of many women impressed by the charismatic *Teresa Billington-Greig when she came to Scotland on behalf of the WSPU in 1906, and defected from the GWSAWS to join it in 1909. After the WSPU-WFL split she remained a member of the WSPU but gave financial support to the WFL. Her militant activity included participation in a window-smashing raid that resulted in a four-month sentence in Holloway prison in 1912, a refusal to pay her taxes in 1913, and firing a blank bullet at a policeman who tried to arrest Mrs Pankhurst at St Andrews Halls in March 1914. She was also one of the most important financial supporters of the women's suffrage campaign. Between 1909 and 1910 she donated £650 to the WSPU, also contributing to the WFL until 1912. In 1914, she gave money to Louisa Garrett Anderson and *Flora Murray to establish the Women's Hospital Corps. She was described by her contemporaries as 'tall and handsome' and a charming presence (Raeburn 1973, p. 224). The part she played remains somewhat hidden in studies of the British women's movement. MKS

• Mitchell Library, Glasgow: Rare Books Collection: 891036/1/1–/1/5 SR 187; GWSAWS executive committee minute books 1902–14.

AGC; Gordon, E. and Nair, G. (2003) *Public Lives: women, family and society in Victorian Britain*; Raeburn, A. (1974) *The Militant Suffragettes*; *SS*.

ALLAN, Jean, n. **Mackie,** born North Ythsie of Tarves, Aberdeenshire, 23 Feb. 1908, died Aberdeenshire 9 April 1991. Educationist and practical thinker. Daughter of Mary Yull, and Maitland Mackie, farmer.

Educated at 'Miss Oliver's' and the University of Aberdeen (MA 1930), Jean Mackie worked as a journalist in London and in adult education in the north of England, before marrying John R. Allan, farmer, writer and broadcaster, in 1934. They had a son, Charlie, and in 1948 she founded St Nicholas School, Aberdeen, a co-educational progressive primary school. Here she introduced a culture-starved post-war generation to music, dance, plays, books, poster paints and big brushes. Scottish Country Dancing replaced 'physical jerks', town children were introduced to cookery, gardening and animal care, and Jean Allan once took a group of 11-year-olds to the Bath Festival (Beecham and Ballet Rambert). She inspired her protégés with enthusiasm for the best things in life and expanded the imagination. AG

• Personal knowledge.

ALTSCHUL, Annie Therese, born Vienna 18 Feb. 1919, died Edinburgh 24 Dec. 2001. Nurse and academic. Daughter of Marie Altschul and Ludwig Altschul.

Educated in Vienna, Annie Altschul moved to London in 1938 with her mother and sister, refugees from Nazi persecution. She worked as a mother's help to learn English, then began nursing, one of the few careers open to refugees. She found general hospital nursing depersonalising and exasperating. Psychiatric nursing at Mill Hill Military Psychiatric hospital was more to her taste. At the Maudsley hospital (1946–64) she became principal tutor and gained a degree in psychology. In 1964, she was encouraged to move to the Department of Nursing Studies at the University of Edinburgh, where she taught for almost 20 years, being appointed professor of nursing in 1976. Her writings and support for therapeutic, humane and non-custodial approaches to mental nursing were influential in the profession. The papers edited for her *Festschrift* (2001) include her forthright comments on a visit to America in 1960–1. Following her retirement in 1983 she pursued many interests and was an active member of the Mental Welfare Commission. BEM

• Royal Coll. Nursing Archives: Altschul papers and oral history interview, T8.

Altschul, A. (1976) *Patient-nurse Interaction.*

The Scotsman, 4 Jan. 2002 (obit.); UK Centre for the history of nursing (2001) *A Festschrift for Annie Altschul.*
www.ukchnm.org

ANDERSON, Janet (Jenny), born 1697, died Edinburgh 3 March 1761. Milliner and maker of grave-clothes, Edinburgh. Daughter of Jean Ellis, advocate's daughter, and James Anderson WS, author of *Diplomata Scotiae.*

Janet Anderson entered the Merchant Company of Edinburgh in 1718. She sold millinery, gloves and accessories, and made grave-clothes. She travelled to London not only to buy goods but to sell goods at fairs. Writing to her brother in July 1718, she reported, 'I heff disposed of the cargoe I brocht with me to good advantage' and that she was bringing a large cargo home (Anderson Papers). Her bills from the 1740s and 1750s, many surviving in family papers, show she long continued in business. Her clients included well-to-do families and everyday Edinburgh customers: she made grave-clothes for Sir John Clerk of Penicuik and the Erskines of Dun, and wedding accessories for Lady Janet Maitland, daughter of the Earl of Lauderdale. ECS

• NLS: MS 29.1.2, vol. 218, Anderson Papers.
ODNB (2004); *WWEE.*

ANDERSON, Margaret, born or baptised Tarland, Aberdeenshire, 14 Dec. 1834, died 2 Oct. 1910. Creator of a roadside museum, Buchan. Daughter of Elspet Grant, and Robert Anderson, crofter, Culsh.

Margaret Anderson's schooling finished at the age of seven when she was employed to herd sheep. Subsequent occupations included domestic service, harvest work and teaching at a dame school.

Despite much illness, including scarlet fever, diphtheria, typhus and rheumatic fever, she took over the running of the family croft when her father and stepmother became infirm. Margaret Anderson was a remarkable woman, despite her lack of education or opportunity. Her interests included fund-raising for missionary work and her museum. From the age of seven, she had begun collecting items of interest including unusual stones, shells, old agricultural and household artifacts. Friends and acquaintants donated additional items, ranging from animal skins from Ngoniland to a haddish cog (a wooden vessel for measuring grain). A 39-page catalogue was printed. She left her museum in the care of Lord and *Lady Aberdeen (see Aberdeen and Temair) who set it up in Tarland, but it was closed down when the room was needed during the First World War. LRM

• *Margaret Anderson's Museum, Cromar* (1908).

Aberdeen, Lord and Lady [Gordon, J. C. and Gordon, I. M.] (1929) *More Cracks with 'We Twa'*, pp. 129–38.

ANDERSON, Margaret Harvie (Betty), Baroness Skrimshire, born Glasgow 12 August 1913, died Worthing, Sussex, 7 Nov. 1979. Politician. Daughter of Margaret Agnes Wilson Shearer, and Colonel Thomas Alexander Harvie Anderson, of Quarter and Shirgarton in Stirlingshire, volunteer soldier, solicitor and magistrate.

An only child, Betty Harvie Anderson was educated at the Quarter village school and at St Leonards School, St Andrews. In 1938, she entered local politics through her election to the Denny district council and in the same year she enlisted in the ATS. During the war she was rapidly promoted, rising to become Chief Commander of the Mixed Heavy Anti-Aircraft Brigade, 1943–6. In 1945, she resumed her political activities, serving successively on the county and town councils of Stirling until 1959, latterly as leader of the Moderate group, with particular interests in agriculture, education and welfare. Having been unsuccessful on three previous occasions, she was returned to Parliament as Conservative MP for Renfrewshire East in 1959, holding the seat until in 1979. In 1960 she married John Francis Penrose Skrimshire, MD, FRCP, a medical consultant, but kept her maiden name in Parliament.

In 1964, to protect indigenous wildlife, she successfully introduced a bill to restrict the importation of animals to the UK. She was an able organiser, serving effectively as an influential member of many parliamentary committees.

She was twice elected by her Conservative colleagues to the executive committee of the backbench 1922 Committee, 1962–70 and 1974–9. Her most important office was as Deputy Speaker of the Commons, 1970–73. Addressing a memorial service in Westminster Abbey in 1979, Enoch Powell described her as 'a Parliamentarian to her finger tips, [who] instinctively understood and participated in every aspect of Parliamentary life . . . the House, with its unerring sense of what is fitting, chose her to be the first woman to sit in the Chair of Mr Speaker' (Carmichael Papers).

From 1966 to 1969 she served on the Royal Commission on Scottish local government that led to the creation of regional local authorities. She signed a note of reservation to the Commission's final report and her advice resulted in significant amendments to the legislation, notably separate councils for the three island groups.

In 1973, she resigned as Deputy Speaker over government policy in favour of a devolved Scottish assembly. She believed it would challenge the sovereignty of the Westminster Parliament and would be ineffective in addressing Scottish problems. Through the cross-party Keep Britain United movement, she campaigned for the issue to be laid before the public in a referendum which led, eventually, to the failure of various attempts in the 1970s to establish a devolved administration for Scotland.

Very much a traditional Conservative in outlook, her conversation tended to be crisp and to the point, but she was respected on all sides. The Labour MP Professor Alan Thomson wrote of her, 'she brought to the House of Commons a refreshing honesty and sincerity, illuminated by a sparkling (if sometimes devastating) sense of humour' (ibid.). In 1979 she was created a life peer, taking the title Baroness Skrimshire of Quarter. TB

• Glasgow City Archives, Mitchell Library, Baroness Skrimshire of Quarter MSS, Constituency Papers TD 1164. Private papers of Mrs Blanche Carmichael, inc. Enoch Powell, MP, memorial address, 5 Dec. 1979.
Begg, T. (2000) *The Kingdom of Kippen*; *Glasgow Herald*, 9 Nov. 1979 (obit.); *ODNB* (2004); *The Scotsman*, 8 Nov. 1979 (obit.); *WWW*, 1971–80.

ANDERSON, Marjorie Ogilvie, n. **Cunningham,** born St Andrews 9 Feb. 1909, died St Andrews 27 May 2002. Scottish medieval historian. Daughter of Eveline Sandeman, and James Cunningham, jute manufacturer.

Marjorie Cunningham was educated at St Leonards School, St Andrews, then read English at Lady Margaret Hall, Oxford. Her career as one of the foremost early medieval Scottish historians began after her return to Scotland, when she attended palaeography classes given in Dundee by Alan Orr Anderson (1879–1958). Anderson was the leading early Scottish medievalist of his generation, having published two key source books in 1908 and 1922. They married in 1932 and settled in Dundee. On their marriage certificate both gave as their profession 'historical research worker', which is what they remained for the rest of their working lives. After working together on the facsimile edition of the *Chronicle of Melrose* (1936), Marjorie Anderson published her first edited volume in 1938 (*The Chronicle of Holyrood*). They then worked on their greatest joint project, an edition and translation of the most important single source for early medieval Scottish history, *Adomnan's Life of Columba* (c. 700). Alan suffered from poor eyesight, and Marjorie became his eyes, reading aloud articles and transcribing the notes which he would speak into a tape-recorder. After his death, Marjorie saw the *Life of Columba* through to publication in 1961.

After Alan's death, Marjorie Anderson moved back to St Andrews where she wrote her greatest work, *Kings and Kingship in Early Scotland* (1973, rev. edn. 1980). It carefully analyses the fragmentary texts, mainly king lists, relating to the kingdoms of Dál Riata (Argyll) and Pictland, and the early kingdom of Alba (Scotland). These texts survive in poor, late copies. To construct a reliable historical framework, the relationships between the different surviving texts had to be painstakingly reconstructed. It is a pioneering work in textual archaeology, setting the highest of standards. The University of St Andrews awarded her a DLitt in 1973. On the occasion of Marjorie Anderson's 90th birthday, a collection of essays, *Kings, Clerics and Chronicles in Scotland 500–1297*, was published and dedicated to her.

The Andersons worked outwith the established academic community, devoting themselves to the unglamorous but essential task of evaluating difficult sources for an obscure historical period. They largely laid the foundations for the flourishing of early medieval Scottish scholarship in the latter part of the 20th century, which Marjorie Anderson lived to enjoy. A memorial lecture was established at St Andrews in the Andersons' names in 2003. ST

• Anderson, M. O., Works as above and (1974) 'St Andrews before Alexander', in G. W. S. Barrow (ed.) *The Scottish Tradition*. See also Taylor (Bibl.) below.
Taylor, S. (ed.) (2000) *Kings, Clerics and Chronicles in Scotland 500–1297* (Bibl.), (2004) *The Anderson Century: 100 years of Scottish medieval scholarship*.

ANDREWS, Sheila Mahala, born Beckenham, 9 Feb. 1939, died Iona 27 Oct. 1997. Vertebrate palaeontologist. Daughter of Mahala Humphrey, crafts teacher, and Alfred J. R. Andrews, GPO overseer.

After her father died in 1941, Sheila (later known as Mahala) Andrews moved to Sydenham with her mother, and attended Beckenham Grammar School for Girls, then Girton College, Cambridge (BSc Zoology 1960). After seven years as research assistant to T. S. Westoll, Professor of Geology at the University of Newcastle-upon-Tyne, she returned to Girton in 1967 to complete her thesis on fossil lobe-finned fish, co-authoring a bench-mark paper (1970, *Trans. RSE*, 68, pp. 207–489). In 1968 she was appointed as Senior Scientific Officer in the Department of Geology at the RSM (now NMS) Edinburgh, becoming a Principal Scientific Officer in 1973. Her work on the group of fossil lobe-finned fish from which the first land vertebrates evolved is one of the principal foundations of research into the origin of amphibians. A wide knowledge of fossil fish led to her outstanding history, *The Discovery of Fossil Fishes in Scotland up to 1845* (1982). (See Gordon-Cumming, Lady Eliza.) These achievements were combined with an astonishing technical virtuosity in the preparation of vertebrate fossil specimens, matched by a talent for drawing and calligraphy. She travelled widely, notably joining the first official palaeontological visit to China in 1979. Her strong Christian faith led her to embrace the religious community on Iona, where she bought a house after her early retirement through ill-health in 1993. JRR

• NMS: Complete list of publications and unpublished memorial, (1997) Reflections on Mahala Andrews.
Andrews, S. M. et al. (1994) 'Westlothiana lizziae from the Visean of East Kirkton, West Lothian, Scotland and the amniote stem', *Trans. RSE Earth Sciences*, 84, pp. 383–412.
Glasgow Herald, 16 Dec. 1997; *The Scotsman*, 1 Dec. 1997; Turner, S. (1998) *Ichthyolith Issues* 19, pp. 11–12 (all obits).

ANGUS, Marion Emily, born Sunderland 27 March 1865, died Arbroath 18 August 1946. Poet. Daughter of Mary Jessie Watson, and Rev. Dr Henry Angus, minister, UPC.

Marion Angus's father took charge of Erskine Church, Arbroath when she was eleven and she spent her youth there, one of six children. On his death in 1902, she moved with her mother and one sister to Aberdeen, where she lived the rest of her adult life, apart from some time in Greenock and Edinburgh, and a spell without a settled home during her much-loved sister's illness. A year before her death she returned to Arbroath to be cared for by a friend.

Marion Angus contributed poetry and stories to journals, including *Pearson's Magazine*, while young, and was published in Hugh MacDiarmid's *Northern Numbers* (1921–2). Her first collection of poems, *The Lilt and Other Poems* (1922) was published when she was 56. Five others followed. Her posthumous *Selected Poems*, edited by Maurice Lindsay (1950), contains a moving personal tribute by the poet *Helen Cruickshank, who first encountered her at a PEN meeting in Edinburgh and who shared her passion for poetry and her love of the Grampian foothills. Marion Angus's poems are mostly written in the Scots of her native north east and show marked influence from ballads and folk song. Critics from her own period and shortly after tended to sentimentalise her poetry. Grierson and Smith say, for example, 'She is the sweetest singer of them all, and has that touch of natural magic and that tragic undertone which, rightly or wrongly, we associate with Celtic blood' (1947, p. 487). But the sadness of Marion Angus's vision is balanced by its toughness, a hard recognition of things as they are. It is a tone that she probably learned from the ballads and it is uncompromising about pain and death. In 'At Candlemas' a young woman, afraid of a witch-like old woman, in no time at all becomes the old witch she is afraid of, asked in turn by a 'blythe bairnie', 'Er' ye the auld witch/O' the Braid hill o' Fare?' And the girl who gives herself to her uncaring lover in 'Mary's Song' knows that the sacramental gift of her body will not win his heart: 'Though he be nae mine as I am his'. Marion Angus's poetry is as austere as it is impressive and its enigmatic stories of women's lives are more often chilling than melting. Of all the Scottish women poets of the first half of the 20th century, she most deserves extensive republication. DAMCM

• Aberdeen Univ. Library: MS 3017/8/1/1, corr. and papers; NLS: MSS 19238, corr.
Angus, M., Works as above and see *HSWW* (Bibl.).
Anderson, C. 'Marion Angus': www.slainte.org.uk/scotauth/angusdsw.htm

Grierson, H. J. C. and Smith, J. C. (1947) *A Critical History of English Poetry*; *HSWW* (Bibl.); *ODNB* (2004); Porter, D. (1987) 'Scotland's songstresses', *Cencrastus* 25, Spring, pp. 48–52.

ANNA OF DENMARK, Queen of Scotland and England,

born Skanderborg Castle, Jutland, 12 Dec. 1574, died Hampton Court, 2 March 1619. Daughter of Sophia of Mecklenburg, and Frederick II, King of Denmark and Norway.

Once dismissed as inconsequential, Anna of Denmark is now recognised for her important contribution to Scottish and English cultural life. Her childhood was happy, surrounded by her family, and her education emphasised cultural pursuits. A skilled linguist, she loved music and dancing. In 1589, James VI of Scotland (1566–1625) chose her as his bride; a dowry of £150,000 Scots was agreed and the proxy marriage ceremony took place at Kronborg Castle on 20 August 1589. Anna sailed for Scotland on 5 September, but severe storms (later blamed on *Agnes Sampson and the North Berwick witches) forced her fleet of 16 ships to land in Norway. In October the couple met for the first time in Oslo, where they married on 23 November. Following a visit to Denmark, they returned to Scotland on 1 May 1590. The Scots, having had no resident Queen since *Mary, Queen of Scots in 1567, celebrated Anna's coronation with great style.

Anna, having mastered the Scots tongue, made a significant impact upon the political world of the court. She meddled in court factions, defending favourites while attacking offenders, including the chancellor, John Maitland of Thirlestane, who had opposed the marriage. James always defended his wife's honour in public, despite her favouring of his enemies, the Earls of Bothwell and Gowrie, and her adherence to Catholicism from the early 1590s, influenced by *Henrietta Stewart, Countess of Huntly. However, the couple were never reconciled over the custody of Prince Henry, born in 1594 after Anna had suffered several miscarriages. Henry lived at Stirling with the Mar family for his own protection. Anna, who was allowed to keep her other six children closer to her, never understood this enforced separation.

Anna's patronage enhanced Scottish culture. She rebuilt Dunfermline Palace in the latest style. She patronised jewellers such as George Heriot and wore the latest fashions. English players were brought to Scotland to establish a theatre, despite Kirk opposition. Foreign musicians and poets flocked to court. When James VI succeeded to the English crown in 1603, the couple moved to the wealthier English court; Anna hosted lavish court masques and collected paintings from European artists. Inigo Jones designed masque sets and altered palaces at Oatlands and Greenwich. Music and poetry were at the heart of Anna's English court.

As she was unable to grasp the complexity of English court factions, Anna's political role declined. The deaths of five of her children, especially Henry in 1612, distressed her, as did the departure of *Elizabeth (see Stewart, Elizabeth, Queen of Bohemia) who married Frederick of the Palatinate in 1613. Around this time she and her husband ceased to be sexually intimate but they remained friends; James was devastated by her death in 1619. Their separation was probably prompted more by Anna's excessive grief and deteriorating health than a dislike of James's preference for the company of favourites. One compensation was her close relationship to the future Charles I, who shared her passion for culture. However, she may have passed on her insistence upon the royal prerogative, with disastrous consequences for the subsequent Stewart monarchy. MMM

• Meikle, M. M. (1999) ' "Holde her at the oeconomicke rule of the house": Anna of Denmark and Scottish court finances, 1589–1603', in E. Ewan and M. M. Meikle (eds) *Women in Scotland, c. 1100–c. 1750*, (2000) 'A meddlesome princess: Anna of Denmark and Scottish court politics, 1589–1603', in J. Goodare and M. Lynch (eds) *The Reign of James VI* (Bibl.); *ODNB* (2004) (see Anne of Denmark); Payne, H. M. (2001) 'Aristocratic Women and the Jacobean Court, 1603–1625', PhD, Univ. of London.

ANNABELLA Drummond, Queen of Scotland,

born before 1367, died probably Scone, autumn 1401. Daughter of Sir John Drummond and his wife.

Inheritance patterns suggest that Annabella Drummond was the daughter of Mary, daughter of William de Montefichet. Annabella married John Stewart, Lord of Kyle (mid-1330s–1406), eldest son and heir of Robert the Steward, before 31 May 1367. The prestigious match was probably arranged through the influence of Annabella's aunt, *Margaret Logie (Drummond), Queen of Scotland, wife of David II. David's nearest male heir was his nephew, Robert the Steward. The King's grant of the earldom of Carrick to John and Annabella in 1368 suggests that he had accepted the likelihood of a Stewart succession. The marriage, however, ensured that Queen Margaret would be succeeded as queen by her own niece. John and Annabella named their eldest son and daughter David and Margaret, suggesting they viewed themselves as the royal heirs. Their other four children included the future James I. In 1371, Annabella Drummond's father-in-law became Robert II. On 19 April 1390, John succeeded, changing his name to Robert III. Political disturbances in the north delayed Robert's coronation until 14 August, Annabella apparently being crowned the following day. Parliament assigned Annabella an annuity of 2,500 merks to support her royal household.

A highly significant and very active political figure, Queen Annabella was also very influential in the career of her son, David, born in 1378, especially after physical infirmity weakened Robert III's political authority. She gave tacit support to a political coup in 1398/9 which established David, who became Duke of Rothesay, as lieutenant of the kingdom. The 15th-century chronicler Walter Bower saw Annabella's death in 1401 as profoundly affecting David who, freed from her moderating influence, began to behave recklessly; his actions alienated his political supporters, and he died a prisoner of his uncle, Robert, Duke of Albany, in March 1402. Annabella herself, however, was commemorated in glowing terms by 15th-century chroniclers. SB

• Boardman, S. (1996) *The Early Stewart Kings*; *ODNB (2004) (Bibl.); Scotichron., vol. 8.

ARCHDALE, Helen Alexander,‡ n. **Russel,** born Nenthorn, Berwick, 25 Aug. 1876, died London 8 Dec. 1949. Suffragette, journalist, feminist campaigner. Daughter of Helen Carter de Lacy Evans, campaigner for medical education, and Alexander Russel, journalist.

Helen Russel's mother, **Helen Evans** (1834–1903), a widow, was one of the first group of five female medical students at the University of Edinburgh, led by *Sophia Jex-Blake. She matriculated on 2 November 1869, but gave up her medical studies two years later ('treachery' according to Jex-Blake) to marry Alexander Russel (1814–76), the Liberal campaigning editor of *The Scotsman*, who had championed the medical women's cause. Widowed again, with three children, she continued to support women's medical education, sitting on the first executive committee of the Edinburgh School of Medicine for Women (1886). Helen Russel, born soon after her father's death, was educated at St Leonards School and the University of St Andrews, one of the first women undergraduates. In 1901 she married Theodore M. Archdale

(1873–1918), Lieut. Col. in the Royal Artillery, and spent her early married life in Lancashire and India. They had two sons and one daughter, and later separated. On her return from India in 1908, she joined the WSPU and became its organiser in several cities, including Edinburgh (at the time of the 1909 suffrage procession). Later she was WSPU prisoners' secretary, organising information and comforts; she worked on *The Suffragette*, and deputised for the Pankhursts when they were in prison in 1912. She was twice imprisoned for militant protests (Dundee, October 1909, initiating one of the first hunger strikes with four others, and London, 1911). Her daughter, Betty Archdale (1907–2000), remembered collecting stones for her mother to use to break Whitehall windows, and visiting her in Holloway Prison. During the war, she worked at WAAC HQ for *Mona Chalmers Watson, then at the Women's Department of the Ministry of National Service, for Lady Mackworth, later Viscountess Rhondda (1883–1958), with whom Helen Archdale had a close personal, political and professional relationship until the early 1930s.

Helen Archdale was the first editor of the political and literary weekly review *Time & Tide*, (1920–6), when it was most strongly feminist, 'broad-ranging, trenchant and critical' (Eoff 1991, p. 120). *Time & Tide* was published by Margaret Rhondda and she, Helen and the children lived together in London and Kent, part of a progressive intellectual circle. Margaret Rhondda founded the Six Point Group in 1921, with Helen Archdale as secretary and later international secretary. Betty Archdale became political secretary. As tensions between differently focused feminisms grew, they founded the Open Door Council in 1926, with *Chrystal Macmillan and *Wilhelmina (Elizabeth) Abbott, to focus on economic emancipation. Helen Archdale also campaigned for the admission of peeresses to the House of Lords. Following a bitter break in 1926, when Rhondda took over the editorship of *Time & Tide*, Helen Archdale became prominent in international feminist activism, working in Geneva from 1927 and lobbying for an Equal Rights Treaty at the League of Nations in the early 1930s. She became secretary of the Liaison Committee of Women's International Organisations, a coalition to promote equal rights, disarmament and women's representation at the League. As first chair of Equal Rights International, founded at The Hague in 1929, she was active in Open Door International, also founded in 1929, and a leading advocate of the equalitarian feminism seen as 'extreme' by the League of Nations. In the late 1930s she was associated with the World Women's Party. She contributed articles to *The Times, Daily News, Christian Science Monitor* and *The Scotsman.* She was described as 'large of mind and body and forthrightness' (MacPherson 2002, pp. 123–4), but the title of her unpublished autobiography, *An Interfering Female,* suggests an ambivalent self-image. SI

• The Women's Library, London: Equal Rights International papers.
DNB (1909) (Russel, Alexander); *Edinburgh School of Medicine for Women, First Report 1886–8*; Eoff, S. M. (1991) *Viscountess Rhondda: equalitarian feminist*; MacPherson, D. (2002) *The Suffragette's Daughter: Betty Archdale*; *ODNB* (2004) (Russel, Alexander); Rupp, L. J. (1997) *Worlds of Women: the making of an international women's movement*; Todd, M. (1918) *Life of Sophia Jex-Blake*; WSM.

ARGENTOCOXOS, wife of, fl. c. AD 210.

The wife of Argentocoxos was the spouse of a tribal leader of the Calidones, subdued in AD 208–10 by the Roman emperor Severus. Historian Cassius Dio described her 'jesting' with the empress after the campaign. The empress remarked upon 'the free intercourse of her sex with men in Britain', men who, Dio reported, 'possess their women in common, and in common rear all the offspring'. Argentocoxos's wife replied 'we fulfil the demands of nature in a much better way than do you Roman women; for we consort openly with the best men, whereas you let yourselves be debauched in secret by the vilest'. Contrasting barbarian societies' primitive morality with Roman vices was a standard literary *topos*; it is unlikely that the conversation occurred. This places the wife of Argentocoxos on shaky historical ground, but the name ('Silver-foot') is genuinely British, and it is possible that the meeting of Argentocoxos and Severus involved their wives. JEF

• Cary, E. (ed.) (1927) *Dio's Roman History*, vol. 9.

ARMOUR, Jean,[‡] m. Burns, born Mauchline 25 Feb. 1765, died Dumfries 26 March 1834. Wife of Robert Burns, poet. Daughter of Mary Smith, and James Armour, master builder.

Jean Armour said that she met Robert Burns (1759–96) on the Mauchline bleaching green. Their relationship was secret until she became pregnant around December 1785. The couple formed an irregular marriage but her parents disapproved and in March 1786 sent her to relations in Paisley for the duration of her pregnancy. She returned to Mauchline in June and gave birth to twins on 3 September 1786. On 5 August 1788, their earlier relationship was regularised by the Mauchline Kirk.

Jean Armour contributed to Burns's work as a listener and critic. She would also sing to him some of the old Scots songs, which he would then adapt or change. She gave birth to nine children by him – four daughters, all of whom died before the age of three, and five sons. As Burns's coffin was carried to St Michael's Kirkyard, Dumfries, on 25 July 1796, Maxwell, her last child, was born. After Burns's death, she remained at Millbrae Vennel (now Burns Street), Dumfries, playing host to numerous visitors. Tennyson was one of many poets who called on her, reading 'Thou Ling'ring Star' on his visit. When Jean Armour died and was interred in the Burns Mausoleum in St Michael's Kirkyard, on 1 April 1834, thousands, including local officials, came to her funeral, as a mark of respect. MB

• Ayrshire Archaeological Society (1996) *Mauchline Memories of Robert Burns*; Bell, M. (2001) *Tae The Lasses*; Hill, J. C. (1961) *The Love Songs and Heroines of Robert Burns*; *ODNB* (2004) (Burns, Robert); Stevenson, Y. H. (1967) *Burns and his Bonnie Jean*; Westwood, P. J. (1996) *Jean Armour*, (2001) *Jean Armour: My life and times with Robert Burns*.

ARMSTRONG, Janet (Jenny), born Fairliehope farm, Carlops, 9 May 1903, died West Linton 20 Nov. 1985. Borders shepherd. Daughter of Margaret (Maggie) Carruthers, and Andrew Armstrong, tenant farm manager.

Jenny Armstrong walked to school at Nine Mile Burn and, as a child, worked the sheep with her father, doing her first lambing at the age of nine. By her twenties she was working a large hill herd with three dogs in difficult Pentlands terrain at over 1,000 feet. She spent all her life as a hill shepherd, often in inclement conditions, at Spital, Carpet, New Hall and South Mains, having moved in the 1940s to Monk's Cottage in the isolated hamlet of Kittleyknowe, which remained her home thereafter. Much of the record of her later life is pictorial: in 1970, when she had retired from the hills but still kept a small flock, the artist Victoria Crowe came to live next door, and Jenny Armstrong became a friend and the focus of the painter's work. Jenny's fast-disappearing way of life and environment were captured in more than 50 paintings and drawings by Victoria Crowe, shown in the exhibition 'A Shepherd's Life' at the SNPG in 2000. These depicted her journey from vigour to illness and from an outdoor life to an indoor one. The exhibition attracted more than 30,000 visitors. VC

• Crowe, V. and Walton, M. (2001) *Painted Insights*; Lawson, J. and Taubman, M. (2000) *Victoria Crowe: 'A Shepherd's Life'*, catalogue and film, NGS; *Scotland on Sunday* 23 Jan. 2000. Private information and archive.

ARRAN, Elizabeth, Countess of *see* **STEWART, Elizabeth, Countess of Arran** (c. 1554–c. 1595)

ARTHUR, Jane, n. **Glen,** born Broomlands, Paisley, 18 Nov. 1827, died Ayr 25 May 1907. Social reformer and supporter of women's emancipation. Daughter of Jessie Fulton, and Thomas Glen, baker and grain merchant.

The third of five children, Jane Glen grew up living alongside her father's bakery in Broomlands, then the family moved to the outskirts of Paisley. On 21 Dec. 1847, she married James Arthur (1819–85), developer of a large manufacturing and wholesale drapery business. They had one daughter and four sons, and resided at the estate of Barshaw, Paisley. Their eldest son, Matthew, became the first Lord Glenarthur (1852–1928). Jane Arthur set up a Dorcas Society around 1863, to provide clothing for convalescents from Paisley Infirmary. In 1866 the Paisley Ladies' Sanitary Association, which promoted public baths, was instituted with Jane Arthur as vice-president. For many years the Arthurs supplied soup and bread to patients destitute following discharge from hospital. James Arthur donated a site for the West Kilbride Convalescent Home, opened in 1868. They contributed to the building of the Paisley model lodging-house and provided mid-morning tea for the inmates of the poor house. The Jane Arthur Fund, which paid for the convalescence of poor patients, was established in 1903.

From the late 1860s, Jane Arthur supported both temperance and the suffrage movement. She held drawing-room meetings and in 1882 was present at a Scottish national demonstration in Glasgow. Her brothers-in-law were on the platform at a public meeting in Paisley in 1871 addressed by Millicent Fawcett. After the 1872 Education Act, Jane Arthur came top of the poll for the Paisley School Board in 1873, the first woman to be elected in the West of Scotland. Following this *The Bailie*, while extolling her virtues, commented critically on her 'inclination to espouse the cause of "the shrieking sisterhood" who rave about "woman's rights" and "woman's wrongs" ', and hoped she would 'remain contented with the ruling power she already exercised'. She joined the organising committee of the GAHEW in 1877 and provided

bursaries for a Renfrewshire student and, later, for a woman medical student. Arthur Street, Paisley, is named after her. CJM

• Paisley Infirmary: Annual Reports 1863–1903; Glasgow Univ. Archives: QMC Collection DC233.
Barclay, J. F. (1953) *The Story of Arthur and Company*, private circulation; *Glasgow Herald*, 27 May 1907 (obit.); *ODNB* (2004); *The Bailie*, 36, 25 June 1873; *Women's Suffrage Journal*, 1 Nov. 1882.

ASQUITH, Emma Alice Margaret (Margot), n. **Tennant,** born Glen, Innerleithen, 2 Feb. 1864, died London 28 July 1945. Political hostess, diarist. Daughter of Emma Winsloe, and Sir Charles Tennant, industrialist and Liberal MP.

One of 11 children in the Tennant family, whose wealth came from the chemical industry in the west of Scotland, Margot Tennant enjoyed a Borders childhood, and was educated privately before she and her sister Laura, witty and unconventional girls, 'came out' in London society. She was 'the best-educated ill-educated woman I ever met', Benjamin Jowett remarked (*DNB* 1950). After Laura's death in childbirth in 1886, Margot Tennant was drawn into the political and intellectual circle nicknamed 'the Souls'. In 1894, she married the widowed Herbert Henry Asquith (1852–1928), MP for East Fife from 1882 for 32 years, then for Paisley, and future prime minister. She became stepmother to the five Asquith children, and had two surviving children of her own after several pregnancies: Elizabeth (1897–1945) and Anthony ('Puffin', 1902–68), later a successful film director.

In 1905, H. H. Asquith became chancellor of the exchequer, and in 1908 prime minister. Margot Asquith kept detailed diaries recording the years at the centre of power. Although 'political judgement was not her strongest suit' (Asquith 1992, intro. p. xii), she presumed to advise politicians, who did not always take kindly to it. Her extravagance, financed by her father, was also unpopular, but she was not frivolous, being a devout Christian. Devotedly loyal to H. H. Asquith, she bitterly resented Lloyd George's ousting him from the leadership in 1916 (of Lloyd George, she said, 'He couldn't see a belt without hitting below it', ibid., p. xxxv). She took little interest in Scottish politics, but spent much time in Scotland, often at her brother's house, Archerfield, near North Berwick, playing golf at Muirfield – once in a 'black afternoon dress and satin toque', (Bennett 1984, p. 354). Her *Autobiography* (1920–2) was frank if not always reliable. Her oft-quoted aphorisms have been exaggerated, but she did say, 'After fox-hunting, the greatest pleasure I have had in life has been intellectual and enduring conversation' (*DNB* 1950). She died in July 1945, just as news came both of her daughter's death and of the Labour landslide. SR

• Asquith, M. [1920–2] (1992 re-edn., intro. Bonham-Carter, M.) *Autobiography*.
Bennett, D. (1984*) Margot: a life of the Countess of Oxford and Asquith*; *DNB* (1950, by L. P. Hartley); *ODNB* (2004) (Bibl.).

ATHOLL, Katharine Marjory Stewart Murray, Duchess of, n. **Ramsay** DBE, born Edinburgh 6 Nov. 1874, died Edinburgh 21 Oct. 1960. First Scottish woman MP, Conservative government minister. Daughter of Charlotte Fanning, and Sir James Ramsay, 10th Baronet of Bamff, Perthshire.

Educated at Wimbledon High School and the Royal College of Music, Katharine Ramsay, like her mother, was a talented musician. Her marriage in 1899 to John, Lord Tullibardine (1871–1942), Unionist MP for West Perthshire 1910–17 and from 1917, 8th Duke of Atholl, took her into public life, initially because she was 'naturally anxious' to aid her husband politically (Atholl 1958, p. 55). The marriage was close, despite Tullibardine's frequent extra-marital affairs, as reflected in the title of their joint autobiography *Working Partnership*.

Her hospital work at Blair Atholl during the First World War was renowned, and she was appointed DBE in 1918. Although she at one time opposed votes for women, she was invited to stand in 1923 for the new seat of Kinross and West Perthshire. Elected, she became Scotland's first woman MP and in 1924 the first Conservative female minister, serving as Under-Secretary at the Board of Education from 1924 to 1929. Apparently it was supposed that she would be 'loyal and decorous' (Hetherington 1989, pp. 108–9). From 1923 to 1929 she focused mainly on domestic questions, though raising the controversial issue of African female circumcision foreshadowed her later focus on three major international issues: forced labour in Stalin's Russia; Indian self-rule; and the plight of Spanish civil war refugees, which she linked with the European fascist threat. Her views on India and Spain set her on a collision course with her party. In May 1935 she resigned the Conservative whip for several months over the passing of the India Act. She believed that self-government would lead to civil war and communal strife and she was concerned about the treatment of girls and women in India (including child

marriages and Hindu temple prostitution). Her position on Spain came as the last straw. De-selected in 1938, the Duchess resigned to fight a by-election on her opposition to appeasement. Dubbed the 'Red Duchess' by Conservative opponents, she found her defeat 'totally unexpected' (Ball 1990, p. 78). In 1939, however, she was elected as Independent candidate for the Scottish Universities, but resigned in 1940 to rejoin the Unionists when Winston Churchill became Prime Minister.

Widowed in 1942, she worked for the Red Cross throughout the war and acted as Honorary Secretary on the Scottish 'Invasion Committee' which was charged with the task of preparing civil resistance and obstruction in the event of invasion. The close of hostilities renewed her concern about the Soviet Union and in 1945 she became Chairman of the British League for European Freedom. In this capacity she became 'totally occupied with Poles and other refugees' (Hetherington 1989, p. 222). From 1955 her health and memory began to fail, although she published *Working Partnership* in 1958. She died after a fall while climbing a wall in 1960. Although her party political career was effectively over by 1938, as an 'accidental trailblazer' (Hetherington 1989, pp. 120–1) she was a pioneering female politician who made an important contribution to the debate on British foreign policy in the inter-war period. CB

• Blair Castle, Blair Atholl: Atholl MSS.
Duchess of Atholl (1932) *Women and Politics*, (1938) *Searchlight on Spain*, (1958) *Working Partnership*.
Ball, S. (1990) 'The politics of appeasement: the fall of the Duchess of Atholl', *Scot. Hist. Rev*., vol. LXIX; Burness, C. (1998) 'Tracing women in Scottish politics since 1880 and the case of an accidental trailblazer: Katharine, Duchess of Atholl', *Scottish Archives*, vol. 4; Hetherington, S. (1989) *Katharine Atholl, 1874–1960: Against the Tide*; Knox, W. W. J. (2006) *The Lives of Scottish Women*; *ODNB* (2004) (see Murray, Katharine Marjory Stewart-).

AUD (aka UNN), the Deep-Minded, born Norway c. 850, died Iceland c. 900. Founding settler of Iceland. Daughter of Yngvild, daughter of Ketil Wether, and Ketil Flat-Nose, Norse ruler of the Hebrides.

Kin to powerful Norwegian chieftains, Aud married Olaf the White, King of Dublin (fl. 853–c. 871). She is said to have left for the Hebrides with her son Thorstein the Red when Olaf was killed. However, the couple may have become estranged before Olaf became king, leading to Aud's earlier return to her father. Thorstein conquered and ruled much of northern Scotland until killed by the Scots. Aud, who was in Caithness, assumed command of Thorstein's household and moved family and possessions to Iceland where she claimed land and distributed portions to her followers; several place-names testify to her presence. Her epithet, 'the Deep-Minded', may refer to the insight she demonstrated in distributing land to good settlers, and the dignity she maintained throughout her life. Aud brought her Gaelic Christianity to Iceland, but one saga gives her a pagan chieftain's ship burial, symbol of the high regard in which she was held. JW

• Magnusson, M. and Pálsson, H. (trans.) (1969) *Laxdaela Saga*; Pálsson H. and Edwards, P. (trans.) (1972) *The Book of Settlements: Landnámabók*, (1973) *Eyrbyggja Saga*.

AUERBACH, Charlotte (Lotte) [Charlotte Austen], born Krefeld, Germany, 14 May 1899, died Edinburgh 17 March 1994. Geneticist. Daughter of Selma Sachs, and Friedrich Auerbach, chemist.

Born into an artistic and scientific family, Lotte Auerbach studied at Berlin, Wurtzburg and Freiburg. Her grandfather, Leopold Auerbach (1828–97), was a neuro-anatomist and discoverer of Auerbach's plexus. She taught until 1933, when Jewish teachers were expelled, then fled from Germany. Through an introduction to Professor Barger of the University of Edinburgh, Lotte Auerbach became a PhD student in the Institute of Animal Genetics. In 1938 she was introduced to the science of mutagenics, by the Nobel laureate Hermann Joseph Müller. With A. J. Clark and J. M. Robson in 1942, she discovered that mustard gas (used in trench warfare) caused genetic mutation in drosophila (fruit flies), and in so doing, founded the study of gene mutation by chemicals (mutagenesis), her particular contribution to science. Her approach was biological rather than chemical, emphasising the complexity of the biological interaction. Mustard gas proving dangerous, she later used other agents and the fungus neurospora, a bread mould, to investigate mutant and non-mutant cells, establishing the principle that increased mutation occurred in stored genes affected by a mutagen, 'replicating instabilities', which affected later generations. An independent-minded scientist, her research was conducted in great depth. Until the age of 70, she directed the Mutagenesis Research Unit of the MRC. She destroyed most of her scientific and personal correspondence and records, but was responsible for a total of 91 scientific publications, as well as a book of fairy stories, *Adventures with Rosalind*, under the pseudonym Charlotte Austen (1947). A supporter of CND, she hated racism. In addition to being FRS (1957) and FRSE, she was awarded the Keith Medal (1947) and the Darwin Medal (1976) and held honorary degrees from Edinburgh, Leiden, Cambridge and Dublin. Her ashes were scattered at Rhu, Arisaig. LS

• Auerbach, C. (1956) *Genetics in the Atomic Age*, (1962) *Mutation. An Introduction to Research on Mutagenesis*, (1962) *The Science of Genetics*, (1976) *Mutation Research Problems, Results and Perspectives.*

Beale, G. H. (1995) 'Charlotte Auerbach', in *Biographical Memoirs of the Fellows of the Royal Society*, 41, pp. 19–42 (Bibl.); Grinstein, L., Biermann, C. A. and Rose K. (1997) *Women in the Biological Sciences: A bibliographical sourcebook*; *ODNB* (2004).

AUST, Sarah, n. **Maese**, m1 **Murray**, m2 **Aust**, born 1744, died London 5 Nov. 1811. Topographical writer on Scotland.

In 1783, aged 39, Sarah Maese married Captain William Murray RN (1734–86), third son of the Earl of Dunmore. Although he died only three years later, it is likely that Sarah Murray acquired her passionate interest in Scotland through her husband. She was 52 when she started a tour of almost 2,000 miles through Scotland and the north of England, an experience she turned into a comprehensive travel guide, published two years later. In the introduction to the *Guide*, the author claims that she provides the traveller with information 'I believe never attended to (in the way I have done) by any of my Predecessors in Tour'; she writes about everything 'worthy of note . . . and by what means they can get at them' (Murray 1799, intro.). From her account, she comes across as a truly intrepid traveller, not put off by primitive hostelling or road conditions, and with a keen eye for the wild, romantic beauties as well as the social conditions of the Scotland of her time. Although she remarried in 1802, to George Aust (d. 1829), a career civil servant, the three editions of her *Guide* were published under the name the Hon. Mrs Murray. MVH

• Murray, Hon. Mrs [1799] *A Companion and Useful Guide to the Beauties of Scotland [etc.]* (1982, W. E. Laughlan (ed.), (1803) *A Companion and Useful Guide to the Beauties in the Western Highlands of Scotland [etc.]*; Murray Aust, Hon. Mrs (1811) [Combined version of the above]; *ODNB* (2004) (see Murray, Sarah).

B

BAILLIE, Lady Grisell,‡ n. **Hume (or Home),** born Redbraes Castle, Berwickshire, 25 Dec. 1665, died Mellerstain 6 Dec. 1746. Poet, household manager. Daughter of Grisell Ker, and Sir Patrick Hume, later Earl of Marchmont.

In 1676, Grisell Hume, aged 11, undertook a dangerous mission when her father's friend, Robert Baillie of Jerviswood, was fined and imprisoned in Edinburgh for rescuing his brother-in-law, the Covenanting Rev. James Kirkton, who was in trouble with the authorities. Anxious to get a message to Robert Baillie, Sir Patrick sent his daughter to Edinburgh Tolbooth, where she delivered his letters to the prisoner and met his son, George Baillie (1664–1738). After Robert Baillie was arrested again in 1683 for complicity in the Rye House Plot, Sir Patrick Hume realised that his own life was in danger and hid in the vaults of Polwarth Church, the troopers having taken possession of his castle of Redbraes. Grisell regularly brought him food, visiting him at midnight with the morsels she had concealed in her lap during her own dinner. When Robert Baillie was executed, Grisell Hume and her family, including her father, fled to Holland and settled in Utrecht, where she met George Baillie again.

After the Revolution of 1688, Grisell Hume was offered and declined a position as maid of honour to Queen Mary II. In love with George Baillie, she knew that she would not see him if she were to settle in London. Instead, she returned to Scotland and married him on 17 September 1692. Attractive, charming and an excellent businesswoman as well as a talented poet, Grisell was his wife for 46 years. They had two daughters and a short-lived son. Living at Mellerstain after her marriage, she put all her father's affairs in order and looked after her brother's interests when he was abroad. Her husband entrusted her with the entire management of his own finances until his death in 1738. After her death in 1746, she was buried at Mellerstain, where her famous household books have been carefully preserved. Noting in meticulous detail her household expenditure from 1692 to 1733, they provide an invaluable source for the social historian. RKM

• Mellerstain: The Earl of Haddington's Archives.

Kerrigan, C. (1991) *An Anthology of Scottish Women's Poetry*; Scott-Moncrieff, R. (ed.) (1911) *The Household Book of Lady Grisell Baillie 1692–1733*; Murray of Stanhope, G., Lady (1821) *Memoirs of the Lives and Characters of the Honourable George Baillie and Lady Grisell Baillie of Jerviswood*; *ODNB* (2004); *SP*; Swain, M. (1970) *Historical Needlework*.

BAILLIE, Lady Grisell, baptised Mellerstain, Berwickshire, 6 June 1822, died St Boswells, 20 Dec. 1891. First deaconess, Church of Scotland. Daughter of Mary Pringle, and George Baillie, 9th Earl of Haddington.

Grisell Baillie grew up at Mellerstain, the Georgian great house near Gordon in the Borders. She was the youngest of 11 children, and the great-great-grand-daughter of another *Lady Grisell Baillie. Although she had many suitors and was known for her beauty, she never married. There were two significant men in her life: her brother, Robert, to whom she was a devoted companion, and Rev. Dr Archibald Charteris who established the order of deaconesses in the Church of Scotland. His vision was to recognise the gifts of women and offer them the opportunity of formal service. Grisell Baillie had covenanted with her brother to share a life of prayer and service, expressed in care for the sick and the children of the parish, raising funds for foreign missions and community improvements such as arranging for better water supplies to the village of St Boswells and for a bridge to be built over the Tweed to shorten the walking distance to church.

Overcoming opposition to this new breed of women within the Church of Scotland, Grisell Baillie undertook the required training and patiently navigated Church bureaucracy until, in 1888, she was 'set apart' (commissioned) in Bowden Church, an occasion which she described as her 'wedding day' (Magnusson 1987, p. 61), becoming the first deaconess in the Church of Scotland. The Church of Scotland Woman's Guild, also an initiative of Dr Charteris and *Catherine Morice Charteris, was formally launched in 1887 and in 1891 held its first conference. Lady Grisell presided, using the occasion to urge members 'to go and work in the vineyard' (Gordon 1912, p. 358) and to launch a campaign for temperance that would prove far-reaching.

After her eldest brother succeeded to the title of 10th Earl of Haddington, she lived with her widowed mother and two unmarried brothers in various houses, eventually settling at Dryburgh Abbey House. She died from influenza shortly after the first Guild conference. Her charismatic character had already helped to launch a movement that would sweep Scotland in the 20th century, releasing the energy and gifts of women within the national church. AT

• Gordon, Rev. A. (1912) *The Life of Archibald Hamilton Charteris, DD LLD*; Magnusson, M. (1987) *Out of Silence*; *ODNB* (2004).

BAILLIE, Isobel Douglas (Isabella, Bella), CBE, DBE, m. **Wrigley,** born Wilton, Hawick, 9 March 1895, died Manchester 24 Sept. 1983. Singer. Daughter of Isabella Douglas, woollen factory worker, and Martin Baillie, baker.

Born on the estates of the Earl of Dalkeith, Isobel Baillie moved with her family to Manchester, where she studied at the High School, taking singing lessons from the age of nine. Her voice was recognised as remarkable early on. She worked briefly as a shop assistant and clerk and, in 1917, married Henry Leonard Wrigley (1891–1957), cotton trader. They had one daughter, Nancy, born in 1918. In 1921, Isobel made her professional debut under Sir Hamilton Harty, who became her mentor, persuading her to alter her name from 'Bella' to 'Isobel', and to continue her vocal training under Guglielmo Somma in Milan (1925). She sang one of Harty's own love songs to him from memory on his deathbed.

Isobel Baillie's first London season in 1923 was an outstanding success. She later performed regularly with Sir Thomas Beecham and Bruno Walter; Toscanini thought highly of her. She was the first British artist to sing in the Hollywood Bowl (1933). Her voice was 'not so much personal as brightly and serenely spiritual, made by her soaring and equable tones' (*Grove's Dict.* 1961) and she specialised in oratorio, giving over a thousand performances of *The Messiah*, and singing the soprano solos in the Brahms *Requiem* and Rachmaninov's *The Bells*, the latter in the composer's presence in Sheffield in 1936. She taught singing at the RCM from 1955 to 1957, was Visiting Professor at Cornell University in 1960, and taught at Manchester College of Music. The list of her recordings is extensive, and her well-written and modest account of her singing career, *Never Sing Louder than Lovely*, is full of

interest. Already CBE (1951), she was made DBE in 1978. JP

• Baillie, I. (1982). Work as above.
(1961) *Grove's Dictionary*; (2001) *The New Grove Dictionary*; *ODNB* (2004); *Who's Who in Music* (1969).

BAILLIE, Joanna, born Bothwell, Lanarkshire, 11 Sept. 1762, died Hampstead, London, 23 Feb. 1851. Playwright and poet. Daughter of Dorothea Hunter, and Rev. James Baillie, Church of Scotland minister.

Joanna Baillie's uncles were William and John Hunter, celebrated surgeons, anatomists and collectors. Her brother Matthew was also set for a career in medicine. She and her sister, her life-long companion Agnes (1760–1861), were educated in the literatures and philosophies of the day, an education reflected in the tone and scope of her poetry, prose and drama. However, she showed, as she put it, an 'uncommon dulness' in learning to read and write, despite being 'an active, stirring child, quick in apprehending or learning anything else' – and remained a poor speller (*SHA* 1999, p. 92). She was at boarding school in Glasgow when, in 1776, her father was appointed Professor of Divinity at the University. The Baillie family moved to Glasgow, but two years later, James Baillie died and his wife and daughters moved to Long Calderwood, the Hunter estate outside Glasgow. Joanna Baillie saw her first play when at school – 'my attention was riveted with delight' – (ibid., p. 99) and she re-enacted scenes with fellow pupils. She also took part in dramatic episodes from Shakespeare for a family audience. In 1783, when William Hunter's death left Matthew Baillie heir to his famous School of Anatomy on Windmill Street, London, they moved south. Shortly after the anonymous publication of Joanna Baillie's first volume of poetry, *Poems* (1790) and Matthew's marriage (1791), the female Baillies went to live in Hampstead, where they remained thereafter. They moved in the literary and intellectual circles associated with the Hunters; Joanna Baillie was close to her aunt, the poet *Anne Home Hunter (1742–1821), who 'turned my thoughts to poetical composition' (ibid., p. 101).

Joanna Baillie published and had produced some of the key plays of the Romantic theatre and was celebrated as the pre-eminent playwright of her generation. Her first play, *Arnold* (1790), does not survive. Her earliest extant dramas are collected in *A Series of Plays* (1798). It includes *Count Basil*, *The Trial* and *De Monfort*, arguably her best plays, as well as the influential preface and other works of theatre theory. A second volume of plays followed in 1802; her *Miscellaneous Plays* in 1804 and another volume in 1812. It is on these early texts that her reputation rests. Her first produced play was *De Monfort*, 29 April 1800, at Drury Lane with John Philip Kemble and Sarah Siddons in the lead roles. A somewhat stilted heroic verse-tragedy, it had limited popular success, but remained in the Kemble repertoire and achieved particular success in Edinburgh as part of his farewell tour in 1817. The city was loyal in its support of Joanna Baillie, celebrated as a Scottish woman of letters. Her friendship with Sir Walter Scott was also influential – he promoted and sponsored her work both in the Scottish capital and in London. Her work had been treated with some hostility by influential reviewers such as Francis Jeffrey – she believed this was because it was discovered that the 'hitherto concealed Dramatist' was a 'private Gentlewoman of no mark or likelihood' (ibid., p. 103).

When she and her sister toured the north in 1808, they were guests of Scott in Edinburgh. Perhaps inspired by her Highland excursion, her next play was *The Family Legend*, which became, along with *De Monfort*, one of her most successful. It was produced, at the insistence of Scott, at the Theatre Royal, Edinburgh, in 1810, with *Harriet Siddons in the lead role, its heroically Ossianic tone coinciding with the patriotic mood of the city, and revived in Newcastle, in Bath (1811) and at Drury Lane. While most of Joanna Baillie's drama is written in verse, a lively alternative is *Witchcraft* (1836). Like *The Family Legend*, it is set in Scotland and is notable for a sustained, distinctive attempt at linguistic realism. In 1836, Baillie's drama-writing career ended with the production of *The Homicide* at Drury Lane and *The Separation* at Covent Garden. Her later works appeared in a three-volume edition of *Dramas*, and her final volume was *Fugitive Verse* (1840). Although few of her plays were performed, her literary reputation was unmatched. Her eloquent letters exemplify the intellectual society of early Romanticism. Before her death she edited her complete works, *The Dramatical and Poetical Works of Joanna Baillie* (1851). AS

• Royal College of Surgeons, London: Hunter-Baillie papers Baillie, J., Works as above, the following, and see Bibls. below, [1790] (1996) *Poems*, J. Wordsworth (ed.), (1789) *A Series of Plays: in which it is Attempted to Delineate the Stronger Passions of the Mind, each Passion being the Subject of a Tragedy and a Comedy*, (1999) *The Collected Letters of Joanna Baillie*, J. B. Slagle, ed.
Carhart, M. S. (1923) *The Life and Works of Joanna Baillie*; Duthie, P. (ed.) (2001) *Plays on the Passions (1798 edition)*; *HSWW* (Bibl.); Lonsdale, R. (ed.) (1994) *Eighteenth-Century Women Poets*; *ODNB* (2004); *SHA*; Slagle, J. B. (ed.) (2002) *Joanna Baillie: a literary life* (Bibl.).

BAKER, Elizabeth, n. **Clendon,** died Jan. or Feb. 1778. Actor and elocution teacher. Daughter of a clergyman.

Elizabeth Baker had married the actor, playwright and theatre historian, David Lionel Erskine Baker (1730–c. 1767) before her Covent Garden debut as Roxana in Nathaniel Lee's *The Rival Queens* (6 October 1762). She was established in Edinburgh by March 1756, when notice was given that she would perform Juliet for Mr Aitken's benefit. She performed regularly in Edinburgh in the winter season of 1767–8, engaging in a protracted newspaper dispute with *Sarah Ward as to precedence on the playbills. Dibdin (1888) notes her as a member of the company from the 1769–70 season through to her retirement at the end of the 1773–4 season. She may have quit the stage after arguing with the actor manager West Digges, but thereafter – and probably before – she pursued a highly successful career as an elocution tutor for Edinburgh society. She hoped for a managerial role in Edinburgh and would have been only the second woman to achieve that – after her early rival, Sarah Ward – but she died before she could acquire the lease of the Theatre Royal, Edinburgh. Her death was marked with a verse remembrance in the Edinburgh *Courant*. Dr Johnson wrote of her as a friend in 1767 and actor-manager Tate Wilkinson admired her abilities. AS

• Dibdin, J. C. (1888) *Annals of the Edinburgh Stage*; Highfill, P. H. Jr., Burnim, K. A. and Langhans, E. A. (c. 1973–93) *A Biographical Dictionary of Actors . . . and Other Stage Personnel in London, 1660–1800*.

BALFOUR, Alison, died Kirkwall 16 Dec. 1594. Healer. Executed for conspiracy to murder by witchcraft.

A purveyor of simple medical remedies, Alison Balfour lived in the Ireland district of the parish of Stenness with her aged husband, surnamed Taillifeir, and her children. She became implicated in the accusations against John Stewart, Master of Orkney, that he planned to murder his brother, Patrick Stewart, the Earl. In early October, 1593,

John Stewart and Patrick Bellenden of Stenness, long Earl Patrick's enemy, were said to have visited her house to ask how 'thay mycht haif bewichit the said . . . Erll . . . and bereif him [of life] be sorcerie and wichcraft'. In December 1594, in Kirkwall Castle under the direction of Henry Colville, parson of Orphir, she suffered 'vehement' torture in that mysterious instrument the caschielawis, being taken insensible from it several times over two days. Besides her torment, she witnessed her husband, said to be over 90, in the 'lang irnis of fiftie stane wecht', her eldest son in the 'buitis with fiftie sevin straikis', and even her seven-year-old daughter in the 'pinnywinkis' or thumbscrews. Henry Colville promised mercy if she co-operated.

She duly confessed, but his promise proved false, and she was condemned to death. Relieved from torture, she immediately and publicly repudiated her admissions, repeating this both at her trial and her execution. She made a public declaration to a notary that she 'would die as innocent of . . . wichcraft as ane barne new borne'. She defended Patrick Bellenden, saying that wax in her possession was for treating his wife's colic. Challenged by Henry Colville, she refused to abide by her confession, made 'aganis her saul and conscience'. She asked for the Lord's mercy and forgiveness, then faced her end 'constantlie'. She was executed at the 'heading hill' at Kirkwall.

Alison Balfour seems to have been the victim of a concerted effort by Henry Colville, acting for the earl, to have John Stewart implicated in grave crimes. Witchcraft, following the North Berwick hysteria which involved *Agnes Sampson and other witches, was potentially the most damaging. At his own trial in 1596, John Stewart denied visiting Alison Balfour, and was cleared of all charges. It is likely that her deposition on the scaffold, produced at Stewart's trial, helped to expose Henry Colville's accusations as the falsehoods they almost certainly were. Not long afterwards, Henry Colville was murdered in Shetland, perhaps on John Stewart's orders. PDA

• Anderson, P. D. (1992) *Black Patie: the Life and Times of Patrick Stewart, Earl of Orkney, Lord of Shetland*; *Crim. Trials*, vol. I.

BALFOUR, Elizabeth (Betty), n. **Anderson,** born on Papa Little, Shetland, 1832, died Houbanster 18 March 1918. Howdie (uncertified midwife), later known as 'Aald Mam o' Houbanster'. Daughter of Margaret (Maggie) Stout and Thomas (Tammy) Anderson, crofters.

Aged 17, Betty Anderson married James (Jeemie) Balfour, fisherman and blacksmith: they had seven sons and four daughters. Her work as howdie was well known, and people consulted her from afar. For one delivery, Jeemie Balfour rowed her out to the island of Muckle Röe. When prolonged labour put the mother's and the baby's lives in danger, he used his smithing expertise to fashion forceps which she used to save them both – apparently the first such delivery in the area. Her own life was tragic: she lost three children early in marriage; a son, grandson and daughter-in-law died of consumption; one daughter died of whooping cough aged four; her son Walter drowned retrieving a lost oar, and Betty dreamed correctly where his body had come ashore. In 1886, her husband and two sons were lost at sea; in 1895, a grand-daughter died in a fire; four grandsons and a great-grandson were later lost at sea. After a stroke, Betty Balfour was bed-ridden for her last five years. LR

• *Shetland Times*, 25 Dec. 1886; Tait, K. (1986) 'Taken by the Sea', *Shetland Life*, Dec., pp. 31–2.
Private information: Kathleen Tait (great-great-grand-daughter).
Additional information, Brian Smith, archivist.

BALFOUR, Lady Evelyn Barbara (Eve), OBE, born Dublin 16 July 1898, died Dunbar 14 Jan. 1990. Pioneer of organic farming, founder of the Soil Association. Daughter of Lady Elizabeth Edith Lytton, and Gerald William Balfour, 2nd Earl Balfour.

Eve Balfour spent six months each year until 1915 at Whittinghame House, East Lothian, home of her uncle, A. J. Balfour, 1st Earl Balfour, prime minister (1902–5). Among her aunts were suffragists Lady Constance Lytton and *Lady Frances Balfour. Educated at home, she was strong-minded from an early age: she became a vegetarian aged eight, after watching a pheasant shoot, and decided to become a farmer after riding out one morning, aged 12, watching the wind ruffling the barley. Her parents encouraged her to read agriculture at the University of Reading in 1915, as one of the first women to do so. She ran a farm in Monmouthshire for the Women's War Agricultural Committee, then, in 1919, she and her sister Mary bought their own farm in Haughley, Suffolk. Over the next few years, she played saxophone in a dance band, acquired a pilot's licence, and with Beryl Hearnden published three detective novels under the pseudonym Hearnden Balfour.

Her interest in what she called biological husbandry developed in the 1930s, after reading *Famine in England* by Lord Lymington, which alerted her to the concept of sustainable agriculture: the bee in the author's bonnet had 'a very interesting buzz and I really [had to] find out more about it' (BBC Radio 4 interview, 25 August 1988). She met Sir Albert Howard, whose book *Agricultural Testament* argued that only healthy soil would produce the right food for human health, and Sir Robert McCarrison, an army doctor in India, who had demonstrated the direct relationship between diet and health. In 1939 with her neighbour Alice Debenham, Eve Balfour set up the Haughley Research Trust on their two farms, to undertake a long-term scientific study of McCarrison's and Howard's claims. The farms were divided into plots, contrasting organic methods of production with chemically dependent methods. By 1943 enough trial evidence was available for her to publish her pioneering book *The Living Soil*: reprinted nine times (rev. edn. 1975), it provoked an avalanche of worldwide correspondence. Meetings with enthusiasts led directly to the formation in 1946 of the Soil Association (SA) with its aim of researching and disseminating information about organic production. Lady Eve became its first president, and the SA took over Haughley, where she worked until it closed in 1970. The postwar UK was committed to intensive agriculture and the farming establishment mocked and ignored Eve Balfour, who was however the inspiration of the modern movement for organic production, with SAs being set up worldwide. Having retired in 1984, she cultivated a large garden in Suffolk, but after a stroke returned to Scotland for her last days, receiving an OBE shortly before she died. A few days later the UK government introduced grants for organic farming. SMD

• MS biography of Eve Balfour by Charles Dowding and Mary Langham.

Balfour, E. B., Work as above, and speech to Annual Meeting of International Federation of Organic Agricultural Movements, Geneva 1977.

Brander, M. (2003) *Eve Balfour, a biography*; Conford, P. (2001) *The Origins of the Organic Movement*; Griggs, B. (1986) *The Food Factor*; *ODNB* (2004); *The Times*, 17 Jan. 1990 (obit.).

website: www.soilassociation.org

BALFOUR, Lady Frances,‡ n. **Campbell,** born Kensington 22 Feb. 1858, died London 25 Feb. 1931. Churchwoman, suffragist and writer. Daughter of Lady Elizabeth Georgiana Sutherland-Leveson-Gower, and Sir George Douglas Campbell, 8th Duke of Argyll.

The tenth of 12 children, Lady Frances Campbell was brought up in Inveraray and Rosneath Castles, and London. She had a hip joint abnormality and from early childhood suffered constant pain and a limp. Her parents, prominent supporters of the Liberal Party, actively involved their children in social reform campaigns. In spite of initial opposition from her father, in 1879 Frances Campbell married into a well-known Conservative family. Her architect husband, Col. Eustace Balfour (1854–1911), was not active in politics but his uncle and brother both served as Prime Minister and Eustace shared their Tory views. Lady Frances was an ardent Liberal and the couple never overcame their political differences, increasingly spending time apart before his death in 1911. They had five children.

It was through membership of the WLUA that Lady Frances Balfour came into contact with feminists, including Eva Maclaren, with whom she helped form the Liberal Women's Suffrage Society (1887). She became an effective public speaker for the cause and, along with her sister-in-law Betty Balfour, tried to win the support of Arthur Balfour (Prime Minister 1902–5). She was deeply involved in the establishment and leadership of the NUWSS and was committed to their constitutional approach to campaigning. She opposed the strategy of the WSPU, although another sister-in-law, Constance Lytton, was imprisoned several times for her militant activities. 'The courage that dares this handling I do admire. There is a fine spirit, but whether it is not rather thrown away on these tactics remains a doubt in my mind.'(Letter to Millicent Fawcett, 29 June 1909, GD433/2/295).

Lady Frances was deeply involved in the Church of Scotland and an avid defender of established Protestant religion and a national Kirk. She was also the prime mover and fundraiser for the rebuilding of Crown Court Church of Scotland, London, for which her husband was architect. She served as President of the Woman's Guild branch there, and hoped that the Guild would promote active citizenship and leadership among Christian women. She was unequivocal in her criticism of institutional religion for failing to offer equality of opportunity. Her commitment to women's rights in church and society came together in her presidency of the Scottish Churches' League for Woman Suffrage (formed 1912), and in her petition (posthumously heard just weeks after her death in 1931) to the General Assembly calling for the ordination of women. Lady Frances served for 15 years as President and Executive Chairwoman of the Lyceum Club, founded in 1904 to provide a welcoming and intellectually stimulating environment for women in London. She received honorary doctorates from the universities of Durham (1919) and Edinburgh (1920).

In church and politics she used her prominence and connections to advantage, but found the restrictions in both spheres, with no right to speak in either the General Assembly or House of Commons, deeply frustrating. A prolific writer of articles and biographies, including *Dr Elsie Inglis* (1918), in print and in speaking she combined passion, polemic and sarcasm to great effect. Of great personal courage, vision and spirit, she confronted the male-dominated institutions to which she was most loyal, forcefully challenging their entrenched inequalities. LO

• NAS: GD433/2, Balfour papers.

Balfour, F., Works as above, and (1911) *Lady Victoria Campbell*, (1925) *A Memoir of Lord Balfour of Burleigh*, (1930) *Ne Obliviscaris*.

Fleming, A. (1931) 'Lady Frances Balfour', *St Columba's (Church of Scotland) Magazine*, March; Huffman, J. B. (1992) 'For Kirk and Crown: the rebuilding of Crown Court Church, 1905–1909', *London Journal* 17/1; Knox, W. W. J. (2006) *The Lives of Scottish Women*; ODNB (2004).

BALFOUR, Margaret Ida, CBE, born Edinburgh 21 April 1866, died London 1 Dec. 1945. Pioneer doctor in India. Daughter of Frances Grace Blaikie, and Robert Balfour, chartered accountant.

On gaining her MBChM at Edinburgh and London in 1891, Margaret Balfour left Britain to become Medical Officer of the *Zenana* (women's quarters) hospital in Ludhiana. *Zenana* hospitals had been established by Christian women missionaries to treat Indian women in purdah – Muslim, Hindu or Sikh – whose religion forbade them to be seen by male doctors. Margaret Balfour was Medical Superintendent of the Women's Hospital at Nahan (1899–1902); of the Lady Dufferin Hospital in Patiala (1903–13); assistant to the Inspector-General of Civil Hospitals in the Punjab (1914–19); and finally Chief Medical Officer of all the Women's Medical Services in India (1920–4). Having dedicated herself to improving the life-chances of Indian women and babies, she published widely on midwifery, infant and puerperal mortality in India. As an expert witness to the Joshi

Committee Enquiry into child marriage in India in 1928, she drew attention to osteomalacia – softening of bones caused by the lack of sunlight in purdah – and to anaemia in pregnancy, also associated with conditions in purdah. A final publication, after 'retirement', was *Maternity Conditions of Women Millworkers in Bombay* (1930). Margaret Balfour also offered health visitor training to the traditional *dais* (midwives) who often inadvertently caused maternal and infant death. She ended her working life as an unpaid octogenarian ARP medical officer in wartime London. 'Beneath her quiet manner and gentle voice there was a core of steel' (Scott 1946). She received the Kaiser-I-Hind medal (1920) and was made CBE (1924). SO

• Balfour, M., Work as above and (1929) Balfour, M. and Young, R., *The Work of Medical Women in India.*

The Lancet, 15 Dec. 1945 (obit.); Oldfield, S. (2001) *Women Humanitarians*; Pollock, J. C. (1958) *Shadows Fall Apart*; Rathbone, E. (1929) *Child-Marriage*; Scott, A. (1946) 'Dr. M. Balfour', *Medical Women's Federation Quarterly Rev.*, Jan. (obit.).

BALLANTINE, Georgina White,[‡] born Caputh 25 Nov. 1889, died Caputh 12 April 1970. Nurse, registrar, salmon fisher. Daughter of Christina White, and James Ballantine, registrar and ghillie.

Between 1914 and 1919, Georgina Ballantine worked as a nurse in Perth, London and Bapaume in France, where she was decorated by the Red Cross. Later she followed her father as registrar in the parish of Caputh. Fame visited her on 7 October 1922, when she was fishing with her father, the local laird's boatman. Using a spinning bait, Georgina Ballantine landed a 64lb salmon on the Glendelvine stretch of the River Tay, the largest recorded salmon taken from a British river with rod and line. A cast was made of the fish before it was donated to Perth Royal Infirmary and a model with supporting display is exhibited in Perth Museum. In 1955, an appreciative fishing syndicate had electricity installed in her riverbank home. In her later years she suffered so severely from arthritis that both legs had to be amputated. EL

• Dunkeld Cathedral Archives: Bell, F. R., 'Diary of a Quiet Life', typescript, n.d.

Paterson, W. and Behan, P. (1990) *Salmon and Women: the feminine angle*.

BALLANTYNE, Nellie Lochhead (Nell), m. **Graham,** born Glasgow 1 Dec. 1898, died Glasgow 21 Feb. 1959. Actor. Daughter of Elizabeth Lochhead, and Peter Ballantyne, dairyman.

Nell Ballantyne grew up in Stirlingshire, where her parents had a farm. In 1918 she went to RADA and, on graduation in 1921, became one of the first members of the Scottish National Players, making extensive tours throughout Scotland with the pioneering company. The company's activities were usually conducted on a shoestring, the actors often living under canvas between engagements. According to Tyrone Guthrie, the company's producer, she would usually do the cooking. In 1925 she married Robert McGregor Graham, manufacturer's agent, and they had a daughter in 1929. They later divorced. Always a utility player rather than a leading actress, she is remembered more for her sunny personality than for her gifts as a performer. The broadcaster Howard M. Lockhart remarked that it was impossible to feel depressed in her company and another colleague, Tom Fleming, told of her popularity in the Gateway company, which she later joined. Nevertheless, her gifts as an actress were not negligible. Her most famous stage role was as Mrs Gellatly in the world premiere of John Brandane's *The Glen is Mine* (25 Jan. 1923) but she became best known for her parts in two radio soap operas. In 1941 she played the mother in the BBC's first series of this kind, *Front Line Family*, and six years later she was the original Mrs McFlannel in the fondly remembered *The McFlannels*. In addition to her stage and radio work, she appeared in several films: *The Shipbuilders* (1943), *Bonnie Prince Charlie* (1948), *Mr Emmanuel* (1949), *Laxdale Hall* (1953), *Rockets Galore* (1958) and *The Bridal Path* (1959). DC
• Campbell, D. (1965) *Six Seasons of the Edinburgh Gateway*, (1996) *Playing for Scotland*; *Glasgow Herald*, 21 Feb. 1959 (obit.).
Private information: Helen Murdoch.

BALLIOL, Dervorgilla *see* **GALLOWAY, Dervorgilla of** (c. 1213–1290)

BANE (or CLERK), Margaret, born before 1567, died Aberdeen 25 March 1597. Midwife.
Margaret Bane, a midwife of Lumphanan parish, Aberdeenshire, was accused of witchcraft, sorcery, enchantment and murder in 1597, when she was probably about 55 years old. She may have married twice, as she had a daughter, Helen Rogie, and a son, Duncan Gardyn. At least eight women tried for witchcraft in 1597 named her as an accomplice. Evidence at her trial indicates that she was consulted widely for advice about childbirth, and her knowledge of midwifery was used as

evidence against her. In a typical incident, it was claimed she transferred the labour pains of a woman to her husband, and that he died as a result. Margaret Bane confessed to some of the items, notably that she had predicted the birth of a male child and that she and her sister, **Janet Spaldarge** (d. 1597), had caused the death of a man. She also confessed that Janet had taught her witchcraft, and that she had become the devil's servant. Other witnesses claimed that she was seen carrying out a ritual at a loch, when she had thrown water, earth and stones over her shoulders. The records indicate that Margaret Bane had been charged 30 years earlier but had not appeared and had remained fugitive from the law. She may have had influence over some people involved in her trials, as it was claimed that she managed to be cleansed ('clengit') of charges brought against her in 1596. She may also have had friends in high places, as Lady Ross of Auchlossan paid 10 merks to the clerks to hide the previous dittay (charge). She was eventually tried at Aberdeen in March 1597, found guilty and executed by burning.
Margaret Bane's association with her sister Janet, burnt for witchcraft in Edinburgh, and others, was a significant element in the verdict, as were the accusations of demonic involvement and malefice (evil harm). However, her midwifery practices and other behaviour were also important. Her daughter, Helen Rogie, was also tried and executed for witchcraft a month after her. JHMM
• Stuart, J. (ed.) (1841–52) *Spalding Club Miscellany*, vol. 1, pp. 140, 145–7, 153–6, 158, 160, 193; Ibid., vol. 5, p. 67.

BANNERMAN, Anne, born Edinburgh 31 Oct. 1765, died Portobello 29 Sept. 1829. Poet. Daughter of Isobel Dick, and William Bannerman, a 'running stationer' (street ballad singer and seller).
Anne Bannerman excelled in the Scottish ballad tradition. Her two collections of poetry, *Poems* (1800) and *Tales of Superstition and Chivalry* (1802), established her as a highly original Scottish poet, appreciated by influential editors such as Bishop Percy, John Leyden (possibly a romantic interest), Dr Robert Anderson, and Walter Scott. Scott praised this 'gifted lady's' poetry in his 'Essay on Imitations of the Ancient Ballad' (1830, quoted Henderson 1902, pp. 16–17), saying it was 'peculiarly fit to be read in a lonely house by a decaying lamp'. Her first volume included an impressive set of visionary poems (e.g. 'The Genii' and 'Ode: The Spirit of the Air') in which the poet assumed the sublime voice thought typical of male

Romantic poets, an accomplishment praised by contemporaries. In *Tales of Superstition*, she concentrated on modern Gothic ballads popularised by writers such as Matthew Lewis, author of *The Monk* (1796). The critical reception was more mixed, many reviewers disapproving of the supernatural horror her work evoked, increasingly thought inappropriate for women poets. Anne Bannerman's mother's death in 1803 left her impoverished. She published a new edition of her poems by subscription (1807), including some new works, such as 'To Miss Baillie,' a tribute to *Joanna Baillie, whom she admired, but sales were insufficient to give her an annuity. She obtained £20 from the Royal Literary Fund in 1805, and became a governess in Exeter in 1807. By the early 1810s, she was back in Scotland, existing at least partially through charitable gifts. In 1824 she visited *Anne Grant. She died an invalid and in debt. AC
• NLS: MSS 971, 3380–2 (Leyden MSS); 22.4.10 and 22.3.11.
Bannerman, A., Works as above and (1807) *Poems*, new edn.
Henderson, T. F. (1902) *Sir Walter Scott's Minstrelsy of the Scottish Border*; *ODNB* (2004).

BANNERMAN, Helen Brodie Cowan, n. **Watson,** born Edinburgh 25 Feb. 1862, died Edinburgh 13 Oct. 1946. Children's writer. Daughter of Jane Cowan, and Rev. Robert Boog Watson.

From 1864, Helen Watson lived in Madeira, where her father, a scientist as well as a minister, taught his seven children. In 1874, the family returned to Edinburgh, where she went to school. She later took an external university degree (LLA St Andrews 1887), and studied languages and philology in Hanover and Italy. In 1889, she married William Burney Bannerman (1858–1924), a doctor in the Indian Medical Service, and spent the next 30 years in India. She first invented stories to comfort her two small daughters, whom she had to leave at a hill station for the hot season while she stayed with her husband in Madras. In 1898, she sent them *The Story of Little Black Sambo*, written, illustrated and bound by her. The next year *Sambo* was published in London, and became an immediate and enormous success. It contains all the ingredients to appeal to small children: a boy hero who outwits four hungry tigers in the Indian jungle, excitement, suspense and a satisfying ending. Short, repetitive sentences are perfectly synchronised with simple bright pictures in a small format, predating *Peter Rabbit* by two years as the first picture-story for young children. The author's lack of copyright resulted in a flood of unauthorised American versions with stereotypical illustrations, which contributed to charges of racism in the 1970s, but the original has remained deservedly popular and in print. Helen Bannerman produced a series of similar but less successful picture books, the last one in 1937. In 1918, the Bannermans returned to live with their four children in Edinburgh. JRR
• NLS: Dep. 325: Bannerman family letters from India to Edinburgh (17 vols 1902–17, incl. watercolour illustrations); Acc. 7690: script 1971 BBC radio programme based on letters; Acc. 8884: Sketch book and printed text, *Sambo and the Twins* (1937).
Bannerman, H., Works as above and see Bibl.
Arbuthnot, M. H. (1957) *Children and Books*; Hay, E. (1981) *Sambo Sahib*; *ODNB* (2004, Bibl.); Tucker, N. (ed.) (1976) *Suitable for Children? Controversies in Children's Literature.*

BARBOUR, Mary,‡ n. **Rough,** born Kilbarchan, Renfrewshire, 22 Feb. 1875, died Govan, Glasgow, 2 April 1958. Housing and Labour activist and councillor. Daughter of Jane (Jeanie) Gavin, and James Rough, carpet weaver.

The third of seven children, Mary Rough began work aged 12 as a thread twister in Elderslie. In 1896, when she was a carpet printer, she married David Barbour (1873–1957), an engineer from Johnstone. They settled in Govan, where he worked in Fairfield Shipbuilding & Engineering Company, and had two sons. She joined the ILP and was involved in her local Socialist Sunday School and the Kinning Park CWG. In 1914, the GWHA was set up by the Glasgow Labour Party Housing Committee and after a series of steep rent rises by landlords, housewives spontaneously refused to pay the increases. By June 1915, effective and organised resistance had developed, particularly in Govan, after the formation of the South Govan WHA, led by Mary Barbour. She organised women's committees who met in kitchens and closes to gather information on impending evictions. By ringing hand-bells and 'ricketies' (rattles) they alerted the women, who came out on to the streets to drive off the sheriff's officers. The rent strike spread to other areas; in Partick, Jean Ferguson also led and organised an effective campaign, while *Helen Crawfurd, Secretary of the GWHA, provided overall leadership, speaking at mass rallies. On 17 November 1915, the strike culminated in a huge demonstration. Thousands of women, supported by engineers and shipyard workers, marched to the sheriff court near Candleriggs, inspired by rousing speeches from Helen Crawfurd,

John Maclean and William Gallacher – who called the women 'Mrs Barbour's Army' (Gallacher 1936, p. 55). As a result, the Rent Restrictions Act 1915 came into force and Mary Barbour 'became a Govan legend' (McShane 1978, p. 75).

In June 1916, with Helen Crawford and *Agnes Dollan, Mary Barbour took part in the founding of the Women's Peace Crusade. In 1920 she stood as Labour Party candidate for Fairfield ward, Govan, and swept in on the new women's vote as the first Labour woman councillor in Glasgow. Devoting her energies to improving women's daily lives, she successfully established municipal baths, wash-houses, laundries and crèches, play areas and free school milk for children. Supported by Dr Norah Wattie, she campaigned for victims of TB and founded the Women's Welfare and Advisory Clinic in September 1926, the first family planning clinic for married women in Glasgow, staffed by women doctors and nurses. She served on Glasgow Corporation as the first woman bailie (1924–27) and was one of Glasgow's first woman magistrates. After her retirement in 1931, she continued to be active in the GHA and in the SCWG. A true pioneering leader on Clydeside, she was held in high regard by her local community. ACa

• Gallacher Memorial Library, GCU, Mary Barbour collection: Election Address, Fairfield Ward, Govan, 2 Nov. 1920; Crawfurd, H. (n.d.) Unpublished Autobiography (copy also in Marx Memorial Library, London); Rent Strikes history; Mitchell Library, Glasgow: *Govan Press* 22 Oct.–5 Nov. 1920, 11 April 1958 (obit.); *Glasgow Bulletin* 23 Jan. 1918. Gallacher, W. (1936) *Revolt on the Clyde*; Horne, R. (1972) 'The great rents victory', *Scottish Marxist*, 2; McShane, H. (1978) *No Mean Fighter*; Melling, J. (1983) *Rent Strikes 1890–1916*; *ODNB* (2004); Sheffield Film Cooperative (1984) *Red Skirts on Clydeside* (Scottish Film Archive); Smyth, J. (1980) 'Working Class Women in Glasgow during the First World War', Diss., Univ. of Glasgow, (1992) 'Rents, Peace, Votes – Working class women and political activity in the First World War', in E. Gordon and E. Breitenbach (eds) *Out of Bounds: Women in Scottish Society 1800–1945*. Private information (Mary Barbour, grand-daughter).

BARLASS, Kate *see* **DOUGLAS, Katherine** (fl. 1437)

BARNARD, Lady Anne, n. **Lindsay,** born Balcarres, Fife, 27 Nov. 1750, died London 6 May 1825. Writer of songs, journals and letters. Daughter of Anne Dalrymple of Castleton, and James Lindsay, 5th Earl of Balcarres.

The eldest of eleven children, Anne Lindsay spent her childhood in Fife. The family often spent the winter in Edinburgh, where Lady Anne was admitted to a social circle which included David Hume, Henry Mackenzie and Lord Monboddo. She moved to London to live with her sister, Margaret, and was courted by, but refused, Henry Dundas, Secretary of State for War in Pitt's first administration. In 1793, she married Andrew Barnard, son of Thomas, Bishop of Limerick: he was 28 and she 43. Andrew Barnard, with Dundas's patronage, was appointed colonial secretary to the Cape of Good Hope. He died at the Cape in 1807 and Lady Anne spent the rest of her life in London.

Lady Anne became famous for her ballad 'Auld Robin Gray', but her letters and journals may prove her most enduring monument. She explains the ballad's beginnings in a song sung by an eccentric family friend, **Sophia Johnston** (c. 1730–c. 1810), in a letter to Sir Walter Scott, 8 July 1823. Before this, her composition was a family secret. 'Auld Robin Gray' tells the story of Jenny, who, believing her lover, Jamie, to have been lost at sea, marries an aged suitor, Robin Gray, to help support her straitened family. Jamie returns after the wedding: Jenny and he meet tenderly and part. The song gives us a movingly stoical speaker, aware of the realities of female lives. Unfortunately, two sentimental continuations followed; in the second, Robin Gray gives his deathbed blessing to the young couple who marry and live happily at last.

Lady Anne's letters to Henry Dundas from South Africa are those of a private individual writing to a great public figure; much of her tolerant advice was good policy. Her letters to her sisters are more social but they too contain precise observation. There are also extensive diaries and journals from the Cape and a journal of her early family life. A volume of poetry by Lady Anne and her sisters, Lady Elizabeth Hardwicke and Lady Margaret Burges (Fordyce), *Lays of the Lindsays*, was originally intended for the Bannatyne Club but withdrawn by Scott at the ladies' request and replaced by one which contained only 'Auld Robin Gray' and its continuations. Lady Anne's awareness of the opinion that it was shameful and presumptuous for women to publish poetic compositions probably inhibited her real talent, if we judge from the first, tough, version of 'Auld Robin Gray'. As it is, we may wonder that the woman who could tell Henry Dundas what he ought to do, hesitated to tell anyone that she had written a song. DAMcM

• NLS: Crawford and Balcarres papers.
Barnard, A., Works as above and see *HSWW* (Bibl.).
Anderson, W. (1863) *The Scottish Nation*; Burman, J. (1990) *In*

the Footsteps of Lady Anne Barnard; Elwood, A. K. C. (1843) *Memoirs of the Literary Ladies of England*; Fairbridge, D. (1924) *Lady Anne Barnard at the Cape of Good Hope, 1797–1802*; Lindsay, A. C. (1849) *Lives of the Lindsays*; Masson, M. (1948) *Lady Anne Barnard*; Mills, G. M. (1950) *First Ladies of the Cape*; *ODNB* (2004); Tytler, S. and Watson, J. L. (eds) (1871) *The Songstresses of Scotland*, 2 vols.

BARNETT, Isobel Morag, Lady, n. **Marshall,** born Aberdeen 30 June 1918, died Loughborough 20 Oct. 1980. Doctor and broadcaster. Daughter of Jane Minty, and Robert McNab Marshall, medical practitioner.

Isobel Marshall grew up in Glasgow, attending Laurel Bank School. She excelled as an athlete and made a name for herself in sporting circles there and at the University of Glasgow, where she qualified as a doctor in 1940. In 1941 she married Geoffrey Barnett, later Lord Mayor of Leicester, who was knighted in 1953. Isobel Barnett's career took a sudden change of direction when she was spotted by the BBC and took part in a programme called *Town Forum*. Immediately popular, she became one of the four original panellists on the long-running television quiz series, *What's My Line?* from 1953 to 1963. With her ladylike manner, elegance and intelligence, she became a national celebrity on the emerging medium of television. As well as having a natural character for broadcasting, adaptable and witty, Isobel Barnett drew attention to herself because of her chic dress style and dramatic jewellery (almost stage props), large bangles, brooches and necklaces. She also wrote books, some for children, worked on radio, and was a sought-after guest speaker and bazaar opener. She served as a magistrate and JP. Latterly much out of the spotlight, she was convicted in 1980 for a very minor shop-lifting offence, and committed suicide a few days later. LS
• Barnett, I. (1956) *My Life Line*, (1965) *Exploring London*, Shell Junior Guide; Barnett, I. and Meadows, J. (1972) *Lady Barnett's Quiz Book: let's have a quiz*.
Gallagher, J. (1982) *Isobel Barnett, Portrait of a Lady*.

BARNS-GRAHAM, Wilhelmina (Willie), m. **Lewis,** born St Andrews 8 June 1912, died St Andrews 26 Jan. 2004. Painter. Daughter of Wilhelmina Bayne Meldrum, and Allan Barns-Graham, landowner.

Wilhelmina Barns-Graham grew up in St Andrews, the eldest child in a minor landed family. Her father opposed her childhood wish to be an artist and only the intervention of her maternal aunt, Mary Niesh, enabled her to attend Edinburgh College of Art from 1931. Her work flourished under the influence of tutors such as William Gillies and John Maxwell. In 1940 she used a scholarship to travel to St Ives, where a close community of modernist artists had emerged, and remained there, working with Ben Nicholson and Barbara Hepworth, and taking a full part in the creativity and politics of St Ives, being 'at the heart of one of the most innovative movements in art' in Britain (Green 2001, p. 274). Wilhelmina Barns-Graham developed as an abstract painter, always willing to experiment, and fascinated by mixing abstract and figurative forms. She did not, however, at that time gain the reputation which was later seen as deserved, but was overshadowed by other, usually male, St Ives artists. She married author David Lewis (b. 1922) in 1949, but the marriage broke down, formally ending in 1963. In 1960, Willie Barns-Graham had inherited Balmungo estate near St Andrews from her supportive Aunt Mary, and began to divide her time between the Fife coast in winter and the Cornish coast in summer. By the late 1970s, renewed attention was focused on the St Ives artists, particularly on their early work. A major exhibition held at the Tate in 1985 gave only a small place to Wilhelmina Barns-Graham, but the retrospective exhibition of her work organised by the City of Edinburgh Museums and Galleries (1989) marked the first significant reconsideration of her career, and the start of a period in which her work received much more critical attention. She produced some of her most confident and admired work in the last years of her long life, when the first major monograph was devoted to her (Green 2001). FJ
• Green, L. (2001) *W. Barns-Graham: a studio life*; *The Guardian*, 29 Jan. 2004 (obit.); *The Scotsman*, 2 Feb. 2004 (obit.); *W. Barns-Graham: retrospective 1940–1989*, exhibition catalogue, 1989, intro. by D. Hall; *Wilhelmina Barns-Graham: an enduring image*, exhibition catalogue, 2000.

BARR, Rev. Elizabeth Brown, born Glasgow 2 Oct. 1905, died Glasgow 23 June 1995. United Free Church of Scotland minister. Daughter of Martha Stephen, and James Barr, UFC minister and Labour MP.

Educated at Bellahouston Academy, Glasgow, Elizabeth Brown Barr graduated MA from the University of Glasgow in 1925. She qualified as a primary school teacher, starting work at Wolseley Street School in 1926. Influenced in her formative years by the traditions and ethos of the United Free Church (UFC), at university she was a member of the Student Christian Movement (SCM), which fostered progressive Christian social ideals, including a measure of gender equality. In 1929, a minority of UFC members (led by James Barr) chose not to enter into union with the established Church of Scotland, and in 1930 the UFC (Continuing) passed a resolution that any member in full communion was eligible to hold any office. For the first time in Britain, ordination to eldership and ministry was open to women in a Presbyterian church. Elizabeth Brown Barr was encouraged to consider this path, and although others urged her to take a 'saner view' she was accepted as a candidate for ministry. She graduated BD and was licensed to preach on 12 September 1933. After ministering in rural Auchterarder (1935–43), she served in Clydebank (1943–55) during and after the ravages of war. She was minister of Glasgow Central UFC, Anderston, 1955–68. In 1966, she also took on Miller Memorial Church, Maryhill, and remained there until her retirement in 1975. In 1960 she was Moderator of the UFC General Assembly: an appointment of symbolic importance during the 400th Anniversary of the Reformation in Scotland. She herself said: 'men and women are one in Christ, and we do wrong to separate them in describing the life, work and witness of the Church' (Thomson 1965, p. 4). LO

• Barr, E. B. (1960–1) 'A woman looks at the ministry', *Reformed and Presbyterian World*, 26.
ODNB (2004); Thomson, D. P. (ed.) (1965) *Women in Ministry* (pamphlet); UFC, *Stedfast* Magazine 1960–1, 1995.

BARRY, James, probably born **Margaret Bulkley**, Dublin c. 1790, died London 25 July 1865. Army medical officer and reformer. Daughter (according to recent research) of Mary Ann Bulkley, and Jeremiah Bulkley, grocer.

Mary Ann Bulkley was rejected by her husband, and with her two daughters appealed to her artist brother, James Barry, in London for help. His death intestate in 1806, and the patronage of his friends the Earl of Buchan and the radical Venezuelan General Francisco Miranda, apparently allowed the child formerly known as Margaret Bulkley to transform her sexual identity and future prospects in registering for a medical degree at the University of Edinburgh in 1809 in the name of Jacobus (James) Barry, with a birth date of 1799. Rose (1977) notes that the name 'James Miranda Steuart Barry' was inscribed in Barry's school books, honouring these patrons, but the middle names were not subsequently used. Under the same name,

in 1812 Barry submitted a dissertation to Edinburgh, and after further study at Guy's and St Thomas's Hospitals, London, passed the army medical board examination, then giving a birth date of 1795.

James Barry's outstanding and controversial career in military medicine, in spite of a slight physique and dandyish appearance, has been frequently related. In 1816, posted to the Cape Colony, Dr Barry became physician to the Governor-General, Lord Charles Somerset, forming a friendship with him which survived ridicule and sexual rumours. As Colonial Medical Inspector from 1822, Dr Barry undertook an extensive programme of medical reform in Cape Town, performing a successful Caesarean section there in July 1826, a feat rarely achieved. From April 1831, Dr Barry was posted as staff surgeon to Jamaica and later St Helena, but following tension over projected reforms, was ordered home and demoted. Reinstated, Dr Barry served in the West Indies and Malta, and in 1855 successfully treated sick and injured soldiers from the Crimea in Corfu, before travelling to inspect the Scutari hospital (and administer a scolding to Florence Nightingale). Posted to Canada as Inspector General of Hospitals in 1857, Dr Barry returned to England for health reasons in 1859. After Barry's death in London, the sensational evidence of the woman who laid out the body, stating that it was female, was immediately circulated, but remains uncertain.

James Barry, or Margaret Bulkley, has appealed to successive generations of historians, novelists, dramatists and film directors, some emphasising his/her Scottish training. One view identifies James Barry with a tradition of cross-dressing women, encouraged by radical and unorthodox patrons, in order to take up a demanding career closed to women. Recent scrutiny of the evidence suggests, however, that James Barry had intersexual characteristics; he or she consciously investigated these in his/her dissertation on hernias in women, a condition that could lead to the discovery of mistaken sexual identity, due to the presence of undescended or partially descended testicles: 'at the heart of his thesis is a close comparative anatomy of the reproductive zones in men and women' (Holmes 2002, pp. 306–7). James Barry's presence in this dictionary may be thought marginal, for the brevity of the Scottish connection (though Barry is often numbered among Scots) and indeterminate sexual identity. But this remarkable life is a reminder of the fluidity of such definitions.

It seems likely that the child brought up as Margaret Bulkley *chose* to live as a male doctor, scientist and humanitarian reformer. JR

• Holmes, R. (2002) *Scanty Particulars. The Life of Dr James Barry*; Kubba, A. K. and Young M. (2001) 'The life, work and gender of Dr James Barry', *Proc. Roy. Coll. Phys. Edin.* 31, pp. 352–6; *ODNB* (2004); Rae, I. (1958) *The Strange Story of Dr James Barry*; Rose, J. (1977) *The Perfect Gentleman: the remarkable life of Dr James Miranda Barry*.

BAXTER, Etheldreda (Ethel), n. **Adam,** born Roseisle, Moray, 22 Oct. 1883, died Elgin 16 August 1963. Businesswoman and cook. Daughter of Elizabeth Farquhar, and Andrew Adam, ploughman.

Ethel Adam was the second of a line of Baxter women whose initiative and skills helped to create the internationally known food company. Born on a farm and trained as a nurse, on 11 November 1914 she married one of her patients, William A. Baxter (1877–1973). His mother, **Margaret Baxter** (n. **Duncan,** 1852–81), and her husband George had a grocery shop in Fochabers through which they sold Margaret's renowned jams and marmalades. Ethel Baxter saw the opportunity to expand, and persuaded her husband to borrow money to open a factory in 1916. While William travelled as a salesman, Ethel worked in the kitchens. She was involved in all aspects of production, from cooking to machinery repairs and the management of workers. She tried out new recipes, looking for better ways to preserve the flavour in canned and bottled products. Her Royal Game soup, created in 1929, became one of the company's best-known products. Under Ethel and William Baxter's direction, the company's product range expanded and was sold to leading London stores such as Harrods and Fortnum and Mason, then to America and throughout the British Empire. Baxter's remained a family firm. Later Baxter women have followed Ethel's example, playing a leading part in the world-wide success of the firm. FJ

• 'Recipe for a Food Giant', in *Scottish Memories*, Sept. 1997; (1980) *Baxters of Speyside*; *ODNB* (2004) (Baxter, William A.).

www.baxters.com

BAXTER, Evelyn Vida, MBE, born Upper Largo, Fife, 29 March 1879, died Upper Largo 1 Oct. 1959. Ornithologist. Daughter of Mary Constance MacPherson, and John Henry Baxter.

Fascinated by birds, Evelyn Baxter wrote her first essay, 'The Redstart', as a child. Although lacking scientific training, she and her life-long friend **Leonora Jeffrey Rintoul** (1875–1953) made recording visits to the Isle of May, where they gathered the first records of rare warblers. Observing resident and migratory birds, they revolutionised bird migration theory by relating it to weather patterns. Their monumental co-authored classic, *The Birds of Scotland*, compiled between 1905 and 1952, included details of species, varieties, habitat and frequency of indigenous and migratory birds. The two women helped establish the Scottish Ornithologists' Club in 1938, becoming joint Presidents. Throughout the Second World War, Evelyn Baxter worked on the Fife Committee of the Woman's Land Army. A life-long interest was the SWRI, for which she travelled across Scotland, giving talks and demonstrations: a scholarship has been established in her name. Her boundless energy was also displayed as 'skip' of a Ladies' Curling Club for fifty years. She was made MBE in 1945, LLD University of Glasgow in 1955, and was the recipient of the British Ornithologists' Union Award in 1959. LS

• Baxter, E. V. and Rintoul, L. J. (1928) *The Geographical Distribution and Status of Birds in Scotland*, (1935) *A Vertebrate Fauna of the Forth*, (1953) *The Birds of Scotland. Their History, Distribution and Migration*. Eggeling, W. J. (1985) *The Isle of May*.

BAXTER, Mary Ann, born Dundee 4 May 1801, died Dundee 19 Dec. 1884. Philanthropist, founder of University College, Dundee (1884). Daughter of Elizabeth Gorrill (or Gorell), and William Baxter, textile merchant and manufacturer.

Mary Ann Baxter, one of eight children, was born into a wealthy family. When she was 54, her brother David became chairman of Baxter's, subsequently the world's largest textile manufacturing firm with a workforce of 4,000. She and David were without dependants; they had 'the means and opportunity to do good' (Dundee *Advertiser*, 1884) and they gave generously. She supported missions in Central Africa, India, China and New Guinea, buying a steamer (called *Ellengowan*, after the family home) to take missionaries to New Guinea, where the Baxter River was named after her. She endowed an independent chapel in Letham, Fife, and a secular school with teacher's salary. She led subscription lists for the Dundee YMCA, the Sailors' Home and Dundee Royal Infirmary children's ward. When family members died, she kept up their subscriptions. With David and her sister Eleanor she funded the creation of the 35-acre Baxter Park for the use of mill-workers.

Always interested in education, she endowed scholarships at the University of Edinburgh. When the idea of a college in Dundee was promoted by John Boyd Baxter, Mary Ann's second cousin and life-long friend, she donated £140,000 of the £150,000 needed to found University College; he was the negotiator but she called the tune. The Deed of Endowment specified that the college should be for 'persons of both sexes and the study of science, literature and the fine arts' – but not divinity. Further, no student, professor or other officer should have to declare their religion (at a time when non-conformists could not graduate at some universities). The college was to be open to the working classes. It should not be part of the University of St Andrews and it should have enough money to be successful. She supervised the constitution, and chose the site and college secretary. She was a devout Congregationalist and an intelligent and determined woman. Her obituaries describe her as quiet and unostentatious. 'She first satisfied herself that she was doing right and then it was a real and manifest pleasure for her to give' (Dundee *Courier* 1884). When she died, she still had a quarter of a million pounds to leave to her nephew. IMH

• Cooke, A. J. (ed.) (1980) *Baxter's of Dundee*, Dundee Univ. Dept. Extra Mural Education; Dundee *Advertiser*, 20 Dec. 1884 (obit.); Dundee *Courier*, 20 Dec. 1884 (obit.); *ODNB* (2004); Southgate, D. (1982) *University Education in Dundee*. Personal information.

BEDDOWS, Charlotte Rankin Maule, n. **Stevenson,** m1 **Watson,** m2 **Beddows,** born Edinburgh 22 Oct. 1887, died North Berwick 22 August 1976. Golfer and hockey player. Daughter of Catherine Maule, and James Stevenson, general merchant.

Charlotte Stevenson had a remarkable career under three names. As a teenager, she played hockey for Scotland from 1905, captaining the team several times; she was president of the SWHA 1925–31. However, she is most remembered for her long and distinguished career in golf. Practically self-taught and playing regularly against men, she developed skills as a long hitter. Aged 17 and still in pigtails, she fought her way to the semi-final of the 1905 Scottish Women's Championship. At 19, she was champion of Craigmillar Park Golf Club and runner-up in the Gibson Cup (Edinburgh Town Council) over the Braid Hills golf course. A member of several local clubs, she won the Scottish

Championship in 1920–2 and 1929, and was runner-up in 1923 and again in 1950, aged 62. While Joyce Wethered and Cecil (Cecilia) Leitch were dominating English golf, she flew the flag for Scotland, playing in the Home Internationals 21 times between 1913 and 1951. Having married optician John Watson, she played in the first Curtis Cup side in 1932, aged 45, as Mrs J. B. Watson. She later married Edward Beddows, Brigadier, RAMC. A life-long golf enthusiast, she organised maintenance of the Gullane course during the Second World War. JLG

• George, J. (2003) 'Women and golf in Scotland', PhD, Univ. of Edinburgh; Low, S. (2003) *Gullane Ladies' Golf Club*; 'Sports and pastimes', *The Ladies' Field*, 9 Oct. 1909; Wilson, E. (1961) *A Gallery of Women Golfers*.

BEGG, Isabella (Isobel), n. **Burn(es)s,** born Mount Oliphant 27 July 1771, died Alloway 4 Dec. 1858. Schoolmistress, sister of Robert Burns. Daughter of Agnes Broun, and William Burness, farmer.

Isabella was the youngest child of the Burness family of four sons and three daughters, and the longest lived. She was the closest to her father and, after his death, Robert Burns, 12 years her senior, became a second father to her. As a child she had a sweet voice and would often sing her brother's songs over to him in order that he could hear how they sounded. On 9 December 1793 she was married at the family home at Mossgiel farm to John Begg, a quarrier in Mossgiel. He died in 1813 after being thrown from his horse, leaving her with six sons and three daughters to raise. To earn her living she opened a school at Ormiston and later at Tranent.

In 1842, admirers of Robert Burns, including Lord Houghton, Thomas Carlyle and Robert Chambers, set up a fund to keep Isabella Begg in her old age and, on the authority of Queen Victoria, she was provided with a pension. In 1843, with her two unmarried daughters, Agnes and Isabella, she moved from Tranent to Bridge House in Alloway, where she remained until her death. Isabella Begg had a remarkable memory and during her lifetime many people came to see her to learn about her brother, whom she outlived by more than 60 years. Her recollections contributed to and influenced many of the later biographies written about Robert Burns, in particular the account by Robert Chambers. After her death, her two daughters took on that responsibility. Visitors came to Bridge House from all walks of life, including several presidents of the USA. MB

• Lindsay, M. (1995) *The Burns Encyclopedia*; Mackay, J. (1992) *Burns*; Ross, J. D. (1894) *Burnsiana,* vol. 3.

BELL, Lily *see* **PEARCE, Isabella Bream (Lily Bell)** (1859–1929)

BERNSTEIN, Marion, born England 1847, died Glasgow 6 Feb. 1906. Writer and music teacher. Daughter of Lydia Pulsford, and Theodore Bernstein, music teacher.

Marion Bernstein and her siblings were born in England. By the 1870s–80s, she was living in Glasgow's West End with her brother and widowed mother, teaching piano and singing. She is now remembered for her writing. Verses commenting on current affairs were published from the 1870s in the *Glasgow Weekly Mail* (*HHGW*, p. 84). In the preface to her poetry collection, *Mirren's Musings* (1876), Marion Bernstein refers to a 'long period of physical affliction': some of this writing is melancholic, in contrast to the self-assured and humorous verse popular in the *Mail*: 'There were female chiefs in the Cabinet/Much better than male I am sure/And the Commons were three parts feminine/While the Lords were seen no more!' (Alexander 2000, p. 81).

No documentary record of involvement with the local Jewish community can be traced. Marion Bernstein's religious beliefs appear from her writing to be more Christian in orientation, so her relation with possible Jewish ethnicity is elusive. She never married; in 1901 she was living with her widowed sister in the city centre (and persuaded the census enumerator to describe her as a 'professor of theory and harmony').

Marion Bernstein had forthright opinions on women's rights and was unafraid of defending them in print. Her views provided a legacy for current political activists in Scotland (ibid., pp. 81–8). LF

• Mitchell Library, Glasgow: copies of *Mirren's Musings*; GPO directories.
Bernstein, M., Verses in T. Leonard (1990) *Radical Renfrew.*
Alexander, W. (2000) 'Women and the Scottish Parliament', in A. Coote (ed.) *New Gender Agenda*; Census, Glasgow.

BETHOC (Beatrice), Daughter of Somerled, died c. 1207. Prioress of Iona. Daughter of Somerled, Lord of the Isles.

Bethoc was sister to Reginald, founder of the Augustinian convent on Iona. Her full title was 'Bethag, daughter of Somhairle, son of GilleBrigde, Prioress of Icollumkill'. She was the nunnery's first prioress, c. 1200 to 1207. The inscription on her tomb, still visible in the 17th century, read '*Behag niin Schorle vic Ilvird Priorissa*' (Steer and Bannerman 1977, p. 90). The Iona Psalter in the NLS may have been owned by Bethoc, since it is claimed to have been illuminated in Oxford in the 13th century and commissioned by an Augustinian canoness with a special interest in Iona saints. KP

• NLS: Iona Psalter, MS 10,000.
McDonald, R. A. (1999) 'The foundation and patronage of nunneries by native elites in twelfth and early thirteenth century Scotland', in E. Ewan and M. Meikle (eds) *Women in Scotland, c. 1100–c. 1750*, (Bibl.); Steer, K. A. and Bannerman, J. W. M. (eds) (1977) *Late Medieval Monumental Sculpture in the West Highlands.*

BETHUNE, Margaret, n. **Peebles,** born Largo, Fife, 2 Oct. 1820, died Largo 10 April 1887. Midwife. Daughter of Margaret Walker, linen worker, and Andrew Peebles, weaver.

In 1844, Margaret Peebles married coal-miner William Bethune. Widowed in 1852 and with two young children and her aged mother to support, she moved from Largo to Edinburgh to seek midwifery training, returning to her family early in 1853. For the rest of her life she was midwife to her community, logging her work in a casebook. Her record of 1,296 labours, all within the parish of Largo, shows that by 1859 she attended the majority of the parish births. Her clients represented most social classes in the village and the local doctor responded to her calls for assistance. An earlier example of a casebook was compiled by **Christian Cowper** of Thurso (before 1766–1843). Mrs Cowper recorded 3,948 deliveries between 1786 and 1843, the first three in Edinburgh, where she may have undertaken training. Her clients represented all ranks of Thurso society, including the Countess of Ross and the daughter-in-law of Sir John Sinclair, who inspired the Statistical Account of Scotland (1791–9). Both casebooks are valuable sources in nursing history. BEM

• NAS: GD1/812/1: M. Bethune, Casebook, 1853–87; Royal College of Physicians of Edinburgh: Manuscripts, Cowper, Christian 1, Casebook.
Mortimer, B. (2002) 'The nurse in Edinburgh c. 1760–1860: the impact of commerce and professionalisation', PhD, Univ. of Edinburgh; *ODNB* (2004).

BIGGAR, Helen Manson, m. **Montlake,** born Partick 25 May 1909, died London 28 March 1953. Sculptor, film-maker, theatre designer. Daughter of

Florence Hadden Manson, and Hugh Biggar, architect or builder.

Helen Biggar was a daughter of the Glasgow Left. Her father was an early member of the ILP and her uncle was John Biggar, Glasgow councillor and Lord Provost. She herself became a member of the CPGB. Serious accidents in childhood left her physically short, with a severe and, at times, debilitating, curvature of the spine. She trained at Glasgow School of Art and on graduation took a studio in Glasgow where she worked as a sculptor.

She is best remembered as the co-director, along with Norman McLaren, of the experimental film *Camera Makes Whoopee* (1935) and the classic agit-prop film *Hell Unlimited* (1936). She also directed a drama-documentary *Glasgow's May Day: Challenge to Fascism* (1938), using a cast drawn from the Glasgow Workers' Theatre Group (GWTG), one of the most adventurous of the left-wing amateur theatre groups active in Scotland in the 1930s. After that collaboration she became an active member of GWTG, designing the group's celebrated production of Jack Lindsay's declamatory poem *On Guard for Spain* (from around 1938). She also designed and co-produced *The Masque of Spain*, a huge pageant involving some 500 performers at Scotstoun Showground on 26 August 1939 in support of the Spanish Aid Committee. GWTG was one of five groups that came together in 1941 to form Glasgow Unity Theatre, where Helen Biggar continued to work and emerged as an influential designer, with productions including a pageant to mark the centenary of the co-operative movement (1944) and *The Lower Depths* (1945). She was a member and then chair of Glasgow Kino, involved particularly with the film society's bid to take their films out to a wider audience.

In 1946, Helen Biggar moved to London and was joined in her Clapham studio by colleagues from Glasgow, artists Robert Frame and her future husband Eli Montlake; they married in October 1948. She continued to design for Glasgow Unity and London Unity, and in 1950 joined Ballet Rambert as wardrobe mistress, becoming costume designer for the company in early 1953. She produced sculpture throughout her life, including 'The kneeling girl' (1945) and 'Mother and child' (1947), and is remembered for her pioneering blend of politics and art. AS

• *ODNB* (2004); Shepherd A. (1978) 'Helen Biggar and Norman McLaren', *New Edinburgh Review* 40, pp. 25–6, (1997) 'Helen Manson Biggar (1909–53)', *Scot. Lab. Hist. Rev.*, 10, pp. 4–6, (1998) 'The Biggar boys', *Scot. Lab. Hist. Rev.*, 11, pp. 12–13.

BILLINGTON-GREIG, Teresa Mary, born Preston 15 Oct. 1876, died London 21 Oct. 1964. Suffragist. Daughter of Helen Wilson, and William Billington, shipping clerk.

Educated in Blackburn, Teresa Billington trained as a pupil teacher in Manchester and became an elementary school teacher there in 1903. Brought up a Roman Catholic, she rejected first Catholicism and then the teaching of Christianity in schools. Emmeline Pankhurst helped her transfer to a Jewish school, to prevent dismissal. Recruited by Emmeline Pankhurst for the WSPU, she began to speak for the women's suffrage cause, and in April 1904 helped organise the Manchester teachers' equal pay league. Pankhurst persuaded Keir Hardie to hire her as an ILP organiser, and for two years she combined this with organising the WSPU's London-based activities, being the first suffragette to go to Holloway Prison. In autumn 1906, she was asked to organise WSPU branches in Scotland. On 8 February 1907, in Glasgow, she married Glasgow businessman and socialist Frederick Lewis Greig (1875–1961). Their pre-nuptial agreement included both adopting the name Billington-Greig. They had one daughter, Fiona (b. 1915).

Teresa Billington-Greig had a considerable impact on the GWSAWS; her powerful speaking rapidly converted *Helen Fraser to WSPU policy. Both women campaigned in the Aberdeen South by-election (February 1907) when the WSPU opposed all Liberal candidates, whatever their views on women's suffrage. When the WSPU Scottish Council was established (June 1907), Teresa Billington-Greig was secretary, *Isabella Pearce treasurer, and Helen Fraser organiser for Scotland. Teresa Billington-Greig favoured a democratic organisation, but Emmeline and Christabel Pankhurst appeared to resent her influence within Scotland. As a result, with Charlotte Despard, she left the WSPU and founded the WFL, for which she campaigned actively throughout Scotland with Isabella Pearce, *Maggie Moffat, *Anna Munro and *Eunice Murray. She campaigned not only for women's suffrage but for full sexual equality, challenging the double standard of morality and the inequitable situation of women in marriage and employment. Her writings analysed male oppression of women, and the misogyny and 'sex prejudice' they faced (McPhee and FitzGerald 1987, p. 115). She left the WFL in December 1910, for not living up to its democratic and non-violent aspirations, putting her case in *The Militant Suffrage Movement* (1911) and in freelance speaking and writing. After briefly separating from her husband in 1913–14, she returned to Glasgow and during the war sometimes substituted for her husband at his billiard works. In 1923, the Billington-Greigs moved to London. She maintained contact with the WFL, occasionally resuming activism, as in 1928 and 1937, and in her final years encouraged the Six Point Group, established in 1921 to continue the campaign for equal rights. Despite her rejection of militant suffragism, Teresa Billington-Greig's impact on the Scottish women's suffrage movement was considerable, and the WFL maintained a strong presence in Scotland long after 1918. J R

• Women's Library, London: Billington-Greig MSS. *AGC*; Eustance, C. (1993) ' "Daring to be free": the evolution of women's political identities in the Women's Freedom League, 1906–1930', DPhil, Univ. of York; Harrison, B. (1987) *Prudent Revolutionaries: portraits of British feminists between the wars*; Holton, S. S. (1986) *Feminism and Democracy: women's suffrage and reform politics in Britain, 1900–1918*; McPhee, C. and Fitzgerald, A. (1987) (eds) *The Non-violent Militant: selected writings of Teresa Billington-Greig*; *ODNB* (2004); *WSM*.

BIRD, Isabella Lucy,‡ m. **Bishop,** born Boroughbridge, Yorkshire, 15 Oct. 1831, died Edinburgh 7 Oct. 1904. Travel writer. Daughter of Dorothy Lawson, and Rev. Edward Bird.

Brought up in English vicarages, Isabella Bird was given a broad education by her parents. From childhood she suffered from a spinal complaint and, in 1854, doctors prescribed a sea-voyage to North America which resulted in her first travelogue. After her father died, with her mother and sister Henrietta she settled in Edinburgh in 1859, which was mostly her home base thereafter. She began her emigration scheme for Highland crofters, established a shelter for itinerant cabmen, and continued writing on religious and literary topics and social conditions.

In 1871, Isabella Bird went on a six-month cruise to North America and Europe which temporarily relieved ill-health and depression, her apparent reaction to staying at home. After a miserable visit to the Antipodes in 1872, she was exhilarated by a hurricane in the South Pacific and daring exploits in Hawaii. Her health improved dramatically. The adventures continued in the Rockies where she went climbing with 'Rocky

Mountain Jim', rode alone over 600 miles in wintry weather through virgin territory, and lived for months in an isolated log cabin. Visiting Japan in 1878, she suffered great privation so that she could reach the Ainu tribe in the wildernesses of Hokkaido. (A permanent exhibition in Nanyo city still commemorates this trip.) In Malaya in 1879, she enjoyed a dinner party with two apes who 'required no conversational efforts' (Bird 1883, p. 307).

Ostensibly travelling for her health, she discovered a way of escaping the confines of conventional society in the wilder parts of the world. Daringly riding astride, wearing a bloomer suit, she preferred a 'journey alone on horseback with only saddle bags and a native as guide' (Bird 2002, p. 101). At last she had found her niche as a travel writer of distinction, justifying her enjoyment of challenging travel as 'a woman's right to do what she can do well' (Checkland 1996). Triumphs and hardships are vividly conveyed and rapturous descriptions of mountains and jungles are accompanied by meticulous practical details of her expeditions. Her popular accounts of the early adventures were based on letters to Henrietta, and are livelier in style than later travelogues after her sister's death in 1880, which much distressed her.

In 1881, she married Dr John Bishop, ten years her junior; he died five years later. In 1887, she trained as a medical auxiliary to help found memorial hospitals to her sister and husband in India, and lectured throughout the UK on the need for medical missions. In 1889, she resumed her travels, spending two years in Tibet and the Middle East. On her return she was consulted by Gladstone about the Christians in Armenia. From 1894, she spent more than three years touring the Far East, taking many photographs. Her last adventure was in Morocco at the age of 70. She died with her trunks packed ready for another journey, finding 'society . . . fatiguing and *clattering*. My soul hankers for solitude and freedom' (Bird 2002, p. 205). The first female Fellow of the RGS (1892) and of the SRGS (1892), Isabella Bishop left her books to the University of Edinburgh and donated several Ainu objects to the RSM. Her tombstone is in the Dean cemetery. J R R

• NLS: MSS 2621–64: Isabella Bird Papers: 1852–1901 (John Stuart Blackie Collection); Archives of John Murray (Publishers); RGS: Photographic negatives of China. Bird, I. L. (1856) *The Englishwoman in America*, (1883) *The Golden Chersonese and the Way Thither*, (1984) (ed. Havely, C. P.) *This Grand Beyond*, (1997) (ed. Checkland, O.)

Collected Travel Writings of Isabella Bird, 12 vols, (2002) (ed. Chubbuck, K.) *Letters to Henrietta*.
Barr, P. (1970, re-ed. 1984) *A Curious Life for a Lady*; Checkland, O. (1996) *Isabella Bird and 'A Woman's Right to Do What She Can Do Well'* (Bibl.); *ODNB* (2004); Stoddart, A. (1906) *The Life of Isabella Bird (Mrs Bishop)*.

BLACKBURN, Jemima, n. **Wedderburn,** born Edinburgh 1 May 1823, died Roshven 9 August 1909. Painter, illustrator, ornithologist. Daughter of Isabella Clerk of Penicuik, and James Wedderburn, Solicitor-General for Scotland.

Born six months after her father's death, Jemima Wedderburn was the seventh child in this well-connected family (her cousin was the physicist James Clerk Maxwell). A delicate child, she was encouraged to draw and treasured a copy of Bewick's *British Birds* given to her at the age of four. She sketched her pets and on a visit to London in her teens met Sir Edwin Landseer (1802–73), who told her he could teach her nothing about painting animals. Her narrative paintings, often including portrayals of herself, form a visual record of her times, later complemented by her memoirs which she began in 1899. She experimented with emerging visual media, including photography, an interest shared with her husband, Hugh Blackburn, Professor of Mathematics at the University of Glasgow (1823–1909). They married on 12 June 1849 and had four children between 1850 and 1865, during which time they moved to Roshven on Loch Ailort. Jemima Blackburn travelled in Europe and North Africa, and contributed to an exhibition of British paintings (New York, Philadelphia and Boston, winter 1857–8). She may have shown at the first exhibition of the Society of Female Artists (London 1857: archives lost during the Second World War). Beatrix Potter met her in 1891 and recalls in her own journal (Potter 1989, p. 215) her delight at receiving a copy of *Birds Drawn from Nature* (1862; 1868) when she was ten. Jemima Blackburn's illustrated account of the newly fledged but blind cuckoo despatching a more mature pipit from its nest verified Edward Jenner's earlier claims and prompted Charles Darwin to revise a paragraph in the 6th edition of the *Origin of Species* (1872). EL
• Blackburn, J., Work as above, and [1899] (1988) *Jemima: the paintings and memoirs of a Victorian lady*, R. Fairley, ed. (1993) *Blackburn's Birds: the bird paintings of Jemima Blackburn*, R. Fairley, ed.
Harris, P. and Halsby, J. (eds) (1990) *The Dictionary of Scottish Painters 1600–1960*; *ODNB* (2004); Potter, B. (1989) *The Journal of Beatrix Potter 1881–1897*.

BLACKWELL, Elizabeth, n. **Blachrie,** baptised Aberdeen 22 June 1707, died London possibly 1758. Botanical illustrator and author.
Daughter of Isobel Fordyce, and William Blachrie, merchant.

Elizabeth Blachrie grew up in Aberdeen but ran away to London and married her second cousin, Alexander Blackwell (1709–47), in about 1728. The elopement may have been related to the fact that Alexander Blackwell's father was the Principal of Marischal College. Her father is thought to have been a stocking merchant, but she was connected to some prominent Aberdeen families. Her cousin, **Barbara Black** (fl. 1749–93), who married Alexander's brother, Thomas Blackwell, c. 1749, left an endowment to Marischal College to establish its first chair of chemistry in 1793.

Alexander Blackwell was imprisoned for debt in 1734, after unsuccessfully trying to practise as a physician and a printer. Elizabeth Blackwell approached a leading physician, Richard Mead, and the Royal College of Physicians for a grant to produce and publish a two-volume book, *A Curious Herbal, Containing 500 Cuts of the Most Useful Plants Which Are Now Used in the Practice of Physick*. She used the advance to pay for her husband's release. The herbal contained 500 botanical copperplate illustrations. Each plant's caption gave the common name (and Latin and Greek where applicable) and associated medical uses. Her drawings were based on plants in the Chelsea Physic Garden. The first volume was so well received that she was permitted to present it in person to the Royal College of Physicians.

On 7 September 1742, her son Alexander was baptised in Saint Paul's, Covent Garden. Her husband became an agricultural adviser to the Duke of Chandos but, in 1743, went to Sweden to serve the King as an agricultural and husbandry improver. He became caught up in the political intrigues of his new country and, in 1747, was executed for conspiring to overthrow the Swedish King and government. Elizabeth Blackwell remained in London with her son until at least July 1747. There is no further record of her, although one historian claims she died in 1758 and was buried in Chelsea Old Church. Her work was acclaimed long after her death and was translated into Latin in 1773 as the *Herbarium Blackwellianum* by the Count Palatine, Dr Christopher Jakob Trew and Christian Ludwig. It was unusual for a woman of her time to produce such a book, as it was intended for and used by a professional medical audience. NK

• Aberdeen City Archives: St Nicholas Parish Registers, Births and Christenings 1707–71; St Paul's, Covent Garden, Parish Registers, Births and Christenings 1653–1837.

Blackwell, E. (1737–9) *A Curious Herbal.*

Bruce, J. (1841) *Lives of Eminent Men of Aberdeen*; Henrey, B. (1975) *British Botanical and Horticultural Literature Before 1800*, vol. 2; *ODNB* (2004) (Bibl.).

BLACKWOOD, Margaret, m. **McGrath,** MBE, born Dundee 1 Oct. 1924, died Edinburgh 28 Jan. 1994. Founder of Disability Income Group Scotland. Daughter of Beatrice Marie Orr, and George Blackwood, actuary.

Margaret Blackwood was diagnosed with muscular dystrophy when she was a pupil at St Margaret's School, Edinburgh. After leaving school in 1943, she failed to complete a watchmaking apprenticeship and later wrote that she spent the next 20 years in despair. 'All my dreams were taken from me . . . I had no aim, no goal. I sank into despair' (*Open Door*, 1991).

In 1965 she learned that Megan du Boisson, suffering from multiple sclerosis, had set up the Disability Income Group (DIG) in England, and wrote to her. In 1966, she established DIG Scotland to campaign for a national disability income. In the same year she lobbied Scottish MPs, organised a march along Princes Street and held a rally in Trafalgar Square. According to the *Edinburgh Weekly* (1968), she had turned from 'vegetating invalid to a warrior in a wheelchair'. The 1970 Chronically Sick and Disabled Persons Act introduced a series of financial benefits for disabled people (including mobility allowance and attendance allowance). Margaret Blackwood was nominated Disabled Scot of 1971 and awarded the MBE in 1972. With help from her mother, Bee, she extended her campaign to housing for disabled people. In 1976, the Margaret Blackwood Housing Association (MBHA) opened in Dundee.

Through DIG, Margaret met and worked with Charles McGrath who was almost completely immobilised by ankylosing spondylitis. They were married in 1978 in the Intensive Care Unit at Perth Royal Infirmary. Charles died two weeks later. FY

• Blackwood, M. (1991) Autobiographical article in *Open Door*, Dec. (former newsletter of MBHA), and on website: www.mbha.org.uk

Darling, S. (1994) Funeral tribute, 'Margaret Blackwood McGrath, an appreciation'; *Edinburgh Weekly*, May 1968;

Leighton, P. (2000) 'Margaret Blackwood McGrath', *Profile 2000.*

BLAIR, Catherine Hogg, n. **Shields,** born Bathgate 8 Jan. 1872, died North Berwick 18 Nov. 1946. Suffragette, artist and founder of the SWRI. Daughter of Susan Jemima Bertram, and James Shields, farmer.

The third of six children, Catherine Shields was educated at Bathgate Academy. She married Thomas Blair in 1894 and they set up home at Hoprig Mains Farm, East Lothian, near Macmerry. They had four children and a happy marriage. A life-long campaigner for fairness and democracy, Catherine Blair was an active member of the WSPU, chairing local meetings and writing countless letters to the press, although she did not participate in militancy because of her young family. Thomas supported her and Hoprig Mains Farm provided a secret refuge for Scottish suffragette prisoners released under the 'Cat and Mouse' Act. Concerned about the social and cultural isolation and welfare needs of women in rural areas, and against considerable opposition, she founded the first SWRI at Longniddry in 1917. As a member of the Council of Agriculture (1916), she persuaded the Scottish Department to fund SWRIs throughout Scotland. She campaigned for the development of rural industries and for economic and social initiatives that would make use of women's potential. In 1919 she founded the Mak'Merry pottery studio as a practical example of a co-operative rural enterprise. Her objective was income generation for poor and isolated rural women rather than leisure activities. She painted and embroidered (including a panel depicting the history of the WRI) and made many of her own designs in needlework, furnishings and pottery. She was also involved in setting up the Lothian Hame Arts Guild of craftswomen. In 1932 Catherine and Thomas retired to North Berwick, where a new Mak'Merry Studio was established.

Among her colleagues was **Agnes Henderson Brown (Nannie)** (fl. 1912, died 1944), a member of the WFL and one of six women who walked from Edinburgh to London on the 1912 suffrage march. She was Honorary Secretary of the Edinburgh branch of the Northern Men's Federation for Women's Suffrage (1913), in which her sister **Jessie Brown** (fl. 1912, d. 1937) was also active. Nannie was the SWRI's organiser, 1917–22, and a member of the EWCA. The sisters were among the first women to be seen on bicycles in Scotland and their home in Castle Terrace became a centre of cultural activity. LRM

• BL: Arncliffe-Sennett Collection, vol. 26 (letter); NAS: HH16/44 (letter) and HH16/40 (letter); Museum of London: Women's Suffrage Fellowship collection, (letter).
Blair, C. (n.d.) *Suffragettes and Sacrilege*, WSPU pamphlet, (1917) *An Appeal to Country Women*, SWRI leaflet, (1925) 'The Scottish Movement', in J. W. R. Scott, *The Story of the Women's Institute Movement*, pp. 214–33; (1940) *Rural Journey: a history of the SWRI from cradle to majority*.
Leneman, L. (1991) 'Northern men and votes for women', *History Today*, Dec., pp. 35–41; Sharon, M. (1987) 'Catherine Blair: living her "splendid best" ', *Scottish Home and Country*, Dec. pp. 742–57; SS; *The Scotsman*, 19 Nov. 1946 (obit.).

'BLAK LADY', THE, fl. 1507–8. Woman at the court of James IV.

The 'Blak Lady' featured prominently in two of the most spectacular events of James's reign: the international tournaments, 'The Jousting of the Wild Knight for the Black Lady', held in Edinburgh in June 1507, then reprised in May 1508. The 'goun for the blak lady' was expensive and gorgeous, comprising damask 'flourit with gold' and bordered with yellow and green Flemish taffeta. She was borne in a 'chair triumphale' from the Castle to the tournament ground, accompanied by costumed attendants (Bawcutt 1992, p. 54). The precise nature of her role during the elaborate tournaments of some days' length is open to conjecture, but it is known that she presided over the ceremonies of entry and that, before jousting, combatants were to touch the White Shield in her keeping. Late-medieval tournaments often employed allegorical plots and took the form of theatrical 'battles' for an unattainable queen of beauty. At the banquet at Holyrood Palace on the final day, in a climactic spectacular, the 'Blak Lady' was spirited away in a cloud by means of an ingenious mechanical device.

The same woman is very probably the subject of William Dunbar's poem, 'Of Ane Black Moir (Moor)', commonly dated 1507–8, since it contains an allusion to the tournaments held in those years. He refers to her having 'landet furth of the last schippis' (arrived on recent ships). Scottish shipmasters the Bartons, favourites of the King, are known to have raided Portuguese vessels and the Portuguese were at the time involved in the African slave trade. A number of black people were living at James IV's court, serving chiefly as musicians and entertainers, but the status and identity of the 'Blak Lady' is uncertain. Court records make general mention of, for example, 'Moris lassis' (Moorish lassies) being conveyed from Dunfermline to Edinburgh, and a 'More las was cristinit' (Moor lass was christened). The names 'Elene Moir (Moor)' and 'blak Margaret' do appear, but it cannot be said with certainty that either was the 'Blak Lady' of Dunbar's poem and the tournaments. BF

• Bawcutt, P. (1992*) Dunbar the Makar*; Dunbar, W. (1998) *The Poems*, 2 vols, P. Bawcutt, ed.; Fradenburg, L. O. (1991) *City, Marriage, Tournament: arts of rule in late medieval Scotland*; Macdougall, N. (1997) *James IV*; Mill, A. J. (1927) *Mediaeval Plays in Scotland*.

BLAZE de BURY, Marie Pauline Rose, Baroness, n. **Stuart [Arthur Dudley],** born Oban c. 1813, interred Paris 28 Jan. 1894. Journalist, critic, novelist, political networker, salon hostess. Daughter of William Stuart, army officer, and his wife, n. Campbell.

Rose Stuart's early life and education remain uncharted. As a single woman she contributed articles pseudonymously or unsigned to *Blackwood's Magazine* and *The Law Review*. Travelling on the continent, she met and married in 1844 Ange-Henri Blaze de Bury (1813–88), French attaché in Weimar. A republican, he refused Second Empire postings and made a distinguished career as historian and critic, in which his wife, who exerted a strong influence over him, occasionally collaborated, as in *Hommes du Jour* (1859). One of their two daughters, Yetta Blaze de Bury (d. 1902/3), also wrote literary criticism. Intelligent, dynamic and charming, Rose Blaze de Bury was fluent in Spanish, French and German, and attracted intellectuals and politicians to her international salons. She was an inveterate traveller with or without her husband, as illustrated by *Voyage en Autriche, Hongrie, Allemagne 1848–49* (1851). Her travel books and studies demonstrated depth and accuracy of knowledge. In 1858–9 she drafted an ambitious plan for Austria's economic development involving a trade pact with Britain: *L'Autriche et ses réformes* (1861). Concurrently, she established an Anglo-Austrian bank of Catholic configuration. From Paris she corresponded with Bismarck and the ambassadors of most European countries and the USA. She wrote for the *Revue des Deux Mondes*, the *Revue de Paris* and on European politics in the *Daily News*. Among her friends were Lord Brougham, Patrick and *Anna Geddes and, in Paris, Paul Desjardins. Her now-forgotten novels included *All for Greed* (1868) and *Love the Avenger* (1869); she also wrote literary studies of Racine (1845) and Molière (1846). DAS

• Blaze de Bury, R., Works as above.
Dictionnaire de Biographie Française; *The Times*, 29 Jan. 1894 (obit.).

BOHEMIA, Elizabeth of *see* **STEWART, Elizabeth, Queen of Bohemia, Electress Palatine** (1596–1662)

BOLLAN, Angela, born Blackburn 5 March 1977, died Stirling 26 April 1996. Subject of government inquiry. Daughter of Ann Bollan, and Jim Bollan, Scottish Socialist Party councillor.

Angela Bollan's family described her as a bubbly person who made friends easily. She was active in art and drama, did voluntary work helping elderly neighbours and, her parents said, 'transcended the gap' between the generations. Her mother was herself on incapacity benefit. Angela's daughter Stephanie was born 2 September 1994. In the last years of her life, Angela was struggling with heroin addiction and was arrested on charges of shoplifting. In April 1996, she was remanded in custody at HMP Cornton Vale for shoplifting toiletries worth £19. Eleven days later, she hanged herself from the bars of her cell.

Angela Bollan's case came to represent the injustice of inappropriate custody for women. Her death was the fourth in a series of eight suicides at Cornton Vale over a three-year period. Most of the women who died were, like Angela, young (under 30) and on remand. Their deaths gave rise to a government inquiry (Inspectorates of Prisons and Social Work Services 1998) which concluded that many female offenders in Scotland were being sent into custody not for the seriousness of their crimes, but for failure to comply with court orders or community penalties. A Scottish Executive Ministerial Group subsequently produced a report addressing the issue (2002). NL
• Inspectorates of Prisons and Social Work Services (1998) *Women Offenders – A Safer Way?*; Scottish Executive Ministerial Group on Women's Offending, (2002) *A Better Way*.
Private information: Jim Bollan.

BON, Ann Fraser, n. **Dougall,** born Dunning, Perthshire, 9 April 1838, died Melbourne, Australia, 5 June 1936. Scottish-Australian philanthropist. Daughter of Jane Fraser, and David Dougall, physician.

In 1858, aged 19, Ann Dougall married a Scotsman, John Bon, and accompanied him to the south-eastern Australian colony of Victoria, where the first colonists had acquired land without

benefit of treaties with or compensation for the indigenous hunter-gatherer owners. John Bon was already well established in pastoralism, and the couple prospered on his extensive holding. Ann Bon gave birth to five children in swift succession, three sons and two daughters, but was widowed in 1868 at the age of 30. Unusually for a woman at the time, she then assumed the management of the property. A devout Presbyterian and humanitarian, she distinguished herself most conspicuously from her peers by her strenuous public interventions to support Aborigines' resistance to increasing state regimes of control and surveillance. While Ann Bon's adherence to goals of 'improvement' and 'civilisation' now appear paternalistic and ethnocentric, many members of indigenous communities nevertheless expressed gratitude for her assistance in thwarting if not defeating the diminution of Aboriginal entitlements and civil rights. Her commitment to this cause and other charitable activities was lifelong. PG
• Barwick, D. (1998) *Rebellion at Coranderrk*; Nairn, B. and Serle, G. (1979) *Australian DNB*, vol. 7 (1891–1939); Nelson, E., Smith, S. and Grimshaw, P. (eds) (2002) *Letters from Aboriginal Women of Victoria, 1867 to 1926*.

BONE, Phyllis Mary, born Hornby, Lancs., 15 Feb. 1894, died Kirkcudbright 12 July 1972. Sculptor. Daughter of Mary Campbell Smith, and Douglas J. Mayhew Bone, GP.

Living with an aunt after her mother's early death, Phyllis Bone attended St George's School, Edinburgh, then ECA and the New College of Art (Diploma in Sculpture 1918) before studying in Paris with the animal sculptor Edouard Navellier. She finally settled in a studio in Belford Mews, Edinburgh. During the First World War, she served as motor driver in the Women's Legion. Her career was launched when she was chosen by Sir Robert Lorimer to be responsible for all the animal sculpture in the Scottish National War Memorial, Edinburgh Castle (1923–8). Other work includes animals on the Zoological Building of the University of Edinburgh, the lion and unicorn reliefs on St Andrew's House, and many public and private commissions, including small bronzes of animals, cast by George Mancini. The first woman elected ARSA, then RSA in 1944, in later life Phyllis Bone relocated to Kirkcudbright near fellow-artists Lena Alexander and *Anna Hotchkis. JH
• NLS: Dep 199: Phyllis Bone papers and inventory of art works, photographs.

Pearson, F. (ed.) (1991) *Virtue and Vision*; Savage, P. (1980) *Lorimer and the Edinburgh Craft Designers*; *SB*. Private information.

BORROWMAN, Agnes Thomson, born Penicuik 7 Oct. 1881, died Clapham, London, 20 August 1955. Pharmacist. Daughter of Margaret Davidson, and Peter Borrowman, shepherd.

The oldest of four children, Agnes Borrowman left school at 16 and served apprenticeships in local chemist shops where, because of the prejudice then existing against women in this field, she always had to work in the back shop. She qualified in 1903 as chemist and druggist, but as a woman was obliged to go to England to find work. As well as managing a pharmacy shop, she studied and became a pharmaceutical chemist in 1909, later carrying out research at the School of Pharmacy. A paper she read to the NAWP was 'one of the most fascinating papers ever read at such a meeting' (*Pharm. Jour.* 1911). Research was poorly paid, so after the death of her father in 1913, she had to return to retail pharmacy to help support younger members of her family. Acquiring a historic pharmacy at Clapham, she made it a valuable training ground for future women pharmacists. Agnes Borrowman was a pioneer in everything to do with the employment of women in pharmacy, and an intrepid fighter where their interests were concerned. The first woman to serve on the Society's Board of Examiners, she was a founder member of the NAWP and a Fellow of the Pharmaceutical Society. Further family commitments included several months nursing a sister in Canada. Latterly in failing health, she remained a fighter for all she believed in. AW
• *Pharm. Jour.*, 1911; ibid., August 1955, p. 155, and Sept. 1955, pp. 191–2 (obits); Shellard, E. J. (1982) 'Some early women research workers in British Pharmacy 1886–1912' (unpub. conf. paper, Univ. of Warwick, April).

BORTHWICK, Jane Laurie, born Edinburgh 9 April 1813, died Edinburgh 7 Sept. 1897. **BORTHWICK, Sarah,** m. **Findlater,** born Edinburgh 26 Nov. 1823, died Torquay 25 Dec. 1907. Hymn writers and translators. Daughters of Sarah Finlay, and James Borthwick, insurance manager.

Both parents were staunch members of the Church of Scotland. Jane, the more prolific sister, spent some months in Switzerland in the 1840s. Her father encouraged her to collaborate with Sarah on producing English translations of pietistic German hymns, first published in the *Free Church Magazine*

in the late 1840s, then collected as *Hymns from the Land of Luther* in four series (1854, 1855, 1858, 1862; enlarged edn. 1884). These works, for which the Borthwick sisters are best known, confirmed their importance as mediators of German hymnody to 19th-century Britain. Of Jane's 61 translations, the best known are 'Be still my soul' and 'Jesus, still lead on'; Sarah's 53 included 'God calling yet', and 'O happy home'. Jane never married, living a life of quiet piety and good works in the family home. In 1861, Sarah married a Free Church minister, Eric J. Findlater (1813–66), and lived in Balquidder, then Prestonpans. Two of her daughters, *Mary and Jane Findlater, became successful novelists. LL
• Andrews, J. S. (1981) *A Study of German Hymns in Current English Hymnals*, (1982–3) 'The Borthwick sisters as translators of German hymns', *Expository Times*, 94, pp. 329–33; Mackenzie, E. (1964) *The Findlater Sisters*; *ODNB* (2004); Routley, E. (1979) *A Panorama of Christian Hymnody*; *The Scotsman*, 9 Sept. 1897 (obit.).

BOSWELL, Margaret (Peggie), n. **Montgomerie,** born Lainshaw, Ayrshire, March 1738, died Auchinleck 4 June 1789. Wife of James Boswell. Daughter of Veronica Boswell, and David Montgomerie of Lainshaw.

Margaret Montgomerie, when aged 31, married her first cousin, James Boswell (1740–95), laird, advocate, author and heir to the Scottish judge, Lord Auchinleck. At 29, Boswell already had a European reputation for his *Account of Corsica* (1768), his private journals recording high and low life, and an illegitimate daughter. Neither a great beauty nor an heiress, Peggie offered a respectable and comfortable alternative to James's whores and grandees. An eminently sensible woman, she presided in James's Court, Edinburgh, and later at Auchinleck House. Five of their seven children reached adulthood: three daughters, the heir, Sir Alexander, poet and antiquarian, and James, scholar and editor of Shakespeare.

James Boswell's correspondence and his journals, which she predicted would leave him 'embowelled to posterity' (*Life of Johnson*, 1773), show his lasting affection for this clever and humorous woman, whose patience he tried through drink, liaisons and London excursions. The undomesticated Samuel Johnson was warily received on his Scottish tour of 1773 (he dropped candle-wax all over her carpet). She remarked 'in a little warmth' of her husband and Johnson, 'I have seen many a bear led by a man, but I never before saw a man led by a bear' (ibid.). Comments on

Johnson's *Journey to the Western Islands* (1775) show her to have been an acute reader. She is the subject of Marie Muir's novel *Dear Mrs Boswell* (1953). IMCG

• Boswell, J. (1957–1989) *The Yale editions of the private papers of James Boswell*, esp. vol. 6; Brady, F. (1984) *James Boswell: The Later Years 1769–1795*; *ODNB* (2004); Pottle, F. A. (1966) *James Boswell: The Earlier Years 1740–1769*.

BOWES-LYON, Lady Mildred Marion,‡ m. **Jessup,** born Glamis Castle 6 Oct. 1868, died St Raphaël, France, 9 June 1897. Composer. Daughter of Frances Smith, and Claude Bowes-Lyon, 13th Earl of Strathmore.

Frances, Lady Strathmore, created a concert party with her 11 children and gave charity concerts in Britain and abroad. Lady Mildred appeared as a singer but not a soloist, apparently overshadowed by her younger sister Lady Maude, a violinist. She suffered 'delicate health' from childhood, and the family was 'practically ordered by medical advisers' to leave Glamis and winter in Egypt (Dundee *Courier*, 1888). In 1890, she married Augustus Jessup, a wealthy American businessman. His lavish reconstruction of the 12th-century Schloss Lenzburg in Switzerland included a music room for his wife alongside the couple's ornate bedroom. In April 1894, her opera, *Etelinda*, written to her husband's libretto, was successfully presented in Florence, conducted by maestro Leopoldo Mugnone. Her local Scottish newspaper recorded that the composer's name was withheld until the success of the performance was assured: on the second night, 'in response to the calls of the audience, Lady Mildred came before the curtain and bowed her acknowledgements'. For a new and anonymous opera to impress the 'fastidious musical public of Florence' and be rewarded with 'enthusiastic approval' (*Kirriemuir Observer*) was an unusual feat. Two years after Lady Mildred's sudden early death, Mugnone conducted more of her music at a concert in 1899, in the new museum at Bordighera, before Emperor Frederick of Germany, indicating his continued high opinion of her. TF

• Glamis Castle Archives: Papers of Lord Strathmore and press cuttings file, courtesy of the archivist, Jane Anderson. Dundee *Courier*, 11 Dec. 1888; *Kirriemuir Observer*, 27 April 1894.

BOYD, Maggie Paton Davidson (Peggy), born Maybole 9 Nov. 1905, died Ayr 21 Sept. 1999. Air ambulance nurse. Daughter of Jessie Paton, and James Boyd, plumber.

The sixth of seven children, Peggy Boyd trained as a nurse (SRN) at Biggart Hospital, Prestwick, and Royal Alexandra Infirmary, Paisley. In 1932 she qualified as a midwife (SCM). With her friend and colleague **Jane Gilmour Govan** (1895–1982), known as Jean, she established Paisley Trained Nurses Association, which developed into Ashtrees maternity nursing home.

From 1 March 1938, Peggy Boyd and Jean Govan became the first dedicated Scottish Air Ambulance nurses. Peggy Boyd flew for the first time three days later, on 4 March, when she accompanied a child with appendicitis from Islay. The nurses often had to fly in inclement weather at a time when aircraft, airfields and navigational aids lacked sophistication. During the Second World War, aircraft windows were blacked out and island air travel required a military permit. Jean Govan was offered an OBE in recognition of her work, but on learning that she was to be the only recipient she declined, saying, 'We are both doing the same work' (Hutchison 1996, p. 110). Wartime conditions meant a shortage of trained nurses for their nursing home, and they withdrew from air ambulance nursing in 1941. Volunteer nurses from Glasgow's Southern General Hospital took over until 1993. The nursing home operated until 1951. Peggy Boyd then spent time in New Zealand, and from her return in 1952 until retiring in 1966, she was a health visitor in Ayr. IH

• *Ayr Advertiser*, 19 May 1983; Hutchison, I. (1996) *Air Ambulance*.
Private information: Janetta Thomson (niece).

BOYD, Mary Syme, born Edinburgh 15 August 1910, died Edinburgh 30 Oct. 1997. Sculptor. Daughter of Clara Lepper of Co. Antrim, and Francis Darby Boyd, Professor of Clinical Medicine at the University of Edinburgh.

While at ECA (1929–33), Mary Boyd was awarded travelling scholarships and studied in Paris (1931–2) under leading *animalier* Edouard Navellier. In 1934, she toured Europe, visiting Denmark, Sweden, Germany, Belgium and France. She sought out examples of modern sculpture, and admired wood carvings in churches, pewter and Danish silver. Her entire professional career was pursued from a house/studio at 14 Belford Mews, Edinburgh, interrupted only by war service with an ambulance team during the London blitz and in Edinburgh. Her notebooks about her European tour and her wartime service are extraordinary testaments. Ecclesiastical subjects influenced by

Eric Gill, allegorical subjects and many naturalistic animal studies were among work exhibited in plaster, bronze, silver, carved wood and stone, at the RSA, SSA and RGIFA. Her work is represented in the NGS, private collections and churches. LAMB
• NGS and RCAHMS Archives: Mary Boyd's notebooks and other papers.
The Scotsman, 8 Nov. 1997 (obit.); 2 Jan. 1998 (feature).

BOYLE, Eleanor Vere (E.V.B.), n. **Gordon,** born Auchlunies, Aberdeenshire, 1 May 1825, died Brighton 29 July 1916. Illustrator. Daughter of Albinia Cumberland, amateur painter, and Alexander Gordon of Auchlunies, son of the 3rd Earl of Aberdeen.

Youngest of nine children, Eleanor Gordon was tutored at home and later learned etching from Thomas Landseer. In 1845, she married Hon. and Rev. Richard Boyle (1812–86), Vicar of Marston Bigot, Somerset, and Chaplain-in-ordinary to *Queen Victoria from 1846 to 1875. They had five children. Under the name 'E.V.B.' or Hon. Mrs Richard Boyle, Eleanor Boyle became a successful illustrator of popular Victorian and Edwardian publications, many of them for children. She specialised in detailed, narrative, magic realist images, some of which, including *Hans Christian Andersen's Fairy Tales* (1872) and *Beauty and the Beast* (1875), were lavishly chromolithographed in editions by Sampson, Low, Marston, Low & Searle of London, in exemplary bindings. She also wrote and illustrated works about gardens and botany, exhibited with the SLA between 1859 and 1879 and also at the Dudley and Grosvenor Galleries. In Somerset, she was a patron of Frome School of Art and a benefactor of her husband's parish, but after his death she lived in reduced circumstances, because of unwise investments by her son-in-law. RA
• Boyle, E. V. (1884) *Days and Hours in a Garden*. Beaumont, R. de (2000) 'Bibliography of E.V.B.', *IBIS Spring Newsletter*, (2002) 'E.V.B. (The Hon. Mrs Eleanor Vere Boyle): an account of her life and a bibliography', *IBIS Jour.*, 2, 29 Nov.; Houfe, S. (1978) *The Dictionary of British Book Illustrators 1800–1914*; *ODNB* (2004); *The Scotsman*, 21 August 1916 (obit.).
www.llansadwrn-wx.co.uk

BRAIDFUTE, Marion, fl. (allegedly) 1297. Literary character.

William Wallace's attack on Lanark in May 1297, burning the town and killing its sheriff, is attested by reliable contemporary sources. The idea that this raid was motivated by Wallace's desire to avenge the execution of a woman is no earlier than Wyntoun's metrical chronicle of the early 15th century. Wyntoun mentions a nameless 'lemman' (paramour), an inhabitant of Lanark executed by the sheriff for having harboured Wallace and helping him to avoid capture. Two generations later, 'Blind' Harry in his poem, *Wallace*, named this person as Marion Braidfute and described how Wallace fell in love with her despite himself, knowing his love would bring her danger, and how she pleaded in vain with him not to put his love for Scotland ahead of his love for her. Both narratives describe a literary character whose existence cannot be corroborated by any contemporary source. JEF
• Amours, F. J. (ed.) (1907) *The Original Chronicle of Andrew of Wyntoun*, vol. 5, pp. 300–4; McDiarmid, M. P. (ed.) (1968) *Hary's Wallace*.

BRECHIN, Ethel, born Edinburgh 1 April 1894, died Edinburgh 23 Feb. 1986. Printing compositor. Daughter of Mary Haig, domestic servant, and George Brechin, butler.

The youngest of nine children, Ethel Brechin went to Canonmills School, then, at 14, following two sisters, she joined the printing-house of Morrison & Gibb as an apprentice hand-setter. This opportunity was briefly open to Edinburgh girls (1880s–1910), and the city's 900-odd female compositors were among the few women in this skilled trade in Britain until the Equal Opportunities legislation of the 1970s. It was better-paid than alternatives such as dressmaking, but since women were still paid less than men, and thus under-cutting male wages, the male union campaigned successfully for a ban on women entrants from 1910. However, Ethel Brechin was able to work out her time to the age of 70, living at home, never marrying, and winning prizes for ballroom dancing. She also loved her work, progressing to monotyping and proof-reading. 'I would have worked weekends if they'd have let me', she said in old age. SR
• Reynolds, S. (1989) *Britannica's Typesetters*. Personal knowledge.

BRIDE (BRIDGET), Saint, possibly born Dundalk or Kildare, c. AD 452, died 525. Reputedly daughter of a bond-maid or slave, and Dubhach, Prince of Ulster and pagan bard.

Although of Irish birth, Bride features strongly in Scottish folklore and is seen as inter-mingling Celtic goddess and Christian saint. The Day of

Bride, 1 February, is the Celtic festival of Spring, linked closely with Candlemas (2 February). For the Gael, she was the patron of poetry, smith-work and healing. Christians revered her as a fertility figure who cared for the home and was aid-woman at births. A much-told legend describes how Bride, transported from Iona to Bethlehem, in the role of inn-keeper's daughter, delivered Mary of the infant Jesus. In the *Gaidhealtachd* she is commonly known as *Miume Chroisd*, foster-mother to Christ, and *Ban-chuidheachaidh*, the aid-woman (or midwife) of Mary. Many Scottish midwives regard Bride as 'their' saint.

Incantations associated with Bride cover issues particularly to do with fertility, the land, and the hearts and lives of the people, especially a happy, safe home with enough food, and safety at birth. Many Scottish churches carry her name. Her cross, traditionally made of woven straw, typifies the star which led Bride to the infant Jesus. LR
• Carmichael, A. (1900) *Carmina Gadelica*; McNeill, F. M. (1959) *The Silver Bough*; Towill, E. S. (1983) *The Saints of Scotland.*

BROADWOOD, Lucy Etheldred, born Melrose 9 August 1858, died Canterbury 22 August 1929. Folk-song collector and singer. Daughter of Juliana Maria Birch, and Henry Fowler Broadwood, piano manufacturer.

Educated privately, Lucy Broadwood became a leading figure in folk-song collection and analysis. She collected folk-songs throughout the British Isles and was a founder member of the Folk-Song Society, holding the honorary secretaryship from its relaunch in 1904 until 1908, editing its *Journal* until 1927, and collaborating with major figures in the field such as Percy Grainger, Gavin Greig, Frank Howes and Frank Kidson. 'The mainstay' of a talk by Ralph Vaughan Williams, for which she sang the examples, she was his 'admired colleague, and an adviser in Ralph's work with folk songs' (U. Vaughan Williams 1964, pp. 62–3). He described her as 'an excellent pianist and a most artistic singer' and wrote of her compositions that though light in texture they showed 'considerable musical imagination' (R. Vaughan Williams 1948, p. 136). Lucy Broadwood was also a poet, artist and cartoonist, contributing to *Punch* and *The Globe*. She was involved in the Broadwood piano manufacturing company, and took an intense interest in the family history. Although she was based in London and the family home at Lyne, her Scottish background was always of importance to

her. In childhood she regularly holidayed in Melrose; in 1906–7 she collected tunes in Arisaig, and she noted tunes from exiled Gaels in London, including Farquhar MacRae and John MacLennan. In 1908–11 she collaborated with *Frances Tolmie, for whose own collection she wrote a note on the Gaelic scale system. Her Gaelic material is on extended loan to the School of Scottish Studies. JP
• Surrey History Centre, Woking: Broadwood papers (material on/of Lucy Broadwood, diaries, journals, photographs: 2185/EB/9); BL and Vaughan Williams Memorial Library: copies of wax cylinder recordings.
Broadwood, L. E. with Fuller-Maitland, J. A. (1893) *English County Songs*, (1911) 'Additional note on the Gaelic scale system', *Journal of the Folk-Song Society* 16, vol. IV/3, pp. 154–5.
Bassin, E. (1965) 'Lucy Broadwood, 1858–1929', *Scottish Studies*, 9, 2, pp. 145–52; Jones, L. W. (1995) 'Lucy Etheldred Broadwood: poet and song writer', *English Dance and Song* 57, 4, pp. 2–3; *ODNB* (2004); Vaughan Williams, R. (1948) 'Lucy Broadwood 1858–1929', *Journal of the English Folk Dance and Song Society* V, 3, pp. 136–8; Vaughan Williams, U. (1964) *R.V.W.*, pp. 62–3, 89–90, 140, 179; Wainwright, D. (1982) *Broadwood by Appointment.*

BRODIE, Margaret Brash, born Glasgow 10 June 1907, died Beith 14 April 1997. Architect. Daughter of Jane Brash, and John Brodie, civil engineer.

Margaret Brodie's parents believed strongly in women's education: her sister Jean studied at GSA and Anne became a dentist. Margaret Brodie went from Glasgow High School for Girls to the Glasgow School of Architecture, one of the few women in the first BScArch cohort in 1926, under the professorship of T. H. Hughes, husband of *Edith Burnet. At the British School of Art in Rome on a scholarship, her fellow students included Robert Mathew and Basil Spence. She graduated with first-class honours in Design (1931), the first student to do so. Her drawings for a proposed Paisley hospital, submitted by Glasgow practice Watson, Salmond & Gray, brought her to the notice of T. S. Tait, dominant partner of Burnet, Tait & Lorne. In 1932, she joined their London office (see Burnet, Edith) and worked on their most influential Scottish commissions: as Tait's senior assistant on St Andrew's House, Edinburgh (1933–9), 'the most impressive work of architecture in Scotland between the wars', (Gifford et al. 1984, p. 441), and as site architect during construction of the Empire Exhibition, Bellahouston, Glasgow (1936–8).

Alongside day-to-day site supervision of more than 150 buildings by disparate, often leading, architects, Margaret Brodie designed the Women of the Empire Pavilion, a 'modest gem' of 'beautifully simple design, cleverly squeezed onto its tight corner' (Baxter 1997, p. 22). A haven for women visitors, with a non-smoking restaurant, its permanent exhibits concerned women's fashions and welfare, in contrast to her own professional contribution to the Exhibition – though apparently she wore 'the largest picture hat' to the opening. During the war, she designed aerodromes in East Anglia for the Air Ministry, then joined Burnet, Tait & Lorne's Edinburgh office. She combined lecturing at GSA with private practice: work included St Martin's Church, Port Glasgow (1957). She advised engineering firms, including Cowan & Linn (Grant's distillery at Grangestone, Girvan, 1963), and sat for 20 years on the Church of Scotland's Artistic Questions Committee. A 'forceful, demanding and kindly' teacher, with a 'pawky sense of humour and highly refined sense of irony' (ibid.), Margaret Brodie spent retirement with her sister Jean in a redesigned 17th-century farmhouse near Lochwinnoch. Her Fellowship of the GSA (1995) (which she dismissed as 'nonsense') honoured 'one of the School's most distinguished female alumni' and 'one of Scotland's leading creative forces of her generation' (ibid.). RC

• Baxter, N. (1997) 'Margaret Brodie', *RIAS Newsletter*, June; Colquhoun, A. (1997) 'Margaret Brash Brodie', *Soc. Arch. Historians of GB Newsletter*, 61, p. 6; Gifford, J., McWilliam, C. and Walker, D. (eds) (1984) *The Buildings of Scotland: Edinburgh*; *Glasgow Herald*, 19 April 1997 (obit.); Kinchin, P. and Kinchin, J. (1988) *Glasgow's Great Exhibitions*; McKean, C. (1987) *The Scottish Thirties: an architectural introduction.* Additional information: Diane Watters.

BROOKSBANK, Mary Watson,‡ n. **Soutar,** born Aberdeen 15 Dec. 1897, died Dundee 16 March 1978. Mill worker, revolutionary, poet and songwriter. Daughter of Roseann Gillan, domestic servant, fish gutter and mill worker, and Alexander Soutar, dock labourer and union activist.

One of five children, in around 1907 Mary Soutar moved with her family to Dundee, where she attended St Andrew's School. Like many others in a city dependent upon female and child labour, she first entered a jute textile spinning mill as a shifter aged 11, an experience reflected in her song, 'Oh, dear me'. By 1912, she was working in the same mill as her mother and taking part in her first industrial dispute. Over three decades, she and her fellow jute workers moved from mill to mill as well as taking casual jobs, fruit picking and cleaning offices. In 1920, she joined the CP, organising the lobbies and demonstrations for unemployment benefits that culminated in riots in Dundee in September 1921. She led local CP campaigns, including resisting the evictions of rent defaulters and representing unemployed workers at Labour Exchange tribunals. On 3 October 1924, she married Ernest Brooksbank (c. 1891–1943), a journeyman tailor. Demonstrations against mass unemployment in Dundee in 1931 that she helped to organise were noteworthy for the presence of working women. When mounted police charged a city centre rally where she was a speaker, she was arrested and charged with incitement to riot. In total, she served three prison sentences as a result of her political activity. During the last of her prison sentences, she began to write poetry.

Mary Brooksbank was expelled from the CP in 1933. She said she doubted the party leadership after hearing reports from women members who had visited the Soviet Union, but tensions also arose locally from her work with the very successful women's section. In 1943, her husband fell seriously ill and died. Five years later she was nursing her sick mother and was no longer in paid employment. At this time she began to write song lyrics as well as poetry. From an early age she had played the violin, appearing in benefit concerts during the First World War, but it was after the Second World War that she gained a reputation as a musician and song writer. In the 1960s and 1970s, supported by the folk singer Ewan MacColl, her songs reached a national audience and she appeared on radio and television in Scotland. Mary Brooksbank continues to be celebrated as a lyricist; in the future her contribution to Scotland's radical tradition may also be recognised: 'Politicians and rulers/Are richly rewarded,/But in one woman's life/Is our history recorded' (Brooksbank 1982, p. 30). GRS

• Dundee Central Library: Lamb Collection; Univ. of Dundee: MS 103/38.
Brooksbank, M. (1966) *Nae Sae Lang Syne: a tale of this city*, (1982) *Sidlaw Breezes*.
Bowman, D. and Bowman, E. (eds) (1967) *Breaking the Fetters: the memoirs of Bob Stewart*; Gordon, E. (1991) *Women and the Labour Movement in Scotland 1850–1914*; Knox, W. W. J. (2006) *The Lives of Scottish Women*; *ODNB (2004)*; Phillips, D. (1967) Appreciation, *The Scots Magazine*, March, reprinted in (1982) Introduction to *Sidlaw Breezes*, pp. 7–10; Smith, G. (1995) 'Protest is better for infants:

motherhood, health and welfare in a women's town, c. 1911–1931', *Oral History*, 23, 1, pp. 63–70.

BROON, Maw, 'born' Dundee 8 March 1936. Matriarch. Brainchild of Robert D. Low, managing editor, and Dudley D. Watkins, illustrator, *Sunday Post*.

For 70 years matriarch of *The Broons* comic strip, Maw Broon sprang into full-grown existence in the Fun Section of the D. C. Thomson newspaper, *Sunday Post*, in 1936. Maw and family, who speak a broad Scots dialect, owe their popularity largely to the talent of Dudley Watkins (1907–69), who was such a successful comic artist that, unusually, he was allowed to sign his strips.

As a Scottish icon, Maw Broon is instantly recognisable; a big woman, wearing pinny and sensible shoes, her hair is scraped into a bun and her bosom is ample. Wife to meek but mischievous Paw, daughter-in-law to roguish Grandpaw and mother to a clan – plain Daphne, glamorous Maggie, lanky Hen, attractive Joe, bookish Horace, the twins and the bairn – Maw epitomises what Scottish society once admired in women: selflessness, dependability and respectability. Maw regulates life for the inhabitants of 10 Glebe Street (in an unspecified town – not Edinburgh); she lives through her family. Apart from forays to the shops, she has no interests of her own; maintaining standards and 'keeping up appearances' is her mission. For visitors, Maw brings out the good china and minds her manners but often things go wrong and she ends up 'affrontit', in the process defying modernity and retaining the affection of generations of readers. CEC/ALS
• *The Broons* (alternate years); website: www.thatsbraw.co.uk

BROWN, Anna, n. **Gordon**, born Aberdeen 24 August 1747, died Falkland 11 July 1810. Singer of traditional ballads. Daughter of Lillias Forbes of Disblair, and Thomas Gordon, Aberdeen professor.

Raised in Aberdeen, Anna Gordon spent time on an estate in the Braemar district with her mother's sister, Anne Forbes Farquharson, who had learned ballads from nurses and servants. She learned her ballads largely from her aunt, but also from her mother, who would have picked them up at Disblair, and from a servant in their Aberdeen house. Also known as 'Mrs Brown of Falkland', having in 1788 married Rev. Andrew Brown (1744–1805), minister of Falkland, Fife, she is the archetypal source of Scots ballads, much as Sir Walter Scott is the archetypal collector and

publisher. She left a group of 42 ballads over which she had complete bardic mastery. During her life, her ballads were eagerly copied by collectors, especially Robert Jamieson and William Tytler. Sir Walter Scott published several in his *Minstrelsy of the Scottish Borders*, and many of them are in Francis Child's collection. She would sing, but was not comfortable with publishing, while Scott readily published ballads that he had not composed. In 1802, she expressed anger at Scott's publication of her name as a source of her often blunt and amorous ballads, written from a female point of view, and this marks a turning point for Scotswomen, newly infected with a fear of impropriety and of publishing. DS
• Harvard Univ.: Brown MSS; NLS: Acc. 11737, Brown MS. Buchan, D. (1972) *The Ballad and the Folk* (Bibl.); Child, F. J. [1882–98] (1965) *The English and Scottish Popular Ballads*; *ODNB* (2004) (see Gordon, Anna); Symonds, D. A. (1997) *Weep Not for Me*.

BROWN, Dorothy *see* **DIORBHAIL NIC A'BHRUTHAINN** (fl. 1644)

BROWN, Marion, born Crawfordjohn, Lanarkshire, 2 July 1843, died Sanquhar 7 Oct. 1915. Telephone exchange operator and correspondent. Daughter of Margaret Glencross (Glencorse), and George Brown, dairyman.

The second of three children, Marion Brown was forced to spend prolonged periods confined to bed and also experienced short-term blindness and speech loss. This originated from an unspecified condition, which she first encountered around the age of five. After her mother died in 1850, George Brown remarried, and Marion Brown spent her youth in the home of her aunt, Agnes Scott (n. Glencross). She became an integral member of the Glencross family where, often bed-bound, she sewed and conducted correspondence with family members, particularly those who had emigrated to Dunmore, Pennsylvania.

Although herself disabled, she later cared for her ageing aunt, Agnes. During this period they lived with Agnes Scott's son, Tam, and his wife, Robina Boyle. Theirs was a large family, and the resulting tensions led to Marion Brown's moving out. Still experiencing mobility problems, she took up her first regular employment in 1892 as Sanquhar's first telephone exchange operator. She had longed to emigrate to the USA and, through her correspondence, maintained the family link with Dunmore for forty years. IH

- 'Correspondence of Marion Brown, Sanquhar, Dumfriesshire, to Dunmore, Pennsylvania, 1852–1903', private collection of L. M. Richards, unpublished 1994 transcription courtesy of P. L. Richards.
Hutchison, I. (2002) 'Disability in nineteenth century Scotland – the case of Marion Brown', *Univ. Sussex Jour. Contemp. Hist.*, 5 (http://www.sussex.ac.uk/history/1-4-1.html)

BROWN, Mary Katherine Barbara (May), n. **Webster,** MBE, born Inverness 21 May 1900, died Earlsferry, Fife, 19 Nov. 1983. General Secretary of Scottish Council of Physical Recreation. Daughter of Mary Hughes, teacher, and William Webster, CBE, political secretary.

May Webster spent her early childhood in Glasgow. Her father was General Secretary of the SLF and the household had a 'very political atmosphere' (Brown 1979, p. 3). She and her sister Muriel attended George Watson's Ladies' College, Edinburgh, where she developed an interest in sport. Both sisters were students at Anstey College of Physical Education, Warwickshire, and Muriel Webster later joined the staff, then became principal. In August 1933, May Webster married Thomas Gow Brown but they divorced seven months later. From the 1930s, she was an influential figure in physical activity promotion in Scotland, for all ages and classes, spending time working among depressed mining communities in Fife. Fitness, fun and friendship were her aims. An officer in both Edinburgh and Glasgow Keep Fit Movements, she helped set up the Scottish Women's Keep Fit Association, was secretary of the RSCDS, and broadcast 'Early Morning Exercises' with the BBC Home Service during the war. In 1945, she became secretary of the new Scottish arm of the Central Council of Physical Recreation, a senior civil service post. Under her leadership, this and its successor, the Scottish Council of Physical Recreation (1953), made significant developments in Scottish sport and physical activity. A 'committed evangelical for women's sports' at a time when most competitive sports were male-dominated (Brown 1999, p. 186), May Brown also introduced new sports such as ski-ing and orienteering. Awarded MBE in 1963, she retired in 1968. IAR
- Brown, M. (1979) *Alive in the 1900s.*
Brown, C. G. (1999) 'Sport and the Scottish Office in the 20th century', *European Sports History Review*, vol. I, pp. 184–202; Scottish Sports Council, *Annual Report* 1983–4, 'Obituary: Mrs M. K. Brown MBE'.

BROWN, Meredith Jemima, born probably Glasgow 1846, died Lisson Grove, London 5 Nov. 1908. Founder and honorary superintendent of the Shaftesbury Institute, London. Daughter of Catherine Dyce (sister of the painter William Dyce), and Rev. David Brown, Free Church minister.

Raised in Aberdeen, Meredith Brown studied music and singing. Following the death of her mother, she went to London, where she determined to alleviate the conditions of poor factory girls and provide a safety net for those who might drift into prostitution. She researched their problems by disguising herself as a factory worker and, with a friend, went round 'low music saloons and gin drinking dens'. She wrote of her experiences in a book, *Only a Factory Girl* (n.d. no copy located), the proceeds of which enabled her to set up the Shaftesbury Institute in Lisson Grove, where poorly paid women could spend a comfortable, teetotal evening and attend classes, and where women arriving in London seeking work could get cheap, safe bed and breakfast. She organised this and related endeavours with success. ATM
- Brown, M., Work as above.
In Memoriam (1897) Aberdeen, p. 114; *In Memoriam* (1908) Aberdeen, p. 20; MacLeod, J. (1910) *Reminiscences*, pp. 79–80; *ODNB* (2004); *WWW*, 1908.

BRUCE, Christian, fl. 1306–57. Scottish resistance leader. Daughter of *Marjory, Countess of Carrick, and Robert Bruce, 5th Lord of Annandale.

During a long, eventful life, Christian Bruce had three husbands: Gartnait Earl of Mar, Sir Christopher Seton (c. 1278–1306) and Andrew Moray of Bothwell (1298–1338), all staunch supporters of the Bruce political faction. She lost two husbands to war and experienced first-hand Edward I's fierce determination to crush her brother, Robert I. Captured at Tain in June 1306 with her sister-in-law, her niece *Marjory Bruce, and *Isobel of Fife, Countess of Buchan, she began a lengthy captivity in the Gilbertine nunnery at Sixhills (Lincolnshire), days after Seton's execution. Imprisoned until 1314, she remained unwaveringly loyal to Robert's cause. In the early 1330s, Christian Bruce and her third husband were active against Edward III, and in 1333 she held the castle of Kildrummy against English forces on Moray's behalf. She remained active in Anglo-Scottish politics until her death. CJN

• Barrow, G. W. S. (1988) *Robert Bruce*; Neville, C. J. (1993) 'Widows of war . . .', in S. S. Walker (ed.) *Wife and Widow in Medieval England*; *Scotichron*, vol. 7; *ODNB* (2004).

BRUCE, Marjory, born 1294, buried Paisley Abbey c. 1317. Daughter of Isobel of Mar (see Elizabeth de Burgh) and Robert I.

Marjory Bruce, with *Christian Bruce and other royal family members, was sent to Kildrummy Castle and then to Tain for refuge in spring 1306, following Robert Bruce's seizure of the throne, but captured soon afterwards. As with several other noblewomen who openly defied him, Edward I ordered her confined to a cage, this one in the Tower of London. He later relaxed this to honourable captivity in the Gilbertine nunnery of Watton (Yorkshire). She was released in 1314, one of several noblewomen, including *Elizabeth de Burgh, her stepmother, exchanged for English prisoners from Bannockburn. That year she married Walter Stewart (c. 1296–1327), whose family had served the crown loyally for generations. In 1315 it was agreed she would inherit the crown if both Robert I and his brother Edward died without male heirs. She died c. 1317, giving birth to the future Robert II. CJN

• Barrow, G. W. S. (1988) *Robert Bruce*; Neville, C. J. (1993) 'Widows of war . . .', in S. S. Walker (ed.) *Wife and Widow in Medieval England*; Nicholson, R. (1978) *Scotland, the Later Middle Ages*; Riley, H. T. (ed.) (1865) *Willelmi Rishanger . . . Chronica et Annales*; *Scotichron*, vol. 6.

BRUNTON, Mary, n. **Balfour,** born island of Burray, Orkney, 1 Nov. 1778, died Edinburgh 19 Dec. 1818. Novelist. Daughter of Frances Ligonier, and Thomas Balfour, soldier and Orkney landowner.

Mary Balfour attended private school in Edinburgh for seven years, returning to Orkney in 1795. Against her family's wishes, on 4 December 1798 she married a visiting minister, Alexander Brunton of Bolton, East Lothian (1772–1854). In 1802, they moved to Edinburgh when her husband became minister of the New Greyfriars Church, and later Professor of Hebrew Languages at the University of Edinburgh. Finding a friend in Yorkshirewoman Mrs Izett, and encouraged by her husband, Mary Brunton read widely, in philosophy, history and literature. In 1811, she published, anonymously, her first novel, *Self-Control*, dedicated to *Joanna Baillie, and in 1814, *Discipline*. These titles may lack appeal to the modern reader, but are unjustly neglected today. Writing from an evangelical perspective, she emphasised that 'the regulation of the passions is the province, it is the triumph of RELIGION' (Brunton [1811] (1986) Preface). Yet her heroines are self-reliant and determined, and become educated in the economic realities of life. Laura Montreville, in *Self-Control*, resists the stratagems of a seducer, searches for employment and, when finally abducted to Canada, implausibly escapes in a canoe. In *Discipline*, wilful, spoilt Ellen Percy, after her father's bankruptcy and suicide, learns to abandon the corrupt fashionable world and to live by moral and religious principle. She too leaves London for Edinburgh looking for work, learns Gaelic (as Brunton herself did), and finds refuge in the Highlands, where, marrying a Highland chief, she identifies with the moral worth and close bonds she finds in 'this faithful romantic race' (ibid., p. 375). Brunton's final unfinished fragment, *Emmeline*, attempted an ambitious and difficult subject, the unhappy life of a woman divorced for adultery and remarried. In May 1819, the anonymous *Blackwood's* reviewer wrote of almost wishing that 'the pure and high soul of the author' had not embarked on 'such a sad tale of profligacy and wretchedness' (Anon. 1819, p. 189). Brunton recorded her travels in England in 1812 and 1815 in her diaries. She was involved in Edinburgh's literary and philanthropic circles with *Eliza Fletcher, and her early death in childbirth was mourned in the Edinburgh press. Contemporaries – including Jane Austen – greatly enjoyed her work. *Self-Control* went through four editions by 1812, 'one of the few unqualified successes [among novels] to come from Scotland before *Waverley*' (Garside 2000, pp. 59, 79); there were two further editions of *Discipline* in 1815. JR

• NAS: GD1/1153, Papers of Alexander Brunton; Orkney Archives, Kirkwall: Balfour papers.
[Brunton, M.]. [1811] (1986) *Self-Control: A Novel*, [1814] (1986) *Discipline*, (1819) *Emmeline, with Some other Pieces* (inc. 'A Memoir of her Life, and Extracts of her Correspondence' by A. Brunton).
Anon. (May 1819) 'Emmeline', *Blackwood's Edinburgh Review*, V, pp. 183–92; Chapman, R. W. (ed.) (1959) *Jane Austen's Letters to her Sister Cassandra and Others*; Garside, P. et al. (2000) *The English Novel 1770–1829: a bibliographical survey of prose fiction published in the British Isles*, Vol. II: 1800–29; *HSWW*; McKerrow, M. (2001) *Mary Brunton. The Forgotten Scottish Novelist*; *ODNB* (2004); Rendall, J. (2005) '"Women that would plague me with rational conversation", aspiring women and Scottish Whigs, c. 1790–1830', in S. Knott and B. Taylor (eds) *Feminism and the Enlightenment*; Smith, S. (1986) 'Men, women and money: the case of Mary Brunton',

in M. A. Schofield and C. Macheski (eds) *Fetter'd or Free? British Women Novelists, 1670–1815*.

BRYSON, Agnes Ann, born New York State, USA, c. 1831, died Ayrshire 13 Dec. 1907. Quaker minister and temperance reformer, Glasgow.

Ann Bryson came to Scotland as a child and made her home in Glasgow for over 40 years. A prominent member of the Society of Friends, she was involved with the women's monthly meeting, acted as an overseer and was recorded as a minister. That commitment was central to her social reform work. Her friend and fellow reformer, **Mary White** (1827–1903), was also a Quaker. Ann and Mary lived 'as sisters' in Glasgow for 34 years (Society of Friends 1909, p. 13). From the 1870s, Ann Bryson, with the help of Mary White, was at the centre of temperance reform in Glasgow. In 1873 she helped to establish the Glasgow Prayer Union branch of the Scottish Christian Union, the largest single-sex women's temperance organisation in Scotland. She was secretary and superintendent of the prison visiting, rescue and evangelical committees. Her most important project was the Whitevale Mission Shelter (originally the Prison Gate Mission) which she established in Glasgow in 1877 and which was used by the SCU as an 'inebriate home' for women: female prisoners were invited upon release to enter the mission in order to become teetotallers. Somewhat retiring when it came to public speaking, Ann Bryson often relied on Mary White to express their opinions; she was, however, renowned as one of the most charitable and influential Quaker women in Scotland. MKS

• Library of the Society of Friends, London: 'Dictionary of Quaker Biography' (folio, n.d.); Glasgow City Archives: TD 955/1/1, Glasgow Prayer Union Minutes (1881–98, 1905, 1914). Bryson, A. (1878) 'Prison Gate Mission, Glasgow', *Monthly Friend*, 9, 110 (July), pp. 104–5.

Smitley, M. (2002) ' "Woman's Mission": the temperance and women's suffrage movements in Scotland, c. 1870–1914', PhD, Univ. of Glasgow; Society of Friends (1909) 'Agnes Ann Bryson', *Annual Monitor*, 96, pp. 12–14; White, M. (1877) 'Proposed "Prison Gate Mission" for Glasgow', *The Monthly Record*, 8, 102 (Nov.), pp. 171–2.

BRYSON, Elizabeth Horne Bain, n. **Macdonald,** born Dundee 19 August 1880, died London c. 1969. Physician, broadcaster. Daughter of Elizabeth Bain, teacher, and Donald Macdonald, sometime cashier and poet.

Despite a family history of poverty, Elizabeth Macdonald graduated, aged 19, from the University of St Andrews with first-class honours in English literature. An early student in the new medical school at University College, Dundee, she graduated MBChB in 1905, completed an MD and published her thesis in 1907. She was not offered a hospital appointment because of her sex. It appeared to be 'the dawn of nothing', she wrote (quoted Dyhouse 1998, p. 335), so she left for New Zealand, entering private practice as an assistant. She was a school medical officer during the First World War, and returned to general practice in 1918 after marrying Dr Robert Bryson (1877–1934), whom she knew from St Andrews. Both their children became doctors.

Elizabeth Bryson was a prominent member of the League of Mothers, founded in 1926 to promote the Christian upbringing of children. A contemporary described her as 'a born organiser and excelling in all things domestic, as a good Scots woman should' (Coates 1969, p. 44). By then she was practising her speciality of gynaecology and diseases of women in Wellington, with her husband's support: 'Women flocked to consult her' (ibid., p. 44). In the 1930s she studied psychology at the Tavistock in London, applying this in her pioneering research on the psychosomatic approach in gynaecology (Bryson 1945). Back in New Zealand in 1939, she broadcast eight radio talks on nutrition for the Health Department. She retired in 1953. Her autobiography (1966) has been used to illustrate both the power of books in the lives of working people (Rose 2001) and the vocational ambitions of women of her generation seeking a medical education (Dyhouse 1998). GRS

• Bryson, E. (1945) 'The psychosomatic approach in gynaeco-logical practice', *Practitioner*, 155, pp. 378–84, (1959) *The History of the League of Mothers in New Zealand*, (1966) *Look Back in Wonder*.

Coates, V. (1969) 'Elizabeth Bryson obituary', *NZ Med. Jour.*, 70, pp. 44–5; Dow, D. (2003), 'The long locum: health propaganda in New Zealand', *NZ Med. Jour.*, 14, March; Dyhouse, C. (1998) 'Driving ambitions: women in pursuit of a medical education, 1890–1939', *Women's History Review*, 7, 3, pp. 321–43; Rose, J. (2001) *The Intellectual Life of the British Working Classes*; Taylor, W., 'A Scotsman's log: graduation stirs a memory', *The Scotsman*, 3 July 1965.

BUCHAN, Anna Masterton [O. Douglas], born Pathhead, Fife, 24 March 1877, died Peebles 24 Nov. 1948. Novelist. Daughter of Helen Masterton, and John Buchan, Free Church of Scotland minister.

Anna Buchan was the second of six children, and her family relationships were deeply significant to her. Her father delighted in fairy stories and read to the children from Scottish classics. In 1888, he was called to John Knox Church in the Gorbals, Glasgow, and the family removed to neighbouring Crosshill. Anna Buchan was educated at Queen's Park Academy, Hutcheson's Grammar School for Girls where she won a prize in English Literature, in Edinburgh, and at Queen Margaret College Glasgow. Through charitable work associated with the manse, she developed habits of generosity – later fuelled by the financial independence writing gave her (Tweedsmuir in A. Buchan, 1950) – and sociability, meeting a range of people from the Gorbals' poor to Glasgow's cultured intelligentsia. Throughout her life, she entertained, conversed and was an excellent listener, able to encourage anyone in difficulty. In 1906, her brother Walter became Clerk to the Town Council in Peebles, which appeared in her fiction as 'Priorsford'. She accompanied him to the Bank House, organising the household there for the rest of her life.

Both parents came to live there. During the nights when she sat up with her mother, during an illness, she began *Olivia in India* (1913), her first novel, based on her visit to her brother William in India in 1907. Her mother survived until 1937, but her father died in 1911; William died in 1912 and her young brother Alastair was killed at Arras in 1917. Anna Buchan did not marry. An early biographer wrote that 'every life has a private agony' (Reekie in A. Buchan, 1950), but whether she was romantically attached to anyone remains a matter of speculation. Her life now revolved around her mother, Walter, and the family of her brother John Buchan (1875–1940), the novelist and diplomat, whom she loved and admired, visiting him in Canada after he had become Governor-General. He understood the pressures she was under as an intelligent woman with no task which matched her abilities. Throughout her life, she was a great lover of theatre and a highly able public speaker at charitable functions, often recounting amusing anecdotes in Scots.

Under the pseudonym 'O. Douglas', Anna Buchan's many novels, often set in the Borders, sold so well that along with A. S. M. Hutchinson, A. E. W. Mason, 'Sapper', and John Buchan, she was among Hodder and Stoughton's 'Big Five' authors (Forrester 1995). Best-known titles include *The Setons* (1917) and *Penny Plain* (1920). She rose at 5 am to do housework so that later in the morning she might write. Her fiction celebrated the circumscribed comfort of settled, female, middle-class existence, and has, perhaps unjustly, sometimes been tagged with the term 'Kailyard'. Her mainly female readers, affirmed by this fiction, identified with its values of female self-effacement, competent service to others, endurance and humour. BD

• Buchan, A. (1950) *Farewell to Priorsford*, (1954) *Unforgettable, Unforgotten.*
Douglas, O., Works as above and see *HSWW* (Bibl.) and website: www.eup.ed.ac.uk
HSWW (Bibl.); Forrester, W. (1995) *Anna Buchan and O. Douglas*; Green, M. (1990) *John Buchan and his Sister Anna*; *ODNB* (2004); Reekie, A. G. (1950) 'A biographical introduction', in A. Buchan, *Farewell to Priorsford*; Tweedsmuir, S. (1950) 'Anna', in A. Buchan, *Farewell to Priorsford.*

BUCHAN, Elspeth, n. **Simpson,** baptised near Banff, 6 Feb. 1740, died Closeburn, Dumfriesshire, 29 March 1791. Founder and 'Friend Mother' of the Scottish religious sect known as the Buchanites. Daughter of Margaret Gordon, and John Simpson, innkeeper.

Elspeth Simpson moved to Glasgow where she met and married on 13 July 1760 a potter, Robert Buchan, and bore him three children, but he reputedly sent her back to Banff where she began to have unusual religious experiences. Returning to Glasgow around 1781, she met a Relief Church minister, Rev. Hugh White of Irvine, to whom she claimed to be 'the woman clothed with the sun' (Revelations 12). Hugh White believed her, took himself to be her 'man-child' (also in Rev. 12), and a band of followers was set up at Irvine in 1783. In 1784, he was deposed by his presbytery, the group was hounded out, and they settled on a farm near Closeburn in Dumfriesshire. With around 50 followers dressed in uniform green frocks, they adopted a celibate life awaiting the 'Second Coming'. Their customs were much mocked. Robert Burns is said to have had a female admirer in the band, and he hinted at sexual perversion and lesbianism. He wrote that Elspeth Buchan 'pretends to give them the Holy Ghost by breathing on them which she does with postures and practices that are scandalously indecent', and they 'lye and lodge all together, and hold likewise a community of women, as it is another of their tenets that they can commit no mortal sin' (Letter to James Burness 1784, quoted in *Dictionary*, 1993, pp. 108–9). When Elspeth Buchan died, the entire band moved to Larghill Farm and then to Crocketford, where a devoted follower took her body, standing vigil the 50th anniversary night of her death in 1841, when she had prophesied to rise. She is reputedly buried with other Buchanites at Crocketford. White took some followers to America, and the sect died out.

Neither the Buchanites nor their leader has been studied in earnest. Elspeth Buchan's claim to be the biblical 'sun-clothed' woman pre-dates the same claim made in 1792 by the better-known Englishwoman, Joanna Southcott (1730–1814), who gave rise to the Southcottian sect. CGB
• Cameron, J. (1904) *History of the Buchanite Delusion 1783–1846*; *Dictionary of Scottish Church History and Theology* (1993) pp. 108–9; *ODNB* (2004); Towill, E. S. (1976) *People and Places in the Story of the Scottish Church*, pp. 51–2, 88; Train, J. (1846) *The Buchanites from First to Last.*

BUCHAN, Isobel, Countess of see **FIFE, Isobel of, Countess of Buchan** (c. 1285–c. 1314)

BUCHAN, Priscilla Jean Fortescue, Lady Tweedsmuir, n. **Thomson,** m1 **Grant,** m2 **Buchan,** born London 25 Jan. 1915, died Potterton House, Aberdeenshire, 11 March 1978. Politician. Daughter of Edythe Mary Unwin, and Brigadier Alan Fortescue Thomson, DSO.

Priscilla Thomson was educated in England, Germany and France. In 1934, she married Major Sir Arthur Lindsay Grant, Grenadier Guards, of Monymusk and had two daughters; he was killed in action in 1944. During the Second World War she carried out welfare work in a munitions factory in Aberdeen that employed large numbers of women. Much later, when she, like many other employees, contracted terminal cancer, her family attributed the cause to the dangerous chemicals to which they had all been exposed. In 1946, a 'strikingly beautiful' widow, she won a by-election for the Conservatives in Aberdeen South, becoming, aged 31, the youngest woman to enter the Commons. In 1948, she married John Buchan, 2nd Baron Tweedsmuir, CBE, CD, son of the celebrated author of the same name and nephew of *Anna Buchan. They had a daughter. She sponsored a private member's bill that became the Protection of Birds Act 1954. The bill, introduced to the Lords by Lord Tweedsmuir, was only the second bill steered through both Houses by a husband and wife. From 1950 to 1953, she was UK representative at the Council of Europe and in 1960–1, UK Delegate to the UN General Assembly. The then Foreign Secretary, Lord Home, later said, 'the years when she served in the United Nations

were difficult and controversial, but she . . . earned the respect of all' (*Scotsman* 1978). From 1962 to 1964 she was Parliamentary Under-Secretary of State for Scotland.

Losing her Aberdeen seat in the 1966 general election, she pursued a business career with the Cunard company until, in 1970, she was created life peeress, Baroness Tweedsmuir of Belhelvie, and returned to politics. She then became Minister of State in the Scottish Office, taking particular interest in the fishing industry. Moving to the Foreign Office, again as Minister of State, she led the British negotiating team in Reykjavik during the so-called 'cod war' dispute over access to the Icelandic fishing grounds.

In 1974, she became the first woman to be appointed Deputy Speaker of the Lords. However, it was as first chair of the Lords' select committee on European affairs that *The Times* thought she would be best remembered. The analytical quality of the Committee's reports on legislative proposals 'gave other European parliamentarians cause to marvel' (*The Times* 1978). Lord Home assessed Lady Tweedsmuir as having 'a natural authority and a clear, disciplined mind', while a junior colleague described her as 'one of the most delightful women in public life, with a breadth of knowledge and incisive understanding' (*Scotsman* 1978). TB
• NLS: Dep. 337, Acc. 9059A and 11884, 11227, 11294, corr. and papers 1930–78, listed NRA 29245; Univ. of Cambridge Library: Dept of Manuscripts, Tweedsmuir of Belhelvie, Priscilla Jean Fortescue, Baroness (1915–78), XII (103), XVII:13 (99, 109, 137, 138, 141, 144, 153).
The Daily Telegraph, 13 March 1978 (obit.); Lord Tweedsmuir (1998) 'Priscilla Tweedsmuir, 1915–1978', *John Buchan Journal*, 18; *ODNB* (2004); *The Scotsman*, 13 March 1978 (obit.); *The Times*, 13 March 1978 (obit.); *WWW*.
Private information: James Douglas-Hamilton (son-in-law).

BUCHANAN, Dorothy Donaldson, m. **Fleming,** born Langholm 8 Oct. 1899, died Sedgemoor, Somerset, 13 June 1985. Civil engineer. Daughter of Marion Vassie, and James Donaldson Buchanan, minister of Langholm Parish.

Surrounded by bridges and other local works of Thomas Telford, Dorothy Buchanan's earliest ambition was to become a civil engineer, although her male relatives were doctors or clergy. She was educated at Langholm Academy, the Ministers' Daughters College and the University of Edinburgh (BSc Engineering 1923), then studied with Nobel Laureate Professor Barkla, but was delayed in graduating by illness. Professor Beare recommended her to contractors S. Pearson & Sons, who would not take her until she had experience. Fortunately, (Sir) Ralph Freeman was recruiting staff for his work as consultant to Dorman Long's on Sydney Harbour Bridge, and appointed Dorothy Buchanan to the design office at £4 a week – the same as the 'boys'. She worked for a while 'running out weights of members, panels, girders etc.', then sought work in the drawing office, to work on the southern approach spans to the bridge.

Having gained the necessary experience, she was taken on by Pearsons' in 1926 and worked on site at the Belfast Waterworks scheme in the Mourne Valley. The site's geological problems involved the novel technique of using compressed air to de-water silty strata, providing further experience. Site work was apparently not a problem, with workers being content to see her as an engineer. She returned to Dorman Long's drawing office to work on the George V Bridge in Newcastle and the Lambeth Bridge in London. In 1930 she left to marry William H. Dalrymple Fleming, electrical engineer, judging that family and professional roles could not be combined with success. She had passed the exams to become the ICE's first female corporate member (1927) and regarded this as a high point in her life. In later years she took up rock climbing and painting. NCB
• *New Civil Engineer*, 6, July 1978.
www.waterni.gov.uk/pdfs/SVALLEY.pdf
Additional information: Dorman Long.

BUICK (or BUIK, BUEK), Mary, m. Watson, born Dundee 4 July 1777, died Kilrenny 28 Feb. 1854. Seafarer, nurse. Daughter of Euphame Watson, and Gideon Buik or Buick.

In 1797, Mary Buick married widower Thomas Watson (c. 1765–1831), a Cellardyke fisherman. He was pressed into the navy, becoming a gunner and quartermaster, and she contrived to be taken on as a nurse on his ship. In April 1801, they were aboard the 64-gun ship HMS *Ardent* off Copenhagen, fighting what Vice-Admiral Nelson considered the most terrific of his 103 engagements (the occasion when he put a telescope to his blind eye). During the battle, Mary Watson gave birth to her daughter, also Mary. In 1803, Thomas Watson was transferred to HMS *Victory* under Nelson's command; Mary Watson and daughter went with him. At the battle of Trafalgar (21 Oct. 1805) he headed a gun crew while she tended the wounded (their daughter was protected by another Cellardyke man, Malcolm McRuvie). At the height of battle, Nelson was

killed. Mary Watson prepared his body for embalming, possibly with another woman, Mary Sperring: they would have undressed and washed him, cut off his hair, and helped lower him into a leaguer (cask) of brandy. After the war, Thomas Watson used his navy prize money to open a public house in Cellardyke, now 7 Shore Street. Mary Watson had several more children, and outlived her husband by 23 years. IMH
• Adkins, R. (2004) *Trafalgar*; Dyke, F. (1930) 'Baby of the Sea Battle', *Weekly Scotsman*, 7 Nov. 1936; *East Fife Observer*, 9 June 1936 (letter); 16 July 1936 (article); Gourlay, G. (1879) *Fisher Life*; Watson, H. (1986) *Kilrenny and Cellardyke*.

BULTER, Rhoda, n. Johnson, born Lerwick 15 July 1929, died Lerwick 7 July 1994. Poet and broadcaster. Daughter of Barbara Thomason, crofter, and Jeremiah Johnson, seaman.

An only child, born in the fishing town of Lerwick, Rhoda Johnson spent two years during the Second World War in the rural parish of Lunnasting. She lived in Lerwick the rest of her life, but the rhythms and discourses of country life had made a deep impression on her. In 1949, she married Dennis Bulter, meteorologist; they had seven children. In 1965, she contributed the first of many Shetland dialect poems to the *New Shetlander* journal, and became a welcome reciter of them at concerts throughout the islands. Her work was often humorous, but with a sad tinge now and again. These different moods are on display in her collections *A Naev foo a Coarn* (1976), *Shaela* (1977), *Link-stanes* (1980) and *Snyivveries* (1986). Rhoda Bulter was an accomplished broadcaster on BBC Radio Shetland, always in her native dialect. Her double-act with Mary Blance as 'Tamar and Beenie', a pair of cute Shetland women, became popular. Her untimely death inspired grief, and Shetland Folk Society put out a volume of dialect verse, *Mindin Rhoda* (1995), in her memory. BS
• Shetland Archives: D1/350 (MSS).
Bulter, R., Work as above.
Thomason, E. (1994) 'Poet patriot', *New Shetlander*, no. 189 (obit.), (1995) *Mindin Rhoda*, introduction and biography.

BURGES, Margaret, born c. 1579, died Edinburgh Jan. 1629, indweller of Nether Cramond, Edinburgh. Indicted for witchcraft.

Although her exact source of income is unknown, Margaret Burges, an urban-dwelling, lower-middle class woman, was in the thick of community business dealings, using curses and threats to pressure her neighbours to bend to her will. She quarrelled with neighbours about cloth, rent and money-lending. She rented land and had tenants in her own right. Her household employed several servants. Her second husband, John Gillespie, a boatman, ferried coal. She was referred to in documents by the nickname of 'Lady Dalyell', a reference to her deceased first husband, John Dalyell, indweller of Cramond.

On 3 October 1628, Elspeth Baird, a confessing witch later burnt in Leith, denounced Margaret Burges as a witch. Burges probably also had a neighbourhood witchcraft reputation in Cramond. The counter-suit of slander she brought against her neighbourhood accusers in the Kirk Session of Cramond on 12 October 1628 failed. For some witchcraft suspects, this strategy stalled witchcraft proceedings – but not this time. Ministers found that it was not slander to call Margaret Burges a witch because compelling evidence suggested that she probably was one. Based on testimony from the slander case, the Privy Council granted a commission of justiciary to try her for witchcraft. Throughout a month of investigations, three threads of evidence came to light. Witnesses from Nether Cramond testified that her behaviour (verbal neighbourhood coercion) resulted in misfortunes. Her 13-year-old female servant 'confest that the said Margaret had kist heir [kissed her] divers tymes beffoir and scho hir lykwayis' (NAS, JC26/9/1). Investigators then found a devil's mark on her leg, which confirmed witchcraft. Malefice (evil harm) and demonic relations were common in Scottish witchcraft trials, but allegations of same-sex affection were unusual. Margaret Burges was tried for witchcraft on 27 January 1629, found guilty and sentenced to death. LM

• NAS: JC26/9, 'Margaret Burges' bundle, items 1–12. *RPC*, 2nd Series, vol. 2, p. 494; Survey of Scottish Witchcraft, www.arts.ed.ac.uk/witches.

BURNET, Edith Mary Wardlaw, m. **Hughes,** born Edinburgh 7 July 1888, died Stirling 28 August 1971. Britain's first qualified woman architect. Daughter of Mary Crudelius, and George Wardlaw Burnet, advocate.

Edith Burnet was the third generation in her family to study architecture, following her grandfather John Burnet and her uncle Sir J. J. Burnet. Her grandmother, *Mary Crudelius, was a campaigner for women's higher education. Edith Burnet studied art and architecture 1907–11, in Paris, Dresden and Florence, then at Gray's School

of Art, Aberdeen (Diploma, 1914), working with the head of department, T. Harold Hughes (1887–1947), whom she married in 1918. They had two daughters. With Harold Hughes and A. C. Bryant, her first professional submission was a competition design for Ottawa Government Buildings (1914). She lectured at Gray's and Robert Gordon's Technical College 1915–19. After her husband's demobilisation, they both resigned from lecturing to concentrate on practice. T. H. Hughes worked briefly in the Glasgow office of Burnet, Tait & Lorne, Edith's uncle's practice. Edith was apparently refused employment in their London office because the toilet accommodation for 'ladies' was inadequate. In 1922, T. H. Hughes became Director of Architectural Studies at Glasgow School of Architecture. Edith Hughes passed her final RIBA exam in 1928. The Glasgow-based phase of her career included a mix of public and monumental commissions (in the family tradition of her uncle's various practices) and a larger number of small, bespoke housing projects in northern Glasgow and Stirlingshire. The latter, sometimes co-designed with her husband, allowed her to develop her interest in 'labour-saving kitchen design' (*RIBA Journal* 1972). In 1926 she lectured on architecture for BBC Scotland. Her marriage was 'uneasy' (McKean 1987), but her husband's influence appears to have been strong: she clearly shared his antipathy to the Modern Movement and respect for classical architecture. Edith Hughes's major works included the 1924 competition design for Coatbridge War Memorial (1926) – a copy of the classical Choragic Monument of Lysicrates, but with open colonnade and no dome, typical of the simplified, low-relief classicism she favoured. Her design for the new Glasgow Mercat Cross (erected 1930) again evoked historical sources. After her husband's death in 1947, she was architect to Lansdowne House School (1951–8); John Watson's School (1958–68); and St Mary's Episcopal Cathedral and Song School (1956–66), all in Edinburgh. The work at St Mary's included design of the screen, wrought-iron gates, replacement font and cathedral furniture. In 1968, she became the first woman to be awarded an honorary fellowship of the RIAS. DMW

• National Monuments Records of Scotland, list of works and biography supplied by Ailsa Tanner (c. 1980); Robert Gordon's Technical College, Governors' Minutes, 1914–20. Glendinning, M. et al. (1996) *A History of Scottish Architecture*; McKean, C. (1987) *The Scottish Thirties, an Architectural Introduction*; *RIBA Journal*, Feb. 1972 (obit.).

BURNETT, Sybil Aird, Lady, n. **Crozier Smith,** born 6 Nov. 1889, died probably Crathes, 6 April 1960. Garden designer. Daughter of William Crozier Smith and his wife.

Sybil Burnett was one of the most influential and respected gardeners in Great Britain in the 20th century. Few records of her life remain, since most family documents were destroyed by a fire at Crathes in 1966. In her youth, she was a successful hockey player, representing the Borders. On 10 July 1913, she married Major General Sir James L. G. Burnett of Leys, Bart (1880–1953), owner of Crathes Castle, Kincardineshire. They had two sons and a daughter. Sybil Burnett became involved in a considerable amount of voluntary work associated with her husband's life as a soldier. She wrote 'The Happy Prisoner', about her life as chatelaine of Crathes Castle, and poetry in memory of the Gordon Highlanders who died in Singapore.

At Crathes she created the now-famous gardens; the Golden Garden was planted later, in the 1970s, with reference to her concept for it. She also redesigned the herbaceous borders in the great garden at Pitmedden. Graham Stuart Thomas considered her 'a very original colour schemer . . . in her central garden she used the soft pinky brown walls as a background . . . She also had the wit, when she made a white garden, to plant a hedge . . . [which] showed up the white flowers' (Thomas 2002, p. 214). Crathes was given to the NTS in 1952. JB
• Burnett of Leys archive, Crathes: Sybil Burnett papers. Taylor, G. C., *Country Life*, 25 Sept. 1937; Thomas, G. S. with Richardson, T. (2002) *The Garden*, vol. 127, Pt 3, March, (RHS Journal). Personal information (James Burnett of Leys).

BURNETT-SMITH, Annie *see* **SWAN, Annie Shepherd** (1859–1943)

BURNS, Margaret,‡ (aka **Matthews**), born Durham c. 1769, died Roslin, near Edinburgh, c. 1792. 'Celebrated beauty' (Kay 1877, p. 399), prostitute.

Margaret Burns's father is thought to have been a wealthy merchant whose second marriage left her and her sisters unprovided for. She resorted to prostitution for the rest of her short life. Arriving in Edinburgh in 1789, aged about 20, she quickly attracted attention at the 'evening promenades'. She was of a slightly later generation than Ranger's 'ladies of pleasure' (1775), who mostly lived in closes off the High Street. Complaints of night-time disturbances at her Rose Street address brought her before the magistrates. The stern Bailie William Creech (1745–1815), Robert Burns's publisher, sentenced her to banishment from the city, on pain of being drummed through the streets plus six months in a house of correction (the normal punishment for prostitution). She appealed, successfully obtaining a bill of suspension, after one witness withdrew his testimony. William Creech became the butt of a mischievous report in a London journal that he was to marry her, followed by an even more equivocal denial. The poet Robert Burns (they were not related) followed her case and wrote of it: 'Cease ye prudes your envious railing/Lovely Burns has charms – confess./True it is she had one failing/Had a woman ever less?' (ibid., p. 400). She lived in 'unenviable notoriety' before going into a 'decline' (ibid.), presumably related to her profession, and retired to Roslin, dying in 1792, still only in her early 20s. She was buried in Rosslyn Chapel graveyard. SR
• Kay, J. (1877 edn.) *A Series of Original Portraits and Caricature Etchings*, vol. 2, pp. 399–401; Leneman, L. (1995) ' "Bad housekeeping" in eighteenth-century Edinburgh', *Scottish Local History*, 33, Feb., pp. 8–10; *ODNB* (2004) (Creech, William); *Ranger's List of Ladies of Pleasure in Edinburgh* (1775, rev. edn. 1978).

BURTON, Mary, born Aberdeen 7 Feb. 1819, died Aberdeen 19 March 1909. Educational and social reformer. Daughter of Elizabeth Paton, and Lieutenant William Kinninmont Burton.

Educated by her mother, who imbued her with admiration for the ideas of Jean-Jacques Rousseau and Mary Wollstonecraft, Mary Burton moved to Edinburgh in 1832 with her widowed mother and brother, John Hill Burton, historian and advocate. She never married, but combined a lifetime's work 'on behalf of women' (Tooley 1896, p. 164) with raising orphaned nephews and nieces 'to see that they were trained alike on the intellectual and practical side of life' (*The Scotsman*, 22 March 1909). This philosophy underpinned her contribution to education. In 1869, she persuaded the directors of the Watt Institution and School of Arts, the first Mechanics Institute and forerunner of Heriot-Watt University, to open its classes to female students. Her niece, Ella Burton, daughter of John Hill Burton and sister of *Mary Rose Burton, was one of the first to enrol. In 1874, Mary Burton became the first woman director. When the Institution became Heriot-Watt College in 1885, she became a life governor. (Heriot-Watt University now has a Mary Burton Centre). In 1884, she was elected to St Cuthbert's Parochial Board, later Edinburgh Parish Council, and in 1885 to the Edinburgh School Board, serving on both until 1897. A leading member of the EWLA, she was a speaker and campaigner for women's suffrage and Irish Home Rule. Mary Burton argued that boys as well as girls should be taught to sew, knit and cook. She also urged that universities should open in the evening to admit working people, and for that reason insisted that the School Board met in the evenings. Her life-long commitment to equality was reflected in her will. She left legacies for prizes for Heriot-Watt College evening class students 'irrespective of age or sex', and to the ENSWS to campaign 'for the admission of women to sit as members of parliament, either at Westminster or in a Scottish Parliament' (*Edinburgh Evening News*, 23 March 1909). AEJ

• Heriot-Watt Univ. Archive: SA1/2/2 Minutes of Directors, Watt Institution and School of Arts, 1869–85; HWC1/1–2 Minutes of Governors of George Heriot's Trust, Heriot-Watt College Cttee., 2 April 1909 (obit.); City of Edinburgh Central Library: YL 353 Minutes of Edinburgh School Board, 1885–97; Edinburgh City Archive: SL/10 Minutes of St Cuthbert's Parochial Board, 17 July 1889.
Edinburgh Evening News, 20–4 March 1885, 28 March–1 April 1891, 22–3 March 1909 (obit., legacy); Jones, A. (2000) 'Rescued from oblivion? The case of Mary Burton and Liberton Bank House', *Scottish Archives*, vol. 6; *ODNB* (2004); Tooley, S. A. (1896) 'A slum landlady. An interview with Miss Hill Burton', *The Young Woman*, vol. IV, p. 164; Tooley, S. A. 'Notable Victorians', *Weekly Scotsman*, 20 Feb. 1932; *The Scotsman*, 22 March 1909 (obit.).

BURTON Mary Rose Hill, born Edinburgh 20 August 1857, died Rome 5 June 1900. Artist. Daughter of Katherine Innes, and John Hill Burton, historian.

The Burton women made a formidable dynasty. Mary Rose Burton's mother, **Katherine Innes** (1829–98), had studied sculpture but abandoned her studies to serve with Florence Nightingale in the Crimea. Upon her return, she married John Hill Burton (3 August 1855) and became a close friend of her sister-in-law and fellow activist *Mary Burton. Katherine Burton was active in the ELEA, and wrote a memoir of its founder *Mary Crudelius. Mary Rose Burton studied mathematics and Latin in the early 1880s with the Edinburgh Association for the University Education of Women, then art in Munich and Paris. She exhibited with the RA, the RSA, and the SSA, among others, and was a founding member of the Edinburgh Lady Artists' Club, formed in 1889 for the benefit of professional, practising artists. Some of her most interesting paintings were based on travels to Japan (two solo exhibitions in London 1895 and 1896) and to Ireland with her friend and fellow artist **Florence Haig** (1855–1952). An intimate friend of Patrick and *Anna Geddes, Mary Rose Burton painted some of the murals for their Ramsay Garden home and for University Hall. The Ramsay Garden murals depicted her grandmother's home, Kilravock Castle, and suggest her love for the north of Scotland: she and her mother actively campaigned to save the Falls of Foyers, near Inverness, from destruction by British Aluminium, but to her great sadness she managed to preserve them only in her drawings and paintings (Helland 1997, p. 127). Like her aunt and her mother, Mary Rose Burton was concerned for the education of women and for women's right to follow a career. She died suddenly during a visit to Italy. JVH

• NLS: Acc. 9557, 10526, 10577, corr.; Strathclyde Univ. Archives, T-GED 9/82 and 1991, corr.
Burton, M. R. H. (1898) 'Photography and colour-printing in Japan', *Studio*, September.
Burton, K. (1874) *A Memoir of Cosmo Innes*, (1879) *A Memoir of Mrs Crudelius*; Helland, J. (1997) 'Artistic advocate: Mary Rose Hill Burton and the Falls of Foyers', *Scot. Econ. and Soc. Hist.*, 17, 2, (2000) *Professional Women Painters in Nineteenth-Century Scotland*.

BURY, Lady Charlotte Susan Maria, n. **Campbell,** m1 **Campbell,** m2 **Bury,** born Argyll House, London, 28 Jan. 1775, died London 31 March 1861. Poet, diarist, popular novelist. Daughter of *Elizabeth Gunning, and John Campbell, 5th Duke of Argyll.

Lady Charlotte Campbell spent much of her privileged upbringing on the Continent, gaining a broad knowledge of art, literature and music. She was presented at court in 1790 and later hosted literary parties in Edinburgh, introducing Walter Scott to Matthew Lewis, author of *The Monk*, to whom she was 'Divinity'. In 1796, she married her impecunious cousin, Colonel Jack Campbell, whose death in 1809 left her with nine children to support. Appointed lady-in-waiting to Princess Caroline in 1810, she left in 1815 with no further contact, except as a defence witness during the 'trial' of Caroline, for adultery, in 1820. Despite her political potential, she believed that women did not have 'the strength and terseness ascribed to male intellect alone'. She travelled frequently and, in 1818, married Rev. Edward John Bury, 15 years her junior, causing disputes with her children. He died in 1832, leaving her with two more daughters.

Lady Charlotte wrote chiefly to support her precarious finances. Her early *Poems on Several Occasions* (1797) reflect both fashionable forms and cosmopolitanism, including sentimental references to the 'lonely cott' of the Scots. The *Three Great Sanctuaries of Tuscany* (1832), in memory of John Bury and illustrated by his engravings, is a poem on medieval monasteries. Primarily, however, she wrote popular novels, the first in 1812, the rest following her second marriage. Her 19 books, produced in 16 years, sold well, pandering to the desire for romantic novels about high society and earning her up to £200 each. Her most successful publication was the *Diary Illustrative of the Times of George IV*, scandalously gossipy insights into court life (Anon. 1838, repr. 1896, 1908 under Bury). Because of the change in tastes, her fiction was little read after her death, but has now attracted renewed attention. DLS

• Bury, Lady C., Works as above and see Bibl.
DBAWW; *HSWW* (Bibl.); *ODNB* (2004); Perkins, P. (2001) 'Bury, Lady Charlotte Susan Maria Campbell, 1775–1861, a critical essay', *Scottish Women Poets of the Romantic Period*, electronic anthology www.alexanderstreet2.com

C

CADELL, Grace Ross, born Carriden 25 Oct. 1855, died Mosspark 19 Feb. 1918. Physician and suffragist. Daughter of Martha Fleming, and George Philip Cadell, coalwork superintendent.

Grace Cadell was one of *Sophia Jex-Blake's first students in the Edinburgh School of Medicine for Women in 1887, but in 1888 was dismissed, along with her younger sister, Georgina, for challenging Jex-Blake's authority. (They brought a partly successful action for damages, heard in 1889.) *Elsie Inglis joined the rebels, and set up an alternative Medical College for Women, in which the Cadell sisters enrolled. When Dr Inglis founded the Medical Women's Club in 1899, Grace Cadell was appointed to the Medical Committee, and in 1904 she also joined the staff of Elsie Inglis's High Street centre, the Hospice, specialising in gynaecology. She was running it in 1911.

An active suffragette, Grace Cadell was president of the Leith Branch of the WSPU in 1907, before aligning herself with the WFL. In 1912, in protest against the withholding of the franchise, she refused to pay taxes, and her furniture was seized and sold under warrant at the Mercat Cross, Edinburgh. Renowned for her tenacity and commitment, her response was to rally her friends and turn the occasion into a suffrage meeting. During the Scottish campaign of attacks on buildings (1913–14) she was one of the medical advisers to women hunger strikers in prison, who were frequently released to her care under the Cat and Mouse Act. Another such was **Mabel Jones** (c. 1865–1923), a Glasgow-based doctor, who wrote damning reports of their condition. Grace Cadell notably treated *Ethel Moorhead after forcible feeding had led to double pneumonia. Her house was known as a place of refuge for suffragettes. She apparently adopted four children, probably on the outbreak of war (*AGC*, p. 256), but died in 1918. RD

• *AGC*; *HHGW*; Lawrence, M. (1971) *Shadow of Swords*; *The Times*, 12 Oct. 1912.

CAIRD, Alice Mona, n. Alison, [G. Noel Hatton], born Ryde, Isle of Wight, 24 May 1854, died London 4 Feb. 1932. Novelist, essayist and campaigner. Daughter of Matilda Ann Jane Hector, and John Alison, engineer.

Mona Caird, whose father was a Scot, said that her conventional upbringing led her to grow up rebelling against traditional attitudes and that she was discouraged as a young writer (*Women's Penny Paper* 1890, p. 421). At 23, she married James Alexander Henryson Caird (1847–1921), son of agriculturalist and MP, Sir James Caird. Although she spent much of her adult life either in London or on the continent, she frequently stayed at Cassencary, the Caird family estate in Galloway, using the area as settings for some of her fiction. She had one son, Alister James Caird.

Mona Caird's first two novels, *Whom Nature Leadeth* (1883) and *One That Wins* (1887), were published under the pseudonym 'G. Noel Hatton'; both express unformed yet powerful views on women's rights as individuals. (It has been claimed that *Lady Hetty* (1875) is her work [Sutherland 1988, p. 99] but that is unlikely.) She acquired notoriety following an 1888 *Westminster Review* essay, 'Marriage', in which she argued that marriage made women little better than legally bound slaves. *The Daily Telegraph* responded under the heading 'Is Marriage a Failure?', bringing a flood of over 27,000 letters. The debate raged and she was 'banned and shunned like the plague in certain circles' (Swan 1934, p. 71). However, Mona Caird was claimed as a champion by women's rights groups, a position supported by the dozens of essays she published before the First World War and her prominent membership in the advanced Pioneer Club.

Her most famous work, *The Daughters of Danaus* (1894), describes a gifted composer who struggles to develop her art in the face of domestic demands. *The Great Wave* (1931), published the year before her death, addresses the tragedy of domination and power, themes that as a staunch pacifist she used throughout her career but that gained particular significance for her during the inter-war period. She also passionately supported anti-vivisection causes and the suffrage movement, although as a pacifist she refused to participate in militant action. Her later years were marked by illness, though the writer Ernest Rhys described her as a woman who, even in suffering, 'defied the omens with superb courage, wit, and gaiety' (Rhys 1940, p. 217). TSR

• Caird, M., Works as above, and (1889) *The Wing of Azrael*, (1891) *A Romance of the Moors*, (1897) *The Morality of Marriage and Other Essays on the Status and Destiny of Woman*, (1898) *The Pathway of the Gods*, (1915) *The Stones of Sacrifice*.
Guilette, M. (1989) Afterword to *The Daughters of Danaus*; Heilmann, A. (1996) 'Mona Caird (1854–1932): wild woman, new woman, and early radical feminist critic of marriage and motherhood', *Wom. Hist. Rev.*, 5,1; *ODNB* (2004); Rhys, E. (1940) *Wales England Wed*; Swan, A. S. (1934) *My Life*; Sutherland, J. (1988) *The Longman Companion to Victorian Fiction; Women's Penny Paper, 1890.*

CAIRD, Janet Hinshaw, n. **Kirkwood,** born Livingstonia, Malawi, 24 April 1913, died Inverness 20 Jan. 1992. Poet, novelist and critic. Daughter of Janet Gilmour, and Peter Scott Kirkwood, missionary.

Janet Kirkwood was educated at Dollar Academy and studied English Literature at the University of Edinburgh. She was awarded a scholarship to study at Grenoble University and the Sorbonne, Paris 1935–6. On 19 July 1938 she married James Bowman Caird, a fellow student. They had two daughters. She taught in Park School in Glasgow in the late 1930s and at Dollar Academy

during the war. After 1945 she worked at home on drafts of her novels and short stories, some of which were broadcast on radio. She returned to teaching at Dollar Academy in the 1950s. After moving to Inverness in 1963, she pursued her writing ambitions, with strong critical support from her husband, himself a writer and authority on Scottish literature. Her novel for children, *Angus the Tartan Partan* (1961), was followed by a series of adult detective novels and the historical novel *The Umbrella Maker's Daughter* (1980), set in Dollar.

Janet Caird's most important contribution is considered by many to be three books of poetry written and published in later life. *Some Walk a Narrow Path* (1977), *A Distant Urn* (1983) and *John Donne, You Were Wrong* (1988) contain short, acutely observed poems, formally influenced by the Imagism which was still influential when she was a student. The poems speak from a woman's perspective of the process and loneliness of ageing. She was an able critic who wrote reviews and articles, especially on women writers, for Scottish journals including *Cencrastus*, *Chapman* and *Scottish Literary Journal*. Her interests extended to archaeology, art and travel. She was a Fellow of the Society of Antiquaries of Scotland and President of the Inverness Association of University Women. MPM

• NLS: Acc. 9670, 9652, 12294, James and Janet Caird Archive.
Caird, J., Works as above and (1961) *Murder Reflected*, (1966) *Perturbing Spirit*, (1967) *Murder Scholastic*, (1968) *The Loch*, (1973) *Murder Remote*.
Contemporary Authors Online, Gale Publishing Co. www.gale-edit.com/cas/; *Scotlit*, No. 7, Spring, 1992; Scottish Poetry Library *Newsletter* No. 19, August 1992; *The Scotsman*, 22 Jan. 1992 (obit.).
Private information: Dr Elisabeth Davenport (daughter).

CALDER, Muriel, m. **Campbell,** born Calder (Cawdor) 13 Feb. 1498, died Calder 1570s. Heiress, progenitor of the Campbells of Cawdor. Daughter of Isabel Rose of Kilravock, and John Calder, son of William, last Thane of Calder, d. 1503.

John Calder had predeceased his father, leaving one child, red-haired Muriel. Her uncle, Hugh Rose, intended to marry her to his grandson, but the Kilravocks got into hot water feuding with the Urquharts of Cromarty. The Campbell Earl of Argyll, Justice General of Scotland, offered leniency on condition that he acquired wardship of Muriel Calder, with the right to marry her to one of his own kinsmen. There have been many retellings of what happened next: how Argyll's emissary, Campbell of Inverliver, sent up the Great Glen to fetch her in 1505, was set upon by enraged Calders and Roses in Strath Nairn, how he stripped his seven-year-old trophy of her clothes, and put these on a haystack in a cart as a decoy, around which four of his own sons perished in furious fighting. When his wisdom was questioned, sacrificing his sons for a 'wee lass who might die next winter', Inverliver is said to have riposted that she would never die 'so long as there's a red-haired lassie by the banks of Loch Awe' (Calder 2003, p. 84). Muriel Calder didn't die. Married in 1510 to Sir John Campbell, son of the Earl of Argyll, she bore him children, including *Katherine Campbell, later Countess of Crawford. Sir John established the Campbells of Calder as a powerful satellite clan, responsible for ousting the Macdonalds from Islay in 1619. Muriel Calder lived in Calder to a ripe old age, but died before Shakespeare's influence transformed the place to Cawdor. ALRC

• Calder, A. (2003) *Gods, Mongrels and Demons*; Macphail, J. R. N. (ed.) (1914) *Highland Papers*, vol. 1; Spalding Club (1859) *Book of the Thanes of Cawdor . . . 1236–1742*.

CALDERÓN DE LA BARCA, **Frances Erskine (Fanny), Marquesa,** n. **Inglis,** born Edinburgh 23 Dec. 1804, died Madrid, Spain, 6 Feb. 1882. Author and teacher. Daughter of Jane Stein, school-teacher, and William Inglis, landowner and Writer to the Signet.

Fanny Inglis was brought up in Edinburgh. In 1828, her father's bankruptcy forced the family to move to Normandy. After his death in 1830 they left for the USA and founded a school in Boston. In 1838 Fanny married the Spanish diplomat Angel Calderón de la Barca (1790–1861). Shortly after their marriage they moved to Mexico where he was appointed Ambassador of Spain. Fanny Calderón de la Barca's letters, based on her journals and compiled as *Life in Mexico* (1843), are considered among the most important documents on 19th-century Mexico. She also wrote *The Attaché in Madrid, or, Sketches of the Court of Isabella II* (1856), published anonymously. Her letters show her wit, curiosity and exuberant love of life. When violent events happen around her, her descriptions are ironic or humorous, never fearful.

Life in Mexico first appeared in Boston and Mexico. A large volume of over 500 pages, with a preface by the historian William H. Prescott, it was reviewed in the *Edinburgh Review* and *North American Review*, which commented: 'In the brilliant gallery of pictures, which our fair author has sketched, sometimes of the city and its inhabitants, . . . at others of its beautiful environs, we know not which to select' (January 1843). *Life in Mexico* was considered to be accurate enough for use as a guide by American officers during the Mexican War of 1847. Fanny Calderón de la Barca witnessed the day-to-day complexity of Mexican life as well as two small uprisings, the copper monetary crisis and a change of president. The most interesting aspect of *Life in Mexico* is her account of the private world of Mexican women, including her privileged access to Catholic nuns. Her descriptions of young girls being given as brides to the church are harrowing and critical.

The Calderón de la Barcas later lived in Washington, but in 1853 political changes in Spain compelled Don Angel to return to Madrid as Minister of Foreign Affairs. In 1861 he died and Fanny went to live in a convent just over the French border. She later accepted a request from Queen Isabella to undertake the education of the young Infanta Isabella. In 1876, she was made a marquesa in her own right and spent the remainder of her life with the royal family in Madrid. JC

• Calderón de la Barca, F. [1843] (1966, 1982, H. T. Fisher and M. H. Fisher, eds) *Life in Mexico*, (1856) *The Attaché in Madrid*. *The North American Review*, 56, 118, Jan. 1843; *ODNB* (2004).

CALDERWOOD, Margaret, of Polton, n. **Steuart,** born 1715, died 1774. Diarist. Daughter of Anne Dalrymple, and Sir James Stewart of Coltness.

Margaret Steuart was the eldest daughter in the family. Her father was Solicitor-General for Scotland (1714–17) and through her mother she was connected with the famous legal family of Viscount Stair. Her brother was Sir James Steuart, a notable political economist whose supposed Jacobite connections forced him to live in exile in Europe for many years following the '45 Rising. She married Thomas Calderwood (d. c. 1773) of Polton, an estate near Edinburgh, in 1735. They had a daughter and two sons and for many years she lived an unremarkable domestic life, her financial abilities manifest in the management of the family estates. Anxiety arising from her brother's continued exile abroad caused her, with her husband, sons and two servants, to travel through England and on to the Low Countries to pay him a visit, joining him in Brussels in 1756. She recorded her experience in a journal in the form of a series of letters home. It was widely circulated among family and friends and later published. The impression it gives, as a later editor commented, is of 'a dominating personality, a delightful companion, and an extremely capable woman' (Fyfe 1942, p. 83).

She was not impressed by much of what she saw: anti-English, anti-Catholic and highly critical of continental manners and customs, she pitied everyone who was not born a Scot. In London, she was distinctly unimpressed by government ministers, describing them as: 'a parcel of old, ignorant, senseless bodies, who mind nothing but eating and drinking, and rolling about in Hyde Park' (*SHA*, p. 45). On her return, she resumed her management of the family estates and never ventured out of Scotland again. She wrote an unpublished novel, *The Adventures of Fanny Roberts*. Her brother was eventually pardoned and returned to Scotland. SN

• Calderwood, M. [1756] (1884) *Letters and journals . . . from England, Holland and the low countries, in 1756*, A. Ferguson, ed.

DNB vol. III (1908); Fyfe, J. G. (ed.) (1942) *Scottish Diaries and Memoirs, 1746–1843*; *ODNB* (2004); *SHA*.

CALDWELL (CALDALL), Christian [John Dicksone], fl. 1660s. Indicted as a cross-dressing witch finder.

On 5 March 1662, Christian Caldwell, while disguised as John Dicksone, burgess of Forfar, initialled a contract with the shire of Moray. The contract stipulated that John Dicksone reside in the shire for one year to identify and examine suspected witches for the devil's mark. At least eight other men of this profession are known. His/her salary of six shillings a day was augmented by six pounds for each person John Dicksone identified who was found guilty of witchcraft. What transpired next is unknown, but Christian Caldwell was interrogated in Edinburgh on 30 August 1662 to answer charges of false accusation, torture, and causing the death of innocent people in Moray. An undated indictment also charged that she 'did counterfoot [her] sex [and] tock on the habit of a man' (NAS, JC26/28/1). Her fate is unknown. LM

• NAS: JC26/28/1–4.

Larner, C. (1981) *Enemies of God: the witch-hunt in Scotland*; MacDonald, S. W. (1997) 'The devil's mark and the witch-prickers of Scotland', *Jour. Roy. Soc. Med.*, 90.

CALLCOTT, Lady Maria *see* **GRAHAM, Maria** (1785–1842)

CAMERON, Elizabeth Jane [Jane Duncan, Janet Sandison], born Renton, Dunbartonshire, 10 March 1910, died Jemimaville 20 Oct. 1976. Novelist. Daughter of Jessie (Janet) Sandison, and Duncan Cameron, policeman.

Elizabeth Jane Cameron was brought up in industrial central Scotland, but spent idyllic childhood holidays at The Colony, her grandparents' croft in the Black Isle, Ross-shire. Her mother died when she was 10 years old, and The Colony, where her baby brother was brought up, became a place of escape from her stepmother. She came to regard it as her real home and it appears in her fiction as 'Reachfar'.

She was educated at Lenzie Academy and graduated MA from the University of Glasgow in 1930. After various secretarial jobs she served in the WRAF, 1939–45. In 1945 she met Alexander (Sandy) Clapperton (1910–58), an engineer, who was unhappily married, and three years later she went with him to Jamaica as his wife, though their partnership was never regularised. She had been writing in secret, though destroying her work, for many years, and began to write seriously in 1956, after Sandy had been diagnosed with heart disease. In some 15 months she wrote seven novels, the first in the long *My Friends* series. They were accepted en bloc before the first was published, a unique event in British publishing at that time. When her partner died in 1958 she settled in Jemimaville in the Black Isle.

The *My Friends* series eventually ran to 19 titles, all published under the pseudonym 'Jane Duncan'. The heroine's name, Janet Sandison, is that of the author's mother. She also published children's stories written for, and fictionally about, her brother's young family. A separate, four-novel series appeared under the pseudonym 'Janet Sandison'; they are, fictionally, the novels that Janet in the *My Friends* series is writing in secret. Although not autobiographical, the *My Friends* novels follow to a large extent the course of her life. A critic suggests that she 'had faced and transformed in fiction the losses and compensations that textured her life' (Hart and Hart 1997, p. 470). MARB

• Duncan, J., Works as above, and (1975) *Letter from Reachfar*. See also (Bibl.).

Hart, L. L. and Hart, F. R. (1997) 'Jane Duncan: the homecoming of imagination', in *HSWW* (Bibl.); *ODNB* (2004).

CAMERON, Jenny (Jean), born Glendessary c. 1698, died Mount Cameron 1772. Jacobite. Daughter

of Jane Cameron, and Hugh Cameron of
Glendessary.

Jenny Cameron lived a quiet life until on
19 August 1745 she rode to the Raising of the
Standard at Glenfinnan at the head of 300
Cameron men. Almost overnight, 'Bonnie Jeanie
Cameron' became the darling of the Whig
propagandists. Among her many alleged exploits,
she is said to have possessed a voracious sexual
appetite (unleashed on sibling, servant, soldier and
sovereign alike), borne several illegitimate children,
and enjoyed a variety of dubious careers as Queen
of the Highland Rovers, a transvestite, and a
smuggler. By the 1750s, Jenny Cameron was a
legend, although at the cost of her good name.

By contrast, another account calls her 'always a
person of the greatest propriety of conduct and
character' (Anon. 1847). After the '45, she kept a
low profile, retreating to the estate of Mount
Cameron, which she purchased in 1751. There she
fostered orphans of the '45, ran a school, and
supported the local Presbyterian parish, despite
being a devout Catholic. She was buried in the
grounds of Mount Cameron. Today, citizens of East
Kilbride remember her as a local heroine and have
marked her burial site with a plaque commemorating her contribution to the Jacobite cause. Two
other 'Jean Camerons' participated in the '45; one,
an Edinburgh milliner, was captured in Stirling and
imprisoned in Edinburgh Castle in 1746. She later
ran a shop in the Lawnmarket (possibly a Jacobite
front) and died penniless in the Canongate. MES
• Anon. (1847) 'A Highland chief one hundred years ago',
from the Dublin Univ. Magazine, September 1847, Clan
Cameron Archives, http://www.clan-cameron.org;
Arbuthnot, A. (1746) Memoirs of the Remarkable Life and
Surprizing Adventures of Miss Jenny Cameron; Craig, M.
(1997) Damn' Rebel Bitches: the women of the '45.

CAMERON, Katharine, m. **Kay,** born Glasgow
26 Feb. 1874, died Edinburgh 21 August 1965.
Artist-illustrator. Daughter of Margaret Johnston
Robertson, and Rev. Robert Cameron of Paisley,
United Presbyterian minister.

Eighth of nine children, Katharine Cameron
was sister to David Young Cameron (1865–1945),
artist and etcher, and a childhood friend of writer
*Anna Buchan. Befriended in her teens by
*Elizabeth Sharp, the anthologist-Celtic Twilight
writer, she conceived art in terms of a 'Gospel'.
One of the *Glasgow Girls (GSA 1899–1901), she
drew illustrations for The Magazine (1893–6) and
The Yellow Book (1886–7) before studying at the

Académie Colarossi, Paris (1902). A skilled etcher,
printmaker and painter, Katharine Cameron
illustrated for T. C. & E. C. Jack, T. N. Foulis, and
Nelson's, and was particularly known for her flower
paintings. She worked from a studio in a house
shared with family in Stirling, then moved to
Edinburgh where her studio was in Forres Street
(1908–28). In 1928, after his divorce, she married
collector and businessman Arthur Kay (1861–1939).
Katharine Cameron designed the cover and dust
jacket for his book Treasure Trove in Art (1939). She
continued to paint into old age. A member of the
GSLA, the RSW (1897–1965) and the SSA (1909),
she exhibited regularly with the RGIFA (1891–1965)
and the RSA (1894–1964), becoming an FRSA in
1950. RA
• NLS: Acc. 8950, Acc. 11164:4; SNPG: PG 2607.
Addison, R. (2000) 'Glasgow Girl: Katharine Cameron',
Scottish Book Collector, 6/9, pp. 4–7; Burkhauser, J. (ed.)
(1990) Glasgow Girls; ODNB (2004); Smith, W. (1992) D Y
Cameron: the visions of the hills.

CAMERON, Mary Margaret, born Portobello
9 March 1865, died Turnhouse 15 Feb. 1921. Artist.
Daughter of Mary Brown Small, and Duncan
Cameron, stationer and steel pen patentee.

A talented linguist, fluent in Spanish, Italian
and French, and an avid traveller, Mary Cameron
studied art in Spain, and in Paris with Courtois and
Rixen. She was awarded an 'Honourable Mention'
in the Paris Salon 1904 for a large portrait of her
sister Flora Cameron but her most ambitious
paintings depicted scenes of Spanish bullfighting:
the French government adopted one of the most
successful of these (Picadors About to Enter the
Bullring, 1901) as a postcard to promote their
opposition to bullfighting in France. She exhibited
widely and participated as a member in a number
of British artists' associations including the SSA,
Women's International Art Club, and the
Edinburgh Lady Artists' Club. Her 'extraordinary'
and 'powerful' pictures (Queen 1910, p. 1101) were
well reviewed and frequently reproduced in the
press. JVH
• Anon. 'Miss Mary Cameron: work of a woman artist in
Spain', Westminster Gazette, 14 June 1910, p. 12; Helland, J.
(2000) Professional Women Painters in Nineteenth-Century
Scotland; 'Round the Galleries – Miss M. Cameron', Queen,
18 June 1910.

CAMERON, Una May, born West Linton,
Peeblesshire, 6 May 1904, died Buckingham, 15
Oct. 1987. Mountaineer. Twin daughter of Jeanie

Dewar, of the whisky family, and Ewen Cameron, landed proprietor.

Una Cameron was educated in Montreux, Switzerland, Cheltenham Ladies' College and the Central School of Arts and Crafts, London. In 1929, after several seasons climbing in the Alps and Dolomites, she attained membership of the Ladies' Alpine Club and became a leading light there (president 1957), due to her climbing achievements all over the world and contributions to its *Journal*. In 1932, with two companion guides, she travelled to Kazbek, Russia, to climb in the Caucasus mountains, a journey recounted in her book, *A Good Line* (1932). During the 1930s she pioneered climbs in the Mont Blanc range from Villa Cameron, the home she had built in Courmayeur. In 1938, during a trip to Ruwenzori, Africa, she became the first woman to climb the two peaks of Mount Kenya. Una Cameron returned to Scotland for the Second World War, driving for the Auxiliary Fire Service, then joining the FANYs. Thereafter, she returned to her adopted home, which she bequeathed to the Valle d'Aosta region. In 2002, the Villa Cameron became the designated site for the Montagna Sicura Foundation, its aim being to promote the safe use and study of the mountains she loved (Bieller 2002, pp. 5, 98). CAO

• Alpine Club Archives, London: G25 Ladies' Alpine Club, application form (1929), climbing lists (1927–39); NLS: Acc. 10384, Una Cameron's climbing diaries, 1931–9:

Cameron, U. (1932) *A Good Line*.

Bieller, C. (2002) *Una Cameron: La Scozzese del Monte Bianco*; Merz, J. (2000) *The Ladies' Alpine Club 1907–1975: Index*, pp. 26–8 (full list of climbs, artwork, photographs and articles for the *LAC Jour.*); *ODNB* (2004); Smith, J. A. (1988–89) 'In Memoriam', *Alpine Jour.*, 93, pp. 323–36. www.fondazionemontagnasicura.org

CAMPBELL, Lady Agnes, born western Highlands c. 1525, died c. 1601. Resistance leader, Ireland. Daughter of Janet Gordon, and Colin Campbell, 3rd Earl of Argyll.

Agnes Campbell's first marriage, in 1545, to James MacDonnell of Dunyvaig and the Glens (d. 1565), united MacDonald and Campbell power in the west of Scotland. Her daughter, *Finola O'Donnell, was born of this marriage. Agnes Campbell played a central role in the operating of ties between Scotland and Ireland in a period of increasing Tudor colonial ambition. Her first husband died a prisoner of Shane O'Neill in 1565. Her direct role in Ulster politics began in 1569 when she arrived in Ireland to marry Turlough

Luineach O'Neill (c. 1530–95), Shane O'Neill's successor as chief. She brought with her a dowry of 1,200 Scottish mercenary troops. She was in a position to command her troops against English colonial forces due to customary Gaelic law which allowed wives to retain considerable control over their dowries. If dowries included troops and ships then those women played an active role in military and political events.

Agnes Campbell was at the centre of a Scottish-Irish network. She was credited with ruling and directing her chieftain husband, and making herself strong in Ireland. Her role in the Desmond rebellion of 1579 to 1583 was described by contemporaries as an attempt to make a new Scotland of Ulster. It was Agnes Campbell who was commissioned to raise munitions from Scottish supporters. She was recorded as being highly educated and intelligent. Sir Henry Sidney negotiated with her in 1579, and she was reported to have spoken Latin in her dealings with English colonial authorities. She was from a cultivated circle of Gaelic-speaking aristocrats, but was also able to communicate fluently in English and Latin.

Agnes Campbell returned to Scotland in 1583 in order to raise financial aid for the Irish rebellion. She was credited by the English as a central figure and cause of the rebellion in Ireland. For the remainder of her life she, together with her daughter, worked to train Scottish mercenaries in Ireland, and acted as a go-between and negotiator. AEK

• NAS: GD 112/39 (1564); National Archives, Kew, Calendar of State Papers, Ireland, vols 29 (1569), 30 (1570).

Knox, A. (2002) 'Barbarous and pestiferous women', in Y. G. Brown and R. Ferguson (eds) *Twisted Sisters*; *ODNB* (2004).

CAMPBELL, Agnes (Lady Roseburn), baptised 1 September 1637, died Edinburgh 24 July 1716. Printer, book trader, businesswoman. Daughter of Isobel Orr, and James Campbell, Edinburgh merchant.

On 26 June 1656 Agnes Campbell married Andrew Anderson (c. 1635–76), son of a leading Glasgow printer. Her husband was appointed printer to Edinburgh Town Council and its college in 1663, becoming a burgess through his wife's right of inheritance from her father. In 1671, he became the King's Printer for Scotland, with a 41-year grant giving him supervision over the other Scottish presses, a monopoly on the printing and importing of bibles and exemption from paper duties. After his death in June 1676, the grant reverted to his heirs. Continuing and extending his business, as 'Heirs of Andrew Anderson', Agnes Campbell became the richest Scottish book maker of her time. In 1678, hers was the largest printing business in Edinburgh with sixteen apprentices, and traded extensively in print and paper in Scotland and Ireland; she also lent money to book traders. Her reputation was significantly damaged by the jealousy of rivals. Her contemporary, James Watson, wrote of her as 'a contentious old woman' (Watson 1713, Preface) who sought to control and reduce all other printers; he also commented on the poor quality of the Andersons' printing. However, she behaved just as her opponents did, frequently going to court against those who contravened her monopoly or even against her own workforce, and printing works of variable quality.

After Agnes Campbell's remarriage to Patrick Tailfer on 22 March 1681, she fought to maintain her independence against her new husband's creditors and, after petitioning Parliament in 1693, was empowered to act independently of him in everything connected with her printing business. In 1704, she purchased an estate at Roseburn, and became known formally as Lady Roseburn. At the age of 72, in 1709, she established the Valleyfield paper mill at Penicuik, and in early 1712 she realised her ambition to become printer to the General Assembly of the Church of Scotland. She had at least eight children, but several died young and the early death of her son James in 1693 meant that the business could not be inherited by her heirs. As the expiry date for the original grant, May 1712, drew near, Agnes Campbell's rivals acted fast; a partnership led by James Watson received a further grant in August 1711, successfully excluding the Anderson company. In her will she left the remarkable fortune of £78,197 (Scots), having inherited from her husband only £7,451 (Scots) in debts. JR

• Campbell, A. (1685) *To the Right Honourable the Lord High Chancellor . . . The humble petition of His Majesties printer and servants*; Campbell, A. and Anderson, J. (1688) *Answers for James Anderson and Agnes Campbell his mother, to the Complaint exhibite against them . . .*, (1712) *A Brief Reply to the Letter from Edinburgh Relating to the Case of Mrs Anderson, Her Majesty's Printer in Scotland.* Fairley, J. A. (1925) *Agnes Campbell Lady Roseburn, relict of Andrew Anderson the King's Printer*; Mann, A. J. (1998) 'Book commerce, litigation and the art of monopoly: the case of Agnes Campbell, royal printer, 1676–1712', *Scot. Econ. and Soc. Hist*, 18, 2, (1999) 'Embroidery to enterprise: the role of women in the book trade of early modern Scotland' in E. Ewan and M. M. Meikle (eds) *Women in Scotland c. 1100–c. 1750*, (2000), *The Scottish Book Trade 1500–1720*; Watson, James (1713), *The History of the Art of Printing.*

CAMPBELL, Anna, fl. 1773. Poet. Daughter of Campbell of Scalpay.

Anna Campbell's one surviving song has assured her a place in the canon of Gaelic literature. On a voyage to visit her, Alan Morrison from Lewis, her fiancé, was drowned. The song, 'Ailein Duinn shiubhlainn leat' ('Brown-haired Alan, I would go with you') is her lament for him, a poem of intense grief in which image after vivid image is created without any trivial commonplaces to disrupt the sequence. The poem ends: 'My prayer to God on the throne/That I do not go in soil or linen/In broken earth or hidden place/But in the spot where you went, Alan.' Legend says a giant wave snatched her coffin overboard on the sea voyage to Rodel in Harris. A more realistic tradition tells that when the ship was caught in a great storm, the funeral party, as a last resort, tipped the coffin into the sea, remembering her prayer. JMACI

• Kerrigan, C. (1991) *An Anthology of Scottish Women Poets*; Sinclair, A. (1879) *An t-Oranaiche (The Gaelic Songster).*

CAMPBELL, Jane Maud, born Liverpool 13 March 1869, died Lynchburg, Virginia, USA, 13 Dec. 1947. Librarian, pioneer of libraries as community centres, especially for migrants. Daughter of Jane Cameron Campbell and George Campbell.

Jane Campbell's family migrated to the USA when she was 12 years old. After her mother's death a year later she returned to Edinburgh. She graduated from the University Ladies' College and the Edinburgh School of Cookery and Domestic Economy, achieving 'Excellent' in cleaning and scullery work. Re-migrating to the US, in 1902 she was appointed Head of Public Libraries in Passaic New Jersey, where 55% of inhabitants were foreign born. She regarded the library as the most democratic and inclusive of public institutions that could 'draw your community together' (SL, address to Norwalk Daughters of the American Revolution, Nov. 1904, p. 10).

Working against prejudice, she made the library an agency of Americanisation and a place where migrant culture was respected. She stocked foreign language books and took advice about acquisitions from locals such as the barber, who considered the *Life of Garibaldi* a book 'every Italian must read and love before he could understand what Washington, Lincoln and Grant meant to Americans' (SL, Long Island Library Club c. 1904, p. 7). Fruitful hybridisations resulted, including a Yiddish-speaking Emerson Literary Society which presented a bust of Shakespeare to the library. Her handling of the youth problem was inspired. When the Jesse James gang lit kerosene on the library windows, she gave the lads a room for meeting, at first leaving them alone, later introducing a quiz, with prizes, on questions of sport. Over time she extended the quiz, enticing the boys to use the whole gamut of reference books – an original form of research training.

Ironically, her attitude to women was less adventurous. While she arranged craft classes for girls and needlework exhibitions to draw in mothers, she did not follow the New York City examples of Mothers' Clubs for women who had 'a devouring desire to "get the English"'' (Rose 1917, p. 16). She was sensitive to the loneliness of professional women, especially at holiday time when 'the only thing to do was to take a large sleeping draught and go to bed' and kept her libraries open for them during public holidays (SL, Talk at Englewood c. 1904, pp. 1–2). In 1910, she went to New York City to work for the North American Civic League and then in 1913 became Educational Director for Work with Immigrants of Massachusetts Library Commission. In 1922, she moved to Lynchburg, Virginia, to join her family, and took initiatives, as Head Librarian, to establish branch libraries in black areas. EY

• Schlesinger Library (SL) of the History of American Women, Radcliffe Institute for Advanced Study, Harvard Univ.: MC382 (Edinburgh School of Cookery Bursar's Certificate, 13 Dec. 1886 and other papers).
Campbell, J. M. (1908) 'Public libraries and the immigrant', *New York Libraries*, pp. 100–5, 132–6, (1913) 'What the foreigner has done for the library', *Library Journal*, 38, pp. 610–15, (1916) 'Americanizing books and periodicals for immigrants', *American Library Association Bulletin*, 10, pp. 269–72.
Jones, P. A. (1999) *Libraries, Immigrants and the American Experience*; Rose, E. (1917) *Bridging the Gulf*.

CAMPBELL, Janet (Jessie), n. **Black,** born Barrhead, Renfrewshire, 26 March 1827, died Alexandria, Dunbartonshire, 10 Feb. 1907. Campaigner and fundraiser for higher education for women. Daughter of Elizabeth Taylor, and James Black, owner of bleaching fields in Barrhead.

In 1846, Jessie Black married James Campbell of Tullichewan Castle (1823–1902), partner in Messrs J. & W. Campbell, wholesale drapers, and cousin of Sir Henry Campbell-Bannerman (Liberal Prime Minister 1905). They had five children. Interested in improving local cultural activities, James Campbell supported his wife's wish to develop facilities for the higher education of women. Through their social connections, Jessie Campbell enlisted the help of John Nichol, Professor of English Literature, to start lectures for ladies in Glasgow in 1868. This successful venture developed into the AHEW and, in 1883, Queen Margaret College for Women. Jessie Campbell remained involved, raising £20,000 to endow the college, the condition insisted upon by *Isabella Elder, who had bought North Park House, Glasgow and given it rent-free as a home for the college. In 1901, Jessie Campbell was awarded the honorary degree of LLD by the University of Glasgow, and is depicted in the memorial window to *Janet Galloway in Bute Hall there. CJM
• Glasgow Univ.: Queen Margaret Coll. Archives.
Book of the Jubilee (1451–1901) (1901) pp. 126–38; McAlpine, C. J. (1997) *The Lady of Claremont House*; *ODNB* (2004).

CAMPBELL, Katherine, Countess of Crawford, born before 1538, died Brechin Castle, 1 Oct. 1578. Matriarch. Daughter of *Muriel Calder, heiress of Calder (Cawdor), and Sir John Campbell, first knight of Calder.

Katherine Campbell married, before 1 October 1539, James, Master of Ogilvy who was killed at Pinkie (November 1547). They had three surviving children, one son and two daughters. No later than 12 November 1550, Katherine married David Lindsay of Edzell, 9th Earl of Crawford, with whom she had five sons and two daughters. In September 1558, she was widowed again, and for the remainder of her life was not required to re-marry. Both her husbands appointed Katherine tutrix testamentary and custodian to their children, giving her an influential role as custodian of the heirs to Airlie and Edzell. As dowager Countess, she devoted her energies to building and maintaining her sons' inheritance, defending her own and her sons' rights against the 10th Earl of Crawford, the Earl of Argyll and a host of others. She arranged marriages for most of the children. Before her death, she dictated a lengthy testament, remembering all her surviving children with personal bequests. MV

• NLS: Acc. 9769 Crawford Muniments, 3/1, 3/2; NAS: GD16 Airlie Muniments; NAS: RD1 Register of Deeds; NAS: CC8/8/7 Register of Testaments; NRA(S) 237 Haigh Inventory.
Bardgett, F. (1989) *Scotland Reformed: the Reformation in Angus and the Mearns*; Lindsay, Lord (1858) *Lives of the Lindsays*, 3 vols; *ODNB* (2004); Verschuur, M. (2006) *A Noble and Potent Lady: Katherine Campbell Countess of Crawford*.

CAMPBELL, Margaret (Mary) (Highland Mary), born Auchamore, Dunoon, c. 18 March 1766, died Greenock c. 20 Oct. 1786. Domestic servant and lover of Robert Burns, poet. Daughter of Agnes Campbell, and Archibald Campbell, seaman.

Tradition states that Margaret Campbell began her working life in 1778 as a servant to the Kirk family in Campbeltown before working for the Rev. David Campbell in Lochranza, Arran. By 1784, she was a dairymaid at Coilsfield, owned by Hugh Montgomerie, before being employed at Mauchline Castle in early 1785 by Robert Burns's friend Gavin Hamilton.

Hugh Montgomerie's household worshipped at Tarbolton Kirk, also frequented by Robert Burns, and it has been suggested that the couple met there. According to Burns, they met in March 1786 after *Jean Armour's parents sent her to Paisley because of her pregnancy, but Burns's brother Gilbert and sister Isabella both stated that he had known Margaret Campbell long before then and that the couple were romantically involved. On 14 May 1786, Robert Burns and 'Highland Mary' parted at Failford and she returned to Campbeltown. Burns wrote years later that they had planned to emigrate to Jamaica and she had returned home to take leave of her family. She and her brother went to Greenock in October, where they lodged with relatives named McPherson at 31 Upper Charles Street. Margaret Campbell died that autumn from typhoid and was buried in the West Highland Churchyard. It was often implied, but never proved, that she was pregnant to Burns. Some also claim she went to Greenock not to meet Burns to go to Jamaica but before taking up a post in Glasgow as housemaid to a Colonel McIvor, which she was to start at Martinmas (11 November). She herself had never spoken of emigration. A statue of 'Highland Mary' stands on Castle Hill, Dunoon. MB
• Ayrshire Archaeological Society (1996) *Mauchline Memories of Robert Burns*.
Bell, M. (2001) *Tae The Lasses*; Bolton, J. (1994) *Love of Highland Mary*; Hill, J. C. (1961) *The Love Songs and Heroines*

of Robert Burns; Munro, A. (1896) *The Story of Burns and Highland Mary*; *ODNB* (2004) (Burns, Robert); Paton, N. R. (1994) *Thou Ling'ring Star*; Ross, J. D. (1894) *Highland Mary*.

CAMPBELL of Canna, Margaret Fay Shaw *see* **SHAW, Margaret Fay** (1903–2004)

CAMPBELL, Marion, n. **Maclellan (Mor Aonghais mhic Eachainn)** born South Uist 4 August 1867, died South Uist 15 Jan. 1970. Daughter of Mary Wilson, and Angus Maclellan, grasskeeper; **MACDONALD, Catherine (Kate),** n. **Campbell,** born 23 June 1897, died 27 May 1977. Daughter of Marion Maclellan, and Neil Campbell, crofter. Tradition-bearers.

Marion Campbell and Kate MacDonald were two of the foremost exponents of Gaelic song and music in South Uist, an island with rich resources of folklore and poetry. Marion Campbell, a monoglot Gaelic speaker, was an accomplished teller of stories, from international folktales to local legends and personal 'memorates'. Among the most prized items in both women's repertoire were heroic ballads of the type on which James MacPherson based his 18th-century 'Ossian'. They were also exponents of the art of *canntaireachd*, chanting of pipe tunes to a syllabic code of vowels and consonants, used in teaching pipe-music. Marion Campbell was over 80 when first recorded; for two decades, she made an enormous contribution to the archives of the School of Scottish Studies at the University of Edinburgh.

Both women had an impressive knowledge of waulking songs (sung while fulling or thickening cloth). Kate MacDonald probably learned additional items from other sources. She was expert at singing *puirt-a-beul* – songs associated with dance tunes – and recorded more than 250 songs. Unusually, she played pipe tunes, although only on the chanter. Traditionally the playing of bagpipes, associated with war, was a masculine art. However, her daughter, Rhona Lightfoot, is one of Scotland's leading pipers. JMACI
• Campbell, J. L. and Collinson, F. (eds) (1977–81) *Hebridean Folk Songs*, vols 2, 3; 'Mór Bean Nill' in J. L. Campbell (2004) *A Very Civil People*, H. Cheape, ed., pp. 31–8; MacDonald, D. A. (1977) 'Kate MacDonald', *Tocher*, 27.

CAMPBELL, Marion, of Kilberry, born Brompton 16 Dec. 1919, died Oban 13 June 2000. Farmer and landowner, writer, archaeologist and councillor. Daughter of Marion Durand, and John Campbell of Kilberry, landowner.

Marion Campbell was brought up on her family's estate in Argyll. She was only eight when, on her father's death in 1928, she first inherited the West Highland castle and 3,500-acre estate of Kilberry, overlooking the Sound of Jura. It was sold three years later to a cousin, but returned to her in 1938. She was educated at Queen Margaret's School, Edinburgh, and by correspondence through the Parents' National Educational Union. During the Second World War, instead of going to university she served with the ATS and the WRNS; during rescue work in a Glasgow air raid, she sustained a back injury that troubled her throughout her life. After 1944, she successfully ran three farms on the estate while pursuing her interest in local history and archaeology.

Marion Campbell's former schoolfriend **Mary Sandeman** (1917–95), who was raised on Jura and had also served in the WRNS during the war, joined her at Kilberry in 1954. This was the beginning of a personal and working partnership which was to last until Mary's death. Mary Sandeman helped start the Mid-Argyll Antiquarian Society, and both women published articles in the society's magazine, *KIST*. They joined the SNP in the 1960s, Marion Campbell serving as chair of the Mid Argyll District Council for four years. Together and with others, they undertook a field survey of the archaeology of Mid Argyll (*Proc. Soc. Antiquaries Scot.* 1962) which is the basis for much later research.

Marion Campbell's energetic promotion of Argyll spurred the opening of Auchindrain museum of farming life in 1967 and the Kilmartin House Museum in 1997. The history and landscape of Argyll informs her best-known book *Argyll: the enduring heartland* (1977), which includes poetry, by herself and others, in Gaelic and English. Having given up farming in the mid-1950s to concentrate on writing and politics, Marion Campbell also published several historical adventures for children, beginning with *The Wide Blue Road* (1957). At a time of stress and depression she found herself having waking dreams in which she seemed to overhear conversations in Gaelic. That led to her adult novel *The Dark Twin* (1973), a mystical romance set in the Scotland of 500 BC, which became a cult novel among students in the USA: American interest led to film rights being taken on this and other work in the 1990s. In 1990 Mary Sandeman and Marion Campbell moved to a small house on the seaward side of the castle. Mary, who was an Elder of the

Kilberry Session of the Church of Scotland, continued to carry out practical work for the church and at the castle (wielding an axe to clear fallen branches on the day before her death in 1995). Marion spent many years researching her biography of *Alexander III, King of Scots* (1999) and also editing letters from her forebears in Jamaica and other colonies to family in Argyll. Both tasks were completed shortly before her death. MARB/EL

• Campbell, M., Works as above, see Davis below, and (1962) (with Mary Sandeman) 'Mid Argyll: an archaeological survey', *Proc. Soc. Antiquaries Scot.* 95, pp. 1–125. Sandeman, M. (1996) *When the years were young*, (ed. Campbell, M.).
Ascherson, N. (2001) Foreword to *Argyll: the enduring heartland*; Colin, B. 'The player', *Scotsman Weekend*, 5 April 1997; Davis, M. (1999) 'Marion Campbell: a bibliography', Argyll & Bute Council; *The Scotsman*, 15 June 2000 (obit.).

CAMPBELL, Mary Maxwell, born Riccarton 19 Nov. 1812, died St Andrews 15 Jan. 1886. Composer. Daughter of Sir D. J. Campbell of Skerrington.

Mary Campbell's place in Scottish music history comes from writing both words and music of the famous 'March of the Cameron Men'. She apparently composed the ballad in 1829, at the age of 16, after hearing the story of Cameron of Lochiel and of how his clansmen, from Lochaber, 'fiercer than fierceness itself', rose to join Prince Charles in 1745. There was a popular edition for pipes alone, as performed by Alexander (MacGregor) Simpson. Mary Campbell (often known as 'of Pitlour, Fife') composed other works for the piano, including a waltz movement and a bolero (in BL) and songs including 'The Mole and the Bat' (1867). PAC

• Cohen, A. I. (1987, 2nd edn.) *International Encyclopedia of Women Composers*; Hixon, D. L. and Hennessee, D. (1975) *Women in Music*; Stern, G. (1978) *Women Composers*; (1913) *Women Composers*.

CAMPBELL, Wilhelmina Allison (Elma), m. **Gibson,** born Cathcart 14 Jan. 1901, died Dalbeattie 28 Feb. 1983. Parliamentary candidate for the National Party of Scotland (NPS). Daughter of Isobel Hunter, and Duncan Campbell, Merchant Navy captain.

A University of Glasgow graduate, teacher and former Conservative debating champion, Elma Campbell rose rapidly on joining the NPS. In 1930 she was Joint Convener of the Women's Section, member of the organisation, finance, press and publications, and bazaar committees, and the

National Council. She was credited with being 'one of our most brilliant speakers', addressing audiences of 'over four thousand in St Andrew's Halls, Glasgow' (*Scots Independent*, Jan. 1930, p. 28). The only NPS woman parliamentary candidate of the inter-war years, she stood twice in Glasgow St Rollox, at the by-election of May 1931 and at the subsequent 1931 general election. Her polls of 15.8% and 13.3% respectively were among the then best nationalist results. A teacher in Greenock, she was refused leave of absence during both campaigns yet still 'attended on average seven meetings each night' (*Scots Independent*, Dec. 1931, p. 22). Her marriage to fellow nationalist Thomas Gibson in March 1932 and his employment in London removed both from the Scottish political scene. CB

• *Scots Independent*, 1930–32.

CAMPBELL, Willielma, Viscountess Glenorchy, n. **Maxwell,** born Kirkcudbright 2 Sept. 1741, died Edinburgh 17 July 1786. Chapel founder. Daughter of Elizabeth Hairstanes, and William Maxwell, medical doctor.

Willielma Maxwell's father died before she was born and she grew up in the home of her stepfather, Lord Alva, later Lord Justice Clerk, in Mylne's Court, Edinburgh. On 26 September 1761 she married John Campbell, Viscount Glenorchy (1738–71), heir to Lord Breadalbane, who gave the Glenorchys virtual control of his estates. When she was 24, a serious illness and a conversation with the clergyman Rowland Hill, led to her conversion to evangelical Christianity. After her husband's death in 1771, she used her considerable wealth to assist religious causes, including the educational work of the SPCK (see Graham, Isabella). She funded the construction of a chapel in Edinburgh, which opened in 1774, and between 1776 and 1786 founded chapels elsewhere, including Buxton, Matlock Bath, Workington, Carlisle, Exmouth, Bristol Hot-Wells and Newton Burhill, Devonshire. Lady Glenorchy was a member of the Church of Scotland, although her Edinburgh chapel was not an established church or a Chapel of Ease. Eventually, the General Assembly accepted that the ministers whom she appointed would be recognised by the Edinburgh Presbytery. Initially, the chapel's pulpit was open to all evangelical clergy, but her increasing commitment to Calvinism led to a break with John Wesley. She appointed Rev. T. S. Jones as minister in 1779 and he served the chapel for 58 years. In 1843, the congregation joined the Free Church of Scotland. Having spent her last years with a niece in George Square,

Lady Glenorchy was buried in her chapel in 1786. When it was demolished in 1844 to make way for Waverley Station, her remains were moved to St John's parish church, and eventually to the Roxburgh Place Chapel (1859). KBER

• Dunlop, A. I. (1989) *The Kirks of Edinburgh 1560–1984*; Jones, T. S. (1822) *The Life of Willielma, Viscountess Glenorchy*; *ODNB* (2004); Scott, H. (1915) *Fasti Eccesiae Scoticanae*, vol. 1, pp. 78–80; Thomson, D. P. (1967) *Lady Glenorchy and Her Churches*.

CARLYLE, Jane Welsh,‡ n. **Welsh,** born Haddington 14 July 1801, died London 22 April 1866. Letter-writer. Daughter of Grace (Grizel) Welsh, and Dr John Welsh (not related).

Jane Welsh Carlyle was known during her life in the private roles of witty story teller and letter writer and as the wife of Thomas Carlyle (1795–1881), the Scottish essayist and historian. She left about 2,000 surviving letters, plus some short prose pieces, 'Much Ado About Nothing' (1849), 'The Simple Story of my Own First Love' (1852), 'Budget of a Femme Incomprise' (1855), an anecdotal notebook (1845–52) and her Journal (1855–6). Educated at local Haddington schools and privately tutored, she learnt Latin and 'strove to "be a Boy" in education' (Carlyle 1881, p. 69) to please her father; she also briefly attended Miss Hall's school, Leith Walk, Edinburgh, 1817–18. After meeting Jane Welsh in 1821, Thomas Carlyle courted her by letter, encouraging her to read German and to write. Jane (and her mother) eventually agreed to the marriage, which took place on 17 October 1826. The Carlyles lived in 21 Comely Bank, Edinburgh, until the move in 1828 to Craigenputtoch, Nithsdale, an isolated moorland household, where Thomas wrote and Jane supported his 'genius'. Later she presented that time as entirely miserable but a triumph for her resourcefulness. In 1834 they left to live in 5 Cheyne Row, London, where she held court to those who came to admire Thomas Carlyle, including literary men and women, intellectuals, many visiting Americans, young radicals from Ireland, and revolutionaries in exile from Europe such as Giuseppe Mazzini. Jane Welsh Carlyle also had her own circle of admirers, including the novelist and reviewer, Geraldine Jewsbury (1812–80), whose writing career she encouraged.

During her early years in London, Jane Welsh Carlyle prided herself on the frugal Scottish organisation of their modest, one-servant household, while Thomas Carlyle made his reputation and earned money with lectures and books. As their social circle widened, she felt herself replaced as the centre of his emotional life by his exaggerated and thoughtless admiration for the aristocratic Lady Ashburton (1805–57). Jane Welsh Carlyle suffered illness and depression. But her letters written at this time contain as much wit in relation to her feelings as to any other of her subjects, and her journal, while recording the intensity of her depression and illness, also records a very active social life of her own. In February 1856, she was one of the signatories of the petition for a married women's property act, a rare public act on her part.

Jane Welsh Carlyle's sudden death (while her husband was away becoming Rector of the University of Edinburgh) led to his collecting all her surviving letters and preparing them for publication after his own death. He thought they equalled and surpassed 'whatever of best I know to exist in that kind' (Carlyle 1881, p. 161), setting the tone for much of the commentary on her work. There are many contemporary and subsequent descriptions of her storytelling abilities. But it was those who recognised her as an accomplished writer whose skill was evident in her letters and other pieces, rather than a 'missing novelist', who came closest to assessing her real worth. *Margaret Oliphant assessed her talk in terms that apply to her writing: 'the power of narration . . . the flashes of keen wit and sarcasm, occasionally even a little sharpness, and always the modifying sense of humour under all' (Oliphant 1990, p. 98). For Virginia Woolf, her letters owed 'their incomparable brilliance to the hawk-like swoop and descent of her mind upon facts' (Woolf 1932, p. 198). Her choice was to write privately, and her reputation rests firmly and justifiably on the skill and power of the life-writing that survives. ABC
• NLS: Corr. Jane Welsh Carlyle.
The Collected Letters of Thomas and Jane Welsh Carlyle (1970–2006, ongoing) (eds) C. R. Sanders, K. J. Fielding, C. de L. Ryals, I. Campbell, A. Christianson, J. Clubbe, S. McIntosh, H. Smith, D. Sorensen, vols 1–34; *Letters and Memorials of Jane Welsh Carlyle* (1883) J. A. Froude, ed.; Carlyle, T. [1881] (1997) *Reminiscences*, K. J. F. Fielding and I. Campbell, eds; Oliphant, M. [1899] (1990) *Autobiography*, E. Jay, ed.; *ODNB* (2004); Woolf, V. (1932) 'Geraldine and Jane', *The Common Reader* (Second series).

CARMICHAEL, Elizabeth Catherine (Ella), m. Watson, born Lismore 9 August 1870, died Edinburgh 30 Nov. 1928. Editor and promoter of Gaelic. Daughter of Mary Frances Urquhart

Macbean, and Alexander Carmichael, collector of Gaelic tales and songs.

Ella Carmichael grew up in Uist, moving to Edinburgh in 1882. A native Gaelic speaker, she assisted her father in the compilation and editing of his great work, *Carmina Gadelica*. Her mother, **Mary Frances Urquhart Macbean** (1841–1928), contributed illustrations to the project. Both parents were granted a Civil List pension in recognition of their contributions to Gaelic. Widowed in 1912, Mary Carmichael moved in with Ella and her husband, W. J. Watson (1865–1948), Professor of Celtic at the University of Edinburgh, whom she had married in 1906. Ella Carmichael Watson prepared the second edition of *Carmina Gadelica*; her preface, written shortly before her death, indicated that she intended to publish further volumes. Her son, James Carmichael Watson, also Professor of Celtic at Edinburgh, later prepared the third and fourth volumes, and edited the poems of *Mairi nighean Alasdair Ruaidh.

As acting editor (and sole editor from 1915) of *The Celtic Review*, Ella Carmichael Watson was largely responsible for preparing it for press. Containing articles on Gaelic literature, history, folktale and dialectology, the *Review* made a lasting contribution to scholarship. She and her brothers also founded the Edinburgh Gaelic Choir and the Celtic Union, a literary and historical society. JMACI
• Carmichael, A. (1928 2nd edn.) *Carmina Gadelica*, E. Carmichael Watson, ed.; *Celtic Review* (1904–16); *ODNB* (2004) (Carmichael, Alexander); Watson, J. C. (1941) 'Mary Frances Macbean', in *Carmina Gadelica*, iv.

CARNEGIE, Susan, n. **Scott,** baptised 1744, died Charleton, Montrose, 14 April 1821. Poor relief campaigner. Daughter of Mary Brown, and David Scott, landowner and Treasurer of the Bank of Scotland.

Educated at home, Susan Scott composed and published poems, sketched, and became fluent in French and Italian. She married the wealthy George Carnegie on 17 March 1769 and settled at Charleton House near Montrose. Her father and husband agreed a marriage contract, which ensured that estates were endowed on her. Eight of her nine children survived infancy, although three of her soldier sons predeceased her, two in India; her husband, 18 years her senior, died in 1799.

Susan Carnegie used her privileged position and forceful personality to improve local conditions. She rose at five each morning to deal with correspondence. She wrote letters and printed anonymous pamphlets encouraging funding for a hospital for the mentally ill who had hitherto been housed in prisons. Aided by the provost, she founded the first asylum in Scotland, built in Montrose in 1781. With no bridges crossing the rivers, there were many drownings locally; she campaigned for a receiving ward and for life-saving procedures. Susan Carnegie founded the Montrose Female Friendly Society in 1808. In 1815, she enlisted Church support to establish a savings bank for labouring classes. The bank, which encouraged small deposits, opened on 3 April 1815, initially operating for one hour each week. In her will she instructed that pensions from her estate should continue during each recipient's lifetime. EL

• Cormack, A. A. (1966) *Susan Carnegie 1744–1821: her life of service*; *ODNB* (2004).

CARRICK, Ellen, c. 1342–c. 1408. Prioress of North Berwick.

Ellen Carrick was Prioress at the nunnery of North Berwick for 28 years from 1379 to 1407. The Carricks were related to the founders of the nunnery, the earls of Fife, through a junior branch of the family, and it is likely that she was a member of this branch. She was elected to the office after the death of Beatrice, former Prioress, on or before 20 September 1379. In 1386, she granted a receipt for the rent of the church of Maybole to Sir Alan Cathcart. This appears to be her only surviving grant. In 1402, she appealed to Pope Benedict XIII, saying that the Bishop of St Andrews had unjustly removed her from her office after a visitation and had made the nuns elect another woman, Matilda de Leys, as Prioress. She pled her case for another five years but in 1407 the case was left undecided. KP

• *HRHS* (Bibl.); Innes, C. (ed.) (1847) *Carte Monialium de Northberwic*.

CARRICK, Marjory, Countess of, fl. 1256–92. Daughter of Neil, Earl of Carrick.

Sole heiress of the lordship of Carrick after 1256, Marjory's early life was typical of that of a noblewoman: in her teens she was married to Adam of Kilconquhar (d. 1271), from a cadet branch of the native family of Fife, who became Earl of Carrick in right of his wife. However, Marjory also demonstrates how medieval noblewomen might play decisive roles in determining their lives. Later chroniclers relate that, in 1272, the widowed Countess won her second husband, Robert Bruce,

lord of Annandale (1243–1304), by seizing him and holding him in honourable captivity until he agreed to marry her; true or not, the couple paid a heavy fine for marrying without royal license. Bruce was also permitted to assume the title of Earl of Carrick in right of his wife. Of their five sons and five daughters, two became kings, Robert I of Scotland and Edward of Ireland, and one a queen, Isobel of Norway. CJN

• Duncan, A. A. M. (1978) *Scotland: the making of the kingdom*; *Scotichron.*, vol. 5; *SP.*

CARSWELL, Catherine Roxburgh, n. **Macfarlane,** m1 **Jackson,** m2 **Carswell,** born Glasgow 27 March 1879, died Oxford 18 Feb. 1946. Biographer, novelist, journalist, editor, critic. Daughter of Mary Anne Lewis, and George Gray Macfarlane, merchant.

The second of four children, Catherine Macfarlane was educated at Park School for Girls, Glasgow. She studied music for two years at the Frankfurt Conservatorium and English Literature at the University of Glasgow (1901–3), where she won Best Essay Prize (1902). She married Herbert Jackson (b. 1867/8) in 1904 and their daughter Diana was born in 1905. However, Jackson proved to be mentally ill and was permanently hospitalised; the marriage was annulled in a pioneering legal case in 1908.

From about 1906, she began reviewing drama and fiction for the *Glasgow Herald*, commenting on the Irish Players (Abbey Theatre) and D. H. Lawrence's early novels. She also began a long-standing affair with painter Maurice Greiffenhagen (1862–1931), Director of Life Classes at Glasgow Art School. She moved to London, possibly in 1912 after her mother died, and suffered the tragic death of her daughter in 1913. After breaking with Greiffenhagen, in 1915 she married an old Glasgow friend, journalist Donald Carswell (1882–1940). Their son, John Patrick Carswell (1918–97), became a writer and editor. The Carswells experienced financial strain, often relying on Catherine's writing after Donald's unsuccessful pursuit of a legal career. They lived mainly in Buckinghamshire and in London (Hampstead).

Catherine Carswell's career with the *Glasgow Herald* was dramatically ended by her unsanctioned review of D. H. Lawrence's controversial *The Rainbow* in 1915. Her close friend, the writer Ivy Litvinov, had introduced her to Lawrence in 1914, beginning a warm friendship that lasted until his death in 1930. Lawrence invited her comments on what became *Women in Love*, and criticised drafts of her own first novel, *Open the Door!* (1920). Begun around 1911, this richly symbolic exploration of emotions and female sexuality won the Melrose prize. A second Glasgow-based novel, *The Camomile* (1922), portrays a young woman becoming a writer. However, her ground-breaking biography, *The Life of Robert Burns* (1930), attracted hostility: 'This morning . . . I had an anonymous letter containing a *bullet*, which I was requested to use upon myself that the world might be left "a brighter cleaner and better place."' (Letter to S. S. Koteliansky 23 Sept. 1930). The book now has considerable status, as does her sympathetic memoir of Lawrence, *The Savage Pilgrimage* (1932). Her biography of Boccaccio, *Tranquil Heart* (1937) claimed he was the first author to write avowedly for women (pp. vii–viii).

A prolific journalist and editor, Catherine Carswell was *The Observer*'s assistant drama critic during the First World War, later writing freelance for many publications including the *Manchester Guardian* during the 1920s and 30s. She also edited poetry and prose collections with Daniel George, co-wrote *The Fays of the Abbey Theatre* (1935) with William Fay, and edited an anthology, *The Scots Week-End* (1936), with Donald Carswell. She shared cultural interests with a wide circle of Scottish and other writer friends, especially *Florence Marian McNeill, with whom she corresponded extensively. Saddened by Donald's sudden death in 1940, Catherine Carswell died six years later. Her son John edited her fragmentary autobiographical writings, published posthumously as *Lying Awake* (1950). CA

• BL: Add. MS 48975, ff. 163–210, letters of Catherine Carswell to S. S. Koteliansky, Koteliansky papers; Mitchell Library, Glasgow: Acc. 898053, corr., Catherine Carswell papers, see also the Robert Burns Collection; NLS: MS 19705, Manuscripts Division, Catherine Carswell; Univ. of Nottingham Library, Dept. of Manuscripts and Special Collections: GB 0159 CC, Papers of Catherine Carswell (D. H. Lawrence correspondence and books); BBC Written Archives Centre, Reading: Catherine Carswell collection. Carswell, C., Work as above, and see Anderson (Bibl.). Anderson, C. (ed.) (2001) *Opening the Doors: the achievement of Catherine Carswell*, (Bibl.); *DLB* Gale, vol. 36; McCulloch, M. P. (1997) 'Sexual politics or the poetry of desire: Catherine Carswell's *Life of Robert Burns*', in K. Simpson (ed.) *Love and Liberty: Robert Burns: a bicentenary celebration*, pp. 289–98; *ODNB* (2004); Pilditch, Jan (2006) *Catherine Carswell: a biography*; *The Scotsman*, 26 Feb. 1946, (Appreciation); *The Times*, 22 Feb. 1946 (obit.).

CATRIONA NIC FHEARGHAIS (Christiana Ferguson), fl. 1745–6. Possibly born in Contin, Ross-shire. Poet.

Catriona nic Fhearghais's father was a blacksmith in Contin and was known for the manufacture of dirks and weapons. She is known for the song 'Cumha do dh'Uilleam Siseal' (William Chisholm's Lament), which she is traditionally believed to have composed for her husband who fell at Culloden. He is said to have carried a banner, *a'Bhratach Choimheach*, for the Chisholms, and not only aided their retreat from the field but mounted a single-handed defence of a barn sheltering his clansmen. The tune is believed to be original, and is published in *The Beauties of Gaelic Poetry* (1904, 2001). It is an emotive work, capturing the personal tragedy and loss that war entails, and has been recorded extensively by various artists, a number of whom draw from oral traditions rather than written sources. ABM

• Mackenzie, J. (1904, repr. 2001) *Sar-obair Nam Bard Gaelach. The Beauties of Gaelic Poetry*, pp. 373–4.

CHAIMBEUL, Fionnghal, fl. 1645–48. Poet. Daughter of Mary Erskine, grand-daughter of the Earl of Mar, and Dugald Campbell of Auchinbreck.

Fionnghal Chaimbeul married Iain Garbh, 7th Maclean of Coll, by whom she had six children, including Hector Roy Maclean. Iain Garbh and Hector Roy fought on the Royalist side at the battle of Inverlochy (1645), in which Fionnghal's brother, Duncan Campbell of Auchinbreck, leader of the Covenanting forces, was killed. Her only extant composition, 'Turus mo chreiche 'thug mi 'Chola' (My journey to Coll was my ruin) is remarkable for her forthright rejection of the clan into which she had married, going as far as to curse her own son while declaring her loyalty to the clan of her birth. Evidence within the poem points to her having been badly treated by the Macleans throughout her marriage. Tradition states that Fionnghal Chaimbeul went mad with grief after Inverlochy, and died around 1648. AF

• NLS: MS No. 50:2:20; pp. 182a–182b.
A Sennachie (1838) *Account of the Clan Maclean*, pp. 308–9; Sinclair, Rev. A. M. (1904–7) 'A Collection of Gaelic Poems', *Trans. Gael. Soc. Inverness*, 26, pp. 238–40; Stevenson, D. (1980) *Alasdair MacColla*, p. 160.

CHALMERS, Margaret, baptised Lerwick, Shetland, 12 December 1758, died after 1823. Carer and poet. Daughter of Kitty Irvine, and William Chalmers, customs officer.

Margaret Chalmers's father was already dead when her only brother was killed at the Battle of Trafalgar in 1805, leaving her with substantial debts and responsibility for her blind and bedridden mother and asthmatic sister. In 1813, she published her *Poems*, but poor editing and long delays impeded its reception. Seizing the 'Thulian quill' – her own phrase – she wrote about the Shetland Islands, noting how Shetland's history was separate from Scotland's, and commenting on wider contemporary issues, often describing how they affected Lerwick and the islands. She corresponded with Scott 1814–5 and sent him copies of some of her poems. She earned enough from *Poems* to reduce the debts but not to discharge them. She was refused a government pension in 1808, but received £10 from the Royal Literary Fund in 1816. Alone and in declining health, she appealed for charity in 1823 then disappears from the record: the date of her death is not known. A flight of steps in Lerwick, 'Miss Chalmers Stairs' (now demolished), was named after her; and her home at 10 Commercial Street still stands.

Margaret Chalmers is one of a number of women poets from humble or straitened backgrounds who developed literary skills, often helped by an educated friend or employer. Their poetry contributed significantly to family income. They share a conviction about their own composi- tions, invariably identifying the source of their muse. **Christian Gray** (1772–c. 1830), a farmer's daughter from Aberdalgie, Perthshire, lost her eyesight in childhood through smallpox. Scripture in particular was read to her and she knitted while walking outside. She composed poetry in Scots and English and memorised it until it could be written down for her. Her published works engage with marriage, slavery, war and religion; she also wrote about her own blindness, aligning herself with Milton, and dealt confidently with the work of Cowper and Ossian. **Christian Milne,** n. **Ross** (1772–c. 1816), domestic servant and poet, was born in Inverness, attended a village school in Auchentoul, and began composing songs in childhood. She went into service at the age of 14 and continued to write in secret until she went to work for the wife of Professor Jack, Principal of the University of Aberdeen, who encouraged her writing. She supported her family through extreme poverty, and developed consumption, aged 18. She married Peter Milne, a ship's carpenter, in 1796 and had eight children. **Susanna Hawkins** (1787–1868), domestic servant and cowherd, was the daughter of

John Hawkins, an Ecclefechan blacksmith. The *Dumfries Courier* began printing volumes of her poems around 1826, larger collections appearing in 1829 and 1838. She became a wandering minstrel in the Borders, selling her own work and seeking out other Dumfriesians. EL

• Shetland Archives, D24/12/43, Chalmers.

Selected works: Chalmers, M. (1813) *Poems*; Gray, C. (1808) *Tales, Letters and other Pieces in Verse*; Hawkins, S. (1829) *Poetical Works*; Milne, C. (1805) *Simple Poems on Simple Subjects.*

Blain, V., Clements, P., Grundy, I. (1990) *The Feminist Companion to Literature in England* (Chalmers, Gray, Milne); *ODNB* (2004) (Chalmers, Hawkins, Milne).

CHALMERS SMITH, Dorothea *see* **SMITH, Dorothea Chalmers** (1872–1944)

CHANCE, Janet, n. **Whyte,** born Edinburgh 10 Feb. 1886, died London 18 Dec. 1953. Sex educator and reformer, founder of Abortion Law Reform Association (ALRA). Daughter of Jane Elizabeth Barbour, and Rev. Alexander Whyte, Moderator of the General Assembly of the Church of Scotland.

After a conventional and comfortable upbringing in a large and talented family in Edinburgh, in 1912 Janet Whyte married Clinton Chance, a stockbroker, and moved to England. They had three children. Their social circle included many well-known intellectual and political names of the day. She was noted for her animated and stimulating conversation and was a catalyst in social events, but she suffered intermit- tently from severe depression. By the mid-1920s, she was deeply involved in the birth control movement and founded a sex education centre in Bow, East London. She commented on the extent of sexual ignorance encountered and in 1931 published *The Cost of English Morals*, a scathing attack on conventional attitudes. Her other published works were *Intellectual Crime* (1933) and *The Romance of Reality* (1934), advancing her rationalist creed, as well as *The Case for the Reform of the Abortion Laws* (1938), and a contribution to ALRA's *Back Street Surgery* (1947). She was one of seven women who in 1936 established ALRA to campaign for the legalisation of safe surgical abortion; she was an active member of the executive and its survival owed much to her generous financial support. She was also active on behalf of Czech refugees, ran a chicken farm during the war, and wrote two series of BBC radio talks.

In 1949, Janet Chance destroyed most of her papers. Following her husband's death, she fell into severe depression and killed herself by jumping out of a window. In a tribute, her long-time colleague Stella Browne commented that 'In her country's stark and stormy past, she might have been another "*Black Agnes of Dunbar"' (*Tributes*, 1954). LAH
• Wellcome Library, London: ALRA and Family Planning Association archives; Library of Congress, Washington DC, and Sophia Smith Collection, Northampton MA: Margaret Sanger papers, corr. Janet and Clinton Chance and Rachel Conrad (their daughter).
Chance, J., Works as above.
ALRA (1954) *Tributes to Janet Chance*; Hindell, K., 'Stella Browne and Janet Chance', *The Listener*, 29 June 1972; *ODNB* (2006 update).

CHARTERIS, Catherine Morice (Katie), n. **Anderson,** born Aberdeen 1835, died Edinburgh 18 Nov. 1918. First President, Church of Scotland Woman's Guild. Daughter of Rachel Johnston, and Sir Alexander Anderson, Lord Provost of Aberdeen.

Katie Anderson was educated at home. In 1863, she married a Church of Scotland minister, Archibald Charteris (1835–1908), Professor of Biblical Criticism at the University of Edinburgh from 1868. In Glasgow and Edinburgh, Katie Charteris organised slum missions, mothers' meetings, Bible classes, and a scheme of home visitation which, typically for the time, combined philanthropy with social control. From 1870, Archibald Charteris was convener of the Kirk's Life and Work Committee, which in 1887 proposed the creation of a national Woman's Guild. Its general object was to unite 'all women who are engaged in the service of Christ in connection with the Church, or desire to give help to any practical Christian work in the parish' (*Church of Scotland Yearbook* 1887, p. 83).

The new movement developed fitfully in the face of considerable resistance, but Katie Charteris, as president 1887–1906, brought energy and commitment to its promotion – especially at the annual conferences held around Scotland. She edited the Church of Scotland's magazine *Life & Work* Woman's Guild supplement, bringing the idea to life for thousands of women. She encouraged them to a life of friendship and purposeful action, highlighting the prejudice and injustice that women, working together, might tackle. By 1906, there were over 40,000 members. Katie Charteris also helped initiate and fund a house for missionary children and a rest home for

deaconesses. A woman of enthusiasm, intelligence and wit, she made a distinctive and enduring contribution to women's position within the national church. LO
• *Church of Scotland Yearbook* (1887); *Life & Work* 1891–1919. Gordon, A. (1912) *The Life of Archibald Hamilton Charteris*; Macdonald, L. Orr (2000) *A Unique and Glorious Mission*; Magnusson, M. (1987) *Out of Silence*; *ODNB* (2004) (Bibl.).

CHEAPE, Lady Griselda Johanna Helen, n. **Ogilvy,** born Cortachy, Angus, 20 Dec. 1865, died London 12 Feb. 1934. Anti-suffrage campaigner. Daughter of the Hon. Henrietta Blanche Stanley, and Sir David Graham Drummond Ogilvy, 5th Earl of Airlie.

Lady Griselda Ogilvy was the youngest of six children of the Angus family of Ogilvy of Airlie. She married James Cheape of Strathtyrum, St Andrews, on 23 December 1897, a match precipitated, it was said, by her dragging him into a 'Ladies Only' railway carriage in Strathmiglo Station. A young niece recalled her as, '. . . awe-inspiring and handsome, tall with wonderful dark eyebrows and white hair' (Cheape 1984). While kind and hospitable, she was also considered eccentric and a strict disciplinarian, with firm views on the upbringing of children, particularly her own three. They were terrified of her 'awful temper', and were dealt corporal punishment liberally; eccentricities included incubating hundreds of hens' eggs in her bed (ibid.). Brought up in the county paternalist tradition with a strong sense of duty, she made the nursing of sick children her special interest, enrolling for training in the Sick Children's Hospital, Edinburgh and the Pendlebury Sick Children's Home, Manchester. She also helped on the wards in the Royal Infirmary, Dundee, and the London Temperance Hospital. Family tradition suggested that her medical skills and a certain dangerous confidence were acquired as a self-appointed auxiliary nurse in the South African War.

She was President of the BWTA, the Open-Air Sanatorium Committee and the Invalid Children's Committee in St Andrews, and served on the Committee of the 'Rescue Home' in Dundee. She is particularly recalled for her leading anti-suffrage role in the Scottish National WASL, founded in 1908, where her platform speeches were said to be so robust and provocative as to cause riots. The WASL amalgamated in 1910 with the Men's National League for Opposing Women's Franchise to form the National League for Opposing Women's Suffrage. With the Earl of Cromer as President and the Countess of Jersey as Vice-President, the

NLOWS was strongly patronised by the British aristocracy and, with its journal, the *Anti-Suffrage Review*, lasted until 1918 and the granting of women's suffrage. Like her privileged aristocratic contemporaries, *Katherine, Duchess of Atholl, and *Violet Graham, Duchess of Montrose, Lady Griselda Cheape found the enfranchisement of women unthinkable. She was President of the St Andrews Branch of the Scottish National WASL, of which the Duchess of Montrose was President. HC/JSC

• Private collection, Cheape, G., 'Memoirs of Sarah Markham' (MS autobiography); Cheape, H. (c. 1984) 'Lady Griselda Cheape of Strathtyrum' (MS memoir).
The Anti-Suffrage Review, 1908–10; *BP* (1999) 106th edn., vol. I, p. 45; Harrison, B. (1978) *Separate Spheres: the opposition to women's suffrage in Britain*; SS.

CHECKLAND, Olive, n. **Anthony,** born Newcastle 6 June 1920, died Swansea 8 Sept. 2004. Historian. Daughter of Edith Philipson, and Robert Anthony, navy cook.

An only child, Olive Anthony became the first graduate in her family, studying geography at the University of Birmingham. There she met and in 1942 married Sydney Checkland (1906–96) who became in 1957 the first Professor of Economic History at the University of Glasgow. In a companionate marriage and a scholarly partnership, she raised five children, first in a garret flat, and later in an official professor's residence at 5 The University. A diminutive figure with a larger-than-life presence beside her tall but often quieter husband, Olive Checkland was active in departmental work, especially with graduates, providing succour and support to political and academic refugees. She made a significant contribution to history writing, although perhaps under-rated in her lifetime. She co-edited with her husband an edition of *The Poor Law Report of 1834* (1974), and with Margaret Lamb *Health Care as Social History* (1982). A string of monographs included: *Philanthropy in Victorian Scotland* (1980); *Industry and Ethos: Scotland 1832–1914* (1989), co-written with Sydney; *Sobriety and Thrift: John Philipson and Family* (1989); *Isabella Bird and a woman's right to do what she can do well* (1996), and *Japanese Whisky, Scotch Blend* (1998). In her books as in her life, she manifested a sense of duty, integrity and liberal freedoms. She wrote histories of pioneering women, philanthropy, health care and moral reform with the feeling and understanding of a bustling campaigner herself, however unfashionable or dated some causes she approved of may have seemed. CGB

• Checkland, O., Works as above, and (1980) *Queen Margaret Union 1890–1980*, (1989) *Britain's Encounter with Meiji Japan 1868–1912*, (1994) *Humanitarianism and the Emperor's Japan 1877–1977*.
The Herald, 2 Oct. 2004; *The Scotsman*, 14 Sept. 2004 (obit.).

CHEVERTON, Charlotte Mary Rose (Lottie), n. **Ramsden,** born Ripon, Yorkshire, 16 Jan. 1960, died Wooler, Northumberland, 17 Sept. 1991. Art teacher, co-founder of Leith School of Art. Daughter of Juliet Ponsonby, and Rt Hon James Ramsden, MP.

Charlotte Ramsden, the youngest of five children, was educated in London, then at Marlborough College, where she was inspired to study art by Robin Child. At the Slade School of Art (1978–81) she received a travelling scholarship to study Christian iconography in Cappadocia, an experience which influenced her later work. In 1982, she married Mark Cheverton, artist and teacher, who was appointed Head of Art at Edinburgh Academy. Lottie Cheverton taught at Fettes College and worked with community groups, in 1985 persuading artists from all over Scotland to donate pictures for display in aid of the Third World ('Art for Africa', Edinburgh City Art Centre). Her encouragement and concern for budding artists led in 1988 to the foundation by the Chevertons of the Leith School of Art, the central philosophy of which was, and is, to offer a creative environment for personal growth and intellectual awareness. Lottie Cheverton was elected a member of council of the SSA in 1989. The road accident in which Mark and Lottie Cheverton died in 1991 brought to an untimely end their artistic careers, but the Leith School remains their legacy. EMS

• 'Freedom within a Framework: the art and teaching of Mark and Charlotte Cheverton', exhibition catalogue, Leith School of Art, August 1992.
The Guardian, 23 Sept. 1991; *The Scotsman*, 19 Sept. 1991 (obit. and article); *The Times*, 20 Sept. and 24 Oct. 1991. Private information: Family, and staff of Fettes College and Leith School of Art.

CHIESLEY (or CHIESLY), Rachel, Lady Grange, m. **Erskine,** baptised Edinburgh 4 Feb. 1679, died Idrigal, Skye, May 1745. Daughter of Margaret Nicholson, and John Chiesley of Dalry.

Rachel Chiesley was apparently very beautiful, and in about 1708 James Erskine, Lord Grange

(1679–1754), younger brother of John, 11th Earl of Mar, fell in love with her. But her father had assassinated Sir George Lockhart, Lord President of the court of session in 1689 and, fearing for his legal career, James Erskine refused to marry her when she became pregnant, until she threatened him with a pistol. According to her, they then lived together for nearly 25 years 'in great love and peace' (NAS, 1506). They had four sons and five daughters.

By 1718, however, her sons' tutor was complaining of Lady Grange's imperiousness and unreasonableness. When the young Alexander Carlyle met her, she was so gorgeously dressed that he thought she must be the Great Scarlet Whore of Babylon. (Invited to tea with her daughters, he noted that they seemed frightened out of their wits by her.) When Lady Grange discovered that her husband had a mistress in London, she followed him about, abused him verbally in public, swore at his relations, drank excessively and allegedly threatened to reveal that he was a Jacobite. Trying to pacify her, he allowed her to manage his estate, but her extravagance meant he had to replace her. Their grown-up children's letters recount in painful detail the violent arguments that disturbed the neighbours in Edinburgh's Cowgate at night.

In 1732, intending to confront her husband, Lady Grange booked a seat on the London coach but a party of Highlanders burst into her house, tied her up, gagged her and carried her off to the Highlands, apparently on Grange's orders. She was taken to the island of Heiskir, then to St Kilda, where she was kept for four years. In 1738 she smuggled out a letter and an expedition set off to rescue her, but she had already been moved elsewhere. She died in 1745, still a prisoner, and was buried at Trumpan, in Waternish, Skye. She was certainly scandalously treated by her husband, but he himself was a victim of the marriage laws of the time, which did not allow him to divorce a partner who had become intolerable not only to him but to his entire family. RKM

• NAS: Mar and Kellie Muniments, GD124/15/1179, 1374–80, 1506, 1524.
Carlyle, A. (1973) *Anecdotes and Characters of the Times*; Grant, I. F. (1959) *The Macleods: The History of a Clan*; Laing, D. (1875) 'Mrs Erskine, Lady Grange, in the Island of St Kilda', in *Proc. Soc. Antiquaries Scot.*, 10; Marshall, R. K. (1983) *Virgins and Viragos*; *ODNB* (2004) (see Erskine, Rachel); Seton-Watson, R. W. (1931) 'The strange story of Lady Grange', *History*, 16.

CHISHOLM, Jane (Jean), fl. 1542–57. Illegitimate daughter of a lady of the Montrose family, and William Chisholm, Bishop of Dunblane.

In pre-Reformation Scotland, it was not uncommon for bishops to have illegitimate children, and significant sums of money were paid to find suitable positions or marriages for these children. Jane Chisholm was one of four of William Chisholm's offspring. In 1542, she married Sir James Stirling of Keir, whose previous marriage to Janet Stirling, heiress of Cadder, had been annulled and its issue made illegitimate. Janet had signed away her birthright and lands to her former husband. When Jane Chisholm married James Stirling, she brought a dowry of £1,000, and through her, James acquired yet more land and property from the Bishop when church lands were sold or disbursed at about the time of the Reformation. The couple had at least one daughter.

Other well-placed bishop's daughters included **Margaret Beaton** (fl. 1545–73), illegitimate daughter of Cardinal David Beaton, who fathered at least eight children with *Marion Ogilvy. Margaret Beaton married David Lindsay (1526/7–74), 10th Earl of Crawford, in 1546, with a dowry of 4,000 marks. She had several children. When the marriage broke up, she went to live with her mother. Archbishop Andrew Forman's illegitimate daughter **Jane Forman** (fl. 1519–50) received roughly £1,000 when she married Alexander Oliphant of Kellie. SEM

• Cockburn, J. H. (1959) *The Medieval Bishops of Dunblane*; MacKenzie, A. (1891) *History of the Chisholms*, pp. 195, 225; Mahoney, M. (1962) 'The Scottish Hierarchy 1513–1565', in D. McRoberts (ed.) *Essays on the Scottish Reformation 1513–1625*, pp. 60–1; *SP*, iii, pp. 29–30, vi, p. 546; Sanderson, M. H. B. (1987) *Mary Stewart's People*, pp. 7, 11–12, 17–18.

CHISHOLM, Mairi Lambert Gooden,‡ of Chisholm, born Datchet, Bucks., 26 Feb. 1896, died Perth 22 August 1981. Ambulance driver and photographer. Daughter of Margaret Fraser, and Roderick Chisholm, chief of Clan Chisholm.

Through a shared love of motorcycles, Mairi Chisholm met (Elizabeth) Elsie Knocker (1884–1978), a trained nurse. In 1914, both women volunteered, initially as dispatch riders, and went with Hector Munro's Flying Ambulance Column (FAC) to Belgium. They drove ambulances, until, chafing under the FAC, they persuaded the Belgian authorities to let them set up a front-line first-aid post in a cellar at Pervyse near Ypres. The only women allowed to work on the western front, they had realised that casualties needed immediate treatment in order to survive further transport. They gave thousands of wounded men first aid, then Mairi Chisholm drove them to hospital by ambulance. Becoming famous as the 'two women of Pervyse', both were made Chevalier of the Order of Leopold, and later awarded the Military Medal. Both women were gassed, Mairi Chisholm twice, and invalided home in 1918. They were assiduous photographers, and their combined collection, running to hundreds of images, makes them 'two of the most important documentarists' of the First World War (Williams 1991, p. 33). Mairi Chisholm's albums depicting daily life at Pervyse are in the NLS. After 1918, the two women parted company. Mairi Chisholm, her health affected, moved to Scotland, where she ran a poultry farm with companion May Davidson, in Cantray, then lived in Connel, Argyll. She retained her love of motoring, and also established the Clan Chisholm society in 1972. She was featured in a BBC TV programme, *Yesterday's Witness* (1977) and an IWM exhibition, 'Women and War' (2003–4). SR

• NLS: Acc. 8006 (1–5): Five albums of photographs and news cuttings; IWM, unpub. memoir, diaries and corr.; film and audio records of both women.
Adie, K. (2003) *Corsets to Camouflage*; Condell, D. and Liddiard, J. (1987) *Working for Victory*; ODNB (2004) (Chisholm, Mairi; T'Serclaes, Elizabeth); Williams, V. (1991) *The Other Observers*.

CHRISTIE, Isabella Robertson (Ella), born Cockpen, Edinburgh, 21 April 1861, died Edinburgh 29 Jan. 1949. Traveller, gardener, landowner. Daughter of Alison Philp, and John Christie, coalmine-owner.

Four years after Ella Christie was born her father acquired the estate of Cowden in the Ochil hills, where she was raised and educated with her younger sister Alice, spending winters in Edinburgh. From the 1870s, the two girls travelled throughout Europe with their father – to Italy, Spain, Germany and the Low Countries. After her sister's marriage and her mother's death, Ella Christie continued to travel, first with her father and later with a friend, to Egypt, Palestine and Syria, and to write about her journeys. Freed of domestic responsibilities after John Christie's death in 1902, her journeys became ever more wide-ranging and ambitious, taking her to India and Tibet in 1904, to China and Japan in 1907, to Central Asia on two separate journeys in 1910 and 1912, and to America in 1914.

In 1916 she became 'directrice' of a canteen called 'La Goutte de Café', established by the French Red Cross at Bar-sur-Aube, and staffed by five Scotswomen during the Battle of Verdun. In 1917, she returned to Cowden but went back to France in 1918–19 to take charge of another canteen at Mulhouse in Alsace. She then resumed her travels and her role as the mistress of Cowden Castle where she created what, in its time, was regarded as one of the best Japanese gardens in the western hemisphere. Inspired by her exploration of Japan in 1907, during which she met and visited gardens with the writer Florence Du Cane and her sister, illustrator Ella Du Cane, she employed a Japanese woman, garden designer Taki Honda from the school of garden design at Nagoya, to transform a once-marshy hollow at Cowden into a traditional Japanese garden, her Shah-rak-uen or 'place of pleasure and delight'. She maintained it with the assistance, latterly, of her devoted Japanese gardener Matsuo. Although the garden was kept up for some years after her death in 1949, neglect and vandalism eventually saw to its destruction. The castle was demolished in 1952. Ella Christie was made FRGS and FSAScot. CHD

• Christie, E. (1925) *Through Khiva to Golden Samarkand*, (n. d.) *A Japanese Garden in Perthshire*; with Stewart, A. (1940) *A Long Look at Life*.
Du Cane, E. & F. (1908) *The Flowers and Gardens of Japan*; ODNB (2004); Pearse, B. (1991) *Companion to Japanese Britain and Ireland*; Stewart, A. (1955) '*Alicella*': *A Memoir of Alice King Stewart and Ella Christie*; Swan, A. (1989) 'Where the Ochils met the Orient', *The Scots Magazine*, vol. 132, no. 1.

CHRISTIE, Madeleine Elsie Jane, m. **Walker,** born Edinburgh 18 Jan. 1904, died London 1 Feb. 1996. Actor and singer. Daughter of Wilhelmina Duncan, and Henry Reid Christie, brewery agent.

Following her education at George Watson's Ladies' College, Edinburgh, Madeleine Christie studied singing at the Central School in London. While there, she was offered the chance of a lifetime, understudying the part of Polly Peachum in *The Beggar's Opera*, with a place in the chorus; but her father, confusing an opera chorus with the variety stage, ordered her home. In 1926, she married David Walker, a lawyer, and moved to Glasgow, raising two children and undertaking amateur work. Her first professional engagement was in 1944 with Glasgow's Park Theatre, following which she joined the Wilson Barrett Company, playing repertory in Glasgow, Edinburgh and Aberdeen. Five years later she moved to the

Glasgow Citizens' Theatre. She played in several roles at the Edinburgh Festival, including 'Sensualitie' in Tyrone Guthrie's production of *The Thrie Estaitis*: later, extensive work for Guthrie took her to Broadway and a tour of North America. Her theatre credits are numerous, and among her films were *Conspiracy of Hearts, Brotherly Love* and *Florence Nightingale*. In broadcasting she ranged from *Mrs Dale's Diary* on radio to *The Pallisers* on television, and was proud to have played the principal role in J. M. Barrie's *The Old Lady Shows Her Medals*, the first play televised from Scotland (19 March 1952). Aged 89, her final engagement was as Sister Godric in the television production *Body and Soul*. DPW

• Personal information (son).

CLANRANALD, Lady *see* **MACLEOD, Margaret, Lady Clanranald** (d. 1780)

'Clarinda' *see* **MCLEHOSE (or Maclehose, M'Lehose), Agnes** (1758–1841)

CLARK, Elizabeth Thomson (Betty) [Joan Ure], n. **Carswell,** born Newcastle upon Tyne 22 June 1918, died Mauchline, 24 Feb. 1978. Playwright and poet. Daughter of Janet Love Thomson, clerkess, and John Carswell, engineering draughtsman.

Betty Carswell was brought up in Wallsend on Tyne. From the age of 12 she cared for her father and siblings when her mother (who was from Greenock) contracted tuberculosis and became a permanent invalid. Betty Carswell left school early and worked as a typist before marrying John Lochhead Clark (b. 1912/13), an accountant and Glasgow businessman. They had one daughter and lived in Glasgow's West End. Betty Clark herself contracted tuberculosis aged 29 and while in hospital she began to write, later joining Edward Scoular's creative writing class at Langside College. Her initial interest was in poetry, but subsequently she turned to playwriting. She used the *nom de plume* Joan Ure to distance her identity as a writer from that of wife and mother: Joan was the name of her sister who had died soon after the Second World War.

She was never a popular dramatist; few of her plays were performed professionally and many were never staged. Productions tended to be by 'fringe' groups, notably Glasgow University Arts Theatre Group and the short-lived Stage Company (Scotland), in whose creation she played a major role. She was also a co-founder of the Scottish Society of Playwrights. Her first theatre production was *Punctuated Rhythms* for the Falcon Theatre in Glasgow in 1962. The Arts Theatre's productions of her work included *Suburban Commentaries* (1964), *Nothing May Come of it: A Revue* (1965), *In this Space in Three by Three* (1966), and *Seven Characters Out of 'The Dream'* (1968). *I See Myself as this Young Girl* was the first play by a Scot to be produced at the Close Theatre in Glasgow (1967). Her best-known pieces are *Something in it for Ophelia* and *Something in it for Cordelia*, both produced at the Edinburgh 'Fringe' in 1971. Several of her stage plays were produced for radio by Stewart Conn. She has been described as 'beautiful if painfully thin . . . exquisitely if eccentrically dressed, wholly self-absorbed and unfailingly manipulative' (McDonald 2002). In his appreciation of her life, Christopher Small celebrated dramas that are 'delicate, allusive and full of wit' (*Glasgow Herald* 1978). He also recorded her as declaring that 'in Scotland the battle of the sexes is a war where everybody has lost'. AS

• Univ. of Glasgow Library Scottish Theatre Archive, Special Collections Department: unpublished scripts, poems, letters, articles and occasional pieces, including Gray's radio transcript.

Ure, J., Works as above, and (1970) *Two Plays*, (1979) *Five Short Plays* (ed. C. Small).

Gray, A. (1985) 'Portrait of a playwright', in J. Kelman, A. Owens and A. Gray, *Lean Tales*; *Glasgow Herald*, 25 Feb. 1978 (obit.); McDonald, J. (2002) ' "Is it not possible to have a poem made out of theatre?": . . . dramas and dramaturgy of Joan Ure', *Int. Jour. Scot. Theatre*, 3.1, June; *ODNB* (2004) http://arts.qmuc.ac.uk/ijost/Volume3_no1/1_mcdonald_j.htm.

CLARK, Grace, m. **Murray,** born Yoker, Glasgow, 29 June 1905, died Ayr 6 May 1995. Entertainer and comedienne. Daughter of Margaret Nelson, and Alexander Clark, ship plater.

Having started out in showbusiness as a concert pianist, Grace Clark met her husband Colin Murray, a singer, during a summer season in Dunbar in 1926. They formed a double act, Clark and Murray, and married in 1931 but did not turn to comedy until after the Second World War. Scottish 'comediennes' (as they were known) were not numerous in the variety era. Two of Grace Clark's best-known predecessors were also in double-acts, Dora Lindsay and Bret Harte, and Doris and Frank Droy. In comedic tradition, they all exploited the dramatic possibilities of 'close-mooth' Glasgow working-class speech. Lindsay and Harte, active in Scotland in the first part of the

20th century, specialised in playing on a contrast between Dora 'the wee shawlie . . . with a mouthful of rhyming slang', and Bret 'the would-be Kelvinsider' (Mackie 1973, p. 101). **Doris Droy** (n. Bell, born c. 1905), who started out as a dancer, was associated with long-running pantomimes at Glasgow's Queen's Theatre in the 1930s and 40s and with her 'Suicide Sal' character in a 1939 revue of that name, a femme fatale who dismisses a boxer with the following: 'He thought that he was strong and sturdy; After I had left him, well, he wasnae worth a curdie' (small coin) (Bruce, p. 116).

Grace Clark and Colin Murray specialised in the arguing husband and wife domestic comedy that was a staple of variety theatre and vaudeville. They gave the act a distinctive Scottish flavour, becoming known as 'Mr and Mrs Glasgow'. Their rapport with their public was honed over the years, certain sketches becoming favourites. They appeared in the first Scottish Royal Variety Performance and were later honoured with the BEM for services to entertainment. Colin Murray died in 1989. FB

• Bruce, F. (2000) *Scottish Showbusiness*; Mackie, A. D. (1973) *The Scotch Comedians*; *The Scotsman*, 8 May 1995 (obit.).

CLARK, Mary, n. Macpherson, born Laggan c. 1740, died Perth c. 1815. Poet. Daughter of Ewen Macpherson, schoolmaster.

Known as Bean T(h)orra Dhamh (the goodwife of Torra Damh) in Badenoch where she lived after her marriage, Mary Clark probably composed many more poems than the seven that survive. Widowed young, she moved in later life to stay with a married daughter in Perth. She is an early representative of the Evangelical Revival that swept through Gaelic Presbyterianism, especially after the New Testament was published in 1767. The movement formalised ideas of social justice, protesting against bad landlordism and opening new perspectives on traditional loyalties bonding chief and clan. Mary Clark's poetry is clear and direct, her expression of Christian faith as forthright as her comments on secular life, but it is her explicit criticism of the idea of a Gaelic Golden Age that is startlingly fresh. The leaders of that society 'placed their foot on the rule of Truth/. . . harnessing the poor and wounding them with malice'. JMACI

• MacRae, A. (ed.) (n.d.) *Mary MacPherson, Bean Torra Dhamh, the Religious Poetess of Badenoch, her Poems and Life*; Rose, J. (ed.) (1851) *Metrical Reliques of 'The Men' in the Highlands*; Sinton, Rev. T. (1906) *The Poetry of Badenoch*.

CLARKSON, Bessie, died Lanark, April 1625.

Bessie Clarkson was a woman of religious conviction whose story was publicised by her Presbyterian minister, William Livingston of the parish of Lanark. For three and a half years, until her death in 1625, she was counselled by him; he referred to her as 'this deare daughter of Abraham'. She is a case study of Puritanism's culture of alienation and guilt, being obsessed with the wrath of God 'that you [Livingston] preached'. Her minister countered that her feelings were actually constructive and beneficial, but she died without surmounting her despair, although she raised eyes and hands heavenward at the end, to his contentment. William Livingston's account of her was first circulated without his permission, probably in manuscript, and then in 1631 in printed form at his own bidding. The popularity of Bessie Clarkson's story is demonstrated by the fact that it was reprinted four times between 1664 and 1698. DM

• Livingston, W. (1631) *The Conflict in Conscience of a deare Christian, named Bessie Clarksone*; Mullan, D. G. (2000) *Scottish Puritanism 1590–1638*.

CLEGHORN, Louisa born c. 1720, died after 1775. Sick-nurse, Edinburgh.

Louisa Cleghorn married Archibald Russell, weaver, in the Canongate, Edinburgh, in 1739. In a court case of 1775, when she was about 55 years old, she stated that it was her business to wait upon sick persons. In this instance she had nursed the widow of a man who had died of a fever, the widow eventually being put in the tolbooth 'delirious' (Edin. Comm. Court Processes). Her statement shows that women saw sick-nursing as continuous employment. It was work in which women with little education or employment skills could earn some money towards the upkeep of the household. ECS

• NAS: CC8/4/644 Edinburgh Commissary Court Processes. Grant, F. J. (ed.) (1915) *Parish of Holyroodhouse or Canongate Register of Marriages, 1564–1800*; WWEE (Bibl.).

CLEPHANE, Elizabeth Cecilia, born Edinburgh 18 June 1830, died Melrose 19 Feb. 1869. Hymn writer. Daughter of Anna Maria Douglas, of an army family, and Andrew Clephane, Sheriff of Fife and Kinross.

Elizabeth Clephane's family moved to Melrose, where she became noted for her philanthropy and good work among the poor, selling her horses to provide money for poor relief. After her death, eight of her hymns appeared in *The Family Treasury*, a religious magazine, between 1872 and 1874, under the heading 'Breathings on the Border'. Two of them became famous, and are still to be found in many hymn books: 'Beneath the Cross of Jesus' (published 1872), and 'There were ninety and nine that safely lay' (published 1874). The latter, made famous by the American evangelist Ira D. Sankey, is said to have been written after the early death in Canada of her oldest brother George, the ne'er do well of the family. A memorial brass to her is in Melrose Corn Exchange. JRW

• Grant, F. (1944) *The Faculty of Advocates in Scotland 1532–1943*; Julian, J. (1892, 1907) *A Dictionary of Hymnology*; Thomson, D. P. (1946) *The Sweet Singer of Melrose*.
Additional information: Alison Robertson.

CLUGSTON, Beatrice, born Glasgow 19 Sept. 1827, died Ardrossan 5 June 1888. Philanthropist. Daughter of Mary Mackenzie, and John Clugston, merchant.

Beatrice Clugston's childhood illness stimulated her life-long sympathy towards the sick. She never married; like many other Victorian middle-class women she devoted her life to philanthropic work. For a period the family lived at Larkhall, Lanarkshire, then, following her father's death in 1855, moved back to Glasgow. Around this time she became a prison visitor and later began visiting patients at the Glasgow Royal Infirmary. In 1864, she founded a Dorcas Society (a group who made clothes and provided small sums of money) to help discharged patients. Conscious that returning impoverished patients to a poor domestic environment significantly impeded their recovery, in 1865 she established the Glasgow Convalescent Home at Bothwell, Lanarkshire, the first such institution in the West of Scotland.

Beatrice Clugston was a prodigious fundraiser, soliciting support from all sections of society, including royalty such as *Princess Louise. It took her only one year to raise sufficient funds for a second convalescent home, the West of Scotland Seaside Convalescent Homes, opened at Dunoon in 1869 and the largest in Scotland with 250 beds. In 1871, following further fundraising, she began the relocation of the Glasgow Convalescent Home to a new, far larger building at Lenzie. She went on to found the Broomhill Homes for Incurables at Kirkintilloch in 1876. She wrote numerous pamphlets to promote her charitable work. In her later years, a fund was raised to provide her with an annuity in recognition of her work. JLC

• Clugston, B. (1871) *West of Scotland Convalescent Seaside Homes, Dunoon. A short account of their present position and capabilities of extension and use.*
Blackie, W. G. (1875) *Miss Clugston and her Work*; Checkland, O. (1980) *Philanthropy in Victorian Scotland*; Cronin, J. (2003) 'The origin and development of Scottish convalescent homes' PhD, Univ. of Glasgow; *ODNB* (2004); Stewart, E. L. 'The incurable Miss Clugston', *Glasgow Herald*, 15 Dec. 1964.

CLUNAS, Maggie Eliza (Lila),‡ born Glasgow 10 August 1876, died Dundee 29 Dec. 1968. Suffragette, teacher, town councillor. Daughter of Elsie Melvin, and Hugh Clunas, dress shop proprietor.

Educated at Bell Baxter High School, Cupar, and Moray House Teacher Training College, Edinburgh, Lila Clunas taught in Brown Street elementary public school, Dundee. A socialist, she joined the WSPU in 1906, moving to the WFL the following year and serving as branch secretary from 1908 to 1912. Both her sisters, Elsie and Jessie Clunas, were members; Elsie was the treasurer. Lila Clunas was active in deputations and heckling and writing to the press, where she showed a sharp wit: 'In this country in the past men have defied the law, and today their names are revered', she pointed out (*Advertiser* 1913). In 1908, she was forcibly ejected from one of Churchill's election meetings; in 1909, on a WFL deputation to Downing Street, she was arrested and charged with obstruction for attempting to present their petition. She was sentenced to three weeks, went on hunger strike and was released early. In 1914, her ejection from a Ramsay MacDonald meeting caused a split between suffrage campaigners and the local Labour Party.

The second half of Lila Clunas's life was spent living with her sister Elsie in Broughty Ferry. In 1943, she was elected to Dundee Town Council as a Labour Party councillor and served until 1964; her interests were in education, libraries and parks. A vegetarian, she was described as a quiet, small, kindly person, but 'apt to surprise her male colleagues with her logic and eloquence' (*Courier & Advertiser* 1968). IMH

• Dundee Local Studies Library: press cuttings; Dundee *Advertiser*, 29 April 1913; Dundee *Courier & Advertiser*, 31 Dec. 1968 (obit.); *WSM*.

COBLAITH, born probably Skye, died 690. Daughter of Cano mac Gartnait (d. 688), probable leader/king of Cenél nGartnait in Skye.

We know nothing of Coblaith aside from the year of her death and a few tantalising references to her family, Cenél nGartnait ('kindred of Gartnait'). Her father was probably the leader of the kindred, which throughout her lifetime seems to have been involved in a protracted struggle with one branch at least of Cenél nGabráin, one of the most eminent and powerful kindreds of 7th-century Argyll. There are almost no references to royal women of the Dál Riata in the early sources, and notice of Coblaith's death in 690 is therefore remarkable. This suggests that she was a particularly notable figure, possibly as a result of a high-profile political marriage, or as a nun. JEF

• MacAirt, S. and MacNiocaill, G. (1983) *The Annals of Ulster (to AD 1131)*.

COCKBURN, Alison n. **Rutherford**, born Fairnilee, Selkirkshire, 8 Oct. 1713, died Edinburgh, 22 Nov. 1794. Songwriter, literary hostess. Daughter of Alison Ker, and Robert Rutherford.

Alison Rutherford was one of six children. Her mother died when she was ten, but by her own account her sisters loved and taught her well. In 1731, she married the advocate, Patrick Cockburn (d. 1753), who became Commissioner for the estates of the Duke of Hamilton. After his death, Alison Cockburn lived mainly in Edinburgh. Her only son, Adam, was born in 1732 and became a captain of dragoons, but died in tragic circumstances in 1780.

She is perhaps most famous for her song, 'I've Seen the Smiling of Fortune Beguiling', to the old Scottish air, 'The Flowers of the Forest', first published in *The Lark*, Edinburgh 1765 (see Elliot, Jean). She also wrote several songs concerning the Jacobite rising of 1745 but, like other upper-class women of her period, she feared print. Her niece, also a poet, **Elizabeth Rutherford** (1729–89), had an 'uncontrollable propensity to rhyme, in which she grew by practice to have considerable aptitude' (Rutherford/Cockburn, 1900, p. 191). Elizabeth married Walter Scot or Scott of Wauchope and was visited in 1787 by Robert Burns to whom she had sent a rhymed epistle: he described Mrs Scott however as 'having all the sense, taste, intrepidity of face and bold critical decision which usually distinguish female authors' (ibid., p. 191).

Alison Cockburn was related to Sir Walter Scott, who admired her, and she was for many years the centre of a distinguished social circle in Edinburgh, being celebrated for her wit and her beauty: her auburn hair apparently survived without artificial aid into old age. Her account of her life, written in 1784 when she was over 70 and dedicated to Rev. Robert Douglas of Galashiels, her usual correspondent, was circulated privately. It remained unprinted until 1900 when it was published by T. Craig-Brown with other texts, giving a notion of her intellectual interests and her social circle, which included David Hume and James Burnett, Lord Monboddo. She wrote to Hume as an intellectual equal and teased him on his atheism. Her letters and the replies circulated among a select group during her lifetime. The moving directness of her autobiography is made possible by its having private rather than public circulation: for example, the convincing, because unembellished, expression of the physical and emotional ties of married love in her account of comforting her dying husband: 'Mr. Cockburn, on whom were the sweats of death, begged me to lie down with him. . . . I stripped instantly and was embraced in his cold wet arms with such affection, dearer than the first embrace' (ibid., p. 9). Her will shows her attentive to all those friends, family and servants who had loved her throughout her life and comforted her in her tragic losses of husband and child. DAMCM

• NAS: GD247/194–243; GD110; NLS: MSS 915, 3188; Edinburgh Univ. Library: La.II.81/2: letters and literary mss. Rutherford or Cockburn, A. [1784] (1900) *Letters and Memoir of Her Own Life; also 'Felix', a Biographical Sketch and Various Songs*, T. Craig-Brown, ed.; *ODNB* (2004). Alison Cockburn's will is at www.scotlandspeople.gov.uk

COKE, Lady Mary, n. **Campbell**, born probably at Inveraray Castle 6 Feb. 1726, died Morton House, Chiswick, 30 Sept. 1811. Journal and letter writer, eccentric. Daughter of Jane Warburton, and John Campbell, 2nd Duke of Argyll.

Lady Mary Campbell was temperamental, poorly educated and indulged in her youth: she appears as a lively, precocious child in Walter Scott's *The Heart of Midlothian*. Married to the 'odious' Edward Coke (1719–53), son of the Earl of Leicester, she was a virtual prisoner until her mother obtained a writ of *habeas corpus*. Having divorced him, she obtained her jointure of £2,500 a year on his death in 1753. She was attached to the Duke of York, younger brother of George III: some rumours suggested they secretly married. Best known as an indefatigable journal writer, mixing with the London elite, her comments on contemporaries were trenchant and acerbic. She operated within the political culture of the day, in which women used their influence in parliamentary politics, seeking positions for friends and family, and where 'gossip' was linked to power. Politically knowledgeable, active within the Scottish aristocracy, though rarely in Scotland, she took a vigorous interest in the Douglas Cause against the Hamiltons (see Gunning, Elizabeth), despite an 'aversion' to 'Scotchmen' (*Journals* 1886–96). Often vocal, against the French she was 'wild & possessed'. Horace Walpole fondly memorialised her in his *Castle of Otranto* (1766): 'No; never was thy pitying breast/Insensible to human woes;/Tender, tho' firm, it melts distrest/For weakness it never knows'. Lady Mary travelled widely. It is said that, 'Eccentric to the end, she slept in a dresser drawer in old age, and died sitting upright wearing a high crowned beaver hat adorned with plumes.' (Holkham Hall website). *Lady Louisa Stuart (1863) described her at 82 as 'still as violent & absurd as ever', with a taste for 'loo, gossip and gardening, but the greatest of these is gossip'. She was buried in the Argyll vault in Westminster Abbey. DLS

• Coke, Lady M., (1889–96 edn.) *The Letters and Journals of Lady Mary Coke (1766–74).*
DBAWW; *ODNB* (2004); Scott, Sir W. (1982 edn.) *The Heart of Midlothian*, pp. 387–8; Stuart, Lady L. (1863) *Some Account of John Duke of Argyll and his Family*, (reprinted in Coke's *Journals*, 1889–96 edition); Walpole, H. (1766) *The Castle of Otranto*; Website Holkham Hall and Estate, North Norfolk, for family tree:
http://www.holkham.co.uk/family/1stearl2ndcreation.html

COMYN, Agnes, Countess of Strathearn, fl. 1296–1320. Daughter of Elizabeth de Quincy, and Alexander Comyn, Earl of Buchan.

Agnes Comyn's life, like that of her sister *Marjory Comyn, Countess of Dunbar, demonstrates both the constraints that matrimonial politics in early-14th-century Scotland imposed on high-born women and, by contrast, the ways in which they might express political convictions usually associated with their male kin. At an early age, Agnes Comyn was married to Malise II, Earl of Strathearn (1261–1317), supporter of the Balliol faction during the unsettled years 1291–6. The marriage, a victory for the Comyn family, created a firm alliance between a native magnate of high standing in national affairs and a political party determined to counter Bruce opposition to the Balliol kingship.

At first the alliance worked well; Malise participated in uprisings against Edward I, joining the expedition that raided south as far as Carlisle in spring 1296, and supporting William Wallace and Sir Andrew Murray. In 1306, however, following his victory at the battle of Methven, Robert Bruce compelled Malise to abandon his loyalty to the Balliol-Comyn group. For this offence, Edward I seized Malise and sent him into captivity in England. Countess Agnes spent several years there with him and, although her confinement was honourable, material conditions were both modest and severe. They were not permitted to return to Scotland until after November 1308. Chastened, Malise remained thereafter an adherent of the pro-English party, but Agnes supported the Comyn-led faction's efforts to oust Robert Bruce. She became actively involved in the dangerous Soules conspiracy of 1320 to restore the Balliol family to the throne and to secure the return of Comyn and other lands forfeited from his political opponents by Bruce after Bannockburn. She was convicted of complicity in the plot and, although her rank and family connections enabled her to escape execution, she was sentenced to perpetual imprisonment. CJN

• Bain, J. (ed.) (1887) *Calendar of Documents relating to Scotland*, vol. 3; Macpherson, D. et al. (eds) (1814–19) *Rotuli Scotiae in turri Londinensi . . .* 2 vols; Maxwell, H. (ed.) (1907) *Scalacronica by Sir Thomas Gray of Heton, Knight*; Neville, C. J. (1983) 'The Earls of Strathearn . . .', PhD, Univ. of Aberdeen, (1986) 'The political allegiance of the Earls of Strathearn . . .', *Scot. Hist. Rev.* 65, 2; Penman, M. (1999) 'A fell coniuracioun again Robert the douchty king . . .', *Innes Review* 50, 1; Riley, H. T. (ed.) (1865) *Willelmi Rishanger . . . Chronica et Annales*; Skene, W. F. (ed.) (1871) *Johannis de Fordun Gesta Annalia.*

COMYN, Marjory, Countess of Dunbar, fl. 1290s. Daughter of Elizabeth de Quincy, and Alexander Comyn, Earl of Buchan.

Marjory Comyn's life, like that of her sister *Agnes Comyn, Countess of Strathearn, shows clearly how the so-called Wars of Independence divided the personal and political lives of the nobility. By spring 1296, Marjory's husband, Patrick, Earl of Dunbar (1242–1308), had declared himself a supporter of the English cause; he left his wife in charge of their strategic castle at Dunbar to join Edward I. Unlike her husband, Marjory Comyn was committed to the Guardian-controlled government of the realm, then dominated by the Comyn family and their followers. In Earl Patrick's absence, she delivered Dunbar to a Scottish raiding party, forcing Edward I to detach from his army a substantial force to recapture the castle.

The English proved victorious, but her actions confirmed Comyn commitment to Scottish independence. CJN

• Barrow, G. W. S. (1988) *Robert Bruce*; Riley, H. T. (ed.) (1865*) Willelmi Rishanger . . . Chronica et Annales*; Rothwell, H. (ed.) (1957) *The Chronicle of Walter of Guisborough*; Young, A. (1997) *Robert Bruce's Rivals: the Comyns, 1212–1314.*

CORDINER, Helen Thomson, m. **Ritchie,** born Peterhead 30 July 1893, died Musselburgh 14 Dec. 1964. Herring gutter. Daughter of Jane Buchan, domestic servant, and Francis Cordiner, fisherman.

Helen Cordiner's mother died from a chronic lung disease, aged 35, in 1898, leaving six children, the youngest six months old. The Cordiner daughters worked at the herring to help their father to support the family. Helen Cordiner attended Buckhaven Primary School, Peterhead, then from age 13 or 14 worked as a herring gutter. Official documents list her occupation as 'fishworker'. In a crew with her sisters, Marjorie and Jane Ann, she gutted and graded herring, standing on quaysides, working in 10 to 12 hour shifts. Female Scottish fishworkers were a highly skilled, mobile workforce who dominated the herring industry: thousands of women travelled around fishing ports, working for curing companies. Each November, end-of-season bonuses were paid to the packer, supposedly for sharing, though Helen was unhappy that Jane Ann as packer kept these bonuses herself. In 1912, Helen Cordiner married Andrew Ritchie, a fisherman she met while working in South Shields. Thereafter they lived in Fisherrow, the fishing community of Musselburgh, with the surviving five of their eight children. She was a tough household manager: if her husband returned from fishing trips without any money, he had to wait at the door for permission to enter the house. Her daughter Jean (1913–2003) worked for a time in the local fishing net mill. MR

• Personal knowledge; private information and family records.

'Countrywoman' *see* **GRIEVE, Jemima Bessie** (1923–96)

COUSIN, Anne Ross, n. **Cundell,** born Hull 27 April 1824, died Edinburgh 6 Dec. 1906. Hymn writer. Daughter of Anne Parker, and David Ross Cundell, a Scottish army surgeon present at the battle of Waterloo.

When Anne Cundell was a small child, the family moved to Leith. She married in 1847 the Rev. William Cousin (1812–83), minister of Chelsea Presbyterian Church, London, then of the Free Church of Scotland, Irvine and after 1859, Melrose. They had six children. In 1854 at Irvine she wrote a celebrated hymn, 'The sands of time are sinking', published in *The Christian Treasury* for 1857. Its title was 'Last Words of Samuel Rutherford', referring to the Covenanter (1600–61) whose last words were 'Glory, Glory dwelleth in Emmanuel's land', which gave Cousin the motif for the last two lines of each verse. It also gave the title to her collection of poems, *Immanuel's Land and other Pieces* (1876). Seven of her hymns were published in *The Service of Praise* (1865) and four in the *Presbyterian Hymnal* of 1876. Part of a stained-glass window to her memory survives in Melrose. JRW

• Beattie, D. J. (n.d., prob. 1934) *Stories and Sketches of our Hymns and their Writers*; Julian, J. (1892, 1907) *A Dictionary of Hymnology*; Kerrigan, C. (ed.) (1991) *An Anthology of Scottish Women Poets*; *ODNB* (2004); Telford, J. (1934) *The New Methodist Hymn Book, Illustrated.*

COWAN (formerly Cohen), Evelyn, m. **Cohen,** born Glasgow 18 Jan. 1921, died Glasgow 8 March 1998. Writer. Daughter of Mary Banks, and Simon Cohen or Cowan, tailor.

The youngest of eleven children of Lithuanian Jewish parents, Evelyn Cowan grew up in the Gorbals. As a young woman, she contributed stories and articles to various publications. She married Paul Cohen, a schoolteacher, in 1950 and they had three sons. She was in middle age when her memoir, *Spring Remembered* (1974), appeared. Her memories of childhood poverty have been deemed sentimental, as compared with her contemporary Ralph Glasser's, but she aimed to write affectionately about immigrant struggles. In her view, being poor did not preclude a secure upbringing: 'It was a world of poverty which to me, was not misery, but rich and happy' (Cowan 1974, p. 10). She is recalled as an energetic and forthright woman, active in Jewish charities. Her novel *A Portrait of Alice* (1976) illustrates her intention not to deceive. Described as a 'taut book of loneliness, despair and rejection' (*Glasgow Herald* 1976), it is set in Glasgow's comfortable suburbs and reflects middle-class living, more representative of Jewish experience in Scotland by the 1970s. Its unflinching gaze at aspects of Jewish life and a middle-aged woman's lot could make uncomfortable reading, but its author was 'unrepentant about its harsh reality' (ibid.). Critical acclaim followed, and another novel was planned but, perhaps because of

ill health, including breast cancer, Evelyn Cowan published nothing further. LF
• Cowan, E., *Works* as above.
Burgess, M. (1999) *The Glasgow Novel*, 3rd edn.; Glasser, R. (1987) *Growing up in the Gorbals*; *Glasgow Herald*, 8 Dec. 1976, p. 9 (interview); *Jewish Chronicle*, 17 April 1998 (obit.).

COWAN, Minna Galbraith, OBE, born Belmont, Paisley, 1 May 1878, died Edinburgh 8 July 1951. Committee woman, author, Unionist candidate. Daughter of Williamina Galbraith, and Hugh Cowan, sheriff.

Born into an eminent legal family, Minna Cowan was educated in Hendon, Glasgow and Girton College (1897–1900). 'Imbued with a great desire to work for women' (*Edinburgh Evening News* 1935), she was an early student for the social science diploma in Edinburgh, where she shared a New Town flat with her brother. Like many educated women of the time, she created a semi-professional career in public life, mixing elected office and committee appointments. A study tour of India resulted in a book arguing for solutions 'on Indian and womanly lines' (Cowan 1912, p. 222). In 1914, she was elected to the Edinburgh School Board. Having been a principal in the WRNS for part of the war, in 1919 she became first convener of the statutory local advisory council of the Education Authority, and was directly elected to the Authority in 1921. Her initiatives included free school meals during the holidays, out-of-school play centres and cutting class size to 50.

In 1923, Minna Cowan became convener of the Higher Education committee, managing the city's nine secondary schools. After co-option to the council Education Committee in 1930, she published an authoritative commentary on the Children and Young Persons (Scotland) Act 1932. Her essay on foreign policy in *Political Idealism* (1924) (by 'four Unionist women', including *Margaret Kidd), argued for a greater role for the League of Nations. She stood as Unionist candidate for Paisley (1929) and as National Government candidate for Edinburgh East (1935), without success. Active in the NCW, she chaired the Edinburgh branch, becoming national president 1946–7 (thereafter international vice-president). During the Second World War, she worked for the Ministry of Food in the East of Scotland, helping develop British Restaurants and writing on the social consequences of evacuation. She made frequent post-war visits to Germany, arguing for social reconstruction and, as NCW president,

establishing links with the German women's movement, seeing women's participation in public life as crucial to its democratic future. She also campaigned for refugees and for the rehabilitation of Greek villages, attending an Athens conference in 1951, shortly before her death. One obituary recalled her 'unflagging enthusiasm in causes that were often difficult to initiate and . . . to sustain' (*Scotsman* 1951). SI
• Cowan, M. G., *Work* as above and (1912) *The Education of the Women of India*, (1926) 'Education' in M. Rackstraw (ed.) *A Social Survey of the City of Edinburgh*, (1933) *The Children and Young Persons (Scotland) Act 1932*, (1944) *Our Scottish Towns: evacuation and the social future*, (1947) 'Sidelights on Germany', *Girton Rev.* pp. 3–5, Lent term.
Edinburgh Evening News, 4 Nov. 1935; *ODNB* (2004); *The Scotsman* and *Edinburgh Evening Dispatch*, 10 July 1951 (obits).

CRAIG, Elizabeth Josephine,‡ MBE, m. **Mann,** born Addiewell, West Lothian, 16 Feb. 1883, died Wexham Park Hospital, Bucks, 7 June 1980. Journalist, cookery writer. Daughter of Catherine Nicoll, and Rev. John Mitchell Craig, of Forfar.

Elizabeth Craig attended Forfar Academy and George Watson's Ladies' College, Edinburgh, later teaching at her village school. In 1912 she joined John Leng & Co., Dundee, gaining experience on the *People's Friend, People's Journal* and *Dundee Advertiser*. Early assignments included interviewing the poet William McGonagall and reporting on a garden party at Glamis Castle, where she encountered the young *Elizabeth Bowes-Lyon (see Elizabeth, Queen and Queen Mother), riding her pony. In 1915, she became one of the first female editors in Fleet Street, on *Woman's Life* magazine. After marrying Arthur E. Mann, an American war correspondent, in 1919, she became a freelance writer and an established authority on food and wine.

She travelled widely, giving her writing a cosmopolitan flavour and in 1923 she published the first of more than 40 books. Elizabeth Craig taught the postwar generation of young middle-class women, now with no servants, how to keep house, budget, cook with electricity and above all to have confidence in the kitchen. During the Second World War she worked with the Ministry of Food and Agriculture, talking to Women's Institutes and other organisations throughout Britain on food rationing and wartime diet. Audiences crowded into her lectures – to receive practical help, but also to enjoy hilarious anecdotes. Among numerous awards she was especially proud of a gold medal at the Frankfurt Book Fair in 1953, Coronation year, for *Court Favourites*. Another successful book was *Collins Family Cookery* (1957). Marguerite Patten defined Elizabeth Craig's appeal thus: 'Her recipes were totally honest. Her readers did not just *like* her – they *loved* her' (personal information). She took pride in replying personally to the hundreds of letters from her worldwide readership.

Elizabeth Craig was a regular contributor to *Queen*, the *Daily Express* and *Sunday Express*; she was *Woman's Journal* cookery editor for 30 years, and wrote for *The Scottish Field* and *People's Friend* into her nineties. She was a popular, outspoken member of Freddie Grisewood's *Brain's Trust*, and on the *Michael Parkinson* show, stunned her host by announcing that her favourite place to make love would be in the Highland heather. Her last book, *Hotch Potch*, was published in 1978 on her 95th birthday, and in 1979 she was made MBE. A free-spirited woman with a generous heart, who inspired women to make the most of their lives, she remained intensely loyal to her Scottish family, old friends, and homeland, retaining her accent to the end. Her ashes were returned to Kirriemuir. EJE

• Craig, E., Works as above and see NLS catalogue [36 listed] Personal information (niece).

CRAIG, Isa, m. **Knox,** born Edinburgh 17 Oct. 1831, died Brockley, Suffolk, 23 Dec. 1903. Poet, feminist and social reformer. Daughter of Ann Braick, and John Craig, hosier and glover.

Raised by her grandmother after the early death of her parents, Isa Craig attended school only until 1840. Yet by 1853, she had joined the staff of *The Scotsman*, writing literary reviews and articles on social questions. In 1856, her first book, *Poems by Isa*, appeared and, with Bessie Parkes, she contributed to the Glasgow-based women's periodical, the *Waverley Journal*. When Bessie Parkes became editor and moved the journal to London, Isa Craig followed to assist and continued her regular contributions after its re-launch in 1858 as the *Englishwoman's Journal*. In 1857, she became Assistant Secretary of NAPSS, the key forum for the discussion of social issues in the mid-Victorian period. She was also committed to the Ladies Sanitary Association associated with NAPSS and founded in the same year, which aimed to give public health a human face. Her work with the secretary of the NAPSS, barrister G. W. Hastings, exemplified the principle of the sexual communion of labour, bringing masculine and feminine

elements into public life to achieve 'a stereoscopic view' and fuller social progress (Cobbe 1861, p. 92).

She left the Association to marry her cousin, London iron merchant John Knox, in 1866 but continued her literary career, writing poetry, including a prize-winning entry in a competition to celebrate the Burns centenary in 1866, and her most highly regarded collection, *Songs of Consolation* (1874). Her *Poems: an Offering to Lancashire* (1863) and *Duchess Agnes . . . and Other Poems* (1864) demonstrated her abolitionist sentiment. She edited *The Argosy* and contributed to *Fraser's Magazine*, *Good Words*, and *The Quiver*, and also published a drama, novels and children's textbooks and histories designed for the education of women, including the *Little Folks' History of England* (1872). EY

• Craig, I., Works as above, and see Alston (Bibl.).
Alston, R. C. (1990) *A Checklist of Women Writers 1801–1900. Fiction, Verse, Drama* (Bibl.); *Cambridge History of English and American Literature* (1907–21), vol. 13; Cobbe, F. P. (1861) 'Social science congresses and women's part in them', *Macmillan's Magazine*, Dec.; *ODNB* (2004); Rendall, J. (1987) ' "A Moral Engine": feminism, liberalism and the *Englishwoman's Journal*', in J. Rendall (ed.) *Equal or Different*; Uglow, J. (ed.) (1998) *Macmillan Dictionary of Women's Biography*, 3rd edn.; Yeo, E. J. (1996) *The Contest for Social Science. Relations and Representations of Gender and Class*.

CRAIK, Helen, born Arbigland, near Dumfries, c. 1751, died Flimby, Cumberland, 11 June 1825. Novelist. Daughter of Elizabeth Stewart, and William Craik, powerful landlord, rumoured also to be the father of John Paul Jones (1747–92).

Helen Craik moved to her family's other property, Flimby Hall, Cumberland, in 1792, a self-exile precipitated by the mysterious death of her lover, a groom on her father's estate. Local sources suggest her family had killed him because they disapproved of the relationship. These dramatic events echo throughout her autobiographical fiction, which focuses on the economic and sexual double standards of British patriarchy, invoking feminist arguments by contemporaries such as Mary Wollstonecraft. Helen Craik published five novels anonymously between 1796 and 1805 with William Lane's popular Minerva Press, and wrote poetry admired by her friend Robert Burns.

Julia de St Pierre (1796) offers a sentimental portrait of a French emigrant woman as virtue in distress. *Adelaide de Narbonne, with Memoirs of Charlotte de Cordet* [sic] (1800) is her most innovative historical novel, possibly the first British fictional account of Marat's assassin, Charlotte

Corday. Drawing on the Gothic romances of Anne Radcliffe and Horace Walpole, Helen Craik fashioned a unique hybrid of historical Gothic, addressing controversial recent events in France, particularly women's active participation in politics. Concern with women's rights is also visible in *Stella of the North* (1802), set in Dumfriesshire, and in *The Nun and Her Daughter* (1805). *Henry of Northumberland* (1800) is Helen Craik's only known novel not set in the recent past. Her obituaries and memorial in St Nicholas Church, Flimby, remember her as an author and a dedicated philanthropist. AC

• Craik, H. Works as above.

Arnott, S. (1923–4) 'The romance of Helen Craik of Arbigland', *Trans. Dumf. & Gall. Nat. Hist. and Antiqu. Soc.*, no. 11; Blakey, D. (1939) *The Minerva Press 1790–1820*; Craciun, A. 'The new Cordays: Helen Craik and British representations of Charlotte Corday 1793–1800', in A. Craciun and K. Lokke (eds) (2001) *Rebellious Heart*; *ODNB* (2004).

CRANSTON, Catherine (Kate) (aka **Miss Cranston),** m. **Cochrane,** born Glasgow 27 May 1849, died Glasgow 18 April 1934. Tea-room owner and patron of the arts. Daughter of Grace Lace, and George Cranston, hotel-keeper.

Kate Cranston's brother Stuart pioneered tea-rooms in Glasgow, but 'Miss Cranston's tea-rooms' became more famous. Kate Cranston was unusual for the time in becoming a businesswoman in her own right. Intending her establishments to be unique, she brought the talented designers, George Walton and Charles Rennie Mackintosh to work on the interiors. Mackintosh remained closely associated with her premises, producing new designs for the existing Argyle and Ingram Street rooms, helping make Glasgow 'a very Tokio for tea-rooms' (Muir 1901, p. 166). The Mackintosh-Cranston partnership excelled, however, in the still partly existing Willow Tea-rooms in Sauchiehall Street (1903), where Kate Cranston's own ideas on the importance of décor for the quality of the customer's experience were implemented. A substantial operation with five tea-rooms, a dining gallery and a billiard room, the establishment was intended to exert a 'civilising' influence on the population of Glasgow. Mackintosh and his wife, *Margaret Macdonald, were given freedom to create the whole building and its contents. The result was one of the finest examples of Art Nouveau in Scotland. 'Miss' Cranston did marry, but when her husband,

John Cochrane (1857–1917), died, she sold the Argyle and Buchanan Street tea-rooms, and in 1919 retired completely. Kate Cranston followed older fashions – she was thought eccentric for her insistence on wearing the outmoded crinoline – but her business acumen and sponsorship of new styles in the arts were never in question. LS

• Burkhauser, J. (ed.) (1990) *Glasgow Girls*, pp. 35–8; Kinchin, P. (1998) *Taking Tea with Mackintosh*, (1999) *Miss Cranston*; Muir, J. H. (1901) *Glasgow in 1901*, pp. 166 ff; *ODNB* (2004).

CRAWFORD, Jane Glen, born Stirling 14 April 1864, died Edinburgh 27 Oct. 1947. First female inspector of domestic economy in Scotland. Daughter of Margaret Glen, and William Crawford, journeyman blacksmith.

Jane Crawford started as a pupil-teacher. Once qualified, she taught senior classes, but resigned in 1892 to train at the Edinburgh School of Cookery. After teaching girls and women in Tranent and then in Dumfriesshire districts, she returned to the School of Cookery as a staff teacher in 1893. There she ran free continuation classes in domestic subjects for over-15s, funded by Edinburgh Town Council. Asked to participate in the newly established examination of schools and students of cookery, she became in 1902 the first Woman Inspector of Domestic Economy appointed by the Scotch (later Scottish) Education Department. In 1910, when two more female inspectors were appointed, she became first Principal Woman Officer. Her duties included inspecting the profes-sional training courses for domestic economy teachers and inspection of all schools in the Southern Division, plus the development of appropriate school-leaving certificates. When she retired in 1925, she was honoured as a key educator of women by representatives of the Training Schools and teachers of domestic subjects throughout Scotland. JMCD

• Begg, T. (1994) *The Excellent Women*; Bone, T. R. (1968) *School Inspection in Scotland 1840–1966*; *Edinburgh School of Cookery Magazine*, Dec. 1925, 11, 25, pp. 2–5.

CRAWFORD, Marion Kirk, ('Crawfie'), m. **Buthlay,** born Kilmaurs 5 June 1909, died Milltimber, Aberdeenshire, 11 Feb. 1988. Royal governess. Daughter of Margaret Jack, and John Inglis Crawford, engineer's clerk.

Marion Crawford grew up in Dunfermline and graduated from Moray House Training College in 1931. Temporary work as governess to local titled families introduced her to the Duke and Duchess of York, who took her on as governess to their daughters for a trial month's period. She remained there, affectionately known as 'Crawfie', for 16 years. In 1936, the Duke of York became King, and she was now governess to Princesses Elizabeth, heir to the throne, and *Margaret Rose (see Snowdon). She attempted to broaden the girls' view of life, taking them on the London underground and starting Brownies and Guides at Buckingham Palace. A dedicated governess, she postponed her marriage to Aberdeenshire banker George Buthlay (1893–1977) until after the Second World War, and left to live with her husband only after Princess Elizabeth's marriage in 1947. Her notoriety came from her memoirs of 1949, published in serial form and then as a book, *The Little Princesses*. Publication of these affectionate but intimate revelations came about as a mixture of pressure from the editors of the *Ladies Home Journal* (USA) and at least partial misunderstandings over royal permission and the contract. Whatever the explanation, Marion Crawford was the first of many palace employees to take her story to the media, and her employers were outraged. Neither the two princesses nor their mother spoke to her again, though two other Scottish nannies, Helen Lightbody (d. 1987) and Mabel Anderson, were later employed by Queen Elizabeth II to care for her own children. Marion Buthlay lived thereafter in a cottage near Balmoral. Her (ghosted) royal column for *Woman's Own* came to grief over a faux pas not of her making. George Buthlay died in 1977, and Crawfie lived alone until 1988, depressed and twice attempting suicide. FJ

• Crawford, M. (1949, re-ed. 1991 with foreword by Jennie Bond) *The Little Princesses*.
ODNB (2004); Pimlott, B. (1996) *The Queen: a biography of Elizabeth II*; *The Royal Encyclopaedia* (1991); Taylor, A., 'Crawfiegate: the original royal scandal', *Sunday Herald*, 27 Jan. 2002. www.channel4.com/history/microsites/R/real_lives/crawfie.html

CRAWFURD, Helen, n. **Jack,** m1 **Crawfurd,** m2 **Anderson,** born Gorbals, Glasgow, 9 Nov. 1877, died Dunoon 18 April 1954. Suffragette and Communist activist. Daughter of Helen Kyle, and William Jack, master baker.

The fourth of seven children, Helen Jack spent her early childhood in the Gorbals. She was educated in Ipswich and London and returned to Glasgow in 1894. Her home background was one of lively religious and political debate; both parents

were active Conservatives. In 1898 she married a local evangelical minister, Alexander Montgomerie Crawfurd (1830–1914), whose anti-war views she shared, but she found church work oppressive, disagreed with biblical attitudes to women and pursued her own study of women's literature. That led to an interest in women's suffrage and in 1910 she joined the WSPU. She was arrested five times, imprisoned in Holloway, London, Duke Street, Glasgow, and Perth prisons and endured three hunger strikes of up to eight days. Of robust character and physique, she acted as Emmeline Pankhurst's bodyguard, but their close relationship ended when Mrs Pankhurst adopted a pro-war stance in 1914. Helen Crawfurd felt betrayed, left the WSPU and after her husband's death joined the ILP and visited Ireland to contact James Connolly and Irish women revolutionaries. In 1915, as Secretary of the Glasgow Women's Housing Association, she led the rent strike and also set up the Glasgow branch of the WIL. In 1916, with *Agnes Dollan and *Mary Barbour she founded and was Secretary of the Women's Peace Crusade in Scotland, launched nationally in Glasgow on 10 June 1917.

She represented the British delegation at the Zurich WIL Congress in 1919, and on return helped John Maclean establish the Scottish Labour College; previously her interest in political education had been pursued in the Glasgow Fabian Society. As Vice-president of the ILP Scottish division, she was invited to Moscow where, after speaking with Lenin, she called for the ILP to affiliate to the Communist International. The ILP did not do so and in 1921 she joined the CPGB and became a member of the national executive. A rousing platform speaker, she was held in great affection and respect. She edited a women's page in *The Communist*. In November 1921, she first stood, unsuccessfully, as a CP candidate for Govan Ward. Throughout the 1920s, as secretary of Workers' International Relief, she travelled nationwide and abroad, raising funds for famine and disaster victims, and in 1926 distributed food to children of striking miners in Fife.

Retiring to Dunoon in 1935, she remained active in anti-fascist campaigning. In 1938, she organised the huge Peace and Empire Conference in Glasgow. In 1944, she married George Anderson (1872–1952), and from 1945 until 1948 served as Dunoon's first woman councillor, strongly supporting the cause of Scottish self-government. Her life and work 'personified all that was best in revolutionary womanhood' (Hunter 1954, p. 4). ACa

• Gallacher Memorial Library, GCU., Helen Crawfurd collection: Crawfurd, H. (n.d.) unpublished autobiography (copy also in Marx Memorial Library, London); 'Mrs Pankhurst, whom does she represent?', *Forward*, 16 June 1919; Election Address, Govan Ward, 1 Nov. 1921; 'A page for women', *The Communist*, 15 July 1922; Hunter, M., Funeral tribute, 1954.

Gallacher, W. (1936) *Revolt on the Clyde*; Liddington, J. (1985) *The Long Road to Greenham*; *ODNB* (2004); *SLL*; *Scottish Women and the Vote*, Strathclyde Regional Council Educ. Dept. (n.d.); Wiltsher, A. (1985) *Most Dangerous Women*.

CRICHTON, Elizabeth, n. **Grierson,** born Rockhall, Dumfriesshire, 1779, died Auchengray, Lanarkshire, 11 Oct. 1862. Philanthropist. Daughter of Margaret Dalzell, and Sir Robert Grierson, 5th baronet of Lag and Rockhall.

The eldest daughter of 11 children, Elizabeth Grierson lived at Rockhall until she married Dr James Crichton (1765–1823) on 14 November 1810, when Friars' Carse, Dumfriesshire, became her home. Widowed and childless in 1823, with an ample provision, she became an outstanding benefactor to psychiatry as co-founder of Crichton Royal Hospital, Dumfries, and remained closely involved with its work. She was the presiding force of five trustees seeking a 'charitable purpose' for the trust fund of £100,000, amassed while Dr Crichton served as physician to the Governor-General and as a trader in India. The trust established a private asylum, now known as Crichton Royal Hospital, in 1839, against local opposition. According to the terms of the Crichton Act (1840) the income was to be devoted to care. Elizabeth Crichton's main interest was in aiding people of her own class in reduced circumstances. By 1938, hospital lands extended to around 405 hectares, with 21 major buildings and exceptional facilities. Mindful of the interests of her husband, her charitable interests also extended to education in Sanquhar, Dumfries and India.

Her godson, the eminent Victorian psychiatrist, Sir James Crichton-Browne (1840–1938), son of the asylum's first physician superintendent, Dr. W. A. F. Browne, described her as 'a prim little lady . . . of a somewhat sombre manner . . . but genial and kindly withal, highly intelligent and well-informed', and recalled her visits to the hospital, 'for monthly meetings or conferences with my father or to make calls on lady patients', and 'picnics she arranged at Friars' Carse, when parties of patients were hospitably entertained . . . (Crichton-Browne 1940, p. 3). Elizabeth Crichton's original proposal had been to found a university college. Nothing came of a scheme to transfer the University of St Andrews, in difficulties in the 1820s, to Dumfries to take advantage of the Crichton fortune. But in fulfilment of that dream, Crichton campus has, since 1999, housed satellite colleges of Paisley and Glasgow universities on the former hospital site. A bronze statue of Elizabeth Crichton by Bill Scott (2000) stands 50 metres north-east of Crichton Memorial Church. MW

• Crichton Royal Hospital, Dumfries: Dumfries and Galloway Health Board Archives.

Anderson, A. (2001) *Crichton University*; *Dumfries Times*, 19 Oct. 1834; Easterbrook, C. C. (1940) *Chronicle of Crichton Royal 1833–1936* with foreword by Sir James Crichton-Browne; *ODNB* (2004).

CRICHTON, Margaret, born 1483, died c. 1546. Customs-collector. Daughter of Margaret Stewart, Princess of Scotland, and William, 3rd Lord Crichton.

The illegitimate daughter of *Margaret Stewart (c. 1460–c. 1503), daughter of James II, Margaret Crichton was probably raised at the royal court. At some point, she had an illegitimate son, David, later Bishop of Ross, and possibly a daughter, Katherine, with Patrick Paniter (Panter) (c. 1470–1519), the king's secretary. Perhaps because of this, around 1506, she made a rather low-status marriage to Edinburgh burgess William Todrik. Widowed in 1507, by 1510 she had married George Halkerston, burgess and custumar (customs-collector) of Edinburgh, and had one son. George died at Flodden (1513); Margaret Crichton and Janet Paterson, widow of Edinburgh's provost and co-custumar, then took over the customs collection. Margaret Crichton was sole custumar for a month in 1516. She had married George, Earl of Rothes (d. 1558), by August 1517. Several children were born but the marriage was dissolved in December 1520. Margaret Crichton kept life-interest in certain lands, but resided mainly in Edinburgh. EE

• *ER*, xiv; *RMS*, iii, no. 2072; *TA*, vols i,vi,vii; *ODNB* (2004) (Panter, David; Panter, Patrick); *SP*, iii, pp. 64–7, iv, pp. 281–9; Wood, M. (ed.) (1953) *Protocol Book of John Foular 1519–28*.

CROALL, Annie Knight, born Guthrie, Montrose, 29 July 1854, died Stirling 1 June 1927. Philanthropist. Daughter of Mary MacKay, and

Alexander Croall, teacher, founding curator of the Smith Institute (now Smith Art Gallery and Museum), Stirling.

Annie Croall was educated in Loanhead, near Montrose, and from 1863 in Derby, England. She arrived in Stirling with her father in 1874 and immediately involved herself in charitable work on behalf of the town's indigent women and children. Driven by her religious calling, she opened the Young Women's Evangelistic Mission in Stirling and organised weekly prayer meetings conducted by women, monthly Bible readings, a lending library, a clothes depot and district visitors for poor families. In 1880, she opened a refuge for homeless and outcast women in Broad Street and in 1883 she moved the refuge to larger premises with a laundry. In the same year she closed the refuge and opened a day nursery and boarding home for destitute and neglected children. In the 1890s she opened the Whinwell Children's Home (WCH) in Whinwell House, Upper Bridge Street.

Described by her obituary writer as Stirling's 'most public-spirited citizen' (*Stirling Observer*), Annie Croall was motivated by her Christian faith. 'The great aim of our work, and the desire of our heart, is their CONVERSION' she wrote of children who found refuge in her home (WCH *Annual Report*, 1898). She was an enthusiastic proponent of child emigration, sending more than 200 children to Canada, Australia and South Africa. The Whinwell Home continued under her direction until her death and remained a children's home until 1980. In the words of her obituary, '. . . The people of Stirling and elsewhere have every reason to be grateful to her for the rescue of so many children'. She is buried in Stirling's Valley Cemetery near the Church of the Holy Rude. LCA

• Stirling Archive Services, PD 41: Whinwell Children's Home; PD 41/1/1, *Annual Reports*.
Croall, A. K. (1923) *Fifty Years on a Scottish Battlefield, 1873–1923*.
Abrams, L. (1998) *The Orphan Country: Children of Scotland's Broken Homes From 1845 to the Present Day; Stirling Observer*, 7 June 1927 (obit.).

CROOKSTONE, Jackie, born Gladsmuir, Lothian, 18 June 1768, died Tranent, Lothian, 29 August 1797. Anti-Militia campaigner. Daughter of Agnes Hogg, and James Crookstone.

Little is known about Jackie Crookstone, apart from the heroic stance she took against the Scottish Militia Act of 1797. The act aimed to supply able

men for Britain's expanding empire, but local miners opposed enforced conscription. On 28 August 1797, the day before the Tranent registrar was to draw up his ballot, Jackie Crookstone organised a protest march, joined by women from Gladsmuir and elsewhere as they marched towards Tranent and Prestonpans. She used her drum to orchestrate continual chants of 'No Militia', intimidating local justices and landowners on the ballot committee. The ballot went ahead on 29 August, amid serious rioting. Soldiers were summoned and killed 11 people in the 'Tranent Massacre'. Dragoons 'mopping up' afterwards were probably responsible for killing Jackie Crookstone. Her body lay in a cornfield for several weeks until discovered by harvesters. Her death was never officially recorded; she was possibly the victim of summary justice for being a female ringleader of the riot. MMM

• Hopkins, B. (2002) 'The enigma of Jackie Crookstone', *East Lothian Life*, 39; M'Neill, P. (1883) *Tranent and its Surroundings*, pp. 124–48.

CRUDELIUS, Mary,‡ n. **M'Lean,** born Bury, Lancs., 23 Feb. 1839, died Edinburgh 24 July 1877. Campaigner for women's higher education. Daughter of Mary Alexander, and William M'Lean from Dumfriesshire, merchant.

Mary M'Lean was partly educated at Miss Turnbull's boarding school in Edinburgh. In 1861, she married Rudolph Crudelius, a German wool merchant working in Leith, and they had two daughters (see Burnet, Edith). Mary Crudelius founded the higher education for women movement in Scotland through the ELEA, which she set up in 1867 and, as secretary, guided closely through its early years with her eye always on her objective: 'My aim is (always *sub rosa* as you know) the throwing open of the University to us, not the organising of a special college for women' (Burton 1879, p. 81). The ELEA sponsored lectures by university professors on the arts curriculum.

Mary Crudelius had begun campaigning quite on her own in 1866. Her letters to school proprietors gaining no response, she turned to the middle class of Edinburgh, who initially treated both her and her proposal with considerable suspicion. Only five years later, however, Professor David Masson could flout the convention of female anonymity to write that 'Mrs Crudelius was so identified with the Association in its origin, and her subsequent labours on its behalf are so well known that I need not hesitate to name her' (*The Scotsman* 1871). She signed the first suffrage petition, but by 1867 had been advised to keep her interests separate, so declined an invitation to join the ENSWS, in order to concentrate on women's higher education. Although strong-willed, she was physically delicate and frequently had to convalesce in the south of England, writing instructions and advice to the executive members of the ELEA. She died aged 38, leaving the Association as her memorial. LRM

• Edinburgh Univ. Library Special Collections: Gen. 1877 (minutes and corr.).

Burton, K. (1879) *A Memoir of Mrs Crudelius*; *ODNB* (2004); *The Scotsman*, letters, 25 Dec. 1871.

CRUICKSHANK, Helen Burness (Nell), born Hillside, Angus, 15 May 1886, died Edinburgh 2 March 1975. Poet and civil servant. Daughter of Sarah Wood, domestic worker at Sunnyside Mental Hospital, Hillside, and George Cruickshank, house steward for the hospital.

Nell Cruickshank was the youngest of three children. She attended Hillside Primary School with her two brothers before moving to Montrose Academy. She was a clever pupil but since the family could not afford to send her to university she sat examinations for the Civil Service. In 1903 she took up an appointment in the West Kensington branch of the Post Office Savings Bank in London, which offered her opportunities for theatre-going and suffrage activity. She was an active member of the Hammersmith branch of the WSPU, marching to Hyde Park Corner in a Civil Service contingent and 'chalking pavements and selling the weekly paper *Votes for Women* in the streets' (Cruickshank 1976, pp. 41–2). She returned to a posting in Edinburgh in 1912.

She began to write poetry during the First World War. In 1922, C. M. Grieve (Hugh MacDiarmid) included her poem, 'The Price o' Johnny', in the third of his *Northern Numbers* anthologies. This initiated a lasting relationship with Grieve/MacDiarmid and the Scottish Renaissance movement. She was a founder member of both Scottish PEN (1927) and the Saltire Society (1936) and became Honorary Secretary of Scottish PEN in 1929. Her house in Corstorphine, Edinburgh, 'Dinnieduff', offered hospitality to many Scottish cultural activists.

Helen Cruickshank never married. As with many women of her time, it was expected that she would provide a home for her mother when her father died; her mother became part of the literary life at 'Dinnieduff'. Three volumes of her poetry were published between 1934 and 1968 and *Collected Poems* appeared in 1971 and 1978. She was awarded the honorary degree of MA by the University of Edinburgh in 1970. Her *Octobiography* was published posthumously in 1976. MPM

• Univ. of Stirling Library Special Collections: Helen Cruickshank Archive; NLS: Lewis Grassic Gibbon papers.

Cruickshank, H., Works as above, and (1934) *Up the Noran Water*, (1954) *Sea Buckthorn*, (1968) *The Ponnage Pool*, (1978) *More Collected Poems*.

Bold, A. (ed.) (1984) *The Letters of Hugh MacDiarmid*, (1988) *MacDiarmid*; *ODNB* (2004).

CULLEN, Alice, n. **McLoughlin,** m1 **Bartlett,** m2 **Cullen,** m3 **Reynolds,** born South Shields 18 March 1891, died Glasgow 30 May 1969. Labour councillor and MP. Daughter of Bridget McKay, and John McLoughlin, railway platelayer.

Alice McLoughlin left Lochwinnoch elementary school aged 14 to be apprenticed as a French polisher, a trade that took her to Canada for several years. She married three times: to Harry Bartlett, waiter; to Pearce Cullen, a GPO sorter, in 1920; and to William Reynolds, headmaster, in 1950, and had three daughters. After working in a fruit shop, in 1930 she opened a dairy in Scotland Street, Glasgow. Active in ILP politics from the 1920s, in 1938 she was elected councillor for Glasgow Hutchesontown. In 1941 she became a Justice of the Peace, and in 1948 she won the Labour nomination for Glasgow Gorbals over stiff competition.

The first Catholic woman to hold a parliamentary seat, she represented Glasgow Gorbals until her death in 1969. She took particular interest in social questions, especially housing and health, and strongly opposed conscription. Her dedication to her constituents won her the title of 'Mrs Gorbals' (*Daily Record*). CB

• *DLabB*, pp. 60–2; Grehan, E., 'The Granny they called Mrs Gorbals', *Daily Record*, 4 Nov. 1968; *Glasgow Herald*, 31 May 1969; *ODNB* (2004); *Scottish Catholic Observer*, 6 June 1969; *The Times*, 2 June 1969.

CULLEN, Margaret, born Glasgow 1767, died Ilfracombe, Devon, 18 Sept. 1837. Novelist. Daughter of Anna Johnston, and William Cullen, Professor of Medicine at Glasgow and later Edinburgh.

Brought up in a family at the heart of the

Scottish Enlightenment, on her father's death Margaret Cullen had to share an annual government pension of £200 with her three sisters, with whom she lived most of her life, mainly in England. Though unknown today, her two novels suggest a reforming outlook and a committed interest in the condition of women. *Home* (1802), directly influenced by the debate on the principles of the French Revolution, was a didactic and provocative attack on the existing laws of marriage and inheritance, influenced by her own awareness of women's financial vulnerability. Widely noticed, it went through four editions between 1802 and 1822. *Mornton* (1814) was less successful but demonstrated her interest in the movement for the humane treatment of animals. Her sister, **Robina Millar** (1768–1844), married John Craig Millar, radical son of Enlightenment philosopher John Millar, and went with him to Pennsylvania in 1795 to found a more congenial community on the banks of the Susquehanna. On his early death, she returned home to live with her sister. Both sisters inspired the early interest of *Frances Wright in the politics of the American republic. JR

• Cullen, M., Works as above.

Rendall, J. (2005) '"Women that would plague me with rational Conversation": aspiring women and Scottish Whigs, c. 1790–1830', in S. Knott and B. Taylor (eds) *Feminism and the Enlightenment*.

CULROSS, Lady *see* **MELVILLE, Elizabeth** (c. 1582–1640)

CUMMING, Constance *see* **GORDON-CUMMING, Constance Frederica** (1837–1924)

CUMMING, Elizabeth, n. **Robertson,** born Knockando 12 May 1827, died Knockando 19 May 1894. Distiller and farmer. Daughter of Jane Inkson, and Lewis Robertson, farmer.

One of five children, Elizabeth Robertson married local whisky distiller, Lewis Cumming, on 20 July 1859, and moved to Cardow, raising three children. The Cardow distillery in Morayshire had humble beginnings as an illicit family operation run by her mother-in-law, Helen Cumming, whose husband John, like others, later obtained a licence under the Excise Act of 1823. No women were recorded as legal distillers at this time, although they were sometimes involved in illicit distilling. Lewis Cumming continued his father's work until his death in 1872. Elizabeth then took over the management of the distillery and farm, to become

one of the handful of female legal distillery proprietors in Scotland.

Under Elizabeth Cumming's administration, the distillery moved to a new site in 1884 and expanded in 1887. She was described as having exceptional good sense and ability, astute business acumen, and untiring perseverance. The local banker noted that she had a personal hand in everything, from bookkeeping and correspondence to supervision of every detail of the farm and distillery. In September 1893 she sold the distillery to John Walker & Sons of Kilmarnock, her son John becoming the managing partner. The distillery developed further, despite economic difficulties, to be known today as Cardhu. A strong adherent of the Church of Scotland, Elizabeth Cumming was of generous disposition, liberal to the poor, and respected by both employees and the local community. Her funeral was one of the largest seen in the district. CL

• Registration records; Cardhu distillery display panels and publicity booklet, *Cardhu*, n.d.

Elgin Courant, 22 May 1894 (obit.); *Moray and Nairn Express*, 26 May 1894 (obit.).

CUNNINGHAM, Elizabeth, Countess of Glencairn, n. **Maguire,** born Ayrshire 1724, died Edinburgh 24 June 1801. Patron of Robert Burns. Daughter of Isabella Maguire, and Hugh Maguire, carpenter and 'sixpenny' fiddler at weddings.

The eldest of five children, Elizabeth Maguire was raised from poverty by the generosity of her mother's cousin, James Macrae, who had returned from India (1731) an exceedingly rich man. He relocated the Maguire family to an estate near Ochiltree and paid for the children's education and 'finishing' at a boarding school. He later secured an advantageous marriage for Elizabeth Maguire to William Cunningham, the impoverished 12th Earl of Glencairn, her dowry including £45,000 in diamonds. As Countess of Glencairn, she overcame her husband's thinly disguised scorn at being married to a 'violer's daughter', to become a respected member of society. Mindful of her lowly upbringing, she set up a school to teach local girls spinning. With her second son James (13th Earl of Glencairn, 1749–91), she was a patron of Robert Burns and orchestrated his smooth passage into Edinburgh society, introducing him to James's former tutor William Creech, who published the extended 'Edinburgh Edition' of his poems. The Countess bought 124 copies, while her son cajoled the gentlemen of the Caledonian Hunt to subscribe to 100 copies. James's death was a great personal loss to Burns, who wrote one of his most poignant laments in his memory. EJG

• Burns, R. (1987) *The Collected Letters of Robert Burns*; Graham, E. J. (2005) *Seawolves*; Mackay, J. A. (1993) *Burns: a biography of Robert Burns*; *SP*, 4, p. 251.

CUNNINGHAM, Lady Margaret, died Malsly Sept. 1623. Writer. Daughter of Margaret Campbell, and James Cunningham, 6th Earl of Glencairn.

Lady Margaret Cunningham wrote about her first husband, Sir James Hamilton of Crawfordjohn, Master of Evandale, whom she married 24 January 1598, in a short memoir, *A Pairt of the Life of Margaret Cuninghame* (1608). She was often forced to turn to her parents, her sister, Anne Cunningham (wife of James Hamilton, 2nd Marquis of Hamilton), and her in-laws for lodging and money. Evandale was physically and emotionally abusive to her; she describes being thrown out of his house one night in 1604, naked, ill, and pregnant, and being carried by two women to the local minister's house for shelter. Evandale had adulterous liaisons, at least one of which produced offspring. Lady Margaret was primary carer to her four children.

After Evandale's death, she became the third wife of Sir James Maxwell of Calderwood, by whom she had another six children. The second marriage was very happy. Like her will and testament and her letters, the three linked sonnets Lady Margaret sent to Evandale in 1607 reflect her ardent Presbyterianism. Her writings circulated in manuscript; the second sonnet was printed anonymously in the 1635 Scottish Metrical Psalter, to be sung to the tune of Psalm 110. The prominent divine Robert Boyd described her as 'that virtuous lady, equal, if not beyond any I have known in Scotland' (Anderson 1851, p. 13). PBG

• NLS: MS 874, ff. 363–84, and MS 906.
Anderson, J. (1851) *Ladies of the Covenant*; *ODNB* (2004); Sharpe, C. K. (ed.) (1827) *A Pairt of the Life of Lady Margaret Cuninghame . . .*; *SP*, 4, pp. 243–5.

CURRIE, Ethel Dobbie, born Glasgow 4 Dec. 1899, died Glasgow 24 March 1963. Palaeontologist. Daughter of Elizabeth Allan, and John Currie, measurer.

After attending Bellahouston Academy, in 1920 Ethel Currie graduated from the University of Glasgow, where she then took two doctorates. Her career was spent as Curator of the geological collections in the University's Hunterian Museum, and she retired as Senior Lecturer in 1962, six months before she died. She catalogued thousands of geological specimens, taught students and prepared many educational exhibits. Under the tutelage of the Honorary Curator, Professor J. W. Gregory, she became an authority on echinoids from Africa and southern Asia and with him published a monograph on mammalian fossils from the Scottish Quaternary (*Hunterian Museum Geology Monograph* 2, 1928). Her work on goniatites (*RSE Trans.*, 62, 1954) proved a key to Scottish Carboniferous stratigraphy. The first woman to win the Neill Prize, for her paper on 'Growth stages in some Jurassic ammonites' (*RSE Trans.*, 61, 1944), she was also one of the first three women to become FRSE in 1949, and in 1952 became the first woman president of the GSG. Modest about her own achievements, she was unfailingly helpful to students, researchers and colleagues. JRR

• Currie, E. D., Works as above.
George, T. N. (1964) *Trans. Geol. Soc. Glasgow*, 25, pp. 98–100; Weir, John (1964) *Yearbook RSE*, pp. 15–17 (obit.).

CUTHBURH, fl. 697–705, born Wessex, died Wimborne, Wessex. Queen of Northumbria, later abbess of Wimborne. Daughter of Cenred of Wessex.

Cuthburh was married by Ine her brother, King of Wessex, to Aldfrith, King of Northumbria (r. 685–705), which included much of what later became southern Scotland. Aldfrith had formerly been a monk on Iona. The strict monastic regimen may have made him shrink from female companionship, and the marriage was probably uncomfortable for both spouses. It addressed two necessities: production of an heir for Northumbria and intimidation of the Mercians, whose kingdom threatened both Northumbria and Wessex. After the birth of their son Osred in 697, but before Aldfrith's death in 705, the marriage was dissolved, and Cuthburh retired, possibly first to the monastery of Barking in Essex, and then to Wimborne in her native Wessex. She and Cwenburh her sister founded a 'double monastery' (monks and nuns) and presided as abbesses. Cuthburh was commemorated as a saint, with a feast day on 31 August. JEF

• *BEHEP*; *ODNB* (2004); Swanton, M. (ed.) (1996) *The Anglo-Saxon Chronicles*, 'A' text, sub anno 718.

D

DALRYMPLE, Christian, born Newhailes, Lothian, 30 Dec. 1765, died Newhailes 9 Jan. 1838. Landowner, diarist. Daughter of Anne Broun of Coalstoun, and Sir David Dalrymple Bt, later Lord Hailes, judge and historian.

Christian Dalrymple's mother died when she was two years old; her father later remarried and her half-sister, Jean, was born in 1777. She grew up in Newhailes House near Musselburgh, where Lord Hailes entertained such figures as David Hume and Samuel Johnson in his magnificent library. He encouraged Christian Dalrymple to explore her literary potential from an early age. From 1798 until her death, she kept a journal which survives, recording the social contacts, household management and travels of a well-off upper-class woman. She inherited the Newhailes estate in 1792, the baronetcy passing to a male cousin. Anecdotal evidence suggests that her father's will was found as she was preparing to leave the house. Since he had successfully pleaded the descent of Scottish titles to and through women in the case of *Elizabeth, Countess of Sutherland, he presumably thought his daughter capable of running Newhailes. She managed the estate well, including negotiating the sale, lease and purchase of land, using the ice house and building a stable block. Despite initially petitioning against the railway, in 1834 she sold some land to the railway company. On tours round Britain, she visited churches, stately homes, the model community at New Lanark and Walter Scott's home at Abbotsford. She visited and corresponded with Lady Eleanor Butler and Sarah Ponsonby in Llangollen, North Wales, attended art exhibitions and the theatre, and associated with many notable figures. Christian Dalrymple's journals reveal a way of life and demonstrate her diligence in preserving the essence of the estate. The long-neglected Newhailes House was opened to the public in 2002 under the auspices of the National Trust for Scotland. EL

• NLS: MSS 25454–25499, Corr., journals and miscellaneous papers.
Dalrymple, C. [1812] (1914) *Private Annals of My Own Time, 1765–1812*, H. Dalrymple, ed.
The Scotsman, 27 May 2002.

DALRYMPLE, Learmonth White (Leah), baptised Coupar Angus 21 July 1827, died Dunedin, New Zealand, 27 August 1906. Campaigner for girls' education. Daughter of Jessie Taylor, and William Dalrymple, ironmongery merchant.

Schooled at Madras College, St Andrews, and fluent in French through European travel, Leah Dalrymple always believed her education inadequate and spoke of her 'hopeless yearning for mental culture' (*Otago Daily Times*, 17 Dec. 1896, supp.). After her mother died in 1840, she cared for her seven younger siblings. In 1853, the family moved to New Zealand to Otago, near Dunedin, settled from Scotland just five years before. There she kept house for her father and three siblings on their farm. The discovery of gold in 1861 brought wealth, population and education to Otago. When a boys' high school opened in Dunedin in 1863, Leah Dalrymple began a seven-year campaign for a high school for girls. Imbued equally with determination and decorum, she gathered together a women's committee, approached the Provincial Council, and wrote around 800 letters to British educationalists, accepting Frances Buss's dictum that girls' education should 'in all essential points . . . be assimilated to that of boys' (Buss to Dalrymple, *ODT*, 10 June 1869). Otago Girls' High School, the first state secondary school for girls in New Zealand, opened in 1871. Leah Dalrymple then transferred her lobbying skills to petitioning for the 'admittance of ladies' to the new University of Otago. In August 1871, Otago became the first university in Australasia to admit women. She also taught Sunday school and supported the kindergarten movement. Moving to Feilding in 1881 to be near her brother, she joined the New Zealand WCTU campaign for women's suffrage, achieved in 1893. DP

• Hocken Library, Dunedin: (HL) Univ. of Otago, Council Minutes, 1871; Letters and Papers, 1871; HL: Otago Provincial Council, Votes and Proceedings, 1864, 1865, 1869; Education Reports, 1869–72.
Grimshaw, P. (1972) *Women's Suffrage in New Zealand*; *Otago Daily Times*, 10 June 1869, 17 Dec. 1896; Page, D. (1990) 'Dalrymple, Learmonth White', *DNZB*, vol. I; Thompson, G. (1921) *History of Otago University*; Trotter, M. (1983) *William and Isabella Trotter* [private, Invercargill, Trotter Family]; Wallis, E. (1972) *A Most Rare Vision*.

DAMER, Anne Seymour, n. **Conway,** born Sevenoaks, Kent, 8 Nov. 1749, died London 28 May 1828. Sculptor and writer. Daughter of Lady Caroline Campbell, daughter of the 4th Duke of Argyll, and Henry Seymour Conway, Field-marshal.

Anne Conway spent much of her youth in the care of her father's cousin, Horace Walpole, who later became an advocate of her talent. She moved in intellectual and aristocratic circles with her mother, who retained her title, Countess of Ailesbury, from her former marriage, and her half-sister, Lady Mary Bruce. In 1767, Anne Conway married Hon. John Damer (1743–76), from whom she later separated, and she was widowed without children in 1776, when he shot himself after accruing large gambling debts. She revived an interest in sculpture, producing works which include the Portland-stone heads of Thame and Isis on Henley Bridge, a statue of George III (Register House, Edinburgh), and a bust of Sir Joseph Banks (BM). Angelika Kauffmann and Sir Joshua Reynolds painted her portrait and Giuseppe Ceracchi sculpted her statue in marble. She spent much time at Inveraray Castle in the company of her Campbell relatives and others, including David Hume, who was for a time secretary to her father. Anne Damer inherited Walpole's gothic mansion, Strawberry Hill, where she acted in private theatricals. She also provided a story from her ancestry which *Joanna Baillie dramatised as *The Family Legend*, the Highland play which launched the new Theatre Royal, Edinburgh, in 1810. She published *Belmour*, a novel (1801), and was identified as the basis for the eccentric character Lady Maclaughlan in *Susan Ferrier's *Marriage* (1818). Anne Damer travelled widely, meeting Nelson in Italy in 1798 and Napoleon in Paris in 1802 during the Peace of Amiens; in 1815, Napoleon gave her a snuff box with his portrait (BM). There was contemporary speculation regarding friendships with women, and her name is often included in modern studies of homosexuality in the 18th century. EL

• Donoghue, E. (1993) *Passions Between Women*; Gunnis, R. (ed.) (1968) *Dictionary of British Sculptors 1660–1851*; Lindsay, I. G. and Cosh, M. (1973) *Inveraray and the Dukes of Argyll*; Noble, P. (1908) *Anne Seymour Damer*; *ODNB* (2004); Yarrington, A. (1997) 'The female Pygmalion', *Sculpture Jour.*, I, pp. 32–44.

DANIELL, Madeline Margaret, n. **Carter,** born Secrole, India, 19 May 1832, died Ashburton 21 April 1906. Education campaigner. Daughter of Helen Gray, and Major Henry Carter.

Educated mainly at the Edinburgh Institution for the Education of Young Ladies, Madeline Carter married Charles Daniell (1833–55), a cavalry officer who died at Lahore in 1855, leaving her with a son. Returning to Scotland, she helped to form the ELEA, campaigning for women's right to higher education. She hosted its inaugural committee meeting, and as honorary secretary, from 1866 to 1869, she provided active support to the president, *Mary Crudelius, who was an invalid. Madeline Daniell undertook much of the ELEA's negotation with sympathetic academics, and was also a founding honorary secretary of the company which established St Leonards School at St Andrews. Her sister, **Helen Evans** (1834–1903), mother of *Helen Archdale (1876–1949), was one of 'the Edinburgh Seven' who joined *Sophia Jex-Blake in her attempt to enter medical school at Edinburgh. Madeline Daniell's later life was spent mostly in England: from 1887 to 1889 she was close friend and companion to the poet Constance Naden (1858–89). A Liberal in politics, she remained an active campaigner for women's rights. TB

• Daniell, M. (1890) 'Memoir' in Naden, C. C. W., *Induction and Deduction (and other essays)*, R. Lewins ed. Burton, K. (ed.) (1879) *A Memoir of Mrs Crudelius*; Grant, J. et al. (1927) *St Leonards School*; *ODNB* (2004) (also Edinburgh Seven).

DARE, Margaret Marie, born Newport on Tay 4 Feb. 1902, died Edinburgh 11 Feb. 1976. Cellist, composer, teacher. Daughter of Elizabeth Lundin Brown, and Joseph Dare, company secretary.

After studies at the GSMD, London, with Warwick Evans, J. E. R. Teague, W. H. Squire and Benjamin Dale, Marie Dare was awarded the Gold Medal for instrumentalists and the Sir Landon Ronald and Guildhall composition prizes. Her career as a soloist began in the First World War Victory Concert at the Albert Hall, in the presence of Queen Alexandra. She worked in Paris with cello virtuoso Paul Bazelaire and, back in England, won the RCM Society of Women Musicians composition prize for her *Piano Trio in F* (1939), subsequently making a debut recital at the Aeolian Hall, presenting her own works. Other concerts followed in Vienna and Budapest. During the Second World War she served in the WRNS and afterwards joined the Reid Orchestra in Edinburgh as principal cellist. For many years she was a member of the Scottish Trio with Wight

Henderson and Horace Fellows, and was professor of cello at the RSAMD.

Marie Dare's earliest known works include *Romance* (1921) and *Le Lac* (1927), both for violoncello and piano, and *Phantasy String Quintet* (1933). She later wrote principally for string instruments (quartets, chamber ensemble) and sacred and secular vocal works for orchestra. Works include compositions for cello quartet: *Chant* (1957); *Aria* (1958); *A Day Dream; Elegy and Rustic Dance* (n.d.), which she recorded with fellow cellists Antonia Butler, Helen Just and Olga Hegedus; *Scottish Rhapsody* for strings (1973); *Red Robert MacIntosh Suite* (1956); *Raasay* (n.d.); *Three Highland Sketches* for string orchestra: *Mist on the Bens – Sea Loch – Strathspey and Reel* (n.d.); and *The White Moth*, a ballet suite with libretto based on an old Scottish folk story. Many of her compositions are still unpublished and in manuscript form at the SMIC, Glasgow. Of particular interest are works for children: *The Penny Wedding: a ballet* (n.d.); *The Pied Piper of Hamelin* (n.d.); and *Thumbeline* (1961/2) with a libretto by Margaret Lyford Pyke from the tale by Hans Christian Andersen. PAC

• Papers of the Society of Women Musicians (1911–72), database at RCM, London; SMIC, Glasgow (MS works). Dare, M., Works as above.

Cohen, A. I. (1987, 2nd edn.) *International Encyclopedia of Women Composers*; Kay, E. (1975, 7th edn.) *International Who's Who in Music*; Kenneson, C. (1974) *Bibliography of Cello Ensemble Music*; www.cello.org

DAVIE, Elspeth Mary, n. **Dryer,** born Kilmarnock 20 March 1919, died Edinburgh 13 Nov. 1995. Novelist and short story writer. Daughter of Lilian McFarlane, and Oliver Dryer, Presbyterian minister.

Elspeth Dryer and her sister spent their early childhood in Surrey while their father worked for the International Peace Movement in London. When Elspeth was nine, the family returned to Scotland and lived in Lasswade near Edinburgh. She was educated at George Watson's Ladies' College, Edinburgh, and spent two years at the University of Edinburgh, where she won a prize for philosophy. She attended Edinburgh College of Art (1938–42) then taught painting in schools in the Borders and Aberdeen. After her marriage to the philosopher George Elder Davie in 1944, they moved to Belfast where he was a university lecturer (1945–69), before settling permanently in Edinburgh. They had one daughter.

Elspeth Davie began to write regularly while in Belfast and her first novel, *Providings*, was published in 1965. She published four novels and five volumes of short stories, of which *The High Tide Talker* (1976) won the Katherine Mansfield Prize in 1978. Her art training is evident in the visual quality of her writing. Her work is notable also for its restraint, conveying contemplation rather than action, with frequent voids or silences, deliberately unrealistic dialogue, and a recurrent theme of travel. She is sometimes criticised for detachment and lack of warmth in her writing, but more often it is recognised that she is depicting the communication gap in everyday life and the alienation and neuroses of modern society. MARB

• NLS: Acc. 10631, MS 19710. Unpublished MSS and diaries. Davie, E., Works as above and see Bibls below.

DLB Gale, vol. 139 (Bibl.); *HSWW* (Bibl.); *ODNB* (2004); *The Scotsman*, 15 Nov. 1995 (obit.).

DAVISON, Euphemia, n. **MacDonald [May Moxon],** born Glasgow 9 Oct. 1906, died Glasgow 26 Nov. 1996. Dancer and supplier of dance troupes. Daughter of Martha McCandlish, and John MacDonald, crane driver.

Born into a theatrical family, Euphemia MacDonald made her first stage appearance in 1917 with her mother and brothers as the 'MacLeans' at the Casino, one of Glasgow's cine-variety venues. They toured Scotland, resulting in an interrupted education spread over 30 different schools. When the family act ended, she continued on her own, then as part of her own troupe of dancers, under the name May Moxon (thought to be her grandmother's). In 1937, she married William Edward Davison, a waiter, and they had one son. A serious leg injury from a car accident in 1934 had ended her dancing career, but May Moxon was determined to stay in the theatre business, and offered to form a troupe for the Galt variety agency. After the success of this first troupe, she went on to supply dancers to theatres across Scotland, notably for a 100-week run at the Glasgow Metropole. This was the hey-day of the 'resident' variety era, when a group of chorus girls was seen as the backbone of the show. May Moxon became a leading supplier of dancers (others were Adeline Calder, Agnes Campbell and Grace Dryburgh) with possibly as many as 1825 'girls' on her books, 60 or 70 at any one time and six to ten dancers per venue. The many costume changes required came from her vast wardrobe. She advertised in local papers: 'When you put an advert in asking for dancers, you would get as many as you wanted, so many girls were wanting to go on the stage. When I think of the girls of years ago, what great wee workers they were' (Devlin 1991, pp. 63–4). The memories of 'Moxon girls' re-iterate the themes of hard work, basic pay and conditions, and camaraderie; 'Sometimes there was four or five in a bed. That sounds ridiculous, but it's true. That happened at Dunfermline, to get it cheap. To get digs for 30 shillings or 25 shillings you shared a bed with four' (May Morrison). With the decline of variety, May Moxon retired in the 1970s. FB

• Devlin, V. (1991) *Kings, Queens and People's Palaces: an oral history of the Scottish variety theatre 1920–1970*; Irving, G. (1977) *The Good Auld Days*; Tudor, F. (1985) 'The dancing years', *The Scots Magazine*, April.
Private information: May Morrison (former Moxon dancer).

DAWSON, Ellen, m. **Kanki,** born Barrhead, Glasgow, 14 Dec. 1900, died Charlotte Harbor, Florida, USA, 17 April 1967. Weaver, trade unionist. Daughter of Annie Halford, weaver, and Patrick Dawson, labourer.

Ellen Dawson lived in Barrhead, probably working in a local textile mill from 1914, until December 1919 when her family moved to Shawforth, north of Rochdale in Lancashire, where she was a spinner in a local mill. In 1921, she and her elder brother were the first of several members of her family to migrate to the United States, settling in New Jersey. A weaver at the Botany Worsted Mill, she was a leader in the 1926 strike of 16,000 Passaic area textile workers and was a prominent organiser in the 1928 New Bedford, Massachusetts, strike of 20,000 workers. From 1928 she was an organiser of the National Textile Workers Union, an American Communist labour union representing unskilled textile workers, primarily women and immigrants. Ellen Dawson was the first woman elected to a national leadership position in an American textile union when she became vice president at the founding convention that year.

In 1929, she co-directed the famous strike at the Loray Mill in Gastonia, North Carolina, which drew national media attention when the local police chief and a prominent woman striker were killed. In retaliation, the US Labor Department arrested her and sought her deportation. Represented by the American Civil Liberties Union, she was acquitted and the Federal judge ordered Labor Department officials to explain why they sought to punish her for her political beliefs. She married Louis Kanki, a labourer from

Hungary, in 1935. Although no longer an activist, she worked in the textile industry until shortly before her death in 1967. DLM

• SS *Cedric* Manifest, May 9, 1921, Ellis Island Passenger Records.
Foner, P. S. (1980) *Women and the American Labor Movement from World War I to the Present*; Georgianna, D. (1993) *The Strike of '28*; Salmond, J. A. (1995) *Gastonia 1929*; *The* (New York) *World*, 24 October 1929; *The* (Passaic) *Herald-News*, 18 April 1967 (obit.); Vorse, M. H. (1927) *The Passaic Textile Strike 1926–1927*.

DEANS, Charlotte, n. **Lowes,** m1 **Johnston,** m2 **Deans,** born Wigton, Cumbria, 1 Sept. 1768, died Bothergate, Carlisle, 14 March 1859. Strolling player. Daughter of Alice Howard, and Henry Lowes, attorney.

Charlotte Lowes was one of three surviving children. Her respectable, comfortable life ended abruptly when she eloped with William Morel Johnston, an actor in Naylor's Company of Comedians, whom she saw performing in a barn in Wigton in 1787. They married in Gretna Green in August that year, and she became an actor in his company. The life was hard, not least because of the disreputable nature of the acting profession and her frequent pregnancies: during this marriage, she gave birth to 12 children. William Johnston died in 1801, and Charlotte returned to the stage with Mr Hobson's Company of Comedians, then in Penrith. In 1803, she married fellow-actor (and nascent manager) Thomas Deans (1781– c. 1859), several years her junior. They set out with four of her surviving children for an engagement in Montrose, where a new northern circuit was being developed. When the Montrose managers failed to pay, the family quit, and worked their way south through Fife and Lanarkshire, performing the standard mixed bill of musical numbers, burlesqued Shakespeare and recitations wherever possible, generally travelling by foot and performing in barns and halls. Charlotte Deans's thirteenth child was baptised in Lanark on 12 February 1805. She had a further four children with Deans, while travelling and performing across central Scotland, the Scottish Borders and the north of England. She toured the Borders between 1808 and 1811, and went on acting into her late 60s. Some of her children also pursued acting careers. Charlotte Deans's memoirs, published in 1837, give distinctive insight into the life of the strolling player. Rona Munro's play *The Maiden Stone* (1995) is partly inspired by her life. AS

• Marshall, F. (ed.) (1984) *A Travelling Actress in the North and Scotland. A Reprint of the Memoirs of the Life of Mrs Charlotte Deans, 1768–1859.*

DEMPSTER, Elizabeth Strachan, born Greenock 23 April 1909, died Edinburgh 17 Jan. 1987. Sculptor. Daughter of Elizabeth Watt, and Duncan Dempster, sugar refiner.

Orphaned, Elizabeth Dempster moved to Edinburgh to be near her guardian, the Very Rev. Dr Charles Warr, and to study sculpting (1930). She enrolled at ECA, joining an illustrious group of instructors and students, including Alexander Carrick, Norman Forrest, Hew Lorimer and Tom Whalen, with whom she maintained collaborative links thereafter. After further training at Regent Street Polytechnic and the Munich Academy, she exhibited at the RSA from 1935. Her first commission was the large, silvered *Seahorse* for the Clyde Navigational Trust (shown at the 1938 Empire Exhibition, Glasgow). Like her contemporaries, she favoured a spare, Romanesque style softened by fluent lines; her interpretation of subjects was original, verging on mystical. Bas-relief depictions of *The Four Elements* (1951), occupying the quadrants of a Latin cross, were an unexpected theme for the War Memorial Chapel in St Giles Cathedral. Her roundels on the NLS façade (1956) are unconventional evocations of the learned disciplines represented by Lorimer's allegorical figures below them. For the Royal Scots Memorial, she supplied straightforward historical images. A proponent of direct carving, she executed the NLS reliefs *in situ* and produced three large oak figures for the St Giles organ-screen unaided. Elizabeth Dempster (ARSA 1960) was remembered by colleagues as combining deep reserve with a delightful sense of humour and profound loyalty. Other works survive in RSA and National Galleries collections. SHH

• RSA Archives (Members' Files): Dean Gallery, Edinburgh. *DSAA.*

DENCE, Marjorie Lillian, MBE, born Teddington, Middlesex, 14 June 1901, died Perth 23 August 1966. Actor and theatre manager. Daughter of Annie Eleanor Searle, and Ernest Martin Dence, brass-founder and company director.

Marjorie Dence discovered her theatrical vocation while studying at the University of London. She joined the university dramatic society, where she met the actor David Steuart. Their relationship was professional rather than romantic, but it was a close and lifelong partnership. In 1934 they were both members of Lena Ashwell's Greater London Theatre Company. In a conversation about starting a repertory theatre, Steuart suggested Perth as an ideal location. By coincidence, shortly afterwards, Perth Theatre was advertised for sale in *The Stage.* Ernest Dence agreed to buy it for £4,000 and appointed his daughter as manager. Marjorie Dence and David Steuart contributed £1,000 of their own money to refurbish the theatre, and engaged a company. On 23 Sept. 1935, their first season began successfully with a performance of *The Rose without a Thorn* by Clifford Bax, and they went on to present a further 18 plays in weekly repertory.

With the outbreak of war in September 1939, Marjorie Dence rose to the occasion: the actors moved into the theatre, sleeping in dressing-rooms and the coffee-bar, and took over all the non-playing functions, such as box office, cleaning and scene shifting. Everyone shared meals in the theatre and any profit was divided equally at the end of a week. Under her management, the Perth company not only survived but extended its activities. Marjorie Dence was a highly respected figure in Perth, becoming a JP. She was made MBE in 1952. Her annual garden party, given at the beginning of each season, was a popular event with the Theatre Club. The last of her parties took place in August 1966, just two days before her sudden and untimely death. Her will stated that the theatre was to be sold to the city of Perth for £5,000, exactly the initial outlay. DC

• Boutcher, R. and Kemp, W. G. (1975) *The Theatre in Perth*; Campbell, D. (1966) *Playing for Scotland*; Hutchison, D. (1977) *The Modern Scottish Theatre*; *ODNB* (2004). Private information: Helen Murdoch.

DER-ILEI, fl. 685, born Pictland. Queen and mother of kings.

The fact that Der-Ilei, whose sons Bridei (697–706) and Naiton (706–24) were Pictish over-kings, was the mother rather than the father of the two children has only recently come to light, though the possibility has been acknowledged for some time. Der-Ilei had two known husbands: Dargart mac Finguine, a dynast of Cenél Comgaill in Cowal, who died in 685, and an otherwise unknown Drostan, apparently a dynast of the Pictish kingdom of Atholl. The chronologies of the children of these marriages suggest that Dargart was her first husband, and Drostan of Atholl her second. Pictish history in the first third of the

eighth century was dominated by the activities and struggles of (and sometimes between) Der-Ilei's sons, but she herself remains enigmatic. JEF
• Anderson, A. O. and Anderson, M. O. (eds) (1961) *Adomnan's Life of Columba*; Clancy, T. O. (2004) 'Philosopher-King: Nechtan mac Der-Ilei', *Scot. Hist. Rev.*, vol. 83, Oct.

DERWENT, Lavinia *see* **DODD, Elizabeth** (1909–89)

DEVINE, Rachel, n. **Blackley,** born Dundee 13 Feb. 1875, died Dundee 13 April 1960. Weaver and trade union leader. Daughter of Rachel McClellan, and John Blackley, yarn dresser.

A founding member of the Dundee and District Jute and Flax Workers' Union in 1906, Rachel Devine served the union for more than 30 years. Women in that union (unlike others) were encouraged to participate at all levels, which was a significant development in an industry employing large numbers of women. As Rachel Devine wryly observed at a joint trade union national women's conference in 1929, 'the difficulty in Dundee was not getting their women to speak, but in getting them to speak and to hold their tongues at the right time' (Lamb Collection).

Rachel Devine was first elected to the union executive as a factory representative in 1909. Her criticism of the union's full-time secretary resulted in her removal as a representative four years later, but she returned to the executive in 1915 and was active in rallying union support for the Dundee rent strikes. In 1923, she was elected vice-president and became president the following year, and one of the union's leading wages and conditions negotiators. After being replaced as president by Jeannie Spence in 1930, she served a second four-year period as vice-president. In 1938, she became a trustee of the union. She was a capable campaigner for working women, with a reputation for combativeness both towards their employers and union leaders. GRS
• Dundee City Archive and Record Centre: GD/JF/1-GD/JF/21, Dundee and District Union of Jute and Flax Workers minute books, 1906–66; Dundee Central Library: Lamb Collection.
Dundee *Courier & Advertiser*, 15 April 1960; Gordon, E. (1991) *Women and the Labour Movement in Scotland 1850–1914*; *ODNB (2004); Walker, W. (1979) *Juteopolis: Dundee and its textile workers 1885–1923*.

DICK, Beetty, born Dalkeith 1693, died Dalkeith 1773. Town crier.

The office of town crier was sometimes performed in small Scottish burghs by 'some old matron' (Kay 1878, p. 365). Beetty Dick was crier in Dalkeith in the mid-18th century. Wearing her distinctive hooded cap (*toy*) and wielding the 'clap' – a plain wooden trencher and spoon – she went the rounds of the town nightly, calling out the arrival of fresh fish, the loss or theft of articles, the availability of hot tripe, and any other intelligence, for the price of one penny per item. Said to be a great favourite with 'the younger portion of the town' (ibid.) who greeted her with acclamation, Beetty Dick never married, and was buried in the Old Churchyard. She was succeeded by a further three female criers, who used handbells, before the magistrates adopted a drum as being 'more dignified' (ibid.). SR
• Kay, J. (1878 edn.) *A Series of Original Portraits and Caricature Etchings*, vol. 2, pp. 365–67.

DICKSON, Katherine Joan Balfour, born Edinburgh 21 Dec. 1921, died London 9 Oct. 1994. Cellist and music teacher. Daughter of Marjorie Balfour Lowe, and J. Douglas Dickson, WS, lawyer.

Joan Dickson was educated at the RCM, London (LRAM 1945) and studied with Ivor James, with Pierre Fournier in Paris in 1947, and with Enrico Mainardi in Rome, Salzburg and Lucerne (1948–51). A professor both at the RCM from 1967 and at the RSAMD from 1954 to 1981, she also taught chamber music and gave many memorable recitals. As a soloist, she appeared at the London Proms, playing Rubbra's *Soliloquy* and the Hindemith Cello Concerto. A distinguished figure in chamber music, she was a founder member of the New Edinburgh Quartet (1953–8), which she left to join the Scottish Trio. She also formed a duo with her sister, Hester. Works were composed for them by Leighton, Wilson and Dunlop, while concerti were composed for Joan by Frank Spedding and David Dorward.

As a teacher her influence was widespread and influential: pupils included Jacqueline du Pré, Murray Welsh, the Prince of Wales and Richard Harwood. Her insistence on technical accomplishment was never allowed to inhibit musicality, and her own performances were often inspired. She could be forceful, even intimidating, but was always open to new ideas. Latterly, she devoted much energy to the European String Teachers' Association. David Donaldson recalled painting her portrait in the Mackintosh studio at the GSA: 'In one of the most beautiful settings

Scotland could produce, I was painting a six-foot picture of a woman wearing a long green dress playing some of the greatest music in the world. It was magic . . . in some ways Joan Dickson was the ultimate' (Smith 1996, p. 68). Joan Dickson was MMus (Durham) and was awarded the Cobbett Medal 1965 for services to chamber music. JP

• RSAMD Alumni Association, *Newsletter* 9, 1996, p. 30; 12, 1997/98, p. 8.

Smith, W. G. (1996) *David Donaldson, Painter and Limner to her Majesty The Queen in Scotland.*

Private information: Hester Dickson (sister); Personal knowledge.

DIORBHAIL NIC A' BHRUTHAINN (Dorothy Brown),
fl. 1644, died Isle of Luing. Poet and songwriter.

Diorbhail nic a' Bhruthainn composed the song 'Alasdair a Laoigh mo chéille' (Alasdair, love of my heart) in praise of Alexander MacDonald or Alasdair Mac Colla, Montrose's general. This is the only extant composition with an ascription to her, although we know that she composed many more. Internal evidence dates the song to late 1643 or early 1644. An ardent Jacobite, she reserved her sharpest satire for the Clan Campbell. In fact, the anti-Campbell sentiments in this song are every bit as strong as, if not stronger than, the royalist or anti-Covenant views expressed. She was buried in the old churchyard in Luing. AF

• MacKenzie, J. (1904) *Sàr-obair nam Bàrd Gaelach*, p. 63; Thomson, D. S. (1994) *The Companion to Gaelic Scotland*, p. 213.

DIXIE, Florence Caroline (Florrie), Lady, n.
Douglas, born London 24 May 1857, died Glen Stuart, Dumfriesshire, 7 Nov. 1905. Traveller, writer. Daughter of Caroline Clayton, and Archibald William Douglas, 8th Marquess of Queensberry.

A twin, youngest of six, Florrie Douglas was born into an ancient but disaster-prone Scottish family, based at Kinmount. Her father died by accident or suicide in 1858; her twin killed himself in 1891; another brother died on the Matterhorn in 1865, and the 9th Marquess, father of Lord Alfred Douglas, was the defendant in the Oscar Wilde case (1895). In the 1860s, her mother converted to Catholicism and fled abroad with the twins for two years, visiting every capital city in Europe. Convent-educated, Florrie Douglas's true love was the outdoors: travel, horse-riding, swimming. In 1875, she married the like-minded, handsome but otherwise unremarkable Sir Alexander Beaumont (Beau) Dixie, Bt. (1851–1924). Two months after the

birth of their second child, in 1878, Lady Dixie set off for South America with her husband, two brothers, and a friend in tow, determined to be the first white woman to visit remote regions. *Across Patagonia* (1880) led to her dispatch as *Morning Post* correspondent to South Africa and another book, *In Defence of Zululand* (1882). She later championed home rule for both Ireland and Scotland, though opposing Land League policy in the former, and claimed to be the victim of an unconfirmed attack by 'Fenians' at Windsor. In the mid-1880s, she and Beau moved permanently to Glen Stuart on the family estate, from where 'books continued to pour out' (Roberts 1981, p. 274). Her advanced views caused her to be thought eccentric and a class traitor: she favoured complete equality for men and women: 'give all human beings fair play and Nature will select her own aristocracy' (*Izra* 1905, quoted ibid., p. 275). She grew to hate blood sports (having once hunted big game) and turned vegetarian. Among other pursuits, she became a member of the Rational Dress society and wrote for the *Agnostic Journal*; with the Scots Patriots, protested against the appellation 'Edward VII' on the King's accession; and presided over a ladies football team, 'the ideal exercise for women'. 'Hard as nails or even a little harder' according to Lady Warwick (ibid., p. 276), Florence Dixie later suffered from arthritis and died aged 48. The inconsolable Beau remarried. SR

• Dixie, F. C., Works as above and see Bibl.

HSWW (Bibl.); *ODNB* (2004); Roberts, B. (1981) *The Mad Bad Line: the family of Lord Alfred Douglas.*

DOCHERTY, Mary, born Cowdenbeath 27 April
1908, died Cowdenbeath 2 Feb. 2000. Communist activist and writer. Daughter of Janet Todd, and William Docherty, miner.

One of three girls, Mary Docherty had first-hand knowledge of the poverty endemic in mining areas in West Fife and of the ignorance and prejudice with which miners' families were treated. Unemployed as a result of his political activities, her father was reduced to selling firewood round the doors. She started in domestic service at 14 and worked in a factory before becoming a full-time CP worker. Involved in politics from an early age, she joined the CP at 18 in the aftermath of the General Strike and remained a dedicated member for over 70 years, campaigning for better conditions alongside Willie Gallacher and Alex and Abe Moffatt.

She began a local children's section of the CP and organised strikes and demonstrations. During a visit to the Soviet Union in 1929, she spent three months in a sanatorium where she was cured of tuberculosis. She retained an enormous love for the country despite its political breakdown, and Lenin was her ultimate hero. *A Miner's Lass* (1991) gives an insight into the poverty and lack of opportunity of working-class women of her generation. Her second book, *'Auld Bob', A Man in a Million* (1996), was a tribute to her guide and mentor, Bob Selkirk, a local councillor and activist. Mary Docherty retired from active political life at 60 but with the publication of her books she was once more in demand as a speaker and until shortly before her death, continued to take part in International Women's Day events. At 91, she was one of the principal speakers at *Red Fife*, a celebration of the kingdom's contribution to political life. LK

• Docherty M., Works as above.

Central Fife Times, 10 Feb. 2000 (obit.).

DODD, Elizabeth [Lavinia Derwent], MBE, born Overton Bush Farm, Borders, 23 Feb. 1909, died Glasgow 26 Nov. 1989. Children's writer and broadcaster. Daughter of Bessie Lamb, and John Dodd, farmer.

Born in the Cheviot Hills, the middle child of five, Elizabeth Dodd attended Edgerton primary school and Jedburgh Grammar School, before keeping house for a minister brother. When he married, she moved to Glasgow to work for Collins Publishers, where she stayed for 30 years, reaching a senior position. She wrote and edited children's books for Collins, adopting the pseudonym 'Lavinia Derwent' for these, as well as for her own work in print, radio and TV. During the Second World War, she worked part-time in a Forces' canteen. Meanwhile, wartime Scotland was cheered by her 'Tammy Troot' radio stories, superbly read by actor Willie Joss on BBC *Children's Hour*. The lovable if conceited hero – 'Ah'm a clever wee troot!' – became a household name, featuring in a newspaper cartoon strip and later in books.

She became a full-time writer in the 1960s, after the success of *Macpherson* (1961), the first of a 13-title series of children's books about a Glasgow errand-boy. In the 1970s, she wrote and presented the STV series *Teatime Tales*. The four-book *Sula* series of novels (1969–76), set on a fictional Hebridean island, was filmed on Tiree for BBC children's television. Seven volumes of memoirs, published 1975–88, provide a lively account of her childhood and early career. Based in Glasgow, she had a wide circle of friends, was a member of the

Soroptimists and several writers' organisations, and was the first woman president of Scottish PEN. A kenspeckle figure on the Scottish literary scene, she dressed '. . . in vivid, stylish colours which defied any attempts at co-ordination yet resulted in individualistic glamour' (*Scotsman* 1989). Her children's books are notable for the liveliness and humour evident in her personality, and *The Adventures of Tammy Troot* (1975) and the *Sula* series have attained near-classic status. MARB

• Mitchell Library, Glasgow: Archive.

Derwent, L., Works as above, and (1975) *A Breath of Border Air*, (1988) *Beyond the Borders*. See also *HSWW* (Select Bibl.). *The Scotsman*, 28 Nov. 1989 (obit.); Strickland, G. (1978) 'Drawn from memory', *Radio Times*, 4–10 March, pp. 15, 17.

DODS, Mary Diana [David Lyndsay, Walter Sholto Douglas], born c. 1790, probably Scotland, died c. 1830. Writer, cross-dresser. Reputed daughter of George Douglas, 15th Earl of Morton (mother unknown).

Mary Diana Dods and her sister, Georgiana Dods Carter, also reputedly the daughter of George Douglas, were raised by Douglas in London and at Dalmahoy House, Ratho. Exceptionally intelligent, Mary was well-read and fluent in French and German. When her father married in 1814, he gave Mary and her sister allowances of £100 each, continued as annuities on his death in 1824. In 1821, the sisters briefly ran a girls' school in London, giving language and piano lessons. That year, Mary Diana Dods began her literary career as 'David Lyndsay', publishing *Dramas of the Ancient World* followed by essays in *Blackwood's Edinburgh Magazine* and short stories in London annuals. A second book, *Tales of the Wild and the Wonderful*, appeared in 1825. Though Blackwood's rejected further submissions, when in 1826 she sent in work under the name of 'Sholto Douglas', it was published.

She may have initially used the name 'Walter Sholto Douglas' for publishing purposes, but around 1825 she formed a relationship with Isabella Robinson (born c. 1810), the daughter of Joshua Robinson, a London builder. When the unmarried Isabella, independent and strikingly beautiful, gave birth to a daughter c. 1826–7, she and Mary named the child Adeline Douglas and established Isabella as Mrs Douglas. In August 1827, Mary Diana Dods donned men's clothing and transformed herself into Mr Walter Sholto Douglas, with wife and child. Their friend Mary Shelley aided this charade and secured false passports for them to travel to Paris, where the couple entered Anglo-French society and she successfully passed as a man. The story of Mary Diana Dods and her guises was a secret until 1980, when uncovered by Betty T. Bennett.

Mary Diana Dods hoped in her male persona to enter the diplomatic corps but was disappointed. So, too, was she disappointed in Isabella Robinson, who openly flirted with men and had a love affair. In 1829, as Douglas, Mary Diana Dods was imprisoned in Paris for debt, where her already ailing physical and mental health rapidly deteriorated. She had probably died by November 1830, when Isabella, as Mrs Douglas, returned to England. In 1839, Isabella Douglas, widow, married the Rev. William Falconer; she died at San Alessi, Italy, in 1869. In 1853, Adeline Douglas married Henry Drummond Wolff as the 'daughter of Walter Sholto Douglas, an officer in HM's Service' (Bennett 1991, p. 231). BB

• Dods, M. D., Lyndsay, D. and Douglas, W. S., Works as above, and see Bennett 1991 (Bibl.).

Bennett, B.T. (ed.) (1980) *The Letters of Mary Wollstonecraft Shelley*, (1991) *Mary Diana Dods, a Gentleman and a Scholar* (Bibl.); *ODNB* (2004).

DODS, Meg *see* **JOHNSTONE, Christian Isobel** (1781–1857)

DOLLAN, Agnes Johnston, Lady, n. **Moir,** MBE, born Springburn, Glasgow, 16 August 1887, died Glasgow 16 July 1966. Labour activist and suffragette. Daughter of Annie Wilkinson, and Henry Moir, blacksmith.

One of 11 children, Agnes Moir left school aged 11 to work first in a factory and then in a telephone exchange. Her experiences made her a socialist and a feminist; she joined the Socialist Sunday School movement, the WSPU, WLL and ILP, and was an active trade unionist. In 1912 she married Patrick Dollan (1885–1963), an ILP propagandist who would later become leader of the Labour Party on Glasgow Corporation and Lord Provost of the city (1938–41). He was knighted in 1941. They had one son, James, who became a journalist.

During the First World War, Agnes Dollan was one of the remarkable group of women who made a distinctive contribution to 'Red Clydeside'. Working with comrades *Helen Crawfurd and *Mary Barbour, she linked the rent strikes agitation with peace campaigns and other issues. They became well-known figures and took prominent roles within the Labour movement, such as speaking on the platform of the 1917 May Day

demonstration at Glasgow Green. Although Harry McShane claimed that Patrick Dollan 'killed her activity' (McShane and Smith 1978, p. 34), Agnes Dollan was particularly active in the immediate post-war years. She was the first woman Labour candidate selected to contest a municipal election in Glasgow, in January 1919. Although unsuccessful, she was elected to the School Board in April and two years later claimed the municipal ward of her home district, Springburn, which she held until illness forced her resignation in 1928. She stood once, unsuccessfully, for Parliament, in 1924, and failed to be re-elected to Glasgow Corporation in the 1930s. She sat on the Labour Party National Executive and campaigned with her husband for the ILP to remain part of the Labour Party. The Second World War saw both Dollans reject their pacifist stance; Agnes's war efforts were rewarded with an MBE in 1946. Later she joined the Moral Re-armament Movement where her antagonism to the Communist Party found expression. Born into an 'Orange' household, she had become a free-thinker in early life, but converted to Catholicism in the 1950s. JJS

• *Glasgow Herald*, 18 July 1966 (obit.); McShane, H. and Smith, J. (1978) *No Mean Fighter*; *ODNB* (2004); *SLL*; Smyth, J. J. (2000) *Labour in Glasgow 1896–1936*.

DONALDSON, Mary Ethel Muir (M. E. M.),[‡] born Norwood, Surrey, 19 May 1876, died Edinburgh 17 Jan. 1958. Author and photographer. Daughter of Mary Isabella Muir, and Alexander Donaldson.

Daughter of an emigrant Scot who had moved from Adelaide to England, M. E. M. Donaldson probably derived the means to research and write six substantial books from family connections with the Donaldson Shipping Line. In *Scottish Biographies* (1938), she described herself as 'author and lecturer' and was often in demand for her illustrated topographical and historical talks.

M. E. M. Donaldson was a pioneer in the expanding field of photography. With bulky plate camera, heavy tripod and equipment, from about 1905 she explored remoter parts of western Inverness-shire and north Argyll, areas largely ignored by travellers and writers. The territory had been dominated by a cadet branch of Clan Donald, and she rationalised her interest as a return to her ancestral land. She was also attracted by the religious affinities of western Inverness-shire, with its strong relict Roman Catholicism and Episcopalianism. She denounced her adopted country's Presbyterianism in her outspoken critique,

Scotland's Suppressed History (1935). Her remarkable and sensitive photographic studies depicted what she saw as disappearing aspects of life and subjects rarely photographed. Her work is remarkable for its aesthetic qualities, its engagement with its topics, and as surviving documentation of west Highland life in the early 20th century. Some books were illustrated by her life-long friend and travelling companion, Isabel Bonus, but according to *Wanderings in the Western Highlands* (1921), watercolour became too expensive. However, photography was already integral to her work, since she selected from 900 negatives to illustrate the book, while apologising for some loss of quality in reproduction.

In 1925, M. E. M. Donaldson built at Sanna in Ardnamurchan a house constructed of local materials: it demonstrated imaginatively how new buildings could harmonise with a landscape which she saw as becoming disfigured with abominable structures of alien materials. In 1935, she sold up and left Sanna for Somerset and later Edinburgh; some disenchantment is evident in surviving unpublished writings (NMS: MS 1979.23). Over 1,000 glass-plate negatives are in Inverness Museum and Art Gallery. Another 123 went to the NMS after being used in the affectionate tribute, *'Herself'* (1979). HC
• NMS: MS 1979.23, Typescript, unpublished 'The building of our home in the Highlands – And much else besides'. Donaldson, M. E. M., Works as above, and (1919) *Tonal Mactonal*, (1926) *Further Wanderings – mainly in Argyll*, (1949) *'Till Scotland Melts in Flame'*.
Dunbar, J. T. (1979) *'Herself': the life and photographs of M. E. M. Donaldson*; *SB*.

DOUGLAS, Alison, born Eskdale c. 1480, died probably Blackadder, Berwickshire, c. 1530. Landowner. Daughter of Elizabeth Drummond, and George Douglas, Master of Angus.

Wife of Robert Blackadder of that Ilk, Alison Douglas was widowed after Flodden Field (1513) and then married David Hume, 4th baron of Wedderburn. Her two daughters, co-heiresses of the Blackadder estate, married her new husband's younger brothers, John and Robert, in 1518. It is likely that the Humes forced their marriages by browbeating Alison. These women typify the landed widows and semi-orphaned daughters exploited in the aftermath of Flodden, despite royal proclamations intended to protect them and their lands.

Alison Douglas's woes persisted because of her kindred with the Douglas earls of Angus. Her

husband was forfeited in 1517 for his associations with Alexander, Lord Home, though his lands were later restored. However, Alison Douglas was fondly remembered by later Hume generations. David Hume of Godscroft called her 'a woman of extraordinary beauty and adorned with piety, goodness and every virtue which procured her honour and esteem from all' (Hume 1839, p. 20). MMM
• Hume of Godscroft, D. (1839) *De Familia Humia Wedderburnensi Liber*; *SP*, i, pp. 186–9, iii, p. 281.

DOUGLAS, Charlotte Ann, OBE, born Auchterarder 29 Dec. 1894, died Perth 27 August 1979. MO, major contributor to Cathcart Report. Daughter of Georgina Cruickshank, and Joseph Douglas, bank manager.

Charlotte Douglas graduated MBChB from the University of Glasgow in 1919. Having obtained a Diploma in Public Health from Cambridge, enabling her to work as a local authority Medical Officer, she completed her MD in Glasgow in 1925. After posts at the City of Bradford ante-natal clinic, as house physician at the Glasgow Royal Maternity and Women's Hospital, and house surgeon at Glasgow Royal Infirmary, she became in 1931 MO for Maternity and Child Welfare of the Department of Health for Scotland, a post she held for 30 years. In the 1930s and 1940s, she travelled Scotland, monitoring maternity and child welfare services, and her series of reports to the Chief MO for Scotland helped lay the foundations for increased Scottish government maternity provision.

With colleague Peter L. McKinlay, Charlotte Douglas conducted the systematic investigation published as the DHS *Report on Maternal Mortality and Morbidity in Scotland* (1935). Its recommendations were endorsed in the DHS Scottish Health Services Committee Report (Cathcart Report, 1936) based on Douglas and McKinlay's statistics. The maternal ill-health and mortality caused by inadequate or intrusive medical care and the lack of medical support revealed in these reports led to the 1937 Maternity Services (Scotland) Act. Wrangles over medical fees meant that some local authorities were slow to implement it, but this comprehensive service for Scotland, with co-ordinated medical attendance by midwife, doctor and consultant, free of charge for those unable to pay fees, was far in advance of that elsewhere in Britain. With medical progress and improved nutrition during wartime, this reform led to a drop in maternal mortality rates from 4.8 per 1,000 births in 1937 to 3.0 per 1,000 in

1944. Charlotte Douglas was made an OBE and retired in 1962. JLMJ

• Douglas, C.A. (1926) 'Ante-natal clinics and their uses', *Jour. Roy. Sanitary Institute*, (1935) DHS *Report on Maternal Mortality and Morbidity in Scotland* (jointly with McKinlay, P. L.), (1959) 'Maternal and infant mortality in Scotland' *DHS Bulletin*.
Jenkinson, J. (2002) *Scotland's Health 1919–1948*; Maclachlan, G. (ed.) (1987) *Improving the Common Weal*; *Medical Directory* (1935); *Medical Register* (1935).

DOUGLAS, Lady Elizabeth, Countess of Erroll, fl. 1587.

Poet. Daughter of Lady Agnes Lesly, daughter of the Earl of Rothes, and Sir William Douglas of Lochleven, Earl of Morton.

Elizabeth Douglas is probably the 'E. D.' who composed two sonnets to the Scottish Renaissance poet, William Fowler (1560–1612). Although another Elizabeth Douglas, wife of Samuel Cockburne of Temple-Hall and daughter of William Douglas of Whittingehame, has also been proposed as 'E. D.', the case for the Earl of Morton's daughter is strengthened by the sonnet which Fowler dedicated to the 'Co[u]ntess of Erroll' since, in 1590, she married Francis Hay, 9th Earl of Errol (c. 1564–1631). These sonnets appear to be her only extant work, composed in December 1587 according to the date of the manuscript in which they are found ('The Triumphs of the Most Famous Poet M. Frances Petrarke Translated out of italian into inglish by Mr. Wm. Fouler P. of Hauicke'). Elizabeth Douglas's marriage may have caused controversy since her husband was a convert to Roman Catholicism; it is not known whether she also converted. As his third wife, she gave birth to three sons and eight daughters. She may have entered royal circles through the political connections of her father during the 1580s and 90s, the culminating period of the Jacobean, or 'Castilian', literary Renaissance of which she seems to have been part, unusually, since most of James VI's court poets were male.

The sonnets appear in the manuscript's opening section, immediately after the King's own dedicatory poem. Devised in the distinctive rhyme scheme of Scottish sonneteers, they are entitled 'E. D. in praise of Mr. Wm. Foular her friend' and 'E. D. in commendatioun of the authour and of his choise'. Fowler's 'choise' related to two women, and one of E. D.'s sonnets transforms Petrarch's flawless Laura into the even more peerless Lady Jean Fleming, dedicatee of Fowler's translation: 'No Laura heir, bot Ladye Ieane it is./O Ladye liwe! Thy foular the extolls/Whose golden pen thy name in fame Inrolls' (ll. 12–14). The poems show Elizabeth Douglas's familiarity with the literary ideals of Scottish Renaissance art; she herself seems the epitome of the learned female courtier. SD

• Edinburgh Univ. Library: MS De.1.10; NLS: MS 2065. *HSWW*; Meikle, H. W. (ed.) (1914–40) *The Works of William Fowler*; *ODNB* (2004) (Fowler, William; Hay, Francis); Travitsky, B. (ed.) (1981) *The Paradise of Women: writings by Englishwomen of the Renaissance*.

DOUGLAS, Lady Frances, n. Scott, born 26 July 1750, died Bothwell Castle May 1817.

Correspondent. Daughter of Lady Caroline Campbell, Baroness Greenwich, and Francis Scott, Earl of Dalkeith.

Born after her father's death, Lady Frances Scott acquired a stepfather in 1755, when her mother married Charles Townsend, the great Whig politician. She grew up in one of the most glamorous political and social circles of the age. She joined the household of her brother, Henry, 3rd Duke of Buccleuch, in 1767, travelling to Scotland for the first time to reside at Dalkeith Palace. Subsequent trips to Ireland, Wales and the Lake District resulted in lively letters and verse journals which were widely circulated among friends and family.

At her brother's home she met Archibald, Lord Douglas (1748–1827), son of Lady Jane Douglas, the figure at the centre of the infamous 'Douglas Cause', an inheritance dispute between the Douglases and the Duke of Hamilton (see Gunning, Elizabeth) which was eventually settled in the allegedly illegitimate Archibald's favour. Lady Frances became Lord Douglas's second wife on 13 May 1783. Her companion on the wedding trip through Scotland was her cousin, *Lady Louisa Stuart, who became a frequent visitor to Bothwell Castle, the Douglas family seat. She later annotated Lady Frances's Journal. Lady Frances raised 12 children, including four step-children. Following her death, Lady Louisa Stuart wrote a 'Memoir' of her for Lady Frances's daughter, the novelist **Caroline Scott** (1784–1857). Intended for private circulation but later published, it paints a vivid picture of her world, and the political and social intrigues characterising such aristocratic families. But the memoir was mainly intended as a record of a kind, clever woman, a good mother and wife, whose main virtues, despite her brilliant connections, were domestic and familial. Her daughter Caroline, who married Captain George

Scott (1770–1841) in 1810, began to write in her 40s. Several educational works appeared under her own name, but her three novels were all published anonymously. SN
• Stuart, Lady L. [n. d.] (1985) *Gleanings from an Old Portfolio, Memoire of Frances, Lady Douglas*, J. Rubenstein, ed. *ODNB* (2004) (Douglas, Frances; Scott, Caroline).

DOUGLAS, Janet, Lady Glamis, died Edinburgh 17 July 1537. Convicted of treason. Daughter of Elizabeth Drummond, and George Douglas, Master of Angus.

Janet Douglas married John Lyon, 6th Lord Glamis, and had four children, but quarrelled with him in 1526 over his failure to support her brother, Archibald, 6th Earl of Angus, in plotting against James V. In 1528, the year her husband died, she was summonsed for helping Angus to organise a rising against the King, and her goods were seized. She was charged in 1532 with poisoning Glamis, but the trial collapsed. She then married Archibald Campbell of Skipnish. Accused of plotting to poison the king, she was burned at the stake on Castle Hill on 17 July 1537 before a large and sympathetic crowd. She seems to have been no mere passive victim of royal hostility but a formidable and energetic protagonist on behalf of the Douglases. RKM
• Cameron, J. (1998) *James V; Crim. Trials*; Fraser, W. (1895) *The Douglas Book*; *ODNB* (2004); *SP*; Tytler, P. F. (1841–3) *History of Scotland 1249–1603.*

DOUGLAS, Katherine (Catherine) [Kate Barlass] fl. 1437. Quasi-historical heroine.

When in 1437 a plot was hatched against the life of James I, who was staying in Perth, the conspirators had removed the bolts from the doors of the royal apartments. James and his wife, *Joan Beaufort, were taken by surprise, but one of Joan's ladies, Katherine Douglas, is said to have thrust her arm into the iron loops where the wooden bolt would have been, to impede the attackers' progress. When they burst in, they broke her arm. She had provided enough time for the King to hide, but he was later found and killed. His protector went down in history as 'Kate Barlass', and her story is often told in books for children, though there are no records of its accuracy. The story was first recounted much later by a mid-sixteenth century historian, who may have elaborated on a more prosaic report from the time that a court lady, Elizabeth (not Katherine) Douglas, accidentally fell into the King's hiding place. SR

• Balfour-Melville, E. M. (1936) *James I King of Scots*; Brown, M. (2000) *James I*, pp. 192–3; Marshall, H. E. (1964 edn.) *Scotland's Story*, pp. 122–3; Mee, A. (n.d.) *The Children's Encyclopedia.*

DOUGLAS, Margaret, born c. 1426, died before April 1475. Heiress. Daughter of Euphemia Graham, and Archibald, 5th Earl of Douglas.

Margaret Douglas's brothers, William, 6th Earl of Douglas, and David, were executed in February 1440. Engineered by their great-uncle, James the Gross, their deaths delivered the entailed Douglas estates to him. Margaret Douglas, however, would succeed to the unentailed lands, mainly in Galloway, on the death of her grandmother, Margaret, daughter of Robert III. For the rest of her life, control of those lands was determined by arranged marriages.

James was determined to re-unite the Douglas heritage and strove to secure a marriage between his son William (1424/5–52) and Margaret. Papal dispensation came in July 1444, by which time William had become the 8th Earl. After William's murder by James II in February 1452, the childless widow regained her inheritance. The new Earl, William's brother James (c. 1425–91), secured papal dispensation and married her in March 1453. Margaret Douglas probably had little choice in the matter. When the family was forfeited in 1455, she fled to England. In 1459, having obtained an annulment, she returned and sought restoration of her inheritance. Unwilling to lose control of the Galloway estates, in 1460, James II married Margaret Douglas to his half-brother, John, Earl of Atholl (c. 1440–1512), who held the former Douglas lordship of Balvenie. The marriage produced at least two children. RO
• Brown, M. (1998) *The Black Douglases*; Dunlop, A. (1950) *The Life and Times of James Kennedy*; Dunlop, A. and MacLauchlan, D. (eds) (1983) *Calendar of Scottish Supplications to Rome*, iv, 1433–1447; *SP.*

DOUGLAS, Lady Margaret, Countess of Lennox, born Harbottle Castle, Northumberland, 8 Oct. 1515, died Stepney, London, 9 March 1578. Daughter of *Margaret Tudor, Queen of Scotland, and Archibald, 6th Earl of Angus.

Margaret Douglas was born as her mother was fleeing to London during the Scottish power struggles following the death of her first husband, James IV. She had quarrelled with her second husband, the Earl of Angus who, after she returned to Scotland in 1517, snatched Margaret from her arms, keeping her in his custody until his exile in 1528. Margaret's uncle, Henry VIII, arranged for her to live in the household of his elder daughter, Mary.

Margaret Douglas had several romantic attachments before marrying, in 1544, Matthew Stewart, 4th Earl of Lennox (1516–71), a descendant of James I. He, too, had been exiled to England. They lived at her residence of Stepney Palace, but shortly before Henry VIII's death in 1547, Margaret quarrelled bitterly with him over her devotion to the Roman Catholic Church. During the reign of Protestant Edward VI she lived mostly at Temple Newsam, her husband's Yorkshire home. Their household became the centre for Roman Catholics in England and when Mary I succeeded Edward, Margaret Douglas was at the centre of affairs again. Mary gave her expensive presents and for a time treated her as her heir. However, after Mary was succeeded by her Protestant half-sister Elizabeth I, in 1558, Margaret withdrew to Temple Newsam.

Her hopes now centred on her elder son, Henry, Lord Darnley, and she worked to promote his marriage to her niece, *Mary, Queen of Scots. When Darnley was murdered at Kirk o' Field in 1567 she was distraught, blaming Mary for his death, but they were eventually reconciled during Mary's English captivity. Mary had restored Lennox to his Scottish estates, and in 1570 he became regent of Scotland, ruling for young James VI. The following year, however, Lennox was assassinated, leaving Margaret bereft. The early death in 1576 of Charles, sole survivor of her eight children, sent her into 'a languishing decay' (Strickland 1851, 2, p. 448). When she died in 1578 she was buried in Westminster Abbey, after a life at the centre of both political and religious events. RKM

• Fraser, W. (1874) *The Lennox*; Fraser, W. (1885) *The Douglas Book*; Phillips, J. (1578) *A Commemoration of the Right Noble and Vertuous Ladye Margrit Duglasis, Countis of Lennox*; *ODNB* (2004); Strickland, A. (1851) *Lives of the Queens of Scotland and English Princesses*, 2.

DOUGLAS, O. *see* **BUCHAN, Anna Masterton** (1877–1948)

DOUGLAS, Walter Sholto *see* **DODS, Mary Diana** (c. 1790–c. 1830)

DRINKWATER, Winifred,[‡] m1 **Short,** m2 **Orchard,** born Waterfoot, near Eaglesham, 11 April 1913, died Taumarunui, NZ, 6 Oct. 1996. Airline pilot and aircraft engineer. Daughter of Emma Banner, and Albert Drinkwater, engineer.

Youngest of three children, Winifred Drinkwater joined the SFC on 2 June 1930 and gained her private pilot's licence shortly after, becoming Scotland's youngest pilot. Her commercial pilot's licence and instructor's certificate followed (1932) and, in 1933, her ground engineer's licence. Joining Midland & Scottish Air Ferries, she flew her first scheduled flight, from Renfrew to Campbeltown, on 27 April 1933. Her first scheduled flight to London, in an open cockpit Fox Moth, was spread over four days in May 1933, but on 4 July she made the roundtrip flight in a flying time of eight and a half hours. She married Francis Short of Short Brothers, aircraft builders, on 19 July 1934 and they moved to Kent where their two children were born. She still flew occasionally, and in 1942 was co-pilot on test flights of the Short Sunderland flying boat and Short Stirling bomber. The family moved to Padstow, Cornwall, where Francis died in 1954. She later married inshore fisherman William Orchard, who died in 1983. After five years back in Scotland, she went to live with her daughter in New Zealand.

Winifred Drinkwater was one of several notable women Pilot Members of the SFC in the 1930s. **Janet Hendry** (1906–2004) became the first woman member on 12 September 1927, causing the Club to resolve the problem 'of ladies not being allowed on the aerodrome' (SFC Minutes). Qualifying for Royal Aero Club Aviator's Certificate No. 8473 on 3 December 1928, she became Scotland's first woman pilot. However, flying was regarded as dangerous and, by 1932, prompted by her brother's death in a car crash, she was on record as lapsed from the SFC. IH

• Mitchell Library, Glasgow: Minute Books, SFC. Allan, J. (2002) *Wings over Scotland*; Clegg, P. V. (1990) *Sword in the Sky*; 'Janet Hendry', *Flight*, 6 Dec. 1928, 21 March 1929; *The Herald*, 19 Oct. 1996 (obit. Drinkwater), 21 Feb. 2004 (obit. Hendry).
Private information: Anne Brewer (daughter), Peter V. Clegg (historian), Joan Short (daughter-in-law).

DRUMMOND, Flora McKinnon,[‡] n. **Gibson [The General, Bluebell],** m1 **Drummond,** m2 **Simpson,** born Manchester 4 August 1878, died Carradale 17 Jan. 1949. Political organiser. Daughter of Sarah Cook, and Francis Gibson, cashier.

Flora Gibson grew up and was educated at Pirnmill on Arran. She left school at 14 and followed a business training in Glasgow, attending economics lectures at the university there. She qualified as a postmistress but was refused entry as her height was below the regulation 5' 2": 'this rejection always rankled' (*WSM*, p. 175). She married Joseph Drummond in 1898 and they moved to Manchester, where she worked for the Oliver typewriter company. Their one child (b. 1908) was named Keir after Keir Hardie. They joined the Fabian Society and the ILP, though she later left the ILP, 'considering that it only paid lip-service to the women's cause' (ibid., p. 175). She joined the WSPU in 1905.

Her talent as an organiser emerged when she undertook publicity for the WSPU after Christabel Pankhurst and Annie Kenney were arrested at Manchester Free Trade Hall in 1905. Moving to London in 1906, Flora Drummond became a leading member of the WSPU central committee, spent time in Glasgow as WSPU organiser, then returned to London as national organiser for the local WSPU branches. Perhaps her greatest contribution to the suffrage movement was the organisation and leading of processions and pageants. Known as 'The General', she rode astride a huge charger, dressed in quasi-military uniform with a peaked cap of purple, white and green. The London crowds nicknamed her 'Bluebell', after the Scottish match, because she was 'more than a match for cabinet ministers' (*HHGW*, p. 100). She was imprisoned nine times, teaching other suffragist inmates Morse code so that they could communicate.

During the First World War, she helped the government recruitment drive and the WSPU industrial peace campaign, opposing strikes and lockouts. In 1923, with Elsie Bowerman she founded the Women's Guild of Empire (WGE), an anti-Communist, anti-fascist organisation. At its peak, the WGE had more than 30 branches. She remained controller until the 1940s. Latterly, she chaired the Six Point Group, was a member of the executive committee of Equal Rights International and in 1947 was a patron of the Suffragette Museum and Record Room. Joseph Drummond left her in 1909 to go to Australia; she married her cousin, engineer Alan Simpson, in 1924. He was killed by a flying bomb at Hammersmith in 1944, after which she moved to Carradale, Argyll. KBB
• *AGC*; *HHGW*; Mitchell, D. (1967) *The Fighting Pankhursts*; *ODNB* (2004); Pankhurst, S. (1977) *The Suffragette Movement*; Tickner, L. (1987) *The Spectacle of Women*; *WSM*.

DRUMMOND, Jane (Jean), Countess of Roxburghe, died London June 1643. First Lady of the Bedchamber to *Anna of Denmark. Daughter of Elizabeth Lindsay, and Patrick, 3rd Lord Drummond.

Jane Drummond accompanied Anna to London in June 1603 and served as a favoured attendant until she 'retired' to Scotland in 1617. Through her close relationship with the Queen, her Catholicism, and her supplying of confidential information to Spain (for which she received a secret pension of approximately £650), she played a significant role at the Jacobean court.

As a Catholic she assisted in the Queen's secret practising of that faith. The Spanish Ambassador reported to Philip III that 'Mass was being said by a Scottish priest, who was simply called a "servant" of [the Queen's] lady-in-waiting, Lady Drummond' (Loomie 1971, p. 308). In serving Spanish interests she embodied pre-1603, pro-Spanish, Catholic Scottish politics, reflecting W. B. Patterson's view that post-1603 English foreign and religious politics originated in James VI's rule in Scotland. One Spanish ambassador described her as 'a prudent person, ready to give help at any time . . .' (Loomie 1963, p. 54). In 1609, her kinsman, James Elphinstone, Lord Balmerino, Lord President, whose nephew married her sister in 1607, found her a staunch supporter when he was sentenced to death for treason. He asked for her help, and her influence with the Queen probably saved his life.

On 3 February 1614 she married Robert Ker, Lord Roxburghe (1569/70–1650) (created Earl 1616) at Somerset House, the Queen's palace. She bore at least three children, two of whom survived. In 1617 she lost her position and returned to Scotland because she failed to inform Anna that her husband had secretly sought the Lord Chamberlainship of Prince Charles's household. She returned to royal service in 1631 when Charles I appointed her governess to Mary, the Princess Royal, and later to his three youngest children. Although she died in London, she was buried in the then ruined chancel of Bowden Parish Church near Kelso on 7 October 1643. HP
• National Archives, formerly PRO: PROB 11/197/140. Fraser, Sir W., *The Elphinstone Family Book*, vol. 2; Loomie, A. J. (1963) 'Toleration and diplomacy', *Trans. Am. Phil. Soc.*, New Series 53, 6, (1971) 'King James I's Catholic consort', *Huntington Library Quarterly*, 34, August; *ODNB* (2004) (see Ker, Jane); Patterson, W. B. (1997) *King James VI and I and the reunion of Christendom*; Payne, H. M. (2001) 'Aristocratic women and the Jacobean court', PhD, Univ. of London.

DRUMMOND, Margaret, born before 1496, died 1502. Mistress of James IV. Daughter of

Elizabeth Lindsay, and John, 1st Lord Drummond, justiciar.

One of six children, Margaret Drummond became mistress of James IV, after the end in 1495 of his relationship with **Marion Boyd** (fl. 1492–1559), with whom he had two children, Alexander and Catherine. Marion, daughter of Christian Mure and Archibald Boyd of Nariston, later married John Mure of Rowallan. Margaret Drummond is first mentioned in royal records in 1496, perhaps having met James on his visit to Drummond Castle in April. During their liaison, she lived briefly at Stirling Castle and at Linlithgow; she was sent back to Drummond Castle early in 1497, perhaps due to her pregnancy, which resulted in the birth of a daughter, Margaret. James' next liaison was with *Janet Kennedy.

Much conjecture surrounds Margaret Drummond's death. Writing a family history in the late 17th century, William Drummond noted that Margaret was poisoned, along with her sisters, Euphemia and Sybilla, for fear the King would never marry while she lived. Modern historians point out there is no contemporary written evidence to support this premise. Interestingly, however, the negotiations for marriage with *Margaret Tudor were completed in 1502 by the Treaty of Perpetual Peace; Margaret and James married in August 1503. SEM

• Drummond, W. [1681] (1881) *The Genealogy of the Most Noble and Ancient House of Drummond*; MacDougall, N. (1989) *James IV*; *ODNB* (2004); *TA*, i, pp. 277, 280, 288, 293, 304, 327.

DRUMMOND, May (aka **Marion** or **Mariana**), born Edinburgh c. 1710, died Edinburgh 1772. Quaker minister. Daughter of John Drummond, merchant, and his wife.

May Drummond became a member of the Society of Friends around 1731, after hearing Thomas Story preach. Her brother, George Drummond, was Provost of Edinburgh and one of the founders of Edinburgh Royal Infirmary. She travelled extensively among English Quakers to raise funds for the hospital. A board in the entrance to the old hospital records that over £370 was raised in this way, much of it due to her efforts. Although her upper-class family strongly disapproved of her joining the Quakers, she was soon formally recognised as a minister and travelled in the ministry throughout Scotland, England and Ireland, drawing large crowds and holding special meetings for young women. She was granted an audience with Queen Caroline and was 'the Quakeress' referred to by Pope in *Epilogue to the Satires* and by other poets. In 1736, she published a pamphlet, *Internal revelation the source of saving knowledge; candidly recommended in several Epistles*.

By the early 1760s, criticisms of May Drummond's ministry and her behaviour began to be made by Edinburgh Quakers. A Minute from Edinburgh Monthly Meeting of February 1765 requires her not to speak in Meetings for Worship and suggests that she was stealing food from Friends' homes, although it is possible that this was malicious gossip. She continued to travel in England, returning to Edinburgh, where she owned property in what was known as 'May Drummond's Close', before her death in 1772. PFB

• Drummond, M., Work as above.

Miller, W. F. (1907) 'Episodes in the life of May Drummond', *Journal of the Friends Historical Society* 4, 2; *ODNB* (2004) Skidmore, G. (1998) *Dear Friends and Sisters: 25 short biographies of Quaker women*; Turner, A. L. (1937) *Story of a Great Hospital: the Royal Infirmary of Edinburgh, 1729–1929*. Derivation of Edinburgh's street names: http://ww2.ebs.hw.ac.uk/edweb/STREETS/

DRUMMOND, Victoria Alexandrina, MBE, born Errol, Perthshire, 14 Oct. 1894, died Kent 25 Dec. 1978. Marine engineer. Daughter of Geraldine Thyssen-Amherst, and Captain Malcolm Drummond.

Victoria Drummond, a goddaughter of *Queen Victoria, grew up at Megginch Castle in Perthshire. After war service (1914–18) in a Perth garage, she worked in a Dundee shipyard, while attending Technical College evening classes. She began her career as an engineer with the Blue Funnel Line in Liverpool and overcame prejudice to become the first British woman to serve as Chief Engineer in the Merchant Navy, and the first to hold a Board of Trade Certificate as a ship's engineer. During the Second World War, she sailed through mines into the Mediterranean to the rescue of part of the British Expeditionary Force. During one voyage her ship, the *Bonita*, was bombed in the Atlantic: after running the engines single-handed during the attack, she arrived back to find herself a heroine. She was awarded the MBE in 1941 and Lloyd's War Medal for gallantry at sea, the first woman to earn it. A canteen, serving food to blitz victims in Lambeth North, was named in her honour. Later she sailed in Atlantic convoys to Murmansk and was involved in the Normandy D-Day landings. It was only in 1962 that she retired from her last ship and wrote the logbook of her life, with details of all her sailings, published in 1994 by her niece, **Cherry Drummond, Lady Strange** (1928–2005), the colourful peer, romantic novelist and campaigner for war widows. LS

• Drummond, C. (ed.) (1994) *The Remarkable Life of Victoria Drummond – Marine Engineer*; *ODNB* (2004); *The Times*, 25 March 2005 (obit. Lady Strange).

DRYSDALE, Anne, born Kirkcaldy, 26 August 1792, died Geelong, Victoria, Australia, May 1853. Pioneer squatter. Daughter of Anne Cunnison, and William Drysdale, town clerk of Kirkcaldy.

Anne Drysdale emigrated to Melbourne in 1840 with capital of £3,000, apparently already experienced in farming. Dr Alexander Thomson of Geelong, son of an Aberdeen shipowner, helped her to secure a licence on a 10,000-acre run at Boronggoop. In 1841, she moved there with another of Thomson's guests, Londoner Caroline Newcomb (1812–74), who had emigrated to Van Diemen's Land in 1833. In 1843 the partners, both Methodists, purchased the freehold property of Coryule, on which by 1844 they were running 6,000 sheep, as well as a few horses and cows. In 1849, they replaced their primitive cottage with a substantial stone house. Despite problems, including defection of labour to the gold fields, the unusual partnership continued until 1852, when Anne Drysdale suffered a stroke, from the effects of which she died 11 months later. Thereafter the enterprise was run single-handedly by Caroline Newcomb. MDH

• State Library of Victoria: MS 9249, diary of Anne Drysdale. Brown, P. L. (ed.) (1941–56) *The Clyde Company Papers*, vols II, pp. 241, 270–1; III, p. 77; V, p. 291, pp. 617–18. Richardson, J. (1986) *The Lady Squatters*. www.zades.com.au/geelong/gdpploo3.htm

DUNBAR, Agnes, Countess of *see* **RANDOLPH, Agnes (Black Agnes of Dunbar)** (born before 1324, d. c. 1369)

DUNBAR, Elizabeth, fl. 1395–1438. Prioress of St Leonard's, Perth. Daughter of Christian (possibly Seton), and George Dunbar, Earl of March.

Elizabeth Dunbar was betrothed to David, Earl of Carrick (later Duke of Rothesay), son of *Annabella Drummond and Robert III. Her father paid a large sum to Robert III for this match but in c. 1400 Rothesay broke the agreement and married Mary, daughter of Archibald, Earl of Douglas, who offered a much larger sum. Rothesay and Elizabeth may have already been married – two

papal dispensations of 1395 and 1397 stated that they had contracted and consummated their marriage.

Robert, Duke of Albany, Governor of Scotland from 1406, was patron of St Leonard's, Perth, and favoured the Earls of March. He may have placed Elizabeth Dunbar at the Augustinian convent as a result of her humiliation by Rothesay. On 23 November 1411, the master of the associated hospital resigned his rights to the 'honorable Lady Elizabeth Dunbar' so that it might be governed by devout women 'religiously associating with chaste bodies' (Perth Museum, MS 65, p. 3). Elizabeth Dunbar was Prioress until 24 April 1438, when she resigned her position. The hospital and convent were granted to the Perth Charterhouse, founded by James I. Nothing further is known about her. KP

• NAS: GD79, King James VI Hospital Perth; Perth Museum & Art Gallery, MS 65, Regarding the Hospitals of Perth. Boardman, S. (1996) *The Early Stewart Kings*; Macdonald, A. J. (2000) *Border Bloodshed: Scotland, England and France at War, 1369–1403*.

DUNBAR, Elizabeth, Countess of Moray, c. 1425–c. 1494. Daughter of Margaret Seton, and James Dunbar, 4th Earl of Moray.

Celebrated as the 'dow [dove] of Dunbar' by poet Richard Holland in 'The Buke of the Howlat' (c. 1450), Elizabeth Dunbar brought the Moray title to her marriage to Archibald Douglas (c. 1442), despite being the younger co-heir. He was killed at Arkinholm on 1 May 1455; on 20 May she contracted to marry her cousin Lord George Gordon (1440/1–1501), later 2nd Earl of Huntly. George Gordon undertook not to force her into 'carnal copulation but of her free will' before the marriage. He also allowed her young son, James, to remain in her care 'withouten bodily harm till his lif', and undertook to ensure that she was 'undistroblit in the posyession of hir erledom of Murra' (*Misc. Spalding* 1849, pp. 128–9). Her daughter Janet is also mentioned in the contract. The notarial copy states that she signed the agreement with her own hand. (The earliest recorded Scottish woman's signature is her sister Janet Dunbar's in 1454.)

Elizabeth Dunbar was divorced by 1459, possibly because the earldom of Moray was not re-granted to George Gordon. He then married Annabella, daughter of James I (see Stewart, Margaret). Elizabeth Dunbar moved west following her third marriage to Sir John Colquhoun of Luss, c. 1463. They had a son, John. After her husband's death in 1478, she sued her stepson Humphrey for withholding her rightful inheritance. The Book of Hours which she probably used in the Rossdhu family chapel, dedicated on 6 April 1469, lists anniversaries of her favourite saints, her father, and other relatives. The book was given to Auckland City Library in New Zealand in 1882. AMCK

• Auckland City Libraries, NZ: Med. Ms G146, Rossdhu Book of Hours: www.aucklandcity.gov.nz/dbtw-wpd/exac/dbtwpub.dll.

Holland, R. (1892) 'The Buke of the Howlat', in F. J. Amours (ed.) *Scottish Alliterative Poems*; McKim, A. (2006) 'The Rossdhu Book of Hours . . .', in A. Barratt and S. Hollis (eds) *Disiecta Membra* (Bibl.); *Misc. of the Spalding Club*, iv, 1849; *ODNB* (2004) (Dunbar family).

DUNCAN, Agnes McMillan, MBE, m. **Nisbet,** born Alexandria, near Glasgow, 22 June 1900, died Glasgow 10 Nov. 1997. Singer, choir mistress. Daughter of Jeannie Jamieson, and William Duncan, engineer.

Agnes Duncan, who left school at 15 to work as a clerk, married in 1932 Matthew Morrison Nisbet, a clerk in Glasgow City Offices. She devoted her life to the West of Scotland choral scene. A member of the Co-operative Choir, she joined the Glasgow Orpheus Choir under the baton of Sir Hugh Roberton, becoming principal solo contralto. The choir gave its last concert in the St Andrews Halls on 11 April 1951. Agnes Duncan then set up the Scottish Junior Singers. Aided by family members, she ran a mixed choir for 7- to 12-year-olds and a choir for girls aged 12 to 21, rehearsing on Saturdays in the old Girls' High School, Garnethill. Their concerts sold out in the St Andrews Halls (later in Woodside Halls and Odeon Cinema). Awarded the MBE in 1967, she was an adjudicator for the Gaelic Mod and other music festivals. An Agnes Duncan trophy is awarded in the Glasgow Music Festivals, as is a Kate Carson prize honouring her daughter Catherine, a speech therapist who carried on her mother's work. Choirs were popular in the Glasgow area, as part of the ethos of self-improvement and civic awareness underpinning left-wing politics of the time. For women, it was also a respectable way of having a night off from domesticity, while the Scottish Junior Singers gave girls from all over Glasgow a chance to travel, singing at concerts throughout the UK. In 1961, they won the BBC *Let the People Sing* competition, and sang regularly on radio and television from the mid-1950s until 1966. LH

• Private information: J. Grant Carson.
Personal knowledge.

DUNCAN, Isabelle (Wight), n. **Clark,** born Dumfries 2 July 1812, died London 26 Dec. 1878. Author. Daughter of Elizabeth Nicolson, and Samuel Clark, lawyer.

Isabelle Clark complained of a lack of rigour in her education, but developed a taste for literature by her early twenties. She married George Duncan (1806–68), minister at Kirkpatrick Durham, in 1833, and had nine children, five of whom survived to adulthood. The family affiliated with the Free Church in the 1843 Disruption and were afterwards associated with English Presbyterian churches, settling in London in 1851.

In 1860 Isabelle Duncan published *Pre-Adamite man: or, the story of our old planet and its inhabitants told by Scripture and science*, a concordist work that attempted to find harmony between scripture and recent developments in the science of geology. Popular in tone, illustrated and written in a gripping literary prose, it is full of facts from recent science. She used pre-Adamism (the theory that God had created a human race before Adam) to help reconcile the biblical creation account with the expanding timescale of geology, proposing that Genesis 1 describes the creation of the pre-Adamites and Genesis 2 the creation of the race of Adam. She sacralised the Ice Age as a pre-Noachic catastrophe that brought the pre-Adamite epoch to an end, contending that the righteous pre-Adamites become the angels and the wicked become demons. Lack of genetic continuity between pre-Adamites and Adamites helped her maintain her Calvinist orthodoxy.

The work generated interest among Scottish and English evangelicals and went through five editions, but was controversial; it appeared anonymously until the final edition in 1866, partly due to her husband's prominent position in the English Presbyterian church. Isabelle Duncan revealed her name then, partly from irritation that most reviewers assumed she was male. However, the work gave some evangelicals an alternative to Darwin's *Origin of Species* (1859), coincidentally released only weeks previously. *Pre-Adamite man*, the first full-length work on pre-Adamism by an evangelical, played an important role in introducing pre-Adamite anthropology and angelology to the English-speaking evangelical world. SS

• Duncan, I., Work as above.

Gould, S. J. (2002) 'The pre-Adamite in a nutshell', in S. J. Gould, *I Have Landed: the end of a beginning in natural history*, pp. 130–46; *ODNB* (2004); Snobelen, S. D. (2001) 'Of stones, men and angels: the competing myth of Isabelle

Duncan's *Pre-Adamite man* (1860)', *Studies in the History and Philosophy of Biological and Biomedical Sciences* 32, pp. 59–104.

DUNCAN, Jane *see* **CAMERON, Elizabeth Jane** (1910–76)

DUNCAN, Mary, n. **Lundie,** born Kelso 26 April 1814, died Cleish, Kinross-shire 5 Jan. 1840. Hymn writer. Daughter of Mary Grey, and Rev. Robert Lundie, minister of Kelso.

Mary Lundie married William Wallace Duncan, minister of Cleish, in 1836, while her younger sister Jane married hymn writer Horatius Bonar, minister in Kelso. Mary Duncan's hymns were written for her children in the last year of her short life and included in a memoir by her mother (Lundie 1841). The hymns were published separately as *Rhymes for my Children* (1842). One entitled 'An evening prayer' and beginning 'Jesus, tender shepherd, hear me', became well known, and was found in many hymn books. JRW
• Barkley, J. M. *Handbook to the Church Hymnary*, 3rd edn.; Julian, J. (1892, 1907) *A Dictionary of Hymnology*; Lundie, M. (1841, 8th edn. 1868) *Memoir of Mrs W. W. Duncan.* Scott, H. (1917) *Fasti Ecclesiae Scoticanae*, vol. 2, pp. 72–3. Additional information: Alison Robertson.

DUNCAN, Ursula Katherine, born Kensington 17 Sept. 1910, died Dundee 27 Jan. 1985. Botanist and landowner. Daughter of Dorothy Weston, and Commander J. A. Duncan.

During Ursula Duncan's infancy, her family returned to Parkhill, Arbroath, the ancestral home. She was educated by a governess, and her academic achievements (BA, MA Classics, external, University of London) were the result almost entirely of self-teaching, intellect and persistence. She was also a pianist of some distinction. She began her botanical studies aged 10, encouraged by her father: they visited remote places, often by bicycle, to study flowers. Already a member of the Wild Flower Society, she made early contacts with eminent botanists by correspondence; their encouragement led to her important work in the fields of bryophytes, lichens and flowering plants.

The most distinguished amateur botanist of her day, Ursula Duncan published in leading specialist journals. Significant publications include her *Bryophyte Flora of Angus* (1966) and *Flora of Easter Ross* (1980), the culmination of years of single-handed work. She also contributed to the production of the *Floras* of Angus and Mull. Generous with help to others, she gave courses at Kindrogan Field Centre. Alongside botanical work, she ran the family estate, including 600 acres of farmland, which she inherited in 1943: the income enabled her to pursue her studies. She received the Bloomer Medal of the Linnean Society and an honorary doctorate from the University of Dundee, a title which she modestly refrained from using. AW
• Obits: (1985) *Jour. of Bryology*, 13; (1986) *Lichenologist*, 18, 4; (1985) *Scottish Newsletter, Botanical Society of the British Isles*, 7; (1986) *Watsonia* 16, 2.

DUNCAN, Victoria Helen Macrae, n. **MacFarlane,** born Callander 25 Nov. 1897, died Edinburgh 6 Dec. 1956. Materialising medium. Daughter of Isabella Rattray, and Archibald MacFarlane, slater and builder.

Helen MacFarlane's tomboyish nature earned her the nickname 'hellish Nell'. Even as a child she claimed clairvoyant and spirit-seeing abilities. In 1914, she became pregnant and went to a women's hostel in Dundee, where, after the birth of her daughter Isabella in 1915, she worked in the jute mills. In 1916 she married Henry Duncan (1897–1967), who became a cabinet maker. Helen Duncan worked in the bleach fields and with the birth of seven more children (six survived childhood), the family lived in poverty. Henry read about mediumship and encouraged his wife to hold sittings with friends. Guests were invited; gradually a small charge was made, then substantial sums. Helen Duncan became famous for her materialisation skills – the ability to produce ectoplasm, a white, allegedly spiritual, substance. Her spirit guides, relaying messages from the dead, were 'Albert' and 'Peggy'. In 1933, a séance was raided and she was fined £10 for fraud, 'Peggy' apparently having been materialised from Helen Duncan's stockinette vest. Despite controversy, her services thrived; famously, in 1941 she apparently materialised a deceased sailor from the ship *Barham* when its sinking was still an official secret. It has been suggested that, consequently, British intelligence services watched and targeted her. In 1944, after another raid, she was tried at the Old Bailey and sentenced to nine months' imprisonment under the Witchcraft Act 1735. Afterwards, she held sittings again. In October 1956 the police raided a séance in Nottingham but found no clear evidence of fraud. There is a continuing campaign to clear her name of the 1944 conviction. A bronze bust of Helen Duncan is in the Smith Art Gallery and Museum, Stirling. FS
• Brealey, G. and Hunter, K. (1985) *The Two Worlds of Helen Duncan*; Cassirer, M. (1996) *Medium on Trial*; Gaskill,

M. (2002) *Hellish Nell, Last of Britain's Witches*; *ODNB* (2004); West, J. D. (1946) 'The trial of Mrs Helen Duncan', *Proc. Soc. Psychical Research* XLVIII, 172: http://www.historic-uk.com/HistoryUK/Scotland-History/Helen Duncan.htm

DUNLOP, Annie Isabella, n. **Cameron,** OBE, born Glasgow 10 May 1897, died Kilmarnock 23 March 1973. Historian. Daughter of Mary Sinclair, and James Cameron, engineer.

Educated in Glasgow, Annie Cameron graduated from the University of Glasgow with an MA in history (1919). She taught in Sunderland and Edinburgh, but returned to historical research in 1922, becoming a leading record scholar. Her doctoral thesis (Edinburgh, 1924) appeared as *The Life and Times of James Kennedy, Bishop of St Andrews* (1950). In 1928, as Carnegie Research Fellow, she attended the Vatican School of Palaeography in Rome. Although initially she found life difficult in the male environment, she formed a life-long association with the Vatican Archives, publicising its rich resources in *Scottish Supplications to Rome* (1934–70) and notes from over 700 volumes. Her frequent visits resulted in her affectionate nickname, *Nonna* (grandmother) of the *Archivo Vaticano*.

After obtaining a DLitt (St Andrews, 1934), she worked in the Scottish Record Office (now NAS) until 1938 when she married George Dunlop, proprietor of the *Kilmarnock Standard*, and moved to Dunselma, Fenwick, Ayrshire. She taught part-time at the University of Edinburgh in 1942 and contributed regularly to the *Standard*. An OBE (1942) and an honorary LLD from St Andrews (1950) followed. Widowed in 1950, she travelled internationally, researching, lecturing and writing, promoting Scottish history through service to historical associations and aiding young scholars. She gifted her books to St Andrews, her house to the Church of Scotland, and paintings to the University of Glasgow. In 1972, Pope Paul VI personally awarded her the Benemerenti medal for services to scholarship. EE

• NLS: Acc. 6528, Papers of Dr Annie J. Dunlop. Dunlop, A., Works as above, and see Bibl. below. Cowan, I. B. (1976) 'Annie I. Dunlop 1897–1973', in C. Burns (ed.) *Calendar of Papal Letters to Scotland of Clement VII of Avignon* (Bibl.); Roy, K. (ed.) (1999) *Dictionary of Scottish Biography I, 1971–5*.

DUNLOP, Frances Anna, n. **Wallace,** born Craigie House, Wallacetown, near Ayr, 16 April 1730, died Dunlop House, Dunlop, Ayrshire, 24 May 1815. Landowner and correspondent of Robert Burns, poet. Daughter of Lady Eleanor Agnew, heiress to the Lochryan Estate, and Sir Thomas Wallace, advocate.

In 1748, Frances Wallace eloped from Dunskey House in Wigtownshire with John Dunlop of Dunlop (1707–85). The marriage was happy and they had seven sons and six daughters. She inherited the Lochryan Estate on her mother's death in 1761. When her husband died on 5 June 1785 she suffered a breakdown lasting more than a year. She was given a copy of Robert Burns's poem 'The Cotter's Saturday Night', and its sentiments touched her heart. In November 1786, she ordered from Burns six copies of *Poems, Chiefly in the Scottish Dialect*. This began a correspondence, and they met at least five times. Although Burns valued her opinion and shared his thoughts with her, Frances Dunlop and he were political opposites and this emerged in a letter dated 12 January 1795 in which Burns referred to the executed French monarchs as 'a perjured Blockhead & an unprincipled Prostitute'. As two of her daughters were married to French royalist émigrés, she found this unacceptable language.

After Burns's death Frances Dunlop and her daughter Eleanor Perochon showed great kindness to his widow *Jean Armour and her family. When Burns's remains were moved from his tomb to the Burns Mausoleum on 19 September 1817, Jean Armour agreed that when Eleanor Perochon died, she could be laid to rest in the vacated tomb of the poet. She died on 10 October 1825 and lies where Burns once lay. MB

• Burns, G. *Narrative Letter to Mrs. Dunlop, 1797*; *ODNB* (2004); Wallace, W. (1898) *Robert Burns and Mrs. Dunlop*.

DUNLOP, Isobel Violet Skelton, born Edinburgh 4 March 1901, died Haddington 12 May 1975. Composer, music teacher, concert organiser. Daughter of Ellen Thompson, and William Dunlop, company secretary.

Isobel Dunlop's name honours her descent from the poet John Skelton. Educated at Rothesay House, Edinburgh, she studied violin with Camillo Ritter, singing with Michael Poutiatine, and composition at the University of Edinburgh under Sir Donald Tovey and Dr Hans Gál. In the 1930s, she taught at Westonbirt and Downham schools and between 1943 and 1948 was Assistant National Officer for the Arts Council of Great Britain. She was an important source of encouragement to younger Scottish composers, taking more than her fair share of administrative work. Although she is best remembered for her work for the Saltire Society, in particular her founding of the Saltire Music Group and Saltire Singers, Isobel Dunlop's contribution as a composer deserves re-evaluation. Her works include a one-act opera, *The Silhouette* (1954), as well as a number of keyboard and vocal works, including cantatas. Her *Fantasy String Quartet*, depicting the four seasons, was commissioned by the University of Glasgow and performed at the 1972 McEwen Memorial concert. JP

• SMIC: Music scores and recordings.

Dunlop, I., Works as above.

Who's Who in Music (1969); *Grove's Dictionary of Music and Musicians* (1954); McLeod, J. (1975) 'Regional report – Scotland', *Composer*, 55, pp. 39–40.

DUNLOP, Marion Wallace- *see* **WALLACE-DUNLOP, Marion** (1864–1942)

DUNNETT, Dorothy n. **Halliday,** OBE, born Dunfermline 25 August 1923, died Edinburgh 9 Nov. 2001. Artist and author. Daughter of Evelyn Millard, and Alick Halliday, mining engineer.

Dorothy Halliday was educated at James Gillespie's High School, Edinburgh, then Edinburgh College of Art and Glasgow School of Art. In 1940 she became assistant press officer for Scottish Government Departments (1940–6) and worked for the Board of Trade Scottish Economics Department, Glasgow (1946–65). On 17 September 1946 she married Alistair M. Dunnett (1908–98), author, playwright and editor of *The Scotsman* from 1956. They had two children. From 1950 she was a professional portrait painter, exhibiting at the RSA. She began to write ten years later, after the death of her father.

The Game of Kings (1961) was the first title in Dorothy Dunnett's series of six novels chronicling the life of the fictional hero Francis Crawford of

Lymond, a 16th-century Scottish soldier of fortune, who, like his author, travelled from his native Scotland to France, Turkey and Russia. As she said, 'the Lymond books became a tremendous cult' (Renton 1989, p. 2). Another series, set in 15th-century Europe, features Niccolo, an apprentice from Bruges, who becomes a successful Renaissance entrepreneur. Niccolo also follows in his author's footsteps, this time to Geneva, Milan, Trebizond and Cyprus. Dorothy Dunnett's historical novels are meticulously researched; their achievement is in the vivid reconstructions of place and period and accuracy of detail, combined with an appeal to a huge and enthusiastic readership. In *King Hereafter* (1982), which began as a work of historical scholarship but due to the pressure of deadlines became a novel, she suggested, controversially, that Earl Thorfinn of Orkney and King Macbeth were the same man. She also published, as Dorothy Halliday, a series of witty thrillers focused on the yacht *Dolly* and its enigmatic master Johnston Johnston, a secret agent and portrait painter. Measures of her popularity are the two-volume *Dorothy Dunnett Companion* (1994, 2002), the Dunnett fanzine, established in 1961, and the association of her fans, the Dorothy Dunnett Readers' Association. She maintained a life-long involvement with the arts in Scotland, later serving as trustee of the NLS and director of the Edinburgh Book Festival. She became Lady Dunnett when her husband was knighted in 1995, and was awarded the OBE for services to literature in 1992. ME

• NLS: Acc. 12135, 12136. Dorothy Dunnett archive.

Dunnett, D. 'Lymond' series (1961) *The Game of Kings* to (1975) *Checkmate*, 'Dolly' series (1968) *Dolly and the Singing Bird* to (1983) *Dolly and the Bird of Paradise*, 'Niccolo' series (1986) *Niccolo Rising* to (2000) *Gemini*.

HSWW (Bibl.); Morrison, E. (ed.) (2002) *Dorothy Dunnett Companion*, vol. 2 (Bibl.); *ODNB* (2005 update); Renton, J. (1989) *The Scottish Book Collector*, Issue 12, pp. 2–4 (interview).

E

EANFLED, born possibly York, Easter 626, died Whitby after 685. Queen of Bernicia, later co-abbess of *Streanaeshalch*/Whitby. Daughter of Aeðilburg daughter of Aeðilberct, and Edwini, King of Deira and Bernicia.

Daughter of a Christian mother and a father about to convert, Eanfled was the first Deiran to be baptised. Her family fled to Kent at her father's death in 633, but she returned in the 640s to marry Oswy of Bernicia (611/12–670), son of her father's enemy. Oswy's kingdom included much of northern England and southern Scotland. Eanfled proved an outspoken and successful queen. Though Oswy had at least one son already by his first wife *Raegnmaeld, it was Eanfled's sons who inherited. Her daughters *Osthryð and *Aelffled were remarkable in their own right. Eanfled openly criticised Oswy when his client killed her kinsman, and opposed his support of unorthodox ecclesiastical practices. This led to the adoption of Roman rather than Celtic practices in the Bernician church at the Council of Whitby. The importance of Eanfled's influence upon Bernicia, and through Oswy's ascendancy upon the spiritual life of much of Britain, was recognised by papal letter. When Oswy died in 670, Eanfled retired to *Streanaeshalch/* Whitby, where AelfflED was a nun; in 680 she and AelfflED became co-abbesses. Eanfled was buried there. Commemorated as a saint, her feast day was 24 November. JEF

• *BEHEP*; Colgrave, B. (ed.) (1927) *The Life of Bishop Wilfrid*; *ODNB* (2004) (Eanflœd).

EARDLEY, Joan Kathleen Harding, born Warnham, Sussex 18 May 1921, died Killearn Hospital, near Glasgow, 16 August 1963. Artist. Daughter of Irene Morrison, and Capt. William Eardley, dairy farmer.

Joan Eardley's father, who had been gassed in the trenches, took his own life in 1929, and the family moved to Blackheath, London. At art school in 1938, her teacher was 'convinced that Joan had a unique career in front of her' (Connell 1975, p. 3). Money was tight, but she applied to Glasgow School of Art in 1939 and studied under Hugh Adam Crawford (1940–3). War work, painting camouflage on ships, interrupted her studies. In 1947, after a summer school tutored by James Cowie, she spent her diploma year in Italy and France. Her travelling companion, Bronwen Pulsford, remembered her persistence: 'she managed to get into places where I would have given up' (SNGMA 1983, p. 2). From the start, Joan Eardley tackled varied subjects, working in the countryside while being attracted to city subjects and keeping in touch with contemporary work. In Glasgow, she exhibited drawings of Italy; and from 1949 worked from a cramped studio there. She was inspired by the Samsons, tenement children who dropped by to see her, and whom she drew, painted and photographed playing. In 1952, photographer (Lady) Audrey Walker began providing photographs of buildings and ephemeral graffiti which Joan Eardley built into her urban

compositions. The realism of her urban works, in oil, pastels and collage, has been compared to that of avant-garde cinema and television (Pearson 1988, pp. 11–12).

In 1950, she discovered Catterline (Kincardineshire), the fishing community with which her name has become identified. From a weather-beaten cottage there, she worked urgently, outside, often in adverse conditions, on large and stormy seascapes in oils, even 'leaving a painting out of doors so that the elements themselves could add the final touches' (Oliver 1984, n.p.). Wide canvases were used to powerful effect when she depicted vegetation and grasses, and the impasto bears traces of seeds. A regular exhibitor in Scotland, she also joined the SSA committee for the De Stael exhibition (1956).

Douglas Hall noted Joan Eardley's 'carelessness of frills' (1977, p. iii). In Glasgow she pushed her easel and paints round in a pram, and was accepted in Catterline as doing an honest day's work, striking up friendly acquaintance with country people. Close friends included Margot Sandeman (later Robson), Audrey Walker, and the painter Angus Neil, her model in the 1950s and the subject of her only known figure painting of an adult: 'Sleeping Nude' 1954–5. (The popular press opined that a 'Girl Artist' was 'fast' to have undertaken, let alone shown, such a work.) Increasing illness in 1962 was faced stoically. Joan Eardley's work was not divided up into periods of subject matter. It was recognised nationally in Scotland in her lifetime, and international recognition had started by the time of her early death: her work was reviewed in New York. An Associate RSA in 1955, she was elected RSA in 1963. Posthumously, Joan Eardley's stature has grown hugely: she has been described as 'world-class' (Hall 1969) and 'a great painter in the European tradition' (Macmillan 1994, pp. 88–9), for her handling and understanding of the 'dramatic intensity' of landscape. HEB

• SNGMA Archive: GMA A09, corr., etc., incl. Pulsford, B. (1983), 'A reminiscence of Joan Eardley' [unpub.]; holdings of Eardley's works presented by her sister.
Connell, C. (1975) 'The life of Joan Eardley, RSA (1921–63)', unpub. thesis, Gray's School of Art; Hall, D. (1969) (intro. Catalogue) *Four Contemporary Scottish Painters: Eardley, Haig, Philipson, Pulford*, Ashmolean, Oxford, (1977) *Exhibition of Paintings by Joan Eardley*, Univ. of Stirling; Macmillan, D. (1994) *Scottish Art in the 20th Century*; Morgan, E. (1962) 'To Joan Eardley', *Lines Review*, 18; Oliver, C. (1964) *Joan Eardley RSA, Memorial Exhibition*, (1984) (Catalogue) *Catterline: Joan Eardley and her Contemporaries*, St Andrews, (1988) *Joan*

Eardley, RSA (Bibl.); *ODNB* (2004); Pearson, F. (1988) *Joan Eardley, 1921–1963.*

EATON, Charlotte Ann *see* **WALDIE, Charlotte Ann** (1788–1859)

ELDER, Isabella, n. **Ure,** born Gorbals, Glasgow, 15 March 1828, died Glasgow 18 Nov. 1905. Philanthropist and supporter of higher education for women. Daughter of Mary Ross, and Alexander Ure, solicitor.

In 1857 Isabella Ure married John Elder (1824–69), who became a famous marine engineer and shipbuilder. His design of the compound engine enabled ships to travel further on less coal, opening up trade throughout the world. His shipyard, John Elder, Fairfield in Govan, employed more than 5,000 men and had the greatest output on the Clyde when he died, aged 45, leaving Isabella Elder the sole owner. She maintained the yard's success for nine months until her brother, John Francis Ure, a celebrated harbour engineer at Newcastle-on-Tyne, took over the management of the business.

A wealthy woman with no children, she used her fortune to benefit others; she was 'a wise benefactress of the public and of learning' (*The Bailie* 1883). At the University of Glasgow she endowed the chair of naval architecture in 1883, and when Queen Margaret College for women was constituted in 1883 she bought North Park House (subsequently BBC Scotland), giving it to the college as rent-free premises. There is no information about her own education but she delivered effective addresses and wrote well-constructed letters. She was especially interested in medical education and in 1890 QMC opened a medical school for which she paid the running costs. Concerned lest women received inferior instruction at QMC compared with men at the university she strove to maintain standards, corresponding with the Principal and informally liaising between the university and the college. In 1901 she was awarded an honorary LLD by the university.

In Govan, she established a School for Domestic Economy in 1885 for poor girls and women, provided the Elder Park and built and financed the Elder Cottage Hospital and Elder Free Library. Always known as Mrs John Elder, she was described as 'a remarkable woman, possessing unusual ability combined with a strong head, a strong will and a most tender and sympathetic

heart' (Macleod 1907). Glasgow's first woman medical graduate, *Dr Marion Gilchrist, signed her death certificate. She is commemorated by a statue in the flower garden of the Elder Park, Govan, where there is also a statue of John Elder, both erected by public subscription, and on the gates erected in University Avenue to mark the fifth centenary of the University of Glasgow. She is also depicted in a stained glass window in the university's Bute Hall. CJM

• Univ. of Glasgow Archives: QMC Collection DC233.
The Bailie, 1883, No. 582; McAlpine, C. J. (1997) *The Lady of Claremont House*; Macleod, D., *Glasgow Herald*, 20 and 23 Nov. 1907; *ODNB* (2004).

ELDER, Margaret Moffat (Madge), born Portobello near Edinburgh, 17 July 1893, died Edinburgh 25 Dec. 1985. Gardener, nurserywoman and writer. Daughter of Margaret Virtue, and John Elder, marine engineer.

Brought up on a farm in Berwickshire, Madge Elder was educated at Gordon village school. Deafness made her completely reliant on lip-reading. In 1912, she was one of the first students to graduate from the Edinburgh School of Gardening for Women in Corstorphine, Edinburgh – Scotland's first horticultural college for women, which opened in 1904 and ran until 1930. Its founders were Lina Barker and Annie Morison, who had graduated from Swanley Horticultural College for Women, Kent, in 1897 and became the first female trainees at the Royal Botanic Garden Edinburgh (RBGE).

Madge Elder graduated with a first-class certificate in horticulture. She worked as a gardener at Fox Covert in Corstorphine and the Priory at Melrose before becoming head gardener at Bowhill, Selkirk home of the Duke of Buccleuch, at that time a convalescent home for wounded officers. Following work at Chiefswood House, Melrose, she opened her own hardy plant nursery. She ran the business for almost 30 years, continuing to work as a freelance gardener specialising in rock garden design. She also wrote regularly for the *Weekly Scotsman* and *The Scots Magazine*. After retiring from gardening in 1948, she published two books on the history and folklore of the Borders, *Tell the Towers Thereof* (1956) and *Ballad Country* (1963). She saw a link between the suffrage movement and pioneering women gardeners: 'a band of young women set on pioneering a new career for women, that of professional gardening . . . We were all of a generation born into the last decade of the

Victorian era, a period when the pioneering spirit in women was strong, and when we joined the Edinburgh School of Gardening for Women in 1910 the suffragettes were at their most militant.' (Elder 1974). FY

• RBGE staff records, 1897.

Elder, M., Works as above, and 'First of the female cultivators', *The Scotsman*, 14 August 1973; (1974) 'We were the pioneers', *The Scots Magazine*, pp. 640–8.

Cowper, A. S. (1992) *Historic Corstorphine*; *The Scotsman*, 31 Dec. 1985 (Appreciation).

ELIOT (or ELLIOT), Grace, n. **Dalrymple,** born probably in Edinburgh c. 1754, died Ville d'Avray, France, 16 May 1823. Courtesan. Daughter of Grisel Brown, and Hew Dalrymple, Edinburgh advocate.

Grace Dalrymple's parents separated in 1758, and some of her childhood was spent in a convent in France or Flanders. In October 1771 she married John (later Sir John) Eliot (1736–86), a Scottish doctor whom she had met at her father's house. Their only child died in infancy and in 1774, following her affair with Arthur Annesley, Viscount Valentia, her husband divorced her in a much publicised case. Grace Eliot then spent some time in France, but returned to England with the 4th Earl of Cholmondley, one of her many lovers. Mixing in high society, she became mistress of the Prince of Wales (later George IV), who may have been the father of her daughter, Georgiana Augusta Frederica Seymour (b. 1782). In 1786, Grace Eliot settled near Paris, where she was for a time mistress of the duc d'Orléans (Philippe Égalité), cousin of Louis XVI. She remained there throughout the French Revolution, and wrote an account of her experiences. Her reliability must be questioned as her *Journal of my life during the French Revolution* (written in 1801, published by her grand-daughter in 1859) contains many inaccuracies, and she undoubtedly exaggerated her experiences. Nevertheless, it is an enthralling and detailed memoir which, given her social position and her friendship with Orléans, also contains much of interest. She certainly spent some time in prison during the Terror. Grace Eliot went back to England after the Revolution, but later returned to France, and died near Sèvres. Interest in her story was revived in 2001 by Eric Rohmer's film *L'Anglaise et le Duc* ('The Englishwoman [sic] and the Duke'), based on her journal. FJ

• Eliot, G. D., Work as above.

ODNB (2004)

ELIZABETH, Angela Marguerite, Queen and **Queen Mother,** n. **Bowes-Lyon,** born probably London 4 August 1900, died Windsor 30 March 2002. Daughter of Nina Cecilia Cavendish-Bentinck, and Sir Claude George Bowes-Lyon, Lord Glamis, later 14th Earl of Strathmore and Kinghorne.

Lady Elizabeth Bowes-Lyon, the ninth of ten children, grew up partly at Glamis Castle, developing a life-long love of Scotland and the outdoors. She met Albert (Bertie), Duke of York (1895–1952) in May 1920. Shy, with a stammer, considered less eligible than his brother, the Prince of Wales, Bertie proposed, and was accepted on the third time of asking. They were married on 26 April 1923 in Westminster Abbey. Her spontaneous gesture of placing her bouquet on the unknown soldier's tomb has been copied by every royal bride since. They had two daughters, Elizabeth Alexandra Mary, born 21 April 1926, and *Margaret Rose (1930–2002) (see Snowdon).

In December 1936, Bertie's brother, now Edward VIII, abdicated to marry American divorcée Wallis Simpson. The Duke of York succeeded as George VI, and his duchess became Queen Consort. Distressed that her shy husband had been thrust into this position, she was determined to support him (and did not forgive the Windsors). Her personality and loyalty enhanced the royal family's image, particularly during the Second World War, when she refused to leave the country or to send her daughters overseas. Remaining in London, they shared some of the privations of ordinary citizens, visiting soldiers, factories and bombsites. When Buckingham Palace was bombed, the Queen was famously reported as saying, 'We can now look the East End in the face'. When, in 1952, George VI died and Princess Elizabeth became Queen, her mother took the title 'HRH Queen Elizabeth the Queen Mother', shortened by press and public to 'the Queen Mother' or 'Queen Mum'. She bought the Castle of Mey, a 16th-century castle in Caithness, where she spent part of each year. Her enthusiasm for her public duties never waned. Privately, she was close to her grandson, Prince Charles. The troubled relationships of the younger generation distressed her, as did the decline of respect for the royal family, but she herself continued to enjoy much admiration. Her extravagance and fondness of gin and horse racing were criticised, but were also the subject of affectionate humour. Her 100th birthday celebrations took place in 2000, and her final public appearance was, stoically, at her daughter

Princess Margaret's funeral. When, soon afterwards, she died herself, long queues formed to pay respects at her lying-in-state. She was buried at Windsor. FJ

• Forbes, G. (2002) *Elizabeth the Queen Mother: a twentieth century life*; *The Observer*, 31 March 2002; *ODNB* (2004) (George VI); Pimlott, B. (1996) *The Queen: a biography of Elizabeth II*; *The Scotsman*, 10 April 2002 (supp.); *The Times*, 1 April 2002; www.royal.gov.uk (official website of the royal family).

ELIZABETH DE BURGH, Queen of Scotland, born probably Down or Antrim, Ireland, before 1302, died Cullen 26 Oct. 1327. Daughter of Margaret de Burgh, and Richard de Burgh, Earl of Ulster.

In 1302, Elizabeth de Burgh married the widowed Robert Bruce (1274–1329), whose first wife Isabel, daughter of Donald, 6th Earl of Mar, had given birth to a daughter, *Marjory Bruce, in the 1290s. Typical of the unions that so often shaped the life cycles of medieval noblewomen, Elizabeth's marriage was arranged primarily to satisfy the diverse political aspirations of her father, her husband, and Edward I of England. Her importance as a political asset became clear in the aftermath of Robert Bruce's seizure of the throne in 1306. Captured at Tain in the company of her sisters-in-law, Mary and *Christian Bruce, her step-daughter, Marjory, and *Isobel of Fife, Countess of Buchan, Elizabeth was sent into confinement in England, first to Burstwick, then to a series of other locations, where she remained a political prisoner for over eight years. She was released only in January 1315, in exchange for valuable English captives taken at the battle of Bannockburn. Elizabeth de Burgh was the mother of Bruce's surviving children, David II, born in 1324, and two daughters. She predeceased her husband. CJN

• Barrow, G. W. S. (1988) *Robert Bruce*; McNeill, T. E. (1980) *Anglo-Norman Ulster*; Neville, C. J. (1993) 'Widows of war: Edward I and the women of Scotland during the War of Independence', in S. S. Walker (ed.) *Wife and Widow in Medieval England*; *ODNB* (2004).

ELLIOT, Jean, born Minto April 1727, died Mount Teviot, Roxburghshire, 29 March 1805. Poet. Daughter of Helen Stewart, and Sir Gilbert Elliot, Lord Minto, Lord Justice.

Jean Elliot is best remembered for the ballad, 'The Flowers of the Forest'. She grew up at home in Minto where she was well educated. In 1745, Jacobite soldiers came to Minto to arrest Sir Gilbert, whom they regarded as a 'Hanoverian Laird', but the 18-year-old Jean was able to implore the soldiers to abandon their investigation while her father hid in a ruined castle.

Ten years later, in the shadow of Culloden, the daughter of the 'Hanoverian Laird' wrote a ballad on a dare from her brother Gilbert, also a songwriter, who wagered a pair of gloves and a set of ribbons if the work demonstrated any artistic merit. Built around one or two surviving lines from an old Scots ballad, Jean Elliot's 'Flowers' is one of three ballads of the same name (one by *Alison Cockburn), and is perhaps the most valuable of the three because 'the Scots vocabulary and rhythm preserve elements of the older tradition' (Kerrigan 1991, p. 6). A tribute to the male population of Ettrick Forest who perished at the Battle of Flodden in 1513, the ballad touchingly sums up the grief felt throughout the nation. Published anonymously in 1755, the ballad became immensely popular and is still often piped at funerals. Jean Elliot also wrote other poems. She moved to Edinburgh with her mother in the 1760s, before returning to Roxburghshire for her remaining years. JJW

• Elliot, G. F. S. (1897) *The Border Elliots and the Family of Minto*; *HSWW*; Kerrigan, C. (ed.) (1991) *An Anthology of Scottish Women Poets*, (1991) 'Reclaiming history: the ballad as a women's tradition', *Études Écossaises* 1; *ODNB* (2004); Tytler, S. and Watson, J. L. (1871) *The Songstresses of Scotland*.

ERMENGARDE de Beaumont, Queen of Scotland, born before 1186, died Balmerino Abbey, Fife, 11 Feb. 1233. Daughter of Richard, Vicomte de Beaumont-sur-Sarthe, France.

In 1186, Henry II of England chose Ermengarde de Beaumont, a distant kinswoman from a relatively insignificant family, to be the bride of William, King of Scots (c. 1142–1214). They were married near Oxford on 5 September 1186, and had three daughters, *Margaret of Scotland, Isabella and Marjory (see Margaret of Scotland), and one son, the future Alexander II. There is little information regarding Ermengarde's political life until 1212, when she may have accompanied William to Durham to mediate with King John. That year, she was unusually active in Scottish affairs, due to William's illness, presiding with Bishop Malveisin over a court case involving Dunfermline Abbey and attaching her seal to the decision. After William's death in 1214, she devoted herself to pious works including founding, in 1229, Balmerino Abbey, where she was buried. KP

• Anderson, A. O. (1922) *Early Sources of Scottish History, AD 500–1286*; Barrow, G. W. S. (ed.) (1971) *Regesta Regum*

Scottorum, ii. Acts of William I, King of Scots; Duncan, A. A. M. (1996) *Scotland: the making of the kingdom*; *ODNB* (2004); Owen, D. D. R. (1997) *William the Lion*.

ERSKINE, Mary, (aka '**Arskine**' etc.) born 1629, died 2 July 1707. Businesswoman, philanthropist, early supporter of female education.

Mary Erskine's first marriage was in 1661 to Robert Kennedy, a writer, who died in 1671; her second was in 1675 to James Hair, a druggist (apothecary), who died in 1683. She had one daughter, Euphame. On the death of her first husband, Mary Erskine became a shopkeeper; on the death of her second, she paid off his debts and became a successful businesswoman. She let property and was a moneylender (also described as a private banker) to businessmen, professionals, and to some women, usually widows continuing their husbands' business, or starting their own. In 1694, she responded generously to a proposal by the Edinburgh Merchant Company to establish a foundation in the Cowgate, Edinburgh, for the schooling of the daughters of Edinburgh burgesses. The aim was to board and educate orphaned, impoverished girls of the city's middle classes. The Merchant Maiden Hospital was founded on 4 June 1694. In 1706, she purchased land and buildings for the Hospital, and on her death in 1707, bequeathed a considerable sum to the foundation, and a similar sum to the Incorporations of Trades who had followed the example of the Company of Merchants to found their own (Trades') Maiden Hospital. Her foundation became the Edinburgh Ladies' College in 1896, then in 1944 Mary Erskine School – one of the oldest girls' schools in the world. Mary Erskine was buried in Greyfriars Churchyard, Edinburgh. JMCD

• Sommerville, M. K. B. (1970, repr. 1993) *The Merchant Maiden Hospital.*
www.scotlandspeople.gov.uk

ESSLEMONT, Mary, CBE, born Aberdeen 3 July 1891, died Aberdeen 25 August 1984. GP and activist. Daughter of Clementina Macdonald, and George Birnie Esslemont, Liberal MP, owners of Aberdeen's first department store.

Mary Esslemont, like her parents, was committed to Liberal causes, becoming life President of the Scottish Young Liberals. She graduated BSc (1914), MA (1915), MBChB (1923) at the University of Aberdeen, taught science in London 1915–19, and took a Diploma in Public Health there in 1924. After working as Assistant MOH at Keighley, Yorkshire, she returned to Aberdeen in 1929 as a pioneering woman GP. Her practice was in the West End, but many of her patients came from the poorer parts of the city and when 'Dr Mary' made home visits to them in winter it was with blankets and a sack of coal in the boot of her car. She was a founding member of the Royal College of General Practitioners, and in 1970 Vice President of the BMA.

Another strand in her life was her attachment to her university. As a mature student, she was elected President of the Student Representative Council in 1922 (there was no other woman President until 1989). She was also the first woman elected to the University Court, from 1946 to 1974, receiving an Honorary LLD in 1954. In her later years, Mary Esslemont was remarkable for her commitment to the cause of women's rights in Scotland, working (voluntarily) for UN International Women's Year in 1975, and thereafter taking an active part in the Scottish Convention of Women (SCOW). SCOW, a voluntary organisation bringing together traditional and more radical women's groups, was instrumental in changing the culture of government in Scotland, being represented on the Scottish Constitutional Convention. 'Dr Mary' was one of its most energetic promoters in the north. This hardworking and influential life led to a CBE in 1955, and to the Freedom of the City of Aberdeen in 1981. JJC

• Univ. of Aberdeen Library, Archives, MS 3179 Mary Esslemont Papers, MS 3620/1–3 Interview (1984), *Roll of Graduates.*
Ritchie, S. (1994) 'Dr Mary Esslemont', *Aberdeen University Review*, LV, 4, 192.
Private information.

EUPHEMIA of Ross, Queen of Scotland, born c. 1329, died 1388/9. Daughter of Margaret Graham, and Hugh, Earl of Ross.

Euphemia of Ross may have been born before her parents obtained a retrospective legitimation of their marriage in November 1329. Her first husband was John Randolph, Earl of Moray (d. 1346). In 1355, she married Robert the Steward (1316–90), who was crowned as Robert II on 26 March 1371. For reasons that are unclear, Euphemia's coronation was delayed until a date between 6 December 1372 and 24 March 1373. Euphemia and Robert had two sons, David and Walter, and at least two daughters, Egidia and Elizabeth. The King also had three sons by his first wife, Elizabeth Mure – John (the future Robert III who married *Annabella Drummond), Robert and Alexander. The place of David and

Walter in the royal succession was stated in an entail of 4 April 1373; only after the failure of the male lines descending from Robert II's first marriage could they or their male heirs succeed. It may be significant that Euphemia was not crowned until shortly before this entail was made. Euphemia's sons were, however, the beneficiaries of substantial royal patronage after 1371, suggesting that she exercised considerable influence as Queen. SB

• Boardman, S. (1996) *The Early Stewart Kings*; *ODNB (2004) (Bibl.).

EVOTA (EVE) of Stirling, fl. 1304. Property owner and garrison-supplier.

Evota of Stirling, who was probably a widow, held a small parcel of land near Stirling. Between 1297 and 1304, Stirling Castle went back and forth between Scottish and English control during the War of Independence; the English retook it on 20 July 1304. At some point during this period, Evota, who it seems had fallen on difficult times, eked out a living by providing the English garrison with victuals and supplies from the surrounding countryside. When her activities were discovered by her fellow townspeople, she was jailed for ten weeks, stripped of her property, and banished from Scotland. She appealed to Edward I of England in July 1304, asking for compensation or the return of her property in view of her services to the English. The King told her to petition his officials in Scotland, but the result is unknown. SEM

• *Calendar of Documents Relating to Scotland* (1888–1986) iv, no. 1800; v, no. 521.

Goldstein, R. J. (1991) 'The women of the Wars of Independence in literature and history', in *Studies in Scottish Literature* 26, p. 275; Marshall, R. (1983) *Virgins and Viragos*, p. 49.

F

FAIRFIELD, Cecily (or Cicily) Isabel (aka **Cissie, Panther) [Rebecca West, Rachel East, Conway Power],**‡ DBE, m. **Andrews,** born London 21 Dec. 1892, died London 15 March 1983. Journalist, novelist, critic, travel-writer, feminist and political commentator. Daughter of Isabella Campbell Mackenzie, governess, pianist and copy-typist, and Charles Fairfield, Irish-born soldier, journalist and entrepreneur.

After Charles Fairfield abandoned the family in 1901 (dying in 1906), their mother took the three children from London to her native Edinburgh, where they lived in Hope Park Square (represented in Rebecca West's novel, *The Judge*) and Buccleuch Place. Cecily Fairfield was educated as a scholarship student at George Watson's Ladies' College, winning 'Best Essay' prize, 1906–7. She campaigned for women's suffrage and at 14 published a letter in *The Scotsman* (16 October 1907) on 'Women's Electoral Claims', writing later: 'Scotland has come out of the militant suffrage agitation very well indeed. There is something magnificently dramatic about the way the Scottish woman . . . has quietly gone about her warfare' (West [1911] 1982, p. 192). Her first, unpublished, novel, 'The Sentinel', written in her late teens, portrays its heroine's sexual and political awakening during suffrage unrest. *The Judge* (1922), featuring a young Edinburgh suffragette, was described by Hugh MacDiarmid as 'unfortunately – the best *Scottish* novel of recent years' (MacDiarmid, [1926], 1995, p. 346).

Cecily was the youngest of three siblings. Her sister **Josephine Letitia (Lettie) Denny Fairfield** (1885–1978) qualified in medicine, Edinburgh 1907, then studied law and became a medical administrator; she supervised women doctors in the First World War and was made CBE in 1919. Winifred (Winnie) Fairfield (1887–1960), to whom Cecily was close, trained as a teacher. All three sisters, young socialists and suffragists, joined the Fabian Society. The family moved back to London in 1910, where 17 year-old Cecily studied for a year at the Academy of Dramatic Art in London and worked briefly as an actor. She soon turned to journalism, publishing her first theatre review in the *Evening Standard* and writing for a new feminist journal, *The Freewoman*. Taking the pseudonym 'Rebecca West' from a strong-willed character in Ibsen's play *Rosmersholm*, she swiftly established a reputation with her often iconoclastic writing; other pieces appeared in the *Daily News* and socialist *Clarion*. Her journalism led to a fateful meeting. After reviewing H. G. Wells's novel *Marriage* (1912), Rebecca West, aged 19, met the famous author, then 46 and married. An intense, troubled, ten-year relationship began in 1913, and their son Anthony

Panther West was born in 1914. Single motherhood was difficult, and the relationship deteriorated; her relationship with Anthony West (1914–87), later a writer himself, also grew recriminatory.

Her first published book, a study of Henry James (1916), was followed by a novel, *The Return of the Soldier* (1918). Eight novels were published during her lifetime, notably *The Fountain Overflows* (1956), drawing on childhood memories. Three more were published posthumously. Rebecca West's non-fiction is particularly celebrated. She contributed to many British newspapers and journals, among them the feminist journal *Time and Tide* in the 1920s. A frequent visitor to the USA, she also wrote for major American publications including *Herald-Tribune*. Her greatest achievement is widely considered to be *Black Lamb and Grey Falcon* (1941), drawing on visits to Yugoslavia in the 1930s and inspired especially by the history, culture and people of Serbia, suffering Nazi occupation when the book was published. Her near contemporary, Scottish ethnographer **Margaret Hasluck**, n. **Hardie** (1885–1948), was carrying out sustained, scholarly work in nearby Albania in the 1930s, and later advised Special Operations Executive (Clark 2000). Rebecca West's reporting of Nuremberg and other treason trials resulted in the highly regarded *The Meaning of Treason* (1947) and *A Train of Powder* (1955). Opposed to fascism, she also spoke out against Communism in the 1950s and is often seen as having grown increasingly reactionary. Yet, helpful to Emma Goldman in the 1920s, she was also generous to other artists and refugees later. Her awards included the Order of Saint Sava 1937, CBE 1949, Chevalier of French Légion d'honneur 1957, DBE 1959 and honorary degrees from New York and Edinburgh universities. She was a Member of the American Academy of Arts and Sciences.

Rebecca West knew many famous people, but always felt an outsider. Her liaisons, some with well-known men, including Max (Lord) Beaverbrook, were generally unhappy. However, marriage in 1930 to a scholarly banker, Henry Maxwell Andrews (1894–1968), lasted until his death. Scottish connections continued through family contact and visits; she also participated in the 1962 Edinburgh Festival forum on censorship and attended the Scottish Writers' Conference that year. She appeared in the film *Reds* (1981) two years before her death, aged 90. She described herself as 'half-Scottish and half-Irish' (letter to Harold Guinzberg, Nov. 1956, West 2000, p. 315). *Family*

Memories, written during her last two decades and published posthumously, shows her lasting preoccupation with 'the rich textures of my mother's ancestry as manufactured by the Scottish tradition' (West [1987] 1992, p. 17). Re-publication and the discovery of unpublished material by this important, wide-ranging writer have helped reinvigorate her reputation. CA

• Beinecke Rare Book and Manuscript Library, Yale Univ. Library: Rebecca West papers; McFarlin Library, Special Collections Department, Univ. of Tulsa, Oklahoma: Rebecca West papers.

West, R., Works as above, and (1982) *The Young Rebecca: Writings of Rebecca West 1911–17*, selected and edited by J. Marcus, (2000) *Selected Letters of Rebecca West*, B. K. Scott, ed. See also Glendinning (Select Bibl.) and www.eup.ed.ac.uk Anderson, C. (2000) 'Feminine space, feminine sentence' in C. Anderson and A. Christianson (eds) *Scottish Women's Fiction 1920s to 1960s*; Clark, M. (2000) 'Margaret Masson Hasluck', in J. B. Allcock and A. Young, *Black Lambs and Grey Falcons*; Devine, E. (ed.) (1984) *The Annual Obituary 1983*; DNB, 1981–5; Glendinning, V. (1987) *Rebecca West* (Select Bibl.; source material); MacDiarmid, H. (1922) 'Following Rebecca West in Edinburgh', reprinted in B. K. Scott (ed.) (1990) *The Gender of Modernism*, (1926) 'Newer Scottish fiction (1)', reprinted in A. Riach (ed. and intro.) (1995) *Contemporary Scottish Studies*; ODNB (2004) (see Andrews, Cicily; Hasluck, Margaret); Rollyson, C. E. (1995) *Rebecca West*; Scott, B. K. (1995) *Refiguring Modernism* vol. 1: *The Women of 1928*; WWW (1991) vol. VIII, 1981–1990.

FENWICK, Margaret Taylor Naysmith, n. Mands, MBE, born Dundee 19 August 1919, died Dundee 8 Feb. 1992. Weaver, trade unionist. Daughter of Hope Stewart, domestic servant, and Alexander Mands, gasworks labourer.

Margaret Mands attended Stobswell School, where she won a bursary but, at 14, she became an apprentice weaver at the SCWS Taybank Works. Her parents and brothers were active trade unionists, and she was conscious of her rights from the very beginning. Aged 15, she discovered that she was paid less than older women doing the same work; she demanded, and won, equal pay. She joined the Dundee & District Union of Jute & Flax and Kindred Textile Operatives, moving on to the Management Committee by about 1948. A fellow weaver remembers her as always standing up for their rights, even when they were not aware they had a grievance: 'She liked to hear herself! But she was a good friend, and always ready for a laugh'. She married Andrew Small Fenwick, jute dresser, in 1938. Her husband worked in the same mill, though he had to go into the army during the war. They had four children. She continued to work as a weaver until January 1961 when she became assistant secretary of the union. The following year the union called its first all-out strike, and the women won a 1% pay rise.

Margaret Fenwick continued campaigning for parity with men throughout her life. In 1971, she became the first woman General Secretary of a British trade union, one of the biggest in Dundee with around 5,000 members. A small but hefty, determined woman, with a perpetual cigarette, she did not take kindly to opposition but, unlike previous union leaders, was prepared to work with employers on issues such as recruitment and government protection for the industry. She served on various jute-related committees, and did much to improve health and safety as well as pay. In 1973, her hard work was acknowledged with an MBE. About five years later, with the jute industry in recession, she retired, but continued to work on industrial tribunals and to serve as a JP until the year before her death. IMH

• Dundee City Archives, Union minute books; Dundee Oral History Project Archive 040, Central Library, Dundee, Interview with Margaret Fenwick.
Dundee Courier & Advertiser 10 Feb. 1992 (obit.); *ODNB* (2004).
Private information (fellow jute worker).

FERGUSON, Christiana *see* **CATRIONA NIC FHEARGHAIS** (fl. 1745–6)

FERGUSSON, Mary Isolen (Molly), OBE, born Stoke, Devonport, 28 April 1914, died London 30 Nov. 1997. Civil engineer. Daughter of Mildred Gladys Mercer, and John N. Fraser Fergusson, MB, maker of early radiography research equipment.

At York College, Molly Fergusson was head girl and was encouraged in her interest in engineering. She graduated BSc Hons in civil engineering from the University of Edinburgh in 1936 and, having returned to her roots, remained in Edinburgh all her working life. As an unpaid indentured trainee with the Scottish firm of civil engineers Blyth and Blyth in 1936, she showed exceptional promise and, after her first year, was paid 30 shillings a week (£1.50). She worked with the senior partner on many important infrastructure projects, including bridges in the Highlands and Islands. She made history by becoming the first female senior partner in a UK civil engineering firm, on 1 January 1948. Molly Fergusson worked with relentless energy on

projects such as the Markinch paper mills and the River Leven water purification scheme, and expected the same dedication from her juniors. The first woman to be elevated to a fellowship of the ICE (1957), on retiring in 1978 she continued with consultancies, using the fees to endow bursaries for young engineers. She was active in the WES and the Edinburgh Soroptimists, was made an OBE in 1979, and was awarded an honorary DSc at Heriot-Watt University (1985) for her work in encouraging women to take up engineering careers. She never married, but took great interest in her nephews and was active in the scouting movement for 35 years. NCB

• Heriot-Watt Univ. Citation for honorary degree of DSc, 1985; *The Scotsman*, 9 Jan. 1998 (obit.); *University of Edinburgh Calendar*, 1936–7.
Personal communications from S. Macartney, Blyth and Blyth, Edinburgh.

FERRIER, Susan Edmonstone, born Edinburgh 7 Sept. 1782, died Edinburgh 5 Nov. 1854. Novelist. Daughter of Helen Coutts, and James Ferrier, Writer to the Signet and later Principal Clerk of Session.

The youngest daughter among ten surviving children, Susan Ferrier was born in Edinburgh's Old Town and grew up in the New Town in George Street. She was probably educated at James Stalker's Academy (a co-educational infants' school) and at home. Her mother died in 1797, followed by the early deaths overseas of three brothers, who were in the army. After her sister Jane Ferrier's marriage in 1804, she kept house for her father.

The Ferriers had literary connections and Susan met Henry Mackenzie, author of *The Man of Feeling*, and Sir Walter Scott, who became a friend; her autograph album contains signatures of Wordsworth, James Hogg and others. Her lawyer brother John Ferrier married the sister of John Wilson (writer 'Christopher North'), Robert Burns addressed verse to her sister Jane, and John Leyden wrote sentimental poetry to her. She accompanied her father, legal agent to the 5th Duke of Argyll, on his business visits to Inveraray. There she encountered Highland landscapes and the Duke's family, forming a friendship with his grand-daughter Charlotte Clavering (1790–1869), niece of Charlotte Campbell (see Bury, Lady Charlotte). In 1809, they began planning a novel together. However, apart from one chapter, Susan Ferrier wrote *Marriage* alone, encouraged by Charlotte, to whom she wrote light-heartedly, imagining her work in print: 'Enchanting sight! Already do I behold myself arrayed in an old mouldy covering, thumbed and creased, and filled with dog's-ears' (Doyle 1898, p. 76).

Marriage was published by Blackwood (1818), anonymously, as Susan Ferrier wished – some characters reputedly had real-life models, such as *Anne Damer. It was attributed by many to Walter Scott; he publicly praised his 'sister shadow', the author of this 'very lively work' (Scott 1819, p. 330), perhaps innocent of her identity. *Marriage* contains conventional didacticism but also robust satire and richly comic characters. Reportedly admired by James Ferrier, who was amazed on learning of his daughter's authorship, the novel was described by *Anne Grant as the 'production of a clever, caustic mind' (Grant 1844, p. 57). Despite its success, Susan Ferrier received only £150. *The Inheritance* (1824) was largely written at Morningside, where the family spent summers. It was well received and, with a contract negotiated by her brother John Ferrier, earned £1,000. Much of her third novel, *Destiny* (1831), was probably written at Stirling Castle where, after her father's death in January 1829, she stayed for a time with Jane, whose husband, General Samuel Graham, was Governor there. Dedicated to Walter Scott, who had negotiated a generous payment (£1,700), this often pungently satirical, now somewhat neglected, work was also enjoyed by Anne Grant.

Susan Ferrier lived in increasing seclusion as her health, in particular her eyesight, declined. In 1830 she visited a London 'oculist' (Doyle 1898, p. 208). Her eyesight was failing so badly she often had to stay in darkened rooms, and writing was difficult: fragments remain of a further novel, 'Maplehurst Manor'. She became deeply religious, joining the Free Church after the 1843 Disruption and supporting charitable causes, temperance, missions and the emancipation of slaves. The novels appeared in editions bearing her name for the first time in 1852. Admired by 19th-century critics, they have attracted fresh interest since the later 20th century. CA

• BL: Susan Ferrier MSS (included in Bentley Papers), Add. 46614 ff.17–22, and Add. 71926, ff.193–4, f.195; NLS: Susan Ferrier Papers, Acc. 8585 (microfilm), letters etc. in other accessions (Accs. 7224, 8304, 10759, 11030).
Ferrier, S. [1818] *Marriage*, 3 vols, (1997) H. Foltinek (ed.), intro. K. Kirkpatrick; [1824] *The Inheritance*, 3 vols, (1984) intro. J. Irvine; [1831] *Destiny*, 3 vols, 'Recollections of Visits to Ashestiel and Abbotsford', *Temple Bar* magazine, 40, Feb. 1874, pp. 329–35; 'Maplehurst Manor', see Yeo below.
Cullinan, M. (1984) *Susan Ferrier*; Doyle, J. A. (ed.) (1898) *Memoir and Correspondence of Susan Ferrier 1782–1854*; Grant, A. (1844) *Memoir and Correspondence of Mrs Grant of Laggan*, vol. III; Grant, A. (1957) *Susan Ferrier of Edinburgh*; HSWW (Bibl.); ODNB (2004); Parker, W. M. (1965) *Susan Ferrier and John Galt*; Scott, W. (1819) *Tales of my Landlord: a legend of Montrose*, 3rd series (4 vols) vol. IV; Yeo, E. (1982) *Susan Ferrier 1782–1854*, NLS Exhibition Catalogue, includes fragments of 'Maplehurst Manor'.

FIFE, Isobel of, Countess of Buchan, c. 1285–c. 1314. Daughter of Anna, possibly daughter of Sir Alan Durward, and Colban, Earl of Fife.

The men of Isobel of Fife's paternal family, who belonged to the long-established native aristocracy, claimed a hereditary right to inaugurate the kings of Scotland at their enthronement. Her own actions following Robert Bruce's victory at Methven in 1306 demonstrate how medieval noblewomen might play decisive roles in the course of their lives. In 1306, Isobel's nephew, heir to the earldom of Fife, was in English captivity; the family of her husband, John Comyn, Earl of Buchan, was reacting in shock to Bruce's murder of their chief representative in the Greyfriars' kirk in Dumfries. When Bruce, anxious to consolidate his kingship claim, arranged his enthronement at Scone, traditional site of Scottish royal inaugurations, Isobel abandoned her husband's faction and, with some of his men and horses, rode to Scone. Several chroniclers, English and Scottish, relate that she performed the rituals traditionally associated with the male representatives of the Fife family. Her actions earned her the enmity of Edward I, now at open war with Robert I. Captured at the sanctuary of Tain in the summer of 1306, together with the king's wife, *Elizabeth de Burgh, and daughter, *Marjory Bruce, Isobel was imprisoned at Berwick Castle in a specially constructed cage of wood and iron, hung out over the walls so 'that all they who pass may see her, and know for what cause she is there' (Palgrave 1837, p. 358; Luard 1890, iii, p. 324; Riley 1865, p. 367). Dubbed a 'faithless conspirator' against the English crown, she was not released from strict confinement at Berwick until 1310, when she was permitted to take up residence in the Carmelite house in the town. Edward II, however, continued to consider her a potentially dangerous figure in the pro-Bruce cause; she was ordered to leave the Carmelites and spent the rest of her life in the custody, if honourable, of an English kinsman of her Comyn husband. CJN

• Luard, H. R. (ed.) (1890) *Flores historiarum*, 3 vols; Neville, C. J. (1993) 'Widows of war . . .', in S. S. Walker (ed.) *Wife* and Widow in Medieval England; Palgrave, F. (ed.) (1837) Documents and Records Illustrating the History of Scotland; ODNB (2004); Riley, H. T. (ed.) (1865) Willelmi Rishanger . . . Chronica et Annales; Skene, W. F. (ed.) (1871) Johannis de Fordun Gesta Annalia.

FINDLATER, Mary Williamina, born Lochearnhead 28 March 1865, died St Fillans 22 Nov. 1963.
FINDLATER, Jane Helen, born Edinburgh 4 Nov. 1866, died Comrie 20 May 1946. Novelists and short story writers. Daughters of Sarah Borthwick (see Jane Borthwick), hymnwriter, and Eric Findlater, Free Church minister.

Mary and Jane Findlater were brought up with an older sister at their father's manse in Lochearnhead and educated by governesses. They were intelligent, quick-tongued girls with striking looks inherited from their father, who was rumoured (they were disturbed to learn in later years) to be the child of 'a Spanish pirate'. They wrote from childhood. Mary said as an old woman, 'I can't remember when we *began* to write, we were always writing' (Mackenzie 1964, p. 18).

When their father died in 1886 the family moved to Prestonpans, living on a tiny income. Both sisters continued to write, and a collection of Mary's poems, *Songs and Sonnets*, was published in 1895. Their breakthrough came with the publication of Jane's first novel *The Green Graves of Balgowrie* (1896). It was well received and they became accepted in literary and intellectual circles. Concern for their mother's health caused them to move to Devon, living in Paignton (1901–23). Admirers of their work included William Gladstone, Ellen Terry and Rudyard Kipling. On a tour of America they met notables including Andrew Carnegie, Frances Hodgson Burnett, William James and Henry James, who later became a close friend.

Both Mary and Jane Findlater published novels individually and wrote short stories. Jane's stories were of particular interest for their strong and sympathetic depiction of farm servants, tinkers and other country people. They collaborated on several books, of which the best known is *Crossriggs* (1908). Though the sisters had always had a very close relationship, this literary collaboration was particularly significant: 'after the turn of the century, the two sisters increasingly relied on each other for support in a changing and violent world' (*HSWW*, p. 303).

During the 1920s their work was going out of fashion. In 1923 they moved to Rye in Sussex, and in 1940 to Comrie in Perthshire, where Jane died in 1946. Mary died in 1963, aged 98. During her last ten years, her 'prodigious memory and . . . astonishing power of re-creating the past in conversational narrative' (Mackenzie 1964, p. xii) gave her biographer an unmatched insight into the sisters' lives. Their work, now out of print, represents the predicament of women writers of their time, exemplifying a 'profound and paralysing internal debate concerning sexual and gender freedoms' (*HSWW*, p. 291). MARB
• Findlater, M., Findlater J., Works as above and see *HSWW* (Bibl.).
HSWW (Bibl.); Mackenzie, E. (1964) *The Findlater Sisters: literature and friendship*; ODNB (2004).

FINDLAY, Jessie, n. **Macmillan,** born Glasgow 30 July 1898, died East Kilbride 10 Nov. 1989. Socialist Sunday School teacher and Labour Party activist. Daughter of Kate Thompson, domestic servant, and John Macmillan, tailor.

The eldest of five children, Jessie Macmillan had a happy childhood in a lively socialist household. She attended Napiershall Street School until she was 15, then worked in shops in Glasgow, eventually being sacked for recruiting women into the Shop Assistants' Union. She took part in the Glasgow rent strike in 1915 and on 31 January 1919 experienced the events of 'Black Friday' when soldiers patrolled the streets of Glasgow after clashes between police and workers in George Square. She attended the Socialist Sunday School (SSS) in Maryhill as a child and later became its most dedicated teacher. Fifty children heard speakers such as James Maxton and John Maclean and were taught not only the principles of socialism but also how to chair and conduct meetings and run the organisation.

In 1922, she married Charles Findlay, a police constable, and devoted her energies to raising her four children. In 1951, she resumed political activities, working for the Co-operative Society, SCWG and the Labour Party in Glasgow. She acted as a sub-agent for Neil Carmichael when he won the significant Woodside by-election in 1962. When she moved to East Kilbride in 1967, her eldest daughter, Edith Findlay, carried on her work in the SSS, becoming its national secretary and editor of the *Young Socialist*. Jessie Findlay worked as her local party fund collector and in 1979 was awarded the Certificate of Merit for outstanding voluntary service to the Labour Party. Due to her lively personality, she was often interviewed for television documentaries on her early experiences as a Clydeside socialist. ACa

• Gallacher Memorial Library, GCU Research Collections: SSS history; People's History Museum, Manchester: Merit Award acceptance speech by Jessie Findlay.
Interview with Edith Findlay by Neil Rafeek, 1995.
Labour Party conference report 1979; Mackie, L., 'How Glasgow Preached Revolution' (interview with Jessie Findlay), *The Guardian*, 20 August 1982; Sheffield Film Co-operative (1984) *Red Skirts on Clydeside* (Scottish Film Archive.)
Private information: Janey Buchan.

FINELLA, fl. c. 995. Assassin. Daughter of Cunchar, mormaer of Angus.

According to contemporary Irish annals, Cinaed mac Máel Coluim (Kenneth II MacMalcolm), King of Alba, was killed in 995 'through deceit'. An early Scottish regnal list elaborates on this, noting (relying perhaps upon information from a 'feud-saga') that the king was killed by his own men in Fettercairn through the treachery of a certain Finella (or Finuela), daughter of the mormaer (similar to earl) of Angus, whose only son had been killed by Cinaed at Dunsinnan. No more than this is known. John of Fordoun's fanciful medieval telling of the tale of Finella, whom he portrays as being in league with Cinaed's rivals, and the impossibly elaborate death-machine she contrived to assassinate the king, is truly fascinating, not least because he was well placed to know local Fettercairn folklore. The story goes that she led the King to a secluded cottage. In the centre of the room stood a statue of a boy with hidden crossbows attached by strings all round. She promised the King 'amazing sport' if he were to touch the statue's head. When he pulled it towards him, the crossbows were released and he died in a hail of arrows. JEF

• Skene, W. F. (ed.) (1871) *Johannis de Fordun Chronica Gentis Scottorum*, iv, pp. 32–3.
Anderson, M. O. (1973) *Kings and Kingship in Early Scotland*; Duncan, A. A. M. (2002) *The Kingship of the Scots, 842–1292*.

FINNIE, Agnes, died Edinburgh 6 March 1645. Shopkeeper and money-lender, Potterrow, Edinburgh. Executed for witchcraft.

Agnes Finnie, widow of James Robertson, ran an apparently profitable business without evidence of male intervention. She sold fish, eggs, cakes, salt and other consumer goods. While she was central to her community, she also generated a great deal of friction. Many were displeased with the quality of her goods and her prices. But the main source of tension was her determination to collect on goods bought on credit and cash loans. Agnes Finnie also cursed in response to social slights, such as when her godchild was not given her name. For over 25 years she responded to her neighbours' complaints with curses, threats and sometimes physical abuse. Her daughter, Margaret Robertson, seems to have acquired her mother's style as she was twice charged with flyting (scolding).

Agnes Finnie was arrested in June 1644. Officials searched her house for wax images, pictures, toads or other witchcraft implements, but found nothing incriminating. After being investigated before the Edinburgh Presbytery, she was placed in the Tolbooth. She complained to the Privy Council about mistreatment and languishing in prison. She was tried on 20 December 1644. Unable to get a confession, corroborating testimony from another witch or any real evidence of demonic involvement, the investigating authorities went to trial solely on the basis of misfortunes allegedly caused by her after curses and quarrels. Her words are exemplary of those attributed to other witchcraft suspects and women charged with slander or flyting. Some of the phrases included: 'Thow sall nevir eat moir in this worald', 'I gar [order] the devill tak ane byt [bite] of the said Bessie', 'Weill, gif I be ane witche, ayther [either] ye or yours sall have better cause to call me soe', 'The devill ryd about the toun with yow and all yours', and 'the devill blaw yow blind' (*Selected Justiciary Cases*, pp. 638–44). Her language was enough for the jury to convict. She was executed on Thursday, 6 March 1645 on the Castle Hill of Edinburgh. LM

• NAS: JC40/9, Witchcraft Papers.
RPC, 2nd Series, vol. 8, pp. 134–5; Smith, J. (ed.) *Selected Justiciary Cases*, vol. 3, pp. 627–75; Survey of Scottish Witchcraft, www.arts.ed.ac.uk/witches

FISH, Elizabeth Mary Jane, born Glasgow 22 Dec. 1860, died Paisley 21 March 1944. First elected woman president (1913) of the EIS. Daughter of Jane McNaughton, and William Fish, chaplain to Sharp's Institution in Perth.

Educated at Sharp's Institution, Elizabeth Fish became a pupil-teacher in Glasgow, came first in Scotland in the Queen's Scholarship examination, and studied at the Glasgow Church of Scotland Training College. She taught for the Glasgow School Board (1881–95), at its Pupil-Teachers' Institute (1895–1907), and in Higher Grade Schools (1907–20). She also ran evening classes for the cure of stammering and lectured in hygiene and physiology. Having graduated LLA from

St Andrews University in 1885, she studied French and Italian (SA medal) and was president of the SMLA for two years. Her final post was as principal teacher of modern languages at Bellahouston Academy (1920–5). Elizabeth Fish held office in the Glasgow branch of the CTA, was president of the Glasgow Local Association of the EIS, was active in the annual Ladies' Meeting of the EIS, and wrote for the EIS paper, *The Educational News*. In the June 1913 EIS presidential election, she polled 4,822 votes against three male candidates, whose combined votes totalled 3,068. She condemned the low pay of women teachers, but although she acknowledged the principle of equal pay, she cautioned against its demand, for fear of alienating the public. JMCD

• *Glasgow Herald*, 22 March 1944 (obit.); *ODNB (2004)*; SB; *Scot. Educ. Jour.*, 27, 3 (1914).

FLEMING, Marjory, born Kirkcaldy 15 Jan. 1803, died Kirkcaldy 19 Dec. 1811. Journal-writer, child author. Daughter of Isabella Rae, and James Fleming, accountant.

Marjory Fleming was raised in Kirkcaldy. A visit to her aunt Marianne Keith's family in Edinburgh, probably in 1809 after her sister's birth, became a prolonged stay. She was tutored by her cousin, Isabella Keith, and between 1810 and 1811 wrote three journals, poems and letters, recording thoughts about Scottish history, lessons, friends, her behaviour, and so on – 'I like to here [sic] my own sex praised but not the other' (McLean 1999, p. 8). She died soon after returning home in July 1811, probably of meningitis. Her writings, preserved by her family, came to the attention of H. B. Farnie who published embellished extracts in 1858, coining the name 'Pet Marjorie'. John Brown extended the extracts in 1863 and began the fictitious story of her great friendship with Walter Scott. The 'child genius' fascinated Victorians; Leslie Stephen wrote her entry for the *DNB* (misnamed Margaret), as its youngest subject. She has continued to intrigue; in 1946, Oriel Malet wrote a fictionalised biography of her and, in 1969, composer Richard Rodney Bennett set some of her poems to music in *A Garland for Marjory Fleming*. Her own writings, published in 1934 and 1999, throw fascinating light on early 19th-century middle-class childhood. EE

• NLS: MSS 1096–1100.
Fleming, M. (1934) *The Journals, Letters & Verses of Marjory Fleming*, A. Esdaile, ed. (facsimile), (1999) *Marjory's Book*, B. McLean, ed.

Gent, F. (1947) 'Marjory Fleming and her biographers', *Scot. Hist. Rev.* 26; Malet, O. [1946] (2000) *Marjory Fleming*; *ODNB* (2004).

FLEMING, Williamina, n. **Stevens,** born Dundee 15 May 1857, died Cambridge, MA, USA, 21 May 1911. Astronomer. Daughter of Mary Walker, and Robert Stevens, carver and gilder.

Soon after her marriage to James Fleming in 1877, Williamina Fleming emigrated to America with her husband. He later abandoned her, leaving her to support herself and her child. In 1881, she was appointed by Harvard College Observatory Director E. C. Pickering to a humble post, copying and routine computing. The work expanded significantly with the founding in 1886 of the Henry Draper Memorial, a fund given by Draper's widow for the examination of the spectra of stars which, in a new observational project, were photographed in their hundreds. E. C. Pickering employed women specifically for this work, and Williamina Fleming was assigned the task of devising an empirical system to classify the stars by their spectra. Her classification, labelling stars according to letters of the alphabet, became the basis of all future systems. In the first four years she catalogued tens of thousands of stars and discovered hundreds of unusual objects. She published some papers in her own name, but much of the catalogue work appeared in the official publications of the Harvard Observatory, for which she also did the proof-reading. Williamina Fleming's efficient supervision of her team of women saw the work expand to become one of the most famous and successful ventures in the history of astronomy, providing one of the earliest opportunities for women in science. In 1899, she was elevated to a post of Curator of Astronomical Photographs, the first woman to hold a formal appointment at Harvard. She was elected an Honorary Member of the Royal Astronomical Society, a rare accolade in that then all-male institution. She was still in office at her death. MTB

• Fleming, W. (1893) 'A field for women's work in astronomy', *Astronomy and Astrophysics*, 12, pp. 638–89, (1907) 'A photographic study of variable stars, forming a part of the H. Draper Memorial'.
Cannon, A. J. (1911) 'Mrs Fleming', *Scientific American*, 102, p. 547 (obit.); Mack, P. E. (1990) 'Strategies and compromises: women in astronomy at Harvard College Observatory, 1870–1920', *Jour. Hist. Astr.* 21, pp. 67–75.

FLETCHER, Christian, fl. 1650–62; **DOUGLAS, Elizabeth,** died Barras 1653, daughter of Jean Fraser, and John Douglas of Barras; **ERSKINE, Lady Mary, Countess Marischal** and **Countess of Panmure,** born 1599, died after 1661, daughter of Marie Stewart, and John, Earl of Mar. Protectors of the Scottish regalia.

In June 1651, faced with Oliver Cromwell's invasion, Parliament gave the Scottish regalia to George Keith, 7th Earl Marischal, for safe-keeping in Dunnottar Castle. When the Earl was captured, he sent the key to the hiding-place to his mother, Lady Mary Erskine, Dowager Countess Marischal. The Countess retrieved the regalia, but with English troops approaching, entrusted them to the castle's commander, George Ogilvie of Barras and his wife, Elizabeth Douglas. With the castle's fall imminent, Elizabeth agreed to hide the regalia without revealing the hiding-place to her husband. In March 1652, Christian Fletcher, wife of James Grainger, minister of nearby Kinneff, gained the besiegers' permission to visit Elizabeth Douglas. The women hid the regalia in bundles of flax, then Christian Fletcher and her maid carried them back through the English encampment to Kinneff. The regalia remained hidden under the church floor until 1660.

When Dunnottar Castle surrendered in May 1652, the Ogilvies were questioned about the regalia's whereabouts. Elizabeth Douglas refused to reveal the hiding-place, even when threatened with torture, saying that the regalia had been taken to France by Sir John Keith, son of the Countess Marischal. The Countess circulated a rumour to this effect. Elizabeth Douglas and her husband were kept in close confinement for seven months, until John Keith was captured in England and, to safeguard the regalia, confirmed the rumour. The couple were allowed to return to Barras. Elizabeth Douglas died shortly afterwards, in 1653, revealing the hiding-place to her husband only on her deathbed. Her role was commemorated in *Lady Caroline Oliphant's song, 'Dunnottar Castle'. When Charles II returned in 1660, both the Countess Marischal and George Ogilvie claimed major responsibility for having kept the regalia safe. The controversy lasted until 1702. Parliament rewarded Christian Fletcher for her part with a payment of 2,000 merks in 1661. EE

• Bell, W. (ed.) (1829) *Papers relative to the Regalia of Scotland*; Howden, C. R. A. (ed.) (1896) 'Papers relative to the preservation of the Honours of Scotland in Dunnottar Castle, 1651–2', in *Diary of Sir Archibald Johnson, Lord Wariston, 1639, and Other Papers.*

FLETCHER, Eliza, n. **Dawson,** born Oxton, Tadcaster, Yorkshire, 15 Jan. 1770, died Grasmere 5 Feb. 1858. Autobiographer, hostess and philanthropist. Daughter of Elizabeth Hill, and Miles Dawson, surveyor and small landowner.

Eliza Dawson, whose mother came from a Yorkshire gentry family and died at her birth, was educated at the Manor School, York. On 16 July 1791, against her father's wishes, she married Scottish advocate Archibald Fletcher, a Gaelic speaker and burgh reformer, and moved to Edinburgh. Until her husband's death in 1828, she remained close to the reforming politics of Edinburgh Whiggism. Her autobiography gives an outstanding account of early 19th-century Edinburgh literary and reforming circles, tracing her own political and philanthropic commitments and chronicling a happy family life. She shared her husband's political sympathies with the early principles of the French Revolution, though not with more radical revolutionary politics. She wrote of the 'strong tide of Tory prejudice' against reformers in Edinburgh in the 1790s, including the rumour that she possessed a miniature guillotine (Fletcher 1875, pp. 65–71). Her attractive personality and political interests allowed her to play a lively though not uncontested role in the circles surrounding the *Edinburgh Review*, founded in 1802. With *Elizabeth Hamilton and *Anne Grant of Laggan, she helped to provide the sociable and conversational contexts in which men such as Francis Jeffrey, Henry Brougham, Dugald Stewart and many others flourished. Her house became 'for many years the centre of attraction to everything that is elegant or enlightened about town' (Grant 1845, I, p. 239).

Eliza Fletcher's autobiography also identifies the close connections between a network of literary women, including Hamilton, Grant, *Joanna Baillie, *Margaret Cullen and *Mary Brunton, and the English dissenters Anna Barbauld and Catherine Cappe. Their common interests included the education of women and philanthropic action. In March 1798, Eliza Fletcher founded the Edinburgh New Town Female Friendly Society, claimed to be the first female friendly society in Scotland, which survived until 1844. An early subscriber to the Edinburgh Magdalen Asylum, founded in 1797, she was a prominent member of the Ladies' Committee of the Society for the Suppression of Beggars, founded in Edinburgh in 1813. Most of her later years were spent in the English Lake District, but she celebrated the passing of the Reform Act for Scotland in Edinburgh in 1832, and regularly visited Edinburgh friends. She also maintained interest in the politics of European nationalisms, corresponding with Giuseppe Mazzini until 1853. She had two sons and four daughters, one of whom, Mary, Lady Richardson, later edited her mother's autobiography, mostly written between 1838 and 1844, with additional correspondence. J R

• NLS: Acc. 3758, 'Autobiography of Mrs Eliza Fletcher (1770–1858)' and corr.
[Fletcher, E.] (1875) *Autobiography of Mrs Fletcher with Letters and Other Family Memorials*, [Richardson, M. (ed.)]; Fletcher, E. (1825) *Elidure and Edward. Two Historical Dramatic Sketches.*
Grant, J. P. (ed.) (1845) *Memoir and Correspondence of Mrs Grant of Laggan*, 3 vols; Rendall, J. (2004) ' "Friends of Liberty and Virtue": women radicals and transatlantic correspondence 1789–1848', in M. Cross (ed.) *Gender, the Letter and Politics*, (2005) ' "Women that would plague me with rational conversation": aspiring women and Scottish Whigs, c. 1790–1830', in S. Knott and B. Taylor (eds) *Feminism and the Enlightenment.*

FLUCKER, Barbara,[‡] n. **Johnston,** born Newhaven 8 Feb. 1784, died Newhaven 18 Feb. 1869. Fishwife. Daughter of Catherine Flucker, and John Johnston, fisherman.

Barbara Johnston married George Flucker in 1806, and had eight children, of whom three died in childhood and one son, James, drowned at sea. Her life illustrates both the hardship and the independence experienced by the fishwives of the fishing village of Newhaven-on-Forth, a close-knit community which in the 1840s was flourishing. The wives had their own income from the fish-sales and ran their households while the men were at the fishing. George Flucker owned his own boat, also possessing two houses, which he left in his will to his wife. Barbara Johnston Flucker's kinswoman, **Elizabeth Johnston** (1823–1901), married in 1842 Daniel Hall, who by 1868 had three fishing boats, one named the *Elizabeth*. Distinctive for its intermarried families and independent style of life, Newhaven was much visited by urban Victorians intrigued by its traditions. The pioneering photographers D. O. Hill and Robert Adamson took a series of photographs in about 1845, which immortalised inhabitants of the village. Barbara Johnston Flucker and Elizabeth Johnston Hall were among the fishwives represented in their flamboyant traditional costume and engaged in the tasks of 'shucking' oysters or carrying heavy creels

of fish on their backs to sell around the houses of Edinburgh. L S

• McGowran, T. (1985) *Newhaven-on-Forth, Port of Grace*; Reade, C. (1852) *Christie Johnstone*; Stevenson, S. (1991) *Hill and Adamson's The Fishermen and Women of the Firth of Forth.*

FOCKART, Janet, born before 1550, died Edinburgh May 1596. Merchant and money-lender. Daughter of Elizabeth Ker, and John Fockart, Edinburgh burgess.

Janet Fockart was a well-known figure in the trading community of Edinburgh. She and her first husband, merchant John Todd, had one son. Her second marriage to prosperous merchant William Fowler (d. 1572) by April 1561, produced three sons and three daughters, including William (1) merchant, William (2) poet in the court circle of James VI, and Susannah, who became the mother of the poet William Drummond of Hawthornden. Her third husband, merchant James Hathoway, committed suicide in 1579. They had no children.

Janet Fockart was left to bring up her seven children and run the family business. In company with other merchants she made trading contracts, once with the Earl of Orkney for produce from his lands in return for a loan. She took bonds as security for payment, which she had done in her own name during William Fowler's lifetime, and received income from letting lodgings. Her payment receipts, in her bold handwriting, survive in various family papers. She went to court personally in pursuit of debtors. From the mid-1580s, she turned to outright money-lending, taking pledges of jewellery and other valuables as security for loans. Her clients included nobility, lairds and the professions, to some of whom she lent as much as £1,000 Scots. She lent to the government, and on one occasion the Court of Exchequer met in her house.

Family relations were not always harmonious. Her son-in-law John Drummond took her to court for failure to pay his wife's tocher (dowry), and her merchant son, William, sued her for allowing the family's property in Fowler's (now Anchor) Close to fall into disrepair. When the Fowler family sought a birth-brieve in the mid-17th century they intentionally or erroneously cut her name out of their genealogy, substituting that of Janet Fisher, Englishwoman. They may not have liked the idea of a money-lender, or wadwife, in their ancestry but they must have benefited from her enterprise. On her death she left moveable estate worth over £22,000 Scots, which despite a quarter-century of inflation was still considerably more than that left by William Fowler from his trade in wine and luxury cloths. MHBS

• NAS: Protocol Book of Alexander Guthrie, B22/1/20 folios 226–7.

*ODNB (2004); Sanderson, M. H. B. (1987) *Mary Stewart's People* (Bibl.).

FORLONG[E], Eliza, n. Jack, baptised **(Betty)** Glasgow 24 Oct. 1784, died Euroa, Victoria, Australia, 5 August 1859. Pioneer pastoralist and sheep classer. Daughter of Jean Mackinnon, and Alexander Jack, teacher.

Eliza Jack married John Forlong, a Glasgow merchant, on 26 November 1804. With a consumptive family, a warmer climate seemed imperative so Eliza Forlong and her sons moved to Hamburg to study the Saxon wool industry. Between 1828 and 1830, she walked through Saxony, personally selecting sheep which she drove to Hamburg for shipment. The Forlongs then emigrated to Kenilworth, Van Diemen's Land. Never content with their grant, they conducted an epistolary war with colonial officials, returning to Britain in 1834 with younger son Andrew to approach English officials. John died, and Eliza returned to Van Diemen's Land to find her elder son William moving to the newly settled Port Phillip District in Victoria. Kenilworth and their Saxon flock were sold. She squatted with William's family on various sheep runs, finally settling at Seven Creeks Station, Euroa. She managed both station and household during William's frequent absences. Although her pioneering and managerial skills were outstanding, it was her ability to select sheep that was unique. The Winton stud, founded on her flock, is Australia's superfine wool parent stud. Today every fine wool sheep in Australia has a genetic trace to Eliza Forlong's Saxon merinos. Memorials include one in the shape of a wool bale at her burial place, a sundial at Kenilworth, the Wool Foundation Eliza Forlonge Medal, and a mural by Tom Thompson in Sydney. MSR

• Archives Office of Tasmania: Forlong file; Euroa (Victoria) Historical Society files.

Argus, Melbourne, 11 August 1859; Clune, F. (1965) *Search for the Golden Fleece*; Massy, C. (1990) *The Australian Merino*; Ramsay, M. S. (2004) 'Eliza Forlong and the Saxon merino industry', *Tas. Hist. Res. Ass. Papers*, vol. 51 no. 3., Sept., pp. 121–35; Wilde, S. (1994) *Eliza Forlonge, her life, her family, her vision*.

Private information: Margaret Higgins, Sydney (descendant).

FORRESTER, Isobel Margaret Stewart, n. McColl, born Glenlyon, Perthshire, 30 June 1895, died Edinburgh 30 August 1976. Pioneer of ecumenism. Daughter of Jeannie Baillie, and John McColl, Free Church of Scotland minister.

Isobel McColl was the older of two children and lived in a Highland manse until 1904, when the family moved to Edinburgh. She was educated at home and later at St George's School, from where she won a scholarship to study English at Lady Margaret Hall, Oxford. From 1917 she taught at St George's and then at Edinburgh Academy. Her brother's death at the Front led to a life-long hatred of war. In 1920, she became Education Secretary for the UFC Girls Auxiliary – a national church organisation influenced by wider movements for social and religious change which became an important forum for young women aged 15–30. In 1922, she married Rev. William Forrester; they had five children. In 1935, he was appointed Professor of practical theology and Christian ethics at the University of St Andrews where, for 25 years, she offered hospitality to people from all over the world (including Germans and Malawians fleeing persecution), led retreats and student missions, and was a leading member of the St Andrews Women's Debating Society. Her commitment to a progressive and global Christianity also found expression in her presidency of the Church of Scotland Women's Foreign Mission. She was a passionate supporter of women's ordination.

Isobel Forrester instigated the inter-church 'Dollarbeg Group' in 1946 to participate in a WCC study on the life and work of women in the church. It met in conference for several years, tackling all the major religious, social and political issues of the day. For the next 30 years she played a key role in the development of ecumenical dialogue and organisation, including chairing the Scottish Churches Ecumenical Association. At her death, she was recalled for 'her intellectual vigour, edged with wit and made lustrous by poetical feeling . . . she was always probing, always questing' (Craig 1976). LO

• Blackie, N. (ed.) (2005) *A Time for Trumpets: Scottish church movers and shakers in the twentieth century*; Craig, Rev. A., Funeral address, 4 Sept. 1976; *ODNB (2004); Small, M. (n.d.) *Growing Together: the ecumenical movement in Scotland 1924–64*.

Private information and family papers.

FORREST-THOMSON, Veronica Elizabeth Marian, m. **Culler,** born Penang 28 Nov. 1947, died Birmingham 26 April 1975. Poet and critic. Daughter of Jean and John Forrest Thomson, rubber planters.

Veronica Forrest Thomson (she adopted the hyphen later) was brought to Scotland with her elder brother in 1948. Her father returned to Malaya but she was raised in Glasgow, the home of her mother's parents. She attended Jordanhill College School, Glasgow, and St Bride's School, Helensburgh, and graduated BA with first class honours in English at the University of Liverpool in 1967. She studied for a PhD at Girton College, Cambridge, 1968–71, and held academic posts at the universities of Leicester (1972–4) and Birmingham (1974–5). She married writer and academic Jonathan Culler in 1971; they divorced in 1974.

Alongside her academic career ran 'a short and incomplete but deeply shaped poetic development' (Prynne memoir). She published her first poetry collection, *Identi-Kits*, in 1967 (under the name Veronica Forrest), but the important collection *On the Periphery* (1976) and her major critical work *Poetic Artifice: a theory of twentieth-century poetry* (1978) were posthumous publications.

The appearance of her *Collected Poems and Translations* in 1990 testified to a growing recognition of 'the extraordinary nature of her work' (Mark 2001, p. 1). Edwin Morgan's ten-poem sequence in tribute to her is prefaced by an appreciation describing the 'raw, moving, almost ballad strain' in her poetry. 'She was a spiky, difficult character of great intelligence and wit, engaging, vulnerable and lonely' (Morgan 1990, p. 373). Her academic supervisor writes of her personal impact: 'She wore outfits of bright green or uncompromising purple and hurled arguments about like brickbats . . . She wore perfume which would give the most hardened logician the staggers' (Prynne). In spite of her untimely death, both her poetry and her critical work are seen as extremely important and influential. MARB

• Forrest-Thomson, V., Works as above.

Mark, A. (2001) *Veronica Forrest-Thomson and Language Poetry*; Morgan, E. (1990) 'Unfinished poems: a sequence for Veronica Forrest-Thomson', *Collected Poems*, pp. 373–80 (includes a short prose appreciation), first published in *The New Divan*, 1977; Prynne, J. H. (1976, 2002) 'Veronica Forrest-Thomson: a personal memoir': www.jacketmagazine.com/20/pryn-vft.html

FORRESTER-PATON, Catherine, born Alloa 1 June 1855, died Grantown-on-Spey 8 August 1914. Temperance campaigner and philanthropist. Daughter of Mary Paton, and Alexander Forrester, merchant and woollen manufacturer.

Catherine Forrester-Paton's parents combined their surnames, possibly because of Alexander Forrester's role in John Paton & Son, founded by Mary Paton's father. Both parents were involved in local welfare through the Townhead United Presbyterian church. Educated at Alloa Academy and Grange House school, Edinburgh, at 15, Catherine Forrester-Paton returned home to care for her parents. In 1883, she inherited their home, Marshill House, and a considerable fortune. Prevented by uncertain health from becoming an overseas missionary, she threw her energies into temperance, nursing and missionary training.

The Townhead branch of the BWTA was established after a visit by US temperance campaigner 'Mother Stewart'. Catherine Forrester-Paton became Secretary for life, later assisted by her housekeeper and companion, Agnes Boe. Under her leadership, activities went beyond temperance and prayer meetings to include cookery classes, laundry demonstrations and lectures on nursing. Tea tents at agricultural fairs and Saturday evenings for young people offered alternatives to the public house. President of the local YWCA, founded in 1880, she ran a Sunday afternoon class for young women in her home, and funded the Women's Missionary Society and other associations.

BWTA meetings raised money from 1886 to fund a nurse for the needy, a model for a district nursing service. In 1899, Catherine Forrester-Paton built and equipped the County Accidents Hospital. She founded possibly the first non-denominational training home for missionary nurses at Westercraigs, Glasgow (succeeded by the Burnbank Lady Missionaries' Training Home) in 1890. Her home became a holiday home for missionaries. BWTA Scottish National President in 1906, she was a popular speaker. She planned and funded the Townhead Institute in Alloa, opened on the site of a tavern, which included a temperance tearoom. SI

• Livingstone, S. (1994) *Bonnie Fechters*; Lusk, I. M. (1997) *Catherine Forrester-Paton of Marshill House, Alloa, 1855–1914* (Bibl.).

FORSTER, Jacqueline Moir (Jackie), n. **Mackenzie,** born London 6 Nov. 1926, died London 10 Oct. 1998. Journalist and pioneering lesbian rights campaigner. Daughter of Margaret Alexander, and Major Kenneth Pirie Mackenzie, RAMC.

After an early childhood spent in India, Jackie Mackenzie studied at St Leonards School in

St Andrews. She joined the Edinburgh-based Wilson-Barrett Repertory Company as an actor. In the 1950s, she moved into film and television, winning the 1956 *Prix Italia* for her television report on the wedding of Prince Rainier and Princess Grace of Monaco. In 1958 she married Peter Forster; the marriage was dissolved in 1962. Although her working life took her south of the border to London and Brighton, she resolutely defined herself as a Scot.

In the 1960s, same-sex attraction was still widely regarded as at best a dire psychological aberration. In 1969, at the dawn of gay liberation, Jackie Forster made a public proclamation of her lesbian identity. 'You are looking', she told a shocked crowd at Hyde Park's Speakers' Corner, 'at a roaring dyke.' (*Times*, 1998). From that point she became one of the most active and high-profile campaigners for lesbian and gay rights and feminist issues. In 1972, she co-founded the influential *Sappho* magazine, along with the social organisation of the same name. She co-scripted the 60-minute television programme about London CHE groups, *Speak for Yourself*, which was shown by LWT on 21 July 1974 as part of Britain's first 'access television' series. She played an active part in the campaign for the 1975 Sex Discrimination Act, was a member of the GLC Women's Committee, a director of the London Women's Centre, and a member of the board of the Lesbian Archive and Information Centre. In 1981, she wrote *Rocking the Cradle: Lesbian Mothers, a Challenge in Family Living*, with Gillian Hanscombe. Until her death, Jackie Forster worked constantly and with considerable wit and style, for social justice and equality for lesbians, gay men, and humankind as a whole. ESG
• Lesbian Archive and Information Centre, Glasgow Women's Library: The Jackie Forster Collection. Films listed: www.sbu.ac.uk/stafflag/people.html
Hanscombe, G. E. and Forster, J., Work as above.
Brighton Ourstory Project, Issue 5, Winter 1998 (obit.); *The Independent*, 31 Oct. 1998 (obit.); *The Times*, 28 Oct. 1998 (obit.).

FRANKLAND, Grace Coleridge, n. **Toynbee,** born Wimbledon, Surrey 4 Dec. 1858, died Letterawe, Argyll, 5 Oct. 1946. Microbiologist. Daughter of Harriet Holmes, and Joseph Toynbee, aurist FRCS.

Educated privately in Germany, then at Bedford College, London, Grace Toynbee married Percy Faraday Frankland (1858–1946) in 1882 and moved with him to Dundee when he took up the Chair of Chemistry in 1888. The Franklands, who had one son, collaborated in their research, Grace Frankland

taking equal recognition for work done and publishing jointly with her husband in *Philosophical Transactions* and in *Proceedings of the Royal Society of London*. She also wrote articles on bacteriological subjects in *Longman's Magazine* and *Nature*. In 1891, the Franklands produced the concept that the organisms characteristic of sewage must be identified to provide evidence for potentially dangerous pollution. They observed and described in detail the process of nitrification carried out by micro-organisms which did not require organic carbon for their growth, but the couple apparently failed to appreciate the extreme importance of their findings. In 1894, they moved from Dundee to the University of Birmingham, and published a biography of Louis Pasteur. They retired to Loch Awe, Argyllshire, in 1919, where Grace Frankland lived thereafter. Her individual contribution was recognised when she was one of the first women to be elected to a Fellowship of the Linnaean Society. She had also represented bacteriology at the Women's International Congress in London in 1899. LS
• Frankland, P. and Frankland, Mrs G. C. (1894) *Micro-organisms in Water, their Significance, Identification and Removal*, (1898) *Life of Pasteur*; Frankland, Mrs G. C. (1903) *Bacteria in Daily Life.*
ODNB (2004); *SB*.

FRASER, Eliza Anne, n. **Slack,** m1 **Fraser,** m2 **Greene,** born Stromness, Orkney, c. 1798, died probably Melbourne, Australia, 1858. Castaway.

In 1835, Eliza Fraser and her husband, Captain James Fraser, left their three children at home in Stromness in the care of the local minister, and sailed to Sydney on the *Stirling Castle*. Shipwrecked in May 1836 off eastern Australia, the Frasers with other crew members survived until the end of June, when they reached Great Sandy Island – later renamed Fraser Island. Some accounts suggest that she gave birth to a child who died while they were adrift. Exhausted, hungry and ill, the party encountered the native people, the Badtjala. The survivors later claimed to have been captured, stripped and forced to work, alleging that the Captain was murdered and the first mate died of burns inflicted by their captors. After their rescue in August, Eliza Fraser, now widowed, became a celebrity, gaining sympathy and financial help from a subscription fund. She remarried in 1837 and returned to Britain with her new husband, Captain Alexander J. Greene. Initially they kept the marriage secret, while she continued to plead destitution. The family later returned to the Antipodes.

Lady Grisell Baillie (1665–1746)
(By William Aikman. In the collection of the Earl of
Haddington, Mellerstain)

Lady Frances Balfour
(By Bassano, taken at the photographer's studio, London,
on 20 November, 1919. National Portrait Gallery London)

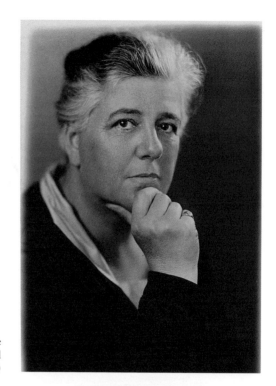

Helen Archdale
(By Harris and Ewing, c. 1932. © Scottish National
Portrait Gallery)

Jean Armour
(Watercolour by Samuel MacKenzie, c. 1820. © Scottish
National Portrait Gallery)

RECORD TAY SALMON
64 lbs.
Length 4ft.6ins. Girth 28ins.
Caught on Glen Delvine Water by Miss Ballantine,
with "MALLOCH" Rod and Tackle

Georgina Ballantine
(Perth Museum and Art Gallery)

Mary Barbour
In her bailie robes, c. 1924
(Supplied by Mary Barbour, grand-daughter)

Isabella Bird
At the Houses of Parliament, London, July 1899
(By Sir John Benjamin Stone. National Portrait Gallery
London)

Mildred Bowes-Lyon
On the day of her marriage in 1890
(From the archive at Glamis Castle)

Mary Brooksbank

Margaret Burns
(From Kay, J. (1877 edn) *A Series of Original Portraits and
Caricature Etchings*, vol. 2. The Trustees of the National
Library of Scotland)

306

Jane Welsh Carlyle
(Edinburgh University Library, Special Collections)

Mairi Chisholm
Mairi Chisholm (right) and Elsie Knocker (the 'two
women of Pervyse'), 1918 (From the Chisholm albums in
the NLS. The Trustees of the National Library of
Scotland)

Lila Clunas
(© D. C. Thomson and Co., Ltd.)

Elizabeth Craig
(Supplied by Elizabeth Evans)

Mary Crudelius
(Edinburgh University Library, Special Collections)

M. E. M. Donaldson
(© The Trustees of the National Museums of Scotland)

Winifred Drinkwater
With an open cockpit Avro Cadet aircraft of Midland
and Scottish Air Ferries (The Peter V. Clegg Collection
via the late Winifred Orange)

Flora Drummond
(By Flora Lion. © Scottish National Portrait Gallery)

Barbara Flucker
(D. O. Hill and Robert Adamson. © Scottish National
Photography Collection/Scottish National Portrait
Gallery)

Anne Grant of Laggan
(By William Bewick. © Scottish National Portrait
Gallery)

Allison Greenlees
(With the drum) and the Cuckoo Patrol, c. 1910
(Girlguiding Scotland)

Jane Haining
(Church of Scotland)

Anne Hamilton, third Duchess of Hamilton
(By Kneller. In the collection of Lennoxlove House,
East Lothian)

Maidie Hart
(Supplied by her daughters)

Gertrude Herzfeld
(By O. Hutchison, presented on the occasion of her
retirement. Reproduced with the kind permission of the
Royal College of Surgeons of Edinburgh)

Florence Horsbrugh
(© D. C. Thomson and Co., Ltd.)

Isabel Wylie Hutchison
In native Greenland dress (From *Women in Modern
Adventures*, by Marjorie H. Tiltman. George Harrap,
1935)

Esther Inglis (Kello)
(By unknown artist. © The Trustees of the National
Museums of Scotland)

Jane Inglis Clark
At the foot of the Crowberry Ridge (From *Jane Inglis Clark: Pictures and Memoirs.* The Moray Press, 1938)

Jessie Jordan
(© D. C. Thomson and Co., Ltd.)

Christina Kay
Centre, with the Junior Class at James Gillespie's Girls' School, 1930. Muriel Camberg (Spark) is 2nd from right on 3rd row, with Frances Niven (Cowell) sitting on her right (Reproduced with the permission of Dame Muriel Spark, and The Trustees of the National Library of Scotland)

Alice Ker
Taken during a BBC interview after attending the last night of the Proms in the Royal Albert Hall, 1942 (Reproduced by kind permission, National Museums Liverpool)

Soon after their rescue, Eliza Fraser and the second mate had both given official reports of their experiences (NSW records). Her experiences were retold repeatedly in newspapers and books, and it became hard to establish what actually happened on the island. Later consideration of the accounts suggests that colonial attitudes, as well as misunderstandings between the castaways and the Aborigines, may lie behind stories of cruel treatment. Eliza Fraser also probably exaggerated her claims to attract attention and financial aid. The story has remained part of Australian popular culture, inspiring paintings (Sidney Nolan), films, a novel (Patrick White) and poetry. Recent academic attention has focused on the portrayal of Aboriginal peoples in the accounts and the alternative narratives handed down among the Badtjala about Eliza Fraser. FJ

• NSW State Records: Colonial Secretary's Correspondence AONSW SZ976, COD 183.

Alexander, M. (1971) *Mrs Fraser on the Fatal Shore*; Behrendt, L. (2000) 'The Eliza Fraser captivity narrative', in *Research School of Soc. Sci. Ann. Rept.*, Australian National Univ.; McNiven, I., Russell, L. and Schaffer, K. (1998) *Constructions of Colonialism*; Wright, J. (2002) 'Desert island risks' in *Scottish Memories*, Nov.

FRASER, Helen Miller [the 'Chieftainess'], m. Moyes, born Leeds 14 Sept. 1881, died Sydney, Australia, 2 December 1979. Suffrage organiser. Daughter of Christiana Sutherland, and James Fraser, tailor's cutter and clothing manufacturer.

The third of ten children, Helen Fraser moved from Yorkshire with her Caithness-born parents to Glasgow, where her father established a wholesale clothing firm, Fraser Ross & Co, and became a city councillor. Educated at Queen's Park Higher Grade School, Langside, her life consisted of 'balls and dances, amateur theatricals, and charitable works' (*AGC*, p. 73). However, in 1904 her father resigned from the council and as managing director of his company, which in 1906 went into liquidation; he died in 1908. With this downturn in family circumstances, she opened a studio, specialising in illustration work and embroidery. After hearing *Teresa Billington-Greig speak in autumn 1906, she became totally committed to women's suffrage. Her family supported her work – her younger sister, actor **Annie Fraser** (b. 1837) was one of the first two Scottish women imprisoned for the cause in Holloway in 1907 with fellow actor *Maggie Moffat; Annie Fraser married Ronald Syme in Glasgow on 20 June 1914.

Soon after joining the WSPU in 1906, Helen Fraser became an organiser. Throughout 1907, she spoke at meetings all over Scotland, establishing new branches, and leading an intensive campaign among holidaymakers in Dunoon, Rothesay and Gourock. A Scottish Council of the WSPU was established with Teresa Billington-Greig as honorary secretary and Helen Fraser as Scottish organiser. In January 1908, the Scottish WSPU headquarters, for which she was largely responsible, opened in Glasgow. However, she resigned from the WSPU later that year when Mrs Pankhurst came to Scotland and told her of the proposed stone-throwing campaign. She said 'I was horrified . . . you don't use violence, you use reason to get the vote. . .' (Harrison tape 1975). She was welcomed into the NUWSS, although the GWSAWS objected to her as organising secretary for Scotland, as she had previously been persuading their members into the WSPU. Her resignation effectively ended the existence of a separate Scottish WSPU, but there was no mass defection to the NUWSS. She continued her speaking tours in a horse-drawn caravan, loaned to her by *Louisa Lumsden, and later worked as an organiser in England, where she became known as the 'Chieftainess'. She remained an NUWSS executive committee member for 14 years.

During the First World War, Helen Fraser worked for the government on the National War Savings Committee and, at the suggestion of Mrs Fawcett, undertook two lengthy speaking tours, on Britain's war effort, in the USA, resulting in her book *Women and War Work* (1918). After the war, she joined the campaign to elect women as Members of Parliament, and was the first woman to be adopted as an official candidate in Scotland, standing unsuccessfully as a National Liberal at Glasgow Govan in 1922 and Hamilton in 1923. She resigned from the Liberal Party in 1925, as they would not take up the task of 'liberating industry and fighting the tyrannies of combinations and unions', to her the 'essential work of Liberalism' (*Glasgow Herald*, 28 Feb. 1925). Later that year, she joined the Unionist Party, finding herself 'increasingly in general agreement with the Unionist programme' (*Glasgow Herald*, 5 May 1925).

She emigrated in 1938 to Sydney, Australia, where her brother James was living, and in 1939 married James Moyes, a divorced Scottish school teacher who had emigrated some years before. Her publications included her autobiography *A Woman in a Man's World* (1971), and *Clothed with Spirit* (n.d.). KBB

• NAS: BT2/4194; New South Wales, Births, Deaths and Marriages: marriage certificate 1939/016620; The Women's Library, London: Harrison tapes collection.
Interview with Helen Fraser Moyes, 19 August 1975 by Brian Harrison (transcribed by Leah Leneman).
Fraser, H., Works as above, and Moyes, H. (1971) *A Woman in a Man's World*.
AGC; *Glasgow Herald*, 28 Feb. and 5 May 1925; HHGW; ODNB (2004); SS; WSM.

FRASER, Janet, n. **Munro,** m1 **Kemp,** m2 **Fraser,** born Glasgow 31 Jan. 1883, died Wellington, New Zealand, 7 March 1945. Community leader, political activist. Daughter of Mary McLean, housekeeper, and William Munro, iron foundry warehouseman.

Growing up in Glasgow, Janet Munro was influenced by the socialist writings of Robert Blatchford, and taught orphaned children. With her husband Frederick Kemp and 5-year-old son Harold, she emigrated in 1909 to Auckland, New Zealand. After meeting fellow-Scot and socialist, Peter Fraser, her marriage ended and she worked alongside him in Wellington during the flu epidemic of 1918. They married in 1919 after her divorce. Janet Fraser supported the recently formed Labour Party and was a founder member of its Wellington women's branch in 1920, joining the Wellington Hospital Board in 1925. Becoming one of the first woman JPs in 1926 was the first of many official appointments. A life-long activist, especially on issues affecting women, children, health and social justice, she was secretary, chair, patron or member of a large number of organisations. With her husband, who became Prime Minister in 1940, Janet Fraser travelled on official delegations, revisiting Scotland in 1935. During the war, she headed the official women's war effort, escorted Eleanor Roosevelt on her 1943 visit, and was instrumental in bringing many Polish refugee children to New Zealand. Significantly, she had an office next to her husband in parliament, acting as political adviser, researcher, gatekeeper and personal support system. They were an effective team. HS

• Bassett, M. and King, M. (2000) *Tomorrow Comes the Song: a life of Peter Fraser*; Stace, H. (1998) 'Making policy as well as tea', in M. Clark (ed.) *Peter Fraser: master politician*; Stace, H., 'Fraser, Janet 1883–1945', in DNZB.
www.dnzb.govt.nz

FRASER, Jessie, m1 **Ryder,** m2 **Pollock,** born c. 1801, died Dalkeith 1 July 1875. Actor, singer and theatre manager.

Local belief has it that Jessie Fraser was the daughter of the owner of the Theatre Royal in Marischal Street, Aberdeen, but parish records contain neither date nor place of her birth. She may have arrived in the city only when her father bought the theatre in 1812. There is little doubt, however, of her great popularity in the city. While still in her teens, she had what we would describe today as 'iconic' status among the young men of Aberdeen and after every performance received a deluge of flowers, letters and verses. One poetic tribute included the lines: 'Her form it is divinely fair/Her eyes sharp as a razor/They've cut into my inmost heart/And there reigns sweet Miss Fraser'.

In 1818, Jessie Fraser married the Welsh actor-manager, Corbet Ryder (1786–1839). Together they formed the company that established the Scottish tradition of touring theatre that continues to this day. Operating from their base in Aberdeen, the Ryder Company barnstormed through northern Scotland, playing annual seasons in Perth, Dundee, Montrose, Arbroath and Inverness. After Corbet Ryder's death, Jessie managed the company with her stepson, Tom. In 1842 she married John Pollock (1813–53) and managed her own company in Her Majesty's Opera House, Aberdeen, until 1853.

Jessie Fraser's acting career is notable for both its longevity and its range, best illustrated by her work in stage adaptations of novels by Sir Walter Scott. In her youth she played a succession of Scott heroines including Diana Vernon in *Rob Roy*, Lucy Bertram in *Guy Mannering*, Amy Robsart in *Kenilworth*. She appeared later in the same plays in other roles: Helen MacGregor, Meg Merrilees and Queen Elizabeth of England. She also excelled in the classics; her favourite role was Lady Macbeth, which she first played, opposite the great English actor William Charles Macready, when she was barely 20 years old. DC

• *Aberdeen Free Press*, 7 July 1875 (obit.); Angus, J. K. (1878) *A Scotch Playhouse: being the historical records of the Old Theatre Royal, Marischal Street, Aberdeen*; Campbell, D. (1996) *Playing for Scotland*.

FRASER, Kate, CBE, born Paisley 10 August 1877, died Paisley 20 March 1957. Physician, mental health pioneer. Daughter of Margaret Coats, of the firm of thread and textiles manufacturers, and Donald Fraser, MD.

Kate Fraser was the fourth daughter in the family. Her father was a GP, examiner in clinical practice for the University of Glasgow, and campaigner against tuberculosis. Her physical exuberance and irascibility, like her father's, earned her the nickname of 'stormy petrel' (Mayes 1995). After Paisley Grammar School, her pleas to study medicine were ignored, and her father enrolled her at Swanley Horticultural College. Determined to become a doctor, she rebelled. Finally giving way, her father thereafter supported her financially. Registering at the arts faculty of Queen Margaret College in 1893, she joined the pioneers of university education for women in Scotland, switched to the Faculty of Science, and graduated BSc with distinction in Physiology in 1900, then MBChB in 1903.

Kate Fraser's early work was with the poor of Glasgow. A resident's post in Crichton Royal Lunatic Asylum exposed her to the challenge of work in mental health. She founded the Paisley Mental Welfare Association in 1907 (the model for the SAMH, 1920), becoming its president. In 1908, she was the first woman School Medical Officer in Govan Parish. Drawing on her postgraduate study in Vienna and Paris, she pioneered Binet-Simon intelligence tests in Britain to help categorise children. Her MD thesis, on syphilis-related mental deficiency in schoolchildren (Glasgow 1913), was highly commended.

Once women could legally become Deputy Commissioners on the General Board of Control for Scotland (after the Mental Deficiency Act, 1913), Kate Fraser applied, becoming the first woman Deputy in April 1914. In 1935, she became a full Commissioner, the first woman to sit on the Board. Aged 68, she was awarded the CBE for her contribution to mental welfare. After retiring in 1947, she remained active in mental health issues, serving on hospital boards, holding office in the SAMH and the Scottish Division of the RMPA. Alongside her international professional reputation, she maintained close relationships with her family and home town. Determined and independent, Kate Fraser was not a domesticated woman, remaining unmarried and being looked after by a long-serving housekeeper until her death. RD

• Mayes, M. (1995) *The Stormy Petrel*; *Medical Directory* (1947); *SB*; *The Times*, 21 March 1957 (obit.).

FRASER, Olive, born Aberdeen 20 Jan. 1909, died Aberdeen 9 Dec. 1977. Poet. Daughter of Elizabeth King, and Roderick Fraser, ironmonger's assistant and farmer.

Olive Fraser's father emigrated to Australia before she was born. Her mother followed a year later, leaving the baby to be brought up by her great-aunt, Ann Maria Jeans, in Nairn. Her parents returned to Scotland when she was about nine years old, but her father maintained no contact, and she suffered a life-long feeling of rejection. She was educated at Millbank School and Rose's Academical Institution in Nairn, gaining an Honours English degree at the University of Aberdeen in 1931 and winning the Calder prize for English verse. She won a scholarship to Cambridge but, possibly for health reasons, did not take it up until 1933, when she went to Girton. Older than the other students, she found it difficult to fit in; she was already showing signs of serious illness, then undiagnosed. She won the Chancellor's Medal for English Verse in 1935, the first woman to do so, but could not keep up with her studies.

During the Second World War, she served with the WRNS and experienced the Merseyside blitz of 1941, with serious effects on her physical and mental health. She was transferred to Naval Intelligence in 1941 and given a compassionate discharge in 1942. Having no settled home after her great-aunt's death in 1944, she occupied a series of temporary jobs and lodgings. She was befriended by Franciscan friars, who supplied practical and spiritual help, and was received into the Catholic Church in 1952; some poems of devotion date from around this time.

In 1951, in a national contest to mark the Festival of Britain, Olive Fraser gained equal first prize for lyrics in Scots. Some of her poetry was published but a planned collection never appeared in her lifetime; most of her work was published posthumously. She suffered a severe mental breakdown in 1956 and a pattern of admissions to mental hospitals, alternating with outpatient treatment, continued for the rest of her life. For much of the time, to her distress, illness or medication made writing impossible. In 1961 she moved to Inverness and in 1963 to Aberdeen where she continued treatment at the Royal Cornhill hospital. In 1968 a doctor there diagnosed her condition as hypothyroidism and prescribed a new course of treatment, with dramatic results. During the following 'wonderful years', as she called them (Fraser 1989, p. 29), she lost excess weight, improved in appearance, regained energy, and was able to write again. Though still on heavy medication, she visited friends, went on holidays and continued to produce striking poetry until her death in 1977. Her friend Helena Mennie Shire edited a selection of her work in 1981 and the collected poems, *The Wrong Music*, in 1989.

*Kathleen Raine's *Temenos* magazine also published some of Olive Fraser's work, in 1988. *The Wrong Music* includes a biographical introduction to this remarkable and little-known poet 'of quite daunting spirit' (*ODNB*, 2004). MARB
• Univ. of Aberdeen Library Archives.
H. M. Shire (ed. and intro.) (1989) *The Wrong Music: the poems of Olive Fraser, 1909–1977*, (1981) *The Pure Account: the poems of Olive Fraser*; *ODNB* (2004).

FULHAME, Elizabeth, fl. 1780–94. Chemist.
Almost nothing is known of Elizabeth Fulhame, except her original contribution to chemistry. Her husband was Irish-born Thomas Fulhame, who enrolled in Joseph Black's University of Edinburgh chemistry class of 1779–80. He graduated as a physician in 1784, and Joseph Black apparently noted that Dr Fulhame had found a new method of manufacturing white lead pigment, c. 1793. Presumably Elizabeth Fulhame was involved in her husband's chemical researches, since she relates in her book (1794) that in about 1780 she became interested in the possibility of making cloths of gold, silver and other metals, by chemical processes. Her husband was sceptical of success, but

she undertook an enormous range of practical experiments and, encouraged by a meeting in 1793 with Joseph Priestley, she published a book summarising her work, *An Essay on Combustion*. In due course, her experiments have also come to be seen as among the early precursors of photography, as she managed to create permanent images using the action of light on various metallic salts. The essay received favourable attention from a number of renowned contemporaries and though she then vanishes from the historical record, later histories of chemistry and photography have acknowledged her work. AM-L
• Fulhame, E. (1794) *An Essay on Combustion with a view to a new Art of Dying and Painting wherein the Phlogistic and Antiphlogistic Hypotheses are proved Erroneous*.
Cornish-Bowden, A. (1998) 'Two centuries of catalysis', *Journal of Biosciences*, 23, pp. 87–92; Davenport, D. A. and Ireland, K. M. (1991) 'The ingenious, lively and celebrated Mrs Fulhame and the dyer's hand', *Bull. Hist. Chem.*, 5, pp. 37–42; *ODNB* (2004); Schaaf, L. J. (1990) 'The first fifty years of British photography: 1794–1844', in M. Pritchard (ed.) *Technology and Art: the birth and early years of photography*.

G

GALLOWAY, Dervorgilla of, (Dervorgilla Balliol), born Galloway c. 1213, died Barnard Castle 28 January 1290. Heiress, religious patron. Daughter of Margaret, daughter of David, Earl of Huntingdon, brother of William the Lion, and Alan, Lord of Galloway.
Dervorgilla was the younger daughter of Alan of Galloway's second marriage and his third surviving legitimate child. The death of their legitimate brother made Dervorgilla and her two sisters heiresses to a landed inheritance centred on Galloway but scattered from Lothian to Northamptonshire. That prospect, and their royal blood, secured Dervorgilla and her sister, Christiana, important marriages. In 1233, Dervorgilla married John Balliol (before 1208–68), lord of Barnard Castle in Teesdale. Following her father's death in 1234, Dervorgilla and John received one third of the Galloway inheritance, despite a rebellion in favour of her illegitimate brother. After 1237, she and her sister fell heirs to the earldoms of Chester and Huntingdon on the death of their uncle, and after 1246, Dervorgilla acquired most of

the inheritance of the childless Christiana. By c. 1260, she possessed properties from Aberdeenshire to Middlesex, making her one of the greatest landholders of the day.
Deeply pious, Dervorgilla expressed her faith through conspicuous religious patronage. In the 1260s, she founded convents in Dundee and Dumfries (Franciscan) and Wigtown (Dominican). Following John's death in 1268, she founded in 1273 the Cistercian abbey of Sweetheart, where she was later buried, and in 1282 she issued statutes that formally instituted Balliol College, Oxford. Several devotional books from her own collection, which she gave to Sweetheart, survive.
Dervorgilla and John Balliol had several children. Their youngest son, John, succeeded to the Balliol lands in 1278. Following the death of Alexander III in 1286 and of *Margaret, Maid of Norway, and his mother in 1290, John Balliol emerged as a competitor for the Scottish throne by virtue of Dervorgilla's descent from David, Earl of Huntingdon, and in 1292 was awarded the kingdom. RO

• Salter, H. E. (ed.) (1913) *The Oxford Deeds of Balliol College.* Brooke, D. (1994) *Wild Men and Holy Places*, pp. 140–9; Huyshe, W. (1913) *Dervorgilla, Lady of Galloway. . .; ODNB* (2004); Oram, R. (1993) 'A family business? . . .' *Scot. Hist. Rev.*, 72, (1999) 'Dervorgilla, the Balliols and Buittle', *Trans. Dumf. and Gal. Nat. Hist. and Antiqu. Soc.*, 73.

GALLOWAY, Janet Anne (or Ann), born Campsie 10 Oct. 1841, died Glasgow 23 Jan. 1909. Educator, administrator. Daughter of Anne Bald, and Alexander Galloway, land surveyor and valuator.

Janet Galloway had a good education followed by residence in France, Germany and Holland: she spoke fluent French and German. Her wide knowledge included history, archaeology, and business methods taught her by her father. Her support for women's education led her to become a secretary of the AHEW and, after her father died in 1883, Honorary Secretary to Queen Margaret College, a post she held until her death. She lived in QMC, accepting no remuneration, but assisting greatly in the preparation of courses, making arrangements with professors and dealing with complaints. She carried this off with 'supreme tact and unwearying patience' (Murray 1914, p. 12). In 1893, she was specially invited to the Great Exhibition in Chicago, representing QMC, and took with her a photograph of the women students of QMC's Medical School, opened in 1890. She knew her students personally and kept in touch later. When QMC was incorporated into the University of Glasgow in 1892, she became a university official, proving a broad-minded and wise administrator. She was awarded Hon LLD by the University of Glasgow in 1907, and a memorial window in Bute Hall depicts her alongside *Isabella Elder and *Jessie Campbell. CJM

• Univ. of Glasgow: Queen Margaret Coll. Archives. McAlpine, C. J. (1997) *The Lady of Claremont House*; Murray, D. (1914) *Miss Janet Ann Galloway and the Higher Education of Women in Glasgow*; *ODNB* (2004).

GALT, Maud, fl. 1648/9. Lesbian accused of witchcraft.

Maud Galt was the wife of John Dickie, wright, in Kilbarchan, with two servants of her own. One of these, Agnes Mitchell, came to the kirk session in September 1649 'with ane peice of clay formed be hir to the liknes of a mans priwie members doing quhat is abominable to think or speik of', complaining of an 'injurie done to hir be the said Mauld'. Agnes Mitchell wanted the case taken to the local laird, but 'was hinderit be sum of thame

for the abominablness of the said act that it sould nevir be hard of'. Two neighbours testified to her complaint; one, Marion Sempill, had intervened in an argument between Maud Galt and Agnes Mitchell to discourage an approach to the laird. The session investigated Maud Galt's 'vyle act in abusing ane of hir servants with ane peis of clay formed lyk the secreit members of ane man', but abandoned the issue in favour of a witchcraft charge. She was evidently an assertive character; several people reported suffering misfortune after crossing her. There is no record of a commission for her trial, so her case may have been dropped. JG

• *RPC*, 2nd series, viii, pp. 198–204.

GARDEN, Mary, born Aberdeen 20 Feb. 1874, died House of Daviot, near Inverurie, 3 Jan. 1967. Opera singer. Daughter of Mary Joss, and Robert Davidson Garden, cashier.

When Mary Garden was nine, the family travelled to America, moving several times, and spending a year back in Aberdeen. She first had singing lessons in Chicago, from 1890, where her potential became clear. Her parents could not afford professional training, but a wealthy Chicago family funded lessons in Paris; she moved there in 1896, studying with Trabadelo and Fugère. Her big break came in 1900: the soprano in Charpentier's *Louise* at the Opéra-Comique was taken ill, and Mary Garden (already well briefed) took over, receiving huge acclaim. She became the Opéra-Comique's leading soprano. In 1901, she created the title role in *Pelléas et Mélisande* by Claude Debussy, with whom she had a close relationship, as with composer-conductor André Messager. Mary Garden's artistic innovation was to sing her roles with the dramatic projection of an actress, thus making her own some 35 roles including *Thaïs* and *Salome*. In 1907, she became a principal soprano with the Manhattan Opera House, and in 1910 moved to the Chicago Opera Company, where she remained until her retirement in 1931. She was 'Directa' of the Chicago Opera Association (1920–2) and spent lavishly, bankrolled by its wealthy president, Harold F. McCormick. Between 1903 and 1931, she made more than 40 recordings, and two films, both directed by Sam Goldwyn: *Thaïs* (1917) and *The Splendid Sinner* (1918). She was awarded the French Médaille de la Reconnaissance after working as a Red Cross nurse in the American hospital at Versailles during the First World War, and the Légion d'Honneur for promoting French music in America. Often in the news, both for her feuds with other divas and for her relationships with men, Mary Garden maintained a high profile after retirement, giving lectures and master classes, and publishing her memoirs. She eventually returned to live in Aberdeen. FJ

• Royal Coll. Music, London (Dept. of Performance History): Garden Collection; Aberdeen City Museums and Art Gallery: stage costume; Newberry Library, Chicago: Garden Collection.
Recordings: Pearl GEMM CD 9067 *Mary Garden: A Selection of Her Finest Recordings.*
Garden, M. and Biancolli, L. (1952) *Mary Garden's Story*; Turnbull, M. T. R. B. (1997) *Mary Garden.*
www.cantabilesubito.de/Sopranos/Garden_Mary/hauptteil_garden_mary.html
Additional information: Michael Turnbull.

GARDINER, Margaret, born Berlin 22 April 1904, died London 2 Jan. 2005. Founder of Pier Arts Centre, Orkney. Daughter of Hedwig van Rosen, and Sir Alan Gardiner, Egyptologist.

One of three children, Margaret Gardiner was raised abroad, then educated at Bedales School. In 1923, she began reading languages at Newnham College, Cambridge. An early romance with anthropologist Bernard Deacon ended with his death from fever in 1927, and for a while she taught school in Gamlingay. Her grandfather's wealth gave her a moderate private income, and when she moved to Hampstead, her circle of creative friends included Barbara Hepworth, Ben Nicolson, W. H. Auden, Solly Zuckerman, Naum Gabo and J. D. Bernal, the microbiologist, who was the father of her son (academic Martin Bernal, b. 1937). She began buying works from artists in the 1930s, always because she liked them, but also at critical junctures when it helped the artist financially and in morale. She acquired a remarkable personal collection, centred on the St Ives group including Hepworth, Nicolson and Gabo, and mostly consisting of small but powerful works. In 1956, on a visit to Orkney with her son, she impulsively bought a cottage on Rousay, and returned there often, founding the Sourin Trust to help Orcadian art students. In 1978, she fulfilled her dream, not an easy one, of donating her valuable collection in trust to Orkney, where it is housed in a former warehouse, the Pier Art Gallery, Stromness – puzzling to southerners, but dazzling to all who have visited it. Margaret Gardiner disliked being called a collector, still less a patron: she was also a campaigner, supporting the Howard League for

Penal Reform, and opposing the Vietnam war. Her generosity was self-effacing, her taste prophetic. SR
• Gardiner, M. (1988) *A Scatter of Memories*, (1988) *Barbara Hepworth: a memoir*, (1988) *The Pier Gallery: the first ten years.*
The Guardian, 5 Jan. 2005 (obit.); *Homecoming: the Pier Arts Centre Collection at Tate St Ives* (2003, catalogue); *The Pier Gallery, Stromness, Orkney* (1978, catalogue); *The Scotsman,* 4 Dec. 2004 (feature).

GARRETT, Edward *see* **MAYO, Isabella** (1843–1914)

GARRY, Flora Macdonald, n. **Campbell,** born Mains of Auchmunziel, New Deer, Aberdeenshire, 30 Sept. 1900, died Comrie 16 June 2000. Poet. Daughter of Helen Mary Metcalfe, writer, and Archibald William Campbell, farmer and journalist.

Flora Campbell, the second of four children, was brought up on the family farm and attended New Deer School and Peterhead Academy. She graduated with honours in English at the University of Aberdeen in 1922, trained as a teacher, and taught in Dumfries and Strichen before marrying, in 1928, Robert Garry (1900–93), later Regius Professor of Physiology at the University of Glasgow. She wrote in English and Scots, but it was her accomplished and creative use of the Doric of her native Buchan that gained her prominence. From the early 1920s, she gave talks on cultural topics and acted in radio dramas. Yet she did not think of writing in dialect until 1941, when she was persuaded by a friend to write the poem 'Bennygoak' in Scots. That became the title of a collection of her verse published by Akros (1974) and an audiotape by Scotsoun (1975). The book had sold out in a week and she found herself in great demand as a speaker and performer of her verse.

In writing in Scots, Flora Garry was continuing a tradition of women dialect poets from the North East such as **Mary Symon** (1863–1938), who also wrote as 'Malcolm Forbes' and 'Forbes Duff'. *Deveron Days* (1933) reflected Symon's native countryside, language and customs, and also contained 'patriotic' verse, written during the First World War, such as the famous 'The Glen's Muster-Roll'. Flora Garry was awarded an honorary degree by the University of Aberdeen in 1999, and there is a plaque to her as 'The Buchan Poetess', in New Deer cemetery. LW
• Garry, F. (1974) *Bennygoak and other Poems*; (1995) *Collected Poems.*

Symon, M. (1933) *Deveron Days*.
Interviews with Flora Garry, and family friends Cuthbert Graham, Sandy Ritchie (c. 1985).
HSWW; *The Scotsman*, 22 June 2000 (obit.); *ODNB* (2004) (Garry; Symon).

GARSCADDEN, Kathleen Mary Evelyn, born Glasgow 18 Feb. 1897, died Glasgow 20 Feb. 1991. Radio and television broadcaster and producer. Daughter of Maggie Vint, and George Garscadden, accountant and businessman.

Educated at Hutcheson's Grammar School for Girls, Glasgow, Kathleen Garscadden studied piano and singing in London under Sir Henry Wood. During this time she visited a widely known fortune-teller, to be told, 'I see you surrounded by hundreds of children, reaching out their arms to you'. She returned home intending to be a professional singer, only to become involved through family interest in the BBC's first radio station in Scotland, which opened in Glasgow in March, 1923. She soon found a niche broadcasting to young people, and the names 'Auntie Cyclone' (see Wood, Wendy), 'Auntie Kathleen' and finally just 'Kathleen' identified a legendary voice that was to span almost 40 years of broadcasts in Scotland. Her programmes were likened to a collage of talent – many well-known broadcasters made their first appearance under her direction: she recalled with pleasure the young Gordon Jackson, Stanley Baxter, Eileen McCallum, the singer Sidney MacEwan and others. Writers, too, were encouraged, including Angus McVicar with his 'Lost Planet' adventures, Don Whyte, author of 'Bran the Cat' stories, and Allan MacKinnon whose 'Boys of Glen Morrach' ran for many years. Retiring from the BBC in 1960, she continued to devote herself to the wellbeing of children, inadvertently fulfilling the prophecy made to her many years before. DPW
• Personal information.
BBC Scotland website: bbc.co.uk/scotland

GEDDES, Anna, n. **Morton,** born Liverpool 19 Nov. 1857, died Lucknow, India 9 June 1917. Music teacher, partner in Patrick Geddes's projects. Daughter of Frazer Morton, Liverpool merchant, and his wife.

Anna Morton had a rigorous upbringing; music was the only indulgence permitted by her Presbyterian father, an Ulster Scot. After boarding-school and a year studying music in Dresden, she became a music teacher. Visiting her sister, wife of James Oliphant, headmaster of an Edinburgh school, she met Patrick Geddes (1854–1932), polymath, scientist, intellectual and town planner, whose ideals she wholeheartedly shared. They married in April 1886, and thereafter Anna was closely associated in all Patrick's projects, as an independent-minded, 'heroic', selfless and 'cheerful' partner (J. Arthur Thomson, quoted Mairet 1957, p. 80). They were deeply attached: her role was often to look after finance and administration, the understated complement to his inspirational ideas. In a rundown tenement in James Court, where they moved to further Patrick's Old Town rehabilitation schemes, Anna Geddes bore her first of their children: all three were educated at home.

After 1891, her inheritance allowed them to move into another building project, Ramsay Garden. During the Summer Meetings organised by Patrick Geddes in the 1890s, Anna looked after many practical details, especially the music, calling on performers such as *Marjory Kennedy Fraser. From their home bases in Edinburgh, Dunfermline or Dundee, she partnered Patrick on many of his foreign travels, including a stint caring for Armenian refugees in Cyprus (1896–7), visiting settlements in the USA, and spending most of 1900 in Paris, where he ran a summer school during the World's Fair. On the second of her working visits to India, where her husband was advising and lecturing in 1917, she died of enteric fever, unaware that their son Alasdair had been killed in France. While Patrick deeply regretted that he might have 'subjected [Anna] to overstrain', her support had been 'the keystone of his career' (Meller 1990, pp. 7–8.) SR
• NLS: MSS 10503 ff. Geddes papers; Univ. of Strathclyde, Geddes papers.
Geddes, Mr and Mrs P. (1897) *Cyprus and its Power to help the East*.
Boardman, P. (1978) *The Worlds of Patrick Geddes*; Kitchen, P. (1975) *A Most Unsettling Person*; Mairet, P. (1957) *Pioneer of Sociology, the Life and Letters of Patrick Geddes*; Meller, H. (1990) *Patrick Geddes*.

GEDDES, Jenny, reputedly alive in 1670. Legendary rioter.

On 23 July 1637, a riot against the Scottish Prayer Book erupted in St Giles' church, Edinburgh. A plaque within the church states that 'constant oral tradition' has it that Jenny Geddes 'struck the first blow' by flinging her stool at the pulpit. A 'Jenet Geddis' was first mentioned in Edinburgh in 1661 but no link with 1637 was made. Edward Phillips claimed that 'Jane or Janet Geddis', who was 'yet living' in 1670 (Baker 1670, p. 473), was responsible for the stool-throwing incident, but no source was given.

Contemporary accounts confirm that women were involved in the riot, but no names were recorded. A suggestion that Geddes came from St Andrews is false. That individual died before February 1637. A source known to Robert Wodrow claimed that the riot ringleader was 'Mrs Mean', Barbara Hamilton, wife of John Mein, an opponent of James VI's religious policies. Women were prominent in nonconformist circles and Barbara Hamilton was particularly well connected. It seems likely, therefore, that 'Jenny Geddes' is the result of blending various local legends. If an energetic female parishioner did lead the 1637 riot, credit should probably go to Barbara Hamilton. LAMS

• Baker, R. (1670) *Chronicle of the Kings of England*; Grant, F. J. (ed.) (1902) *Commissariot Record of St Andrews Register of Testaments 1549–1800*; Hewison, J. K., 'Jenny Geddes: who was she?', *The Scotsman*, 30 March 1932; Lothian, M. (1995) *The Cutty Stool*; *ODNB* (2004); Stevenson, D. (1972–4) 'Conventicles in the Kirk, 1619–37 . . .', *Records of the Scottish Church History Society*, 18; Wodrow, R. (1842–3) *Analecta*, 4 vols.

GILBERTSON, Jenny Isabel, n. **Brown,** born Glasgow 28 Oct. 1902, died Shetland 8 Jan. 1990. Film-maker and teacher. Daughter of Mary Dunn Wright, and William Brown, iron and steel merchant.

After studying at Laurel Bank School and the University of Glasgow, teacher training and a secretarial course with journalism, Jenny Brown decided that educational film-making was for her after watching an amateur film of Loch Lomond. She bought a 16mm camera and practised filming squirrels in Kensington Gardens and barges on the Thames at Westminster Bridge. In January 1931 she went to Shetland where she had spent several summer holidays with crofter friends as a child. By autumn that year, she had made *A Crofter's Life in Shetland*. John Grierson, whose film, *Drifters*, about North Sea herring fishers, laid the foundation for documentary film-making in Britain, advised her on technique, so she bought a 35mm Eyemo camera. Returning to Shetland, she made five documentary films and *The Rugged Island* (1934), a story of the harsh life of crofting families at that time. She also married the 'romantic lead', Shetlander Johnny Gilbertson (1908–67).

During a 1934–5 lecture tour of Canada with *The Rugged Island*, she made *Prairie Winter* with Canadian film-maker Evelyn Spice. In 1940 she and Johnny Gilbertson set up a small Shetland hosiery business. From 1947 she taught in the local school until retiring in 1967. During that time they had two daughters, Helen and Ann, and she broadcast several short radio talks, wrote scripts for schools radio and two radio plays. A further film on Shetland, *People of Many Lands – Shetland*, made with the Scottish documentary film-maker Elizabeth Balneaves, was broadcast by the BBC in October 1967. In 1970, Jenny Gilbertson returned to Canada where she made *People of Many Lands – the Eskimo* for the BBC and *Jenny's Arctic – Part 1* for the Canadian Broadcasting Company. To film *Jenny's Dog Team Journey* in 1975 she travelled 300 miles over inhospitable Arctic terrain. In 1977–8, at the age of 76, she spent 13 months in Grisefiord, 900 miles north of the Arctic Circle, to make *Jenny's Arctic Diary*, recording the life of the Inuit community.

Jenny Gilbertson was remarkable in that all her films were what she described as a 'one-woman job'. She wrote the script and did the filming, sound, lighting and direction herself. She was particularly keen to film people coping with harsh environments before their way of life disappeared. Her films have a very special quality; she identified with and was clearly accepted by the people being filmed. ARW

• Crichton, R. (1999) *Jenny Gilbertson: documentary film-maker* (programme notes for screening *The Rugged Island*, Stirling Univ.); Gilbertson, J. (n.d.) Autobiographical notes, Scottish Screen Archive; McBain, J. (n.d.) Draft obituary of Jenny Gilbertson, Scottish Screen Archive; *ODNB* (2004). Private information.

GILCHRIST, Anne Geddes, OBE, born Hulme, Lancs., 8 Dec. 1863, died Lancaster 24 July 1954. Folklorist and song collector. Daughter of Jane Helen Thomson, and George Gilchrist, bank cashier.

Described as 'a pure-blooded Scot on both sides of her family', like her colleague *Lucy Broadwood she was a descendant of piano-maker John Broadwood, and related to Rev. Neil Livingston, whose 1864 edition of Millar's 1635 *Psalter* inspired Anne Gilchrist to undertake seminal research and classification of early psalm tunes. She studied at the RAM and Trinity College, London, but had begun to memorise Scottish folk tunes from the age of six, influenced by her parents' singing. She collaborated closely with Frank Kidson, notably on Orkney melodies and songs from the Borders, and joined the editorial board of the *Journal of the Folk-Song Society*. She described her collections as small in bulk but 'catholic', and wrote 'To me, as to the true folk-singer, tune and words are interdependent – texts without tunes are deaf, and tunes without texts, blind' (Gilchrist 1942, p. 63). She was awarded FSA, OBE, and the Gold Badge of the EFDSS. J P

• Vaughan Williams Library, Cecil Sharp House, London: Collection of Gilchrist's publications.
Gilchrist, A. G. (1911) 'Note on the modal system of Gaelic tunes', *Jour. Folk-Song Soc.*, IV, 3, no. 16 (pp. 150–3, repr. as volume 1997), (1936) 'Ten songs from Scotland and the Scottish Border', *Jour. Eng. Folk Dance and Song Soc.*, III, 1, pp. 46–71, (1942) 'Let Us Remember . . .' *English Dance and Song*, 6, 6, pp. 62–3.
Dean-Smith, M. (1958) 'The work of Anne Geddes Gilchrist, OBE, FSA, 1863–1954', *Proc. Roy. Music Assoc.*, 84th Session, pp. 43–53; Howes, F. (1954) 'Anne Geddes Gilchrist', *Jour. Eng. Folk Dance and Song Soc.*, VII, 3, p. 202 (obit.).

GILCHRIST, Marion, born Bothwell, Lanarkshire, 5 Feb. 1864, died Glasgow 7 Sept. 1952. Physician. Daughter of Margaret Williamson, and William Gilchrist, farmer.

Marion Gilchrist was sent to Hamilton Academy, before working on the family farm. She then gained her LLA (St Andrews) via the arts faculty at Queen Margaret College, University of Glasgow (1890), but immediately transferred to study medicine, to which women had just been granted admittance. In protest against a ruling that excluded women from certain clinical demonstrations, she gathered the class tickets of her fellow female students and returned them. Notwithstanding, she excelled at her studies, and in 1894 she and **Alice Lilian Louisa (Lily) Cumming** (1870–1945 m. Robson) became the first women in Scotland to gain the university medical qualification MBChM.

Marion Gilchrist specialised in ophthalmology, practising in Glasgow, where she shared consulting rooms with her friend Dr Katherine Chapman for many years. A keen supporter of the suffrage movement, she joined the Glasgow WSPU in 1907, along with *Janie Allan, *Margaret Irwin and *Grace Paterson. In later years, she energetically supported women in the professions. In 1914, she was appointed Assistant Surgeon at the Victoria Infirmary and later Ophthalmic Surgeon at Redlands Hospital for Women, which she served for many years. The first woman to chair the Glasgow division of the BMA, she was a Trustee of the Muirhead Trust which helped women to enter medical careers. Marion Gilchrist was far from narrow in her interests, which included music and art and a varied social life. R D

• Gilchrist, M. (1926) 'Amblyopia with haemorrhages due to tobacco & lead poisoning', *BMJ*, vol. 1, 12 June, p. 990, (1926b) 'Some medical legal aspects in ophthalmology', *Trans. Ophthalmology Soc.*
AGC; *BMJ*, 20 Sept. 1952 (obit.); *Glasgow Herald*, 5 Dec. 1994; *HHGW*.

GILLESPIE, Margaret, n. **Duncan,** born New Deer, Aberdeenshire, 12 Dec. 1841, died South Africa 1913. Singer of traditional songs. Daughter of Elizabeth Birnie, and William Duncan, millwright;
ROBERTSON, Isabel (Bell), born Denhead of Boyndlie, Aberdeenshire 1 Feb. 1841, died New Pitsligo 19 August 1922. Informant on traditional songs. Daughter of Jean Gall, and James Robertson.

The second of 11 children, Margaret Duncan was the sister of Rev. James Bruce Duncan who collected 466 songs from her for the folk-song collection he compiled jointly with Gavin Greig. Margaret Gillespie was the most prolific informant of the collection. She married James Gillespie, a slater, in 1867. After his death she moved to Glasgow where she worked as a sewing machinist and then took in lodgers, one of them James Matthew Brown, who noted down many of her songs on behalf of her brother, James. Her sources included her family and neighbours in her childhood, and others she encountered when she worked as a house servant. James Duncan began collecting from her in 1905 and continued until her departure in 1909 for South Africa, where her two sons lived. Her grand-daughter, Ursula Gillespie, recalled that she was known in the family for being a splendid dancer and playing the piano by ear. She 'had a very nice voice, not high nor low'.

Another major informant for the Greig-Duncan collection, contributing 398 songs, was Bell Robertson, who had received little formal education and worked as a housekeeper. Unlike Margaret Gillespie, she was not a singer and gave no tunes, but her ballad repertoire was particularly rich. Her principal source was her mother who had learned songs from *her* mother. Bell Robertson, who also wrote devotional poetry, lived near Greig's home at Whitehill: she was first an informant for Greig, then after his death for Duncan. Her memory was exceptional and she is the sole source for many of the songs in the collection. K M C

• Robertson, B. (1910) *Poems and Songs.*
Buchan, D. (1997, 2nd edn.) 'The Ballads of Bell Robertson', *The Ballad and the Folk* (ch. 18); Campbell, K. (2007) *Songs from North-East Scotland: a selection for performers from 'The Greig-Duncan Folk Song Collection'; ODNB* (2004) (Greig, Gavin; Robertson, Bell); Shuldham-Shaw, P., Lyle, E. B. et al. (eds) (1981–2002) *The Greig-Duncan Folk Song Collection,* 8 vols. (see Petrie, E., 'Mrs Margaret Gillespie' and 'Miss Bell Robertson' in vol. 8).

GILLON, Mary, m. **Armistead,** born Edinburgh 17 July 1898, died Perth 2 Jan. 2002. First World War tram conductress (clippie). Daughter of Agnes Ewing, and Allan Anderson Gillon, fishmonger.

When Mary Gillon left school at the age of 14 she worked at her father's fish shop in Portobello, before joining the staff of the Buttercup Dairy. At the age of 17 she joined Edinburgh's cable tram services as a clippie. 'It was April or May 1916 I went on . . . they started to ask for conductresses for the trams as what men there were there, they trained as drivers so they couldn't be taken away, and that's when they started putting the girls on.' Her usual run was on the Waterloo Place to Joppa route, frequently with the same driver. Her uniform was provided but she bought long boots to protect her legs when her skirt became wet on the outside steps. The shifts were nine hours long and the back shift didn't finish until 11.35pm. At each terminus she had three minutes to check the seats and floor for lost property and litter, turn the seat backs to face the direction of travel, change the points and pull down the step for the passengers to board. There was no time allowed for a proper break; tea and sandwiches were eaten on the uncovered platform. On cashing up at the end of the shift, any shortages had to be paid for out of her wages. As many women did, she left after the war, in August 1919. 'I look back on it as a very nice time, but it was understood that if your conductor came back, you gave up your shift.' She went to work at the Craigmillar Creamery and on 12 June 1924 she married George Armistead, a joiner and motor lorry driver. HEC
• People's Story Oral History Archive T122/88, Canongate Tolbooth, Edinburgh.

GLAMIS, Janet, Lady *see* **DOUGLAS, Janet, Lady Glamis** (d. 1537)

GLASGOW GIRLS: this name was given posthumously to women artists of the period c. 1880–c. 1920 associated with the Glasgow School of Art (GSA). The label, modelled on that of the 'Glasgow Boys' (see McEwan 1994, pp. 234–5) was coined in part ironically, to draw attention to a remarkable generation of women students who specialised in painting, drawing, design, embroidery and crafts but who, it was argued, had been all but eliminated from art history. Research by *Ailsa Tanner, American-born **Jude Burkhauser** (1947–98) and more than a dozen colleagues, resulted in an exhibition with this title in 1988 and a definitive collection of essays (Burkhauser 1990). The GSA had been open to women since the 1850s, but particular impact was made by the post-1880 intakes. The percentage of women students was 28% in 1881, 35% in 1891, 42% in 1901. Their success was largely due to the encouragement of the incoming headmaster in 1885, Fra Newbery (1853–1946), and his wife, *Jessie Rowat Newbery. Fra Newbery, who stayed at the GSA until 1918, began appointing female staff and encouraged design and crafts as much as easel painting and sculpture. Jessie Newbery wrote: 'I believe that the design . . . of a pepper pot is as important in its degree as the conception of a cathedral' (ibid., p. 74).

Among the 'Glasgow Girls' are numbered several who have separate entries here: designers *Margaret and Frances Macdonald, painters *Katharine Cameron, *Norah Neilson Gray, *Anna Hotchkis, *Jessie M. King, *Bessie MacNicol, embroiderers *Ann Macbeth and *Kathleen Mann. Others generally associated with the School include painters **Mary Armour** (1902–2000), **Lily Blatherwick** (1854–1934), known particularly for flower painting and printmaking, **Stansmore Dean** (1866–1944), **Margaret and Mary Gilmour** (1860–1942 and 1872–1938), **Eleanor Allen Moore** (1885–1955) and **Mary Viola Paterson** (1899–1981); costume designer **Dorothy Carleton Smyth** (1890–1933) and her sisters Rose and Olive; painter and embroiderer **Helen Paxton Brown** (1876–1956); illustrator **Annie French** (1872–1965); designer and enamellist **Margaret De Courcy Lewthwaite Dewar** (1878–1959); and the **Walton** sisters, **Constance** (1865–1960), Hannah and Helen.

Most of these artists worked in more than one medium, and a striking feature of these years is the number of sisters who worked together. The period of their training coincided with Art Nouveau, Symbolism, Japonism and the Celtic revival. Elements of all of these can be seen in the so-called 'Glasgow style', associated with Charles Rennie Mackintosh (1868–1928), who was married to Margaret Macdonald, and his circle. Middle-class

Glasgow in its expansionist phase had money to spend on the decorative artworks, textiles and furnishings produced by young designers. These women, whose output ranged very widely, were among the first to have their own studios, to live rather independent lives as 'new women' and, above all, to experiment in all kinds of media. Their importance as individuals is varied: their works are scattered, and few of them have received much posthumous recognition, although several had undoubted talent. Their careers were often disrupted by marriage (sometimes, inhibitingly, to other artists), children, illness, lack of resources and inability to find patrons. But they made a substantial collective contribution to Scotland's participation in European art and design at the turn of the century, and prepared the way for later women artists. S R

• Arthur, L. and Macfarlane, F. C. (1980) *Glasgow School of Art Embroidery 1894–1920*; Burkhauser, J. (ed.) (1990) *Glasgow Girls* (Bibl.); Callen, A. (1979) *Angel in the Studio*; DSAA; Dewar, M. De C. L. (1950) *History of the Glasgow Society of Lady Artists*; *ODNB* (2004) (see 'Glasgow Girls'); Tanner, A. (1992) *A Centenary Exhibition to Celebrate the Founding of the Glasgow Society of Lady Artists in 1882.*

GLENORCHY, Lady Willielma *see* **CAMPBELL, Willielma, Viscountess Glenorchy** (1741–86)

GLOAG, Helen, born Muthill, Perthshire, Jan. 1750, date and place of death unknown. According to Perthshire tradition, 'Empress of Morocco'. Daughter of Ann Key, and Andrew Gloag, blacksmith.

Helen Gloag was brought up at Mill of Steps. It seems she did not get on with her stepmother. Aged 19, the story goes, she left Perthshire with friends, intending to emigrate to South Carolina. The following tale was thereafter developed in Perthshire (and credited by antiquarian Robert Chambers). The vessel carrying her to America is hijacked by Sale corsairs. At their base in Morocco, she joins the harem of the 'Emperor', Sultan Sidi Muhammad, and bears him two sons, later involved in the succession crisis after his death, when another son, Mulay al-Yazid, rules briefly (1790–1). Meanwhile, her brother trades with Morocco, bringing gifts for her family and a local farmer, John Bayne, and assuring them of her prosperity. There is no documentary evidence that she got to Morocco at all. Sidi Muhammad did have white wives and concubines, but Dr Lempriere, who visited Sidi's harem in 1789, saw no sign of a Scottish sultana. Perhaps Helen Gloag invented her own Perthshire legend to cover up some less savoury career in the Mediterranean, yielding the fine china (not a Moroccan product) which she apparently did send home. ALRC

• Calder, A. (2003) *Gods, Mongrels and Demons*; Chambers, R. (1868) *Traditions of Edinburgh*; Lempriere, W. (1793) *A Tour from Gibraltar to Morocco*; McKerracher, A. (2000) *Perthshire in History and Legend*; Rogers, P. G. (1992) *A History of Anglo-Moroccan Relations to 1900*; Shearer, J. (c. 1860) *Antiquities in Perthshire.*

GLOVER, Jean, born Townhead, Kilmarnock, 31 Oct. 1758, died Letterkenny, Ireland, in or after 1801. Travelling actor and singer. Daughter of Jean Thomson, and James Glover, weaver.

Jean Glover was educated at the parish school. She was never meek and blossomed into a splendidly beautiful 'wild child'. Dressed in a buff jacket, a linsey-woolsey petticoat and with her hair in a snood, she attended the local fairs and races. She enjoyed playing with fire and when asked to join one of the travelling shows leapt at the chance. She fell in love and eloped with the leader of the troupe, a Mr Richard – actor, conjurer and all-round scoundrel. The players performed historical displays and Jean Glover was acknowledged to be their best actor and singer, known for her renditions of Scots songs, particularly 'Green Grow the Rashes'. Before one performance in Irvine c. 1795, dressed in scarlet, tinsel and glass beads, she played the tambourine to attract customers. One old woman is reported as saying, 'Weel dae I remember her, and thocht her the brawest leddy I had ever seen step in leather shoon' (MacIntosh 1910, p. 31).

Tradition has it that Robert Burns took down the words of Jean Glover's song 'Ower the Muir Amang the Heather' after hearing her perform it in the Old Commercial Inn, Kilmarnock, and sent it to James Johnson for inclusion in the *The Scots Musical Museum* (1792). Burns liked neither Jean nor her husband and added a footnote to Johnson: 'This song is the composition of a Jean Glover, a girl who was not only a whore; but also a thief, and in one or other character has visited most of the correction houses in the west . . . I took the song down from her singing as she was strolling through the country with a sleight-of-hand blackguard'. Others were a little kinder and said that though she 'rugged and reived' (robbed), Jean Glover was no worse than any other in her situation and she was always faithful to her 'ne'er-do-weel' husband. She died in Ireland while on tour and was performing up until two months before her death. MB

• MacIntosh J. (1910) *The Poets of Ayrshire*; Paterson, J. (1840) *The Contemporaries of Burns*; Stenhouse, W. (1853) *Illustrations of the Lyric Poetry and Music of Scotland*; Tytler, S. and Watson, J. L. (1871) *The Songstresses of Scotland.*

GORDON, Jane Maxwell, Duchess of *see* **MAXWELL, Jane, Duchess of Gordon** (c. 1749– 1812)

GORDON, Isabella, OBE, born Keith 18 May 1901, died Carlisle 11 May 1988. Marine biologist. Daughter, out of wedlock, of Maggie Lamb, domestic servant, and James Gordon, general labourer.

After Keith Grammar School, Isabella Gordon entered the University of Aberdeen, where in 1923 she obtained the first Kilgour Research Scholarship to study sea fans. The next two years were spent at Imperial College studying sea urchin embryology, followed by two years in the USA on a Commonwealth Fund Fellowship at Woods Hole Laboratory, Palo Alto Marine Station, and Yale University. In 1928, she was appointed curator of Crustacea, the first woman on the full-time permanent staff of the BM (Natural History). The 'Grand Old Lady of Carcinology' (study of crustacea), (Holthuis, 1989, p. 93) retired in 1966. Her numerous publications, mostly on decapod crustaceans and sea spiders, and her helpfulness towards researchers had established her as an internationally respected carcinologist. A highlight of her career was a month-long visit in 1961 to Japan as the guest of Japanese scientists; she gave a public lecture in honour of the Emperor Hirohito, also a marine biologist. She was awarded the OBE that year. Although traditional in her work as curator, manager and researcher at the museum, 'as an unmarried woman scientist in what was still . . . a male-dominated world, she was conscious of her trail-blazing role' (Rice 1988, p. 704). JRR

• Gordon, I. (1932) 'Pycnogonida', *Discovery* Rep., 6, pp. 1–138, (1953) 'On a new crab from Cadaques, NE Spain', *Eos. Madrid*, 28, 4, pp. 303–14, (1961) 'Crustaceans, Japan and I', *Contemp. Japan*, 27, 1, pp. 115–26, (1974) 'Crustacea', *Encycl. Brit.*, pp. 310–19. See also Bibl.
Holthuis, L. B. and Ingle, R. W. (1989) 'Isabella Gordon', *Crustaceana*, 56, pp. 93–105, (Bibl.); Rice, A. L. (1988) 'Dr Isabella Gordon', *Jour. Crustacean Biology*, 8, 4, pp. 703–5.

GORDON, Jane (Jean), Countess of Bothwell (1566–67), **Countess of Sutherland** (1573–1629),

born 1545, died Dunrobin 14 May 1629. Daughter of Elizabeth Keith, and George, 4th Earl of Huntly.

After the collapse of her father's rebellion in 1562 against *Mary, Queen of Scots and his death, Jane Gordon and her mother were given places at court. The family's restoration included an alliance, promoted by the Queen, between Jane's brother George Gordon, later 5th Earl of Huntly, and James, 4th Earl of Bothwell (1534/5–78), part of which was Jane's marriage to Bothwell on 22 February 1566, her tocher (dowry) of £8,000 Scots going to clear his debts. The wedding was a Protestant ceremony. However, to satisfy those Catholics involved, Archbishop John Hamilton granted the couple a dispensation to marry, since they were related within the Catholic prohibited degrees (Parliament removed these restrictions in 1567). The marriage was unhappy – Bothwell's attachment to Queen Mary probably pre-dated Lord Darnley's murder on 10 February 1567 – and Countess Jane was granted a divorce by the secular Commissary Court on 3 May 1567 on the grounds of his adultery with her servant, Bessie Crawford. Archbishop Hamilton, whose consistorial authority Mary had restored for the purpose, pronounced the marriage annulled on 7 May because no dispensation had been procured. His own dispensation was suppressed in the interests of all concerned, not least Jane Gordon, who wished release and who retained it. It was discovered among Sutherland papers at Dunrobin in the 1800s.

Jane Gordon returned north in 1567. She married Alexander, 12th Earl of Sutherland (1552–94), on 13 December 1573; they had seven children. Due to Sutherland's ill-health, and after his death, she managed the vast Sutherland estates while bringing up her grandchildren. In 1599, she married Alexander Ogilvy of Boyne, suitor of her youth and widower of Mary Beaton (see Maries, The Four). Her many surviving letters testify to her energy. She remained a Catholic, sheltering missionary priests at Dunrobin, and was buried in Dornoch Cathedral with honours usually given to a Sutherland earl. Contemporaries praised her conduct throughout the tragedy of her early life, and her son paid tribute in his history: 'a vertuous and comelie lady, judicious, of excellent memorie and of great understanding above the capacitie of her sex; . . . she brought to a prosperous end many hard and difficult bussiness . . .' (Fraser 1892, p. 168). MHBS

• NLS: Sutherland Muniments (Deposit 313).
Fraser, W. (1892) *The Sutherland Book*, 2 vols (incl. Sir Robert Gordon's *History*); *ODNB* (2004) (see Gordon, Jean);

Stewart, J. (1874) *A Lost Chapter in the History of Mary, Queen of Scots Recovered*; Sanderson, M. H. B. (1987) *Mary Stewart's People* (Bibl.).

GORDON, Jean, born c. 1670 into one of the gypsy tribes of Kirk Yetholm, died Carlisle 1746.

Tall, hawkfaced and swarthy, Jean Gordon was the inspiration for Meg Merrilees in Sir Walter Scott's novel *Guy Mannering*. She married Patrick Faa, one of the 'royal' gypsies, and they had nine sons. Patrick Faa was convicted of fire-raising and general misdemeanours and banished to Queen Anne's American colonies for life in 1714. Jean Gordon was to lose all her sons, one by murder and eight on the gallows, mainly for the crime of being 'evil-doing gypsies'. In 1732, in her 60s, she was charged at Jedburgh Court with 'being an Egyptian, common vagabond and notorious thief' and plea bargained that she would leave Scotland forever. She survived in the north of England until 1746. Known as a staunch Jacobite, she was ducked in the river Eden by a Hanoverian mob until she drowned, it is said crying out 'Chairlie Yet'. WE
• NAS: Jedburgh Minute Books and Court Records 1714–32. Gordon, A. (1980) *Hearts upon the Highway*; Lang, J. (1913) *North and South of the Tweed*.

GORDON, Mary Clark, n. **Gilmour,** born Glasgow 16 May 1882, died Pasadena, California, USA, 23 August 1963. Hollywood character actor. Daughter of Mary Gibbons, and Allan Gilmour, salesman and storeman.

In her teens, Mary Gilmour sang in the local church choir before becoming a professional contralto, working under her maiden name. Based in Glasgow, she toured Britain and America, often working with Sir Harry Lauder. On 8 December 1908, she married William Gordon, yarn salesman, and in 1910, she had a daughter, Molly. Her husband abandoned her at the end of the First World War. As soon as the war was over, with her daughter and her mother she left Scotland for San Francisco, where her two brothers had settled. She hoped to continue her singing career there. When the family arrived, her mother became ill and her plans to tour were put on hold. The three generations of women moved to Hollywood and, needing to make money quickly to support her family, she took a job as cook in the Robertson-Cole Studio (which later became the famous RKO Studios).

From 1925 Mary Gordon supplemented her income by working as an extra in silent movies.

Her distinctive Glaswegian accent led to a role in *The Little Minister* (1934), which was set in Scotland, and to the job of tutoring the star, Katharine Hepburn, in a Scottish accent. From then until her retirement in 1950 she was one of Hollywood's best-loved character actors. She worked in more than 200 films, often playing Irish mothers as well as Scottish ones. Her films include *The Bride of Frankenstein* (1935), *Bonnie Scotland* (1935) and *Fort Apache* (1948), but her most famous role was as the housekeeper, Mrs Hudson, in the long-running Sherlock Holmes series of films. A popular volunteer at the Hollywood Canteen, entertaining troops during the Second World War, Mary Gordon had the honour of spending her last days in the Motion Picture Home which was set up by the studios to care for those who had devoted their lives to the movies. AK
• Interview with Molly Dutton (Mary Gordon's daughter), 1994.
Katz, E. (1994 edn.) *The Macmillan International Film Encyclopedia*; Quinlan, D. (1995) *Quinlan's Film Character Actors*.

GORDON CATHCART, Emily Eliza Steele, Lady, n. **Pringle,** m1 **Gordon,** m2 **Cathcart,** born 1845, died Margate, Kent, 8 August 1932. Controversial Hebridean landowner. Daughter of John Robert Pringle and his wife.

Emily Gordon assumed possession of the islands of Barra, South Uist and Benbecula in 1878 on the death of her first husband, John Gordon, son of the notorious evictor and emigrationist, Colonel John Gordon of Cluny. In December 1880, in St George's, Hanover Square, London, she married Sir Reginald Archibald Edward Cathcart Bt. The harsh estate regime continued under their joint control until his death in 1916. An absentee proprietor, living in the south of England, Lady Cathcart rarely visited her Hebridean properties and was disliked by both her tenants and the Congested Districts Board (CDB) appointed in 1897 to tackle continuing problems of Highland land hunger and poverty. The CDB's 15-year lifespan was punctuated by land raids, notably on Barra and Vatersay, as crofters reacted against her refusal to assign more land for their use. Repeated occupations led to the CDB's purchase of part of Barra in 1900 and Vatersay in 1909.

Lady Cathcart was criticised for her support for emigration, perceived as the estate management's weapon against unwanted Catholic tenants. In 1883, while the Highland land war was raging, she and

Ranald Macdonald, the unpopular estate factor, orchestrated a short-lived scheme to send families to Wapella and Regina in Canada's Northwest Territories. Parsimonious treatment of the colonists engendered bad publicity into the 20th century, as did a belief that Lady Cathcart's share interests in the Canadian Pacific Railway and Hudson's Bay Company lay behind the scheme. Renewed attempts to encourage the emigration of young people from her estates in 1911 failed, while the plan of the Scottish priest and emigration agent, Andrew MacDonell, to create a colony of Hebridean Catholics in Alberta in the 1920s was tarnished by a perception that he was collaborating with an anti-Catholic, pro-emigration landowner. Lady Cathcart was living near Ascot at the time of her death. Her will included a provision for establishing the Long Island Emigration Fund, but such was the depth of hostility that the trustees refused to implement her wishes. MDH

• Scottish Catholic Archives: DA66/77/3, MacColl, priest, Ardkenneth, South Uist to Bishop of Argyll and the Isles, 27 Sept., 28 Oct. 1883; Saskatchewan Archives Board: R-2.999, reel 1, bundle 138, Lady Cathcart's Canadian Crofters' Reference Book, 1893–1921.
Cameron, E. A. (1996) *Land for the People?*; Campbell, J. L. (ed.) (1936) *The Book of Barra*.

GORDON-CUMMING, Constance Frederica, born Altyre, Morayshire, 26 May 1837, died Crieff 4 Sept. 1924. Travel writer and explorer. Daughter of *Lady Eliza Maria Campbell (see Gordon-Cumming, Lady Eliza) and Sir William Gordon-Cumming.

Constance Gordon-Cumming was the twelfth child of wealthy landowners in Altyre and Gordonstoun, with strong family and business ties to Britain's colonies. Her childhood was spent shuttling between Scotland and England, receiving a sporadic private education. Between 1868 and 1880 she embarked on a series of national and international tours, mainly to visit friends and family, from which she would produce 13 published travel books. Her first work, *From the Hebrides to the Himalayas* (1876, later revised), was a rather unwieldy account of her sojourn across the Hebridean islands and her travels through India and the Himalayas. The explorer *Isabella Bird, with whom she shared common interests and a friendly rivalry, read the book proofs while Constance Gordon-Cumming was living in Fiji between 1875 and 1877 (later recounted in *At Home in Fiji*, 1881). Subsequent works chronicled with increasing clarity her experiences in exotic locations, including the USA,

Tahiti, Samoa and Tonga. In 1880 she retired to Crieff, continuing to write books and contributing articles to leading periodicals, including *Blackwood's Magazine, Contemporary Review, Cornhill Magazine, Leisure Hour, Good Words* and *Cassell's Family Magazine*. At its best her writing responded to her surroundings sympathetically and generously, offering candid insights into exploitative colonial behaviour where she saw it. In general, her work was characterised by a mixture of conventional religiosity, anthropological interest, vivid description and generalised commentary, with some class affectation. DF

• NLS: Blackwood papers, MS 4000–4940; MS series 30,000; Reading Univ.: Chatto & Windus papers.
Gordon-Cumming, C., Works as above, and see (Bibl.).
DLB Gale, vol. 174; *HSWW* (Bibl.); *ODNB* (2004).

GORDON-CUMMING, Lady Eliza Maria, n. **Campbell,** probably born 1798 in Inveraray, died Altyre, near Forres, 21 April 1842. Fossil collector and illustrator. Daughter of Lady Charlotte Maria Campbell (daughter of 4th Duke of Argyll), and John Campbell of Shawfield and Islay.

In 1815 the beautiful Eliza Campbell married Sir William Gordon-Cumming of Altyre and Gordonstown. Despite having 13 children, this exceptional woman obviously took her mother's advice to 'avoid growing into a squashy milk cow . . . [and] not let women prose to you all day long about cake and candles and clothes' (NLS: Dep 175/164/1). Her many accomplishments included painting and horticulture; she designed the gardens at Altyre House, produced new varieties of plants by crossing, and went salmon fishing. Her 'artistic talent . . . was fired . . . by frequent visits from such artists as Sir Edwin Landseer' (Gordon-Cumming 1904, p. 38) and advice from Benjamin West. Sir Henry Raeburn portrays her holding a pencil and George Saunders' portrait (Private Collection) shows her with a sketchbook as well (Smailes).

In 1839, a geologist 'introduced her to the delights of . . . collecting the beautifully preserved fossil fishes' (Andrews 1982, p. 25) in a small quarry near Nairn. Louis Agassiz visited Altyre in 1840 to see her large collection. Her generous gifts to him and to other geologists are now in Neuchatel University, the NHM, Oxford, Paris and elsewhere. The Altyre Collection of Middle Old Red Sandstone fishes (NMS) was a major source for Agassiz's 1844–5 monograph on fossil fish, for which she also drew several plates. Although he praised

her 'precision of detail and . . . artistic talent', her watercolours were later taxed with 'many confident inaccuracies' (ibid., p. 31). During her last pregnancy, she was 'severely injured in stopping a bolting horse in a gig wherein sat a terrified woman' (Gordon-Cumming 1904, p. 43) and died less than a month after the baby's birth. Her daughter *Constance Frederica Gordon-Cumming became an encyclopaedic travel writer. JRR
• NLS: Dep 175, Gordon-Cumming of Altyre Papers (quoted with permission).
Andrews, S. M. (1982) *The Discovery of Fossil Fishes in Scotland up to 1845*; Gordon-Cumming, C. F. (1904) *Memories*; *ODNB* (2004) (see Cumming, Constance Frederica Gordon).
Personal communication: Helen Smailes.

GORMLA (Gormshuil Mhór), fl. 17th century (traditionally), Lochaber. Witch figure.

Gormla is the leading Gaelic witch figure, others being less well known outside their localities. A woman of the same name is associated with Skye, perhaps due to the vagaries of tradition or the name being the cognomen of more than one person. Gaelic nomenclature groups all witches under the term *banabhuidseach* (a loanword from English 'witch'). Possibly Gaelic tradition vaguely reflects a system of shamanism, with its own hierarchy. The elements of Gormla's name ('deep blue' and 'noble') have produced in some dialects *Gormshuil* – 'the blue-eyed'. Such witches are formidable characters, with definite prestige, feared but treated with respect, perhaps enjoying some of the immunity protecting poets in Gaelic society. In tradition Gormla Mhór gives valued advice to Cameron of Lochiel, head of his clan, and is also one of the witches who bring about the death by drowning of MacLeod of Raasay in 1671. JMacI
• Black, R. (ed.) (2005) *John Gregor Campbell's The Gaelic Otherworld*; Camshron, A. (1957) 'Gormshuil Mhór na Maighe', *An Gaidheal*, March; McKerracher, A. (1994) 'The Great Gormshuil' *The Scots Magazine*, April, pp. 374–81; MacKellar, M. (1889–90) 'Legends and traditions of Lochaber', *Trans. Gael. Soc. Inverness*, 16.

GOWDIE, Isobel, fl. Auldearn 1662. Confessed witch.

The year 1662 produced some of the worst witch-hunting in Scottish history; one of the most infamous cases occurred in the village of Auldearn, Nairnshire. The trial of Isobel Gowdie is unusual in that her confessions were allegedly given voluntarily and no torture was used. However, the use and nature of judicial torture in Scottish witchcraft trials are contentious subjects. It is likely that her elderly body was pricked with a long needle to search for the witch's mark (a spot insensitive to pain) and she may have been kept awake for days while being interrogated.

Some aspects of her confession reflected beliefs held a century earlier. She interspersed witchcraft, fairy lore and diabolism to a degree unparalleled in any other known Scottish witch trial. She affirmed she was a member of a coven of thirteen people, each with a named spirit to wait upon her, and spoke of riding through the air on 'cornstraws' with her companions, attacking people whom the devil had instructed them to harm. Continental confessions often spoke of infant sacrifice and cannibalism, but Isobel Gowdie reported dancing, drinking and eating fine meats. She also said that a woman, Jean Martin, named 'Maiden' by the devil, was so called because the 'devil always takes the Maiden in his hand next to him, when we dance' (*Crim. Trials*, p. 606). Martin regretted several deaths, which she believed she had caused with arrows supplied by the devil.

Other aspects are more unusual. Isobel Gowdie admitted meeting with the fairies on several occasions: 'we went in to the Downie-Hills; the hills opened, and we came to a fair and large braw room' (ibid. p. 611). The presence of large bulls bellowing indicated wealth and status to an agricultural community. She witnessed the manufacture of elf arrowheads by diminutive, hump-backed 'elf-boys'. She reported the fairies' names and dress; her own sprite, 'The Red Reiver', was clothed in black. Such details seem to have annoyed her interrogators who tried to alter her words with a demonic twist or stopped writing down parts that did not fit their own prejudices. Although Auldearn was slow to experience the full force of the Presbyterian system, Isobel Gowdie's confession demonstrates the tenacity of witch and fairy traditions, despite almost a century of intensive persecution. Her ultimate fate is unknown. An orchestral work by James MacMillan, 'The confession of Isobel Gowdie', was premiered in 1990. LFH
• *Crim. Trials*, vol. iii, pp. 602–16.
Henderson, L. and Cowan, E. J. (2001) *Scottish Fairy Belief: A History*; *ODNB* (2004).

GRAHAM, Helen, m. **Tovey-Tennent,** born Edinburgh 8 June 1806, died London 14 June 1896. Diarist. Daughter of Jane Ferrier, and

Brigadier-General Samuel Graham, sometime Deputy-Governor, Stirling Castle.

The eldest of four children, Helen Graham corresponded with her aunt, novelist *Susan Ferrier. Her mother was celebrated beauty **Jane Graham** (1767–1846), who inspired Robert Burns's verse, 'To Miss Ferrier' (1787). Jane Graham rescued and made drawings of 16th-century carvings from Stirling Castle, published, with her drawings and accompanying illustrations by the renowned architect Edward Blore, as *Lacunar Strevelinense* (1817).

Apart from a period in Ireland (1808–13), where her father was posted, Helen Graham was raised in Scotland and educated at home, mainly by her mother, learning French, Italian and Latin. She kept at least eight volumes of (mainly unpublished) diaries. The earliest ones (1820–1) concern English travels. The most interesting (1823–6, published 1957) vividly depict early 19th-century Scottish domestic life and manners – too rarely portrayed in that period's fiction. She records meeting Walter Scott and family, and describes Edinburgh gatherings involving other well-known figures, with well-selected (sometimes Scots) dialogue. Sharing Susan Ferrier's eye for absurdity, she describes church attendance together: 'Dr Grant or rather (as Aunt Susan says) "Grunt", preached, and she desired me to cough pretty loud, if I saw her head "nid-nid-noddin" of which she was afraid. A sermon was announced to be preached for the benefit of indigent old men. Aunt Susan told me as we came out that she heard of a boy who, asked where he had been, replied he had been at church to hear a sermon about "indigestible old men".' The later diaries run from 1826 to 1854, the last ones being fragmentary. After marrying Colonel Hamilton Tovey-Tennent in 1836, she lived near London. CA

• NLS: Acc. 8585, Ferrier papers.

Irvine, J. (ed.) (1957) *Parties and Pleasures, the diaries of Helen Graham, 1823–1826*, intro. Marion Lochhead.

Family papers.

GRAHAM, Isabella, n. **Marshall,** born Lanarkshire 29 July 1742, died New York, USA, 27 July 1814. Educator and poor-relief worker. Daughter of Janet Hamilton, and John Marshall, tenant farmer.

Isabella Marshall grew up at Elderslie, Ayrshire. She used a legacy from her grandfather for her education, attending boarding school for seven years. Her devout family had close connections to the local minister, Rev. Dr John Witherspoon, later President of Princeton. In 1765, she married John Graham, a Paisley doctor and surgeon for the Royal American Regiment. When the regiment travelled to British North America in 1767, the couple left behind two sons from John Graham's first marriage, as well as their son; the infant died shortly afterwards. A daughter was born in Montreal and two more in Fort Niagara where the family lived for four years. John Graham planned to buy land and settle in the Mohawk Valley but the American Revolutionary War intervened. In 1772, the regiment was ordered to Antigua where John Graham died in November 1774; a son was born posthumously. Distraught, Isabella Graham and her children returned from Antigua to Scotland, where she cared for her impoverished father and taught school in Paisley. After a business venture failed, friends including *Willielma Campbell, Lady Glenorchy, helped her establish a successful school in Edinburgh in 1779–80. She also founded 'The Penny Society', a fund for mutual relief in sickness, which became The Society for the Relief of the Destitute Sick.

When Dr Witherspoon visited Scotland in 1785, he suggested that Isabella Graham move to America. Aided by a legacy from Lady Glenorchy, she and her daughters moved in 1789 to New York, where she opened a school. Her charitable ventures included organising the Society for the Relief of Poor Widows with Small Children (1797), one of the first of its kind in America. In 1798, with her daughters married and her son dead, she retired from teaching, and spent the next decade as director of the Society. She opened Sunday schools, worked with the Bible Society, was involved with her daughter Joanna Bethune in founding the Orphan Asylum Society in 1806, and served as superintendent of the Magdalen House (1811). In 1814, shortly before her death, she helped found the Society for the Promotion of Industry Among the Poor. EE

• Bethune, J. (ed.) [1816] (1843) *The Power of Faith, Exemplified in the Life and Writings of the Late Mrs Isabella Graham*; E. T. James et al. (eds) (1971) *Notable American Women 1607–1950* (Bibl.); Religious Tract Society (1832) *The Life of Mrs Isabella Graham of New York*.

GRAHAM, Margaret Manson, born Orphir, Orkney, 26 April 1860, died Aro-Chuku, Nigeria, 14 Oct. 1933. Missionary-nurse. Daughter of Isabella Manson, and John Graham, weaver and crofter.

One of five children, Margaret Graham trained as a teacher in Orphir and later as a nurse in

Glasgow. In 1895, she joined the Women's Foreign Mission Committee (WFMC) in Old Calabar, Nigeria, where her nursing skills saved the lives of many sick crew members on British trading ships. Subsequently, she became the first matron of Duketown Hospital. In 1901, a military campaign was launched against the Aro tribe and she tended the casualties at Itu, the Aro heartland Aro-Chuku, and Bende. She received the Africa General Service medal with clasps and in 1906 was appointed a Serving Sister on the Roll of the Order of the Hospital of St John of Jerusalem.

Distressed by the Aro subjugation, Margaret Graham again offered nursing service two years into retirement, specifying the Aro people. Her work varied from dressing ulcers and stitching knife wounds to rescuing twins and training women in child welfare. Twin births were regarded with superstition so she supervised the building of a sanctuary for outcast women and babies. Another new venture was a dispensary, for which she funded medicines. She adopted an orphan, Okorafo, and trained an Aro chief's descendant, Lazarus Okoroji, as dispensary assistant. Fledgling missionaries were teased by her but quickly respected her devotion to the Aros, despite the gruelling conditions. She worked with two other women missionaries, **Agnes Siddons Arnot** (n. Young) (1881–1953) and Susan McKennell from Armagh, Ireland. Agnes Arnot, from Kinross, Principal of the Slessor Memorial Home, was a former assistant to *Mary Slessor and had returned to the field after her husband's death. She helped outcast women to earn a livelihood by teaching them to embroider on linen, using traditional Aro female designs.

Margaret Graham was nominated 'Orkney's Own Missionary' in 1924. She continued her work even when, with a broken leg, she had to be carried. Drumbeats broadcast her death and she was buried next to Mary Slessor. There are memorials to Margaret Graham in Nigeria and Orkney. RL

• Maurice Gray papers (privately held); NLS: Letterbooks and Minutes of the WFMC; Orkney Archives: Records of Paterson Church, Kirkwall, Orphir Public School, Kirbister, Orphir School Log Books.
Interview with Rev. R. M. MacDonald (1995) by author.
Arnot, A. S. (1934) 'A Calabar heroine. The inspiring career and personality of Margaret Manson Graham', *Life & Work*, Feb.; Beattie, J. A. T. (1978) *The River Highway: a personal record of the Scottish Mission in Nigeria from 1927 to 1957*, The Church of Scotland Overseas Council; *The Orcadian*, 1 March 1956 and 14 Oct. 1993; Mowatt, H. (1956) 'Sister Graham: a great Orkney lady, she gave her life to Nigeria', *The Orcadian*, 1 March; Paterson Church *United Free Church Quarterly Record*, April 1924.

GRAHAM, Maria (Lady Callcott), n. **Dundas,** m1 **Graham,** m2 **Callcott,** born Cockermouth 19 July 1785, died Kensington 28 Nov. 1842. Author and traveller. Daughter of Ann Thompson, of an American loyalist family, and Rear-Admiral George Dundas.

Maria Dundas was well educated at the Miss Brights' school in Abingdon, with frequent visits to the Richmond house of her uncle, David Dundas, who introduced her into London literary society. In February 1805, visiting another uncle, James Dundas, in Edinburgh, she met leading literary and academic figures, including Henry Mackenzie, Dugald Stewart, Thomas Brown and Francis Jeffrey. Her academic interests apparently led Brown to christen her 'metaphysics in muslin' (Gotch 1937, p. 75). In 1809, sailing with her father to India, she met Lt Thomas Graham of Fintry, and they married on 9 December. Her travel writing was intellectually and politically ambitious, incorporating a thoughtful historical awareness of the different societies she observed. In her *Journal of a Residence in India* (1812), and even more in the scholarly *Letters on India* (1814), she wrote not only of everyday life but of the history, languages, religions and antiquities of India, drawing on the work of contemporary orientalist scholars, including Scottish friends Sir James Mackintosh, John Leyden and Colin Mackenzie, and scandalising some readers (ibid., p. 154).

On returning to Scotland, the Grahams established a home in Broughty Ferry for a number of years. She published the first book in English on Poussin. Later, sailing with her husband to South America, and remaining there after his sudden death in April 1822, she kept detailed journals of her visits to Brazil and Chile, which she published with extensive historical introductions. She strongly sympathised with the Chilean struggle against Spain and with the efforts of her friend Admiral Lord Cochrane to forward Chilean independence. Her famous, important and closely observed description of the elevation of the land during the 1822 earthquake in Chile was to lead to a major attack on her in 1834 by G. B. Greenough of the GSL, but she was vindicated by the observations of Charles Darwin from the *Beagle* in 1836. In Brazil, having met the Empress Leopoldina, she was governess to the royal children for about 12 months from April 1824. On 20 February 1827, she married the artist (later Sir) Augustus Wall Callcott (1779–1844), returned to literary London, and continued her writing career in history, art history, and books for children. She was a pioneer writer on Giotto and other Italian primitives. Her best-known later work, *Little Arthur's History of England* (1835), displayed a patriotic spirit consistent with her earlier support for a nationalist politics in South America. It was reprinted and updated many times, most recently in 1962. JR

• Location Register of English Literary Manuscripts and Letters: Eighteenth and Nineteenth Centuries, 1995, vol. I, pp. 158–9, for full list of archive holdings [BL, NLS, Bodleian, etc.] for Maria Graham.

[Callcott, M. G.] (C. E. Lawrence, (ed.), 1936 [rev. 1962]) *Little Arthur's History of England . . .* The century edition; Graham, M. (1835) 'On the reality of the rise of the coast of Chile, in 1822, as stated by Mrs Graham', *Amer. Jour. for Science and Arts*, 28, pp. 239–47.

Creese, M. R. S. and T. M. (1994) 'British women who contributed to research in the geological sciences in the nineteenth century', *Brit. Jour. Hist. Science*, 27, pp. 23–54; Gotch, R. B. (1937) *Maria Lady Callcott* (Bibl.); Kölbl-Ebert, M. (1999) 'Observing orogeny – Maria Graham's account of the earthquake in Chile in 1822', *Episodes*, 22, no. 1, pp. 36–40; Mavor, E. (1993) *The Captain's Wife*; *ODNB* (2004); O'Leary, P. (1989) *Sir James Mackintosh, the Whig Cicero*.

GRAHAM, Violet Hermione, Duchess of Montrose, GBE, m. **Graham,** born London 10 Sept. 1854, died Abbots Langley, Herts, 21 Nov. 1940. Anti-suffragist and philanthropist. Daughter of Jane Seymour, and Sir Frederick Graham of Netherby.

On 24 July 1876 Violet Graham married Douglas Graham, 5th Duke of Montrose (1852–1925); they had three sons and two daughters. Committed to philanthropy, the Duchess was President of the Soldiers' and Sailors' Families Association in Scotland from 1900, and from 1909 President of the Scottish Red Cross and Vice-President of the Territorial Nursing Service. She also took particular interest in Govan, founding the West Govan Child Welfare Association, the Montrose Holiday Home for poor children on Loch Lomond, and the Montrose Maternity Home. She also presided over the Training Home for Midwives and Nurses and the Elder Cottage Hospital there. She was awarded an LLD by the University of Glasgow for her philanthropic work. The *Anti-Suffrage Review* (*ASR*) recorded that such extensive experience in organisations helping women made her an 'invaluable acquisition' to the anti-suffrage cause, leading the way in 'womanly service for her country' (*ASR* June 1910). Like *Lady Griselda Cheape, she was deeply hostile to the cause of women's suffrage. Branches of the Women's Anti-Suffrage League (WASL) were founded in Scotland in 1909, and in May 1910, on the formation of the Scottish National WASL, the Duchess, as President, circulated an appeal 'to convince women of the danger to the state if votes were given to large numbers of inexperienced women debarred by nature and circumstances from the requisite political knowledge' (*ASR* May 1910). Active until the League dissolved in 1918, she was one of the first women to be awarded the GBE in that year, and one of the first women JPs appointed in 1920. JR

• *Anti-Suffrage Review*, 1909–10, 1918; Checkland, O. (1980) *Philanthropy in Victorian Scotland*; *Glasgow Herald*, 23 Nov. 1940 (obit.); *The Times*, 23 Nov. 1940 (obit.), *The Times*, 7 Dec. 1940.

GRAHAMSLAW, Helen, of Newton, fl. c. 1570–c. 1600. Heiress. Daughter of John Grahamslaw of Newton.

By 1586, Helen Grahamslaw's eight brothers had all been murdered by the Turnbulls as part of a vicious Border bloodfeud. Her father decided to dispose of his estates in a dignified manner, selling his lands to Robert Ker, a political ally and younger son of Robin Ker of Ancrum, for £4,000, reserving a life rent to himself, and arranging Helen's marriage to Robert. This helped ensure that his ancestral lands would not be overrun by the avaricious Turnbulls. They continued to harass Helen Grahamslaw and her new husband, stealing sheep belonging to her in 1588. Robert had died by 1600, at which time animosity still raged between his wife and the Turnbulls. The Turnbulls were brought to account only after the Union of the Crowns. MMM

• NAS: Lothian MSS, GD40/1/379/4, GD40/3/382; Register of Deeds, RD1/24/1 fos 1823.

Crim. Trials, vol. ii, pp. 370–5, 378–81, 419–21, 442; *RMS*, v, no.1058.

GRANGE, Rachel, Lady *see* **CHIESLEY, Rachel** (1679–1745)

GRANT, Anne, of Laggan,[‡] n. **Macvicar,** born Glasgow 21 Feb. 1755, died Edinburgh 7 Nov. 1838. Letter writer, essayist and poet. Daughter of Duncan Macvicar, army officer. Her mother was of the family of Stewart of Invernahyle in Argyllshire.

Soon after Anne Macvicar's birth, her father joined the army and was sent with his regiment to North America. Aged 3, she and her mother joined him and settled near Albany, New York, where they lived for most of the following decade. As a child she attracted the attention of Catalina (or Margaretta) Schuyler, a member of a prominent New York family, who provided most of her formal education. In 1768, the family returned to Glasgow and in 1773 moved to Fort Augustus where her father became Barrack-Master. In 1779 she married Rev. James Grant (d. 1801), an army chaplain, scholar and minister of the Highland parish of Laggan, where they lived for the following 23 years. There she learnt Gaelic and 'found all the virtues of simplicity and family values that she felt were increasingly being threatened elsewhere in Britain and Europe' (*SHA* p. 66). Between 1780 and 1799, they had 12 children, all of whom she outlived, except her youngest son, John, who became the editor of her posthumous *Memoir and Correspondence* (1844). In 1801, her husband died suddenly, leaving her with eight children to support and no income other than two pensions totalling about £40. In 1803, she began her literary career with the publication, by subscription, of a volume of poems. Soon afterwards she began to collect the letters she had written to friends from Fort Augustus and Laggan, publishing them as *Letters from the Mountains* (1806). Characterised by 'vivacity and strong sense' (*DNB* vol. VIII, p. 377), the letters made her reputation.

In 1803 she moved to Woodend, a village near Stirling, and in 1806 to Stirling, taking live-in pupils to supplement her income. There she wrote *Memoirs of an American Lady* (1808), an account of the Schuyler family that includes her own childhood memories of America before the revolution, of Indian tribes and Dutch settlers. She moved to Edinburgh in 1810, where she published *Essays on the Superstitions of the Highlanders of Scotland* (1811), possibly her most important work, and in 1814 the last of her major publications, *Eighteen Hundred and Thirteen: a poem*. Despite the deaths of her adult children and a fall followed by disability, she played an important role in Edinburgh literary life, as hostess, prolific correspondent and occasional translator of Gaelic poetry. A High Tory, she nevertheless had Whig friends and knew many leading women writers,

including *Elizabeth Hamilton, *Eliza Fletcher and *Joanna Baillie. Sir Walter Scott described her as 'a woman whose tongue and pen are rather overpowering' although 'an excellent person, notwithstanding' (ibid., p. 377). In 1826, he and others procured a government pension of 100 shillings that, with several legacies from old friends and pupils, made her last years comfortable. Contemporary appreciation of her work was significantly influenced by the respect she commanded for her courage and virtue, her deep faith, 'extraordinary good sense, and . . . uncommon powers of mind' (Wilson 1876, p. xviii). She was also recognised as a thoughtful observer of minority cultures. MVH
• Grant, A., Works as above and see Bibls.
Corvey Women Writers on the Web (CW3)
www2.shu.ac.uk/corvey/CW3/ (Bibl.);
DNB, vol. VIII; Grant, J. P. (ed.) (1844) *Memoir and Correspondence of Mrs Grant of Laggan*; *HSWW* (Bibl.); *ODNB* (2004) (Bibl.); Perkins, P. (1999) *Biography of Anne Grant*, Corvey CW3; *Survey of Reception of the Works of Anne Grant*, Corvey CW3; *Critical Essay on the Work of Anne Grant*, Corvey CW3; *SHA*; Wilson, J. G. (1876) Introduction to *Memoirs of an American Lady with Sketches of Manners and Scenery in America*.

GRANT, Elizabeth, of Rothiemurchus, m. **Smith,** born Edinburgh 7 May 1797, died Baltiboys, Co. Wicklow, Ireland, 16 Nov. 1885. Diarist. Daughter of Jane Ironside, of Durham, and Sir John Peter Grant of Rothiemurchus.

Much of Elizabeth Grant's childhood, 1802–12, was spent in southern England, but holidays were spent on her father's estate, The Doune, Rothiemurchus, Inverness-shire, and from 1812 to 1814 the family resided there. In 1814, financial difficulties took them to Edinburgh, where an early love affair was ended by her parents because of a family feud. The Grants travelled to Europe, but by 1820 returned to Rothiemurchus; in 1826, to help out family finances, Elizabeth began to write for *Fraser's Magazine* and others. In September 1828, her father's appointment as judge at Bombay took the family to India where, in June 1829, she married Colonel Henry Smith (1780–1867). On the Baltiboys estate in Ireland, which he had inherited, the couple embarked on a programme of improvements, interrupted by two years in France, 1843–5 with their three children.

From 1845, Elizabeth Smith began to write memoirs, for her family rather than for publication, vividly recreating her early years, especially the life of Rothiemurchus and the Highland community. She recalled, unsentimentally and in detail, the domestic lives of local households, the countryside and its hardships, and the working practices of Highland men and women such as the timber floaters of the Spey. She recreated harvest home in Rothiemurchus, the gaiety of the Kinrara home of *Jane Maxwell, Duchess of Gordon, and her own 'coming out' at Inverness in 1814. She wrote, too, of the different social worlds of Edinburgh in the early years of the century, of fashion, literature and the law, providing a lively record of parties, theatre and opera-going. The memoirs include sharp words on colonial society and enthusiasm for her experiences of India. From 1840 to 1885, she kept a diary intermittently of her life in Ireland: only selections from the 1840s have been published, as an important record of the famine years, 1845–9. Her perspective is that of a conscientious, improving, resident landlord, but also a 'benevolent patrician' (*HSWW*, p. 214), convinced of the rightness of the policy of evictions and the move to larger farms. The same complacency appears in her articles of the 1840s in *Chambers's Edinburgh Journal*. Selections from her memoirs were published after her death by her niece, Lady Strachey, as *Memoirs of a Highland Lady* (1897); immediate success rapidly meant three more editions. The full text was published by Canongate, 1988, 1992. J R

• Grant, E. (1849–50) 'Mrs Wright's Conversations with her Irish Acquaintances', *Chambers Edinburgh Journal*, XIII, XIV [1897, 1898] [1988] (1992) *Memoirs of a Highland Lady*, (1991) *The Highland Lady in Ireland*, (1996) *A Highland Lady in France*; Thomson, D. and McGusty, M. (eds) (1980) *The Irish Journals of Elizabeth Smith 1840–1850*.
HSWW (Select Bibl.); *ODNB* (2004) (see Smith, Elizabeth).

GRANT, Isabel Frances (Elsie), MBE, born Edinburgh 21 July 1887, died Edinburgh 19 Sept. 1983. Historian and folk museum pioneer. Daughter of Isabel Mackintosh of Balnespick, and Colonel Hugh Gough Grant CB.

Elsie Grant was raised in London by her grandfather, Field-Marshall Sir Patrick Grant, and aunt, Frances Gough Grant, following her parents' posting to India. Educated privately, she often recalled childhood visits to the British Museum. The most formative influences, however, came from a visit to Stockholm and Oslo which included the pioneering museum projects of Skansen in Sweden's Nordiska Museum and Norway's Sandvig Collection at Lillehammer. These earliest European 'folk museums', together

with a 'costume gallery' in the Rijksmuseum in Amsterdam, inspired in her the vision of a museum for the Highlands and Islands to preserve their vanishing material culture, Gaelic traditions and values.

Elsie Grant's writing career was encouraged by John Maynard Keynes, for whom she worked as a researcher. He published several of her articles in *The Economic Journal* and two of the Supplements (1926, 1928) appeared under her name. Her contribution to modern scholarship, especially Highland history, is still recognised and respected. Her first two major books, *Everyday Life on an Old Highland Farm, 1769–82* (1924, 1981) and *The Social and Economic Development of Scotland before 1603* (1930) expanded the paradigm of Scotland's academic history. Her first book closely analysed the farm accounts of William Mackintosh of Balnespick, her ancestor, and described the social and economic context of Dunachton in Badenoch, an open-field farmtown held in runrig. Of particular significance is her sympathetic evaluation of the benevolent tacksman, a class conventionally vilified for its perceived role in the decline and collapse of Gaelic society.

Travel and research, including conversations with an older generation and extensive fieldwork in Badenoch and Strathspey, led to her involvement in the Highland Exhibition staged in Inverness in 1930, when 2,100 artefacts were collected for a 'national folk museum'. When this failed to develop, Elsie Grant used a personal legacy to establish a folk museum in the disued Free Church in Iona in 1935. Later she moved the rapidly growing collection to Pitmain House in Kingussie, where the Highland Folk Museum opened in 1944 as *Am Fasgadh* ('The Shelter'). With four reconstructed buildings, it illustrated the complex history of farming and fishing, crofting and domestic life, local varieties and regional variations between Mainland Scotland and the Hebrides. *Highland Folk Ways* (1961) stands as a handbook for this pioneering enterprise.

The University of Edinburgh awarded Elsie Grant the honorary degree of LLD in 1948 for her creation of *Am Fasgadh*; when she retired to Edinburgh in 1954, it was run by the four Scottish universities until taken over by Highland Region in 1975. Awarded an MBE in 1959 for her contributions to scholarship, she continued to publish, especially on Highland social history and the medieval Lordship of the Isles. Her hospitable Edinburgh house in Heriot Row was a meeting place for scholars at her frequent and congenial soirées. HC

• Grant, I. F., Works as above, and (1935) *The Lordship of the Isles*, (1980) *Along a Highland Road*, and see Bibl. below. Cheape, H. (1986) 'Dr I. F. Grant (1887–1983): The Highland Folk Museum and bibliography of her written works', *Rev. of Scot. Culture*, 2 (Bibl.); Noble, R. (1977) 'The changing role of the Highland Folk Museum', *Aberdeen Univ. Rev.*, 47; *ODNB* (2004).

GRANT, Isobel, fl. 1637. Quasi-historical figure involved in a notorious case of murder. Daughter of Grant of Tulloch (aka Fear Thulach, aka McJokkie).

Isobel or Iseabail Dhubh Thulach had apparently given her affections to a MacGregor 'ruffian' known as Iain Dubh Gearr. Both the Grants and MacGregors were drawn into a fight near her homestead with a rival suitor for her hand. The subsequent decreet alleges that a number of men, some of them MacGregors, set upon one John Steuart, near Tulloch in Strathspey, 'shot him through the thighs, broke his thigh bones, cut off his fingers and cut off his head and danced and made merry about him a long time' (McLean 1994–6, p. 125). It is assumed that Isobel is the daughter referred to in the charge, preceding the decreet. This refers to 'Johne Grant alias McJokkie in Tulloch, his two sons and daughter' (ibid.). This event is thought to lie behind the composition of the famous Reel of Tulloch. A variant of the tale (for which lyrics and tune survive) has Isobel Grant running off with one of the MacGregors, and dancing the Reel of Tulloch with him over the body of one of her brothers whom he has just killed, the brother having pursued them to break up the dangerous liaison with an outlaw. JP

• McLean, D. P. (1994–6) 'The Reel of Tulloch in fact and fiction', *Trans. Gael. Soc. Inverness*, vol. LIX, pp. 118–128.

GRANT, Mary, born Kilgraston, Perthshire, 16 March 1831, died London 20 Feb. 1908. Sculptor. Daughter of Lady Lucy Bruce, and John Grant, JP.

Despite initial family opposition, Mary Grant's traditional upper-middle-class education was followed by training with master sculptors in Florence, Paris and London. Having made her debut at the RSA (1864), she moved to London where she established an independent studio and exhibited at the RA from 1866 to 1882. Two passions dominated her career: 'to make a mark on time' and 'to do something for the Glory of God in the way of art' (Copeland 1995). Her statue *Saint Margaret of Antioch* satisfied both ambitions. At the

urging of the Prince of Wales, she exhibited it at the Paris Exposition (1878) to resounding praise, and later presented it to her spiritual adviser, Bishop C. C. Grafton, for St Paul's Cathedral, Fond-du-Lac, Wisconsin.

Considered a 'pioneer . . . amongst women' by her nephew (*DSAA* p. 246), she also appears to have advocated female suffrage, being the putative author of *The Franchise: an educational test* (1878) and the sculptor of the *Henry Fawcett Memorial* (1886), subscribed to by his grateful countrywomen. Works survive at Kilgraston, in the SNPG (bust of Lord Advocate Henry Erskine), in St Giles (medallion of A. P. Stanley) and in St Mary's (Episcopal) Cathedral, Edinburgh (*Crucifixion*). SHH

• Royal Archives, Windsor Castle: Corr. Mary Grant, RA VIC/Add. T149 (access by gracious permission of Her Majesty The Queen); St Paul's Cathedral Archive: Corr. Mary Grant, Journal of Bishop C. C. Grafton. Grant, M., Works as above, and (1885) 'The Women's Fawcett Memorial Fund', *Englishwoman's Review*, passim; (1899) 'Miss Mary Grant', *Ladies' Field*, 15 July, pp. 248–9. Copeland, J. (1995) ' "A Mark on Time": the diary and letterbook of Mary Grant, sculptor, 1830–1908', Diss. for Archb. Dipl. Readers, Lambeth, pp. 25, 63; *Dictionary of Women Artists*; *DSAA*; Hurtado, S. H. (2002) 'Genteel mavericks: women sculptors in Victorian Britain', PhD, Univ. of Manitoba, Canada (copy in Courtauld Inst., Bibl.); *The Times*, 29 Feb. 1908 (obit.).

GRANT, Mary Pollock (May), born Partick 2 December 1876, died Tunbridge Wells, August 1957. Missionary, suffragette and policewoman. Daughter of Eliza Muirhead, and Rev. Dr Charles Martin Grant, Minister of St Mark's, Dundee.

May Grant attended Dundee High School, and worked as a Church of Scotland missionary in Scotland and from 1905 in India. As a militant suffragette and WSPU member in Dundee, she first came to public attention when she was imprisoned (using the alias Marion Pollock) following an attempt to disrupt a meeting with Lloyd George in Aberdeen Music Hall. After her release, she revealed her true identity as a clergyman's daughter at a meeting in Dundee on 18 December 1912, where she called on her sisters to help their oppressed fellow women by fighting for political power. She maintained her high profile throughout 1913–14, writing regularly to the press and frequently being ejected from public meetings. She worked as a VAD nurse during the First World War, subsequently joining the women's police service, first in munitions factories and then in London. She was involved in civil defence work during the Second World War. Mary Grant took an active interest in politics and was known as an excellent platform speaker. She was twice a Liberal candidate for English constituencies in Parliamentary elections. In the 1930s she became a Christian Scientist, and for 20 years was in practice as a healer, until disabled by a stroke in 1953. LO

• AGC; Dundee Courier, 17 August 1957 (obit.); Leneman, L. (1992) 'The Scottish churches and votes for women', Records of the Scottish Church History Society, 24, p. 129.

GRAY, Elizabeth, n. **Anderson,** born Alloway 21 Feb. 1831, died Edinburgh 11 Feb. 1924. Fossil collector. Daughter of Mary Hamilton Young, and Thomas Anderson, innkeeper, farmer.

Second of eight children, after school in Girvan and Glasgow, Elizabeth Anderson became interested in the local fossils, thanks to her father, a keen naturalist. In 1856, she married Robert Gray, Glasgow banker and amateur ornithologist. Their joint interest in natural history focused on the Girvan fossils. Their four daughters and two sons helped collect specimens every summer holiday, even after their move to Edinburgh (1874). The original Gray Collection was presented to the Hunterian Museum, University of Glasgow, in 1866 and attendance at a newly instituted class in geology for women helped Elizabeth Gray to appreciate the scientific importance of her fossils. Her material formed the basis for many significant publications, notably Prof. C. Lapworth's *Girvan Succession* (1882). He later stressed its importance as 'the very first collection in which the exact localities and horizons of every individual fossil . . . [were] written down at the time of collection' (letter to Mrs Gray, 10 June 1914, NHM) and in which the part and counterpart of each fossil were kept together.

Elizabeth Gray collected on demand for several specialists, but her main concern was to have her specimens named, published with illustrations, and returned to her quickly. Widowed in 1887, she resolutely continued collecting, with her three unmarried daughters, until her death. Further collections were acquired by the RMS (1889), the BGS, the NHM (1920), and elsewhere. Her huge collections from the Lower Paleozoic around Girvan included unusual fossil groups and new species, several of which were named after her. For her substantial contribution to geology, she was made an honorary member of the GSG (1900) and

awarded the Murchison Geological Fund (1903). JRR

• NHM: Mrs Gray Archive (Corr.).
Bull. BM (NH) (1989) 17, 2, pp. 167–258; Cleevely, R. J., Tripp, R. P. and Howells, Y. (1989) *Mrs Elizabeth Gray (1831–1924)*; Creese, M. R. S. (1998) *Ladies in the Laboratory*; Horne, J. (1925) in *Trans. Geol. Soc. Edin.*, 11, p. 392 (obit.); *ODNB* (2004); *The Scotsman*, 12 Feb. 1924 (obit.).

GRAY, Norah Neilson, born Helensburgh 16 June 1882, died Glasgow 27 May 1931. Artist. Daughter of Norah Neilson, and George William Gray, merchant.

One of seven children, of whom one sister, Margaret, became a lecturer at the University of Glasgow, and another, Tina, a surgeon, in 1901 Norah Neilson Gray enrolled at GSA, graduating and joining the staff in 1906 to teach fashion design. She staged a solo exhibition in Glasgow in 1910. While serving as an orderly in the *Scottish Women's Hospital at the Abbaye de Royaumont in 1918, she documented both staff and patients in paintings, one now in the IWM. After the war, she enjoyed an international reputation as an exhibitor, particularly in Paris (Bronze medal 1921, Silver 1923). Her talent was recognised in Scotland in 1921 when she became the first woman on the hanging committee of the RGI. Particularly gifted at depicting children, she showed the traditional Glasgow genius for design in portraiture, also producing book illustrations and watercolour landscapes (RSW 1914). Several works are owned by Glasgow Art Galleries. Her premature death put an end to a successful career in full flow. NJI
• Burkhauser, J. (ed.) (1990) *Glasgow Girls*, pp. 200–6; Crofton, E. (1997) *The Women of Royaumont*, p. 304 and cover; *ODNB* (2004) (see Glasgow Girls); Simpson, J. S. (1921) 'Miss Norah Neilson Gray', *Scottish Country Life*, March, pp. 100–1; Tanner, A. (1985) *Norah Neilson Gray 1882–1931*.

GREENLEES, Allison Hope,[‡] n. **Cargill,** born Hillhead, Glasgow, 13 August 1896, died Edinburgh 4 August 1979. Pioneer of Girl Guiding in Scotland. Daughter of Mary Grierson, and John Cargill, East India merchant.

Allison Cargill provided the spark that ignited the Girl Guide Association in Scotland. Following the chance purchase of a 1908 instalment of Baden-Powell's *Scouting for Boys*, she knew that its programme was what she wanted. 'Why only for boys?' she thought. With five friends from Laurel Bank School, Glasgow, she formed the Cuckoo

Patrol, affiliated in 1909 to the 1st Glasgow Scout Group. In 1910, Guiding became 'official' and the Cuckoo Patrol became the Girl Guide Thistle Patrol. Allison Cargill went on to St James School, Malvern, where Guiding flourished with a strong Scottish connection. She later worked enthusiastically to introduce Guiding in Glasgow, and when the First World War intervened, used her experience to help raise the Glasgow Battalion of the WVR. After the war, the original spark became a blaze and as Division Commissioner, N. E. Glasgow, she enrolled 30 Guides at a time. In 1922, she married Dr Greenlees, headmaster of Loretto School, and they had a son and daughter. Alongside commitment to the school, she continued Guiding, latterly as Midlothian County Commissioner and chair of the Scottish Finance Committee, both for 23 years. In 1939, she received the Silver Fish, Guiding's highest award, and in 1953 became President of the Council for Scotland. East Lothian's Brownie House is named Allison Cargill House. SGA

• Archives of Girlguiding Scotland (SHQ, 16 Coates Crescent, Edinburgh).

GREENLEES, Georgina Mossman, m. **Wylie,** born Glasgow 13 May 1849, died London 6 Feb. 1932. Artist. Daughter of Ann Anderson, and Robert Greenlees, portrait painter.

Georgina Greenlees was a prize-winning student at Glasgow School of Art, where she taught from 1874 until her resignation in 1881. She was the moving force behind the 1883 founding of the Glasgow Society of Lady Artists (GSLA) and became the Society's first president. Known for her accomplished landscape paintings which frequently depicted touristic Scotland, particularly the areas around Loch Lomond to the north and Kilmacolm to the south, she also painted scenes of continental Europe and the south of England. After her resignation from the GSA, she taught art privately in her Glasgow studio and exhibited regularly with the Glasgow Institute of the Fine Arts as well as at other venues in Scotland and England. She married Graham Kinloch Wylie on 14 October 1885. In addition to her landscape pictures, she painted images of women such as her *Itinerant Musician* (1883), a rare portrayal of a female violinist, and genre scenes such as *Favourite Air* (1883). Georgina Greenlees and Helensburgh artist Lily Blatherwick (see Glasgow Girls) were the first two female members elected to the SSWCP when the Society formed in 1878. JVH

• Helland, J. (1997) 'Locality and pleasure in landscape: a study of three nineteenth-century Scottish Watercolourists', *Rural History: Economy, Society, Culture*, 8, 2, (2000) *Professional Women Painters in Nineteenth-Century Scotland*.

GREGORY, Helen (Ella), born Edinburgh 11 April 1898, died Edinburgh 17 April 1946. Medical missionary. Daughter of Helen Williamson, and Thomas Gregory, dental surgeon.

After attending Brunstane School for Girls, Helen Gregory qualified at the University of Edinburgh Medical School (MBChB, 1921), then obtained a diploma from the London School of Tropical Medicine (1922). Becoming a medical missionary with the Baptist Missionary Society, she worked in its hospital in Berhampore for more than 17 years (latterly as assistant superintendent), and was awarded the Kaisar-i-Hind Medal. Returning to Edinburgh in 1941, she was unable to go back to India due to illness. On her death, she was described as possessing medical skill of a high order, and many accomplishments, with 'a radiant charm of personality that drew the hearts of Indian and European alike with a magnetic power' (*Scottish Baptist Magazine* 1946). A memorial Prayer Hall was erected to her at Berhampore Hospital. One sister, **Andrina Gregory** (1896–1966), qualified as a nurse from Edinburgh College of Domestic Science, and privately nursed Sir Arthur Conan Doyle. Another, **Margaret (Margot) Gregory** (1904–52), a graduate of ECA, shared a flat with artists Edward and Valerie Gage and Archie Watt. She became Captain of the 19th Company Edinburgh Division, Girl Guides, then District Commissioner, Crewe Toll, and joined the Guide International Service Team involved in the post-war reconstruction of Germany, driving large army trucks. The wider Gregory family numbered some 36 doctors and dentists, all grandchildren of Hannah Steer and John Gregory, an Edinburgh silversmith. CBMG

• *Scottish Baptist Magazine*, May 1946.
Personal knowledge and family records.

GREIG, Jane (or Jean) Stocks, born Cupar, Fife, 12 June 1872, died Melbourne, Australia, 16 Sept. 1939, medical practitioner; **GREIG, Janet Lindsay (Jenny),** born Broughty Ferry 8 August 1874, died London 18 Oct. 1950, medical practitioner; **GREIG, Clara Puella,** m. **Hack,** born Broughty Ferry 23 Dec. 1877, died Brighton, Victoria, 9 June 1957, tutor; **GREIG, Grata Flos,** born Broughty Ferry 7 Nov. 1880, died Moorabbin, Victoria, 31 Dec. 1958, barrister and solicitor. Daughters of Jane Stocks Macfarlane, and Robert Lindsay Greig, merchant.

This remarkable group of sisters emigrated to Victoria in 1889 with their parents. Jane and Janet studied medicine at the University of Melbourne, both graduating MB, BS by 1896, when they were among the founders of the Queen Victoria Hospital, the first women's hospital in Victoria. Jane was on the honorary medical staff until 1910, Janet for 52 years, until 1948. In 1910, Jane Greig was the first woman to receive the Diploma of Public Health from the University of Melbourne and was appointed MO to the Victorian Education Department, becoming Chief MO in 1929 and retiring in 1937. Janet was a consulting physician in Collins Street for more than 30 years. The first woman anaesthetist in Victoria, she was admitted to the Royal Australasian College of Physicians in 1940; the pathology building at the Queen Victoria Hospital is named after her. Clara entered the University of Melbourne and began a BSc, but left in 1901 to open a tutorial college for university students. In 1910, she married C. A. Hack, patent attorney. Grata was the first woman in Australia to enter a law faculty at the University of Melbourne (1897), the first to graduate LLB (1903) and to be admitted to the bar (1905). She worked for many years as a solicitor, retiring in 1942. Stella, their Australian-born sister (1889–1913), graduated LLB from the University of Melbourne in 1911, but died two years later from tuberculosis. MA

• Royal Australasian Coll. Surgeons Archives: Records for Jane S. Greig and Janet L. Greig.
ADB (1993) Nairn, B. and Serle, G. (eds), vol. 9, pp. 101–3; Kelly, F. (1982) ' "The woman question" in Melbourne, 1880–1914', PhD, Monash Univ., Victoria; Kirk, D. and Twigg, K. (1994) 'Regulating Australian Bodies: eugenics, anthropometrics and school medical inspection in Victoria, 1900–1940', *Hist. Edu. Rev.*, 23, 1; Neve, M. H. (1980) '*This Mad Folly!' Australia's Pioneer Doctors.*

GRIERSON, Ruby Isabel, born Cambusbarron, Stirlingshire, 24 Nov. 1903, died at sea 17 Sept. 1940. Documentary film-maker. Daughter of Jane Anthony, English teacher, and Robert Morrison Grierson, schoolmaster.

Overshadowed by her more famous brother, John Grierson (1898–1972), the founder of British documentary film-making, Ruby Grierson was an influential figure in the early documentary movement. She was the second youngest of eight children in a politically conscious, intellectual family. Her mother had been a suffragette and was an active ILP member and Ruby inherited her passions and beliefs. There were lively family debates on all sorts of topics, in which social and political concerns were prominent. All the children attended the local school, where their father was headmaster, and she and all but one of her siblings went on to the University of Glasgow.

Ruby Grierson's strong political views and pacifism informed her work. She was a teacher before joining her brother at the Empire Marketing Board film unit, a government organisation, in the early 1930s. Her films dealt with the daily hardships of life and in *They Also Serve* (1940) she focused on the role of the housewife during the Second World War. She was both pugnacious and committed, reflected in the choice of subjects such as *Housing Problems* (1937) and *Peace Film* (1936), the latter the object of a bid by the authorities to have it banned. She had a reputation as a meticulous researcher. *Documentary Newsletter* said in 1937: 'Her co-direction of *Today We Live* established her as one of the few directors whose passion and sympathy was the life and spirit of ordinary people and she has formed the real main artery of documentary progress'. *Housing Problems* was noted for the spontaneity and honesty of its interviews, influencing subsequent work. In her documentary *The Zoo and You* (1938) she had the original notion of filming from the perspective of the animals.

She died in action. She was commissioned by the Canadian government to make a film on the evacuation of children to Canada and when the liner *The City of Benares* was torpedoed in mid-Atlantic she was among those lost. A flamboyant figure in her wide trousers, frequently holding a long cigarette holder as she manoeuvred her cameras, she was remembered for her 'good humour, her fierce enthusiasms and her physical and spiritual energies' (Hardy 1979, p. 113). Kirsty Wark, whose company made a 1994 BBC Scotland documentary on her work, believes that 'modern film-makers have a lot to learn from Ruby Grierson's simplicity and clarity'. Her sister **Marion Anthony Grierson**, m. **Taylor** (1907–98) was also a film-maker with EMB, and editor of the periodical *World Film News* 1936–8, before she turned to social work in Edinburgh. She said that Ruby Grierson believed that films could change the world. RM

• Ellis, J. C. (2000) *John Grierson: life, contributions, influence*; *Glasgow Herald*, 8 Nov. 1994; Hardy, F. (1979) *John Grierson: a documentary biography*; *The Scotsman*, 3 Nov. 1994; *Ex-S: re-shooting history*, broadcast, BBC1, Nov. 1994. Private information.

GRIEVE, Jemima Bessie, n. **Skea** **['Countrywoman']**, born Shapinsay, Orkney, 28 June 1923, died Shapinsay, Orkney, 19 May 1996. Writer. Daughter of Margaret Skethaway, postmistress, and John Skea, crofter and poet.

The elder of two sisters, born and brought up on the family farm of Ostoft, Shapinsay, Bessie Skea attended school on the island of Shapinsay and from the age of nine wrote 'bits and pieces' of poetry and prose (*Orcadian* 1996, p. 5). In 1942, she married James Grieve and they had three children. After a short time living in Rousay and Birsay, the family settled in Harray. In March 1958, Bessie Grieve's work was first published in *The Orkney Herald* under the byline 'Countrywoman'. Her personal thoughts and descriptions of contemporary country life in the islands, with specific reference to natural history and the antics of her cats, were juxtaposed and intermingled with memories of her childhood. After the cessation of that newspaper, her work was published in *The Orcadian* from 1961 until her death. Several published works included her column, short stories, poetry and anecdotes. Her perceptive and poetic writing style ensures that she will be remembered as a writer of great clarity and one of Orkney's foremost literary figures, alongside her friends George Mackay Brown and Ernest Marwick. SJG
• Grieve, J. B. (1962) *A Countrywoman's Calendar*, (1964) *Waves and Tangles*, (1983) *A Countrywoman's Diary*, (1993) *Island Journeys, A Countrywoman's Travels*, (1958–61) 'Countrywoman', in *The Orkney Herald*, (1961–96) 'Countrywoman's Diary', in *The Orcadian*.
The Orcadian, 23 May 1996 (obit.).
Private information (family members)

GRIEVE, Mary Margaret, [Mary Lyon], OBE, born Ayr 11 April 1906, died Berkhamsted 19 Feb. 1998. Journalist, Editor of *Woman* magazine. Daughter of Annie Stark, nurse, and Robert Grieve, fundholder.

Mary Grieve, the second of three children, spent much of her childhood in bed through illness and was educated at home. Aged 16, she briefly attended school in Glasgow before training as a secretary and studying journalism in London. She returned to Glasgow to work on *Scottish Home and Country*, the magazine of the SWRI, and as a social reporter on the popular daily, *The Bulletin*. In 1935, she published, under the pseudonym 'Mary Lyon', her only work of fiction, *Without Alphonse: the diary of a Frenchwoman in Scotland*. In 1936, she returned to London to work on the recently established monthly magazine *Mother*. Its publisher,

Odhams, launched the weekly, *Woman*, in 1937. After a disastrous start, the editorial team from *Mother* was brought in to save the situation and Mary Grieve became associate editor of *Woman*. When the male editor left to join the RAF in 1940, she was made editor and remained in that post for the rest of her working life.

Mary Grieve advised the Ministry of Information on women's role in wartime, and ensured that *Woman* responded constantly to women's concerns, from rationing through post-war austerity to the consumer-oriented 1960s. Using the new colour photogravure process, the magazine became enormously popular and influential, its circulation peaking at almost 3.5 million in 1957. She introduced a letters page, the 'Evelyn Home' agony column, and a consumer advice department backed by practical testing. She became a member of the Council for Industrial Design (1952–60), the National Council for Diplomas in Art and Design (from 1960) and the council of the Royal College of Art (from 1963). On her retirement in 1962, she was made OBE for services to journalism. She had inspired a generation of woman journalists including **Ruby Turberville** (1922–2003), features writer with the *Press and Journal* in her native Aberdeen before becoming women's editor of the Aberdeen *Evening Express* in the 1960s. Ruby Turberville championed a range of women's issues, loved to meet her readers, and carried her enthusiasm into a subsidiary career as a public speaker.

In her retirement, Mary Grieve published her autobiography, *Millions Made My Story* (1964). She edited textbooks aimed at preparing girls for life after school and, with a friend, ran a business, Dove Delicacies, making paté and supplying it to local shops and restaurants, until her activity was curtailed by a severe stroke in 1978. MARB
• Grieve, M., and Lyon, M., Works as above.
Knight, A. (2003) 'Ruby Turberville' *Scottish PEN Newsletter* 26 (obit.); *ODNB* (2004); *The Times*, 26 Feb. 1998 (obit.).

GRIMOND, Laura Miranda, n. **Bonham Carter**, born London 13 Oct. 1918, died Orkney 15 Feb. 1994. Councillor and Liberal Party activist. Daughter of Lady Violet Bonham-Carter, n. Asquith, and Sir Maurice Bonham Carter.

Laura Bonham Carter came from one of the most prominent political families in the British Isles. Her grandfather, Herbert Asquith, was Prime Minister 1908–16, both parents were politically active and 'she grew up in a household that sparkled with ideas and intellect' (Anderson et al. 2000, p. 86). Educated at home in London, she spent time in Paris and Vienna before her debutante season. In 1938, she married Jo Grimond (1913–93), leader of the UK Liberal party 1956–67. They had four children. The family moved to Orkney in 1951 after Jo Grimond was elected MP for Orkney.

Although she was active within the Liberal Party at a national level, most of Laura Grimond's political work was undertaken locally in Orkney (Girl Guides, Woman's Guild, Mental Health Association). In 1974, she was elected Councillor for Firth and Harray and served until 1980, chairing the Housing Committee for part of that time. She was held in high regard and built up warm relationships with the Orkney people. With her feeling for landscape and buildings, she was central to the establishment of local conservation organisations flourishing today: the Orkney Heritage Society, Blide Trust, Hoy Trust and Sanday Development Trust. She believed that conservation was beneficial for everyone living in the area, not just for posterity. The Orkney Heritage Society established the Laura Grimond Award in her memory, for completed or restored buildings blending well with their surroundings. 'In her determination to help others . . . and put their welfare above her own, she was rather like one of the noblest and finest characters in Scottish literature' (Howie Firth, funeral tribute, ibid., p. 89). Laura and Jo Grimond were given the Freedom of Orkney in August 1987. HEK

• Anderson, J., Foulkes, B., Tait, C., Williams, R. & Wallace, R. (eds) (2000) *Jo and Laura Grimond: a selection of memories and photographs 1945–1994*; *ODNB* (2004) (Grimond, Joseph).
Personal information.

GRUOCH, Queen of Scotland (Lady Macbeth), fl. early–mid 11th century.

Although her reputation as Lady Macbeth is anachronistic, Gruoch is one of the most famous women of medieval Scotland, yet little is known of her. A grand-daughter of Cináed (Kenneth) II or III, she married Gillacomgain, mormaer of Moray (d. 1032) and, after his death, his cousin Macbeth, King of Scots 1040–57. Since Macbeth may have slain Gillacomgain, this marriage might represent an attempt to end the internecine strife within the Cenél Loairn. Gruoch's son by Gillacomgain, Lulach, briefly succeeded Macbeth in the kingship in 1057–8.

During Macbeth's reign, Gruoch and her husband jointly granted land to the Culdees of Loch Leven; in this document, Gruoch is styled 'daughter of Bodhe . . . queen of Scots' (Lawrie 1905, no. 5). This reference may be indicative of her status and influence within the kingdom of Scots. RAM

• Aitchison, N. (1999) *Macbeth: man and myth*; Anderson, A. O. (ed.) (1922) *Early Sources of Scottish History* AD 500 to 1286; Cowan, E. J. (1993) 'The historical MacBeth', in W. D. H. Sellar (ed.) *Moray: province and people*; Lawrie, A. C. (ed.) (1905) *Early Scottish Charters Prior to AD 1153*; Hudson, B. T. (1994) *Kings of Celtic Scotland.*

GUNN, Isabel, n. **Fubister,** born Tankerness, Orkney, 1 August 1781, died Stromness 7 Nov. 1861. Hudson's Bay Company labourer, cross-dresser. Daughter of Girzal Allan, and John Fubister.

Isabel Fubister entered the exclusively male employment of the Hudson's Bay Company (HBC) under the alias 'John Fubister'. She sailed for Hudson Bay on the *Prince of Wales* in 1806, her true identity known only to John Scarth of the Orkney parish of Firth, an experienced hand with the HBC. She was posted as a labourer to Fort Albany on the west coast of James Bay and worked with Scarth in the brigade of boats, making regular trips with trade goods up the Albany River and returning with furs. In the summer of 1807 she was sent with a brigade on the long and difficult route up the Albany to Lake Winnipeg and then south up the Red River to the HBC post at Pembina, a distance of more than 1,500 miles. John Scarth was not on the trip.

On 29 December 1807, at the fur-trading post of the North West Company trader Alexander Henry, 'John Fubister' was taken ill and requested permission to remain in the house. Henry was startled to find 'Fubister' in labour and shortly after delivered of a son, the first white child born in the North West. Isabel (now calling herself Gunn) returned to Fort Albany the following June, where she was employed as a washerwoman until she could be sent back to Stromness in October, 1809. John Scarth is registered as the child's father. She lived as a pauper in Stromness with her son James until her death in 1861. A version of her story is told in the novel *Isobel Gunn* by Audrey Thomas (1999). GH

• Skaill Papers, Kirkwall Library.
Bolus, M. (1971) 'The son of I. Gunn', *Beaver*, 302 (Bibl.); Coues, E. (ed.) (1897) *New Light on the Early History of the Greater Northwest . . . 1799–1814*; Gough, B. (ed.) (1988)

The Journal of Alexander Henry the Younger, 1799–1814; *ODNB* (2004).

GUNNING, Elizabeth, Duchess of Hamilton, Duchess of Argyll, born near Huntingdon, Dec. 1733, died London 20 Dec. 1790, buried Kilmun, Argyllshire. Leader of society. Daughter of Bridget Bourke, daughter of Viscount Mayo, and John Gunning of Castlecoote.

Daughter of an impoverished Irish gentleman, Elizabeth Gunning was a leading figure in Scottish aristocratic society and the London court. Elizabeth Gunning and her sister Maria arrived in London in 1750. Both great beauties, and painted by fashionable portrait artists and engraved for the popular market, they were the 'pin-ups' of the age. The two sisters made spectacular marriages. Elizabeth married James, 6th Duke of Hamilton (1724–58), in 1752 and had three children. After James's death, a marriage in 1759 to John Campbell, Marquis of Lorne (1723–1806), heir to the Duke of Argyll, produced five children, including the author *Lady Charlotte Bury. Twice a Duchess, Elizabeth Gunning was mother to the 7th and 8th Dukes of Hamilton and the 6th and 7th Dukes of Argyll.

In 1761, she became Lady of the Bedchamber to Queen Charlotte. Following Argyll's death, she was made peeress in her own right as Baroness Hamilton of Hameldon. During the Wilkes Riots in London in 1768, she bravely refused to 'illuminate' the windows of Argyll House in support of the rioters, despite intimidation. As mother of the Duke of Hamilton, from 1761 to 1769 she was involved in prosecuting the 'Douglas Cause'. **Lady Jane Douglas** (1698–1753), sister of the childless 1st Duke of Douglas, had secretly married Colonel John Stewart (1687–1764) in 1746, leaving soon after for France. There she had twin sons in 1748; she claimed the surviving twin, Archibald, was his uncle's heir, displacing Elizabeth Gunning's first husband and their son. Scepticism about Archibald's true identity, since his mother was 50 when he was born, led to a lengthy court case over who was the rightful heir. Lady Jane's son eventually won the right to inherit the Douglas estates over the Hamilton children. (He married Lady Frances Scott, see *Douglas, Lady Frances.) When Johnson and Boswell visited Inveraray Castle in 1773, Elizabeth Gunning cold-shouldered Boswell, a lawyer for the victorious Douglas side. SN

• Boswell, J. (1936) *Journal of a Tour to the Hebrides*; Hicks, C. (2001) *Improper Pursuits: the scandalous life of Lady Di Beauclerk*; *ODNB* (2004) (see Campbell, Elizabeth (Bibl.); Douglas, Lady Jane (Bibl.)).

GUTHRIE, Helen, born 1574. Presbyterian petitioner. Daughter of an Aberdeen saddler.

In June 1592, 18-year-old Helen Guthrie approached James VI as he was going hunting. She handed him a letter of complaint and, kneeling, lambasted him for being a bad Christian. It was not unusual for Scots to approach the monarch personally, but James was taken aback by her zeal. In her letter she asked James to repent and prevent 'the sinnes raigning in the countrie, swearing, filthie speeking, profanatioun of the Sabbath'. James apparently swore at her, asking if she was a prophetess. She replied that 'she was a poore simple servant of God' (Calderwood 1844, p. 169). She was then sent to *Anna of Denmark, who received her more kindly. Helen Guthrie's actions were prompted by Presbyterian concerns that the royal households were not godly enough; her supporters knew that the King always listened to kneeling female petitioners. MMM

• Calderwood, D. (1844) *The History of the Kirk of Scotland*, vol. v, T. Thomson, ed.; Cameron, A. I. (ed.) (1932) *The Warrender Papers*, ii, pp. 170–4.

H

HAINING, Jane Mathison,[‡] born Lochenhead, Dunscore, Dumfriesshire, 6 June 1897, died Auschwitz 17 July 1944. Missionary. Daughter of Jane Mathison, and Thomas Haining, farmer.

Jane Haining was brought up in a deeply religious home in rural Dumfriesshire and this early influence, together with the practical housekeeping skills learned of necessity after the death of her mother, may have prepared the ground for her future calling as a Church of Scotland missionary. Academically able, she attended Dumfries Academy and then worked as a secretary for the thread manufacturers, J. & P. Coats, in Paisley. Her life outside work revolved around her church, the United Free Church, Queen's Park West in Pollockshields. After hearing a talk on missionary work among Eastern European Jews, she declared to a friend, 'I have found my life's work'

(McDougall 1998, p. 13). This conviction sustained her over four years of training and waiting for a suitable opportunity. It came in 1932 with her appointment as matron to the Jewish Mission Girls' Home in Budapest. Having learned Hungarian, she won the trust of her young charges, many of whom came from difficult backgrounds and broken families.

Life was fulfilling for her, as she coped calmly with frequent domestic crises, but she became aware of increasing hostility towards Jews in Hungary and rising fear among her charges. She was on home leave when war was declared and she arranged to return immediately to Hungary. With the worsening situation, all staff were recalled, but she remained at her post despite repeated cables from Edinburgh. 'If these children need me in days of sunshine, how much more do they need me in days of darkness?', she wrote (McDougall 1998, p. 24). The mission became a refuge and she was in grave danger by early 1944 when the Germans occupied Hungary. Denounced and arrested by the Gestapo, her care for her Jewish charges was enough to send her, in April 1944, by cattle truck to Auschwitz. Although passed fit for work and not gassed on arrival, by July she was dead. In 1997, she was posthumously recognised at Yad Vashem in Jerusalem as Righteous Amongst the Nations, the only Scot to be so honoured. AT
• McDougall, D. [1949] *Jane Haining*, (1998) amended and reprinted, I. Alexander, ed., for the Church of Scotland Board of World Mission; *ODNB* (2004).

HALDANE, Elizabeth Sanderson, CH, born Edinburgh 27 May 1862, died Auchterarder 24 Dec. 1937. Social reformer, political activist and writer. Daughter of Mary Burdon-Sanderson, and Robert Haldane, WS.

Born into a well-established Perthshire family, Elizabeth Haldane was brought up in an atmosphere of religious and social commitment. She was the only daughter and was educated by tutors alongside her brothers until her early teens, when she attended classes for girls in Edinburgh. When her father died in 1877, she became her mother's companion, and after Mary Haldane (1825–1925) died, she wrote of 'that dreadful feeling of unwantedness when one has been necessary for so many years . . .' (Letter to Violet Markham, 25 May 1925). Her early 20s were the one time when her life was not 'brimming full and running over' (Haldane 1937, p. 73). Her energy found an outlet in Liberal politics, shared with her oldest brother, Richard Haldane, and in the initiation of a housing scheme in Edinburgh which came about through a meeting with philanthropist Octavia Hill in London.

The family spent summers at Cloan, in Perthshire. Needing something to occupy 'my spare time in the country and give me the sense of not wasting it', with Frances H. Simson she began a three-volume translation of Hegel's *History of Philosophy*, which was published in 1892, the first of her 12 published books. Writing on Victorian women writers, nursing and Scotland's history and gardens followed. While at Cloan she also founded the Auchterarder Institute and Library, of which she remained secretary for 53 years. The work was given financial support by her neighbour, Andrew Carnegie, who drew her into the work of the Carnegie UK Trust; she became the first woman trustee in December 1913. She was convinced of the importance of education and was elected first to the local School Board and then to the County Education Committee.

Judging from her diaries, she found politics engrossing. She campaigned for her brother Richard Haldane from his first election in 1884, often speaking at women's meetings. She had 'advanced views' on women's rights from an early age and was a supporter of suffrage, 'though hating militancy' (Ibid., pp. 55, 271) and working through the WLF. She was close to and influenced her niece, *Naomi Mitchison. Richard Haldane never married and when in London, Elizabeth acted as his hostess. He trusted her with his private views and, on occasion, with the sight of 'secret papers' (Diary, 23 February 1912). He became a member of the government in 1906, so Elizabeth met and discussed political and philosophical questions with all the leading politicians of the day. The respect in which her views were held is apparent from her correspondence, her giving evidence to the Poor Law Commission in 1907 on the position of women in Scotland, and her appointment to the Royal Commission on the Civil Service in 1912. In 1911, she was among the first women to receive an LLD from the University of St Andrews. She refused, despite her family's urging, a paid post as an insurance commissioner for Scotland, because it would have taken up too much of her time. Her interest in nursing, fostered by her membership of the board of management of the Edinburgh Infirmary, led to her extensive contribution to proposals by the Local Government Board on nurse training, and to a significant role in setting up nursing services for time of war attached to the Territorial Army. She was made Companion of Honour (CH) in 1917, and in 1920 she became the first Scottish woman JP.

In the 1920s, Elizabeth Haldane and her brother drew nearer to Labour, and their circle of friends, which had for many years included Beatrice and Sidney Webb, was now extended to Labour politicians. Richard Haldane became a member of the 1924 Labour Government. After his death in 1928, Elizabeth Haldane continued her wide-ranging activities and also travelled extensively, visiting Egypt in 1934 and Persia in 1936. JA

• NLS: MSS 6010–6068, corr., MSS 20240–20244, Diaries; LSE: Markham 25/26, 7.

Haldane, E. Works as above (and see website www.eup.ed.ac.uk), (1937) *From One Century to Another*. Alberti, J. (1990) 'Inside out: Elizabeth Haldane as a women's suffrage survivor in the 1920s and 1930s', *Women's Studies International Forum* 13, pp. 117–23; Mitchison, N. (1973) *Small Talk*, (1975) *All Change Here*, (1979) *You May Well Ask*; *ODNB* (2004).

HALIBURTON, Marion (Mariot), Lady Home, born probably Dirleton Castle c. 1500, died probably Dunglass c. 1563. Daughter of Margaret Douglas of Pumpherston, and Patrick, Lord Haliburton.

Marion Haliburton's marriage to George, 4th Lord Home, c. 1518, brought a third of the lucrative Dirleton (East Lothian) estates into Home ownership. Supporters of the Franco-Scottish alliance throughout the 1540s, the Homes paid a heavy price for their loyalty, as their goods were all destroyed by the end of 1545. When Lord Home was injured and the Master of Home captured around the time of the Battle of Pinkie (1547), Lady Home was compelled to give some assurance to England's Protector Somerset. Being pragmatic, she wrote to Somerset that 'I dare not let my lord my husband see your last writing about the rendering of Home [Castle] and the pledges'. (*L&P. Henry VIII*, p. 501). This is perhaps why the strategically important castle capitulated with ease in 1547, though it was recaptured by Franco-Scottish forces in 1548. Lady Home quickly reverted to the Scottish side, giving good intelligence to *Mary of Guise. Her treachery, committed to protect her family, was never discovered. MMM

• Bain, J. (ed.) (1898) *Calendar of the State Papers relating to Scotland*, i, p. 36; Cameron, A. L. (ed.) (1927) *The Scottish Correspondence of Mary of Lorraine*, pp. 280–1, 291–2, 295–7; Gairdnar, J. and Brodie, R. H. (eds) (1907) *Letters and Papers, foreign and domestic, of the reign* of Henry VIII, xx, pt 2;

Meikle, M. M. (2004) *A British Frontier? Lairds and Gentlemen of the Eastern Borders, 1540–1603*; *ODNB* (2004) (Hume, George); *RMS*, iii, 1480, 1764; *SP*, iv, pp. 377, 460.

HALKETT, Anne, Lady *see* **MURRAY, Anne** (1623–1699)

HAMILTON, Anne,[‡] 3rd Duchess of Hamilton *suo jure*, born Whitehall Palace, London 16 Jan. 1632, died Hamilton Palace 17 Oct. 1716. Daughter of Lady Mary Feilding, and James Hamilton, 3rd Marquis and later 1st Duke of Hamilton.

Anne Hamilton's mother, one of Queen Henrietta Maria's ladies of the bedchamber, died in 1638 after giving birth to six children in five years. Her eldest child had already died and the others were all said to be delicate, so their father, Charles I's leading Scottish adviser, moved them from Whitehall to the healthier air of Chelsea. Even so, only Anne and her younger sister, Susanna, survived. Their lives were further disrupted by the outbreak of civil war, and the Duke, fearing for the future and believing that the family needed a man at its head in such troubled times, drew up a will leaving all his titles and estates to his younger brother William, Earl of Lanark. He sent Anne to be brought up at Hamilton Palace by his own mother, Anna Cunningham, 2nd Marchioness of Hamilton, while Susanna remained in London with the children's other grandmother, Susan, Countess of Denbigh.

For the next five years, Anne watched her elderly grandmother run the vast Hamilton estates. The Marchioness died in 1647 and in 1649 Anne's father was executed by the Cromwellians. Her uncle became 2nd Duke of Hamilton, but in 1651 he was fatally wounded at the battle of Worcester and in accordance with his will Anne became 3rd Duchess of Hamilton in her own right. She was 19 years old, and in theory Scotland's greatest heiress, but all her estates had been confiscated, her father and uncle had contracted enormous debts and her kinsman the Earl of Abercorn claimed that everything was rightfully his, on the grounds that the family titles were entailed on the male line. In fact, Anne's uncle had broken the entail, but the lawsuit with Abercorn dragged on for years. Her situation seemed desperate, and for a time she had to take refuge in a small house near Hamilton Palace.

On 29 April 1656, Anne married William Douglas, Earl of Selkirk (1634–94). This love-match was surprising, for he came from a well-known

Roman Catholic family and Anne's father had stipulated that she must marry a Protestant. Gradually, they managed to pay the fines allowing them to reclaim the estates. At the Restoration, Charles II gave Duchess Anne the £25,000 sterling his father had owed hers, creating her husband Duke of Hamilton for life, at her request. While raising seven sons and six daughters, the Duke and Duchess embarked on an ambitious rebuilding programme at Hamilton Palace, laying out extensive gardens and improving their estates.

The Duke died in 1694 but the Duchess persevered with their plans. She rebuilt Hamilton burgh school and schoolhouse, provided a large new almshouse in the town, and established a woollen manufactory and a spinning school. She introduced coal mining, a salt pan and a ferry boat on her island of Arran, sending an ambulatory preacher there. She gave silver communion cups to the churches on her estates and was strongly supportive of the Presbyterian church. Although she insisted that she was above party politics, she did donate money to the Darien Scheme and opposed the Union of the Parliaments of 1707. Dying at the age of 84, she was buried in Hamilton Parish Church and was long remembered in the west of Scotland as 'Good Duchess Anne'. RKM
• Lennoxlove, The Hamilton Archives; NAS: The Hamilton Muniments, GD406.
Marshall, R. K. (2000) *The Days of Duchess Anne* (Bibl.); *ODNB* (2004).

HAMILTON, Elizabeth, born Belfast 25 July 1758, died Harrogate 23 July 1816. Novelist, educationalist, moral philosopher. Daughter of Katherine Mackay of Dublin, and Charles Hamilton, Scottish merchant in Belfast.

The youngest of three children, whose father died a year after her birth, Elizabeth Hamilton was sent in 1762 to live with her Scottish uncle and aunt near Stirling. She was educated from the age of 13 mainly by her aunt who, though sympathetic, once advised her 'to avoid any display of superior knowledge' (Benger 1818, I, p. 50). In 1785, a contribution she sent to Henry Mackenzie's *Lounger* was accepted, followed by others. Her brother Charles, an orientalist, returned from India, encouraged her ambitions and 'taught her to explore her own talents' (ibid., p. 109). She joined him in London and was introduced into literary and political circles before his death in March 1792. His inspiration was evident in her *Translation of the Letters of a Hindoo Rajah* (1796), which mocked the follies of British

society through the eyes of an Indian visitor. She wrote in an anti-Jacobin spirit against the ideas of the French Revolution, yet with a progressive concern to improve women's education and other aspects of her own society. The same ambiguity is present in her *Memoirs of Modern Philosophers* (1800), which more directly and comically satirised radical ideas, but also supported Mary Wollstonecraft's educational views and female philanthropy.

In her *Letters on the Elementary Principles of Education* (1801–2, I, p. vii) (her major interest), Elizabeth Hamilton suggested to women readers that any approach to the subject without 'some knowledge of the principles of the human mind, must be labour lost'. She acknowledged the influence of Dugald Stewart, Professor of Moral Philosophy at the University of Edinburgh. With his encouragement, she moved to Edinburgh in 1804 and, with *Eliza Fletcher, played an active role in literary society there, holding her own successful Monday morning levees. It was probably Eliza Fletcher who described her as 'correcting the vulgar prejudices against literary women' and as 'giving a new direction to the pursuits of her own sex' through her philanthropic interests (Benger 1818, I, p. 179). Her *Memoirs of Agrippina* (1804) was a semi-fictional didactic biography, less successful than *The Cottagers of Glenburnie* (1808), which drew on her Perthshire upbringing to relate humorously the cleansing and civilising of the McClarty family.

Having been governess to the daughters of Lord Lucan (1804–5), Elizabeth Hamilton published *Letters Addressed to the Daughters of a Nobleman* (1806). In the mis-titled *Series of Popular Essays* (1813) she wrote again on the powers of the mind. Her own distinctive addition to these was the propensity to magnify the idea of self, which could foster the ambition forged by the spirit of party. She further suggested that the sexes could be considered as two parties, a concept which led her to a surprisingly radical analysis of masculine power. She looked forward to the spread of education in a morally progressive society. She also wrote Scots poetry, including the once popular 'My ain fireside' and the cheerful 'Is that Auld Age that's tirling at the pin?'. She did not marry but lived mainly in her later years with her widowed sister, Katherine Blake. JR
• Hamilton, E., Works as above, and see Bibl. below.
Benger, Miss [E. Ogilvy] (1818) *Memoirs of the late Mrs Elizabeth Hamilton. With a selection from her correspondence*

and other unpublished writings (2 vols.); Grogan, C. (2000) 'Introduction', to Elizabeth Hamilton, *Memoirs of Modern Philosophers* (Bibl.); Kelly, G. (1993) *Women, Writing and Revolution 1790–1827*; *ODNB* (2004); Perkins, P. and Russell, S. (1999) 'Introduction', to *Translation of the Letters of a Hindoo Rajah* (Bibl.); Rendall, J. (1996) 'Writing history for British women', in C. Campbell-Orr, (ed.) *Wollstonecraft's Daughters*; Thaddeus, J. F. (1994) 'Elizabeth Hamilton's domestic politics', *Studies in Eighteenth-Century Culture* 23, pp. 265–84; Tytler, S. [*Henrietta Keddie] and Watson, J. L. (1871) *The Songstresses of Scotland*, vol. 1, pp. 291–328.

HAMILTON Janet, n. **Thomson,** born Carshill, Lanarkshire, 14 Oct. 1795, died Langloan, Lanarkshire, 30 Oct. 1873. Poet, spinner. Daughter of Mary Brownlee, and James Thomson, shoemaker.

When Janet Thomson was about two years old, the family moved to Hamilton and, when she was seven, to Langloan, where her parents were farm workers on the Drumpellier estate. She worked from the age of seven, recalling her experience in *Rhymes and Recollections of a Handloom Weaver* (1844). She spun yarn for sale and, later, worked at the tambour-frame. Self-taught, she read widely in the village library, including *Paradise Lost*, the works of Allan Ramsay, Fergusson, Burns, Pitscottie's historical work, and Plutarch's *Lives*. In 1809, she married John Hamilton (1783/4–1878), a shoemaker. They had ten children, three of whom died in her lifetime. She continued her self-education, reading *Blackwood's Edinburgh Magazine* and the works of Shakespeare while she nursed the children; she taught all her children to read and to spell.

She began to write in 1849. From 1855, she was blind; her son James transcribed her work, and read it back to her so that she could make corrections. Her works include *Poems and Essays* (1863), *Poems of Purpose and Sketches in Prose* (1865) and *Poems and Ballads* (1868). A wide scope of interest is evident in her work, from local to national and international affairs. Often, her sympathies focus on women workers. 'A Lay of the Tambour Frame' expresses sympathy for those who were 'slave in all but the name' and did not have a union; she demands a fund to aid 'sisters in need'. 'Oor Location', while primarily a temperance poem (a frequent theme), is an eloquent expression of 19th-century industrial life, with 'A hunner funnels bleezin', reekin'', written in articulate Scots. She capably defends the language in 'A Plea for the Doric'. She does not, however, criticise the British status quo. She admired British royalty, as is evident in 'Lines. Suggested by Seeing the Train Containing the Queen and Suite pass through Coatbridge . . . 1862'. Equally, her deeply felt Christian belief, expressed in, for example, 'The Fruits of the Spirit', suggests that she thought faith compensated for weariness in this life. Even so, she hated exploitation. Her essay, 'Reminiscences of the Radical Time 1810–20', expresses a dislike for 'would-be insurgents' but implies a great deal of sympathy for those who lacked the 'privileges' of 'paternal and enlightened government'. 'Freedom for Italy 1867' expresses her admiration for Garibaldi, and demands action: 'Slaves of the Papacy! when will ye know/That, to be free, yourselves must strike the blow?'. Janet Hamilton is summed up by George Eyre-Todd in *The Glasgow Poets* as 'one of those remarkable women in humble life of whom Scotland has produced so strong a crop' (1906, pp. 226–7, quoted *HSWW*, p. 255). VB

• Monklands Library Services (1984) *Janet Hamilton: selected works*.

Hamilton, J., Works as above and see *HSWW* (Bibl.). Bold, V. (forthcoming) 'Danaus' daughters', *Nature's Making: James Hogg and the Autodidacts*; Finlay, W. 'Reclaiming Local Literature: William Thom and Janet Hamilton', in D. Gifford (ed.) (1988) *The History of Scottish Literature*, vol. 3; *HSWW* (Bibl.); Wright, J. (1889) *Janet Hamilton and other Papers*; *ODNB* (2004); Young, J. (1877) *Pictures in Prose and Verse, or, Personal Recollections of the Late Janet Hamilton*.

HAMILTON, Mary Agnes (Molly), n. **Adamson,** CBE, born Manchester 8 July 1882, died London 10 Feb. 1966. Writer, broadcaster and politician. Daughter of Margaret Duncan, schoolteacher, and Robert Adamson, university professor.

Molly Adamson's father was Professor of Logic at Owen's College, Manchester, 1876–93. He later took up posts in Aberdeen and Glasgow. The eldest of six children, Molly was educated mainly at Glasgow High School for Girls. She inherited her parents' academic abilities as well as their radicalism and feminism. From 1901, she spent three years at Newnham College, Cambridge, specialising in economics and gaining first-class honours. She moved to Cardiff to assist the Professor of History at the University College of South Wales, leaving in September 1905 to marry a colleague, Charles Hamilton. Molly Hamilton had published several books, on history and fiction, by 1913, when the couple separated. Thereafter, she pursued a successful career in journalism.

Initially a radical Liberal, her pacifist commitment led her to join the ILP in 1914 and she became assistant editor of the ILP's *New Leader* during the mid-1920s. Her main political influences were Ramsay MacDonald and Norman Angell, the latter dedicated to building up the League of Nations from 1919. In 1929 she was returned as MP for Blackburn. She championed equal pay and the removal of marriage bars for women in professions such as teaching. Women's employment rights were a life-long interest. She also served as parliamentary private secretary to Clement Attlee, and was appointed delegate to the League of Nations. She would certainly have progressed further within Parliament had she not been defeated at Blackburn in the 1931 General Election. Her socialism hardened as a result of the unemployment crisis and Ramsay MacDonald's decision to join with the Conservatives to form the National Government.

Remaining politically active after 1931, and committed to the League of Nations, she was a vocal critic of appeasement. During the 1930s, her pacifism turned into dedicated anti-fascism and ultimately support for war against Germany. Meantime, she continued to make her living from writing and broadcasting. Her output was eclectic, ranging from novels to political biographies, notably her acclaimed 1938 study of Arthur Henderson (Foreign Secretary 1929–31), a close friend. An able and effective speaker, she appeared regularly on radio and served on the BBC's Board of Governors from 1932 to 1936. After three years as an alderman on the LCC, she was a civil servant between 1940 and 1952, working on government information and propaganda. She was made CBE in 1949. Up to her death Molly Hamilton continued to be a prolific writer and in 1944 and 1953 published two autobiographical volumes, *Remembering My Good Friends* (1944) and *Uphill All the Way* (1953). IEM

• Hamilton, M., Works as above, and see website for extracts from writings:
www.spartacus.schoolnet.co.uk/Whamilton.htm
BDBF(2); *DLabB*, vol. 5 (Bibl.); Harrison, B. (1986) 'Women in a men's house: the women MPs, 1919–1945', *Historical Journal*, 29; *ODNB* (2004).

HAMILTON, Lady Mary *see* **WALKER, Lady Mary** (1736–1821)

HANNAY, Jane Ewing, n. **Wilson,** CBE, born New Abbey, Dumfries, 8 Feb. 1868, died Edinburgh 14 April 1938. Teacher, women's welfare and employment campaigner. Daughter of Jane Ewing Brown, and the Rev. James Stewart Wilson.

Jane Wilson was educated at St Leonards School, St Andrews, where she was captain of games and head of school, and at Girton College, Cambridge, where she passed the Classical Tripos in 1889. From 1890 to 1899 she taught Classics and German at St Leonards. She resigned her teaching post on her marriage in 1899 to Robert Kerr Hannay (1867–1940), historian, and their only child was born the following year. In 1911, the Hannays moved to Edinburgh. There Jane Hannay became publicly prominent during the First World War when, despite the initial doubts of the authorities, she was involved in the organisation of voluntary women's patrols (the forerunners of women police) and was honorary secretary of a training school for policewomen and patrols established in Glasgow. In 1918, she was elected to the first executive committee of the EWCA. She was a JP, and member of a number of public bodies, including the Edinburgh Local Employment Committee (set up in 1916 to assist the Home Office and Board of Trade), two trade boards, a Ministry of Labour committee (on the supply of female domestic servants and the effect of the unemployment insurance scheme), and the Central Committee on Training and Employment of Women. She was vice-chairman of the Scottish equivalent of CCTEW at her death. In 1920 she was appointed (with *Elizabeth Sanderson Haldane) a member of the Scottish Savings Committee set up by the Treasury, and for this work she was awarded the CBE in 1933.

Jane Hannay was also an active member of the Church of Scotland. She served on the Women's Association for Foreign Missions Committee from 1915 and was elected to the influential General Assembly Home Mission Committee in 1930, the first year when women were admitted. She was seen by contemporaries as a pioneer worker for women's welfare. LRM

• NAS: GD333/7/1 and GD333/7/21 (EWCA papers); St Leonards School Archives (Minutes and reports). Church of Scotland, *Reports on the Schemes of the Church of Scotland with legislative Acts passed by the General Assembly,* 1914, passim; *Evening News*, 15 April 1938 (obit.); Ford, P. and Ford, G. (eds) (1951) *A Breviate of Parliamentary Papers, 1917–1939*; *ODNB* (2004); *SB*; *St Leonards School Gazette*, June 1938, p. 2 (obit.); *The Scotsman*, 27 August 1919, and 'The late Mrs Hannay', 19 April 1938. Private information.

HARDEN, Janet (Jessy), n. **Allan,** born Edinburgh 25 Feb. 1776, died 1837. Diarist. Daughter of Margaret Learmonth, and Robert Allan, banker and proprietor of the *Caledonian Mercury.*

The Allan family lived at 28 Queen Street in Edinburgh's New Town, and their social set included the notable Edinburgh families of the day. Jessy Allan was interested in art and her friends included the artist Alexander Nasmyth, and his talented painter daughters, *Jane Nasmyth and her sisters. When Jessy Allan's elder sister, Agnes Ranken, left Scotland for India with her military husband, Jessy began a detailed journal of her daily life to keep Agnes up-to-date with family affairs. Covering 1801–11, with contributions from other relatives including her father, the 32 small volumes constitute a unique record of early-19th-century New Town society.

In 1803, Jessy Allan married John Harden (1772–1847), a talented amateur artist. Their early married life was spent in Queen Street, then they moved to Brathay Hall near Windermere, where they were part of the literary social circle that included the Wordsworths. To complement his wife's journal, John Harden undertook a series of delightful drawings of domestic and family life in Edinburgh and the Lake District. Both drawings and journal are housed in the National Library of Scotland. SN
• NLS: MSS 8832–63, Jessy Harden's Journal; MSS 8866–8, John Harden's Drawings.
Brown, I. G. (1995) *Elegance and Entertainment in the New Town of Edinburgh.*

HARDIE, Agnes, n. **Pettigrew,** born Glasgow 6 Sept. 1874, died London 24 March 1951. Labour MP for Glasgow Springburn, 1937–45. Daughter of Margaret Drummond, and John Pettigrew, Poorhouse Assistant Governor.

Details of her early life and education are unknown but in her teens Agnes Pettigrew was employed as a shop assistant. In c. 1893, she helped organise Scottish shoe workers and went on to become the first female organiser of the shop assistants' union. An ILP member, in 1907 she became a platform speaker gifted 'in unfolding practical Socialism to women taking up politics for the first time' (Haddow 1920, p. 63). In c. 1909, she was elected to Glasgow School Board and became the first female member of Glasgow Trades Council. In 1909 she married George Hardie, half brother of Keir Hardie and later Labour MP for Glasgow Springburn, with whom she had a son.

She was a pacifist and linked with the Women's Peace Crusade during the First World War; in the Second World War, she opposed the introduction of conscription for men in 1939 and women in 1941. In 1919, she was appointed as Women's Organiser for the Labour Party in Scotland, a post that she held until 1923 when she moved to London with her newly elected husband. On his death in 1937, she replaced him as MP for Glasgow Springburn. Elected at the age of 63, she retired in 1945.

Although hardly a typical housewife herself, she became known as the 'housewife's MP' on account of her voluble attacks on the price of meat or shortage of potatoes (Vallance 1979, p. 85). Her selection as Labour candidate for Springburn was attributed to her marital connections but in her own life she pioneered a path for women as a political organiser and elected representative. CB
• *Glasgow Herald,* 31 March 1951 (obit.); Haddow, W. M. (1920) *Socialism in Scotland: its rise and progress;* Vallance, E. (1979) *Women in the House, A Study of Women Members of Parliament; SLL.*

HARDIE, Margaret ('Midside Maggie'), n. **Lylestoun,** born c. 1625 Westruther, Berwickshire, died after 1660. Tenant farmer.

In 1643, Margaret Lylestoun married Thomas Hardie, who farmed the Midside part of Tollishill Farm, part of the estates of the Earl of Lauderdale. Seven years of bad weather followed. The local story has it that when the rent was due, Thomas Hardie was ready to give up and seek work elsewhere. However, his young wife went to beg an interview to see whether the Earl would let the rent 'stand over'. At Thirlstane Castle, she was given a hearing by the reluctant Earl. She told of the lean years and the deep snowdrifts on the Midside of Tollishill. The Earl told her to bring a snowball on Midsummer's Day and he would forego his rent. Thomas and Maggie Hardie collected a large amount of snow in a deep cleuch on the hill and were able to produce the promised snowball on Midsummer's Day. For once, the Earl kept his word. Thereafter, the Hardies prospered.

The Earl, a staunch loyalist, was captured at the Battle of Worcester and confined in the Tower of London for nine years. His tenants in Lauderdale saw no reason to pay rent to a rebel landlord, except for those at the Midside of Tollishill. Here, Maggie Hardie put aside the rent money in gold coins which she baked into a bannock and set off on foot to London. She gained access to the Tower

and presented the Earl with the bannock. On breaking it, gold coins fell to the floor. With these, he obtained his freedom and on the Restoration of Charles II, returned to Lauderdale where he presented Maggie Hardie with a silver girdle (now in the National Museum of Scotland, Edinburgh). He gave Maggie and Tom Hardie their farm rent-free for the remainder of their days. WE
• NAS: Lauderdale Estate Records 1643–1700.
Lang, J. (1913) *North and South of the Tweed.*

HARGRAVE, Letitia, n. **Mactavish,** born Edinburgh 1813, died Sault Ste Marie, Upper Canada, Sept. 1854. Northern pioneer. Daughter of Letitia Lockhart, and Dugald Mactavish, sheriff of Argyllshire.

The eldest of nine children, grandchildren of Lachlan, Chief of Clan Tavish, Letitia Mactavish grew up at Kilchrist House, near Campbeltown, and completed her education at a ladies' finishing-school. She married James Hargrave in January 1840 and they sailed to Canada later that year. Her husband was a chief trader in charge of York Factory, at that time the Hudson's Bay Company's most northern supply post, on the bleak and barren shores of Hudson Bay. She was the first European wife to go with her husband to such an isolated post and she spent altogether ten years in a place of 'solitude, swamps, infernal fried suckers and salt geese' (Macleod, 1947, p. cvi), giving birth there to five children, and surviving scurvy and the epidemics of measles which sometimes decimated the native population. The letters written to her family in Scotland give a vivid picture of life at an isolated fur-trade post. GH
• Macleod, M. A. (ed.) (1947) *The Letters of Letitia Hargrave.* Van Kirk, S. (1980) *'Many Tender Ties': women in fur-trade society, 1670–1870.*

HARRIS, Amelia, born Fearn, Angus, 7 April 1815, died Edinburgh 16 Jan. 1891; **HARRIS, Jane,** born Fearn 18 Jan. 1823, died Edinburgh 2 Sept. 1897. Singers and preservers of traditional songs. Daughters of Grace Dow, and David Harris, minister.

Amelia and Jane Harris spent most of their lives together, living finally in the Morningside district of Edinburgh. Norval Clyne, an Aberdeen lawyer who met them in 1873, remarked about Amelia Harris in a letter of 27 August: 'She is personally an exceedingly pleasant lady, with means apparently sufficient to enable her to live comfortably and ramble here and there, as she and her sister have

just been doing' (Lyle et al. 2002, p. xxvi). In Lerwick, they heard an inspiring lecture by William Edmonstoune Aytoun, Professor of Rhetoric and Belles Lettres at the University of Edinburgh; it gave their lives the focus that enabled them to leave their heritage of song to posterity. They sent him the words and music of their ballads and songs in 1859, and later, when the Aytoun materials had been lost sight of, they prepared another manuscript for Francis James Child of Harvard University, Amelia Harris writing the words and Jane Harris the music. Their songs had come down to them from their mother, who had learnt them by the age of ten from a nurse called Jannie Scott. The tradition of passing songs down through the female line, sung in the home, is a familiar one, but for the first time in Scotland these women, recognising the cultural value of what they knew, took steps themselves to make the songs available to the world at large. Previously, women's songs had been taken down by collectors, one notable case earlier in the century being **Mary Storie**, n. **Macqueen** (born c. 1801, emigrated to Canada 1828), who was the wife of William Storie, a weaver at Lochwinnoch in Renfrewshire, and belonged to a traveller family. Her parents were Elizabeth Copeland and Osburn Macqueen. In 1827, she sang for Andrew Crawfurd and Andrew Blaikie a repertoire of 47 songs, including a number that came to her from her mother, her grandmother and her great-grandmother. EBL
• Child, F. J. (ed.) *The English and Scottish Popular Ballads,* 1882–98; Lyle, E. (ed.) (1975, 1996) *Andrew Crawfurd's Collection of Ballads and Songs;* Lyle, E., McAlpine, K. and McLucas, A. D. (eds) (2002) *The Song Repertoire of Amelia and Jane Harris.*
Audio sources: *Mary Macqueen's Ballads sung by Jo Miller,* STS 01; Katherine Campbell, *The Songs of Amelia and Jane Harris* (2004) SPRCD 1041.

HART, Constance Mary (Judith), n. **Ridehalgh, Baroness Hart of South Lanark,** DBE, born Burnley, Lancs, 18 Sept. 1924, died London 8 Dec. 1991. Socialist, Labour MP. Daughter of Lily Lord, schoolteacher, and Harry Ridehalgh, linotype operator.

Judith Ridehalgh was brought up in Wharley and educated at Clitheroe Royal Grammar School and the LSE, where she took a first in sociology in 1945. As a teenager she adopted the name Judith. Her marriage in 1946 to scientist Anthony Hart (1917–99) produced two sons, Richard and Steven. Her family, she frequently acknowledged, provided both political and personal support. She was a life-long socialist and member of the 'hard left' of the Parliamentary Labour Party, with a strong power base in the NEC. As such, she consistently opposed party policy despite being a member of government or of the shadow cabinet for most of her career.

She fought, unsuccessfully, Bournemouth West in 1951 and South Aberdeen in 1955. In 1959, a landslide year for Macmillan's Conservative Party, Judith Hart, an Englishwoman in a traditional area of Scotland, took the Tory-held seat of Lanark, latterly Clydesdale. She held it for nearly 30 years, until she retired from the Commons in 1987. For some years in the early 1980s, she was the sole Scottish woman MP. Her constituency straddled the grim Lanarkshire coalfield and she worked indefatigably, always elegantly dressed and coiffed, against pit closures and to ameliorate their effects. Described by Barbara Castle in her obituary (*Guardian* 1991) as dynamic, physically attractive, courageous and challenging, she campaigned for nationalisation, public-sector job-creation and school pupils with disabilities, and against the EEC, the sale of arms to Chile, and the Falklands war. She took a firm line against Ian Smith and arranged scholarships for black Rhodesians to study in Britain. It was largely due to her efforts that the tawse was outlawed in Scottish schools.

Judith Hart was Paymaster General in Harold Wilson's cabinet from 1968 to 1969, but it is for her determined work as Minister for Overseas Development (1969–70, 1974–5, 1977–9) that she is most remembered, her name known and respected in remote corners of the least developed countries. She articulated, long before it became fashionable, the connection between the economic and fiscal policies and actions of the First World and the condition of the Third. Judith Hart was instrumental in achieving the Lomé Convention (1975). She spoke at the first Aldermaston march in 1958 and was a moving force in the World Disarmament Campaign. Her work was recognised in numerous ways, including the Chilean Order of Merit for her support in the struggle against Pinochet. The South African security services attempted to smear her and British Intelligence took some interest. In 1979, to the consternation of many friends, she became a Dame of the British Empire (DBE). In 1988, she was made a life peer and was active in the Lords until prevented from continuing by symptoms of the cancer from which she died. Donald Dewar memorialised Judith Hart as an influential figure in Scottish politics who devoted her life to fighting poverty both in the UK and in the developing world (*Scotsman* 1991). LH

• Hart, J. (1968) *Minorities in our Society*, Address to National Council of Social Service, (1973) *Aid and Liberation*, (1975) *Administering an Aid Programme in a Year of Change*: a personal diary/address to the Royal Commonwealth Society, (1977) *New Perspectives in North-South Relations: a radical view of world poverty and development*, (1978) *Interdependence*, (1979) *The Rights of Man*: Sir David Owen memorial lecture (NLS).

Castle, B., *The Guardian*, 9 Dec. 1991 (obit.); Dewar, D., *The Scotsman*, 9 Dec. 1991 (obit.); *DLabB*; Hansard, 9 Dec. 1991; *ODNB* (2004); *Who's Who of Women in World Politics* (1991). Private information: Keith Harwood, Clitheroe Royal Grammar School; Tony Benn. Personal knowledge.

HART, Jennifer Marianne (Maidie),[‡] n. **Bridge,** born Brookfield, Renfrewshire, 15 Dec. 1916, died Edinburgh 7 Nov. 1997. Campaigner for equality, development and peace. Daughter of Jennifer Gibson, and Norman Cressy Bridge, consultant electrical engineer.

Maidie Bridge was educated at St Columba's school, Kilmacolm, and the University of St Andrews, where she graduated with first-class honours in English. She married William Douglas (Bill) Hart in 1941. They had two daughters, Constance and Jennifer. From early days in the playgroup movement, through work with the Church of Scotland – she was President of the Woman's Guild in the 1970s – to ecumenical involvement with the World Council of Churches (WCC), she followed her belief that women, too, are made in the image of God. After attending the WCC Vienna conference on human rights in 1982, she became a founder member of the Ecumenical Forum of European Christian Women. She also served as a Vice-President of the British Council of Churches (BCC) 1978–81, and of Scottish Churches Council (SCC) 1982–86. As an Executive member of the UK Women's National Commission (the independent advisory group to the UK Government on women's issues) she chaired the Steering Committee for the UN International Women's Year 1975 events in Scotland. Out of these joint activities came the foundation of the Scottish Convention of Women (SCOW) in 1977, linking traditional organisations, women's movement groups and individual women in work on equality issues. SCOW's work was carried forward after 1992 by bodies including the Scottish Joint Action Group, Women's Forum Scotland, Engender, the Network of Ecumenical Women in Scotland

(NEWS) and the now government-supported Scottish Women's Convention.

Maidie Hart was a quiet revolutionary, determined that women's voices should be heard in decision making and their experience acknowledged and valued. She worked to bring a gender perspective to international conferences, to the Church of Scotland, particularly in her work with former Moderator Bill Johnston on the Community of Women and Men in Church and Society, and to devolution for Scotland (SCOW was a member of the Scottish Constitutional Convention). At a women's workshop, on a peace march or talking to government ministers (she was never intimidated by high office), her gift was to bring people together. A committed Christian, she was an Elder of the Church of Scotland from 1974, serving in Edinburgh and Dirleton. She is commemorated by a wooden bench, designed by the late Tim Stead, beside the chapel in the garden at Scottish Churches House, Dunblane. KMD/AH
• NLS: SCOW Archive.
Hart, M. and Davies, K. (1990) 'The Scottish Convention of Women', in S. Henderson and A. Mackay (eds) *Grit and Diamonds: Women in Scotland making history*.
Blackie, N. (ed.) (2005) *A Time for Trumpets: Scottish church movers and shakers in the twentieth century*; Breitenbach, E. and Mackay, F. (eds) (1998) *Women and Contemporary Scottish Politics*; *Glasgow Herald*, 15 November 1997 (obit.); *Life & Work*, Jan. 1998 (obit.); *The Scotsman*, 21 Nov. 1997 (obit.). Private information.

HARTSIDE, Margaret, fl.1590s–1610s. Chamberer to *Anna of Denmark.

Margaret Hartside's royal service ended in 1607 when she and her husband, John Buchanan, sergeant of the king's buttery, returned to Scotland, but her subsequent arrest for allegedly stealing jewels worth £400 from Anna, her trial at Linlithgow on 31 May 1608, and her curious punishment, provide fascinating insights into the dangers of indiscretion in high places. Depositions suggest the charge was a pretext to silence various indiscreet speeches she had made about the sovereigns. The charge was reduced from theft to 'detaining' the jewels. By king's warrant of 20 July 1608, she was declared Infamous, required to repay the jewels' value to Anna, and exiled for life to Orkney. Her husband shared her fate for complicity, although his partial liberty was restored in 1611. Shortly after Anna's death in March 1619, the king lifted Margaret Hartside's doom and restored her liberty. HP

• NAS: Treasurer's Accounts, E21/75.
Fraser, W. (1889) *Memorials of the Earls of Haddington*; *Crim. Trials*, vol. 2; *RPC*, vols 8, 11.

HASTIE, Annie Harper, n. **Williamson,** born Carriden, Bo'ness, 13 Feb. 1922, died Falkirk 18 Sept. 2002. Baker. Daughter of Annie Martin, domestic servant, and David Williamson, blacksmith.

Annie Williamson attended Carriden Primary School and Bo'ness Academy, where discipline was strict, with the belt in frequent use. Leaving school in 1937, she played acoustic guitar in a band, 'The Georgians', with her brother and sister, while working in domestic service and as a doctor's receptionist. During the Second World War, she travelled to 'secret' munitions work in London and Scotland. She commented, 'We weren't supposed to know it was Dumfries, but we all kent!', reflecting that the experience gave young women a sense of identity and broader horizons. But her world mostly pivoted around the community of Bo'ness. After a stint at Paton and Baldwin's, in 1949 she married local baker William Hastie. She worked in the shop and kept accounts until the bakery closed in 1988, while raising three sons, including twins. She is widely remembered for her local activities, which included the Townswomen's Guild, the Red Cross, the WRVS, the Churchwomen's Guild, and the SWRI. Always reliable, she helped with charity events and catering, carrying Christmas parcels to the 'old dears' on foot at an advanced age, and was a fixture at the Rotary Club, the local theatre, and the golf club. Through a Rotary exchange programme, she befriended a Dutch girl, who called Annie Hastie her 'Scottish mum'. She engendered much local affection through her activities and genuine kindness: people came on to the street to pay respects as the family returned from her funeral. Annie Hastie would have said she was just an ordinary woman doing what needed to be done, but she represents all those small-town women who, through their energy, keep many a community running. DLS
• Hastie, A. Manuscript notes about Bo'ness.
Interviews with Annie Hastie, family and friends.

HATTON, G. Noel *see* **CAIRD, Alice Mona** (1854–1932)

HAWARDEN, Clementina, Viscountess, n. **Elphinstone Fleeming,** m. **Maude,** born Cumbernauld House, 1 June 1822, died London 19 Jan. 1865. Photographer. Daughter of Catalina

Alessandro of Spain, and Admiral Charles Elphinstone Fleeming, C.-in-C. Gibraltar, Governor of Greenwich Hospital, MP for Stirlingshire.

After a traditional private education in fine arts and languages, in 1845 Clementina Elphinstone Fleeming married Cornwallis Maude, Lifeguards officer and heir to an Irish peerage (Hawarden), to which he succeeded in 1856. They had eight surviving children. Life on the Dundrum estate in Co. Tipperary enabled her to begin a photographic career, unusual in the 1850s, early years in the development of photography. At least partly self-taught, she produced 850 photographs, almost exclusively in wet collodion negative-albumen print technique. Initially using a stereoscopic camera, she created studies of the Tipperary landscape, in which her family and household often were placed. She collaborated with the artist Sir Francis Seymour Haden and he produced etchings from her photographs. The work for which she is most familiar, however, derived from after 1859 when the family moved to a house in South Kensington, ideally suited for photography. Lady Hawarden used light-flooded first-floor rooms to capture costume portraits and amateur theatrical tableaux featuring her daughters. This period coincided with the development of the South Kensington Museum; the Hawardens belonged to the influential arts people of that milieu.

Lady Hawarden presented her photographs at the 1863 and 1864 exhibitions of the Photographic Society of London, was awarded silver medals and elected to the Society. Her work was admired and bought by Charles Lutwidge Dodgson (Lewis Carroll). She was a supporter of women artists and of the Female School of Art, in aid of which she sold photographs. She was planning to help establish the United Association of Photography when her death from pneumonia at 42 put an untimely end to a flourishing career. She ranks with Julia Margaret Cameron among the few Victorian women photographers to achieve excellence and recognition. LS
• Dodier, V. (1999) *Clementina, Lady Hawarden*; Lawson, J. (1997) *Women in White*; *ODNB* (2004); Ovenden, G. (ed.) (1974) *Clementina, Lady Hawarden*.

HAY, Helen Ann, born Montrose, 14 Jan. 1867, died Arbroath, 27 April 1955. Artist. Daughter of Elizabeth Middleton Ross, and William Hay, bank accountant, farmer.

A student of Arts and Crafts under John Duncan at Patrick Geddes's 'Old Edinburgh School of Art' (c. 1893–7), Helen Hay produced illustrations for Geddes & Colleagues publications *The Evergreen* (Spring 1895) and *Lyra Celtica* (1898). She painted friezes for the Edinburgh Room, Outlook Tower, Castle Hill, from designs by artists including James Cadenhead. She produced paintings for Dr Fletcher and Rev. Millar Patrick while working as Secretary of the School (c. 1898–1901). In a George Street studio, 'Designer and Decorator' (1901), she also advertised as an 'Art Metal Worker' (1903–12). She designed a booklet of Burns' poems (1912) and may have exhibited watercolours with the RSA (1930s and 1940s) as well as silversmithing. RA
• NLS: MSS 10589–90 Geddes papers; Strathclyde Univ. Archives: Geddes papers and issues of *The Evergreen* (1895–98).
Gordon Bowe, N. and Cumming, E. (1998) *The Arts and Crafts Movements in Dublin and Edinburgh 1880–1925.*

HAY, Helen (Eleanor, Helenor), Countess of Linlithgow, born before 1570, died Cumbernauld, 1627. Royal tutor, death-bed convert to Protestantism. Daughter of Jean Hay, and Andrew Hay, 8th Earl of Erroll.

When most of the Scottish nobility had become Protestant, Helen Hay remained openly and defiantly Roman Catholic. Her connection with James VI's court is first recorded after she married a Protestant, Lord Alexander Livingston (d. 1621), later first Earl of Linlithgow, in January 1584. In 1594, Alexander carried the towel at the christening of Prince Henry. James VI placed his two daughters in the care of the Livingstons from 1596 until 1603; Princess Margaret died young, but *Elizabeth (see Stewart, Elizabeth, Queen of Bohemia) lived with them long enough for them to be responsible for her early education. Helen and Alexander had five children. As early as 1587, the ministers of the reformed church complained to the King about her Catholicism and began their aggressive attempts to convert her, threatening excommunication if she did not conform. These attempts continued well into the 17th century. Late in life, Helen Hay appears to have relented. Her daughter, Margaret, Countess of Wigtown, summoned Mr John Livingston to her mother's deathbed. From this meeting resulted her conversion document, *The Confession and Conversion of My Lady C. of L.* The minister may have written the conversion himself and merely had her sign it, but the core of the piece was probably written or dictated by her, with John Livingston serving as editor. The *Confession*, printed in 1629, circulated widely. Helen Hay's documented conversion signified a coup for the reformed church. P B G

• Hay, H. (1629) *The Confession and Conversion of the Right Honorable, Most Illustrious and Elect Lady, My Lady C of L.* Johnston, G.P. (1929) 'Introduction', *The Confession and Conversion of My Lady C. of L.*; *SP*, 3, p. 572; 5, pp. 543–6; *ODNB* (2004) (see Livingstone, Helen).

HENERY, Marion, n. **Jenkins,** born Cambuslang 29 April 1910, died Coatbridge 15 Sept. 2001. Typist, Communist activist, hunger marcher. Daughter of Mary Robertson, farm servant, and Robert Jenkins, stonemason.

The family lived in Cambuslang, where Marion Jenkins, the youngest of eight, attended Socialist Sunday School. Aged 14, she took a commercial course at Skerry's College, Glasgow, before working for a carpet manufacturer and then for the United Mineworkers of Scotland. She became full-time organiser for the YCL in Scotland in 1931. In 1932 she helped organise the women's contingent on the hunger march to London, which started from Lancashire. In 1933–4 she attended the Lenin School in the Soviet Union. She married Joe Henery, a miner, in 1935; they had three children. In 1937, unable to get work, they moved to Welwyn Garden City, then settled in Auchinloch, Kirkintilloch, during the war.

Marion Henery was very active in the SCWG and in 1956 she took over responsibility for the CP Scottish Women's Advisory Committee. Between 1956 and 1969 she organised classes and weekend schools for women. Working as secretary of the Geriatric Unit at Stobhill Hospital, she was active in NALGO and in the mid-60s campaigned on cervical cancer detection. In retirement, she became Secretary of the Scottish Old Age Pensioners Campaign and continued working for CND. She stayed in the CPGB until its end in 1991. N R

• Questionnaire returned to NR, 1994; Author interviews 6 April 1994 and 17 Nov. 1995.
MacDougall, I. (ed.) (1986–91) *Voices of the Hunger Marches: personal recollections by Scottish hunger marchers of the 1920s and 1930s*, vols 1, 2.
Private information.

HEPBURN, Jane (Janet), Lady Seton, c. 1480– c. 1558. Religious patron. Daughter of Janet Douglas, daughter of the Earl of Morton, and Patrick Hepburn of Hailes, Earl of Bothwell.

Jane Hepburn married George, 3rd Lord Seton, before December 1506. He died at Flodden Field in 1513; she survived him by 45 years and became known as a 'wise and noble lady' (Maitland 1828, p. 38). She was possibly the founder of the Dominican convent of Sciennes, Edinburgh, sometime before 20 January 1518. The building was certainly erected at her expense and she continued to give generously to it. She also helped to rebuild Seton Collegiate Church in the 1520s, endowing two chaplains in the 1540s. Sciennes may have been founded for her own benefit, since she retired there once her sons were able to manage the family estate, and remained there until her death. She was buried in Seton Church beside her husband. K P

• Maidment, J. (ed.) (1841) *Liber Conventus Saint Katherine Senensis Prope Edinburgh*; Maitland, R. (1828 edn.) *Historie or Chronicle of the house of Seytoun*; Seton, G. (1896) *A History of the Family of Seton*, vol. ii; *SP*.

HERBISON, Margaret McCrorie (Peggy), born Shotts 11 March 1907, died Lanark 29 Dec. 1996. Teacher, government minister. Daughter of Jane McCrorie, and John Herbison, miner.

Peggy Herbison was brought up with her five brothers in the close-knit Lanarkshire mining community of Shotts. Deeply committed to her roots, she made the town her life-long home base. She progressed from Dykehead Public School to Bellshill Academy and the University of Glasgow (MA, 1928), later teaching English and history at Allan Glen's, one of Glasgow's foremost boys' schools. She absorbed her parents' Christian socialist politics and by 1944 was known in Labour Party circles as an impressive public speaker. Miners from the Party's Baton Colliery branch invited her to become parliamentary candidate for North Lanark, where the sitting Unionist MP was an old Etonian ex-army officer. She demurred, telling the miners to 'find a man' (Hollis 1997, p. 121), but won the seat convincingly in the general election of July 1945. Because she was relatively young and small in stature, she was known as 'the miners' little sister' at Westminster.

Peggy Herbison sat uninterruptedly on Labour's National Executive from 1948 to 1968, and served as party Chair 1956–7. In 1950, she was the first woman Labour MP from a Scottish constituency to achieve ministerial office, as Under-Secretary of State in the Scottish Office. In October 1964, Harold Wilson appointed her Minister of Pensions and National Insurance in the new Labour Government, a post using her social security expertise. She also became a Privy Councillor. Fulfilling the Party's election pledge, she removed the stigma attached to means-tested national assistance but, by 1966, financial constraints were curtailing Labour's welfare reform programme, limiting family allowances and state pensions. Peggy Herbison was unable to accept budgetary impositions and in July 1967 resigned as Minister. She did not contest North Lanark in 1970, encouraging future Labour leader, John Smith, to stand instead. However, she maintained a high profile in Scotland during the 1970s, considering her greatest honour to be her year (1970–1) as Lord High Commissioner, the monarch's representative at the General Assembly of the Church of Scotland: she was the first woman incumbent. The University of Glasgow awarded her an honorary LLD in 1970.

John Smith's biographer categorised Peggy Herbison as 'austere, religious and right-wing' (McSmith 1994, p. 42), echoing the view of Roy Hattersley, her PPS. Her unmarried status, which she used as a kind of weapon, possibly led to such snap judgements. Yet Janey Buchan in a tribute at the time of her death suggested that her 'sweet little-lady look' was misleading, and had been carefully cultivated to project a respectable stereotype (*Scotsman* 1996). Significantly, she refused Harold Wilson's offer of a life peerage, as she disapproved of the unelected House of Lords. IEM

• Motherwell Heritage Centre, Peggy Herbison Files: transcript, Helen Liddell's funeral tribute, Jan. 1997.
1901 Census return; *DLabB*, vol. 10; *Glasgow Herald*, 26 July 1967, 28 Jan. 1970; *Herald*, 22 July 1995, 30 Dec. 1996 (obit.), 31 Dec. 1996 (Appreciation); Hollis, P. (1997) *Jennie Lee: a life*; McSmith, A. (1993, 1994) *John Smith: a life, 1938–1994*; Mann, J. (1962) *Woman in Parliament*; *ODNB* (2004); Stenton, M. and Lees, S. (1981) *Who's Who of British Members of Parliament*, vol. IV, 1945–1979; *The Scotsman*, 31 Dec 1996.

HERSCHEL, Margaret Brodie, n. **Stewart,** born Dingwall 16 August 1810, died Collingwood, Kent, 3 August 1884. Hostess, correspondent. Daughter of Emilia Calder, and Dr Alexander Stewart, Church of Scotland minister and Gaelic scholar.

Aged 18, Margaret Stewart, a woman of beauty, talent and piety, was introduced to John Herschel (1792–1871), astronomer, mathematician and polymath, one of the most renowned scientists in Europe. They married on 3 March 1829. The marriage, described as one of 'unclouded happiness', produced a remarkable family of nine daughters and three sons. Though not herself a scientist, Margaret Herschel shared her husband's joy in astronomy and his interests in music and botany, to which she contributed illustrations: her South African botanical drawings (1833–8) were later published. She had a serene influence on her husband and their children whose education at home embraced practical and artistic skills as well as academic learning. Her hospitable and perfectly managed home in Kent – *Mary Somerville called it 'a house by itself in the world' – was open to a wide circle of friends, scientific and literary. A wonderful correspondent, her lively letters to other 'scientific wives' and family members, especially Caroline Herschel, Sir John's aunt and astronomer-collaborator of his father Sir William, form a valuable part of the Herschel heritage. MTB

• Buttmann, G. (1974) *The Shadow of the Telescope, a Biography of John Herschel*; Crowe, M. et al. (eds) (1998) *Calendar of the Correspondence of Sir John Herschel* (inc. 338 letters to or from Margaret); *ODNB* (2004) (Herschel, Sir John); Warner, B. (ed.) (1991) *Margaret Herschel: letters from the Cape 1834–1838*.

HERZFELD, Gertrude Marian Amalia,[‡] born London 1 June 1890, died Edinburgh 12 May 1981. First woman surgeon in Scotland. Daughter of Mathilde Winternitz, and Michael Herzfeld, stockbroker.

The daughter of Austrian immigrants, Gertrude Herzfeld spent almost all her professional life in Edinburgh, gaining her MBChB degree in 1914. She was house surgeon to Sir Harold Stiles at the Royal Hospital for Sick Children, Edinburgh, and after wartime posts at the Cambridge Military Hospital and Bolton Royal Infirmary, returned to Scotland in 1920. That year, she became the second female Fellow of the RCSE (the first, Alice Headwards Hunter, did not practise) and the first female honorary assistant surgeon at the Sick Children's Hospital. By 1925, she was full surgeon there, serving for 20 years. From 1920 to 1955 she was also surgeon at the Bruntsfield Hospital for Women and Children, staffed entirely by women. She carried out a wide range of procedures in paediatric and gynaecological surgery, and was noted for her precision and good teaching. Involved in the foundation of the Edinburgh School of Chiropody, she was medical adviser to the Edinburgh Cripple Aid Society. Gertrude Herzfeld joined the BMA in 1915, chaired the Edinburgh City Branch (1960–2), and was National President of the Medical Women's Federation (1948–50). She published widely, in the *Lancet* (1920) and elsewhere, on such diverse topics as rupture of the intestine, uterine prolapse, congenital talipes (club foot), and malformations of the newborn.

Unmarried, she spent her retirement in Edinburgh and died a few weeks before her 91st birthday, having blazed the trail for female surgeons in Scotland. HMD

Herzfeld, G. M. A. (1920) 'Traumatic rupture of the intestine without external injury', *Lancet*, 1, p. 377, (1950) 'Injuries and malformations of the newborn', *Practitioner*, 164, pp. 52–60.

Birrell, G. (1995) *A Most Perfect Hospital: the centenary of the Royal Hospital for Sick Children at Sciennes*; *BMJ* 282, 1981 p. 883 (obit.); Creswell, C. H. (1926) *The Royal College of Surgeons of Edinburgh*; Masson, A. H. B. (1995) *Portraits, Paintings and Busts in the Royal College of Surgeons of Edinburgh*; Young, D. G. (1999) 'The Scots and paediatric surgery', *Journal of the RCSE*, 44, 4, pp. 211–15.

HESKETH, Marianne Edith Frances, n. **Richards** MBE, born London 15 May 1930, died Dervaig, Mull, 24 April 1984. Actor, theatre manager. Daughter of Rita Frances Turner, and Percival Thomas Richards, prison officer.

Marianne Richards met her husband, John Barrie Hesketh (b. 1930) in London while they were training to be actors. After working in English theatre for several years, they moved to Scotland in 1960, where John Hesketh took up a post with the Scottish Community Drama Association. Three years later, they settled in Dervaig on the Isle of Mull and opened a guesthouse. For their guests' entertainment, in 1966 they converted a byre beside their house into a theatre: thus was born Mull Little Theatre, the smallest professional theatre in Britain. They closed the guesthouse in 1970 to concentrate on the theatre, which they ran until Marianne Hesketh's death in 1984.

Although the theatre was tiny and they were the sole performers, Mull Little Theatre achieved wide recognition through British and European tours undertaken in addition to the annual summer seasons on Mull. Marianne Hesketh adapted a number of plays, including Strindberg's *Miss Julie* and Chekhov's *The Bear*, to allow them to be played as two-handers. Together they wrote a satire, 'Willy Nilly' (unpublished), and a full-length play, *Ostrich*, a comedy about academia. In 1983 they were both made MBE for their achievements. A small professional drama company, independent of the original, still operates from a base in Dervaig under the new name of The Mull Theatre. BF

• Hesketh, M. and Hesketh, J. B. (1988) *Ostrich*.
Hesketh, J. B. (1997) *Taking Off: the story of the Mull Little Theatre*.

HEWAT, Elizabeth Glendinning Kirkwood, born Prestwick 16 Sept. 1895, died Edinburgh 13 Oct. 1968. Missionary, historian, ecumenicist and advocate of women's equality in the Church of Scotland. Daughter of Elizabeth Glendinning, and Kirkwood Hewat, UFC minister, Prestwick.

Elizabeth Hewat was educated at Wellington School, Ayr, and the University of Edinburgh. She had outstanding intellectual gifts, graduating MA in history and philosophy before taking a post as assistant lecturer in history at the University of St Andrews. From 1922 to 1926, she taught at the UFC Women's Missionary College, Edinburgh – an institution with a progressive tradition in education and inclusive community. One of the first women to study theology at New College, she was the first to graduate BD (1926). Intending to work as a missionary, she believed she should be ordained in order to equip herself fully. Her case led to a debate on women's ordination during the 1926 UFC General Assembly. The proposer argued that she had come top of her class, making it difficult to argue that she could not be put on the same level as the men. Although the motion failed, Elizabeth Hewat joined her sister in China, where she combined work as a teaching missionary with scholarly research comparing Hebrew and Confucian Wisdom literature. She returned to Scotland to complete her PhD and worked as unpaid assistant at North Merchiston Church, Edinburgh. Moving to Bombay, she became Professor of History at Wilson College, 1935–56. An elder in the United Church of North India, she frequently conducted worship in the Chapel, the Scots Kirk, and elsewhere. For many years she was editorial assistant and contributor to the *International Review of Missions*.

After returning to Scotland, she wrote the official history of Church of Scotland Missions, served as National Vice-President of the Woman's Guild, and undertook extensive speaking and writing commitments. In 1966, she received an honorary DD from the University of Edinburgh. She was a passionate supporter of CND, deeply involved in the growing international ecumenical movement and a life-long advocate of equality in church and society. She wrote in 1931, 'women in the church hold a subordinate position; and women of today ask why . . . Of one thing they are certain, and it is this, that it is not Christ who is barring the way' (Hewat 1931, p. 145). LO

• Hewat, E. (1931) *Life & Work*, New Series No. 16, April.
Magnusson, M. (1987) *Out of Silence*; Macdonald, L. A. O.

(2000) *A Unique and Glorious Mission: Women and Presbyterianism in Scotland c. 1830–c. 1930*; Sherrard, M. (ed.) (1993) *Women of Faith.*
Private information.

'Highland Mary' *see* **CAMPBELL, Margaret** (1766–86)

HILL, Amelia, n. **Paton,** born Dunfermline 1820, died Edinburgh 5 July 1904. Sculptor. Daughter of Catherine McDiarmid, folklorist, and Joseph Neil Paton, damask designer.

Amelia Paton enjoyed a free-spirited childhood, roaming the grounds of her Dunfermline home, where she received an informal education in natural science, Highland folklore and antiquities, and lessons from a Quaker governess. Surprisingly, despite the family's involvement with art and design (her younger brothers Joseph Noel Paton and Waller Hugh Paton became painters), she 'had no tuition in drawing and painting' (Tooley 1895, p. 364). Using makeshift tools, she taught herself to model, presumably later refining her technique through casual instruction at friends' studios. At 40, she launched her career with the exhibition of two busts (RSA 1860), having moved to Edinburgh with her brothers the previous year. Thereafter she showed more than 60 sculptures, mostly portraits, at the RSA, RA, and Glasgow Institute until 1882. In 1862, she married David Octavius Hill (1802–70), pioneer of photography, and their childless marriage was 'one of mutual comradeship in art' (Tooley 1932), he being her mentor and enthusiastic promoter, she providing vital assistance with his painting of the Disruption. As one of an emergent, indigenous school of sculpture, she created an oeuvre comprising idealised figures from national literature (*The Mermaid of Galloway*); portraits memorialising men of science and letters (*Sir David Brewster*); Free Church clergy (*R. S. Candlish*); national heroes (*Regent Murray*) and other Scottish notables (*Countess of Elgin*). There are some busts in the SNPG and several works were commissioned for monuments, the most celebrated being the statue of David Livingstone (Princes Street Gardens, Edinburgh). Excluded from RSA membership, she helped found the Albert Institute in Shandwick Place (1877), an alternative art society that welcomed aspirant artists regardless of gender: its exterior figures of Painting and Sculpture are by her. A woman of varied interests, she propagated exotic plants, decocted herbal remedies, studied phrenology, and collected Roman and Scottish antiquities. SHH

• NLS: Acc. 11315; MS 2628 ff. 18, 19; MS 1749 f. 54; Dep. 351; MS 10291 f. 143; MS 2629 ff. 1, 248, 249, corr. D. O. Hill, J. Noel Paton, Amelia Hill; RSA letter collection: corr. Hill and '1928 folder'.
Gifford, W. (1904) 'Mrs D. O. Hill', *Englishwoman's Review,* 5 Oct., pp. 280–2 (obit.); Hurtado, S. H. (2002) 'Genteel mavericks: women sculptors in Victorian Britain', PhD, Univ. of Manitoba, (copy in Courtauld Inst., London, Bibl.); *ODNB* (2004); Tooley, S. A. (1895) 'A famous lady sculptor: an interview with Mrs D. O. Hill', *The Young Woman,* 35, (1932) 'Notable Victorians', *Weekly Scotsman,* 13 Feb., p. 6.

HODGE, Hannah, born Lochgelly 6 Jan. 1751. Coalminer. Daughter of Bessie Adamson and William Hodge, coal-miners.

Born at a time when miners and their families were still bonded slaves, Hannah Hodge is one of the very few coal-mining women about whom anything is known. She married William Cook but, as was common, retained her maiden name. Shortly after their fifth child was born, her husband was killed and she took over his job as a coal and stone miner, continuing until her children were old enough to support her.

Hannah Hodge carried her two youngest children underground in a basket and took time out from work to breastfeed her baby. The older children carried the 'redd' or waste matter out of the pit on their backs and Hannah worked with men at the coal face. She 'brought more coal to the bank than any other miner' (Cook MSS). She not only had to dig coal but carry it to the surface as well, a job she would previously have done for her husband. Hannah Hodge's grandson Archibald, born in 1833, wrote down details of conversations he remembered hearing as a child. They included working in areas where the air was so bad that no lamp would burn and illumination came from 'fish heads', and tales of a trial of strength between Hannah and another female miner in which they each carried four hundredweights (about 200 kilos) of coal. LK
• Cook, A. 'Bygone life in Lochgelly, stray memories of an old miner', MSS in possession of the Cook family.
Cook, A., Brown, P., Westwater, A. (1954) *One Hundred Years of The Jenny Gray Pit.*

HOGG, Jane Donaldson, n. **MacLaren [Atalanta],** born Macduff 18 Aug. 1834, died Stirling 12 Feb. 1900. Journalist and newspaper proprietor. Daughter of Margaret Donaldson, and Alexander MacLaren, bank agent.

Jane MacLaren was a teacher in Stirling before marrying James Hogg (1823–76), editor of the

Stirling Journal and Advertiser, in 1858. They had six daughters and one son. Widowed in 1876, 'within a week' she had decided to conduct the printing business and two newspapers (including the *Bridge of Allan Reporter*), with the assistance of a manager (Johnston 1900). From 1885 she wrote a 'Ladies' Column' as 'Atalanta', proving 'a born journalist' (ibid.). One of her three surviving daughters, **Anna Porteous Hogg** (1862–1909), married Thomas Johnston, editor of the *Stirling Journal*, in 1887 and became co-editor of both papers from 1900 to 1912, continuing their tradition of Conservatism. Both Jane Hogg's other daughters, Harriet Hogg and Margaret Murray Hogg, were headmistresses of St Hilda's School for Girls, Stirling.

Jane Hogg flourished in later life. She was the first woman elected (three times from 1888) to Stirling School Board 'especially charged . . . with the care of the female education', where she 'more than justified her election' (*Stirling Observer* 1900, p. 4). She was also known for her business sense and eloquent advocacy of charitable causes. She was local Hon Treasurer of the Scottish Domestic Servants' Benevolent Association, assisting *Carrie Johnstone of Alva, and an active church member and organist. A founder member of Stirling Natural History and Archaeological Society (SNHAS) in 1878, she contributed five papers on local history to their *Transactions*, which she also edited. MAMC

• Elliot, B. J. (1979) '*The Stirling Journal and Advertiser*: a history', *Stirling Journal and Advertiser* Index, vol. 2, pp. 1–2; Johnston, T. W. R., 'The Late Mrs Hogg', *Stirling Journal and Advertiser*, 16 February 1900, p. 4; Kidston, R. and Morris, D. B. (eds) (1900) 'The Late Mrs Hogg', *Trans. SNHAS*, 6, II, pp. 63–4; *Stirling Observer and Advertiser*, 'The Late Mrs Hogg', 16 February 1900 (anonymous appreciation); 'The Late Mrs Hogg', reprinted from *North Parish Church Magazine*, 9 March 1900, p. 4.

HOLM, Helen, n. **Gray,** born Jordanhill, Glasgow, 14 March 1907, died Ayr 14 Dec. 1971. Golf champion. Daughter of Violet Warren, and Thomas Gray, Professor of Chemistry.

Helen Gray first came to prominence in 1928 when she won the inaugural Lanarkshire Ladies' Championship, a feat which she repeated in 1929 and 1932. After her marriage to farmer Andrew Holm, she won the Scottish Ladies' Amateur Championship in 1930, captured it on four further occasions (1932, 1937, 1948, 1950) and was runner-up five times. Success in the 1934 Ladies' British Open Amateur Championship at Royal Porthcawl paved the way for international honours and she

was a member of the Curtis Cup team that halved the match against the USA at Gleneagles in 1936. She also won the British title in 1938 and took part in two further Curtis Cups (1938, 1948), but turned down the opportunity of playing in the first post-war challenge on American soil in 1950 because she felt her son Michael was too young to be left. In 1951, having previously played against both teams, she was non-playing GB captain in matches against France and Belgium. Renowned for her mental and physical toughness, she continued to compete after a thrombosis in late 1951 nearly ended her career, and represented Scotland in the home internationals of 1955 and 1957, thereby completing a total of 14 appearances for her country. The Helen Holm Trophy, played over her home course of Troon, was instituted in 1973, two years after her death. JK

• Cossey, R. (1984) *Golfing Ladies*; George, J. (2003) 'Women and golf in Scotland', PhD, Univ. of Edinburgh; Mair, L. (1992) *One Hundred Years of Women's Golf*; ODNB (2004).

HOOD, Morag Macleod, born Glasgow 12 Dec. 1942, died London 5 Oct. 2002. Actor. Daughter of Helen Kelso, and Thomas Hood, master of works, Glasgow theatres.

Morag Hood was educated at Bellahouston Academy, Glasgow and the University of Glasgow. Without any formal drama training, she gained experience as anchor for a Scottish Television current affairs programme aimed at teenagers, and scored several exclusives, including an interview with the Beatles. She made her stage debut with a walk-on role in *Wedding Fever* by Sam Cree, at the Glasgow Metropole in 1964. Following seasons in Scottish repertory theatres (Dundee Rep, Pitlochry Festival Theatre and the Royal Lyceum), she performed at Liverpool Playhouse and the Bristol Old Vic. Her London West End debut was in 1968 as Clarice in Goldoni's *The Servant of Two Masters*.

Morag Hood had an emotional power that belied her slight frame. Her role as Natasha in the marathon BBC TV production of *War and Peace* in 1972 brought her to the attention of a wider public; she was chosen for the part out of 1,000 candidates. Her performance over more than 20 episodes was widely acclaimed, maturing from love-struck teenager to the wife of Pierre Bezuhov (played by Anthony Hopkins). Other notable work followed: in Lorca's *The House of Bernarda Alba* at Greenwich Theatre (1973) and as Juliet at Liverpool Playhouse (1974). She joined the National Theatre in 1976, playing Gasparina in Goldoni's *Il Campiello* as well as the title part in Feydeau's farce *The Lady from*

Maxim's. Pat Marmont, her agent, described her as having 'the elegance and poise of a dancer . . . [S]he was like a piece of prize porcelain' (*Guardian* 2002). She never married but was surrounded by the offspring of friends and family. Morag Hood also acted in television series such as *Families*, *Dr Finlay's Casebook*, *Coronation Street*, *Heartbeat*, *Bergerac* and *Z-Cars*. Latterly, she was the downtrodden wife in the bodice-ripper *A Sense of Guilt*. She had few film roles but in 1998 returned to Scotland to play Robert Duvall's wife in the football epic, *A Shot for Glory*. RM

• *The Guardian*, 10 Oct. 2002 (obit.); *The Stage* 17 Oct. 2002 (obit.); *The Times*, 15 Nov. 2002 (obit.).

HOPEKIRK, Helen, m. Wilson, born Edinburgh 20 May 1856, died Cambridge, MA, 19 Nov. 1945. Pianist and composer. Daughter of Helen Croall, and Adam Hopekirk, music seller.

Showing early promise as a pianist, Helen Hopekirk was taught by George Lichtenstein. She played Beethoven's 5th Piano Concerto with the Edinburgh Amateur Orchestral Society in 1876, and also performed with A. C. (later Sir Alexander) Mackenzie. At her father's dying wish, she studied at the Leipzig Conservatoire under Maase, Reinecke, Jadassohn and Richter, making her Gewandhaus debut in 1878, playing the Chopin F minor Concerto, and meeting Liszt. Her London debut was at the Crystal Palace under Manns in 1879, playing the second Saint-Saëns Concerto. She met Clara Schumann, Grieg and Rubinstein, whose playing she particularly admired and whom she recalled replacing the artificial roses in her hat with real ones from his table. In 1882, she married London music critic William A. Wilson, who devoted himself to furthering her career. Theirs was a happy marriage without issue.

From 1883 to 1886, after playing in Boston to acclaim, Helen Hopekirk stayed in the USA for three seasons, appearing in over 60 recitals and concerts. In 1887, she studied piano in Vienna with Leschetizky who described her as the finest woman musician he had ever known. She also studied composition with Nawratil and played with Ysaÿe. From 1897 to 1901 she was an influential teacher in the New England Conservatory, then taught privately, taking US citizenship in 1918. She and her husband returned to Scotland in 1919, expecting a musical renaissance which did not take place. She resumed teaching and performing in America, though greatly affected by her husband's illness and death in 1926. Her last performance was a recital of her own works in Steinert Hall, Boston, in 1939. As a composer, her output is varied. It includes a fine early *Violin Sonata* and outstanding settings of Heine's *Der Nordsee*. She premiered her *Concertstück* in Edinburgh in 1894 and 1904 in Boston, and her *Concerto in D major for Piano and Orchestra* in Boston in 1900. The score and parts are missing. Her music is romantic, poetic and grateful to play, and exhibits occasional influences of Scottish folk music, which she regarded as an important element in musical education. She admired *Marjory Kennedy-Fraser's work, but unlike Kennedy-Fraser, her piano writing can occasionally be repetitive. Her songs were very popular in their day. JP

• Hopekirk, H. (1905, 1992) *Seventy Scottish Songs Selected and Arranged by Helen Hopekirk*, (1909) *Iona Memories, Sundown*. Ammer, C. (1980) *Unsung: A History of Women in American Music*, pp. 91–3; Hall, C. H. (1954) *Helen Hopekirk 1856–1945* (privately printed: includes repertoire and performances); Hutton, F. (1922) Review of 'Iona Memories', *The Scottish Musical Magazine*, IV, 1 Sept., p. 11; Johnson, F. H. (1931) *Musical Memories of Hartford*, pp. 245–6; Muller, D. and Steigerwalt, G. (eds) (1993) Hopekirk, Helen (1894) *Concertstück in D minor*; Muller, D. (1995) 'Helen Hopekirk, pianist, composer, pedagogue', Diss., Hartt School of Music, USA (Bibl. and listings of works); Anon. (1920) 'Vignettes I: Helen Hopekirk', *Scottish Musical Magazine* I, 6, 2 Feb., pp. 168–9.

HOPPRINGLE (or Pringle), Isabella, born before 1505, died Coldstream 26 Jan 1538. Prioress of Coldstream, spy. Daughter of Adam Hoppringle of that ilk.

A member of the prominent Border family of Pringle who provided the Cistercian convent of Coldstream with prioresses from 1475 to 1588, Isabella Hoppringle was prioress c. 1505–38, succeeding her aunt Margaret Hoppringle. She was considered as 'one of the best and assured spies' that the English had in Scotland (Rogers 1879, p. xxiv). In 1509, the convent was granted a license to hold communications with Englishmen in times of war and peace. Isabella Hoppringle switched allegiance several times between England and Scotland depending on which posed the more serious threat to the convent. She is said to have strongly supported Scottish rule but was also attached to English interests, due to the convent's closeness to the border. Local tradition says Dame Isabella and her nuns helped gather the dead from Flodden Field, burying them at the convent. In 1515, when *Margaret Tudor lived nearby, the prioress was 'an intelligent and congenial companion' to her (ibid., p. xxi). Margaret persuaded England to protect the convent from English troops. Margaret's patronage led James V to grant lands and money to Coldstream in 1525.

On Dame Isabella's death, **Janet Pringle** (fl. c. 1537–60) succeeded her, as Prioress and spy, but could not prevent the priory's burning by the English in 1545. She married her kinsman James Pringle of Langmuir in the 1550s. **Elizabeth Lamb** (fl. 1546–73), prioress of the Cistercian house of St Bothan's, was more successful in saving her convent. She was reprimanded for assisting the English army in 1546 to protect herself and the priory's tenants and servants, but was later exonerated for her actions. She was still listed as prioress in 1573, although another prioress, Elizabeth Hume, had been granted the priory in 1566. KP

• NAS: GD110, Hamilton-Dalrymple of North Berwick Muniments; GD158, Humes of Marchmount.
HRHS; Innes, C. (ed.) *Carte Monalium de Northberwic*; Meikle, M. (1997) 'Victims, Viragos and Vamps: women of the sixteenth-century Anglo-Scottish frontier' in J. C. Appleby and P. Dalton (eds) *Government, Religion and Society in Northern England, 1000–1700*; Rogers, C. (ed.) (1879) *Chartulary of the Cistercian Abbey of Coldstream*; Sanderson, M. (2002) *A Kindly Place?*

HORNE, Janet, died Dornoch 1722 or 1727.

The incident commonly regarded as ending Scottish witch persecutions is the famous 'last execution' for witchcraft, that of Janet Horne in Dornoch. The witch's stone in Littletown supposedly marks the site, but no court records survive. The first known report, by Edmund Burt (1727), stated that a mother and daughter were condemned; the daughter escaped but the mother was burned in a pitch barrel. James Fraser reported great uproar over witchcraft in the area. Other references are much later. In 1819, C. K. Sharpe sensationalised the event, which he dated to 1722, describing the witch being accused of riding her daughter, transformed into a pony, and composedly warming herself beside the execution fire against the cold. The name Janet Horne, accepted by most modern commentators, is a later attribution. Probably a woman, perhaps called Janet Horne, was executed at Dornoch in the 1720s for witchcraft, but the date and circumstances remain uncertain. LFH

• Cowan, E. J. and Henderson, L. (2002) 'The last of the witches? The survival of Scottish witch belief', in J. Goodare (ed.) *The Scottish Witch-Hunt in Context* (Bibl.).

HORSBRUGH, Florence Gertrude, Baroness Horsbrugh,‡ MBE, born Edinburgh 13 Oct. 1889, died Edinburgh 6 Dec. 1969. Politician. Daughter of Mary Harriet Stark Christie, and Henry Moncrieff Horsbrugh, chartered accountant.

The youngest of three daughters, Florence Horsbrugh was educated at Lansdowne House, Edinburgh, St Hilda's, Folkestone and Mills College, California. As a young woman during the First World War, she organised travelling canteens, for which she was made MBE in 1920. Active in the Unionist party, she was elected to Parliament in 1931 for one of the few remaining two-member seats, in Dundee; she saw it as an opportunity to elect a woman and a man. It was an unusual result for Dundee, not only because she was the city's first woman MP but also because she was a Unionist. She held the seat until 1945. 'A tall, striking figure', she was an outstanding speaker with a 'resonant, well-modulated voice' (Pugh 1992, p. 193). In 1936, she was the first woman to reply to the King's Speech and, in so doing, the first politician to be televised. She successfully introduced two private member's bills, the first to curb meths drinking (1937); the second the Adoption of Children (Regulation) Act 1939 – of particular concern were children sent abroad to be adopted. She was Parliamentary Secretary, Ministry of Health (1939–45), only the fourth woman to occupy government office, responsible for developing arrangements for the evacuation of children and other priority groups from cities threatened by bombing. She retained oversight of this programme throughout the Second World War. Through the Scottish Special Housing Association, she supported the development of five large purpose-built camps to accommodate children from the Scottish cities. In 1944, she was injured during an air raid on London, but it did not prevent her from spending much of the last year of the war assisting in drafting the scheme for a national health service, and she also became Parliamentary Secretary, Ministry of Food, in 1945. That year, she became the first Scottish woman Privy Councillor and was awarded LLD by the University of Edinburgh. In 1946, the RCSE recognised her work with an honorary fellowship, the first such award made by the college to a woman.

Defeated in the 1945 election, she returned to Parliament in 1950 as member for Moss Side, Manchester. She was appointed Minister for Education in 1951; it became a Cabinet post in 1953, and she became the first woman member of a Conservative Cabinet. She resigned from office in 1954, possibly because education was not a priority for the government, and she was forced to plan for reduced expenditure. Throughout her career, she was active in international affairs: at the League of Nations 1933–6 and in 1945 as a member of the delegation to the San Francisco conference that drafted the UN Charter. She was delegate to the Council of Europe and the Western European Union, 1955–61. Florence Horsbrugh was made a life peer in 1959.

She was described as 'one of the best-equipped party politicians of all the women in Parliament' (*The Times* 1969). Her fellow MP – and opponent – *Jean Mann saw both sides: 'One has a cold, stern appearance, formidable in controversy; detached and inflexible – complete party politician. At close quarters, another Florence emerges: kind, warm-hearted, unstuffy and genial; interested in knitting-patterns and getting home to her fireside' (Mann 1962, p. 24). TB

• Begg, T. (1987) *50 Special Years: A Study in Scottish Housing*; *DNB* 1961–70; Mann, J. (1962) *Woman in Parliament*; *ODNB* (2004); Pugh, M. (1992) W*omen and the Women's Movement in Britain*; *The Times*, 8 Dec. 1969 (obit.); Watson, N. (2000) 'Daughters of Dundee. Gender politics in Dundee: the representation of women 1870–1997', PhD, The Open University.

HOTCHKIS, Anna Mary, born Crookston, Paisley, 30 May 1885, died Kirkcudbright 14 Oct. 1984. Artist and traveller. Daughter of Mary Anne Young, and Richard James Hotchkis, Major, Argyll and Sutherland Highlanders.

Anna Hotchkis and her sister Isobel (1879–1947) studied at GSA from 1906 to 1910, and afterwards at the Munich Academy of Fine Art. Between 1912 and 1916, Anna Hotchkis attended ECA. She settled in Kirkcudbright on the recommendation of her tutor, Robert Burns, joining a coterie of artists based there. She painted mostly landscape, architecture and flower subjects in oils, watercolours and pastels, exhibiting in Kirkcudbright, Edinburgh, Glasgow and London. Widely travelled, she was particularly interested in Chinese art. She taught at Yenching University, Beijing (1922–4) and travelled extensively in China (1926–37). With her American companion, Mary Mullikin, she produced two illustrated books (Mullikin and Hotchkis 1935, 1973) and in 1938 they exhibited their Chinese paintings at The Corcoran Gallery, Washington DC. JOS

• Corcoran Museum of Art: Typescript: ' "Special Exhibition of paintings in tempera, wash and water colour by Mary Augusta Mullikin and Anna M. Hotchkis", The Corcoran Gallery of Art, Washington DC, 8–30 Oct. 1938'. Mullikin, M. A. and Hotchkis, A. M. (1935, Beijing) *Buddhist Sculptures at the Yun Kang Caves*, (1973, imprint Hong Kong) *The Nine Sacred Mountains of China*. Bourne, P. (ed.) (2000) *Kirkcudbright, 100 years of an artists' colony*; Burkhauser, J. (ed.) (1990) *Glasgow Girls*; *Glasgow Herald*, 9 Sept. 1982; *The News*, 12 Feb. 1981.

HOUSTON, Caterina (or **Catherine) Rita Murphy Gribbin (Renée),** m1 **Balharrie,** m2 **Aherne,** m3 **Stewart,** born Johnstone, Renfrewshire, 24 July 1902, died Surrey 9 Feb. 1980. Comedienne and actor. Daughter of Elizabeth Houston and James Houston (formerly Gribbin), variety performers.

Born into a showbusiness family, Renée Houston made her professional debut at 14, playing for three seasons with Fyfe & Fyfe's Rothesay Entertainers, working with veteran comic Charlie Kemble. At 18 she and her younger sister **Billie Houston** (Sarah McMahon Gribbin, 1906–72) stood in for their parents at a theatre in Airdrie, and the Houston Sisters were born. In their act, gamine Billie played a boy to her more feminine elder sister's girl, although Renée's precocious ability to charm, and sometimes shock, an audience belied her Bo-Peep image. After appearing in pantomime with Tommy Lorne at the Pavilion Theatre, Glasgow, a week's try-out at Shoreditch in October 1925 led to a booking at the London Coliseum, where *The Era's* critic found the sisters 'a clever pair who speak like Scots and sing like Americans' (20 Jan. 1926). Their success led to an appearance in the 1926 Royal Variety Command Performance and established them as one of Britain's leading variety acts. In 1935, when Billie's ill health ended the partnership, Renée Houston began a solo career, scoring a personal triumph in the musical comedy *Love Laughs* at the London Hippodrome. The following year, while working on the film *Fine Feathers*, she met the love of her life, American actor Donald Stewart, who became her third husband. They formed a successful variety partnership, touring South Africa in 1938 and appearing in a further Royal Command performance. From the 1950s, Renée Houston worked increasingly in the theatre, acting opposite Charles Laughton in *The Party*, appearing on television in *Dr Finlay's Casebook* and becoming a sought-after screen character actor, with appearances in nearly 40 films ranging from

A Town Like Alice (1956) and The Horse's Mouth with Alec Guinness (1958) to Polanski's Cul de Sac (1966) and several of the 'Carry On' series. Latterly an outspoken panellist on the long-running radio series 'Petticoat Line', she was described by Albert Mackie as 'probably the most talented comedienne Scotland ever produced' (Mackie 1973, p. 104). Writing in the Glasgow Herald, John Easton summed her up as 'one of the most abrasive, petulant, outrageous, controversial, ebullient and lovable characters on the British stage'. PM
• Houston, R. (1974) Don't Fence Me In.
Bruce, F. (2000) Scottish Showbusiness, Music Hall, Variety and Pantomime; Devlin, V. (1991) King's, Queen's and People's Palaces: an oral history of the Scottish variety theatre; Easton, J. Glasgow Herald, 11 Feb. 1980; Irving, G. (1977) The Good Auld Days: the story of Scotland's entertainers from music hall to television; Mackie, A. D. (1973) The Scotch Comedians, pp. 104–5; The Era, 20 Jan. 1926, p. 16; The Scotsman, 11 Feb. 1980 (obit.); The Times, 28 June 1935, 11 Feb. 1980 (obit.).

HUGHES, Agnes Paterson (Nan), n. **Hardie,** born Cumnock, Ayrshire, 5 Oct. 1885, died Mauchline, Ayrshire, 27 June 1947. Campaigner, local politician. Daughter of Lillias Balfour Wilson, and James Keir Hardie, journalist and Labour MP.

The Hardie family moved from Lanarkshire to the mining town of Cumnock after Keir Hardie was appointed trade union organiser for the Ayrshire miners in 1881. Nan Hardie attended school locally, but her parents could not afford to educate her further. A serious illness in 1902 undermined her health; in later years she suffered from debilitating bouts of depression, possibly aggravated by her father's prolonged absences to pursue his political career. Although London-based from the 1890s, Keir Hardie insisted that the family should remain in Cumnock to provide him with a retreat from campaigning pressures. Money was always a problem, making life for his wife and daughter very insecure.

Keir Hardie was proud of his daughter's socialist commitment, but did little at a practical level to draw out her political talents. She was treated as an unpaid secretary in his career as MP for Merthyr Tydfil from 1900. However, through this Welsh connection she became close to the Hughes family of Abercynon, especially Aggie Hughes and her brother Emrys (1894–1969). Her work with them against conscription helped re-energise her after a period of depression around the time of her father's death in 1915. Her regard for Emrys Hughes was heightened by his wartime

stance as a conscientious objector – he was imprisoned for nine months in 1916. She married him in 1924, after he had come to Scotland to work as a journalist for the socialist weekly, Forward.

The couple continued to live in Cumnock, where Emrys Hughes encouraged his wife to establish her own political identity. She was elected as a Labour councillor for Cumnock and Holmhead in 1933 and two years later succeeded her husband as Provost (1935–47). She helped to initiate reforms that gave Cumnock a socially progressive reputation, especially in the provision of council housing. However, from 1939 the war may have intensified her depressive tendencies, not least because there was a tension between her commitment to pacifism and service to the community (Benn 1992). She continued to be a popular civic leader, but her mental and physical health deteriorated. In 1946, Emrys Hughes was elected Labour MP for South Ayrshire in a parliamentary by-election. His success may inadvertently have precipitated Nan Hughes's death the following year, as her ultimate fear was abandonment. IEM
• Benn, C. (1992) Keir Hardie, (Bibl.); Forward, 5 July 1947 (obit.); ODNB (2004) (see Hardie, Agnes Paterson); SLL.

HUGONE, Katherine, fl. 1598–1602. Assault victim.

In December 1598, Katherine Hugone, who lived in a cottage at Burnside of Saling, suffered a vicious assault for some unknown reason. Alexander Rowan of Sandiedub and his accomplices 'put violent hands in hir persoune, and sett hir bair erse upoune ane reid hett girdill (red-hot griddle), standand upoun ane ingill (fire), held her perforce thairon quhill (until) ane grit pairt of the flesche of hir hipis was brunt' (Dalyell 1798, p. 56). Indicted for murder in 1602, he audaciously argued that the case should not be heard because she was not burnt to death. The Lord Advocate disagreed, saying the crime deserved death. He continued proceedings against Alexander Rowan for all his crimes, including animal theft and shooting one Christian Hamilton in the head. Justice prevailed for Katherine Hugone and other victims, as he was executed on the Castle Hill of Edinburgh. Onlookers commented that a cruel man was hanged for his violence towards women. MMM
• 'Diary of Robert Birrell, 1532–1605', in Dalyell, J. D. (ed.) (1798) Fragments of Scottish History; Crim. Trials vol. ii, pp. 391–3.

HUME, Anna, fl. 1629–44. Writer. Daughter of Barbara Johnstoun of Elphinstone, and Sir David

Hume of Godscroft, humanist, historian and Latin poet.

Anna Hume's only known work, *The Triumphs of Love: Chastity: Death* (1644), is the first known example of printed secular writing by a Scottish woman. A partial translation of the medieval philosophical allegory, *I Trionfi*, by Petrarch, into highly wrought English couplets, it is dedicated to Princess Elizabeth of Bohemia, daughter of *Elizabeth of Bohemia (see Stewart, Elizabeth). Little is known of Anna Hume's life but she belonged to a scholarly family; her brother composed mathematical treatises. Intellectually, she appears close to her prolifically published father. After his death, she confessed to the poet William Drummond of Hawthornden her alarm that her father had left unpublished papers to be dealt with; nevertheless, she helped orchestrate the publication of his *History of the Houses of Douglas and Angus*. When the *History* finally appeared in 1644, so did her translation, published by the same Edinburgh printer. The daughter had gained a literary presence of her own, demonstrating the creative skill that William Drummond, in a letter to her, had already observed (NLS: MS 2061).

The *Triumphs* are an impressive blend of skilful imitation and sophisticated invention. At the end of each *trionfo* is a prose commentary or, in her words, an 'Annotation', providing an explanatory gloss of linguistic, historical, or cultural points which she feels may interest her reader. She is especially concerned to comment on the representation of Petrarch's allegorical women, often with elegant wit. These 'Annotations' may have been intended to instruct and entertain the Princess Palatinate, nicknamed 'la Grecque' for her well-established intellectual reputation. She bestows lavish praise on the Princess but, in the absence of documentary evidence, it is difficult to prove whether this attests Elizabeth's actual literary patronage or whether Anna Hume herself visited The Hague, where the exiled Elector and Electress had created a distinguished court culture. Her alliance with the Princess provokes speculation about cultural connections between Scottish and European women in the Renaissance.

Above all, Anna Hume's fascination lies with the figure of Laura, the beautiful virgin beloved by Petrarch. In a dedicatory poem, she proclaims that she has 'tane [taken]' her '[f]rom the dark Cloyster, where she did remain/Unmarkt, because unknown'. Symbolically, she presents Princess Elizabeth with a newly unveiled or rediscovered Laura, sealing her

Triumphs as one of the most interesting and 'proto-feminist' works of Renaissance women's writing. SD

• NLS: MS 2061.
Hume, A. (1644) *The Triumphs of Love: Chastitie: Death translated out of Petrarch by Mris Anna Hume.*
Dunnigan, S. M. (2004) 'Daughterly Desires: representing and re-imagining the feminine in Anna Hume's "Triumphs"', in S. M. Dunnigan et al. (eds) *Woman and the Feminine in Medieval and Early Modern Scottish Writing*; *HSWW* (Bibl.); *ODNB* (2004); Reid, D. (ed.) (1996) *David Hume of Godscroft's The History of the House of Douglas*, 2 vols.

HUMPHREYS, Elizabeth Margaret Jane (Eliza) [Rita], n. Gollan, m1 Booth, m2 Humphreys, born Gollanfield, Inverness-shire, 14 June 1850, died Bath 1 Jan. 1938. Novelist. Daughter of Jane Plumb, and John Gilbert Gollan, landowner and businessman.

Eliza Gollan, the second of three children, was born on the family estate in Inverness-shire but brought up and educated (largely at home) in Australia, where her father had business interests. The family returned to London when she was 14 years old. In 1872 she married Karl Booth, a musician. The marriage ended unhappily and she later married the Anglo-Irish professional singer William Ernest (Desmond) Humphreys. This marriage lasted until her death. She had three sons by her first husband and a daughter by her second.

From 1877 onwards, Eliza Humphreys, under the pseudonym 'Rita', was the author of some 120 books, plays and essays. She began by writing light, sometimes 'daring', popular fiction and was compared to Marie Corelli. Later she used her novels to express her own opinions and beliefs. In spite of her own professional success, and though she founded the Writers' Club for Women in 1902, she disapproved of the contemporary New Woman movement, attacking it in such novels as *A Husband of No Importance* (1894) and *Souls* (1903). Unconvinced by the claims of organised religion, she took up theosophy, addressing problems of belief in *Calvary* (1909), which, with two other novels, was filmed.

After the First World War, literary fashions changed and her work fell out of favour. In addition, her husband became an invalid, forcing her to apply to charitable organisations for aid, sometimes unsuccessfully because her writing did not meet the necessary standard. In 1930 she received an award from the Royal Bounty Fund: Queen Mary was an enthusiast for her novels. She wrote an autobiography in old age, two years before her death. MARB

• 'Rita' [E. M. J. Humphreys], Works as above, and (1906) *Saba Macdonald*, (1936) *Recollections of a Literary Life*; *ODNB* (2004).

HUNTER, Anne n. **Home,** born Greenlaw, Berwickshire 1742, died London 7 Jan. 1821. Poet, ballad- and song-writer. Daughter of Mary Hutchinson, and Robert Boyne Home, surgeon.

The seventh of nine children, in 1771 Anne Home married John Hunter (1728–93), the distinguished Lanarkshire anatomist and surgeon. Of their four children, two survived childhood. As hostess for John and his brother William in London, she kept house for an array of servants, relatives and students. Her conversation parties were notable for their unaffected character, and she was friendly with the bluestocking circle. Having written poetry from her youth, she was recognised as a lyricist and poet, and in 1792, Joseph Haydn, with whom she was friendly, began setting her verses to music. His first set of *Canzonettas* includes at least six of her songs. Known as 'Haydn's muse' (Nares 1848), she produced many songs, which Haydn's music brought to a wide audience. These were 'very popular among the cultivated circles of society', while her poems also 'deservedly gained for her the reputation of a woman of genius', according to her niece *Joanna Baillie, who credited her with 'a considerable influence on my mind' (Baillie, n.d.). Anne Hunter published *Poems* in 1802, and a second volume in 1804, dedicated to the memory of Susan, daughter of Archibald Macdonald, the Lord Chief Baron, whose etchings illustrate it. John Hunter's death in 1793 left Anne dependent on others for support, ameliorated by the sale of his effects in 1799 and a pension, connected to the Hunterian museum, London. Her poems covered not only family and lost love, but history, patriotism and current social issues, including lyrics for a collection of national songs. Her work is now benefiting from re-examination by scholars. DLS
• Wellcome Institute for the History of Medicine Library: Hunterian Society Deposit, MS 5613/68.
Hunter, Mrs. J. (1802) [Anne Home] *Poems*, (1804) *The Sports of the Genii.*
Baillie, J. (n. d.) 'Memoirs written to please my Nephew, William Baillie'; Currie, J. M. (2001) 'Poet and lyricist Anne Hunter: more than "Haydn's Muse" ', in N. Kushigian and S. Behrendt (eds) *Scottish Women Poets of the Romantic Period*, 2001; *DBAWW* (1985); *HSWW* (Bibl.); Nares, R. (1848) 'Memoir of Mrs. John Hunter, by Archdeacon Nares' in J. B. Nichols (ed.) *Literary History of the Eighteenth Century*, vol. 7; *ODNB* (2004) (Hunter, Anne; Hunter, John).

HUNTER, Margaret Annie, n. **Anderson,** born Bridgeton, Glasgow, 11 Nov. 1922, died London 21 Feb. 1986. Communist activist. Daughter of Margaret Rippey, and James Anderson, milk salesman.

The youngest of five children, Margaret Anderson was involved with the Young Pioneers in the Gorbals district of Glasgow, joining the YCL at 14. Growing up in Polmadie, she attended Queen's Park High School, followed by work as a typist with British Oxygen. In 1940, she was Secretary of the Knightswood Branch of the CP, employed at Barr and Stroud engineering company and a member of the T&G. Tall and striking, she spoke regularly at lunch-time factory meetings, where she met James Hunter (b. 1921), also a Communist. They married in 1946.

Margaret Hunter became a full-time secretary for the CP in Glasgow, standing in Dalmarnock ward in local elections in 1947 and 1949. In the 1950s she became a CPGB Scottish organiser, part of the Scottish Secretariat. She helped organise the Party's 1958 celebrations to mark the bi-centenary of the birth of Robert Burns. She also stood in the Gorbals in the 1964 and 1966 General Elections. In 1964, she became party National Women's Officer, campaigning on women's issues, sitting on the NEC, organising weekend schools and co-ordinating the work of the Women's Advisory Committee. On a delegation to the GDR, she became seriously ill and her political career was cut short. NR
• Univ. of Manchester, Communist Party Archive: Communist Party publications: *Women Today*, 1950s; *Comment*, 1960s/70s.
Interviews: Pat Milligan, 1994; James Hunter, 1995. *ODNB* (2004).

HUNTLY, Henrietta, Countess of *see* **STEWART, Henrietta, Countess of Huntly** (1573–1642)

HURD, Dorothy Iona, n. **Campbell,** m1 **Hurd,** m2 **Howe,** born Edinburgh 24 March 1883, died Yemassee, South Carolina, USA, 20 March 1945. Amateur golfer. Daughter of Emily Mary Tipper, and William Campbell, metal merchant.

Dorothy Campbell claimed she was 'an entirely self-taught golfer' (Holme 1925, p. 28). One of nine siblings, she was playing matches against her older sisters at the age of five. She joined the North Berwick Ladies' Golf Club, aged 13, and had a handicap of nine. Her father died when she was 16, and she and her mother moved to North Berwick.

In June 1903, she played in the inaugural Scottish Ladies Championship, held at St Andrews, and reached the semi-finals. The founding of the Championship and then the SLGA in 1904 owes much to London-born **Agnes Grainger** (fl. 1900s) of the St Rule Club, who had seen Scotland beaten at Deal in 1902, and realised that if Scottish golfers were to hold their own against golfers of other countries, they must gain wider match-play experience.

Between 1905 and 1912, Dorothy Campbell was many times a champion in women's amateur golf, with wins in the Ladies' Championships of Scotland, Britain, America and Canada. She represented Scotland internationally seven times and Britain twice. Her style of play 'was unmistakably North Berwick' and she was said to possess 'a wonderful and most useful calm, unruffled temperament' (Stringer 1945, p. 41). Throughout her career, her mashie 'Thomas' and her putter 'Stella' were among her favoured clubs. In 1910, Dorothy Campbell moved to Canada, then to Pittsburgh, Pennsylvania, in 1913, when she married Jack V. Hurd. The couple had one son but divorced in 1923. Dorothy Campbell Hurd had been in semi-retirement since her marriage, but returned to amateur competition in 1924 after spending ten months transforming her grip and swing. Aged 41, she was the unexpected, and oldest, winner of the US Ladies' Championship. She returned to Scotland to play several times. Her second marriage to Edward Howe (1937) ended in divorce in 1943, and she died accidentally in 1945, falling under a train in the USA. With ten national titles, Dorothy Campbell Hurd was 'the first woman to dominate international golf' (World Golf Hall of Fame Profile: www.wgv.com; inducted 1978). IAR

• Minutes of the St Rule Ladies' Golf Club.
Dey, J. (1934) 'The amateur golfer', in S. Baddiel (1990) *Golf – The Golden Years*, pp. 82–6; Dunlop-Hill, N. (1930) *History of the Scottish Ladies' Golfing Association 1903–1928*; George, J. (2003) 'Women and golf in Scotland', PhD, Univ. of Edinburgh; Holme, E. (1925) *The Best of Golf*; Julius, M. E. (1998) *For the Good of Golf and St Andrews: the St Rule Club, 1898–1998*; *ODNB* (2004) (see Campbell, Dorothy); Stringer, M. (1924) *Golfing Reminiscences*; Stringer, M. E. (1945) 'Mrs Edward Howe (Dorothy Campbell Hurd)', Personal News Service, F & H 1945, p. 41.
www.kirkwood.co.uk; www.golfjournal.org/greatamateur; www.usamateur.org/history/records; www.wgv.com; www.north.berwick.co.uk

HUSBAND, Ann (Agnes), born Tayport 20 May 1852, died Dundee 30 April 1929. Councillor, social reformer, suffragist. Daughter of Agnes Lamond (or Lomand), and John Husband, master mariner.

Agnes Husband ran a dressmaking business in Murraygate, Dundee, with her sister Kitty (Catherine Husband, 1853–1940). An early and prominent member of the ILP, she was, after several unsuccessful efforts, one of the first two women elected to Dundee Parish Council in 1901 (with *Mary Lily Walker), where she served conscientiously until 1928. She pressed for a more humane approach to the poor, through both the council and Dundee Social Union. Elected to the Dundee School Board in 1905, she championed better care and education for children, arguing for free school books and meals, and was a pioneer in the nursery schools movement. She also worked on the Dundee Distress Committee (as convener), the Dundee Insurance Committee and at least five other committees concerned with health, education and young people. In 1904, she participated in the inaugural meeting of Dundee WSS. She joined the WSPU in 1906 but three years later became president of Dundee WFL and a member of the national executive. Asserting the claims of women and their competence to participate in the administration of public affairs, she saw more women on the council as an effective way of promoting women's suffrage. She influenced many of Dundee's younger suffragettes and was keen to include working-class women. After the First World War she was on the executive of DWCA. In 1926, she was the fifth Dundonian woman to be given the Freedom of the City. She was hard-working and serious: 'You won't find Miss Husband 'midst the gay and giddy throng . . . but you *will* find her where distress is . . .' the ILP paper *The Tocsin* commented (April 1909, p. 8). IMH

• Dundee City Archives: Dundee Council minutes and Corporation diaries.
AGC; Whatley, C. (ed.) (1992) *The Remaking of Juteopolis: Dundee circa 1891–1991*.

HUTCHISON, Isabel Wylie,[‡] born Carlowrie, Kirkliston, 30 May 1889, died Carlowrie 20 Feb. 1982. Writer, Arctic traveller, botanist. Daughter of Jean Wylie, and Thomas Hutchison, wine merchant.

The third in a family of five, Isabel Hutchison was taught at home by governesses and at Miss Gamgee's School (later Rothesay House) in Edinburgh, where she excelled in botany. Shy and introspective, she composed poems on long, solitary walks. Her first poems were accepted for publication in 1911, winning for her prizes and recognition.

In 1924 Isabel Hutchison visited Iceland where she made a difficult and celebrated walk across the island; her article about Iceland in the *National Geographic Magazine* began a long association with the country. She then visited Greenland as a plant collector; she returned twice more and spent a year in a village north of the Arctic Circle. In 1933, she travelled around the north coast of Alaska in small trading vessels, completing the journey by dog-team at the Arctic village of Aklavik on the Mackenzie River in Canada. On her final northern trip in 1937, she travelled to the Aleutian Islands, reaching Attu at the farthest end of the archipelago, and also to the Pribiloff Islands in Bering Strait. On these journeys she collected plants for the RHS, the Royal Botanic Gardens at Kew and Edinburgh, and the BM. She also brought back native artefacts for the Museum of Archaeology and Anthropology at Cambridge and the RSM.

In addition to six books of poetry, including two verse dramas, she wrote four books on her northern travels and contributed articles to a wide range of journals and newspapers, some in French and Gaelic. She was also proficient in Danish, German and Italian, and during her stay in Greenland learned enough of the native language to get by. Employed as a censor during the Second World War, she was a frequent broadcaster and lectured on her northern travels throughout Britain. She also exhibited water-colour landscapes at the RSA. She was awarded the Mungo Park medal by the Royal Scottish Geographical Society in 1935, the Danish Freedom Medal in 1946 and the honorary degree of LLD by the University of St Andrews in 1949.

After the war, Isabel Hutchison continued to write for the *National Geographic Magazine*, including accounts of three 'strolls' across the length of Britain and over the Brenner Pass from Innsbruck to Venice – in her sixties with a knapsack on her back. With her sister, Hilda Hutchison (1892–1979), who had earned her doctorate of music at the Sorbonne, she spent her declining years at Carlowrie, the home in which they were born. GH

• NLS: Acc. 4775, 8138, 9713, Papers, diaries and corr. of Isabel Wylie Hutchison.
Hutchison, I. (1923) *Original Companions*, (1930) *On Greenland's Closed Shore*, (1934) *North to the Rime-Ringed Sun*, (1935) *Arctic Nights' Entertainments*, (1937) *Stepping Stones from Alaska to Asia*.

Hoyle, G. (2001) *Flowers in the Snow: the life of Isabel Wylie Hutchison*; Tiltman, M. H. (1935) *Women in Modern Adventure*.

HUTCHISON, Mary, n. **Casey,** born Edinburgh 18 Jan. 1915, died Edinburgh 1 Oct. 1994. National president, Scottish Co-operative Women's Guild. Daughter of Catherine Sinclair, printer's machinist, and Michael Casey, confectioner.

One of three girls, Mary Casey grew up in the south side of Edinburgh. After leaving school she worked as an upholsterer. In 1938, she married Laurence Hutchison, a foreman joiner, and they had three daughters. She joined the Craigmillar Branch of the SCWG in the early 1960s, and found that the Guild offered opportunities not available elsewhere for the education and self-development of working women. Mary Hutchison attended classes in business procedure run by the SCWG, and, in response to local demand, started a youth club with the support of the St Cuthbert's Co-operative Association Education Committee, which paid for her training in youth work. She won a scholarship to attend the Co-operative College at Stamford Hall, Loughborough. From 1979 to 1983, she was SCWG national president, travelling to international conferences in Moscow and Germany. She stood six times as a Labour Party candidate in Portobello in the local elections. She gave credit to the SCWG: 'I know I have had a very interesting life because of the Co-operative movement. If I had never joined the Women's Guild, I would have had a much poorer life'.

The Guilds in Scotland were organised in local sections. Presidents of the East of Scotland regional section (IV) of the SCWG included **Annie (Nan) Sutherland,** (1913–98, president 1972–6) and **Ella Williamson,** (1916–2000, president 1986–8), both of whom, like Mary Hutchison, have left recorded memories in the People's Story Museum Archive Edinburgh. HEC

• People's Story Oral History Archive: Mary Hutchison T 22a/87; Ella Williamson T15/87; Nan Sutherland T11/87.

HUTTON, Sibilla (Sibbie), born before 1773, died Edinburgh 1808. Milliner and shopkeeper. Daughter of Sibilla Tunnock, brewer's daughter, and the Rev. William Hutton, Secession minister in Dalkeith.

A well-known Edinburgh shopkeeper, portrayed twice in Kay's *Original Portraits*, Sibilla Hutton had a shop in the Royal Exchange. This building housed several shops and a coffee house. She advertised in Edinburgh newspapers, travelled to London to buy goods and make contacts, and attended law courts personally to pursue clients' bills. Her sister Nellie (Mrs Kidd) had a 'Haberdashery and Millinery Warehouse' in Princes Street; in 1785 she intimated she 'boarded young ladies as well as carrying on her other business' (*Edinburgh Evening Courant*, December 1785).

Sibilla Hutton set up in London in 1790, but later returned to Edinburgh. *The Scots Magazine* recorded her death. She exemplified the single woman of professional background who ran her own business to earn her living. ECS

• Kay, J. (1878 edn.) *A Series of Original Portraits and Caricature Etchings*; *ODNB (2004); WWEE (Bibl.).

I

INGEBJORG ('mother of earls', *jarlamóðir*), Queen of Scotland, Countess of Orkney, fl. c. 1025–70. Daughter of Bergliot daughter of Halvdan, and Finn Arnesson of Giske.

Ingebjorg was probably born on Giske, an island in Romsdal Fjord, west Norway. Most of her family were strong supporters of Olaf Haraldsson (St Olaf) in his struggle to maintain power in Norway. He was the brother of Ingebjorg's grandfather, Halvdan son of Sigurd Syr. Olaf probably arranged her marriage to Earl Thorfinn of Orkney, in the late 1020s, to help tie the Earl into his circle. Thorfinn and Ingebjorg named their eldest son Paul, the first Christian name in the family, perhaps reflecting their commitment to the new religion. The comment in *Orkneyinga Saga* that the Earl loved Paul and his brother Erlend dearly is unusual, suggesting a close family relationship. So does the remarkable story of Thorfinn's flight from his burning house, when he broke through a wooden partition wall and '. . . escaped carrying his wife Ingebjorg in his arms' (Palsson and Edwards 1978, Ch. 28), a rare personal detail.

According to the saga, after Thorfinn's death in the early-mid 1060s, Ingebjorg married Malcolm III of Scotland (r. 1058–93), and bore a son, Duncan. Duncan's legitimacy has been doubted – a later chronicler refers to him as a bastard. However, he was important enough to be taken as a hostage to England by King William (the Conqueror) after his 1072 expedition to Scotland. The absence of any other record of the marriage must reflect the fact that Malcolm's second marriage, to Margaret, (see Margaret, Saint, Queen of Scotland) established the medieval Scottish royal line. It has been questioned whether Ingebjorg's marriage to Malcolm was possible, and there has been unwarranted surmise that it must have been Thorfinn's daughter, rather than wife, who was meant. Ingebjorg may also have borne Donald, mentioned in one Irish source as Malcolm's son.

In 1066, the earls Paul and Erlend joined Harald Hardraada's army. They survived the defeat at Stamford Bridge and returned to Orkney. After William's victory at Hastings, the survivors of the Anglo-Saxon royal house fled to Scotland. Malcolm decided to marry Margaret in 1070/1, and it is unclear whether Ingebjorg died or was put aside in favour of Margaret. She was certainly eclipsed as Scottish queen by her saintly successor. In the Durham martyrology she is commemorated as *Ingeberga comitissa* (Countess Ingebjorg) perhaps in pious remembrance by either Malcolm or their son Duncan. Her designation as Countess in this source may also suggest that her marriage to Malcolm was not recognised as completely regular. BEC

• Palsson, H. and Edwards, P. G. (trans.) (1978) *Orkneyinga Saga*.
Crawford, B. E. (with Clancy, T. O.) (2001) 'The Formation of the Scottish Kingdom', in R. A. Houston and W. W. J. Knox (eds) *The New Penguin History of Scotland*, pp. 84–6; Duncan, A. A. M. (2003) *Kingship of the Scots*, Ch. 3;
Wall, V. 'Queen Margaret of Scotland, 1070–93: burying the past, enshrining the future', in A. Duggan (ed.) (1997) *Queens and Queenship in Medieval Europe*, pp. 27–38.

INGLIS, Elsie Maude, born Naini Tal, India, 16 August, 1864, died Newcastle upon Tyne, 26 Nov. 1917. Doctor, pioneer of *Scottish Women's Hospitals abroad. Daughter of Harriet Thompson, and John Forbes Inglis, magistrate.

Elsie Inglis, second daughter and seventh child, spent her childhood in India until the family settled in Edinburgh in 1876. Educated there and in Paris, for a time she stayed at home to help her father, to whom she was devoted; his death in 1894 devastated her. In 1886 it became possible to attend, as a home student, the Edinburgh School of Medicine for Women founded by *Sophia Jex-Blake, from whom, however, Elsie Inglis and others soon parted company. After further study in Glasgow, she gained the Triple Qualification Licentiateship of the Royal Colleges of Physicians and Surgeons of Edinburgh and the Faculty of Physicians and Surgeons of Glasgow in 1892. After working as house surgeon in the Elizabeth Garrett Anderson Hospital for Women in London, and gaining midwifery experience at the world-famous Rotunda Hospital in Dublin, Elsie Inglis set up medical practice in Edinburgh in 1894, in partnership with **Jessie McGregor** (d. US 1906; MBChM 1896, MD 1899 with gold medal). Jessie McGregor was elected a Fellow of the Edinburgh Obstetrical Society in 1901, and emigrated to America in 1905. Elsie Inglis went on in 1899 to acquire her MBChM from the University of Edinburgh, now that it was open to women. She lectured on gynaecology in the Edinburgh Medical College for Women, which she had helped found, and travelled to Vienna and the USA to gain further experience. Back in Edinburgh, she established the Hospice in the High Street, a nursing home and maternity centre: within five years it was a recognised training centre for midwives. (Women could not yet take posts in the Edinburgh Maternity Hospital.) By 1910, the Hospice was amalgamated with the Bruntsfield Hospital for Women and Children, under her direction.

Elsie Inglis's medical reputation might have rested solely on the care of women and children, but the First World War brought a new challenge. Not satisfied with her role as Commandant of the 6th Edinburgh VAD, she approached the authorities with plans for incorporating women into the RAMC. Her initial offer to serve as a surgeon was declined by the War Office – she was told: 'My good lady, go home and sit still' (Lawrence 1971, pp. 97–8). She then proposed setting up hospitals staffed fully by women, a project supported by the SFWSS. The *Scottish Women's Hospitals for Home and Foreign Service movement played a key role in wartime medical services. Lacking support at home, the women offered their services to the Allies, and hospitals were quickly established in France, Greece and Serbia, eventually gaining support from the Admiralty and Foreign Office. Elsie Inglis visited the hospital at Royaumont in France before travelling in spring 1915 to Kragujevac in Serbia, where she remained for some months, until her unit was imprisoned following the Serbian retreat. After her release, she returned to Scotland, and agreed to set up a hospital in Russia. She had barely arrived in Dobrudja in Romania when the Allies were forced into retreat, and her hospital was handed over to the Russian Red Cross at Reni. Elsie Inglis remained there before rejoining the Serbian division in autumn 1916. During most of her time in these centres, she had to cope with the effects of endemic disease and recurrent outbreaks of typhoid, as well as primitive conditions and the difficulty of obtaining adequate medical supplies. She herself became increasingly ill during 1917, but survived a hazardous journey back from Odessa, only to succumb three days after arriving at Newcastle. Her body lay in state in St Giles in Edinburgh, and British and Serbian royalty attended her funeral. She had been awarded the Serbian Order of the White Eagle (First Class) in 1916, a mark of the esteem in which she was held by the Serbs, whose cause she consistently supported.

As well as for her war work, Elsie Inglis is remembered for her contribution to the health of women and children, for which the Elsie Inglis Memorial Maternity Hospital, opened in 1925 (now closed), is a visible memorial. She was also prominent in the campaign for female suffrage, being a member of the WFL, and in Liberal politics, as Vice-President of the Central Edinburgh Women's Liberal Association and a convinced Home Ruler. She campaigned for equal opportunities for male and female students, and helped found Muir Hall of residence for female students at the University of Edinburgh. A somewhat austere and reserved figure, Elsie Inglis needed all her considerable determination to enter the unwelcoming male-dominated world of medicine. Her obituary in the *BMJ* on 17 December 1917 described her as a 'born leader, entirely patriotic and free from self-seeking'. HMD

• Mitchell Library, Glasgow: Papers of the Scottish Women's Hospitals for Home and Foreign Service movement, deposit 1922.

Balfour, F. (1918) *Dr Elsie Maude Inglis*; *BMJ*, 17 Dec. 1917 (obit.); Cahill, A. F. (ed.) (1999) *Between the Lines: letters and diaries from Elsie Inglis's Russian Unit*; Crofton, E. (1997) *The Women of Royaumont*; *Edinburgh Medical Journal* New Series XX, 1916, pp. 60–4 (obit.); Knox, W. W. J. (2006) *The Lives of Scottish Women*; Lawrence, M. (1971) *Shadow of Swords: a biography of Elsie Inglis*; Leneman, L. (1994) *In the Service of Life*, (1998) *Elsie Inglis*; McLaren, E. S. (ed.) (1919) *A History of the Scottish Women's Hospitals*; ODNB (2004).

INGLIS, Esther,[‡] n. **Langlois,** born c. 1571, died Leith 30 August 1624. Calligrapher. Daughter of Marie Presot, calligrapher, and Nicolas Langlois, schoolmaster.

Esther Langlois was probably born in London. Her Huguenot parents fled there from France

c. 1569, before they moved to Edinburgh, where her father was Master of the French School (1580–1611) under King James VI's patronage. Esther Langlois was probably trained by her mother (d. 24 August 1574), an accomplished calligrapher. She married Bartholomew Kello (d. 1631), a clergyman, c. 1596, but from at least 1604 used an anglicised form of her maiden name professionally (Langlois = English: Inglis). Bartholomew Kello was appointed Clerk of passports and other foreign correspondence under James VI: the warrant conferring this position suggests that Esther Inglis made fair copies for him. She was by then producing calligraphic manuscripts of her own, containing specimens of writing styles, as in a 1591 New Year's gift to Elizabeth I, *Discours de la Foy*. Texts in later gift-books are drawn from the Bible (Psalms, Proverbs and Ecclesiastes) or French poetry. In 1599, she presented books to Elizabeth I, Prince Maurice of Nassau, the Earl of Essex and Anthony Bacon. Bartholomew Kello may have been engaged in the secret negotiations for James's succession to the English throne, and the couple appears to have moved to London with King James's court c. 1604. Appealing for patronage, Esther Inglis presented manuscripts to Prince Henry, *Queen Anna, and their circles. For a while in 1606/7 she moved from a black-and-white style copied from printed books to the use of coloured flowers from pattern books but in 1624 gave Prince Charles an elaborate manuscript of 50 *Emblemes Chrestiens*, based on Georgette de Montenay's printed work. She often included self-portraits in her books, and made some of their bindings. Four of her six children survived to adulthood, Samuel succeeding his father as rector of Spexhall, Suffolk. About 57 calligraphic manuscripts by Esther Inglis are known to exist. GZ

• NLS: MSS 2197, 8874, 20498, 25240; Acc. 7633, 11624, 11821; NAS: GD 18/4508; Univ. of Edinburgh Library: MS La.III 75, 249, 439, 440, 522.
Frye, S. (2002) 'Materializing authorship in Esther Inglis's Books', *Jour. Medieval and Modern Studies*, 32, pp. 469–91; Jackson, D. J. (1937) *Esther Inglis, Calligrapher 1571–1624*; Laing, D. (1865–6) 'Notes relating to Mrs Esther Inglis', *Proc. Soc. Antiquaries Scot.*, 6; *ODNB* (2004); Scott-Elliot, A. H. and Yeo, E. (1990) 'Calligraphic manuscripts of Esther Inglis . . . a catalogue', *Papers of the Bibliographical Society of America*, 84, 1; Tjan-Bakker, A. (2000) 'Dame Flora's blossoms: Esther Inglis's flower-illustrated manuscripts', in P. Beal and M. J. M. Ezell (eds) *English Manuscript Studies*, 9; Ziegler, G. (2000) ' "More than feminine boldness": the gift books of Esther Inglis', in M. E. Burke et al. (eds) *Women, Writing and the Reproduction of Culture*.

INGLIS CLARK, Jane Isabella (Janie),‡ n. **Shannon,** born 1859/60, possibly abroad, died Edinburgh 9 March 1950. Rock climber and mountaineer, co-founder of the Ladies Scottish Climbing Club. Daughter of Isabella Struthers Wilson, and David Shannon, tea planter.

Married in 1884 to Dr William Inglis Clark (1856–1932) and living in Edinburgh, Jane Shannon had always been 'a good walker and enthusiastic hill lover' (Inglis Clark 1938, p. 26) but did not begin rock climbing until 1897. She found that she possessed a natural aptitude for difficult routes, demonstrated by her subsequent participation in six first ascents of Ben Nevis between 1897 and 1904, as well as many other climbs made in Scotland with her husband and leading male exponents of the day. She also climbed and ski-toured for several seasons in the Swiss Alps, the Dolomites and Tyrol. The idea of a climbing club exclusively for women had long been in her mind, but became a realistic proposition when her daughter, **Mabel Jeffrey** (1885–1967), was old enough to be her 'lieutenant' (Inglis Clark 1929, p. 6). The Inglis Clarks' two children had been encouraged to climb, and Mabel gathered climbing friends around her. With family friend **Lucy Smith** (d. 1970), daughter of Edinburgh lawyer William C. Smith, mother and daughter founded the LSCC in 1908, the first of its kind to promote independent climbing for women. During the First World War, Jane Inglis Clark was VAD Commandant (Red Cross). A parish and county councillor in Edinburgh (1919–38), she was also a JP. In later years, she saw women's increased participation in mountaineering as indicative of the broader movement to emancipation, and was proud of her role as a pioneer. *Pictures and Memories* (1938) indicates her belief in women's capabilities and right to self-fulfilment. A memorial hut for climbers in Allt a'Mhuillinn, Coire Leis, Ben Nevis commemorates the Inglis Clarks' son Charles, who died in the First World War. CAO

• Alpine Club Archives, London: G25 Ladies' Alpine Club, application form and climbing lists (1924).
Inglis Clark, J. (1929) 'The Club in Early Days: 1908–1914', *LSCC Jour.*, 1, pp. 5–9, (1938) 'Second Ascent of Abraham's Route' *LSCC Jour.*, 2, pp. 24–6, (1938) *Pictures and Memories*. Glover, G. T. (1933) 'In Memoriam William Inglis Clark', *Scot. Mountaineering Club Jour.*, 20, 115, pp. 3–7.

INVERARITY, Eliza, m. **Martyn,** born Edinburgh 23 March 1813, died Newcastle upon Tyne 27 Dec. 1846. Singer. Daughter of Helen McLagan, and James Inverarity, merchant.

Great-niece of the poet Robert Fergusson (Farmer 1947, p. 445), Eliza Inverarity studied with tenor Alexander Murray in Edinburgh, and made her debut during one of his concerts in 1829, performing later in other Scottish cities. In 1836, she married the bass Charles T. Martyn. Together they performed in England and Scotland in operatic productions; Eliza was successful as Amina, the sleepwalking heroine in Bellini's *La Sonnambula* (1838). Both signed contracts to visit the USA with the Touring John Templeton Opera Company and Eliza Inverarity attracted attention for her performances as Leonora in Beethoven's *Fidelio* in New York (1839). Like many other popular singers of her day, she composed chamber songs and ballads, probably presented during special gala events, benefits, or in the drawing rooms of the wealthy. Her career ended with her premature death from tuberculosis. PAC

• Cohen, A. I. (1987, 2nd edn.) *International Encyclopedia of Women Composers*; Crawford, R. (ed.) (1997) *Robert Burns and Cultural Authority*; Farmer, H. G. (1947) *A History of Music in Scotland*; *ODNB* (2004); Smith, S. G. (1952) *Robert Fergusson, 1770–1774, Essays by Various Hands*; Stern, G. (1978) *Women Composers*.

IRVINE, Jessie Seymour, born Dunnottar, Kincardineshire, 26 July 1836, died Aberdeen 2 Sept. 1887. Reputedly hymn tune composer. Daughter of Jessie Nicol, and Alexander Irvine, minister of Crimond, Aberdeenshire.

Jessie Irvine was possibly the composer of the tune 'Crimond', made famous by Sir Hugh Roberton and the Glasgow Orpheus Choir as a setting for Psalm 23. In many books, the tune appears as 'melody attributed to Jessie Seymour Irvine', although when it first appeared in William Carnie's *The Northern Psalter and Hymn Tune Book* (1872), it was attributed to David Grant (1833–93). In 1911, Jessie Irvine's sister Anna claimed that the tune had been written by her sister and that David Grant had only harmonised it, but her recollection was disputed by others. The matter is still in some doubt, though Sir Ronald Johnson (1988) came down firmly in favour of Grant, after assessing the evidence, as had Barkley (1979). JRW

• Barkley, J. M. (1979) *Handbook to the Church Hymnary*; Johnson, R. (1988) 'How far is it to Crimond?', *Bulletin of the Hymn Society*, 12, 3, pp. 38–42; Scott, H. (1926) *Fasti Ecclesiae Scoticanae*; Wyness, J. F. (1958) *'Crimond' –The Full Story of a Psalm Tune Controversy*.

IRWIN, Margaret Hardinge, CBE, born at sea, 13 Jan. 1858 (registered Broughty Ferry), died Glasgow 21 Jan. 1940. Trade union and suffrage activist. Daughter of Margaret Hunter Cappon, and Captain James Ritchie Irwin, master mariner.

An only child, Margaret Irwin was educated privately and at the University of St Andrews (LLA 1880), having studied German, French and English Literature. Moving to Glasgow, she attended classes at Glasgow School of Art and studied political economy at Queen Margaret College. In 1891 she began her lifetime's work on improving working women's conditions, probably influenced by early experience in the Dundee area with its poor living conditions, large female workforce and active labour movement. She became full-time organising secretary of the Women's Protective and Provident League, a philanthropic organisation sponsored by Glasgow Trades Council, and in 1895 Secretary of its offshoot, the Glasgow, then the Scottish, Council for Women's Trades (SCWT). As Assistant Commissioner to the Royal Commission on Labour, she provided detailed reports on women's working conditions, for example in laundries, shops, tailoring and sweated trades, published by SCWT and welcomed by the Trades Councils. Women's participation at their conferences greatly increased. By 1895, the SCWT represented 100,000 members affiliated to 16 Trades Councils.

Margaret Irwin was a driving force on the STUC provisional committee, becoming Secretary two months after its inauguration in March 1897. This was described as 'a stroke of great good fortune for the fledgling congress' (Aitken 1997, p. 7). Although never a trade union member, she was recognised as a leading authority on women workers, possessing an unrivalled knowledge of industrial organisation that was used to advantage in STUC deputations to Parliament and in committee procedures and reports. An active member of GWSAWS, her first motion at the first STUC Congress in 1897 was on women's suffrage. She resigned as STUC Secretary in 1900 but continued as SCWT delegate until 1910. She was particularly concerned with women's exploitation in homework, an area she called 'terra incognita', toiling alone up dilapidated tenement stairs to discover the slum housing conditions of women working for a pittance, and their families. She reported on the differences between English and Scots women textile workers at the Women's Industrial Council in London. In 1910, she gave evidence to the Select Committee, House of Lords, on closing hours of shops and restaurants, after achieving basic amenities for shop girls of seating and toilet facilities. That year, she initiated a government inquiry into the poor housing of seasonal agricultural workers. In 1918, she designed a model artisan dwelling for Glasgow Corporation health committee, a maquette of which was exhibited by the SCWS. In the 1920s, she wrote articles on women's work for the *Glasgow Herald*. She was made CBE in 1927.

In her later years she owned and ran a fruit farm in Blairgowrie, Perthshire, employing women in model conditions. She was also active in land settlement schemes and work schemes for unemployed girls. A woman of strong intellect, shrewd, determined and visionary, Margaret Irwin's contribution to the reform of laws affecting working women was long-lasting. ACa

• Univ. of Glasgow library; Mitchell Library, Glasgow; Gallacher Memorial library; STUC Archives in GCU research collections (all contain material relating to Margeret Irwin).

Irwin, M. H., *Glasgow Herald*, 9 July 1918 (Housing), 11 Oct. 1920 (Report to SCWT), 14 Jan. 1921 (Small-holdings for women), 10 Nov. 1921 (Women's labour), 16 Dec. 1921, (Defence of Trade Boards Act), 14 April 1924 (Work for unemployed girls); www.eup.ed.ac.uk (Bibl.)

Aitken, K. (1997) *The Bairns o'Adam: story of the STUC*; Canning, A. (1997) 'Margaret Irwin', in *Scottish Marxist Voice*, Issue 6; *Glasgow Herald*, 22 Jan. 1940 (obit.); Gordon, E. (1991) *Women and the Labour Movement in Scotland 1850–1914*; Lewenhak, S. (1973) 'Women in the leadership of the STUC 1897–1970', in *Scot. Lab. Hist. Soc. Jour.* No. 7, July, (1977) *Women and Trade Unions*; *ODNB* (2004); Tuckett, A. (1986) *The Scottish Trades Union Congress: the first 80 years 1897–1977*.

Private information: Henry McCubbin.

ISEABAIL NÍ MHEIC CAILEIN, n. **Stewart?,** fl. 1490s. Poet. Daughter of John Stewart, Lord of Lorn.

Most probably to be identified as Isabella, Countess of Argyll, wife of Colin Campbell, 1st Earl of Argyll, Iseabail had eight children, including Archibald, 2nd Earl of Argyll. She composed two courtly love poems using classical bardic language; only three such *dánta grádha*

survive from Gaelic Scotland. With these poems, 'Atá Fleasgach ar mo Thí' (There's a young man in pursuit of me) and 'Is Mairg Dá nGalar an Grádh' (Woe to the one whose sickness is love) she was following a European fashion of the time, imported to Scotland via Ireland. Doubt has been cast on the ascription of these poems and especially of her third extant work, 'Éistibh a Luchd an Tighe-se' (Listen, members of this household), to Iseabail, due to their subject matter, but these doubts arise from reading the poems as fact-based compositions rather than as imaginative poetic exercises. AF

• *An Gàidheal* (1871) 1, p. 297; *Guth na Bliadhna*, (1913) 10, p. 346; Kerrigan, C. (1991) *An Anthology of Scottish Women Poets*, p. 14; Ó Rathille, T. (1984) *Dánta Grádha*, p. 74; Thomson, D. S. (1983) *The Companion to Gaelic Scotland*, p. 139; Watson, W. J. (1978) *Bàrdachd Albannach O Leabhar Deadhan Liòs-Moir*, p. 307.

IURMINBURG, fl. 672–85. Queen of Bernicia.

Iurminburg married Ecgfrith, King of Bernicia (645/6–85), a kingdom which included parts of southern Scotland, after the dissolution of his marriage to *Aeðilthryð, who had retired into monastic life about 672, but before he became king of all Northumbria after 679. Saint Wilfrith's supporters blamed her for the souring of his relationship with Ecgfrith, who exiled him in 678 and imprisoned him in 680. They interpreted her serious illness of c. 680 as divine punishment for having 'shot poisoned arrows of speech from her quiver into the heart of the king' (Colgrave 1927). Fleeting glimpses of Iurminburg as Queen suggest she was active in Bernician (and later Northumbrian) politics. Ecgfrith also benefited from her sister's marriage to the King of Wessex. She was at Carlisle when she heard of Ecgfrith's death in battle in Pictland in 685; like other Northumbrian queens, Iurminburg retired to monastic life and became a respected abbess. JEF

• Colgrave, B. (ed.) (1927) *The Life of Bishop Wilfrid*.

J

JACOB, Violet Augusta Mary Frederica, n. **Kennedy-Erskine,** born Dun, near Montrose, 1 Sept. 1863, died Kirriemuir 9 Sept. 1946. Writer and painter. Daughter of Catherine Jones, and

William Henry Kennedy-Erskine, 18th Laird of Dun.

Violet Kennedy-Erskine was the eldest of three surviving children. Her father died when she was a child, in 1870, and her 16-year-old sister died suddenly and traumatically in 1883. She was raised by her Welsh mother and educated at home, the House of Dun (now NTS), 'Balnillo House' in her novel *Flemington*. Her writing often draws on the history of her ancient, landed family, which she recorded in *The Lairds of Dun* (1931), and on the landscapes and people of Angus. In 1894, she married Arthur Otway Jacob (1867–1936), an Irishman serving in the British Army. After their son Harry was born in 1895, they spent several years in India with Arthur Jacob's regiment, a happy period recorded in Violet's diaries and letters to her mother from Indore State. She nursed in Mhow military hospital but also enjoyed considerable freedom, meeting rulers of the Central Indian States and riding on the plains. Five volumes of her Indian flower paintings are held at the Royal Botanic Garden, Edinburgh.

Returning to Britain in 1901, she lived mainly in English garrison towns, apart from a spell in Egypt (1903–4). However, on leave and after retirement, the Jacobs frequently stayed near Llanigon in the Welsh borders. Her first, well-received novel, *The Sheepstealers* (1902), depicts social unrest in 1840s Wales (the 'Rebecca riots'). Her Scottish fiction with its vivid Scots dialogue is especially outstanding. *The Interloper* (1904), set in early 19th-century Angus, found contemporary success, and John Buchan described the powerful *Flemington* (1911) as 'the best Scots romance since *The Master of Ballantrae*' (NLS, MS 27416). *Flemington* depicts personal and political turmoil in 'this tormented country' during and after the 1745 Jacobite Rising, when, as one character remarks: 'Whiles, it's no sae easy tellin' havers frae truth' (1998 edn., pp. 335, 361).

Violet Jacob nursed during the First World War. Her son, Harry, died at the Somme in 1916, aged 20, and after this tragedy she wrote only short prose and poetry. Her poetry was mainly in Scots at this time, drawing on ballad and folksong traditions. The successful *Songs of Angus* (1915) appealed to exiled Scots, especially soldiers, and three further volumes followed. *The Scottish Poems of Violet Jacob* (1944) was reprinted several times; various poems have been much anthologised and some set to music. In 1920, she moved to Ludlow in Shropshire, but regularly visited Angus, the setting of *Tales of My Own Country* (1922) and *The Lum Hat and Other Stories* (1982). The Jacobs often wintered abroad in the 1930s because of Arthur Jacob's health. After his death in 1936, she returned

to Angus, making her final home at Marywell House, Kirriemuir. CA

• Montrose Public Library: David Waterson corr., Archives, MS X/510/8 (13 letters from VJ), letters to James Christison, librarian; NLS: Acc. 9277 and MSS 27411–16 (manuscripts and letters of VJ), MS 26190 (Marion Lochhead file, ff. 234–7, letters (n.d.) to Lochhead, and concerning Jacob's work), MS 26706 (Helen Cruickshank file, f. 82, poems by VJ); RBGE: 5 vols watercolour paintings by VJ, 4 vols 'Indian Flowering Plants', and 1 vol. 'Indian Convolvuli'. Jacob, V., Works as above and see *HSWW* (Bibl.).
Bing, S. (1993) 'Autobiography in the work of Violet Jacob', *Chapman* 74–5, Autumn/Winter, pp. 98–109; Caird, J. (1984) 'The poetry of Violet Jacob and Helen Cruickshank', *Cencrastus* 19, Winter, pp. 32–4; Gordon, K. H. (2000) 'Voices from the "cauld east countra": representations of self in the poetry of Violet Jacob and Marion Angus', PhD, Glasgow Univ.; *HSWW* (Bibl.); *ODNB* (2004); *The Scotsman*, 11 Sept. 1946 (obit.).

JAFFRAY, Grissel, died Dundee Nov. 1669. Last woman executed as a witch in Dundee.

Grissel Jaffray married James Butchart, maltman and burgess of Dundee. The Commission for her trial is dated 11 November 1669 and her execution is confirmed by the Council Minute Book entry for 23 November. The following year, Margaret Coul and several others accused of witchcraft were banished, after Grissel Jaffray had denounced them at her execution. Nothing else is known of her, although a later writer (*People's Journal* 1904) suggests she may have been Aberdonian and had one son, a skipper in foreign trade. Local legend tells that he sailed in on the day of her execution and when he discovered the source of the smoke and flames visible from the river, turned his ship about and was never seen again. Another legend suggests that James Butchart was also charged with witchcraft in January 1669, held in the Tolbooth and subsequently released. It is known that he was admitted to Dundee's hospital after Grissel Jaffray's death. C-MW

• Dundee City Archives: Dundee Council Book, VI, 1669–1707; McManus Galleries, Dundee: Stockdale, D. 'List of Known Cases of Witchcraft in the Dundee Area', 10 June 1996; NAS: PC1/40 p. 283.
Larner, K. et al. (1977) *A Source Book of Scottish Witchcraft*; *People's Journal*, 22 October 1904.

JAMIESON, Christina [John Cranston], born Sandness, Shetland, 30 June 1864, died Nelson, New Zealand, 23 March 1942. Writer and suffragist.

Daughter of Barbara Laing, and Robert Jamieson, schoolmaster.

Christina Jamieson was educated in the parish of Sandness on the west coast of Shetland, where her father was the schoolmaster and where she was a pupil-teacher. Unlike her brothers, several of whom became noted academics, she was expected to remain at home. Following the example of her father, a contributor to *The Scotsman*, she started to write both fiction and factual items about Shetland for several papers, sometimes as 'John Cranston'.

In 1899, after her father's death, she moved with her mother to Lerwick. In October 1909, she was one of the founding members of the – determinedly non-militant – Shetland Women's Suffrage Society. As secretary, she negotiated affiliation to the NUWSS and was frequently seen as the public face of the Shetland society, travelling to London to take part in a suffrage procession with a Shetland banner that she had designed. Her approach to suffrage was rooted in the economic and social conditions of Shetland. She was acutely aware of the plight of Shetland women, the 'real inhabitants of Shetland' she argued, 'who alone maintain continuous life on the isles' (Jamieson 1991, p. 31). With the men so often away at the fishing, it was women who ran the crofts and such was 'the general feeling of equality' that 'Shetland men as a rule "don't see why women soodna vot"' (ibid., p. 33). She herself believed that the women's 'constant industry and self-dependence, their patient, unselfish, faithful rearing of men . . . their high moral and religious character' (ibid., p. 33), entitled them to the vote.

Christina Jamieson was fondly remembered as one of Shetland's most 'notable and talented women' (Sill 1992, p. 4). A member of Lerwick School Board in 1916 and two years later its Chair, she also sat on the county committee on secondary education and the education authority. With her social conscience and an adventurous political streak, she was always willing to aid individuals or groups striving to improve the lot of ordinary people. In later years, like her contemporary *Jessie Saxby, she turned her attention to Shetland folklore, founding the Shetland Folklore Society in 1930. With her nephew Bertie Jamieson, she transcribed and edited extracts from the Kirk Session records of Walls and Sandness, published in two volumes as *The Hjaltland Miscellany* (1937 and 1939). Seeking relief from asthma, she emigrated to New Zealand in 1935. LCA

• Shetland Archives, D.1/32: Minute book of the Shetland Women's Suffrage Society, 1909–19.
Jamieson, C. (1991) 'The Women of Shetland', *New Shetlander*, 177, pp. 31–3 (originally published in *The Shetland News*, 22, 29 Jan. 1910).
AGC; *ODNB* (2004); Sill, R. (1992) 'Christina Jamieson (1866–1942): a notable Shetlander', *New Shetlander*, 179, March, pp. 11–14.

JEX-BLAKE, Sophia Louisa, born Hastings, Sussex, 21 Jan. 1840, died Sussex 7 Jan. 1912. Doctor and campaigner for women's medical training. Daughter of Maria Cubitt, and Thomas Jex-Blake, retired barrister.

Educated at home until the age of eight, Sophia Jex-Blake then attended six boarding schools in eight years. Described by a fellow-pupil as 'excessively clever' (Roberts 1993, p. 11), she was unhappy with the lack of educational opportunities available to her as a woman. From 1858 she attended Queen's College, London, qualifying as a teacher, and offered her services free to organisations providing education to impoverished women and children. In 1862, she took a temporary post in Mannheim, Germany, but was unhappy there. Only after travelling to America in 1865 did she fall 'desperately in love with medicine, . . . to an extent I could not have believed possible' (Todd 1918, p. 183). Refused entry to Harvard because she was a woman, she enrolled at the Women's Medical College, New York, in March 1868, but returned to Britain soon after, following her father's death.

Still determined to become a doctor, she applied to the University of Edinburgh in March 1869, but was refused entry on the grounds that she was the only female applicant. Undeterred, she recruited four other women, including **Helen Evans,** later Russel (1834–1903). All four passed the matriculation examination and were admitted to the medical school in November, a pivotal moment in women's history. It was particularly significant since Elizabeth Garrett Anderson had earlier failed to gain admittance to the same school. Two more women, including Mary Anderson Marshall, joined the following year, becoming the '*septem contra Edinam*', as Sophia Jex-Blake called them. They met hostility both from the male students, in the form of violent demonstrations including the famous 'riot at Surgeons' Hall', and from the professoriate of the university, which effectively barred them from classes and refused to allow them to graduate. Sophia Jex-Blake brought an action of declarator against the university to force it to allow graduation, but the decision was upheld in 1873, bringing to a halt the pioneering campaign at Edinburgh. She continued to work towards her goal, establishing the London School of Medicine for Women in 1874, but was thought too divisive to be its head. She eventually passed the medical degree examination in January 1877 at Berne University, Switzerland, and obtained her licence to practise in May that year. Returning to Edinburgh in the 1880s, she practised privately and founded the Edinburgh Hospital and Dispensary for Women and Children (later the Bruntsfield Hospital). In 1886, she founded the Edinburgh School of Medicine for Women, where she taught classes, also lecturing in midwifery at the School of Medicine of the Royal Colleges. She supported the Russell Gurney Enabling Bill (1876), which allowed medical examination boards to admit women as candidates – an essential step in the registration process, as outlined in the 1858 Medical Act. She wrote several essays in favour of female physicians (see also Jex-Blake 1873), and this combination of theory and practice did much to raise the profile and acceptability of female doctors. She retired to Sussex in 1895, with her long-term friend and colleague **Margaret Todd** (1859–1918), a Scot who had graduated in 1894 from Sophia Jex-Blake's Edinburgh School but who now continued her literary career, having published one bestseller, *Mona MacLean* (1892), under the pseudonym 'Graham Travers'. Margaret Todd wrote a further three novels. Her last work was a biography of Sophia Jex-Blake, and she shortly afterwards committed suicide.

Sophia Jex-Blake provoked strong reactions among her contemporaries: she was described by Louisa Martindale as 'brilliant, hot-tempered and resourceful' (Bonner 1995, pp. 125–6), precisely the characteristics that brought success. Others were less complimentary: Elizabeth Blackwell saw her as 'a dangerous woman from her power and want of tact' (ibid.). Some even blamed her high-profile campaign for the failure at Edinburgh, feeling that a more restrained effort would have brought lasting results. However, her tenacity was undoubtedly crucial in the campaign to gain a place for women in medicine. NRS

• NLS: Blackwood Papers (Todd).
Jex-Blake, S. (1872) *Medical Women: Two Essays*, ([1873] 1987) 'The Medical Education of Women', in D. Spender (ed.) *The Education Papers. Women's quest for equality in Britain, 1850–1912*.
Achterberg, J. (1990) *Woman as Healer*; Bonner, T. N. (1995) *To the Ends of the Earth. Women's search for education in medicine*; Finkelstein, D. (2002) *The House of Blackwood: author-publisher relations in the Victorian era*; ODNB (2004) (see Blake, Sophia Jex-; also 'Edinburgh Seven'); Roberts, R. (1993) *Sophia Jex-Blake*; Sutherland, J. (1988) *The Longman Companion to Victorian Fiction*; Todd, M. (1918) *The Life of Sophia Jex-Blake*.
Additional information from David Finkelstein.

JOAN Beaufort, Queen of Scotland, born England, died Dunbar 15 July 1445. Daughter of Margaret Holland, co-heiress to the earldom of Kent, and John Beaufort, Earl of Somerset.

Joan Beaufort married James I (1394–1437) at Southwark in February 1424. The marriage may have been a love-match but was arranged primarily as part of negotiations for James's release from his eighteen-year English captivity. Joan was well-connected (half-cousin to Henry VI and niece of the bishop of Winchester, later Cardinal Beaufort) but had no right of succession to the English throne: she provided a link to the newly freed Scottish king but could not transmit any rights to her husband or children.

Joan Beaufort arrived in Scotland at the end of March 1424 and was crowned at Scone on 21 May. She and James had six daughters, including *Margaret Stewart, Dauphine of France, and twin sons, one of whom died in infancy. Evidence of her political activity as consort is slight, limited largely to acts of intercession, but James clearly regarded her as an important ally. He twice arranged for the political community to swear oaths of loyalty to her as his consort, in 1428 and 1435. Loyalty to a queen was assumed to be inseparable from that owed to the king, so the two oaths effectively gave Joan her own identity in government.

Following the assassination of James I on 21 February 1437, she played a leading political role for some weeks, but soon returned to a more limited position as guardian of the young king, James II. Intense factionalism saw even this role eroded. In the summer of 1439, Joan married James Stewart of Lorne (d. 1451), with whom she had three sons. Joan and her new husband sought to regain effective custody of King James at Stirling but were captured on 3 August by the captain of Stirling Castle, Alexander Livingston. The Queen was released on 31 August after renouncing custody of her children to Livingston. She and her allies continued to oppose the Livingston faction but with little success, particularly after Livingston's alliance with the 8th Earl of Douglas in 1443. With her allies under attack, she took refuge in the castle

of Dunbar in June 1445, where she died the following month. The focus of opposition to the Douglas-Livingston dominance died with her. FD
• Brown, M. (1994) *James I*, (1998) *The Black Douglases*; Downie, F. A. (1998) '"Sche is but a womman": the queen and princess in Scotland, 1424–63', PhD, Univ. of Aberdeen (Bibl.); *ODNB* (2004) (Bibl.).

JOAN of England, Queen of Scotland, born 22 or 24 July 1210, died Havering, Essex, 4 March 1238. Daughter of Isabella of Angoulême and King John I of England; **MARGARET of England, Queen of Scotland,** born Windsor 2 Oct. 1240, died Cupar 26 or 27 Feb. 1275. Daughter of Eleanor of Provence and Henry III of England.

Joan of England spent much of her early life in France, as she was contracted to marry Hugues, later Lord of Lusignan, in 1214; however, he married her mother in 1220. Joan was returned to England and married Alexander II (1198–1249) on 19 June 1221. Though Joan's marriage was important for Anglo-Scottish relations, she seems to have had little influence on political life, due to her youth, childlessness, and perhaps the dominance at court of her mother-in-law *Ermengarde de Beaumont. Joan undertook a pilgrimage to Canterbury in 1237, remained in England and died the following year.

Joan of England's niece, Margaret, married the young Alexander III (1241–86) on 26 December 1251. Her early years in Scotland were unhappy but she maintained a close relationship with her father. She was influential in persuading her father to intervene in Scottish political affairs in 1255. From 1260, Alexander assumed control of the government. The royal couple travelled frequently to England and Margaret gave birth there in 1261, to their first child, Margaret, later Queen of Norway. Two sons followed; their early deaths precipitated a succession crisis when Alexander III died in 1286, and Margaret's grand-daughter, *Margaret, 'Maid of Norway', died in 1290. CAA
• Duncan, A. A. M. (1975) *Scotland: the making of the kingdom*; Giles, J. A. (ed.) (1853) *Matthew Paris's English History*; *ODNB* (2004) (see Joan; Margaret of England; Marie de Coucy); *Scotichron.*

JOHNSTON, Anne (Annie), born Barra 10 Feb. 1886, died Barra 6 March 1963. Gaelic folklorist. Daughter of Catherine McNeil, and Angus Johnston, fisherman.

One of eight children, Annie Johnston took an early interest in the culture and traditions of Barra, soaking up stories and songs heard from her

mother and talented neighbours. She spent her whole life in Barra, and as a teacher instilled an interest in their folklore in the children of Castlebay school, at a time when the stories of Aesop, the brothers Grimm and Hans Christian Andersen were familiar to school children whose own tradition had equally exciting versions memorised by their own people. Among the collectors who came to her door for information about 'Celtic' traditions, becoming increasingly fascinating to the outside world in the early 20th century, were the American Alan Lomax, Dr John Lorne Campbell of Canna, and his wife *Margaret Fay Shaw. Campbell's recordings of Annie Johnston and her siblings were passed on to the School of Scottish Studies, after 1951, forming a precious part of the archives.

Annie Johnston and her brother Calum contributed to *Marjorie Kennedy-Fraser's famous three-volume *Songs of the Hebrides*. Children's lore, proverbial sayings, bird calls, cradle-songs and representations of other song types might never have been known had it not been for the Johnstons and those who recorded them. Annie Johnston introduced collectors to the 'waulking song', a genre unique to Gaelic Scotland, used to accompany the shrinking of homespun cloth by beating it, soaked, on to a board. Several women sat around the board, singing songs with a distinctive beat, as a means of regulating the hand movements. Annie Johnston sang them herself, and encouraged other women to display their repertory. The School of Scottish Studies published a boxed cassette of songs and stories by Annie and Calum Johnston in 1980. MMacL
• Recording: *Calum and Annie Johnston*, CTRAX 9013, [1980 Greentrax Recordings, Edinburgh].
Béaloideas, vols 1, 4 and 6; Campbell, J. L. and Collinson, F. (1969–81) *Hebridean Folksongs*, 3 vols; *Gairm*, nos. 2, 6, and 10; Kennedy-Fraser, M. (1909–21) *Songs of the Hebrides*, 3 vols; *Tocher* (School of Scottish Studies), no. 13 (1980).

JOHNSTON, Elizabeth see **FLUCKER, Barbara** (1784–1869)

JOHNSTON, Ellen, born Hamilton c. 1835, died Barony Poorhouse hospital, Springburn, c. 1873. Poet and autobiographer. Daughter of Mary Bilsland, and James Johnston, stonemason.

Ellen Johnston, known as 'The Factory Girl', was one of the small number of 19th-century working-class women poets. Her father emigrated to America when Ellen was a baby and eight years later her mother, believing him dead, remarried. Ellen's life of extreme hardship included flight from home after abuse by her stepfather, poor health resulting from work in factories in Glasgow, Belfast, Manchester and Dundee, and single parenthood (she had an illegitimate daughter in 1852), yet she managed to write from an early age. She enjoyed some middle-class patronage, particularly from the Rev. George Gilfillan and Alexander Campbell, editor of the *Penny Post*, and two editions of her poems were produced on subscription in 1867 and 1869. The second edition acknowledges 'the gift of Five Pounds from Her Majesty Queen Victoria, and the grant of Fifty Pounds from the Royal Bounty Fund . . . which enabled me to furnish a home and discharge the pecuniary obligations I had unavoidably contracted for my maintenance in Glasgow, while suffering from a delicate constitution and factory life, to which I have long been a victim' (Johnston 1869, v).

Ellen Johnston's poetry is often sentimental (especially when she writes in English rather than Scots) and technically conservative, but a voice of true feeling gleams through, and she is often radical. She celebrated Garibaldi's visit to Britain, comparing him to Wallace who 'purchased Scotland's freedom with the ransom of his life'. Her poems provoked poetic addresses from other working men and women to which she replied, establishing a culture of compliment. 'The Last Sark', her most anthologised poem, is radical in feeling and forthright in expression; until recently its fame unfairly relegated her other verse. Both editions of her poems include an autobiography which is the only real source of information about her life. The second version omits reference to her child and removes the detail of her persecution by her female fellow workers after her successful case for wrongful dismissal against the Verdant Factory, Dundee. Possibly she thought she would present a more pleasing image with these omissions. Yet what makes Ellen Johnston's story so moving is that her real sufferings emerge clearly. Her allusions to abuse by her stepfather are shrouded in sentimental cliché but her sheer endurance rescues her story from self-pity. Given the absence of any real moral, educational and financial support, her achievement is remarkable.

Wilson reported that Ellen Johnston died in the Barony Poorhouse in 1873 (Wilson 1873, p. 525). Klaus (1998) suggests a date of 1874. DAMCM
• Johnston, E. (1867, 1869) *Autobiography, Poems and Songs of Ellen Johnston, the Factory Girl.*

Boos, F. S. (2003) 'The "Queen" of the "Far-Famed Penny Post" ', *Women's Writing*, 10, no. 3, pp. 503–26; *DLB* Gale, vol. 199, pp. 188–93; Klaus, H. G. (1998) 'Factory Girl', *SSL*, 23; *ODNB* (2004); Wilson, J. G. (1873) *The Poets and Poetry of Scotland*, vol. 2; Zlotnick, S. (1991) ' "A thousand times I'd be a factory girl" ', *Victorian Studies*, vol. 35 no. 1.

JOHNSTON, Euphemia, n. **Alexander, born 1824** Inveresk, died after 1867. Lady's nurse. Daughter of Jean Brackenridge, and James Alexander.

The eldest of six children, Euphemia Alexander married Alexander Johnston in June 1844 in Edinburgh. By 1851, she was widowed and living with her three young daughters and her elderly aunt in Edinburgh. She may have attended the Maternity hospital as a pupil midwife that year; she certainly made the acquaintance of Professor James Simpson and impressed him with her competence. In her regular entries in the annual Post Office Directory of Edinburgh, she described herself as a 'lady's nurse'. Following a recommendation by Simpson, she attended Princess Christian (daughter of *Queen Victoria) at the birth of her first child in 1867. From then on, her career continued among élite women able to afford her fee of 25 guineas. Her career path contrasts with that of other women who gained midwifery or nursing expertise in Edinburgh such as *Margaret Bethune. BEM
• Mortimer, B. (2002) 'The nurse in Edinburgh c. 1760–1860: the impact of commerce and professionalisation', PhD, Univ. of Edinburgh (lists primary sources).

JOHNSTONE, Caroline Elizabeth Mary (Carrie), born Alva, Clackmannanshire, 25 July 1849, died Alva 4 July 1929. Philanthropist. Daughter of Hon. William Augusta Ann Norton, and James Johnstone, landowner.

Born into a prominent local family living at Alva House, Carrie Johnstone became locally well-known as a benefactor of many causes and an active citizen, although it is suggested that her 'excessive spending' (Dovey 2002, p. 9) led to the decline of the ample establishment at Alva House, the sale of the house furnishings and eventually the house's dilapidation. She moved to Myretoun House, where she lived with her companion of many years, Miss L'Estrange.

Typical of philanthropic middle-class women in the late 19th-century, Carrie Johnstone was involved in many national and local charities, including serving as President of the Scottish Domestic Servants' Benevolent Association and working with the Alva Mothers' Union and Child

Welfare Society. A gifted public speaker, she was President of the Alva Women's Unionist Association and a member of the Clackmannanshire Central Committee for Maternal and Child Welfare. She also took a close personal interest in local families' welfare. A fountain in her memory, funded by public subscription, was erected in 1951 in Johnstone Park (the park was a gift to the town from her father). SI

• *Alloa Advertiser,* 17 Nov. 1951, p. 4; *Alloa Journal,* 6 July 1929 (obit.); Dovey, N. (2002) *Alva 1900–2000.*
Additional information: Alloa Library, Morag Cross.

JOHNSTONE, Christian Isobel [Meg Dods], n. **Tod,** m1 **M'Leish,** m2 **Johnstone,** born Edinburgh 12 June 1781, died Edinburgh 26 August 1857. Journalist and woman of letters. Daughter of Jean Campbell, and James Todd, medical student.

Early in life, according to the *Biographical Dictionary of Eminent Men of Fife* (1866), Christian Isobel Tod married a man called M'Leish from whom she later obtained a divorce: the circumstances surrounding this remain obscure. In 1815, she married John Johnstone (1779–1857), a schoolmaster at Dunfermline. She may have been the author of *The Saxon and the Gael* (1814), a novel of social comedy. In 1815 she published anonymously her best-known novel, *Clan-Albin: A National Tale.* She and her husband became editors of the *Inverness Courier* in 1817 and, after what seems to have been a successful period in Inverness, the Johnstones moved in 1824 to Edinburgh where Christian wrote her third novel, *Elizabeth de Bruce* (1827). She also joined her husband in editing the *Edinburgh Weekly Chronicle,* the weekly *The Schoolmaster* and the monthly *Johnstone's Magazine.* In 1834, she formed with William Tait her most important literary connection. She began to assist in the management of the popular *Tait's Edinburgh Magazine,* which, in opposition to *Blackwood's Magazine,* supported radical politics: in the same year *Johnstone's Magazine* merged with *Tait's.* Although not, strictly speaking, the editor, she had entire charge of the literary department, and was a regular contributor.

Christian Johnstone befriended and supported the radical poet, Robert Nicoll, and many other young writers and she employed an unusually high number of women to write for the magazine. She edited a number of fiction contributions to *Tait's* and other periodicals, including some of her own, as *The Edinburgh Tales,* 1845–6. Among other writings are *Nights of the Round Table* (1832), and

the *Cook and Housewife's Manual,* by 'Mrs Margaret (Meg) Dods' (1826), which subsequently went into 11 editions. She also published *The Diversions of Hollycot; or, The Mother's Art of Thinking* (1828), an instructional work for children which includes an account of the life of the exemplary Scottish heroine, *Lady Grisell Baillie (1665–1746). Throughout her career as journalist and editor she was a thorough professional with a strong sense of the commercial possibilities of the craft. She died aged 76, a few months before her husband. They were buried in Grange Cemetery, Edinburgh, where an obelisk was erected to their memory. DAMCM

• Johnstone, C., Works as above, and see Bibls. below.
A Highland Newspaper: The First Hundred and Fifty Years of 'The Inverness Courier', 1817–1967; *HSWW* (Bibl.); *DNB* vol. X (1908); McMillan, D. (2002–3) 'Figuring the Nation: Christian Isobel Johnstone as novelist and editor', *Études Écossaises* 9, pp. 27–41; Monnickendam, A. (2003) 'Introduction' to *Clan-Albin: A national tale,* ASLS, v-xxi (Bibl.); *ODNB* (2004); *The Wellesley Index to Victorian Periodicals, 1824–1900:* (includes authors and Bibls.), 5 vols, 1966–89.

JOHNSTONE, Dorothy, m. **Sutherland,** born Edinburgh 25 Dec. 1892, died Bodelwyddan, North Wales, 15 July 1980. Artist and art educator. Daughter of Jessie Hunter Heron, and George Whitton Johnstone, RSA, artist.

In 1908 Dorothy Johnstone enrolled for the Drawing and Painting course at ECA. A precociously gifted student, she obtained her Diploma in 1912, along with a maintenance bursary and a studio in the College. She joined the teaching staff in 1914. From 1915 summers were spent in Kirkcudbright painting alongside other female artists such as Anne Finlay (1898–1963). She first exhibited at the RSA in 1912 and the next year showed *Marguerite,* a virtuoso portrait of her younger sister **Rona Johnstone** (1902–2003, later a successful dance teacher), who inspired much of her early figure work. She exhibited with the dynamic Edinburgh Group (1919, 1920, 1921), as one of its three female members, and at the RA in London, until 1923. In 1924 she had a joint exhibition in Edinburgh with her close friend *Cecile Walton, and married fellow Edinburgh Group exhibitor David MacBeth Sutherland. She had to give up her teaching post on marriage, entering a new phase of her life as 'artist's wife and portrait painter' (Sturrock 1980, p. 32). Her son Iain (b. 1925) and daughter Anne (b. 1928) both feature in her work.

In 1933, she relocated to Aberdeen where her husband was Head of Gray's School of Art, settling in Cults in 1939 and exhibiting regularly with the AAS. Her work largely consisted of portraiture and figure painting, focusing almost exclusively on women and children, but she also produced landscapes. Her long and productive career (SSA 1931, ARSA 1962) lost some of its momentum after her marriage and the premature end of her role as a gifted art educator. NJI

• ECA Archives: student records 1908–20; Board of Management Reports, minute books 1908–13; RSA Archives: Sturrock, M. N. (1980) 'Dorothy Johnstone, ARSA', in *One Hundred and Fifty-Third Annual Report of the Council of the RSA*, pp. 31–2.
Aberdeen Art Gallery & Museums (1983) *Dorothy Johnstone, ARSA, 1892–1980, A Memorial Exhibition* (catalogue); Bourne, P. (2000) *Kirkcudbright: 100 years of an artists' colony*; Kemplay, J. (1983) *The Edinburgh Group*; Stephens, J. W. (1924) 'Cecile Walton and Dorothy Johnstone', *The Studio*, vol. 88; Taylor, E. A. (1920) 'The Edinburgh Group', *The Studio*, vol. 79.

JORDAN, Jessie,‡ n. **Wallace,** m1 **Jordan,** m2 **Baumgarten,** born Glasgow 23 Dec. 1887, died Hanover 1954. Spy. Daughter, out of wedlock, of Elizabeth Wallace, domestic servant.

Jessie Wallace grew up in Perth. She met a German waiter, Frederick Jordan, in Dundee, and in 1907, when he was 18 and she was 19, they moved to Hanover, marrying in 1912. A daughter was born in 1914. When Frederick died of pneumonia during the First World War, Jessie Jordan stayed on, working as a hairdresser in Hamburg. She returned to Perth in 1919, but by April 1920 was back in Germany: she married her husband's cousin, Baur Baumgarten. The marriage did not last, and she returned to Scotland in 1937. It was at this point that she claimed to have been asked by a friend's husband to verify information for the Germans. The hairdressing business she set up in Dundee was used by German agents in the USA and Britain as a forwarding address. She received letters and documents which she then sent to a chemist's shop in Amsterdam. An assistant in the salon, Mary Curran, became suspicious at the mail arriving for her employer, and informed the police, who put Jessie Jordan under surveillance. She was arrested on 2 March 1938. The charges included not only receiving and forwarding censored mail, but taking photographs and making sketches of classified coastal and military locations. Found guilty of spying, Jessie Jordan spent most of the Second World War in prison. An editorial in a Dundee newspaper commented at the time: 'It does not appear that Mrs Jordan took to spying because of love of Germany or hatred of Britain, or even from desire to make money from it. She has apparently been chosen as an instrument by agents aware of her personal history, and in a position to put her under some form of pressure to do what was required of her' (*Dundee Courier* 1938). After the war she was repatriated to Germany, where she died in 1954. Documents relating to her arrest were released by MI5 in April 2000 (PRO). FJ

• PRO: KV2/193–4; NAS: Trial records 1938.
The Daily Telegraph, 20 April 2000; *Dundee Courier and Advertiser*, 17 May 1938; Mahoney, M. H. (1993) *Women in Espionage*; Watson, N. (1997) *Daughters of Dundee*.

K

KAY, Christina,‡ born Edinburgh 11 June 1878, died Midhope, West Lothian, 23 May 1951. School teacher. Model for Miss Jean Brodie in Muriel Spark's *The Prime of Miss Jean Brodie*. Daughter of Mary Ann MacDonald, and Alexander Kay, cabinet maker.

Christina Kay led an apparently uneventful life, but one that would inspire one of the great characters of 20th-century literature: Miss Jean Brodie (Spark 1961). From the age of five, she was a pupil at James Gillespie's School for Girls, one of Edinburgh's merchant company schools, where she would later teach. Between 1897 and 1899, she completed her teacher training at the Church of Scotland college in Edinburgh, where her conduct was described as 'exemplary'. An only child and a devout Christian, Christina Kay was born and lived in the same flat, at 4 Grindlay Street, Edinburgh, almost all her life. Her father died when she was 15, and she lived with her mother, caring for her until her death in 1913. She never married. Her pupils believed, probably correctly, that like many other women of her generation she lost her fiancé in the First World War.

Christina Kay devoted her life to teaching at Gillespie's. Since in her early years very few women could take degrees, as younger colleagues could, she remained a 'class mistress', without promotion. But she was an inspirational teacher to her classes of 11- to 12-year-olds, sharing with them her passion for the arts. In 1929–30 they included the young Muriel Camberg (later Spark) whose literary success she predicted. Muriel Spark's *Curriculum Vitae* (1992, pp. 56 ff.), vividly recalling Miss Kay, makes it clear that Jean Brodie was based on 'that character in search of an author'. Christina Kay would exhilarate her pupils by speaking in 'dazzling non-sequiturs' (ibid., p. 59) of her foreign travels, particularly to Italy, and the great art she saw there, reproductions of which adorned her schoolroom walls. She admired Mussolini, as many contemporaries did, and a picture of his Fascisti was also given wall space. Miss Kay called her entire class the 'crème de la crème' but she also had favourites, including Muriel Camberg and her friend Frances Niven, whom she took to exhibitions, theatre and ballet. Most of her pupils found her teaching unforgettable. Perhaps from shyness, Miss Kay kept her coming retiral in 1942 secret, but a tribute in the school magazine said that 'service like hers must surely be unique'; the tribute spoke of her love of ancient Greece and therefore of perfection in all things, 'for the gods see everywhere'. She was buried, as she wished, in Abercorn Churchyard. ED

• NAS: registration records; Moray House Archives; James Gillespie's High School records; *JGHS School Magazine*, 1942. Spark, M. (1961) *The Prime of Miss Jean Brodie*, (1992) *Curriculum Vitae.*
Private information from former pupils, including Dame Muriel Spark and Frances Cowell (n. Niven).

KEDDIE, Henrietta [Sarah Tytler], born Cupar 4 March 1827, died London 6 Jan. 1914. Novelist. Daughter of Mary Gibb, and Philip Keddie, lawyer and coalmaster.

Henrietta Keddie, seventh of eight children, was educated at home by an older sister, apart from a few months' schooling in Edinburgh. When their father's mining interests resulted in financial disaster for the household, several of the sisters opened a small private school for girls in Cupar, where Henrietta taught from 1848 to 1870. She had already begun writing and her first novel, *Phemie Millar*, was published under her own name in 1854. Most of her work thereafter appeared under the pseudonym 'Sarah Tytler'. Her success allowed her to become a full-time writer and she moved to

London in 1870 with her sister Margaret, moving in literary circles and becoming acquainted with other women writers, such as Mrs Craik and *Margaret Oliphant. Much of her prolific production (she published well over 100 titles) consisted of historical romances for girls. Two adult novels are notable: *St Mungo's City* (1884), a novel of manners set in middle-class Victorian Glasgow, and *Logie Town* (1887), a loving portrait of her native town of Cupar.

Henrietta Keddie collaborated with the Edinburgh writer **Jean Logan Watson** (1835–85) in editing *The Songstresses of Scotland* (1871), an anthology of Scottish women songwriters. Jean Watson wrote guidebooks and local history, biographies of Scottish religious leaders and one of Hugh Miller, and novels, including *Bygone days in our village* (1864) and *Heiress of Ravensby: a tale of reformation times* (1882). She was known for 'racy dialect and unconventional manners' and was 'of a commanding presence, with traces of a dark beauty probably derived from a strain of gypsy blood of which she boasted, forthgoing in all her impulses, trenchant in utterance' (*Scots Pictorial* 1898, pp. 354–5).

Following her sister's death, Henrietta Keddie moved to Oxford in 1884, and continued to write, using the Bodleian Library for her historical research and acquiring a new circle of friends among the women students. Her autobiography, *Three Generations* (1911), contains, as the title suggests, much information about her family, but little about her own busy and successful writing career. MARB

• Keddie, H., and Tytler, S., Works as above and see *HSWW* (Select Bibl.).
Burgess, M. (1997) 'Rediscovering Scottish women's fiction', in *HSWW* (Bibl.); *ODNB* (2004); 'Scots worthies: Henrietta Keddie ("Sarah Tytler")', *Scots Pictorial*, 1 Jan. 1898.

KEER, Honoria Somerville, born Toronto, Canada, 26 Dec. 1883, died London 20 March 1969. Surgeon for the *Scottish Women's Hospitals during the First World War. Daughter of Eliza Somerville, and Major-General Jonathan Keer, ex-HM Bengal Staff Corps.

Honoria Keer graduated MBChB from the University of Glasgow in 1910. After civilian posts at Glasgow Royal Asylum, Gartnavel, and as House Surgeon at Kilmarnock, she joined the Girton and Newnham Unit of the SWH abroad from December 1915. After service in France and Salonika, she became MO (head) of the unit for

Serbian refugees in Ajaccio, Corsica, in April 1918. She was awarded the French Croix de Guerre and the Médaille des Epidémies, having also received the Serbian Order of St Sava. Honoria Keer then worked as a GP in Lanark, before obtaining a Diploma in Tropical Medicine (London) in 1924. She spent most of the next 10 years as Lady Medical Officer at Massey Street Dispensary in Lagos, Nigeria, before retiring prematurely to Bayswater in London in 1934, illness abroad having resulted in recurrent hearing problems. During the Second World War, she worked actively for the WVS in civil defence, and was responsible, among other things, for the Queen's letter to householders. She was described by a SWH colleague, Isabel Emslie, as 'a strange mass of contradictions: serious, reserved, and with very correct old-world manners; . . . at the same time . . . her sly wit was a constant joy' (Leneman 1994, p. 37). JLMJ

• Univ. of Glasgow Archive: DC171, Honoria Keer papers. Alexander, W. (1987) *First Ladies of Medicine*; Leneman, L. (1994) *In the Service of Life*; McLaren, E. S. (ed.) (1919) *A History of the Scottish Women's Hospitals*; *Medical Directory* (1919–20); *Medical Register* (1969).

KEILLER, Gabrielle Muriel, n. **Ritchie,** m1 unknown, m2 **Style,** m3 **Keiller,** born North Berwick 10 August 1908, died Bath 23 Dec. 1995. Golf champion and art collector. Daughter of Daisy Hoare, and James (Jack) Ritchie, rancher.

Gabrielle Ritchie's birth in Scotland was unexpected, her parents being on a golfing holiday. Brought up in Rutland with her two brothers, and privately educated, she took up golf early, and had a flourishing career in the 1930s and 1940s. She won the Ladies' Open in Switzerland, Luxembourg and Monaco in 1948, and was selected for England several times as 'one of the longest hitters in the country' (Calvocoressi 1997, p. 9). During the Second World War, she drove ambulances for the LCC. She had been twice married briefly and had a son, and it was as Mrs Style that in 1947 she met Alexander Keiller (1889–1955), heir to the Dundee marmalade fortune. Having 'run away to France' (Murray 1999, p. 109), they married when his divorce came through in 1951 and were a devoted couple until his death from cancer in 1955, Gabrielle being his fourth wife. Alexander Keiller had sold his family shares in 1918, and devoted his wealth largely to his passion for archaeology, including the excavation of Windmill Hill and Avebury.

After her husband's death, Gabrielle Keiller had his reports edited, and worked at the BM as a volunteer in the archaeology department. She gave up golf, converted to Catholicism, and began a second career as a serious art connoisseur, having inherited both from her husband and from her American connections. After visiting Peggy Guggenheim in 1960 in Venice, where she saw Eduardo Paolozzi's work, she became a patron to Paolozzi and Richard Long among others. Advised notably by Roland Penrose, she was also a remarkable collector of Dada and Surrealism, amassing major works of art and thousands of catalogues, letters, manuscripts, books, journals and ephemera, some of which were exhibited anonymously at the SNGMA in 1988 ('The Magic Mirror'). Having been an active member of SNGMA's Advisory Committee, with an 'acerbity of eye which does not go to sleep' (ibid., p. 17), she bequeathed her entire surrealist collection to the Gallery. It is now in the Dean Centre, Edinburgh. A perfectionist, tall and elegant, Gabrielle Keiller was personally modest – but commissioned Andy Warhol to do a portrait of her dachshund, Maurice. Her ashes are buried alongside her husband's in the walls of Gairn Castle, on his former estate at Morven, Deeside. SR

• Calvocoressi, R. (1997) 'Gabrielle Keiller, a biographical sketch', in E. Cowling, et al., *Surrealism and After*; Cowling, E. (1988) *The Magic Mirror*, catalogue; Gere, C. and Vaizey, M. (1999) *Great Women Collectors*; Murray, L. J. (1999) *A Zest for Life*.

KEILLER, Janet, n. **Mathewson,** born Dundee c. 1737, died Dundee 23 July 1813. Shopkeeper, associate in marmalade family.

The most persistent account of the origin of the Keiller marmalade business is that a cargo of Seville oranges, storm-bound in Dundee, inspired Mrs Keiller to try out her recipe for quince marmalade on a new fruit. Some such chance is not impossible, but the Keillers were mainly confectioners throughout Janet Keiller's life. In 1762, she had married John Keiller (1737–1804). They had eight children and Janet Keiller kept a shop in Seagate, 'like many other female establishments of the time' (Mathew 1998, p. 2), based on domestic production of cakes, biscuits, jams, jellies and sweets. Recipes for orange marmalade already existed, but the Keillers appear to have promoted a chopped-peel Scottish variety, 'chip marmalade', lighter than most, and set up a company in about 1797, in the name of their son James (1775–1839). Keiller's was 'in considerable measure run by women in its first decades' (ibid., p. 11), but

marmalade was only a small part of their confectionery business until well into the 19th century. The success of the breakfast delicacy was probably mostly due to good marketing and branding, contributing to Dundee's reputation as the home of 'jam, jute and journalism'. SR
• Mathew, W. M. (1998) *Keiller's of Dundee: the rise of the marmalade dynasty* (Abertay Hist. Soc., no. 38, Bibl.); *ODNB* (2004) (Keiller, John M.).

KEITH, Annas (Agnes, Anna), Countess of Moray, Countess of Argyll, died 16 July 1588. Daughter of Margaret Keith of Inverugie, and William Keith, 4th Earl Marischal.

Probably born at Dunnottar Castle, Annas Keith was well educated, later becoming known for her Protestantism. In an unusual love match, she married Lord James Stewart, Earl of Moray (1531/2–70), close adviser to his half-sister *Mary, Queen of Scots. John Knox preached at the ceremony on 8 February 1562 in St Giles, Edinburgh, in the presence of the Queen who provided a lavish banquet at Holyrood Palace. Two daughters survived into adulthood. During 1565, when Moray rebelled, the pregnant Annas, unable to join him in exile, remained in their home in St Andrews Priory defending his interests. Having been prominent at court, in 1567 she became the foremost woman in the country when Moray became Regent. After he was assassinated in January 1570, his widow demonstrated remarkable resilience, efficiently running the Moray estates and tenaciously defending her daughters' inheritance. In spite of long-running, acrimonious disputes with Queen Mary and Regent Morton, she retained certain royal jewels acquired by Moray as part payment of his expenses as Regent.

In late January 1572, she married Colin Campbell (c. 1542–84), who became Earl of Argyll in 1573. Annas was the dominant partner, Argyll being 'overmuch led by his wife', according to one commentator (Rogers 1873, p. 35). The couple had two sons and a daughter; Annas helped nine-year-old Archibald when he succeeded in 1584. She was buried in Moray's tomb in St Giles, Edinburgh. Through her forceful personality and her position as Countess of Moray and Argyll, Annas Keith made a significant impact upon national and regional affairs. Her correspondence also demonstrates that she was able to overcome Moray's murder and the all-too-common experience of the death of a child. JEAD
• NRAS 217: Moray Muniments, Darnaway Castle.

Historical Manuscripts Commission Sixth Report; Rogers, C. (ed.) (1873) *Estimate of Scottish Nobility*; *SP*, 6, pp. 48–50; Thomson, T. (ed.) (1853) *Registrum Honoris de Morton*.

KENMURE, Vera Mary Muir, n. **Findlay,** born Glasgow 13 Feb. 1904, died Aberdeen 27 Dec. 1973. Minister and first woman ordained to a pastoral charge in a Scottish mainstream denomination. Daughter of Viola Craig, and John Findlay, measurer.

Vera Findlay became Dux in English at Hillhead High School, Glasgow and a prize-winner in classics at the University of Glasgow. As a student she began seriously to consider ministry in the Congregational Church, encouraged by the Principal of the Scottish Congregational College, where she studied with distinction 1926–8. A gifted preacher, she so impressed the deacons of Partick Congregational Church that they called her to be their pastor before she had completed her BD degree at the University of Glasgow. Ordained on 1 November 1928, in 1929 she applied for recognition as a minister of the Congregational Union of Scotland (CUS), stimulating great debate about women's ordination within Scottish Protestant churches. On 29 April 1929, the CUS carried a constitutional amendment allowing 'minister' to apply equally to women and men. She remained at Partick until 1934. By that time she had married Colin Kenmure, CA: some of her congregation (a minority) were implacably opposed to having a married woman as minister, and objections came to a head when she became a mother. In dramatic circumstances, she tendered her resignation, declaring 'a married woman makes an ideal minister. If she is a mother, so much the better, because her gift of understanding is thereby increased' (*Sunday Chronicle* 1934). Many agreed; they started a new church, led by Vera Kenmure, and in 1936 joined her when she was called to Hillhead Congregational Church. She also served at Pollokshields (1954–68) and regularly preached in pulpits of several denominations. She chaired the management committee of the Scottish Congregational College and, as President of the CUS 1952–3, attended the Church of Scotland General Assembly, although initially refused entrance because of her sex. LO
• Family papers.
Escott, A. (1990) 'True valour', in K. McCarra and H. Whyte (eds) *A Glasgow Collection*; *ODNB* (2004); *Sunday Chronicle*, 25 March 1934.
Private information.

KENNEDY, Janet, Lady Bothwell, c. 1480–1547. Mistress of James IV. Daughter of Elizabeth Gordon, and John, Lord Kennedy.

Janet Kennedy married first c. 1493, aged about 12, Alexander Gordon of Lochinvar, with whom she had a daughter, also called Janet. By 1497, she was the mistress of Archibald Douglas (c. 1449–1513), 5th Earl of Angus. She later claimed to be married to him but she was in fact in 1497 still married to Alexander Gordon. In 1498, she received from the Earl various lands including the barony of Bothwell and its castle, but within a year had become the mistress of James IV (1473–1513). This was probably the reason for the quarrel between James and the Earl and the latter's political eclipse for the next eight years. James was the father of Janet Kennedy's son, the Earl of Moray, and at least two daughters. He gave her Darnaway Castle but only as long as she remained 'without another man' (*RMS*, ii, no. 2585). In 1505, she was described as the spouse of Sir John Ramsay of Trarinzean, an intimate courtier of James's but also an English spy and traitor. By 1513, all these men were dead and Janet Kennedy spent the next 30 years looking after the rights of herself and her children. She retained the barony of Bothwell and also acquired a house in the fashionable Cowgate in Edinburgh. She was litigious and always prepared to play the system to her own advantage. Her life demonstrates that the concept of marriage in late medieval Scotland was a fluid one – and that although the country was Catholic, divorce, which could be obtained on the grounds of consanguinity, was, in practice, easy and common. ICMB

• *RMS*, ii.

Barnes, I. (2007) *Janet Kennedy* (Bibl.); Calderwood, A. (ed.) (1993) *Acts of the Lords of Council*; *ER*; *RSS*; *SP*; *TA*.

KENNEDY-FRASER, Marjory, n. **Kennedy,** m. **Fraser,** born Perth 1 Oct. 1857, died Edinburgh 22 Nov. 1930. Folksong collector, arranger and singer. Daughter of Elizabeth Fraser, and David Kennedy, singer.

Initially educated by her father, by 1870 Marjory Kennedy was providing piano accompaniment for his recital tours of Scots song. In 1871, the family, with 11 children, formed a successful vocal group, in which she sang contralto. Their world tour, 1872–9, took in the Antipodes, North America and South Africa. Marjory Kennedy studied voice production with Gambardella in Milan and Marchesi in Paris. In 1887, she married Alec Yule Fraser, who died in 1890, leaving her with two children, David and

Patuffa Kennedy-Fraser (b. 1888), the latter named by a visiting friend. Teaching song and piano in Edinburgh, she also assisted her brother-in-law, Tobias Matthay, with *The Act of Touch* and studied at the Reid School of Music. Her interest in Gaelic song began in 1882, but it was in 1905, at the suggestion of the artist John Duncan, that she found her true calling: collecting folk-song on Eriskay in the Outer Hebrides.

Many regard Marjory Kennedy-Fraser's involvement with Hebridean song as unfortunate (see *ODNB*, 2004). True, she altered her material, conflated different versions and adapted words from other songs (not always appropriately), and her arrangements have, for some, too much Celtic mist about them. But she was one of the first to make field recordings and was absolutely honest about what she was doing (stating in print that there was no substitute for the tradition as sung traditionally). Her arrangements were sensitive to the modal character of the material, varied in texture, and inspired leading composers such as Granville Bantock and F. G. Scott. Her work was more temperately judged by Campbell and Collinson, the two leading experts in the field, and by *Frances Tolmie, one of her chief informants.

Her *Songs of the Hebrides,* published in three volumes (1909–21), have become minor classics. Advanced in style for art-songs of the period, they contain important introductory material, including significant contributions from her Gaelic-speaking collaborator, Kenneth MacLeod, with whom she worked from 1908, and whose contribution is also open to criticism and praise. The famous song 'The Road to the Isles' was written by him in 1915, at her request for a tramping song for British troops in the First World War, setting a tune their informant, Calum Johnston (see Johnston, Annie), picked up in Barra. Much of the success of the *Songs of the Hebrides* was due to Marjory Kennedy-Fraser's performances, at home and abroad, with her daughter Patuffa on the clarsach. Patuffa, who later married J. C. F. Hood, also assisted on field trips and studied at the Matthay School in London. Marjory Kennedy-Fraser continued as chief music critic for the Edinburgh *Evening News*. In 1917, she wrote a libretto for Bantock's opera *The Seal-Woman*, produced in Birmingham under Sir Adrian Boult in 1924, in which she took the role of Mary MacLeod. The opera incorporated many of the tunes she had published, and was subsequently broadcast. JP

• Kennedy-Fraser, M. (1909, 1917, 1921, repr. 1922) *Songs of the Hebrides,* vols I, II, III, (1913) *Sea-Tangle, Some More Songs* of the Hebrides, (1922) *Hebridean Song and the Laws of Interpretation,* (1922) *Scots Folk Song,* (1923) *The Kennedy-Fraser Collection of Part-Songs,* (n.d., c. 1925) *From the Hebrides,* (1929) *A Life of Song.*

Campbell, J. L. (1958) 'Songs of the Hebrides', *The Scots Magazine,* Jan., pp. 307–14; Campbell, J. L. and Collinson, F. (1981) *Hebridean Folksongs,* vol. III, pp. 324–36; Lindsay, M. (1957) 'Songs of the Hebrides'; *Marjory Kennedy-Fraser – tributes . . . together with the memorial services in London & Edinburgh,* 1930, 1931; *The Scottish Field,* Nov. 1957, pp. 42–4; *ODNB* (2004).

KEPPEL, Alice Frederica, n. **Edmonstone,** born Woolwich 29 April 1868, died Italy 11 Sept. 1947. Mistress of Edward VII. Daughter of Mary Elizabeth Parsons, and Sir William Edmonstone, 4th Bt and naval commodore.

Alice Edmonstone grew up in the two family homes of Duntreath Castle and 11 Ainslie Place, Edinburgh. The youngest of nine children, she married George Keppel (1865–1947), son of the Earl of Albemarle, in 1891, and moved to London. It was probably in 1898 that she met the Prince of Wales. She quickly became his mistress, and continued as such when he became King in 1901 and until his death in 1910. He was alleged to be the father of her second daughter, Sonia, born in 1900. Mrs Keppel's position as royal mistress was widely acknowledged. Queen Alexandra disliked but unwillingly put up with her, and George Keppel appears to have accepted the situation uncomplainingly. Alice Keppel and Edward VII often attended functions together, and spent an annual holiday in Biarritz where they could almost behave as husband and wife. Mrs Keppel's position gave her considerable wealth and a certain amount of political influence. After the King's death she was no longer welcome among the royals. She travelled abroad, then returned to London as a society hostess. In the 1920s, her daughter Violet (Trefusis) conducted a very public lesbian affair with Vita Sackville-West, causing her embarrassment. In 1925, the Keppels bought a villa in Tuscany where they lived the rest of their lives, with the exception of the wartime years. Having returned to Italy, they both died there in 1947 and are buried in Florence. FJ
• Lamont-Brown, R. (2001) *Edward VII's Last Loves: Alice Keppel & Agnes Keyser; ODNB* (2004); Souhami, D. (1996) *Mrs Keppel and her Daughter.*

KER, Alice Jane Shannan Stewart,‡ n. **Ker,** born Deskford, Banffshire, 2 Dec. 1853, died London 20 March 1943. Doctor, health educator and suffrage campaigner. Daughter of Margaret Millar Stevenson, and William Turnbull Ker, Free Church minister.

Alice Ker was the eldest of nine children. Her mother came from a well-to-do middle-class family – two of Margaret Stevenson's five sisters, the 'Stevenson aunts' *Louisa and *Flora, were influential philanthropists and women's rights campaigners in Edinburgh. At 18, Alice Ker attended University Classes for Ladies in Edinburgh, where she met the women who, under the leadership of *Sophia Jex-Blake, fought for medical education for women. The University of Edinburgh did not issue degrees to women students, so in 1873 she enrolled for classes begun in London by Sophia Jex-Blake. In 1876, she became a Licentiate of the King and Queen's College of Physicians, Ireland, and the thirteenth woman on the British Medical Register. After a year in Berne, Switzerland, her first post was as House Surgeon to the Children's Hospital in Birmingham. In 1884, she became a GP in Leeds, then moved to Edinburgh where the Edinburgh Royal College of Surgeons admitted women to the Conjoint Examinations in 1886, and her name is among the 119 entrants (only one other was female) who passed the finals that year, achieving her aim of qualifying in Britain.

In 1888, Alice Ker married her cousin, Edward Stewart Ker (1839–1907), and moved to Birkenhead, where he was a shipping merchant. In 1890, they had a son, who died in infancy, and two daughters, Margaret and Mary, were born in 1892 and 1896. Soon she had a thriving medical practice, the only woman doctor in the area. She became MO to female staff of the Post Office, to the Birkenhead Lying-In Hospital, the Birkenhead Rescue Home and the Caledonian Free Schools, Liverpool. She was involved with social reform through the Ladies' Sanitary Association and the Ladies' Temperance Association and in 1891 joined the NUWSS. She gave lectures to working-class women in Manchester on sexuality, motherhood and birth control, which were published as *Motherhood: A Book for Every Woman* (1891). She tried to be as frank as Victorian mores allowed and with her interest in female hygiene and healthy lifestyles for women on a low budget she was an early exponent of preventive medicine. She was also a vegetarian and anti-vivisectionist.

Her husband's sudden death in 1907 left her with sole financial responsibility for the family. Through Fabian and Socialist friends in Liverpool,

Alice Ker and her 17-year-old daughter Margaret became active in the WSPU. In 1912, she took part in a window-smashing raid in London, for which she received a two-month sentence in Holloway Prison. There she wrote a series of letters to her daughters about her motives for taking part in the raid and her life in prison. Margaret Ker, a university student, was herself sentenced to three months in Walton Goal, Liverpool, for militant action. In November 1916, Alice Ker moved to London where she continued in practice, taking school and baby clinics well into her 70s. To her many commitments she added theosophy and, after the First World War, the women's peace movement. MVH

• Museum of London: Suffragette Fellowship collection; The Women's Library, London: GB 9/29, 'Autograph Letters Collection, Letters of Rosa May Billington and Dr Alice Ker', 1912–70; Dr Alice Ker's diaries 1872–1942 (family papers).
Ker, A. Works as above, and (1884) *Lectures to Women*.
Stevenson, L. (1914) 'Recollections of the public work and home life of Louisa and Flora Stevenson', printed for private circulation.
AGC; Helmond, M. van (1992) *Votes for Women: the events on Merseyside 1870–1928*; Jex-Blake, S. (1886) *Medical Women*; Lytton, C. (1914) *Prisons and Prisoners*; *ODNB* (2004); Waller, P. J. (1981) *Democracy and Sectarianism: a political and social history of Liverpool 1868–1939*.

KER, Dame Elizabeth ('Old Lady Buccleuch'), born c. 1478, died Catslak Tower, 19 Oct. 1548. Victim of a bloodfeud. Daughter of Isabel Hay of Yester, and Walter Ker of Cessford.

Dame Elizabeth Ker married first Sir Walter Scott of Buccleuch (d. 1504) and second Philip Rutherford of that Ilk (d. c. 1498). She had been a widow for 44 years and was 70 years old when in 1548 her tower at Catslak in Ettrick Forest was attacked by an English army, assisted by the Kers of Cessford, and she was burned to death. The Kers intentionally targeted Scott lands as part of an ongoing bloodfeud. The Scotts had also reverted to supporting the Scottish crown, unlike the Kers who remained pledged to England. Elizabeth Ker's own kinship to the Kers of Cessford and her advanced age were shamefully ignored. The Kers were indicted, but never punished, and the bloodfeud persisted until 1598. MMM

• NAS: GD224/529/1/108, Buccleuch Muniments.
Meikle, M. M. (1997) 'Victims, viragos and vamps . . .', in J. C. Appleby and P. Dalton (eds) *Government, Religion and Society in Northern England 1000–1700*, p. 174; *SP*, ii, 228, vii, pp. 331–2, 367 (Bibl.)

KERR, Isabella (Isabel),‡ n. **Gunn**, born Enzie, Banff, 30 May 1875, died India 12 Jan. 1932. Medical missionary. Daughter of Mary Garden, and John Bain Gunn, farmer.

After graduating MBChB (Aberdeen), Isabel Kerr went out to Hyderabad with her Wesleyan missionary husband, Rev. G. M. Kerr, a former joiner, in 1907. Having learned to speak Telugu, she set up wayside dispensaries and travelled from village to village by bullock cart. On discovering the extent of suffering from leprosy in Nizamabad, she opened her first home for lepers at Dichpali in 1915, at first offering only palliative care. Funded by a wealthy Hindu, the home served every religion and caste. In 1921, Isabel Kerr was enabled to do pioneering curative treatment of leprosy by intramuscular injections of hyndocarpus oil, following the discoveries of Leonard Rogers and Edwin Muir. In addition to her teaching work at Dichpali and her later clinic in Hyderabad, Isabel Kerr travelled hundreds of miles, reaching Muslim women lepers secluded in *Zenanas* (women's quarters). It is estimated that of her 2,800 patients, more than a thousand had their disease arrested. She was awarded the Kaiser-I-Hind gold medal (1923). SO

• *Aberdeen Press and Journal*, 24 Dec. 1932; Oldfield, S. (2001) *Women Humanitarians*; Monahan, D. (1938) *The Lepers of Dichpali*; Rogers, L. and Muir, E. (1925) *Leprosy*; *The Times*, 24 Dec. 1932.

KERRIGAN, Rose, n. **Klasko,** born Dublin 11 Feb. 1903, died London 10 July 1995. Communist activist.

Rose Klasko was born into a Jewish family, the second of five children. Her father, a tailor, came from Siberia and her mother from Lithuania. The family moved to Glasgow where she attended Stow School during the day and Hebrew School in the evenings. She also attended the Socialist Sunday School, listened to debates at Glasgow Green and quickly became involved in political work. At the outbreak of the First World War she was hounded at school for being anti-war. She was active in the rent strikes led by *Mary Barbour. Rose Klasko worked from age 14 and experienced anti-Semitism before finding employment in a department store at Trongate, from which she was sacked because of her anti-war views. Later, she learned tailoring from her father. She was present on 31 January 1919 at the demonstration in George Square in support of the 40-hour strike that became a battle with the police, with many injured.

Greatly influenced by the Russian Revolution, Rose Klasko was a foundation member of the CPGB in January 1921. In 1926, she married Peter Kerrigan (1899–1977), NUWM organiser and industrial organiser of the CPGB. They had three daughters. Both were involved in the National Minority Movement and she was a member of the TGWU and of the SAU. As a young married woman, she supported *Marie Stopes's work in family planning, strongly aware of the restricted role women had, even in socialist politics. Rose Kerrigan, her husband and their three-year-old daughter, also Rose, visited the Soviet Union in 1935, where she worked in an office while Peter Kerrigan was working for the Communist International. They moved to London in 1939. There she worked for Prudential Insurance, organising a women's branch of the union. In 1987, Rose Kerrigan visited Cuba. In 1993, she appeared in *Time Gentlemen Please*, a BBC Scotland documentary about women in the early 20th century, and in 1996 a short film *A Red Rose* was made about her. N R

• GCU, Gallacher Memorial Library: Rose Kerrigan archive. Interview with Audrey Canning, 21 August 1987; Interview with author 9 July 1995; Questionnaire returned to author 1995.

A Red Rose, National Film and Television School, 1996; Gallacher, W. (1978) *Revolt on the Clyde*; *Glasgow Herald*, 20 July 1995 (obit.); *Granma* [Cuban political weekly] 18 April 1987; *Scottish Marxist*, No 2, Winter, 1972; *The Guardian,* 19 July 1995 (obit.).

KESSON, Jessie, n. **MacDonald,** born Inverness 29 Oct. 1916, died London 26 Dec. 1994. Novelist and radio playwright. Daughter (out of wedlock) of Elizabeth MacDonald, domestic servant turned occasional prostitute.

Born in a workhouse, Jessie MacDonald's early life was spent in Elgin's model lodging house and an Elgin slum made famous in her first and best-known novel, *The White Bird Passes* (1958). Her childhood was spent in poverty and in fear of the 'Cruelty Man' and she was eventually removed from her mother, who was charged with neglect, and sent to an orphanage at Kirkton of Skene where she remained until she left school at 16. Her mother, whom she dearly loved and who taught her poetry, contracted syphilis and was institutionalised until her death in 1949.

Jessie MacDonald was an excellent scholar, but was not allowed the university education she yearned for. She failed at farm and shop work and

endured miserable years in a hostel in Aberdeen, before a breakdown led to a traumatic year in a mental hospital. Sent to convalesce near Loch Ness, she met and in 1937 married Johnnie Kesson (1905–94) and the two spent some years as farm workers in the North East of Scotland, in wretched tied cottar houses in conditions she described in her fiction. She began writing, often about her early life, for Scottish magazines in 1941 and for the BBC in Aberdeen in 1945, where her radio plays were well respected by the time the Kessons and their two children moved to London in 1951.

Her husband was never strong, and Jessie Kesson took on a range of difficult jobs – night carer, cleaner, running old people's homes – as well as others she preferred, such as psychodrama with disturbed teenagers, deputy head of a further education institution, artist's model, and part-time producer on *Woman's Hour*. Her play *The Childhood* (1949) resulted in a Scottish Home Department investigation into the policy of boarding out the children of problem parents as far away as possible from their influence. Her novel *Glitter of Mica* (1963) is an unhappy tale of farm workers, detailing oppressive conditions and sexual frustration. *Another Time, Another Place* (1983) shows that a young woman charged to look after Italian prisoners of war on a farm in the Black Isle is more a prisoner than they are. She often used radio to hone subjects for her fiction. The play *Somewhere Beyond* (1961) is a fictional rendering of her unhappiest teenage years; it seemed to exorcise them, freeing her to choose less personal subjects, such as the novella *Where the Apple Ripens* (1985). *The White Bird Passes* was successfully dramatised for television in 1981, while *Another Time, Another Place* (1983) was made into a prize-winning film. More important for the education-hungry writer, she was awarded honorary degrees by the universities of Dundee (1984) and Aberdeen (1987).

Nursing her increasingly frail husband, she died only six weeks after him in 1994. She had famously invented her own epitaph: 'Here, very much against *her* will, lies JK'. But a stone did not seem appropriate; their ashes were scattered at Abriachan, where they met, and a rowan tree was planted as a memorial. I M

• NLS: Acc. 7845, Jessie Kesson papers; Univ. of Reading Library: Chatto & Windus archive; BBC archive, Caversham.

Kesson, J., Works as above and see *HSWW* (Bibl.).
Anderson, J. (2001) 'That great brute of a bunion! The construction of masculinity in Jessie Kesson's *Glitter of Mica*',

Scot. Studies Rev., 21, Spring; *HSWW* (Bibl.); Murray, I. (2000) *Jessie Kesson: writing her life*; Norquay, G. (2000) 'Borderlines: Jessie Kesson's *The White Bird Passes*', in C. Anderson and A. Christianson (eds) *Scottish Women's Fiction, 1920s to 1960s*; *ODNB* (2004).

KESWICK, Margaret (Maggie),‡ m. **Jencks,** born London 10 Oct. 1941, died London 8 July 1995. Garden designer, writer, inspiration for the Maggie's Centres. Daughter of Clare Elwes, and Sir John Keswick, businessman.

As the only child of Sir John Keswick, Taipan (MD) of the Jardine Matheson business empire, Maggie Keswick's education took her from Shanghai and Hong Kong to Britain, where she read English at the University of Oxford. After a brief foray into the fashion business, she went on to study at the Architectural Association in London, where she met Charles Jencks, post-modern architect and writer, whom she married in 1978. In that year, she published *The Chinese Garden: history, art and architecture,* still widely regarded as the standard work on Chinese gardens. As well as contributing to *The Oxford Companion to Gardens* (1986), she also edited a history of Jardine Matheson (1982). Her upbringing in China and her fascination with meaning and function in landscape were reflected in the garden that she and Charles Jencks went on to develop at her family home of Portrack, near Dumfries, after 1988.

Having survived breast cancer in 1988, she was diagnosed with inoperable cancer in 1993. Her determination to fight the disease led her to try a number of alternative therapies before her death in the summer of 1995. Having seen for herself the problems of providing appropriate care for cancer patients within the NHS, she decided to do what she could to provide a more caring and patient-oriented environment for their treatment. During a brief period of remission in 1994, she worked on plans for a new Cancer Caring Centre at the Western General Hospital in Edinburgh (opened in 1996) and went on to publish *A View from the Front Line* (1994). Together with her *Blueprint and Constitution for a Cancer Caring Centre* (1995), this has served as the inspiration for the growing number of Maggie's Centres being developed in Scotland, all of them notable for their architecture and landscape setting. CHD

• Keswick, M., Works as above and (2003) *The Chinese Garden: history, art and architecture*, with an introduction by Alison Hardie.

Jencks, C. (2003) *The Garden of Cosmic Speculation.*

KEYZER, Isabella, n. **Mitchell,** born Dundee 29 August 1922, died Dundee 18 July 1992. Weaver and welder. Daughter of Isabella Campbell, confectionery worker and part-time cleaner, and Thomas Mitchell, foreman baker and trade unionist.

Bella Mitchell left school aged 14; after training and working as a canvas weaver, she entered a munitions factory in 1941. She then trained as a welder and worked in the Caledon shipyard in Dundee until she was made redundant at the end of the war. In 1949, she migrated to Holland with her husband, Dirk Keyzer, adjutant, Royal Dutch Navy, and their son, before returning with her family in 1957 and joining the largely female workforce in Dundee's expanding light engineering sector. In the mid-1970s, dissatisfied with assembly line work, she took a welding course at Dundee Technical College and subsequently found employment with a small firm. Her aim of returning to shipyard welding was less easily fulfilled and she began to resort to applying to the yards as 'Mr I. Keyzer'. Finally, she found work with the same company who had employed her during the war – a victory she considered important not only personally, but also for women's rights generally. She later said, 'they were all expecting this young dolly bird to come doon, and doon comes this fat grey-haired wifie' (DOHP).

Bella Keyzer was an articulate socialist feminist who appeared in a number of television programmes recorded in the late 1980s. She said that her reflections on the gendered construction of skill and occupation were a result of her working experiences. In 1992, Dundee District Council presented her with a special award in recognition of her work to promote women's equality in Dundee. She always insisted that she was an atypical representative of women in Dundee. GRS

• Dundee Central Library, Wellgate Centre, Dundee: Dundee Oral History Project Archive, Interview with Bella Keyzer, DOHP 022, interview by Elizabeth Feeney, recorded 14/11/1985 and 25/11/1985.

Holdsworth, A. (1988) *Out of the Dolls' House: the story of women in the twentieth century*; *ODNB* (2004); Smith, G. (1990) 'None Can Compare', in B. Kay (ed.) *The Dundee Book.*

KIDD, Margaret Henderson, DBE, m. **Macdonald,** born Carriden, Bo'ness, 14 March 1900, died Cambridge 22 March 1989. Pioneer lawyer. Daughter of Janet Gardner Turnbull, teacher, and James Kidd, solicitor, MP for West Lothian.

At a time when few careers were open to women, Margaret Kidd, the eldest of nine children, benefited from her father's example, making her own career in the law. After attending Linlithgow Academy, she graduated in law at the University of Edinburgh in 1922, and the following year was the first woman to be admitted to the Scottish Bar. Becoming a member of the Faculty of Advocates, she was the second British woman to practise as an advocate. Until 1949, Margaret Kidd remained the only female representative on the faculty, but never prosecuted for the Crown. She defended capably, often in poignant family cases, such as that of a mother who had accidentally smothered her child. In a brief sortie into politics at the request of the Unionist Party, she stood for a by-election in 1928 in West Lothian, but lost to Independent Labour candidate Manny Shinwell.

She married in 1930 Donald S. Macdonald (d. 1958), a fellow lawyer, and they had one daughter. Active in other fields, Margaret Kidd in 1946 became a reporter for the *Scots Law Times* and editor of the Court of Session Reports until 1976. In 1948, she became the first woman QC (Scotland) and was later Sheriff Principal of Dumfries and Galloway (1960–6) and Sheriff Principal of Perth and Angus (1966–74). She was created DBE in 1975. Keeper of the Advocates' Library for 14 years, she eventually received the title of 'Father [sic] of the Scottish Bar', as well as honorary degrees from Dundee (1982) and Edinburgh (1984). A strong personality, she paved the way for other women in her profession. LS

• Cowan, M. G., Williamson, M. G., Kidd, M. H., Martin, J. (1924) *Political Realism by Four Scottish Unionists*; *ODNB* (2004); *SB*; *The Times*, 26 March 1989 (obit.); *Who's Who*.

KING, Ellen Elizabeth, m1 **MacPherson,** m2 **Pearson,** born Renfrew 16 Jan. 1909, died Chester area Feb. 1994. Swimming champion. Daughter of Florence Pearson, and Benjamin King, storekeeper.

Ellen King was described as one of the world's greatest all-round swimmers in 1928. She was one of the few Scottish women to win Olympic medals that year: silver in both the 100 yards backstroke and the 100 yards freestyle relay at the Amsterdam Olympic Games. As women's captain of the Scottish team at the 1930 inaugural Empire Games, Hamilton, Canada, she won silver in the 100 yards freestyle and bronze in the 400 yards freestyle. In total, Ellen King won six British swimming championships, two Olympic and two Commonwealth medals and set two world records. In 1927, she set a world best of

3 minutes, 2 seconds in the 200 yards breaststroke and the following year a world best of 1 minute, 57.2 seconds in the 150 yards backstroke. In 1945, she married Bobby McPherson, taxicab hirer, who died in 1957. Ellen King taught swimming in Edinburgh schools until her retirement in 1974. That year she remarried, to Alfred Pearson, a retired builder. One of only five women to appear among the first 50 athletes to be inducted into the Scottish Sports Hall of Fame in 2002, she was arguably the best all-round swimmer of her era. GJ

• 'Scotland's 100 Greatest Sporting Moments', Part 2, *Scotland on Sunday*, 16 Sept. 2001, p. 18.
'History' at www.cgcs.org.uk
Additional information: Anne Lynas Shah.

KING (or Kean), Jessie, born Glasgow 27 March 1861, died Edinburgh 11 March 1889. Childminder. Daughter of Grace Liddell, and James Kean, warper.

Jessie King moved, following her mother's death, from Glasgow to Edinburgh where she worked as a laundress. She met and moved in with the much older Thomas Pearson. In 1887, her three-week-old child died. She then 'adopted' at least three babies; all either disappeared or were found dead in suspicious circumstances. The discovery of the third on waste land prompted her arrest. In court, Jessie King was described as a small, slight woman, dressed respectably and older in appearance than her 27 years. She was found guilty of murder and sentenced to hang on 11 March 1889, an unusually harsh punishment. She had given birth to another child just a few months before her arrest and tried to end her own life in prison.

Jessie King was labelled a callous baby-farmer, a woman who took in babies for money with the intention of killing them, a concern that lay behind the introduction of the Infant Life Protection Act 1872. It is likely, however, that she was a vulnerable working-class woman whose solution to her financial and emotional instability was to take advantage of desperate mothers of illegitimate babies and the lax adoption laws. LCA

• NAS: JC26/1408 High Court Process; AD14/89/146 precognition.
Abrams, L. (1998) *The Orphan Country: children of Scotland's broken homes, 1845 to the present day*; Arnot, M. L. (1994) 'Infant death, child care and the state: the baby-farming scandal and the first Infant Life Protection Legislation of 1872', *Continuity & Change*, 9, pp. 271–311.

KING, Jessie Marion,‡ m. **Taylor,** born Bearsden 20 March 1875, died Kirkcudbright 3 August 1949.

Illustrator and designer. Daughter of Mary Ann Anderson, and Rev. James W. King.

Jessie M. King studied at Queen Margaret College and GSA, quickly achieving recognition for her imaginative book illustration in a distinctive rhythmic linear style which regularly featured in *The Studio* magazine, and for which she received a gold medal at the Turin International Exhibition in 1902. Often based on legends and fairy tales, her work was also exhibited in Berlin, Calcutta and Cork. From 1899, she taught design for the bookbinding course at GSA; in 1904 she took temporary charge of the Embroidery Department and in 1907 taught ceramic design. The most commercially successful of the designers associated with the Glasgow Style, her diverse work included silver, jewellery and textiles, some of which was sold by Liberty & Co., as well as gesso panels, wallpapers, posters, bookplates and costumes for masques and pageants. Later she designed interiors and mural decoration.

In 1908, she married Ernest Archibald Taylor (1874–1951) but, always independently minded, she retained her own name, unusually for the time. They had one daughter. Ernest Taylor's career as a designer took them to Manchester and in 1911 to Paris, where they established a small studio gallery. During this time, Jessie M. King discovered the technique of batik, which she continued to develop after their enforced return to Scotland on the outbreak of the First World War. They settled in Greengate Close, Kirkcudbright, which became a focus for her many friends in the GSLA with whom she regularly exhibited. Here she produced quantities of decorated ceramics as well as watercolour paintings. Summers were spent on Arran where she and her husband held sketching classes. Her reputation has risen steadily after a long period of eclipse. LA

• Univ. of Glasgow Library, Special Collections: Jessie M. King Collection.

Burkhauser, J. (ed.) (1990) *Glasgow Girls*, pp. 133–9; Cumming, E. (ed.) (1992) *Glasgow 1900 Art & Design*; *ODNB* (2004); (1977) *The Private Library*, second series, 10, 3, Autumn, 'Towards a checklist of books illustrated by Jessie M. King'; White, C. (ed.) (1989) *The Enchanted World of Jessie M. King*.

KING, Mary, n. **Kerr,** born Bellshiel, near Swinton, Berwickshire, 12 Dec. 1905, died Edinburgh 25 May 1998. Bondager and domestic servant. Daughter of Isabella Paxton, domestic servant, and Andrew Kerr, ploughman.

The eldest of eight children, Mary Kerr was born out of wedlock; her parents married soon after her birth. The family lived in a series of tied cottages without running water, as her father moved from farm to farm in the Borders. After village school at St Abbs and Coldingham, she left at 13 to become first a domestic helper, then a bondager to her father at Temple Hall Farm, Reston, where he was first ploughman: 'Ah didnae sign any papers, nothing like that. . . . Ah wid jist be telt, "Ye're gaun tae work oot." And that wis that'. The work included singling (thinning) turnips, planting and digging potatoes, mucking out byres, repairing sacks, driving a cart, stooking sheaves at harvest and loading. As a bondager, she worked the same hours as the men: 6am to 6pm or longer, six days a week, for 13s (65p), rising after three or four years to £1. But the farmer never handed her her wages: they went into her father's pay packet. After moving to a farm near Duns with the family, she left home at 19 to become a kitchen maid, making way for her sisters to replace her as bondager. In 1928, she married a local woodcutter and they had four children, one of whom died in infancy. Mary King had to give up her job on marriage, but later worked part-time in the fields. One of very few Scottish bondagers whose life has been recorded in depth, she said in retrospect, 'Ah think the fields wis hard, awfy hard work, and gey often in a' weathers'. IMacD

• Interview with Mary King by Ian MacDougall, 1997 (source of all quotations). MacDougall, I. (2001) *Bondagers*, Scottish Working People's History Trust; Robertson, B. (1990) 'In bondage: the female farm worker in south-east Scotland', in E. Gordon and E. Breitenbach (eds) *The World is Ill-Divided*.

KINNEAR, Georgina, born Edinburgh c. 1826/27, died Edinburgh 26 April 1914. Governess and headmistress. Daughter of Mary Smith, and John Gardiner Kinnear, Glasgow merchant.

Educated at home, Georgina Kinnear, then in her 30s, was permitted by her parents to accompany family friends to The Hague and then to St Petersburg in 1860. After becoming fluent in Russian, she was governess to the family of Nicolai Milyutin, radical politician in the liberal government of Tsar Alexander II, who reputedly consulted her about British political methods (Murray 1914, p. 529). The secondary and higher education of women and girls had become of particular interest to her and she returned to Britain permanently in 1874 to promote this. After gaining experience at Cheltenham Ladies College, in 1877 she was appointed, at *Louisa Lumsden's request, as a founder member of staff at St Andrews School for Girls (later St Leonards School). In 1880 she was appointed the first headmistress of The Park School, Glasgow, where she remained for 20 years. A stimulating and original teacher, and an ardent Liberal and reformer, she was 'a charming but formidable woman, full of new ideas of a woman's place in the world' (Lightwood 1980, p. 29). LRM

• NAS: ED17/97 (school inspection reports); Univ. of Leeds, Brotherton Library Special Collections: MS 851 (20th century corr. about Kinnear).

Kinnear, G. (1904) *The Use of Words.*

Lightwood, J. (1980) *The Park School, 1880–1980*; Murray, M. (1914) 'Georgina Kinnear', *The Journal of Education*, July, pp. 529–30; *ODNB* (2004); *The Park School, Glasgow, 1880–1930* (1930).

KNIGHT, Annie Cargill, n. Murray, born Torphins, Aberdeenshire, 10 April 1906, died Dunfermline 4 Nov. 1996. Nurse in Spanish Civil War. Daughter of Anne Cargill, and George Wilson Murray, tenant farmer.

One of eight children – two brothers, Tom and George, fought in the International Brigades – Annie Murray finished training as a nurse at Edinburgh Royal Infirmary in 1936, just as the Spanish Civil War began. She had already been politically active, getting nurses to protest at conditions in the Infirmary, and she joined the Communist Party that year. 'I went to Spain', she said, 'because I believed in the cause of the Spanish Republican government'. One of the first British volunteers to arrive there, via the British Medical Aid Association, she was a nurse with Republican forces, at first at a small hospital in Huete, then with a Spanish medical group at a hospital in Barcelona, where she worked with Dr Quemada for the rest of the war, sometimes in hospital trains under bombardment. Most of her patients were Spanish Republican troops or International Brigaders, but included North African prisoners of war. Annie Murray left Barcelona as Franco's troops entered it, and recalled seeing atrocities caused by booby-trapped bombs during the retreat. The Spanish war 'had a terrific impact on me', she recalled. Later she worked in London, in civil defence, in nursing, and then in the Post Office until her retirement. In 1948, she had married Frank Knight, and they moved in 1978 to Cairneyhill near Dunfermline, dying within a few months of each other. IMacD

• MacDougall, I. (1986) *Voices from the Spanish Civil War* (and recorded interviews with subject), (2000) *Voices from Work and Home*; *The Herald*, Nov. 1996 (obit.).

KNIGHT, Mary Joan,‡ OBE, born Walton-le-Dale, Lancs., 27 Sept. 1924, died Perth 20 Dec. 1996. Theatre director. Daughter of Mary Cottam, and Henry Knight, market gardener.

Joan Knight directed from the age of five, producing plays at home on rainy days. Leaving school at 15, she became a Ministry of Agriculture and Fisheries secretary and also volunteered for the Land Army. Despite her youth, she directed for many amateur societies around Preston, qualified as LRAM and taught English and Drama at St Anne's College, St Anne's-on-Sea. In 1951, she took Bristol Old Vic Theatre School's one-year special technical course. Her stage management career started with Midland Theatre Company (1952–5), followed by Perth Theatre where she first directed professionally in 1957. Thereafter, she directed widely in the English regions, first directing a company of her own at Whitby (1958–60) and then becoming artistic director at the Castle Theatre, Farnham (1960–4). After further freelance years, including directing Patrick Stewart's 1965 Shylock at Bristol Old Vic, in 1968 she became artistic director of Perth Theatre (see Dence, Marjorie). She remained industrious and in demand, also running, for example, the Ludlow Festival for three years in the late 1960s, directing, among others, a well-remembered 1969 *Romeo and Juliet*, and resolving a crisis in 1976 and 1977 by serving as Pitlochry Festival Theatre's director of productions. She directed for most major regional playhouses. Her range is demonstrated by the fact that in addition to work at the Royal Court Theatre, invited there by Bill Gaskill to join his directing team, she was responsible for six annual West End re-directions of *The Mousetrap*. Early in her Perth career, Laurence Olivier offered her a National Theatre directorship, but she believed her art was best fulfilled by long-term commitment within a community. Even after her 1993 retirement, she directed, in her three remaining years, six plays at Pitlochry, concluding with a memorable production of Bridie's *Mr Bolfry* starring Jimmy Logan, nephew of *Georgina Allan.

Joan Knight was a renowned mentor. Important figures in all branches of theatre learned their crafts under her care. An attentive and perceptive director, she had the rare skills required to bring new drafts to full production. Committed to her art form's development, she served on the SAC drama and several other committees, becoming a council member (1980–6). She was also a governor of Queen Margaret University College (QMUC) (1983–8) and board member of Perth College (1993–6). She was made OBE in 1985. In the early 1990s, Lord Palumbo, then Chairman of the ACGB, with the support of the SAC twice strongly recommended her for a DBE; metropolitan myopia may have blocked both proposals. During her lifetime, theatre directors were predominantly Oxbridge-educated men. Setting her own mould, Joan Knight shaped Scottish and British theatre both directly and through her myriad protégés. She was made Hon DLitt by QMUC in 1996. IB

• Interviews with Christopher Denys, Isobel Lister (QMUC), Professor Clive Perry, Jeanette Tosh (Perth College), Antony Tuckey, Helen Williamson (Pitlochry Festival Theatre), Joyce Whiteside.
The Scotsman, 23 Dec. 1996 (obit.).
Personal knowledge.

L

LAIDLAW, Margaret, m. **Hogg,** born Ettrick 1730, died Ettrick 1813. Tradition-bearer. Daughter of Bessie Scott, and William Laidlaw, tenant farmer.

Margaret Laidlaw is remembered through the writing of her son, James Hogg (1770–1835). She was the eldest daughter of William Laidlaw ('Will o' Phaup'), an authority on traditional culture (as was her brother William), who was the tenant of Old Upper Phawhope, in Ettrick. In 1765, she married Robert Hogg (c. 1729–92), the tenant farmer of Ettrick House and Ettrick Hall, and they had four sons.

Her most famous appearance is in James Hogg's *Familiar Anecdotes of Sir Walter Scott* (1834), as a commentator on Scott's editing of her songs in *The Minstrelsy of the Scottish Border* (1802–3): 'they war made for singing, an' no for reading; and they're nouther right spelled nor right setten down' (Bold 2000, pp. 116–17). Scott wrote that Margaret Laidlaw, 'sings, or rather chants . . . with great animation' (ibid., p. 122). James Hogg was surprised at the extent of his mother's repertoire, leading Elaine Petrie to argue that her passive repertoire was activated by the Minstrelsy collection (Petrie 1983, pp. 34–8).

James Hogg's brother William, in the *New Monthly Magazine* of 1836, says their mother was a skilled narrator of 'tales and songs of spectres, ghosts, fairies, brownies, voices, &c. These had been both seen and heard in her time in the Glen of Phaup'. She was a deeply religious woman, and made sure her children knew their psalms.

There are tantalising glimpses of Margaret Laidlaw in James Hogg's work, in the spirited mother of 'The Marvellous Doctor' in *Blackwood's Edinburgh Magazine*, 21 (1827) and the reductive Scots-speaker of 'The Love Adventures of George Cochrane' in *Winter Evening Tales* (1820) vol. 1. She instructed him to set 'Athol Cummers' in *Songs* (1831): 'O man, it's a shame to hear sic a good tune an' nae words till't. Gae away ben the house, like a good lad, and mak' me a verse till't' (p. 191). In 1813, Hogg described his mother as 'the best friend that ever I had' (Miller 2003, p. 15) and his affection is reflected in 'A Last Adieu', in *Blackwood's* 1 (1817). Margaret Laidlaw was a profound influence on the writer of *The Private Memoirs and Confessions of a Justified Sinner* (1824). VB

• Bold, V. (2000) ' "Nouther right spelled nor right setten down": Scott, Child and the Hogg Family Ballads' in E. J. Cowan (ed.) *The Ballad in Scottish History*; Hogg, J. (1827) 'The shepherd's calendar', *Blackwood's Edinburgh Magazine*, 21, pp. 440–5; [1834] (1972) *Memoir of the Author's Life and Familiar Anecdotes of Sir Walter Scott*, D. S. Mack, ed.; Miller, K. (2003) *The Electric Shepherd*; Petrie, E. (1983) 'Odd characters: traditional informants in James Hogg's family', *Scottish Literary Journal*, 10, 1.

LAIDLAW, Robena Anna (later **Anna Robena),** m. **Thomson,** born Bretton, Yorkshire, 30 April 1819, died London 29 May 1901. Pianist. Daughter of Ann Keddy, and Alexander Laidlaw, merchant.

Robena Laidlaw was born into a well-placed Borders family, intimate with Sir Walter Scott. In 1827 they moved to Edinburgh where she studied with Robert Müller, continuing her studies in Königsberg in 1830. In her teens she performed in Berlin, Leipzig and, in 1832, at Paganini's farewell concert in London: he wrote of the 'prodigious effect she produced', professing 'never to have heard [the piano] treated so magnificently' (Patterson 1903, p. 91). Further study followed in London. In 1837, she became intimate with Schumann, who suggested she transpose her first names as being 'more

musical'. She was the dedicatee of his *Fantasiestücke*, Opus 12: 'I have not asked for permission to make this dedication, but they belong to you, and the whole "Rosenthal" with its romantic surroundings, is in the music' (ibid., p. 98) – a reference to a walk in the Rose Valley when Schumann gave her a flawless rose. Of her personality, he wrote that it 'united English solidity and natural amiability', and of her playing, in the Leipzig Gewandhaus, that it was 'thoroughly good and individual' (*Neue Zeitschrift für Musik*, 11 Sept. 1837). Following a tour in Prussia, Russia and Austria, Anna Laidlaw was appointed pianist to the Queen of Hanover, but settled in London in 1840. In 1852, she married George Thomson, a fellow Scot, and this ended her career. They had four daughters. JP
• Farmer, H. G. (1947) *A History of Music in Scotland*, pp. 449–50; Nauhaus, G. (1987) *Robert Schumann Tagebücher*, Band II 1836–54, pp. 22, 33 and note, 279, 303, 319; *ODNB* (2004); Patterson, A. W. (1903, rev. edn. 1934) *Schumann*, pp. 90–9.

LAMOND, Mary, born Edinburgh 22 Feb. 1862, died 15 March 1949. Deaconess and president, Church of Scotland Woman's Guild. Daughter of Elizabeth Thomas Deans, and William Lamond, Advocate.

When Mary Lamond succeeded Lady Polwarth as president of the Woman's Guild in 1920, she had already served the church as a deaconess for 26 years, including time as head of the training house for the order, which provided residential training courses for women preparing for full-time mission work at home and abroad. A woman of considerable administrative skills, she had previously been secretary of the Guild for six years and had also edited its supplement to the Church's magazine, *Life & Work*. Her organisational abilities were instrumental in streamlining this burgeoning movement and in giving it much-needed cohesion. The grouping of guilds in Presbyterial Councils, the tradition of national office bearers paying visits to all councils, and the large annual meeting continue to the present day. Her presidency (1920–32) spanned the years of the general strike and depression and she responded to the consequent social deprivation by mobilising the practical skills of Guild members in providing food, linen and clothing for the needy. She was also determined that women's voices should be heard and organised courses in public speaking for Guild members, as well as encouraging participation in group discussions. Her experience and clear thinking helped to merge the two women's organisations of

the denominations involved in the union of 1929. In retirement she remained open to new challenges, reading history and learning Hebrew in order to study the psalms. AT
• Church of Scotland Guild (1957) *Through the Years: some aspects of guild life and work*; Magnusson, M. (1987) *Out of Silence.*

LARNER, Christina (Kirsty), n. **Ross,** born London 22 Nov. 1933, died Glasgow 27 April 1983. Historian. Daughter of Nella Wallace, and John Ross, senior civil servant.

The daughter of highly educated parents, Christina Ross gained her PhD from the University of Edinburgh in 1962. She subsequently became senior lecturer and, briefly, Professor in the Department of Sociology at the University of Glasgow. She had married Professor John Larner, a historian of Renaissance Italy, in 1960, and they had two sons.

Christina Larner acquired an admirable academic reputation during her lifetime: in 1982, she was asked to give the Gifford lectures. However, particular acclaim has come to her posthumously for her work on European and particularly Scottish witchcraft. Her growing reputation is based largely on two books: the first, *A Source-book of Scottish Witchcraft* (1977, 2005), was compiled jointly with Christopher Hyde Lee and Hugh V. McLachlan, and is still the most authoritative general reference work on the topic. Even more significant is *Enemies of God* (1981), a book in which she addressed what have become the acknowledged central questions regarding witchcraft accusations and prosecution, with particular reference to Scotland in the 16th and 17th centuries. She considered witch-hunting as a sort of women-hunting, and argued that it was a '. . . rearguard action against the emergence of women as independent adults . . .' (1981, p. 101). Kirsty, as she was known socially, loved playing the cello, fly-fishing for trout and drinking malt whisky. After long and recurrent periods of illness, borne with inspiring stoicism, she died aged 49. HMCL
• Larner, C., Works as above and (1982) *The Thinking Peasant* (The Gifford Lectures), (1983) *Witchcraft and Religion.* Private information: John Larner and Gavin Larner.

LAUDERDALE, Elizabeth, Duchess of *see* **MURRAY, Lady Elizabeth, Countess of Dysart** (baptised 1626, d. 1698)

LAWS, Margaret Troup, n. **Gray,** born Aberdeen, 4 Feb. 1849, died Edinburgh 17 Sept. 1921. Teacher, translator, missionary. Daughter of Mary Gordon, and Charles Gray, clerk.

The fifth of nine children, Margaret Gray grew up in a household where learning was encouraged. A dictionary and an atlas were kept at the ready on the family dinner table. She attended the Sunday school at St Nicholas Lane United Presbyterian church, run by Janet Melville, which produced several missionaries, including her future husband, Robert Laws (1851–1934). Having trained and worked as a teacher, Margaret Gray became engaged to Robert Laws in 1875 and, after a long engagement while he became established as a medical missionary, they married in Africa in 1879. Their only child, Amelia Nyasa Laws, born 1886, was sent back to Scotland for her education at the age of eight. For most of her 40 years at Livingstonia, Nyasaland (now Malawi), Margaret Laws concentrated on teaching, studying the Chinyanja language, and producing religious and educational material in that language. During visits to Scotland she was in great demand as a speaker. She returned to Scotland in failing health and died there. ATM

• Univ. of Aberdeen, Special Archives: Six boxes of uncatalogued material relating to Laws family; Univ. of Edinburgh, New College Archives: Laws papers.

Laws, R. (1886) *Women's Work in Livingstonia*; McIntosh, H. (1993) *Robert Laws, Servant of Africa*; Thomson, D. P. (1975) *Women of the Scottish Church.*

LEE, Janet (Jennie), Baroness of Asheridge,‡ m. **Bevan,** born Lochgelly, Fife, 3 Nov. 1904, died London 16 Nov. 1988. Politician, writer and lecturer. Daughter of Euphemia Greig, cook and hotel manager, and James Lee, coal miner, hotel manager and ILP activist.

Brought up in Fife, one of two surviving children, Jennie Lee was educated at Beath Secondary School and the University of Edinburgh, graduating MA and LLB and with a teaching certificate and diploma in education. An ILP activist, she won the North Lanark Labour selection over the miners' nominee, overturning a Tory majority at the 1929 by-election and becoming the youngest woman elected to the House of Commons. Beautiful and passionate, she made an immediate impact, linking herself with figures of the left such as James Maxton, Ellen Wilkinson, and Frank Wise, a married man with whom she fell in love. After Frank Wise's sudden death in 1933, she married leading Labour politician Aneurin (Nye) Bevan (1897–1960) in October 1934, inaugurating a long partnership.

Defeated at the 1931 National Government landslide, Jennie Lee became involved in bitter disputes involving party discipline versus principle. She could not bear to leave the ILP over the break with Labour, an attitude that led Nye Bevan to call her 'my Salvation Army lassie' (Brown 1988, p. 310). The decision sidelined her as Bevan became better known. Although she kept her own name, '[over] the years, the balance in their marriage changed' to the point of what Barbara Castle called 'Nyedolatry' (Hollis 1997, p. 84). Failure to recapture North Lanark in 1935 took her out of Scottish politics, but in 1945 she was elected MP for Cannock and closely supported Nye Bevan in his role as leader of the Labour left and Minister of Health after 1945, sharing in his victories and defeats. His death in 1960 devastated her and 'she felt that he had been murdered [by attacks upon him]' (*DNB* 1991, p. 260). When later she was promoted by Harold Wilson, the most notable of her political appointments was as first Minister for the Arts from 1964 to 1970. She gave the arts a public profile for the first time. She was also the chief architect of the Open University, set up in 1971, the lasting legacy of this controversial and charismatic politician who had lost her Cannock seat in 1970.

Jennie Lee did not identify with the promotion of women in politics *per se*, stating, 'I shall always vote on policy issues, not on the sex of the candidate' (Lee 1981, p. 168). However, her suppression of her own career in favour of Bevan's was 'all the more remarkable because as a woman in politics she had always laid claim to a "male" life, public, itinerant, and unencumbered by family responsibilities' (Hollis 1997, p. viii). At the same time she had the benefit of support from her Scottish family, most notably her mother, 'Ma Lee', who lived with and cared for her for many years both before and after Nye's death. She became a life peer in 1970, and was awarded an honorary LLD from the University of Cambridge in 1974. CB

• Open Univ. Library Archival Collection, Walton Hall: Jennie Lee corr.

Lee, J. (1939) *Tomorrow is a New Day*, (1981) *My Life with Nye.*

Brown, G. (1988) *Maxton*; *DNB* (1991); Hollis, P. (1997) *Jennie Lee: a life*; *ODNB* (2004).

LEIGH, Margaret Mary, born Oxford 17 Dec. 1894, died Inverness 7 April 1973. Author and farmer. Daughter of Alice Maud Bayliss, and Henry Devenish Leigh, Oxford don.

After her father's death in 1903, Margaret Leigh and her mother remained in Oxford. She attended the High School, and won a classical scholarship to Somerville College in 1913. After completing her studies, in 1919 she was appointed lecturer in Classics at the University of Reading, a life-long dream. However, as a woman, she considered her chances of promotion limited and left academia in 1924. Moving with her mother to Plockton, Wester Ross, she developed a strong interest in agriculture and in the Highlands and islands. After returning to Oxford to do a Dip. Agric., she applied her knowledge to farming and reclaiming derelict holdings in the western Highlands and on Bodmin moor in Cornwall. Her autobiography, *The Fruit in the Seed* (1952), charts her spiritual journey and eventual conversion to Catholicism in 1948; in 1950 she entered a Carmelite convent. Her writing career started with fictional works, but she gained acclaim with books of an autobiographical cast. *Spade among the Rushes* (1949, 1996) recounted her attempt to bring a croft back into cultivation in Moidart. She also wrote essays on agricultural and environmental matters: her analysis of crofting (Leigh 1928–9) is one of the earliest scientific studies exploring the origins of the socio-economic situation of the Highlands. Her work is illustrative of the line of thought supporting the regeneration of the Highlands and the value of the traditional way of life of the crofting population. LG

• Leigh, M., Works as above and (1922) *The Passing of the Pengwerns*, (1928–9) 'The Crofting Problem, 1790–1883', *Scot. Jour. Agric.* xi, pp. 4–21, 137–47, 261–73, 426–33; xii, pp. 34–9, (1935) *Highland Homespun*, (1937) *Harvest of the Moor*, (1938) *Love of the Destroyer*, (1938) *My Kingdom for a Horse*, (1941) *Driftwood and Tangle*.

LENEMAN, Leah, born De Kalb, Illinois, USA, 3 March 1944, died Edinburgh 26 Dec. 1999. Historian and cookery writer. Daughter of Lisa Leneman, and David Leneman, artist.

Leah Leneman grew up in Los Angeles, the daughter of Jewish émigré parents. Educated in a private English/Hebrew school, then state school, she embarked on an acting career in the early 1960s, first in New York, then in Islington, London (Tower Theatre). She was influenced by the Vedanta movement of Hinduism to become a vegetarian and later a vegan and, taking up cookery writing, was a regular contributor to and editorial assistant for *The Vegetarian*. She published seven popular cookbooks, including *The Amazing Avocado* (1984), many of the recipes taste-tested by Graham Sutton, her partner from 1976.

Leah Leneman was also one of the pioneers of women's history in Scotland. A temporary job at Aviemore and adult education classes developed her interest in Scotland's history, and after taking A-levels, she enrolled as a mature student at the University of Edinburgh in 1975. Her PhD was published as *Living in Atholl 1685–1785* (1986). A prolific researcher and writer, she thereafter earned her living through research grants and publications (apart from a few spells at the NAS). Writing in an accessible style, she introduced to a wide audience many aspects of Scottish social history from the 17th to the 19th centuries. Collaboration with *Rosalind Mitchison on an innovative study of illegitimacy, *Sexuality and Social Control 1660–1780* (1989), led to further work on Scottish women's history, including books on women's suffrage, the *Scottish Women's Hospitals, *Elsie Inglis, marriage and divorce. Facing breast cancer from 1991 with courage, she continued writing, including her posthumously published life-story. EE

• Leneman, L., Works as above, and (2000) 'A personal history', *Wom. Hist. Rev.*, 9, (2003) *Promises, Promises*. See also Bibl. below.
Nenadic, S. (2000) 'Leah Leneman (1944–99): an appreciation', *Wom. Hist. Rev.*, 9; *The Scotsman*, 12 Dec. 1999 (obit.) (Bibl.).
Private information.

LENNOX, Agnes, fl. 1839–1841. Chartist leader.

Agnes Lennox was the chairwoman of the Gorbals Female Universal Suffrage Association of Glasgow, founded in 1839, which brought women into the Chartist movement, and provided soirées and temperance teas. She was known for singing the Chartist song of liberty. The group also served the cause of self-improvement; its members wrote useful essays and instructed each other 'in political and scientific subjects'. The women primarily defined themselves as the wives, daughters and mothers of Chartist men, and the men who addressed them denounced the necessity for women to work in factories. Agnes Lennox proclaimed, 'It is a bitter slavery many have to endure in these factories – there "many a flower is born to blush unseen/And waste its fragrance midst the factory steam" '(*True Scotsman* 1840). However, she asserted women's right to participate in politics and male Chartists supported her. The *Glasgow Constitutional* insulted her as 'Miss Impudence' and a 'Brazen-faced Jade' (1839), but she vigorously defended herself as a 'young virtuous female' in a letter to the newspapers. The male Operative Masons Universal Suffrage Society also wrote to applaud Agnes Lennox against these insinuations. Her leadership became known as far as away as Birmingham, where 'her example was referred to when young ladies blushed and hesitated to take the chair at meetings' (*Scots Times* 1841). Another young woman (and daughter of a Chartist), known only as **Miss Muir** (fl. 1840s), was the leader of the Calton and Mile End Female Chartist Association in Glasgow. Initially apologetic about speaking in public, Miss Muir too asserted herself: 'I have ventured to step over that false delicacy in which the conventional prejudices of society have enshrouded women' (*Scots Times* 1840). She asked, 'is it indelicate for a starving woman to say she was in want?' In fact, she argued, it was immoral for a mother to fail to protest 'while her children are crying for bread' (ibid.). AKC

• Lennox, A. *Glasgow Constitutional*, 20 Nov. 1839; *Scottish Patriot*, 3 August, 14 Sept., 30 Nov. 1839; *Scots Times*, 17 Jan., 29 Feb., 6 May, 30 Sept. 1840, 4 March 1841; *True Scotsman*, 7 Dec. 1839, 3 Oct. 1840.
Muir, Miss, *Scots Times*, 17 June, 18 Nov., 30 Dec. 1840.
Clark, A. (1995) *The Struggle for the Breeches: gender and the making of the British working class.*

LESLIE, Beatrix (or Beatrice), born c. 1577, died 3 Sept. 1661. Midwife. Executed for witchcraft.

Little is known about Beatrix Leslie's life, apart from her marriage to William Moffat, until she was accused in 1661, at the age of 84, of causing the collapse of a coal pit through witchcraft. She described how, as a midwife, she used salt and a knife in protective rituals during childbirth and, from her advanced age, it would seem that her skills had proved useful for years. However, she does appear to have been argumentative. Several disputes with her neighbours were reported. It was said she uttered curses, as a result of which several women claimed to have suffered harm and loss. As the accusations brought against her included malefice (evil harm) and demonic witchcraft, the witch-pricker, John Kincaid, was involved and Beatrix Leslie was subjected to ordeals such as pricking to prove the existence of the devil's mark, and 'bierricht'. During the latter ritual, suspects were brought near to, or touched, the body of their supposed victim and, if guilty, the corpse would bleed. Beatrix Leslie confessed to several aspects of demonic witchcraft, including meeting the Devil in the shape of a brown dog and as a young lad. She said she was given a new name, 'Bold Leslie', and agreed to be his servant, but claimed she had not renounced her baptism. She was investigated and tried with five other women. Found guilty, she was ordered to be executed by being strangled and burnt on 3 September 1661.

Although Beatrix Leslie's midwifery skills were significant enough to be mentioned in her trial, they had little to do with her accusations of witchcraft. These were more likely the result of her quarrelsome attitude, followed by harm. Two other factors were important in her trial. One was her confession, albeit as a result of ordeal, to demonic pact, and the other was being part of a group of accused people. 1661 was a year of high intensity for prosecutions in the Lothians, and she may have been unlucky to have been tried at this time. JHMM
• NAS: JC2/10, ff 10v-17v; JC2/11, Books of Adjournal; JC26/27/9 items 4, 5, 9, 13, 19, 20, High Court Process Notes.

LESLIE, Euphemia, born c. 1508, died Elcho 7 Sept. 1570. Prioress of Elcho. Possibly daughter of Mr Walter Leslie, parson of Menmuir, or a Leslie of Rothes.

Sister to Master Robert Leslie, advocate, Euphemia Leslie was involved in a famous legal case. On 6 November 1526, she sought papal dispensation because of her illegitimate birth as the daughter of an unmarried woman and a priest, and her age, since she was only 18, in order to become Prioress of Elcho. It was granted, but litigation ensued for the office with her predecessor, Elizabeth Swinton. In 1527, with the help of her brother and an army of 80 men, she invaded the priory, causing much damage. Elizabeth Swinton, confined to her chamber and fearing for her life, was compelled to resign. Litigation continued, however, and Euphemia Leslie did not receive office until 14 January 1529.

As Prioress, she granted tacks (land leases) to her brother and others. A document addressed to John Swinton was written in her own hand and includes her signature and those of ten nuns. She managed the convent's affairs, including dealing with an English invasion in 1547 and subsequent financial difficulties, until her death. She was the only Scottish prioress to leave a will and testament; it includes a list of pensions owed to the remaining nuns. KP
• NAS: GD12, Swinton Charters; Commissary Court of Edinburgh, Register of Testaments; Perth Museum and Art Gallery: PMAG 1983-4, Elcho Nunnery Archive.
HRHS; Perkins, K. (2001) 'Death, removal and resignation: . . . office of Prioress in late medieval Scotland', in Y. Brown and R. Ferguson (eds) *Twisted Sisters* (Bibl.).

LESLIE MACKENZIE, Lady *see* **MACKENZIE, Helen Carruthers** (1859–1945)

LEWIS, Agnes Smith,‡ n. **Smith, GIBSON, Margaret Dunlop,** n. **Smith;** born Irvine 1843, died Cambridge 29 March 1926 and 11 Jan. 1920 respectively. Travellers, scholars of Semitic languages. Twin daughters of Margaret Dunlop, and John Smith, solicitor of Irvine.

Their mother's early death made for an isolated childhood that laid the foundation of Agnes and Margaret Smith's intense attachment to each other throughout their life. When they were 23, their father's sudden death gave them independence and a very considerable fortune. They ignored prevailing social restrictions and in 1868 set off, unchaperoned, on the first of their journeys to the Near East. On their return they started to study Greek, the first of many languages they were to master. Agnes Smith also produced three novels of minor literary value. Margaret Smith married James Y. Gibson (1826–86, minister and translator) and Agnes Smith married Samuel Lewis (1836–91, classicist, librarian of Corpus Christi College, Cambridge), but each was widowed after a few years. They spent the rest of their lives together in 'Castlebrae', the house built by Agnes Lewis's husband in Cambridge. Here they became part of a wide circle of academics and developed their own academic interests, acquiring proficiency in Syriac, Arabic and Hebrew.

In 1890, they set off for St Catherine's Monastery at Mt Sinai, a journey of 10 days by camel from Cairo. A letter from the leading scholar James Rendel Harris admitted them to the monastery's famous library, where they made a most outstanding discovery, a version of the Old Syriac Gospels, dated to the 5th century AD. Further expeditions to the Middle East followed and even greater discoveries. Leaves of a Hebrew manuscript purchased in Cairo proved to be the Hebrew version of the Jewish text of Ecclesiasticus in the Septuagint, until then only known in Greek and Syriac translations. Their pioneering research and publications in what was a male-dominated field of academic pursuit gave the sisters a place in scholarship that continues until today. For their achievements, they received doctorates from Halle, St Andrews, Heidelberg and Trinity College, Dublin, though not from Cambridge, despite having been active members of the academic community there. They encouraged young scholars and endowed Westminster College, which opened in 1899. Their portraits, showing them robed in doctoral gowns, still hang in the hall of the College. MVH

• Gibson, M. D. (Selected) (1893) *How the Codex was Found*, (1894) *A Catalogue of the Arabic manuscripts in the Convent of St Catharine on Mount Sinai*.
Lewis, A. S. (Selected) (1870) *Eastern Pilgrims*, (1879) *Effie Maxwell*, 3 vols, (1884) *Glimpses of Greek Life and Scenery*, (1894) *A Translation of The Four Gospels from the Syriac of the Sinaitic Palimpsest*, (1913) *Light on the Four Gospels from the Sinai Palimpsest*, (1894) *A Catalogue of the Syriac manuscripts in the Convent of St Catharine on Mount Sinai*.
ODNB (2004) (Lewis, Agnes; Gibson, Margaret); Price, A. W. (1985) *The Ladies of Castlebrae* (Bibl.).

LIEBENTHAL, Dora Tertia, born Edinburgh 10 July 1889, died Edinburgh 4 March 1970. Concert organiser. Daughter of Agnes Shillinglaw, and Louis Liebenthal, German grain merchant, Leith.

Tertia Liebenthal, born into a musical household and educated at St George's School, spent a year in Berlin in 1906, visiting relatives and attending finishing school. Inspired by Donald Tovey, she played the violin in the Reid Orchestra for several seasons, during the 'golden age of Edinburgh music-making' (*ODNB* 2004, Tovey). She became best-known in the musical world as a concert organiser, after writing to *The Scotsman* in 1941 suggesting that a concert series might comfort people in the dark days of the war. The suggestion was taken up, and the Trustees of the National Gallery provided the space on Wednesday lunchtimes. At first a committee was formed, but soon Tertia Liebenthal, a formidable talent scout, ran the concerts as 'an inspired autocracy' (*Scotsman*, 1965), contacting both well-known and up-and-coming musicians: Kathleen Ferrier gave a recital in Edinburgh in 1943, at the outset of her career; other national figures included Peter Pears, Solomon, John Ogdon, and Scottish performers such as *Joan Dickson. Conrad Wilson remarked that it was enjoyable to say of a star musician in London that he or she had been spotted 'years ago' by Miss Liebenthal (*Scotsman*, 1963). Hers was perhaps the only concert series started by artillery – the Edinburgh one o'clock gun. The concerts continued after the war, the 600th being performed in 1965, without one having been cancelled. Tertia Liebenthal died in the RSA building in 1970. At Festival time, she kept open house in her life-long home in Regent Terrace for musicians from all over the world. A bronze bust of her (after Diona Murray) is in the SNPG. SR

• NLS: MSS 21564-71, Liebenthal family papers.
Glasgow Herald, 19 April 1966; *The Scotsman,* 28 Oct. 1963
and 11 Dec. 1965; *ODNB* (2004) (Tovey, Donald).

LILIAS of Ancrum, fl. allegedly 1545. Border folk heroine.

The only known reference to Lilias is on a memorial stone near the site of the Battle of Ancrum Moor (February, 1545). The inscription reads:

> Fair maiden Lilliard lies under this stane;
> Little was her stature, but great was her fame;
> Upon the English loons she laid mony thumps,
> And when her legs were cuttid aff, she fought on her
> stumps.

As no other sources mention a female warrior, Lilias is probably fictitious. The stone, first mentioned in the mid-19th century, may be linked to renewed interest in Border folklore after Walter Scott published his Border Ballads. A local myth recalled that while Lilias watched the battle, she saw her lover killed. In anguish she took a sword and fought bravely before dying herself. The Scots won this Border battle, a rare victory amidst the terrible 'Rough Wooing' of Scotland by Henry VIII. MMM

• Cowan, E. J. (2000) 'Sex and violence in the Scottish ballads', in E. J. Cowan (ed.) *The Ballad in Scottish History,* p. 109; Lamont-Brown, R. (1996) *Scottish Folklore,* pp. 53-4; *New Statistical Account of Scotland* (1845), iii, 244.

LINDSAY, Christian, fl. 1588. Cook, possibly poet.

In 1586, Christian Lindsay, a member of the royal household, married William Murray, Master of the Carriage to James VI. In August 1588, she was awarded a lifetime annual pension of four measures of barley for providing oatcakes and bread for the king. She has more recently excited critical attention as possibly having been an early Scottish female poet. A sonnet bearing the name 'Christiane Lyndesay to Robert Hudsone' is appended, in the Ker MS, to Alexander Montgomerie's sonnet sequence 'To Robert Hudsone'. The name Christian Lindsay is also associated with poetry in James VI's poem, 'The Admonition of the Master Poet', written in or before 1584. These references do not prove that Christian Lindsay was a well-known female court poet – it may be that Montgomerie is ventriloquising and using 'Christian Lindsay' as a nom de plume – but the possibility that she may have been recognised as a poet is intriguing. It is also not certain that the Christian Lindsay who wrote the poems is the same Christian Lindsay who baked for the king although, as she was at court during the 1580s, she seems to be the most likely candidate. PBG

• Univ. of Edinburgh Library, De.3.70, f.68v 'Christen Lyndesay to Robert Hudsone'.
Juhala, A. (2000) 'The household and court of King James VI of Scotland, 1567–1603', PhD, Univ. of Edinburgh, p. 175; Heijnsbergen, T. van (2000) 'Performing the female: Christian Lindsay and male adaptations of female voices', in N. Royan and T. van Heijnsbergen (eds) *Public Literature and Performance in the Sixteenth Century,* p. 88, n. 58.
Private information: Amy Juhala.

LINKLATER, Marjorie, n. **MacIntyre,** born Edinburgh 19 March 1909, died Kirkwall, Orkney, 29 June 1997. Campaigner for arts, heritage, environment. Daughter of Ida van der Gucht, and Ian MacIntyre, politician and lawyer.

One of six children, Marjorie MacIntyre was educated at St George's School, Edinburgh, and Downe House, Berkshire. She studied at RADA in London, and acted in small parts in the West End. Her beauty is evident in a portrait by Stanley Cursiter (Linklater Rooms, University of Aberdeen). In 1933 she met and married the novelist Eric Linklater (1899–1974) in Edinburgh. They lived together in Orkney, then in 1947 moved to Easter Ross, where they brought up their family of four children. Active in local drama groups, and member of the SAC (1957–63), Marjorie Linklater became involved in politics as an independent county councillor. Following her husband's death in 1974, she moved back to Orkney and for the next 25 years was an active 'green' campaigner against plans to mine uranium and the dumping of nuclear waste in Orkney waters. She became agent for the veteran SNP MEP, Winnie Ewing, who said of her: 'If I could have a wand and be in power in Scotland, I would have urged that she be an ambassadress'. She chaired the Orkney Heritage Society, helped restore the 8th-century chapel of St Boniface on Papa Westray and was founder-chair of the Pier Arts Centre (see Gardiner, Margaret) and honorary vice-president of the St Magnus Festival. She initiated the Johnsmas Foy, a celebration of writing, and the Orkney Folk Festival. She was able to attend the last concert of the 1977 St Magnus Festival shortly before her death. Her memory is honoured in Orkney by the annual Marjorie Linklater Writing Award. MDL

• NLS: Linklater papers. Family papers, diaries and photographs held by Alison, Kristin, Magnus and Andro Linklater.
Parnell, M. (1984) *Eric Linklater;* Obits in *Glasgow Herald, The Orcadian, The Scotsman, The Times,* July 1997.

LISTON, Esther Wilson, n. **Murray,** born Newhaven, Edinburgh, 11 August 1896, died Newhaven 15 April 1989. Fishwife. Daughter of Esther Murray, fishwife, and Henry Murray, fisherman.

One of three children, Esther Murray was educated at Newhaven and Couper Street schools, leaving at 15 when she was apprenticed to a seamstress, then to a butcher. In 1923 she married George Liston, fisherman. He had served in the First World War, returning with damaged health, and died in 1932, leaving her to raise two sons, aged seven and five, on an 18 shilling weekly pension. Necessity sent her to the creel, something she had learned from her mother. She spoke of the weight of the creel – a basket filled with fish carried on the back, suspended from a linen strap around the forehead: 'At first I felt as if my neck was breaking. It's an art you know. I used to practise with a two-stone box of kippers, then I got used to it' (*Newhaven* 1998, p. 37). Three mornings a week, she would get up at 6am to go down to the crowded harbour where fishwives bought crates of fish at auction, divided them, then went into Edinburgh to sell them, each on her own territory.

Esther Liston also sang with the Fisherwomen's Choir, started in Newhaven in 1927, which performed in Scotland, London and in Norway. Through hearing her sing, the sculptor Julian Allen asked her to sit for a bronze bust (presented to the Newhaven Heritage Museum in 1995). Her life represents that of many women in fishing communities, some of whose names, photographs, traditional costumes and songs are displayed in the museum (see also Flucker, Barbara). BBC Scotland described her as the 'last working fishwife that went out with the creel' (1953) well before her retirement in her late seventies. The last surviving Newhaven fishwife is thought to have been **Frances Milligan,** n. **Clements** (1908–2000), who 'left school on the Friday when I was fourteen year old and on the Tuesday I had the creel on my back'. AWP

• Interview by author with George Liston, July 2002; Newhaven Heritage Museum, staff and volunteers; People's Story Museum, Edinburgh, Oral History Archive Tapes: Esther Liston T267/94 and N1, Frances Milligan T271/94. City of Edinburgh Council, (1998) *Newhaven: Personal Recollections & Photographs.*

LISTON, Henrietta, Lady, n. **Marchant,** born Antigua 1751, died Edinburgh 1828. Diarist and travel writer. Daughter of Sarah Marchant, and Nathaniel Marchant, merchant and planter.

Born into a large Scottish family in the West Indies, Henrietta Marchant had at least seven brothers, three of whom attended the University of Glasgow. In February 1796, she too was in Glasgow, to marry the Scottish diplomat Sir Robert Liston (1742–1836). They went to the United States, where her husband was ambassador, and from where she sent a series of lively letters home, then travelled in the Caribbean from December 1800 to April 1801. Her detailed journal recounts her impressions of Antigua, Dominica, Martinique, St Vincent, Montserrat and St Kitts, offering insight into the social lives of the white élite on the islands, but largely silent on the condition of the enslaved. In 1804, the Listons retired to Millburn Tower near Edinburgh, where Henrietta Liston, who collected botanical specimens, created an American garden. A late posting to Constantinople followed, and the Listons finally retired in 1821 to Millburn Tower, where Lady Liston died in 1828. DJH

• NLS: MS 5704, Liston Papers.

Innes, W. A. (1913) *The Matriculation Albums of the University of Glasgow*; *ODNB* (2004) (Liston, Sir Robert); Perkins, B. (1954) 'A diplomat's wife in Philadelphia: letters of Henrietta Liston 1796–1800', in *William and Mary Quarterly*, 11, pp. 592–632.

LITTLE, Janet ('the Scotch Milkmaid'), m. **Richmond,** born Nether Bogside, Ecclefechan, baptised 13 August 1759, died Loudoun Castle 15 March 1813. Poet. Daughter of George Little.

Not much is known about Janet Little's upbringing. She worked in domestic service for the Rev. Johnstone, then as head dairymaid at Loudoun Castle in Ayrshire, where her employer was Susan Henrie, daughter of Robert Burns's patron, *Frances Dunlop. After the Henries' lease expired, she continued to run the Loudoun dairy. In 1792, Janet Little married labourer John Richmond (c. 1741–1819) and became stepmother to his five children. In the same year she published her *Poetical Works,* which sold about 800 copies by subscription. Patronised by Frances Dunlop, she experimented in various poetic styles, from formal English ('To a Lady, A Patroness of the Muse on her Recovery from Sickness') to satires on pastoral life ('The Fickle Pair'). She was accomplished in the Scots language, as in the Ramsayan 'On Seeing Mr – baking cakes' or the Fergusson-influenced 'On Hallowe'en'. She greatly admired Burns, and commemorated an apparent meeting with the 'bard', 'On a Visit to Mr Burns'. Her originality (and self-consciousness) is evident in 'Given to a

Lady who asked me to write a poem'. There, the 'rustic country quean' is told to mind her dairy rather than to write, 'Does she, poor silly thing, pretend/The manners of our age to mend?' Faced with such hostility, 'My hand still trembles while I write'. More of her poems were published after her death (Paterson 1840). Janet Little was a fine poet, whose literary reputation deserves to be rescued. VB

• Little, J. (1792) *The Poetical Works of Janet Little, The Scotch Milkmaid*.

Bold, V. (1993) 'Janet Little, "The Scotch Milkmaid" and "Peasant Poetry"', *Scot. Lit. Jour.*, 20: 2; Brown, H. (1950) 'Burns and the Scotch Milkmaid', *Burns Chronicle*, 2nd series, 25, pp. 15–20; Landry, D. (1990) *The Muses of Resistance*, p. 237; *ODNB* (2004); Paterson, J. (1840) *The Contemporaries of Burns*.

LIVINGSTON, Jean (aka **Lady Warriston),** born Stirlingshire 1579, died Edinburgh 5 July 1600. Murderer. Daughter of Margaret Colville, and John Livingston, younger of Dunipace.

Jean Livingston married John Kincaid of Warriston in 1594. The marriage was unhappy, possibly involving physical abuse. In 1600, Jean and her nurse, Janet Murdo, decided on John's murder, and approached Robert Weir, a servant of Jean's father. On 1 July 1600, after John Kincaid had retired, Weir, who had been hidden in the house, strangled him. The murderer escaped (until 1604), but the noise caused alarm; the next morning officers arrested Jean Livingston, Janet Murdo and two servants, Barbara Barton and Agnes Johnston. Jean and Janet were found guilty on 3 July and sentenced to be strangled and burnt on 5 July. The servants, charged as accomplices, were acquitted (although a 17th-century history erroneously reports that one was burnt). Jean Livingston's father, having recently returned to royal favour, made no attempt to save her, although the family urged that the execution be changed to an early-morning beheading, and for Janet Murdo to be burnt at the same time on Castle Hill to distract attention. Before the trial, a minister visited Jean Livingston and urged her to repent, with little effect. Afterwards, however, she became penitent and spent the day in prayer with him. He recorded her conversion and her execution at the Girth Cross in Canongate. The ballad 'The Laird of Waristoun' commemorates these events. EE

• Edinburgh City Archives: SL150/1/7 Regality Court Book of Canongate.

Brown, K. M. (1992) 'The laird, his daughter, her husband and the minister', in R. Mason and N. MacDougall (eds)

People and Power in Scotland; *ODNB* (2004); Sharpe, C. K. (ed.) (1827) *Memorial of the confession of Jean Livingston, Lady Wariston . . . July 1600*.

LOCHHEAD, Marion Cleland, MBE, born Wishaw, Lanarkshire, 19 April 1902, died Edinburgh 19 Jan. 1985. Writer, social historian. Daughter of Helen Watt, and Alexander Lochhead, draper and clothier.

Marion Lochhead graduated in English Literature and Latin at the University of Glasgow (MA 1923). Becoming a teacher, she turned to poetry and other writing in the 1920s. She said, 'I began as a poet, with an increasing interest in biography and social and domestic history' (*DLB* Gale 1981, p. 289). Her biographical work includes *John Gibson Lockhart* (1954) and *Elizabeth Rigley, Lady Eastlake* (1961). Her historical interests led to her important *The Scots Household in the Eighteenth Century* (1948) and to works on Victorian domestic life and childhood, anticipating current interest in women's history. She also contributed poems, articles and reviews to *The Scotsman* and to various journals. Her first collection, *Poems*, was published in 1928, followed by three further collections. She wrote five novels in the 1930s, including *Anne Dalrymple* (1934) and *Island Destiny* (1936). She had no children, but her interest in the imaginative capacities of childhood can be seen in *The Renaissance of Wonder in Children's Literature* (1977) published when she was in her mid-70s. A friend described her as having 'the rare ability to meet all ages at their own level, moving effortlessly from the childlike belief in the Other Country with its innate innocence to the sharpness of her undoubted intellect' (*Scotsman* 1985). She also edited *Scottish Tales of Magic and Mystery* (1978), *Scottish Love Stories* (1979) and *Magic and Witchcraft of the Borders* (1984).

Marion Lochhead was a devout member of the Scottish Episcopal Church and edited its *Diocesan Gazette* for many years. Her obituary in *The Scotsman* calls her 'a most exceptional friend' and she was close to other women writers including *Helen Cruickshank. She was a founder member of Scottish PEN, a fellow of the RSL (1955) and an MBE (1963). MPM

• NLS: , MSS 26190–3, Marion Lochhead Archive, Acc. 7783, 9507, 11588; Motherwell Heritage Centre (Local Studies division).

Lochhead, M., Works as above, and see *HSWW* (Bibl.) and www.eup.ed.ac.uk

Cruickshank, H. (1976) *Octobiography*; *DLB* Gale (1981);

HSWW (Bibl.); *The Scotsman*, 21 Jan. 1985 (obit.); *The Times*, 26 Jan. 1985 (obit.).

LOFTUS, Marie, m. **Brown,** born Glasgow, 24 Nov. 1857, died Hendon, London, 7 Dec. 1940. Music hall comedian and pantomime principal boy.
LOFTUS, Marie Cecilia Brown (Cissie), m. **McCarthy** born Glasgow 22 Oct. 1876, died New York, USA, 12 July 1943. Mimic and actor. Daughter of Marie Loftus, and Ben Brown, variety artist.

Marie Loftus was born in Glasgow of Irish parents, reputedly in Stockwell Street, where she made her first stage appearance, dancing at Mrs Baylis's Scotia Music Hall, and earning 3s 6d a week. She made her début at Brown's Royal Music Hall, Glasgow, in March 1874, and her first London appearances at the Oxford Music Hall in April 1877. As 'The Hibernian Hebe' and 'The Sarah Bernhardt of the Music Halls', she became one of the British music hall's highest-paid female stars, reputedly commanding £100 a week by the late 1890s, and touring to the United States and South Africa. She was also a leading pantomime principal boy, appearing at the Theatre Royal Glasgow as Robinson Crusoe in 1889 and 1900 and Sinbad the Sailor in 1895, and in Augustus Harris's 1892 Drury Lane production of *Little Bo-Peep*.

A full-figured, strikingly handsome woman, Marie Loftus was a 'serio-comedienne', a now-forgotten genre of performer who sang both comic and sentimental songs. She was enormously popular in Glasgow. After one performance at the Britannia in Trongate in 1894, more than 1,000 people waited for her outside the hall and six extra constables had to be called to disperse the crowd. A gifted burlesque artist, her material ranged from coquettishly risqué songs such as 'Sister Mary wants to know' to sentimental ballads such as 'A Thing you can't buy with gold' and 'To err is human, to forgive divine'. Recalling her, the author J. J. Bell wrote: 'Glasgow never had a greater favourite . . . In the spotlight, singing "That is Love", she looked – to me, at 18 – beautiful. To this day you can still hear people humming the tune of that song of more than forty years ago – her memorial' (Bell 1932, p. 134).

Her daughter Cecilia was a highly talented mimic and actor. After a convent education, she appeared at the Oxford in July 1893 at the age of 16, where her imitations of stage and music hall personalities caused a sensation. After eloping with her first husband, the novelist Justin Huntly McCarthy, she appeared in New York from 1894 in both legitimate drama and vaudeville, and subsequently appeared in London with Irving in *Faust* at the Lyceum, in the title role in *Peter Pan* and in the first Royal Music Hall Command Performance in 1912. She also acted in about a dozen films. PM

• Bell, J. J. (1932) *I Remember*; Busby, R. (1976) *British Music Hall: an illustrated who's who from 1850 to the present day*; *Glasgow Evening News*, 13 Nov. 1894; 'Marie Loftus at Home', *Glasgow Harlequin*, 17 Dec. 1895 pp. 8–9; *Glasgow Herald*, 14 Dec. 1940 (obit.); *Illustrated London News*, 15 Sept. 1923; Maloney, P. (2003) *Scotland and the Music Hall, 1850–1914*; Parker J. (ed.) (1916) *Who's Who in the Theatre*, ['Who's Who in Variety' supplement] 3rd edn.; 'Miss Marie Loftus' *The Sketch*, 26 Dec. 1894, p. 401.

LOG, Lucky Margaret ('Lucky'), n. **Laird,** m1 **Log,** m2 **Hare,** born Ireland c. 1788, died probably Australia, date unknown. Wife of William Hare, one of the two murderers who supplied Edinburgh anatomists with bodies.

Lucky Log was a tough woman who had worked on the Union Canal as a navvy with her first husband, James Log. They settled in Edinburgh when the canal was finished, and after her husband's death, she maintained their lodging-house in the Grassmarket, and took in William Hare, another Irish labourer. She was known legally as Mrs William Hare in 1828, and she may have been the instigator of the first few successful attempts to murder old, ill, or drunken lodgers in her establishment. She undoubtedly intended to remain in control of the gang, but was displaced as a result of her husband's growing friendship with William Burke. She and William Hare turned king's evidence, so escaped prosecution. She has faded from historical accounts of the scandal and trial, perhaps because commentators hesitated to recognise evil in female form. DS

• Barzun, J. (ed.) (1974) *Burke and Hare*; *Edinburgh Evening Courant*, Nov. 1828–March 1829; Edwards, O. D. (1980, 1993) *Burke and Hare*; (1829) *Trial of William Burke and Helen M'Dougal Before the High Court of Justiciary, at Edinburgh, December 24, 1828, for the Murder of Margery Campbell, or Docherty*; *ODNB* (2004) (Burke, William); *West Port Murders* (1829, repr. 2001).

LOGAN, Ella *see* **ALLAN, Georgina Armour** (1913–69)

LORIMER, Jean ('Chloris'), m. **Whelpdale,** born Craigieburn, Moffatt, 1775, died Edinburgh 11 Sept. 1831. Friend and contemporary of Robert Burns. Daughter of Agnes Carson, and William Lorimer, farmer.

In autumn 1790, Jean Lorimer's family rented Kemys Hall, two miles from Ellisland, Nithsdale, where Robert Burns and *Jean Armour farmed. The families became good friends. Jean Lorimer attracted many suitors, one being Andrew Whelpdale from Cumbria, whom she met in 1793 and eloped with to marry at Gretna Green. Within a few weeks he fled Scotland to avoid his creditors, leaving her to return to her father's house, penniless: although he deserted her, she never divorced him. He died in Langholm, Dumfries, in 1834.

In August 1795, the Lorimers gave up Kemys Hall and moved into Dumfries, where the Burns family lived. Jean Lorimer lived with her father until his death on 25 October 1808, then worked as a seamstress and a governess in the north of England before moving to Edinburgh c. 1816. Rumour, and letters written in the 1850s by Thomas Thorburn and James Hogg, suggested that she was a vagrant but those who knew her well denied the accusations.

In 1825 she was brought to public attention as a friend of Burns by an Edinburgh newspaper. Following this publicity she was offered the post of housekeeper to a gentleman in Blacket Place. Many people came to visit and talk with the 'Lassie wi' the lint-white locks'. A few years later, she developed tuberculosis and moved to a small flat in Middleton's Entry, Potterrow, supported by her ex-employer until her death. In 1901, to commemorate her memory, the Ninety Burns Club erected a Celtic cross over her grave in Preston Street Cemetery. Although Jean Lorimer and Robert Burns were not romantically involved, his esteem for her was high and he dedicated more songs to her than to any other woman. MB
• Adams, J. (1893) *Burns's Chloris*; Hill, J. C. (1961) *The Love Songs and Heroines of Robert Burns*; Bell, M. (2001) *Tae The Lasses*.

LOUISE, Princess Caroline Alberta, [Myra Fontenoy], Duchess of Argyll, born Buckingham Palace 18 March 1848, died Kensington Palace 3 Dec. 1939. Painter and sculptor. Daughter of *Queen Victoria, and Prince Albert.

Educated privately by artists Mary Thornycroft and Edward Courbould, Princess Louise broke royal precedent, attending public classes from tutors (e.g. J. E. Boehm, L. Alma-Tadema) at London's National Art Training School (1868). She commissioned Edward Godwin to design her studio in Kensington Palace. The princess was thought in the family to have 'Bohemian tendencies' and 'to chase anything

in trousers' (Longford 1991, p. 52). Her terracotta self-portrait (NPG, n.d.), sculptures, sketches, portraits, designs for uniforms, jewellery and lace, as well as her journalism (as 'Myra Fontenoy'), display her artistic bent. Her main sculptures include a bust of Queen Victoria (1869, Kensington Palace) and a memorial to Canadian soldiers of the Boer War (1905, St Paul's Cathedral). In 1871, she married John Douglas Sutherland Campbell, Marquis of Lorne (1845–1914), 9th Duke of Argyll (1900), Governor-General of Canada (1878–83). As the wife of a Scottish Marquis, and later Duchess of Argyll (1900–14), she acquitted her duties to his Scottish estates. There were times when she found marriage to John Campbell difficult. They had no children. Some have suggested that he was homosexual and that their interest in the arts kept them together. On the Duke's death in 1914, however, she suffered a nervous breakdown. Princess Louise had redesigned uniforms for the Argyll and Sutherland Highlanders (1892) and became their colonel-in-chief in 1919. She maintained a home at Roseneath (Rosneath), Dunbartonshire, which she visited regularly thereafter. She played a part in public life as first president of the NUHEW (1872), patroness of the LWS, president of the National Trust and more than 20 hospital trusts, and during the First World War carried out many good works. As an unconventional member of the royal family, she attracted both admiration and censure at different times. RA
• Duff, D. (1940, 1971) *The Life Story of HRH Princess Louise, Duchess of Argyll*; Longford, E. (1964) *Victoria RI*, (1991) *Darling Loosy*; *ODNB* (2004); Stamp, R. (1988) *Royal Rebels*; Tuttle, C. (1978) *Royalty in Canada*; Wake, J. (1988) *Princess Louise*.

LOVI, Isabell, fl. 1805–1827. Inventor and business-woman.

Isabell Lovi, widow of Angelo Lovi, glass-blower, took over and developed her late husband's business in Edinburgh from 1805 to 1827. Angelo Lovi (born Milan c. 1756) had arrived in Britain via Rotterdam in May 1772. By July 1798, he was living at 16 Niddry Street. He figures in the Edinburgh street directory in 1804, the year he died, as a 'glass-blower' at 82 South Bridge, and is known to have made barometers and sets of specific gravity beads. Nothing is known of Isabell Lovi's family circumstances – not even whether she was a Scot herself. In 1805, however, she took out a patent with an advocate, J. R. Irving, for an 'Apparatus for determining the specific gravity of fluid bodies', involving developments to the hydrostatic bubbles invented by Alexander Wilson in the mid-1750s. These beads, which were to be used for precise measurements in industries as diverse as bleaching and distilling, came in sets accompanied by a short instruction booklet (Lovi 1805). In 1813, perhaps in an effort to market the device more widely, she produced another set of 'Directions', and a Committee of the Highland Society later approved its use in ascertaining the richness of milk. She made her final appearance in the street directories in 1827. Of the four known sets of 'Mrs Lovi's beads', one is in the Castle Museum, York; one in the Science Museum, London (Inv. 1948–23), and one is in a private collection; the other is in the Royal Museum of Scotland. AM-L

• British patent 2826, 9 March 1805; Edinburgh City Archives: 'Register of Aliens 1798 [–1803]', f.22; RMS, inv. T.1962.115 (beads).

Lovi, I. (1805) *A Short Introduction to the Use of the Patent Aerometrical Beads*, (1813) *Directions for using the Patent Aerometric Beads*.

Clarke, T. N. et al. (1989) *Brass & Glass: scientific instrument-making workshops in Scotland*; Morrison-Low, A. D. (1991) 'Women in the nineteenth-century scientific instrument trade', in M. Benjamin (ed.) *Science and Sensibility: gender and scientific enquiry 1780–1945*; (1817) *Trans. Highland Soc.*, 5, pp. 181–6.

LOW, Helen Nora Wilson [Lorna Moon], m. **Hebditch,** born Strichen, Buchan, 16 June 1886, died Albuquerque, New Mexico, 1 May 1930. Novelist and Hollywood screen-writer. Daughter of Margaret Benzies, and Charles Low, plasterer and hotel landlord.

Nora Low received an elementary education at the local Episcopal school but was also influenced by her father, an atheist and socialist. A voracious reader, she constructed her own romance when in 1907 she secretly married a commercial traveller from Yorkshire, William Hebditch (1878–1960), who had stayed at her parents' Temperance Hotel. After emigrating with him to Alberta, Canada, she left him for another Yorkshireman, Walter Moon (1890–1971), moving first to Winnipeg then to Minneapolis where she worked as a journalist. She had a child with each man but left these domestic ties behind and moved to Hollywood, where she wrote film scripts for Cecil B. DeMille and quickly achieved successes such as *Mr Wu* (1927). She was regarded as one of Hollywood's top three screen-writers. Studio and publishers' publicity from this time reveals that she invented a number of different and exotic identities for herself in this new

environment. She also became the mistress of Cecil B. DeMille's brother, William de Mille (1878–1955), and bore him a child, Richard. During the pregnancy she was diagnosed with tuberculosis and gave the child (who remained ignorant of his parentage until adulthood) up to adoption by Cecil B. DeMille. While being treated she produced short stories, collected as *Doorways in Drumorty* (USA, 1925; Britain, 1926). A novel, *Dark Star* (1929), followed. She died of tuberculosis in a sanatorium in New Mexico, still pursuing her writing career and resolutely refusing to allow her role as invalid to be used in publicity material. Her ashes were brought back to Scotland and scattered on the hill above Strichen.

Lorna Moon's fiction drew on her early experiences in Strichen, moving between dark comedy, satire and melodrama in its depiction of farming and fishing communities in north-east Scotland. Her short stories demonstrated her eye for detail – the intricate hypocrisies of small-town life – while her novel, ambitious but uneven, suggested her dramatic potential. Although successful commercially in America and Britain, she was regarded as controversial in her home village and remained critically neglected until the late 20th century. Her fiction has a freshness of style and candour in the representation of small-town communities and an energetic critique of the ways in which women's lives are shaped by moral and social policing, making her one of the significant voices in 20th-century fiction of the north-east of Scotland. GN

• Lilly Library, Indiana: Corr.; Private collection, Richard de Mille; Strichen Public Library: Lorna Moon archive.

Moon, A., Works as above.

Norquay, G. (ed.) (2002) *The Collected Works of Lorna Moon*. de Mille, R. (1998) *My Secret Mother, Lorna Moon*; *ODNB* (2004).

LOWE, Helen Millar, MBE, born Duns 10 Dec. 1897, died Edinburgh 6 Nov. 1997. Accountant, millionaire. Daughter of Margaret Trotter, and James Lowe, coal merchant.

Helen Lowe left Berwickshire High School at 16 to work as a clerk in the Post Office Bank in London, earning her father's disapproval. She later trained in accountancy in Edinburgh, becoming one of the first women chartered accountants in Scotland. Having 'put up her plate' in Queen Street, she ran her own firm almost until her death, aged 99. A strong character, Helen Lowe advised many societies and charities, particularly those for women and the elderly, and campaigned unsuccessfully for the continuation of the Bruntsfield Hospital. She never married, a wartime engagement having ended in 1918, and lived frugally in her parents' house. She joked to her gardener that she could not afford a foreign holiday, but on her death (intestate) left £7 million from property and investments. She was awarded the MBE in 1964. SR

• *The Scotsman, Evening News, Daily Record*, 11 Nov. 1997 (obits).

Private information and family records.

LUMSDEN, Louisa Innes, DBE, born Aberdeen 31 Dec. 1840, died Edinburgh 2 Jan. 1935. Educational pioneer, suffragist, animal welfare campaigner. Daughter of Jane Forbes of Echt, and Clements Lumsden, Aberdeen advocate.

The youngest of seven children, Louisa Lumsden was educated at private schools in Cheltenham, Brussels and London, before returning to the family home, Glenbogie, for several years. She was one of the first five students at Hitchin College (1869–72) and, with **Rachel Cook** from St Andrews (later Mrs Scott, 1848–1905, educational campaigner, suffragist and editorial collaborator on the *Manchester Guardian*), one of the first three women to pass the Classical Tripos (1873). First resident tutor in Classics, Girton College (1873–75), Louisa Lumsden resigned in disagreement with Emily Davies and the Girton executive committee over students' grievances and her own status. She became Classical Tutor at Cheltenham Ladies College 1876–77, then first headmistress at St Leonards School, St Andrews, 1877–82. Failing to be elected Mistress of Girton in 1884, she returned to the family home in Aberdeenshire, serving on two rural school boards. In 1894 she became the first Warden of University Hall for Women, University of St Andrews. She hoped to turn it into a Scottish Girton, but problems with the governing committee led to her resignation in 1900, although she was mollified by an honorary degree in 1911.

Single-minded, uncertain-tempered, forthright and geographically restless, she struggled in the institutional posts she considered it her patriotic duty to accept. Her problems were exacerbated by an intense homoerotic friendship with Constance Maynard (1849–1935, later Principal, Westfield College), which began at Girton and continued when they were teachers at Cheltenham and St Leonards. Constance Maynard was intensely devout, while Louisa Lumsden was not, although she later became a vice-president of the SCLWS.

She travelled widely, often with her sister *Rachel Lumsden. Her forte was public speaking. From 1908 president of the AWSS and later on the executive committee of the SFWSS, she campaigned for women's suffrage and women's rights throughout Scotland, alongside women such as *Elsie Inglis and *Frances Balfour. She loved animals and campaigned widely for animal welfare and anti-vivisection, editing *Our Fellow Mortals* for 11 years. Intensely Scottish and intensely patriotic, in 1914 she addressed wartime recruitment meetings and worked in the chemistry laboratories at St Andrews for the Ministry of Scientific Warfare. When in her 80s, she worked for the Unionist Party and Women's Rural Industries, and was created DBE in 1925. The Lumsden Wing, University Hall, University of St Andrews, was opened in 1962. She was working on a poem the day she died. LRM

• Girton College Archives: Corr.; Museum of London, Suffragette Fellowship Collection: 75/16/18, Corr.; St Leonards School Archives; Univ. of St Andrews Archives: UY3778; Westfield College Archives: Constance Maynard's autobiography & diaries.

Lumsden, L. I. (1875) 'Woman's work, II. Girls' schools', *The Ladies' Edinburgh Magazine*, 1 (7 & 8), pp. 208–20, 238–46, (n.d.: 1884) *On the Higher Education of Women in Great Britain and Ireland,* (1911) 'The position of woman in history', in *The Position of Women: actual and ideal,* (1933) *Yellow Leaves: memories of a long life.*

Banks, O. (1990) *Biographical Dictionary of British Feminists*, vol. 2: Supp. *1900–45*; Firth, C. B. (1949) *Constance Louisa Maynard*; MacDonald, L. A. O. (2002) *Unique & Glorious Mission; ODNB* (2004); *The Scotsman*, 4 Jan. 1935 (obit.); Vicinus, M. (1985) *Independent Women*; Walker, L. (ed.) (1996) *Dame Louisa Lumsden.*

LUMSDEN, Rachel Frances, born Aberdeen 17 April 1835, died Aberdeen 22 April 1908. Pioneering nurse. Daughter of Jane Forbes of Echt, and Clements Lumsden, advocate.

The fifth of seven children, when her sister *Louisa Lumsden left for Hitchin College in 1869, Rachel Lumsden trained as a nurse at the Hospital for Sick Children, Great Ormond Street, London and worked at King's College Hospital. In 1877, she was appointed superintendent of the new Aberdeen Hospital for Sick Children, later being elected an honorary president and attending the meetings of the all-male executive committee. In 1885, she was appointed (at her own insistence, unpaid) as superintendent, head nurse and housekeeper/matron at the Aberdeen Royal Infirmary. The superintendent had previously always been a man. By 1891 she had initiated a three-year training course, reputedly the first in Scotland. She advised on the Jubilee extension scheme, and on retirement in 1897 received an album signed by 63 Aberdeen doctors, and a message from the Queen. A member of the Council for Queen Victoria's Jubilee Institute for Nurses (QVJIN) (1891–7) and Scottish representative on the executive committee of the BNA, founded in 1887 by Ethel Manson (see Stewart, Eliza) she actively supported the key demand of state registration of nurses.

Rachel Lumsden was succeeded as unpaid superintendent of the Children's Hospital by her elder sister, **Katharine Maria** (1831–1912). Almost blind, Katharine Lumsden had cared for their widowed mother until her death in 1883. Like Rachel, an able administrator, she organised fund-raising bazaars and house-to-house collections to finance the hospital. Honorary secretary of the Aberdeen District Nursing Association for almost 20 years, she also succeeded Rachel in QVJIN, 1897–1912. An active, philanthropic figure, Katharine Lumsden campaigned for causes such as fireguards in the home and for an Aberdeen crematorium (she was herself cremated). She contributed to *Blackwood's Magazine* and *Chambers's Journal*. LRM

• *Annual Reports of the Directors of the Aberdeen Hospital for Sick Children*; Northern Health Services Archives, Aberdeen: ARI, (R)AHSC and ADNA collections.
Aberdeen Daily Journal, 24 April 1908 (obit. Rachel Lumsden), 2 Dec. 1912 (obit. Katharine); *Aberdeen Free Press*, 2 Dec. 1912; Levack, I. D. and Dudley, H. A. F. (1992) *Aberdeen Royal Infirmary*; Lumsden, L. I. (1933) *Yellow Leaves: memories of a long life*; Pedersen, S. (2002) 'Within their sphere? Women correspondents to Aberdeen daily newspapers 1900–1914', *Northern Scotland*, 22, pp. 159–66; Webster, K. (1988) 'Rachel Frances Lumsden of Glenbogie', *Aberdeen Postgraduate Medical Bulletin*, 22(1), pp. 18–20.

LUSK, Janet Theodora, OBE, born Oxford 27 April 1924, died Edinburgh 20 June 1994. Social worker. Daughter of Mary Theodora Colville, and Rev. David Colville Lusk, Church of Scotland minister.

The youngest of five children, Janet Lusk spent her early years in Oxford; her father was a chaplain to the university. In 1933, the family moved to Edinburgh, where David Lusk became minister of West Coates Church. She attended St Leonards School, St Andrews until 1942, when she joined the ATS. Following wartime service, she studied French and Spanish at the University of Edinburgh. She

began her social work career at Edinburgh Children's Holiday Home before undertaking a postgraduate childcare course at the University of Birmingham (1955–6). Returning to Scotland, she was a caseworker at the Guild of Service, Edinburgh, working with 'unmarried mothers' and adoptive parents. In 1960, she worked with the University of Edinburgh to launch the first childcare course in Scotland, with placements at the Guild. In 1962, she was appointed Director of the Guild of Service, a post she held until retirement in 1984. She died following a road accident.

Janet Lusk pioneered professional practice in social work with children and families, in Scotland and across the UK. She was acknowledged as the leading authority on adoption in Scotland in the 1960s and 70s, and served on several key committees including the Houghton Committee on Adoption, on which she was the sole Scottish social work representative. She was awarded the OBE in recognition of her work. She is remembered by her sister and many friends as a keen gardener and needleworker and a wonderful companion. VEC

• Interviews with Janet Lusk, 1990, and Rev. Mary Levison (sister), 2003.
Cree, V. E. (1995) *From Public Streets to Private Lives: the changing task of social work*; *The Scotsman*, 2 July 1994 (obit.).

LYALL, David *see* **SWAN, Anne Shepherd (Annie)** (1859–1943)

LYLE, Agnes, of Kilbarchan, born 1775, died after 1825. Traditional ballad singer. Daughter of Mr Lyle, weaver.

The only source for the few known facts about Agnes Lyle's life is the Tory antiquary William Motherwell, author of *Minstrelsy Ancient and Modern* (1827). His search for items brought him to the active ballad community of Kilbarchan, where he visited her repeatedly, gathering a repertoire that included 22 complete ballads. Her stock of songs, the subject of *The Ballad Matrix* (McCarthy 1990), was representative of the broader ballad repertoire of south-west Scotland, including the popular 'Twa Sisters' (Child 10F), 'Mary Hamilton' (Child 173B) and 'Gypsy Laddie' (Child 200C), as well as the rare 'Lord William' (Child 254A), of which hers is the only known complete version, text and air. The structure and technique of her ballads is the epitome of the traditional singer's art. But the consistent rearrangement of plot, character and diction to create a picture of the honest Scots working class betrayed by the perfidious gentry expresses the radical politics of a region and era polarised along class lines. The gentry, after the French revolution and the Napoleonic wars, had come to identify with the crown and fear the working class, while the working class, stirred by post-war depression in the weaving industry, increasingly embraced political radicalism. These unusual ballads demonstrate how a creative singer could freely reframe traditional materials to meet new situations and express a view. Whatever she thought of the Tory gentleman who came to visit, the weaver's daughter trusted him with her subversive songs, weeping openly as she sang of forbidden love and class perfidy. WBM

• Glasgow Univ. Library: MS Murray 501, Motherwell Manuscript; Harvard Univ. Library: MS 25241.56F: Motherwell Ballad Notebook Facsimile.

Child, F. J. (ed.) (1882–98) *The English and Scottish Popular Ballads*; McCarthy, W. B. (1990) *The Ballad Matrix*; Motherwell, W. (1827) *Minstrelsy Ancient and Modern*.

LYNDSAY, David *see* **DODS, Mary Diana** (c. 1790–c. 1830)

LYON, Mary *see* **GRIEVE, Mary Margaret** (1906–98)

LYON, Sibilla, born before 1738, died Edinburgh 9 May 1754. Rouping-woman. Daughter of John Lyon of Whytewell in Angus.

Sibilla Lyon married Charles Dickson, an Edinburgh goldsmith and son of Charles Dickson of Cannonside, Provost of Forfar. They had three children. In poor circumstances after her husband's death in 1738, she petitioned the goldsmiths' incorporation for financial help and was granted £12 Scots per quarter. From the 1730s to 1800 the names of rouping-women (pronounced rooping), who valued the household effects of the deceased, appear regularly in Edinburgh testaments. It is not known why these women's names were recorded. Earlier, the practice was simply to record that the valuation was made by 'skillful persons'. After 1800, those who did valuations were increasingly called 'auctioneers', and were often men. Sibilla Lyon was recorded as rouping between 1741 and 1754. Her testament was recorded on 22 August 1754. ECS

• NAS: CC8/8/115/1, Edinburgh Commissary Records, Register of Testaments; GD1/482/2, Records of Edinburgh Goldsmiths' Incorporation; *WWEE* (Bibl.).

M

MACADAM, Elizabeth, born Chryston, near Glasgow, 10 Oct. 1871, died Edinburgh 25 Oct. 1948. Social worker. Daughter of Elizabeth Whyte, and Thomas Macadam, Presbyterian minister.

Elizabeth Macadam's childhood was spent partly in Canada before she and her sister returned to Scotland and lived for some years in Edinburgh. In 1898, she was awarded a Pfeiffer scholarship to train in social work at the Women's University Settlement in Southwark, London, and in 1902 became the first salaried warden of the Victoria Women's Settlement in Liverpool, a position she held until 1910. She proved an imaginative and capable head. She pioneered many Liverpool medical and educational services for women and children at the settlement and inspired local well-off young women and female students to staff them. Yet she believed firmly that social work should be a profession and not simply a pastime and in 1904 launched a visionary training programme, combining lectures on poverty and politics with supervised practical work. In 1910, the University of Liverpool absorbed this programme and hired Elizabeth Macadam, as lecturer, to run it.

Elizabeth Macadam's success caught the attention of Seebohm Rowntree, who brought her to London early in the First World War to train welfare workers for factories run by the Ministry of Munitions. In 1919 she left Liverpool permanently to become secretary to a new, London-based Joint Universities Council for Social Science, which was to co-ordinate training programmes. The move caused a personal crisis, for she had developed a close friendship with Eleanor Rathbone, by then a Liverpool city councillor. Rathbone was determined not to hamper Macadam's career and in 1919 the two women bought a house in Westminster. But in the end it was Eleanor Rathbone who profited more from the move: the Westminster house became the base for her blossoming political career and Macadam's organising skills were an asset to many Rathbone campaigns. In the 1920s, when Rathbone served as President of NUSEC, Macadam became an officer and the editor of its paper; after

Rathbone's election as MP in 1929, Macadam helped to manage her complex parliamentary career. Practical where Rathbone was abstracted, straightforward where Rathbone was diffident, Elizabeth Macadam struck some observers as an ideal 'political wife'. Nevertheless, she always remained abreast of developments in social work, in 1934 publishing what remains the best account of the changing relationship between voluntary services and the state between the wars, *The New Philanthropy*. After Eleanor Rathbone's death in 1946, Elizabeth Macadam returned to Edinburgh. SP

• Victoria Women's Settlement, Annual Reports; Univ. of Liverpool Library, Special Collections and Archives, records of the School of Training for Social Work.

ODNB (2004) (Macadam, Elizabeth; Rathbone, Eleanor); Pedersen, S. (2004) *Eleanor Rathbone and the Politics of Conscience*; Simey, M. (1992) *Charity Rediscovered: a study of philanthropic effort in nineteenth-century Liverpool*.

MCALISTER, Mary Agnes Josephine, n. **McMackin,** CBE, born Glasgow 26 April 1896, died Glasgow, 26 Feb. 1976. Labour councillor and MP. Daughter of Winifred Deeney, and Charles McMackin, publican.

Educated at the Franciscan Convent, Glasgow, Mary McMackin trained as a fevers nurse at Knightswood Hospital, Glasgow. She married Joseph Alexander McAlister, a window-cleaning contractor, and they had four daughters. During the Second World War she served in the Civil Nursing Reserve and Postal Censorship. She was a councillor with Glasgow City Council (1945–58) and a JP (1947–51). Her nursing background shaped her interest in health issues, and she was Convener of the Health and Welfare Committee (1952–5). In March 1958, she captured the Glasgow Kelvingrove seat from the Conservatives, defeating Katharine Elliot, widow of Walter Elliot, Unionist MP for Kelvingrove (1950–8), in what Elliot referred to as 'a good clean women's fight' (*Daily Record* 1958). Although the by-election was seen as 'symbolic' (*Glasgow Herald* 1958), she lost the seat at the 1959 general election. Afterwards she retained an interest in public life, holding positions on the National Assistance Board (1961–6), and the Supplementary Benefits Commission (1966–7) (Department Chairman 1967). CB

• *Daily Record*, 14 March 1958; *Glasgow Herald*, 14 and 20 March 1958; *WWW, 1971–80* (1981).

MACARTHUR, Mary Reid, m. **Anderson,** born Glasgow 13 August 1880, died London 1 Jan. 1921. Trade unionist and Labour activist. Daughter of

Anne Elizabeth Martin, and John Duncan Macarthur, draper.

Mary Macarthur was the eldest of three surviving daughters. Her father was a prominent Conservative citizen and businessman. After leaving Glasgow High School she spent a year in Germany and on her return became a book-keeper in the family business in Ayr, where the family had moved in 1895; it was then that she first became interested in the trade union movement. In 1901, she joined the SAU and soon became secretary of the Ayr branch. She was elected to the Union's National Executive, the first woman to be a member, and quickly rose to the position of president of the Scottish National District. In 1903, she moved to London, where she became secretary of the WTUL, a role she continued to undertake until her death. Through the WTUL, she campaigned for better working conditions for women workers, including homeworkers, organised strikes and worked to establish trade boards and minimum wage rates. In 1904 and 1908 she was a delegate to the International Congress of Women in Berlin and the USA. In 1906, she was involved in the formation of the Anti-Sweating League, which established wage boards and set minimum wage rates. That year, she became secretary of the NFWW, an organisation that in Scotland alone had a membership of around 2,000 women before the First World War. In 1907, she founded the *Women Worker*, a monthly newspaper for female trade union activists. She continued to protect the interests of women workers during the war, particularly those working in munitions, not only through the NFWW, which recruited widely during 1914–18, but also as a member of the War Emergency Workers National Committee and as honorary secretary of the Wartime Central Committee of Women's Training and Employment.

Mary Macarthur was an active member of the ILP in London and on its National Council from 1909 to 1912. In 1911, she married Will Anderson, also an active member of the ILP and an MP (1914–18). They had one daughter. Mary Macarthur was one of the three main speakers at the memorial service for Keir Hardie in Glasgow in October 1915. In 1918, she stood as a parliamentary candidate for Stourbridge, Worcestershire, but was narrowly defeated, probably due to her anti-war stance and support for the Russian Revolution. She was elected to the NEC of the ILP (1919–20). Will Anderson died of influenza in 1919, after which she continued to campaign for the rights of women workers, attending ILO conferences in Switzerland and the

USA. Two years later she died of cancer, a death described as 'a tragic loss not only to her friends but to the cause of all that is sane & wise in the Labour Movement' (Markham 1921). YGB

• Smillie, R., Ramsay Macdonald, J., and MacArthur, M. (1915) *Memoir of James Keir Hardie MP and Tributes to his Work* (pamphlet from memorial service held in St Andrews Hall, Glasgow, 3 Oct. 1915).

Bondfield, M. (1950) *A Life's Work, etc.*; Hamilton, M. A. (1925) *Mary Macarthur: a biographical sketch*; Markham, V., Letter to E. S. Haldane, 2 Jan. 1921, in J. Alberti (1990) 'Inside out: Elizabeth Haldane as a women's suffrage survivor in the 1920s and 1930s', *Women's Studies International Forum*, vol. 13, 1–2, p. 122.

MACBETH, Ann, born Bolton 25 Sept. 1875, died Patterdale 23 March 1948. Embroiderer and teacher. Daughter of Annie MacNicol, and Norman Macbeth, engineer.

The eldest of nine children, Ann Macbeth enrolled at Glasgow School of Art in 1897. On completing her studies in 1901 she became assistant to *Jessie Newbery. She exhibited at the Glasgow International Exhibition of 1901 and the following year won a silver medal at the Turin International Exhibition of Decorative Arts. Her striking embroidery work was highly regarded and given regular coverage in *The Studio*. In 1904 she took over the classes for teachers, and began teaching metalwork in 1906, bookbinding from 1907 to 1911, and ceramic decoration from 1912. She also designed for Alexander Morton & Co., Donald Bros. of Dundee, and Liberty's. Ann Macbeth became head of the Embroidery Department in 1908 and, in 1911, with educational psychologist Margaret Swanson published *Educational Needlecraft*, a textbook which won international acclaim and influenced needlework teaching for many years. She received honorary diplomas from Paris, Tunis, Ghent, Budapest and Chicago. Moving to Patterdale in 1920, Ann Macbeth taught handicrafts through the Women's Institute in an attempt to alleviate local hardship. She had a strong work ethic and her prolific output included books, painted ceramics and embroideries, which she regularly exhibited with the GSLA. LA

• Swanson, M. and Macbeth, A. (1911) *Educational Needlecraft*.

Burkhauser, J. (ed.) (1990) *Glasgow Girls*; Cumming, E. (ed.) (1992) *Glasgow 1900 Art & Design*; Macfarlane, F. C. and Arthur, E. (1980) *Glasgow School of Art Embroidery 1894–1920*; *ODNB* (2004) ('Glasgow Girls'); Swain, M. (1974) 'Miss Ann Macbeth (1975–1948)', *Embroidery 25*, pp. 8–11.

MACBETH, Lady *see* **GRUOCH, Queen of Scotland (Lady Macbeth)** (fl. early/mid-11th century).

MCCALLUM, Janet Hutchinson (Jennie), m. **Richardson,** born Dunfermline 27 July 1881, died South Africa 1946. Suffragette. Daughter of Janet Hutchinson, and John McCallum, stone mason.

The eldest of 13 children, Jennie McCallum is one of a very small number of Scottish women suffrage activists to come from a working-class background about whom there is any information. Her father was employed in the construction of the Forth Rail Bridge. She worked in the Dunfermline linen industry, where she was a leading figure in the TWU and became involved in the women's rights movement. A member of the WFL, she spoke at meetings throughout Scotland. In October 1908, she was one of 14 demonstrators arrested for creating a disturbance outside the House of Commons while other suffragettes disrupted the Ladies' Gallery. She was imprisoned in Holloway for a month and on her return to Dunfermline could get no further employment in the linen industry. On 17 December 1915, when she was secretary of the TWU, she married Harry Richardson, an engine fitter. They had two sons and a daughter and later emigrated to South Africa. LK

• *AGC*; 'Dunfermline suffragette', *Dunfermline Press*, 2 March 1968.

MACCALZEAN, Euphame, born before 1558, died Edinburgh 25 June 1591. One of the North Berwick witches. Daughter of Thomas MacCalzean, Lord Cliftonhall, advocate and Senator of the College of Justice.

As daughter and heir of Lord Cliftonhall, Euphame MacCalzean was connected by birth and marriage to the powerful Edinburgh legal community. She married Patrick Moscrop, an advocate's son, and had at least five children. Moscrop appears to have taken her surname. There is some evidence that the marriage was not sanctioned by the Kirk, and may have been Catholic.

Euphame MacCalzean was a pivotal figure in one of the most important episodes of Scottish witch-hunting, the North Berwick Witch Trials of 1590–1. Her trial had important political and legal ramifications, and the allegations against her provide insight into the construction of witches as 'unnatural' women who subverted the natural order. She was alleged to have been one of the witches, including *Agnes Sampson and others, who tried to use magic to kill James VI. She was an important link between the North Berwick Witch Trial and incriminating the Earl of Bothwell in plots against the King. The charges against her portray her as a domineering and forceful woman who, in addition to seeking the King's death, used her magic in attempts to gain her husband's love, then to try to kill him and his relatives, and even to avoid the pains of childbirth. The evidence makes connections between the 'treason' of a woman attempting to kill her husband, and the treason of the witches in their attempts at regicide.

Despite an apparently spirited defence by several notable lawyers, Euphame MacCalzean was executed in 1591. Her sentence of being burned alive was harsh – most witches were strangled before being burned. There was a partially successful attempt to clear her name after her death, and some of her property was returned to her heirs in 1592. Her trial and execution may have helped introduce many of the current demonological ideas into Scotland, and set an important precedent. In the trial of *Issobell Young in 1629, the prosecutor cited her case as precedent for allowing women's testimony in cases of witchcraft. SAM

• Chambers, R. (ed.) (1859) *Domestic Annals of Scotland from the Reformation to the Revolution*; Normand, L. and Roberts, G. (eds) (2000) *Witchcraft in Early Modern Scotland: James VI's daemonology and the North Berwick witches*; *ODNB* (2004) (North Berwick witches); Yeoman, L. (2001) 'Hunting the rich witch in Scotland: high status witch suspects and their persecutors, 1590–1650', in J. Goodare (ed.) *The Scottish Witch-hunt in Context*.

MCCRAE, Georgiana Huntly, n. **Gordon,** born London 15 March 1804, died Melbourne, Australia, 24 May 1890. Painter. Illegitimate daughter of Jane Graham, and George Gordon, Marquis of Huntly.

Acknowledged by her father and baptised as a Gordon, Georgiana was educated by French émigrés in Somers Town, London. Exceptionally gifted in painting and drawing, she studied under such masters as John Varley and Charles Hayter. Aged 12, she had a landscape accepted by the Royal Academy; aged 16, she won the Society of Arts silver medal for her portrait of her grandfather, Alexander, 4th Duke of Gordon, who took her to live at Gordon Castle, Morayshire, in the early 1820s. Her privileged life ended with her grandfather's death in 1827, when her father became 5th Duke of Gordon. The new Duchess, who had

no children, dismissed Georgiana to earn her living as a portrait painter in Edinburgh, which she did with considerable success. At Gordon Castle on 25 September 1830, she married Edinburgh lawyer Andrew Murison McCrae. He emigrated to Australia in 1838 and Georgiana followed in 1841 with their four sons. In Melbourne, Andrew McCrae's legal practice failed. He took up land at Arthur's Seat, on the Mornington Peninsula, where the last of their five daughters was born. In spite of near-bankruptcy, Andrew McCrae forbade his wife to paint portraits for money, a decision she bitterly resented. From 1851, when their pastoral venture failed, the couple lived apart. A legacy, promised by her father, was withheld by the Duchess. Georgiana McCrae is remembered for some fine portraits and landscapes now held in Australian galleries, and for the beauty, intelligence and quick wit that made her an influential figure among artists, musicians and writers. An unwilling emigrant, she made a remarkable contribution to the cultural life of colonial Melbourne. BN

• Fisher Library, Univ. of Sydney: McCrae Papers; State Library of Victoria: McCrae Family Papers; National Trust of Australia (Victoria) Collection: McCrae Papers (Harry F. Chaplin Collection).

McCrae, H. (ed.) (1934) *Georgiana's Journal*; Niall, B. (1994) *Georgiana: a biography of Georgiana McCrae*.

MACDONALD, Agnes, born Edinburgh 8 Sept. 1882, died Edinburgh 16 Oct. 1966. Suffrage and women's citizenship campaigner. Daughter of Euphemia Henderson, and Alexander Macdonald, wine and spirit merchant.

Fifth of six children and the only daughter, Agnes Macdonald was brought up to be a 'daughter of the house who stayed home' (*Dispatch* 1962), despite her mother taking over the business in 1893. She later said she joined the WSPU because she was one of 'too many women running around with no training to do anything' (ibid.). In March 1912, she was imprisoned in Holloway for two months for window smashing, an experience she found instructive for her later social work.

A founder member in 1918 and until 1939 the paid secretary of the EWCA, Agnes Macdonald remembered the organisation as busy and effective, 'Meetings all over the country, constant efforts to get things done. And we did get things done!' (ibid.). The ambitious programme included campaigns for more women councillors and MPs; for equal pay and an end to the marriage bar; for pre-school nurseries, improvements to public health and social housing; against child sexual abuse; and for a national maternity service. After retiring, she did Quaker relief work for European refugees and was a governor of a progressive school for delinquent boys. SI

• Macdonald, A., *Evening Dispatch*, 12 Dec. 1962.
Innes, S. (1998) 'Love and Work: Feminism, family and ideas of equality and citizenship, Britain 1900–39', PhD, Univ. of Edinburgh; *ODNB (2004).

MACDONALD, Ann Smith (Annie), n. **Johnston,** born Barony, Lanark, 20 Nov. 1849, died Edinburgh 21 Oct. 1924. Artistic bookbinder. Daughter of Lucy Leitch, and Fred Johnston, bank cashier.

Brought up in Lanark and Glasgow, Annie Johnston in 1880 married William Rae Macdonald, secretary of the Scottish Metropolitan Life Assurance Company and later Carrick Pursuivant and Albany Herald. Their bourgeois Edinburgh circle included the first SNPG curator, John Miller Gray, and, through him, the artist *Phoebe Anna Traquair. John Gray and Annie Macdonald took 'pleasure in searching out and enjoying old bindings in libraries . . . Then we wished to try it ourselves' (Sutherland 1899, p. 420). Walter B. Blaikie allowed evening access to his printing workrooms at T. & A. Constable, where Annie Macdonald developed a method of embossing leather 'worked on the book after it is covered, with one small tool' (Anstruther 1902). Her uncoloured, medievalist figurative bindings were accepted for the Women's Work section of the 'Victorian Era' exhibition (Earl's Court, London 1897) where they were seen by London bookseller-publisher Frank Karslake (Sutherland 1899, p. 420). Their discussions led to the 1898 formation of the Guild of Women Binders, a British exhibiting collective including the dozen-strong ESU group, which exhibited throughout Britain and at the 1900 Exposition Universelle in Paris. EC

• Anstruther, G. E. (1902) *The Bindings of Tomorrow*; Callen, A. (1979) *Angel in the Studio*, pp. 191–2; *Catalogue of Exhibition of Artistic Bookbinding by Women* (1898); 'Studio-Talk', *The Studio* (1898), p. 112; Sutherland, D. M. (1899) 'The Guild of Women Binders', *The Magazine of Art*, pp. 420–3; Tidcombe, M. E. (1996) *Women Bookbinders 1880–1920*, pp. 117–18; Waller, A. C. (1983) 'The Guild of Women-Binders', *The Private Library*, 3rd series, vol. 6: 3, pp. 99–131.

MCDONALD, Camelia Ethel, born 24 Feb. 1909, Bellshill, died Glasgow 1 Dec. 1960. Anarchist envoy to Spanish civil war, printer. Daughter of

Daisy Watts, and Andrew McDonald, coach painter.

One of nine children, Ethel McDonald attended Motherwell High School, and at 16 joined the ILP and left home. After several jobs, she became secretary to the charismatic Guy Aldred (1886–1963) and later to the anti-parliamentary and anti-fascist United Socialist Movement he founded in Glasgow. In October 1936, with Guy Aldred's companion **Jane (Jenny) Patrick** (1884–1971), Ethel McDonald went to Spain at the request of the CNT-FAI (anarchist federation). They could barely ask for a cup of coffee in Spanish, but Ethel McDonald was soon making broadcasts in English on behalf of the Barcelona Anarchist radio station: 'her Scottish voice was a special attraction and her broadcasts aroused comment as far afield as the USA' (John Caldwell quoted Hodgart n. d., p. 11). Together the two women experienced the May Days in Barcelona in 1937, when the communists attacked the anarchist headquarters: 'we [were] filling cartridge clips for the soldiers and preparing meals for them' (ibid., p. 14). Three hundred of their comrades were killed. Guy Aldred published the women's accounts in his *Barcelona Bulletin* in Glasgow. Jenny Patrick returned home, but Ethel McDonald remained through further persecution of the anarchists. She visited anarchists in prison, helped others escape, and became known as the 'Scots Scarlet Pimpernel' and the 'Bellshill Girl Anarchist'. Imprisoned for several days herself, she spent further weeks in hiding, unable to exit Spain legally. Consular intervention got her out and she was welcomed back to Glasgow, telling the press: 'I went to Spain full of hopes and dreams . . . I return full of sadness, dulled by the tragedy I have seen' (ibid., p. 19). Thereafter, she helped run the anarchist Strickland Press with Guy Aldred, Jenny Patrick and John Caldwell. Ethel McDonald was 'equally at ease with a spanner, a sewing machine or a paintbrush' (*ODNB* 2004). She died of multiple sclerosis. A film of her life has been discussed (*Sunday Herald*, 2005). SR

• Mitchell Library, Glasgow: McDonald corr. and papers. Caldwell, J. T. (1988) *Come Dungeons Dark: the life and times of Guy Aldred*; Hodgart, R. M. (n. d., Kate Sharpley Library) *Ethel MacDonald* [sic]: *Glasgow woman anarchist*; *ODNB* (2004) (MacDonald [sic], Ethel; Aldred, Guy; Patrick, Jenny); *Sunday Herald*, 13 Feb. 2005.

MACDONALD, Cicely (c. 1660–c. 1729) *see* **SILEAS NIGHEAN MHIC RAGHNAILL** (c. 1660–c. 1729)

MACDONALD, Flora, n. **MacDonald,** born Milton, South Uist, 1722, died Penduin, Isle of Skye, 4 March 1790. Jacobite heroine. Daughter of Marion MacDonald, minister's daughter, and Ranald MacDonald of Milton, tacksman.

Related to her own chief and the Campbells of Argyll, Flora MacDonald's family had high social standing. Her father died around 1724 and her mother remarried in 1728. They remained at Milton, moving to Armadale on Skye when her eldest brother married in 1745 and took over the Milton farms.

After Culloden, Prince Charles Edward Stewart was in hiding in South Uist. To secure his escape, in June 1746 Flora MacDonald visited her brother in South Uist, and travelled back to Skye with the Prince disguised as her maid. Her stepfather, Hugh MacDonald, although a government officer, is assumed to have had Jacobite sympathies and to have engineered her visit, providing her with a passport to cross the Minch. *Margaret MacLeod, Lady Clanranald, supplied provisions for the crossing. Despite a £30,000 price on his head, the Prince gained freedom, but Flora MacDonald was captured on 12 July 1746 and taken by prison ship to Leith then onwards to London where she was held in a messenger's house. Supporters raised £1,500 for her and an amnesty secured her release after a year's imprisonment. She stayed a year in Edinburgh before returning to Skye in July 1748 to a muted reception – many Highlanders had suffered while she became rich and celebrated. She spent the next two years between London and Edinburgh, then returned to Skye to marry Allan MacDonald of Kingsburgh (1722–92) on 6 November 1750. While trying new farming methods at Kingsburgh and Flodigarry, during his work as factor for *Lady Margaret Macdonald of Sleat and her family, MacDonald lost his wife's fortune and, having overspent his chief's money, was dismissed as factor in 1766. Although now struggling with increasing rents, Flora MacDonald charmed Johnson and Boswell when they visited in 1773.

Flora and Allan MacDonald had five sons and two daughters; when the family emigrated to North Carolina in 1774, John (15) and Frances (8) were left behind. While her husband, on the British side in the American Revolution, was imprisoned from April 1776, Flora MacDonald broke her arm, contracted fevers and was looted of the silver and books she had brought from home. Allan MacDonald was paroled after eighteen months and

Flora followed him to New York in April 1778, then Nova Scotia, where she spent a bitter winter and injured her good arm. In October 1779, she sailed for London where, quite ill, she stayed for six months before travelling to Edinburgh to see her son John, then to Skye to be reunited with Frances. She lived at Dunvegan Castle, where her daughter Anne was a guest. Before Allan MacDonald returned in 1785, she learned that two of their sons had been lost at sea. John gave his parents an allowance in 1788 and they leased Penduin. A few months before her death, Flora MacDonald dictated a description of the events of 1746, and of her time in America. EL

• Douglas, H. (2003) *Flora MacDonald: the most loyal rebel* (Bibl.); MacDonald, A. R. (1938) *The Truth about Flora MacDonald*; Macleod, R. H. (1995) *Flora MacDonald: the Scottish heroine in Scotland and North America*; *ODNB* (2004).

MACDONALD, Louisa, born Arbroath 10 Dec. 1858, died Marylebone, London, 28 Nov. 1949. Scholar, pioneering college principal, Australia. Daughter of Ann Kidd, and John Macdonald, WS and town clerk.

The family's 11th child, Louisa Macdonald was first educated by older sisters, a brother who taught her Latin, and a tutor. After attending a London finishing school and doing well in the Edinburgh Local examinations, she and her sister Bella matriculated at the University of London, which had recently admitted women. Louisa Macdonald graduated from University College London with first-class honours in Classics and honours in German (1884), later acquiring an MA in Classics, while Bella graduated in medicine. After visiting the USA and her brother in Australia, Lousa Macdonald returned to a fellowship at UCL. She taught, undertook research in classical archaeology at the British Museum, travelled, and worked voluntarily on educational reform and women's rights. This excellent preparation, rare for women at the time, gave her a strong advantage when she was selected in 1891 from 65 candidates (eight Australian) to be Foundation Principal of The Women's College within the University of Sydney. She remained in that influential role until 1919, establishing the college's strong academic reputation and collegiate life reminiscent of Girton and Newnham. She was assisted by her life-long friend Dr Evelyn Dickinson, 'new woman', medical graduate and college honorary physician. Louisa Macdonald played a major part in Sydney life, befriending Rose Scott and Maybanke Anderson, central figures in Australian feminism, and other leading Sydney citizens. On retirement she returned to London, retaining close ties with the college. She was both a pioneer of women's education in Australia and a witty commentator on Sydney life, glimpsed through her letters to Eleanor Grove, former principal at College Hall, London. AM

• Macdonald, L. (1949) *The Women's College within the University of Sydney.*
Beaumont, J. and Hole, W. V. (1996) *Letters from Louisa*; Hole, W. V. and Treweeke, A. H. (1953) *The History of The Women's College within the University of Sydney*; Mackinnon, A. (1997) *Love and Freedom: professional women and the reshaping of personal life.*

MACDONALD, Margaret, born Tipton, Staffordshire, 5 Nov. 1864, died London 7 Jan. 1933; **MACDONALD, Frances Eliza,** born Kidsgrove, Staffordshire, 24 August 1873, died Glasgow 12 Dec. 1921. Artist designers. Daughters of Frances Grove Hardeman, and John Macdonald, engineer.

Margaret and Frances Macdonald moved to Glasgow with their family upon the retirement of their Glaswegian father, and enrolled in classes at the Glasgow School of Art. By 1894, they had formed an alliance with a group of students that included their future husbands, architect Charles Rennie Mackintosh and designer James Herbert McNair. Frances married McNair on 14 June 1899, Margaret married Mackintosh on 22 August 1900. Their partnerships with each other and with their husbands proved artistically successful as they collaborated on various projects. Together they became known as 'The Glasgow Four', their work being associated with 'The Glasgow Style' (see Glasgow Girls). Early work by the Macdonald sisters was nicknamed the 'Spook School' by hostile critics. The *Studio*, however, commended the metalwork jointly designed and produced by them in the 1896 Arts and Crafts Exhibition (London) for its novelty, sense of decoration and 'break with tradition', while at the same time noting its eccentricity (*Studio* 1897, p. 89). The collaboration of the four resulted in the highly acclaimed 'rooms' designed for the Vienna Secession (1900) and the Turin Exhibition of Modern Decorative Art (1902), including furniture, metalwork, textiles, gesso panels and paintings.

After 1900, Frances Macdonald tended to focus mostly on watercolours: between 1910 and 1915, she produced a series of enigmatic paintings with titles such as *Man makes the beads of life but woman must thread them* (Hunterian Art Gallery, Glasgow), depicting elongated, emaciated women. Her sister, who was elected a member of the RSSPWC in 1898, produced equally enigmatic watercolours, with themes frequently related to flower lore (*Dancer of the Rhododendrons*, 1910, untraced) or mysticism (*Silver Apples of the Moon*, 1912, untraced, the title of which is a line from a poem by W. B. Yeats). She also made sumptuously elegant gesso panels of mysterious aspect: *O Ye that Walk in Willow Wood*, 1903, refers to Dante Gabriel and Christina Rossetti, and *The Seven Princesses*, 1909 (Vienna), refers to Maeterlinck's play of that name. These panels, as well as her equally accomplished and elegant *The May Queen*, 1900 (Glasgow Museums), were made for interior spaces designed by Mackintosh and, in the case of *May Queen* and *Willow Wood*, graced the walls of *Kate Cranston's popular Glasgow tea-rooms. Frances Macdonald had lived in Liverpool following her marriage to James McNair, but in 1908 the couple, who had one son, returned to Glasgow, where she taught at the GSA for a year or two. She seems to have ceased producing art by 1916, and her early death at 48 remains, like many of her pictures, shrouded in mystery. Margaret Macdonald Mackintosh moved south during the war, and she and her husband lived on and off in France during the 1920s: he died in 1928. She retained her Chelsea studio and died there in 1933. Only in recent years has the striking contribution of the Macdonald sisters to the Glasgow Style been fully recognised. JVH

• J. Burkhauser, J. (ed.) (1990) *Glasgow Girls*; Cumming, E. (ed.) (1992) *Glasgow 1900 Art & Design*; Helland, J. (1993) 'Frances Macdonald: the self as *fin-de-siècle* woman', *Woman's Art Journal*, 14, 1, (1994) 'The critics and the arts and crafts: the instance of Margaret Macdonald and Charles Rennie Mackintosh', *Art History*, 17, 2, (1996) *The Studios of Frances and Margaret Macdonald*, (2001) 'A sense of extravagance: Margaret Macdonald's gesso panels, 1900–3', *Visual Culture in Britain*, 2, 1; *ODNB* (2004); Robertson, P. (1983) *Margaret Macdonald Mackintosh*; White, G. (1897) 'Some Glasgow designers and their work (Part 1)', *Studio*.

MACDONALD, Margaret, of Sleat, n. **Montgomerie,** born Eglinton c. 1716, died 30 March 1799. Estate manager. Daughter of Susanna Kennedy of Culzean, and Alexander, 9th Earl of Eglinton.

Lady Margaret Montgomerie married Sir Alexander Macdonald of Sleat on Skye, whose family was of Jacobite inclination, on 24 April 1739. During the uprising, she was reputed to have helped Prince Charles Edward Stewart escape when *Flora MacDonald brought him to her house, and acted bravely to protect her property and avoid confiscation. Widowed in 1747, she successfully took on the responsibility for running the estate and raising several children.

In 1752, before the departure of her two elder sons, James and Alexander, for an English education, she commissioned the Edinburgh artist William Mosman to paint a double portrait, known as *The Macdonald Boys*. This charming tartan extravaganza showing one boy holding a golf club and the other a shotgun, set against the Skye landscape, is commonly reproduced on shortbread tins and 'Highland' products today. The untimely death in 1766 of her adored eldest son James, a promising classical scholar, caused Lady Margaret to erect a monument to his memory on Skye. Boswell's and Johnson's visit in 1773 inspired melancholy speculation on the death of a genius and the grief of a mother and clan. SN

• Boswell, J. [1773] (1936) *Boswell's Journal of a Tour to the Hebrides with Samuel Johnson*; Douglas, H. (1993) *Flora MacDonald: the most loyal rebel*.
SNPG, *The Macdonald Boys*.

MACDONALD, Mary, n. **MacDougall,** born Ardtun, Isle of Mull, 1789, died Ardtun 21 May 1872. Gaelic poet and hymn writer. Daughter of Anne Morrison, and Duncan MacDougall, farmer.

Mary MacDougall married crofter Neil Macdonald. Her best-known poem is probably 'Leanabh an aigh', verses of which were roughly translated as 'Child in the manger' by Lachlan MacBean for his *Songs and Hymns of the Scottish Highlands* (1888) and set to the Highland melody called in hymn books 'Bunessan', after the village near Ardtun. The translation was included with this tune in the *Revised Church Hymnary* of 1927, and in many books since, though without the pungent second verse, contrasting the Christ child with the children of earthly kings ('Monarchs have tender, delicate children/Nourished in splendour, proud and gay . . . But the most holy Child of salvation/Gently and lowly lived below'). A devout Baptist, Mary Macdonald wrote hymns and poems which she sang at her spinning wheel: one, a satirical poem on tobacco, was written because she thought her husband smoked too much. In many hymn books her dates are wrongly listed as 1817–1890. JRW

• Anon. (1999) *Companion to Rejoice and Sing*; Milgate, W. (1982) *Songs of the People of God*.

MCDOUALL, Agnes, n. **Buchan-Hepburn,** born East Linton 27 Sept. 1838, died Logan 15 March 1926. Gardener and plant collector. Daughter of Helen Little, and Sir Thomas Buchan-Hepburn.

The second of five children, Agnes Buchan-Hepburn was born into a family of keen gardeners and plant collectors. During her childhood at Smeaton Hepburn, East Linton, her father expanded the woodlands, planting new conifers discovered by Scottish plant hunters such as David Douglas and Robert Fortune. When she married James McDouall, landowner, in 1869, she moved to his ancient family estate at Logan, near Stranraer, taking her own collection of roses, lilies and shrubs, as well as important connections with plant hunters. Although the plant collection at Logan was later to become famous under her sons, Kenneth and Douglas, Agnes McDouall was their inspiration and she was the first to exploit the garden's potential for growing tender exotic plants. She is credited with starting the collection of Southern Hemisphere species by planting Logan's first eucalyptus tree, *Eucalyptus urnigera*, beneath the ruin of Castle Balzieland in the walled garden.

The walled garden, now Logan Botanic Garden, became part of the Royal Botanic Garden Edinburgh in 1969. Agnes McDouall's tree was cut down in 1994 when it became unsafe. She is buried in Kirkmaiden Churchyard near Drummore. FY

• Affleck, D. (2000) 'Smeaton Hepburn Gardens, East Linton', *Caledonian Gardener*, RCHS, pp. 56–7; Bennell, A. (2003) *Logan Botanic Garden, Royal Botanic Garden Edinburgh*; (1987) *An Inventory of Gardens and Designed Landscapes*, vol. 5; Smith, W. Wright (1945) 'Obituary Kenneth McDouall', *The Gardeners' Chronicle*, p. 34; Williamson, D. (1901) 'Logan Gardens, Wigtonshire', *The Gardeners' Chronicle*, p. 126.

MCDOUGALL, Lily Martha Maud, born Glasgow 25 July 1875, died Edinburgh 21 Dec. 1958. Artist and hostess. Daughter of Matilda Milne, and William Henrie McDougall, banker.

Lily McDougall grew up in Glasgow and Bonnyrigg, Midlothian. She studied at the Royal Institution, Edinburgh and at The Hague School of Art, Antwerp. In 1904, she entered the Carrière Academy, Paris and worked in the studio of Jacques-Emile Blanche under Lucien Simon. Returning to Edinburgh, she joined the many women in Scotland striving to become accepted as professional artists in a male-dominated sphere. Exceptionally, her father supported her by founding in 1924 the SSWA, which enabled women in

Scotland to exhibit their work. She became a regular exhibitor and, by 1914, she had a studio at 45 Frederick Street, Edinburgh. In 1923 an adjacent studio was rented by William MacTaggart, William Crozier, and later William Gillies. A generation older than these rising artists, she was an influential figure who offered them encouragement and support. The impact of her own painting, especially portraits and flower subjects which were full of panache and relied on rich impasto and dense colours, was acknowledged by Gillies. In 1940, she and her younger sister, Rose, a violinist, moved to Eskbank, near Dalkeith. Thereafter the sisters became famous for their tea parties and dinners for artists, musicians, actors and writers, which became part of the Edinburgh social calendar. In 1955, the Scottish Gallery celebrated Lily McDougall's 80th birthday with a one-woman show, and a memorial exhibition was held there in 1959 after her death. JOS

• RSA archives: typescript list, works available for exhibition 1955.
Carolan, A. (ed.) (1999) *Review, 75 Years of Visual Arts Scotland*; *Memorial Exhibition of Paintings by the late Lily M. M. McDougall (1875–1958), 2–14 March 1959, Scottish Gallery* (catalogue); *The Scotsman*, 23 Dec. 1958 (obit.); Soden, J. and Keller, V. (1998) *William Gillies*.

MACDOUGALL of MacDougall, Margaret Hope Garnons, born Athlone, Ireland, 21 Jan. 1913, died Oban 22 Dec. 1998. Historian and collector. Daughter of Colina MacDougall, and Alexander James MacDougall, Chief of the Clan MacDougall.

Hope MacDougall was the youngest of three sisters brought up at the clan seat, Dunollie Castle, Argyll. She was educated by a governess, at a French school in Edinburgh and boarding school in Yorkshire. During the Second World War she assisted nursing staff at Cortachy Castle, Kirriemuir, and worked on a farm, later becoming a gardener in Forfar, for six years. She returned home on her father's death in 1953 to care for her mother, who died in 1963.

Hope's eldest sister, **Coline Helen Elizabeth MacDougall of MacDougall** (1904–90), moved into Dunollie in 1966, on becoming the first woman Chief of the Clan MacDougall. Coline was a collector of Chinese jade with historical interests, and when in 1966 Hope McDougall moved to nearby Ganavan House, she too began to collect systematically, having developed her interest in social history earlier. Over the next 35 years she established the MacDougall Collection, a museum

collection of national significance, backed by a large archive of photographs and documents. Her mentor was *Isabel Grant, founder of *Am Fasgadh*, later the Highland Folk Museum at Kingussie. The MacDougall Collection, now held at Dunollie House, Oban, covers the working and domestic lives of the people of the Highlands and Islands, with comparative material from elsewhere and important sub-groups such as treen (decorative wooden objects) and wooden spoons. Hope MacDougall also had a keen sense of Highland lineage: she preserved many items from life in the 'big house' and took on the role of clan historian. Her *Kerrera: Mirror of History* (reprinted 2004), is the definitive book on a clan land gifted by her direct ancestor, Somerled.

A notable local figure, she was renowned for clearing old shops as they closed, for beach-combing, midden-searching, and befriending local people on her collecting tours from Arran to Shetland. Hope MacDougall was also a birdwatcher and a keen dawn bather, all year round and well into her 70s. She lived a frugal life, grinding flour on a quernstone and weaving her own MacDougall tartan. She made only three trips abroad: two to the Holy Land and one to the Faroes, for the collection.

The middle sister, **Jean Louisa Morag Hadfield** (1910–99), was an expert on natural textile dyes, and contributed to the collection. She also researched the correspondence of the Clan MacDougall chiefs between 1715 and 1864, following the discovery of bundles of letters in the attic, during preparations for the wedding of her daughter, Morag, the current Clan Chief: all three sisters collaborated on the resulting book *Highland Postbag* (1984 reprinted 2003). CG

• MacDougall Collection archive and Clan MacDougall archive, Dunollie House, Oban, Argyll.
MacDougall, M. H. G., Works as above.
Private information (Madam MacDougall of MacDougall, 31st Chief of the Clan MacDougall).

MACFARLANE, Helen, [Howard Morton], journalist and translator, fl. 1850–1.

Traceable only through her articles, published between April and December 1850 in the papers of Chartist George Julian Harney, when it is likely that she was around 30, Helen Macfarlane remains quite obscure. She is believed to have been born and brought up in Scotland. Her wide reading in philosophy and literature, including French and German originals, which informs her writing, suggests a middle-class background, as does her travelling on the Continent. She was an appalled eye-witness of the ruthless repression following the Vienna uprising of March 1848. In 1850, she returned to Britain and had settled in Burnley by the end of the year, where she probably lived with 33-year-old William Macfarlane, calico printer, and his wife Agnes, both born in Scotland. The explicit socialism adopted by some Chartist leaders was akin to her own vision of a society, to be achieved by revolution, in which everybody would enjoy equal political and social rights regardless of class, race or gender. Her socialism was suffused with a Christianity in which Jesus figured as a prototypical proletarian. It was also influenced by Marx, Engels and Hegel, whom she was the first to publicise in English, inserting translated passages into her articles. Her name disappeared from Harney's *Democratic Review* after June 1850 and articles by one 'Howard Morton' began to appear. Schoyen's suggestion (1958, p. 204) that this was her pen-name is now generally accepted. Marx and Engels, who knew her personally, commissioned her to produce the first English translation of their *Communist Manifesto*, serialised in Harney's *Red Republican*. After an insult by Harney's wife, Mary Cameron (the daughter of a radical Ayrshire weaver), at the New-Year's-Eve party of the internationalist Fraternal Democrats in 1850, no more articles by Helen Macfarlane appeared. This was deplored by Marx, who considered her 'the only collaborator on [Harney's] spouting rag who had original ideas – a rare bird, on his paper' (ibid. p. 215). 'Howard Morton' was last heard of in April 1851, donating money for revolutionary Polish and Hungarian refugees facing deportation. JS

• Macfarlane, H., Work as above and see Black (Bibl.) and www.eup.ed.ac.uk

Anon. (1975) 'Helen Macfarlane, chartist and marxist', *Quarterly Bulletin of Marx Memorial Library*, 74; Black, D. (2004) *Helen Macfarlane: a feminist, revolutionary journalist and philosopher in mid 19th-century England* (Bibl.); *Marx Engels Collected Works* [1963] (1976) Marx to Engels, Letter 23.2.1851, 27; Schoyen, A. R. (1958) *The Chartist Challenge: a portrait of George Julian Harney*; Schwarzkopf, J. (1991) *Women in the Chartist Movement*.

MACFARLANE, Jessie, m. **Brodie,** born Edinburgh 20 Jan. 1843, died Edinburgh 18 August 1871. Itinerant preacher. Daughter of Mary Maxwell Turner, and Archibald McFarlane, clothier.

Jessie Macfarlane grew up in a Presbyterian household. In 1859, at the beginning of a period of evangelical revival, she heard the influential lay preacher Brownlow North. She attended revival meetings throughout 1860 and converted late that year. In 1861 she began extemporary preaching to women's meetings and missions around Scotland. Although unusual, it was considered acceptable in revivalist circles for women to engage in public preaching to other women. Jessie Macfarlane's ministry entered a new and controversial phase when she began to admit men to her meetings, challenging conventions that respectable women played no public role in mixed society and that women should keep silent in church. When she also undertook religious instruction of new converts and spoke to mixed Christian audiences, these traditions were further confronted. She was supported by Gordon Forlong, an Aberdeen lawyer who was a leading light in the Plymouth Brethren. He believed there was scriptural warrant for female preaching and actively promoted Jessie Macfarlane's ministry. This view was not shared by her fiancé, who broke off their engagement. In 1864 she published a pamphlet, *Scriptural Warrant for Women to Preach the Gospel*, in which she claimed that the role of prophetess, mentioned in scripture, remained valid. Her emotional style of millennialist preaching was effective both in Scotland and, from 1866 to 1869, in major English cities.

Jessie Macfarlane was only one of several itinerant female preachers working for the Brethren during the 1860s. They were mostly young, single, working-class and strong-minded. **Isabella Armstrong** (born 1840) began preaching in her native County Tyrone at the age of nineteen. When she came to Scotland in 1863 she was based at Newmains Assembly, preaching to hundreds every week. She was considered an 'eloquent' challenge to those who were antipathetic to 'petticoat preachers'. In 1866 in a tract in defence of her ministry (*A Plea for Modern Prophetesses*) she argued that women are created equal with men, and that Christ has freedom in whom he chooses as the instruments of salvation. Female preachers were a distinctive feature of popular lay revivalism, and constituted a serious provocation to religious and social norms of the mid-Victorian era. They helped to contribute to changing perceptions and possibilities for women. Isabella Armstrong went on to engage in temperance and suffrage activity, but Jessie Macfarlane, who married Dr David Brodie on 31 Oct 1869, suffered ill-health and died in 1871. LO

• Anderson, O. (1969) 'Women Preachers in mid-Victorian Britain', *Historical Journal*, 12; Dickson, N. (1993–5) 'Modern prophetesses: women preachers in the 19th century Scottish Brethren' *Records of the Scottish Church History Society*, 25; Macdonald, L. A. O. (2000) *A Unique and Glorious Mission*; *ODNB* (2004).

MCGHIE, Mrs, fl. 1770s, Aberdeen. Innkeeper.

The New Inn, Aberdeen, was prominently located in the Castlegate, adjoining the Tolbooth and Masonic Lodge. From June 1763, it was operated by John McGhie and, after his death in about 1770, it was regularly identified in the *Aberdeen Journal* as 'Mrs McGhie's House'. It appeared even more commercially active during her tenure, benefiting from its location in Aberdeen's commercial district. Senior members of the community regularly used it to conduct business. Alexander Carlyle, of the Edinburgh literati, described it in 1769 as, 'a very good house – handsome rooms, very good service' (LHPS n. d.), as did Samuel Johnson in August 1773: 'we found a very good house and civil treatment' (Johnson, 1924 edn., p. 12). Operating a 'civil' business with a good reputation, women like Mrs McGhie established themselves in Scotland's commercial communities. DLS
• *Aberdeen Journal*, 1758–73; Carlyle, A. (n. d.) *Journal of a Tour to the North of Scotland*, Local History Pamphlet Series (LHPS); Defoe, D. [1726–7] (1987) *The Complete English Tradesman*; Johnson, S. [1775] (1924) *Journey to the Western Isles of Scotland*, R. W. Chapman, ed.; Keith, A. (1972) *A Thousand Years of Aberdeen*.

MACGOUN, Hannah Clarke Preston, born Edinburgh 19 June 1864, died Edinburgh 20 August 1913. Artist, illustrator. Daughter of Isabella Clarke, and Rev. Robert William MacGoun of Greenock.

The sixth of eight children and profoundly deaf from birth, Hannah MacGoun followed her sister Janet to Edinburgh Trustees' Academy (1887–92) where tutor Robert McGregor guided her interest in painters of the Dutch and Barbizon schools. 'Highly Commended' in her final year, she travelled to Germany and Holland, meeting Bernardus Blommers and Josef Israels. The Church of Scotland Magazine *Life & Work* gave Hannah MacGoun her earliest commission, illustrating poems by her father (1894). More work followed, for publishers Oliphant Anderson & Ferrier (1896) and T. N. Foulis (1905–13). Harriet Warrack used her drawings for an anthology of poems, and she illustrated many children's books (full list in *DSAA*, p. 359). John Hogben (1914, pp. 12–13) referred to her as 'the Scottish Kate Greenaway' and Sir James

Caw noted her ability to paint children, although she also produced many images of elderly people and of the Scottish clergy, in the social realist vein of Herkomer. She exhibited at the Scottish National Exhibition (1908), the RGIFA (1898–1914) and the SSA (1909–13). Her portraits of children from the Nelson, Haldane and Morison families appear in catalogues for the RSA (1885–1914). RA
• Addison, R. (2000) 'Spirited activity: Scottish book design and women illustrators, 1890–1920', *Jour. Scot. Soc. Art History*, 5, pp. 59–68, (2004) 'Women in book illustration in Edinburgh 1886–1945', PhD, ECA; *DSAA*; Elphick, I. and Harris, P. (2000) *T. N. Foulis*; Helland, J. (2000) *Professional Women Painters in Nineteenth-century Scotland*; Hogben, J. (1914) 'Hannah McGoun', *Life & Work*, Jan. 1914, pp. 12–13 (obit.).

MACGREGOR, Margaret Ann Kinniburgh, n. Burns, baptised Edinburgh 11 Nov. 1838, died Glasgow 20 Jan. 1901. Bible Woman and Lady Mission Superintendent. Daughter of Jeanie Marshall, and James Burns, clerk.

Margaret Burns attended Moray House School in Edinburgh. She belonged to Lothian Road United Presbyterian Church, but experienced an evangelical conversion during the Revival that swept Scotland 1859–61. After marriage, she and her husband Thomas Macgregor moved to Govan and joined St Mary's Free Church. She was soon involved in the church's Sabbath School and outreach work. In 1869, she began holding meetings for local mothers in her home and visiting the sick. Her work grew as she ran evangelical, gospel, and kitchen meetings and Bible classes for young men and women. She moved to new premises in Harmony Row in 1883, just before her husband's death, her work now funded by *Isabella Elder. As Lady Superintendent for Fairfield Works Mission, Margaret Macgregor took responsibility for a panoply of initiatives. Sewing and kitchen meetings were key elements in the mission strategy – offering women skills, materials and company in carrying out traditional domestic duties, in an atmosphere of Bible studies, 'improving' readings and prayer. The mission was run on non-denominational lines, seeking co-operation with local Protestant congregations. A nursery offered childcare for women mill-workers and widowers. Margaret Macgregor made great personal efforts to enable numerous women and children to enjoy a summer holiday in the country.

Her gifts as an orator and expounder of Scripture were widely acknowledged, and her organisational resourcefulness, combined with her faith and compassion, endeared her to the community. She persistently struggled, against the odds, to provide quality of life in the midst of poverty. Trusting in a loving God herself, she tried to embody that love in her ministry. Margaret Macgregor typified the increasing reliance of Victorian evangelical Protestantism on the labours of women. LO

• Ferguson, J. (1904) *Set Apart: being the life-work of Margaret A Macgregor, Superintendent of the Fairfield Works Mission*; Macdonald, L. A. O. (1999) *A Woman of Many Parts*, The 2nd Margaret Macgregor Memorial Lecture; Thomson, D. P. (c. 1975) *Women of the Scottish Church*.

MCIAN, Frances Matilda (Fanny), n. **Whitaker,** m1 **McIan,** m2 **Unwin,** born Bath c. 1814, died London 7 April 1897. Artist, painter of Highland scenes. Daughter of Sarah Hawkins, upholsterer, and William Whitaker, cabinetmaker.

Fanny Whitaker's early education is unclear, but she eloped to Bristol in 1831 with Robert McIan (1803–56), an actor from Inverness-shire (stage name, 'Robert Jones'). Swept off her feet by this Scottish Highlander, she identified with his dramatic initiatives. In London, he joined the Highland Society, while she worked as an art tutor and illustrator. Both painted and exhibited together, romantic Jacobite subjects being a significant element in their repertoire. Fanny McIan's *Highland Refugees from the '45* (1845) became a popular print. Other paintings, *Soldiers' wives awaiting the results of the Battle of Prestonpans* (1849) and *Highland Emigration* (1852), reflected some of the common emotional experience of Highland families. As Head of the Female School at London's Government School of Design (1842–57), Fanny McIan was respected for her professional expertise. She was elected honorary associate of the RSA (1854), only the second woman to achieve this distinction. Meanwhile, Robert McIan produced illustrated books, *Clans of the Scottish Highlands* (1845, 1847) and *Picturesque Gatherings of the Scottish Highlanders* (1848). After his death, Fanny McIan remarried in 1858, acquiring property in Argyll on the death of her second husband, Richard Unwin (1820–64). Although she was not Scottish-born, her association with Highland subjects was firmly fixed in the public mind. RA

• RSA catalogues (1840s).

Morse, B. (2001) *A Woman of Design, a Man of Passion*; *ODNB* (2004).

Private information.

MCILROY, Anne Louise, DBE, born Lavin House, Co. Antrim, c. 1875, died Girvan, Ayrshire, 8 Feb. 1968. Obstetrician, gynaecologist. Daughter of James McIlroy, GP, and his wife.

Louise McIlroy was one of the first female Glasgow medical students, graduating MBChB from the all-women Queen Margaret College in 1898, and studying in London, Vienna and Berlin. Her career was a series of firsts: the first woman MD (1900, commended) from the University of Glasgow and first female resident at Glasgow Royal Infirmary (1899); by 1910 she had served as house surgeon at the Glasgow Samaritan Hospital and gynaecologist at the Victoria Infirmary. The first woman senior assistant to the Muirhead Professor of Obstetrics at the University of Glasgow, she also obtained the LM Dublin in 1901 and the DSc from Glasgow in 1910 and London in 1934.

During the First World War, Louise McIlroy was Médecin Chef at the *Scottish Women's Hospital, Troyes, France, and then in Salonika and Serbia. A natural leader, showing great 'steadiness of purpose' (Leneman 1994, p. 178), she held out against interference from influential outsiders, fought off illness and pioneered several initiatives. She always wore a thistle badge on her French army cap. She ended the war as a surgeon with the RAMC in Constantinople, receiving the Croix de Guerre and two Serbian medals. Louise McIlroy spent the rest of her career chiefly in London as consultant and Professor of Obstetrics and Gynaecology at the Royal Free Hospital, while holding posts at Bermondsey and the Marie Curie Hospital for Women. She published more than 20 research articles and wrote a textbook on pregnancy. During the Second World War, now well into her 60s, she served as gynaecological surgeon in Slough and as obstetric war consultant for Buckinghamshire. Created DBE in 1929, she was appointed to the BMA General Council and to fellowships of the Royal College of Physicians, England (1923) and the Royal College of Obstetricians and Gynaecologists (1929). She had honorary degrees from Glasgow and Belfast, and among other administrative roles was vice-president in 1912 of the Glasgow Obstetrical and Gynaecological Society and secretary of the Glasgow and West of Scotland Association of Registered Medical Women (founded 1904). Sharp-minded, with 'a ready wit' (ibid., p. 30), she worked until the age of 70, retiring to Turnberry, Ayrshire. JLMJ

• McIlroy, A. L. (1924) *From a Balcony on the Bosphorus*, (1936) *The Toxaemias of Pregnancy*.

Alexander, W. (1987) *First Ladies of Medicine*; *BMJ*, 17 Feb. 1968, 1(589), p. 451; Jenkinson, J. (1993) *Scottish Medical Societies 1731–1939*; Leneman, L. (1994) *In the Service of Life*; *ODNB* (2004).

MCINNES (or MACINNES), Helen Clark, m. **Highet,** born Glasgow 7 Oct. 1907, died New York, USA, 30 Sept. 1985. Novelist. Daughter of Jessie McDiarmid, and Donald McInnes, joiner.

Helen McInnes and her brother were brought up in Helensburgh, where she attended Hermitage School. She graduated MA in French and German at the University of Glasgow in 1928. After working with Dumbarton County Libraries, she gained a diploma in librarianship at University College London in 1931. At the University of Glasgow – anecdotally, in her first week there – she met classical scholar Gilbert Highet (d. 1978), whom she married on 22 September 1932. Moving to Oxford where he held a fellowship, they worked together on translations and spent their summers travelling in Europe. They had one son. In 1937, they moved to New York, where Gilbert Highet was professor of Latin and Greek at Columbia University. They became American citizens in 1952. In 1973, both received the Wallace Award of the American Scottish Foundation, awarded to Americans of Scottish descent distinguished in fields including education and literature.

She published 21 espionage thrillers under the name Helen MacInnes. Her first novel, *Above Suspicion* (1941), drew on her observations of the growing Nazi movement during the 1930s, particularly on her honeymoon in Bavaria. *Assignment in Brittany* (1942) is said to have been used to train Allied personnel to work with the French underground, and *The Unconquerable* (1944) was such a convincing portrayal of the Polish resistance that she was called to Washington to reveal her sources. Though her husband served as a British intelligence officer in the Second World War, she denied having access to inside information, claiming that she based most of her stories on newspaper reports. She supplemented this with extensive travel in Europe and her novels are noted for their accurate depiction of the history, culture and social conditions of the areas in which they are set. They have been criticised as formulaic (two more experimental mainstream novels were poorly received by critics) but her choice of theme arises from a life-long concern, dating from her reading of George Orwell, about totalitarian regimes. MARB

• Princeton Univ. Library, Princeton, NJ, USA: Archive; Univ. of Glasgow Archives.
MacInnes, H., Works as above and see *HSWW* (Bibl.).
DLB Gale, 87, pp. 284–94; *HSWW* (Bibl.); *ODNB* (2004); *The Times*, 2 Oct. 1985 (obit.).

MACINTYRE, Sheila, n. **Scott,** born Edinburgh 23 April 1910, died Cincinatti, Ohio, 21 March 1960. Mathematician. Daughter of Helen Myers Meldrum, and James Alexander Scott, science teacher.

Sheila Scott attended Trinity Academy and The Edinburgh Ladies' College before taking her MA in mathematics and natural philosophy (University of Edinburgh, 1932). She moved to Girton College, Cambridge, and carried out research with Mary Cartwright, leading to the paper 'On the asymptotic periods of integral functions' in the *Proceedings of the Cambridge Philosophical Society* (1933). Having returned to Scotland in 1934 and taught at several schools, including St Leonards, St Andrews, she married mathematician Archibald James Macintyre in 1940 and was appointed assistant lecturer at the University of Aberdeen where her husband also taught. There she completed her PhD, supervised by Edward M. Wright, on 'Some problems in interpolatory function theory' (1947). Between 1947 and 1958 she published another ten papers while bringing up her two children, and became FRSE in 1958. Sheila Macintyre also prepared a German-English mathematical dictionary and was an active member of the EMS and the MA. In 1958, she and her husband accepted visiting research professorships at the University of Cincinnati, where she taught until her early death from cancer. Considered a brilliant original mathematician, she was remembered too as a superb teacher and helpful colleague, whose clarity of mind made her an exceptionally able lecturer. LS
• Cartwright, M. L. (1961) 'Sheila Scott Macintyre', *Jour. of the London Math. Soc.*, 36, pp. 254–6; Cossar, J. (1960–1) 'Sheila Scott Macintyre', *Proc. of the Edin. Math. Soc.*, 12, p. 112; Fasanelli, F. D. (1987) 'Sheila Scott Macintyre', in Campbell, P. and Grinstein, L. (eds) *Women of Mathematics*, pp. 140–3; Wright, E. M. (1961) 'Sheila Scott Macintyre', *Year Book of the RSE*, pp. 21–3.

MCIVER, Margaret (Maggie) ('The Barras Queen'), n. **Russell,** born Bridgeton, Glasgow, 9 May 1879, died Cambuslang 31 May 1958. Entrepreneur, founder of the Glasgow 'Barras' market and Barrowland Ballroom. Daughter of Margaret

Hutcheson, French polisher, and Alexander Russell, policeman.

Maggie Russell is said to have had her first taste of business aged 12 when she was asked to look after a family friend's fruit barrow in Parkhead, in the East End of Glasgow. She later opened a small fruit shop in Bridgeton, also in Glasgow's East End, and met her future husband and business partner, James McIver, at the local fruit market. In the early 1920s, they started up a small business in the Calton district of Glasgow, hiring out horses and carts to local hawkers (mainly women) on a daily basis. After the First World War there was an increased volume of traffic on city thoroughfares and renewed attempts by the Corporation to discourage street trading. The McIvers began organising Saturday markets on land they acquired on the site of the present Barras and the market grew quickly to become one of Glasgow's most famous institutions. It soon had more than 300 barrows. The original market was covered in 1926, as Maggie McIver was concerned for the welfare of the hawkers and customers in poor weather.

When her husband died, of malaria contracted during the war, Maggie McIver, left to raise nine children, had to think up new ways of raising income – a ballroom was the solution. Every year, she had treated her stallholders and their families to a Christmas meal, drink and dance in the local St Mungo's Hall. Finding it already booked one year, she built a ballroom above the enclosed market. It was opened on Christmas Eve, 1934, in a city and period described as 'dancing daft' (*Herald* 1955). It attracted many big bands and during the Second World War was popular with American servicemen, who introduced the jive and the jitterbug to the city. The sign over the door, of a man pushing a barrow, became such a landmark that it was referred to in a German propaganda broadcast by 'Lord Haw-Haw' (William Joyce), and was removed. In June 1958, Maggie McIver, by now a multi-millionaire, died, and in September that year, the ballroom was destroyed by fire. The Barras business remains in her family, and the market, which continues to be dominated by female stallholders, operates every Saturday and Sunday, attracting huge crowds. The rebuilt ballroom is one of the city's premier rock concert venues. YGB

• *Glasgow Herald*, 25 Jan. 1955; *The Herald*, 13 August 1999; *HHGW*; *Sunday Herald*, 12 April 2001.
The Glasgow Story – culture and leisure: www.theglasgow-story.com
The History of the Barras Market: www.glasgowbarrowland.com/market/history.htm

MACKAY, Barbara, Lady Reay, born Scourie c. 1615, died c. 1690. Poet. Daughter of Ann Corbett of Arkboll, and Hugh MacKay of Scourie.

The second wife of a Highland chieftain, John MacKay, 2nd Lord Reay (c. 1612–80), Barbara MacKay, like her father and her husband, was a staunch Royalist and an early proponent of Presbyterianism in Strathnaver. When her husband was imprisoned in 1649 for fighting under Montrose, Barbara pleaded his cause with Oliver Cromwell, who promised not to pursue John if he escaped, which she then helped him to do. She went to London in 1664 to ask for Charles II's support in an ongoing land dispute against the Gordons. Her lively household included a tutor, a harper, a piper, and a fool. When Hugh Fraser, 8th Lord Lovat, visited Lord and Lady Reay at Balnakeil House in Durness in 1669, he was entertained with activities as varied as fishing, hawking, hunting, archery, jumping, wrestling and dancing. At the end of his visit, Lord Lovat reported that Lady Reay gave him a silk plaid and trousers and a doublet, all of her own work, and the Rev. James Fraser called her 'the prettiest, wittiest woman that ever I knew here . . . a great historian, a smart poet, and for virtue and housekeeping, few or none her parallel' (Fraser 1905, p. 450). The MacKays had at least six children. After her eldest son and heir, Donald MacKay, was killed in a gunpowder accident, Barbara MacKay helped educate her grandson, George, 3rd Lord Reay. Her principal poetry manuscript, containing ten largely religious poems, is dedicated to the Countess of Caithness. Her best known poem, 'Anagramme on his Ma[jes]ty', mingles religious and political ideas, encouraging Charles II to be a good king. She also wrote a eulogy to Lord Lovat (ibid., pp. 509–10), who died in 1672. PBG

• NAS: GD84, Papers of the MacKay Family, Lords Reay; NLS: Adv. MS.19.3.4 'Anagramme on his Ma[jes]ty'; Wodrow Quarto xxvii, ff 9v–28 'To the Right Honourable the Countess off Caithness'.
Fraser, J. [1676–c. 1699] (1905) *Chronicles of the Frasers*, W. MacKay, ed.; Mackay, A. (1906) *The Book of MacKay*; *SP*, 7, pp. 169–74.

MACKAY, Janet, of Bighouse, c. 1731–c. 1768. Wife of murder victim. Daughter of Elizabeth Mackay, heiress of Bighouse, Sutherland, and Hugh Mackay, second son of Lord Reay.

Raised in Tongue House, 18-year-old Janet Mackay finished her education in Edinburgh where she met Colin Campbell of Glenure, a man in his 40s with four illegitimate daughters. In February 1749 he was made government factor on a forfeited Jacobite estate; in May 1749 the couple married and settled at Glenure House. They had two daughters. Janet Mackay was pregnant when Colin Campbell was killed in Appin in 1752, a murder made famous in R. L. Stevenson's *Kidnapped*.

After the murder, Janet Mackay returned to her family home to await the birth of her child; a son would inherit the estate. To her great disappointment, the child born was a girl and Glenure passed to her brother-in-law Duncan Campbell. Janet Mackay secretly married her sister's stepson, Charles Baillie, younger of Rosehall. Her father turned her out, and the couple spent several years in Yorkshire before returning north in 1756 to be with her children. Duncan Campbell was slow to provide for the upkeep and education of her daughters. Her father took up her cause, causing a rift between the Mackay and Campbell families. Charles Baillie was killed in Louisbourg, New France, in 1758. Janet Mackay moved to Edinburgh where she married a merchant, Alexander Hart. Her eldest surviving daughter, Louisa, succeeded to Bighouse. MB-J

• NAS: GD170, Campbell of Barcaldine Papers.
Gibson, R. (2003) *The Appin Murder in their Own Words.*

MACKAY, Margaret, born c. 1722, died Strathnaver 18 June 1814. Victim of the Sutherland Clearances.

In 1814, Margaret Mackay (also incorrectly referred to as Mrs Chisholm), was living with her daughter Henrietta and son-in-law William Chisholm, a sub-tenant and tinker, at Badinloskin, an isolated holding in the midst of the common grazings of Rosal in Strathnaver. Aged over 90, she had been bedridden for some years. Her father and grandfather had been ground officers on the Sutherland estate in the parish of Farr.

The tenants of Rosal agreed with Patrick Sellar, factor for the Marquess and Marchioness of Stafford (*Elizabeth Sutherland, Duchess-Countess of Sutherland) and incoming sheep farming tenant, that William Chisholm should be removed. Sellar later claimed that he was of ill repute. On 13 June 1814, the family was evicted by a party acting under Patrick Sellar's orders. The roof was thrown down and the house set on fire, apparently while Margaret Mackay was still inside. Carried out by another daughter, Janet, and taken

to a small bothy, she died five days later. Sellar was accused of causing her death but acquitted at his trial. The event became one of the most notorious in the history of the Highland Clearances. MB-J

• NAS: CS232/S/23/2 Court of Session process.
Adam, R. J. (ed.) (1972) *Papers on Sutherland Estate Management 1802–16*; Richards, E. (1999) *Patrick Sellar and the Highland Clearances.*

MCKECHNIE, Sheila Marshall, DBE, born Camelon, Falkirk, 3 May 1948, died London 2 Jan. 2004. Campaigner. Daughter of Christina Marshall, and Hugh McKechnie, baker.

Sheila McKechnie grew up in Falkirk. She was greatly influenced by her family, who gave her the confidence and spirit she used to great effect in her campaigning career. Her mother remarked that she could 'start a fight in an empty house' (*Guardian*, 2004). Head girl at Falkirk Grammar School, she was the first person in her family to go on to university, reading politics and history at the University of Edinburgh. There, she joined in the widespread questioning of authority in the late 1960s, becoming an outspoken feminist and campaigner for student representation in university policy-making (a thorn in the side of the university establishment at the time, she was made Alumna of the year in 1991, a generation later). After an MA in industrial relations at Warwick and research work at Oxford, where she was on the board of radical feminist *Red Rag*, she worked with various trade unions until her appointment as director of Shelter (1985–94), the campaigning organisation for housing the homeless. Under her guidance, Shelter restructured, heightened its campaigning profile and increased its turnover tenfold.

Appointed director of the Consumers' Association in 1995, she was involved in establishing the FSAgency and in changing laws on competition, foodstuffs labelling and advertising to children. She campaigned (notably against CAP) at a European level as President of the European Union Consumer Group, and served on the Bank of England board. She was extremely critical of financial institutions. Friends and colleagues found her fiercely loyal and kind, and her partnership with Alan Grant lasted 27 years. Eventually the value of her forthright, confrontational manner, questioning injustice wherever she saw it, was publicly recognised. She was made OBE in 1995 for services to housing and the homeless, and DBE in 2001 for services to consumers. The FSAgency has set up an annual Award for community food initiatives in her memory. KMD

• McKechnie, S. and Wilson, D. (1986) *Homes above All: housing in Britain.*
The Guardian, 5 Jan. 2004 (Appreciation and obit.); *The Herald*, 7 Jan. 2004 (Appreciation); *The Scotsman*, 6 Jan. 2004 (obit.).
Private information.

MACKELLAR, Mary, n. **Cameron,** born Fort William 1 Oct. 1834, died Edinburgh 7 Sept. 1890. Poet and folklorist. Daughter of Allan Cameron, baker.

Mary Cameron married a sea captain, John Mackellar. The couple travelled around Europe by sea for some years, surviving several shipwrecks. In 1876, Mary Mackellar settled in Edinburgh, soon afterwards obtaining a judicial separation from her husband. She taught Gaelic to *Marjory Kennedy-Fraser. From 1880, she earned her living as a writer, publishing *Poems and Songs in Gaelic and English* (1880), and translating *Queen Victoria's second series of *Leaves from Our Journal in the Highlands* into Gaelic. An accomplished versifier, her Gaelic poetry flows easily. She was honorary bard to the Gaelic Society of Inverness, 1876–90, delivering several important lectures. Expert in the lore of her native Lochaber, her description of women's waulking (fulling or thickening) of cloth and the accompanying choral songs, and her account of transhumance (moving cattle to summer pastures), are unique witnesses to activities fast disappearing. Occasionally she evokes a sense of Arcadian life for previous generations, but that does not diminish her work's great value. JMACI

• Mackellar, M., Works as above and (1885–6) 'Unknown Lochaber bards', *Trans. Gael. Soc. Inverness*, 12, (1886–7) 'The Waulking Day, with Songs', ibid., 13, (1887–9) 'The Sheiling and its Tradition and Songs', ibid., 14, 15, (1889–90) 'Legends and Traditions of Lochaber', ibid., 16.
ODNB (2004).

MACKENZIE, Agnes Mure (Muriel),‡ CBE, born Stornoway 9 April 1891, died Edinburgh 26 Feb. 1955. Author and historian. Daughter of Agnes Drake, and Murdoch Mackenzie, physician.

A graduate of the University of Aberdeen, Agnes Mure Mackenzie lectured in English Literature at Aberdeen and Birkbeck College, London. She published 40 works of literary criticism, fiction, poetry, and history and was a popular public speaker whose lectures were published by the Saltire Society, of which she was Honorary President (1942).

A study of *The Women in Shakespeare's Plays* (1924), her DLitt dissertation at Aberdeen, was followed by *The Process of Literature* (1929). Her interests then turned to her native land. She published *An Historical Survey of Scottish Literature* (1934*)* and *Scottish Pageant* (1946–52), a four-volume anthology of documentary sources; the third was dedicated to her sister Jean Mackenzie, MA, her devoted lifetime companion. Despite spending most of her adult life in London, her love of the Hebrides was strong. Evocative descriptions of Lewis inform two poems, 'Island Moon' and 'Aignish on the Machair', and the novel *The Quiet Lady* (1926). The sisters endowed a prize in their brother's memory at the Nicolson Institute, Stornoway, where all three were educated.

Both novels and drama followed her first novel *Without Conditions* (1923), but Agnes Mure Mackenzie's greatest contribution was to Scottish history. Strongly nationalist in sentiment, she raised national consciousness with her lecture on the Declaration of Arbroath, whose significance had been neglected. She explored the contribution made by Gaelic Scotland, especially in *Robert Bruce* (1938, 1979), and spanned Scottish history in six volumes from *The Foundations of Scotland* to *Scotland in Modern Times* (1938–41*)*. She was made CBE in 1945 for services to Scottish history. Her work has perhaps been unduly overlooked in recent times, although she received an honorary LLD from Aberdeen in 1951, and the Saltire Society established a History Book Prize in her memory in 1965. JMN

• NLS: MSS 9172–9225.
Mackenzie, A. M., Works as above. See *ODNB* (2004) (Bibl.).
The Scotsman, 28 Feb. 1955 (obit.); 'An appreciation', letter; *The Stornoway Gazette*, 4 March 1955 (obit.).
Private information: Colin Scott Mackenzie, DL, June 2002.

MACKENZIE, Barbara, of Kintail, born c. 1595, died Strathnaver c. 1630. Survivor of domestic abuse. Daughter of Jean Ross of Balnagown, and Kenneth Mackenzie, Lord Kintail.

Barbara Mackenzie married Sir Donald Mackay of Farr (1591–1649) in 1610. They had six children, including John, 2nd Lord Reay, who married *Barbara Mackay. In January 1617, Barbara Mackenzie asked the Privy Council to pursue her husband for adultery and cruelty. He had begun an affair with Marie Lindsay, sister of the 12th Earl of Crawford, while in Edinburgh; she bore him a son. Donald Mackay brought Marie Lindsay back to his home at Durness, and 'without pitie or compassioun' (*RPC*, xi, p. 3) dragged his heavily pregnant wife from bed, dumping her in an outhouse with no roof, candles, or fire. Barbara Mackenzie was fed bread and water and had only a young kitchen lass to help with the baby's birth. Donald Mackay was warded in Edinburgh's tolbooth and Barbara Mackenzie took refuge with the Earl of Dunfermline. Husband and wife were later reconciled, Donald Mackay paying a 2000 merk fine for adultery in 1620. No more is heard of Marie Lindsay, who had herself been named as a survivor of abuse in 1611, when a household servant was accused of her abduction and rape. Despite his behaviour to his family, Donald Mackay distinguished himself in royal service in the Thirty Years' War, being made Lord Reay in 1628. In 1629, he took his family to Denmark. He apparently did not remain faithful to his wife, becoming involved in bigamy. In 1631, around the time of Barbara Mackenzie's death, Rachel Winterfield claimed that he had married her and was the father of her son. She began legal proceedings for maintenance; the marriage was recognised as lawful in 1637, although Donald had married Elizabeth Thomson soon after Barbara Mackenzie's death. He was jailed temporarily for non-payment of maintenance to Rachel Winterfield and her child in 1642. MMM

• *ODNB* (2004) (Mackay, Donald, first Lord Reay); *RPC*, ix, p. 300, xi, pp. 2–3, 23–4, 28; xii, p. 293; *RPC*, 2nd ser., vi, p. 440; vii, p. 309; *SP*, iii, p. 31; vii, pp. 168–70, 503–4.

MACKENZIE, Helen Carruthers, n. **Spence,** CBE, born Mortlach, Banffshire, 13 April 1859, died Edinburgh 25 Sept. 1945. Public health campaigner. Daughter of Mary McDonell, and William Spence, merchant tailor, provost of Dufftown.

Helen Spence was a pupil teacher at Mortlach village school, then at the Church of Scotland Training College, Aberdeen. In 1892, she married Dr (later Sir) W. Leslie Mackenzie (1862–1935), first Medical Inspector of Schools at the Local Government Board for Scotland. Their subsequent careers were dedicated to improving the physical condition of Scottish schoolchildren, influencing many important educational reforms in the early 1900s. For a Royal Commission (1903) they conducted a pioneering investigation of the physical condition of children in Edinburgh. Helen Mackenzie organised the studies, wrote the findings and was present while her husband examined each child. Having demonstrated conclusively that

children from poorer areas were smaller, lighter and less healthy than children from middle-class or rural communities, they called for routine medical inspections of school children and the training of teachers in health and hygiene.

In 1903–4, Lady Leslie Mackenzie (as she was known) gave evidence before an interdepartmental committee on young people's health: many of her recommendations were adopted in the 1908 Education (Scotland) Act. Among her numerous welfare initiatives, she assisted in the establishment of special schools for mentally handicapped children and campaigned for children's medical care, rural district nursing services and continuation classes for young women. She helped her friend *Elsie Inglis to obtain better maternity hospital facilities in Edinburgh, and sat on the Edinburgh School Board and the Council of the Edinburgh College of Domestic Science (now Queen Margaret University College), chairing it from 1943 to 1945. In recognition, in 1933 she was appointed CBE and received an LLD from the University of Edinburgh. A gifted public speaker, she gave speeches 'marked by directness and candour, and spiced with a characteristic humour that gripped attention' (*Scotsman* 1945). TB

• *Parl. Papers* (1903) Royal Commission on physical training (Scotland), vol. 30, Cd. 1507–8; *Parl. Papers* (1904) 'Inter-departmental committee on physical deterioration: list of witnesses and evidence', 32.54, 275–8, Cd. 2186 (evidence of Mrs Leslie Mackenzie).
Begg, T. (1994) *The Excellent Women*; (1945) *Edinburgh College of Domestic Science Magazine*, Oct.; *ODNB* (2004); *The Scotsman*, 3 July 1937 and 26 Sept. 1945 (obit.).

MACKENZIE, Isabel, Countess of Seaforth, born c. 1640, buried Holyrood 18 Feb. 1715. Estate manager. Daughter of Margaret Erskine, and Sir John Mackenzie of Tarbat.

Isabel Mackenzie married in 1658 Kenneth Mackenzie, 3rd Earl of Seaforth (1635–78), who, it was said, received 'neither beuty, parts, portion, relation' (Mackay 1905, p. 421). After his death in 1678, a new title to the estate was established in her person. She played a central role in dealing with the Seaforth family's financial, personal and political crises. The continual struggle made her feel that her 'trublls shall neuer end till my tym end' (Fraser 1876, p. 146). After her son's marriage, she was known as the Countess Dowager; after 1701 and her eldest son's death she became the Countess Dowager 'elder' to distinguish her from his widow Frances. Difficulties with Frances, who gained possession of the estate in 1706, forced her to take refuge from her creditors in the sanctuary of Holyrood. MB-J

• Fraser, W. (1876) *The Earls of Cromartie*; Mackay, W. (ed.) (1905) *Chronicles of the Frasers: the Wardlaw manuscript*; Warrand, D. (1965) *Some Mackenzie Pedigrees*.

MACKENZIE, Penelope, born Tangier c. 1675, died 1743. Estate manager, supporter of Catholicism in the Highlands. Daughter apparently of a German woman, and Col. Alexander Mackenzie.

Probably due to family connections, Penelope Mackenzie was sent from Tangier, where her father was stationed, to the Jacobite court in exile at St Germain, where she won much admiration for her charm and beauty. There she met the young Captain of Clan Ranald, Allan MacDonald (Ailean Dearg), who had been badly wounded while in French service, following his flight from Scotland after the battle of Killiecrankie (1689). The love-match determined the rest of her life. She accompanied her husband home to South Uist in 1696 after he made peace with the authorities, a step facilitated by her sister's marriage into the influential Villiers family. The couple probably brought with them 'the african secretarie', ancestor of the present-day Buies (Bowies) in South Uist. Oral tradition reports her dissatisfaction with the existing clan stronghold in Borgh – 'like a hen-house' – and that she made her husband build her a snug little mansion at Ormacleit. The elegant court he gathered, with bard, piper, and harper, not only represents a last bastion of classical Gaelic culture, but was a focus for renewed Jacobite intrigue. Allan MacDonald died from a wound sustained at the Battle of Sheriffmuir (1715), reputedly on the day his Ormacleit mansion burnt down.

With his brother and heir in exile, the burden of ensuring the return of the forfeited Clan Ranald estates rested upon Allan's widow. Combining a charm offensive with astute, relentless lobbying in London and more forceful tactics in Uist, Penelope Mackenzie and lawyer siblings John and Alexander Mackenzie won the support of the Duke of Argyll, superior of many Clan Ranald lands. In 1727, the estates returned to MacDonald control. Her widow's jointure and her excessive generosity laid a heavy burden upon the already badly indebted Clan Ranald finances, continuing beyond her death. Penelope Mackenzie is notable for her political intriguing and networking and her cultural patronage, but also as a supporter of the Roman Catholic mission, enabling it to consolidate its hold on the 'heartland' Clan Ranald territories. Penelope remains a common name for girls in South Uist. DUS

• NAS: E648/13/4; GD201/1/198-9, 212, 217, 219, 221, 228, 259; /4/41; /5/21, 23, 29, 37, 39, 46, 54, 982; NLS: MS 1303 fos. 7–182; MS 1304, fos. 6–187 *passim*.
Clark, J. T. (ed.) (1900) *MacFarlane's Genealogical Collections* I, p. 90; Hopkins, P. (1998) *Glencoe and the end of the Highland War*, pp. 391, 398–9; Macdonald, A. and Macdonald, A. (1900–4) *Clan Donald*, ii, pp. 340–5, 349; iii, p. 233; Mackenzie, A. (1881) *History of the MacDonalds and Lords of the Isles*, pp. 421–4, 427–8; Stewart, Jr., J. A. (1982) 'The Clan Ranald: history of a Highland kindred', PhD, Univ. of Edinburgh.

MACKINNON, Georgina Russell (Gina), n. **Davidson,** OBE, born Wick 1 March 1884, died Linlithgow 11 April 1973. Chairman of Drambuie. Daughter of Maggie Dean Russell, and John Davidson, fish food processor.

Gina Davidson arrived in Edinburgh c. 1910 to work as a school teacher, and met Malcolm MacKinnon at St Oram's Highland Church. They married in 1915, and had two children, Margaret (b. 1916), who became a doctor, and Norman (b. 1923), later Managing Director of Drambuie. Malcolm MacKinnon had come from Skye in 1900 to work in the whisky business, but in 1909 he began mixing commercial quantities of the old MacKinnon liqueur 'Drambuie', and in 1914 established the Drambuie Liqueur Company Ltd. Gina MacKinnon's two brothers became directors of the company in the 1920s. In the 1930s, she ran the household at Hillwood House, Corstorphine, which became the company's headquarters in 1998, but when Malcolm MacKinnon died in 1945, aged 62, she became Chairman (sic) of the company. The 1950s and 1960s were the heyday of her involvement: sales took off and Drambuie became the most widely distributed liqueur in the world, selling in more than 150 countries. Gina MacKinnon travelled widely, sometimes accompanied by her personal bagpipers, appearing in newspapers and magazines and on radio and TV. She began the tradition, which is continued today, whereby the mixing of the secret essence at the heart of Drambuie is known only to a female member of the family, who prepares the mixture in a private laboratory once a month. To the US press, she became known as 'the canny wee granny with the $2m secret'. In 1964, she was awarded the OBE for services to British exports. She passed on the

Drambuie secret to her daughter-in-law on her retirement to a mansion outside Linlithgow, and enjoyed a successful second career as a prize-winning breeder of Jersey cattle. RP
• Robin Nicholson, Curator, The Drambuie Collection; The Drambuie Liqueur Company Ltd.

MACKINNON, Nan (Nan Eachainn Fhionnlaigh), born Kentangaval, Barra, 12 Dec. 1902, died Vatersay 24 June 1982. Tradition-bearer. Daughter of Mary MacPhee, and Hector MacKinnon, fisherman.

Nan Eachainn Fhionnlaigh spent much of her life, apart from five years on the mainland, in Vatersay, having moved there with her family when she was four. From 1940, she looked after her late sister's children. Her immense repertoire of songs, stories and miscellaneous lore was first recorded by Donald MacPherson, a native of Barra, and later by the School of Scottish Studies, University of Edinburgh. She contributed more than any other individual to the School's archives of Scottish Gaelic material – some 600 songs and around 1,000 proverbs (often accompanied by explanatory comment), anecdotes, adages and idiomatic phrases, all carried in her memory.

Some songs came from the now deserted island of Mingulay, where she had family connections. Her singing style was unique, with slow rhythm and minimal volume. Her voice was minor in tone, yet intense, giving the impression of a strangely pitched wind instrument. Some musicologists considered her style highly idiosyncratic; others suggested she was a unique exponent of an otherwise lost art. JMacI
• McDermitt, B. (1983) 'Nan MacKinnon', *Tocher*, 38. Private information.

MACKINTOSH, Lady Anne, ('Colonel Anne'), n. **Farquharson,** born 1723, died Leith 2 March 1787. Jacobite. Daughter of Margaret Murray, and John Farquharson of Invercauld.

Anne Mackintosh was 22 years old at the outbreak of the 1745 Jacobite Rising. Her husband, Aeneas (Angus), whom she married in 1741, was chief of the clan Mackintosh. A captain in the Black Watch, he was absent from home, meeting his military commitments to the Hanoverian government, when his wife raised his relatives and tenants in support of Prince Charles Edward Stewart and the last attempt to regain the British throne for the Stewarts. Despite contemporary propaganda portraying her as a warlike Amazon,

she never led men into battle, handing over command of the 300-strong Lady Mackintosh's Regiment to her husband's cousin, Alexander MacGillivray of Dunmaglass. In February 1746, while giving hospitality to Prince Charles Edward Stewart and his retinue at Moy Hall, Inverness-shire, she played a pivotal role in the Rout of Moy, a ruse which pitted five men against 1,500. Government commander Lord Loudon, bent on seizing the Prince, was fooled into retreating in the erroneous belief that his quarry was being guarded by a substantial force.

Tradition has it that Anne Mackintosh's greeting to her husband when he was captured by the Jacobites and given into her custody in February 1746 was a polite, 'Your servant, Captain'. He is alleged to have replied, 'Your servant, Colonel,' acknowledging the nickname which her raising of the clan had earned her. After the Jacobite defeat at Culloden in April 1746, she was arrested and detained in Inverness for six weeks, but then released without charge into her husband's custody. Following his death in 1770, she moved to the Lowlands. A recently erected plaque marks her gravesite in North Leith Churchyard. MEC
• Blaikie, W. B. B. [1916] (1975) *Origins of the 'Forty-Five*; Craig, M. (1997) *Damn' Rebel Bitches: the women of the '45*; Macdonald, F. (1987) *'Colonel Anne' – Lady Anne Mackintosh*; *ODNB* (2004).

MACKINTOSH, Elizabeth, [Josephine Tey, Gordon Daviot], born Inverness 25 July 1896, died London 13 Feb. 1952. Novelist and dramatist. Daughter of Josephine Horne, teacher, and Colin MacKintosh, fruiterer.

One of three sisters, Elizabeth MacKintosh was educated at Inverness Royal Academy, and Anstey Physical Training College, Birmingham (1914–17). She taught near Liverpool and in Tunbridge Wells, but returned to Inverness to care for her mother, who died in 1926, and her invalid father, and took up writing as an alternative career. Her early short stories and first detective novel, *The Man in the Queue* (1929), together with three other novels, appeared under the pseudonym 'Gordon Daviot'; she had spent family holidays at Daviot, near Inverness. Success as a dramatist, under the same name, came with *Richard of Bordeaux*, first produced in 1932. A year later, John Gielgud, who remained a life-long friend, played the title role.

She adopted a second pseudonym for *A Shilling for Candles* (1936), and as 'Josephine Tey', her great-grandmother's name, became well known for her literate and unconventional detective stories. Still known as Elizabeth MacKintosh in Inverness, she herself preferred the name Gordon Daviot: her entry in *Who's Who* was, at her request, under that name, as was her death notice in *The Times*. Extremely shy, she attended no functions and never gave interviews. Readers have searched for clues to her life in her novels; *Miss Pym Disposes* (1946) takes its setting from her college years, but nothing further can be reliably established. John Gielgud admitted that though they were friends for many years, he did not know her intimately; he thought she might have lost a close friend or lover in the First World War. According to a schoolmate, she had an obsessive fear that her life would be too short to write everything she wanted to (MacDonald 1982). She apparently dismissed her detective novels as her 'yearly knitting' (Gielgud 1953, p. 1). Nevertheless, these eight novels are highly regarded – her hero Alan Grant is an early example of the fallible, self-doubting detective. Most notable perhaps are *The Franchise Affair* (1948) and *The Daughter of Time* (1951); in the latter, Grant investigates the case of the Princes in the Tower and concludes (controversially for some) that Richard III was not guilty of their murder.

Her premature death in 1952 shocked her theatre friends. Gielgud wrote: 'I learned afterwards that she had known herself to be mortally ill for nearly a year, and had resolutely avoided seeing anyone she knew. This gallant behaviour was typical of her and curiously touching, if a little inhuman too' (ibid.). MARB

• NLS: Acc. 4771: papers.
Daviot, G. and Tey, J., Works as above, and see Bibls below. The BL catalogue also lists works.
Butler, P. J. (2002) 'The mystery of Josephine Tey': www.r3.org/fiction/mysteries/tey_butler.html
Gielgud, J. (1953) Foreword to *Plays by Gordon Daviot*; *HSWW* (Bibl.); MacDonald, M. A. (1982) *By the Banks of the Ness: tales from the history of Inverness and district*; Morris, V. B. (1989) 'Josephine Tey (Elizabeth MacKintosh, Gordon Daviot)', *DLB* Gale, 77, 'British mystery writers, 1920–1939', pp. 284–96 (Bibl.); *ODNB* (2004); Williamson, A. (1982) 'Gordon Daviot (Elizabeth MacKintosh)', *DLB* Gale, 10, 'Modern British dramatists 1900–1945', pp. 139–41.

MACLACHLAN, Jessie Niven, m. **Buchanan,** born Oban 18 June 1866, died Glasgow 13 May 1916. Gaelic and Scots singer, 'the Scots Prima Donna'. Daughter of Margaret Niven, and Alexander MacLachlan, auctioneer.

Jessie MacLachlan's soprano voice attracted her first audiences at Highland gatherings throughout Argyllshire. Largely self-taught, she began to achieve fame as a 'sweet singer of Gaelic ballads'. In 1887, she married Robert Buchanan, a prominent Glasgow musician who became her constant accompanist on the piano, but she continued to sing under her maiden name. In September 1892, she was commanded by *Queen Victoria to sing Scottish and Gaelic songs at Balmoral Castle, the first artist to do so since Gaelic as a language had been proscribed. She appeared at the inaugural National Mòd in Oban in 1893 and, by 1899, had had her voice recorded on a German-invented disc. She made two world tours, singing to large audiences of expatriate Gaels and Scots in Australia, New Zealand, Canada and the USA. The outbreak of the First World War found Jessie MacLachlan and her husband in France: their hazardous journey home on board a tramp steamer via Spain contributed to her death shortly before her 50th birthday at the height of her fame. Now largely forgotten, in her day Jessie MacLachlan's world reputation as a Scottish artist was possibly exceeded only by that of Harry Lauder. MM/MVH

• *Badenoch Record*, 23 Sept. 1921; *Campbeltown Courier*, 20 May 1916 (obit.); *Glasgow Star*, 12 March 1904, 'Miss Jessie N. Maclachlan. An interesting talk with the Scottish prima donna'; *John O'Groats Journal*, 23 Sept. 1921; *Press and Journal*, 10 March 2001; *The Times*, 15 May 1916 (obit.).

MCLACHLAN (MACLAUGHLAN), Margaret, born c. 1614; **WILSON, Agnes,** born c. 1678; **WILSON, Margaret,** born c. 1667. 'The Wigtown Martyrs'.

One of the most contentious and mythologised episodes of the Covenanting persecutions alleges that two women, Margaret McLachlan and Margaret Wilson, were executed by drowning at Wigtown on 11 May 1685. This case represents a classic example of ongoing tensions between oral tradition and documented corroboration. The legend was designed to embarrass the Government by highlighting atrocities supposedly committed by its servants. The two women and Margaret Wilson's younger sister Agnes, were, according to Robert Wodrow, tried on 13 April 1685 before the Justiciary Court at Wigtown. The story goes that Agnes was freed on payment of £100 sterling, an unrealistically enormous sum. The others were tied to stakes between the high and low water mark, Margaret McLachlan being placed further out to encourage Margaret Wilson to recant. Instead, the younger woman sang the 25th psalm and read from Romans while her sister in Christ expired. Margaret Wilson was held above the rising waters one last time but refused the opportunity to save herself and so perished.

Wodrow's allegation that they were indicted for being present at the battles of Bothwell Bridge and Aird's Moss is quite untenable; Agnes Wilson was only seven at the time. Moreover, the Privy Council explicitly refused to prosecute anyone aged 16 and under. A petition on the 70-year-old Margaret McLachlan's behalf admits she was justly condemned because she refused to disown the Apologetical Declaration (of 1684, threatening death to all opponents of the Covenant) and had declined abjuration of the Covenant. She acknowledged that the said declaration was traitorous and was willing to abjure. Probably a similar plea was entered for the 18-year-old Margaret Wilson; both women received a reprieve on 30 April. The evidence suggests the executions never occurred.

Women were prominent in the cause of the Covenant, but only two were executed for treason between 1660 and 1688. Lord Fountainhall commented on their hanging in 1681, and Sir George Mackenzie wrote extensively about women and the law. If the Wigtown women had been executed these writers would have discussed what would have been a highly publicised case. Another controversy concerns the graves. There is no evidence that Margaret Wilson's gravestone at Wigtown was in existence before 1730. Indeed, residing as she did in nearby Penninghame, why would she have been buried in Wigtown? It is a similar story with Margaret Mclachlan who came from Kirkinner. The 'new' monument to the Wigtown Martyrs was dedicated as recently as 1938. EJC

• Cowan, E. J. (2002) 'The Covenanting tradition in Scottish history', in E. J. Cowan and R. J. Finlay (eds) *Scottish History: the power of the past* (Bibl.); Napier, M. (1863) *The Case for the Crown in re the Wigtown Martyrs Proved to be Myths*; Stewart, A. (1869) *History vindicated in the case of the Wigtown Martyrs*; ODNB (2004) (Wilson, Margaret); Wodrow, R. [1721–2] (1823) *The History of the Suffering of the Church of Scotland.*

MACLAGAN, Christian, born near Denny, baptised 26 July 1811, died Stirling 10 May 1901. Archaeologist and philanthropist. Daughter of Janet Colville, and George MacLagan, distiller.

The third child of a literary family, Christian MacLagan was brought up in Stirlingshire and moved to Stirling c. 1820. Her widowed mother

and clerical grandfather inspired her interest in history and religion. She followed 'the pope of Stirling', the Rev. Dr Alexander Beith, into the Free Church on the Disruption of 1843, holding to the literal truth of the Bible which influenced her self-taught archaeological theories. She believed that megalithic circles and tombs were remnants of circular houses and forts and that, as with the Bible, a message would reveal itself on scholarly examination of the architectural 'language'. She described hill forts and Neolithic monuments in Brittany and Sardinia and carefully recorded hundreds of early medieval gravestones with rubbings. She published her findings, interspersed with anthropological comment, at her own expense. Her ideas were eccentric even to her contemporaries, but her publications preserve valuable records of now-eroded sites.

Christian MacLagan shared her home, 'Ravenscroft' in Stirling, with a companion, Jessie Hunter Colvin (1825–90), a minister's daughter and also an antiquary, who predeceased her. Christian MacLagan was acutely aware of her academic disadvantage, denied access to learned societies and research libraries because of her sex. She was elected as the second Lady Associate of the Society of Antiquaries in 1871. The first was Lady John Scott (*Alicia Ann Spottiswoode). When Christian MacLagan was denied equal membership with men she bequeathed her catalogued rubbings to the British Museum. She spoke and exhibited drawings and models at the Stirling Natural History and Archaeological Society, the British Association (aged over 80), and corresponded with Dr James Young Simpson and other notable academics. When, on occasion, she felt slighted, she could carry resentments for years. In one case, she generously funded a Free Kirk in Stirling and then looked for a congregation to accept the building. After a disagreement and court case in 1875–6, she repossessed the church. Later rejoining the Church of Scotland, her more positive nature showed in charitable contributions to Sunday Schools, church missions, workers' housing, and her own servants' welfare. MAMC

• MacLagan, C. (1872) 'On the round castles and ancient dwellings of the valley of the Forth . . .', *Proc. Soc. Antiquaries Scot.* pp. 29–44, (1875) *The Hill Forts, Stone Circles and other Structural Remains of Ancient Scotland*, (1881) *Chips from Old Stones*, private printing, G. Waterston, (1894) *What Mean these Stones?*, (1898) *Catalogue Raisonné of the British Museum Collection of Rubbings from Ancient Sculptured Stones.*

Cook, W. B. (1903) 'The Late Miss C. MacLagan', *Stirling Antiquary*, III (1900–3), pp. 219–21; Elsdon, S. M. (2004) *Christian MacLagan*; *ODNB* (2004); *The Scotsman*, 13 May 1901 (obit.); *Stirling Journal & Advertiser*, 17 May 1901 (obit.).

MCLAREN, Agnes, born Edinburgh 4 July 1837, died probably Antibes 1913. Physician and Catholic campaigner, suffragist. Daughter of Christina Gordon Renton, and Duncan McLaren, draper, Liberal politician.

Agnes McLaren was brought up by her stepmother, *Priscilla Bright McLaren. Drawn early into charitable work and campaigning, she was secretary of the EWSS from 1869, and toured Scotland on its behalf with *Jane Taylour in the early 1870s. Having befriended *Sophia Jex-Blake, she decided to become a doctor in order to help women and children. Her family were not keen but, at the age of 38, she enrolled to study medicine in Montpellier, graduating in 1878 and obtaining a licence (Dublin 1879). She settled in Cannes, practising medicine, and in 1898 joined the Catholic Church. From then on, she campaigned for Catholic nuns to be trained as nurses and doctors for medical missions abroad, particularly in India. Canon law forbade this. Agnes McLaren raised funds for a Catholic hospital in Rawalpindi, where a lay doctor was appointed. She made several journeys to Rome to plead with the Vatican, but died before a religious Society of Catholic Medical Missionaries could be achieved. Her protégée, Anna Dengel, had more success in the 1920s and canon law was reversed in 1936, allowing religious to train in obstetrics and as doctors. Agnes McLaren, who regularly returned to Edinburgh, was spoken of as combining 'strong purpose with instinctive aloofness . . . shyness . . . and old world grace' (Todd 1918, p. 324). SR

• Women's Library, London: nominal files; NLS: MSS 24810–15, McLaren papers.
AGC; Burton, K. (1946) *According to the Pattern*; Spender, C. (1946) 'The fulfilment of a dream', *The Catholic Citizen*, 22, 4, April; Todd, M. (1918) *The Life of Sophia Jex-Blake*.

MCLAREN, Priscilla, n. **Bright,** born Rochdale, Lancs., 8 Sept. 1815, died Edinburgh 5 Nov. 1906. Women's rights campaigner. Daughter of Martha Wood, and Jacob Bright, cotton manufacturer.

Fifth of 11 children, Priscilla Bright belonged to a famous campaigning Quaker family in England, and married into one of the best-known Presbyterian Liberal dynasties in Scotland. Educated at schools in York and Liverpool, she had an early encounter with prison reformer Elizabeth Fry. Having helped her widowed brother, John Bright, to bring up his daughter, she met through him the Edinburgh draper and Liberal politician, Duncan McLaren (1800–86). They married in 1848, and she lived thereafter in Edinburgh, where her husband was city provost (1851–4) and MP for the city (1865–81). The McLaren clan was large: Priscilla became stepmother to five children, and had a further three herself. Her grandchildren included sculptor **Ottilie McLaren**, later **Wallace** (1875–1947). Both of her brothers, her husband, two sons, one stepson and a grandson became MPs during her long lifetime.

Priscilla Bright McLaren was a life-long supporter of women's rights, taking an energetic part in many campaigns, and being connected by family or friendship with many leading activists. In 1870, both she and her husband supported Josephine Butler's campaign against the Contagious Diseases Acts. At about the same time, they supported the efforts to have women admitted to Edinburgh's medical school. Priscilla Bright McLaren actively campaigned for the abolition of slavery (over which she was in touch with *Elizabeth Pease Nichol) and for temperance. Above all, she became identified with the radical campaign for women's suffrage. Having supported John Stuart Mill's 1867 amendment, she was the first president of the EWSS, set up after its defeat. (She was still going strong in this role in the 1890s.) Her stepdaughter, *Dr Agnes McLaren, became joint secretary with *Eliza Wigham. Two thousand signatures were collected in Edinburgh and more petitions followed (*AGC*, p. 12). The Bright brothers were on opposite sides in this battle, John being against and Jacob for women's suffrage. Priscilla Bright McLaren wrote that John 'ought to keep silence when he sees all his women relations for women's suffrage' (Holton 1996, p. 64). She became exasperated with the Gladstonian Liberals' failure to support it in the 1880s, and reported that her husband looked 'very sorrowful' (ibid., p. 66). 'Generally liked and conciliatory' (ibid., p. 59), Priscilla Bright McLaren favoured setting up an international movement, and was active in Edinburgh, inclining towards the militant wing, although she died before the WSPU got going. In extreme old age, she sent a deathbed letter to suffrage activists in prison, praising their 'noble courage and self-sacrifice' (*Times* obit. 1906). She died in the family home, Newington House (now demolished). SR

• NLS: MSS 24810–15, McLaren papers; MSS 21502–40 Wallace papers.
AGC; Holton, S. (1996) *Suffrage Days*; *ODNB* (2004); *The Times*, 7 Nov. 1906 (obit.).

MCLEAN, Agnes, n. **Bell,** born Glasgow 15 March 1843, died Edinburgh 23 Jan. 1940. Scottish Cooperative Women's Guild Leader. Daughter of Minnie McNicol, and Peter Bell, shoemaker.

In 1870 Agnes Bell married Alexander McLean, baker. She was called 'Mother' of the SCWG, since, as a later Guild leader, President Annie Buchan, observed, 'Mrs. McLean was to our Women's Guild what the Rochdale Pioneers were to the Co-operative movement' (*Annual Report* 1905, p. 8). Founder-member of the first Guild branch, in Kinning Park Glasgow (1890), Agnes McLean was elected the first President of the SCWG in 1893, and three times again during her long years on the Central Council. With her splendid voice and stirring addresses, she helped organise branches all over the country. She wanted the Guild to practise 'mutual aid' among women, and 'develop the latent talent that only wanted a chance to show that the "hand that rocked the cradle" was directed by a brain' (Buchan 1913, p. 13).

Like other pioneers, she had to negotiate gender prejudice. She was represented as an impeccable housekeeper to justify her public activity: 'Mr McLean will tell you, behind his wife's back, that more than once she has been up at four in the morning so that the washing might be got through before she left for a meeting. Critics of the guild please note' (*Scottish Co-operator (SC)*, 21 March 1903). In 1898, her husband was victimised as part of a traders' boycott against co-operative societies, and the family moved to Edinburgh. She had a daughter, and a son who was killed in action in 1917.

In the on-going tension between 'industrial' work (sewing and other home-craft) and 'intellectual' work, Mother McLean trod a careful path. She wanted women to develop citizenship skills (hear lectures, write papers, speak in public), but realistically combined this with the 'industrial' work that attracted members. Thus a woman could 'bring cloth for a suit for a boy to the Guild meeting and have it cut and fitted, and sewn with the machine' while also taking tea, singing songs and listening to a lecture (*SC* Oct. 1893). During Agnes McLean's lifetime, the SCWG grew from 14 branches with 1,491 members to become one of the largest-ever women's organisations, boasting 421 branches and 32,854 members in 1939. Even more remarkable, the Guild attracted the hardest group to organise: married, working-class women. Mother McLean was judged 'one of the greatest working-class women who has ever been in this country' (President Mrs Small, *SC*, 25 Jan. 1941). Her memorial fund refurbished four bedrooms at the Seamill Convalescent Home and presented a grandmother clock to the Abbotview Home. EY

• Mitchell Library Glasgow: The Scottish Co-operative Wholesale Society Archive, printed and MS sources, catalogued under 'CWS Additions'.
Buchan, A. (1913) *History of the Scottish Co-operative Women's Guild 1892–1913*; *Edinburgh News*, 23 Jan. 1940 (funeral notice); Scottish Co-operative Women's Guild (1894–1920) *Annual Reports* 1–50; *Scottish Co-operator (SC)* 1893–1940, 3 Feb. 1940 (obit.).

MCLEAN, Agnes,[‡] born Glasgow 4 Dec. 1918, died Glasgow 25 April 1994. Trade unionist, councillor, dancer. Daughter of Sarah Ann (Sally) McLean, and Colin McLean, shipyard worker.

Agnes McLean was born into a family committed to socialist politics: her father was a follower of John MacLean. She and her sister Sadie attended Proletarian Sunday School and then Socialist Sunday School. She started work at 14 as a bookbinder at Collins publishers where, after faster working methods were introduced, she successfully fought for a halfpenny rise. She began work at the Rolls Royce aero-engine plant at Hillington on Christmas Day 1939, later joining the AEU. She led a brief strike action over equal pay in 1941 and a more effective strike in December 1943, furthering the cause of women throughout the labour movement. In 1954, Agnes McLean was the first woman elected to serve on the AEU executive. By 1968, she was on a women's committee organising factories on the Hillington estate in support of British-wide action for equal pay. In 1977, she left Rolls Royce to look after her mother and did not return to full-time employment. She joined the CPGB in 1942 and served on the Scottish and national committees of the party. In 1961, she visited the Soviet Union and was impressed by what she saw. That year, she was arrested in a mass sit-down at the Polaris nuclear base at Holy Loch. She left the CP in 1969 and joined the Labour Party, becoming a councillor for Glasgow District Council and subsequently Strathclyde Regional Council during the 1970s. She was the first convener of the Region's Women's Committee.

Ballroom dancing had long been Agnes McLean's passion – it allowed her to express herself, though one negative encounter associated with it was the apartheid practised by the US army, which she experienced during the war. In 1993, she went to Cuba to trace the origins of the rumba, resulting in the BAFTA Scotland award-winning BBC programme, *In Cuba They're Still Dancing*. NR

• GCU, Gallacher Memorial Library: Papers inc. funeral oration, Jane McKay, 29 April 1994.

Duffy Meets, Radio Clyde, 4 April 1989, interview with Agnes McLean; Interview with Agnes McLean by Lesley Dougall, 7 Oct. 1993, for BA (History) Univ. of Strathclyde, 1994; Interview with Marion Robertson, 1994; with Sadie Fulton, 1994. Questionnaire returned to author 1994.

Braybon, G. and Summerfield, P. (1987) *Out of the Cage: women's experiences in two world wars.*

MCLEHOSE (or MacLehose, M'Lehose, Meiklehose), Agnes ('Clarinda'), n. **Craig,** born Saltmarket, Glasgow, 26 April 1758, died Edinburgh 22 Oct. 1841. Correspondent of Robert Burns. Daughter of Christian McLaurin, and Andrew Craig, surgeon.

Agnes Craig was the third of four daughters (and possibly one son). Her mother and siblings died before she was 14. An attractive and charming girl, she was voted top of the 'Toast List of 1773' at the 'Glasgow Hodge-Podge Club', an association for professional men. Worried by this 'honour', in 1774 her father sent 'Pretty Miss Nancy' to an Edinburgh boarding school. After returning home, she married Glasgow lawyer James McLehose (1752–1812) on 1 July 1776. They had four sons. James McLehose was a violent drunk and she left him in December 1780, returning to her father's house in the Saltmarket. Her father was very ill and died on 13 May 1782. In August of that year, having recovered custody of her three surviving sons, she moved to Edinburgh where she rented a first-floor flat over General's Entry, Potterrow.

On 4 December 1787, Agnes McLehose met Robert Burns at a soirée given by Miss Erskine Nimmo at Alison Square. They agreed to meet on 8 December, but Burns fell from a carriage before the day and injured his knee, which left him housebound. To pass the time, he began writing letters from his lodgings at 2 St James Square. His first letter to her was on 8 December. Later in December, Agnes suggested using 'Clarinda' and 'Sylvester' as names in their future correspondence, mainly to protect her reputation in case the letters fell into the wrong hands. Thus began the 'Sylvander-Clarinda' correspondence. They finally met on 4 January 1788 when Burns limped his way to her home to keep the belated rendezvous. Six weeks later, on 18 February, Burns left Edinburgh to return home to Mossgiel in Ayrshire and his eventual marriage to *Jean Armour. Agnes McLehose and Burns were to meet again only twice before his death, in March 1788 and on 6 December 1791. It was after this last meeting, as she prepared to leave for Jamaica to salvage her marriage, that Burns penned his immortal poem to her, 'Ae Fond Kiss'.

She neither divorced her husband nor re-married after his death in Jamaica on 16 March 1812. Only one of her four children survived to adulthood and he died two years before her. She is buried in the Canongate Cemetery, Edinburgh. On 22 January 1937, the Clarinda Burns Club dedicated a plaque to her memory near the Potterrow, where her house once stood, but only after questions had been raised at Westminster as to whether she was of good enough character to receive this honour. Her relationship with Burns had for many years been deemed by some to be immoral, but there is no evidence for anything other than a strong attraction and fondness between the couple. MB

• MacLehose, W. C. (1843) *The Correspondence of Burns and Clarinda*; Ross, J. D. (ed.) (1929) *The Poems of Clarinda.*
Bell, M. (2001) *Tae The Lasses*; Brown, R. L. (1968) *Clarinda*; Campsie, A. (1989) *The Clarinda Conspiracy*; Donald, T. F. (1900) *The Hodge-Podge Club*; Hill, J. C. (1961) *The Love Songs and Heroines of Robert Burns*; ODNB (2004) (see MacLehose, Agnes); O'Rourke, D. (2000) *Ae Fond Kiss*; Ross, J. D. (1897) *Burns's Clarinda.*

MACLEOD, Anna MacGillivray, born Kirkhill, Inverness-shire, 15 May 1917, died Edinburgh 13 August 2004. Professor of brewing. Daughter of Margaret Ingram Sangster, and Alasdair MacGillivray MacLeod, United Free Church minister.

A daughter of the manse, Anna MacLeod had two brothers. She attended Invergordon Academy and Mary Erskine's School, Edinburgh, where she was dux in 1924. After graduating with first-class honours in botany from the University of Edinburgh in 1939, she taught first at Moray House Training College, then became lecturer at Heriot-Watt College, where she remained until retirement in 1977. While there, she gained her PhD (Edinburgh), published research on barley germination and malting, became Professor of Brewing (1975), and encouraged her postgraduate

students. Anna MacLeod was one of the best-known scientists and technologists in the malting, brewing and distilling industries, worldwide. Having been elected FRSE in 1962, she was later editor of the important *Journal of the Institute of Brewing*, chaired the Institute's Scottish section in 1966, and became President of the (international) Institute of Brewing in 1970. In 1976, on receiving the Horace Brown Medal, she gave a lecture entitled '*Rerum Cognoscere Causas*', reflecting her egalitarian view that the people of the world will be better off for knowing how nature works. She received an honorary DSc from Heriot-Watt University in 1993. A respected and successful woman in a male-dominated industry, Anna MacLeod disliked humbug. When asked to explain the differences between beers and Scotch whiskies, she replied: 'Drink the stuff!' (water, no ice, with Scotch). GP
• *The Scotsman*, 6 Sept. 2004 (obit.).
Personal knowledge.

MACLEOD, Catherine (Kitty) (Ceit NicLeòid), m1 **MacLennan,** m2 **Gregson,** born Kasauli, India, 4 Sept. 1914, died Haddington 7 May 2000. Singer. Daughter of Anna MacLeod, primary school-teacher, and Kenneth MacLeod, soldier.

Kitty MacLeod was born in India to Lewis parents. Her mother tongue was Gaelic, her second language Urdu, later supplanted by English when the First World War forced repatriation of army families. Her formal education was at Lionel School in Lewis and the University of Edinburgh, but she attributed her remarkable knowledge of the Gaelic language and culture to the 'taigh ceilidh' – thatched houses where people gathered to share tales, legends, history, songs, proverbs, riddles and folklore from oral tradition.

At university she outshone fellow students (including Sorley MacLean and Norman MacCaig), winning gold medals for both Celtic and Moral Philosophy. It was as a singer that she made her biggest impact, both for her unique style and her knowledge of Gaelic song traditions (including such songs as the lament of *Anna Campbell). Still a student, she won the Mòd Gold Medal in 1936 and was recorded by Parlaphone Records, which distributed worldwide. She popularised 'An Aitearachd Ard' ('The high swelling of the sea'), arguably the most recorded, frequently requested Gaelic song, and composed and recorded the melody for 'Oran Chalum Sgaire'. Leading European and North American artists have recorded it, but without credit to her.

Kitty MacLeod was featured in Scotland's first colour film documentary, *The Western Isles* (1942). Other films included the Hollywood movie *Rob Roy* (1953) in which she sang and acted with her sister Marietta (d. 1983). Both sisters recorded songs for the School of Scottish Studies in Edinburgh. Kitty MacLeod married twice, first Murdoch Dubh MacLennan from Lewis, and secondly, on 26 February 1998, Ernest Renaud Lewtas Gregson, an Edinburgh doctor. While she dutifully followed a career in school teaching until retirement in 1974, her enduring influence continues far beyond the classroom to traditional singers world-wide; she has been ranked equal to Sorley MacLean in her influence on Gaeldom. MGtB
• Bennett, M. 'The life and songs of Kitty MacLeod', lecture, Celtic Connections festival, Glasgow, 31 Jan. 2003; *ODNB* (2004); *The Scotsman*, 9 May 2000 (obit.).

MACLEOD, Fiona *see* **SHARP, Elizabeth Amelia** (1856–1932)

MACLEOD, Flora Louisa Cecilia, DBE, m. **Walker,** born London 3 Feb. 1878, died Ythan Lodge, Aberdeenshire, 4 Nov. 1976. Chief of Clan MacLeod. Daughter of Agnes Mary Cecilia Northcote, and Sir Reginald MacLeod of MacLeod, 27th Chief.

Raised in London and Edinburgh, Flora MacLeod also spent time at the family seat, Dunvegan Castle. On 5 June 1901, she married Hubert Walker (1870–1933), correspondent for *The Times*. The couple had two children. Flora MacLeod was active in voluntary aid and welfare in England; from the 1920s she increasingly worked in Skye. Sir Reginald MacLeod died in 1935 and Flora succeeded him soon thereafter, being unanimously accepted as the 28th Chief by the Clan MacLeod Society on 17 March 1936. Positive international response to the recently founded *Clan MacLeod Magazine* inspired her to visualise a world-wide MacLeod community. She spent the early 1950s travelling, inaugurating clan societies in the USA, Canada, Australia and New Zealand. Societies later emerged in France, Germany, and South Africa. As a Chief 'who lived, thought and felt internationally rather than parochially', Flora MacLeod 'gave a new and abiding sense of identity to those proud to bear a Highland name' (Grant 1981, p. 617).

In 1953, Flora MacLeod was made DBE. She spent the next twenty years encouraging preservation of the history, folklore, and genealogy of Clan MacLeod. She lived at Dunvegan until 1972, when she moved to Ythan Lodge to live with a grandson. Dame Flora was buried alongside previous chiefs in the ruins of Duirinish Church, Dunvegan Castle. MES

• Grant, I. F. (1981) *The MacLeods*; Morrison, A. (1986) *The Chiefs of Clan MacLeod*; *The Times*, 6 Nov. 1976 (obit.); *ODNB* (2004); Wolrige Gordon, A. (1974) *Dame Flora*.

MACLEOD, Margaret, Lady Clanranald ('Lady Clan'), m. **MacDonald,** born Berneray, Harris, before 1720, died Ormiclate, South Uist, 9 September 1780. Jacobite. Daughter of Margaret Mackenzie, and William MacLeod 1st of Luscantyre.

Little is known about Margaret MacLeod's life before c. 1720, when she married Ranald MacDonald, 'Old Clanranald', 17th Captain of Clanranald and 4th of Benbecula. Lady Clanranald was much loved by her husband's kinsmen and was affectionately referred to as 'Lady Clan'. Despite her husband's outward devotion to the Hanoverian monarchy, Lady Clanranald was dedicated to the Jacobite cause, a loyalty she instilled in her children. Indeed, her son, Ranald MacDonald ('Young Clanranald'), gathered the Clanranald men at the Raising of the Standard at Glenfinnan on 19 August 1745.

Lady Clanranald's lasting historical contribution came after Culloden. By late June 1746, Charles Edward Stewart had already successfully evaded the Hanoverian troops for two months, hiding in an uninhabited hut on Old Clanranald's land in South Uist. The net, however, was closing around him. Hugh MacDonald (stepfather of *Flora MacDonald) came up with an escape plan: the Prince would travel to Skye as 'Betty Burke', Flora MacDonald's Irish lady's maid. Lady Clanranald took charge of the preparations, directing the creation of a suitable gown for Charles Edward Stewart and providing food for the crossing. After this adventure, however, and a brief imprisonment in Southwark, Lady Clanranald kept a low profile for the rest of her life. MES

• Craig, M. (1997) *Damn' Rebel Bitches: the women of the '45*; Douglas, H. (1993) *Flora MacDonald: the most loyal rebel*; Douglas, Sir R. of Glenbervie (1798) *The Baronage of Scotland*, p. 392; Grant, I. F. (1963) *The Clan Donald*; MacKinnon, Rev. Dr. D. and Morrison, A. (1968) *The MacLeods – The Genealogy of a Clan*, section II, pp. 35–6. Personal communication: Jim Ayars, Associated Clan MacLeod Societies.

MACLEOD, Mary *see* **MÀIRI NIGHEAN ALASDAIR RUAIDH** (c. 1615–c. 1707)

MACMILLAN, Chrystal Jessie, born Edinburgh 13 June 1872, died Edinburgh 21 Sept. 1937. Suffragist, internationalist, lawyer. Daughter of Jessie Chrystal Finlayson, and John Macmillan, tea merchant.

The family, including Chrystal Macmillan's eight brothers, lived in Corstorphine Hill House, now the Fellows' house, Edinburgh Zoo. From 1888, she attended St Leonards School, St Andrews, and in 1892 was among the first women admitted to the University of Edinburgh, where she took a first-class degree and, after a brief period in Berlin, an MA in mental and moral philosophy. A committed suffragist, she was secretary to the Women Graduates of the Scottish Universities Committee, which argued that members, as graduates, had the right to the parliamentary franchise within the university electorates, which returned four MPs. When their case was rejected by the Court of Session, she and four others raised £1,000 to appeal in November 1908 to the House of Lords, where Chrystal Macmillan, labelled a 'modern Portia', acted as senior counsel (*AGC*, p. 69) and though unsuccessful, generated much publicity and sympathetic support. An active campaigner within Scotland, she was vice-president of ENSWS, and after moving to London a member of the NUWSS executive. A committed internationalist, on 31 July 1914, with Millicent Fawcett and Rosika Schwimmer, she drafted and delivered to the Foreign Secretary and relevant ambassadors an international women's manifesto appealing for conciliation and arbitration. Opposed to the war, she resigned from NUWSS and made international contacts leading to the Women's International Congress at The Hague in April 1915: she was one of only three women from the UK able to attend. She became secretary of the Women's International Committee for Permanent Peace, in Amsterdam, later the WILPF, and visited Scandinavia, Russia and the United States on its behalf. In May 1919, after the International Congress of Women in Zurich, she and others took its resolutions, critical of the peace terms, to the victors at the Paris peace conference.

After 1918, she entered the Middle Temple and was called to the bar on 28 January 1924. An equal rights feminist, in 1923 she was a founder of the Open Door Council, which campaigned against legal restrictions on women's employment and, in 1929, president of Open Door International, which campaigned internationally on the issue. Like *Wilhelmina (Elizabeth) Abbott, she participated in the debates about protective legislation in the Council of NUSEC, resigning over the issue in 1927. She took an interest in many aspects of women's legal status, including the right to retain their nationality on marriage. She stood, unsuccessfully, as Liberal candidate for Edinburgh North in 1935. SI/JR

• MS: Wallace, J. (1996) Standard Grade History Investigation on Chrystal Macmillan, Boroughmuir High School, Edinburgh.

AGC; Alberti, J. (1989) *Beyond Suffrage. Feminists in War and Peace*; ODNB (2004); Wiltsher, A. (1985) *Most Dangerous Women: feminist peace campaigners of the first world war*; WSM.

MCMILLAN, Margaret,‡ CBE, CH, born Westchester Co., NY, USA, 19 July 1860, died Harrow on the Hill 29 March 1931; **MCMILLAN, Rachel,** born Westchester Co. 25 March 1859, died Deptford 25 March 1917. Educational and social reformers. Daughters of Jean Cameron, and James McMillan, estate manager.

Widowed in 1865, Jean McMillan returned to her parents' home in Inverness with daughters Margaret and Rachel, who both attended Inverness High School and Academy in the 1870s. Rachel stayed at home to nurse her grandmother until 1888, but Margaret went to Frankfurt-am-Main in 1878 to study music and acting, acquiring there her conviction that 'oral culture' and a liberal education were vital for elementary schoolteachers and their pupils. After working as a governess (1879–87), she joined her sister in London in 1889, where they worked as junior superintendents in homes for working girls. Rachel converted Margaret to Christian Socialism, and they joined the Fabian Society, Labour Church, SDF, ILP, and later the Labour Party. Their support for the 1889 London dock strike alienated Margaret's benefactor, Lady Meux.

The McMillan sisters moved to Bradford in the 1890s, invited by the local ILP to campaign for a better physical environment for working-class youth. Rachel returned south to qualify as a health visitor and hygiene teacher, working in Kent. Margaret remained in Bradford, collaborating on the first medical inspection of elementary schoolchildren in Britain (1893), joining Bradford School Board for the ILP, and becoming first president of Bradford's Froebel Society (1901). She was notably critical of the narrow training of elementary schoolteachers, comparing them unfavourably to the university-educated Scottish dominie. Rejoining

Rachel, she was appointed by the LCC to manage a school group in Deptford (1903–18). Financed by the American philanthropist Joseph Fels, the sisters opened a health clinic in Bow, moving it to Deptford in 1910 to serve several schools. There they also established camps for girls (1911) and boys (1912) aged from six to 14, and a pioneer open air nursery and training centre (incorporating a Mothers' Club) in 1914. Both camps and the nursery supplied meals as well as garden space and play activities. During the First World War, the sisters created a nursery for munitions workers' children in Peckham (named after Rachel, who died in 1917). Margaret continued to run the nursery and served on the LCC (1919–22). As president of the NSA (1923), she resigned in 1929 over provision for working-class children. With Conservative MP Nancy Astor, she founded the Rachel McMillan College for training nurses and teachers in Deptford in 1930.

A prolific writer and charismatic speaker, Margaret McMillan remained active in Socialist Sunday Schools, the WEA and lecture tours, writing journalism and children's fiction. Her works on education influenced the 1906 Provision of School Meals Act and the development of school medical inspections. Both sisters had campaigned for female and adult suffrage: Margaret sought to mediate between the WSPU and the ILP in 1907, and campaigned against the 'Cat and Mouse' Act (1913). Made CBE in 1917, she became a CH in 1930. The sisters are buried in the same grave and were commemorated by the college and the [Margaret] McMillan Library in Bradford. JMCD

• Greenwich Univ. Library: McMillan family and other papers.

Lowndes, G. A. N. (1960) *Margaret McMillan*; Moriarty, V. (1998) *Margaret McMillan*; ODNB (2004); Steedman, C. (1990) *Childhood, Culture and Class in Britain* (Bibl.); *WWW* (2nd edn. 1967), vol. III, *1929–1940*.

MCMURTRIE, Mary Margaret, n. **Mitchell,** born Skene, Aberdeenshire 26 June 1902, died Aberdeenshire 1 Nov. 2003. Artist, plantswoman, historian. Daughter of Jane Philip, and George Mitchell, schoolmaster.

Mary Mitchell was one of the first female students of Gray's School of Art in Aberdeen (DA 1923). After graduating, she married Rev. John McMurtrie, minister of Skene Parish Church. At the Manse, they brought up their four children and restored the garden. After the death of her husband in 1949, Mary McMurtrie started a nursery specialising in alpine and old garden flowers. For 40 years she worked to conserve and distribute Old Pinks and Double Primroses, which she also recorded in her watercolours. She became internationally recognised and acclaimed as one of the best flower painters of her day, never losing sight of a flower's overall appeal while remaining botanically accurate. She was keenly interested in the conservation, buying and restoring of Balbithan House, Aberdeenshire, in the early 1960s. She always researched for authenticity, finding skilled local craftworkers, and her work influenced other restorations in the area. Mary McMurtrie wrote articles for *The Scots Magazine*, *The Countryman*, and the Deeside Field Club on local history and the countryside of her youth, and, for *The Statistical Account of Scotland*, volume 4, she completed the account for the Parish of Skene. She also wrote and illustrated *Wild Flowers of Scotland* (1982) and *Scots Roses* (1998), as well as the wild flowers, shrubs and trees of the Algarve, Portugal (1973–95, 1997, 1998). She continued to work until her 102nd year, completing *Old Cottage Pinks* (2004) shortly before her death. EAH/EMH

• RBGE: originals of *Scottish Wild Flowers*.

McMurtrie, M. M., Works as above, and (1973–95) *Wild Flowers of the Algarve*, vols I–IV; (1997) *Shrubs of the Algarve*; (1998) *Trees of Portugal*; (2001) *Scottish Wild Flowers*.

Alfonso, M. da L. R. and McMurtrie, M. M. (1991) *Plantas do Algarve*. See also www.eup.ed.ac.uk

Beck, C. and Hopkinson, C. (1999) 'Mary McMurtrie, horticultural who's who', *Gardens Illustrated*, 42; Boyd, P. (2004) 'Mary McMurtrie, painter of Scots roses', *Historic Rose Journal*, 28; Clark, T. (1992–3) 'Mary McMurtrie, painting and garden conservation', *Historic Garden*, Winter; Hellyer, A. G. L. (1978) 'The gardens of Balbithan House, Kintore', *Country Life*, Nov. 1978.

MACNEIL, Aithbhreac *see* **AITHBHREAC INGHEAN COIRCEADAIL** (fl. 1460)

MCNEILL, Florence Marian, MBE, born Holm, Orkney, 26 March 1885, died Edinburgh, 22 Feb. 1973. Writer and folklorist, cultural and political activist. Daughter of Janet Dewar, and Rev. Daniel McNeill, Minister of Holm West United Free Church.

One of three daughters, 'Flos' McNeill grew up in Orkney and was educated at Kirkwall Burgh School and the University of Glasgow, where she was part of a lively student community that included the future playwright 'James Bridie' (O. H. Mavor) and future politicians James Maxton and Walter Elliot. She graduated in 1912 and for a time taught English in schools for girls in France and Germany. She was organiser for the SFWSS 1912–13, and secretary of the Association for Moral and Social Hygiene in London, 1913–17.

She was part of the literary and cultural revival movement in Scotland, working as a researcher and, from 1929, principal assistant on the *Scottish National Dictionary*. That year saw the publication of her most popular book, *The Scots Kitchen*; its success encouraged her to work full-time as an author and journalist (writing as F. Marian McNeill). She was a founder member of Scottish PEN and became a vice-president of the recently formed Scottish National Party in the 1930s. She founded the Clan MacNeill Association of Scotland in 1932 and from 1944 to 1945 was a member of the Scottish Secretary of State's Advisory Committee on Rural Housing. She lived mainly in Edinburgh but counted among her recreations Gaelic music and travelling in the Highlands and Islands.

As a writer Marian McNeill is now best remembered for *The Scots Kitchen* and for her four-volume study of Scottish folklore, *The Silver Bough* (1957–68). She also had ambitions to be a novelist and her correspondence with *Catherine Carswell demonstrates the struggle and determination that eventually produced the semi-autobiographical *The Road Home* (1932). Her correspondence with others involved in the Scottish cultural revival is a legacy of equal significance with her published writings and public activities, giving a first-hand account of Scottish affairs in the inter-war period. She was also at the centre of a lively correspondence among women friends which offers insight into the difficulties women experienced in their attempts to balance a domestic role with public writing ambitions. Letters to her demonstrate her friends' warm appreciation of her kindnesses and consideration. In 1962, she was made MBE for services to Scottish culture. It seems that in her later years, 'her fortunes as an author waned, and when she died in 1973 she was in sadly constrained and lonely circumstances' (Sanderson 1989, p. xi). MPM

• NLS: F. Marian McNeill archive; Willa and Edwin Muir corr.

McNeill, F. M., Works as above, and (1920) *Iona: a history of the island*, (1956, 1992) *The Scots Cellar*, (1989) *The Silver Bough* (vol. I), S. Sanderson, ed. and intro. See also website: www.eup.ed.ac.uk

Carswell, C. (1950, 1997) *Lying Awake: an unfinished autobiography and other posthumous papers*, J. Carswell, ed. and

intro.; Cruickshank, H. (1976) *Octobiography*; *HSWW*
(Bibl.); Royle, T. (1993) *Mainstream Companion to Scottish
Literature*; *SB* .

MACNICOL, Elizabeth (Bessie), m. Frew, born
Glasgow 15 July 1869, died Glasgow 4 June 1904.
Painter. Daughter of Mary Ann Matthews, and
Peter MacNicol, schoolmaster.

Bessie MacNicol had a supportive and
affectionate family background, though marked by
the deaths of four siblings, including her twin sister,
in early childhood. She studied at the GSA under
Fra Newbery (1887–93, see Glasgow Girls), and at
the Académie Colarossi in Paris in 1893–4. The next
year, she exhibited *A French Girl* at the Glasgow
Institute, and began to receive public acclaim. In
1896, Bessie MacNicol visited the artists'
community at Kirkcudbright, where she began a
friendship with E. A. Hornel, whom she painted.
Her letters to him are among the few records, other
than her paintings, which survive. Her work was
for a while influenced by him, and her use of
colour and textures is closely related to the Glasgow
Boys. She was not afraid to work in areas
considered more suitable for men, as in her nude
painting, *Vanity* (1902). She also painted many
costume pieces, the first of which was *A Girl of the
'Sixties* (1898). In 1899, she married Alexander Frew
(1861–1908), gynaecologist and painter. Bessie
MacNicol used the studio at the back of their
Glasgow house to create larger-scale paintings. By
this time she had built up a considerable reputation
and had exhibited in Germany, Austria, Russia and
the USA. She died in childbirth, aged only 34. FJ
• Broughton House Collection, Kirkcudbright:
Correspondence.
Burkhauser, J. (ed.) (1990) *Glasgow Girls*; *Glasgow Herald*,
7 June 1904 (obit.); Macmillan, D. (1990) *Scottish Art
1460–1990*; *ODNB* (2004); Tanner, A. (1998) *Bessie MacNicol,
New Woman*.

MACPHAIL, Katherine Stewart, OBE, born
Coatbridge 30 Oct. 1887, died St Andrews 21 Sept.
1974. Doctor. Daughter of Jessie Edmonstone
Mitchell, and Donald Macphail, GP.

Not long after qualifying MBChB (Glasgow,
1911), Katherine Macphail joined a *Scottish
Women's Hospital Unit in wartime Serbia, where
she found wounded men dying of gangrene,
paratyphoid, enteric fever and typhus. Invalided
out herself with typhus, she rejoined the defeated
Serbs, then after brief internment, accompanied the
Serb Refugee Relief Unit to Corsica and Salonika.

At the end of the war, she attended refugee women
and children in Macedonia, returning to Belgrade
after the Armistice to help fight a typhus epidemic.
There she opened a hospital for sick street children
in a disused army hut, using her own money before
support came from the newly founded Save the
Children Fund. By 1934, 170,000 children had been
treated in what had become the first children's
hospital in Yugoslavia. Katherine Macphail later
built a specialist home for children with tubercular
diseases of the bones and joints, which was closed
in 1941 when Yugoslavia was again invaded and
she herself was interned. She worked for two years
in Lanarkshire, then in 1944 returned with
UNRRA to reopen the children's hospital, which
she handed over to the new Communist
government in 1947. SO
• Krippner, M. (1980) *The Quality of Mercy*; Leneman,
L. (1998) *In the Service of Life*; Wilson, F. (1944) *In the
Margins of Chaos*.

MACPHERSON, Annie Parlane, born Campsie,
Stirlingshire, 2 June 1825, died 27 Nov. 1904. Social
worker, pioneer of child migration. Daughter of
Helen Edwards, and James Macpherson,
shoemaker, teacher.

Educated at the Home and Colonial Training
College in London, Annie Macpherson undertook
evangelical mission work in the East End and in
Cambridge. She established her first orphanage in
Spitalfields in 1864, then became convinced that
emigration was the answer. In 1870, she
accompanied a party of 100 boys to Canada,
settling them on farms in Quebec and Ontario.
Further receiving homes were acquired at
Belleville, Galt and Knowlton, and from 1870 to
1920 more than 14,000 children were brought to
Canada. Recruits were trained in a London home
opened by Lord Shaftesbury, being taught
marketable skills while their supervised passage and
relocation was being arranged. Annie Macpherson's
sisters, Rachel Merry and Louisa Birt, were respectively involved with British receiving centres and
Canadian distributing homes, and her pioneering,
though not uncontroversial, work provided the
theoretical rationale and practical model for
Thomas Barnardo, William Quarrier and other
like-minded evangelicals. Through a chance
meeting in Toronto, Annie Macpherson also
inspired the founding, back in Edinburgh, by
William and **Margaret Blaikie** (1823–1915) of Mrs
Blaikie's Orphan and Emigration Home in 1872,
but this home closed in 1892, partly because of

questionable recruiting methods, partly because of duplication of effort with that of *Emma Stirling.
MDH

• Univ. of Liverpool, Social Work Archives: D715/1–2, Committee Minute Books, 1873–1933; D715/3–4, Annual Reports, 1873–1907; D715/5–15, Miscellaneous, 1903–73. Macpherson, A. (1866) *The Little Matchbox-Makers,* (1870) *Canadian Homes for London Wanderers.*
Birt, L. M. (1913) *The Children's Home Finder*; Blaikie, W. G. (1901) *An Autobiography: 'Recollections of a Busy Life'*; Harper, M. (1992) 'Halfway to heaven or hell on earth? Canada's Scottish child immigrants', in C. Kerrigan (ed.) *The Immigrant Experience*, pp. 165–83; Harper, M. (2003) *Adventurers and Exiles*; *ODNB* (2004); Wagner, G. (1982) *Children of the Empire.* http://ist.uwaterloo.ca/~marj/genealogy/children/Organizations/anniem.html

MACPHERSON, Margaret Hope, n. **MacLean,** born Colinton 29 June 1908, died Portree 21 Oct. 2001. Crofter, author, political activist. Daughter of Sheena Macaulay, and Norman MacLean, minister.

Margaret MacLean was educated in Edinburgh. After marrying Duncan MacPherson, a crofter from The Braes on Skye, she moved to the Highlands, where she raised her family. In the 1960s, she became a writer of children's fiction, often inspired by Highland culture and history. Her fictional account of the 1880s Land War, *The Battle of the Braes* (1970), draws on her family's long-standing connections with The Braes area, where her grandfather was schoolmaster during the crofters' rebellion. Her deep concern for the crofting districts was translated into local politics. A long-time member of the Labour Party, she sat on Inverness-shire County Council (1945–9), and was secretary of the Skye Labour Party (1961–84). In 1951, her knowledge of the Highlands' socio-economic situation earned her a place on the Commission of Enquiry into Crofting Conditions. In a note of dissent to the final report, Margaret MacPherson expressed her disillusion with its conclusions, arguing that it 'did not go far enough to remedy the evils of which we had all become aware' (*Report* 1954, p. 89). Believing that the cause of the crofting problem lay in private ownership, she remained strongly opposed to crofters' purchasing their own holdings, preferring the notion of community ownership. LG

• MacPherson, M., Work as above, and (1963) *Shinty Boys,* (1965) *The Rough Road,* (1967) *Ponies on Hire,* (1968) *The New Tenants,* (1972) *The Boy on the Roof,* (1985) 'Crofters and the Crofters' Commission' in *Land and the People*, Scottish Socialist Society.
Report of the Commission of Enquiry into Crofting Conditions, 1954.

MACPHERSON, Mary see **MÀIRI MHÒR NAN ÒRAN** (1821–98)

MACRUAIRI, Amy, fl. 1318–50. Dispossessed heiress and religious patron. Daughter of Ruairi MacRuairi of Garmoran.

Amy MacRuairi, whose father was recognised as Ri Innse Gall (King of the Hebrides), married her third cousin, John MacDonald of Islay (d. c. 1387), chief of Clan Donald. Although their marriage was legitimate in Gaelic eyes, the couple had it confirmed by papal dispensation in 1337. Amy's brother Ranald MacRuairi, who in 1318 had succeeded his father in the Clan Ruairi lordship of Garmoran, despite the objections of his aunt *Christiana MacRuairi, was assassinated in 1346. Amy MacRuairi inherited the Clan Ruairi territories and titles, consolidating the two lineages and creating a focus for both Gaelic and Scottish political ambition.

In circumstances which remain obscure, Amy MacRuairi and her three sons were systematically dispossessed of much of their land and power: her marriage was annulled in 1350 so that John MacDonald could marry Margaret, daughter of Robert Stewart, heir to the throne. In 1354 he was inaugurated as Ri Innse Gall. He continued to exercise lordship over Amy MacRuairi's lands and in 1372 his father-in-law, now Robert II, granted him Garmoran. In 1373, John granted Garmoran to Amy's eldest son, Ranald, but his other lands and titles went to the eldest son of his second marriage, Donald, Robert II's grandson.

Tradition relates that Amy MacRuairi took to religious life and patronage: the oratory known as the Temple of St Michael in Grimsay, North Uist, and the castles of Borve, Benbecula and Tiorim, Moidart, are all ascribed to her. She is reputedly buried in Iona, where an Order of Benedictine nuns had been founded by *Bethoc, daughter of Somerled, her ancestor. CGP

• Boardman, S. (1996) *The Early Stewart Kings*; Brown, M. (2004) *The Wars of Scotland 1214–1371*; Steer, K. A. and Bannerman, J. (1977) *Late Medieval Monumental Sculpture in the West Highlands*; 'The Book of Clanranald' in A. Cameron (1894) *Reliquiae Celticae*; MacDonald, A. and MacDonald A. (1896–1904) *The Clan Donald.*

MACRUAIRI, Christiana, of the Isles (of Mar), fl. 1290–1318. Supporter of Robert Bruce. Daughter of Alan MacRuairi of Garmoran.

Although Christiana MacRuairi had two half-brothers, she was the sole legitimate heir of Alan MacRuairi, chief of Clan Ruairi and lord of Garmoran which included large parts of the western Highlands and Islands. Her marriage in the 1290s to Duncan of Mar, younger son of Donald, Earl of Mar, made her the sister-in-law of Robert Bruce, husband of Isabel of Mar. Although Christiana and Duncan gave homage to Edward I when he conquered Scotland in 1296, Christiana of the Isles raised men and ships in the Hebrides to help Robert Bruce's bid for the throne in 1306/7. In 1309, Bruce, now king, confirmed Christiana's resignation of Garmoran to her half-brother Ruairi MacRuairi, in what was probably a family attempt to keep the lordship in the MacRuairi male line. If Ruairi had no male heirs, Christiana's own son Ruairi would succeed. If neither man had heirs, the lands would return to Christiana. When Ruairi MacRuairi died in 1318, his son Ranald succeeded him, despite Christiana's attempt to grant the lands to Arthur Campbell. Garmoran later passed to Christiana's niece, *Amy MacRuairi. Christiana MacRuairi's continuing Bruce connections were shown in her patronage of Inchaffray Abbey, also favoured by Robert I. EE

• Barrow, G. W. S. (1988) *Robert Bruce*; Brown, M. (2004) *The Wars of Scotland 1214–1371*; Duncan, A. A. M. (ed.) (1988) *The Acts of Robert I*; McDonald, R. A. (1997) *The Kingdom of the Isles.*
Private information: R. A. McDonald.

MAIR, Sarah Elizabeth Siddons (Sally), DBE, born Edinburgh 22 Sept. 1846, died Wendover, Bucks., 13 Feb. 1941. Campaigner for women's education and rights. Daughter of Elizabeth Harriot Siddons, and Arthur Mair, army major and town councillor.

Sally Mair lived all her life in Edinburgh's New Town. She was the great-grand-daughter of the actor Sarah Siddons, and grand-daughter of the actor-theatre manager *Harriet Murray (see Siddons), and Henry Siddons, who managed the Theatre Royal in Edinburgh. The family enjoyed the growing city's advantages and were proud of their theatrical and literary connections. After a loss of money on railway shares, Elizabeth Harriot Mair gave readings from Shakespeare in her drawing-room four afternoons a week.

In 1865, at the age of 18, Sally Mair founded the Edinburgh Essay Society – a young ladies' literary circle that evolved into the influential Ladies' Edinburgh Debating Society (1865–1935). When it began there were no women on school boards or town councils, in university or Parliament. In 1866, the society debated parliamentary votes for women. Although it voted against the idea, its position changed in later years. The group acted as a seedbed of reforming activity. Its membership included most women who were active in most causes in Scotland at the time. Their focus was broadly literary and educational, but became more social and political over time. The group published a magazine of stories, poetry and non-fiction, *The Attempt,* which became *The Ladies' Edinburgh Magazine,* edited by Sarah Mair, with Helen Reid (d. 1895), daughter of its publisher Reid & Son. The society's work was, unusually, recorded by the daughter of one of its early members, Lettice Milne Rae. Meeting weekly on Saturday mornings to debate a range of formally chosen topics, it had around 100 members. Probably more than 600 women were members over its duration. For many it was valuable training for further education and public life. Sally Mair was admired as its leader and as a gifted speaker. She was also one of the founders of the Edinburgh Association for the University Education of Women, St George's School and Training College, and Masson Hall. In 1906, she became president of ENSWS and in 1910 president of the SFSS. With *Elsie Inglis, she proposed the formation of the *Scottish Women's Hospitals. After 1918, she was honorary president of the ENSEC, and vice-president of EWCA. She was awarded an honorary doctorate by the University of Edinburgh (1920) for her work for women's higher education. Made DBE in 1931, at the age of 95, she was still active in women's causes. In 1936, she wrote that: 'My life has been a long and very happy one . . . I have watched, and, to a small extent shared in . . . the Awakening of Women' (Rae 1936, p. 7). SI

• Hamilton, S. (1987) 'Women and the Scottish universities c. 1869–1939: a social history', PhD, Univ. of Edinburgh; Kelman, K. A. (2002) 'Female "self culture" in Edinburgh: the Ladies' Edinburgh Debating Society', PhD, Queen Margaret Univ. College, Edinburgh; *ODNB* (2004); Rae, L. M. (1936) *Ladies in Debate*; SB.

MAIREARAD NIGHEAN LACHLAINN, born Mull c. 1660. Clan Maclean poet.

Mairearad nighean Lachlainn may not have been a Maclean by birth. The evidence points to one parent being a Maclean, the other a Clanranald

MacDonald. Some traditions state that Mairearad was married with children but that her children all predeceased her. She composed several poems, mainly concerned with the diminishing power of the Clan Maclean under the leadership of Sir John Maclean, which eventually led to the clan losing the Isle of Mull. Her most famous work is her lament for Sir John Maclean, 'Gaoir nam ban Muileach' (The Cry of the Mull Women). She is reputed to have been buried face downwards, as was her contemporary *Màiri nighean Alasdair Ruaidh. AF

• Black, R. (ed.) (2001) *An Lasair*, pp. 60–72; *The Celtic Review*, October 1911, p. 200; Maclean Sinclair, A. (1898) *Na Bàird Leathanach*, vol. 1; (1892) *The Gaelic Bards from 1715 to 1765*; MacGill-eain, S. (1985) *Ris a' Bhruthaich*, W. Gillies ed., p. 162; Thomson, D. S. (1974) *An Introduction to Gaelic Poetry*, p. 141.

MÀIRI MHÒR NAN ÒRAN (Màiri nighean Iain Bhàin/Mary MacPherson), born Sgèabost, Isle of Skye, 10 March 1821, died Portree, 7 Nov. 1898. Poet. Daughter of Flòraidh Nèill MhicAonghais (Flora MacInnis), and Iain Bàn MacAonghais Oig (John MacDonald), crofter.

Màiri nighean Iain Bhàin became known throughout the Highlands and Islands as Màiri Mhòr nan Òran ('Great Mary of the Songs') as a result of her popular compositions which captured the hearts of Highland people and gave voice to the land agitations of the 19th century. Her early life was spent in Skye. Sometime around 1843–5, she began her married life with Isaac Mac a'Phearsain (d. 1871) in Inverness. She is said to have had seven children, although records show only six. In 1871, she was widowed; the need for employment led to a series of events pushing her forward into the public eye, despite great personal difficulties.

In 1872, Màiri Mhòr was employed in Inverness as a nurse to the family of Captain Turner, Royal Engineers. Upon his wife's death, she was accused of theft and was sentenced to 40 days' imprisonment. By her own account and other traditional accounts she was innocent; however, in her own words, 'Se na dh'fhulaing mi de thàmailt a thug mo bhàrdachd beò' ('My suffering brought life to my poetry') (Meek 1977, p. 9). Her subsequent compositions reflect both her own personal straits and those of her contemporary Highlanders.

Màiri Mhòr continued her nursing career with further training and moves to Glasgow and Greenock. The lively Highland community of the time provided opportunities to popularise her works and she became the foremost poet of the Highland Land Reform Association, known as the Highland Land League. Through the Land League her songs became known throughout the Highlands and Islands, while the associated political movement provided opportunities for travel. Upon retirement she returned to Sgèabost, and died after a short illness in 1898 in Portree. She was interred in Chapel Yard, Inverness, alongside her husband. She left a legacy of poetry notable as commentary of the time, expressed in clear language imbued with symbolism drawn from the land and history. In 2002, Highland Council established the Mary MacPherson Gaelic Song Fellowship (Caidreachas òrain Gaìdhlig Màiri Mhòr) for the research and development of Gaelic song. ABM

• *Màiri Mhòr nan Òran*, Greentrax Recordings CDTRAX 070.
Meek, D. E. (1977) 'Gaelic poets of the land agitation', *Trans. Gael. Soc. Inverness*, 41, (1977) *Màiri Mhòr nan Òran* (Bibl.); MacLean, S. (1962) 'The poetry of the Clearances', *Trans. Gael. Soc. Inverness*, 38; *ODNB* (2004) (see MacPherson, Mary); Thomson, D. (1974) *An Introduction to Gaelic Poetry*.

MÀIRI NIGHEAN ALASDAIR RUAIDH (Mary MacLeod) born Rodel, Harris c. 1615, buried Rodel c. 1707. Poet. Daughter of a kinswoman of the MacDonalds of Clan Ranald, and Alexander Roy MacLeod.

Màiri nighean Alasdair Ruaidh (she would not have recognised the English version of her name), scion of an aristocratic family, had connections with the island of Berneray, Harris, and the castle of Dunvegan in Skye. Her poetry mainly addresses leading men of the Clan MacLeod. Her exact position in Dunvegan is unclear. Some say she enjoyed privileges similar to those of an official bard, yet for a time after 1660 she was compelled to leave Dunvegan. This, tradition explains, was because, as a nursemaid, her overweening praise of the children might bring ill luck. Others suggest that composing panegyrics was the exclusive prerogative of male poets: Mairi was exiled for usurping their position. The most plausible explanation is political. Acts of the Lowland parliament that singled out bards for fomenting unrest culminated in the Statutes of Iona in 1609; the MacLeod chief had been a signatory and his successors were influenced by the edict. In Berneray, Sir Norman MacLeod, son of the Clan chief, gave her a house near his own. Sir Norman was a patron of learning and Màiri benefited from the cultural environment.

At her own behest she was buried face down 'beul nam breug a chur foidhpe' (with her lying mouth undermost) (Watson 1934, p. xix). It is unlikely that this gesture was intended as poetic justice for daring to compose a type of poetry reserved for males. Rather, she regretted the fulsome praise she had bestowed on her patrons, one of whom had rewarded her with exile. Màiri nighean Alasdair Ruaidh was essentially a praise-singer whose reputation is based on her innovations to the imagery and metrical structures of traditional vernacular oral verse. She was a leading representative of a movement of resurgence in song-poetry at a time when written Classical Gaelic was falling into disuse. JMACI

• *Gaelic Songs of Mary MacLeod* [1934] (1965) J. C. Watson, ed.

Matheson, W. (1951–2) 'Notes on Mary MacLeod (1) her Family Connections (2) her Forgotten Songs' *Trans. Gael. Soc. Inverness*, 41; *ODNB* (2004).

MAITLAND, Mary (Marie), born before 1586, died 1596. Manuscript owner and poet. Daughter of Mariota Cranstoun, and Sir Richard Maitland of Lethington, poet and courtier.

Mary Maitland exemplifies the role that Scottish Renaissance women of the aristocratic and upper middle classes played in the composition, creation, and transcription of literary manuscripts. She is associated with the manuscript volume known as the Maitland Quarto, a substantial collection of Scottish poems, social, moral, political, and amatory in nature, from the period c. 1550–86. Her signatures, and the date 1586, appear on the flyleaf, denoting possible ownership, but also implying that she may have transcribed, and even composed, some poetry. Her text suggests that it served as a family commonplace book, both celebration and commemoration of the distinguished Maitland family. An early editor even suggested that Mary Maitland was a kind of Miltonic daughter, helping her aged father in his own literary pursuits. In the same year that the book was completed, she married Alexander Lauder (d. c. 1622), heir to Sir William Lauder of Hatton. Her son George Lauder became a political and military poet.

Mary Maitland's creative influence may be detected in the presence of several female-voiced lyrics, such as the translation of a French poem about an unhappily married woman. The extraordinary poem of erotic and spiritual love between women, 'As phebus bricht', invites speculation whether she herself was the author of this and other anonymous poems, for the convention of anonymity in a manuscript collection was frequently 'exploited' by a female transcriber.

Several lyrics are directly addressed to Mary Maitland. One playfully puns on her name, 'Marie thocht in this wod did appeir/mait land and gold scho gave aboundantlie'. In this visionary poem, 'Marie' appears to the dreamer in a beautiful garden, signifying virtue and chastity. The lyric simply inscribed 'to your self' celebrates Mary Maitland as part of a triumvirate of female poets, alluding to the poetic crown of immortality which will be hers once the labour of the book's compilation is complete. The specific allusion to 'sapphic songe' implies that she is being praised for her gifts as a lyricist and, given the Renaissance understanding of Sappho, strengthens her association with the lyric of female eroticism. The manuscript richly suggests the scope and nature of women's creative role in Renaissance manuscript compilation, even if it does not resolve all the questions it provokes. SD

• Pepys Library, Cambridge: PL 1408.

Craigie, W. A. (ed.) (1919–27) *The Maitland Folio Manuscript*, (1920) *The Maitland Quarto Manuscript*; *HSWW*; Newlyn, E. S. (2004) 'A methodology for reading against the culture: anonymous, women poets, and the Maitland Quarto Manuscript (c. 1586)', in S. M. Dunnigan et al. (eds) *Woman and the Feminine in Medieval and Early Modern Scottish Writing*; *ODNB* (2004); *SP*; Traub, V. (2002) *The Renaissance of Lesbianism in Early Modern England*.

MALCOLM, Lavinia, n. **Laing,** born Forres, probably 1847, died Dollar 2 Nov. 1920. Councillor and campaigner, Provost, 1913–19. Daughter of Janet Kynoch, and Alexander Laing, tinsmith and ironmonger.

Lavinia Laing's family in Forres included merchants, shopkeepers and craftworkers: her grandfather, John Kynoch, was Provost (1848–55), her father a councillor. The Laings and Kynochs were Liberals and United Presbyterians, and Lavinia inherited their radical outlook and commitment to public service. In 1883, when she married Richard Malcolm (1840–1926), she was a schoolteacher in Edinburgh, but moved to Dollar where her husband was a master at Dollar Academy, one of Scotland's most prominent schools. The town had grown around the Academy, founded in 1818. By the 1880s, there were some 800 scholars and the Malcolms accommodated boarders at their home. Their only son, Richard, died in 1895: thereafter,

Lavinia Malcolm became a leading figure in the Clackmannan and Kinross Women's Liberal Association; she was a dedicated campaigner for the extension of the parliamentary vote.

Both Malcolms were active in local government. Dollar became a police burgh in 1891 and Richard Malcolm served as Provost, 1896–9. In 1907, the Liberal Government allowed women to stand as councillors in burgh and county elections. Lavinia Malcolm was the only successful woman candidate returned unopposed for both the town and parish councils of Dollar. In 1909 she was elected to the local School Board and in 1913 became Provost of the burgh, on the unanimous vote of councillors. The circumstances were slightly unusual, involving a controversy over the new town hall that prompted the resignation of the serving Provost and others. However, she remained Provost until 1919, her term extended because of the war, and by the time of her death in 1920 she had achieved further recognition as one of the first women to attend the Convention of Scottish Burghs and to be appointed JP. Scotland's first female civic leader, Lavinia Malcolm strongly identified herself as a role model for others, arguing that women should make the most of public service opportunities to show that they were sufficiently responsible to play an equal part in parliamentary affairs. IEM

• Douglas, R. (1934) *The Annals of the Royal Burgh of Forres*; Hollis, P. (1987) *Ladies Elect: Women in English local government, 1865–1914*; *ODNB* (2004) (Bibl.); *Glasgow Herald*, 6, 7 Nov. 1907, 11 Nov. 1913, 3 Nov. 1920 (obit.); *The Scotsman*, 3 Nov. 1920 (obit.).

MANN, Janet (Jean), n. **Stewart,** born Polmaddie, East Renfrewshire, 2 July 1889, died Greenock 21 March 1964. Councillor and MP. Daughter of Annie Morrison, and William Stewart, iron-moulder.

Jean Stewart attended Kinning Park School and Bellahouston Academy before training in accountancy. In 1908, she married William Lawrence Mann (1878–1958), chair of the Rothesay ILP branch, and went to live and work on the island of Bute. The couple had six children. She became ILP branch secretary and stood unsuccessfully for the Rothesay Town Council in 1923 and 1924. After moving to Glasgow she was elected to Glasgow Corporation for Provan in 1931 and served until 1938. She became a bailie (1934), a senior bailie (1937–8) and eventually chair of the magistrates' committee. She also took an active

interest in housing issues as convener of the city's housing committee between 1935 and 1938, organising secretary of the Town and Country Planning Association (Scotland) and a member of the Housing Advisory Council of the Secretary of State for Scotland. She favoured low-rise council housing.

In the 1931 and 1935 General Elections she stood unsuccessfully as the ILP candidate for West Renfrewshire. Parliamentary success came in 1945 when she was returned as Labour MP for Coatbridge, a constituency she represented at Westminster until 1959 (together with Airdrie after 1950). In Parliament she continued her interest in housing and other areas of social concern, largely those affecting women in working-class households. From 1953 to 1958 she was on the NEC of the Labour Party as an independent right-winger and was active on its policy sub-committee on housing. In 1958, the year in which her husband died, she resigned from the NEC and did not stand for re-election in the General Election of the following year. However, she was a councillor for Gourock from 1958 to 1964. A backbencher throughout her parliamentary career, she attended a great many foreign conferences and in later life was received by a number of dignitaries, including Eleanor Roosevelt during a trip to the USA. YGB

• Mann, J. (ed.) (1941) *Re-planning Scotland. Expert evidence on pre-war conditions in Scotland and post-war speeches delivered at planning conference, Largs, 1941* (Prepared on behalf of the Town and Country Planning Association Scotland), (1962) *Woman in Parliament.*
Brown, Y. (2001) 'Women and society c. 1770s onwards', in M. Lynch (ed.) *Oxford Companion to Scottish History*; *ODNB* (2004); *SLL.*

MANN, Kathleen, m. **Crawford,** born Kent 30 Nov. 1908, died Killearn, Stirlingshire, 11 Jan. 2000. Illustrator and textile artist. Daughter of Rosamond Mann, and Archibald Mann, businessman.

Precociously talented, Kathleen Mann studied costume design at Croydon School of Art (1924–8). Having developed her interest in peasant dress at the Royal College of Art, she wrote and illustrated *Peasant Costume in Europe* (1931). In 1930, she was appointed Head of the Embroidery Department at Glasgow School of Art, where she revitalised the department. Introducing a more spontaneous approach, she encouraged work on a large scale. Her growing reputation in the forefront of embroidery design led to recognition by *The Studio* magazine; her work was featured in a special number, *Modern Embroidery* (1933). She was obliged to resign on marriage to her colleague Hugh Adam Crawford RSA in 1934; they had two sons and subsequently she wrote and illustrated several books. Her husband's career took her to Aberdeen where she taught a variety of subjects, but by 1955 she had abandoned textiles in favour of painting. LA

• Mann, K. (1931) *Peasant Costume in Europe*, (1937) *Appliqué Design and Method*, (1937b) *Embroidery Design and Stitches*, (1939) *Design from Peasant Art*, (1952) *China Decoration*. Arthur, L. (ed.) (1994) *The Unbroken Thread, a Century of Embroidery and Weaving at Glasgow School of Art*; Hogarth, M. (ed.) (1933) *Modern Embroidery*, Special Spring No., *The Studio*.

MANN, Selma, born Windau, Latvia, 24 Nov. 1891, died London March 1989. Active Zionist.

Selma Mann came from a Latvian Jewish family and attended university in Geneva, then in 1910 at Edinburgh, where she met her doctor husband (formerly known as Teitelman). They had one son. She became involved in charitable work among Glasgow's Jewish community and is chiefly remembered for two notable contributions. Encouraged by Rebecca Sieff, creator of England's Federation of Women Zionists, which became the worldwide Women's International Zionist Organisation (WIZO), Selma Mann was founder-president of the first two WIZO branches in Scotland. She initiated further Scottish branches, and Scotland quickly became a centre for Zionist fundraising by women. In 1935, she formed a Glasgow-based 'Care of Children Committee', one of many agencies assisting Jewish child refugees in the UK. As convener, she was instrumental in bringing more than 300 children to Scotland from Nazi-controlled Europe. She later moved to London, and continued to take a prominent role in WIZO while maintaining links with Glasgow members. She remained honorary president of the Glasgow Central Group until her death. LF

• Scottish Jewish Archives Centre, Glasgow: Documents relating to Glasgow WIZO.
Fleming, L. (2005) 'Jewish women in Glasgow c.1880–1950: gender, ethnicity and the immigrant experience', unpublished PhD thesis, Univ. of Glasgow; *Jewish Chronicle*, 24 March 1989 (obit.); *Jewish Echo*, 17 March 1989 (obit.); *Zionist Yearbook 1960*.

MANSON, Mary Jane, n. **Ninian,** born Mid Yell, Shetland, 10 March 1897, died Westsandwick, Shetland, 19 May 1994. Crofter, knitter, storyteller. Daughter of Janet (Jessie) and John Ninian.

Mary Ninian was born into a fishing-crofting family. After marrying Robert Manson she moved to a croft at Westsandwick, where alongside croft work, from spring lambing and peat-raising to autumn potato harvest, she produced hosiery: hand-knitted items that could be exchanged at merchants' stores for tea, sugar and drapery. Barter-truck lasted in Shetland well after its prohibition under the 1887 Truck Amendment Act. It perpetuated the exploitation of hand-knitters who never received a fair price for their goods, but also led to the emergence of an active network of women producers with a strong female identity. Mary Manson was taught Fair Isle patterns by an aunt, a valuable skill since Fair Isle hosiery commanded high prices. She recalled evenings spent carding and spinning wool with friends, and was proud that one of her shawls was presented to the Princess Royal on her marriage in 1922. Royal patronage – notably the Prince of Wales's Fair Isle golf sweaters in the 1920s – stimulated demand. Hand-knitting remained a staple home industry in Shetland until the 1960s, when it was largely displaced by machine production. Mary Manson's fame as a storyteller was demonstrated in oral history interviews shortly before she died. Combining autobiography and folklore, she encapsulated a lost way of life, in a form that empowered the female narrator as a keeper of social memory in the islands. LCA

• Shetland Archives: 3/3/77/1–3, interview with Mary Manson, 30 Jan. and 17 August 1982, 3/1/397: interview with Netta Inkster, 9 April 2001; British Parliamentary Papers, C555: Commission to Inquire into the Truck System, 2nd report (Shetland), 1872.
Abrams, L. (2005) *Myth and Materiality in a Woman's World*; Fryer, L. (1995) *Knitting by the Fireside and on the Hillside*.

MARGARET Logie, Queen of Scotland, n. **Drummond,** born Perthshire c. 1330, died Marseille, France, c. 1373. Daughter of Malcolm Drummond, minor Lennox and Perthshire lord.

Margaret Drummond was the first Scotswoman since the 11th century to marry a reigning King of Scots, David II (1324–71), and the first Scots Queen to face divorce. David had married **Joan 'of the Tower'** (1322–62), daughter of Isabella of France and Edward II of England, in July 1328, under the peace which closed the first phase of the Wars of Independence. Their marriage was never happy: without issue, David took mistresses after his release from English captivity (1346–57). His liaison with the shadowy **Katherine Mortimer**

(d. 1360) – probably daughter of Sir Roger Mortimer of Inverbervie and wife of Sir William Ramsay of Colluthie, whom David imposed as Earl of the disputed region of Fife – caused Joan to return to England and a religious life in 1358. Katherine's perceived influence upon David's pro-English policies proved tragic. On about 24 June 1360 she was murdered on the orders of the Earl of Angus and other great lords: she was interred in Newbattle Abbey, Lothian.

David now took up with Margaret Drummond, wife of Sir John Logie of Logie (d. c. 1363) in Strathearn, by whom she had a son, John, born c. 1350. David exploited the network of lands and offices run by Margaret's Drummond kinfolk in Stewart-dominated Perthshire. Queen Joan's death on 7 September 1362 and her burial in the Grey Friars, London, freed David to marry Margaret, 'who had lived with him for some time' (Maxwell 1907, pp. 173–4), but only after her first marriage was annulled or John Logie died. Their plans provoked a rebellion led by the Stewart heirs to the throne in spring 1363. David combined the submission of these rebels with marriage to Margaret at the Bishop of St Andrews' manor of Inchmurdoch near Crail in about May 1363. Queen Margaret was gifted Perthshire lands and customs revenue from Aberdeen and Inverkeithing, a bounty she expanded aggressively to judge from her dispute with Glasgow's bishop over clerical provision, her bond with Sir John Kennedy of Dunnure c. 1366 (who promised to warn her of any plots against her) and her ambitious procurement for her son of the royal lands of Annandale. She pressed David into stripping the Earl of Ross of his lands and briefly arresting the heir presumptive, Robert Steward. But by mid-1368, David had moved to annul this issueless marriage (one 15th-century chronicler even accused Queen Margaret of pretending to be with child) and marry instead Agnes Dunbar, sister of the Earl of March and niece of *Agnes Randolph ('Black Agnes'). Queen Margaret's appeal to the papacy prevented this match and threatened interdict upon Scotland. Her claim to recover a fortune in lands, gold coin and jewels continued after David's unexpected death on 22 February 1371: the new king, Robert II, was spared only when Queen Margaret died at Marseille on her way to the Pope at Avignon. The papacy paid for her burial. Her son, John Logie, was stripped of his lands thereafter. MP

• NAS: Vatican Transcripts, RH2/6.

Maxwell, H. (trans.) (1907) *Sir Thomas Gray's The Scalacronica*; *ODNB* (2004) (Margaret [n. Drummond]); Penman, M. (2004) *David II, 1329–71*; *Scotichron.*; *SP*.

MARGARET, 'Maid of Norway', Queen-designate of Scots, born Norway (possibly Bergen) c. 1282, died Orkney, October 1290. Daughter of Margaret, daughter of Alexander III, and Erik II, King of Norway.

Alexander III's death on 18 March 1286 left his grand-daughter Margaret as his sole direct heir. Her right to inherit the Scottish crown had been established in parliament in 1284, but divisions within the governing community threatened to cause civil war; this was narrowly averted by the committee of Guardians elected in April 1286. Perhaps even earlier, negotiations had begun for Margaret's marriage to Edward, son of Edward I of England. The Treaties of Salisbury (6 November 1289) and Birgham (18 July 1290) ensured mutual support for Margaret's inheritance and effected the marriage contract, hedged about by elaborate safeguards for Scottish independence. The treaties were rendered ineffectual, however, by Margaret's death in Orkney during her passage to Scotland. The resulting dynastic crisis led to decades of Anglo-Scottish warfare. NHR

• *ODNB* (2004); Reid, N. H. (1982) 'Margaret "Maid of Norway" and Scottish Queenship', in *Reading Medieval Studies*, 8 (Bibl.).

MARGARET of Denmark, Queen of Scotland, born Denmark c. 1457, died Stirling 14 July 1486. Daughter of Dorothea of Brandenburg, and Christian I of Denmark .

The marriage of Margaret of Denmark and James III (1452–88) on 13 July 1469 brought the Orkney and Shetland islands to the Scottish crown. Christian I had pledged the Northern Isles to Scotland because of his financial difficulties over paying his only daughter's dowry, and the Scottish parliament annexed the isles in 1472. Margaret was awarded a generous dower (provision for widowhood) by the Scots, including one third of the royal revenues, the castle of Stirling and the palace of Linlithgow.

Unlike her two predecessors, *Joan Beaufort and *Mary of Guelders, as Scottish Queen, Margaret does not appear to have enjoyed a close working partnership with her husband. Only one grant issued in the King's name was made with her consent, suggesting that the two did not often discuss royal business. This single grant is not representative of an otherwise unrecorded daily administrative partnership but was issued in extraordinary circumstances, rewarding John Dundas for his part in liberating James III from Edinburgh Castle in 1482.

The King's capture at Lauder Bridge and his imprisonment in Edinburgh marked the highpoint of Margaret's political involvement. She had been appointed guardian of James, heir to the throne, and custodian of Edinburgh Castle for five years from 1478, making her influential in the negotiation of a resolution to the 1482 crisis. Her custody of the heir ensured that the King's brother, Albany, had to seek her advice about how to proceed, and she had access to James III through Lord Darnley, whom she paid as keeper of Edinburgh. The relatively prompt and bloodless end to the crisis is testament to her political acumen and her insistence that government continue in the King's name. Margaret's role during 1482 may not have been welcomed by her husband. James III resided largely in Edinburgh after his release, while Margaret remained in her dower castle of Stirling with her three sons. She retained their custody, probably for security reasons, and control of their education until her death in 1486. James III sought to have her canonised in 1487, but this public relations campaign was undermined by a rumour (circulated in Denmark by the rebels supporting the future James IV in 1488) that one of the King's men had poisoned the Queen. FD

• Chandler, S. B. (1953) 'An Italian life of Margaret, Queen of James III,' *Scot. Hist. Rev.* 32; Macdougall, N. (1982) *James III*, (1997) *James IV*; *ODNB* (2004) (Bibl.); Riis, T. (1988) *Should Auld Acquaintance Be Forgot . . . Scottish-Danish Relations c. 1450–1707.*

MARGARET of Scotland, Countess of Kent, m. de Burgh, born before 1195, buried London 1259; **ISABELLA of Scotland, Countess of Norfolk,** m. **Bigod,** fl. 1209–53; **MARGARET of Scotland, the younger (Marjory), Countess of Pembroke,** m. **Marshal,** born before 1214, died London 17 Nov. 1244. Daughters of *Ermengarde de Beaumont and William the Lion.

The marriages of William the Lion's daughters demonstrate the unequal nature of 13th-century Anglo-Scottish relations. All three were promised royal marriages but had to settle for less prestigious matches and, as a result, have attracted little attention from Scottish historians. Margaret of Scotland was the eldest daughter; her mother was either a daughter of Adam de Whitsome, possibly

William's first wife, or Ermengarde de Beaumont, mother of her two sisters, Isabella and Margaret the younger. Declared heir to the throne in 1195 during marriage negotiations with Saxony, she was replaced by her brother Alexander, born 1198. In 1209, the Anglo-Scottish Treaty of Norham arranged for Margaret to marry Prince Henry of England and Isabella to marry his brother Richard. The sisters went to England but neither marriage occurred. In October 1221, Margaret married Hubert de Burgh (c. 1170–1243), Justiciar of England, a disparaging match as he was not ennobled as Earl of Kent until 1227. He fell from favour in 1232; Margaret took sanctuary until 1234 at Bury, but took independent action by arranging, probably without her husband's knowledge, the marriage of their daughter Megotta (Margaret) to the Earl of Gloucester. When Henry III discovered the marriage in 1236, it was dissolved. Megotta died in 1237, but the secret marriage had alienated the King, and the de Burghs' role in public life had ended by 1239. Widowed in 1243, Margaret lived out her remaining years as an English noblewoman.

In May 1225, Isabella married Roger Bigod (c. 1212–70), son and heir of the Earl of Norfolk. In 1245, he repudiated her on grounds of consanguinity, but the church declared the marriage valid in 1253, forcing him to reunite with her. Alexander II attempted to negotiate a marriage for his sister Margaret the younger with Richard in 1227 and Henry III in 1231, but the English magnates rejected the matches. In August 1235, she married Gilbert Marshal, Earl of Pembroke, and was widowed in 1241. CAA

• Duncan, A. A. M. (1975) *Scotland: the making of the kingdom*; Giles, J. A. (ed.) (1853) *Matthew Paris's English History*; Giles, J. A. (ed.) (1849) *Roger of Wendover's Flowers of History*; *ODNB* (2004) (Margaret of Scotland, Countess of Kent); *Scotichron.*; *SP.*

MARGARET Rose, Princess *see* **SNOWDON, The Princess Margaret Rose, Countess of** (1930–2002)

MARGARET, Saint, Queen of Scotland, probably born Castle Reka, Hungary, c. 1046, died Edinburgh 16 Nov. 1093. Daughter of Agatha of West Friesland and Edward 'the Exile' of England.

Margaret's father, Edward 'the Exile', son of the English king, Edmund 'Ironside', fled into exile in Hungary after the Danish conquest of England in 1016 and married Agatha, daughter of Liudolf, Margrave of West Friesland. They returned to England in 1056, during the reign of Edward the

Confessor, with their children, Edgar 'the Aetheling', Margaret and Christina, expecting that Edward 'the Exile' would succeed the childless Confessor. However, Edward himself died shortly after his return, and his family was caught up in the Norman conquest of 1066. Duke William's victory at Hastings put Agatha and her children in peril, since Edgar was an obvious rallying point for disaffected Anglo-Saxons. In 1068, the family fled into exile again and sailed north; they are traditionally believed to have landed at the bay of St Margaret's Hope on the north side of the Firth of Forth. Malcolm III (r. 1058–93) became protector of these symbols of resistance to the new Norman political regime by taking Margaret for his second wife, in 1070/1. What happened to his first wife, *Ingebjorg, is unclear.

Malcolm and Margaret had at least six sons and two daughters. Margaret's biography (written by her confessor, Turgot, after her death) (Metcalfe 1895), gives evidence of the couple's close personal relationship. Turgot records stories about Malcolm's tolerance of Margaret's 'pious plundering' of his wealth to give to the poor and how Malcolm upbraided her in jocular fashion. Such contemporary written evidence is rare; though the biography is a product of ecclesiastical learning and Latin culture, it nonetheless provides precious glimpses of daily events at court and of Margaret's relationship with her children. It was written as a 'model of queenship', commissioned by her daughter *Matilda (Edith), wife of Henry I and Queen of England.

Margaret's reputation as a spiritual woman, full of religious zeal, who devoted her life to good works, grew after her death in November 1093, following news of the death of her husband and their eldest son Edward three days earlier, in an ambush at Alnwick. Margaret was eventually canonised, and on 19 June 1250 her remains were translated from a tomb in Dunfermline Abbey to a shrine in the Lady Chapel there (marked today by a plaque). Having the founding mother of the MacMalcolm dynasty recognised as a saint brought the crown enormous prestige. Her shift, 'Sanct Margaretis serk', was used to help later Scottish queens in childbirth. Her Gospel Book survives in the Bodleian Library, and a bone is held in the Ursuline convent of St Margaret in Edinburgh.

Yet Turgot's biography has been detrimental to Margaret's reputation, partly because it stresses her piety and the extent of her religious commitments. Some readers have reacted against the importance accorded to her as a 'moderniser' of the Scottish church, which Turgot says she tried to reform. However, the picture of her standing up to the churchmen whom she summoned to councils for the purpose of combating the 'defenders of a perverse custom' (ibid., p. 55), with Malcolm as interpreter, indicates a spirited and educated woman. Concerned with the external dignity of the court, she reformed the personnel and 'increased the splendour of the royal palace' (ibid., p. 53). Up-to-date dress and lavish adornment were introduced and she set up a workshop in her own quarters, where needlewomen produced liturgical vestments and undoubtedly fine garments. She also encouraged the import of merchandise. Turgot says that Margaret did all this only because 'she was compelled to do what the royal dignity required of her' (ibid., p. 53). More importantly, she set a pious example for her family. She established a free ferry across the Firth of Forth for pilgrims to St Andrews. She strongly influenced the Scottish religious and cultural scene, patronising ancient ecclesiastical centres and introducing reformed ideas of cult and worship, especially at the dynastic centre of Dunfermline, where she founded Holy Trinity with Benedictine monks from Christ Church, Canterbury.

Turgot's account is certainly fulsome in its praise (and perhaps a little boring in its adulation) and some have reacted against the hagiographical appreciations of earlier biographies. However, lack of sympathy for a woman in a foreign land who strove to meet the highest religious ideals and introduce the latest ecclesiastical innovations should not mar appreciation of the outstanding personal achievements of this 11th-century queen. As the last representative of the Anglo-Saxon royal house, she perpetuated the bloodline and preserved its cultural identity by giving royal Anglo-Saxon names to five children; three of her sons became kings of Scots and one of her daughters became queen of England. BEC

• Bartlett, R. (ed. and trans.) (2003) *The Miracles of Saint Æbbe of Coldingham and Saint Margaret of Scotland*; Crawford, B. E. (with Clancy, T. O.) (2001) 'The formation of the Scottish Kingdom', in R. A. Houston and W. W. J. Knox (eds) *The New Penguin History of Scotland* (Bibl.); Huneycutt, L. L. (2003) *Matilda of Scotland: a study in medieval queenship*; Metcalfe, W. M. (trans.) (1895, 1990) *Lives of the Scottish Saints*. *ODNB* (2004); Wilson, A. J. (1993) *St Margaret Queen of Scotland* (Bibl.).

MARGARET Tudor, Queen of Scotland, born
Westminster Palace, London, 28/29 Nov. 1489, died
Methven Castle, Perthshire, 18 Oct. 1541. Daughter
of Elizabeth of York, and Henry VII of England.

Margaret Tudor was brought up at Richmond
Palace with her two brothers, Arthur and the future
Henry VIII. On 24 January 1502, aged 12, she was
betrothed to marry James IV, King of Scots
(1473–1513), and after a proxy wedding a year later
she travelled north. Her wedding took place at
Holyrood Abbey on 8 August 1503. William
Dunbar marked the occasion with his poem, 'The
Thistle and the Rose'. James was twice his bride's
age but treated her kindly and as long as her father
was alive there was peace between Scotland and
England. When her brother Henry VIII succeeded
to the English throne in 1509, the situation
changed; he attacked France and the French asked
James IV for help. Ignoring Margaret's pleas, James
invaded England, only to be killed at Flodden on
9 September 1513, leaving her to rule as regent for
the young James V, born in 1512. A second son was
born in April 1514. She forfeited this position when,
less than a year later, she married Archibald
Douglas, 6th Earl of Angus (c. 1489–1557). John
Stewart, Duke of Albany and heir presumptive,
replaced her, ruling the country in the French
interest. He not only turned against the Douglases,
but demanded possession of the young king and his
brother in 1515; Margaret handed them over then
fled to England, giving birth to Angus's daughter at
Harbottle Castle on her way south. She took the
baby, *Lady Margaret Douglas, to London,
spending the winter at Henry VIII's court.

In spring 1517, Henry sent Margaret north
again. Albany was about to visit France, and this
was the opportunity for her to resume power,
ruling in the English interest with the help of her
husband. She fell out with him, however, and to
her brother's fury decided to divorce him. When
Albany returned in 1521 he exiled Angus to France
and he and Margaret governed Scotland together.
Their joint rule could have remedied Scotland's
internal problems, but Margaret was financially
dependent on Henry VIII, who successfully put
pressure on her to inform him of Albany's military
plans. Frustrated by the Scots' refusal to follow him
across the border to besiege Wark Castle, Albany
left Scotland in May 1524. Margaret was in power
once more, and redoubled her efforts to divorce
Angus, having fallen in love with Harry Stewart
(c. 1495–1553/4), later Lord Methven. Henry VIII
made vigorous efforts to prevent the Pope from

granting the divorce, Angus arrived back in
Scotland, and by 1526 Margaret's government had
collapsed. When her divorce was finally granted in
1527, Margaret married Harry Stewart. By 1528
James V was old enough to rule for himself. He
found his mother as trying as everyone else did,
and when he discovered nearly ten years later that
she was attempting to divorce Lord Methven in
order to remarry Angus, he put a stop to her plans.
In the late 1530s she largely retired from public life,
dying at Methven Castle in 1541 after suffering a
stroke. She was buried in the Carthusian monastery
in Perth. Often criticised for her impulsive
behaviour and her matrimonial adventures, Queen
Margaret nonetheless deserves greater recognition
for her determination, her pragmatic outlook and
her remarkable talent for self-preservation. RKM
• Buchanan, P. H. (1985) *Margaret Tudor, Queen of Scots*;
Fradenburg, L. O. (1991) *City Marriage, Tournament: arts of
rule in late medieval Scotland*, (1998) 'Troubled times:
Margaret Tudor and the historians', in S. Mapstone and
J. Wood (eds) *The Rose and the Thistle*; Marshall, R. K.
(2003) *Scottish Queens 1034–1714*; *ODNB* (2004).

MARIES, The Four: Mary SETON, died Rheims after
1615, daughter of Marie Pieris, and George, 4th
Lord Seton; **Mary BEATON,** born c. 1543, died 1597,
daughter of Jeanne de la Reinville, and Robert
Beaton of Creich; **Mary LIVINGSTON,** died 1585,
daughter of Lady Agnes Douglas, and Alexander,
5th Lord Livingston; **Mary FLEMING,** born 1542,
died c. 1600, daughter of Janet Stewart, and
Malcolm, 3rd Lord Fleming.

Chosen as maids of honour to *Mary, Queen of
Scots when she went to France as the fiancée of the
future François II in 1548, the four Maries were at
first relegated by Henri II to a convent at Poissy.
Soon reunited with their mistress, they remained
with her, accompanying her back to Scotland in
1561. Elegant and sophisticated, at the centre of the
Scottish court, they were close friends and
confidantes of the Queen, who arranged their
marriages. In 1565, Mary Livingston married John,
son of Robert, 3rd Lord Sempill (d. 1583); Mary
Beaton married Alexander Ogilvy of Boyne in 1566,
and in 1567 Mary Fleming and William Maitland
of Lethington (1525/30–1573), the Queen's Secretary
of State, were married. Some time after his death in
1573, Mary Fleming married George Meldrum of
Fyvie. Mary Seton remained unmarried and was
with the Queen when she surrendered at Carberry
in 1567. She and Mary Livingston attended Queen
Mary at Lochleven Castle, and after her escape to

England in 1568, Mary Seton joined her, sharing her captivity for the next 15 years. Christopher Norton wished to marry Mary Seton, but was executed after his involvement in the Northern Rising against Elizabeth I. When Andrew Beaton, master of the royal household, fell in love with her, she rejected him on the grounds that she had taken a vow of chastity. Eventually, her health failed and she retired in 1583 to the Abbey of St Pierre aux Dames in Rheims, where Queen Mary's aunt, Renée de Lorraine, was abbess. She died there.

A popular ballad about the Four Maries replaced the real Mary Fleming and Mary Livingston with the imaginary Mary Carmichael and Mary Hamilton (allegedly executed for conceiving an illegitimate child). In fact, none of the Maries suffered this fate but the idea of the four small girls who were faithful attendants of Mary, Queen of Scots has always caught the public imagination and secured them their place in history. RKM

• Duncan, T. (1905) 'The Queen's Maries', *Scot. Hist. Rev.*, 2; *ODNB* (2004) (see Queen's Maries); Seton, G. (1896) *A History of the Family of Seton*, 2 vols; *SP*; Strickland, S. A. (1873) *Life of Mary, Queen of Scots*.

MARISHALL, Jean [Jean Marshall], born Scotland fl. 1765–89. Author and playwright.

Jean Marishall published her first novel, *The History of Miss Clarinda Cathcart and Miss Fanny Renton* (1765, repr. 1975) under the name 'Jean Marshall'. Then living in London, she used her social connections to persuade the Duchess of Northumberland to present the novel to its dedicatee, the Queen, but she was disappointed that the book brought her only fifteen guineas. *The History of Alicia Montague* (1767, repr. 1975), attained more success. Although these novels were conventional romantic works, her heroines were enterprising and resourceful. Of the former, Pam Perkins observes, 'when Clarinda is, apparently inevitably, abducted by a scheming aristocrat, it is a thorough familiarity with romances that enables her confidante Nancy to solve the mystery of her disappearance, while everybody else is left helpless and bewildered' (Perkins 2001, p. 10). In the latter she suggests that women would be less likely to be seduced if they could establish themselves in independent trades. Her work, although obscure, is of interest in that she asserted the necessity for women's financial independence, downplayed domesticity, criticised male oppression of women, and envisioned utopian social reform.

She found less success as a playwright. She met the famous theatrical impresario Samuel Foote, hoping to have her comedy *Sir Harry Gaylove* (1772) produced, but her Scottish accent seems to have put him off. Her attempt at establishing a periodical publication also failed. According to a brief memoir, she was a private teacher in Edinburgh for several years before publishing her next work, *A Series of Letters* (1789), in which the memoir is included. In it she attacks the legitimacy of the court, critiques genteel marriage and male arrogance, asserts middle-class values and proposes a humanitarian criminal law and planned economy. Like *Elizabeth Hamilton, she published her ideas on education as letters supposedly addressed to a former pupil, and states that she has been influenced by the Scottish system of education. Perkins suggests that Marishall is innovative 'in suggesting that the education of men ought to be more like that of women' (ibid.). A reviewer in *The Scots Magazine* praised her judicious comments but deprecated her critique of domesticity. AKC

• Marishall, J., Works as above.
ODNB (2004); Perkins, P. (2001) 'Planting seeds of virtue: sentimental fiction and the moral education of women', *Cardiff Corvey* 6, www.cf.ac.uk/encap/corvey/download/cc06_n02.pdf; (1789) 'Review of *A Series of Letters*', *The Scots Magazine* 51.

MARLEY, Hilda Gertrude (Sister Marie Hilda in religion**),** born Bishop Auckland 13 Oct. 1876, died Glasgow 19 Nov. 1951. Educator, psychologist. Daughter of Marie Simonds, and George Marley, miller.

Youngest of seven children, Hilda Marley was educated at convent schools in South Africa and England. She entered the teaching order of Notre Dame de Namur in Belgium in 1898, becoming a Sister in 1901. From 1904 to 1930, she lectured at Notre Dame Training College, Dowanhill, Glasgow, specialising in psychology and mental testing in the 1920s. In 1931, with Robert Rusk of Jordanhill College, she founded Notre Dame Child Guidance Clinic in Glasgow. The clinic's motto was *Dirupisti vincula mea* ('You have freed me from my chains'). Funded by local sources and the EIS, she implemented and developed ideas from Montessori, Bowlby, Dewey, Klein, Pestalozzi and Winnicott, using visual aids, play-therapy, individualised learning and psycho-drama. The clinic's services to children were free and non-denominational. A woman of purposeful vision, spiritual strength and good humour, despite deafness, Sister Marie

Hilda was aware, ahead of her times, of the interplay between emotional deprivation, poverty and ill-health. She drew on the work of the Tavistock Clinic in London, and was in demand as a lecturer in Britain and abroad. Appointed to the Scottish Advisory Council on the Treatment and Rehabilitation of Offenders in 1944, she published a textbook on her therapeutic work. Her Scottish legacy remains in two Glasgow clinics: one for primary-school age children (Athole Gardens) and one for teenagers (Fern Tower). JF

• Marley, Sister Marie Hilda, SND (1944) *Child Guidance.* Fitzpatrick, T. A. (1994) *No Mean Service*; *ODNB* (2004); Sister Jude, SND (1981) *Freedom to Grow: Sister Marie Hilda's vision of child guidance.*

MARSHALL, Henrietta Elizabeth, [H. E. Marshall], born Bo'ness 9 August 1867, died Hampstead, London, 19 Sept. 1941. Author of popular history books, including *Our Island Story.* Daughter of Catherine Jane Pratt, and John Marshall, Northern Ware manufacturer.

H. E. Marshall, known as 'Leeby' to friends and relatives (Skelton), was born into a wealthy family with eight children, and well-educated: in the 1880s, she was a pupil at Laurel Bank Boarding School, Melrose. She was briefly (1901–4) warden of Queen Margaret Hall in Glasgow. In 1905–8, she was living in Oxford, and may have spent some time later in Australia, possibly as a governess. She is known to have spent the years 1913–1917 in Redlands, California, writing a book on US history (1919): the A. K. Smiley Library there holds autographed copies of her works. Her histories, aimed mostly at a young audience, were hugely popular: some 34 are listed in the British Library catalogue, and print runs went into thousands. Her best known was a history of Britain, *Our Island Story* (1905, re-issue 2005). She also wrote *Scotland's Story: a child's history of Scotland* (1906). Her Scottish background emerges in the preface to this book, written as if to a little girl: 'you know *we* were defeated sometimes, Caledonia' (1906, p. vii, our italics). But she ended it with an optimistic view of the Union, suggesting that Scotland's history thereafter was shared with 'the glory of the Empire'. The books were all authored as 'H. E. Marshall', initials behind which the author deliber- ately hid her full name, which did however become known to library cataloguers. Records of royalties paid by her publishers to 'Miss Marshall' in 1912 are in the Jack/Nelson archives. Engagingly written, her books, *Our Island Story* in particular,

shaped the view of history of many generations of children, including historian Antonia Fraser, and the book was reissued in 2005 by Civitas following a press campaign (McKie, 2004; Clare 2005; www.civitas.org.uk). H. E. Marshall was not, however, well-off in her later years. SR

• BL catalogue; NAS: birth records; Census of Scotland 1881, 1891; University of Edinburgh, Special Collections, Nelson archive, no. 619 [T. E. Jack, Royalties].

Marshall, H. E., Works as above and (1907) *Stories of Roland Told to the Children*; (1908) *Our Empire Story*; (1908) *Stories of Beowulf Told to the Children*; (1909) *The Child's English Literature*; (1919) *This Country of Ours, The Story of the United States*; (1937) *Kings and Things.*

McKie, D., 'History after lights out', *Guardian*, 9 Dec. 2004; Clare, J., 'Wonderful response to history appeal', *Daily Telegraph*, 22 June 2005; *ODNB* (update 2006).

Extra research findings: Moyra Ashford, USA, and Robert Whelan, Civitas.

Personal knowledge: Dr Martin Skelton.

MARSHALL, Jean *see* **MARISHALL, Jean** (fl. 1766–89)

MARSHALL, Sheina MacAlister, OBE, born Rothesay 20 April 1896, died Millport 7 April 1977. Marine biologist. Daughter of Jean Colville Binnie, and John Marshall, MD.

Graduating from the University of Glasgow in 1919, Sheina Marshall held a Carnegie Fellowship there (1920–2), and joined the SMBA's Millport station on the Clyde as a naturalist in 1924. With her long-time collaborator, Andrew P. Orr, she 'established Millport as a major centre' (Yonge 1977, p. 66) for plankton and other research. They co-authored 12 papers on the lifecycle of the copepod *Calanus finmarchicus*, of vital economic significance to western Scotland as part of the food chain for the herring, since it converted phytoplankton into protein and fat suitable as food for shoaling fishes and other creatures. In 1927, she joined the Great Barrier Reef expedition of (later Sir) Maurice Yonge, studying coral formations. During the Second World War, she investigated the production of agar (used in the preparation of vaccines) from native seaweeds, after Japanese sources became unavailable. In 1955, she and Orr published their major study of *Calanus finmarchicus*. One of the first five women admitted to the RSE (1949), she was elected to the RSL in 1963. After her formal retirement in 1964, Sheina Marshall remained active in research at Millport, presiding over the staff tea table, for which she embroidered a teapot cover with copepods. She travelled latterly with her sister **Margaret Marshall,** OBE, Hon LLD (d. Jan. 1995), formerly Matron of Edinburgh Royal Infirmary and, during the war, Principal Matron for Emergency Medical Services in Scotland. Their younger sister, **Dorothy Nairn Marshall,** MBE (1900–92), was a prominent amateur archaeologist and museum curator on Bute. In addition to her pioneering work on food chains, Sheina Marshall is remembered as hospitable, dignified and generous – she bequeathed her house for the use of the Directors of Millport. MAMC

• Marine Biological Station, Millport archive: Sheina Marshall's notebooks, papers and offprints.

Marshall, S. M. and Orr, A. P. (1955) *The Biology of a Marine Copepod: Calanus finmarchicus*; Marshall, S. M. (1987) *An Account of the Marine Station at Millport.*

McLaughlin, P. A. and Gilchrist, S. (1993) 'Women's contributions to carcinology', in F. Truesdale (ed.) *History of Carcinology*, pp. 165–206; *ODNB* (2004); Russell, Sir F. (1978) 'Sheina MacAlister Marshall 1896–1977', *Biographical Memoirs of FRS*, vol. 24, pp. 369–89; Yonge, Sir M. (1977) 'Sheina MacAlister Marshall – Millport 1922–77', *Scot. Marine Biol. Ass. Ann. Rept*, 31 Mar. 1977, pp. 66–9 (Bibl. to 1977).

Private information: Prof J. A. Allen, Millport, and Mr I. Gibbs, Bute Museum.

MARTIN, Catherine Edith MacAuley, n. **Mackay,** born Isle of Skye, March 1847, died Adelaide, South Australia, 15 March 1937. Writer. Daughter of Janet Mackinnon and Samuel Nicholson Mackay, crofters.

Catherine Martin used several pseudonyms, including 'M. C.', 'C. M.', 'Ishbel', 'Helen Derwent', 'Mrs Alick MacLeod', 'Mrs Frederick Martin', 'Mrs C. E. M. Martin'. The Mackay family emigrated to South Australia from their poor croft in 1855. Catherine Mackay grew up in the south east of South Australia at the end of the frontier era. She supplemented her private education with intensive study of the literature of German Romanticism. While running a school in Mount Gambier with her sisters, she began publishing verse, serial and short stories in the local press from 1865. In Adelaide, from 1877, she worked as a clerk and then as a writer, but also travelled in Europe for long periods. In 1882, she married Frederick Martin: they had no children. Her major works, some published anonymously or pseudonymously, were marked by a great intellectual independence. *The Explorers and Other Poems*

(1874) memorialised the ill-fated Burke and Wills expedition and explored her 'epic struggles of faith' (Ackland 1994, p. 95). Her best-known book, *An Australian Girl* (1890), has been described as 'one of Australia's most important, distinctive and ambitious nineteenth-century novels' (Giles 1998, p. 98). It describes the struggles of Stella Courtland, an Australian 'New Woman', in a context both of national identity and social change. *The Incredible Journey* (1923) has been seen as challenging negative stereotypes of Aboriginal women as mothers. MA

• M. C. (1874) *The Explorers and other poems*; Anon. (1890) *An Australian Girl*, (2002) *An Australian Girl*, R. Campbell, ed. (contains biographical essay by Allen, M.); McLeod, Mrs A. (1892) *The Silent Sea*, 3 vols; Martin, C. E. M. (1923) *The Incredible Journey.*

Ackland, M. (1994) *That Shining Band*; Giles, F. (1998) *Too Far Everywhere.*

MARY of Guelders, Queen of Scotland, born Guelders c. 1433, died 1 December 1463. Eldest daughter of Catherine of Cleves, and Arnold, Duke of Guelders.

The marriage potential of Mary of Guelders was of particular interest to her uncle, the Duke of Burgundy, who lacked legitimate daughters to offer in marriage. In 1446, five years after the failed attempt of the French king to arrange her marriage, Mary became a resident of the Burgundian court. Her residency in the household of Isabel of Portugal, the politically astute duchess of Burgundy, provided her with a form of political apprenticeship. Mary was put forward as a possible bride for Albert, Duke of Austria, before Burgundy negotiated her marriage to James II (1430–60). The marriage, with its accompanying alliances with Burgundy, Guelders and Brittany, was a political coup, broadening Scotland's diplomatic options and raising its European profile without endangering the long-standing French alliance.

Mary's marriage and coronation were celebrated at Holyrood on 3 July 1449. She and James had five sons and three daughters, including a son and daughter who died in infancy. The Queen was promised an annual income of £5,000, generated largely by her extensive dower lands, and undertook an extensive building programme. She founded a hospital and church at Fail, Ayrshire, in the late 1450s, ordered the construction of a defensive castle at Ravenscraig in 1460, and was responsible for works at Falkland and repairs at Stirling during the minority of her son, James III. Her greatest project was the foundation in 1460 of Holy Trinity collegiate church and hospital in Edinburgh.

The Queen's political skill was demonstrated during the years immediately after James II's death in 1460. Mary and the regency council continued his flexible policy with regard to the Lancastrian-Yorkist conflict in England, and relied upon men who had been appointed by, or had served, James II. In her own right, Mary undertook negotiations with both Lancastrian and Yorkist leaders, received letters and embassies from European rulers, and was described as the leader of the dominant party in government. Bishop Kennedy, who succeeded her as leader of government, opposed her power in parliament, but Mary was able to withstand the criticism that a woman could not, and should not, govern. Her early death in 1463 meant that this key period in the development of the Scottish queen's role was relatively brief. FD

• Downie, F. A. (1998) ' "Sche is but a womman": the queen and princess in Scotland, 1424–63', PhD, Univ. of Aberdeen; Dunlop, A. I. (1950) *The Life and Times of James Kennedy, Bishop of St Andrews*; Macdougall, N. (1982) *James III*; McGladdery, C. (1990) *James II*; *ODNB* (2004) (Mary of Gueldres).

MARY of Guise, Queen of Scotland, born Bar-le-Duc, Lorraine, 20 Nov. 1515, died Edinburgh 11 June 1560. Queen Dowager, Regent of Scotland. Daughter of Antoinette de Bourbon, and Claude, Duc de Guise.

Mary of Guise was the eldest child of the newly created house of Guise, a scion of the princely house of Lorraine and, arguably, the most powerful dynasty of 16th-century France. Her early life was spent as a Poor Clare at the Convent at Pont-au-Mousson under the tutelage of her grandmother, Philippa de Gueldres, but at the age of 14 she was removed by her uncle, who thought her better suited to a life at court. She became a favourite of François I who helped arrange her marriage in 1534 to Louis, Duc de Longueville (1510–37), Grand Chamberlain of France. They had two children, François and Louis. During her second pregnancy, however, her husband died, the first of many deaths that marred Mary's personal happiness. Her infant also died. A second marriage was quickly negotiated with James V (1512–42), François I's recently widowed son-in-law. James had married **Madeleine of France** (1520–37) in January 1537, but the ailing princess had died in July after only six weeks in Scotland. James and Mary of Guise were married by proxy on 9 May 1538. Scotland's new Queen

arrived at St Andrews the following June. She bore three children in quick succession: James (1540), Robert (1541) and *Mary (1542). A week after Robert's birth, however, the couple suffered a double blow – both princes died within hours of each other. When James V died suddenly on 14 December 1542, Scotland's new queen was barely one week old.

Mary Queen of Scots' sovereignty, Guisean lineage and Catholic claim to the English throne made her a figure of extraordinary dynastic importance. She alone could unite the kingdoms of Scotland, England and Ireland under one Catholic crown. Marriage dominated her reign as it brought with it notions of British imperialism and possible control of the entire British Isles. Mary of Guise, now Queen Dowager of Scotland, was naturally keen to protect and advance her daughter's dynastic interests. This was the pretext for her entry into Scottish politics during the 1540s, in opposition to the proposed dynastic union of the English and Scottish crowns contracted in the treaties of Greenwich (1543). During the English invasions known as the 'rough wooings', Mary of Guise staunchly upheld French interests and secured French financial and military assistance against the English. The treaty of Haddington (1548) arranged Mary's betrothal to the Dauphin François, with whom she was sent to live as an absentee monarch for safety. Surprisingly, her mother remained in Scotland until the Anglo-Scottish conflict was over, returning to France in 1550. The Scots who accompanied her, however, wanted the Queen Dowager to replace James, 2nd Earl of Arran and Duc de Châtelherault, as regent once Mary's minority ended. She reluctantly agreed and returned to Scotland in 1551 – days after her eldest son, François, died in her arms at Dieppe.

Mary of Guise became Queen Regent in April 1554. An effective, astute and well respected politician, she aimed to strengthen royal power and impose law and order. In 1558, she saw the completion of her dynastic policies with the marriage of Mary and François and, more impressively, gained parliament's consent to grant the crown matrimonial to the dauphin. The year 1559, however, witnessed the outbreak of the Reformation rebellion. Until that time, religion had been a secondary consideration for Mary of Guise, who adopted a tolerant and accommodating position towards the reform movement. The dubious legality of Elizabeth I's 1558 accession in Catholic eyes, and Henri II's subsequent campaign to advance the Catholic claim of Mary Queen of Scots to the English crown, however, forced her to take a harder line towards Protestantism. Her religious proclamation ordering all Scots to return to Catholicism (March 1559) sparked a chain of events that eventually led to the end of France's influence in Scotland. Consistently believing that the true aim of the rebellion was not religion but the subversion of authority, Mary of Guise had her suspicions confirmed by the Lords of the Congregation's 'Act of Suspension' (October 1559) deposing her as regent, and England's military intervention in 1560. France's failure to come to her aid saw her administration begin to crumble. Only with her death would its collapse be complete. Mary of Guise died at Edinburgh Castle on 11 June 1560. Fearing demonstrations of support for her cause if she was buried at Holyrood, the Protestant lords left her body for many months in St Margaret's Chapel. She was finally buried in 1561 at the Convent of St Peter, Rheims. PER

• Cameron, J. (1998) *James V*; *ODNB* (2004); Ritchie, P. E. (2002) *Mary of Guise in Scotland, 1548–1560: a political career* (Bibl.).

MARY, Queen of Scots, born Linlithgow 8 December 1542, died Fotheringhay, England, 7 February 1587. Daughter of *Mary of Guise and James V.

Mary's father died on 14 December 1542, embroiled in war with England. As the new Queen, Mary's betrothal to the future Edward VI was first agreed but then renounced; Anglo-Scottish war, the 'rough wooing', resumed. Following their disastrous defeat at Pinkie in 1547, the Scots sought French military aid, agreeing to Mary's delivery to France in 1548 and betrothal to the Dauphin, François (1544–60). Mary embraced French court life, where her beauty, charm, wit and grace were warmly appreciated. She married François on 24 April 1558. As a great-grand-daughter of Henry VII, Mary's Tudor blood became crucial when the Catholic Mary of England was succeeded by the Protestant Elizabeth in November 1558. Henri II of France had Mary adopt the English royal arms, which Elizabeth never forgave. When Henri II died in 1559, Mary became Queen of France, as wife of François II.

Meanwhile, in Scotland, where Mary of Guise was regent, the throne was rocked by a successful Protestant, anti-French uprising (1559–60), supported by England. Nevertheless, Mary, widowed in late 1560, returned from France to Scotland on 19 August 1561, having agreed with the Protestant leaders including Lord James Stewart, her illegitimate half-brother (whom she created Earl of Moray), that she would accept the Protestant regime while retaining a private Catholic Mass. Mary's lavish court and progresses were popular, but her regime's stability rested on détente with England. She negotiated with Elizabeth for the English succession. When Mary offered to make a suitable marriage, Elizabeth in 1564 offered her own favourite, Leicester – but without a firm promise of the succession. Instead, on 29 July 1565, Mary married her cousin Henry, Lord Darnley (1545/6–67), son of *Margaret Douglas, Countess of Lennox, and next in the English succession. Elizabeth was furious and Moray raised an unsuccessful rebellion. Mary's chances of agreement with England had all but vanished, irreparably weakening her position now that her enemies could expect English backing. Darnley proved an incapable consort, being violent and irresponsible, and the marriage broke down within months. When Mary decided to forfeit (confiscate the lands and goods of) the exiled Moray and his friends, their sympathisers (notably the Earl of Morton) gained Darnley's support for a coup. They captured the pregnant queen in Holyroodhouse on 9 March 1566 and killed her confidant David Riccio. Mary escaped and rallied supporters, including James Hepburn, Earl of Bothwell (1534/5–78), who restored her at the price of rehabilitating Moray.

Mary's son, later James VI and I, was born on 19 June. Later that year she suffered from physical illness, exacerbated by depression at the Darnley problem and the faction-ridden state of Scottish politics. The murder of Darnley on 10 February 1567 looks like Bothwell's and Morton's attempt to reconcile their differences through an honourable revenge killing. Mary suffered a nervous breakdown after the murder. The idea of a Mary-Bothwell love affair, beloved of dramatists and novelists, rests only on the discredited 'Casket Letters' and is contradicted by all contemporary evidence. Bothwell's political bid to marry the Queen gathered the support of Morton and many others. Mary, however, rejected Bothwell's proposal. On 24 April, he made the disastrous mistake of abducting and raping her, thus forcing her into marriage on 15 May to save her honour. Other nobles were horrified, especially since this benefited nobody but Bothwell. An uprising followed, and Mary surrendered at Carberry on 15 June. The core of the anti-Bothwell coalition, now revealed as also anti-Mary, imprisoned her in Lochleven Castle, and deposed her on 24 July. Moray became regent for the infant James VI.

Mary escaped on 2 May 1568 and gathered wide support, but Moray defeated her at Langside on 13 May. Failing to recognise that she still had many allies, Mary crossed to England to seek Elizabeth's aid. Elizabeth distrusted Mary's Catholic connections and recognised Moray as a friend. Reluctant to sanction rebellion, however, she tried to negotiate a conditional restoration. But Moray produced the fabricated 'Casket Letters', openly accusing Mary of murder, and leading Elizabeth to support him over his sister. Kept a prisoner in England, Mary pursued every possible route to freedom – offering concessions to Elizabeth, and simultaneously engaging in Catholic plots for her overthrow. The first, the Ridolfi plot of 1571, shattered her credibility with the Anglo-Scottish Protestant establishment. When her attempt to rebuild it with her 'Association scheme' for joint rule of Scotland with her son James (1581–4) failed, her plotting resumed. Convicted of complicity in the Babington plot in 1586, she was executed, despite Elizabeth's reluctance, on 7 February 1587.

Mary's posthumous reputation has varied widely: martyr for Catholicism; murderous adulteress; fallible but sympathetic victim; or romantic heroine. With the abandonment of the idea of her complicity in Darnley's murder, her political failure can be seen as the result of the impossible circumstances in which she found herself. JG

• Donaldson, G. (1983) *All the Queen's Men: power and politics in Mary Stewart's Scotland*; Fraser, A. (1969) *Mary Queen of Scots*; Guy, J. A. (2004) *My Heart is My Own: a life of Mary Queen of Scots*; Lynch, M. (ed.) (1988) *Mary Stewart: queen in three kingdoms*, (1990) 'Mary queen of Scots: a new case for the prosecution', *Jour. Ecc. Hist.* 41 (review of Wormald, see below); *ODNB* (2004) (Bibl.); Wormald, J. (1988) *Mary Queen of Scots: a study in failure*.

MASON, Elliot Cranston, born c. 1888, died Newchapel, Surrey, 20 June 1947. Actor and occasional director. Daughter of Mary Mason, and George Mason, photographic dealer.

Elliot Mason began her career with the influential amateur company, The Scottish National Players, appearing in their opening programme (13 January 1921) as Anna MacDougall in the premiere of John Brandane's and A. W. Yuill's *Glenforsa*. Between 1921 and 1933, she acted in some 74 productions and stage-managed or directed

others. Her roles included Morag Gillespie in George Blake's *The Mother* (13 April 1921), Mrs Duncan in Brandane's *The Glen is Mine* (25 January 1923), Maggie Groundwater in James Bridie's *Sunlight Sonata* (20 March 1928), and Miss Soulis in his *The Dancing Bear* (24 February 1931). A member of the company committee, she was one of their donors. Elliot Mason was also the director of Neil M. Gunn's play, *The Ancient Fire*, premiered at the Lyric Theatre Glasgow on 8 October 1929. An ambitious work, it mixed a realistic depiction of working-class Glasgow with a mystical section set in the Highlands. Contemporary reviews were rather damning, focusing on Gunn's lack of dramaturgical experience, though Mason's production was described as 'excellent' (Scottish Theatre Archive).

Like many of her contemporaries, Elliot Mason used the Players project as a way into a professional career. Her independent means supported her theatrical apprenticeship, which led to a move to London and roles in the West End as well as on film. Her film appearances included Mrs McNiff in *The Ghost Goes West* (René Clair, 1936), Mrs McCosh in *On Approval* (Clive Brook, 1944), Mrs Hemmings in *Vacation from Marriage* (Alexander Korda, 1945), and Mrs Lennox in *The Captive Heart* (Basil Dearden, 1948). Elliot Mason was a niece of *Miss Kate Cranston who ran a thriving Glasgow teashop business and the aunt of fellow actor Hal D. Stewart. AS

• *Glasgow Herald,* 21 June 1949 (obit.), 1 July 1949; Marshalsay, K. A. (1991) 'The Scottish National Players: in the nature of an experiment, 1913–34', PhD, Univ. of Glasgow.

MASSON, Rosaline, born Edinburgh 6 May 1867, died Edinburgh 7 Dec. 1949. Campaigner and writer. Daughter of **Emily Rosaline Orme** (c. 1835–1915), and David Masson, Professor of English Literature at the University of Edinburgh.

Rosaline Masson's parents were supporters of female suffrage and women's entry into higher education. In 1866, her mother signed the women's suffrage petition: she subscribed to ENSWS, joining its committee in 1874 and becoming joint honorary secretary (with *Eliza Wigham) in 1877. David Masson (1822–1907) was on the platform of the first public meeting on female suffrage in Edinburgh (January 1870) and at the 1871 meeting addressed by J. S. Mill. He supported the ELEA from its foundation. Rosaline and her elder sister, **Flora Masson** (1856–1937) campaigned for female enfranchisement and joined the LEDS (Flora from 1881, Rosaline from 1890), thereby meeting other campaigners such as *Sarah Siddons Mair and *Flora and Louisa Stevenson. In 1913 Rosaline Masson became honorary secretary of the CUWFA. She addressed meetings of the NUWSS (1912–13), and held office in the Edinburgh branch of its successor, the NSEC.

Rosaline Masson was a prolific writer in various genres, including Scottish history, biography (Robert Louis Stevenson), literary criticism, travel literature (Edinburgh), and memories of famous people, notably *Poets, Patriots and Lovers* (1934), a collection of earlier articles. Flora Masson edited her father's work after his death in 1907, and wrote on the Brontës and Charles Lamb. Both sisters wrote for the *Cornhill Magazine, Chambers's Journal, Blackwood's Magazine* and *The Scotsman* newspaper. Flora, a friend of Florence Nightingale, had trained as a nurse at the Nightingale School. She worked in hospitals in London and Oxford, returning to Edinburgh in the 1900s to care for her parents. She was awarded the Royal Red Cross First Class in 1919 for her war work as matron, then Commanding Officer, of the Red Cross hospital at Whitehill, Rosewell, Midlothian. The sisters lived together at 20 Ann Street, Edinburgh. JMCD
• Masson, R., Works as above.
AGC; Edinburgh Evening News, 2 Oct. 1937 (obit. Flora); *The Scotsman*, 2 Oct. 1937; *The Weekly Scotsman*, 18 Feb. 1933; *WSM; WWW* (4th edn., 1967), vols III and IV.

MASTERTON, Margaret, born 1709, died Edinburgh 6 July 1737. Shopkeeper. Daughter of Elizabeth Bowie, and George Masterton, tanner burgess.

Margaret Masterton was apprenticed at 16 to Janet Justice, shopkeeper in the High Exchange, Edinburgh, where many women had small shops. Her indenture stipulated she was to live at home, serving her mistress '. . . faithfully minding on her Chop in the Exchange and in shewing [sewing] all such needlework as she shall happen to be imployed in or is capable of . . .' (Register House Papers series). She established her own Lawnmarket shop, selling fabric and accessories, gloves, ribbons and children's clothes, and continued trading after marrying William Yuill, stabler, in 1735. Her sister Katherine also married a stabler, William Tennent. Both men became burgesses through their wives. In 1737, Margaret Masterton and William Yuill drew up a post-nuptial marriage contract, providing for their daughter Elizabeth, born on 2 May. Margaret Masterton died soon afterwards. ECS

• NAS: RH9/17/298, Register House Papers series (Apprentice Indenture); CC8/4/639/1, Edinburgh Commissary Court Processes; CC8/8/99, Edinburgh Commissary Court, Register of Testaments; Edinburgh Central Library: (microfilm) Edinburgh Old Parish Register, May 1737. *WWEE.*

MATILDA (Edith) of Scotland, born c. 1080, died Westminster 1 May 1118. Queen of England. Daughter of *Margaret, Saint, Queen of Scotland, and Malcolm III 'Canmore'.

Matilda and her sister **Mary of Boulogne** (c. 1082–1115) were educated at West Saxon nunneries and were probably among the most cultured women of their day. Controversy over whether or not Matilda had taken the veil did not prevent her from marrying Henry I of England (1068/9–1135) in 1100. Contemporary writers noted the union's dynastic significance, since, through her mother, Matilda was descended from the pre-Norman royal dynasty. The marriage also affected Matilda's siblings, especially the future David I, whose fortunes rose and who became a close confidant of Henry I. Arguably, Matilda's marriage helped to consolidate the nascent 'Canmore dynasty'.

Matilda was prominent on the Anglo-Norman and European scene. She corresponded with the Pope and Archbishop Anselm and was active in government, administering the kingdom during Henry's frequent absences. She supported the establishment of the Augustinian canons in England and Scotland, becoming known as 'Mold the gode quene'. She was particularly noted for piety and devotion to the poor and lepers, founding a leprosarium in 1101 at St Giles-in-the-Fields, Holborn, near London. She was a renowned patroness of the arts. The work most often associated with her is a *Life of Margaret* (her mother), written early in Matilda's reign, possibly as instruction for the young queen.

Matilda and Henry had two children. When Matilda died in 1118, her lavish funeral was attended by many notables. She was buried at Westminster Abbey. Their daughter, Empress Maud, claimed the English throne after Henry's death in 1135, pitting herself against Stephen of Blois and his wife, Matilda of Boulogne, daughter of Mary, who had married Eustace of Boulogne (d. after 1125) in 1102. A Scottish king-list, which paid considerable attention to Matilda and Mary, remarked of them that: 'By their marriages, by the ingenuousness of their customs, by the greatness of their knowledge, by their generous distribution of temporal things to the churches, they fittingly adorned the dignity of their race' (Anderson 1922, vol. i, pp. 54–5). RAM

• Anderson, A. O. (ed.) (1922) *Early Sources of Scottish History AD 500 to 1286*, (ed.) (1908) *Scottish Annals from English Chroniclers AD 500 to 1286*; Huneycutt, L. (1989) 'The idea of the perfect princess' *Anglo-Norman Studies* 12; (2003) *Matilda of Scotland*; *ODNB* (2004); Ritchie, R. L. G. (1954) *The Normans in Scotland*; Schmitt, F. S. (ed.) (1940–4) *The Letters of St Anselm*; Wright, W. A. (ed.) (1887) *The Metrical Chronicle of Robert of Gloucester*.

MAUD (Matilda) de Senlis, Queen of Scotland, formerly **Countess of Huntingdon,** born between 1071 and 1075, died 1130 or 1131. Daughter of Judith, niece of William I of England, and Waltheof, Earl of Northumbria.

Following her father's death in 1076, Maud became heir to extensive English lands, mainly in Huntingdonshire and Northamptonshire. These lands were held by her mother, Countess Judith, until Maud's betrothal, c. 1086, and subsequent marriage to Simon de Senlis, son of a Norman baron and a supporter of Henry I. There were two sons from this marriage, Simon (II), later Earl of Northampton, and Waldef, abbot of Melrose, and a daughter, Matilda. Maud de Senlis and her husband supported various monastic establishments, particularly the Cluniac foundation at Northampton and the convent at Elstow founded by her mother Judith. Her association with the priory at Daventry was continued by her daughter Matilda. Simon de Senlis died in 1111 at La Charité-sur-Loire, on his second Crusade.

In December 1113 or early 1114, Maud de Senlis married David (c. 1085–1153), future King of Scots. The lands and titles received by David as a result of this marriage, and the family associations that Queen Maud brought to the union, had an important impact on the claims of successive generations of Scottish kings. Their son, Henry, born in the early years of the marriage, was himself the father of two kings, Malcolm IV (r. 1153–65) and William (r. 1165–1214). Throughout her marriage to David, Maud continued to support the religious foundations she had patronised with her first husband and was also joint grantor, or witness, to several of David's charters involving other establishments. She was buried at Scone in Perthshire. KAM

• Anderson, A. O. and Anderson, M. O. (eds) [1922] (1990) *Early Sources of Scottish History*; Barrow, G. W. S. (1973) *The Kingdom of the Scots*, (1999) (ed.) *The Charters of King David I*; Forrest, S. S. (1952) 'Earl Waltheof of Northumbria', *Archaeologica Aeliana*, 4th series, 30; Green, J. (1997) *The Aristocracy of Norman England*.

MAXWELL, Alice Maude, born Cardoness 17 Nov. 1856, died Edinburgh 5 Feb. 1915. Deaconess. Daughter of Louisa Shakerley, and Sir William Maxwell of Cardoness, baronet.

Alice Maxwell had a comfortable upbringing as member of a rural landed family, prominent in the parish church. She nursed her father in his final years. In the 1880s, moves to organise women's work in the Church of Scotland culminated in the national Woman's Guild (1887). *Catherine Charteris was the first President of the Guild, and her husband Archibald its founder. He included a new Order of Deaconesses at the apex of his scheme; the intention was to encourage 'ladies of social standing' to devote themselves to full-time service on behalf of the church. Alice Maxwell's minister recommended her as a suitable superintendent for the proposed Deaconess Institute. She accepted with some reluctance, and on 13 January 1888 became the second woman to be 'set apart' as a DCS (the first was *Grisell Baillie). Her task was to develop training to prepare women for a distinctive 'female ministry', under an ethos deeply influenced by Florence Nightingale's vision of nursing as both a science and a Christian occupation for women. Until retirement in 1911, Alice Maxwell developed a programme of theoretical education linked with practical work in the slums of the Pleasance, Edinburgh, and helped establish new missions and institutions, including the Deaconess Hospital (1894). Quiet but forceful, she opened up significant new fields of opportunity and social service for some women, while confirming the ultimately subordinate and class-defined character of the new order. This was illustrated in her 1904 call for volunteers from women who were free of domestic ties to offer their efforts and money to build up the church. LO

• Macrae, Mrs H. (1919) *Alice Maxwell, Deaconess*; Magnusson, M. (1987) *Out of Silence*; Macdonald, L. A. O. (2000) *A Unique and Glorious Mission*.

MAXWELL, Jane, Duchess of Gordon,‡ m. **Gordon,** born Edinburgh c. 1749, died London 14 April 1812. Political hostess, agricultural reformer. Daughter of Magdalen Blair of Blair, and Sir William Maxwell of Monreith, Bart.

Brought up in her parents' house in Hyndford's Close, Edinburgh, Jane Maxwell was a boisterous child. A favourite anecdote tells how she and her sister Betty (later *Lady Eglinton Wallace of Craigie), as small girls rode pigs from a nearby wynd. She grew up to be a great beauty and on 28 October 1767 married Alexander, 4th Duke of Gordon (1743–1827), reputedly one of the most handsome young men of his time. They had two sons and five daughters, but she did not content herself with staying quietly at Gordon Castle. Intelligent and witty, although criticised for her coarse speech, she famously assisted her husband in raising the 89th Regiment of Foot in 1769, and she greatly enjoyed the time they spent at the house they rented in Pall Mall, London. The Duke was a leading supporter of William Pitt and the Duchess soon became a confidante of the prime minister, at the centre of Tory society and delighting and shocking her friends with her unconventional remarks. She was also active in the management of the Gordon estates and was influenced by contemporary ideas on agricultural improvement. She was involved in plans to introduce flax growing and the linen industry, in establishing the village at Kingussie, and in instituting the Badenoch and Strathspey Farming Society in 1803.

An enthusiastic matchmaker, she failed to marry her eldest daughter to Pitt himself but, thanks to her efforts, three daughters married dukes and the fourth a marquis. In 1802, she went to Paris in an unsuccessful attempt to interest Eugène de Beauharnais in her youngest daughter, Georgiana. When she returned, her enemies declared that she had boasted that she hoped to see Napoleon have breakfast in Ireland, dinner in London and supper at Gordon Castle. This earned her a good deal of unpopularity and by 1804 she had become estranged from her husband, who had a large family by his mistress, Jane Christie of Fochabers. The Duchess then led a peripatetic existence, dividing her time between London, Edinburgh, where she was regarded as the arbiter of fashion, and a small house in the Highlands at Kinrara where she entertained visitors including *Elizabeth Grant of Rothiemurchus. She died aged 63 in Pultenay's Hotel, Piccadilly, surrounded by her children, and at her own request was buried at Kinrara. A highly successful political and society hostess, she has rightly been remembered as a woman of unusual character and ability. RKM
• Craven, M. (1906) *Famous Beauties of Two Reigns*; Guild, J. W. (ed.) (1864) *An Autobiographical Chapter in the life of Jane, Duchess of Gordon*; *ODNB* (2004) (see Gordon, Jane); Robinson, M. (c. 1900) *Beaux and Belles of England*; *SP*; Wraxall, N. W. (1836) *Posthumous Memoirs of his own Time*.

MAXWELL, Lady Winifred, Countess of Nithsdale, n. **Herbert,** born Powis Castle, Wales, 1672, died Rome May 1749. Jacobite. Daughter of Elizabeth Somerset, and William Herbert, 2nd Marquess, 3rd Baron Powis.

Winifred Herbert was born into the Welsh landowning aristocracy. When William of Orange took the throne in 1688 her devoutly Catholic parents accompanied the Stewart royal family into exile, her mother, Lady Powis, being appointed governess to the infant Prince of Wales, later known as the Old Pretender. Joining the Stewart court at St Germain in 1691, Winifred Herbert became a lady-in-waiting to Mary of Modena and in 1699, aged 27, married William Maxwell, 5th Earl of Nithsdale (1676–1744). Returning to Scotland to live with him at his family seat of Terregles, she suffered repeated miscarriages and stillbirths. One son and one daughter survived to adulthood.

When her husband was sentenced to death for treason for his part in the 1715 Jacobite Rising, Lady Nithsdale petitioned King George I for clemency. Fearful that this would not be granted, she hatched the plot which freed her husband from the Tower of London on 22 February 1716, the eve of the day planned for his execution. Its boldness and success made her famous in her own time. With the aid of two women friends, she disguised her husband in female clothes and led him out past the guards, handing him over to her maidservant and life-long companion Cecelia Evans. She returned to Scotland to retrieve family belongings before joining her husband in France in September 1716, miscarrying during the difficult voyage. Lord and Lady Nithsdale spent the rest of their lives at the Stewart court-in-exile in Italy. Appointed governess to Prince Henry, younger brother of Prince Charles Edward, Lady Nithsdale played an important role in the early upbringing of both children. MEC
• Maxwell Stuart, F. (1995) *Lady Nithsdale and the Jacobites*; *ODNB* (2004); Tayler, H. (1939) *Lady Nithsdale and her Family.*

MAYO, Isabella, n. **Fyvie [Edward Garrett],** born London 10 Dec. 1843, died Aberdeen 13 May 1914. Writer, Tolstoyan and anti-racism campaigner. Daughter of Margaret Thomson, and George Fyvie, baker from Aberdeenshire.

One of eight children, five of whom died young, at 16, Isabella Fyvie began working to pay off a family debt of £800, obtaining jobs from the Langham Place employment register as secretary, law writer and author. The debt cleared, in 1870 she married John Ryall Mayo, a London solicitor (d. 1877). Their happy married life was cut short by his death and in 1878 she moved to Aberdeen. Her published work (often under the name of 'Edward Garrett') included poetry, articles, short stories and novels, much of it first appearing in the religious press.

In 1887, she discovered Tolstoy's writings and felt an immediate affinity. Thereafter she gave her energies to Tolstoyan causes: anti-militarism, anti-racism, anti-imperialism, anti-vivisection, anti-violence, anti-industrialism, vegetarianism and human brotherhood. She began writing for various co-operative society journals and *New Age* periodical. By 1903, she was editing Vladimir Grigor'evich Chertkov's translations of Tolstoy, appending her own notes and applying Tolstoy's analysis to Britain. In 1910, Chertkov delegated her to correspond with Mohandas Gandhi via his close friend, Herman Kallenbach.

In 1893, the British anti-lynching society, the Society for the Recognition of the Brotherhood of Man, was founded at a meeting at her house attended by anti-racist reformer Catherine Impey (1847–1923) and black American journalist and campaigner Ida Bell Wells-Barnett (1862–1931). Catherine Impey and Isabella Mayo fell out when Catherine unexpectedly proposed to George Ferdinands, a Sri Lankan boarding with Isabella, whom she regarded as a son. He remained with Isabella Mayo until her death, but the split damaged the new society and its journal, *Fraternity*. In 1894, she was elected to the Aberdeen School Board, the first female member of any public board in the city. Her opposition to the Boer War resulted in her house being stoned. She was secretary of the Aberdeen branch of the Scottish Society for the Prevention of Vivisection, founded in 1911 (now Advocates for Animals). She was buried in Coldharbour churchyard, Surrey, with her husband. LRM
• Univ. of Victoria, Canada: Special Collection, SC079. Mayo, I. F., Works as above and see Bibls. below. *Aberdeen Daily Journal*, 14 May 1914 (obit.); *Aberdeen Free Press*, 14 May 1914 (obit.); Diack, W. (1939) *A History of the Trades Council and the Trade Union Movement in Aberdeen*; *HSWW* (Select Bibl.); Hunt, J. D. (1998) 'Isabella Fyvie Mayo: a Scottish friend of Gandhi', *The Gandhi Way*, 55,

Spring, pp. 10–12; Onslow, B. (2000) *Women of the Press in 19th-Century Britain* (Select Bibl.); *ODNB* (2004); Ware, V. (1992) *Beyond the Pale: white women, racism and history*.

MEG of Abernethy, fl. 1390s. Harper. All that is known of this musician is from three references in the Aberdeen Burgh Records for the years 1398–1400, in one of which she is described as 'Meg of Abernethy, harper'. It is not known which Abernethy is referred to, the Abernethy in Perthshire or that near Grantown-on-Spey. The entries are significant, however, in that they indicate that it was possible for women to join the ranks of professional harp players. JP
• Dickinson, W. C. (ed.) (1957) *Early Records of the Burgh of Aberdeen, 1317, 1398–1407*, pp. 86–91.

MELVILLE, Elizabeth (Lady Culross), born Halhill near Collessie, Fife, c. 1582, died probably at Culross 1640. Poet. Daughter of Christian Boswell, and Sir James Melville of Halhill, ambassador, minor statesman and memoirist.

Nothing is known of Elizabeth Melville's clearly extensive education, presumably received at home. She married John Colville, second son of Alexander, Commendator of Culross, before 5 February 1597, and was described in February 1599 as a 'faithfull, vertuous ladie, a tender youth' and a prolific and distinguished poet, by the poet-pastor Alexander Hume ([1599] 1902, p. 3). By 1603, she appears to have been living in Culross and was known as 'Lady Culross, younger'. John Colville was apparently a poor manager, and Lady Culross's financial circumstances were always straitened. She had at least four children, but religion remained the centre of her life; she admitted that her constant travelling to preachings and communion services meant she neglected her family. Her son Alexander became a distinguished minister in Scotland and France, Samuel became a minor satirical poet, while James frequented the court. Her daughter predeceased her.

Lady Culross was one of several aristocratic women committed to the radical, presbyterian wing of the Kirk. She appears to have been a friend of Robert Bruce, the minister of Edinburgh banished in 1600, and wrote a sonnet of comfort to Knox's son-in-law, John Welsh, when he was in prison before banishment in 1606. She helped launch the careers of radical ministers David Dickson in 1621 and John Livingstone in 1630; letters to the latter, and to her son James, have survived. She also corresponded with the well-known religious writer, Samuel Rutherford. In 1603 she published her most important poem, *Ane Godlie Dreame*, many times republished down to 1735 and the probable prototype of Bunyan's *Pilgrim's Progress*. Some of her sacred songs set to secular melodies circulated in manuscript. A large manuscript collection of her early verse was discovered in 2002. She wrote in Scots, with technical mastery, in many verse forms. Her subject is the sufferings (and occasional glimpses of joy) experienced by the Calvinist Elect as they endure the misery of human existence in expectation of heaven. Her extant work, some 4,000 lines of verse, establishes her as a significant early modern woman writer. J R B

• Melville, E. (1603) *Ane Godlie Dreame, compylit be M. M. gentilwoman in Culros.*
ODNB (2004); Reid Baxter, J. (forthcoming) *Elizabeth Melville, Lady Culross: Poems and Letters* (Bibl.); Hume, A. [1599] (1902) *Hymns and Sacred Songs*, A. Lawson, ed.

MELVILLE, Frances Helen, OBE, born Edinburgh 11 Oct. 1873, died Edinburgh 7 March 1962. Academic, educational administrator, suffragist. Daughter of Helen A. Kerr, and Francis Suther Melville, Assistant Clerk of Session.

Educated at George Watson's College and the University of Edinburgh (MA, 1897), Frances Melville's first post was as philosophy tutor at the latter (1896–9). She succeeded *Louisa Lumsden as Warden of University Hall, St Andrews, in 1900, and in 1909 was appointed Mistress of Queen Margaret College, University of Glasgow. The post carried responsibility for all women students in the university, and she held it until the college closed in 1935. She was the first woman to be awarded a BD degree in Scotland (St Andrews, 1910). President of the BFUW and a member of the Glasgow and West of Scotland Provincial Committee for the Training of Teachers, she also chaired the committee of the Queen Margaret College Settlement Association for 24 years. The most senior woman academic in Scotland, she was an important constitutional suffragist, holding posts in several suffrage societies. In 1906, she was one of five women who initiated the Scottish women graduates' lawsuit, which they pursued up to the House of Lords.

During the First World War, Frances Melville undertook a range of responsible advisory activities relating to war work and women's training. She later joined the GSEC, the WCA, the Soroptimist Club (president 1931–2), and was vice-president of the Fellowship of Equal Service, founded c. 1930 to secure the ordination of women and equal opportunity in church life. As Independent candidate in the Scottish Universities' by-election 1937, she came second in a four-cornered contest including *Chrystal Macmillan. In retirement at Dalry, Kirkcudbrightshire, she drove her car with uncharacteristic abandon around the country lanes for the LDV during the Second World War. A sought-after public speaker, Frances Melville was critical of society's 'acquiescence in a double burden of education for women, and a double-faced ideal' (Melville 1911, p. 134). Her fine academic and outstanding administrative abilities, refined culture and impressive personality enabled her to be firmly and at times publicly critical of the universities and other masculinist institutions, while retaining their confidence and respect. She was the first Scottish woman graduate to receive the honorary degree of LLD (Glasgow, 1927). A women's hall of residence was named after her, and the Frances Melville medal is still awarded to students of philosophy. L R M

• Univ. of Glasgow Archives: DC233 (typescripts, corr. with Phoebe Shervyn, 1924); Univ. of St Andrews Dept. of Rare Books and Muniments: UY 37781 (memoranda, corr.).
Melville, F. (1902) 'University education for women in Scotland: its effects on social and intellectual life', (1911) 'The education of woman', in *The Position of Women: Actual and Ideal*, pp. 118–34.
AGC; *The Alumnus Chronicle of the University of St Andrews*, VIII, 1957–62, pp. 45–6; Dyhouse, C. (1995) *No Distinction of Sex? Women in British universities 1870–1939*; *Glasgow Herald*, 8 March 1935, 16 Nov. 1935, 8 March 1962 (obit.); MacDonald, L. A. O. (2000) *A Unique and Glorious Mission*; *ODNB* (2004); *SB*; *St Andrews Citizen*, 8 June 1935; *The Times*, 14 March 1962 (obit.); http://titan.glo.be/~bea/glashome.html

MENTEITH, Isabella, Countess of, fl. 1234–60. Daughter of Maurice, Earl of Menteith.

Isabella, Countess of Menteith, heiress to her father, had delivered the earldom to her husband Walter Comyn by 1234. One of the kingdom's most powerful magnates, Walter Comyn died in November 1258. She soon married Sir John Russell, an obscure English knight, apparently against the rival offers of Scottish nobles. A group of Scottish nobles led by the Comyns accused her of murder and had the pair imprisoned. Fleeing to England by 1260, they petitioned the Pope, who sent an envoy to York, but his summons was met with disdain by the Scottish king and aristocracy. Walter 'Bailloch' Stewart, whose wife Mary was probably Isabella's cousin, then gained the earldom. Isabella's further

efforts with Henry III and the Pope to reclaim the earldom and prove her innocence did not succeed. Her daughter married into the Comyn family.
MHH

• Anderson, A. O. (ed.) (1908) *Scottish Annals from English Chroniclers*; Bliss, W. H. (ed.) (1893) *Calendar of Entries in the Papal Registers: Papal Letters, vol. 1, 1198–1304*; Duncan, A. A. M. (1975) *Scotland: the making of the kingdom*; Fraser, W. (1880) *Red Book of Menteith*, vol. 2.

MENTEITH, Joanna, Countess of Strathearn, fl. 1323–1366. Daughter of Sir John Menteith.

Joanna Menteith's life is remarkable chiefly for the unusual circumstances under which she twice became Countess of Strathearn. Her first marriage, c. 1323, was to Malise IV, Earl of Strathearn (c. 1277–c. 1328). Soon after his death (without issue by her) in 1329 or 1330 she married John Campbell, Earl of Atholl (d. 1333), who was killed at the battle of Halidon Hill in 1333. In 1339 she obtained papal dispensation to marry Sir Maurice Moray of Drumsagard (d. 1346), a prominent Strathearn landholder. When the last Gaelic Earl of Strathearn was forfeited, David II awarded the title to Sir Maurice, and Joanna thus became Countess of Strathearn for a second time. Although she later married William, Earl of Sutherland (d. 1370/1), until her death around 1366 she most often identified herself with the lordship of Strathearn.
CJN

• Neville, C. J. (1983) 'The Earls of Strathearn . . .', PhD, Univ. of Aberdeen; *SP.*

MILLER, Christina Cruickshank (Chrissie), born Coatbridge 29 August 1899, died Edinburgh 16 July 2001. Research chemist. Daughter of Jessie Copland, and Alexander Miller, stationmaster.

Rubella at age five left Chrissie Miller with impaired hearing. She was good at maths, but the option of school-teaching was barred by her deafness, and a magazine article suggesting industrial analytical chemistry as a career for girls led her to study chemistry at both the University of Edinburgh and Heriot-Watt College. She followed the compressed courses laid on during wartime (1917 to 1920), graduating with BSc (distinction) and diploma. Her first doctorate was with Sir James Walker, thanks to Carnegie funding (1921–24). In difficult conditions (the chemistry building was still under construction), she used her own glass-blown equipment. Devoting herself thereafter to the microanalysis of rocks and metals, she went on to produce in 1928 the first-ever sample of pure

phosphorus trioxide, and to explain the characteristic glow. This work earned her the RSE Keith Prize: the citation included an expert view that it was 'the most important advance made in the last 20 years'. Chrissie Miller graduated DSc before she was 30 (her secret ambition) with a much-praised thesis. But she had lost an eye in a lab explosion, so chose to continue as lecturer and then director of the inorganic laboratory at Heriot-Watt, where she supervised a procession of good research students. As teacher and supervisor, she was scrupulous and exacting, inspiring logical thinking and intense debate and, according to one student, 'switching off her hearing aid only in the most extreme of situations' (RSE website). During the Second World War she worked for the war department on gas detection and sample analysis. In 1949, she was the only chemist among the first five women Fellows of the RSE, and in 1951 the only woman among the 25 Foundation Fellows of Heriot-Watt College. She had to take early retirement in 1961 because of hearing problems and family commitments (her mother and sister were semi-invalids). Had she been less self-effacing, some thought, she would have been Britain's first professor of analytic chemistry. SR

• Chalmers, R., *The Guardian*, 30 July 2001 (obit.), and longer version on RSE website: www.royalsoced.org.uk/fellowship/obits/2004/ccmiller Rayner-Canham, M. F. and Rayner-Canham, G. (1998) *Women in Chemistry.*

MILLER, Elizabeth (Betsy), born Saltcoats, Ayrshire, 11 June 1792, died Saltcoats 12 May 1864. Shipmaster and owner, Saltcoats and Ardrossan. Daughter of Mary Garret, and Captain William Miller, merchant and mariner.

The eldest of eight children, Betsy Miller was first employed in the family timber-exporting business as the on-shore clerk and book-keeper. The tragic drowning of her two brothers in separate incidents left the family with a large trading brig, the *Clytus*, without a master. Faced with rapidly mounting debts, her aged father gave way to her request to take over command of the brig in 1827. For over thirty years, Captain Betsy Miller sailed between Ayrshire and Ireland in all seasons. As the first woman to be certified by the Board of Trade, her abilities were honourably mentioned in the House of Commons during the debate on the Merchant Shipping Act (1834). Local legend has it that when faced with almost certain shipwreck in Irvine bay during the great winter storm of 1839, she calmed her panicking crew with the jibe: 'Lads, I'll gang below and put on a clean sark [chemise] for I wud like to be flung up on the sauns [sands] kin' o' decent – Irvine folks are nasty noticing buddies!' (Jack 1989, p. 48). She relinquished her command to her younger sister Hannah when she was 71, having restored the family fortunes. EJG

• *Lloyd's Register of Shipping* (1835–45).
Ardrossan & Saltcoats Herald, 14 May 1864 (obit.); Carragher, P. C. (1909) *Saltcoats: old and new*; Jack, W. (1989) 'The Captain was a Lady', *The Scots Magazine*, Oct.

MILLER, Lydia Falconer, n. **Fraser [Mrs H. Myrtle],** baptised Inverness 25 Jan. 1812, died Lochinver 11 March 1876. Editor, writer. Daughter of Elizabeth Lydia Macleod, teacher, and William Fraser, small merchant.

Lydia Fraser was educated at Inverness Royal Academy from 1820, and in the arts as a 'lady boarder' with George Thomson, Edinburgh (1827–8). From 1830, she ran a small school in Cromarty, and in 1837 married poet, stonemason and geologist Hugh Miller (1802–56). Lydia Miller bore five children and wrote children's books about natural history and religion. From 1840, she assisted Hugh Miller as editor of *The Witness*, which supported the Disruption. Theirs was an intellectual partnership: her novel *Passages in the Life of an English Heiress* (1847) argued the Free Church cause. After the devastating blow of her husband's suicide in 1856, she sought to ensure his reputation. Despite poor health, she worked as his literary executor, publishing his manuscripts, revising works and collaborating with his biographer, Peter Bayne, producing 'lucid and well-informed editorial apparatuses' (Shortland 1996, p. 47). Whether Hugh Miller's suicide was at all related to marital stress is a matter of dispute. It has been argued variously that her 'strong views on the intelligence and self-sufficiency of women . . . would certainly have played havoc with Miller's sense of self' (ibid., p. 47); that she played the tragic heroine (Rosie 1981); and that she was intelligent, loyal, courageous and remarkable (Sutherland 2002).

Lydia and Hugh Miller's oldest surviving child was the writer **Harriet Miller Davidson** (born Cromarty 25 Nov. 1839, died Adelaide, South Australia, 21 Dec. 1883). Harriet Miller had a gift for improvisation in music and poetry. At Oliphant's School, Edinburgh, she excelled at versifying, but left on her father's death to care for her mother, returning to school in London

(1857–9). She married Rev. John Davidson (1834/5–81), Free Church minister, in 1863, and bore five children. She published verse and two temperance novels before the family migrated to South Australia in 1870, where John Davidson was at Chalmers Church and later the University of Adelaide. Writing verse, fiction, children's stories, essays and reviews while running a school, she commented that the mother and artist engages 'in a vain struggle between her emotional and intellectual natures' (1880, p. 617). Two serials, *Man of Genius* and *Sir Gilbert's Children,* explored her family's story: her father's suicide 'haunted her' (obit., 1883). Her own daughter, Lydia Miller Middleton (1864–1934), writer, wrote, 'She was really an Intellectual. The joy of her life lay in the use of her wits. She was a fine talker, of the Victorian era, when talking was a fine art' (Private letter). MA

• NLS: MSS relating to Lydia F. Miller, MS 7516, 5139, 7527, 7528; Acc. 10097, vol. I, no. 103; MSS relating to Harriet M. Davidson, MS 7528, 7516; [Williamson, H. M.] 'Life of Hugh Miller', unpub. MS (c. 1872), NLS, S 7527; Univ. of Adelaide, Barr Smith Library: Davidson papers.
Miller, L., Work as above, and as Myrtle, Mrs H. (1845) *A Story Book of the Seasons: Spring* (and 16 other children's books); (1902) 'Mrs Hugh Miller's Journal', edited by her grand-daughter [Lydia Miller Mackay]; *Chambers's Journal*, 6th Series, April–July 1902; Anon. [Lydia F. Miller] (1847) *Passages in the Life of an English Heiress*; Davidson, H. M. (1867) *Isobel Jardine's History*, (1880) 'Girls', *The Adelaide Observer*, 10 April, p. 617 [and other writings].
Allen, M. (1999) 'The author's daughter, the professor's wife, Harriet Miller Davidson', *Jour. Hist. Soc. South Australia*, 27 (Bibl.); Bayne, P. (1871) *The Life and Letters of Hugh Miller*; Calder, A. (1993) 'The Disruption in fiction', in S. J. Brown and M. Fry (eds) *Scotland in the Age of Disruption*; *ODNB* (2004); Rosie, G. (1981) *Hugh Miller: outrage and order*; Shortland, M. (ed.) (1996) *Hugh Miller and the Controversies of Victorian Science*; Sutherland, E. (2002) *Lydia, Wife of Hugh Miller of Cromarty*; *The Adelaide Observer*, 22 Dec. 1883 (obit.).

MILLIGAN, Jean Callander, born Glasgow 9 July 1886, died Glasgow 28 July 1978. Advocate of traditional Scottish dance. Daughter of Isabella Aitchison, teacher, and Dr James Milligan, Rector, Glasgow High School for Girls.

The fifth of six children, Jean Milligan was educated at her father's school, then qualified in physical training at Kingsfield College, Dartford. Appointed to Dundas Vale Training College (later Jordanhill) in 1909, she immediately showed interest in traditional dance and music. After war service as a VAD in Malta, she became principal PT instructor at Jordanhill, and was influential in the national development of physical education in Scotland, until her retirement in 1948. In 1923, she met **Ysobel Stewart** of Fasnacloich (1882–1968), head of training for Girl Guides in Scotland, who was keen to promote Scottish country dancing among young people. With others, they convened a meeting in Glasgow in November 1923, forming the Scottish Country Dance Society. With Jean Milligan as inspirational principal teacher and technical adviser, the Society produced instruction books, devised a teacher-training programme, and founded a St Andrews Summer School, held annually since 1927 (except in wartime) and now hosting some thousand dancers. Jean Milligan compiled the popular *101 Scottish Country Dances* (1956, 1963) and a manual, *Won't You Join the Dance?* (1982, rev. edn.). After 1945, she travelled to promote Scottish country dancing worldwide, encouraging new branches of the Society, and still dancing even after operations on her knees. In 1973, she was voted *Evening Times* Scotswoman of the Year, and in 1977 the University of Aberdeen awarded her an LLD. She was 'a woman with a vision and with the ability and tenacity to . . . make it become reality' (the Earl of Mansfield in MacFadyen and Adams 1983, p. 7). By its 80th anniversary in 2003, the RSCDS had 166 branches and 448 affiliated groups in 41 countries. JTH

• Milligan, J. C., Works as above, and (1924) *The Scottish Country Dance* and other books.

MacFadyen, A. and Adams, F. H. (1983) *Dance with Your Soul*; MacFadyen, A. (1988) *An Album for Mrs Stewart*.

MILNE, Lennox Carruthers, OBE, m. **McLaren,** born Edinburgh 9 May 1909, died Haddington 23 June 1980. Actor. Daughter of Jessie Josephine Thomson, and Robert Rose Milne, stockbroker's cashier.

Growing up in Portobello, Lennox Milne trained for the stage at Edinburgh College of Drama and RADA. After graduation, she worked for a short time as a producer of schools programmes for the BBC but was soon offered work by the various repertory companies that were becoming established in Scotland. She appeared in all Tyrone Guthrie's productions of *The Thrie Estaitis* at the Edinburgh International Festival and in many plays by Robert McLellan. She gave distinguished performances on radio and television and, at the Gateway Theatre during the 1953 Edinburgh festival, she gave her first performance in *The Heart is Highland,* a solo play written for her by Robert Kemp. It gained her the first drama award to be given by the SAC (1954), was seen throughout Scotland and later had a successful North American tour. In 1968, she played the headmistress in the Broadway production of *The Prime of Miss Jean Brodie* (see Kay, Christina), repeating her performance at the Royal Lyceum Theatre, Edinburgh, later that year.

Always an active, practical woman, Lennox Milne was one of the co-founders of the Edinburgh Gateway Company in 1953 (with Tom Fleming and Robert Kemp) and for the next 12 years, in her work as actor, director and administrator, the theatre in Leith Walk became pivotal in all her activities. In its first season, she took part in the play *One Traveller Returns* and shortly afterwards married the author, Moray McLaren. Appointed a member of the SAC in 1965, she was also one of the first directors of Radio Forth. After her husband's death in 1972, she moved to Haddington where, in her final years, she devoted much energy to the Lamp of Lothian Charitable Trust. DC

• Campbell, D. (1996) *Playing for Scotland*; Edinburgh Gateway Company (1965) *Six Seasons of the Edinburgh Gateway.*

MINER, Mary Gill (Mae, Pat), n. **McKenzie Campbell,** born Leith 17 June 1910, died California, USA, 9 August, 1991. Restaurant worker and emigrant. Daughter of Mary Jane Gill, m. McKenzie, domestic worker, and Daniel Campbell, iron worker and commercial traveller.

At the time of her birth, Mary McKenzie Campbell's parents were not married to each other but to different spouses, with whom they both had children. They left their spouses and moved in together in 1914, taking Mary and her younger sister Peggy with them but leaving the four McKenzie children and seven Campbell children with the other parents. They then had another child, Colin. Faced with a another pregnancy in 1917 and living in poor accommodation with very limited means, her mother had an abortion, illegal at that time, and died as a result. Daniel Campbell died seven years later of tuberculosis.

Orphaned at age 14, Mary left school to become a waitress at Fairley's dancehall and café in Edinburgh, living in lodgings. In 1930, she emigrated alone, in steerage, to the USA. She found work as a waitress in New York, Connecticut and Florida before marrying John Daniel Miner

(1917–92), a merchant seaman, in 1941. They had three children. The family moved twice then settled in northern California in 1961. After some time spent caring for her invalid mother-in-law and the children, Mary Miner returned to restaurant jobs. Her husband left the family in 1966, moving out of state to avoid paying alimony and child support. Mary Miner continued working until she was 77 years old, when the all-night café in which she was employed was closed down.

Most of her 13 siblings, like many other Scots of the time, also left Scotland, for Canada, India, England, New Zealand, Australia and the USA. In her life she faced considerable hardship, but was known for her resilient spirit, hard work, strong faith and wry wit. Among her favourite sayings was, 'There's never a bad that couldn't be worse'. vm

• Miner, V. (2001) *The Low Road: a Scottish family memoir*. Personal information, Valerie Miner (daughter).

MITCHEL (or MITCHELSON), Margaret, fl. 1638. Prophetess. Possibly daughter of James Mitchelson, minister of Yester.

Margaret Mitchel rose briefly to fame around the time of the 1638 Glasgow General Assembly, when she predicted the success of the National Covenant. She was close to the minister Henry Rollock who was spellbound by her. Archibald Johnston of Wariston heard of her from Rollock on 13 September 1638: the final notice in his diary is on 22 January 1639. He wrote that she 'was transported in heavinly raptures and spak strainge things for the happy succes of Gods cause and Chryst croune in this kingdome' (Johnston 1911, p. 393). Some noblemen found Christian conviction in listening to her, though she was noted disparagingly in James Gordon's *Scots Affairs* and in the *Large Declaration* which stated that she was a minister's daughter and that 'she hath been for many yeeres distracted by fits' (*Large Declaration*, p. 227). She was, however, the object of an 'incredible concourse' (ibid., p. 227) in Edinburgh. dm

• Gordon, J. (1841) *History of Scots Affairs, from 1637 to 1641*, 3 vols, J. Robertson and G. Grub, eds; Johnston of Wariston, A., (1911) *Diary 1632–1639*, G. M. Paul, ed.; *A Large Declaration concerning the late tumults in Scotland* (1639) pp. 226–8; *ODNB* (2004) (see Mitchelson, Margaret).

MITCHELL, Lillias Tait, born Leith 24 March 1884, died Edinburgh 24 Sept. 1940. Suffragette campaigner. Daughter of Annie Alexander and Alexander Mitchell, timber merchant.

Lillias Mitchell joined the WSPU in 1907/early 1908 after attending, with her mother, a suffrage meeting in Edinburgh at which Emmeline Pankhurst spoke; she later recalled 'I shall never forget the blazing warmth of that meeting' (*AGC*, p. 73). Of the following years she wrote, 'I lived and moved and seemed to have my being in working for votes for women' (ibid.). Imprisoned in Holloway for two weeks in 1910, by 1911 she was WSPU organiser in Aberdeen. In March 1912, after a window-smashing raid in London, she was sentenced to four months' imprisonment and went on hunger strike. When released, she continued to lead militant protest from Aberdeen, painting the marker flags on Balmoral golf course in WSPU colours and confronting the Prime Minister, H. H. Asquith, on the Dornoch golf course. Taking over the campaign in the English midlands, with Mary Richardson she planted a bomb in a Birmingham railway station, and helped attack the Castle Bromwich racecourse. When arrested, she again went on hunger strike at Winson Green Prison, Birmingham, in May 1914. Loyal to the Pankhursts, she was 'a model WSPU organiser' (ibid., p. 117). After the war she joined the EWCA, wrote for *The Scotsman* and was secretary to the Edinburgh and South Area of the YWCA. jr

• *AGC*; *SS*; *WSM*.

MITCHISON, Naomi Mary Margaret,‡ n. **Haldane,** CBE, born Edinburgh 1 Nov. 1897, died Carradale 11 Jan. 1999. Author, political activist and councillor. Daughter of Louisa Kathleen Trotter, and John Scott Haldane, physiologist.

Naomi Haldane and her elder brother Jack grew up in Oxford, although summer visits to the Haldane family estate at Cloan, Perthshire, were a vital part of their childhood. She was educated at the Dragon School, Oxford, and began a degree course in science at the Society of Home Students (later St Anne's College), Oxford. She married Gilbert Richard (Dick) Mitchison (1890–1970) in 1916, and had seven children, two of whom died young, and, eventually, 19 grandchildren. She was born into upper-middle-class privilege but created a life for herself that was experimental and adventurous. As a young married woman with a husband at the Front, she worked as a VAD nurse in London in 1915. Her first novel, *The Conquerors,* was published in 1923. She was an active socialist and stood unsuccessfully for parliament for the Scottish Universities in 1935. In 1932, she travelled to Russia with the Fabian Society, a trip that also allowed her to visit the scenes of her recently published novel, *The Corn King and the Spring Queen.* Although her early fiction was set in the Classical world, it clearly embodies both the richness of her own life and the political issues of her time. It also reflects the Mitchisons' openness about relationships.

In 1937, the Mitchison family moved to Carradale on the Mull of Kintyre, where she involved herself with Highland affairs. Throughout the Second World War she kept a diary for the Mass-Observation archive, detailing life in Carradale. She ran the home farm, gardening, farming and fishing. She wrote and produced plays locally, and also wrote her monumental Scottish novel *The Bull Calves* (1947), drawing on her Scottish ancestry and her concerns about gender and nation. She was a long-standing member of Argyll County Council (1945–65), a member of the Highland Panel (1947–65) and served on the Highlands and Islands Advisory Council (1966–75).

In 1960, a meeting with Linchwe, chief of the Bakgatla, led to her involvement with the Bakgatla people in Botswana. She was recognised as tribal adviser and *Mmarona* (mother) to the Bakgatla in 1963. For 25 years she visited Botswana regularly and her African experiences shaped her writing.

She wrote more than 70 books, published between 1923 and 1991, including, as well as her major achievement in historical fiction, children's books, three books of poetry, several plays, collections of short stories and social and political non-fiction. In 1962, she moved into science fiction with *Memoirs of a Spacewoman.* Her last book, *Sea Green Ribbons,* was published in 1991. In her later years she divided her time between Carradale and London. Her writing expresses her passionate concern for justice and social equality; Neil Ascherson commented in her obituary, 'If intelligent people shouted long and loud enough at governments, she believed, truth would prevail' (*Guardian* 1999). Her novels are about individuals with lives that are personally both difficult and rewarding, but who have in common a social role and a social conscience. Like Naomi Mitchison, Kirstie in *The Bull Calves* and Erif Der in *The Corn King and the Spring Queen* are undefeated women who retain their sense of adventure and their belief that kindness and truth should, and will, prevail, in the face of all difficulty and disillusionment. ME

• The Mitchell Library, Glasgow: Archives and Special Collections, Misc corr. and MSS; NLS: Acc. 4549, 5912, 7721, 8503, 9186, corr. and literary MSS; NRA: see website for other archive sources, www.nra.nationalarchives.gov.uk
Mitchison, N., Works as above and see Bibls. below.
Calder, J. (1997) *The Nine Lives of Naomi Mitchison* (Bibl.); *HSWW* (Bibl.); *ODNB* (2004) (also lists archive sources); *The Guardian,* 17 Jan. 1999 (obit.).

MITCHISON, Rosalind Mary (Rowy), n. **Wrong,** born Manchester 11 April 1919, died Edinburgh 20 Sept. 2002. Historian, teacher. Daughter of Rosalind Grace Smith, and Edward Murray Wrong, mathematician.

Rosalind Wrong, grand-daughter of Canadian historian George Wrong, was educated in Oxford and London. She took a double first in mathematics and modern history at Lady Margaret Hall, Oxford, in 1942. In 1947, with her marriage to Murdoch Mitchison, who became Professor of Zoology at the University of Edinburgh, she joined and contributed to the Haldane-Mitchison network (which included *Naomi Mitchison), so active in British scientific and literary life and the intellectual and political life of the labour movement.

Between 1947 and 1967 she combined raising four children with several different university teaching posts. At the University of Edinburgh she was lecturer, then reader, in economic history and gained a personal chair in social history in 1981. An inspiring teacher, she combined modern social history with an insistence on archive research and narrative. She was active in many historical societies including the Scottish History Society (serving as President), and the Social Science Research Council, as well as providing leadership for the East Lothian Historical Association. Rowy Mitchison made a major contribution to Scotland's historical literature, notably in the widely read *History of Scotland* (1970), her studies on the Poor Law, and joint research with *Leah Leneman on early modern illegitimacy, including *Sexuality and Social Control* (1989). She was made FRHistS and FRSE. Her publications were an innovatory part of the renaissance of Scottish historical writing since 1960. RJM

• Mitchison, R., Works as above, and (1962) *Agricultural Sir John,* (1980) (ed.) *The Roots of Nationalism,* (1991) *Why Scottish History Matters,* (2000) *The Old Poor Law in Scotland, 1574–1845.*
Fraser, W. H. (2003) 'Rosalind Mitchison (1919–2002) and John Butt (1929–2002): an appreciation', *Scot. Econ. and Soc. Hist.,* 23/1; Leneman, L. (ed.) (1988) *Perspectives in Scottish Social History* (Bibl. to 1988); *The Guardian,* 4 Oct. 2002 (obit.).
Private information.

MOAR, May (Marjory), n. **Hectorson,** born Unst 1825, died Baltasound 2 July 1894. Awarded medals for bravery by RNLI and RHSoc. Daughter of Williamina Anderson and Laurence Hectorson.

May Hectorson, one of six children, was orphaned by her father's death by drowning in 1826. Fostered out to the island of Yell, she married David Moar, a fisherman, in 1847. On 9 September 1858 she was out in the fields when she and two other women saw a four-oared sail-boat capsize in a gale and the upturned vessel drift towards rocks with the four men clinging to the hull. Oral accounts tell of her fashioning a rope from a cow's tethers and attaching a buoy. ' "If some o' you will guide weel this rope" . . . dashing from her face her woman's tears, "I'll gang ower the banks and save the men, wi' God's help" ' (Saxby 1892, p. 11). She was lowered down the cliff to a ledge; two men caught the line she threw and came ashore, the other two clung to the wreckage and drifted to shelter. The local minister sent accounts of the rescue to the RNLI and the Royal Humane Society and May Moar was awarded the medals in recognition of her bravery.

In 1867, she and her family were evicted from their home during the Yell clearances and in 1881 her husband was drowned during the Gloup fishing disaster of 20 July when 58 men were lost. May returned to her home island of Unst. Her bravery was the subject of the short story *Daughter of Sea Kings* by Shetland writer *Jessie Saxby. Her RNLI medal was discovered in a dyke at Unst and is now in the Shetland Museum.

Grace Petrie (1819–1917) was also recognised for bravery by the Royal Humane Society following her rescue, along with her sister-in-law Helen Petrie, of two men from a sinking boat in 1856. They are also said to have rescued a father and son in similar circumstances in 1859. LCA

• 'Museum Corner' *New Shetlander*, 196, Summer, 1996, pp. 10–11; Robertson, M. S. (1991) *Sons and Daughters of Shetland 1800–1900*; Saxby, J. M. E. (1892) *Heim-Laund and Heim-Folk*.

MOFFAT, Maggie Liddell, n. **Linck,** born Spittal, Northumberland, 7 Jan. 1873, died Capetown, South Africa, Feb. 1943. Actress and suffragette. Daughter of Margaret Liddell Dowie, and Gottlob Frederick William Linck, seaman.

Maggie Linck was the sixth of seven children. Most of her siblings had been born in Glasgow, and the family returned there shortly before the father died in 1878. The Lincks were musical, and she herself sang. She worked as a drapery saleswoman for some years however, before embarking on an acting career. She met photographer, actor and playwright Graham Moffat (1866–1951) when auditioning for his troupe, the Glasgow Junior Dramatic Club, and they married in 1897. They had one daughter, Winifred, who later worked in their company 'Mr and Mrs Graham Moffat and their company of Scottish players'.

Maggie Moffat's interest in the WSPU was sparked when her husband overheard a man say: 'Would we be discussing women's claims now, if these women had not behaved outrageously?' (Moffat 1955, p. 51). She joined the WSPU in 1907 and was arrested during a deputation to the House of Commons. Sent to Holloway for two weeks, she was one of the first two Scottish women to be imprisoned for the cause; the other was actress Annie Fraser, younger sister of *Helen Fraser. After his wife's imprisonment, Graham Moffat formed the Glasgow Men's League for Women's Suffrage, for 'the husbands and brothers of active suffragettes and other male sympathisers', who often received 'cruel comments' (Moffat 1955, p. 52; *HHGW*, p. 105). When the WSPU split in October 1907, Maggie Moffat moved to the WFL, following the lead of *Teresa Billington-Greig, and became treasurer of its Scottish council.

Graham Moffat wrote several plays, including the hugely successful *Bunty Pulls the Strings*, a 'sabbatarian comedy', which opened at the Haymarket (11 July 1911) and changed their lives; after 617 performances, it transferred to Broadway in 1912 and toured the English-speaking world. Theatre work left the Moffats little time to devote to the suffrage cause, but they always made 'their views clear when interviewed in the Press' (*AGC*, p. 266). Maggie and Graham Moffat retired to South Africa in 1936. KBB

• *AGC*; Campbell, D. (1996) *Playing for Scotland*; *HHGW*; Moffat, G. (1955) *Join Me in Remembering*.

MONCRIEFF, Marianne Isobel, n. **Dunlop,** born Glasgow 21 Dec. 1874, died Edinburgh 28 Sept. 1961. Glass designer and entrepreneur. Daughter of Margaret Waters Ure and Matthew Dunlop.

John Moncrieff Ltd was established as The North British Glassworks in Perth in the 19th century. Marianne Dunlop, who in 1897 married John Moncrieff Jnr, had a remarkable sense of design which radically altered the company's production. When cheap foreign competition reduced demand after 1918, the firm decided to concentrate on domestic fine glass production. Marianne Moncrieff took charge as artistic director, introducing an art-based style made by a Spanish family of skilled artisans, the Ysarts, and innovative production methods; she created a patternbook for the glass blowers. The product, 'Monart Ware', became world-famous. Launched in 1924 at the British Industries Fair, a year before the Arts Deco Paris Exhibition, it was similar in style. Determined that Monart's Scottish identity would be prominent, Marianne Moncrieff advertised it with a Scottish thistle. Early bowls and vases were followed by lamps and lampshades in simple round shapes, often using a feather motif. She forged a link with Liberty's fabrics, matching glass with their shades, and deriving most of the colour sources from the continent. 'Gold-dust', 'silver-dust', and a dark rich red were popular at first, but changing taste later inspired a palette of pastel hues. Fashionable Monart glassware was exported worldwide. Scottish glass suffered depression during and after the Second World War, but revived in different forms thereafter (Caithness, paperweight production). The art of glass engraving owed its renaissance to another woman, **Helen Monro Turner** (1901–77), who taught a new generation at ECA after 1943 (Blench 1983, 1989). LS

• Blench, B. J. R. (1983) 'Scottish glass: 1945 to the present day', *Jour. Glass Studies*, 25, pp. 207–11, (1989) 'Impassioned vision – Helen Turner and the teaching of glass design', *Jour. Decorative Arts Soc.*, 13, pp. 39–52; Fleming, A. (1938, repr. 1977) *Scottish and Jacobite Glass*; Vaughan, M. T. (1994) 'Scottish art glass: Marianne Isobel Moncrieff (1874–1961)', in J. Seddon, and S. Worden (eds) *Women Designing*.

MONTGOMERIE, Norah Mary, n. **Shargool,** born West Dulwich 6 April 1909, died Edinburgh 19 Feb. 1998. Folklorist and artist. Daughter of Letitia Collins, tailoress, and John Shargool, accountant.

Born into a musical family, Norah Shargool was educated at a convent boarding school in Folkstone. She worked in London as a freelance magazine illustrator to finance art school. Influenced by her great-grandmother, Clara Saunders Lewis, who had sung Scottish folk songs to her as a child, she moved to Dundee to become an illustrator with D. C. Thomson. In 1934, she married poet, teacher and folklorist William Montgomerie, who shared her life-long commitment to collecting and preserving Scottish traditional culture.

In the mid-1940s, when William Montgomerie began to record Scots ballads, Norah collected street songs, rhymes, sayings, games and riddles. Together they produced a remarkable collection which she illustrated. When Scottish publishers showed no interest, Norah Montgomerie sent the manuscript to poet laureate Walter de la Mare, whose delight ensured publication of *Sandy Candy and other Scottish Nursery Rhymes* (1948). Thus began a series of child lore books, the product of ground-breaking work which pre-dates that of the internationally known Opies by at least 15 years. With no provision for the Scots language in the school curriculum, the Montgomeries assiduously promoted its use through such books as *The Well at the World's End* (1956) and *A Book of Scottish Nursery Rhymes* (1965). Their anthologies aimed to attune the young to the pleasure of Scots language and poetry in general, so that in adulthood they might appreciate the richness of traditional balladry.

Norah Montgomerie also wrote her own books, many with her colour illustrations. As a mother of two children herself, she enthusiastically encouraged and gave confidence to many who, influenced by teachers and parents who sought to eliminate Scots dialects, had lost their native speech. Her passionate commitment, creativity and work (largely funded from the family purse) were life-long and continue to bear fruit. MgtB

• Montgomerie, N., Works as above and (1961) *Twenty-Five Fables*, (1962) *To Read and to Tell*, (1964) *The Merry Little Fox and other Animal Stories*; (1959) with K. Lines, *Poems and Pictures*.
Private information: Dian Montgomerie Elvin.

MONTROSE, Duchess of *see* **GRAHAM, Violet, Duchess of Montrose** (1854–1940)

MOON, Lorna *see* **LOW, Helen Nora Wilson** (1886–1930)

MOORE (or MUIR), Jane (Jean), n. **Watson/ NicWalter,** born Cardross c. 1635, died London 1695. Tobacconist, philanthropist.

Jane, sometimes Jean, Watson was said by local tradition to have been of humble birth and to have been employed initially as a domestic servant. Following a minor theft from her employer she fled Cardross, found her way to Leith, married a man by the name of Moore or Muir and with him travelled to London. Following her husband's death in London, she ran a successful tobacconist's business in Wapping. Her interesting will, proved in the Prerogative Court of Canterbury in 1695, reveals her considerable wealth, including her

'Negro servants', and that she moved within a circle of expatriate Scots.

Moore's Bridge, which carries the busy A814 road across the Auchinfroe Burn in the village of Cardross, is a permanent memorial to her. Although now largely a Victorian reconstruction, the bridge still bears the date 1688, the year in which she funded its construction. She also gave a bell to the parish kirk, with two fine mortcloths. Her greatest act of charity, however, was her bequest of £500 sterling for the poor of Cardross. Known as 'Mrs Moore's Mortification', the bequest is still available for community causes in the village, more than three centuries after her death. MM

• NAS: Will of Jane Moore, proved 3 Oct. 1695.
MacLeod, D. (1891) *Historic Families, Notable Families and Memorabilia of the Lennox*; Maughan, W. C. (1897) *Annals of Garelochside*.

MOORHEAD, Ethel Agnes Mary,‡ born Maidstone, Kent, 28 August 1869, died Dublin 4 March 1955. Artist, suffragette and editor. Daughter of Margaret Humphreys, and George Moorhead, army surgeon.

The third of six children in an Irish Roman Catholic family, Ethel Moorhead was convent educated. Her sister Alice Moorhead (see Thomson, Emily) and three brothers became doctors, two in the army. The family lived in India, Mauritius and South Africa, until the parents settled in Dundee in 1900. Alice Moorhead paid for her sister to train as an artist in Whistler's studio, Atelier Carmen, in Paris, some time between 1898 and 1901. Ethel Moorhead returned home to look after her parents until they died. She had a studio in Dundee, and first exhibited there in 1901; her paintings were considered 'the gems of the collection' (*Advertiser* 1901). From until 1918 she exhibited at Glasgow Institute of Fine Arts, the RSA, Walker Gallery, Liverpool, and New England Art Club, as well as in London and Dublin. She painted mostly portraits, but also landscapes of the Irish countryside. Her early work was conventional but she later painted what she called 'daubs' in Fauvist style.

When her father died in 1911, Ethel Moorhead joined the WSPU. Using a string of aliases she smashed windows in London and a showcase at the Wallace Monument in Stirling; threw an egg at Churchill and pepper at the police; attacked a teacher with a dog whip; wrecked police cells, and was involved in several arson attempts. The 'most turbulent' of suffragettes (*AGC*, p. 266), she achieved notoriety in the Scottish press but held no formal post in the WSPU, acting on her own initiative. She defended militancy in the local press: 'We, indeed, owe it to the women who had reasoned for 40 years and done nothing that we have got nothing. How beggarly appear arguments before a defiant deed' (*Advertiser* 1912). Never one to suffer injustice quietly, she refused to recognise the jurisdiction of the courts, and complained so vehemently about treatment that the Secretary of State had to answer a question in parliament.

She was imprisoned several times. Following her arrest with *Dorothea Chalmers Smith in July 1913 for attempted arson, she became the first Scottish suffragette to be force-fed – the focus of considerable protest. Released under the 'Cat and Mouse Act', an experience she describes in 'Incendiaries' (1925), she was held responsible by the police for four further fires. She was caught and imprisoned again and once more went on hunger strike, adding thirst and sleep strikes. She was near to death before she was released. It is virtually certain she was the woman who escaped when her close friend **Frances (Fanny) Mary Parker** (1875–1924) was arrested in July 1914 attempting to set fire to Burns's cottage. Fanny Parker was born in New Zealand, a niece of Lord Kitchener. She was a WSPU organiser in Dundee (1912) and Edinburgh (1913). She also spoke for and organised tours for the Scottish University Women's Suffrage Union. She was imprisoned five times and force-fed three times (see Cadell, Grace). Ethel Moorhead and Fanny Parker worked together for the WFL National Service organisation during the First World War, campaigning for women war workers to be properly paid. Later, Fanny Parker was Deputy Controller of the WAAC in Boulogne.

In 1922, Ethel Moorhead met a young poet called Ernest Walsh in Claridges. He became her protégé, and together they travelled round Europe. When Fanny Parker died in 1924, Ethel Moorhead used her legacy to start a quarterly arts journal with Ernest Walsh. *This Quarter* published writing by Gertrude Stein, Ezra Pound, Ernest Hemingway and James Joyce, and art by Brancusi and Picabia, as well as work by Ethel Moorhead and Ernest Walsh. After Walsh died in 1926, she edited the third and fourth editions. During these years it was said in the family that she had various affairs with Bohemians of the time, but no details are known. Although the family had been wealthy, she was left nothing by her parents, and it seems likely that she lived mainly on money from her brothers. In later life, she was supported financially by her niece. It seems her latter years were unhappy. She died in a nursing home in Dublin. IMH

• Dundee Local Studies Library: newspapers including *Celtic Journal, Piper o' Dundee, Wizard of the North*.
Moorhead, E. (1925) 'Incendiaries', *This Quarter*, 2.
AGC; Dundee *Advertiser*, 17 April 1901, 11 March 1912;
Leneman, L. (1993) *Martyrs in our Midst*; McAlmon, R. and Boyle, K. (1966) *Being Geniuses Together, 1920–30*; *WSM*.
Private information.

MORICE, Margaret, n. **Kennedy (or Kennerty),** baptised Aberdeen 21 August 1718, died Aberdeen 1799/1800. Baker. Daughter of Janet Buchan, and Thomas Kennerty, tailor.

Like many tradeswomen, Margaret Kennedy Morice shared her husband's business, managing the bakery for 27 years after his death in 1770, and retaining the family tenement, located centrally on Castle Street. As 'Margaret Morice and Co.' she took apprentices, generally from families of good standing, between 1776 and 1794, collecting premiums comparable to those of male bakers. She deliberately kept the name Morice, to retain the prestige and commercial identity developed when the partnership had built up a substantial and respected undertaking. The bakers' guild commonly allowed widows to keep trading, and in this case no artificial measures were needed to prop up the well-regarded business. She reverted to her family name of Kennedy in 1794. Between 1739 and 1750, she bore seven children. Few survived her, and none joined the business, the eldest, David, becoming an advocate. DLS

• Aberdeen City Archives: *Listing* and *Enactment Books 5*.
Register of Indentures, 1622–1878; St Nicholas, Aberdeen, Baptism and Burial Records.
Bain, E. (1887) *Merchant and Craft Guilds, A History of the Aberdeen Incorporated Trades*; Henderson, J. A. (ed.) (1912) *History of the Society of Advocates in Aberdeen*.

MORRIS, Margaret, born London 10 March 1891, died Glasgow 29 Feb. 1980. Dancer, artist, educator, founder of the Margaret Morris Movement (MMM). Daughter of Victoria Maundrell, acting teacher, and William Bright Morris, artist.

Margaret Morris was brought up in France until she was 5 years old: she began performing in public, aged 3, reciting French verse. She had no formal education but was bi-lingual and gained an appreciation of painting, literature and music from her parents' circle. She spent three years with Ben Greet's Shakespeare Company as a child actor and took lessons with John d'Auban, ballet master at Drury Lane Theatre. She joined Frank Benson's company as an ingenue but soon returned to dancing. She adapted the six Greek positions (learned from Raymond Duncan, brother of Isadora), incorporating her own exercises and some modified balletic positions, to create a system of movement that became the basis of her future work.

John Galsworthy, with whom she had a brief affair, and his wife, Ada, were instrumental in the establishment of Margaret Morris's first dance school in 1910. In 1913, she took a troupe of dancers to the Marigny Theatre in Paris where she visited the Scottish artist John Duncan Fergusson (1874–1961). His enthusiasm for Diaghilev's Russian Ballet and for Indian and Cambodian art influenced the choreography and costuming of her dances. He moved to London at the outbreak of the First World War, and they jointly founded the Margaret Morris Club, a centre for artists, writers, musicians and dancers. Their relationship became mutually inspirational. In the 1920s, Margaret Morris became increasingly interested in the application of her system of movement to physical education, medicine and sport. After some initial resistance, her techniques became influential. She qualified as a physiotherapist in 1930 and worked with many international sportsmen and women, in tennis, golf, fencing and rugby. As a result of her work at the Army Training School at Aldershot, she was encouraged to found a men's training college, which under the auspices of the Basic Physical Training Association, was launched at Loughborough College in 1939.

Seven 'MMM' schools were established in England, Scotland and France, where she and John Duncan Fergusson regularly spent summers. After the outbreak of the Second World War, all the schools closed except the one in Glasgow, where they settled. In 1940, she founded the Celtic Ballet Club, which gave monthly performances of her dances including *The Forsaken Mermaid* and *The Skye Boat Song*. In 1947, she formed a small professional company, Celtic Ballet of Scotland, which toured to France, Spain and the USA. Appearances at festivals in Russia, Austria and Czechoslovakia added to the company's reputation, but her dream of creating a national Scottish dance company remained elusive. After financial losses from a further tour, the Glasgow school closed in 1961. Following John Duncan Fergusson's sudden death that year, she devoted much of her time to writing and broadcasting. New MMM schools again flourished with her support, and at the time of her death in 1980, there were classes in Great Britain, Canada, USA, Switzerland, France, West Germany, the West Indies and South Africa. The annual international summer schools, which began in 1917, are still a focus for the movement. JBIM

• Morris, M. (1925) *Margaret Morris Dancing*, (1928) *The Notation of Movement*, (1937) *Basic Physical Training*, (1943) 'Celtic Ballet', *Dancing Times*, 398, p. 89, (1954) 'Celtic Ballet at Jacob's Pillow', *Dance and Dancers*, 15, 8, p. 29, (1955) 'Celtic Ballet College', *Dancing Times*, 542, p. 91, (1967) *My Galsworthy Story*, (1969) *My Life in Movement*, (1972) *Creation in Dance and Life*, (1974) *The Art of J. D. Fergusson*. Galsworthy, J. (1913) *The Dark Flower*; Goodwin, N. (1979) *A Ballet for Scotland*; Jeayes, I. (1960) 'Margaret Morris Jubilee', *Dancing Times*, 603, p. 173; Lawson, J. (1964) *History of Ballet and its Makers*; *Margaret Morris Movement*, film by Scottish Arts Council and Educational Films of Scotland, 1973; *ODNB* (2004); Trewhitt, B. and Hastie J. (c. 1985) *Margaret Morris, 1891–1980*; White, J. W. (1980) *Margaret Morris*.
Private information: Jim Hastie, President and Artistic Director, MMM.

MORRISON, Agnes Brysson Inglis (Nancy),
[N. Brysson Morrison, Christine Strathern], born Scotstownhill, near Glasgow, 24 Dec. 1903, died London 27 Feb. 1986. Novelist and biographer. Daughter of Agnes Brysson Inglis, charity fund-raiser, and Arthur Mackie Morrison, engineer.

One of six children, five of whom became published writers, Nancy (as she was known in the family) attended Park School in Glasgow and completed her education at Harvington College in London. Their mother, **Agnes Brysson Morrison** n. **Inglis** (1866–1934), originated the Flag Day movement in Glasgow in September 1914 and personally supervised 400 subsequent flag days throughout Britain, for which she was awarded the CBE in 1920. In their youth, Nancy and her elder sisters, Mary and Peggy, adopted the pen surname 'Cost'; 'Ann Cost' was Nancy's pen-name in the early 1920s. However, only **Peggy Morrison** (1897–1973) maintained the pseudonym throughout her life. Peggy studied at Glasgow School of Art and worked with Sir Frank Benson's Company of Shakespearean Players. She published 18 novels and a collection of short stories under the name 'March Cost'. Mary Morrison also wrote short stories which appeared in *Argosy* and *Tatler* under the pen name 'M. N. Thomas'. Their brother Tommy Morrison wrote screenplays and novels as both T. J. Morrison and Alan Muir. Another brother,

John Morrison, also wrote, including a history of Iona and the Iona Community of which he was a founder member.

Nancy Brysson Morrison lived most of her life in Glasgow, sharing a home with Mary Morrison in Hillhead, but moved to London in later life. All her work was originally published under the authorship of N. Brysson Morrison, something she insisted on, possibly in the hope of receiving an unprejudiced reception. Some of her novels are set in Glasgow and Edinburgh, while others evoke the landscape and people of Perthshire and Aberdeenshire, where she spent many holidays. Her work has a preoccupation with the past, exemplified in *The Winnowing Years* (1949), for which she won the first Frederick Niven Award. It outlines three centuries of the history of the fictional parish of Drumban, based on factual details about the village of Carmunnock, near Glasgow, where her parents are buried. Between 1930 and 1974, she published ten novels, of which only *The Gowk Storm* (1933, 1988) has remained in print, five historical biographies, three religious texts and various short stories. Her historical novels question traditional approaches to historical narrative by highlighting earlier class, gender and ideological skewing. Focusing on those people previously omitted from conventional historical fiction – women, the poor, religious dissidents and social outcasts – her work offered a modern interpretation of Scotland's past. She fictionalised the Highland Clearances when they were considered unsuitable material for such treatment, offered early psychological and feminist interpretations of history and explored the changing position of women in Scottish society. She also published 27 romances under the pseudonym 'Christine Strathern'. MS

• NLS: MSS 27287–27373, 27400, 27403–4, 27410. Morrison, N. Brysson, Works as above. See also *HSWW* (Bibl.) and www.swhn.org
'N. Brysson Morrison: a case for reappraisal', *Chapman*, no. 106, pp. 95–100; *Glasgow Herald*, 2 August 1934 (obit.); *HSWW* (Bibl.); Hunter, S. (1953) 'The Writing Morrisons', *The Scots Magazine*, June; *ODNB* (2004); Seenan, M. (2000) 'The watcher at the crossroads: ideological negotiations in the fiction of N. Brysson Morrison', PhD, Univ. of Glasgow; (2002) 'The writing Morrisons', *The Scots Magazine*, August; *The Times*, 27 March 1986 (obit.).

MORRISON, Euphemia Flora Nicholson (Effie), born South Snizort, Skye, 28 Jan. 1917, died Glasgow 24 Sept. 1974. Secretary, broadcaster and occasional actor. Daughter of Annie Mackenzie, and Rev. Norman John Morrison, Free Church minister.

During radio's heydey in the 1940s and 1950s, Effie Morrison's voice was one of the most familiar in Scotland. She was recruited by the Drama Department of the Scottish Home Service as one of a group of pioneer actors. However, she never gave up her day job as a secretary in a Glasgow office. Apart from performing in a wide range of radio drama, from *Children's Hour* and schools broadcasting to *Saturday Night Theatre,* her scriptwriting and literary skills were demonstrated in her witty *Kirsty Morag Letters.* She scored her greatest success as an actress playing Chris Guthrie in Lewis Grassic Gibbons's *Sunset Song* and *Cloud Howe,* transmitted in the early 1950s.

Her theatrical roles were surprisingly few. With the Edinburgh Gateway Company, she played Mrs Noah in a cycle of Mystery plays entitled *That Old Serpent* (1961) and appeared at the 1961 Edinburgh Festival as Alison in Tom Fleming's production of Robert Kemp's *Let Wives Tak Tent.* She disliked appearing in front of an audience, feeling that this restricted her creativity; in a radio studio she felt free to be young or old, saint or sinner. It is perhaps ironic that she is often remembered today for her most famous television role, Mistress Niven in the original series of *Doctor Finlay's Casebook.* DC
• Edinburgh Gateway Company (1965) *Six Seasons of the Edinburgh Gateway.*

MOUAT, Elizabeth (Betty),‡ born Levenwick, Shetland, 1825, died Dunrossness, Shetland, 6 Feb. 1918. Spinner and handknitter. Daughter of Margaret Harper, and Thomas Mouat, shoemaker and fisherman.

Betty Mouat was a typical, and in most ways unremarkable, Shetland woman who became famous for her lone drift to Norway on the sailing vessel *Columbine* in January 1886, when she was 59 years old. Like many of her contemporaries in Shetland, where women significantly outnumbered men because of the high male mortality rate and long absences occasioned by the fishing industry, she never married. She lived with her half-brother, contributing to the household income by her fine knitting which she exchanged for goods in Lerwick's stores. On a boat trip to Lerwick to sell shawls and to seek medical advice regarding a recent stroke, a heavy swell swept the skipper and his crew overboard, leaving her to drift alone. Sustained by one bottle of milk and two biscuits, she survived eight days and nine nights before the

Columbine ran aground off the Norwegian coast, where she was attached to a rope and hauled ashore by local fishermen. The story soon reached the British and continental press and her own account of the voyage was printed in *The Scotsman* (24 February 1886); it said that 'at no period of her trying experience does she seem to have given way to anything like violent grief, but rather . . . endured her dreadful trial . . . with remarkable calmness and resignation'. On her arrival in Edinburgh, hundreds queued to see her, and her return to Shetland was greeted by crowds on the dockside. Her fame ensured that her shawls were highly valued thereafter.

Betty Mouat's experience fascinated a nation unacquainted with the hard lives of Shetland women and her adventure was romanticised in prose and poetry, including the poem, 'The Wreck of the Columbine' by William McGonagall: 'Oh! heaven, hard was the fate of this woman of sixty years of age/Tossing about on the briny deep, while the storm fiend did rage . . .' She continued to receive visitors until her death at the age of 93. Her memorial is in the churchyard at Dunrossness and her former cottage in nearby Scatness is now a camping bothy. LCA
• Shetland Archives: D1/134, scrapbook cuttings.
Grant, R. (1973) *The Lone Voyage of Betty Mouat*; Manson, T. M. Y. (1996) *Drifting Alone to Norway.*

MOXON, May *see* **DAVISON, Euphemia** (1906–1996)

MUIR, Wilhelmina Johnston (Willa),‡ n. **Anderson [Agnes Neill Scott],** born Montrose 13 March 1890, died Dunoon 22 May 1970. Writer and translator. Daughter of Elizabeth Gray Anderson, dressmaker, and Peter Anderson, draper.

Willa Anderson (then known as Minnie) had two brothers and attended Montrose Academy. After graduating first class in Classics at the University of St Andrews, 1910, she taught Latin and educational psychology in London. She met Orcadian poet Edwin Muir (1887–1959) in Glasgow in 1918 and they married the following year. They lived in London until 1921, in Prague, Germany, Italy, Montrose, and France from 1921 to 1926, then mainly in England from 1927 to 1935. Their son Gavin was born in 1927. To finance themselves, from 1925 to 1938 they taught, and translated from German and Czech, including Franz Kafka's *The Trial* (1937). In *Belonging* (1968), Willa Muir's memoir of her husband, she indicates that sometimes she did most of the translation, as the more fluent linguist, and at other times they shared the work. She also translated alone under the name 'Agnes Neill Scott'.

She published *Women: An Inquiry*, in 1925, exploring feminist ideas of the time, and the polemic *Mrs Grundy in Scotland* in 1936. She described her first novel, *Imagined Corners* (1931), as 'Quite pre-Marxian! But a good picture of the world I grew up in' (Journal 1948); it was reviewed as 'a memorable contribution to the cartography of Scotland' (*Glasgow Herald* 1931). Her second novel, the powerful *Mrs Ritchie* (1933), was darker and less autobiographical. She also wrote short pieces, radio talks, and two unpublished autobiographical novels, 'Mrs Muttoe and the Top Storey' (finished 1940) and 'The Usurpers' (1951–2).

The Muirs lived in St Andrews and Edinburgh between 1935 and 1945; after the war they lived in Prague and Rome, at Newbattle Abbey, Dalkeith and spent a year at Harvard, USA. Because her parents were from Shetland, Willa Muir saw herself as a 'displaced person': 'I grew up not fitting into Angus tradition and therefore critical, resentful, unsure. Hence my secret desire to *own* a house' (Journal 1947–8). They bought their only house in Cambridgeshire in 1956. Edwin Muir died in 1959. Willa Muir's last published works were *Living with Ballads* (1965) and *Belonging*. Displaced once more, she lived mainly in London from 1963, then in Dunoon from 1969.

Willa Muir's feminism and her intellectual interests are apparent in all her writing, published and private. Intellectual, passionate, insecure, inextricably connected with Edwin Muir during her life, she can now be assessed in her own right. Her novels, journals and letters illuminate an intellectual, European life as well as giving detailed and moving insight into growing up female in Scotland. A B C

• NLS: MSS 19670, 19674–19700, 19703, Willa Muir Letters (inc. Kathleen Raine, Tom Scott) and Verses; Univ. of St Andrews Library: MS Deposit 9/1–8, Willa Muir Notebooks (including Journals, 9/5), Miscellaneous Papers (including 'Mrs Muir's Reminiscences', 26 Feb. 1963, 9/2), and Letters (inc. Anna Mill, Edwin Muir, A. S. Neill, 9/8). Muir, W., Works as above and see *HSWW* (Bibl.). *Glasgow Herald*, 2 July 1931 (Review of *Imagined Corners*), 23 May 1970 (obit.); *ODNB* (2004).

MUNRO, Ailie, n. **Edmunds,** born Swatow, South China, 24 August 1918, died London 9 May 2002. Teacher, author and folk music scholar. Daughter of Dorothy Paton and the Rev. Frederick Edmunds, teacher-missionaries.

Ailie Edmunds's family moved to Edinburgh when she was seven. An avid reader from an early age, she became fascinated with literature through hearing stories of Beowulf and Grendel from her primary school teacher, Miss Rivington. She trained as a music teacher and taught in Paisley, where she supplemented class singing sessions with recordings by the great traditional singers *Jeannie Robertson and Jimmy MacBeath. Her appreciation of music was eclectic, spanning classical, blues, jazz and the dustbowl ballads of American folksinger Woody Guthrie, which chimed with her strong socialist and feminist beliefs.

In 1968, she joined the School of Scottish Studies in Edinburgh, where she worked in research, recording and lecturing on Scots song for 15 years. At the suggestion of composer Ronald Stevenson, she prepared the first commercially published study of Scottish folk music, *The Folk Music Revival in Scotland* (1984). Like other song collectors, she roamed the country seeking song variants and canvassing opinions, which she later collated. Alive to developments within traditional music, she updated the book in 1996. She was a consultant on the eight-volume *Greig-Duncan Folk Song Collection* and was proud to see its publication inspire the Edinburgh International Festival to take folksong out of the Fringe and grant it official status with a 21-concert series in 1995. RPA

• School of Scottish Studies Archives. Munro, A. Edmunds (1996) *The Democratic Muse*. *The Herald*, May 2002 (obit.); SSS Archive (2005) *TOCHER*, 58, pp. 50–6 (Appreciation). Private information.

MUNRO, Anna Gillies Macdonald,[‡] m. **Munro-Ashman,** born Glasgow 4 Oct. 1881, died Padworth, near Reading, 11 Sept. 1962. Suffragette, campaigner for women's rights. Daughter of Margaret Ann MacVean, and Evan Macdonald Munro, schoolmaster.

Anna Munro grew up in Edinburgh and remained there with her father and sister Eva after her mother's death in 1892. She campaigned for socialist James Connolly to be elected to Edinburgh Town Council in 1895, joining the Scottish Socialist Federation. Her life-long socialism dated from her experience of 'the extreme poverty, squalor and overcrowding in Edinburgh Cowgate' (Autobiographical notes). Through the Wesleyan Methodist Sisters of the People (whom she admired for their socialism rather than their religious faith), she spent three years among women working in the sweated trades in Shoreditch, London. By 1905 she was back in Scotland, living with her uncle, the Rev. Jacob Primmer, in Dunfermline. In October 1906, she joined the WSPU, becoming Dunfermline organiser, but with *Isabella Pearce, *Maggie Moffat and others, disillusioned with the WSPU for what they regarded as its betrayal of democratic principles, she followed *Teresa Billington-Greig into the WFL. In January 1908, she attempted to deliver a petition to the King on his way to open Parliament, and was imprisoned in Holloway for six weeks for demonstrating outside the house of the Secretary of State for War.

She became organising secretary of the Scottish Council of the WFL in February 1908; by 1913, there were ten WFL branches in Scotland (the WSPU had three). From 1910, she was on its national executive, campaigning across Britain. On 4 April 1913, she married Sydney Ashman, leather-worker, socialist and conscientious objector. In May, she was arrested while defying the government ban on speaking in Hyde Park; later, in a BBC talk, she recalled her thrill at receiving from Sydney a message sewn into a banana. She also described having to use communal bathwater and one-size prison uniforms.

Anna and Sydney Munro-Ashman lived at Thatcham and after 1929 at Padworth, and had a son and daughter. In 1915, she was elected president of the Reading WFL branch. She remained on the WFL executive after 1918, as president (1925–6) and treasurer (after 1933), until the WFL disbanded in 1961. She was a close friend of Charlotte Despard, former president of the WFL and a committed international socialist. She helped lead the WFL campaign for equal suffrage in the 1920s, speaking at an important rally in Hyde Park in July 1926 and writing of 'the joy of those who put on the armour for the . . . long warfare for the full political equality of women and men' (Eustance 1998, p. 348). As WFL delegate to the IWSA conference in Paris, 1926, she supported the case for economic equality and the removal of all restrictions on women's work. In the 1950s, she addressed UN seminars in Geneva and Paris on racial prejudice and juvenile delinquency. Once, writing to her husband, she said, 'Did you know when the socialist ideal first formed in a favourable aspect I thought people only had to hear it to embrace it. That is a good many years ago now. . .'. JR

• MS autobiographical notes, private collection.

AGC; Eustance, C. (1998) ' "Daring to be Free": the evolution of women's political identities in the Women's Freedom League 1907–30', DPhil., Univ. of York; ODNB (2004); WSM.
Private information: Bob Ashman.

MURE, Elizabeth, of Caldwell, born Caldwell, Renfrewshire, c. 1715, died c. 1791. Memoirist and estate manager. Daughter of Anne Stewart, and William Mure of Duncarnock.

One of four children, Elizabeth Mure came from a family of literate and improving landowners. Her generation embraced the 18th century. Her only brother, William (1718–76), was an MP and perhaps David Hume's oldest friend. She took over the family estate on William's death in 1776, until his son came of age, and returned it to profitability after his spending on improvements. She was an educated commentator on 18th-century Scotland. Her memoir (1790, in Mure of Caldwell, 1854) displays her knowledge of manners, religious and civic controversy, literature, women, education, and the economy – unsurprisingly, since Caldwell was at the heart of a developing linen industry and a centre of dairy production. She should be read in the context of Adam Smith, *Lady Grisell Baillie, and the great ministers of the age (as she thought): Hamilton, Wishart, Hutchison, Craig, Clark, and Leishman. From her years at Caldwell and her brother's house in Abbeyhill, outside Edinburgh, she has left us very little. But she thought keenly: 'May not even the love of Liberty become the disease of a State; and Men be enslaved in the worst way by their own passions?' (ibid., p. 270). DS

• NLS: Mure of Caldwell Papers: Ch. 2635–3799; MSS 4941–5018; NAS: GD1/481/1; GD1/481/5.
Mure, E. (1790) 'Memoir', in W. Mure of Caldwell (ed.) (1854) Selections from the Family Papers Preserved at Caldwell, I, pp. 259–72.
Crawfurd, G., and Robertson, G. (1818) The Shire of Renfrew; Marshall, R. K. (1983) Virgins and Viragos: a history of women in Scotland; Symonds, D. A. (1997) Weep Not for Me: women, ballads, and infanticide in early modern Scotland.

MURRAY, Anne, Lady Halkett, born London 4 Jan. 1623, died Dunfermline 22 April 1699. Writer. Daughter of Jane Drummond, royal governess, and Thomas Murray, Provost of Eton College.

Anne Murray is currently best remembered for collaborating with Colonel Joseph Bampfield (then a Royalist spy) to procure female clothing to disguise the Duke of York, later James VII and II, for his escape from St James's Palace in 1648.

Fearing retribution, she left London and arrived in Edinburgh in June 1650. When the English occupation of Scotland began, she accompanied the Countess of Dunfermline to Fyvie. En route, she attended to soldiers wounded at the Battle of Dunbar and, later, argued with Richard Overton about the execution of Charles I. On her return to Edinburgh in June 1652, Anne Murray was introduced to Sir James Halkett of Pitfirrane (d. 1670). Due to a combination of debt and anxiety about her prior relationship with Joseph Bampfield, she initially resisted James Halkett's proposals. Although the exact nature of their relationship is unknown, she had previously agreed to marry Joseph Bampfield, unaware that his first wife was still alive. Eventually, she married James Halkett privately at her sister's house in Kent on 2 March 1656, then the couple returned to Scotland.

According to her own account, the marriage was a happy one, although only one child survived infancy. She was devastated by James Halkett's death on 21 September 1670, which she mourned and recalled in numerous diary entries until her own death, 29 years later. Antagonistic relations with her step-son, Sir Charles Halkett, led to her removal to Abbot House in Dunfermline in February 1671. The persistent rumours relating to Joseph Bampfield prompted her to write her autobiographical *Memoirs*. Most criticism focuses on this text and consequently places Lady Halkett within the conventions of either autobiography or romance. A more extensive account of her life can be found in the 14 volumes of extant manuscript *Meditations*, written from 1650 to 1699 (NLS: MSS 6489–6502). There she predominantly depicts herself as an exemplary widow: 'A Widow indeed'. Plagued by debt, she maintained herself by taking in aristocratic boarders. She was active in the local community as a midwife, physician, and herbalist. Her religious beliefs were central to her life. Her writing records an active involvement in contemporary social, religious and political events, both locally and nationally. SLT

• BL: Add. MS 32376; NAS: GD29; NLS: Acc. 6112; NLS: MSS 6407, 6409, 6489–6502.
Halkett, A., Lady, Works as above, and see Bibls.
Loftis, J. C. (ed.) (1979) *The Memoirs of Anne, Lady Halkett and Ann, Lady Fanshawe*; Trill, S. (ed.) (2006) *Lady Anne Halkett: memoirs and selected meditations* (Bibl.).
HSWW (Bibl.); *ODNB* (2004) (see Halkett, Anne); Stevenson, D. (1996) 'A lady and her lovers: Anne, Lady Halkett', in D. Stevenson (ed.) *King or Covenant? Voices from Civil War*.

MURRAY, Lady Charlotte, *suo jure* **Viscountess of Strathallan,** born Dunkeld 2 August 1754, died Bath 4 April 1808. Gentlewoman and botanist. Daughter of Charlotte Murray, and John Murray, 3rd Duke of Atholl.

Charlotte Murray was the eldest of seven surviving children. Her paternal grandfather was the Jacobite general, Lord George Murray, while her maternal grandfather was his elder brother, the Hanoverian James Murray, 2nd Duke of Atholl. Educated in London, Charlotte Murray never married but later was styled Viscountess of Strathallan in her own right. Although she spent much of her life in England, she visited Scotland regularly and returned for an extended period in the early 1790s to look after the children of her brother John, 4th Duke of Atholl, following the death of his first wife, Jane Cathcart, in 1790. A 1767 portrait of the Duke and Duchess and their children by Johann Zoffany, set against the background of the River Tay at Dunkeld, shows Charlotte Murray in her early teens, clutching a floral wreath. She went on to live the comfortable life of a gentlewoman, eventually settling in the genteel surroundings of Bath. She was buried in Bath Abbey. Although little is known of her education, it is clear that she was an accomplished botanist. In Bath she compiled *The British Garden: A Descriptive Catalogue of Hardy Plants* (1799), intended as an accessible introduction to the subject, which she describes as 'open to almost every curious mind . . . and conducing to health, by affording a continual and engaging motive for air and exercise' (Murray 1799, i. p. vi). Based on the comparatively new Linnaean classification and using English names wherever possible, her book was described at the time of its publication as 'an instructive companion to young botanists' (cited in Henrey 1975, p. 584). CHD

• Blair Castle, Atholl Archives: Boxes 49, 59, 65, letters 1762–95; NLS: Acc. 4562 MSS *The British Garden* with collection of pressed flowers (Acc. 4567); NLS: MSS 3590–3, Graham of Balgowan papers.
Murray, C., Work as above.
Fussell, G. E. (1950) 'Lady botanists of the nineteenth century: The Rt. Hon. Lady Charlotte Murray', *Gardeners' Chronicle*, 2; Henrey, B. E. (1975) *British Botanical and Horticultural Literature before 1800*, ii, p. 584; Stewart-Murray, J. (1907) *Chronicles of the Atholl and Tullibardine Families*, vols 3, 4.

MURRAY, Lady Elizabeth, Countess of Dysart, *suo jure,* also **Lady Tollemache, Duchess of Lauderdale,** baptised London 28 Sept. 1626, died

Ham, Surrey, 5 June 1698. Heiress, royalist agent, courtier and patron. Daughter of Catherine Bruce of Clackmannan, and William Murray, 1st Earl of Dysart.

Elizabeth Murray was admired for her beauty and intellect, although later detractors noted she was 'violent in everything she set about . . . She had a restless ambition, lived at a vast expense, and was ravenously covetous' (Burnet 1723–4, p. 245). In 1648, she married Sir Lionel Tollemache (1624–69), with whom she had several children, including *Elizabeth Tollemache, later Duchess of Argyll. During the Interregnum she controversially befriended Cromwell, yet was also a key member of the secret Sealed Knot society, working for the restoration of Charles II in 1660, for which she was awarded a crown pension. At her father's death in 1655, she inherited the title of Countess of Dysart, being formally recognised as such in 1670. An important early patron of the artist Peter Lely, she commissioned from him portraits of various Scots, royalists and family members for her gallery at Ham House.

After her first husband's death, in 1669 she married John Maitland, 2nd Earl of Lauderdale (1616–82), a minister in Charles II's Cabal cabinet, four months after his first wife's death. The same year they were created Duke and Duchess of Lauderdale, and were sent to Scotland, where the Duke was Lord High Commissioner. Her cousin, the architect William Bruce, was employed to embellish the Lauderdales' Scottish homes, Lethington (Lennoxlove), Brunstane, and Thirlestane. Her corruption and political machinations equated her with her husband's despotic rule in Scotland, which lasted until he suffered a stroke in 1680. Much lampooned, she was the inspiration for the character Widow Blackacre in Wycherley's comedy, *The Plain Dealer* (1674). DAHBT

• Burnet, G. (1723–4) *Bishop Burnet's History of His Own Time*; Cripps, D. (1975) *Elizabeth of the Sealed Knot*; *ODNB* (2004); Paterson, R. C. (2003) *King Lauderdale: the corruption of power* (Bibl.); Taylor, D. A. H. B. (2002) ' "Ravenous Covetousness", Sir Peter Lely's portraits of the Duchess of Lauderdale', *History Scotland* vol. 2/2.

MURRAY, Eunice Guthrie, MBE, born Cardross, Dunbartonshire, 21 Jan. 1878, died Cardross 26 March 1960. Author, suffrage campaigner. Daughter of *Frances Stoddard (see Murray, Frances), author and antiquarian, and David Murray, lawyer and historian.

Third of four children, Eunice Guthrie lived all her life in Cardross, in a progressive and hospitable family. Her sister **Sylvia Winthrop Murray** (1875–1955), her constant companion and support, studied at Girton, became a missionary before working in their father's law firm, and joined both the NUWSS and the WFL. Eunice Murray was educated at St Leonards, but did not go to university. Voluntary work with the League of Pity, in a settlement and for temperance, drew her towards politics, with family support; her mother described her as likely to succeed because 'you are one who steers straight for the object ahead' (Murray 1920, p. 262). Having found local apathy and hostility to the suffrage cause in Cardross, she joined the WFL in 1908, becoming secretary for the 'Scottish scattered' (outside the cities). A leading speaker, she was president of the Glasgow branch and in 1913 of the Scottish Council of the WFL, and wrote several pamphlets, including *Prejudices Old and New* (1910). She joined a WFL delegation to Churchill in 1909, and spoke at the 1910 suffrage march in Edinburgh. From the WFL tea room and bookshop in Sauchiehall Street, Glasgow, she took part in its summer campaign 'doon the watter', in Rothesay. One listener felt that if everyone heard her speak, 'the vote would be won without delay' (*Glasgow Herald* 1913, quoted *AGC*, p. 152).

Although not openly critical of the WSPU, Eunice Murray disagreed with arson and favoured democratic decision-making. On 17 November 1913 she was charged with obstructing police at Downing Street and noted on the corner of the summons that the Scotsmen who saw the PM were not arrested; 'I as a Scottish woman was, when I went to see Asquith' (Women's Library). During the First World War, Eunice and Sylvia Murray did weekend relief work in munitions in Glasgow, and Eunice was absent on unspecified war work. In 1915, she requested an interview with the Secretary for Scotland, proposing an emergency measure granting women votes because of their war effort. After a political novel, *The Hidden Tragedy* (1917), she wrote more fiction, local history, a memoir of her mother and, notably, works on women's and social history. Breaking with traditional approaches to Scottish history, her *Scottish Women of Bygone Days* (1930) discussed social and domestic life, funeral practices, witchcraft, women's education and early struggles for emancipation. *A Gallery of Scottish Women* (1935) was in the Scottish tradition of brief lives. Lectures to the SWRI resulted in a book on Scottish historical costume, trades and tradition, illustrated by dolls in costumes she made herself (*Scottish Homespun* 1947). In 1918, she stood unsuccessfully for Glasgow (Bridgeton) as an Independent – the first woman to stand for parliament in Scotland. She came third. In December 1919, she was elected councillor in Dunbartonshire, where she worked on education, health and housing and campaigned for sex equality measures. She hated complacency: 'A good cause is an inspiration . . . So many people are content with things as they are – this is one of the hazards of life' (diary, July 1896, quoted Mayhall, p. 81). SI

• Univ. of Glasgow Library: Murray Collection; Women's Library: Autograph Letters collection (vol. XX); Metropolitan Police summons, 17 Nov. 1913; Unpub. diaries (private collection).

Murray, E. G., Works as above, and (1920) *Frances Murray, a Memoir by her Daughter.*

AGC; http://special.lib.gla.ac.uk/collection/murray.html; Mayhall, L. E. N. (2000) 'The making of a suffragette: the uses of reading 1890–1918', in G. Behlmer and F. Leventhal (eds) *Singular Continuities,* pp. 75–88; *ODNB* (2004).

MURRAY, Flora, CBE, born Cummertrees, Dumfries, 8 May 1869, died Penn, Bucks., 28 July 1923. Doctor and suffrage campaigner. Daughter of Grace Harriet Graham, and Captain John Murray RN, landed proprietor.

Flora Murray qualified MBChBS in 1903 (MD 1905) at the University of Durham, after training in London. In 1908 she became assistant anaesthetist at the Chelsea Hospital for Women, and joined the WSPU. She organised a first-aid unit to treat women injured in militant suffrage actions – notably on 'Black Friday' in November 1910. With her companion Louisa Garrett Anderson (1873–1943), daughter of Elizabeth Garrett Anderson, the first woman to qualify as a doctor in Britain, she worked at a nursing-home in Notting Hill Gate treating hunger-striking suffragette prisoners on release. She personally attended Emmeline Pankhurst and campaigned against forced feeding. In 1912, she and Louisa Garrett Anderson founded the Women's Hospital for Children in Marylebone.

In August 1914, the two women offered a fully equipped surgical unit to the French Red Cross. Their first hospital was in the new Hotel Claridge in Paris, where Flora Murray was Médecin Chef and Louisa Garrett Anderson chief surgeon. In treating the wounded, heavy surgery and acute sepsis were the norm. As the 'first women to break

down the prejudice of the British War Office' (Crawford 2002, p. 262), they were asked to organise a British Army hospital near Boulogne, then to run the Endell Street Military Hospital in London, with 17 wards. From March 1916 to October 1919, Flora Murray was Doctor-in-Charge (rank equivalent to Lieutenant-Colonel). She advised *Mona Chalmers Watson on forming the WAAC. All their hospitals were officered, staffed and run by women, except for a few male orderlies. Flora Murray wrote a vivid account of their experience (Murray 1920), dedicated to Louisa Garrett Anderson, 'Bold, cautious, true and my loving comrade'. They are buried in adjacent graves in Penn. SI

• Univ. of Durham Library: Archives and Special Collections.

Murray, F. (1920) *Women as Army Surgeons* [1914–19]

Crawford, E. (2002) *Enterprising Women*; Marlow, J. (ed.) (2000) *Votes for Women*; *ODNB* (2004) (Chambers, Helen); *WSM*.

MURRAY, Frances Porter, n. **Stoddard,** born New York, USA, 23 Feb. 1843, died Cardross 3 April 1919. Suffragist. Daughter of Frances Stoddard, and Arthur Stoddard, merchant and carpet manufacturer.

The Stoddard family moved to Scotland in 1844, living first in Glasgow and then in Renfrewshire. Frances Stoddard was educated largely at home, but went to finishing school in London in 1861. In 1867, she and her sister Alice spent 18 months visiting relatives in the USA, where they met Harriet Beecher Stowe; there she was introduced to 'women's rights', about which she vacillated. Only much later in life did she become a committed suffragist. In June 1872, after a lengthy courtship, she married David Murray (1842–1928), a prominent Glasgow lawyer and medieval historian. She had been reluctant to give up her independence, and indeed never wore a wedding ring on the grounds that wives should not do so unless their husbands did the same. The Murrays travelled extensively together, both before and after their marriage, sharing hobbies such as archaeology, geology and botany. They both took a keen interest in the GAHEW and Frances Murray attended lectures for women held at the University of Glasgow. She was also active for many years in delivering lectures and organising concerts, particularly in Cardross, where they had settled.

They had one son and three daughters, the eldest of whom, *Eunice Guthrie Murray, became a prominent member of the WFL, writer and historian. Another sister, **Sylvia Winthrop Murray** (1875–1955) was also active in the WFL and went to China as part of the China Inland Mission, later working in her father's firm. Like many women of her class and generation, Frances Murray encouraged her daughters to press for and take up opportunities that she had been denied. She urged Eunice, who was speaking at suffrage rallies, to 'Go ahead my daughter – you possess on both sides fighting blood' (Murray 1920, p. 235). In 1910, she joined Eunice at a suffrage demonstration in Edinburgh and led one of the processions. Looking back on her already long life in 1917, she wrote in defence of the Victorians, noting that whereas in her youth, little higher education and few careers were open to women, 'The Victorian Era burst through this bondage, and now we have schools and colleges for girls and women' (ibid., p. 264). As a young woman, in 1877, Frances Murray had said, 'Before I die I look forward to the fulfilment of sex equality' (ibid., p. 164). She lived to vote in the 1918 election. EG/GMN

• Murray, E. (1920) *Frances Murray: a memoir – by her daughter.*

MURRAY, Sarah *see* **AUST, Sarah** (1744–1811)

MYLNE, Margaret, n. Thomson [P. M. Y.], born Colinton, Midlothian, 2 Dec. 1806, died London 15 Jan. 1892. Writer on the situation of women. Daughter of Margaret Millar, and Professor John Thomson of Edinburgh.

Grand-daughter of John Millar, Professor of Civil Law at Glasgow and Enlightenment historian, Margaret Thomson grew up in the liberal academic circles around her father and her uncle, Professor James Mylne of Glasgow. She recalled how the Reform Act of 1832 had inspired her life-long support for women's suffrage. Watching the Whig success at the Edinburgh hustings with her family and *Eliza Fletcher in 1832, she had felt: 'as soon as ever I understood the

benefits expected from a £10 franchise, I began to wish that female householders should have it too, thinking it only fair' (Mylne 1872, p. iii). In 1841, Dr James Young Simpson and the editor of the *Westminster Review*, William Hickson, persuaded her to publish in that journal, using the pseudonym 'P. M. Y.', a pioneering article, 'Woman and her Social Position', ostensibly a review of major works on the subject by such as Sydney Smith, Anna Jameson, Caroline Norton and Harriet Martineau. She identified the progress of western civilisation with the gradual, if still incomplete, equalising of the condition of the sexes, in the spirit of her grandfather's writings. Ten years before Harriet Taylor Mill's better-known essay on 'The Enfranchisement of Women', Margaret Thomson celebrated the passing of 'the distinguishing and opprobrious epithet of blue-stocking' (P. M. Y. 1841, p. 24), called for women who exercised the duties of citizens to enjoy the right to vote, and demanded the reform of the laws affecting married women. She married her cousin, John Millar Mylne, WS, in Edinburgh in 1843. They had two daughters and later moved to London. Margaret Mylne signed the petition for women's suffrage presented to the House of Commons in 1866, and in 1872 recorded her continuing commitment to that cause in her introduction to a new edition of her 1841 article. JR

• P. M. Y. (1841) 'Woman and Her Social Position', *Westminster Review*, 35, pp. 24–52, (1840, 1841) Reviews, ibid., 34, pp. 502–4 and 35, pp. 534–5; Mylne, M. (1872) 'A Letter to My Friends', *Woman and Her Social Position. An article reprinted from the Westminster Review, No. LXVIII, 1841.* [Fletcher, E.] (1875) *Autobiography of Mrs Fletcher with Letters and Other Family Memorials*, M. Richardson, ed.; (1892) *Englishwoman's Review*, CCXIII, pp. 95–6 (obit.); Rendall, J. (2005) ' "Women that would plague me with rational conversation": aspiring women and Scottish Whigs, c. 1790–1830', in S. Knott and B. Taylor, (eds) *Feminism and the Enlightenment.*

N

NAIRNE, Carolina, Lady *see* **OLIPHANT, Carolina, Lady Nairne** (1766–1845)

NAN EACHAINN FHIONNLAIGH *see* **MACKINNON, Nan** (1902–82)

NASMYTH, Jane, born 29 March 1788, died 11 May 1867; **NASMYTH, Barbara,** born 15 April 1790, died 21 Feb. 1870; **NASMYTH, Margaret,** born 11 April 1791, died 3 Nov. 1869; **NASMYTH, Elizabeth,** m1 **Terry,** m2 **Richardson,** born 2 Sept. 1793, died 10 July 1862; **NASMYTH, Anne,** m. **Bennett,** born

13 Nov. 1798, died 28 Jan. 1874; **NASMYTH, Charlotte,** born 17 Feb. 1804, died 26 July 1884. All born Edinburgh, died Putney. Landscape artists. Daughters of Barbara Foulis, and Alexander Nasmyth, landscape artist.

Alexander Nasmyth (1758–1840) was the foremost Scottish landscape artist of his day. All six daughters and their brother Patrick became landscape artists. Elizabeth married Daniel Terry (1789–1829), the actor, in 1815; her second husband was dictionary author Charles Richardson (1775–1865), whom she married in 1835. Anne married William Bennett (d. 1866), a Manchester engineer, in 1838. After Alexander Nasmyth's death in 1840, a collection of 155 works by father and children was sold at auction. The four unmarried sisters and their mother moved to England to join their siblings. Their father's will and the aid of their wealthy brother, engineer James, ensured the sisters' financial independence.

Alexander Nasmyth was central to the development of the emerging commercial art world of early-19th-century Edinburgh. The art classes at his house at 47 York Place included classes for 'ladies', taught by his daughters. The eldest, Jane, nicknamed 'Old Solid' by the family, also helped her father in his business affairs. Among the pupils was *Mary Somerville. Barbara and Anne also ran classes in London. In addition to providing art instruction, the daughters were studio assistants to their father. All exhibited in their own right in public art institutions in Manchester, London and Edinburgh. Most of their works were small and finely detailed landscape paintings in oil or watercolour. Barbara's work focused mainly on Scottish subjects, while Jane and Margaret painted both English and Scottish landscapes. Elizabeth contributed designs to Walter Scott's armoury. Anne concentrated on Highland scenery, while Charlotte's painting was the most flamboyant and wildest of the sisters' works. SN

• Cooksey, J. C. B. (1991) *Alexander Nasmyth*; *DSAA*; *ODNB* (2004) (Nasmyth family) (Bibl.).

NEIL, Annie Innes Clydesdale (Andy),‡ m. **Dundas,** born Glasgow 2 Dec. 1924, died Glasgow 11 Dec. 2004; **NEIL, Christina Marion Smith (Chrissie),**‡ born Glasgow 22 August 1927, died Glasgow 9 Sept. 1991. Rally champions. Daughters of Annie Neil, draftswoman, and George H. Neil, flesher and pig farmer.

Both Andy and Chrissie Neil went to Glasgow High School for Girls. When the Second World War broke out, Andy Neil, aged 15, jumped at the chance to leave school and work on the farm, learning to drive, and regularly driving her father's trucks to the meat market in the East End of Glasgow. She never did sit a driving test. She loved working with the pigs, and was proud that she could lift as heavy loads as the men. Chrissie Neil, being younger, was evacuated to Pitlochry with her school, went on to graduate in French at the University of Glasgow, and also joined the family business, in the office. When Andy Neil developed an interest in competitive rally driving, she persuaded Chrissie to take an intensive driving course. Chrissie passed her test in under a week and the Neil sisters entered the world of rallying, Andy as driver and Chrissie as navigator. Joining the Lanarkshire Car Club, and going on to win a string of Scottish and British awards, they added a touch of glamour to the rally circuit. Ladies' teams were unusual, let alone sisters. At the peak of their rallying, Andy set her heart on a Morgan sports car, for which there was a lengthy waiting list. But after Peter Morgan saw her performing competitive road trials, he promised them the next Morgan off the production line, and they won further awards in 'Toots' the Morgan. The Neil sisters entered the Monte Carlo Rally twice, in 1954 and 1955 (Chrissie entered alone in 1958, when Andy, who had married Frank Dundas, was expecting her first child.) They always had a tremendous send-off from the RAC in Glasgow, and successfully finished the Monte both times, a significant achievement before seat belts and crash helmets. The sisters took on the running of the pig farm when their father became ill, later selling up to create a small industrial estate on the site. Andy went on to have a successful career in sales, and Chrissie became an international fashion designer, trading as Smith Innes. CM

• *The Herald*, 17 Dec. 2004 (obit. Andy Neil).
Personal knowledge.

NEILL, Elizabeth Grace, n. **Campbell,** born Edinburgh 24 May 1846, died Wellington, NZ, 18 August 1926. Founding nursing reformer in New Zealand. Daughter of Maria Grace Cameron, and James Archibald Campbell, landowner.

Grace Campbell grew up on the shores of Loch Awe, and never lost her Highland identity, despite later moving south. After training as a nurse with the Anglican sisterhood of St John in London, she married Dr Channing Neill in 1879, which led to estrangement from her father. In 1886 the Neills, with their son (born 1882), moved to Australia. Widowed in 1888, Grace Neill made a living through journalism and her own typewriting business. This led to her appointment to a Queensland Royal Commission on Labour Conditions. She then moved to New Zealand, where she became the first female inspector of factories. However, it was in another pioneering role, as female inspector of hospitals and charitable institutions, that Grace Neill was best known. Trained under the Nightingale ethos, she made her mark as a nursing reformer between 1895 and her retirement in 1906. She established the first national scheme for state examination and registration of nurses in 1901, and for midwives in 1904, going on to establish the state-run St Helen's Maternity hospitals to train midwives. Tall, red-headed and cigarette-smoking, Grace Neill was the first woman to gain a senior position in New Zealand's public service, a founder member of the ICN in 1899, and an honorary member of the Matrons' Council of Great Britain. When she died in 1926, obituaries testified to her strong character, intellectual qualities and keen sense of humour. MT

• Alexander Turnbull Library, Wellington: A. E. I. Bennett Collection, Folders 176, 211; Archives New Zealand, Wellington: Seddon Papers, 3/60.
Evening Post (Wellington) 31 August 1894, 19 August 1926; Neill, J. O. C. (1961) *Grace Neill*; Tennant, M. (1978) 'Mrs Grace Neill, in the Department of Asylums, Hospitals and Charitable Institutions', *NZ Jour. Hist.*, April, pp. 3–16; (1992) 'Neill, Elizabeth Grace 1846–1926', *DNZB*, vol. II [updated, 2003]: http://www.dnzb.govt.nz/

NEWBERY, Jessie, n. **Rowat,** born Paisley 28 May 1864, died Corfe Castle, Dorset, 27 April 1948. Embroiderer and designer. Daughter of Margaret Hill, and William Rowat, shawl manufacturer.

The eldest of four children, Jessie Rowat was educated in Paisley and at an Edinburgh boarding school. Following a visit to Italy, she attended GSA where she met and, in 1889, married the Headmaster, Francis H. Newbery (1855–1946). In 1894 she began to teach embroidery, effectively establishing a department and putting it on the artistic map. Embroidery became part of the diploma course in applied design at GSA and in 1901 special classes were introduced for the training of teachers. Jessie Newbery's radical views created new aesthetic standards, encouraging simplicity of

design, good craftsmanship and the use of easily available materials. The department won international renown. Her creative individuality was expressed in the clothes she made for herself and her children, embroidering distinctive collars, yokes, belts and cuffs that influenced many of her students. Her work, which frequently used the women's suffrage colours of green, white and violet, was exhibited in Britain, France, Germany, Italy and the US and in many art magazines of the period, notably *The Studio, Das Eigenkleid der Frau* and *Moderne Stickerein.* Though best remembered for embroidery, she also taught enamelling, mosaic work and book decoration in the 1890s, and designed stained glass, metalwork and a carpet for Alexander Morton & Co. She retired in 1908, but continued embroidery and her active support of the WSPU. **Mary Newbery** (1890–1985), the younger of her two daughters, studied painting and design at GSA, then in Paris. She married Archibald Sturrock and lived in Edinburgh where, in later life, she enjoyed popularity as a painter of flowers in watercolour. LA

• Arthur, E. (1980) 'Glasgow School of Art embroideries, 1894–1920', *Journal of the Decorative Arts Society*, 4, pp. 18–25; Burkhauser, J. (ed.) (1990) *Glasgow Girls*; Cumming, E. (ed.) (1992) *Glasgow 1900 Art & Design*; Macfarlane, F. C. and Arthur, E. (1980) *Glasgow School of Art Embroidery 1894–1920*; *ODNB* (2004) (see Glasgow Girls); Swain, M. (1973) 'Mrs Jessie R. Newbery (1864–1948)', *Embroidery* 24, pp. 104–7, (1978) 'Mrs Newbery's dress', *Costume* 12, pp. 64–73.

NEWBIGIN, Marion Isabel, born Alnwick 23 Sept. 1869, died Edinburgh 20 July 1934. Geographer. Daughter of Emma France, and James Lesslie Newbigin, pharmacist.

Marion Newbigin was one of eight children: all five sisters were given as good an education as possible – and became feminists; the sons were told to make their way in the world unaided. She studied at University College, Aberystwyth and at the University of Edinburgh (BSc 1893, DSc 1898 by University of London external degree). A student at Edinburgh's extra-mural School of Medicine for Women, she later lectured in biology and zoology at Edinburgh, at Bedford College, London, and at Patrick Geddes's Edinburgh summer schools. She was highly regarded as editor of the RSGS *Scottish Geographical Magazine* from 1902 to 1934: 'it is difficult to over-estimate the part which Dr Newbigin played in encouraging original work' (Taylor 1934, p. 367). She also made important original contributions, notably in plant and animal biology and geography, climatology, the political geography of the Balkans and regional geography, and helped to analyse collections dating from the Challenger expedition of 1872–6. The claim that she should be credited with laying 'the foundations of scientific method' on which all Scottish geography was built (Adams 1984, p. 10) is, however, unwarranted. Her early training in biology, and in zoology and oceanography underlay her holistic views of human-nature relationships, views reflected in unjustly neglected books (1898, 1901) and in later works of synthesis (1929, 1936). Her work, highly regarded by contemporaries, has continuing resonance, demonstrating commitment to the scientific understanding of the natural world, and to the need to think geographically in order to be a responsible global citizen. CW

• NLS: MSS 7782–3, Newbigin papers; RSGS Membership archive: corr., uncatalogued MSS.
Newbigin, M. (1898) *Colour in Nature: a study in biology*, (1901) *Life by the Seashore: an introduction to natural history*, (1929) *A New Regional Geography of the World*, (1936) *Plant and Animal Geography*.
Adams, I. et al. (eds) (1984) *The Making of Scottish Geography: 100 years of the RSGS*; Maddrell, A. M. C. (1997) 'Scientific discourse and the geographical work of Marion Newbigin', *Scot. Geog. Mag.* 113, 1, pp. 33–41; *ODNB* (2004); Taylor, E. G. R. (1934) 'Obituary: Dr Marion Newbigin', *Geog. Journ.*, 84, p. 367.
Private information (family).

NEWTON, Janet, of Dalcove, fl. c. 1520–c. 1566. Heiress. Daughter of James Newton of Dalcove.

Janet Newton was James Ker of Mersington's ward. He brutally exploited his legal right to determine her marriage during the 1530s, objecting when she sought to marry Adam Ker of Shaw. For the right to 'mary quhat partey she plesis' (NAS, GD239/2/1/8) and be 'infeft in' (put in legal possession of) her father's lands, he demanded she pay him a £2,000 Scots penalty within a month. Janet Newton was forced to sell a third of her lands to him and mortgage the rest. This was a heavy price, but the methods used by her unscrupulous guardian were not illegal. To make matters worse, Dalcove was attacked by the English in 1544 and 1545. Janet Newton was still trying to buy back her lands in 1550. Widowed before 1554, she married Ralph Haliburton. Her son Thomas Ker of Dalcove succeeded her rather more peaceably. MMM

• NAS: GD239/1/2, GD239/2/1/2, 8, Papers of the Don family of Newton; NAS: RD1/6 fo. 222, Register of Deeds; *RMS*, iii, nos. 1364, 2033; *RSS*, iii, no. 2330.
Anderson, J. and Angus, W. (eds) (1911) *Protocol Book of Sir William Corbet*, nos. 56, 79; Maley, T. and Elliot, W. (eds) (1993) *Selkirk Protocol Books 1511–1547*, pp. 118–19.

NICHOL, Elizabeth Pease, n. **Pease,** born Darlington 5 Jan. 1807, died Edinburgh 3 Feb. 1897. Abolitionist and suffragist. Daughter of Elizabeth Beaumont, and Joseph Pease, wool manufacturer.

Elizabeth Pease was born into a north-east England Quaker family with a tradition of involvement in the major social issues of the day. She was actively engaged throughout her life in many campaigns. She founded a Women's Abolition of Slavery Society in Darlington, not least because women were frequently excluded from the public meetings of the anti-slavery groups, and she was also involved in the campaign in support of the Reform Act of 1832.

On 6 July 1853, she married John Nichol (1804–59), Professor of Astronomy at the University of Glasgow, and moved to Glasgow; the marriage resulted in her disownment by Quakers, as John Nichol was not a member of the Society of Friends. She moved to Edinburgh shortly after her husband's death in 1859, but continued her active involvement in the social concerns of the day. She was treasurer of the ENSWS, on which she worked with *Eliza Wigham and her sister Jane, having already met Eliza during the anti-slavery campaign. Along with some 239 other female householders, she claimed the vote in 1868. She was also involved in the efforts to open up medical education to women. In 1873, she became a member of the first school board to be established in Scotland as a result of the Education Act, and shortly afterwards established the Scottish branch of the anti-vivisection society formed in London by Frances Power Cobbe. Elizabeth Cady Stanton, US campaigner for women's rights, records that, on a visit to Edinburgh in 1882, she met Elizabeth Pease Nichol and the two Wigham sisters for the first time since the Anti-Slavery Convention of 1840: 'Yet I knew Mrs Nichol at once: her strongly marked face was not readily forgotten' (Stanton [1898] 1971, p. 354). Elizabeth Pease Nichol's Edinburgh home was apparently a port-of-call for many American and English reformers and philanthropists and Stanton also notes that 'Though over eighty years of age, [she] was still awake to all the questions of the hour, and generous in her hospitalities as of yore.' (ibid., p. 355). PFB

• Stanton, E. C. [1898] (1971) *Eighty Years and More: reminiscences, 1815–97*, also at http://digital.library.upenn.edu/women/

Hall, C., McClelland, K., Rendall, J. (2000) *Defining the Victorian Nation: class, race, gender and the British Reform Act of 1867*; Orde, A. (2000) *Religion, Business and Society in north-east England: the Pease family of Darlington in the nineteenth century*; *ODNB* (2004); Stoddart, A. M. (1899) *Elizabeth Pease Nichol*; WSM.

'NICNEVEN' (or Nicnevin, Nicniven), a name or soubriquet used by several witches from the 1560s onwards.

Meaning in Gaelic 'little daughter of the holy one', 'Nicneven' may indicate a claim to supernatural abilities. (A possible link to 'Nemain', a shadowy war-goddess of early Irish mythology, cannot be substantiated without earlier Scottish references.) A 'Nic Neville' was executed in St Andrews in 1569. However, several records associate the name with Monzie or Crieff. John Burgh, a folk healer convicted of witchcraft in 1643, said that his knowledge was 'learned be him frome a wedow woman namet Neane VcClerich, of thrie scoir of yeiris of aidge, quha was sister dochter to Nik Neveing that notorious and infamous witche in Monaie, quha for hir sorcerie and witchcraft was brunt four scoir of yeir since or thairby' (Smith 1974, p. 598). 'VcClerich' ('clerk's, or priest's, daughter') may have been another soubriquet, but she was a real person and her aunt evidently was too. The apparent existence of two 'Nicnevens' in the 1560s indicates that the name was already traditional, and its origins are now lost.

The name next appeared in Alexander Montgomerie's celebrated poem, 'Flyting with Polwarth' (c. 1580). In this ribald, comic account of the birth and upbringing of his poetic antagonist, Patrick Hume of Polwarth, the infant Polwarth was suckled by 'Nicneven' amid much burlesque witch and fairy lore. One version of the poem mentioned 'Kait of Creife'. This may be connected with a tradition, recorded in the 19th century, about a lucky blue stone then held by the Grahams of Inchbrakie. 'Kate McNiven' of Monzie, a witch about to be executed, spat out the stone for the laird in gratitude for his intercession. In the late 20th century, a new 'Nicneven' tradition was created when the neo-pagan movement adopted her as a 'Celtic goddess'. JG

• Hanham, A. (1969) '"The Scottish Hecate": a wild witch chase', *Scottish Studies*, 13; Henderson, L. and Cowan, E. J. (2000) *Scottish Fairy Belief: a history*; Simpson, J. (1995) '"The weird sisters wandering": burlesque witchcraft in Montgomerie's 'Flyting', *Folklore*, 106; Smith, J. I. (ed.) (1974) *Selected Justiciary Cases, 1624–1650* vol. iii.

NITHSDALE, Winifred, Countess of *see* **MAXWELL, Lady Winifred, Countess of Nithsdale** (1672–1749)

NOBLE, Mary Jessie McDonald, born Edinburgh 23 Feb. 1911, died Lasswade, Midlothian, 20 July 2002. Plant pathologist, mycologist. Daughter of Helen Graham Millar, and John Noble, pharmacist.

Mary Noble was educated at Mary Erskine School, Edinburgh 1920–9, and at the University of Edinburgh 1929–35. After an honours degree in botany, her PhD was on the mycological aspects of seed pathology, winning the Gunning Victoria Jubilee Prize. Having joined the plant pathology service of the Board of Agriculture, now the SASA, she was concerned with the health of flax fields during the Second World War (linen was used to cover aircraft wings). She was later in charge of seed pathology and mycology. From 1950, she was a member of the ISTA, work which continued after her retirement in 1971. She presided over the first International Symposium of Seed Pathology in 1978, and travelled widely, giving talks and workshops in developing countries. At home she gave much support to Suntrap, the gardening advice centre in Edinburgh.

Mary Noble was instrumental in producing the authoritative *Handbook of Seed-borne Diseases* (4th edn., ISTA, 1990), and the ISTA *Handbook of Seed Health Testing*, as well as many papers on a variety of plant diseases. Vice-president of the British Mycological Society in 1958, she edited its journal 1972–8. In 1975, she began research on Charles McIntosh, naturalist and postman, whose importance to Scottish cryptogams and connection with Beatrix Potter was unrecognised. She reinstated Beatrix Potter's reputation as a mycologist and co-authored *A Victorian Naturalist – Beatrix Potter's drawings from the Arnitt collection*, lecturing and writing widely thereon. She became FRSE 1958, Companion of the Imperial Service Order 1968, and received the Neill Medal in 1973. JM

• Noble, M. Works as above.

(2003) *BSS News*, 80, March; Hadley, G. (2003) 'Mary Noble (1911–2002): an appreciation', *The Mycologist*, 17, 2, Feb.; *The Scotsman*, 8 August 2002 (obit.).

O

O'DONNELL, Finola (Inion Dubh, 'the dark daughter'),
born western Highlands c. 1552, died c. 1610. Daughter of *Lady Agnes Campbell, and James MacDonnell of Dunyvaig and the Glens.

Finola O'Donnell is credited, along with her mother, with establishing a Scottish-Irish network central to mid-16th century revolt against the English. In August 1569 she went to Ireland to marry the Ulster chief Hugh O'Donnell (d. 1593). This act, together with the marriage of her mother to Turlough Luineach O'Neill, brought together the O'Neills and the O'Donnells, previously rivals, and united the Ulster clans against the English colonisers. Finola O'Donnell possessed a dowry of 1,200 Scottish mercenary troops whose presence, swelling the ranks of Irish rebels, the English viewed with alarm. Although ultimately these alliances were not strong enough to repel the colonial forces, the two women were at the centre of the Scottish-Irish network, working to keep Ulster independent from English rule in Dublin.

Finola O'Donnell's activities were monitored throughout the late 16th century. Her own testimonies provide evidence of female agency in networks and rebellion. In 1588, she stated that she would hire the Spaniards to stir up wars against the English. The threat of Spanish invasion was rightly feared by the English in this period. In 1590, she had plans to overthrow the English sheriff of Donegal. However, by 1600, Irish rebellion was weakening, and despite mercenary support, the Irish and Scottish forces were outnumbered by the English. Nevertheless, she and her supporters waged an aggressive campaign against English governors, assassinating several English officials. After the Flight of the Earls from Ireland in 1606, the O'Donnell clan left Ireland for Spain. The eventual defeat of the Irish rebels also marked the end of a period when Ireland could call upon Scottish military aid. AEK

• PRO (National Archives), Kew, Calendar of State Papers, Ireland, vols 29 (1569), 30 (1570), 3 (1588–92).
Knox, A. (2002) ' "Barbarous and Pestiferous Women": female criminality, violence and aggression in sixteenth- and seventeenth-century Scotland and Ireland', in Y. G. Brown and R. Ferguson (eds) Twisted Sisters; ODNB (2004) (Campbell, Agnes).

OGILVY, Marion, lady of Melgund,
born probably Airlie before 1503, died Melgund June 1575. Mistress of Cardinal David Beaton. Daughter of Janet Lyle, and James, 1st Lord Ogilvy of Airlie.

Born of her father's fourth marriage, Marion Ogilvy was poorly provided for at his death in 1504 (except as an alternative bride in her sister's marriage contract of 1503, not implemented). Her association with David Beaton (c. 1494–1546), then abbot of Arbroath, may have begun around 1525 when she wound up her late mother's affairs at Airlie. She became the mother of Beaton's eight recorded children, rearing them at Ethie, his castle near Arbroath. She built up considerable property, held from the abbey, frequently appearing in court to defend her rights. An able manager of her affairs, she used a seal and could write. When her sons studied in France she sent them money through an Italian banker. In 1543 the Cardinal obtained a secular property, the barony of North Melgund near Brechin, settling it on her 'in liferent' and on their oldest son heritably. Melgund Castle, which he built or rebuilt for his family, displayed the armorial bearings of them both, like those of a landed married couple. She was with Beaton in the castle at St Andrews the night before his assassination on 29 May 1546. After his death, her houses were attacked and papers stolen, but were returned after successful court action.

In spring 1547 Marion Ogilvy married William Douglas (otherwise unknown) but was widowed by 18 September; Douglas may have died at the battle of Pinkie (9 September). She spent the rest of her life managing affairs at Melgund, joined in 1572 by her daughter Margaret (see Chisholm, Jane), estranged from her husband, David, 10th Earl of Crawford. The castle was a rallying point for *Queen Mary's Angus supporters after her escape from Lochleven in 1568. Several relatives were prosecuted as Catholic recusants. When Marion Ogilvy died, she left over £3,000 Scots, including £1,000 in ready money. She asked for burial in the Ogilvy aisle of Kinnell church. Less than two weeks later, her family formally made peace with the Cardinal's surviving assassin, John Leslie of Parkhill.

Marion Ogilvy exemplifies many landed women who managed their affairs single-handed. Her association with the Cardinal, differing little outwardly from marriage, offended those who deplored the double standard by which prelates prosecuted those advocating married clergy, yet lived in open disregard of the rule of clerical celibacy. MHBS

• Sanderson, M. H. B. (1987) *Mary Stewart's People* (Bibl.), (2001) *Cardinal of Scotland: David Beaton c. 1494–1546*; **ODNB* (2004).

OLIPHANT, Carolina, Lady Nairne [Mrs Bogan of Bogan], m. **Nairne,** born Gask, Perthshire, 16 August 1766, died Gask 26 Oct. 1845. Songwriter. Daughter of Margaret Robertson, and Laurence Oliphant, laird of Gask.

The Oliphant family was old and distinguished. Carolina Oliphant's grandfather and father were Jacobites. One of seven children, she was educated at home and read widely: she admired Thomas Campbell and Robert Burns (although not the more robust pieces) and persuaded her brother Laurence to subscribe to the 1786 edition of Burns. She was equally familiar with Scotland's song traditions, performed music to a high standard, and painted. In 1806, she married her second cousin, Major William Nairne (1757–1830), born in Ireland to a Perthshire Jacobite family. They moved to Edinburgh, latterly to Caroline Cottage in Western Duddingston where their son, William Murray Nairne, was born in 1808. She became Baroness Nairne in 1824 when the act of attainder affecting her husband's title was reversed. After his death, she spent 12 years in England, Ireland and, from 1834, continental Europe, with her son, her sister Mrs Keith, and her niece, Margaret Harriet Steuart. During this time she suffered the deaths of her niece, the poet Caroline Oliphant, her nephew Charles Steuart, and Lord Nairne, her only child. In 1843, she returned to Gask where she had a stroke and declined in health. She is buried in the chapel there.

Celebrated as 'The Flower of Strathearn', Carolina Oliphant is now remembered for her songs, although none appeared under her name while she was alive, for reasons of respectability. Her work shows knowledge of traditional idioms in words and music, making it eminently suitable for performance. It appeared in her lifetime under the pseudonym of 'Mrs Bogan of Bogan' in Robert Purdie's six-volume *The Scottish Minstrel* (1821–4). The writer was first named, with Mrs Keith's approval, in *Lays from Strathearn, by Carolina, Baroness Nairne, author of 'The Land o' the Leal, etc.' arranged . . . by Finlay Dun* (1846). Many pieces

deal with Scotland's past. The Jacobite 'Will ye no come back again?' laments the loss of 'Bonnie Charlie'. 'Castell Gloom' represents a country seat ruined through civil war. Despite her family's Episcopal affiliations, Carolina Oliphant wrote several Covenanting pieces: 'The Pentland Hills' condemns 'fell Claverhouse' and mourns the 'brave and martyr'd men' who fell at Rullion Green. 'Dunnottar Castle' celebrates the actions of Elizabeth Ogilvy in saving the Scottish regalia from Cromwell (see Fletcher, Christian). She often celebrated working people such as 'The Pleughman'. 'Caller Herrin' honours those who put their lives in danger at sea: 'Darkling as they faced the billows,/A' to fill the woven willows'. It has obvious sincerity although, like 'The Pleughman', its narrator is somewhat sanitised. There are also timeless pieces like the comic 'The Laird o' Cockpen' set to 'When she cam' ben, she bobbit' – Mistress Jean initially responds to the proposal with a decisive 'Na', later realising she was 'daft'. Carolina Oliphant's deeply held religiosity (an assiduous reader of devotional works and charitable donor, she was sympathetic to the Free Church) is evident in pieces such as the melancholic 'The Land o' the Leal', set to 'Hey tuttie tattie', commemorating Mrs Campbell Colquhoun's 'bonnie bairn'. Carolina Oliphant's work was long popular in performance. Despite a sentimental vein perhaps less appealing to a modern audience, its range and ambition merits renewed attention. VB

• NLS: MS 981: Corr. etc.

Oliphant, C., Work as above.

Davis, L. 'Gender, genre and the imagining of the Scottish nation: the songs of Lady Nairne', online *Scottish Women Poets of the Romantic Period*:
www.alexanderstreet2.com/SWRPLive/bios/S7038-D001.html
HSWW (Bibl.); Kerrigan, C. (1991) *An Anthology of Scottish Women Poets*; *ODNB* (2004); Rogers, C. (1869) *Life and Songs of the Baroness Nairne*.

OLIPHANT, Margaret, n. **Oliphant Wilson,** born Wallyford 4 April 1828, died Windsor 25 June 1897. Writer. Daughter of Margaret Oliphant, and Francis W. Wilson, clerk.

Margaret Oliphant's literary aspirations were encouraged by her mother, from whom she inherited a deep understanding of Scottish culture, particularly of the ballad tradition. The family moved to Lasswade near Edinburgh, Glasgow and Liverpool, where she wrote her first novel, aged 17. Her autobiographical notes contain cameos of her youth in an introverted, lower-middle-class

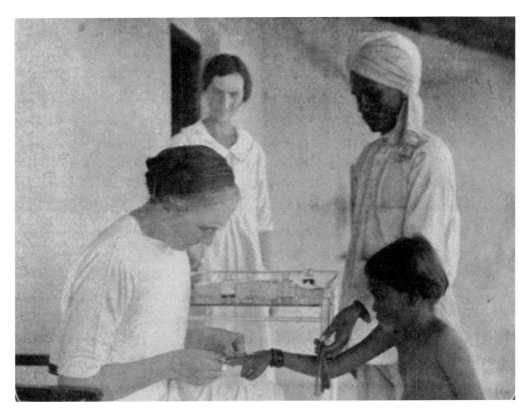

Isabella Kerr
Treating a child, c. 1930 (Supplied by Sybil Oldfield)

Maggie Keswick
At home in London, 1984 (photographed by her friend
Sophie Litchfield; supplied by Charles Jencks)

Jessie M. King
(By James Craig Annan. © Scottish National Photography Collection/Scottish National Portrait Gallery)

Joan Knight
On the occasion of her graduation with an Hon DLitt
awarded by Queen Margaret University College,
Edinburgh (Lesley Donald Photography)

Jennie Lee
At the time of the Bristol Central by-election, when standing as an Independent Socialist Candidate (© Robert
Capa/Magnum Photos. Held in the Scottish National Photography Collection/Scottish National Portrait Gallery)

Agnes Lewis (left) and Margaret Gibson (right) (the Smith sisters)
(Portraits painted in 1920 by John Peddie, a Manchester-based artist, using photographs which had been taken in a St
Andrews studio. By permission of the Senatus of Westminster College, Cambridge)

Agnes Mure Mackenzie
(By Bassano 1934. National Portrait Gallery London)

Agnes McLean
(© The Trustees of the National Museums of Scotland)

Margaret McMillan
(By Bassano, 18 July 1930. National Portrait Gallery
London)

Jane Maxwell, Duchess of Gordon
(By Angelika Kauffmann. © Scottish National Portrait
Gallery)

Naomi Mitchison
(© The Trustees of the National Museums of Scotland)

Ethel Moorhead
(© Martin Emmerson)

Betty Mouat
(Courtesy of Shetland Museum)

Willa Muir
(By Nigel McIsaac. © Scottish National Portrait Gallery)

Anna Munro
(Supplied by Bob Ashman. With thanks to Margaret
Ridgway)

The Neil sisters, Annie (Andy) (left) and Christina (Chrissie)
Taken at the finishing line of the 1954 Monte Carlo Rally (Supplied by Candy Munro)

Doris Reynolds
Taken c. 1930 (With thanks to Jill Reynolds)

Jeannie Robertson
(© The Trustees of the National Museums of Scotland)

Dr Winifred Rushforth
(By Victoria Crowe 1982, oil on board, 24″×28″
collection. From the Scottish National Portrait Gallery. ©
Victoria Crowe)

Flora McBain Sadler
On the occasion of her marriage to Donald H. Sadler,
Superintendent of HM Nautical Almanac Office, on 22
December 1954 (Supplied by George Wilkins)

Margaret Fay Shaw
(Courtesy of the estate of Margaret Fay Shaw Campbell)

Tibbie Shiel
(Supplied by Walter Elliot)

Vera Speirs
In her lumberjill uniform (Supplied by Mrs Victoria
Coyle, Brantford, Ontario, Canada)

Elizabeth Stewart, Queen of Bohemia
(By the studio of Michel van Miereveld. © Scottish
National Portrait Gallery)

Margaret Tait
(By Gunnie Moberg, Orkney. Held in the Scottish
National Photography Collection/Scottish National
Portrait Gallery. © Gunnie Moberg)

Margaret Thomson
Taken in 1949 (With kind permission of her niece,
A. Sharp)

Agnes Toward
(Reproduced by kind permission of The National Trust for Scotland)

Bessie Watson
Taken on 9 October 1909 at the time of her playing in the WSPU pageant, Princes Street, Edinburgh (City of Edinburgh Museums, The People's Story)

Christian Watt
(From *The Christian Watt Papers* by D. Fraser, Paul Harris, 1983)

Rebecca West (Cecily Fairfield)
(By George Charles Beresford, 1912. National Portrait
Gallery London)

Doris Zinkeisen
Self-portrait, exhibited 1929 (© The estate of Doris Clare
Zinkeisen/National Portrait Gallery London)

household. She returned to Scotland for various short periods, but her identity as a Scot 'ran through everything' and some of her best novels are situated in her birth country. Her first published novel, featuring an astute Scottish spinster, *Passages in the Life of Margaret Maitland* (1849), brought her literary acclaim and an introduction to the publishing house of Blackwood. On the day of her wedding in 1852 to her artist cousin Frank Oliphant (1818–59), she received the proofs of her novel *Katie Stewart*. It began a 45-year relationship with Blackwood's and her beloved 'Maga' – *Blackwood's Edinburgh Magazine*. Although she contributed to other literary journals, it was to its editor, John Blackwood, that she turned for financial support when her husband died of tuberculosis in 1859, leaving her with two young children, pregnant with her third child and £1,000 in debt. Her writing moved from being a source of pleasure and interest to the only means by which she fed, clothed and educated her children and later the children of her bankrupt brother. Her notebooks chart the life of a spirited, resourceful woman who experienced a series of bereavements that fell like 'hammer blows'. Despite her long association with Blackwood's, recognised when she was asked to write *Annals of a Publishing House* (1897), and despite continual petitioning, her burden was never eased with an editorship.

For the rest of her life, Margaret Oliphant sustained herself and her extended family with her writing, often sacrificing fine tuning for the sake of pressing deadlines. She published more than 90 novels, 50 short stories, around 300 articles and 25 works of non-fiction, including translation, biography and travel writing. She wrote so much that she wore a groove in her right forefinger from overwork. In 1888 she reflected, 'I don't think I have ever had two hours undisturbed (except at night, when everyone is in bed) during my whole literary life'. Her literary work was often carried out while tending a sick child. All her children predeceased her: three died in infancy, her 10-year-old daughter Maggie died suddenly in 1864, and her sons Cyril ('Tiddy') and Francis Romano ('Cecco') in their early 30s, in 1890 and 1894.

At the end of her life Margaret Oliphant's ambivalence about the worth of her literary talent damaged her literary reputation. While there are examples of obvious hack work, there are also notable successes. Her biography *The Life of Edward Irving* (1862) was praised by Thomas Carlyle. Also acclaimed was the series of novels

about the fictional town of Carlingford, offering a perceptive social critique of English domestic and clerical life and giving special attention to the lives of women. She broke new ground with her heroines, sensible Scottish single women, such as the eponymous *Kirsteen* (1890). Her stories of the supernatural, published in two collections *A Beleaguered City* (1880) and *A Little Pilgrim in the Unseen* (1882), were important and original, subverting Victorian gender roles, and are an expression of her deeply held non-denominational Christian beliefs and familiarity with Scottish Celtic folklore. Her story 'The Library Window' (1896) is one of the finest Scottish short stories ever written.
AMCMS

• NLS: MSS 21501–23000: corr., papers, diaries of Margaret Oliphant; MSS 23218/19: Original notebooks with autobiographical reminiscences; NLS microfilm, *Blackwood's Edinburgh Magazine*; BL: Add. 54919, corr. with publishers Bentley and Macmillan; Princeton Univ., corr. with American publishers.
Oliphant, M. [Mrs], Works as above, and (1990, 2002) *The Autobiography of Margaret Oliphant*, E. Jay, ed.; [Carlingford series]: (1861) *The Executor*; (1863, 1986) *The Rector* and *The Doctor's Family*; (1863, 1986) *Salem Chapel*; (1864, 1987) *The Perpetual Curate*; (1866, 1989 and 2002) *Miss Marjoribanks*; (1876) *Phoebe, Junior*; see also Clarke (1986 and 1987) and NLS catalogue for full lists.
Clarke, J. S. (1986) *Margaret Oliphant (1828–1897): A Bibliography*, Victorian Research Guides 11, St Lucia: Univ. of Queensland; Clarke, J. S. (1997) *Margaret Oliphant (1828–1897), Non-Fictional Writings: a bibliography*, Victorian Research Guide 26, St Lucia: Univ. of Queensland; HSWW (Select Bibl.); Jay, E. (1995) *Mrs Oliphant: 'A Fiction to Herself'*; Kamper, B. (2001) *Margaret Oliphant's Carlingford Series*; ODNB (2004); Scriven, A. (2003) 'Molten sapphires, moments that speak: Margaret Oliphant's journals', *Folio* 6, Spring, pp. 10–12; Williams, M. (1986) *Margaret Oliphant: a critical biography*.

ORABILIS (or **ORABILA**), **Countess of Mar**, fl. 1172, died before 30 June 1203. Daughter of Nessi, son of William.

Orabilis, heiress to the extensive estate of Leuchars in north-east Fife, was the first 12th-century woman to bring lands in Scotland north of the Forth to a prominent Anglo-French baron, perhaps a fitting role for someone named after a character from a chivalric *chanson de geste*. She married Robert de Quincy (d. 1197), and their son Saher de Quincy became first Earl of Winchester and inherited the Fife estates. Between 1172 and 1188, however, Orabilis and de Quincy were divorced and she married Adam son of Duncan, probably a relative of the Earl of Fife. By 1188, she had remarried again, calling herself 'Countess of Mar' in a charter relating to St Andrews. Her husband was almost certainly Earl Gilchrist. Orabilis was also a religious benefactor, granting lands to St Andrews and Inchaffray in her own right. MHH

• (1841) *Liber Cartarum Prioratus Sancti Andree in Scotia*; Lindsay, W. A. and Dowden, J. (eds) (1908) *Charters, Bulls and Other Documents relating to the Abbey of Inchaffray.*

O'ROURKE, Mary [Master Joe Petersen], m. **Lethbridge,** born Helensburgh 26 July 1913, died Glasgow 24 Dec. 1964. 'Boy' soprano, variety singer. Daughter of Hannah Irvine, and James O'Rourke, mason's labourer.

One of a large family, Mary O'Rourke began singing at talent competitions in Glasgow with her elder brother Joe, who possessed a remarkable counter-tenor voice and also had a career in variety, before dying at the age of 35 in 1945. At 17, she went to London to live with her aunt Minnie Irvine and her husband Edward Stebbings. In his youth, Stebbings had performed on the halls as 'Master Edward Frisby' and was training his son for a similar career. When the son's voice broke in 1933, Edward Stebbings persuaded Mary O'Rourke to impersonate a boy's voice under his tutelage. By this time, she had married George Lethbridge (May 1933) and was pregnant. When initial recordings, issued under the name 'Master Joe Petersen, the Phenomenal Boy Singer', proved successful, she went on to make nearly 60 records between 1933 and 1942. Most were issued on the Rex and Eclipse labels and included some attributed to 'Master Wilfred Eaton' and 'Michael Dawney'. She appeared in variety throughout the UK, Germany and Holland, always rigorously maintaining the deception, professionally, that she was a boy.

In 1952, following the break-up of her marriage, she returned to Glasgow, where she was hugely popular. At the height of her fame, when she regularly packed the Metropole in Stockwell Street, her performances always followed the same formula:

the auditorium would go dark, and a spotlight would appear on the curtains as they parted to reveal a small boy, singing his signature, 'Choirboy', in a remarkable voice of great purity. Another favourite number was 'Skylark', about a boy whose mother has died asking a passing skylark to take a message to her in heaven, which 'Master Joe' delivered to devastating effect. The illusion, reliant on Mary's slight figure, was completed by close-cropped dark hair, a white Eton collar, bow tie and black velvet suit. However, her increasing alcoholism led to professional decline. In 1963, she appeared at the final night of the Glasgow Empire and on STV's *One O'Clock Gang*, but the following year she was singing at the Palace bingo hall in the Gorbals. PM

• Wappat, F. (1994) *Master Joe Petersen.*
'Lismor' Records, Master Joe Petersen, LISMOR LCOM 5233 (2002).

OSTHRYð, fl. 675–97, born Bernicia, died Mercia. Queen of Mercia. Daughter of *Eanfled and Oswy, Queen and King of Bernicia.

Osthryð grew up in Bernicia, which included lands in northern England and southern Scotland. Married to Aeðilred of Mercia, probably by her brother Ecgfrith, Osthryð became Queen of her people's greatest enemies. Her murder by Mercian nobles in 697 implies she had to deal with resentment throughout her queenship. However, she seems to have been both active and influential. Aeðilred shook off Ecgfrith's domination in 679. The death of Osthryð's brother in this war may have inspired her to be a force in the unlikely peace that followed, and was maintained even when Bernicia was left vulnerable after Ecgfrith's death in 685. She witnessed the foundation charter of Peterborough c. 680. A steadfast supporter of the cult of her uncle Oswald (who died fighting Aeðilred's father), Osthryð showed strength of character, though she aroused Mercian resentment by selecting a Mercian monastery to house his relics. JEF

• *BEHEP*; Colgrave, B. (ed.) (1927) *The Life of Bishop Wilfrid*, cap 40; Swanton, M. (ed.) (1996) *The Anglo-Saxon Chronicles*, 'E' text, sub anni 675, 697.

P

PAGAN, Isobel, born near Nith-head, 1741, died 1821. Poet.

In Isobel Pagan's *Collection of Poems and Songs*, published c. 1805, she states that she was born 'near four miles from Nith-head' in the south west of Scotland and educated for 'ten weeks, when I was seven years old,/With a good old religious wife'. She also indicates that she was convivial by nature: 'I sing a song with mirth and glee,/And sometimes I the whisky pree' and that she ran a howff at Muirkirk, where she raised her illegitimate child.

High spirits and thoughtful qualities are equally present in her work. She composed in Scots, and was known as 'Wicked Tibbie' for her satirical skills (her work was transcribed by a tailor, William Gemmell). Her lyric version of 'Ca' the yowes to the knowes', collected in *The Scots Musical Museum* (Johnson 1787–1803) by Robert Burns, has a subversive quality. Her heroine is not taken in by lovers' tricks and, in the tradition of Allan Ramsay's cautious lover Jenny in *The Gentle Shepherd* (1725), wants hard currency before she offers herself: 'gowns and ribbons meet'. On a more dignified note, pieces like 'The Crook and the Plaid' elevated those considered to be socially lowly into spiritually high positions. A shepherd lad is compared with the Biblical shepherd David: 'when he came to be a king, and left his former trade,/'Twas an honour to the laddie that wears the crook and plaid' (ll. 23–4). While Isobel Pagan's work has, hitherto, largely been considered as an appendix to Burns's, its imaginative range deserves more detailed critical consideration. VB

• Pagan, I. (1803) *A Collection of Poems and Songs on Several Occasions*; Johnson, J. (1787–1803) *The Scots Musical Museum*, vol. III, Song 264 (6 vols, reissued as 2 vols, 1962).
Bold, V. (1997) 'Beyond "The Empire of the Gentle Heart": Scottish women poets of the nineteenth century', in *HSWW*; (Forthcoming) 'Danaus' Daughters', in V. Bold *Nature's Making: James Hogg and the Autodidacts*; Paterson, J. (1840) *The Contemporaries of Burns, and the More Recent Poets of Ayrshire*, pp. 113–23, (1847) *The Ballads and Songs of Ayrshire*, pp. 63–6.

PARKER, Agnes Miller, m. **McCance,** born Irvine 25 March 1895, died Greenock 15 Nov. 1980. Artist-wood-engraver. Daughter of Agnes Harriet Mitchell, and William McCall Parker, analytical chemist.

The eldest of eight children, after Whitehill Higher Grade School in Glasgow Agnes Miller Parker attended the GSA (Diploma 1916) and tutored until 1920. In 1918, she married fellow-artist William McCance (1894–1970). Both received praise as Scottish modernists, particularly from Neil Gunn and Hugh MacDiarmid. Agnes Miller Parker taught art at Gerrards Cross (1920–8) and Clapham (1928–30) and taught herself engraving, learning enough from Gertrude Hermes and her husband, Blair Hughes Stanton, to receive the Walter Brewster Prize for Engraving, Chicago (1929). A lively social life included friendship with *Naomi Mitchison and Marjorie Spring Rice. Agnes Miller Parker's first published illustrations accompanied *How it Happened: Myths and Folk Tales* by Rhoda Power (1930) as linocuts. More complex wood engravings appeared in the edition of *Esope's Fables* (1931), published while William McCance and Blair Hughes Stanton worked for Gregynog Press (1930–3). Thereafter, Agnes Miller Parker designed many book illustrations. She became an Associate of the RSPEE (1940) and subsequently a Fellow (1953). In 1955, she left her husband. She lived in Glasgow, taught art in a city school, and went on sketching trips with artist Louise Annand. She retired to a house she built with her brothers on Arran (1962) where, according to *Who's Who*, she could keep cats, swim and fish, and where she is buried. RA

• Manchester Metropolitan Univ. archives; NLS: Papers, book-plates and etching tools.
Addison, R. (1998) 'Fine lines: Agnes Miller Parker', *Scottish Book Collector*, 6/2, pp. 16–19; *ODNB* (2004); Rogerson, I. and Dreyfus, J. (1990) *Agnes Miller Parker, Wood Engraver and Book Illustrator, 1895–1980*; *Who's Who*.

PATERSON, Grace Chalmers, born Glasgow 25 Dec. 1843, died Edinburgh 26 Nov. 1925. Founder of Glasgow School of Cookery. Daughter of Georgina Smith, and William Paterson, merchant.

Grace Paterson campaigned for improving the domestic education of working-class girls and women, and was a friend and supporter of *Janet Galloway and the founders of Queen Margaret College, Glasgow, and of *Christian Guthrie Wright, founder of the Edinburgh School of Cookery. She was the first (non-teaching) principal of the Glasgow School of Cookery (1875–1908). One of the early teachers there was **Margaret Black**, n. **McKirdy** (1830–1903), writer of a number of books on cookery, laundry and housekeeping, all published by William Collins, who was a director of the GSC. Margaret Black had qualified at the National School of Cookery in Kensington in 1874, and went on to found the West End School of Cookery in 1878. After her death in 1903, her niece, Mary McKirdy, succeeded her as principal, and the two schools eventually merged in 1908 to form the Glasgow and West of Scotland College of Domestic Science (later part of Glasgow Caledonian University). Grace Paterson and Margaret Black were early elected members of the School Board of Glasgow, Paterson in 1885, Black in 1891, and each was active in a number of causes, including temperance and women's suffrage. Grace Paterson joined the WSPU in 1907. In that year, the Lord Provost of Glasgow commended Grace Paterson's services to the community as a pioneer of women's work in the west of Scotland. JMCD

• GCU Archives: Mitchell Library, Glasgow, *Minute Books of the Glasgow and West of Scotland Association for Women's Suffrage.*
Glasgow Herald, 28 June 1906, 26 Nov. 1907, 30 Nov. 1925 (obit. Paterson); *HHGW*; Miller, E. (1975) *Century of Change 1875–1975*; Thompson, W. and McCallum, C. (1998) *Glasgow Caledonian University: its origins and evolution*; *GASHE [Gateway to Archives of Scottish Higher Education]* entries on M. Black and G. Paterson by J. O'Brien: www.gashe.archives.gla.ac.uk/contact.html

PATON, Mary Ann, m1 **Lennox,** m2 **Wood,** born Edinburgh Oct. 1802, died Chapelthorpe, Yorks., 21 July 1864. Singer. Daughter of George Paton, writing-master and amateur violinist, and his wife, n. Crawford.

Mary Ann Paton's great-uncle was a founder of the Aberdeen Musical Society, and she first performed in public, aged eight, as a singer, pianist and harpist. Two other sisters were singers. The family moved to London, and she joined the Haymarket Company, making her debut as Susanna in Mozart's *Le Nozze di Figaro* on 3 August 1822. At the height of her career, she had a vocal range from a low D to an E above the stave. Acknowledged as the leading soprano of the day, she sang both traditional operatic roles and new works, including Weber's *Freischütz* and operas by M. W. Balfe (1808–70). In April 1826, at Covent Garden, she created, to acclaim, the role of Reiza in Weber's *Oberon*, conducted by the composer. In

1824, she married Lord William Pitt Lennox (1799–1881), but they divorced in 1831, and she married the tenor Joseph Wood (1801–90). The Woods undertook two successful operatic tours in the USA (1833–6 and 1840). She is said to have introduced Bellini's operas and Italian bel canto to the USA. Mary Ann Paton is the subject of 14 large-scale portraits in the NPG's collection in Bodelwyddan Castle, North Wales, including those by Sully, Woolnoth, Hunt and Lane. They show her in costume for roles including Mandane in Thomas Arne's *Artaxerxes*. Mandane's spectacular aria, 'The Soldier, tir'd of War's Alarms', was a showpiece for sopranos all century, and one of her 'warhorses'. Like another famous soprano, Jenny Lind, she composed a number of sacred solos. PAC

• Cohen, A. I. (1987, 2nd edn.) *International Encyclopedia of Women Composers*; Kennedy, M. (1997, 2nd edn.) *The Oxford Dictionary of Music*; Moore, F. L. (1961) *Crowell's Handbook of World Opera*; *New Grove Dictionary of Music and Musicians* (2001, see under Wood); *ODNB* (2004); Stieger, F. (1977) *Opernlexikon*.

PEARCE, Isabella Bream [Lily Bell], n. **Duncan,** born Glasgow 5 May 1859, died Glasgow 11 Dec. 1929. Socialist propagandist and suffrage campaigner. Daughter of Margaret Fraser, and John Thomson Duncan, mercantile bookkeeper.

Isabella Duncan married Charles Bream Pearce (c. 1839–1905), wine importer for an American organisation, the Brotherhood of the New Life. She was active in the 1890s in the Glasgow ILP and was vice-president of the Glasgow Labour Party, president of the Glasgow Women's Labour Party and a member of the Cathcart School Board. She and her husband were friends of the ILP leader Keir Hardie, supporting his newspaper, *Labour Leader*, financially. As 'Lily Bell', between 1894 and 1898 she contributed a column, 'Matrons and Maidens', which covered all aspects of women's emancipation, with a hardhitting feminist analysis and critique of male power over women. She criticised socialist men for treating women's emancipation as marginal rather than central to the socialist project. Hardie, however, dismissed her as 'hopeless' in 1898, though whether for her journalistic skills or her opinions is not known (FJC, C1898/11).

Isabella Pearce was an early advocate of women's suffrage, on which she spoke at ILP annual conferences in the early 1890s, and after 1900 suffrage was more central to her politics. A leading member of the Glasgow branch of the militant WSPU, in June 1907 she became honorary treasurer of its Scottish Council, and shortly afterwards joint honorary secretary of the Scottish WSPU; between 1906 and 1908 she edited a women's suffrage column in *Forward*, the influential local socialist newspaper, again as 'Lily Bell'. In contemporary debates about the precedence of class or sex for socialists, she argued strongly that 'sex autocracy is even more tyrannical than class autocracy' (*Forward*, 18 May 1907). Her commitment to suffrage may explain why she appears to have played less of a role in socialist politics after 1908; she was a friend of Elizabeth Wolstenholme Elmy and, like Elmy, contributed articles and letters on the suffrage movement to the *Westminster Review* in 1907–8, and *The Freewoman* in 1911–12. JBH

• LSE: Francis Johnson Collection (FJC), BLPES. Pearce, I. D. (1907) *Westminster Review*, 168, pp. 17–22, 622–4, (1908) *Westminster Review*, 169, pp. 444–51, *Labour Leader* 1894–8, *Forward* 1906–8.
AGC; Hannam, J. and Hunt, K. (1999) 'Propagandising as socialist women', in B. Taithe and T. Thornton (eds) *Propaganda*; Kazama, M. (1988) 'Seeking after the "New Morality": *The Freewoman*, a radical feminist journal, Nov. 1811–Oct. 1912', MA, Univ. of York; Lintell, H. (1990) 'Lily Bell: socialist and feminist, 1894–8', MA, Bristol Polytechnic; *WSM*.

PENNY, Margaret n. **Irvine,** born Aberdeen 1812, died Aberdeen 1891. Northern pioneer. Daughter of Helen Colvile (or Collie), and George Irvine, weaver.

Margaret Penny was the first Scottish woman to accompany her husband north on a wintering expedition to Baffin Island. Only a dozen British women were known to have sailed on whalers, mostly to the South Seas. With her husband Captain William Penny of the whaling ship *Lady Franklin*, she sailed from Aberdeen in June 1857, returning to the home port on 22 August 1858. Her diary records daily events, descriptions of the land, and her many contacts with the Inuit: 'Dec. 15th . . . I was on shore in several of their edloos [igloos] . . . can now crawl out & in as well as any Esquimaux & eat mactac [narwhal skin, an antiscorbutic] with pleasure' (Ross 1997, p. 117). At the end of the voyage the shareholders of the whaling company recognised her contribution to the expedition by presenting her with a silver tea service, now in the collection of the City of Aberdeen Art Gallery and Museum. Margaret Penny returned for a second winter in the Arctic in 1863. GH

• Druett, J. (1991) *Petticoat whalers: whaling wives at sea 1820–1920*; Ross, W. G. (1997) *This Distant and Unsurveyed Country: a woman's winter at Baffin Island, 1857–68*.

PHILLIPS, Mary Elizabeth, born St Mary Bourne, Hampshire, 15 July 1880, died Hove 21 June 1969. Feminist, suffragette. Daughter of Louisa Elizabeth Simms, and William Fleming Phillips, doctor.

The family moved to Glasgow where Mary Phillips first became involved with feminism, organising for the GWSAWS. A convinced socialist, realising that constitutional tactics were not for her, she threw in her lot with the WSPU. In November 1907, Christabel Pankhurst invited her to become a WSPU organiser, helping with Scottish campaigns. She also wrote a regular column on suffrage for the Glasgow socialist paper, *Forward*. She was sent to London, possibly for further WSPU training, and served her first imprisonment of six weeks for her part in a raid on Parliament. She found this inspiring, writing to fellow organiser Annot Robinson that she could not 'look back on Holloway without pleasure!' (8 April 1908, Robinson Papers). Other aspects of WSPU work were more challenging, and lengthy periods as a district organiser helped overcome the loneliness of itinerant campaigning. She returned to prison in June 1908 and July 1909, going on hunger-strike, but Christabel Pankhurst dissuaded her from further time in gaol, following WSPU policy for organisers. In July 1913, Christabel Pankhurst, from her exile in France, dismissed Mary Phillips from the WSPU. Although she claimed financial motivation, she appears to have begun to doubt her loyalty. Under the pseudonym of Mary Paterson, Mary Phillips then worked for Sylvia Pankhurst in the East End of London during the First World War, then acted briefly as an organiser for the United Suffragists.

After the war, she worked for the New Constitutional Society for Women's Suffrage, the WIL and the Save the Children Fund, but gave up organising in 1928 to edit a daily news service for the brewing trade. In later life she was an active member of the Six Point Group. Also committed to the Suffragette Fellowship, she wrote her own version of the suffrage campaign in a short pamphlet published in 1957. KC

• Manchester Central Library: Annot Robinson Papers; Museum of London: Suffragette Fellowship Collection; Private collection: Mary Phillips Papers.
Phillips, M. (1957) *The Militant Suffrage Campaign in Perspective*.

Hesketh, P. (1992) *My Aunt Edith: the story of a Preston suffragette*; *ODNB* (2004); Raeburn, A. (1973) *The Militant Suffragettes*; *WSM*.

PICKFORD, Lillian Mary, born Jubbalpore, India, 14 August 1902, died Edinburgh 14 August 2002. Neuro-endocrinologist. Daughter of Lillian Alice Minnie Wintle, and Herbert Arthur Pickford, colonial businessman.

Educated at Wycombe Abbey School and Bedford College, London (BSc Physiology 1925), Mary Pickford became research assistant and demonstrator at University College London. She worked as house physician in Stafford General Infirmary, then as a locum GP, before a Beit Memorial Fellowship at Cambridge (1936) enabled her to work with E. B. Verney. In 1939, she became Lecturer in Physiology at the University of Edinburgh Medical School, where she spent the rest of her career (Reader 1952, Professor 1966). Her DSc (1957) was from London, where, during the Second World War, she had spent vacations working as a medical officer during air raids.

Mary Pickford was an outstanding and respected teacher. Her research contribution was to the understanding and regulation of kidney function. Aware that trauma could lead to kidney failure, she emphasised the importance of the antidiuretic hormone, ADH. Her work relating to oxytocin, responsible for uterine contraction and the let-down of milk, was of particular significance to women's health. With Sybil Lloyd, she investigated the actions of hormones on the brain. She officially retired in 1972, but continued to carry out research abroad. She wrote more than 60 papers, some for *The Lancet* and the RSE, and chapters in books. She became FRS in 1966, FRSE and FRCP in 1977, and Hon DSc (Heriot Watt) in 1991. Mary Pickford returned in 1982 to Edinburgh, where she died on her 100th birthday. A keen amateur painter, she enjoyed being confused with the famous actress of the same name. LS
• Pickford, L. M. (1967) *Physiology – the part and the whole* [Univ. of Edinburgh Inaugural Lecture, 8 May], (1969) *The Central Role of Hormones*.
Bindman, L., Brading, A., Tansey, T. (eds) (1992) *Women Physiologists*; *The Guardian*, 27 August 2002 (obit.).

PIRIE, Jane, born c. 1784, fl. 1821. Teacher, litigant in court case concerning lesbianism.

Jane Pirie's family lived in Edinburgh. Her maternal grandfather was a Presbyterian minister and her father wrote religious works. She too was a deeply religious Presbyterian. After working as a governess 1801–9, she opened a fashionable private school for girls at Drumsheugh, Edinburgh, in partnership with **Marianne Woods** (born c. 1783, fl. 1821) with whom she had formed a close, if tempestuous, friendship. From 1798 to 1802, Marianne Woods had lived with her uncle, a comedy actor at the Edinburgh theatre, and his wife, Ann Quelch Woods, who had played alongside Sarah Siddons in 1784. In 1810, Jane Pirie and Marianne Woods were accused of 'lewd and indecent behaviour' and all their pupils left. Facing financial ruin, and with nothing remaining to save but their name, they sued Dame Helen Cumming Gordon of Gordonstoun, grandmother of one of their pupils, for libel. The case was heard behind closed doors and all involved were sworn to secrecy. Jane Pirie and Marianne Woods won their case in 1812, but Dame Helen appealed to the House of Lords. Jane Pirie remained in Edinburgh, unable to find employment, while Marianne Woods obtained a post at Camden House Academy, London, where she had taught previously. The House of Lords dismissed the appeal in 1819, but the fight over damages lasted until 1821. Jane Pirie's whereabouts after that are unknown. The case inspired Lillian Hellman's play, *The Children's Hour* (1934). LRM
• Signet Library, Edinburgh, Roughead Collection: Session papers, Case of Miss Marianne Woods and Miss Jane Pirie against Dame Helen Gordon Cumming.
Edinburgh Weekly Journal, 21 July 1819; Faderman, L. (1985) *Scotch Verdict*; *ODNB* (2004).

PIRIE, Mary, born Aberdeen 20 Jan. 1822, died Portsoy, Banffshire, 8 Feb. 1885. Botanist and teacher. Daughter of Clementina Anderson, and William Pirie, carpet manufacturer.

One of ten children, Mary Pirie developed a passion for botany. In 1860 she published her principal work on flowers, grasses and shrubs, mostly indigenous or imported to Britain. It includes poems and line drawings which may be her own. Her preface indicates a didactic approach: 'With a view of directing the attention, and encouraging a love for the useful with the beautiful, in the Floral Kingdom, I have endeavoured in [this] work . . . to render popular a science which I fondly love . . .'. Mary Pirie lived latterly in Portsoy, where she ran a small private school. Her second published work, *Familiar teachings on natural history* (1864), demonstrates her concern with inspiring children with her own love of nature. For many years she contributed a column of lively notes on botany and natural history to the local newspaper, *The Banffshire Reporter.* LS

• Pirie, M., Works as above, and (1860) *Flowers, Grasses and Shrubs, a popular book on botany.*
Anon. (1908) 'Notes and Queries', *Aberdeen Journal*, 1, 15; Ogilvie, M. and Harvey, J. (eds) (2000) *The Biographical Dictionary of Women in Science.*

PIRRET, Ruth, born Milton, Glasgow, 24 July 1874, died South Kensington, London, 19 June 1939. Nuclear and engineering chemist. Daughter of Violet Brown, and the Rev. David Pirret, United Presbyterian minister.

One of a large family, Ruth Pirret graduated on 2 April 1898, the first woman to be awarded a BSc from the University of Glasgow. She appears then to have taught at Kilmacolm High School, in Newcastle upon Tyne, and in Arbroath. The work for which she deserves greatest recognition happened between 1909 and 1911 when she collaborated with the nuclear chemist Frederick Soddy, in the University of Glasgow's physical chemistry department. Together they published two key papers reporting their research on the ratio of radium to uranium in uranium-bearing metals, thus shedding light on the disintegration theory of radioactivity. Such a high profile in nuclear studies was rare for a woman, but while Frederick Soddy was to become a Nobel Laureate in 1921, Ruth Pirret's career continued as vice-warden of Ashbourne House Hall, University of Manchester. Her later activities are obscure, but in 1924 she published a paper with Guy Dunstan Bengough on the chemical processes of metal corrosion. G. D. Bengough was Principal Scientific Officer at the Chemical Research Laboratory and it seems possible that Ruth Pirret was by then a government research scientist. In London she shared a house with her sister **Mary Janet Pirret** (1876–1942), MBChB, MD, DPH, an early medical graduate and MOH. LS

• Soddy, F. and Pirret, R. (1910) 'The ratio between uranium and radium in minerals', *Philosophical Magazine*, 20, pp. 345–9; Pirret, R. and Soddy, F. (1911) 'The ratio between uranium and radium in minerals II', ibid., 21, pp. 652–8; Bengough, G. D., May, R. and Pirret, R. (1924) 'The causes of rapid corrosion of condenser tubes', *North East Coast Institution of Engineers and Shipbuilders.*
Ogilvie, M. and Harvey, J. (eds) (2000) *The Biographical Dictionary of Women in Science*; Rayner-Canham, G. W. and M. F. (1990) 'Pioneer Women in Nuclear Science', *Amer. Jour. Physics*, Nov., pp. 1036–43.

PORTER, Jane, born Durham 1776, died Bristol 24 May 1850; **PORTER, Anna Maria,** born 1778, died 1832. Historical novelists. Daughters of Jane Blenkinsop, and William Porter, army surgeon.

After their father's death in 1779, their mother moved her younger children to Edinburgh, where they were apparently raised in the company of Walter Scott among others. Anna Maria Porter published the first of more than 14 works of fiction and poetry in 1793–5, *Artless Tales*. Jane Porter followed suit in 1803 with *Thaddeus of Warsaw.* Popular, it was translated many times, and she was elected a canoness of the Teutonic order of St Joachim. By then the Porters were in Surrey where, in 1810, Jane published the William Wallace story as *The Scottish Chiefs*, establishing a type of Scots historical fiction four years before Walter Scott, and inspired by popular accounts: 'I was hardly six years of age when I first heard the names of William Wallace and Robert Bruce – not from gentlemen and ladies, . . . but from the maids in the nursery, and the serving man in the kitchen' (Porter 1831, p. 3). For Jane Porter, the warrior past was both transmitted by women, and embodied in them, particularly in a servant, Luckie Forbes, 'that dear old woman; so shrewd, yet simple-minded . . . reading her Bible, which she did every day. I do not recollect ever seeing any other book in her house; though she knew the history of Scotland, . . . as accurately as if the top of her *muckle kist*, on which her Bible lay, had been filled with historic chronicles' (ibid., p. 4). Both sisters were relentlessly productive, publishing historical novels, writing plays, and contributing to periodicals. They collaborated on *Tales round a Winter Hearth* (1826), and Jane Porter published a novel-memoir written by her brother under her name, *Sir Edward Seaward's Diary*, in 1831. Her work remained popular, though it was far from universally admired (*ODNB* 2004). If their mother had hoped to foster her children's talents by moving to Edinburgh in 1780, she succeeded: one brother was a painter, another a surgeon. But Anna Maria died of typhus in 1832, and Jane led a nomadic existence thereafter, not having made much money from her writing. DS

• Univ. of Durham Library: Archives and Special Collections, Porter corr.; The Lilly Library, Indiana Univ.: Porter MSS. Porter, A., Works as above, and see Bibls.; Porter, J. (1810, 1831) *The Scottish Chiefs*, Works as above, and see Bibls. *HSWW* (Bibl.); *ODNB* (2004) (Bibl.).

PULLINGER, Dorothée Aurélie Marianne, MBE, m. **Martin,** born St Aubin-sur-Scie, France, 13 Jan. 1894, died St Peter Port, Guernsey, 28 Jan. 1986. Aero and automobile engineer and entrepreneur. Daughter of Aurélie Bérénice Sitwell, and Thomas Charles Pullinger, engineer.

The eldest of 12 children, Dorothée Pullinger was born in France, where her father had gone to work in 1890. After returning to Britain, he worked for several automobile manufacturers: Sunbeam, Humber and, finally, Arrol's at Paisley. She attended Loughborough Girls Grammar School, then joined her father, who was managing director at the Arrol Johnston car works until its closure in 1931. She did drawing-office work, and converted German designs from metric to imperial measurements for UK use. When Arrol Johnston built a plant at Tongland, Kirkcudbright, making spare parts for aero engines, she helped design the Beardmore-Halford-Pullinger aero engine, known as the Beardmore. Moving to Vickers in Barrow-in-Furness, she started a women's apprenticeship scheme and managed the female munitions workers, who had their own football team. After the First World War, she returned to Tongland,

where Galloway cars were produced with an all-female workforce, using the suffragette colours of violet, green and white for the cars' badge. The Galloway (10/20 CV, 4 cylinders, capacity 1528cc) remained in production until 1925. After her marriage in 1924 to Edward Marshall Martin (1895–1951), she undertook the sales side of the operation but, annoyed at accusations of stealing a 'man's job', she and her husband opened a large laundry in Croydon. In 1940, Nuffield recruited her to organise women recruits to munitions. She managed 13 factories during the Second World War and was the only woman on a post-war government committee formed to recruit women into factories. Made an MBE, she became a member of the Institute of Personnel Management. There is a plaque to her memory at Vickers, Barrow-in-Furness. NCB

• *ODNB* (2004); Websites about Galloway car factory: www.old-kirkcudbright.net/books/tongland/factory.htm
www.coloracademy.co.uk/Subjects/Transport/Transport5.htm
www.ideahobby.it/DB-Auto/galloway.html
Private information: Lewis Martin (son).

Q

QUAILE, Barbara Helen, n. **Renton,** born Edinburgh 28 March 1906, died Glasgow 15 Feb. 1999. Hospital matron. Daughter of Ida Sandeman, and David Renton, solicitor.

Educated at St Trinneans School, Barbara Renton trained as a nurse at the Royal Infirmary of Edinburgh (RIE). She joined the College of Nursing in 1932, obtained her Diplomas in nursing (London 1936) and midwife teaching (1939) and registered as a Sister Tutor in 1946. As Miss Renton, she was the youngest Scottish matron when appointed to the 2,000-bed Emergency Hospital at Bangour in 1940. After the war, she became Matron

of the Victoria Infirmary in Glasgow (1946–55) then Lady Superintendent of the Royal Infirmary of Edinburgh. She retired to marry Kenneth Quaile, a Glasgow stockbroker, in 1959. Later voluntary work included membership of the Western Region Hospital Board, Chair of the governors of Queen's College Glasgow, and divisional president of the Bearsden Red Cross. Her career illustrates commitment to public service and continuing professional education. BEM

• Quaile, B. H. (n.d.) *The Story of the Royal Infirmary of Edinburgh Nurse Training School 1872–1972.*
The Scotsman, 5 March 1999 (obit.).

R

RADCLIFFE, Mary Ann, n. **Clayton,** baptised Nottingham 18 June 1746, died Edinburgh, in or after 1810. Writer. Daughter of Sarah Clayton, and James Clayton, retired merchant.

Mary Ann Clayton's father, an Anglican, died when she was three: her mother was a Catholic

and, after arbitration, it was decided that the child should be brought up an Anglican. However, her mother sent her to the Bar Convent school, York, from 1758. Her guardians later fought her mother's favouring of Mary Ann's Catholic suitor, Joseph Radcliffe (born c. 1715), sending her to London and putting her money in Chancery, but she eloped with Radcliffe and married him on 2 May 1762, bearing him eight children. Her picaresque *Memoirs* tell the story of her struggle for survival, after her fortune was managed by trustees and her husband's businesses failed. She ran a coffee house, kept a shop, took in lodgers and sewing, and acted as a chaperone and a governess.

From 1781 to 1783 Mary Ann Radcliffe was housekeeper for her former schoolfriend Mary Stewart, Countess of Traquair, at whose Peebles home she met the sympathetic liberal Catholic priest Alexander Geddes. She afterwards remained in Edinburgh, where she ran a boarding-house, saw her eldest daughter married, and found schools or places for her sons, returning to London in 1789. Her *Female Advocate; or An Attempt to recover the Rights of Women from Male Usurpation* (1799), though disavowing 'the Amazonian spirit of a Wollstonecraft' (p.xi) discussed the declining job market for women, which might leave unprotected women with little recourse but prostitution. In 1802, she published two issues of *Radcliffe's New Novelists' Pocket Magazine*. The authorship of several Gothic novels, *The Fate of Velina de Guidova* (1790), *Manfroné* (1809) and *Radzivil* (1814) has been ascribed to her, probably wrongly. She is often confused with the English Gothic novelist Ann Radcliffe. Friends urged her to return to Edinburgh, where after the failure of several business attempts, she published her *Memoirs* by subcription in 1810, revealing her poverty and appealing for help in her final years. JR

• Radcliffe, M. A. (1810) *The Memoirs of Mary Ann Radcliffe in Familiar Letters to Her Female Friend.*
Blain V., Clements P., Grundy I. (eds) (1990) *Feminist Companion to Literature in English*; Coleridge, H. J. (1887) *St Mary's Convent, Micklegate Bar, York (1686–1887)*; Luria, G. (1994) 'Introduction' to Radcliffe, M. A. *The Female Advocate*; *ODNB* (2004).

RAE, Jane, m. **Coates,** born Denny 20 Dec. 1872, died Clydebank 12 May 1959. ILP activist and councillor. Daughter of Elizabeth Cossens, and Livingston Rae, ironmonger.

Jane Rae became well known as a Clydebank activist through her involvement in the all-out strike that paralysed the giant Singer Sewing Machine works in Clydebank in 1910–11. She worked in the needle-making department and was among those who felt deeply aggrieved by the increased workloads, wage-rate undercutting and imposition of American scientific management methods (including job timing, work reorganisation and use of the stop-watch) at the factory. She became actively involved in the dispute and found herself, with 400–1,000 others (press accounts vary) sacked for standing up for their rights – a common enough experience for those active in trade unions or in socialist politics at the time. She was described by one of her fellow Singer employees, Bill Lang, as 'a fiery customer . . . involved in everything'. She was a strikingly tall, strong-willed, studious woman who was, according to her brother John Rae, 'an intellectual, interested in the progress of society . . . she always wanted to improve the social conditions of the working people'. A contemporary labour activist was **Frances (Fanny) Abbott** (1892–1971) who worked at Singer's in 1910–11 and was involved from the 1910s with the ILP and later with organising the Women's Section of the Labour Party.

Jane Rae joined the ILP around this time, inspired, her family recalled, by a Keir Hardie speech. By 1913, she was secretary of the Clydebank branch. Thereafter, her wide-ranging political activities included involvement in the suffrage campaign (chairing a meeting for Emmeline Pankhurst at Clydebank Town Hall), the Co-operative movement and the anti-war movement during the First World War. The period from then until 1928 was her most active in politics. She was elected as a local councillor in Clydebank in 1922: among her particular interests were temperance and education. In these years she involved her whole family in political campaigning – chalking the streets, protesting outside pubs and parading with umbrellas painted with political slogans. Her niece, also Jane Rae, recalled that 'she would go out with her school bell and get all the children out, like the Pied Piper. Jane in front and all the children all following'. Among her successes in local politics was a policy of not having any pubs licensed within sight of schools in Clydebank. She also became a JP. Her brother recalled that she used her position to protect women who had suffered domestic violence.

After her mother died in 1929, Jane Rae married a long-time Australian friend, Alfred Coates, a builder, and emigrated to Australia. They returned about a decade later and settled in the Channel Islands where she witnessed the hardships, 'disappearances' and brutalities meted out to Russian prisoners of war at the time of its occupation by the Nazis. Her family recall that she destroyed all her socialist literature and records of past political involvement at this time as a precaution. Jane Rae returned to Clydebank around 1946–7, after the death of her husband. AMCI

• Quotations from oral evidence in possession of the author: John, Anne, Jane (niece) and Norman Rae, 3 Nov. 1988; Bill Lang, 17 May 1988; Amy Summers (Frances Abbott's daughter), 15 Jan. 1989.

Clydebank Press, 17 June 1913, 17 Sept. 1971; Glasgow Labour History Workshop (1989) *The Singer Strike, Clydebank, 1911*; Gordon, E. (1991) *Women and the Labour Movement in Scotland, 1850–1914*; Green, W. (1983) 'Jane Rae', *Clydebank Local History Journal*, 4, Autumn; Hood, J. (1988) *The History of Clydebank*; Kenefick, W. and McIvor, A. (eds) (1996) *Roots of Red Clydeside, 1910–1914*.

RAEGNMAELD, born probably Rheged, fl. mid-7th century. Possibly Queen of Bernicia. Daughter of Royth map Ru[n].

The 9th-century *Historia Brittonum* notes that Oswy (611/12–670) of Bernicia, a kingdom which included much of northern England and southern Scotland, had two wives: *Eanfled (his second wife) and 'Rieinmelth', a daughter of Royth map Ru[n]. Elsewhere, this text asserts that Ru[n] map Urbgen baptised Eanfled's father Edwini, an achievement which Bede credits to Roman missionaries. It seems likely that Raegnmaeld, whose name appears as such in the Durham *Liber Vitae*, was a great-grand-daughter of Urbgen (Urien) of Rheged. Nothing is known of her career except that she and Oswy had at least two children: Alchfrith, later King of Deira (655–c. 666), and *Alchfled; possibly Aldfrith, King of Northumbria (685–705), was also their son. The circumstances surrounding the end of the marriage are mysterious, including whether Raegnmaeld died or was set aside; it is possible that she and Oswy were still married when he became King in 642. JEF

• Morris, J. (1980) *British History and Welsh Annals*, cc 57, 63; Surtees Society (1841) *Liber Vitae Ecclesiæ Dunelmensis*.

RAFFLES, Frances Rachel (Franki), born Salford 17 Oct. 1955, died Edinburgh 6 Dec. 1994. Photographer and co-founder of the Zero Tolerance campaign against violence against women. Daughter of Gillian Posnansky, director, Mercury Gallery, London and Edinburgh, and Eric Raffles, textiles manufacturer and farmer.

Brought up in London, the third daughter of four children, Franki Raffles studied at the University of St Andrews (1973–7) and thereafter made Scotland her home. At university she was a strongly committed member of the women's liberation group and her Marxism-feminism shaped her life and work. She also retained a Jewish cultural identity. In 1978, she moved to Lewis where she and her partner, Martin Sime, restored the 169-acre farm at Calanais and kept sheep. She taught herself photography, leading to her first exhibition, *Lewis Women*, in the Stills Gallery in Edinburgh. She separated from her partner and in 1982, with her daughter, Anna, moved to Edinburgh where she worked as co-ordinator of the Scottish Joint Action Group and began to build a career as a freelance photographer and designer for mainly public sector clients, including the Edinburgh District Council women's committee. She also developed innovative uses of photography with children and adults with learning difficulties. With Evelyn Gillan and Susan Hart she developed the Zero Tolerance campaign for the women's committee, a ground-breaking initiative challenging attitudes to male violence against women and children, launched in 1992. Her approach eschewed images of abused women in favour of images of women and children in domestic settings, apparently comfortable and secure, underlining the familiar but hidden nature of abuse. She helped found the Zero Tolerance Trust to take on that work.

She became a lesbian and in 1983 met Sandy Lunan (b. 1954), who remained her partner until the end of her life. The following year, with Anna they made a year-long journey, mainly by train and local buses, through the Soviet Union, to China, Tibet, Nepal and India, recorded in an exhibition in Edinburgh and London. Other trips with her camera included Zimbabwe, Australia, Mexico and the Dominican Republic. Franki Raffles died giving birth to twin daughters; she was survived by her three daughters, a son, and the daughter she brought up with Sandy Lunan. At the time of her death she was working on 'Lot's Wife', a photographic series on the lives of Soviet-Jewish women immigrants to Israel. Malcolm Chisholm, MP (now MSP), paid tribute in the House of Commons to the 'brilliant designer' of the Zero Tolerance campaign (Hansard 5C). SI

• Raffles, F. (1988) *Photographers with special needs*. *Edinburgh Evening News*, 8 Dec. 1994 (obit.); Gillan, E. (1995) 'The strength of one voice', *The Scotsman*, 28 Sept. 1995; Gillan, E. and Samson, E. (2000) 'The Zero Tolerance campaign', in J. Hamner, and C. Itzin (eds) *Home Truths About Domestic Violence*; Hansard 5C, 29 March 1995, col. 944; *ODNB* (2004).

Private information: Emma Feather, Evelyn Gillan, Sandy Lunan, Greg Michaelson, Martin Sime. Personal knowledge.

RAGNHILD SIMUNSDATTER, fl. 1299, Papa Stour, Shetland.

Ragnhild Simunsdatter was possibly the tenant of a farm called *Brekasætre* (Bragaster) on the island of Papa Stour. The farm was the centre of a fiscal dispute, discussed in a letter written in 1299 by the *lawthingmen* (judicial representatives) of Shetland to Duke Hakon of Norway, who held Shetland as part of his possessions, having divided the kingdom with his brother King Erik in 1284. The dispute had occurred between Ragnhild, probably a widow, given that she spoke on her own behalf at a meeting, and the ducal official, Lord Thorvald Thoresson, on Papa Stour at Easter 1299, and was concerned with the re-assessment of the arable land there. An angry Ragnhild thought that the new arrangements cheated the Duke of some of his due income.

The document, now in the Arnamagnæan Institute, Copenhagen, describes how Ragnhild made a statement in the *stofa* (log-timbered building) on the ducal farm, where a public meeting was taking place. (The probable site was discovered in an excavation at the Biggings in the 1980s.) She stated that *Brekasætre* was not rented with the ducal farm of Uphouse and the Duke was not getting full rent as a result. Thorvald countered by reminding her that many individuals had already been sent by Duke Hakon to deal with this matter. Her response was direct and quoted verbatim: *all* of those who had dealt with this had betrayed the Duke. She thus accused the powerful Thorvald and other ducal representatives of treachery. This was compounded the next day when Ragnhild called Thorvald 'Judas' in public. To clear his name, a document was drawn up at the summer Shetland *lawthing* assembly, setting out the facts, with a deposition about the rates of rent and tax paid from Papa Stour. The results are unknown, although Lord Thorvald continued to act as the ducal (later royal) representative in Shetland. One can only wonder what ensued for Ragnhild.

This remarkable record of a woman standing up to a powerful official in a remote island shows that women in the medieval Scandinavian world had greater freedom than their sisters in the feudal societies of Europe. To appear at a public meeting and to make such statements on her own behalf – apparently fearless of the consequences – is very rare evidence of a woman playing a dramatic role, and whose accusation was taken very seriously indeed. BEC

• Ballantyne, J. and Smith, B. (eds) (1999) *Shetland Documents 1195–1579*; Crawford, B. E. and Ballin Smith, B. (1999) *The Biggings, Papa Stour, Shetland*; Øye, I. (2002) 'Ragnhild Simunsdatter and women's social and economic position in Norse society', in B. E. Crawford (ed.) *Papa Stour and 1299*.

RAINE, Kathleen Jessie, CBE, m1 **Davies**, m2 **Madge,** born Ilford 14 June 1908, died London 7 July 2003. Poet, editor, Blake scholar. Daughter of Jessie Wilkie, and George Raine, teacher and Methodist lay preacher.

Kathleen Raine's epic life-journey had strange beginnings in this strict Methodist household, but one softening influence was her Scottish mother and her Scots tongue, her border ballads and songs: from her Kathleen drew spiritual and artistic inspiration and a powerful, life-long affinity with Scotland and Scottish culture. Schooling was interrupted during the First World War, when she was sent to live in Bavington, Northumberland, seeding her passion for nature. On a scholarship to Girton College, Cambridge, she studied natural sciences and psychology. Her hasty marriage to Hugh Sykes Davies ended when she eloped with Charles Madge, co-founder of Mass Observation, with whom she had a son and a daughter. Domestic life was not for her, however, and the marriage was dissolved. *Stone and Flower*, her first book of poetry, was published in 1943. In 1949 she fell in love with Gavin Maxwell, whose homosexuality left that passion ever unrequited. She often stayed with Maxwell at his house at Sandaig, Wester Ross. A bitter quarrel led her, famously, to lay a curse on him, and a series of tragedies followed. In 1956 she fled to Cambridge, then London, lecturing and developing a career as critic and scholar specialising in William Blake and W. B. Yeats. She returned frequently to Scotland. In 1980, aged 72, she began *Temenos*, a 'journal of the arts and the imagination', supported by, among others, Prince Charles. The magazine ran to 13 fat editions, and led to the founding of the Temenos Academy in 1990. She was closely associated with the Scottish Poetry Library from its beginning.

Active to the end, Kathleen Raine was a unique, patrician spirit, defiantly individual, proudly élitist, and always true to the universality of her vision of life as noble and, at least potentially, enlightening for all. She received many honorary degrees, prizes and honours, including the Queen's Gold Medal for Poetry, (1992), Commander of the Ordre des Arts et des Lettres, and CBE (2000). JMH

• Girton College Archives: papers of Kathleen Raine; interview with Joy Hendry (1994) *Agenda*, 31, 4 and 32, 1. Raine, K. J., Work as above, and [poetry] (1946) *Living in Time*, (1949) *The Pythoness*, (1952) *The Year One*, (1956) *Collected Poems*, (1965) *The Hollow Hill*; [criticism] (1973) *Yeats, the Tarot and the Golden Dawn*, (1979) *Blake and the New Age*; [autobiography] (1973) *Farewell Happy Fields*, (1975) *The Land Unknown*, (1977) *The Lion's Mouth*, (1991) *India Seen Afar*; (2002) 'The Supreme Companionship', *Chapman* no. 100–101.

Private information from Kathleen Raine.

RAMSAY, Christian (Christina), Countess of Dalhousie, n. **Broun,** born Coalstoun 28 Feb. 1786, died Edinburgh 22 Jan. 1839. Plant collector. Daughter of Christian McDowal, and Charles Broun, advocate.

In May 1805, Christian Broun married George (Ramsay), 9th Earl of Dalhousie (1770–1838), who fought at Waterloo and became Governor-General of Nova Scotia, 1816, Governor-in-Chief of Canada, 1819–28 and later Commander-in-Chief of India. George was a former schoolfellow of Sir Walter Scott, who described him as 'steady, wise, and generous' and Christian Broun as 'an amiable, intelligent and lively woman' (*Journal*, 30 March 1829). Only their third son survived to become the 10th Earl (later achieving distinction as Governor-General of India, and Marquis of Dalhousie and the Punjab). Like several early women plant collectors, Lady Dalhousie was enabled to travel by following her husband on his postings. She made collections of plants in Nova Scotia and in Simla, Penang and other parts of India from 1816 to 1828. Her correspondence from 1826 to 1833 with W. J. Hooker, afterwards Director of Kew Gardens, records that she sent him many of her plants. She presented her Indian herbarium, consisting of about 1,200 specimens, to the BSE c. 1836, and she is commemorated in the plant genus *dalhousiea*. She died suddenly, aged 53, in Dean Ramsay's house. He later wrote of her that she 'was eminently distinguished for a fund of the most varied knowledge, for clear and powerful judgement, for acute observation, for a kind heart, a brilliant wit' (Ramsay 1924 edn., pp. 224–5). AW

• Desmond, R. (1977) *Dictionary of British and Irish Botanists and Horticulturalists*; Gibbs, Hon. V. (ed.) (1916) *The Complete Peerage*, vol. IV; Hooker, J. D. and Thomson, T. (1855) *Flora Indica*, p. 70; Nelmes, E. and Cuthbertson, W. (eds) (1931) *Portraits and Biographical Notes, Curtis's Botanical Magazine, Dedications 1827–1927*, pp. 27–8; *ODNB* (2004); Ramsay, E. B. (1857, 1924) *Reminiscences of Scottish Life and Character*; Smith, W. W. (1970) *The Royal Botanic Garden 1670–1970*, p. 115; *Trans. Bot. Soc. Edinburgh* (1836–7) p. 50, 1837–38, p. 40, 1838–39, p. 52.

RANDOLPH, Agnes (Black Agnes of Dunbar), Countess of Dunbar and March, born before 1324, died c. 1369. Defender of Scottish independence. Daughter of Isabel Stewart, and Thomas Randolph, Earl of Moray, Regent of Scotland.

Known as 'Black Agnes' because of her dark complexion, Agnes Randolph was a member of a family active in the cause of Scottish independence. Her father and her brother John both served as regents; John was captured by the English shortly after becoming co-regent in 1335. Agnes Randolph had married Patrick, Earl of Dunbar and March (d. 1369), by 1324. As Governor of Berwick, captured by the English in 1333, Earl Patrick swore allegiance to Edward III who gave him permission to re-fortify his castle of Dunbar. In 1335, Patrick switched allegiance and Dunbar became a centre of the struggle against English occupation. Edward III was suspicious of Agnes's role in fostering Scottish resistance. A force of 20,000 men, under the Earl of Salisbury, was sent to take the castle, arriving on 13 January 1338. In Earl Patrick's absence, Dunbar's defence was undertaken by his wife.

Black Agnes's defence of Dunbar has become one of the most famous stories of the Wars of Independence. In one of many colourful episodes recounted by medieval chroniclers, after a bombardment, Agnes or one of her ladies appeared on the battlements to wipe away the dust with white handkerchiefs as an act of defiance. Salisbury tried to force Black Agnes to surrender by threatening to execute her brother, but she retorted that this would make her Countess of Moray. Moreover, as the castle was her husband's, she had no power to surrender it. A song was penned by one of the English soldiers: 'Come I early, come I late, I find Annes at the gate' (Wyntoun 1903–14, vi, pp. 90–1). Local allies helped her supply the castle at night. After five months, the besiegers withdrew to join Edward III in France for what became known as the Hundred Years War. The hugely expensive siege, one of the last English military actions of the Wars of Independence, resulted in no gain. When John, Earl of Moray, died in 1346, his lands were divided between Agnes and her sister Isabella. Agnes and Patrick took the titles Earl and Countess of Moray, as Agnes had predicted to Salisbury, although as the couple were childless the title passed to Isabella's descendants, including *Elizabeth Dunbar, after their deaths. EE

• Amours, S. J. (ed.) (1903–14) *The Original Chronicle of Andrew of Wyntoun*, vi, pp. 80–91; Ewan, E. (2003) 'Agnes of Dunbar', in R. Pennington (ed.) *Amazons to Fighter Pilots* (Bibl.); *Liber Pluscardensis* (1877–80) F. J. H. Skene, ed.; *ODNB* (2004) (Dunbar, Patrick); *RMS*, i, nos. 149, 265; *SP*; *The Chronicle of Lanercost* [1913] (2001) H. Maxwell (trans.).

RAPHAEL, Sylvia, n. **Daiches,** born Sunderland 21 Feb. 1914, died Kingston upon Thames 6 Oct. 1996. Scholar and translator. Daughter of Flora Levin, and Rabbi Dr Salis Daiches.

Sylvia Daiches moved to Edinburgh, aged five, when her father became rabbi of the city's Hebrew Congregation. She would later hold the traditional male role of Warden at Westminster Synagogue. From an intellectually remarkable family, she excelled at George Watson's and the University of Edinburgh, graduating with first-class honours in French (1936). She completed her Oxford BLitt in French philology in half the normal two years. The war prevented further research: her war service was at the Treasury in London, alongside another exceptional graduate, Iris Murdoch. Sylvia Daiches met the academic David Raphael at Oxford, and they married in 1942, going on to have two daughters. She gave up a promising post at UCL to accompany her husband to New Zealand. In Glasgow, where she was resident from 1949 to 1972, she was at first denied an established post at the university because of her married status, but was appointed during the 1960s. Although her initial interest was linguistics, Sylvia Raphael was also a lover of literature, and completed distinguished translations of works by Balzac (nearest to her heart, reissued by Penguin 2005), as well as by George Sand and Mme de Staël, mostly for OUP in the 1990s. The professional and personal esteem in which she was held can be gauged from her tombstone in Edinburgh's Piershill Cemetery: 'a fine scholar and an even finer person'. ED

• Daiches, D. (1975) *Was: a pastime from time past*, (1997) *Two Worlds*, (1997) 'Sylvia Raphael', *Edinburgh Star*, 26, Feb.; France P. (ed.) (2001) *The Oxford Guide to Literature in English Translation*; *ODNB* (2004) (Daiches, Salis); Raphael, D. (1997) 'Tribute', *Westminster Synagogue Newsletter*, Feb.; UNESCO, *Index Translationum*.
Personal knowledge. Private information.

READ, Katharine (Catherine), born Dundee 3 Feb. 1723, died 15 Dec. 1778, returning from India. Portraitist and pastellist. Daughter of Elizabeth Wedderburn, and Alexander Read, laird and merchant.

Katharine Read has been described as the first professionally trained woman artist in Scotland (Macmillan 2000, p. 110). After training in Edinburgh, France and Italy, she was a successful portraitist in London for some 20 years. Her uncle, John Wedderburn, was executed for his part in the '45 at about the time that she moved to France to continue training under the pastellist De La Tour, and during her Italian stay, Katharine Read made use of some key figures surrounding the exiled Jacobite court in order to pursue her training and provide patronage. Unusually, she apparently undertook her 'Grand Tour' unaccompanied by a family member. Her example probably inspired a younger portraitist, **Anne Forbes** (1745–1840) of Edinburgh, grand-daughter of William Aikman, whose family financed her training in Italy, where she was taught by Gavin Hamilton: although she did not make her mark in London, she enjoyed later success in Edinburgh. Katharine Read did very well in the English capital, painting prominent figures, including both the Hanoverian royal family and the republican historian, Catherine Macaulay. In the 1770s, she exhibited at the RA. Patronage came from the Scottish nobility in London, and her best-known portrait (now in Inveraray Castle) was of *Elizabeth Gunning, Duchess of Hamilton and Argyll; it was engraved many times. Remaining close to her family, she also painted several relatives. Having supported her niece Helena Beatson, later Lady Oakley, also a promising artist, she travelled with her to India, to pursue her own career and, successfully, to seek a husband for her niece. But Katharine Read suffered from ill health there, and died on the journey home. Most of her paintings, signed with the spelling 'Katharine', are privately owned. LLin

• NLS: MSS, Acc. 3081: Forbes correspondence; unpub. MS: Torrance, D. R. (1985) 'Katharine Read of Drumgeith', in 'The Reads of Auchenlick [etc.]'.
Archer, M. (1979) *India and British Portraiture 1770–1825*; Gaze, D. (1997) *Dictionary of Women Artists*, 'Katharine Read' by D. Taylor, pp. 1143–5 and 'Anne Forbes', by K. Sloan, pp. 537–9; Ingamells, J. (1997) *A Dictionary of British and Irish Travellers in Italy 1701–1800*, pp. 804–5; Macmillan, D. (2000) *Scottish Art 1460–2000*; Manners, Lady V. (1931) 'Catherine Read: the "English Rosalba"', *The Connoisseur*, 88, pp. 376–86, and two further articles ibid., (1932) 89, pp. 35–40, 171–8; *ODNB* (2004) (Read, Katharine; Forbes, Anne); Steuart, A. F. (1905) 'Miss Catherine Read, Court Paintress', *Scot. Hist. Rev.*, 2, pp. 38–46.

REDPATH, Anne, OBE, m. **Michie,** born Galashiels 29 March 1895, died Edinburgh 7 Jan. 1965. Artist. Daughter of Agnes Milne, and Thomas Brown Redpath, textile designer.

Her family having moved to Hawick in 1901, Anne Redpath attended Hawick High School until 1913, receiving encouragement from the art master, John Gray. Her parents allowed her to enrol at ECA if she also attended Moray House to gain a teacher's certificate, and she qualified as a primary school teacher in 1917. The following year, she received her Diploma in Drawing and Painting, a bursary, a year's post-graduate study, and in 1919 a travelling scholarship. She journeyed through Belgium to Paris, and then to Florence and Siena, where she discovered Italian quattrocento painting. Returning to Scotland, in 1920 she married James Beattie Michie (1891–1958), an architect with the Imperial War Graves Commission. They settled in St Omer and she continued to paint and exhibit locally in northern France, where two sons were born: Alastair (1921) and Lindsay (1924). A third son, David, was born in 1928 in southern France. During this period, most of her creativity went into the children's upbringing. The family returned to Hawick in 1934, following the bankruptcy of James Michie's employer. He moved to London in search of work and thereafter the family drifted apart. Anne Redpath re-embarked on her career, working mostly on landscapes and still life subjects. She resumed exhibiting at the RSA in 1935 (having exhibited as a student in 1919). President of the SSWA (1944–7), she held her first solo exhibition in 1947 in Gordon Small's gallery in Princes Street, Edinburgh. During the late 1940s she was a member of the Hanover Street Group, an informal grouping of artists who met to exchange ideas and encourage each other.

In her still life paintings, Anne Redpath employed the miscellanea of objects collected over a lifetime. Calling up such varied references as Bonnard, Matisse and Islamic miniatures, her work is both highly decorative and personal, for example *The Indian Rug* (1940s SNGMA). After two painting trips to Skye in the 1940s, she started to travel seriously in the 1950s. These journeys were pivotal in the inspiration for her art. She travelled to Spain via Paris and Collioure (1951) and visited Brittany (1953), Corsica (1954), the Canary Islands (1959) and Portugal (1961). The visual impact of stark living conditions, extreme climates, regional architecture and, in Portugal especially, of the intensely ornate gold altarpieces is reflected in her work. Her early pastel palette intensified to one of strident colours and strong contrasts, and her brushwork reflected the energy of her response to the landscape.

From the 1950s, Anne Redpath became a central figure in the art scene in Scotland, and her home at 7 London Street, Edinburgh (now marked with a plaque) was an important artists' meeting place. She won formal recognition through her election as associate (1947) and later academician (1952) of the RSA. Between 1950 and 1963, she had five one-woman exhibitions in the Scottish Gallery, and gradually acquired recognition in England (OBE 1955, ARA 1960). Her work is held in many collections, including the RSA and SNGMA. JOS

• Bourne, P. (1989) *Anne Redpath 1895–1965*; Bruce, G. (1974) *Anne Redpath*; Dickson, T. E. (1960) 'Anne Redpath', *The Studio*, March, vol. 159, no. 803; Hartley, K. (ed.) (1989) *Scottish Art since 1900*; Long, P. (1996) *Anne Redpath 1895–1965* (catalogue); McCullough, F. (1963) 'Anne Redpath', *Scot. Art Rev.*, IX, 2; Mullaly, T. (1965) Introduction to catalogue *Anne Redpath – Memorial Exhibition, Edinburgh*; *ODNB* (2004); Westwater, R. H. (1955) 'Anne Redpath', *Scot. Art Rev.*, V, 3.

REEKIE, Stella Jane, born Gravesend 29 July 1922, died Glasgow 28 Sept. 1982. Missionary and inter-faith worker. Daughter of Jane Reekie and Arthur Reekie.

Educated in Gravesend, Stella Reekie trained as a nursery nurse in Golders Green. She joined the Red Cross in 1943, which took her to Belgium and to the horrors of Belsen in 1945, where she worked to rehabilitate Jewish children. Later she worked in the children's ward of the Red Cross TB hospital in Bad Rehburg. Back in Britain in 1949, she joined the Church of Scotland, in 1951 becoming a missionary in Karachi in Pakistan, where she spent 17 years. Returning from Pakistan to Scotland in 1968, she helped run a support group for refugees from Central Europe. In 1969, she was appointed by the Church of Scotland to work with Asian immigrant women in Glasgow, developing ways of meeting their needs and those of young people through co-operative projects and educational programmes. She supported a health clinic for immigrant children and established a permanent summer project for them. She also served on the Glasgow Community Relations Council. In 1972, an 'International Flat' was established where Stella Reekie lived and opened the doors to all. Her work included setting up a Sharing of Faiths Group that provided a forum for Muslims, Buddhists, Sikhs, Hindus, Jews, Christians, Baha'is and others to work together. The continuing growth of the inter-faith movement in Scotland is due in no small measure to the vision of Stella Reekie, who dedicated her life to establishing tolerance and understanding across ethnic and religious divides. M B S

• Adamson, J., Ramsay, K., and Craig, M. (1984) *Stella: the story of Stella Jane Reekie, 1922–1982.*

REID, Marion, n. **Kirkland,** born Glasgow 25 March 1815, died Shepherd's Bush, London, 9 March 1902. Author. Daughter of Janet Finlay, and James Kirkland, a Glasgow merchant.

On 7 January 1839, Marion Kirkland married Hugo Reid (1809–72), a progressive educationalist, in Edinburgh. In June 1840, as the only Scotswoman present at the World Anti-Slavery Convention in London, she watched as a group of American woman delegates were refused the right to participate, after a lengthy debate, and met their leader, Lucretia Mott (Stanton et al. 1881, vol. 3, p. 838n.). Influenced by this debate, Marion Reid's *Plea for Woman* (1843) was probably the first work in Britain or the USA to give priority to achieving civil and political rights for women, and was particularly influential in the USA in the first years of the women's suffrage movement (Ferguson 1988). Aware of an earlier radical tradition, Marion Reid, like Mary Wollstonecraft, cited Talleyrand (following Condorcet), as indicating that the democratic principles of the French Revolution had not yet been applied to half the human race (ibid., p. 22). She criticised Sarah Lewis's *Woman's Mission* (1839) and the anonymous female author of *Woman's Rights and Duties* (1840) for their stress on the power of women's influence and advocacy of a separate 'woman's sphere'. While women's responsibilities might remain primarily domestic, she argued, this did not unfit them for civil and political rights, which would 'ennoble and elevate the mind' (ibid., p. 24). Exercising rights would enable women's interests to be represented, and their grievances redressed. Such grievances included the laws oppressing married women, and the failure to provide girls with a good education, not as future wives and mothers but for their own fulfilment.

Marion Reid's arguments foreshadowed some of John Stuart Mill's in his *Subjection of Woman* (1869). In the only serious review of her work, *Christian Isobel Johnstone recognised the allusion to Wollstonecraft, but suggested that economic independence for women was an even higher priority than political rights. In the USA, the first edition was followed by three more (1847, 1851 and 1852) entitled *Woman, her Education and Influence,* with an introduction by Caroline Kirkland (unrelated). After posts in Liverpool and Nottingham, Marion Reid's husband became Principal of Dalhousie College, Halifax, Nova Scotia (1855–60) and she probably accompanied him there. The couple had one daughter. Much later, in 1888, the Finnish feminist Aleksandra Gripenberg recorded a meeting with her, recalling 'how interested and fresh she was in all our questions, having watched their progress for many years' (McFadden 1999, p. 21). J R

• Reid, M., Works as above.

Ferguson, S. (1988) 'Foreword' to Marion Reid, *A Plea for Woman*; Johnstone, C. I. (1844) 'Mrs Hugo Reid's Plea for Woman', *Tait's Edinburgh Magazine*, vol.II. o.s, 15 n.s., pp. 423–8; Kirkland, C. (1852) 'General Introduction' to Mrs H. Reid, *Woman, Her Education and Influence*; McFadden, M. (1999) *Golden Cables of Sympathy*; Midgley, C. (1992) *Women Against Slavery*; *ODNB* (Reid, Hugo); Stanton, E. C., Anthony, S. B. and Gage, M. J. (eds) (1881) *History of Woman Suffrage*, 6 vols.

RENTON, Dorothy Graham, n. **Robertson,** born Perth 7 April 1898, died Perth 28 Jan. 1966. Plantswoman. Daughter of Robina Conacher, and William Robertson, medical practitioner.

Dorothy Robertson grew up in Edinburgh, where her regular visits to the Royal Botanic Garden widened her enthusiasm for and knowledge of plants. In 1922 she married John Taylor Renton (1891–1967), a chartered land agent. They purchased land from Orchardbank Nursery in Perth, built their house, Branklyn, and started to develop the garden. Forty years later it was described by Harold Fletcher, at that time Regius Keeper of the RBGE, as 'the finest garden under two acres in Europe' (RCHS award 1960). Dorothy Renton was the plant expert, her husband the garden designer. They were influenced by the rock gardener Reginald Farrer and by Gertrude Jekyll but developed in their own style a unique garden of rock and scree features, peat walls and narrow winding paths, creating many microclimates. Dorothy Renton acquired an international reputation for her skill in raising rare and difficult plants, many of which were new to science, particularly those from seeds collected from the Sino-Himalayan region. The Rentons were founder members of the Alpine Garden Society in 1929 and of the Scottish Rock Garden Club in 1933.

Dorothy Renton's expertise earned her many Awards of Merit from the RHS, including the

Veitch Memorial Medal in 1954 for her work in introducing and cultivating rare plant species. She also received medals from the Scottish Rock Garden Club, the Alpine Garden Society and, in 1960, the RCHS Gold Medal. In 1962, the Rentons were jointly awarded the Lyttel Trophy, the Alpine Garden Society's highest award.

Dorothy Renton was involved with the Red Cross for 30 years until her retirement in 1962, becoming President of the Perth Division during the Second World War. She was awarded the voluntary long service medal, to which a Clasp was added in 1957. Since they had no children, Branklyn was bequeathed to the NTS in 1967. BM
• *Alpine Garden Society Bulletin*, 1966, 34 (2) (obit.); Fletcher, H. R. (1969) *The Story of the Royal Horticultural Society, 1804–1968*, p. 521; Hellyer, A. G. L. 'A living tapestry created', *Country Life*, 12 August 1976, pp. 406–7; Mitchell, R. J. (1992) *Branklyn Garden*, NTS Guidebook; *Perthshire Advertiser*, 29 Jan. 1966 (obit.); 'Scottish horticultural medal awards', *RCHS Yearbook, 1960*, pp. 47–9; Roper, L. 'A plant lover's paradise', *Country Life*, 2 June 1966; Scottish Rock Garden Club, *Journal*, 1966 (obit.).

REYNOLDS, Doris Livesey,‡ m. **Holmes,** born Manchester 1 July 1899, died Hove 10 Oct. 1985. Geologist, first woman FRSE. Daughter of Louisa Livesey, and Alfred Reynolds, textile merchant.

After obtaining first-class honours in geology (Bedford College London, 1920; DSc London 1937), Doris Reynolds established an international reputation as a brilliant, if unconventional, petrologist. On a field trip to Ardnamurchan, while teaching geology at University College London (1931–3), she met Arthur Holmes (1890–1965), Professor of Geology at the University of Durham. She was offered a lectureship at Durham where they worked closely together, generating consid-erable gossip. They married in 1939 after Arthur Holmes' first wife died, moving in 1942 to Edinburgh, where he was appointed Regius Professor of Geology. He considered that the university was getting 'two for the price of one', for Doris Reynolds was never given a salaried post at Edinburgh. As an Honorary Research Fellow, she made a huge contribution to that department over 20 years, lecturing, supervising PhD students and researching 'her hobby' (Hawkes unpub.).

In the 1940s, Doris Reynolds developed the theory of 'granitisation' to explain the origin of granites: fluids migrating upwards through the Earth's crust soaked into overlying rocks, chemically turning them into granite (Reynolds 1946).

A feature of this theory was the 'basic front', a halo of dark minerals around the altered rock (Reynolds 1947a). Norman Bowen, leader of the opposing hypothesis – that granites evolved from basalts – described her theory as a basic *af* front (Lewis 2000, p. 212). The ensuing 'Granite Controversy' (Reynolds 1947b) dominated petrological research for two decades. Although her granitisation theory eventually proved incorrect, her work had the merit both of provoking research – 'erecting wickets to be bowled at' as Arthur Holmes put it – and of drawing attention to the role of fluids within the Earth's crust, the importance of which was recognised only later. She was the first woman FRSE (1949) and was awarded the GSL Lyell medal (1960). As with her work, she was controversial in her relationships, polarising people into loving or hating her. After Arthur Holmes died in 1965, she revised his famous textbook *Holmes' Principles of Physical Geology* (1978), bought a car and learnt to drive. CLEL
• Royal Holloway Univ. of London Archives: Papers of Dr Doris Reynolds, PP21; (see PP21/6, 4 August 1943, for Hawkes, unpub).
Reynolds, D. L. (1946) 'The sequence of chemical changes leading to granitisation', *Geol. Soc. of London Q. J.*, 102, pp. 389–446, (1947a) 'The association of basic "fronts" with granitization', *Science Progress*, 35, pp. 205–19, (1947b) 'The granite controversy', *Geol. Mag.* 84, pp. 209–23, (1950) 'The geology of Slieve Cullion, Foughill and Carrickcarnan', *Trans. RSE*, LXII, 1, 4, pp. 85–143, (1954) 'Fluidization as a geological process, and its bearing on the problem of intrusive granites', *Amer. Jour. Science*, 252, pp. 577–614. Black, G. P. (1986) 'Dr D. L. Reynolds (1899–1985)', *Geol. Soc. [of London] Annual Report*, 32–3 (obit.); Lewis, C. (2000) *The Dating Game*; *ODNB* (2004) (see Holmes, Arthur).

RIACH, Nancy Anderson Long, born Motherwell 6 April 1927, died Monte Carlo 15 Sept. 1947. Champion swimmer. Daughter of Agnes Nicol White, teacher, and Charles Fraser Riach, police inspector.

Nancy Riach was the most famous of a long line of stars from the Motherwell Amateur Swimming and Water Polo Club of the 1930s and 1940s, coached by David Crabb. The club's other national swimmers included Cathie Gibson and Margaret Bolton (the latter Nancy's friend from Dalziel High School in Motherwell). One of only five women to appear in the first 50 Scottish athletes in the 2002 Scottish Sports Hall of Fame, Nancy Riach held 28 Scottish and British swimming records – freestyle, breaststroke and backstroke – by the time she was 17. From a devout home, she, like Scottish sprinter Eric Liddell, refused to compete on Sundays. Her career was cut tragically short at the age of 20: in Monte Carlo for the European Championships of 1947 with the British swimming team, preparing for the 1948 Olympics, she contracted polio and died before her parents reached the hospital. On her death, she was hailed by the chairman of the UN Swimming Committee as 'the finest swimmer that the British Empire had ever produced' and the 'finest ambassador of sport that Scotland or any other country within the British Empire had ever turned out' (*Hamilton Advertiser* 1947). Scotland mourned her when she was buried at Airdrie. The Nancy Riach Memorial Award remains one of the most coveted annual awards in Scottish swimming. GJ

• *Glasgow Herald*, 15 Sept. 1947; *Hamilton Advertiser*, 20 Sept. 1947; *ODNB* (2004); Walker, G. (1994) 'Nancy Riach and the Motherwell Swimming Phenomenon', in G. Jarvie and G. Walker, *Scottish Sport in the Making of the Nation*, pp. 142–54.

RITA *see* **Humphreys, Elizabeth** (1850–1938)

RITSON, Muriel, CBE, born Greenock 2 Jan. 1885, died Edinburgh 8 July 1980. Career administrator and civil servant. Daughter of Agnes Jane Catto, and John Fletcher Ritson, railway agent.

Educated at Greenock Academy and in Germany, Muriel Ritson was a social worker and rent collector for the Glasgow Workman's Dwellings Company (1908–11). As secretary of the WFS and Honorary Treasurer of the GWCA, she became familiar with health insurance work. Having been on several committees dealing with public health during the First World War, she joined the Commission of Investigation which visited France, in connection with the WAAF (*Glasgow Herald*, 1919). By the time of her appointment in 1919 as the only woman member of the six-strong Scottish Board of Health, which administered and directed Scottish health policy (1919–28), Muriel Ritson was prominently associated with social work in Glasgow. In 1929 she moved to the new Department of Health for Scotland as Assistant Secretary and later Controller of Health and Pensions Insurance, until 1945. For the year before her retirement in 1946, she was Scottish Controller of the Ministry of National Insurance. She sat on the Ryan Committee (Health Insurance) and the Committee on Admission of Women to the Diplomatic and Consular Service. Undoubtedly her most high-profile appointment, however, was as Scottish representative on the Beveridge Committee (Social Insurance and Allied Services, 1941–2). She was awarded the CBE in 1936. JLMJ

• *Glasgow Herald*, 17 July 1919 p. 6; Jenkinson, J. (2002) *Scotland's Health 1919–1948*; *WWW*, vol. 7 (1980).
Private information: Muriel Ritson's surviving relatives in Australia.

ROBERTS, Jean Barr McDonald, n. **Weir,** DBE, born Glasgow, 20 Dec. 1895, died Glasgow, 26 March 1988. Glasgow town councillor, 1929–66; first woman Lord Provost, Glasgow, 1960–3. Daughter of Mary Nevin, and Walter Weir, railway engine fitter.

Jean Weir was born and brought up in the Springburn district of Glasgow, an industrial community famous for the manufacture of railway locomotives. She was educated locally, at Albert School, and then at Whitehill School in Dennistoun. Between 1914 and 1916 she was a student at Glasgow's Dundas Vale Teacher Training College, thereafter teaching at Bishop Street Elementary School and for a time in a special school for children with disabilities. She left the profession in 1922 when she married Cameron Roberts (1889–1964), a mathematics teacher and later headmaster. The couple had one daughter.

Jean Roberts, having grown up in a socialist family, was, along with her husband, an active member of the ILP. In 1929, she was encouraged to stand as a Glasgow Corporation councillor for Kingston, a docklands district immediately to the south of the River Clyde. Her educational expertise helped to win the ward for Labour, as schooling was one of the responsibilities absorbed by the Corporation under local government reorganisation in 1929. Although Glasgow then had the largest municipal administration in the United Kingdom outside London, she was only the tenth female councillor elected since 1920 and the sixth to represent Labour. The party gained municipal control in Glasgow for the first time in November 1933, and Jean Roberts rose to prominence in assorted positions, becoming Senior Magistrate in 1936. From 1952, she was the first woman to serve as City Treasurer and then, from 1955, as Labour Group leader.

Jean Roberts had been nominated as a candidate for Lord Provost, Scottish equivalent of Lord Mayor, as early as 1949, but was not successful until 1960. She was aware that she had broken

centuries of convention to become the city's first female civic leader, but was still determined to embrace the ermine-robed ceremonial attached to the post. Her shrewd blend of traditionalism and progress meant that during her three years of office she became well known and widely respected. Yet it is revealing that it took her 31 years to achieve Glasgow's chief municipal honour. Her status as a woman Lord Provost also remained unique in Scottish local government until the 1980s.
Jean Roberts was made DBE in 1962 and served as Chairman of Cumbernauld Development Corporation between 1965 and 1972. IEM
• Univ. of Glasgow Archives, Acc. 44/32, Senate Orations File, Dame Jean Roberts (1977).
Glasgow *Evening News*, 27 April 1933; Glasgow *Evening Times*, 4 May, 6 May 1960; *Glasgow Herald*, 5 May, 7 May 1960, 18 May 1962, 11 August 1964, 23 June 1977; *ODNB* (2004); Sinclair, K. 'Passing of a piece of history', *Glasgow Herald*, 29 March 1988 (Appreciation); *WWW 1981–90* (1991).

ROBERTSON, Anne Strachan, born Glasgow 3 May 1910, died Glasgow 4 Oct. 1997. Archaeologist, numismatist, museum curator. Daughter of Margaret Purden and John Anderson Robertson, teachers.

Anne Robertson was brought up in Glasgow, one of four sisters, and studied Classics at the University of Glasgow and archaeology at the University of London. From the early 1930s, frequent scholarships enabled her to participate in Mortimer Wheeler's excavations, to work at the British Museum and to produce specialist numismatic publications. At a time when there were few professional, let alone female, archaeologists, she excavated Roman military sites on the Antonine Wall and worked at the Hunterian Museum, producing a series of important reports spanning 40 years, including a scholarly catalogue of the Roman Imperial coins in the Hunter Coin Cabinet (1962–82). She was appointed Under-Keeper of the Hunterian Museum and Curator of the Hunter Coin Cabinet in 1952. Continuing a tradition of meticulous and detailed scholarship inherited from George Macdonald and other pioneers, Anne Robertson became a doughty, if formal, doyenne of Roman studies. Among many professional distinctions, she received the Medal of the Royal Numismatic Society (RNS), the Huntington Medal and the Dalrymple lectureship. She was also FRSE, FMA, FRNS, FSA and FSAScot. She showed her enthusiasm for public participation in archaeology

by her long involvement with Glasgow Archaeological Society and the Scottish Field School of Archaeology. She became Professor of Roman Archaeology, one of the first women to be given professorial rank at the University of Glasgow, in 1974, a year before her retirement. MAMC
• Robertson, A. S., Selected publications: (1960) *The Antonine Wall* (5th edn. 2001), (1961–82) *Catalogue of Roman Imperial Coins in the Hunter Coin Cabinet*, vols 1–5, (1961) *Sylloge of Anglo-Saxon Coins in the Hunter Coin Cabinet* (British Academy), (2002) *Romano-British Coin Hoards*.
The Herald, 11 Oct. 1997 (obit.); *The Independent*, 15 Nov. 1997; Keppie, L. J. F. (1997) 'Obituary, Anne S. Robertson', *Proc. Soc. Antiquaries Scot.*, 127, pp. xiii–xvii.

ROBERTSON, Christina, n. **Saunders,** born Kinghorn, Fife, 17 Dec. 1796, died St Petersburg 30 April 1854. Painter at Russian court. Daughter of a coach painter.

Christina Saunders seems to have been encouraged to paint by her uncle, artist George Sa(u)nders (1774–1846). Working from his address in London, she quickly made a name for painting portraits, cabinet pictures and miniatures. In 1823, she married James Robertson, artist, and they had four surviving children. In 1828, she moved to her own studio in Argyle Street and exhibited regularly at the RA (1823–44). Her distinguished sitters included the Drummond-Burrells, the Marchioness of Lothian, the Duke and Duchess of Buccleuch, the Duke and Duchess of Northumberland and the de Rothschilds. Although one critic relegated her to the 'little boudoir school' (Bird et al. 1996, p. 41), her reputation was sufficiently established by 1829 for the RSA to elect her as the first woman honorary member. She painted several fashionable Russian ladies and their children in Paris (1837), and commissions from the Tsar's family and other Russian Europhiles followed. Christina Robertson was resourceful, as well as sharp-tongued and hump-backed, according to some reports (SNPG: Scottish file). She travelled to Russia (1839–40), to occupy rooms in the Peterhof Palace in St Petersburg. She was made honorary member of the Imperial Academy of Arts in 1841 for her royal portraits, and made regular visits to the city, having a studio on Nevsky Prospect in 1849. A watercolour portrait of her friend the artist Vladimir Ivanovich Gau (1816–95) survives in the State Russian Museum there, as does a pencil portrait of Christina by her daughter Mary (1846).

Christina Robertson, whose husband predeceased her, died in St Petersburg and was buried in the Volkov Cemetery (1854). Her capacity to paint to order has left prolific evidence of the pre-Revolutionary Russian aristocracy in the State Hermitage Museum and several other Russian museums (Stavropol, Omsk, Alupka, Simferopol, Tashkent, Voronezh, Moscow). Neglected after her death, her modern reputation was boosted by an exhibition in Edinburgh and St Petersburg in 1996. RA

• SNPG: Scottish File 5, also Christina Robertson, 'Three Unknown Children' c. 1830–5, SNPG 3267; V & A: Account Book and Self-Portrait.
Bird, A. (1977) 'A painter of Russian aristocracy', *Country Life*, 6 Jan., pp. 32–3; Bird, A. et al. (1996) *Christina Robertson: a Scottish portraitist at the Russian court*, exhibition catalogue; *ODNB* (2004); Pomeroy, J. et al. (2003) 'An imperial collection: women artists from the State Hermitage Museum'.

ROBERTSON, Edith Anne, n. **Stewart,** born Glasgow 10 Jan. 1883, died Glasgow 31 Jan. 1973. Poet, biographer, dramatist. Daughter of Jane Louisa Faulds, and Robert Stewart, civil engineer.

Edith Anne Stewart was educated at Glasgow High School for Girls and in London and Germany. In 1919 she married the Rev. Professor James Alexander Robertson; they had three daughters. She was a member of PEN and a keen walker and gardener. In the foreword to her *Collected Ballads and Poems* (1967) the writer and critic Douglas Young celebrates the religious qualities of her poetry and praises her use of Scots. '[The poems] bring the reader constantly into touch with an exceptionally rich personality, of the finest sensibility, and with an atmosphere of poetic timelessness, truly that of the great old Scots ballads' (Robertson 1967, p. [i]). It is, paradoxically, in her translations of Gerard Manley Hopkins's poems into Scots that Edith Anne Robertson is most original: here, her religious sense, which was never narrowly sectarian, could reveal itself, as could her sensitivity to the possibilities of Scots: 'In God's guid time, in God's guid kennin. Heaven's smile/'s nae wry smile, – cud be shy smile – sae skies gangrel gait/Foilzies mirk bens – lichtens a loesome mile.' ('Til My Ain Hert,' *MSWP*, pp. 39–40). She also wrote biography and drama, including an unpublished play (in NLS) celebrating the piety, courage and resilient femininity of *Lady Janet Douglas, burned at the stake in 1537. DAMCM

• Univ. of Aberdeen Library, Personal papers and manuscripts, AUL MS 3406/1/1–14, MS 2794; NLS: MSS 26977–26984, corr. and literary papers.
Robertson, E. A., Works as above, and see Bibl. *MSWP* (Bibl.).

ROBERTSON, Hannah, n. **Swan,** born 2 Oct. 1724, died Edinburgh in or after 1807. Autobiographer, writer on fancy work and cookery. Daughter of Anne Huntingdon of Carlisle, and a Mr Swan, allegedly illegitimate son of Charles II.

In her picaresque autobiography (1791), Hannah Robertson recounted a comfortable childhood. On her mother's remarriage, for her own amusement, she acquired skills in embroidery, drawing and flower-making. She married Robert Robertson on 21 October 1749 in Perth. After his financial failure, she briefly managed the Free Masons' Tavern in Aberdeen, but returned to Perth to teach school. In 1766, she published *The Young Ladies' School of Arts*, dedicated to the Countess of Fyfe, instructing servants, and young ladies, 'especially young women who have no fortunes, or may be left in low circumstances', in cookery ('Jamms, Pickles', etc.) and a variety of skills and accomplishments ('Filigree . . . Japanning'). In the expanded edition of 1767, she appealed to 'Scots Ladies' to redress their backwardness in housekeeping in the spirit of improvement. After her husband's death in 1771, she taught school in Edinburgh and York; published further editions; and in 1782, with her daughter, opened a shop in Grosvenor Square, London, popular with ladies. After successive family disasters, she published her life history, helped by subscriptions from patrons. Back in Edinburgh c. 1794, she sought to support her grandchildren by teaching, flower-making and from sales of her books; Lord Buchan recorded that, having survived her husband and nine children, 'an object of great commiseration', she was in February 1807 living in poverty, with failing eyesight, in East Lochend Close, Canongate. JR

• Robertson, H. (1766, 1767, 1776) *The Young Ladies' School of Arts*, (1791) *The Life of Mrs Robertson (A Tale of Truth as well as of Sorrow)*, (1806) *The Ladies' School of Arts . . . Likewise a Narrative of the Author's Life, Addressed to a Friend*, NLS copy H.17.e.19, with MS note by Lord Buchan, 10 Feb. 1807.

ROBERTSON, Regina Christina (Jeannie),[‡] n. **Stewart,** MBE, born 17 April 1908, died Aberdeen 13 March 1975. Traditional singer. Daughter of Maria Stewart, hawker, and Donald Robertson, pedlar; husband and wife according to the customs of the travelling people.

Jeannie Robertson eloped in 1927 with Donald Higgins (1907–71), whose widowed father had married her elder sister. Such complex relationship patterns were not rare among the travelling people, who wintered in towns but took to the roads in spring, the men working with metal or with animals, the women, like Jeannie's mother, typically hawking goods. As seasonal labourers, picking berries and lifting potatoes, in their camps they shared fiddle and pipe music and songs handed down from ancient tradition. Donald Higgins was a fine piper. Jeannie Robertson's daughter, **Lizzie Higgins** (1929–93) became an outstanding singer in her own right. But her mother, who learnt her songs from her own mother, Maria, was by common consent the finest traditional singer discovered through the Scottish Folk Song Revival of the 1950s. She always sang unaccompanied, eschewing instrumental backing.

Hamish Henderson, of the then recently founded School of Scottish Studies at the University of Edinburgh, was in 1953 in quest of traditional singers. Travelling people directed him to Jeannie Robertson's house in Aberdeen's Gallowgate. Through Henderson, and the portable tape recorder, this retiring middle-aged housewife was heard on the BBC Scottish Home Service, and invited to sing in the Edinburgh International Festival. Jeannie Robertson toured the clubs which burgeoned in the Scottish Folk Song Revival and travelled as far as London, but declined invitations to the USSR and USA. Fees from concerts and LPs – not much – provided comforts for her ailing husband. In 1968, she became the first traveller to receive an honour (MBE) from the monarch. Her repertoire included bawdy and lyrical songs as well as great traditional ballads. Her version of the ancient 'My Son David' had enormous tragic power. With her dark eyes, raven hair and sharp mind, she maintained her dignity in any company, so that her auditors provisionally had to believe, as she did, that every word she sang in her ballads was true history. ALRC

• Tapes held in the School of Scottish Studies, Univ. of Edinburgh.

Henderson, H. (1992) *Alias McAlias*; Munro, A. (2nd edn., 1998) *The Democratic Muse, Folk Music Revival in Scotland*; *ODNB* (2004) (see Robertson, Christina Jane); Porter, J. and Gower, H. (1995) *Jeannie Robertson: emergent singer, transformative voice*.

ROSE, Elizabeth, of Kilravock, m. **Rose,** born Kilravock Castle, Nairnshire, 8 March 1747, died Kilravock 1 Nov. 1815. Diarist and letter-writer, clan chief. Daughter of Elizabeth Clephane, and Hugh Rose of Kilravock.

Educated at home, Elizabeth Rose read widely in English and Scottish literature, and corresponded with her uncle, Dr John Clephane, friend of David Hume, and her cousin, the novelist Henry Mackenzie. On 19 June 1779, she married Captain Hugh Rose of Brea, MD, who died the following year. In 1782, on the death of her brother Hugh, 18th Baron of Kilravock, she succeeded to the title, finally confirmed by the House of Lords in April 1787; her only child, Hugh, succeeded her. Her extensive journals, and reading-lists with extracts, kept intermittently from 1771 to her death, offer an opportunity to study the activities, reading and self-representations of a landed gentlewoman close to several leading Enlightenment figures, including Henry Mackenzie, Lord Kames and James Beattie. The lists are wide-ranging, including religious and devotional literature, works on education, conduct, travel, history and moral philosophy, poetry, plays and novels. She was a literary confidante of Mackenzie, who informed her on the progress of his novels: having sent her chapters from *A Man of Feeling*, he commented 'I am proud of having drawn a female character so much to your liking' (Oct. 1769, Drescher, p. 25). But they did not always agree on the position of women: 'You are hard on me for my idea of inferiority in your sex', he wrote in 1771 (ibid., pp. 67–8, cited Moran, p. 89). JR

• NAS: GD1/726, GD125: Elizabeth Rose, corr., journals, and reading lists.

Drescher, H. W. (1967) *Henry Mackenzie. Letters to Elizabeth Rose of Kilravock. On Literature, Events and People*; [Innes, C.] (1848) *A Genealogical Deduction of the Family of Rose of Kilravock*, Spalding Club of Aberdeen, vol. 18; Moran, M. C. (1999) 'From rudeness to refinement: gender, genre and Scottish enlightenment discourse', DPhil, Johns Hopkins University.

ROSS, Marion Amelia Spence, born Edinburgh 9 April 1903, died Dunfermline 3 Jan. 1994. Physicist. Daughter of Marion Amelia Spence Thomson, and William Baird Ross, organist and music teacher.

Marion Ross graduated with honours in mathematics and natural philosophy from the University of Edinburgh. After teacher training, she taught mathematics for two years in Surrey. In 1928, she was appointed to Assistant Lecturer posts in the Physics and Music Departments at Edinburgh, where she pioneered a new course in acoustics, still a part of the BMus course. She followed her own line of investigation, using techniques of X-ray diffraction, with experimental work done in Manchester during the vacations, in collaboration with Sir Lawrence Bragg. She gained her PhD in 1943, under Charles Barkla, a Nobel Prize winner. Her first major paper was on crystal structure, published with Arnold Beevers, on determinations using Fourier methods and the new Patterson method; important examples were the alums, copper sulfate pentahydrate, and b-alumina, $NaAl_{11}O_{17}$. Originally studied as a troublesome impurity in Al_2O_3 production, it is now an important solid-state ionic conductor, and two sites in the structure are known as Beevers-Ross and anti-Beevers-Ross sites.

During the Second World War, Marion Ross taught mathematics in Falkirk Technical School then spent four years with the Admiralty in Rosyth, working on underwater acoustics, fluid flows and hydrodynamics, becoming Head of the Research Group. At the end of the war, invited to return to the University of Edinburgh as a lecturer, she set up a laboratory to study high-energy physics using emulsions, which produced major results on the calibration of emulsions. In 1965, she established the Fluid Dynamics Unit and as its first director made important findings in the stability of boundary layers, retiring as an emeritus reader. She was elected FRSE and on her retirement a prize was founded to honour her name. NCB

• *The Scotsman*, 13 Jan. 1994 (obit.). www.cpa.ed.ac.uk/bulletinarchive/1993–1994/06/ obituaries.html; www.ph.ed.ac.uk/fluids/Homepage.html; www.ecanews.org/beev.htm

ROUGH, Alison, born c. 1480, died Edinburgh 3 Sept. 1535. Merchant and property-holder. Executed for murder.

By 1507, Alison Rough had married Jasper Mayne, an Edinburgh notary and merchant who was active in royal service and acquired a large number of urban properties, many of them held jointly with his wife. Jasper Mayne was killed at Flodden in 1513, leaving his widow, like many other women, to provide for the future of her children. Alison Rough was involved in numerous legal disputes over her properties, unpaid merchant debts, and other affairs, making her more publicly visible than most contemporary women. Marriage to Thomas Lauriston ended in divorce c. 1517. In 1528, she secured her son John's marriage to the wealthy widow Margaret Martin, who had been

Jasper Mayne's client. Her son Adam entered the priesthood and returned property earlier granted to him to his mother. She used these lands and a substantial cash sum as a rich dowry for her daughter, **Katherine Mayne** (c. 1513–c. 1565), attracting the twice-widowed but well-connected Edinburgh burgess, Alexander Cant. Alison Rough moved into her daughter's and son-in-law's home after their marriage in late 1531.

In 1533, Alison Rough and her son John were embroiled in a bitter inheritance dispute; he claimed his sister Isabel was illegitimate, a claim Alison denied. Alexander Cant, angered by delays in the dowry payments, sued his wife and mother-in-law. In 1535, a property Katherine Mayne had brought to her marriage was claimed by another man; on 31 August, Alexander, Katherine and Alison lost a court case over the property. That night, tempers flared and Alexander Cant was killed by his mother-in-law and wife. Mother and daughter were condemned to death; Katherine Mayne's pregnancy delayed her execution. After the birth, she fled to England, married the Protestant exile Alexander Allan (Alesius), and moved to Germany. Thirty years later she granted an Edinburgh property to the daughter she had left behind. Alison Rough was executed by drowning on 3 September 1535. A six-year legal struggle ensued as the town and the King fought over her forfeited goods.

Alison Rough's story is told today in an exhibition in The Real Mary King's Close, which lies underneath Edinburgh City Chambers. **Mary King** (fl. 1616–44) married a local merchant, Thomas Nimmo, in 1616; the couple had four children. Widowed in 1629, Mary and her young family moved before 1635 to what had been known as Alexander King's Close, where she rented a house along with a shop on the High Street. Her testament, drawn up in September 1644, shows that she was a successful tailor and cloth merchant. EE

• Edinburgh City Archives: Inventory of Charters; NAS: CS 5,6, Court of Session Records; CH 5/3/1, Act Book of Archdeaconry of Lothian; B22/1/5–7, Protocol Book of Vincent Strathauchin.

Ewan, E. (2003) 'A woman's life in late medieval Edinburgh', *Women's History Magazine*, 45; Continuum Group (2003) *The Real Mary King's Close Official Guide*; Thomson, T. (ed.) (1833) *A Diurnal of Remarkable Occurents*; Wood, M., Macleod, W. and Durkan, J. (eds) (1930–85) *Protocol Book of John Foular*, 4 vols.

ROYDS, Mabel Alington, m. **Lumsden,** born Little Barford, Beds., 3 April 1874, died Edinburgh

22 Nov. 1941. Artist-printmaker. Daughter of Hester Frances Alington, and the Rev. Nathanael Royds, Anglican parson.

Mabel Royds was fifth of 11 children. She found the progressive Slade School of Art (1892–7), where women could attend life classes, preferable to art training at the RA Schools, despite the offer of a scholarship. She went to Paris (c. 1898–1906), befriended Walter Sickert, and supplemented an allowance with graphic design work. She taught briefly in Toronto (1906–7) before becoming a design tutor at ECA. In 1913, she married Ernest Lumsden (1883–1948), etching tutor, and on the outbreak of war travelled to India, initially joining her sister. When their baby daughter required urgent medical treatment, Mabel Royds and Ernest Lumsden returned to Edinburgh, where Mabel resumed her life as artist and printmaker. Among her best works are prints of Indian and Nepalese subjects (1920s, Aberdeen Art Gallery) and flower prints (1930s, SNGMA). She painted a mural for St Mary's Church, Hamilton, and taught intermittently at ECA where her daughter was a student (1930–3). She exhibited with the RSA and the SSA. RA

• Unpub. MS (family ownership): Barton, M. (1989) 'Mabel Royds by her Daughter'; ECA Archives: Letter Books and Prospectuses 1907 ff.

Furst, H. (1924) *The Modern Woodcut*; Lawrie, S. (1996) 'Edinburgh College of Art 1904–1969: a study in institutional history', PhD, ECA/HW; Salaman, M. C. (1919) 'Modern British woodcuts and lithographs by British and French artists', *The Studio Special Edition*, (1927) *The Woodcut of Today at Home and Abroad*; Somerville, E. and Ross, M. (1920) *Stray-Aways*.

RUDDICK, Edith, m. **Brill,** born Dunfermline 2 March 1918, died Glasgow 12 July 1996. Theatre, television, film and radio actor. Daughter of Rachel Nankin, and Jacob Ruddick, draper.

Edith Ruddick was the youngest of seven children of Jewish parents who fled from Russia in 1901. She began her acting career at Dunfermline High School and, after contacting John Gielgud who auditioned her, won a scholarship to RADA. She graduated in 1938 and soon after the start of the Second World War was asked to join a semi-professional company based in St Andrews, which later became famous as the Byre Theatre. She joined the innovative Unity Theatre in Glasgow and from 1942 worked with BBC Radio, writing scripts, plays and sketches as well as broadcasting. In 1948, she took part in David Lyndsay's *The Thrie*

Estaitis at the Edinburgh Festival. Other ground-breaking work included a 1969 performance of *Romeo and Juliet* with teenagers from Easterhouse as Montagues and Capulets.

In 1941, she married Jack Brill (1909–92), musician, actor and, later, clothing manufacturer in Glasgow, and they had two sons. Her work also included teaching speech and drama and a series of television acting roles, but problems with her eyesight led her to work in a Citizens' Rights office, which provided a source of inspiration for her writing and introduced her to the Playback Service for blind people. She recorded many books and newspapers for this service. Her last major role was in *Local Hero*, the 1983 Bill Forsyth film, and her last television role, shortly before she died, was in an episode of *Dr Finlay's Casebook*. LK

• Ruddick, E. (1995) *My Mother's Daughter*.

Private information.

RUSHFORTH, Margaret Winifred,[‡] n. **Bartholomew,** OBE, born Duntarvie, West Lothian, 21 August 1885, died Edinburgh, 29 August 1983. Medical practitioner, psychoanalytic therapist, pioneer of therapeutic group work. Daughter of Agnes Bartholomew, and John Bartholomew, farmer.

The middle child of five, Winifred Bartholomew was educated at Edinburgh Ladies' College, after which she studied medicine at Edinburgh, graduating MBChB in 1908. After a year in general practice in Dundee, she travelled to India as a medical missionary and lived and worked in India for 20 years. Within a year of her arrival in India she met her future husband, Frank Victor Rushforth (d. 1945), a financial expert working for the Imperial Finance Service. They married in Bombay in 1915 and had four children. Her interest in psychology and psychoanalysis was stimulated in part by her work with groups of mothers of young children in Calcutta. In 1929, she embarked on a year's psychoanalytic training at the Tavistock Clinic in London. The following year, her husband retired from his work in India and they moved to Edinburgh. After undergoing two years of personal analysis, she established her own psychoanalytic therapy practice in Edinburgh. In 1939, she founded the Davidson Clinic, which provided psychoanalytically informed family therapy, child psychotherapy and adult psychotherapy for 34 years. The clinic remained independent of the NHS; patients paid fees according to their means and many paid no fee at all. The clinic ran annual summer schools and other educational events, attended by a wide range of professionals, through which its ideas were communicated.

Religion and spirituality were central to her life and work. She always valued the Christian tradition into which she was born and she was also powerfully drawn to eastern religious traditions, including Sufism and Buddhism, which helped to underpin her holistic understanding of body, mind and spirit. She was a pioneering figure in the human potential and creative group movements. In the early 1970s, she was instrumental and inspirational in the creation of an alternative community at the Salisbury Centre in Edinburgh. In 1978, five years after the closure of the Davidson Clinic, her daughter **Diana Bates** (1918–98), doctor and psychotherapist, established with colleagues a new therapy centre in Edinburgh, Wellspring, which embodies a distinctive growth-oriented ethos bequeathed at least in part by Winifred Rushforth herself. 'The Dreamer', a sculpture by Chris Hall sited in George Square Gardens, Edinburgh, is dedicated to her. LB

• Rushforth, W. (1984) *Ten Decades of Happenings*. For other works see: www.eup.ed.ac.uk

RUSSELL, Jessie, born Glasgow 1850, died after 1881. Poet, dressmaker.

Orphaned at an early age, Jessie Russell was raised in Torthorwald, Dumfriesshire, by her maternal grandparents. Her mother had hoped Jessie would be a teacher but on the death of her grandfather she entered domestic service, aged 14. She learned dressmaking, married a Clyde shipyard carpenter in 1873, and spent her adult life in Partick. Her poems appeared in the *Glasgow Weekly Mail* and other local newspapers, and were collected in *The Blinkin' o' the Fire and other poems* (1877). They show her to have been a fiery, moralistic poet, probably influenced by her Cameronian family. Her politics are always on the side of the worker and, in particular, of women. 'Woman's Rights *versus* Woman's Wrongs' (pp. 29–31) defends women 'struggling for daily bread' and condemns the physical violence they often face from men. Like *Janet Hamilton she points out that women have far fewer rights than men: 'Workmen's wages have risen, but so has the price of bread,/While female work is so poorly paid, can women be clothed or fed?'. This poem provoked a response from *Marion Bernstein and, in her reply, 'A Recantation' (p. 31), Jessie Russell makes a plea for female suffrage. In 1881, the

Glasgow Weekly Mail reported that she had not written any poetry for a few years due to 'an increasing little family and the trials and vicissitudes of married life' (cited Leonard 1990, p. 306). Like that of Bernstein and Hamilton, Jessie Russell's work is spirited and spiritual; she is particularly intriguing in her Scots language poetry. VB
• Russell, J., Work as above.
Bold, V. (1997) 'Beyond the "Empire of the Gentle Heart": Scottish women poets of the nineteenth century', in *HSWW*; (forthcoming) 'Danaus' daughters', in *Nature's Making: James Hogg and the Autodidacts*; Leonard, T. (ed.) (1990) *Radical Renfrew*.

RUTHERFORD, Alison *see* **COCKBURN, Alison** (1713–1794)

RUTHERFORD, Mistress, born early 1600s, died after 1633. Author of a spiritual autobiography.

Mistress Rutherford's family connections are uncertain, though she may have been a granddaughter of Thomas Foulis, Edinburgh goldsmith. Her date of death is unknown, although an Elizabeth Rutherford was banished from Edinburgh and Leith in 1674, along with the widows of covenanting leaders John Livingston and Robert Blair, for vehemence in the presbyterian cause.

Everything known of Mistress Rutherford derives from her narrative (14,500 words), a copy of which exists only in the hand of the noted ecclesiastical historian Robert Wodrow. It describes her early life in and around Edinburgh, her spiritual development and presbyterian commitment, marriage (husband not named), migration to Ulster, relations with ministers (including Blair) and the death of her husband and first child (c. 1633). Her autobiography is one of the earliest examples of a genre that expanded rapidly during the Restoration and beyond. DM
• Univ. of Edinburgh Library: Laing MSS, La.III.263, Wodrow Octavo 33, no. 6.
Mullan, D. G. (1997) 'Mistress Rutherford's narrative: a Scottish puritan autobiography', *Bunyan Studies*, 7, (2004) 'Mistress Rutherford's autobiography', *Scot. Hist. Soc. Misc.* xiii.

RUTHVEN, Katherine, Lady Glenorchy, died 1584. Estate manager and Protestant patron. Daughter of Janet Haliburton, and William Ruthven, 3rd Lord Ruthven.

Katherine Ruthven was raised at Ruthven Castle (Huntingtower) near Perth and probably given a Protestant education alongside her five brothers and six sisters. In 1551, she married 'Grey Colin' Campbell, 6th Laird of Glenorchy (1499–1583) whose main base lay at Balloch Castle at the east end of Loch Tay, Perthshire. Katherine Ruthven was a supporter of the Protestant Reformation and patronised Protestant ministers. She played an important role in running the extensive Glenorchy estates stretching across the Central Highlands, and most probably understood and spoke Gaelic. She was well-known at the court of *Mary, Queen of Scots and was a close personal friend of William Maitland of Lethington, the Queen's Secretary, and of leading royal advisers including the earls of Argyll, Morton, and Moray, and Moray's wife, *Annas Keith. Unusually in the early modern period, some of her correspondents addressed her as 'Kait' or such affectionate titles as 'luffing ant [aunt]' (Dawson 1997, p. 26). She was involved in all aspects of family strategy and business, taking a leading role in the marriage negotiations of her children, especially Duncan, her eldest son and heir. However, after he succeeded in 1583 the two were at loggerheads regarding the dower portion owed to her as a widow and control over the family. Along with her husband, Katherine had re-established control over the family and, with their four surviving sons and four daughters, secured the lineage of the house of Glenorchy (later earls of Breadalbane). Katherine Ruthven's lively and interesting personality shines through her correspondence, providing a fascinating glimpse into the world of a 16th-century noblewoman who moved easily between Highland and Lowland society. JEAD

• NAS: GD112/39 Breadalbane Collection Correspondence. Dawson, J. (ed.) (1997) *Clan Campbell Letters, 1559–83*; *Breadalbane Letters, 1548–83*: http://www.div.ed.ac.uk/ Breadalbane/index; Dawson, J. (1999) 'Clan, kin and kirk: the Campbells and the Scottish Reformation', in S. Amos et al. (eds) *The Education of a Christian Society*; Innes, C. (ed.) (1855) *The Black Book of Taymouth*.

RYND (or RHIND), Jonet (Janet), c. 1504–53. Co-founder, Magdalen Hospital, Cowgate, Edinburgh, merchant.

Janet Rynd was a member of a well-established family in pre-Reformation Edinburgh. By 1520, she had married Michael McQueen, burgess, merchant, and holder of various public offices, who founded the Magdalen Chapel in the 1530s. After he died (c. 1536), Janet Rynd oversaw the realisation of her husband's original plans, and enlarged the institution by adding a hospital. Her Catholic civic piety is made clear through her involvement with the hospital. She was also a successful businesswoman, selling iron to James IV in 1540, and engaging in protracted but ultimately successful negotiations with the Hammermen's Guild, giving them patronage of the Magdalen Chapel in exchange for residence in a house in Niddry's Wynd. Janet Rynd's tomb lies in the chapel, a rare survival for a woman of her class and time. MC

• Lynch, M. (1981) *Edinburgh and the Reformation*; *RMS*, vol. 3; Smith, J. (ed.) (1906) *The Hammermen of Edinburgh*; *TA*, vol. 5, 7; Wood, M. (ed.) (1940–1) *The Protocol Book of John Foular*.

S

SADLER, Flora Munro,‡ n. **McBain,** born Aberdeen 4 June 1912, died Aberdeen 25 Dec. 2000. Mathematician and astronomer. Daughter of Isabella Webster, domestic servant, and John McBain, dairyman's carter.

Flora McBain graduated with honours in physics and mathematics from the University of Aberdeen in 1934. She held posts there from 1934 to 1937 as demonstrator in medical physics and then as lecturer in applied mathematics, while researching into radium sources for cancer treatment. With her professor, J. A. Carroll, she took part in a successful expedition to observe the total eclipse of the sun in Omsk, Siberia (19 June

1936). In 1937, despite being advised initially that a woman had little chance, she was appointed to a post at the Nautical Almanac Office, becoming the first woman scientist to hold a senior post (eventually Principal Scientific Officer) at the Royal Observatory, Greenwich, of which the Nautical Almanac Office was part. In 1949, the Observatory moved from Greenwich to Herstmonceux in Sussex where she worked until her retirement in 1973. Apart from during the Second World War, when the Almanac Office carried out special tasks for the Services, Flora McBain's work involved the computation of astronomical and navigational tables, her special field being the motion of the moon and the prediction of eclipses of stars. Her work, entailing international collaboration in which she represented Britain, had wider significance in determining the variation in the rotation of the Earth and the establishment of time. The first editor of the Royal Astronomical Society's professional journal, she was also the first woman secretary of that society, from 1949 to 1954, the year she married her colleague Donald H. Sadler (1908–87), Superintendent of the Nautical Almanac Office, in what was described as 'the astronomical romance of the decade'. MTB

• *ODNB* (2004) (Sadler, Donald); Tayler, R. J. (ed.) (1987) *History of the Royal Astronomical Society*, vol. 2, 1920–1980; Wilkins, G. A. (2001) 'Flora Munro McBain 1912–2000', *Astronomy and Geophysics*, 42.4, p. 34. Private information.

ST CLAIR-ERSKINE, Lady Millicent Fanny, Duchess of Sutherland, m1 **Sutherland-Leveson-Gower,** m2 **Fitzgerald,** m3 **Hawes,** born Dysart House, Fife, 20 Oct. 1867, died Orriule, France, 20 August 1955. Social reformer, writer. Daughter of Blanche Adeliza Fitzroy, and Robert Francis, 4th Earl of Rosslyn.

Married on 20 October 1884 to Cromartie Sutherland-Leveson-Gower (1851–1913), 4th Duke of Sutherland (from 1892), with whom she had four children, Millicent, Duchess of Sutherland was a well-travelled and renowned society hostess who took a close interest in the welfare of the people on her husband's extensive estates and was responsible for several practical schemes. Her reconstitution of the Sutherland Home Industries in 1886 led to her Presidency of the Scottish Home Industries Association (later Highland Home Industries). She founded the Sutherland Benefit Nursing Association, Sutherland Technical School, and Sutherland Gaelic Association. Her Staffordshire initiatives, particularly in the Potteries, earned her the sobriquet 'Meddlesome Millie'. She established and ran a hospital unit, the Millicent Sutherland Ambulance (1914–18), for which she was awarded the French Croix de Guerre and Belgian Royal Red Cross. Subsequently she lived in France. She wrote widely. The novel *That Fool of a Woman* (1925) reflects her experiences from marriages to Percy Desmond Fitzgerald in 1914 (dissolved 1919) and George Ernest Hawes in 1919 (dissolved 1925). MB-J

• St Clair-Erskine, M., Works as above and, as Stafford, Marchioness of (1889) *How I Spent My Twentieth Year, being a Short Record of a Tour Round the World, 1886–7*, as Sutherland, Millicent (1899) *One Hour and the Next*, (1902) *The Winds of the World*, (1914) *Six Weeks at War*. See also Bibl. below.

Beaton, E. (1991) 'The Sutherland Technical School: pioneer education for crofters' sons', *Rev. of Scot. Culture*, 7; *ODNB* (2004) (see Sutherland-Leveson-Gower, Fanny); Stuart, D. (1982) *Dear Duchess: Millicent Duchess of Sutherland 1867–1955* (Bibl.).

SAMPSON, Agnes, died Edinburgh 28 Jan. 1591. Midwife and healer. One of the North Berwick witches.

Agnes Sampson lived at Nether Keith near Haddington. A widow, middle-aged or older, she was accused of being part of a witches' conspiracy to kill James VI. This launched a major witch-hunting panic. Popular accounts of her rely on the sensationalised pamphlet *Newes from Scotland* (1591); her confessions and trial records give a fuller picture. Her medical practice was extensive, including clients from the common folk and lairds' wives in East Lothian and Midlothian. Her reported cures had a large magical element, including curing diseases induced by fairies and witches. She apparently took one man's witch-induced illness on herself and tried to transfer it to a dog or cat, but it landed on another man who died. She used a prayer in divination (a metrical version of the Apostles' Creed, learned from her father): if she halted once when reciting it, the person was bewitched, if twice, they would die.

The Haddington church presbytery suspected Agnes Sampson of witchcraft in 1589. In November 1590 a story of treasonable witchcraft broke in nearby Tranent, and she was arrested. After being tortured, her head squeezed in a twisted rope, and searched intimately for the devil's mark, she 'immediately confessed whatsoever was demanded of her' (Normand and Roberts 2000, p. 314). On 4/5 December she made a series of confessions, some before the King, at Holyroodhouse. These included raising storms to prevent the voyage of James's Queen, *Anna of Denmark, to Scotland in 1589, a Hallowe'en witches' convention at North Berwick, and a plot to bewitch the King by using toad's venom on some of his linen. This last line of investigation was dropped, perhaps because it might incriminate the wrong people. According to *Newes* she convinced James of the genuineness of the witches' conspiracy by recounting his conversation with his wife on their wedding night. This is not recorded in her confessions, and since parts of

Newes are clearly fictionalised it need not be taken literally.

Further confessions in January 1591 helped incriminate higher-status witches whom the investigation was now targeting – Barbara Napier, *Euphame MacCalzean and (through them) the Earl of Bothwell. Having served her purpose, Agnes Sampson was tried and convicted of witchcraft on 27 January 1591, and next day died penitently, strangled and burned at the Castle Hill in Edinburgh. JG

• Normand, L. and Roberts, G. (eds) (2000) *Witchcraft in Early Modern Scotland: James VI's Demonology and the North Berwick Witches*; *ODNB* (2004) (North Berwick witches); Wormald, J. (2000) 'The witches, the devil, and the king', in T. Brotherstone and D. Ditchburn (eds) *Freedom and Authority: Scotland, c. 1050–c. 1650*.

SANDISON, Janet *see* **CAMERON, Elizabeth Jane** (1910–76)

SANDISON, May, n. **Innes,** born or baptised Alvah, Aberdeenshire, 3 August 1825, died Fyvie, 13 July 1888. Embroiderer. Daughter of May Gauld, and Robert Innes, mason crofter.

May Innes went briefly to the local school before being sent out to herd cattle, and later went into service, subsequently marrying her employer's coachman, Robert Sandison. They took a croft at Steinmanhill, near Fyvie. Despite a growing family, she also helped on the farm, once building 134 yards of stone dyke. Naturally artistic and entirely self-taught, she became famous locally for her beautiful art embroideries, many of them designed by herself, although her cottage chimney smoked so badly the door had to be left open for her to see to do the work. For *Lady Aberdeen, she completed an embroidery heirloom originally designed by Ann, Jacobite Countess of Aberdeen. *Queen Victoria was another customer. Work of May Sandison's design was exhibited posthumously at the Chicago International Exhibition of 1893. Examples of her work are at Haddo House. LRM

• Aberdeen, Lord and Lady [Gordon, J. C. and Gordon, I. M.] (1929) *More Cracks with 'We Twa'*, pp. 120–8.

SAWYER, Mairi Thyra, n. **Mackenzie,** m1 **Hanbury,** m2 **Sawyer,** born West Derby, 1 March 1879, died Edinburgh 23 July 1953. Gardener. Daughter of Minna Amy Edwards Moss, and Osgood Hanbury Mackenzie, landowner.

Mairi Mackenzie's parents separated acrimoniously: accounts vary about whether and when she lived with her mother, but from an early age she doted on her father – the visionary landowner who from 1862 created Inverewe garden, Wester Ross. She came to share his love of gardening and field sports. History has painted her in his shadow, but Inverewe garden was her life's work as much as his. It is to Mairi and her then husband, landowner Robert Hanbury (1867–1933), whom she married in 1907, that Scotland owes the garden's survival and development after her father's death in 1922. With Ronald Sawyer (d. 1945), a farmer and agricultural improver whom she married in 1935, she re-built Inverewe House on the site of her father's mansion, ruined by fire in 1914.

Mairi Sawyer was described as quiet, unassuming, retiring but also charming, and her 'courteous reception of all her visitors added greatly to their enjoyment and appreciation of the property' (*Inverness Courier*, July 1953). Her personal life was touched by tragedy: both her children died in infancy and both husbands predeceased her. Knowing her beloved garden faced an uncertain future, from 1950 she negotiated its transfer to the NTS, handing over management in May 1953. She died suddenly two months later of a heart attack – friends said of a broken heart – while convalescing from a routine eye operation. DD

• NTS: Inverewe archives: Margaret Cuthbert, 'Memories of Inverewe', c. 1990; Dawn MacLeod, 'Some random notes . . . Mairi Sawyer and Inverewe in her time', 29 September 1988; other papers.
Sawyer, M. (1949) Chapter on Inverewe Garden in Mackenzie, O. [1922] (1949) *A Hundred Years in the Highlands*, (1950) 'Inverewe', *RHS Journal*, 75, 11, pp. 436–44, (1953) *Inverewe: an illustrated Guide to Inverewe Garden*. Cowan, M. (1964) *Inverewe: A Garden in the North West Highlands*; *Inverness Courier*, 24 July 1953 (obit.); MacLeod, D. (1958) *Oasis of the North*, (1982) *Down-to-Earth Women*.

SAXBY, Jessie Margaret, n. **Edmondston,** born Halligarth, Unst, Shetland, 30 June 1842, died Wulver's Hool, Unst, 27 Dec. 1940. Author and folklorist. Daughter of Eliza Macbrair, writer, and Laurence Edmondston, doctor.

Jessie Edmondston received no formal education but was immersed in the literary and scientific atmosphere fostered by her parents. Her mother, Eliza Macbrair (c. 1802–69), was the daughter of a Glasgow merchant and author of *Sketches and Tales of the Shetland Islands* (1856). In 1859, Jessie Edmonston married her father's assistant, Henry Linckmyer Saxby (1836–73), with whom she had five sons, and a daughter who died young. The couple lived in Inveraray, Argyllshire until Henry's death in 1873. Jessie then moved to Edinburgh, before returning to Unst in 1890.

She was a prolific writer from an early age. Her first published work was *Lichens from the Old Rock* (1868) and she wrote poetry, prose, romantic fiction and dialect verse, much with a Shetland theme. Her prodigious output was necessary to support her family. As well as producing 47 books, she contributed to magazines and journals including *The Boy's Own Paper*. Back in Unst, she immersed herself in Shetland folklore, publishing *Shetland Traditional Lore* (1932) aged 90.

In her poetry and fiction, Jessie Saxby created a romantic, tragic-heroic image of Shetland womanhood: the stoic widow of the man lost at sea; the hardy crofter; the heroic survivor – an image encapsulated in the figure of Britta Inkster in 'The Brother's Sacrifice' which appeared in the collection *Daala-Mist: Or, Stories of Shetland* (1876). In 1894 she was involved in a public controversy about the morals of Shetland women. In a letter to the *Shetland Times* (9 June), she intervened in a breach of promise case being heard in Lerwick sheriff court. The female complainant had asserted that it was customary for courting couples to sleep with one another before marriage. Jessie Saxby saw this as a gross attack on the morals of Shetland womanhood. 'Why are Shetland men silent when the morality of their countrywomen is impugned by Scots?' she inquired, 'I assert that a purer and more lasting love has its home in Shetland than in any other part of "religious" Scotland'. Her reward was to be honoured as a 'sister' in a poem published anonymously in the *Shetland Times* (14 July). Addressed to her, the poem concluded: 'Sister! For that one noble word/So promptly said, so bold and true,/The women of your island race/For years to come will honour you.'

A political liberal, Jessie Saxby was a temperance supporter and a suffrage campaigner with the Shetland Women's Suffrage Society, as well as a writer and advocate for Shetland. On her 90th birthday, admirers presented her with an illuminated address praising her for embodying 'for thousands in every quarter of the world the very spirit of Shetland'. LCA

• Shetland Archives D.11/135/2: (Bibl.).
Saxby, J., Works as above and see Bibl.
ODNB (2004); *Shetland Times*, 11 Jan. 1941 (obit.).

SCÁTHACH (Scáthach of Skye) fl. (allegedly) c. 500 BC; **AÍFE (Aífe of Alba)** fl. (allegedly) c. 500 BC. Legendary warrior women of Alba.

In the Middle Irish tale, 'The Wooing of Emer', the hero Cú Chulainn travels to Scáthach's realm across the Irish Sea to obtain training in feats of arms from her. Scáthach lives in a fortress on an island (often identified as Skye in popular tradition) and trains the few young warriors who are strong enough and clever enough to penetrate her fortress. She teaches Cú Chulainn a variety of martial arts, and particularly instructs him in the use of the deadly *gae bolga*, a type of barbed spear that enters as a single point but expands and tears the flesh if removed. During his training, Cú Chulainn joins Scáthach and her army in battling the rival female chieftain of a neighbouring territory, Aífe. Cú Chulainn is granted the right to fight Aífe in single combat on Scáthach's behalf. He overcomes Aífe through a combination of physical strength and trickery, and grants her mercy on three conditions: that she make peace with Scáthach; that she sleep with him, and that she bear him a son. She agrees, and a truce is negotiated between the two sides. Aífe becomes pregnant with Cú Chulainn's son, and the hero leaves a ring and a name for him before he departs. Before the hero leaves Alba, Scáthach foretells Cú Chulainn's future triumph in the great epic battle, the Táin (The Cattle Raid of Cooley). The hero's son appears again in a related tale, 'The Death of Aífe's Only Son', in which the seven-year-old boy travels across the sea to Ireland to challenge the heroes there, refusing to reveal his identity. Cú Chulainn fights the boy and kills him with the *gae bolga*, thus slaying his only son, who laments 'there is something Scáthach didn't teach me' (Kinsella 1970, p. 44). JAF

• Kinsella, T. (trans.) *The Táin* (1970) 'The Wooing of Emer' and 'The Death of Aífe's Only Son'.

SCHAW, Janet, born Lauriston, Edinburgh, c. 1737, died 1801. Diarist and travel writer. Daughter of Anne Rutherford, and Gideon Schaw.

Little is known of Janet Schaw's life, apart from what is revealed in her journal of her travel from Scotland to the Caribbean and North Carolina between 1774 and 1776. The journal, which was discovered in 1927, provides a detailed contemporary account of those places. She sailed from Burntisland, Fife, in October 1774 with her brother Alexander and the children of John Rutherford of North Carolina, who had been at school in Scotland. Her journal indicates her attitudes to contemporary issues: noticeably uncomfortable attending Anglican church services, she disapproved of the rebellious Americans and displayed unthinking racial prejudice, not unusual at the time, towards enslaved Africans. In the colonies, she encountered many Scotswomen, some on plantations, others running shops and farms. She also met old friends, some from leading Scottish aristocratic and mercantile families, which suggests that she was well-connected in Scotland. She probably lived in Edinburgh's New Town, and her journal is her legacy. DJH

• Schaw, J. (1921, 1934, 1939 edns) *Journal of a Lady of Quality, being the Narrative of a journey from Scotland to the West Indies, North Carolina and Portugal*, E. W. Andrews and C. M. Andrews, eds.
HSWW.

SCHIREHAM, Marjory de, fl. 1326–31. Customs collector.

Marjory de Schireham was Scotland's earliest recorded woman custumar, a collector of the king's customs on certain exports. Most towns had two custumars; Marjory de Schireham and Alan de Balmossy were the custumars for Dundee from 1327 to 1331. Marjory may have been related to other Schirehams living in Dundee. She received a royal pension for six years from 1326, although the reason for this is unknown. No further female custumars held office until 1513, when several women, including *Margaret Crichton, took up the office following the deaths of their husbands at the Battle of Flodden. EE

• *ER*, vol. i.

SCOTA, fl. (allegedly) c. 500 BC.

Eponymous ancestor of the *Scoti*, Scota originated as a pseudo-historical figure, typical of medieval European origin mythology. The Latin term *Scoti* was used to refer to Gaels from both Ireland and northern Britain, and Scota first appeared as their ancestor in the 'first' (and far earlier) recension of the 11th-century *Lebor Gabála Érenn* ('Book of the Takings of Ireland'). She became and remained a mainstay of the origin legends of the *Scoti* of northern Britain, although as an instrument of medieval political rhetoric this pseudo-history was amended frequently. Recent work has revolutionised our understanding of how the origin myth and Scota's place within it developed between *Lebor Gabála* and John of Fordoun's later *Chronica Gentis Scottorum*. Usually Scota was presented as a daughter of

Pharaoh, Moses' antagonist, and wife or mother of Gáedel Glas, ancestor of the Gaels. Her descendants migrated to northern Britain but the details of the migration changed from source to source. JEF

• Broun, D. (1999) *The Irish Identity of the Kingdom of the Scots in the Twelfth and Thirteenth Centuries; Lebor Gabála Érenn*, in Koch, J. T. (ed.) (1995) *The Celtic Heroic Age*, pp. 213–66; Skene, W. F. (ed.) (1871) *Johannis de Fordun Chronica Gentis Scottorum.*

SCOTT, Agnes Neill *see* **MUIR, Wilhelmina Johnston (Willa)** (1890–1970)

SCOTT, Anna, Duchess of Buccleuch, *suo jure*, **Duchess of Monmouth,** born Dundee 11 Feb. 1651, died London Feb. 1732. Heiress. Daughter of Margaret Leslie, and Francis Scott, 2nd Earl of Buccleuch.

Anna Scott was born in Dundee, where her family, one of Scotland's wealthiest, sought refuge from the English invasion. The family seat of Dalkeith was seized by the English after Earl Francis' death in 1651. Margaret Leslie married David Earl of Wemyss in 1653 and raised Anna and her sister Mary, Countess of Buccleuch, in Wemyss Castle, Fife. Mary's death in 1661 made Anna Countess of Buccleuch. Margaret Leslie proposed to Charles II that Anna marry his illegitimate son, James Crofts (1649–85), who took the surname Scott for their marriage on 20 April 1663. James became Duke of Monmouth, and Buccleuch a dukedom. In 1666 Anna was made Duchess of Buccleuch in her own right.

The marriage was unhappy, with Monmouth consistently unfaithful and politically incompetent. When he fled to France in 1683, his wife publicly dissociated herself from his actions. In 1685, Monmouth raised an unsuccessful rebellion against James VII and II, proclaiming himself the rightful king. Duchess Anna voluntarily accompanied her children to the Tower. On Monmouth's execution day, she secured a statement from him that he acted alone; this, and her friendship with the royal family, helped her preserve the Buccleuch inheritance. Anna Scott remained Duchess of Buccleuch for life, refusing to pass on the title before death to her son, as *Anne, Duchess of Hamilton had done. In 1688 she married Charles, 3rd Baron Cornwallis (1655–98). From 1701 she extensively rebuilt Dalkeith Castle (now Palace) as a home suitable for those of royal blood. She returned to London in 1714, but was buried in St Nicholas Church, Dalkeith.

Royal friendship helped another noblewoman, Anna Scott's kinswoman, **Anna Mackenzie** (c. 1621–1707), dowager countess of Balcarres, whose second husband Archibald Campbell, Earl of Argyll (1629–85), supported Monmouth's rebellion. In 1681 when Argyll was sentenced to death for disobedience to the Crown, Anna's daughter, Sophia Lindsay, smuggled him out of Edinburgh Castle dressed as a page. Mother and daughter both endured short imprisonment during the Monmouth rebellion, and Argyll was executed, but Anna Mackenzie, who had actively supported the Stewarts under Cromwell, retained royal favour, helping her preserve the interests of both her Balcarres and Argyll families. EE

• Fraser, W. (1878) *The Scotts of Buccleuch*; Lee, M. (1996) *The Heiresses of Buccleuch*; Lindsay, A., Lord (1849) *Lives of the Lindsays*, vol ii, (1868) *A Memoir of Lady Anna Mackenzie*; *ODNB* (2004) (Scott, Anna; Mackenzie, Anna); *SP*.

SCOTT, Edith Agnes Kathleen (aka **Lady Scott** and **Lady Kennet**), n. **Bruce**, m1 **Scott**, m2 **Young**, later **Kennet**, born Lindrick, Notts., 27 March 1878, died London 24 July 1947. Sculptor. Daughter of Jane Skene, and Lloyd Stewart Bruce, Anglican clergyman.

Of Scottish descent, and the youngest of 11 children, Kathleen Bruce was orphaned at the age of eight, and sent to live with her great-uncle, historian William Forbes Skene (1809–92), in Edinburgh. Strictly reared in this bachelor household, she made up for it by determining to become a sculptor, training at the Slade, then from 1901 in Paris, at the Académie Colarossi. She later wrote, 'to say that a lass perhaps not out of her teens had gone off prancing to Paris to study art was to say that she had gone irretrievably to hell' (Kennet 1949, pp. 23–4). She had some tuition from Rodin and has left vivid descriptions of his studio. In 1903, she volunteered for relief work in Macedonia, later returning to Paris, then London, where she met the explorer Captain Robert Falcon Scott (1868–1912). They married in 1908 and had one son, the wildlife expert Peter Scott (1909–89). She learnt of Captain Scott's death in the Antarctic on her arrival in New Zealand to meet him. Her bronze statue of him stands in Waterloo Place, central London.

Kathleen Scott carried out war work, and in 1922 remarried, to politician Edward Hilton Young (1879–1960), later Baron Kennet. Their son, Wayland Young (b. 1923), became a journalist. 'By far my highest ability has been that of a father chooser', she later claimed (Lees-Milne 1996, p. 5), and indeed her husbands and sons were all achievers. Kathleen Scott was well connected and talented. Her prolific sculpture, largely done between the wars, consists of figurative work: lifelike portrait busts of the eminent, and statues, mostly of male subjects. She was one of very few successful women sculptors of the mid-20th century, but her resolute opposition to the modernist aesthetic has deprived her of art historians' attention. With her 'silhouette like carved granite' (Lees-Milne 1996, p. 2) she was a striking, independent, though non-feminist figure, admired by many. SR

• Musée Rodin, Paris: Corr. (as Kathleen Bruce). Kennet, K. (1949) *Self-portrait of an Artist*. Lees-Milne, J. (1996) *Fourteen Friends*; *ODNB* (2004); Stocker, M. (1999) 'The tool's trace; Kathleen Scott, sculptor of men', unpub. conference paper, Sussex, (1999) 'My masculine models: the sculpture of Kathleen Scott', *Apollo*, 150, pp. 47–54.

SCOTT, Isabella Mary, m. **Gibson,** born Edinburgh 1786, died Edinburgh 28 Nov. 1838. Harpist, composer, teacher. Daughter of William Scott, teacher, and his wife, and related to Sir Walter Scott.

Isabella Scott, who in 1818 married Patrick Gibson, landscape painter, ran a boarding school for young ladies in Edinburgh and taught music. The composer Robert A. Smith, musical conductor of St George's Church, Edinburgh, consulted her during the creation of his own works. In return, he published some of hers in his *Scottish Minstrel* series (6 vols 1821–4), including her most popular song, 'Loch na Garr' (1822) to a text by Lord Byron, arranged with symphonies and accompaniment for the harp or piano.

Isabella Scott's music was among the first to provide the (concert) harp, then fairly new to Scotland, with a Scottish repertoire. Her other arrangements for the harp or piano include 'The Bouquet' (1805), 'Mount and go' (1815), 'O say that my Heart's too small' (1815), 'Ye Banks and Braes of Bonnie Doon' (1820), 'Kenmure's on and away' (1820). She also composed hymns and sacred songs published in several collections. PAC

• Brown, J. D. and Stratton, S. S. (1897) *British Musical Biography*; Cohen, A. I. (1987, 2nd edn.) *International Encyclopedia of Women Composers*; Garvey Jackson, B. (1994) *Say Can you Deny me?*; Hixon, D. L. and Hennessee, D. (1975) *Women in Music*; Johnson, D. (1972) *Music and*

Society in Lowland Scotland in the Eighteenth Century; Rensch, R. (1989) *Harps and Harpists.*

SCOTT, Jean (Janet), Lady Ferniehurst, born Selkirkshire c. 1548, died Jedburgh after 1595. Factrix and Catholic intermediary. Daughter of Grisel Betoun of Creich, and Sir William Scott of Kirkurd.

Jean Scott was a young child when in the early 1550s her father died and her grandfather, Sir Walter Scott of Buccleuch, was murdered in a bloodfeud with the Kers. A pawn in the manoeuvrings to pacify the feud, she was contracted to marry George Ker of Faldonside in 1565. The marriage did not occur, but in 1569 she became the second wife of Sir Thomas Ker of Ferniehurst (d. 1586). In 1577, she was paid 1,000 merks as compensation for the failure of the 1565 contract.

Despite its bloody background, the marriage was a success, preventing Jean's brother, Walter Scott of Buccleuch, from killing her husband. The couple's daughter and three sons included Robert Ker, Earl of Somerset, a favourite of James VI. Lady Ferniehurst converted to Catholicism after 1569, becoming an important protector of Catholic priests. She proved an able factrix of her husband's estates during his political exile from 1573 for supporting *Mary, Queen of Scots, attending the royal court to plead his case. She corresponded with Mary in England and actively promoted Mary's cause in Scotland. Sir Thomas returned to public life 1583–5, but died in disgrace in March 1586. She continued to administer his estates, incurring the wrath of her step-son, Andrew Ker of Ferniehurst, in 1595. She died some time later, still defending her husband's reputation and upholding Catholicism in the family. RG/MMM

• NAS: GD40/2/9, Lothian Muniments.
Grant, R. (1999) 'Politicking Jacobean women: Lady Ferniehurst, the Countess of Arran and the Countess of Huntly, c. 1580–1603', in E. Ewan and M. M. Meikle (eds) *Women in Scotland c. 1100–c. 1750;* Meikle, M. M. (2004) *A British Frontier? Lairds and Gentlemen of the Eastern Borders, 1504–1603; ODNB* (2004); *SP,* ii, p. 231, iv, pp. 62–72.

SCOTT-MONCRIEFF, Agnes Millar (Ann), n. **Shearer,** born Kirkwall, Orkney, 11 Jan. 1914, died (assumed) February 1943. Poet, short-story writer, children's writer. Daughter of Jeannie Moir Murison, and John Shearer, tailor and hotel-keeper.

Ann Shearer grew up in Orkney and attended Kirkwall Grammar School. Her mother died when she was 10 years old. She started as a journalist on

The Orcadian newspaper aged 17, and moved south to work in Fleet Street in 1932. She began an archaeology course at the University of Edinburgh but left after one term to marry the writer George Scott-Moncrieff, whom she had met in London, in March 1934. They had two sons and a daughter.

Their first home was a cottage in Peeblesshire, let in return for farm work, where they both followed writing careers. Ann was at first more successful than her husband, publishing two children's books during the 1930s. They moved successively to Temple in Midlothian and to a cottage in Badenoch. Ann became a Roman Catholic in 1940 and was joined by her husband. In 1941 they moved to Haddington, their circle of friends including many of the writers of the Scottish Literary Renaissance. Ann contributed poems and short stories to newspapers and magazines, wrote for BBC radio, and published the children's novel *Auntie Robbo* (1941), which has been reissued in paperback and translated into Swedish. Increasing ill-health was exacerbated by the stresses of freelance writing and of family life in wartime. She travelled north early in 1943 and was last seen alive in Nairn in February of that year.

Contemporary tributes speak of her potential greatness as a writer. Her fellow Orkney writer, Edwin Muir, wrote a moving poem on her death. Her daughter thinks (L. Scott-Moncrieff 1987) that 'something of her personal impact' can be found in George Scott-Moncrieff's novel, *Death's Bright Shadow.* In it, an important character is described thus: 'The blazing youthful expectancy of her whole face and bearing . . . In some ways she was fantastically young, and then again so old' (Scott-Moncrieff, G. 1948, pp. 40, 68). MARB

• Scott-Moncrieff, A., Works as above, and (1934) *Aboard the Bulger,* (1936) *The White Drake.*
Glasgow Herald, 10 March 1943 (obit.); Muir, E. (1987) 'Ann Scott-Moncrieff', *Chapman* 47–8, Spring, p. 112 with tributes by Scott-Moncrieff, L., pp. 83–4, Davie, E. and Jamieson, M., pp. 113–14; *The Scotsman,* 11 March 1943 (obit.); Scott-Moncrieff, G. (1948) *Death's Bright Shadow.*

SCOTTISH WOMEN'S HOSPITALS (SWH) for Foreign Service

This movement was the brainchild of *Dr Elsie Inglis. It arose from her frustration that no use was made by the British War Office of women doctors when war broke out in 1914. The first generation of women through the medical schools were often unable to find jobs after qualifying. While minimally trained women volunteers were accepted as first-aiders or orderlies (known as VADs), the RAMC did not accept women doctors. Elsie Inglis suggested to the SFWSS that it might finance a hospital unit, fully staffed by women, for the Red Cross. But the Red Cross, too, came under the War Office and the offer was refused. Approaches were made instead to Allied governments and several accepted. The units were initially planned to consist of two doctors, 10 nurses, an administrator, cooks and clerk, and would cost about £5,000. Appeals for funds started slowly: the first £1,000 was raised by 30 October 1914. The first French unit, seen off from Edinburgh by *Sarah Siddons Mair, went over in December, and was housed in the abbey of Royaumont, about 25 miles from Paris. Under Englishwoman Frances Ivens, Royaumont functioned throughout the war, and was depicted in paintings by *Norah Neilson Gray (see Crofton 1997). The second unit, soon followed by a third, went to Serbia in January 1915, and almost immediately encountered a typhus epidemic which killed several of its staff. The Girton and Newnham unit (50% Scottish, 50% English) was based at Chanteloup, near Troyes. Eventually about 14 units of the SWH were raised and worked in the field, attached to every Allied force in the west, except the British. (The War Office did later accept the participation of Scot *Dr Flora Murray at an all-woman hospital in London.) The Scottish identity of the SWH was maintained, with headquarters in Edinburgh, chaired for the SFWSS by **Nellie Hunter** (fl. 1914–18) with treasurer **Jessie Laurie** (fl. 1914–18), but in truth the initiative was supported both with funds and personnel from England as well (and Elsie Inglis would have preferred the name 'British Women's Hospitals'). A large number of Scottish women doctors chose to work with these units. They included *Louise McIlroy, present throughout the war, **Mary Gordon** (1861–1941), **Isabel Emslie, Lady Hutton** (1887–1960), **Lydia Henry** (1891–1985), *Honoria Keer, **Helen Lillie** (1890–1977) and **Agnes Savill** (1875–1964). Together with nurses and voluntary orderlies, Scotswomen made up about half of all the hospital staff. S R

• Mitchell Library, Glasgow: Archives of the Scottish Women's Hospitals.

Crofton, E. (1997) *The Women of Royaumont*; Hutton, I. (1928) *With a Woman's Unit in Serbia, Salonika and Sebastopol*; Hutton, I. (1960) *Memories of a Doctor in War and Peace*; Leneman, L. (1994) *In the Service of Life*, (1998) *Elsie Inglis*; *ODNB* (2004) (Gordon, Mary; Inglis, Elsie; Hutton, Isabel Emslie, Lady; McIlroy, Louise); Ross, I. (1988) *Little Grey Partridge*.

SHARP, Elizabeth Amelia, n. **Sharp,** born Paisley 7 May 1856, died probably abroad 1932. Editor, writer. Daughter of Agnes Farquharson, and Thomas Sharp.

Following a secret engagement, Elizabeth Sharp married her cousin, writer William Sharp (1855–1905), in London in 1884. Their relationship developed through collaborative writing and independent projects associated with literature, music, art and Gaelic folklore. When Elizabeth Sharp edited *Lyra Celtica* (1896), her husband wrote an introduction and notes. When William Sharp wrote *Progress of Art in the Century* (1906), he included a section on music by his wife. A life-long friend of suffragist *Mona Caird, Elizabeth Sharp championed women as writers: she compiled two anthologies of women's poems (Sharp 1887b: binding by *Phoebe Traquair; and Sharp 1891). The Sharp couple were also party to an extraordinary literary deception, lasting several years. William Sharp created a female alter ego, under the pseudonym **Fiona MacLeod**: 'Fiona', a version of Fionn, was combined with the surname of Seumas MacLeod, a Gaelic fisherman and storyteller. He was inspired to do this through his relationship with Edith Wingate Rinder (a Celticist and a relative of Caird's) who 'unlocked new doors' (*DNB* 1909, p. 223) after their meeting in Rome in the 1880s. He invented a life for his 'cousin' Fiona MacLeod, later backed up by an entry in *Who's Who* (1905). The deception was remarkably effective, winning widespread interest in and praise for 'her' publications – including *The Sin Eater* (1895), contributions to Patrick Geddes's *Evergreen* (1895–6), *The Washer of the Ford* (1896), *Green Fire* (1896), and other novels, *Shorter Stories* (1897), and poems *From the Hills of a Dream: mountain songs and Highland runes* (1897). Identified with 'Celtic romance and dream and the glamour of the mysterious', (William Sharp, letter of 12 Aug. 1893, www.sas.ac.uk), the writings were sometimes produced in states of spiritual and mesmeric trance, productive of psychological strain. The story is William's not Elizabeth's, but after his death, she wrote a *Memoir* (1910) giving an account of their combined lives and of 'Fiona MacLeod'. Art critic for the *Glasgow Herald* for a while, Elizabeth Sharp gave up journalism in 1902, when her husband became increasingly ill. She maintained strong links with Scotland, visiting relatives in Glasgow, holidaying in Scotland, and identifying with her husband's literary output. The Sharps had no children, travelled widely, and were often apart, but Elizabeth's support for her husband was constant. RA

• NLS: MSS 15941 (105–99), 11972; Strathclyde Univ., Geddes archives: corr.

Sharp, E. A., Work as above, and (1887a) *Sea Music*, (1887b) *Women's Voices*, (1891) *Women Poets of the Victorian Era*, (1893) *Great Musical Composers*, (1904) *Rembrandt*, (1906) *The Progress of Art in the Century – append. A history of music in the nineteenth century*, (1910) *William Sharp (Fiona MacLeod), a Memoir compiled by his wife.*

Alaya, F. (1970) *William Sharp – Fiona MacLeod 1855–1905*; *DNB* (1909); *ODNB* (2004) (Sharp, William).

SHAW, Christian, of Bargarran, born Bargarran, Erskine, Renfrewshire, 1686, died after 1737. Entrepreneur and alleged victim of witchcraft. Daughter of Christian McGilchrist, and John Shaw, Laird of Bargarran.

With her mother and sisters, Christian Shaw set up and ran the Bargarran Thread Company, which laid the foundation for the cotton industry in Paisley. Traditionally, she has also been thought of as 'The Bargarran Imposter', a malicious child who made fraudulent accusations against seven people, subsequently executed as witches in Paisley in 1697. However, contemporary scholarship would tend to exonerate her. That she was mentally ill or that she was maligned and was not the author of the words and deeds attributed to her are now the predominant views.

Christian Shaw was only 11 years old at the time. It is said that she fell into fits, during which she was deaf and blind, at the mere mention of the names of the accused witches. They were also said to torment her by nipping and biting her, while being invisible to all others present apart from Christian. She was one of many supposed witnesses against the accused witches. There were other children who were reported as having had fits and other experiences similar to hers. What was peculiar about Christian Shaw as a child was that a book was written about her experiences as a demonstration to non-believers of the reality of the devil and the power and mercy of God (Anon. 1698).

In 1719, Christian Shaw married the Rev. John Millar, minister of Kilmaurs. When, two years later, he died, Christian worked on the process of bleaching linen yarn perfectly white and producing very fine and very strong sewing thread from it. When she succeeded in this, she organised the production, distribution and sale of it under the name of 'Bargarran Thread'. The thread was marketed with the family coat of arms – three gold cups with a sky-blue background – as its trademark in an attempt to differentiate it from the imitation 'Bargarran Thread' that appeared on the market. She seems to have retired from business when, in 1737, she married William Livingstone, a glover, in Edinburgh. HMCL

• NAS: JC10/4, pp. 1–81; JC26/81/D9; PC1/51, pp. 136–9.

Anon. (1698) *A True Narrative of the Sufferings and Relief of a Young Girle*; McLachlan, H. V. and Swales, J. K. (2002) 'The bewitchment of Christian Shaw. . .', in Y. G. Brown and R. Ferguson (eds) *Twisted Sisters* (Bibl.); Wasser, M. (2002) 'The western witch-hunt of 1697–1700. . .' in J. Goodare (ed.) *The Scottish Witch-hunt in Context*; Young, W. 'Parish of Erskine', in J. Sinclair (ed.) [1791–99] (1973) *The Statistical Account of Scotland.*

SHAW, Clarice Marion, n. **McNab,** born Leith 22 Oct. 1883, died Troon 27 Oct. 1946. Labour activist, councillor and MP. Daughter of Mary Deas Fraser, compositor, and Thomas Charles McNab, weaver.

As a young woman, Clarice McNab taught music in Leith. She became involved with the Socialist Sunday Schools and later was national president for 25 years. Following its recruiting tour of Scotland, she joined the WLL, c. 1910. She served on its executive committee and was head of its Scottish district (1917–18). That position gave her a seat on the executive committee of the Scottish Advisory Committee (later Council) of the Labour Party. She was elected to Leith School Board and, in 1913, to Leith council, becoming the first Labour woman member of a town council in Scotland, and later a bailie. Her interests included child welfare and public health, women's rights, equal pay for women teachers, and girls' employment. She was also director of the Leith Co-operative Association.

In 1918, she married Benjamin Shaw (1865–1942), first secretary of the Scottish Labour Party, and moved to Glasgow and, in 1921, to Troon, where she was also elected to the town council. Her step-daughter, **Mary Marjorie Annie Shaw (Marjorie)** (1904–84) was a gifted linguist and graduate of the University of Glasgow (1927) who was *Times* correspondent in Russia during the Second World War and later taught languages at St Denis's School, Edinburgh.

In 1918, when the WLL disbanded, Clarice Shaw remained active in women's organisations in the Labour Party at UK level and in Scotland. An extrovert and outstanding orator, she was known as an efficient and conscientious administrator. She became secretary to the Scottish Joint Committee of Labour, Co-operative and Trade Union Women, formed in 1934. She retained her seat on the Scottish Labour Party Council executive, which she chaired 1939–40, thus presiding at the 1940 Silver Jubilee conference where a presentation marked her unbroken yearly re-elections to the executive. She also served on Ayr County Council, 1932–6, where she chaired the Public Health Committee for a time, campaigning for state hospital and maternity provision and for nursery schools. After standing unsuccessfully for Ayr Burghs in the 1929 and 1931 general elections, she achieved a long-held ambition when she won Kilmarnock in 1945. However, she was prevented by illness from taking her seat, which she reluctantly resigned in September 1946. She died the following month. Her successor was Willie Ross, who had been one of her Sunday school pupils. CC

• Reports of the Annual Conference of the Labour Party; Labour Party Archives and Study Centre, John Rylands Library, Manchester Univ.: *Women's Labour League Secretarial Correspondence and Related Papers*; NLS: Acc. 12250 Marjorie Shaw papers.

Collette, C. (1989) *For Labour and for Women: the Women's Labour League, 1906–18*; *DLabB*, vol. VIII; *Glasgow Herald*, 28 Oct. 1946 (obit.); *ODNB* (2004); *SLL*; Socialist Sunday School Union (1910) *Socialist Sunday School Hymnbook*.

SHAW, Helen Brown, n. **Graham,** MBE, born Glasgow 2 June 1879, died Glasgow 20 April 1964. Politician and activist. Daughter of Annie Gillespie, and David Graham, wine merchant.

Educated privately, on 18 September 1902 Helen Graham married Major David Shaw of the 6th Cameronians (b. 1875/6), who was killed in action in 1915. They had a daughter and a son. During and after the First World War, Helen Graham was active in many war charities, notably as a member of the War Pensions Committee (1915), chair of the Lanarkshire Prisoners of War Relief Committee (1915) and member of the Food Control Committee (1917), and was made MBE in 1920. She was District Commissioner of the Lanarkshire Girl Guides (1919–36) and Vice-Chairman WVS (1938–46). After serving on Lanarkshire Education Authority, she became the first woman to be elected to Lanarkshire County Council, 1930–2. Following unsuccessful attempts in 1924 and 1929, she was elected as National Unionist (Conservative) MP for Bothwell in 1931, holding the seat until her defeat in 1935. As an MP, she lobbied for modernisation of the Lanarkshire

mines and for new industries and infrastructure. In 1938, she became district administrator for the WVS for ARP, West of Scotland. Her son, Gavin, who followed her into politics as president of the Bothwell Unionist Association, was killed in action in 1943. TB

• *Motherwell Times*, 25 Jan. 1935; *SB*; *The Scotsman*, 22 April 1964 (obit.); *ODNB* (2004).

Additional information: Motherwell Heritage Centre.

SHAW, Margaret Fay,‡ m. **Campbell,** born Glenshaw, near Pittsburgh, USA, 9 Nov. 1903, died Fort William 11 Dec. 2004. Writer, photographer and recorder of Hebridean life. Daughter of Fanny Maria Patchin, and Henry Clay Shaw.

Margaret Fay Shaw was intensely proud of her American origins and Scottish descent. Orphaned when young and brought up by sisters and relatives, she made little progress in formal education. In 1921, she travelled to Scotland to finish her schooling at St Bride's, Helensburgh. Hearing *Marjory Kennedy-Fraser, doyenne of the 'Celtic revival', in concert, she determined to learn more about such music. Cycling tours of Britain, no mean feat in the 1920s, included the Hebrides and eventually South Uist, for which she formed a life-long attraction.

Taught piano to professional level but with a possible career blighted by rheumatism in wrists and hands, she returned to the Hebrides. She lodged with the sisters Màiri and Peigi MacRae, gifted singers and tradition-bearers, near Lochboisdale (1929–35), learnt Gaelic, and transcribed the community's songs and traditions. Published in the meticulously edited and beautifully illustrated *Folksongs and Folklore of South Uist* (1955, 1977, 1986, 1999), they provide extraordinary testimony to the island's wealth of oral tradition. Honorary doctorates from the universities of St Francis Xavier (Nova Scotia), Edinburgh, Aberdeen and the National University of Ireland later recognised her contribution.

In 1935 Margaret Fay Shaw married John Lorne Campbell (1906–96), fellow student of Gaelic language and oral tradition. After he bought the island of Canna in 1938, they set up a hospitable home, entertaining friends and scholars and continuing their recording and writing, with visits to record the Gaelic of Nova Scotia. The Campbells presented Canna, with its important Celtic Studies archives, to the NTS in 1981. Widowed in 1996, Margaret continued living in Canna and entertaining friends and scholars. HC

• Campbell, M. S., Works as above, and (1947) 'Hunting folk songs in the Hebrides', *Nat. Geog. Mag.*, vol. 91, (1956) 'Gaelic Folksongs from South Uist', in *Studia Memoriae Belae Bartók Sacra*, (1993) *From the Alleghenies to the Hebrides*. *The Independent*, 15 Dec. 2004 (obit.). Private information.

SHAW, Winnie, m. **Wooldridge,** born Clarkston, Glasgow, 18 Jan. 1947, died Woking, Surrey, 30 March 1992. Tennis star. Daughter of Winifred Mason, former tennis champion, and Angus Shaw, journalist.

Coached by her mother, Winnie Shaw swept up every Scottish title open to her while still at Hutcheson's Grammar School. After winning the British Junior Hardcourt Championship in 1964, she moved to London at the age of 17. A gutsy senior debut at Wimbledon 1965 against champion Maria Bueno led to selection for both the Wightman and Federation Cups in 1966. She ultimately represented Great Britain on 26 occasions. Her best tennis was played in the early 1970s. A singles quarter-finalist at Wimbledon (1970, 1971) and a semi-finalist at the Australian Open (1970, 1971), she was the only Scot, in the open era, to contest Grand Slam finals: the French mixed doubles (1971 with Toomas Lejus of the USSR) and women's doubles (1972 with Nell Truman). Her best-known performance came at Wimbledon in 1972, when she and fellow-Scot Joyce Williams lost a doubles semi-final in three sets to Billie-Jean King and Betty Stove. Then suddenly, it was all over. She married tennis player Ken Wooldridge, retired from the international circuit, and took up golf, representing Scotland in 1983. She was Surrey champion in 1987 and 1990 but, collapsing on the course at Wentworth in 1991, she was found to have an incurable brain tumour and died a year later. She was a gifted sportswoman and one of the finest tennis players Scotland has ever produced. JK

• *The Independent*, 1 April 1992 (obit.); *Scotland on Sunday*, 23 June 2002, Scottish Sports Hall of Fame.

SHEPHERD, Anna (Nan), born East Peterculter 11 Feb. 1893, died Aberdeen 27 Feb. 1981. Writer and teacher. Daughter of Jane Smith Kelly, and John Shepherd, mechanical engineer.

Nan Shepherd was brought up with her elder brother, Frank, in the family home of 'Dunvegan', Cults, Deeside, and spent most of her life there. She was educated at Cults School and Aberdeen High School for Girls before going on to study at the University of Aberdeen, where she graduated (MA 1915). She lectured in English at the Training Centre for Teachers (later the College of Education), Aberdeen, from 1915 until her retirement in 1956. Although she was involved in literary activities throughout her life, her novels *The Quarry Wood* (1928), *The Weatherhouse* (1930) and *A Pass in the Grampians* (1933) were published in one burst of creativity and were met with critical acclaim both in Britain and the USA. They are notable both for their use of Scots and their perceptive rendering of female experience. All three novels have a strong sense of place and of the life of small communities. Set in the north-east of Scotland, they illustrate the tensions between traditional and changing ways of living. In particular, *The Quarry Wood* follows a young woman's struggle for formal education and her growing understanding that wisdom is based on more than academic learning.

Nan Shepherd continued to write articles and reviews and numbered among her friends *Willa Muir, *Jessie Kesson, whose early writing she encouraged, and Hugh MacDiarmid. She was also a friend of the poet Charles Murray, whose last poems she prepared for publication in 1969, and of the writer and historian *Agnes Mure Mackenzie, publishing a portrait of her in 1955. She edited the *Aberdeen University Review* (1957–63), writing articles for it on topics including women in the early days of the university. She was awarded an honorary LLD from the University of Aberdeen in 1964.

Nan Shepherd was a keen traveller and hill-walker, reflected in her only collection of poems, *In the Cairngorms* (1934), and in *The Living Mountain: A Celebration of the Cairngorm Mountains of Scotland* (1977). Both works explore connections between the power of nature and the life of the mind. Her novels were out of print for many years but critical interest in them has revived since their recent re-publication. There is a stone dedicated to her in Makars' Court, Lady Stair's Close, Edinburgh. AML

• NLS: MSS 26256, 26073–4, 26706, 26900, 27438–45, Nan Shepherd papers; Univ. of Aberdeen, Letters, Special Collections and Archives: MS 2750/1–42 and MS 3017/8/1/1–3.
Shepherd N., Works as above and see *HSWW* (Bibl).
Anderson, C. and Christianson, A. (eds) (2000) *Scottish Women's Fiction, 1920s to 1960s*; Forrest, V. (1986/7) 'In Search of Nan Shepherd', *Leopard Magazine*; *HSWW* (Bibl.); *ODNB* (2004); Watson, R. (1996) 'Introduction', *The Grampian Quartet*.

SHEPHERD, Lady Mary, n. **Primrose, of Dalmeny,**
born Barnbougle Castle, Dalmeny, 31 Dec. 1777,
died London 7 Jan. 1847. Philosopher. Daughter of
Mary Vincent, and Neil Primrose, 3rd Earl of
Rosebery.

Lady Mary Primrose was raised at Barnbougle
Castle and educated according to the traditional
curriculum of the 'Scotch plan' by a Mr Pillans,
who taught Latin, geography, mathematics, history
and philosophy. She and her four siblings were avid
readers and talkers who exchanged essays in the
form of letters. Lady Mary took an interest in
philosophical analysis, and by the age of 27,
according to her daughter, she had written
numerous manuscripts exposing errors in the
reasoning of Hume and Priestley. On 11 April 1808,
she married Henry John Shepherd (c. 1783–1855),
son of the prominent London lawyer, Sir Samuel
Shepherd. They had three children and she became
an active member of London society, hosting
leading thinkers of the day. Her social circle
included, among others, David Ricardo, William
Whewell, Charles Babbage, *Mary Somerville and
Richard Whately. Lady Mary's two published
books, *An Essay upon the Relation of Cause and
Effect, controverting the doctrine of Mr. Hume* (1824)
and *Essays on the Perception of an External Universe*
(1827), addressed the theories of Berkeley, Reid,
Hume, Stewart, Brown and Lawrence. In
responding to Hume, Lady Mary developed an
original defence of the causal relation, drawing on
both rationalist and empiricist principles. William
Whewell is said to have used one of her books as a
text at Cambridge, and Robert Blakey included a
summary of her philosophy in his *A History of the
Philosophy of Mind* (1848). A short memorial of her
life was published in the *Gentleman's Magazine* of
August 1847. J M C R
• Shepherd, Lady M., Works as above, and McRobert, J.
(ed.) (2000) *The Philosophical Works of Lady Mary Shepherd*,
2 vols (Bibl.).
Anon. (1847) 'Lady Mary Shepherd', *Gentleman's Magazine* 28,
August, p. 209; Blakey, R. (1848) *A History of the Philosophy of
Mind: Embracing all Writers on Mental Science from the Earliest
Period to the Present Time*, 4 vols; *ODNB* (2004).

SHEPPARD, Catherine Wilson (Katherine or **Kate),**
n. **Malcolm,** m1 **Sheppard,** m2 **Lovell-Smith,** born
Liverpool 10 March 1848, died Christchurch, NZ,
13 July 1934. Suffragist, New Zealand. Daughter of
Jemima Souter, and Andrew Malcolm, clerk.

Born to Scottish parents, Kate Malcolm
apparently spent much of her childhood in Nairn,
living with an uncle who was a minister in the Free
Church of Scotland. After her father's death, the
family emigrated in 1868 to Christchurch,
New Zealand, where she and her siblings joined in
the philanthropic and cultural life of the town.
Active in the Congregational Church, she married
Walter Sheppard (1836–1915), a storekeeper, in 1891.
They had one son. A strong prohibitionist, Kate
Sheppard joined the New Zealand WCTU when it
was founded in 1885. As Superintendent of the
WCTU's Franchise Department, she led the
campaign for women's suffrage in New Zealand. In
the face of strong opposition, displaying courage,
tenacity and tact, she addressed public meetings,
edited a franchise page for a fortnightly temperance
paper, wrote articles and pamphlets, organised three
nationwide petitions, lobbied politicians, and
provided guidance for suffrage campaigners
throughout the country.

On 19 September 1893, New Zealand became
the first country in the world to give the parliamentary vote to women, both European and
Maori. On subsequent visits to Britain, Kate
Sheppard met suffrage leaders, and was a valued
speaker at meetings in England and Scotland. Back
in New Zealand, she helped found the NCW, and
campaigned for further social reforms, also
preparing reports on the position of women in
New Zealand, and on the effects of women's
suffrage, for the ICW. In later life, she endured ill-
health and bereavement. Her son, who had married
the daughter of *Margaret Sievwright, died in 1910;
her husband died in 1915 and her grandchild in
1930. In 1925, she married William Lovell-Smith
(1852–1929), who predeceased her. Kate Sheppard is
remembered in New Zealand on Suffrage Day,
19 September, each year. Her face appears on the
New Zealand $10 note, a street in the capital is
named after her, and her Memorial stands on the
banks of the Avon River in Christchurch. J D
• Canterbury Museum, Christchurch, New Zealand:
K. W. Sheppard papers.
Devaliant, J. (1992) *Kate Sheppard*; *DNZB* (1993); Grimshaw,
P. (1972) *Women's Suffrage in New Zealand*; *ODNB* (2004);
Page, D. (1993) *The Suffragists*.

SHIEL, Isabella (Tibbie),‡ m. **Richardson,** born
Ettrick 1782, died Yarrow 23 July 1878. Innkeeper.
Daughter of Mary Shiel, and Walter Shiel.

Tibbie Shiel, a second daughter, had little
education and worked on local farms. She married
Robert Richardson, a molecatcher, in 1806 and set
up house in the Yarrow Valley, in the Scottish

Borders. They moved into a cottage near St Mary's Loch with their three sons and three daughters. It was a simple building, two downstairs rooms and a floored attic. Robert died the next year and Tibbie Shiel, now the sole provider for the family, opened a small inn offering wholesome food and cheap lodgings for those who wished to fish the neighbouring lochs and burns.

In her childhood, Tibbie Shiel had worked with *Margaret Laidlaw, mother of James Hogg, the Ettrick Shepherd, and so knew the poet well. James Hogg had also moved into the Yarrow Valley when he received the farm of Altrieve Lake from the Duke of Buccleuch at a nominal rent. He was a frequent visitor at the inn and Tibbie Shiel summed up her friend: 'for aa the nonsense he wrote, Hogg was a gey sensible man in some things' (Craig-Brown 1886, p. 392). Hogg was a good publicist for Tibbie Shiel's establishment and when Christopher North first visited in 1829, he based his *Noctes Ambrosianae* on the inn. It became a place for celebrities to meet, talk and write. Tibbie Shiel's descendants live in nearby Henderland Farm. Tibbie Shiel's Inn is still open for custom in the same idyllic setting. WE

• Craig-Brown, T. (1886) *History of Selkirkshire*; North, C. (Prof J. Wilson) [1822–35] (1876) *Comedy of the Noctes Ambrosianae*; Russel, J. (1894) *Reminiscences of Yarrow*.

SHORT, Maria Theresa, m. **Henderson,** born Edinburgh before 1788, died Edinburgh 15 Jan. 1869. Observatory owner. Daughter of Jacobina Downie, and Thomas Short, optician and scientific instrument maker.

Part of a scientific family, Maria Short claimed the Great Telescope made by her uncle, James Short (1710–68). Her father had never completed his own attempt to use it as the centrepiece for an Observatory on Calton Hill. On his death in 1788, the Telescope fell into the possession of Edinburgh Council. A child at the time, Maria Short reappeared from Ireland in 1827 to reclaim it. Her plans met council opposition and she raised money by public subscription. The Telescope having been returned to her in 1828, she opened her successful 'Popular Observatory' on Calton Hill in 1835. In 1843, she married Thomas Henderson. After conflict with the council and rivalry from another observatory, Maria Short was evicted in 1850, but in 1856 opened 'Short's Observatory' on a new site on Castle Hill, home of the current Camera Obscura. Still known as 'Short's Observatory', it was taken over by an instrument-maker named Hart in 1861.

Patrick Geddes rented it and made it his Outlook Tower in 1896. Doubts have been raised about Maria Short's parentage (her age at death was recorded as 'about 70', which may be inaccurate) and her claim to the Telescope, but she successfully fought off such challenges during her lifetime. FJ

• NLS: MS 1553 f252, 257; 1861 Census; Edinburgh City Archive.
AOC Archaeology Group, *Calton Hill Conservation Plan*, August 1999 (http://download.edinburgh.gov.uk/calton); Brück, H. A. (1983) *The Story of Astronomy in Edinburgh*; Wallace, V. (1992) 'Maria Obscura', *Edinburgh Review*, 88.

SIDDONS, Harriet, n. **Murray,** born Norwich 16 April 1783, died Edinburgh 24 Nov. 1844. Actor, singer and theatre manager. Daughter of Ann Acres and Charles Murray, actors.

Harriet Murray was born into the leading acting dynasty of British theatre. Her mother (formerly the wife of Jonathan Payne) was an actor (fl. 1770–99), and her father was the son of the prominent Jacobite Sir John Murray of Broughton. Her own reputation combined a celebrated London and provincial acting career and a distinguished tenure as patentee and manager in Edinburgh. The date of her debut is uncertain, either 1791 at Bristol in a performance of *King John* for her father's benefit, or in Bath on 1 July 1793. She appeared as Titania at Bath in 1792 and 1793 and was Palmyra in James Miller and John Hoadly's *Mahomet the Imposter* in Birmingham on 28 August 1797. She made her London debut on 12 May 1798 as Perdita and joined the Covent Garden company for the 1798–99 season, where she continued in high-profile roles until 1804–5.

She married Henry Siddons (1774–1815), the eldest son of celebrated actor Sarah Siddons (1755–1831), on 22 June 1802. They had four children who reached maturity – Sarah, Henry, William and Elizabeth, who was the mother of *Sarah Mair. In autumn 1802, Harriet and Henry Siddons went over to the Drury Lane house, appearing in the major roles of the day until the end of the 1808–9 season when they left London for Edinburgh where Henry had obtained the patent (the licence to play legitimate drama) in the major house, the Theatre Royal. Henry Siddons first appeared as patentee on 14 November 1809 when he acted the Duke, opposite Harriet as Juliana, in John Tobin's *The Honeymoon*.

For the next six seasons Harriet Siddons worked assiduously for the Edinburgh company, appearing in some 100 roles and turning down the opportunity to act opposite Edmund Kean at Drury Lane. Henry Siddons died of tuberculosis in 1815. Harriet took over the management of the Edinburgh house, assisted by her brother, the actor William Henry Murray. Their management was associated with the emergence of the national drama, the often-patriotic stage adaptations of the novels of Sir Walter Scott, and forged a tradition of respectable, legitimate playing in the Scottish capital, where she was celebrated as 'our own Mrs Siddons'. Her last benefit was on 29 March 1830, when she played Lady Townly in Colley Cibber's *The Provok'd Husband* and spoke a farewell address written for her by her long-term supporter Sir Walter Scott. She appeared in a handful of other benefit roles for colleagues in the remainder of that season before retiring completely from the stage. Harriet Siddons and her husband are buried in Greyfriars churchyard, Edinburgh. AS

• Dibdin, J. C. (1888) *Annals of the Edinburgh Stage*; Highfill, P. H. Jr., Burnim, K. A. and Langhans, E. A. (c. 1973–93) *A Biographical Dictionary of Actors . . . and Other Stage Personnel in London, 1660–1800*; *ODNB* (2004) (Henry Siddons).

SIDGWICK, Eleanor Mildred (Nora), n. **Balfour,** born Whittinghame, East Lothian, 11 March 1845, died Woking 10 Feb. 1936. College principal, mathematician. Daughter of Lady Blanche Gascoyne Cecil, and James Maitland Balfour, MP.

Nora Balfour was the eldest of eight children, whose father died when they were very young. Several had eminent careers, Arthur Balfour (1848–1930) later becoming prime minister. She herself had a talent for mathematics, having been well taught privately, but never followed a degree course, although she later collaborated with her brother-in-law Lord Rayleigh on measurements of electricity. Other 'unqualified' Scottish women mathematicians included her contemporaries **Flora** and **Jane Sang** (fl. 1850–90s), who helped their father Edward Sang (1805–90) to compile his famous logarithm tables.

Nora Balfour married Henry Sidgwick (1838–1900), teacher of philosophy at Trinity College, Cambridge. It was a marriage conducted as an intellectual and affectionate partnership. Henry Sidgwick had helped found Newnham College for women students, and Nora Sidgwick taught mathematics there, while maintaining their home as an intellectual centre. She became vice-principal in 1880, and the college's financially far-sighted principal in 1891. Nora Sidgwick imposed her rational and benign vision of women's education on Newnham, instituting what has been called its 'golden age' (*ODNB* 2004), although women would not be allowed to graduate from the University of Cambridge in her lifetime. She served on a Royal Commission for secondary education and supported the suffrage campaign, though disapproving of militant action. She and her husband were both closely involved with the Society for Psychical Research, generally taking a sceptical view of the paranormal: she gave short shrift to Madame Blavatsky, for example. Widowed in 1900, she retired as principal in 1910 but maintained links with Newnham and received honorary degrees from Edinburgh and St Andrews among others. SR

• Sidgwick, A. and E. (1906) *A Memoir of Henry Sidgwick*. *ODNB* (2004) (both Sidgwicks and Sang, Edward); Sidgwick, E. (1938) *Mrs Henry Sidgwick, a Memoir*.

SIEVWRIGHT, Margaret Home, n. **Richardson,** born Pencaitland, East Lothian, 19 March 1844, died Gisborne, NZ, 9 March 1905. Political activist, feminist, New Zealand. Daughter of Jane Law Home, and John Richardson, estate factor.

Growing up in and near Edinburgh, Margaret Richardson acquired a thorough knowledge of classical writings and the Bible and an enthusiasm for liberal humanist ideals. All her life she retained a love of learning and a commitment to improving society, especially conditions for women and children. After teaching in Ragged Schools in Edinburgh, she trained as a nurse, and campaigned against the Contagious Diseases Acts both in Britain and later in New Zealand, calling them 'iniquitous laws'. The repeal of discriminatory legislation was part of her vision for an 'ethical world' (Sievwright c. 1902, pp. 2–4). Aged about 33, Margaret Richardson left Britain for Dunedin, New Zealand, probably by invitation. Her personal contacts there introduced her to networks of prominent intellectuals, liberals and political activists, including widower William Sievwright, a solicitor from Lerwick, whom she married in Wellington in November 1878. In 1883, the couple settled in isolated Poverty Bay near Gisborne, with their three young children (two from William Sievwright's former marriage). Through reading and correspondence, Margaret Sievwright stayed in contact with developments in international feminism and, with the help of her sympathetic husband, acquired a deep knowledge of the law. She built a small school on the family property, provided local nursing assistance and led political discussion groups from home.

Active in Gisborne as a temperance and women's suffrage campaigner, Margaret Sievwright achieved national and international renown as a feminist leader once New Zealand women won the right to vote in 1893. She wrote prolifically for women's political journals and, as vice-president, then president (1901–5) of the New Zealand NCW, she lobbied actively for a wide range of humanitarian statutory reforms. Although softly spoken and retiring by nature, she was probably the most radical and visionary of early New Zealand feminists, many of whom were Scottish by birth or parentage. Her views on women's economic independence within marriage and her pacifism during the Boer War earned her opprobrium in the press, but she was widely loved and respected. Her daughter Wilhelmina married the son of Margaret's fellow-campaigner *Kate Sheppard. A memorial was dedicated to Margaret Sievwright in Gisborne in 1906, with NCW and ICW support. RMCC

• National Register of Archives and Manuscripts, NZ (www.nram.org.nz): various references: NRAM: W20, W28, W115, W141, Y980.
Sievwright, M. H. (c. 1902) *The Removal of the Civil and Political Disabilities of Women*, Articles in contemporary journals: *Daybreak*, the *Prohibitionist*, the *White Ribbon*. Devaliant, J. (1992) *Kate Sheppard*; McGrannachan, M. (1993) *A Fair Field and No Favour*; *DNZB* (updated 16 Dec. 2003): www.dnzb.govt.nz; 'White Ribbon', *Jour. NZWCTU*, 15 March 1905 (tributes by Sheppard, K. W. and A. W. [Ada Wells]).

SILEAS NIGHEAN MHIC RAGHNAILL (Sìleas na Ceapaich, Cicely MacDonald), c. 1660–c. 1729.
Jacobite and Clan Donald bard. Daughter of Mary Cameron (or MacMartin), and Gilleasbuig, Chief of the MacDonalds of Keppoch.

Sìleas na Ceapaich was a poet from the higher strata of Gaelic society, well acquainted with the forms of bardic elegy, who adopted many of the characteristics of the classical style when composing songs on the deaths of important people in her life. This is particularly evident in her lament for Alasdair of Glengarry, which contains the longest list of kennings and related images in Scottish Gaelic verse as well as ending with a classical *dúnadh*.

Sìleas na Ceapaich was opposed to the 1707 Union of the parliaments, describing it in one of her earliest poems as 'uinnein puinnsein' (a poisoned onion) served up to the Scots. She

composed several songs connected to the Jacobite Rising of 1715, including 'Do Rìgh Seumas' (To King James), late 1714 or early 1715, and at least one poem composed after the battle of Sherrifmuir.

She composed several hymns and religious poems, and two songs, probably those later condemned as 'coarse and indelicate' (Ó Baoill 1972, pp. 125–6) in which she gives advice on sexual morality: 'Comhairle air na Nigheanan Òga' (Advice to Young Girls) and 'An Aghaidh na h-Obair Nodha' (Against the New Work). In the first song, she uses her own experiences in order to outline the pitfalls of a too ready belief in the flattery of young men. This has led to the suggestion that she herself had an illegitimate child, Gilleasbuig, before her marriage to Alexander Gordon of Camdell in 1685, by whom she had at least five and possibly nine children. The second song was composed as a direct response to MacKenzie of Gruineard's 'An obair nogha' (The New Work) in which the poet praises sexual licence in explicit terms, using female characters to illustrate his case. Sìleas na Ceapaich describes the consequences which girls will have to face if they succumb to the new fashion being promoted by Mackenzie's song: pregnancy, abandonment, disgrace and the disapprobation of the Church. AF

• Ó Baoill, C. (ed.) (1972) *Bàrdachd Shìlis na Ceapaich: poems and songs by Sìleas MacDonald*.
Black, R. (ed.) (2001) *An Lasair*; Kerrigan, C. (1991) *An Anthology of Scottish Women's Poetry*; MacGill-eain, S. (1985) *Ris a'Bhruthaich*, W. Gillies, ed., p. 235; *ODNB* (2004) (see NicDhòmhnaill, Sìleas); Thomson, D. S. (1990) *An Introduction to Gaelic Poetry*, pp. 135–6.

SIMON, Edith Margarete, m. Reeve, born
Charlottenburg, Berlin, 18 May 1917, died Edinburgh 7 Jan. 2003. Artist and writer. Daughter of Grete Simon and Walter Simon.

In 1932, this Jewish family moved to London, although Edith Simon returned briefly to Berlin to complete her education before attending the Slade and the Central School of Art. In early years she made a living from book illustration and jacket design. Her first book was published in 1937, and her translation of Arthur Koestler's *The Gladiators* in 1940. In 1942, marriage to Eric Reeve, a scientist, led to a move to Edinburgh, where she combined her writing career with care of their three children. She published a total of 17 books (history, novels, and biography). She re-focused on the visual arts and, as well as painting, experimented with diverse materials and techniques. Self-imposed disciplines such as resin for sculpture and continuous-line drawing led to greater freedom of expression. She devised a method of using a scalpel to cut through layers of paper to expose colours, create shadows and produce likenesses which rivalled paint in their complexity. The aim was never to make a pretty picture but to engage and hold the viewer. Visitors to 30 annual exhibitions in Edinburgh were encouraged to ponder the depth of the work and converse with the artist. Edith Simon excelled at one-line drawings, figurative depictions, innovative sculpture, and multi-layered paper-cuts. Works are held by the University of Edinburgh Student Centre, St Mary's Cathedral and the City Art Centre. EMS

• Demarco, R., 'Edith Simon', *Glasgow Herald*, 24 Feb. 2003; 'Edith Simon: Signals', Edinburgh Festival Exhibition Catalogue, Aug. 1991 (Bibl.); Goodwin, I. [Edith's younger sister] and Sutherland, G. (2005) *Moderation Be Damned*; *The Scotsman*, 30 Jan. 2003 (obit.).

SINCLAIR, Catherine, born Edinburgh 17 April 1800, died London 6 August 1864. Children's writer. Daughter of Lady Diana Macdonald, and Sir John Sinclair, agriculturist and statistician.

The Caithness flags in the pavement outside their house were known as 'the Giants' Causeway' (Walford 1984, p. 18) as the Sinclair children were extremely tall. Catherine Sinclair, the seventh of 13 children, acted as her father's secretary from 1814 until his death in 1835, and his famed lack of humour may have influenced her early conventional, moralising novels for children and adults. In her greatest success, *Holiday House* (1839), based on stories told to her nieces and nephews, she deliber-ately portrays children who are 'noisy, frolicsome [and] mischievous' (Sinclair 1839, p. vii) but good-hearted and likeable. The more subtle moral tone is masked by their high-spirited adventures and a 'Nonsensical Story', in which a giant 'was obliged to climb on a ladder to comb his hair' (ibid., p. 172). It was judged 'the most original children's book written up to that time and one of the jolliest and most hilarious of any period' (Darton 1932, p. 220), and it marked the transition of children's stories from improving tales to the subversive views of Lewis Carroll. Although *Holiday House* remained in print for 100 years, her best seller was a popular series of coloured *Picture Letters* for children (1861–4).

Catherine Sinclair was well known in Edinburgh for several philanthropic ventures: establishing soup kitchens, an industrial school for girls, public benches, and the first public drinking-fountain in the city – all referred to on the 60-foot gothic stone memorial to her on the corner of North Charlotte Street and St Colme Street. Her niece *Lucy Walford, also a novelist, describes Catherine Sinclair's charm of manner and witty conversation, and the unmarried Sinclairs' hospitable household at 133 George Street as a centre of Edinburgh society. JRR

• NLS: MS 24640: original hand-illustrated copy of *Holiday House*; Corr.; BL: MSS 46651–2: Accounts & Corr.; Add. MSS 44393 and 46117.
Sinclair, C. [1839] (1976 facsimile reprint) *Holiday House: a book for the young* (Bibl.).
Darton, F. J. H. (1932, 3rd edn. 1982) *Children's Books in England*, pp. 219–21; *DNB* (1897 edn. lists most of 35 books); Hunt, P. (ed.) (2001) *Children's Literature: an anthology 1801–1902*, pp. 49–54; *ODNB* (2004); Shattuck, J. (1993) *The Oxford Guide to British Women Writers*; *The Times*, 15 August 1864 (obit.); Walford, L. [1910] (1984) *Recollections of a Scottish Novelist*.

SINCLAIR, Isabella Janet (Bell), born 1776, died Wick 3 May 1795. Journeywoman mantua-maker. Daughter of Elizabeth Sinclair of Dun, and William Sinclair of Mey.

Bell Sinclair was one of eleven surviving Sinclair children. Their mother died on 13 June 1785, their father on 9 February 1792, leaving the family unprovided for. She learned mantua-making in Thurso from Miss Betty Sinclair but she was advised against setting up business there because there was not enough work for local mantua-makers. A friend told her that anyone hoping to set up needed experience in Edinburgh (NAS: GD139/366/4): she went there in 1794, working for the Misses Sinclair and other mantua-makers. She wrote home that she had become acquainted with all the new fashions, yet she made no profit, as she only 'worked for her meat' (ibid., GD139/370/2). Although she intended to marry a Mr Sutherland and move to the West Indies, severe illness forced her to return home to Wick, where she died of consumption, aged 19. She exemplifies the woman of gentry background who had to undertake paid work for her living. ECS

• NAS: GD139, Sutherland of Forse Muniments.
WWEE.

SINCLAIR, Margaret Anne [Sister Mary Francis of the Five Wounds], born Edinburgh, 29 March 1900, died Warley, Essex, 24 Nov. 1925. Venerable Poor Clare nun. Daughter of Elizabeth Kelly, and Andrew Sinclair, street-sweeper.

The third of six surviving children, Margaret Sinclair was described as 'a bit of a sport' (O'Rourke 1930, p. 7) and a satisfactory pupil. At age 14 she began full-time work as a french polisher with Waverley Cabinet Works, Edinburgh, and between 1918 and 1923 she worked for Sheerwinter, the Civil Service Stores and McVitie and Price. In 1919 she started a relationship with ex-serviceman, Patrick Lynch, but ended it in 1922. The following year she entered as extern sister London's Poor Clare Colettine order at Notting Hill (a rigorous enclosed order whose extern sisters were the link to the outside world). She took as her name in religion Sister Mary Francis of the Five Wounds. Throughout her youth she exhibited a deep spirituality and had maintained regular religious observance, even as a worker.

In 1926, soon after her early death from tuberculosis, a campaign was launched for her beatification and canonisation; in 1930 her cause became official with Rome and in 1978 she was declared Venerable by Paul VI. Although popularly portrayed as an active trade unionist, it is more likely that her membership was discreet. Nevertheless, it was the image 'Margaret Sinclair, factory worker', coupled with her ordinariness and humble background, that attracted a significant following among the working classes in Scotland and beyond. Originally buried at Kensal cemetery, London, she was moved to Mount Vernon cemetery, Edinburgh, in 1927 and in 2003 her body was placed in the side chapel of St Patrick's Church, Edinburgh. SKK

• Scottish Catholic Archives, Edinburgh; Margaret Sinclair Archive, St Patrick's Church, Edinburgh.

Barry, D. E. (1952) *The Story of Margaret Sinclair*; *ODNB (2005 update); O'Brien, F. (1989) *The Cheerful Giver: Margaret Sinclair*; O'Rourke, M. R. (1930) *Margaret Sinclair*; *The Times*, 11 July 2003.

Private information: Raymond Burnett (nephew); Poor Clares, Humbie, East Lothian; Fr Richard Reid, Edinburgh.

SKEA, Isabella Low, n. **Chalmers,** born Bridge of Don 16 Jan. 1845, died Aberdeen 7 Oct. 1914. Headmistress, campaigner for women's rights. Daughter of Isabella Low and George Chalmers, tenant farmers.

Isabella Chalmers was encouraged by her schoolmaster and trained at the Church of Scotland Normal College in Edinburgh c. 1866. Returning to Aberdeen, she became Girls' Head, then overall Headteacher of East Parish Sessional School (afterwards St Paul Street Public Elementary School), and was the fifth woman to become a Fellow of the EIS. Having created a model example in her own school, she was particularly interested in the development of school libraries. She opposed 'payment by results' for teachers as educationally unsound, but her own pupils' performance made her one of the highest paid teachers in Aberdeen in the 1870s. Married to William Skea, a printer/journalist (25 Dec. 1884), she firmly believed that marriage need not interfere with a woman's career. The Skeas had no children but provided a home for three of her nieces. In the 1880s, she campaigned for university education for women, and wrote a series of textbooks, the 'Combined Class Series'. In the 1890s, she campaigned for better pay and pension rights for women teachers and actively supported 'fresh air' holidays for Aberdeen's slum-dwelling children. St Paul Street School was extended several times before being demolished and rebuilt as a 1,000-pupil, mixed-sex Public Elementary in 1896. Isabella Skea retired in 1908. ATM

• Aberdeen City Archives: school log books; Aberdeen Central Library, Local Studies collection: textbooks; Univ. of Aberdeen Local Collections: pamphlets.

Aberdeen Daily Free Press, 10 Oct. 1881; *Aberdeen Daily Journal*, 24 Dec. 1908, 8 Oct. 1914; *Aberdeen Journal*, 31 Dec. 1896, 18 Oct. 1897; *Aberdeen Today*, 1907; Moore, L. (1991) *Bajanellas and Semilinas*; Northcroft, D. (2003) *Scots at School.*

SKENE, Lilias, n. **Gillespie,** born Kirkcaldy 1626/7, died Aberdeen 21 June 1697. Quaker author, prophet, poet. Daughter of Lilias Simson, and John Gillespie, minister of Kirkcaldy.

Lilias Gillespie's father, grandfathers, and two famous covenanting brothers, Patrick (1617–75) and George Gillespie (1613–48), were ministers. By her own account she was devout from an early age. In 1646, she married Alexander Skene (1621–93), later a burgh magistrate and authority on Scottish urban government, and moved to Aberdeen. Between 1647 and 1665 she bore ten children, seven surviving. Her eldest son, John Skene (c. 1649–90), became deputy governor of West New Jersey, and possibly America's first freemason. In 1666, she converted to Quakerism, six years before her husband. She marked the change by adopting his surname, contrary to Scottish custom but in keeping with the English forms of the Society of Friends.

Quakers afforded women public roles: Lilias Skene served on disciplinary committees and in

1682 helped found Scotland's first Quaker school at Aberdeen. In 1677, she travelled to London on Quaker business, but declined, for reasons unclear, an invitation to continue to Germany on a missionary tour with George Fox, William Penn, and fellow Scots Robert Barclay, George Keith and his wife Elizabeth Johnston. When Quaker men in Aberdeen were imprisoned between 1676 and 1679, Lilias attended to the prisoners and their businesses, and led outlawed meetings for worship. She was not arrested, but the Privy Council increased her husband's fine by half to account for her 'transgressions' (NAS: CH10/3/35, f. 23).

Writing was at the heart of Lilias Skene's activism. In poetry and prose she reworked personal experience for didactic effect, whether cautionary or inspirational. Her surviving or known prose dates from the crisis of 1676–9, when she joined the literary campaign to win the prisoners' release and gain toleration for Friends. To that end, she wrote a series of letters, now lost, to Elisabeth, Princess of the Rhine (cousin of Charles II), and in 1677 addressed a stinging prophetic sermon (published in 1753) to the magistrates of Aberdeen, demanding that they let her people go. In 1678, she responded to a Presbyterian critic by publishing a letter of pious rebuke. Her poems date from 1665 until just before her death in 1697. In 1878, William Walker published selections from a manuscript since lost: his full transcription of all 33 poems survives in his papers at the University of Aberdeen. G D

• Univ. of Aberdeen Library Historic Collections: MS 2774, William Walker Papers; NAS: CH10/3/35, '. . . the Most Material Passages . . . Of Sufferings and Persecution at Aberdene'; CH10/3/36, '. . . Record of the First Rise and Progress of . . . Quakerism, In and About Aberdeen'. Skene, L. (1679) 'An expostulatory epistle', in R. Barclay, *Robert Barclay's Apology For the True Christian Divinity Vindicated. . . .*; writings in J. Besse, (1753) *A Collection of the Sufferings of the People Called Quakers*, ii, pp. 522–3. DesBrisay, G. (2004) 'Lilias Skene: a Quaker poet and her "Cursed Self"', in S. Dunnigan et al. (eds) *Woman and the Feminine in Medieval and Early Modern Scottish Writing* (Bibl.); *ODNB* (2004); Walker, W. (1887) *The Bards of Bon-Accord, 1375–1860.*

SKINNER, Mabel (Mabs), n. **Parrot,** born London 17 Nov. 1912, died Inverness 9 August 1996. Communist activist and councillor. Daughter of Fred Parrot, shopkeeper, and his wife.

One of ten children, Mabel Parrot came to Inverness from the Midlands in 1930 to work as a domestic servant. In 1936, she married Tom Skinner, a panel beater, and they moved to West Molesey in Surrey. They had four children. Mabel Skinner joined the CPGB in 1941, became secretary of Molesey Branch and sat on the Women's Advisory Council (later Committee) in the 1940s. During the war they sent their children to stay in the Merkinch area of Inverness and settled there themselves in 1947. She became Secretary of the local CP branch from the late 1940s and sat on the Scottish Committee of the CPGB (1966–76). Having stood as a candidate seven times, Mabel Skinner finally won a council seat in May 1968, the first Communist councillor on Inverness Town Council. She was Convener of Social Work and played a major role in getting a community centre for the Merkinch area. She worked in shops, such as Lipton's, and was an organiser for USDAW. She was also involved in the Anti-Apartheid Movement, CND and the Scotland-USSR Society and was active during the miners' strike of 1984–5. Her cultural interests included membership of Inverness Musical Society and *An Comunn Gaidhealach* and she was on the board of the 7:84 Theatre Company. N R

• Mabs Skinner interview (with author) 15 April 1994, Inverness; Questionnaire returned to author 1994; Telephone interview between Tom Skinner and author 24 March 1998.
Aberdeen Press and Journal, 13 August 1996 (obit.); Election leaflet, 1965 (copy courtesy of Frieda Gostwick); *Inverness Courier,* 13 August 1996 (obit.); *Morning Star,* 25 March 1970; *The Scotsman,* 13 August 1996 (obit.).

SLESSOR, Mary Mitchell, born Gilcomston, Aberdeen, 2 Dec. 1848, died Use Ikot Oku, Nigeria, 13 Jan. 1915. Missionary. Daughter of Mary Mitchell, weaver, and Robert Slessor, shoemaker.

Mary Slessor, the second of seven children, had a childhood scarred by her father's alcoholism, which cost him his job in Aberdeen. The family moved to Dundee in 1859, where the burden of providing for them all fell on Mary and her mother after the deaths of three of her siblings. From the age of 11, Mary Slessor was a half-timer in Baxter's mill and at 14 she was weaving 12 hours a day at the power loom. Her formal education took place mainly in factory schools; she was largely self-taught. Her mother, deeply religious, sent the children to Sunday School at the United Presbyterian Church (UPC); she was interested in foreign missions, especially that of Calabar in West Africa. Mary Slessor graduated from Sunday School to Bible Class, becoming part of home missions and teaching in the Sabbath School. By her mid-20s she was an articulate and well-read Christian who had adopted the values of middle-class Victorian society.

The death of David Livingstone (1873) and the wishes of her mother encouraged her to apply to the UPC Foreign Missions Board to train as a missionary. She set sail for Calabar, Nigeria, 'the white man's grave', on 6 August 1876. Over the next 39 years she carved out a reputation as the most celebrated Scottish missionary since David Livingstone. In doing so, she pushed the boundaries of Victorian femininity and acceptable behaviour to the limits. The poverty of her upbringing allowed her to strike an immediate rapport with the peoples of Calabar, especially the women. She refused to wear a bonnet or shoes and learnt by ear the local Efik language. Her lifestyle played havoc with her health and she wrote of being covered in boils, her hair falling out and going temporarily blind. Although she never married, she was engaged for a time to another Scottish missionary, Charles Morrison.

Mary Slessor pushed into the interior of the country in her attempt to Christianise native populations. She decided early on that if the 'unacceptable' aspects of Calabar tribal society, such as twin murder, drunkenness and ritual sacrifices, were to be eradicated, she had to co-operate with the imperial authorities. She adopted twins herself. In recognition of her work, in 1892 she was appointed British vice-consul of the Okoyong territory and in 1913 was elected an Honorary Associate, Order of St John of Jerusalem. Although she believed in the superiority of British values, it is not straightforward to consider her as contributing to the racism of 19th-century colonialism. In her view, British superiority lay only in the knowledge of God; once the Africans had embraced Christianity, that superiority would evaporate. She nurtured women's independence and was the moving force in setting up industrial and farming settlements to provide training. Her work among the peoples of Calabar converted few to Christianity but her integrity left an enduring legacy encapsulated in her title there, 'Mother of all the peoples'. WWJK

• Dundee City Archives: Letters; Dundee Museums and Art Galleries: Corr., diaries, papers.

Buchan, J. (1980) *The Expendable Mary Slessor*; Knox, W. W. J. (2006) *The Lives of Scottish Women*; Livingstone, W. P. (1915) *Mary Slessor of Calabar*; McEwan, C. (2000) *Gender, Geography and Empire: Victorian women travellers in West Africa*; ODNB (2004).

SMALL, Ann Hunter (Annie), born Redding, near Falkirk, 26 Dec. 1857, died Edinburgh 7 Feb. 1945. Missionary and college principal. Daughter of Nathina Hunter and the Rev. John Small, Free Church of Scotland missionaries in Poona.

Annie Small spent her childhood in Arbroath, in India and at school in London then, aged 19, returned to Poona as a missionary in her own right. She developed a great love of Indian people, culture and languages, and became highly regarded for her knowledge of Indian religions and musical traditions. Unusually perceptive about the imperial pretensions of Victorian Britain, she later reflected: 'I criticised hotly our British acquisitiveness, restlessness, our talk of commerce while intending conquest, our hypocritical profession of desire for the good of India' (Wyon 1953, p. 194). Poor health forced her to return to Scotland in 1892. She was somewhat disillusioned at the state of church life, especially the official disregard of women, which she thought bordered on contempt.

An opportunity to challenge this arose when the Women's Foreign Mission Committee invited her to become principal of the new Women's Missionary College (WMC), later St Colm's College, to provide specialised mission training for women. Annie Small thereafter demonstrated practical commitment to overcoming divisions and injustice in church and community. From 1894 to 1913 she led a pioneering institution, offering for the first time anywhere in the world dedicated professional education for female missionaries. She developed an innovative curriculum, based on progressive scholarship, methods and practical work, and in the context of an encouraging residential community.

The WMC attracted students from many countries and became a model institution, commended by the 1910 Edinburgh World Missionary Conference – a key ecumenical event at which Annie Small and the college were active and influential. She combined passion for her Scottish Presbyterian heritage with an ecumenical spirit, rooted in her love of Iona. Always open to new ideas, she engaged passionately with key issues – not least the place of women in church and society. After retirement, she experimented in models of community living, maintained a worldwide circle of friends, and went on writing and lecturing into her 70s. A commonsense visionary, she called for women to be unconventional explorers in the service of the gospel. LO

• St Colm's International House, Edinburgh: St Colm's Collection (archives of WMC).

Small, A. H. (1944) *The Church of Scotland Women's Missionary College, St Colm's, Edinburgh.*

Macdonald, L. A. O. (2000) *A Unique and Glorious Mission*; *ODNB* (2004) (Bibl.); Stewart, M. (1972) *Training in Mission*; Wyon, O. (1953) *The Three Windows: The Life of Annie Hunter Small.*

SMITH, Ann Lorrain (Annie), OBE, born Everton, Lancs., 23 Oct. 1854, died Kensington, London, 7 Sept. 1937. Lichenologist, mycologist. Daughter of Margaret Lorrain Brown, and the Rev. Walter Smith.

In 1848, Annie Smith's father, Free Church minister at Half Morton, Dumfriesshire, had been translated to St Peter's (Scotch) Church, Liverpool. The family returned to Half Morton in 1856. Annie, the fourth of their nine children, may have had her interest in botany kindled by the Rev. J. C. Meiklejohn, a friend of her father. After 1888, Annie L. Smith became a paid but 'unofficial worker' (women could not be on the permanent staff) in the Cryptogamic Herbarium in the botanical department of the BM (Natural History). Apart from a short period when she assisted Dr William Carruthers of Moffat with studies in seed testing, her connection with the Herbarium was unbroken up to her 80th birthday. The first woman president of the British Mycological Society (1907) and a council member of the Linnean Society (1918–21), she completed a *Monograph of British Lichens* (started by the Rev. J. Crombie), which became a standard work (1911, 1918, 1926). Her *Handbook of British Lichens* (1921) provided a key for the identification of species, while her major publication, *Lichens* (1921, re-pub. 1975), included anthropological and ecological notes as well as taxonomic data. Annie L. Smith became recognised as the British authority on lichens, contributing many records and articles to journals about these and other cryptogams. On her retirement in 1934, she was awarded the OBE. EMS

• Smith, A. L., Works as above.

Ainsworth, G. C. (1996) in J. Webster and D. Moore (eds) *Brief Biographies of British Mycologists*; *Dumfries & Galloway Standard*, 15 Sept. 1937; Ewing, Rev. W. (ed.) (1914) *Annals of the Free Church of Scotland: 1843–1900*; Gepp, A. and Rendle, A. B. (1937) *Jour. Bot. Lond.* 75, (obit.); Liverpool Record Office; *ODNB* (2004) (place and d.o.b. corrected here). Private information: written family record.

SMITH, Dorothea Chalmers, n. **Lyness (Lynas),** born Glasgow 1872, died Glasgow 21 May 1944.

Pioneer doctor and militant suffragette. Daughter of Lavinia Bannister, and William Crawford Lyness, property owner and merchant.

Among the first cohort of female medical students at Queen Margaret Medical School, opened in 1890, Dorothea Lyness graduated MB from the University of Glasgow in 1894, and worked in the Glasgow Samaritan Hospital for Women. On 16 June 1899 she married the Rev. William Chalmers Smith (1864–1935), Minister of Calton Parish Church in the East End of the city. They had four daughters (two of whom became doctors) and two sons. Dorothea and her younger sister Jane developed an active interest in the women's suffrage campaign, and she joined the militant WSPU in 1912. On 24 July 1913, Dorothea Chalmers Smith and her audacious accomplice, *Ethel Moorhead, were apprehended with fire-lighting equipment in a mansion house at 6 Park Gardens. Arrested and held on remand at Duke Street Prison, they went on hunger strike. After five days, she was released under the Cat and Mouse Act, but did not return to the jail when her licence expired. She was later found at Tighnabruich, indicted and released on bail to appear at the High Court on 15 October. At the trial, the women calmly declared their intention to defend themselves against the charge of housebreaking with intent to set fire. They were found guilty and sentenced to eight months imprisonment amid chaotic scenes as supporters shouted, 'Shame! Shame!' and threw apples. After five days on hunger strike, Dorothea Chalmers Smith was discharged under licence to return home. To her husband's dismay, police placed the house under 24-hour watch after she failed to return to prison as required. She escaped on 19 November and was never apprehended.

Her notoriety proved too much for the Kirk Session of Calton Parish Church, who demanded that the minister either control or divorce his wife. Unlike some other clergymen married to suffragettes, William Chalmers Smith was less than supportive of his wife's actions, and Dorothea eventually left him. After the divorce, she was forbidden to see her sons, who remained with their father. Dorothea Chalmers Smith successfully resumed her career as a doctor, specialising in childcare and public health, and was remembered fondly in Glasgow for her medical work and her kindness. LO

• *AGC*; *HHGW*; *SS*.
Private information.

SMITH, Janet Buchanan Adam, OBE, m1 **Roberts,** m2 **Carleton,** born Glasgow 9 Dec. 1905, died London 11 Sept. 1999. Biographer, critic and anthologist. Daughter of Lilian Buchanan, and George Adam Smith, Presbyterian minister and academic.

Janet Adam Smith, the sixth child in her family, was brought up in Aberdeen, where her father was university principal: a childhood friend was *Janet Teissier du Cros, n. Grierson. She was educated at Cheltenham Ladies' College and Somerville College, Oxford (BA 1927). She began work with the BBC in 1928 and was assistant editor of *The Listener* 1930–5, meeting the young poets of the day and compiling an anthology of their work, *Poems of Tomorrow* (1935). She displeased Lord Reith, BBC Director-General, by publishing a W. H. Auden poem which he found incomprehensible. In 1935, she married the poet Michael Roberts (1902–48), who shared her love of mountain climbing, and moved to Newcastle, where he was a teacher. During wartime evacuation to Penrith, housebound with young children (they shared the house with poet *Kathleen Raine), she wrote *Mountain Holidays* (1946) about her climbing experiences. Later, they moved to London. Michael Roberts developed leukemia and died in 1948.

Janet Adam Smith brought up her four children in a home which was also an intellectual centre for her friends. In 1949, she resumed her journalistic career with the *New Statesman* and was its literary editor 1952–60, becoming a freelance writer and broadcaster in 1960. She married John Carleton (1908–74), a headmaster, in 1965. Among her numerous publications are *John Buchan: a biography* (1965), the standard biography for many years, and the anthologies *The Faber Book of Children's Verse* (1953) and *The Faber Book of Comic Verse* (rev. edn. 1974). Her critical writings included reviews for journals including *The New York Review of Books*. She collaborated in the translation of several mountaineering memoirs. A past president of the Ladies' Alpine Club, she was one of the first woman committee members when the Alpine Club admitted women in the 1970s. She was vice-president 1978–80 and elected an honorary member in 1993. She was a trustee of the NLS 1950–85 and president of the Royal Literary Fund 1976–84. She received an honorary degree of LLD from the University of Aberdeen in 1962 and was made OBE in 1982. MARB

• Smith, J. B. Adam, Works as above and see *The New York Review of Books* (Bibl.): www.nybooks.com/authors

'Michael Roberts' www.online.northumbria.ac.uk/faculties/art/humanities/cns/m-roberts.html; *ODNB* (2004); *The Times*, 13 Sept. 1999 (obit.).

SMITH, Madeleine Hamilton, m. **Wardle,** born Glasgow 29 March 1835, died New York, USA, 28 April 1928. Defendant in murder trial. Daughter of Elizabeth Hamilton, and James Smith, architect.

Madeleine Smith grew up in Glasgow, the daughter of a prosperous architect. She went to school in London 1851–3, and returned to a busy social life both in the city and at the family's country home at Rhu on the Clyde. Early in 1855, she met Emile L'Angelier (c. 1826–57), a warehouse clerk from Jersey, and they began a secret relationship. About 250 of Madeleine Smith's letters to her 'dear sweet pet of a husband' survive. The couple continued to meet and correspond clandestinely after her parents had forbidden any marriage on the grounds of Emile L'Angelier's financial and social unsuitability. However, by early 1857 she had agreed to marry William Minnoch, a family friend, and asked L'Angelier to return her letters. He refused, and continued to meet her at the family house in Blythswood Square. In the early hours of 23 March 1857, he died suddenly at his lodgings of arsenic poisoning. Madeleine Smith was arrested for his murder: the trial, which took place in July 1857, was a national sensation. Her youth, appearance and social status excited great interest; but the greatest furore was caused by the uninhibited nature of the letters read out in court. The prosecution was unable to show that she had had the opportunity to give L'Angelier the arsenic that killed him, and to public jubilation the jury returned a verdict of Not Proven.

After returning briefly to Rhu, Madeleine Smith went to live in England and married George Wardle in London in July 1861. They settled in Bloomsbury and had two children. Through Wardle's work as a close associate of William Morris, they moved in circles that included Rossetti, Burne Jones and Bernard Shaw. Madeleine Wardle became an active socialist and served on committees with, among others, Eleanor Marx. The Wardle marriage broke down in about 1890, and in 1893 she went to New York, where her son had already settled and where she lived for a further 35 years. EG/GMN

• NAS: JC 26/1031/1, Letters of Madeleine Smith to Emile L' Angelier.

Hartman, M. S. (1972–3) 'Murder for respectability: the case of Madeleine Smith', *Victorian Studies*, 16; Knox, W. W. J. (2006) *The Lives of Scottish Women*; MacGowan, D. (1999) *Murder in Victorian Scotland: the trial of Madeleine Smith*; *ODNB* (2004).

SMYTH, Jessica Piazzi (Jessie), n. **Duncan,** born Aberdeen 1815, died Ripon 24 March 1896. Amateur geologist and astronomical observer. Daughter of Jannet Young, and Thomas Duncan, lawyer.

Brought up in Clova near Rhynie, Aberdeenshire, Jessie Duncan later attended the geology courses of Alexander Rose in Edinburgh, which included field excursions, and embarked on geological tours in England, Ireland, and continental Europe. Through her scientific interests she met Charles Piazzi Smyth (1819–1900), the brilliant, if eccentric, Astronomer Royal for Scotland and professor at the University of Edinburgh. They married on Christmas Day, 1854. Thereafter she was his indispensable amanuensis on astronomical expeditions abroad: to Tenerife on a pioneering test of 'mountain astronomy', to Egypt for a survey of the Great Pyramid, and to Mediterranean locations to observe the sun. A modest person whose name is rarely mentioned in the formal reports, her contribution to science was subsumed under that of her husband. MTB
• Library of the Royal Observatory Edinburgh: Archives. Brück, H. A. and Brück, M. T. (1988) *The Peripatetic Astronomer: the life of Charles Piazzi Smyth*; *ODNB* (2004) (Smyth, Charles Piazzi).

SNODGRASS, Catherine Park, born Bonnyrigg 17 July 1902, died Edinburgh 13 Dec. 1974. Geographer, planner and political commentator.

Educated at Eskbank Girls' School, George Watson's Ladies' College and St George's School in Edinburgh, Catherine Snodgrass graduated MA from the University of Edinburgh in 1924 and obtained her PhD in 1931 for work on Scotland's physical environment and agriculture. She lectured in geography at the University of Edinburgh from 1936 to 1957. Her work, undeservedly neglected, falls into three broad periods and types. In the late 1930s and early 1940s she concentrated upon land use planning, culminating in involvement with L. Dudley Stamp's Land Utilisation Survey and in membership of the Scottish Reconstruction Committee. In the 1950s, she made significant contributions to the *Third Statistical Account of Scotland*. Her later work focused upon Scottish

nationalism and the geography and politics of self-government. CW
• Univ. of Edinburgh, Department of Geography Archives: Snodgrass Papers (DG 6).
Snodgrass, C. (1946) 'Part 30: Fife' in L. D. Stamp (ed.) *Land of Britain: the report of the Land Utilisation Survey*, (1953) 'East Lothian' and 'Edinburgh' in *Third Statistical Account of Scotland*, (1960) *Scotland in the Modern World: a plea for freedom, self-government and full participation*.

SNOWDON, The Princess Margaret Rose, Countess of, born Glamis Castle 21 August 1930, died London 9 Feb. 2002. Daughter of *Queen Elizabeth (see Elizabeth, Queen and Queen Mother) and King George VI.

Margaret's position was transformed when her father, the Duke of York, became king in 1936. She and her sister, Elizabeth, were educated by their Scottish governess *Marion Crawford. A lively little girl, her later role in the 'Margaret set', whose activities and relationships were much reported in the press, created the image of a somewhat wayward member of the royal family. Her life illustrates the difficulties of being close to the throne. Her love for Group Captain Peter Townsend, her father's equerry but a divorcé, caused a constitutional crisis: could Elizabeth, as Queen and Head of the Anglican Church, permit the marriage? In 1955, Princess Margaret released a public statement to say she would not marry Capt. Townsend. In 1960, she married photographer Antony Armstrong-Jones (b. 1930, Earl of Snowdon 1961). With their two children, David and Sarah, they lived in London, mixing with celebrities in music, arts and fashion. The marriage ended in divorce in 1978, and Princess Margaret's private life was then and later the subject of press scrutiny. In her middle years, she was patron of more than 80 associations, being particularly fond of the ballet and the arts. In later years, she spent much time on the Caribbean island of Mustique, carrying out fewer public engagements. She also suffered from poor health, associated with smoking and drinking, had a bad scalding accident, and several strokes. Among her Scottish links, she was Colonel-in-Chief of the Royal Highland Fusiliers (Princess Margaret's Own Glasgow and Ayrshire regiment), which provided the pall-bearers at her funeral. FJ
• Crawford, M. (1991 rev. edn.) *The Little Princesses*; *The Guardian*, 9 Feb., 11 Feb. 2002 (obit.); *Scotland on Sunday*, 10 Feb. 2002 (obit.); Warwick, C. (2002) *Princess Margaret*; www.royal.gov.uk (official website of the royal family).

SOMERVILLE, Euphemia Gilchrist, n. Gibb, born Dollar 19 Sept. 1860, died Edinburgh 27 Sept. 1935. Councillor and campaigner on health and welfare issues. Daughter of Margaret Scott McMinn, and William Gibb, draper.

Euphemia Gibb was educated at Dollar Academy. In 1893, she married Alexander Somerville (1841/2–1907), retired East India merchant and widower with three daughters; they had three more children. After his death in 1907, the family moved to Edinburgh. Having organised voluntary health visitors on behalf of Glasgow City Council, Euphemia Somerville was asked to develop a similar scheme in Edinburgh and in 1908 started the Edinburgh Voluntary Health Workers' Association. Her life-long work was to create links between voluntary work and public service.

Elected to Edinburgh Council for Merchiston Ward in 1919 as an Independent, she was supported by the EWCA, of which she was an active member. Only the second woman councillor in the city and a member of the Education, Public Health, Housing and Town Planning and Public Parks Committees, she held her seat until her death in 1935. She spent a month in the Craiglockhart Poorhouse, to 'obtain first-hand information on this side of Social Service' (*A Child Lover*, p. 11), and later took a social work diploma at the University of Edinburgh. She became the city's second woman bailie, or magistrate, in 1932, and was particularly concerned about prostitution. In 1928, she launched the Edinburgh Welfare Housing Trust to build 'good houses for the very poor'. By 1934, the Trust had built on four city sites. Accounts hint that her determination over housing, particularly slum clearance, bordered on the obsessive. On her death it was said that, 'the vast new housing schemes that now detract from the landscape around Edinburgh' were her reward (*The Scotsman* 1935) – an ambiguous legacy but a response to housing conditions of the time. She pioneered (1930–2) progressive approaches to the care and treatment of the mentally ill and disabled, but she was best known in the city for the Toddlers' Playgrounds. The 19 playgrounds offered supervision, 'exercise, fresh air, and happy occupation' (*A Child Lover*, p. 18). Euphemia Somerville also campaigned for council nursery schools, the first of which was built in 1930 and is still open. She was inspired by 'practical Christianity' and her experience of child poverty in Glasgow was said to be the motivation for all her work. SI

• Anon. (1937) *A Child Lover*; Innes, S. (1998) 'Love and Work: feminism, family and ideas of equality and citizenship, Britain 1900–1939', PhD, Univ. of Edinburgh; *ODNB* (2004); Stewart, J. (1925) 'Kindergarten schools', in Edinburgh Corporation Education Committee, *Organisation of Education in Edinburgh*, chapter XI, pp. 76–7; *The Scotsman*, 28 Sept. 1935 (obit.); *The Scotsman*, 1 Dec. 1937.

SOMERVILLE, Mary, n. Fairfax, m1 Greig, m2 Somerville, born Jedburgh 26 Dec. 1780, died Naples 29 Nov. 1872. Writer on science. Daughter of Margaret Charters, and Lieutenant (later Vice-Admiral) William George Fairfax.

Mary Fairfax was born in the manse at Jedburgh, where her maternal aunt was wife of the minister, the Rev. Dr Thomas Somerville. Her father being at sea and her mother unwell after her confinement, Mary was suckled by her aunt (later her mother-in-law). The four Fairfax children were brought up in Burntisland in a house which is still standing. In her *Personal Recollections*, Mary Somerville describes her childhood, schooling and early life in Fife, Musselburgh and Edinburgh. Her unconventional desire to learn geometry, algebra and the classics was already well established, though not encouraged, by 1804, when she married her cousin, Samuel Greig (1778–1807), son of Admiral Sir Samuel Greig, who had gone to Russia in 1763 to organise Catherine II's navy. Samuel junior, who was Russian consul in London, died, aged 29, leaving his wife with two young children. Widowed and back in her parents' home, she had the means and the independence to pursue her studies, with guidance from Scottish mathematicians, before her second marriage in 1812 to another cousin, William Somerville (1771–1860), an army doctor. This was a happier union than the first. After a brief period in Edinburgh, the family settled in London where William became Physician at Chelsea Hospital (1819). Over the next two decades, the Somervilles played a significant part in the intellectual life of London: their acquaintance embraced the worlds of science, arts and politics. From 1840, the family spent most of their time in Italy, for William's health. By then, Mary Somerville had embarked, in her late 40s, on her career as a writer on science.

Her first work, the translation and English edition of *La Mécanique Céleste* by the French astronomer and mathematician, Pierre-Simon Laplace (1749–1827), was undertaken at the suggestion of Henry, Lord Brougham. *The Mechanism of the Heavens* was published in 1831 to general acclaim: this work, which could not have been translated without specialist knowledge, did much to assist the modernisation of mathematics in Britain, and was a recommended text in Cambridge. Mary Somerville's most ambitious work was *On the Connexion of the Physical Sciences* (1834), which ran to nine British editions in her lifetime. This book, incorporating astronomy, physics, meteorology and geography, reached a wider non-specialist audience, but also assisted specialist research – the astronomer John Couch Adams said that a suggestion in that work inspired him to calculate the orbit of Neptune. James Clerk Maxwell described *The Connexion* as one of those 'suggestive books, which put into definite, intelligible and communicable form, the guiding ideas that are clearly already working in the minds of men of science, so as to lead them to discoveries, but which they cannot yet shape into a definite statement' (Maxwell 1890, p. 401). Mary Somerville's *Physical Geography* (1848) also went through nine British editions and *On Molecular and Microscopic Science* (1869) was published when she was in her 80s. She down-played her achievement: 'Although I had recorded in a clear point of view some of the most refined and difficult analytical processes and astronomical discoveries, I was conscious that I had never made a discovery myself, that I had no originality' (*Queen of Science*, p. 145).

In her personal life, Mary Somerville belied male fears that education made women unwomanly or narrow: she wrote for the press, taught her own small children, read widely and was very fond of society. Into extreme old age she remained tart about any assumption of female inferiority. Her politics were Liberal from early on; she advocated female education and supported female suffrage. Her memoirs are remarkable for their wit and perception. When she died in Naples, obituaries appeared in newspapers and journals throughout Europe and America: the *Morning Post* obituary called her, with complete confidence, 'the Queen of science' (2 Dec. 1872). She had received numerous honours in her lifetime, and Somerville College, established in 1879 as the first women's college in Oxford, was named after her. Her successful public life had its private tragedies: three of her six children died in childhood. It is hard, given all that was stacked against her, to speak too highly of Mary Somerville's achievement: her life proved that Victorian women *could* understand science.

DAMCM

• NRA: Mary Somerville's papers, various locations. www.nra.nationalarchives.gov.uk/nra
Somerville, M., Works as above and 'Personal Recollections', in D. McMillan (ed.) (2001) *Queen of Science: the personal recollections of Mary Somerville*, augmented from MSS.
McKinlay, J. (1987) *Mary Somerville, 1780–1872*; Maxwell, J. C. (1890) *Scientific Papers*, ii, p. 401; Neely, K. (2001) *Science, Illumination and the Female Mind*; ODNB (2004); Patterson, E. C. (1983) *Mary Somerville and the Cultivation of Science, 1815–1840*.

SOULE, Caroline Augusta, n. **White,** born Albany, New York, 3 Sept. 1824, died Shawlands, Glasgow, 6 Dec. 1903. Writer, Universalist missionary to Scotland; first woman ordained as a minister in the UK. Daughter of Elizabeth Merselis, and Nathaniel White, mechanic.

Educated at Albany Female Academy, Caroline White became unpaid principal of the girls' department of a secondary school founded by the Universalist Church in Clinton, New York. She married Henry Birdsall Soule, a Universalist minister, in 1843 and had five children. She helped him edit the *Connecticut Odd Fellow* and wrote short stories for the *Hartford Times* and for Universalist magazines. When he died of smallpox in 1852, she returned to teaching, but also made an income from editing and writing, including a biography of her husband (1852) and a collection of moral stories (1855). In 1854, to live less expensively, the family moved to a log cabin in Boonsboro, Iowa, where she wrote three novels, two of which were *The Pet of the Settlement* (1860) and *Wine or Water* (1862). She moved back to New York State in 1864 to have treatment for an eye problem. In 1869, she became a founder of the earliest national organisation of American church women, the Women's Centenary Aid Association (WCA), serving as President until 1880. In 1874, aged 49, she preached her first sermon. Her first formal pastorate was in Elizabeth, New Jersey, in 1876.

On holiday in 1875, Caroline Soule visited Scotland where she helped to organise the Scottish Universalist Convention, preached and gave public lectures. In 1878, the WCA sent her to Scotland as their 'evangel', the church's first foreign missionary. She preached throughout the UK and worked in Dunfermline before settling for the next 20 years in Glasgow, where she established the St Paul's Universalist Church. On 27 March 1880, she was ordained by the Scottish Universalist Convention, an ordination later acknowledged in the USA,

where she assisted the WCA and preached 1882–6. Returning to Glasgow, she served her church of some 120 members (also acting as minister in Dundee 1886–7) until her retirement in 1892. SI
• New York City Public Library: Caroline A. Soule Papers. *American National Biography* (1999); Hill, A. M. (2003) 'The obscure mosaic of British Universalism: an outline', *Trans. Unit. Hist. Soc.* 23/1, April; Seaburg A. (1967) 'Missionary to Scotland: Caroline Augusta Soule', *Trans. Unit. Hist. Soc.* 14/1, Oct., 'Caroline Soule':
http://www.uua.org/uuhs/duub/articles/carolinesoule.html
Additional information: Andrew M. Hill.

SPEIRS, Vera Muriel,‡ m. **Laracy,** born Glasgow 24 Sept. 1921, died Brantford, Ontario, Canada, 24 Jan. 1995. 'Lumberjill' during Second World War. Daughter of Rosina Crombie, and Archibald Speirs, pharmaceutical salesman.

The eldest of three children, Vera Speirs was an excellent student at local schools in the Charing Cross district, though motherless from the age of seven. After school, she worked as a secretary for a Glasgow steel company. In November 1942, like many young Scotswomen, Vera Speirs joined the Women's Timber Corps, a recently formed branch of the Women's Land Army. After a month training in Brechin, Angus, learning the rudiments of the lumber business, she was posted to Advie, Morayshire, as a feller and crosscutter. Here the WTC Lumberjills lived in cold, damp wooden huts in a remote, densely forested area of the Highlands. Full uniforms were issued upon arrival. Camp life was rugged, the work (8 am to 5 pm weekdays with a half-day on Saturday) was arduous and dangerous: felling, crosscutting with 6 ft saws, loading and hauling timber by horse or to the railway siding by tractor and bogey. The women were supervised by male gaffers, who assisted with extra heavy lifting. Vera Speirs became a 'horsewoman', dragging trees through the forest to the crosscutters (and suffered a hand injury there). When Advie camp closed, WTC members transferred to Dunvegan House, Grantown on Spey. On 27 June 1945, in Glasgow, Vera Spiers married Canadian Thomas Laracy, whom she had met at Advie: he was from the Newfoundland Forestry Unit, a civilian group who came to help the war effort in Britain. They left for Newfoundland in July 1946 and moved to Brantford, Ontario, eventually having four children. The Lumberjills, although a uniformed body subject to the same rules as all service personnel, were not recognised at war's end as veterans, a bitter disappointment to the members. RE

• (1945) 'Meet the Members' (ISBN 1 670423 3 48) at www.members.shaw.ca/relder1/
Personal knowledge: RE, T/855 Lumberjill WTC.

SPENCE, Catherine Helen, born Melrose 31 Oct. 1825, died Adelaide, South Australia, 3 April 1910. Writer, journalist and social reformer. Daughter of Helen Brodie, and David Spence, banker, lawyer and clerk.

The fifth of eight children, Catherine Spence began her education in Melrose and expected to go to high school in Edinburgh, but her father's ruinous investments saw the family emigrating to South Australia in 1839. There she worked as a governess, 1843–6, and ran her own school, 1846–c. 1850. Her first novel, *Clara Morison* (1854), tells the story of a young Scottish orphan making her way in South Australia. This was followed by *Tender and True* (1856), *Mr. Hogarth's Will* (1865), *The Author's Daughter* (1868), *An Agnostic's Progress* (1884) and serials in the local press. Leaving Presbyterianism in 1856 to become a Unitarian, she felt 'the cloud was lifted from the universe' (Spence 1910, p. 28). From 1878, she preached in the Adelaide Unitarian church. She wrote prolifically in the press, initially under her brother's name, but from 1878 was an important member of outside staff of the *Register* newspaper, contributing over 1,500 articles, including leader articles and reviews over a broad array of areas to the press. Her fiction and her journalistic work were now infused with scientific meliorism and social science. Visiting Britain, including Melrose, in 1865–6, she enjoyed participating in circles of writers and social reformers.

A key figure in the Boarding Out Society (1872), which supervised the care of state children in private homes, she was appointed to the State Children's Council in 1887 and the Destitute Board in 1897. She supported free public education, was the first woman appointed to a local School Board (1877), and campaigned for the Advanced School for Girls, opened in 1879. *The Laws We Live Under* (1880) was the first Australian social studies textbook. During the 1890s, she campaigned for electoral reform along proportional representation lines, speaking publicly in Australia, and during 1893–4 in the US and Britain. She joined the WSL only in 1891, becoming a vice-president. The first Australian woman to run for election, she was a candidate for the Federal Convention (1897). She lived with her mother until the latter's death in 1887.

Catherine Spence pioneered many areas, as a writer, journalist, political commentator, social reformer and political candidate. Widely known on her death as 'The Grand Old Woman' of Australia, her memory was largely lost until feminist historians reclaimed her as a foremother: in 2001 she figured on the Australian $5 note produced to commemorate the Centenary of Federation. More recent critiques have pointed to other sides of her career: as a middle-class reformer seeking to control the poor, and as a white woman deeply implicated in colonialism. MA

• State Library of South Australia: Private Record Group 88: records of C. H. Spence; National Library of Australia, Canberra: Spence papers MSS 41; Mitchell Library, Sydney NSW: Spence corr. and papers, 1856–1909 ML MSS 202; Spence diary 1894, in private hands.

Spence, C. H., Works as above and (1878) 'Some Social Aspects of South Australian Life, by a Colonist of 1839'; [1879 unpub.] (1984) *Handfasted*, (1884) *An Agnostic's Progress from the Known to the Unknown*, (1910) *Autobiography*, (1994) *Tenacious of the Past: the recollections of Helen Brodie*, J. King, J. and G. Tulloch, eds.

Bibl. at www.slsa.sa.gov.au/spence/

Magarey, S. (1985) *Unbridling the Tongues of Women*; *ODNB* (2004).

SPENCE, Catherine Stafford, born Lerwick 16 July 1823, died Lerwick 21 Sept. 1906. Teacher and translator. Daughter of Jane Fea, and Dr William Spence, army staff surgeon.

Fifth of twelve children, Catherine Spence was educated by Moravians in the Lerwick Subscription School, and became a life-long teacher. Unmarried, she taught in private schools, some her own: she was a governess for several years to a Shetland clergyman, and headmistress briefly at a reformatory in Perth. In 1875, she was female principal of the Church of Scotland College at Madras, India, and in the 1880s taught at a Board School in New Zealand. In her late 60s, she returned to Shetland, and became headmistress at schools in West Yell and Gulberwick. Her log book for Gulberwick survives: each entry, unusually, is an account of her teaching methods, and her efforts to teach Scandinavian history to pupils. Catherine Spence was a gifted translator, from Danish, Dutch, Italian and other languages. She tackled theology and novels and, in old age, Jakob Jakobsen's great dictionary of the Norn language in Shetland. Her book *Earl Rognvald and his Forebears* (1896) is an attractive introduction to Shetland's Viking history. A local newspaper celebrated Catherine Spence's ability 'to fight the world almost unaided and alone. . .'[B]y sheer force of character, which

strenuous work, a hard fight, and high ideals inevitably produce, [she] has left a name and memorial' (*Shetland News*, 1906). BS

• Shetland Archives: CO5/5/34: Log book, Gulberwick school, 1893–1907; D3/2-4 (MS translations).

Spence, C., Works as above, and (trans.) (1894) *Ployen's Reminiscences*.

Shetland News, 29 Sept. 1906 (obit.); *Shetland Times*, 29 Sept. 1906 (obits).

SPOTTISWOODE, Alicia Anne (Lady John Scott), m. **Scott,** born Spottiswoode, Berwickshire, 24 June 1810, died Spottiswoode, 12 March 1900. Composer and collector of songs. Daughter of Helen Wauchope of Niddrie-Marischal, and John Spottiswoode of Spottiswoode, lawyer.

Alicia Anne Spottiswoode was the eldest of five children. She was well educated, at her father's insistence, and displayed a talent for both music and poetry. On 16 March 1836, she married Lord John Montagu Douglas Scott (1809–60), brother of the Duke of Buccleuch. Although the Spottiswoodes were already well connected, the marriage propelled her further into Scotland's high society. She was widowed in 1860. A philanthropist, she bequeathed £2,000 to local trustees for the benefit of 'the moral and respectable poor on the estate of Spottiswoode' (Hall and Barry 1997, p. 78).

A collector of songs and poems, she composed several works including 'Durisdeer' and the pro-Jacobite poem, 'Shame on ye Gallants'– an ode to Prince Charlie – and, some scholars argue, 'Loch Lomond'. She is best remembered for 'Annie Laurie', originally penned in the 1690s by William Douglas of Fingland. Douglas had tried, unsuccessfully, to woo young Anna Laurie of Maxwelton by writing two stanzas in her honour. More than 140 years later, Alicia Spottiswoode, aged 25, came across the poem in a book of Scottish ballads. She reworked Douglas's original, added a third stanza, and set the words to the melody of her own ballad, 'Kempie Kaye'. Published anonymously in 1838, without the author's permission, 'Annie Laurie' grew in popularity throughout the 19th century, was the most popular song sung during the First World War, and is perhaps Scotland's best-known love song. JJW

• Cunningham, A. (1825) *The Songs of Scotland, Ancient and Modern*; Warrender, M. (ed.) (1911) *Songs and Verses by Lady John Scott*; Hall, D. and Barry, T. (1997) *Spottiswoode: life and labour on a Berwickshire estate, 1753–1793*; *ODNB* (2004) (see Scott, Alicia Anne); Palmer, R. (1990) *What a Lovely War! British Soldiers' Songs from the Boer War to the Present Day*.

STEEL, Flora Annie, n. **Webster,** born Harrow-on-the-Hill 2 April 1847, died Minchinhampton 12 April 1929. Novelist and campaigner for women's rights in India and Britain. Daughter of Isabella Macallum, and George Webster, Sheriff-Clerk of Forfarshire.

Sixth of 11 children, Flora Annie Webster moved to Burnside, Forfar, when she was nine. She was educated mostly at home; she believed her mother provided a wider education than any contemporary girls' institution. From an established Anglo-Indian family, she treasured her Scottish roots. After marrying Henry William Steel (1840–1923) in December 1867 she travelled to India. Unable to have any more children after the difficult birth of her daughter, Mabel, in 1870, and disdainful of traditional memsahib roles, she eagerly campaigned for women's rights to education, employment and health care, wrote for newspapers and, whenever Henry Steel fell ill, performed his duties. Despite fraught relations with local government, she served as first female Inspector of Schools and on the Punjab Educational Board from 1885 to 1888.

Her profound belief in the imperial mission underpinned unrelenting criticism of anything failing to meet her exacting standards, whether by corruption or penny-pinching officialdom, especially the failure of most Britons to learn local languages and the policy of regularly moving officials, resulting in superficial contacts between the races. She criticised even the Vicereine Dufferin's campaign to bring female doctors to India, as consolidating the power of purdah over Indian women.

In India, she translated anthologies of Punjabi folktales, lavishly illustrated by Lockwood Kipling. With Grace Gardiner, she co-authored *The Complete Indian Cook and Housekeeper*, advising on everything from correct memsahib-servant etiquette to house construction. Returning to Britain in 1889, she began writing fiction, becoming known as the female Kipling. Almost alone among contemporaries, she tried to analyse both sides of the Anglo-Indian relationship. Her finest book, *On the Face of the Waters* (1896), provides one of the most balanced fictionalised accounts of the 1857 Rebellion by an Anglo-Indian.

A suffragist, she campaigned in both countries: in protest she refused to pay rent, resulting in Heinemann purchasing a manuscript copy of *On the Face*, which was sold by bailiffs in 1913. Her last years were spent writing her very candid autobiography, *The Garden of Fidelity* (1930). A complex woman, she exemplified the conflicting motivations of Victorian feminists. Unfairly classed now as India's Mrs Beeton, Flora Annie Steel deserves to be remembered more for her fiction and the campaigning zeal she retained throughout her life. P B

• Steel, F. A., Works as above and see *SWHA* (Bibl.). Brantlinger, P. (1988) *Rule of Darkness: British literature and imperialism 1830–1914*; *Glasgow Herald*, 'Portrait of a Gifted Scotswoman', 21 Nov. 1929; *HSWW* (Bibl.); *ODNB* (2004); *SWHA* (Bibl.).

STEIN, Grace *see* **WALLACE, Grace Jane** (1804–78)

STEPHEN, Jessie, MBE, born Marylebone, London, 19 April 1893, died Bristol 12 June 1979. Domestic servant, suffragette and trade unionist. Daughter of Jane Miller, and Alexander Stephen, tailor.

Jessie Stephen was the eldest of 11 children. The family stayed in Edinburgh for six years, then moved to Glasgow in 1901. She was educated at North Kelvinside School and, after gaining a scholarship, at 15 she became a pupil teacher. Her father's unemployment forced her to work as an errand girl, then in a factory, before going into domestic service because the 'board and lodging helped the money wage' (*Spare Rib*, 32, p. 11).

Her father was an ILP member and all the children attended the Socialist Sunday School. Aged 12, Jessie Stephen was selling *Labour Woman* outside the St Andrew's Hall in Glasgow; she became vice-chair of her local ILP branch, Maryhill, at 16, 'the youngest age you were allowed to join as a full member' (ibid.). She joined the WSPU, attending branch meetings and demonstrations and participating in acid attacks on post boxes, unsuspected in her servant's clothes. 'Dressed in my maid's uniform I . . . dropped in my little package, walked away again and reached home without interruption' (Stephen [n.d.], p. 49). As part of a delegation of 12 women from Glasgow WSPU, she lobbied the House of Commons and was received by David Lloyd George. Jessie Stephen saw the vote 'as only the means to an end' (ibid., p. 12), and was a life-long campaigner for women's rights, the Labour Party, the Co-operative Society and the trade union movement.

She experienced first-hand how employers treated maidservants as slaves, and organised her fellow workers into the new Scottish Domestic Workers' Federation, affiliated to Glasgow Trades Council before being integrated into the Domestic Workers' Union of Great Britain (DWU). Because of her political activities, employment opportunities dried up, so she moved to London where the DWU assisted her. She returned to Glasgow during the First World War, but Sylvia Pankhurst recruited her to establish new branches of the Workers' Suffrage Federation (WSF) in England. She worked with the WSF until 1917, then became women's organiser of the Bermondsey ILP and was elected to Bermondsey Borough Council in 1922. She also worked with *Mary Macarthur and the NFWW, becoming secretary of the domestic workers' section in December 1918.

Leading an independent lifestyle, Jessie Stephen became a journalist with a regular women's column in the *Glasgow Herald*. She lectured in Canada and the USA in the 1920s, was active in the Workers' Birth Control movement, ran her own secretarial agency and joined the National Union of Clerks in 1938. In 1952, she became a councillor in Bristol and was the first woman President of the Bristol Trades Council, an office she retained into her late seventies. She was awarded the TUC Gold Badge in 1955 and was made MBE in 1977 for her work in the trade union movement. KBB

• GCU, Gallacher Memorial Library: Jessie Stephen, 'Submission is for Slaves', unpublished autobiography (n.d.). *ODNB* (2004); Smyth, J. J. (2000) *Labour in Glasgow 1896–1936: socialism, suffrage, sectarianism*; *Spare Rib*, 32 (1975), pp. 10–13; *WSM*.
Additional information: Audrey Canning.

STEVENSON, Flora Clift, born Glasgow 30 Oct. 1839, died St Andrews 28 Sept. 1905; **STEVENSON, Louisa,** born Glasgow 15 July 1835, died Edinburgh 13 May 1908. Feminists, educationalists and philanthropists. Daughters of Jane Stewart Shannan, and James Stevenson, businessman.

Flora Stevenson was the youngest of six daughters; four, herself included, stayed single. Early years were spent in South Shields, where their father was a senior partner in the Jarrow Chemical Company. On his retirement, the family settled in 13 Randolph Crescent, Edinburgh, where she spent the rest of her life. She was educated in a private school, but was committed to improving the education of working-class children as well as middle-class girls. Flora Stevenson and Phoebe Blyth were the first women elected to a school board (1873) after the 1872 Education (Scotland) Act. She won a further nine elections and in 1900 was the first woman to chair the Edinburgh School Board. She represented the Board on the Burgh Committee on Secondary Education (1892–9) and

the Edinburgh Educational and the George Heriot Trusts (1899) and became an Honorary Fellow of the EIS (1892). She insisted that girls should compete on the same terms as boys, questioned the time devoted to domestic subjects in the girls' curriculum, and suggested that boys would benefit from such subjects. Her resistance to the introduction of cookery into Edinburgh's Board Schools was successfully opposed by *Christian Guthrie Wright and by her sister, Louisa Stevenson, Honorary Secretary and Treasurer respectively of the Edinburgh School of Cookery (1875–91). Louisa Stevenson chaired its successor, the Edinburgh School of Cookery and Domestic Economy (1892–1905).

Flora and Louisa Stevenson were early members of the Ladies' Debating Society (established by *Sarah Siddons Mair in 1865 as the Edinburgh Essay Society), and founder members of the ELEA (1867), which campaigned for women's entry to university. They supported *Sophia Jex-Blake in founding a women's medical school. With their elder sister Elisa Stevenson (1829–1904), they were members of ENSWS (1867). Flora Stevenson addressed the first public meeting of the GWSAWS (1902). The Stevensons held to the Free Church of Scotland principles of self-help and private charity, and believed that women should play a role in public bodies. One of the first two women elected to the Edinburgh Parochial Board, Louisa Stevenson was re-elected six times to the Board of Managers of Edinburgh Royal Infirmary. Flora Stevenson held a number of posts in the 1890s: Director of the Edinburgh Philosophical Institution and the Royal Blind Asylum and School, and Vice-president of the WFTU, the NUWW and the WLUA. The University of Edinburgh made her an Honorary LLD in 1903, and her sister Louisa Stevenson in 1906, for their services to female higher education. The Edinburgh School Board named a school in Flora Stevenson's honour at Comely Bank; it opened in 1902 and still flourishes as a primary school. In 1905, just before her death, she was presented with the Freedom of the City of Edinburgh. JMCD

• *AGC*; Begg, T. (1994) *The Excellent Women: the origins and history of Queen Margaret College*; Corr, H. (1998) 'Reclaiming Scottish women's lives in education: the life of Flora Stevenson', *Gender and Scottish Society. Politics, Policies and Participation* (Conference, 31 Oct. 1997); *Glasgow Herald*, 13 April 1906 (obit. FS); 14 May 1908 (obit. LS); *ODNB* (2004) (Stevenson, Flora; Stevenson, Louisa); *The Scotsman*, 28, 30 Sept. 1876; *WWW* (1966) vol. 1 (1897–1915).

STEVENSON, Louisa *see* **STEVENSON, Flora** (1839–1905)

STEWART, Eliza, (later Isla), born Dryfesdale, Dumfriesshire, 21 August 1855, died Shalford, Surrey, 6 March 1910. Matron, nurse leader, educationist and activist. Daughter of Janet (Jessie) Murray, and John Hope Johnstone Stewart, farmer and journalist.

Isla Stewart was educated at home, then trained in 1879 as a special probationer at the Nightingale School of Nursing, London. Following posts as matron in a smallpox and a fever hospital for the Metropolitan Asylum's Board, she was appointed matron of St Bartholomew's Hospital, London (1887–1910). Her predecessor there was Scottish-born **Ethel Manson** (1857–1947), who had moved to England as a child, and was matron of Barts for six years before marrying Dr Bedford Fenwick in 1887. The two women remained close friends and allies thereafter; both were instrumental in achieving reforms in nursing, campaigning for state registration and founding the ICN in 1899. Ethel Fenwick founded the first professional nursing journal, *The Nursing Record,* later *The British Journal of Nursing.* In nurse education, Isla Stewart advocated discipline, supervised practical nursing experience and the importance of moral values. She published a textbook, *Practical Nursing,* in 1899. As matron, she consolidated Ethel Fenwick's reforms and improved working conditions for nurses. In the fight for registration, opposed by Florence Nightingale and not achieved until 1919, Isla Stewart's cool diplomacy restrained her friend Ethel Fenwick's impetuosity. Isla Stewart contributed significantly to the development of professional awareness among nurses. Her grave is in Moffat. BEM

• *ODNB* (2004) (Fenwick, Ethel; Stewart, Eliza); McGann, S. Y. (1992) *The Battle of the Nurses*; *Nursing Record/Brit. Jour. Nursing, 1888–1947,* online at: www.rcn.org.uk/historicalnursingjournals

STEWART, Elizabeth, Lady Lovat, Countess of Lennox and March, Countess of Arran, c. 1554–c. 1595. Courtier and political leader. Daughter of Elizabeth Gordon, and John, 4th Earl of Atholl.

Elizabeth Stewart played a unique role, participating equally with her third husband in governing the realm in the last years of James VI's minority. She had six children with her first husband, Hugh Fraser, 5th Lord of Lovat (d. 1577). On 6 December 1578, she married Robert Stewart (1522/3–86), Earl

of Lennox (and Earl of March from 1580). However, she became pregnant with the child of James Stewart (c. 1545–96), son of Lord Ochiltree, and had her marriage publicly annulled on the grounds of her elderly husband's impotency (despite rumours that he had an illegitimate child). On 6 July 1581, she married James, who had become Earl of Arran a few months earlier, possibly due to her influence. They had at least three other children.

From mid-1583 until July 1585, the couple enjoyed a political ascendancy at court. Contemporaries recognised them as equal partners. Arran became Chancellor in 1584; by February 1585 it was rumoured that the Countess had been made 'Lady Comptroller', presiding over justice courts, although there is no official record of this. Although the absence of a queen consort or dowager helps explain Elizabeth Stewart's prominent role, it earned her much dislike, especially when her enemies died and she plundered the deposed *Mary Queen of Scots' possessions. Rumours circulated that she consulted with witches and even used sorcery herself. Arran's downfall came in late 1585 and he lost his earldom. Retiring to Elizabeth's jointure lands from her marriage to Lord Lovat, the couple plotted unsuccessfully to return to power. Elizabeth Stewart died c. 1595; her husband was murdered shortly afterwards. RG/EE

• Grant, R. (1999) 'Politicking Jacobean women: Lady Ferniehurst, the Countess of Arran and the Countess of Huntly, c. 1580–1603', in E. Ewan and M. Meikle (eds) *Women in Scotland c. 1100–c. 1750; ODNB* (2004).

STEWART, Elizabeth, Queen of Bohemia, Electress Palatine,‡ born probably Dunfermline 19 August 1596, died London 13 Feb. 1662. Daughter of *Anna of Denmark, Queen of Scots, and James VI.

Born two years after her brother, Prince Henry Frederick, Elizabeth was named after her godmother, Elizabeth I of England. She was sent to live with Lord and Lady Livingstone, her guardians, at Linlithgow Palace, where she stayed until her father inherited the English throne in 1603. When she moved south, her new guardians were Lord and Lady Harington at Combe Abbey, Wiltshire. There she had her own household and was taught reading, writing, French, Italian, dancing and music. In 1605, Guy Fawkes plotted to blow up her father and brothers in parliament and place her on the throne instead, but the assassination attempt was discovered and the conspirators executed. When she was 12, Elizabeth was given apartments in the palaces of Whitehall and Hampton Court, and visited London more frequently. Since her birth there had been talk of her marriage, and a long list of suitors expressed an interest in her. Anxious to preserve the balance of power in Europe, James decided to marry her to Frederick, the young Protestant Elector Palatine (1596–1632). The marriage articles were signed in spring 1612 and in October Frederick arrived in London. He and Elizabeth fell deeply in love. Although the marriage arrangements had to be postponed when her adored elder brother died in November 1612, the young couple were betrothed on 27 December and married on St Valentine's Day, 1613.

In April, they left for Frederick's castle of Heidelberg. The first of Elizabeth's 13 children, Frederick Henry, was born there the following January. In 1618, however, the longstanding religious crisis reached a climax and the Protestants of Bohemia wrote to ask Frederick to become their king; theirs was an elective monarchy, and until then they had been ruled by Roman Catholics. Frederick was anxious to help the Bohemians, but he knew the dangers of accepting their throne. The Catholic Holy Roman Emperor would never tolerate a Protestant monarch in his realms. In the end Frederick agreed, some said to please Elizabeth, and they set out for Prague, where they were crowned in November 1619.

Their enemies referred to them as 'the Winter King and Queen', saying that when spring came they would melt away with the snow. Frederick's reign lasted slightly longer, but on 8 November 1620 his army was defeated by imperial forces at the Battle of the White Mountain and he and Elizabeth were forced to flee. Her cheerful courage in the face of danger earned her the admiration of all their supporters. They eventually found refuge with Frederick's uncle, the Prince of Orange, at The Hague. Despite many attempts, Frederick never succeeded in regaining his possessions. He died in 1632. Although her eldest son was restored to the Palatinate in 1648, Elizabeth lived in increasingly penurious circumstances and in 1661, after the Restoration, she finally returned to London, where she died less than a year later. Roman Catholics compared her to Helen of Troy, blaming her for starting the Thirty Years' War, but for Protestants she was their iconic 'Queen of Hearts' and when her grandson eventually succeeded to the British throne in 1714 as George I, she was remembered as the vital dynastic link between the house of Hanover and the royal Stewarts. RKM

• Baker, L. M. (ed.) (1953) *The Letters of Elizabeth, Queen of Bohemia*; Marshall, R. K. (1998) *The Winter Queen* (Bibl.); *ODNB* (2004) (Elizabeth, Princess [Elizabeth Stuart]).

STEWART, Helen D'Arcy, n. **Cranstoun,** born 13 March 1765, died Edinburgh 28 July 1838. Hostess and poet. Daughter of Maria Brisbane, and the Hon. George Cranstoun.

Helen Cranstoun is known to have written several poems, among them 'The tears I shed must ever fall', which was included, with four lines added by Robert Burns, in *The Scots Musical Museum* (Johnson 1792). Her future husband's admiration for this lyric was said to have been the cause of their meeting. On 26 July 1790, Helen Cranstoun married, as his second wife, Dugald Stewart (1753–1828), Professor of Moral Philosophy at Edinburgh University. It was an outstandingly happy and successful marriage. Stewart 'never considered a piece of his composition to be finished until she had reviewed it' (Stewart 1828, Appendix, p. 2). They had a son and daughter, and between 1796 and 1806 the Stewarts accommodated as boarders a succession of young men of rank who came to study at the University of Edinburgh. Helen D'Arcy Stewart became a virtual foster-mother to several of them, including John William Ward, 1st Earl of Dudley and Foreign Secretary under Canning and Wellington, whose letters to 'Ivy' (Romilly 1905) were addressed to Helen Stewart; Hon. Henry Temple, Viscount Palmerston, later Foreign Secretary and Prime Minister; and his brother William. Other young men who frequented the Stewarts' home at various periods included Rev. Sydney Smith; Lovell and Henry Edgeworth, brothers of the writer Maria, who greatly admired Helen D'Arcy Stewart; Walter Scott; and the poet Thomas Campbell, who noted that she 'addresses me by the endearing name of *son*' (Beattie 1850, II, p. 287). Another visitor was Count Purgstall, who married her sister, **Jane Anne Cranstoun** (c. 1760–1835), believed to have suggested the character of Diana Vernon in *Rob Roy*. As Countess Purgstall, Jane lived mainly in Austria (cf. Grierson 1932, pp. 504–8). The Stewarts were famous for entertaining a mix of aristocrats, lawyers, intellectuals, students and visitors to Edinburgh, especially while living in Lothian House and Whitefoord House in the Canongate. Many attested that the success of these evenings owed much to Helen D'Arcy Stewart's warmth and unpretentiousness. She was also a lively letter-writer. Helen Stewart survived her husband by ten years: theirs is the only sealed tomb in Canongate Kirkyard. DGM

• Beattie, W. (1850) *Life and Letters of Thomas Campbell*; Grierson, H. J. C (ed.) (1932–7) *The Letters of Sir Walter Scott*, VI, pp. 504–8; Johnson, J. (1787–1803) *The Scots Musical Museum*; Macintyre, G. (2003) *Dugald Stewart: the pride and ornament of Scotland* (Bibl.); *ODNB* (2004); Romilly, S. H. (ed.) (1905) *Letters to 'Ivy' from the First Earl of Dudley*; Stewart, M. (1828) *Memoir of the late Dugald Stewart, Esq.*

STEWART, Henrietta, Countess and Marchioness of Huntly, born France 1573, died France 2 Sept. 1642. Courtier and defender of Catholicism. Daughter of Katherine de Balsac, and Esmé Stewart, Duke of Lennox, favoured courtier of James VI.

Raised in France, Henrietta Stewart was James VI's close female relative – she was the daughter of James's cousin and a descendant of James II. She was engaged to marry George Gordon, 6th Earl of Huntly (1561/2–1636), in 1581. The Privy Council granted 5,000 merks to bring her from France for a magnificent wedding at Holyrood on 21 July 1588. Loved by James as a daughter, she became a confidante of *Anna of Denmark. Henrietta Stewart's strong connection to the Jesuits influenced the young Queen. She gave Anna a Catholic catechism and influenced her in her decision to convert to Catholicism in the early 1590s.

The Countess's connections with James ensured that, despite her religion and her husband's intrigues, she was never far from royal favour; she was present at the birth or baptism of three royal children. At Princess Margaret's baptism the Earl and Countess were made Marquis and Marchioness of Huntly. They had at least five sons and four daughters. The Marchioness actively looked after the family's estates, and energetically interceded for her husband's interests during his banishments.

After 1603, the absentee monarchs did not protect the Marquis from the Kirk, which had long detested his Catholicism. He was excommunicated, reconciled, and then lapsed again. Henrietta Stewart, however, never recanted; she lived quietly in Aberdeenshire, protected by her royal connection. Widowed in 1636 and persecuted by the Covenanting kirk, she fled to France in 1641. RG/MMM

• Grant, R. (1999) 'Politicking Jacobean women: Lady Ferniehurst, the Countess of Arran and the Countess of Huntly', in E. Ewan and M. Meikle (eds) *Women in Scotland c. 1100–c. 1750* (Bibl.); *SP*, iv, pp. 541–5, v, p. 356.

STEWART, Isabella (Belle), n. **Macgregor,** BEM, born near Caputh, 17 July 1906, died Blairgowrie 4 Sept. 1997. Traditional singer and songwriter. Daughter of Martha Stewart and Donald (Dan) MacGregor, travelling people.

Belle Macgregor was born in a tent on the banks of the Tay, the daughter of a travelling family. She grew up in Blairgowrie in a 'single-end', taken by her mother when her father died, and went to school there. She learned her father's songs through her brothers, Donald and Andy. When she was a teenager she went with her brothers to Ireland, pearl-fishing, and married her second cousin Alec Stewart in Ballymoney in 1925. They had two sons and three daughters. Alec served as a piper in the Black Watch in the Second World War. Belle found the life of a traveller in Ireland difficult, and she and Alec finally settled in Blairgowrie. In Ireland, however, she had learned many songs, which she sang all her life. At weddings and special occasions the Stewarts had a tradition of making up family songs, which was how Belle began writing her own songs, which include 'The Berryfields of Blair' and 'Whistling at the Ploo'.

Blairgowrie journalist Maurice Fleming 'discovered' the Stewart family, living in a cottage in Rattray, in the early 1950s. That led to years of visits by scholars and collectors including Hamish Henderson and Ewan MacColl. After the first Blairgowrie Festival in 1966, the Traditional Music and Song Association of Scotland was founded. Belle Stewart became world-famous as a traditional singer. According to Maurice Fleming, more than one authority regarded Belle Stewart as one of the finest folk artists in these islands. She sang ballads, broadsides and music hall songs, including 'The Twa Brithers', 'The Bonnie Hoose o'Airlie', 'The Queen amang the Heather' and 'Betsy Bell'. When Ewan MacColl involved Belle's family in the Radio Ballad, 'The Travelling People', their reputation grew and their performance context widened. They were invited abroad, to Europe and the USA. Belle Stewart had become a matriarch of song, charming audiences everywhere. She received the British Empire Medal (BEM) for services to folk music in 1985. On her 90th birthday, Blairgowrie gave her the most prestigious venue in the town for the party. SMDoug

• Douglas, S. (ed.) (1992) *The Sang's the Thing: voices from Lowland Scotland.*
Personal knowledge.

STEWART, Lucy, born Aberdeen 4 Feb. 1901, died 3 Dec. 1982. Singer. Daughter of Betty Townsley, dealer and businesswoman, and James Stewart, ex-army, piper and fiddler.

Lucy Stewart was one of a musical family of 14 in Aberdeen who later lived on a croft in Fetterangus. Her brother James played drums in Aberdeen's Tivoli Theatre. Her youngest sister, Jean (born 1911), was a pianist, fell in love with the accordion, had her own dance band and became well known as a broadcaster. Lucy, the stay-at-home daughter who never married, virtually brought up her two nieces, one of whom, the singer Elizabeth Stewart, learned Lucy's ballads and songs by osmosis. In the family, Lucy, who is now considered one of the great source singers of the Folk Revival, was not classed as a musician at all. She was the one in the background cooking and cleaning for the rest of the family, which she was happy to do. She was a handsome woman with a wonderful voice and a great family heritage of song. Elizabeth Stewart describes her as both shy and easy-going. She sang about the house, to help with the work and to keep up her spirits. All the travelling Elizabeth Stewart and her sister did was on a horse and cart with their aunt. Even when Jean settled in Fetterangus, she still had a dance band and taught in schools and farmhouses and from her home(s), so Lucy Stewart continued to fulfil the role of mother-figure and general factotum.

In the 1960s, Kenneth Goldstein, a Fulbright scholar (later President of the American Folklore Society), was introduced to the Stewarts of Fetterangus. He recognised and recorded Lucy's singing, which later appeared on disc. Her repertoire included 'The Laird o'Drum', 'The Battle of Harlaw', 'I Aince Loed a Lass', 'The Lass o'Bennachie', 'The Lass o'Glenshee', 'Mill o'Tifty's Annie' and 'Plooman Laddies'. Lucy Stewart never sang in public so did not become as well known as some of her relations, but she now has an international reputation. SMDOUG

• Douglas, S. (1992) *The Sang's the Thing: voices from Lowland Scotland.*

Private information: Elizabeth Stewart.

STEWART, Margaret, born 25 Dec. 1424, died Châlons, France, 16 Aug. 1445; **Isabella,** died 1494; **Eleanor,** died 20 Nov 1480; **Joanna,** died after 1486; **Mary,** died 20 March 1465; **Annabella,** fl. 1444–71. Princesses of Scotland. Daughters of *Joan Beaufort and James I.

These Stewart princesses were valuable commodities on the European marriage market. The eldest, Margaret, married Louis (1423–83), heir

to Charles VII of France, on 25 June 1436. The Dauphin disliked his wife, but Margaret was a favourite of the French king and queen and well regarded by her contemporaries. A member of court literary and musical circles, she devoted much time to writing poetry, though none survives.

Isabella married Duke Francis I of Brittany on 30 October 1442. Widowed in 1450, with two daughters, she resisted plans for her remarriage by James II, Charles VII and the Bretons, preferring life on her dowager estates of Succinio. Isabella became a noted patron, collecting at least four Books of Hours (two probably made at her direction) and commissioning at least one devotional work.

Eleanor was invited to the French court as a possible bride for the King of the Romans. She eventually married Sigismund, Archduke of Austria-Tyrol, by proxy on 8 September 1448. Politically active and capable, she acted as regent during Sigismund's absence in the mid-1450s. Her letter collection and literary patronage reveal her literacy in Scots, German, Latin and French. She owned devotional works and romances and was responsible for a French-German translation of the romance *Pontus und Sidonia.*

Joanna's betrothal to the third Earl of Angus in 1440 was later dissolved. She accompanied Eleanor to France in 1445 but did not marry there. James II recalled her to Scotland in 1458. She married James Douglas of Dalkeith (d. 1493), first Earl of Morton, before 15 May 1459 and bore four children. Later accounts reported her to have been mute.

Mary became Countess of Buchan in her own right and married Wolfaert van Borselen, son of the Lord of Veere, Admiral of the Burgundian fleet, in 1444. Their two sons died young.

Annabella was betrothed to Louis, Count of Geneva, son of the Duke of Savoy, on 14 December 1444. After living in the Duchess of Savoy's household from 1445 until 1456, her betrothal was dissolved, probably at James II's request. She left Savoy unwillingly, returning to Scotland with Joanna in 1458. Before 15 May 1459, Annabella married George Gordon, Master of Huntly (1440/1–1501), who had divorced *Elizabeth Dunbar, Countess of Moray. Annabella was divorced in 1471, after bearing several children. FD

• Downie, F. A. (1998) '"Sche is but a womman": the queen and princess in Scotland, 1424–63', PhD, Univ. of Aberdeen, (1999) '"La voie quelle menace tenir": Annabella Stewart, Scotland, and the European marriage market, 1444–56', *Scot.*

Hist. Rev., 78; Dunlop, A. I. (1950) *The Life and Times of James Kennedy, Bishop of St Andrews*; *ODNB* (2004) (see Margaret of Scotland) (Bibl.).

STEWART, Margaret, born c. 1460, died c. 1503. Princess of Scotland. Daughter of *Mary of Guelders and James II.

As a young child in 1464, Princess Margaret was sent to the convent of Haddington for 'education' until her marriage was arranged. A marriage to the English Duke of Clarence was proposed in 1477, and in March 1478 to Earl Rivers, brother-in-law of the English king, Edward IV. Parliament granted a contribution of £20,000 Scots. Despite further negotiations in 1482, Margaret never left Scotland. For 'personal reasons' of the princess – and possibly rumours that she was of 'unfavourable character'– the marriage was opposed. In fact, she had been seduced by the already married William, 3rd Lord Crichton. In 1483, she gave birth to an illegitimate daughter, *Margaret Crichton. She was at court in 1493, but by 1494 had moved to the convent of Elcho, which received £67 annually for her expenses. In 1503 she is recorded as being in Hamilton, perhaps having left the convent due to illness. KP

• Bain, J. (ed.) (1881–8) *Calendar of Documents Relating to Scotland*, vol. 4; *ER*; Nicholson, R. (1974) *Scotland: the later Middle Ages*; Rymer, T. (ed.) (1704–35) *Foedera, Conventiones, Literae*, vol. 12; *TA*, vol. 1.

STEWART, Margaret, of Ochiltree, c. 1548–1611. Wife of and assistant to John Knox. Daughter of Agnes Cunningham, and Andrew Stewart, 2nd Lord Ochiltree.

Margaret Stewart was only 16 or 17 years old when in March 1564 she married the minister and Protestant reformer John Knox (c. 1514–72) who was then about 50 years old. His first wife had been the Englishwoman **Marjory Bowes** (d. Dec. 1560), daughter of Elizabeth (n. Aske) and Richard Bowes, captain of Norham Castle on the English Border. John Knox was a good friend of Elizabeth Bowes who encouraged his marriage to her daughter, probably in spring 1556, despite her husband's opposition to the match. She accompanied the couple to Geneva in 1556. Well-educated, Marjory Bowes acted as secretary for her husband. A happy marriage ended with her early death. Elizabeth Bowes cared for her two grandchildren in Scotland from 1562 until 1564, and stayed in contact with John Knox and his family until her own death in 1568.

John Knox's second marriage was deemed a very godly match as Margaret Stewart came from a strongly Protestant family. Few remarked on the big age-gap between them, but the disparity in their social status was commented upon as she was a noblewoman and he of mercantile stock. Moreover, as *Mary, Queen of Scots pointed out, Margaret Stewart was distantly related to the royal family. It was neither a platonic marriage, nor a marriage of convenience, for they had three daughters. In Margaret Stewart's view, she had married the hero of the Reformation. Like his first wife, she acted as secretary to her husband; she also nursed him in his final years. Two years after John Knox's death, in January 1574, she married the fervently Protestant Border laird, Sir Andrew Ker of Faldonside. Margaret Stewart no doubt remarried for godly reasons, but she would also have wanted protection for her young children. She had several more children by her second husband. MMM

• NAS: CC8/8/33, CC8/8/48, fos 71r-v, Edinburgh Commissary Court, Testaments.
Newman, C. M. (1990) 'The Reformation and Elizabeth Bowes: a study of a sixteenth-century northern gentlewoman', in W. J. Sheils and D. Wood (eds) *Women in the Church*; *ODNB* (2004) (Bowes, Elizabeth; Knox, John); *SP*, vi, p. 514.

STEWART, Mary, born Scotland before 16 May 1452, died Scotland c. May 1488. Princess of Scotland. Daughter of Mary of Guelders and James II.

The young Mary Stewart was considered a valuable marriage commodity. When *Mary of Guelders met Margaret of Anjou, the Lancastrian Queen of England, in 1460, she suggested her daughter marry Prince Edward, heir to the throne. Lancastrian defeat in the Wars of the Roses ended the proposal. Mary's limited dowry made a foreign marriage difficult. In October 1466, a commission of Lords appointed by Parliament arranged her marriage to Lord Thomas Boyd, who was made Earl of Arran. Her brother, James III, distrusting the Boyds, opposed the marriage. When the Earl arrived back in Scotland from Denmark in 1469 with James's bride, *Margaret of Denmark, Mary warned him of danger and together they fled to Denmark, then to Bruges. The Earl of Arran and several relatives were charged with treason in November 1469. Mary Stewart later returned to Scotland and married James, Lord Hamilton, in 1474. It is not known whether her first marriage was ended by divorce or by Arran's death, c. 1474. Mary had a son and daughter with Thomas Boyd and another son and daughter with Lord Hamilton. ECH

• MacDougall, N. (1982) *James III*; Nicholson, R. (1974) *Scotland in the Later Middle Ages*; TA, vol. 1.

STEWART, Olga Margaret, n. **Mounsey,** born Edinburgh 1 July 1920, died New Abbey, Dumfries, 6 August 1998. Botanist and botanical artist. Daughter of Marjory Brookfield from Nova Scotia, and James Mounsey, lawyer.

One of two daughters, Olga Mounsey was educated at schools in Edinburgh and Kent before studying architecture at ECA. At the outbreak of war in 1939, she was in Nova Scotia where she remained until 1943, studying engineering for a year at Dalhousie University, then working as a draughtswoman at Halifax naval dockyard for the National Research Council of Canada. Returning to Edinburgh, she worked for the Royal Navy. In 1946, she married Frank Stewart, an Edinburgh lawyer, who was later Scottish consul for the principality of Monaco. By her own account, she started drawing flowers in 1947 while pregnant with her first child (she had four children, one of whom became a professional botanist). It remained a hobby until she joined the Wildflower Society in 1965 and the BSBI in 1967. She quickly became an expert field botanist, in 1975 being appointed botanical recorder for Kirkcudbrightshire (where the family had a holiday home) and publishing her checklist of *Flowering Plants of Kirkcudbrightshire* in 1990. Her botanical illustrations appear in many BSBI publications, in Mary M. Webster's *Flora of Moray, Nairn and East Inverness* (1978) and in Princess Grace of Monaco's *My Book of Flowers* (1980). She also enjoyed curling, and represented Scotland on a tour of western Canada in 1967, continuing to play in Edinburgh until 1996. JM

• Haines, C. M. and Stevens, H. (2001) *International Women in Science*, p. 302; Jermy, A. C. (1999) 'Olga Margaret Stewart 1920–1998', *Watsonia*, 22, 4; (1999) 'In Memoriam: Olga M. Stewart 1920–1998', *BSBI Scottish Newsletter*, 21. Private information: Frank Stewart, husband.

STEWART SMITH, Janet Eliza (Jane), n. **James,** born Edinburgh 1839, died Edinburgh 1 Dec. 1925. Artist, illustrator, amateur historian. Daughter of Eliza Cuthbertson, and William Henry Spinks James, corn merchant.

In 1862, Jane James married John Smith (later John Stewart Smith), an Edinburgh carver, gilder and picture dealer. Shortly afterwards, she began

recording the early morning life of Edinburgh's Old Town in some 60 watercolours to 'catch the reverberating echoes of the past as they linger round the old historic buildings' (Butchart 1951, p. xx). These vivid paintings in the picturesque tradition, not made for sale, were given to Edinburgh Public Library (CPL) in 1932 by her friend Catherine Roberts, a retired dressmaker. Until the later 1890s, the Stewart Smiths lived in south Edinburgh, which prompted her to research, write and illustrate *The Grange of St Giles* (1898). After her husband's death in 1921, she wrote a second book, *Historic Stones and Stories of bygone Edinburgh* (1924) 'in affectionate remembrance of our 59 years of happy wedded life'. Illustrated 'with pen, pencil and camera' by her, the books were designed and printed by T. & A. Constable, published at her own expense, and still provide useful antiquarian references. EC

• Stewart Smith, J. E., Works as above.
Butchart, R. (1951) *The Edinburgh Scene: catalogue of prints and drawings in the Edinburgh Room (CPL)*.

STEWART-MURRAY, Lady Dorothea, m. **Ruggles-Brise,** born London 25 March 1866, died Vence, Alpes-Maritimes, 28 Dec. 1937, on a visit to France. Music collector. Daughter of Louisa Moncreiffe, and John, 7th Duke of Atholl.

The eldest daughter of the Duke of Atholl, a promoter of Gaelic language and culture, Lady Dorothea Stewart-Murray grew up with her two brothers and two sisters in a family with a strong interest in local song and folklore. Her sister *Lady Evelyn Stewart-Murray was an avid collector of Gaelic tales and poetry. Lady Dorothea began collecting Scottish music in her girlhood and continued her collecting throughout her busy life. Her family had earlier been the patrons of the great fiddler Niel Gow and his music and that of his family, which formed an important part of the collection. He wrote tunes for members of the Duke of Atholl's family and for family occasions.

Dorothea Stewart-Murray married an English army officer, Harold Ruggles-Brise, on 5 February 1895 and went to live in London, where her collecting continued unabated. Knowledgeable and skilled, she gathered most of the 18th- and 19th-century song and tune collections for all the instruments, including pipes, fiddle and harp, along with poetry and ephemera, including some interesting MS material. In London she had a busy social life, as her husband climbed the promotion ladder. She also kept in touch with her family in Perthshire, which she often visited. She bequeathed her collection of over 600 books and manuscripts to the Sandeman Library (now the A. K. Bell Library) in Perth. SMDOUG

• A. K. Bell Library, Perth: Atholl Collection.
Douglas, S. (comp.) (1999) *The Atholl Collection Catalogue*, Perth and Kinross Libraries.

STEWART-MURRAY, Lady Evelyn, born Blair Castle 17 March 1868, died Easter Moncreiffe 20 July 1940. Gaelic folktale collector. Daughter of Louisa Moncreiffe, and John, 7th Duke of Atholl.

Like her siblings, including *Dorothea Stewart-Murray, Lady Evelyn Stewart-Murray was a Gaelic speaker and surrounded by Gaelic from childhood. Her father was fluent and enthusiastically supported the language; all estate workers spoke Gaelic. By the age of 19, her life-long interest in Gaelic had developed strongly. From 1887 to 1891 she collected tales and songs from the Perthshire Gaels. Her serious academic study grew so intense that her parents became deeply concerned for her health. Her mother, apparently indifferent to Gaelic, disapproved of what she saw as an obsession which distracted her from the normal life of an aristocratic girl. Even her father, delighted at her ardent affection for Gaelic, demurred at her overstudy. A highly strung, headstrong girl, she suffered severe psychosomatic illnesses when not allowed to follow her chosen career. In December 1891, aged 23, she was sent to Switzerland in the hopes of restoring her health. Not wishing to return home, she settled in Belgium until the Second World War when she moved to London. Shortly before her death, her brother brought her to his home at Easter Moncreiffe. Lady Evelyn was a brilliant needlewoman; her collection of embroidery and lace, which she had sent home from Europe for the opening of Blair Castle to the public in 1936, can still be seen there today.

Lady Evelyn's magnum opus is a collection of 250 tales, legends and songs. Her methods show her competence and a scientific approach: the salient characteristics of Perthshire Gaelic – a dialect now dead – are faithfully recorded. The work, the only 19th-century collection by a woman, and the only one covering that region, is her enduring monument. JMACI

• School of Scottish Studies, Univ. of Edinburgh: Lady Evelyn Stewart-Murray Collection.

Anderson, J. (ed.) (1991) *Chronicles of the Atholl and Tullibardine Families, vol. 6 (1907–1957)*; *ODNB* (2004); Robertson, S. and Young, P. (1996) *Daughter of Atholl.*

STIRK (STARK), Hellen (Ellen, Elena), died Perth 27 Jan. 1544. Executed for blasphemy. Daughter of John Stirk, skinner burgess.

Hellen Stirk was married to James Ranaldsone, a skinner burgess of Perth. The couple had one son and two daughters. She was drowned in the Tay in January 1544 for blasphemy and for her association with five men of Perth (including her husband), who were accused of breaking the Acts of Parliament by disputing upon the scriptures.

The specific charge against Hellen Stirk was that she had refused to call upon the Virgin Mary in childbirth, thereby tarnishing the reputation, and discrediting the merits, of the mother of Christ. She witnessed the executions of the men, and although she requested to die with her husband, this was refused and she was led to the river to be drowned. She was carrying her daughter, some reports say suckling the child. The baby was handed to a wet nurse before her mother was consigned to the river. Hellen Stirk's father took custody of the orphaned children, recovered the family's forfeited goods, and administered their affairs until his own death in 1551. MV

• A. K. Bell Library, Perth and Kinross Council Archive: B59/12/3, Perth Burgh Court Records, Register of Decreets, Nov. 1547 to Nov. 1552; NAS: B59/1/1, Protocol Book of Sir Henry Elder; Perth Museum and Art Gallery: The Convener Court Book of Perth, item 34.
Calderwood, D. [1678] (1842) *The History of the Kirk of Scotland*, T. Thompson, ed.; Foxe, J. [1559] (1838) *The Acts and Monuments of John Foxe*, S. Cattley, ed.; *RSS*, vol. 3 no. 609.

STIRLING, Emma Maitland, born Edinburgh 1838/9, died Coatesville, Pennsylvania, USA, 2 Sept. 1907. Child philanthropist, anti-cruelty campaigner. Daughter of Elizabeth Willing, and John Stirling, landed gentleman.

Emma Stirling grew up in St Andrews, the youngest of 11 children, six of whom died during her youth. Of strong Christian convictions, she published moralistic children's literature. Receipt of an inheritance brought her to Edinburgh, where in 1877 she opened the Stockbridge Day Nursery, for working mothers, and Infant Home, for motherless children. In 1878, the latter was renamed the Edinburgh and Leith Children's Aid and Refuge Society. Expanding into care of abused children, she opened a Shelter from Cruelty, which eclipsed local efforts to establish an Edinburgh SPCC. By 1886, she had opened two further boys' homes, two girls' homes and a training farm, catering in all for 300 children. Extension of her work to Canada in 1886 was prompted by the need for a cheap outlet for increasing numbers. Hillfoot Farm at Aylesford, in Nova Scotia's Annapolis Valley, was purchased, and in 1887 Emma Stirling moved to Canada. Small parties were sent out until April 1895, when Hillfoot was destroyed by an arsonist, after which she moved to the USA. She was unpopular with her Edinburgh colleagues, whom she had abruptly abandoned in 1887, with parents whose children she removed without consent, and with Nova Scotians who resented her patronising and litigious attitude. This has contributed to the loss from the record of a prickly, perhaps injudicious, but forceful pioneer. MDH

• NAS: GD 409/1, RSSPCC Fonds, Minutes of Meeting of the Directors of the Edinburgh & Leith Children's Aid and Refuge.
Stirling, E. M. (1868) *The History of a Pin*, (1892) *Our Children in Old Scotland and Nova Scotia*.
Girard, P. (2000) 'Victorian philanthropy and child rescue: the career of Emma Stirling in Scotland and Nova Scotia, 1860–95', in M. Harper and M. E. Vance (eds) *Myth, Migration and the Making of Memory*, pp. 218–31; *ODNB* (2004).

STIRLING, Jane Wilhelmina, born Kippenross House, Dunblane, baptised 8 April 1804, died Calder House, Mid Calder, 6 Feb. 1859. Pupil and friend of Frederic Chopin. Daughter of Mary Graham of Airth, and John Stirling, 6th Laird of Kippendavie and Kippenross.

The youngest of 13 children, Jane Stirling was cared for by her elder widowed sister, Katherine Erskine, after her parents died. Attractive, a skilful pianist and harpist, with a strong personality, she is said to have received more than 30 marriage proposals. In 1826, she and Katherine travelled to Paris where they joined the Protestant community, both sisters being Francophiles and fluent in French. Chopin agreed to give Jane Stirling piano lessons in about 1842. He was still with George Sand at the time, but when they parted, Jane Stirling took on a role in his life as virtual business manager and concert agent. In April 1848, she arranged for Chopin to perform in London, Glasgow, Edinburgh and Manchester. His letters tell of a bewildering round of visits to Scottish stately homes during this tour. He was already unwell, however, and returned to Paris in November, dying 11 months later from tuberculosis.

Jane Stirling, who apparently cherished an unrequited love for Chopin, gave him financial support and is thought to have arranged and paid for his funeral out of her own pocket. She bought his effects when they were auctioned in Paris, shipping some of his furniture to Calder House, where she set up a Chopin Room in his memory. Her grave is in Dunblane Cathedral. MB

• Bone, A. E. (1960) *Jane Wilhelmina Stirling*; Eisler, B. (2003) *Chopin's Funeral*; Jorgenson, C. and J. (2003) *Chopin and the Swedish Nightingale*; Szulk, T. (2001) *Chopin in Paris*; Walker, A. (1972) 'When Chopin came to Scotland', *Scottish Field*, August, pp. 20–21.

STIRLING GRAHAM, Clementina, born Seagate, Dundee, 4 May 1782, died Duntrune House, Angus, 23 August 1877. Impersonator, author, translator, beekeeper. Daughter of Amelia Graham and Patrick Stirling Graham.

Clementina Stirling Graham's father added the surname Graham in 1802, in order to inherit Duntrune House. In 1844, her brother William died and she became heiress to the estate. Well-connected as part of the Graham clan, whose forebear was John Graham of Claverhouse ('Bonnie Dundee'), she was cousin to the 9th Countess of Airlie, and godmother to her cousin's grand-daughter Blanche Ogilvy, future mother of Clementina Churchill. While young, it seems she lost the man she loved, possibly at sea, and never married. One obituarist wrote: 'Clementina Stirling Graham was an heiress, beautiful and intelligent – why did she never marry?' concluding 'perhaps for those very reasons' (DCL archives). In 1829, she received the Highland Society Award for her translation of Jonas de Gélieu's *The Bee Preserver*, and taught local farmers how to extract honey without killing the bees. Well known in Edinburgh for her wit and her impersonations, she captivated such literary and legal giants as Sir Walter Scott, Lords Jeffrey, Gillies and Cockburn, and successfully duped the then Mr Jeffrey in 1821, by calling on him as the elderly 'Lady Pitlyal'. She is credited with the remark: 'The only way to deal with temptation is to give in to it'. When friends persuaded her to write her memoirs, her book *Mystifications* was published privately in 1859 and by Dr John Brown in 1865. It became a bestseller ('no parlour complete without it') and went into five printings. HK

• Dundee Central Library (DCL) archives: Box 398, local history dept., newscuttings and biog. notices; Univ. of Dundee Archives: MS 113, Corr. of Clementina Stirling Graham; other corr. in private hands.

Graham, C. S., Works as above.
ODNB (2004).

STOPES, Charlotte Carmichael [Leitea Reseda], n.
Carmichael, born Edinburgh 6 Feb. 1846, died
Worthing, Sussex, 6 Feb. 1929. Shakespearean
scholar, suffragist, dress reformer. Daughter of
Christine Brown Graham, and James Ferrier
Carmichael, landscape painter.

The youngest of five children, Charlotte
Carmichael attended Mr Oliphant's School and the
Normal School, Edinburgh, passing the
government teacher training examination. In 1867,
after attending Edinburgh Ladies' Educational
Association classes, she was the first Scottish
woman to be awarded Ordinary and Honours
Certificates of Arts. She taught at Miss Brooke's
Huntley School, gave private classes and worked as
a governess. After publishing some early stories in
Chambers' Juvenile Series, she joined the Edinburgh
Essay Society (renamed Ladies' Edinburgh Literary
Society in 1869), formed by *Sarah Siddons Mair,
contributing to its journal, *The Attempt*, under the
pseudonym 'Leitea Reseda'.

In 1879, she married Henry Stopes, FGS
(1851–1902), amateur archaeologist, civil engineer
and brewery designer. They travelled in the Middle
East, returning to Edinburgh where their daughter,
*Marie Stopes, was born (1880). The family then
settled in London and a second daughter, Winifred,
was born (1884). Both Charlotte and Henry Stopes
regularly presented papers at British Association
meetings. Charlotte organised a Shakespeare
Reading Society, a Logic Class, and home meetings
on women's suffrage and rational dress. An active
member of the Rational Dress Society (1888–97),
she was also a committed suffragist from the 1870s,
joining the NUWSS (1906) and the WSPU (1908)
and lecturing on suffrage throughout Britain,
including Scotland (1896). She was a prolific
Shakespeare scholar, specialising in his social
background, a vice-president of the Elizabethan
Society and member of the New Shakespeare
Society. The British Academy awarded her the Rose
Crawshaff prize for *Shakespeare's Industry* (1916) and
an Honorary Fellowship. She is buried in Highgate
Cemetery, London. KHB

• BL: Marie Stopes MSS Coll. and Add. MSS coll.,
Elizabeth Wolstenholme Elmy Papers; UCL: GB 010, Add.
MSS 157, Charlotte Carmichael Stopes, corr. and papers
1888–1926.
Stopes, C. C. (1894) *British Freewomen: their historical
privilege*, (1907) *The Sphere of 'Man' in relation to that of
'Woman' in the Constitution*, (1916) *Shakespeare's Industry*. (For
Bibl., see BL catalogue.)
Boas, J. S. (1931) 'Charlotte Carmichael Stopes', *Trans. Roy.
Soc. Lit.*, X; Briant, K. (1962) *Marie Stopes: a biography*; Hall,
R. (1977) *Marie Stopes: a biography*; *ODNB* (2004); Tooley, S.
'Flints, suffrage and higher education', *Woman's Signal*, 6 June
1894; *WSM*.

STOPES, Marie Charlotte Carmichael, m1 **Gates,**
m2 **Roe,** born Edinburgh 15 Oct. 1880, died
London 2 Oct. 1958. Pioneer of birth control.
Daughter of *Charlotte Carmichael, campaigner for
women's education, and Henry Stopes, architect
and archaeologist.

Marie Stopes was educated at St George's
School in Edinburgh, chosen for its quality of
education, and later moved to North London
Collegiate School, which also offered girls a broad
curriculum. At University College London, she
gained a BSc in botany and geology in 1902, and
two years later she was awarded a PhD in Munich
for her work on fossilised plants. Marie Stopes
continued her outstanding academic career,
becoming a lecturer in botany at the University of
Manchester in 1904, and the youngest DSc in the
country a year later. From 1907 to 1908 she spent
18 months carrying out research at the University of
Tokyo. As her scientific career flourished (including
later war work on the composition of coal), she was
also writing poetry and fiction. In March 1911, she
married Reginald Ruggles Gates (1882–1962), a
botanist whom she had met in Canada. Her
unhappy marriage became the catalyst to the
campaigning and writing for which she is best
remembered. In 1914, she had her marriage
annulled on the grounds that it had never been
consummated, alleging that her ignorance about
sex meant she took two years to realise that her
husband was impotent and she was still a virgin.
Whether or not her claims were accurate, the
experience undoubtedly inspired *Married Love*
(1918), her book about sex and equality in the
marriage relationship. She could not at first find a
publisher, but Lt Humphrey Verdon Roe
(1877–1949), soon to be her second husband (1918),
financed its publication. It was a huge success, and
later that year she published *Wise Parenthood*,
dealing more explicitly with birth control.

Marie Stopes already knew Margaret Sanger,
the US birth control pioneer, and with Humphrey
Roe, who shared her interests, opened the UK's first
birth control clinic in London in 1921. More clinics
followed, and she continued to promote birth

control in her writing and in public speaking, becoming a famous, if controversial, figure. She came into opposition with members of the medical profession and the Catholic Church, notably being involved in a much-publicised libel case in 1923, but successfully broke many taboos by introducing public discussion of the issues, which included eugenics. Her son, Harry, was born on 27 March 1924 when she was over 40 (a previous child was stillborn). Her private life, never calm, included some estrangement from husband and son, and several later relationships. Her forceful personality often made it hard for her to work closely with others involved in family planning; her later writings never matched the popularity of *Married Love* and *Wise Parenthood*, nor were her literary ambitions particularly fulfilled, but she was undoubtedly a major force in the spread of contraception in Britain, at a time when few dared speak of it. FJ

• Stopes, M., Works as above, and see Bibls.

Hall, R. (1977) *Marie Stopes*; Rose, J. (1992) *Marie Stopes and the Sexual Revolution* (Bibl.); *ODNB* (2004) (Bibl.).

STRATHERN, Christine *see* **MORRISON, Agnes Brysson Inglis (Nancy)** (1903–1986)

STRONG, Rebecca, n. **Thorogood,** OBE, born Aldgate, London, 23 August 1843, died Chester 24 April 1944. Hospital matron, pioneer of nurse training. Daughter of Mary Westell, and John Thorogood, innkeeper.

Rebecca Thorogood, although born in England, spent most of her life in Scotland. She married Andrew Strong (1841–65), an instrument maker, but was widowed with a daughter by the age of 23. In 1867, she trained at the Nightingale School of Nursing, St Thomas's Hospital, London. In 1873, she was appointed Matron of Dundee Royal Infirmary with a remit to improve the training of its nurses and in 1879, she became Matron of Glasgow Royal Infirmary (GRI), where a course of lectures on medical and surgical nursing had just started. Seeing the point of systematic training, she persuaded the GRI Board to drop fees for the lecture course, to attract more probationers. She also obtained approval for introducing nurses' uniform. When plans for a new nurses' home were delayed, she left to set up a private nursing home in 1884, but was reappointed in 1891. In 1892, she collaborated with William Macewen, the world-renowned brain surgeon at GRI, to devise a new systematic training course with regular examina-

tions. Introduced in 1893, the course included three months' preliminary training, a more advanced programme of lectures, clinical and surgical demonstrations and ward work, then two years as a probationer, before certification. The scheme became a model for nurse training in hospitals internationally. Known as 'Mamma' to the medical staff at GRI, Rebecca Strong retired in 1907 but maintained an active interest in nursing, co-founding the Glasgow Scottish Nurses' Club in Glasgow (1918) and chairing the inaugural dinner of the GRI Nurses' League (1921). She continued to attend conferences and give interviews well into old age. She was awarded the OBE in 1939. JLMJ

• Jenkinson, J. et al. (1994) *The Royal: the history of Glasgow Royal Infirmary*; Maclachlan, G. (ed.) (1987) *Improving the Common Weal*; McGann, S. (1992) *Battle of the Nurses*; *ODNB* (2004).

STUART, Lady Louisa, born London 12 August 1757, died London 4 August 1851. Writer. Daughter of Mary Wortley Montagu (daughter of the celebrated Lady Mary Wortley Montagu), and John Stuart, 3rd Earl of Bute, Prime Minister to George III in the 1760s.

Lady Louisa Stuart was the youngest of 11 children, and remained a life-long companion to her mother. Her parents' position in aristocratic society meant that her early years were mostly spent in England, either in London or in the magnificent but sombre Luton Hoo in Sussex. Only when freed from parental restraint by her mother's death in 1794 could she indulge her love of travel and of Scotland. She continued to live mostly in London – a modest house in Gloucester Place – but made frequent journeys to visit her extensive circle of family and friends north of the border. Though she lived a life of private domesticity, never venturing into the public glare of print, Lady Louisa Stuart was a gifted writer, maintaining a lively correspondence with female friends and with her sister Caroline, who married into the Irish peerage. She was also a correspondent of Walter Scott. She wrote a memoir of her friend and cousin, *Frances Scott, Lady Douglas, and another of the famous *Lady Mary Coke. Her numerous writings, many published after her death, reveal both wit and intelligence in this excellent observer of the grand but narrow social world in which she lived. In particular, she wrote about the experience of women in this milieu, in a life spanning both Georgian and Victoria eras. SN

• Stuart, L. (1985) *Memoire of Frances Lady Douglas*, (1901–3) *Letters . . . to Miss Louisa Clinton*, J. Home, ed., (1863). *Some Account of John Duke of Argyll and his Family* (reprinted in Coke, Lady M. (1889–96) *Letters and Journals*); see also BL catalogue.
Clark, Mrs G. (ed.) (1895–9) *Gleanings from an Old Portfolio*, 3 vols; *ODNB* (2004).

SUTHERLAND, Elizabeth, Countess of Sutherland, *suo jure,* **Marchioness of Stafford, Duchess of Sutherland, Duchess-Countess of Sutherland,** m. **Leveson-Gower,** born Leven Lodge near Edinburgh, 24 May 1765, died London 29 Jan. 1839. Landlord associated with the Sutherland Clearances. Daughter of Mary Maxwell, and William, Earl of Sutherland.

Elizabeth Sutherland succeeded as Countess of Sutherland as an infant and was brought up in Edinburgh by her maternal grandmother, Lady Alva. There were two other claimants to the peerage but the House of Lords found in her favour in 1771. On 4 September 1785, she married George Granville Leveson-Gower (1758–1833), Viscount Trentham, who, in 1803, inherited the Bridgewater Canal, making him one of the country's richest men, and succeeded as Marquess of Stafford. The couple had eight children and spent some time in Paris during the Revolution, when he was ambassador 1790–2. They became Duke and Duchess of Sutherland in 1833, just before George's death.

In 1799, the Countess raised a regiment, the 93rd Sutherland Highlanders, from her Scottish lands. Difficulties with this prompted the formulation of a far-reaching plan to develop the Sutherland estates and increase the rental income, involving clearing the interior for sheep and the better lowland ground for arable farms. Those cleared were to be resettled elsewhere on the estate where they would acquire new 'habits of industry'. Considerable investment was made in establishing villages, infrastructure, and industrial development. Remarkable in scale, the Sutherland Clearances also attracted considerable criticism, particularly for the manner in which they were carried out, including the death of *Margaret Mackay in the 1814 Strathnaver clearance. Although much opprobrium attached to the estate managers, the Countess herself has been described as 'the principal source of energy and intellect behind the Sutherland clearances' (Richards 2000, p. 120), though increasingly subject to the commissioner James Loch's influence. Known in the north as *Ban-mhorair Chataibh*, the Great Lady of Sutherland, she was,

nevertheless, apparently described in 1820 as a 'benign Princess over her very considerable territory' (Richards 1982, p. 345). M B-J

• Lynch, M. (ed.) (2001) *The Oxford Companion to Scottish History*; *ODNB* (2004) (see Gower, Elizabeth Leveson-) (Bibl.); Richards, E. (1982) *A History of the Highland Clearances*, (2000) *The Highland Clearances*.

SUTHERLAND, Margaret Sinclair (Greta), m. **Macdonald,** born Wick, Caithness, 2 May 1891, died Yarmouth 9 Nov. 1923. Herring packer. Daughter of Margaret Rosie, and Robert Sutherland, sawyer.

One of nine children, Greta Sutherland attended Wick North Primary School. Wick was then known as 'the herring capital of Europe', and she joined the fishworkers as a packer. She would negotiate a pre-season contract with a curing company on behalf of the gutting 'crew' of three women, who processed the fresh catches (see Cordiner, Helen). Two women gutted and graded, while the packer, bent almost double into a wooden barrel, salted and packed the fish to Crown Brand standards, then topped up barrels at the end of the pickling process, and received an end-of-season bonus. Efficient packing was essential to successful preservation and work was rigorously inspected. Greta Sutherland and her sister Barbara worked at local herring fishing stations, and she also travelled south to work. In 1910, she married Donald Macdonald, carter (1885–1915); two of their four children died in a measles epidemic in 1912. He enlisted in 1914, but died from injuries sustained at Loos: his was the first military funeral of the war in Wick. Widowed, Greta Sutherland returned to work. Aged 32, she contracted meningitis, and died in Yarmouth, two weeks before the herring season ended, leaving a daughter and son. The Factories Acts did not cover outdoor employment: inadequate facilities and crowded accommodation increased the possibility of disease. She is buried in Wick Cemetery, beside her husband. M R

• Fairrie, A. [1983] (1998 rev. edn.) *History of Queen's Own Highlanders (Seaforth and Cameron)*; *John O'Groats Journal*, 15 Oct. 1915.
Private information.

SUTHERLAND, Mary Elizabeth, CBE, born Banchory 30 Nov. 1895, died East Kilbride, 19 Oct. 1972. Trade unionist and Labour Party activist. Daughter of Jessie Henderson and Alexander Sutherland, crofters.

Despite deputising for her sick mother, who died in 1911, Mary Sutherland won bursaries to Aberdeen Girls' High School and the University of Aberdeen, graduating in 1917 and qualifying to teach in 1918. However, she soon moved into politics, as organiser (1920–2) of the Scottish Farm Servants' Union and working on the left-wing weekly, *Forward* (1923). In 1924, she became Labour Party woman's organiser for Scotland. In 1932, she took over from Marion Phillips as Labour Party Chief Woman's Officer, secretary to the Standing Joint Committee of Industrial Women's Organisations (SJC) and editor of *Labour Woman*, moving to London. She held the posts until her retirement in 1960. The SJC combined Labour Party, trades union and Co-operative women, tackling issues such as married women's right to work, equal pay, social policy and war-time evacuation.

Mary Sutherland's engagement in socialist internationalism was life-long. She had been delegate to the International Federation of Landworkers, meeting in Vienna, in 1922. In 1933, she became British correspondent to the Women's Advisory Committee of the Labour and Socialist International (LSI). After the Second World War, she became chair of the International Council of Social Democratic Women (successor to the LSI committee), and continued to attend meetings after her retirement. When she retired, Labour Party women's organisation was changed. Bessie Braddock MP moved the tribute to her at the 1960 Labour Party conference. Suffering a stroke, she returned to Scotland to live near her family. In memory of her work, her name was added to the Marion Phillips International Fund. CC

• Univ. of Manchester, John Rylands Library: Labour Party Archives and Study Centre, Mary Sutherland papers and SJC papers.

Collette, C. (2000) 'Questions of gender: Labour and women', in B. Brivati and R. Heffernan (eds) *The Labour Party: a centenary history*; Graves, P. M. (1994) *Labour Women: women in British working class politics, 1918–1939*; *ODNB* (2004); *SLL*.

SUTHERLAND, Millicent, Duchess of *see* **ST CLAIR-ERSKINE, Lady Millicent Fanny** (1867–1955)

SWAIN, Margaret Helen, n. **Hart,** MBE, born Parbold, Lancs., 13 May 1909, died Edinburgh 27 July 2002. Historian of Scottish embroidery, tapestries, and furniture. Daughter of Isabella Johnston, nurse, and John Hart.

Margaret Hart was educated at Notre Dame Convent, Wigan, and in 1929 trained as a nurse at St Bartholomew's Hospital, London, where she met Richard (Dick) H. A. Swain (d. 1981), a bacteriologist, whom she married in 1937. They had three children. In 1947, the family moved to Edinburgh, where Dick Swain had a university post, just before the first International Festival. Margaret Swain had been taught to embroider by her Irish grandmother before she could read, and her historical interest was aroused by the embroidery she found in Scotland. Her first book was *The Flowerers: the Story of Ayrshire White Needlework* (1955). Thereafter she wrote many articles in academic journals, such as *The Burlington Magazine, Costume*, and others including *Scottish Home and Country*, aiming to make people aware of the rich heritage of Scottish textiles and furniture. She lectured widely in Scotland and abroad. A pioneer in the history of embroidery in Scotland, as an outsider, Margaret Swain had an eye for what was important. She was a consultant to the national museums in Edinburgh, to the NTS, to many privately owned houses, and to the Palace of Holyroodhouse. Despite tinnitus and deafness, she enjoyed music and working for others, including the Samaritans. She was awarded Hon MA from the University of Edinburgh (1981) and MBE (1989). NEAT

• Swain, M., Work as above, and (1970) *Historical Needlework*, (1983) *The Needlework of Mary Queen of Scots*, (1980) *Figures on Fabric*, (1986) *Scottish Embroidery*, (1988) *Tapestries and Textiles at the Palace of Holyroodhouse in the Royal Collection*, (2001, privately printed) *Nursing: A Family Tradition*.

Costume, 37, 2003 (obit.); *The Independent*, 14 Sept. 2002 (obit.); *The Scotsman*, 27 August 2002 (obit.). Private information and personal knowledge.

SWAN, Annie Shepherd, [Annie S. Swan, David Lyall], CBE, m. **Burnett-Smith,** born Edinburgh 8 July 1859, died Gullane 17 June 1943. Popular novelist and journalist. Daughter of Euphemia Brown, and Edward Swan, potato merchant.

Annie Swan attended a dame school in Edinburgh and later Queen Street Ladies' College. Her novels are imbued with the values of her evangelical upbringing. She began writing in her teens, and a story, 'Wrongs Righted', appeared in *The People's Friend* magazine in 1881. Her reputation was established with her novel *Aldersyde* (1883). Her mother died in 1881 and her father remarried, to Barbara Leitch, in 1883. Family life was disrupted by the new marriage and soon afterwards, on

27 December 1883, Annie Swan married James Burnett-Smith (1857–1927), a schoolteacher. They lived at Star, Markinch, in Fife, before moving to Edinburgh where James Burnett-Smith pursued his ambition to train as a doctor. After his graduation they moved to London, where their two children were born. In 1910 their son died aged 18, after shooting himself accidentally.

Annie S. Swan was one of the most commercially successful writers of her day. Her novels upheld the ideology of domesticity and the value of hard work, suiting the tastes of a newly literate readership. She was also the agony aunt in 'Over the Teacups' in *The British Weekly*. Her prolific output of over 200 novels was the result of rising at 6 am and writing 3,000 words a day (she never redrafted) – and always meeting copy deadlines. Though she referred to her husband as the 'head of the household', she was liberated from the usual constraints of marriage by her earning power – throughout their marriage she and her husband had separate bank accounts. *The Pendulum* (1926), with its critique of nonconformist values, caused consternation to many readers who had valued her fiction because it upheld their conscientious morality.

Swan knew she was no literary author, but took great satisfaction from her readers' estimate of the difference her fiction made to their lives. Her writing made her a celebrity and she undertook numerous speaking engagements, often for social or moral causes. On one occasion, after speaking to women in the East End of Glasgow, she noted, 'I had to pass through a large crowd to reach my car. Many toil-worn hands were thrust out to grasp mine, and one woman, with a shawl over her head, said unsteadily, "Ye canna dee yet, for *we* couldna dae without ye"' (Swan 1934). In 1918 she was asked by the Ministry of Information to tour the USA to explain the extent of British food shortages, and she stood unsuccessfully as a parliamentary candidate for the Liberals in the 1922 election in Maryhill, Glasgow. After James Burnett-Smith died in 1927, she moved to Gullane, East Lothian, with her daughter. She was awarded the CBE in 1930. BD

• NLS: Acc. 6003.

Swan, A. S., Works as above, and (1881) *Wrongs Righted*, (1887) *The Gates of Eden*, (1891) *Maitland of Laurieston*, (1914) *Meg Hamilton*, (1932) *The Luck of the Livingstones*, (1934) *My Life*; see also *HSWW* (Bibl.).

ODNB (2004).

T

TAIT, Margaret,‡ m. **Pirie,** born Kirkwall, Orkney, 11 Nov. 1918, died Kirkwall 16 April 1999. Film-maker. Daughter of Mary Ibister, and Charles Tait, agricultural merchant.

Margaret Tait studied medicine at the University of Edinburgh, graduating in 1941 and serving in the RAMC (1943–6). In the late 1940s she developed a passion for film and went to study in Rome (1950–2). Returning to Scotland, she could not find a place in the British film industry, where there were few opportunities for women to direct. Between 1952 and 1998 she made 32 films, of which all but three were self-financed, initially by locum work. In addition to raising the money, Margaret Tait worked as a one-woman crew. Occasionally she had the help of her life-long partner, Alex Pirie, whom she married in 1968 and who is credited as producer on *Where I am is here* (1964). Margaret Tait described herself as a 'film poet' (Curtis 1999) rather than a documentarian. Her films sometimes seem like a picture of the past (e.g. *Land Makar* 1981) but her intention was not so much to document as to create visual poems from

sound and image. She developed a very singular style, which is being increasingly recognised as a unique voice within European avant-garde film. In 1993, she had the opportunity, aged 74, to direct her first feature film, *Blue Black Permanent*, based on a script she first started to write in the 1940s. Filmed in Edinburgh and Orkney, 'it is beautiful, ingenious, and extraordinarily sad, all at once' (EIFF Catalogue 2004). She made her last film, *Garden Pieces*, in 1998, the year before her death. In addition to film-making she published stories and poetry and painted. MJG

• Orkney Archives: the Tait Papers; Scottish Screen Archive.

Tait, M. (1959) *Origins & Elements*, (1960) *Subjects & Sequences*, (1960) *The Hen & The Bees: legends & lyrics*.

Select Filmography (not mentioned above): (1955) *A portrait of Ga*, (1956) *Calypso*, (1958) *Happy Bees*, (1966) *Hugh MacDiarmid – A Portrait*, (1966) *The Big Sheep*.

Curtis, D. (1999) 'Britain's oldest living experimentalist . . . Margaret Tait', *Vertigo*, 9, Summer; *Edinburgh International Film Festival* Catalogue 2004; Sandhu, S. 'Edinburgh Reports: unique vision of a film poet', *The Daily Telegraph*, 23 August 2004; Todd, P. (1999) 'A deeper knowledge than wisdom', *Vertigo*, 2, 9, Autumn/Winter, (2004) *Subjects and Sequences*; www.luxonline.org.uk

TANEU (also **Thenew)** born Lothian, fl. (traditionally) 5th century. Daughter (traditionally) of Leudonus, King of Lothian.

According to two 12th-century Lives of St Kentigern, his mother Taneu was the daughter of a 'semi-pagan' king of Lothian. The confused chronology and dubious historicity of the different elements of these Lives stem no doubt from their relative lateness and disconnection from the period they purport to describe. Whether or not there was ever an historical Taneu is matter for speculation. Taneu was condemned to death by her father for becoming pregnant out of wedlock, but having been saved by divine intervention, she was set adrift in the Forth, and landed at Culross where she gave birth to Kentigern. It seems that the Lives' authors were presented with (and appalled by) an older tradition in which Taneu conceived Kentigern while remaining a virgin. Her name is commemorated (in corrupted form) by St Enoch's Cross in Glasgow. JEF
• Forbes, A. P. (ed.) (1874) *Lives of S. Ninian and S. Kentigern*; Jackson, K. H. (1958) 'The sources for the life of St Kentigern', in N. K. Chadwick (ed.) *Studies in the Early British Church.*

TANNER, Ann Ailsa Louise, n. **Robertson,** born Kilmarnock 23 June 1923, died Helensburgh 19 Nov. 2001. Artist and researcher. Daughter of Eleanor Allen Moore, artist, and Robert Cecil Robertson, doctor.

In 1925, Ailsa Robertson's family moved from Scotland to Shanghai. Their privileged lifestyle and servants enabled her mother **Eleanor Allen Moore** (1885–1955), an accomplished artist who had studied at Glasgow School of Art, to concentrate on recording the landscape and daily life around her. In August 1937, British women and children were evacuated to Hong Kong, and Ailsa Robertson was sent to complete her schooling in Edinburgh. From 1942 to 1945 she worked for the Women's Land Army in Tighnabruaich. After study at the University of Edinburgh and College of Art (MA and Diploma 1950) she became Assistant Curator of Prints and Drawings at Kelvingrove Museum and Art Galleries, Glasgow, where she met her future husband, Philip H. Tanner. As was customary then for women public employees, she resigned on marriage in 1956.

Ailsa Tanner was active in the artistic life of Helensburgh, where the family lived with their three children. She continued to paint, exhibiting with the Helensburgh Art Club, GSLA, RGI(FA) and the RSW. Through her pioneering research into Scottish women artists, she became very knowledgeable about them, arranging exhibitions and contributing substantially to research on the *Glasgow Girls, of whom her mother had been one. LA
• Tanner, A. (1982) *A Centenary Exhibition to Celebrate the Founding of the Glasgow Society of Lady Artists*, (1994) 'Women's Forum cont.', *Chapman*, 77, (1998) *Bessie MacNicol, New Woman.*
Burkhauser, J. (ed.) (1990) *Glasgow Girls: women in art and design 1880–1920*; Paling, B. (2002) *Ailsa Tanner 1923–2001,* exhibition catalogue.

TAYLOUR (or **TAYLOR), Jane Elizabeth,** born Inch, Stranraer, baptised 23 June 1827, died Saffron Walden, Essex, 25 Feb. 1905. Suffrage and women's movement campaigner. Daughter of Maria Angus and Nathaniel Taylor.

From December 1869, Jane Taylour toured north-east England and throughout Scotland, giving public lectures campaigning for women's suffrage and equality of opportunity for women in education and employment. She was accompanied on some of her lecture tours in Scotland by *Mary Hill Burton or *Agnes McLaren. In July 1873, when she had delivered more than 150 public lectures in Scotland, she was presented with a substantial testimonial. She was the first Honorary Secretary of the Galloway branch of the NSWS (1870–2), joint Secretary of ENSWS (1873–6, with Agnes McLaren), an executive member of the central committee of NSWS (1875), and remained interested in women's suffrage all her life.

In 1871 she was appointed an agent for the Scottish Commercial Fire and Life Insurance Company. She left her home in Belmont in about 1872, staying in Edinburgh until at least 1875. In 1891, she settled in Saffron Walden, Essex, where, in 1895, she was Secretary of the local branch of the BWTA and was influential in obtaining the appointment of women to the local Board of Guardians. In 1901, she was recorded as living with Rachel P. Robson of Saffron Walden. She was interred in the Society of Friends' burial ground. LRM
• *AGC*; *Aberdeen Journal*, 17 May 1871; *Argyllshire Herald*, 18 Feb. 1871; *Galloway Advertiser and Wigtownshire Free Press*, 16 Dec. 1869, 2 Feb. 1871, 22 June 1871.
Blackburn, H. (1902) *Women's Suffrage: a record of the women's suffrage movement in the British Isles*; NUWSS (1899) Report

of the Executive Committee presented at the AGM held in Westminster Town Hall, 21 July; *Saffron Walden Weekly News*, 5 March 1905 (obit.); *WSM*.

TEISSIER DU CROS, Janet, n. **Grierson,** born Aberdeen 26 Jan. 1905, died Ganges, France, 14 Oct. 1990. Writer, broadcaster, concert pianist. Daughter of Mary Letitia Ogston, and Sir Herbert J. C. Grierson, professor of literature.

Janet Grierson, the youngest of five daughters, spent her early years in Aberdeen, where a childhood friend was *Janet Adam Smith. In 1915, the family moved to Edinburgh, where Janet attended St George's School and developed a notable talent for music. Her piano tutor was composer Sir Donald Tovey, who encouraged her to continue her studies in Vienna in 1923. She also studied theory of music at the University of Edinburgh. She married François Teissier du Cros, a civil engineer (later a research physicist), on 9 December 1930, and settled in France. In 1939 her husband enlisted and she, with two young sons, moved in with his parents at Mandiargues in the Cévennes, but political differences within the family soon made this untenable. She spent the rest of the war alone with her children – a third son was born in 1942 – in a remote village, visited only occasionally by her husband, who was taken prisoner early in the war and released on parole. Her memoir *Divided Loyalties* (1962) describes the difficulties and privations of her life in occupied France.

After the war the family settled in Paris, where a daughter was born in 1946 and where Janet worked as a translator. She contributed a regular 'Paris Letter' to BBC radio *Woman's Hour* and the *Glasgow Herald* from the 1950s. In the early 1960s, she became a Catholic, partly because of the Church's regard for art and music. When her husband retired in 1972, the couple moved to the family house at Mandiargues. She suffered from arthritis and osteoporosis from the late 1960s and eventually walked with crutches, but retained the ability to play the piano and to write. Her memoir of childhood and adolescence, *Cross Currents*, was posthumously published in 1997. MARB

• Teissier du Cros, J. (1962) *Divided Loyalties: a Scotswoman in occupied France* (see also 'Afterword' by Janet Adam Smith in Canongate Classics edition, 1992), (1997) *Cross Currents: a childhood in Scotland.*

TEY, Josephine *see* **MACKINTOSH, Elizabeth** (1896–1952)

THOMSON, Emily Charlotte, born in India c. 1864, died Dundee 21 August 1955. Medical practitioner. Daughter of Emily Plumb Ogilvie, and Alexander Thompson, schools inspector.

Together with **Alice Margaret Moorhead** (1868–1910), Emily Thomson was among the first women in Scotland to gain admission to the male-dominated professional medical societies. Educated in Edinburgh, Rouen and Dublin, in 1891 Emily Thomson obtained the Triple Qualification of the three Scottish Licensing authorities, the RCPE, RCSE and the FPSG. She also obtained the Dublin Licentiate in Medicine in 1892. Her contemporary and GP partner, Alice Moorhead, sister of the suffragette *Ethel Moorhead, had similar qualifications, although Emily Thomson additionally qualified MBChM in Edinburgh in 1899.

After short appointments elsewhere, the two women became the first female GPs in Dundee, initially in the Nethergate and, by 1901, in Tay Square. Alice Moorhead worked mainly with poorer patients while Emily Thomson worked with the better-off and was involved in the founding of Dundee Women's Hospital, in 1896, with *Mary Lily Walker. In 1893, they successfully applied for membership of the Forfarshire Medical Association, and eventually both were members of the BMA. *Elizabeth Bryson remembered moving, as an overawed locum, into their big house with housemaid, cook and chauffeur. 'Dr Emily', described by Bryson as 'vivid, dark, business-like, capable' (Bryson 1966, p. 213) was one of Dundee's first woman car drivers. 'Dr Alice', who was 'fair, blue-eyed, soft spoken, with a touch of Irish gaiety' (ibid.), served on the parish council (1908). At the age of 41 she married Dr Hamilton Langwill and moved to Leith. She died in childbirth the following year. Emily Thomson retired to Arbroath. Her life is the subject of a novel by Eileen Ramsay, *Butterflies in December* (1995). JLMJ

• Univ. of Dundee Archives: Forfarshire Medical Association Annual Report, 29 June 1893; Margaret Menzies Campbell papers (MS 15/92).

Bryson E. (1966) *Look Back in Wonder*; *Dundee Courier & Advertiser*, 22 August 1955 (Thomson, obit.); Jenkinson, J. (1993) *Scottish Medical Societies 1731–1939*; *Medical Directory* (1908); *Medical Register* (1955).

Additional information: Mary Henderson.

THOMSON, Helen Mitchell, m. **Moon,** born Dundee 8 Feb. 1883, died Dundee 2 Nov. 1973. Prison wardress, Calton Jail, Edinburgh. Daughter of

Mary Thomson, power loom weaver, and John Thomson, cloth lapper.

Helen Thomson was one of two sisters and grew up in the Upper Hilltown area of Dundee. After she left school she worked in the Overgate Mission where the minister saw her aptitude for social work and urged her to become a prison wardress. Keen to move away from Dundee, she started work at Calton Jail, Edinburgh, just before the First World War. She joined a team of women, many of whom were Gaelic speakers from the Highlands and Hebrides. The female prisoners at the time included suffragettes, and the humiliating experience of force-feeding was described to her by another wardress. Other inmates included prostitutes and political prisoners such as James Maxton, John McLean and Willie Gallacher. Helen Thomson helped run the prison bible class, which was well attended as it offered the prisoners the opportunity to leave their cells. During her time in Edinburgh, she also played the organ for the Carruber's Close Mission. In 1921, she returned to Dundee where, on 21 August, she married John Moon, a railway goods checker. They had two daughters. Necessity forced her out to work in the jute mills where one of her jobs was making sandbags. She was an active member of the Woman's Guild at the local church and was involved in running an 'old folks' club. HEC

• Interview with Mary Moon, daughter of Helen Thomson.

THOMSON, Margaret Henderson,‡ n. **Hunter,** MBE, born Edinburgh 20 August 1902, died Huntly 16 June 1982. Doctor, war heroine. Daughter of Margaret Robertson, and George Alexander Hunter, solicitor and banker.

The third of six children, Margaret Hunter was educated at Edinburgh Ladies' College (later the Mary Erskine School) and the University of Edinburgh, where she qualified MBChB (1926), as did her younger sister. After general practice in Lanarkshire, she married rubber planter and agricultural researcher Daniel Stewart Thomson (1899/1900–1971). When war broke out, they were at the Experimental Rubber Station near Kuala Lumpur. Margaret Thomson was attached to the Malaya Medical Services, organising first-aid classes. After the fall of Singapore in February 1942, she left on the last allied ship, the SS *Kuala*, tending the injured. The ship was dive-bombed, and she spent hours in the sea before being picked up. Although suffering from a thigh wound, she helped row for hours in a swamped lifeboat. On first Kebat, then

Senajang Island, she took charge of the wounded and performed emergency operations, using driftwood to make splints and cleaning wounds in the sea. She helped evacuate the injured to hospital on Sinkep Island. Her own wound turned septic and she was stretchered to Sinkep, but made the sea voyage to Sumatra, then began the long overland trek with other women survivors before the advancing Japanese. She was captured and imprisoned for the rest of the war, first in Djambi jail and later in a Sumatran jungle POW camp. Another Scotswoman in the Irenelaan camp, musically trained **Norah Chambers,** n. **Hope** (1905–89), created a choir, which sang orchestral works arranged by herself and Sunderland-born missionary Margaret Dryburgh (d. 1945), to keep up morale. Death depleted the choir's ranks and Margaret Thomson saw her patients die, as Red Cross medical supplies were hoarded by camp guards. She was awarded the MBE 'for her resolution and disregard of self, her sacrifice and admirable courage' (*London Gazette*, August 1943). After the war, Margaret Thomson and her husband, an emaciated survivor of the Burmah Railway, returned to the rubber station in Kuala Lumpur, where she ran a health clinic for estate workers. They left Malaya permanently c. 1950, and spent the rest of their lives as innovative farmers near Huntly, Aberdeenshire. Although later consulted for the BBC drama, *Tenko*, Margaret Thomson did not watch it or like talking about the camp to outsiders. SO

• Stanford Univ.: MSS of vocal arrangements.
Brooke, G. (1989) *Singapore's Dunkirk*; *Daily Herald*, 3 July 1943; Hall, C. (1989) 'Music gave them the will to survive', *Music Maker*, Sept.–Oct., pp. 24–7; *ODNB* (2004); Smyth, J., Brig. (1970) *The Will to Live*; Warner, L. and Sandilands, J. (1982) *Women beyond the Wire*.
Additional information: John Purser.

TOD, Isabella Maria Susan, born Edinburgh 18 May 1836, died Belfast 8 Dec. 1896. Campaigner for women's rights. Daughter of Maria Isabella Waddell of Co. Monaghan, and James Banks Tod, Scottish merchant.

Isabella Tod, of Presbyterian background, was educated at home by her mother, who had a profound influence on her. By the 1860s, she and her mother were living in Belfast, where Isabella Tod appears, for a time, to have earned a living writing leaders for the Belfast newspaper the *Northern Whig*. Her first foray into public life came in 1867 when her paper on the education of girls was read at a meeting of the National Association for the Promotion of Social Science. She then became active in a committee to support changes in the married women's property laws. In 1867, she helped establish the Ladies' Institute in Belfast which initially provided lectures to young women in arts subjects, but also campaigned successfully to have women take examinations drawn up by the Queen's University, Belfast. She was a leading figure in promoting the secondary education of girls and was instrumental in having girls included in the Intermediate Education (Ireland) Act of 1878.

In 1871, she organised the first suffrage society in Ireland, the North of Ireland Women's Suffrage Committee. She campaigned on the issue of suffrage throughout Britain and her speeches were widely reported in the daily newspapers. At local level, her campaigning won women in Belfast the municipal franchise in 1887. Isabella Tod was also active in the temperance movement and acted as vice-president of the British Women's Temperance Union from 1877 to 1892. She was a significant force in the split that occurred in the BWTU, which led to the formation of the Women's Total Abstinence Union, of which she was vice-president until 1896.

In 1886, Isabella Tod threw herself into the campaign against Home Rule for Ireland, believing it would destroy the country and fatally damage the relationship between Ireland and the rest of the United Kingdom. The resulting crusade not only lost her a number of suffrage friends but also seriously damaged her health. ML

• Victoria College, Belfast: MS Ladies' Institute Minute Book, 1867–97; LSE Archives: K. Courtney, diary/letter to M. Courtney, 3 Sept.–19 Oct. 1890, vol. xxv, Courtney Papers, BLPES.
Armour, N. (2004) 'Isabella Tod and Liberal Unionism', in A. Hayes and D. Urquhart, *Irish Women's History*; Bourke A. et al. (eds) (2002) *The Field Day Anthology of Irish Writing*, vol. 5 (Bibl.); Brown, H. (1998) 'An alternative imperialism: Isabella Tod, internationalist and "good Liberal Unionist"', *Gender and History*, 10:3; *Englishwoman's Review*, 15 Jan. 1897; Luddy, M. (1995) 'Isabella M. S. Tod (1836–96)', in M. Cullen and M. Luddy (eds) *Women, Power and Consciousness in 19th-Century Ireland*; *ODNB* (2004); *Wings*, July 1893 pp. 217–19; *The Witness*, 11 Dec. 1896; *Women's Penny Paper*, 12 Oct. 1889.

TOLLEMACHE, Elizabeth, Duchess of Argyll, born July 1659, died Campbeltown 9 May 1735. Estate manager, philanthropist. Daughter of *Elizabeth Murray, Countess of Dysart, later Duchess of Lauderdale, and Sir Lionel Tollemache.

The eldest surviving daughter from her mother's first marriage, Elizabeth Tollemache spent her youth at Ham House, London, and family homes in Suffolk. In 1678, she was married to Archibald Campbell, Lord Lorne, eldest son of the 9th Earl of Argyll, in a match intended to strengthen relations between her parents and Argyll. Her generous marriage settlement of most of his estates of Kintyre in jointure was probably due to her parents' influence with Charles II. Lorne recovered the forfeited title of Earl of Argyll in 1689, after the accession of William and Mary, and was created 1st Duke of Argyll in 1701, two years before his death. Two sons became Dukes of Argyll and a daughter married the Earl of Bute. Another daughter, *Lady Charlotte Bury, became a novelist and diarist.

The marriage was not happy and the couple separated in 1696. Duchess Elizabeth moved to Campbeltown where, from her residence, 'Limecraigs', she managed her Kintyre estates. Her business acumen is evident from the many references to her in the Minutes of Campbeltown Town Council. She was the first to recognise the town's potential as a seaport, suggesting the building of quays and harbour and subsequently subsidising the first packet service between Campbeltown and Glasgow. She helped build the 'Lowland Church' that still stands today. Her residence, the 'Duchess Well' near the gate of the manse, and a large silver communion vessel gifted by her to the church, are surviving testimony to her strong bond with Campbeltown. MVH

• Cripps, D. (1975) *Elizabeth of the Sealed Knot. A biography of Elizabeth Murray Countess of Dysart*; Mactaggart, Col. C. (1986) 'The Limecraigs Duchess', *Kintyre Antiq. and Nat. Hist. Soc.* 15; *ODNB* (2004) (Campbell, Archibald, 1st Duke of Argyll).

TOLMIE, Frances, born Uignish Farm, Duirinish, Isle of Skye, 13 Oct. 1840, died Dunvegan, Isle of Skye, 31 Dec. 1926. Folklorist and song collector. Daughter of Margaret Hope MacAskill, and John Tolmie, tacksman.

The Tolmies of Uignish were a distinguished Skye family, but Frances's father died in 1844, and it was from her mother's people, the MacAskills, at Talisker and later Rubha an Dùnan, that she first acquired Gaelic songs. In her early 20s she began actively collecting from women who escorted her in her work as a distributor of wool. She had excellent Gaelic and a sound knowledge of Irish Gaelic, as well as some Manx and Welsh, and was encouraged by Alexander Carmichael of *Carmina Gadelica* fame, who was a family friend (see Carmichael, Ella). After periods as a governess in Edinburgh and with her brother's family in Nairn, she moved to Cambridge, studying briefly at Newnham, where she was described as a 'tall, rather gaunt' figure with red hair that reached the ground when she was seated (Bassin 1977, p. 63). There followed 20 years (1874–95) in the Lake District as companion to Harriet Rigbye, on whose death Frances Tolmie became heir and executrix with a comfortable inheritance. She then joined her sister in Oban, and later Edinburgh, returning to Skye only after the latter's death. The fruits of her labours were published in 1911 in the *Journal of the Folk-Song Society*, with the encouragement of *Lucy Broadwood. With the original Gaelic and the substantial annotations, these form one of the single most important and reliable sources of Gaelic song. She notated the tunes and words as she had heard them, and her more correct versions compare favourably with those of *Marjory Kennedy-Fraser. JP

• Tolmie, F. (1911) 'One hundred and five songs of occupation from the Western Isles of Scotland', *Jour. of the Folk-Song Society*, 16, 3rd part of vol. IV., pp. iv–xiv, 143–276 (reprinted as volume, Llanerch 1997); recordings of Tolmie's singing, made by Marjory Kennedy-Fraser, SSS, Univ. of Edinburgh. Bassin, E. (1948) 'Frances Tolmie', *Jour. Eng. Folk Dance and Song Soc.*, vol. V, no. 3, pp. 141–4, (1951) 'The Tolmie Manuscripts', ibid., vol. VI, no. 3, pp. 61–8, (1977) *The Old Songs of Skye – Frances Tolmie and her Circle*; Broadwood, L. E. (1927) 'Frances Tolmie', *Folk Song Journal*, p. 50 (obit.); *ODNB* (2004).

TOMNAT, died probably in Lorne 695. Queen of Cenel Loairn.

Nothing is known of Tomnat aside from the year of her death, although this is of itself quite remarkable given an almost complete lack of reference to royal women of the Dál Riata in the early sources. She was the wife of Ferchar, evidently Ferchar the Tall (*fota*), King of Cenél Loairn of Lorne in northern Argyll, who was latterly over-king of the Dál Riata. The reference suggests that she was a key figure, probably as a result of a high-profile marriage, in the power politics that saw her husband, who died in 697, capture the over-kingship as early, perhaps, as the mid-670s. It is uncertain whether Tomnat was the mother of either of Ferchar's sons, Ainbcellach and Selbach, who dominated Dál Riata in the subsequent generation. JEF

• MacAirt, S. and MacNiocaill, G. (eds) (1983) *The Annals of Ulster (to AD 1131)*, AU 695.

TOWARD, Agnes Reid,‡ born Glasgow 19 Sept. 1886, died Glasgow 1975. Shorthand typist, tenement dweller. Daughter of Agnes Reid, dressmaker, and William Toward, metal merchant.

Agnes Toward spent most of her life in the Garnethill area of Glasgow. She attended Garnethill Public School, then studied shorthand and typing at the Glasgow Athenaeum Commercial College in Buchanan Street (1905–6). In 1914, she joined a shipping company, Prentice, Service & Henderson, as a shorthand typist and remained with them till she retired in 1960, aged 74. From 1911 until 1965, Miss Toward lived in a tenement flat at 145 Buccleuch Street in Glasgow. When she died in 1975, her flat was bought by Anna Davidson who sold it seven years later to the NTS. The flat is now preserved as a typical example of the type of tenement flat many Scottish people lived in during the late 19th and early 20th centuries. Miss Toward had kept many items which other people would have thrown away, such as household bills, recipes, dressmaking items, books from her schooldays, postcards and letters including copies of her own letters to friends. Together, they build up a picture of her life. Of particular interest is her correspondence, kept up during both world wars, with a former colleague, Mr Collins, which provides a fascinating insight into office life in the first half of the 20th century. LRH

• Hepburn, L. (2003) *The Tenement House*; Ritchie, W. K. (1997) *Miss Toward of The Tenement House*.

TRAIL, Ann Agnes (Agnes Xavier), born Panbride, Forfarshire, 16 Feb. 1798, died Edinburgh 3 Dec. 1872. Artist, pioneering nun and educator. Daughter of Catherine Biss and the Rev. David Trail.

Ann Trail's father's family had ministered at Panbride for three generations, the longest held charge in a single family in the Church of Scotland. She was the second of 11 children. Educated at home, she then taught her younger siblings. Following a spell in northern England, she taught at an Irish charity school for two years and did charity visiting. After training as an artist and receiving commissions in London, in 1826 she left to travel extensively in Italy, including some time spent with the artist David Wilkie. After rejecting several suitors, she became a Catholic in June 1828. Returning home in 1829, she was influenced by the prominent Cambridge movement converts,

Ambrose Philips de Lisle, the Passionist Rev. Ignatius Spencer and the exuberant Rev. James Gillis, later vicar-Apostolic of the Eastern District and, with a fellow Scotswoman, Margaret Clapperton, she decided to enter the Ursuline novitiate in Cavagnes, France, in 1833. She took the name Agnes Xavier.

In 1834 she, seven French nuns and two lay sisters founded the first post-Reformation convent in Scotland at St Margaret's, Greenhill, Edinburgh, where she spent the rest of her life. In 1842, her convent held the first Quarant'Ore and the first modern Corpus Christi procession in Scotland, long before they were introduced into England. Her wide-ranging interests and connections throughout the Catholic world drew her into the full vigour of the Catholic revival. She taught, gave drawing classes and executed many fine miniatures, of which several remain in St Margaret's. After a stroke late in life she gradually retired and died on the feast day of her patron, Francis Xavier. BA
• Scottish Catholic Archives, Edinburgh; St Margaret's Convent, Edinburgh; Sacra Congregazione di Propaganda Fide, Rome.
Trail A. A. (1897) *Conversion of Miss Trail, a Scotch Presbyterian, written by herself*, (1886) *The Revival of Conventual Life*.
Anon. (1897) *History of St Margaret's Convent, Edinburgh*; *ODNB* (2004).

TRAQUAIR, Phoebe Anna, n. **Moss,** born Dublin 24 May 1852, died Edinburgh 4 August 1936. Artist, mural decorator and craftworker. Daughter of Teresa Richardson, and William Moss, surgeon.

One of seven children, Phoebe Anna Moss studied between 1869 and 1872 at the School of Design run by the RDS, which assigned her to illustrate the research papers of Dr Ramsay Heatley Traquair (1840–1912), a Scots palaeontologist. They married on 5 June 1873, moving in 1874 to Edinburgh, where Ramsay was appointed Keeper of Natural History at the MSA. Determined to be a professional artist-craftsperson, Phoebe Traquair had turned from small-scale embroidered work to large stitched figurative panels by 1886. Despite, or because of, a demanding home life with three children, she began to create public art, decorating the tiny new chapel of the Royal Edinburgh Hospital for Sick Children, a commission arranged through the philanthropic ESU. In 1892, the Union negotiated her commission for the Catholic Apostolic Church for their Mansfield Place church (today the Mansfield Traquair Centre). Meantime,

she painted the Song School, a choir practice room of St Mary's Episcopal Cathedral (1888–92). In all these, she wished to unite the arts and spiritually benefit her community. She also decorated two English buildings, the church of St Peter in Clayworth, Nottinghamshire (1904–5) and the Manners Chapel at Thorneyhill, Hampshire (1920–2), in her late Pre-Raphaelite style.

From the late 1880s, Phoebe Anna Traquair worked in both commercial book art and private manuscript illumination. John Ruskin lent her medieval manuscripts to copy in 1887. Her principal publisher was T. & A. Constable for whose proprietor, Walter B. Blaikie, she later designed garden gates and railings. Her 1890s manuscripts illuminated the poetry of Rossetti, Tennyson and the Brownings. After 1900, she turned to the fashionable field of enamelwork set as jewellery or ornaments. With her friend *Annie Macdonald she was a member of the GWB, which met in the Dean Studio, where she also rented a studio from 1890 until the Traquairs moved to Colinton in 1906. A member of the SGH and the ACES, London, from the 1890s, she also showed work at the RSA (which eventually elected her an honorary member in 1920) and in charity and professional exhibitions across Scotland. On the advice of designer Walter Crane, she showed a tooled bookcover at the 1893 Chicago World's Fair (Cumming 1993, p. 31). Her embroideries *The Progress of a Soul* (NGS, 1893–1902: Cumming 1993, pp. 65–6) were exhibited at the World's Fair at St Louis in 1904. Her architect friend Robert Lorimer commissioned enamelled stallplates for the Thistle Chapel, Edinburgh, a piano decoration for Frank Tennant (both worked in 1909–10) and three post-war memorial altarpieces for Glasgow churches. Her elder son, Ramsay, articled to Lorimer, designed some of her enamelled ornament settings, later becoming an authority on Canadian silver. In recent years, Phoebe Anna Traquair has regained recognition as a multi-talented creator, one of the most important in her generation in Scotland. EC
• NLS: Acc. 8122–29: Corr. and papers of Phoebe Anna Traquair.
Armour, M. (1897) 'Beautiful modern manuscripts', *The Studio: Special Winter Number*, pp. 47–55, (1897) 'Mural decoration in Scotland', *The Studio*, pp. 100–6; Baldwin Brown, G. (1889) 'Some recent efforts in mural decoration', *The Scottish Art Review*, Jan., pp. 225–8; Callen, A. (1979) *Angel in the Studio*; Caw, J. L. (1900) 'The art work of Mrs Traquair', *The Art Journal*, pp. 143–8; Cumming, E. (1987) 'Phoebe Anna Traquair HRSA (1852–1936) and her

contribution to arts and crafts in Edinburgh', PhD, Univ. of Edinburgh, (1993) *Phoebe Anna Traquair 1852–1936*, (2005) *Phoebe Anna Traquair*; *ODNB* (2004).

TRIDUANA, fl. between the 6th and 8th centuries. Nun and probably abbess, southern Pictland.

Little can be said with confidence about Triduana, patron saint of Restalrig near Edinburgh, where her relics were venerated in the later middle ages. Her feast day was 8 October. The 16th-century Aberdeen Breviary makes her a Greek nun who came to Scotland with St Regulus, the man credited with having brought Christianity and St Andrew's relics to the kingdom. This story is not historical; more useful are Triduana's associations with retreats at Rescobie near Forfar and Dunfallandy near Pitlochry, which hint at an aristocratic Pictish woman who became a nun and abbess. Legend has it that Triduana was desired by a king called Nectan (a common Pictish name). To preserve her modesty she tore out her eyes and sent them to him, having learned that his passions had been aroused by their 'most superb beauty'. Her relics were considered particularly efficacious for curing eye ailments. JEF
• MacDonald, A. A. (2000) 'The Chapel of Restalrig: royal folly or venerable shrine?', in L. A. J. R. Houwen et al. (eds) *A Palace in the Wild*.

TROTTER, Menie, of Mortonhall, born Midlothian c. 1740, died after 1828. Noted conversationalist.

Menie Trotter left no writing, but accounts of her conversation survive. Henry Cockburn (1779–1854), Whig contemporary of Walter Scott, recalled in his memoirs 'a singular race of excellent Scotch old ladies' as they were in 1810. He particularly singled out Miss Menie Trotter, whose 'understanding was fully as masculine' as her attire. Cockburn gave one story to make his point.

On one of her friends asking [Miss Trotter], not long before her death, how she was, she said, 'Very weel – quite weel. But, eh, I had a dismal dream last night! a fearfu' dream!'[. . .] Of a'places i'the world, I dreamed I was in heeven! And what d'ye think I saw there? Deil ha'et but thoosands upon thoosands, o'stark naked weans! That wad be a dreadfu' thing! for ye ken I ne'er could bide bairns a'my days!' (1974, p. 61)

Cockburn went on to say that 'all these female Nestors' were truly pious, but would hardly be deemed so in his own day, for 'the very freedom and cheerfulness of their conversation and views'.

*Anne Grant of Laggan described Miss Trotter in 1828 as 'a stately form and firm, energetic and high-principled', despite her great age, and serving food from her own farm 'well-dressed and excellent' (1844, III, pp. 144–6). Cockburn's outspoken ladies included **Sophia Johnston** of Hilton, (c. 1730–c. 1810). Raised without forcible education, like Rousseau's Emile, she taught herself carpentry and blacksmithing, preferred men's clothing, learnt to read and write later in life, and discussed everything. Cockburn recalled 'her talk intelligent and racy, rich in both old anecdote, and shrewd modern observation, and spiced with a good deal of plain sarcasm; her understanding powerful; all her opinions free, and very freely expressed . . .' (1974, p. 55). DS
• NLS: Acc. 11880, papers of Dr Neil Ker relating to research on the Trotter family.
Cockburn, H. [1874] (1974) *Memorials of His Time*, K. Miller, ed.; Grant of Laggan, Mrs [Anne] (1844) *Memoir and Correspondence of Mrs Grant of Laggan*, 3 vols; Lindsay, Lady A., 'Sophia (Suff) Johnston of the Hilton Family', in A. W. C. Lindsay, (1849) *Lives of the Lindsays: a memoir of the house of Crawford and Balcarres*; Symonds, D. A. (1997) *Weep Not for Me: women, ballads, and infanticide in Early Modern Scotland*.

TROUT, Jennie (or Jenny) Kidd, n. **Gowanlock,** born Kelso, 21 April 1841, died California, USA, 10 Nov. 1921. Canada's first licensed woman physician. Daughter of Elizabeth (probably Kidd), and Andrew Gowanlock.

Jennie Gowanlock's family emigrated to Stratford, Canada, in 1847. Accredited as a teacher in 1861, she taught until 1865 when she married Edward Trout, influential publisher of Toronto's *Monetary Times*. He encouraged her to pursue medical studies, her decision prompted by prolonged bouts with 'nervous ailments'. Jennie Trout pioneered Canadian women's long struggle to enter the medical profession. Despite huge barriers, she and a colleague gained admission to the Toronto School of Medicine in 1871, conditional on launching no complaints. The male students' and professors' indecencies and pranks rendered this unworkable and she finished her degree at Pennsylvania's Women's Medical College, 1872–5. When the Canadian profession refused to acknowledge her foreign degree, she passed all their examinations (1875).

Edward Trout's media connections prominently publicised her as Canada's first licensed woman physician. Inundated with requests from women seeking a female physician, she operated a private practice and free women's dispensary, and founded the Therapeutic and Electric Institute for women's health care. These demands strained her health and forced retirement in 1882. When women were expelled from studying medicine at Queen's University for challenging male students' discriminatory behaviour, Jennie Trout, continuing her activism for women's equality, personally encouraged them, contributing $10,000 and scholarships to establish the Women's Medical College of Kingston (1883–93), with women as trustees and professors. Little is known after her emigration to the USA, where she devoted her life to Bible study. A Canadian 40 cent stamp (1991 issue) commemorated her life. LJ

• Dembski, P. E. P. (1985) 'Jenny Kidd Trout and the founding of the Women's Medical Colleges at Kingston and Toronto', *Ontario History*, 77, p. 3, September (Bibl.).

TWEEDSMUIR, Priscilla, Lady *see* **BUCHAN, Priscilla** (1915–78)

TYTLER, Ann Fraser, born c. 1781, died 3 Sept. 1857. Writer. Daughter of Ann Fraser, and Alexander Fraser Tytler, writer and professor of universal history at the University of Edinburgh, later Lord Woodhouselee.

In middle age Ann Fraser Tytler began to write stories for the children of her youngest brother, Patrick Fraser Tytler, the historian (1791–1849). Her first and most successful novel, *Leila; or The Island* (1833), was in the fashionable genre of Robinsonnades: eight-year-old Leila Howard is shipwrecked along with her father, nurse and pet dog and cat on what proves to be an idyllic uninhabited island. This was followed by two stories about twins, *Mary and Florence; or Grave and Gay* (1835) and *Mary and Florence at Sixteen* (1838), and then by two Leila sequels, *Leila in England* (1842) and *Leila at Home* (1852). Popular on both sides of the Atlantic until at least the 1880s, these books are full of happiness, religious in spirit, and not particularly concerned with moral instruction. As fiction they are characterised by a well-sustained narrative thrust and quite lively dialogue. At the end of her life Ann Fraser Tytler contributed with reminiscences to a biography of her brother Patrick. DGM

• Tytler, A. F., Works as above.

Avery, G. (1965) *Nineteenth Century Children: Heroes and Heroines in English Children's Stories 1780–1900*; Burgon, J. W. (1859) *The Portrait of a Christian Gentleman - a Memoir of Patrick Fraser Tytler, author of 'The History of Scotland'.*

TYTLER, Sarah *see* **KEDDIE, Henrietta** (1827–1914)

U

URE, Joan *see* **CLARK, Elizabeth Thomson (Betty)** (1918–78)

URE, Mary, born Kelvinside, Glasgow, 18 Feb. 1933, died London 3 April 1975. Actor. Daughter of Edith Swinburne, and Colin McGregor Ure, engineer.

Educated in Glasgow and at the Mount School, York, Mary Ure was an actor of skill, range and beauty, frequently cast in vulnerable roles. She trained at the Central School of Speech and Drama in London, making her debut at the Manchester Opera House in 1953 in Alan Melville's *Simon and Laura*. Her potential was swiftly recognised, and she made a dazzling West End debut at the London Arts Theatre in 1954 in Anouilh's *Time Remembered*. In 1955 she played Ophelia to Paul Scofield's Hamlet, appearing in this production in Moscow on stage and television. Her most memorable roles came at the Royal Court Theatre, London, in the spring of 1956 – Abigail in the first British production of *The Crucible* by Arthur Miller, and Alison in John Osborne's *Look Back in Anger*. She also played Alison in the film version (opposite Richard Burton) and on the New York stage. Mary Ure married John Osborne (1929–94) in 1957; a tempestuous union, it ended in divorce five years later, when their son was one year old. By this time, she had fallen in love with Robert Shaw (1927–78), appearing with him in the Elizabethan comedy *The Changeling* at the Royal Court in 1961. They married in 1963 and had four children.

Mary Ure played leading roles with the Royal Shakespeare Company at Stratford. Her films included *Storm Over the Nile* (1955), *Sons and Lovers* (for which she received an Academy Award Nomination in 1960), *Custer of the West* (1967) and *Where Eagles Dare* (1968). She claimed, however, that her preference was for the theatre and that she appeared in films to please her husbands. She returned to the stage in 1975, giving a powerful performance in Don Taylor's *The Exorcism* at the Comedy Theatre, London. On the evening of the first night of this production, a cocktail of whisky and tranquillisers led to her untimely death. DC

• *ODNB* (2004); *The Scotsman*, 6 April 1975 (obit.).

URQUHART, Mary Sinclair (Molly), m. **McIntosh,** born Glasgow 21 Jan. 1906, died Glasgow 5 Oct. 1977. Actor and theatre director. Daughter of Ann McCallum, post office clerk, and William Urquhart, sea-going engineer.

Molly Urquhart was the eldest of three surviving daughters of parents from Tiree and Wester Ross. Two sisters died in infancy and she had two younger siblings. She lived all her life in Glasgow, in the West End and, after marriage, in Ibrox, enjoying a career of local, national and international activity and success. She attended Dowanhill Primary School and Church Street School before working in a local shop and then passing an exam to join the GPO. As a teenager, she acted in the flourishing Glasgow amateur sector with the St George Players and with Glasgow's two influential 'little theatres', the Tron and the Curtain. She began working professionally in 1932 as a member of a Howard and Wyndham company. On 1 August 1934, she married police officer William McIntosh (1900–59); they had one son, James. In 1936, she appeared at Gourock with the Sheldon Brown Rep and was a member of the repertory company at the Festival Theatre, Cambridge, appearing in character roles in productions of Somerset Maugham, Emlyn Williams and Ivor Novello.

In 1939, she founded the MSU (Molly Sinclair Urquhart) Theatre in Rutherglen, a venture she managed, directed for and acted with until 1944. Based in the converted Congregational Church in East Main Street, the theatre opened with Merton Hodge's *The Wind and the Rain* on 2 May 1939. The company was a significant training ground for local amateur talent, including Gordon Jackson, Duncan Macrae and Nicholas Parsons, who went on to professional careers. The MSU project coincided with the launch of the Citizens' Theatre, Glasgow (1943), where almost all of MSU's nascent professionals were later employed. Molly Urquhart made her own Citizens' debut in its first season, as Molly Cudden in J. B. Priestley's *Bull Market*, and her London debut in 1945 at Sadlers Wells as Mrs Grant in James Bridie's *The Forrigan Reel*. Subsequent roles included Jeanie in *Dr Angelus* at the Phoenix opposite Alistair Sim (1947), and Dame Sensualitie in the modern production of Lindsay's *Ane Satyre of the Thrie Estaitis* at the Assembly Hall in Edinburgh (1948). Her appearances in the Citizens' pantomimes, most famously in *The Tintock Cup* in 1949–50, were extremely popular. In the 1950s, she combined performances in the *Five Past Eight Shows* and standard rep work in Glasgow, Edinburgh and London. Film work included notable roles in *Geordie* (1955), *The Nun's Story* (1958) and *The Sundowners* (1960). In later life, her focus returned to the amateur sector and charitable ventures and she was a champion of community-based activities in the Cessnock, Ibrox and Pollokshields areas of Glasgow. AS

• Univ. of Glasgow, Scottish Theatre Archive: Molly Urquhart Collection.
Murdoch, H. (1981) *Travelling Hopefully: the story of Molly Urquhart*; *ODNB* (2004).

V

VEITCH, Marion, n. **Fairlie,** born Edinburgh or Lanark 1638/9, died Dumfries May 1722. Memoir-writer.

Around 1706, Marion Veitch recorded her life story and her personal relationship with God, noting her godly (but un-named) parents and that she was 'well educated'. She may have been the Marion Fairlie, daughter of Euphan Kincaid, and James Fairlie, shoemaker, baptised in Canongate Kirk, Edinburgh, 20 December 1639. By 1645, she

was living in Lanark. She married the minister William Veitch (1640–1722) on 23 November 1664. Following the failed Covenanters' rebellion at Pentland Hills in 1666, William Veitch went into exile in England to avoid persecution. Marion Veitch fled back to Lanark, then to Edinburgh; this enforced separation was one of many they endured during their marriage. Between 1672 and 1685, Marion Veitch and the children lived in the north of England, then briefly in Edinburgh, then again in England. William lived with the family only sporadically, between stints in prison and visits to London and Rotterdam. Shortly after James VII granted religious tolerance in 1685, the Veitches returned to Scotland. William and Mary Veitch had ten children; four died young. Two sons, William and Samuel, were prominent members of the failed Darien Expedition. At her husband's last church, St Michael's in Dumfries, a refurbished joint gravestone bears witness to Marion's support of her persecuted husband and to William's death, within one day of his wife's. PBG

• Veitch, M. [1706] (1846) *Memoirs of Mrs William Veitch [by herself], Mr Thomas Hog of Kiltearn, Mr Henry Erskine and Mr John Carstairs*, Committee of the General Assembly of the Free Church of Scotland.

Anderson, J. (1851) *Ladies of the Covenant*, pp. 159–180; Veitch, W. (1825) *Memoirs of Mr William Veitch and George Brysson, written by themselves*, T. McCrie, ed.; *ODNB* (2004).

VICTORIA, (Alexandrina Victoria), Queen and Empress, born Kensington Palace, 19 May 1819, died Osborne House, Isle of Wight, 22 Jan. 1901. Daughter of Victoria of Saxe-Coburg-Saalfeld, and Edward Augustus, Duke of Kent, fourth son of George III.

Queen Victoria was not 'Scottish' in any obvious dynastic way, but began the Hanoverian royal family's links with Highland Scotland which have been maintained to the present day. Princess Victoria was regarded as an heir to the British throne from early on, since there were few other legitimate descendants of George III in her generation. When on 20 June 1837, her uncle William IV died, she succeeded, removing the need for a regency, since she was just 18. She was crowned in 1838. Her initial prime minister, Lord Melbourne, the first of ten, was one of her early advisers. When in 1840 she married her cousin, Prince Albert of Saxe-Coburg (1819–1861), he became a major influence in her life politically and personally. They had nine children, all of whom survived (see Louise, Princess), and who became linked by marriage to much of European royalty.

The royal couple made their first visit to Scotland in 1842; in 1848, they bought the Balmoral estate, and rebuilt the castle during the 1850s. Alternating with Osborne House in the Isle of Wight, it became their retreat from London. Travelling up every year by train, they 'embraced Scottishness wholeheartedly' (*ODNB* 2004), dressing their children in kilts, and enjoying rural life.

In 1861, Prince Albert died, probably from typhoid fever, a bereavement which devastated the Queen, prompting a withdrawal from public duties for several years. During this period, she became increasingly close to an attendant at Balmoral, John Brown (1826–83), who became the 'chief focus of her emotional life' (ibid.), and 'her best friend' (Longford 1964, p. 456). There were even rumours of marriage (unproven, and not seriously thinkable). He became a close confidant until his death in 1883, which was deeply mourned by Queen Victoria: she put up a memorial to him at Balmoral, where there was also a large monument to Prince Albert. The Queen had evolved an unshakeable calendar, dividing her time between Windsor, Osborne House and Balmoral: she regularly came to Scotland in May, returning in August and staying until November. Affairs of state had to be dealt with by the communications of the time, not always easy when she was in residence at the far end of Loch Muick.

Queen Victoria again became interventionist in public affairs in her later years and did not always maintain neutrality in her dealings with her prime ministers, especially Disraeli (whom she favoured) and Gladstone (whom she did not). She welcomed her title of Empress of India (1877) and celebrated her golden and diamond jubilees (1887 and 1897), becoming the longest reigning monarch in the history of the British Isles, and lending her name to the age. Her funeral cortege on 2 February 1901 was watched by thousands. Balmoral retained its importance as a residence for later generations of the royal family, who have adopted a kind of alternative Scottish identity (kilts, outdoor sports), which however artificial originally, appears to be heartfelt. SR

• Queen Victoria (1868) *Leaves from the Journal of our Life in the Highlands*, A. Helps, ed., (1884) *More leaves from the Journal of a Life in the Highlands, from 1862 to 1882*, and see *ODNB* (Bibl.).

Arnstein, W. A. (2003) *Queen Victoria*; Longford, E. (1964) *Victoria RI*; *ODNB* (2004) (Bibl.).

VIOLANTE, Signora, m. possibly **Larini,** born 1682, died Edinburgh 1741. Rope dancer, tumbler, actor, manager and dance teacher.

Italian, or possibly French but married to an Italian, Signora Violante was a celebrated figure in early 18th-century Edinburgh. There is speculation that she was in Edinburgh from 1719, but her connection with the city is probably later. She was in London in spring 1720, working with

De Grimbergue's French company performing pantomime, *commedia dell'arte* pieces and other entertainments. She was particularly noted for a rope dance with flags that was separately listed on some playbills. Signora Violante returned to London in spring 1726, performing in *commedia dell'arte* at the Haymarket, and stayed on as a tumbler and rope dancer. She ran a season of 70 nights at the Haymarket in 1726–7 with a programme of acrobatics, pantomime and dancing. Her children were among the performers, including two daughters; one, the dancer Rosina Violante, later became the wife of George Richard Escourt Luppino.

Signora Violante was in Dublin in 1727 and then in Edinburgh, where the magistrates refused her company permission to perform. Thereafter, it performed throughout Britain, and possibly in Paris, with entertainments including a pirated version of *The Beggar's Opera* in Dublin in which

the teenage Peg Woffington appeared. In 1735, Signora Violante performed in Edinburgh, where she settled, and continued her rope dancing turn in a variety of venues, as well as keeping 'a much Frequented [dancing] School for the Young Ladies', which Alexander Carlyle, minister of Inveresk and chronicler of Lothian society, attended in his youth (Carlyle 1973, p. 25). She was described as a 'virago' (Arnot 1779, p. 366) and styled an 'evil genius' by Lee Lewes (Lewes 1805, vol. 3, p. 28), but defended in James Dibdin's history of Scottish theatre (Dibdin 1888, p. 35). Notice of her death 'lately' appeared in *The Scots Magazine* in June 1741. AS

• Arnot, H. (1779) *The History of Edinburgh*; Carlyle, A. (1973) *Anecdotes and Characters of the Times*, J. Kinsley ed.; Dibdin, J. C. (1888) *Annals of the Edinburgh Stage*; Highfill, P. H. Jr., Burnim, K. A. and Langhans, E. A. (c. 1973–93) *A Biographical Dictionary of Actors . . . and Other Stage Personnel in London, 1660–1800*; Lewes, C. L. (1805) *Memoirs of Charles Lee Lewes*; *ODNB* (2004).

WADDELL, Roberta Johanna (Bertha), MBE, born Uddingston 17 June 1907, died Cambuslang 17 August 1980. Theatre writer, actor, director and manager; **WADDELL, Janet Jane (Jenny),** born Uddingston 13 August 1905, died Uddingston 7 January 1984. Theatre director and costume designer, musical accompanist. Daughters of Jean Leadbetter Swan, primary headmistress, and John Jeffrey Waddell, architect.

The Waddell sisters' parents were profoundly interested in the arts. As youngsters, the sisters saw Anna Pavlova dance and Forbes Robertson and Ellen Terry act. Governess-educated, they learned dance, singing and piano, later attending drama and speech classes in Glasgow. Both joined local amateur companies and then the Scottish National Players. Bertha Waddell played, aged 15, a lead role at the Athenaeum in Glasgow, going on to become LRAM. Meantime, Jenny Waddell developed as a musical accompanist. Complementary talents helped them establish the first professional company specifically for children, launched in 1927 in the McLellan Galleries, Glasgow, as the Scottish Children's Theatre (later The Children's Theatre, Bertha Waddell's Children's Theatre). Positive reactions to their first performances led to their beginning to tour, initially to Bearsden, Hamilton and Stirling. Directors of Education noticed them

and, beginning with Lanarkshire, they were invited to perform in schools during the day, an important recognition. In 1930, CUKT awarded them £300. Their touring developed on a seasonal basis into schools and public halls throughout Scotland and sometimes beyond. They often spoke of being invited to perform for Princesses Elizabeth and *Margaret (see Snowdon) at Glamis in 1933 and 1935 and at Buckingham Palace in 1937, and for new royal children in 1953, 1955 and 1967. The SAC supported their company, and by their retirement in 1968, which they spent in the family home near Blantyre, whole generations of Scottish children had enjoyed their work.

Bertha Waddell took the lead and, with her sister, developed a very particular style. Shows began with a sound effect and Bertha's head appearing through the curtains, announcing 'Item Number One'. Each performance comprised some dozen or more individually introduced scenes, usually based on folk tales or nursery rhymes. Some used mime or puppets, and music and song were central to the aesthetic. Design was simple, suited to touring constraints. In the 1950s, children's drama began to involve children themselves, engaging them with social and educational issues, and the Waddells' themes and modes came to seem old-fashioned. Bertha Waddell, while defending their values, wanted their scripts to be destroyed after her death (it is not known whether this was done), believing people would laugh at them. Yet the Waddells were the first to address British children's theatre provision creatively, and their pioneering work is fondly remembered. IB

• Casciani, E. (1980–1) 'Item Number One', *The Scots Magazine*, vol. 114, pp. 391–8; McKeever, J. (1982) 'The Bertha Waddell Children's Theatre', *Scottish Theatre News*, August, pp. 32–3.
Personal knowledge.

WALDIE, Charlotte Anne, m. **Eaton,** born Hendersyde Park, near Kelso, 28 Sept. 1788, died London 28 April 1859. Writer. Daughter of Ann Ormston and George Waldie.

Charlotte Waldie is known for her highly successful travel journal, first published in 1817 in the immediate aftermath of the Napoleonic Wars. Its title, *Narrative of a Residence in Belgium during the Campaign of 1815 and of a Visit to the Field of Waterloo (by an Englishwoman)*, secured immediate attention. In it, she described a trip she made to Brussels in 1815 with her brother John and younger sister Jane. She witnessed the panic and chaos that beset so much of Western Europe following Waterloo, and gave descriptions of the battlefield, with all its horrors, just a few weeks after the event. It was seen as one of the foremost contemporary accounts 'by other than military writers' (*DNB* 1909). She subsequently published two novels and the three-volume *Rome in the Nineteenth Century* (1820), with accounts of historical buildings and monuments, which went into six editions and was considered, 89 years later, as still useful to travellers. She married banker Stephen Eaton (d. 1834) in 1822. They lived at Ketton Hall in Rutland and had two sons and two daughters. Her sister **Jane Waldie** m. **Watts** (1793–1826) studied painting with Alexander Nasmyth (see Nasmyth, Jane) and also published an account of her travels in Italy. SN

• Eaton, C. A., Works as above, and (1827) *Continental Adventures*, (1831) *At home and abroad; or, Memoirs of Emily de Cardonnell by the author of 'Rome in the nineteenth century'*; Waldie, J. (1820) *Sketches Descriptive of Italy in the Years 1816 and 1817*.
DNB vol. XX (1909); *ODNB* (2004) (see Eaton, Charlotte Anne); *SHA*.

WALFORD, Lucy Bethia, n. **Colquhoun,** born Portobello, Edinburgh, 17 April 1845, died London 11 May 1915. Novelist and artist. Daughter of Frances Sara Fuller Maitland, poet and hymn writer, and John Colquhoun, naturalist, author and former military officer.

Lucy Colquhoun, seventh of nine children, was raised in a Presbyterian family with artistic and literary connections; her aunt *Catherine Sinclair and her grandmother Lady Janet Colquhoun were both religious writers. Her childhood was spent in Edinburgh, Oxford and Dunbartonshire. Educated at home by foreign governesses, from an early age she proved an avid reader of writers such as Charlotte Yonge, *Susan Ferrier and, in particular, Jane Austen. Austen, she later said, was to 'exercise an abiding influence over all my own future effort' (Walford 1910, p. 142). She successfully entered work for the RSA annual exhibition in 1868 and several years following. In June 1869, she married Alfred Saunders Walford (d. 1907), a young magistrate. They moved to Essex and, in 1900, to London. They had two sons and five daughters.

In 1874, William Blackwood & Sons, Edinburgh, published Lucy Walford's first novel, *Mr. Smith: a Part of His Life*. A popular work of domestic-centred fiction, it was praised by contemporary critics such as Coventry Patmore and admired by *Queen Victoria. Over the next 30 years she produced 45 further books and wrote for literary journals and newspapers, including *Blackwood's Edinburgh Magazine, Cornhill Magazine*, the *London Magazine* and *World*. From 1889 to 1893 she was the London correspondent for the New York-based *The Critic*, taking over the position from W. E. Henley. She continued to produce and publish work until shortly before her death. DF

• NLS: Blackwood Papers; Waddesdon Manor, Bucks: Kylin archive.
Walford, L. B., Works as above, and (1910) *Recollections of a Scottish Novelist*; see also *HSWW* (Bibl.).
Finkelstein, D. (2002) *The House of Blackwood*; *ODNB* (2004); Schlueter, P. and Schlueter, J. (eds) (1998) *An Encyclopedia of British Women Writers*.

WALKER, Ethel, DBE, born Edinburgh 9 June 1861, died London 2 March 1951. Painter and sculptor. Daughter of Isabella Robertson, and Arthur Abney Walker, proprietor.

Ethel Walker's family moved to London when she was nine. She began painting early with little formal training. Much later, aged 38, she attended Putney, Westminster and the Slade schools of art, becoming a pupil of Walter Sickert and Wyndham Lewis. Success came late in her long life, which she spent between Chelsea and Robin Hood's Bay on the Yorkshire coast, a subject for marines, such as *Seascape: Autumn Morning* (1935). Considered by some critics one of the best marine painters of her age, she was also known for watercolours of nudes and sensitive flower studies. She admired and emulated the Impressionists, particularly Pissarro. Prominent works are her watercolour, *The Judgement of Paris*, the visionary *Nausicaa* (1920), and portraits, notably *Vanessa*. From 1936, she was a member of the London Group. Contemporaries considered Ethel Walker 'energetic, witty and wild about small dogs' (*DSAA*, p. 588). Her work was exhibited widely during her lifetime at the RA and the Lefevre Gallery, London, and at the RSA. The Tate held a retrospective exhibition of works by Ethel Walker, Gwen John and Frances Hodgkins in 1951. LS

• Birmingham City Museum and Art Gallery (1950) *Six Contemporary Painters: Coldstream, Hitchins, Hodgkins, Piper, Vaughan, Walker*; Corrymella Scott Gallery (1999) *Ethel Walker*; *DSAA*; National Gallery of British Art (afterwards Tate Gallery, now Tate Britain) (1952) *Ethel Walker, Frances Hodgkins, Gwen John*; *ODNB* (2004).

WALKER, Helen, born Dumfriesshire c. 1710, died Irongray, Dumfriesshire, 1791. Supposed model for Jeanie Deans in Sir Walter Scott's *The Heart of Midlothian* (1818).

In his 'Introduction' to the 1830 edition (Scott 1994, pp. 537–42), Scott described receiving a letter about Helen Walker's story: she became the original of Jeanie Deans, a canny yet principled model of womanhood. In the novel, after refusing to lie on oath, Jeanie Deans walks to London in 1738 to secure from the Duke of Argyll a reprieve for her young sister, convicted of infanticide. The 'sister' did exist: Isobell Walker almost certainly killed her newborn child in Cluden, Dumfriesshire, in 1736. Villagers, especially midwives, were outraged. But no one like Helen Walker exists in court records, and the cause of the Great Seal Warrant of Remission that saved Isobell Walker from the gallows is currently unknown. The rumours that Scott heard about Helen, the 'wily body' (ibid., p. 539) believed by locals to know about the case, are all that survive. The memorial stone that Scott set up for Helen Walker is in the Kirkpatrick-Irongray churchyard. DS

• NAS: JC12/5, Isobell Walker.

Crockett, W. S. (1912) *The Sir Walter Scott Originals*; Scott, Sir W. [1818] (1994) *The Heart of Midlothian*, T. Inglis, ed.

WALKER, Lady Mary (aka **Lady Mary Hamilton**), n. **Leslie,** born Melville House, Cupar, Fife, 8 May 1736, died Exeter c. Feb. 1821. Novelist. Daughter of Elizabeth Monypenny of Pitmilly, and Alexander Leslie, 5th Earl of Leven.

On 3 January 1762, Lady Mary Leslie married Dr James Walker (1731–before 1804) of Inverdovat, Fife, whose estate had heavy debts. The marriage was unhappy and financially troubled, and James Walker left his wife in the 1770s. Moving to London, Lady Mary attempted to support the family through writing fiction. The ambivalence of her purpose is indicated in the full title of her first novel, *Letters from the Duchesse de Crui and others, on subjects moral and entertaining, wherein the character of the female sex, with their rank, importance, and consequence, is stated, and their relative duties in life are enforced, by a lady* (1776). In this and the equally lengthy and epistolary *Memoirs of the Marchioness de Louvoi* (1777), plot and character were subordinated to moral instruction for young ladies. The *Critical Review* noted her eagerness to display familiarity with classical and historical texts, especially those dealing with the situation of women (Garside, I, p. 250). She consistently advocated improvement of women's education.

Her best-known novel, *Munster Village* (1778), is remembered for its portrayal of a utopian village community, architecturally designed to foster industry and learning, created by an enlightened, mature aristocratic woman, delaying marriage to fulfil her aims. Other themes (the need for women to be self-supporting, a plea for divorce and tolerance towards women's sexuality) may be related to Lady Mary's unconventional life. She had ten children, of whom three died young; according to her grandson, Baron Adolphe Thiebault, only the first four were James Walker's children.

By 1779, when he went to Jamaica to try to redeem his debts, Lady Mary was relying on her mother's financial help, but by 1781 had met wealthy Jamaican plantation owner, George Robinson Hamilton (d. 1797), with whom she went to live in France. On 4 December 1786, she wrote to her nephew of being 'the happiest woman in the world' and of George Hamilton's support for her family (NAS GD26/13/689). They could not marry, though Mary Walker took his name. Contacts with Britain became difficult during the revolutionary war. The couple were imprisoned as aliens near Lille for 16 months in 1794–5. In 1797, George Hamilton bequeathed Mary Walker his whole estate, including the 775-acre Jamaican plantation, 'Success', for her lifetime but in trust, to ward off any 'interference' by James Walker. She met English scholar Sir Herbert Croft (1751–1816) near Lille in 1803, and they set up a scholarly household together, as friends, near Amiens in 1805, later described by Croft's secretary, Charles Nodier, who translated *Munster Village* and helped Lady Mary write a novel in French, *La famille du duc de Popoli* (1810). In 1815, she visited the Jamaican estate, returning to live with her youngest daughter in London, and later near Exeter, where she died in 1821. JR

• NAS: GD 26/13, 674, 688–9: Leslie-Melville Papers; Yale Univ. Beinecke Library: Lady Mary Hamilton Papers, James Marshall and Marie-Louise Osborn Collection.
Walker, Lady M., Works as above, and (1782) *Life of Mrs Justman*, 2 vols [no surviving copy].
Babchi, B. (2004) *Pliable Pupils and Sufficient Self-Directors*; Baylis, S. (1987) 'Introduction' to Lady Mary Hamilton, *Munster Village*; Dahan, J. R. (1995) *Charles Nodier, Correspondance de Jeunesse*, 2 vols; Forster, A. (1996) *Index to Book Reviews in England 1775–1800*; Fraser, Sir W. (1890) *The Melvilles, Earls of Melville and the Leslies, Earls of Leven*, 3 vols; Garside P. et al. (2000) *The English Novel, 1770–1829*, 2 vols; *Gentleman's Magazine* (1821) vol. 91, p. 283; *Jamaica Almanac* (1840), at http://jamaicanfamilysearch.com 14/10/04; Johns, A. (2003) *Women's Utopias of the Eighteenth Century*; Munk, W. (1878) *Roll of the Royal College of Physicians of London*, 9 vols; *ODNB* (2004); Oliver, R. (1964) *Charles Nodier* (1964); Rees, C. (1996) *Utopian Imagination in Eighteenth-Century Fiction*.

WALKER, Mary Lily, born Dundee 3 July 1863, died Dundee 1 July 1913. Social reformer. Daughter of Mary Allen, and Thomas Walker, solicitor.

Educated privately at Tayside House girls' school, Mary Lily Walker was a brilliant student at University College, Dundee, from 1883, studying Latin, maths and sciences. In 1888, some young professors, appalled at the condition of Dundee's poor, founded the Dundee Social Union (DSU). Mary Lily Walker joined and was appointed superintendent of housing for the Union's 102 houses. In London, she learned the social worker's trade from Octavia Hill in Southwark and the Grey Ladies Settlement in Blackheath. She wore the grey habit for the rest of her life. Returning to Dundee and the DSU in 1889, she established a Grey Lodge Settlement in Wellington Street and began transforming the social profile of Dundee. She entered local government, researched and publicised the facts about industrial conditions, health and housing among poor workers, and intervened directly. In 1901, one of the first two women elected to the Dundee Parish Council (the other was *Agnes Husband), she served on the Distress and the Insurance Committees, and was frustrated by resistance from male colleagues. In the voluntary sector, she moved as an equal with men. In 1904, with Mona Wilson she produced a large-scale statistical report for the DSU, *Report on Housing & Industrial Conditions & Medical Inspection of Schoolchildren*, which shocked people into action and helped change current perceptions of the poor as having only themselves to blame.

To address high rates of infant mortality, following a French example, she opened restaurants for nursing mothers; the service was free if babies were breastfed, weighed weekly, and mothers did not go out to work for three months. Within five years, infant mortality fell from 246 to 183 per 1,000. Mary Lily Walker started baby clinics and home visiting of infants (later taken over by the far-seeing MOH); she helped establish a dispensary, a women's hospital, milk depots, school dinners and an after-school club. She opened a class for disabled children and raised funds for transport to it. At Grey Lodge, girls' and boys' clubs flourished and the foundations for Dundee's nursery schools were laid; in 1907 she organised Country Holiday and Recreation Committee holidays for over 3,000 children.

A member of the Advisory Committee of the National Health Insurance Commission for Scotland, she took the lead in the Dundee Insurance Committee set up after 1911. Her 1913 survey of Dundee housing for the Scottish Housing Commission, showing evidence of overcrowding, was cited in the SHC Report of 1917. Mary Lily Walker never lost her passionate concern for the poor or her capacity for innovation, and never took 'no' for an answer. Her work was one of the main reasons why Dundee became the first city in Scotland to develop a municipal infant health service, influencing social reformers throughout Scotland. IMH

• Walker, M. L. (1912) 'Work among Women', in British Association *Handbook to Dundee and District*.
Baillie, M. (2000) 'The Grey Lady: Mary Lily Walker of Dundee', in L. Miskell et al. (eds) *Victorian Dundee: image & realities*; Grey Lodge Settlement Association (1999) *Grey Lodge – A Century of Care & Concern*; Paterson, M. (1935) *Mary Lily Walker; Some Memories*; Thompson, D. (1938) *Fifty Years Ago and Now*; Valentine, M. O. (1921) *Dundee Social Union & Grey Lodge Settlement*.

WALKINSHAW, Clementina, (Clementine), (aka **Countess of Albestroff),** probably born Glasgow, c. 1720, died Fribourg, Switzerland, 27 Nov. 1802.

Jacobite and paramour of Charles Edward Stewart. Daughter of Katharine Paterson, and John Walkinshaw of Barrowfield, merchant and landowner.

A staunch Jacobite, Clementina Walkinshaw's father had forfeited his lands and substantial fortune for supporting the Stewart cause in the abortive 1715 Rising. His youngest daughter, named after Clementina Sobieska, wife of James, the 'Old Pretender', was probably born at Camlachie House, one of the few remaining properties on the Walkinshaw estate in Glasgow's East End. Little is known of her formative years. Raised as a Roman Catholic, she may have received a convent education in Belgium or France.

By 1738, she had returned to Scotland. During the 1745 Jacobite Rising she met Charles Edward Stewart (1720–88), charismatic son of the Old Pretender, probably in January 1746. The precise nature of their relationship at this time has been much debated, and it is not clear how far the couple maintained contact after the Battle of Culloden. By accident or design their acquaintance was renewed in 1752 and they began living together as Count and Countess Johnson in Ghent. Their daughter, Charlotte, was born in October 1753.

Financial insecurity and constant fear of British government surveillance made the couple's life together difficult, leading to Charles Stewart's alcohol addiction and propensity to violence. In 1760, Clementina left him, living in France and then Switzerland as the Countess of Albestroff. Charles Stewart legitimated his daughter in 1784 and made her Duchess of Albany, fuelling rumours that he and Clementina had been secretly married. Although Charlotte renounced any claim to the throne, Jacobite preoccupation with bloodline has elevated Clementina Walkinshaw's importance in the Stewart dynastic saga. IEM

• Berry, C. L. (1977) *The Young Pretender's Mistress: Clementine Walkinshaw (Comtesse d'Albestroff), 1720–1802* (Bibl.); Craig, M. (1997) *Damn' Rebel Bitches: the women of the '45*; Douglas, H. [1995] (1998) *The Private Passions of Bonnie Prince Charlie*; McLynn, F. [1988] (2003) *Bonnie Prince Charlie*; ODNB (2004); 'Senex' [R. Reid] et al. (1884) *Glasgow Past and Present*, vol. 2.

WALLACE, Eglinton or **Eglantine (Lady Wallace),** n. **Maxwell,** born Monreith, Wigtownshire, c. 1754, died Munich 28 March 1803. Dramatist, author, exile, reputed spy. Daughter of Magdalene Blair, and Sir William Maxwell; sister to *Jane Maxwell, Duchess of Gordon.

After her parents separated, Eglinton Maxwell lived with her mother in Edinburgh in some poverty. On 4 September 1770, now using the spelling 'Eglantine', she married Thomas Dunlop (1750–1835), grandson of Sir Thomas Wallace of Craigie, Bt, whose name and title passed to Dunlop (1770). They had two sons, but in 1778 she divorced her husband for adultery and, helped by Henry Dundas, claimed her jointure from the estate, later receiving a government pension of £120. Boswell's journals mention kissing the charming Lady Wallace in Edinburgh (29 September 1778) but later refer to her 'indelicate effrontery' (9 May 1780). In 1787, in London, she published *A Letter to a Friend, with a Poem called the Ghost of Werther*: a response to Goethe's Charlotte, containing a plea for enlightened education for women. She also published a comedy, *Diamond Cut Diamond*, translated from A.-J. Dumaniant's *Guerre ouverte, ou Ruse contre Ruse* (never performed). In March 1788, she allegedly entered the gallery of the House of Commons in male dress, and she had an affair with a 'fortune-hunting colonel' in Bath (quoted O'Quinn, website). These reports influenced the riotous reception at Covent Garden of her play, *The Ton* (1788), attacking aristocratic corruption and arguing for female education and divorce.

In 1789, visiting France, she was arrested as a spy and demanded an apology from Lafayette. In *Lady Wallace's Letter to Capt. William Wallace* (1792) she again called for the reform of aristocratic behaviour, and analysed the causes of the French Revolution. Her *Conduct of the King of Prussia and General Dumourier* [sic] (1793) recounted her visit to the Austrian Netherlands, then annexed by the French under Dumouriez. Her admiration for Dumouriez was satirised: in Liège 'the civic crown was placed on his head by the fair hands of our English amazon, Lady Wallace' (*Flower of the Jacobins*, 3rd edn., 1793, p. 74). Her *Supplement to the Conduct of the King of Prussia* (1794), *Sermon Addressed to the People* (c. 1794) and *Lady Wallace's Address to the Margate Volunteers* (1795) supported Pitt and the British constitution, but she still called for a reformed aristocracy. *The Whim* (1795), reversing the roles of servants and masters, was banned, but its message admired by the radical Thomas Holcroft (*Monthly Review*, n.s. 19 (1796), pp. 94–6). After 1798, she lived in different German states, and sent regular observations to Dundas and his agent William Wickham. She was again arrested as a spy by the French in Munich in February 1800, but was helped to escape by a French officer. She left as her heir her 'dear and unprotected George Edward Hamilton Gordon', possibly her illegitimate son. JR

• NAS: CS 224/124 and GD51/1/639/1–11 (Corr. with Dundas); NLS: MS 11730, Acc. 11612 and 11730; Will, 3 Aug. 1803, Documents Online PROB 11/1398.
Wallace, Lady E., Works as above.
Leneman, L. (1998) *Alienated Affections*; O'Quinn, D., 'Introduction to Wallace's *The Ton*', in *British Women Playwrights around 1800*, at
www.etang.umontreal.ca/bwp1800/essays/oquinn_ton_intro. html; *ODNB* (2004); Roger, C. (ed.) (1889) *The Book of Wallace*, 2 vols; Yale Edition, *Private Papers of James Boswell*.

WALLACE, Grace Jane, n. **Stein (Lady Wallace),** m1 **Don,** m2 **Wallace,** born Edinburgh 20 Feb. 1804, died probably Aberdour 12 March 1878. Translator. Daughter of Grace Bushby, and John Stein, distiller and MP.

In 1824, Grace Stein married the older widower Sir Alexander Don (c. 1779–1826), MP for Roxburghshire and a friend of Sir Walter Scott, who remarked that Don's wife played the harp 'delightfully' (*Letters* 9, p. 228). They had two children, their son becoming the actor Sir William Henry Don who later sold his father's Berwickshire estate to pay debts. After Sir Alexander's death, Grace married in 1836 Lieutenant-Colonel, later General, Sir James Maxwell Wallace (1783–1867). As Lady Wallace, she began translating from the German in the 1850s, at first concentrating on children's books and contemporary women writers such as Elise Polko and Marie Petersen. She translated and prefaced a life of Schiller, and later translated for the publishers Longman a series of letters by the great composers – Mendelssohn (1862 and 1863); Mozart (1865) and Beethoven (1866) – which for a time were the standard editions. SR

• Scott, Sir W. (1932–79) *Letters*, 12 vols; *DNB* (1903); *ODNB* (2004).

WALLACE-DUNLOP, Marion, born Leys Castle, Inverness, 22 Dec. 1864; died Guildford 12 Sept. 1942. Illustrator, suffrage campaigner. Daughter of Lucy Dawson, and Robert Henry Wallace-Dunlop, of the Bengal Civil Service.

Marion Wallace-Dunlop studied at the Slade School and lived mostly in London, while identifying strongly with her Scottish roots, having been named after *Marion Braidfute, alleged wife of William Wallace. She illustrated two children's books, *The Magic Fruit Garden* (1899) and (with

M. Rivett Carnac) *Fairies, Elves and Flower Babies* (1899), and exhibited in Scotland, London and Paris. She became best known, however, as a suffrage activist. Always an active campaigner for the vote, she joined the militant WSPU in 1908, and was the movement's first hunger striker in July 1909, in Holloway, pioneering this form of protest. She helped design several of WSPU's pageant-like processions, on which the Edinburgh demonstration of 1909 was based. She faced prison again in 1911 after a window-smashing campaign. In 1916 she adopted a baby girl and cultivated a domestic lifestyle at Peaslake in Surrey. RA

• Beckett, J. and Cherry, D. (1988) *The Edwardian Era* (exhibition catalogue, Barbican); Houfe, S. (1978) *The Dictionary of British Book Illustrators 1800–1914*; Rosen, A. (1974) *Rise up Women!*; *ODNB* (2004) (see Dunlop, Marion Wallace-); *WSM*.

WALTON, Cecile, m1 **Robertson,** m2 **Gildard,** born Glasgow 29 March 1891, died Edinburgh 23 April 1956. Artist and illustrator. Daughter of Helen Henderson, and Edward Arthur Walton, RSA, artist.

Immersed in art from childhood, Cecile Walton attended ECA, 1908–10, meeting there her close friend *Dorothy Johnstone. She also studied in Paris and Florence. In 1912, she obtained her own studio in Torphichen Street, Edinburgh, marrying the artist Eric Robertson (1887–1941) in 1914. Her sons Gavril (b. 1915) and Edward (b. 1919) both feature in her work, including her striking picture *Romance* (1920, SNPG). The only woman to exhibit with the Edinburgh Group in 1913, she was one of their most fêted members at subsequent shows in 1919, 1920 and 1921. She exhibited at the RA and the RSA, winning the latter's Guthrie prize in 1921. Much admired for her imaginative figure paintings, with their 'decorative effect and skill of execution' (*Scotsman*, 1921), she also produced children's book illustrations. From 1926, she diversified into theatre design in Cambridge, her first marriage ending in divorce in 1927. The 1930s were spent organising the BBC Scottish *Children's Hour*; her second marriage, to BBC producer Gordon Gildard (b. 1899/1900) in 1936, ended in divorce in 1948, after which she settled permanently in Kirkcudbright. Her painting, having declined in output and inspiration, had begun to attract attention again, particularly her North African watercolours, at the time of her death. NJI

• ECA Archives: registers; NLS: Acc. 10425, unpub. memoir by Walton, C. (1950) 'More Lives than One'.

Walton, C. and Robertson, E. W. (1949) *The Children's Theatre Book for Young Actors and Dancers.*
Bourne, P. (2000) *Kirkcudbright: 100 years of an artists' colony*; Kemplay, J. (1983) *The Edinburgh Group*, (1991) *The Two Companions*; *ODNB* (2004); *The Scotsman*, 4 July 1921; Stephens, J. W. (1942) 'Cecile Walton and Dorothy Johnstone', *The Studio*, vol. 88.

WARD, Sarah, n. **Achurch,** born 1726/7, died 9 March 1771. Actor and theatre manager. Daughter of Thomas Achurch, actor, and his wife.

Sarah Ward's father was based in York. Her mother may have been the 'Mrs Achurch' appearing on a London playbill, 31 May 1734. The couple had at least four daughters. Sarah, aged 17, married actor and minor playwright Henry Ward (fl. 1734–58). Her theatrical career began in the mid-1740s at York. She and her husband transferred to Thomas Este's Taylor's Hall Company in Edinburgh in 1745. Following internal disputes, the company split into two groups, one led by Sarah Ward, which expanded to include Lacy Ryan and West Digges (c. 1725–86), and opened at the new Canongate theatre in Edinburgh on 16 November 1747, after an unsuccessful attempt to perform in Aberdeen. Sarah Ward then made her London debut at Covent Garden in 1748 as Cordelia to James Quin's Lear, and at Drury Lane in 1749, as Cordelia to David Garrick's Lear. (Garrick, however, found her intractable and unteachable.)

In 1752, she returned to Edinburgh with John Lee's company, now including Digges, with whom she began a long affair. In September 1752, she joined Thomas Sheridan's Smock Alley Company, and 1755 saw her return to Edinburgh, appearing as Mrs Sullen in *The Beaux' Stratagem*. In a complicated financial dispute, John Lee lost control of the Edinburgh theatre. James Callender was briefly appointed business manager, and West Digges, having rejoined the Edinburgh Company in September 1756, controlled 'artistic policy'. It was during this season, on 14 December, that Sarah Ward appeared as Lady Barnet (the character later re-named Lady Randolph) to Digges's Norval in the premiere of John Home's *Douglas*. It was one of her most popular and celebrated roles. She remained in Edinburgh until May 1758. After a season in Dublin, her relationship with West Digges finally ended and she returned to Covent Garden remaining there for the next twelve seasons. It is uncertain how many children Sarah Ward had: at least three with Henry Ward, of whom two, Thomas and Margaretta, became actors. She had

six or more children with West Digges, although how many survived to maturity is unknown. AS
• Dibdin, J. C. (1888) *The Annals of the Edinburgh Stage with an Account of the Dramatic Writing of Scotland*; Highfill, P. J. Jr., Burnim K. A. and Langhans, E. A. (1973–93) *A Biographical Dictionary of Actors . . . and other Stage Personnel in London, 1660–1800*, 16 vols (Bibl.); Lawson, R. (1917) *The Story of the Scots Stage*; *ODNB* (2004); *WWW in the Theatre* (14th edn.).

WARENNE, Ada de, c. 1123–c. 1178. Daughter of Elizabeth of Vermandois, and William de Warenne, Earl of Surrey.

Ada de Warenne's marriage to Henry (c. 1115–52), son of David I of Scotland, was part of the diplomatic manoeuvering around the Treaty of Durham (1139), made between Scotland and the supporters of Stephen of England. The couple had three sons and three daughters. Ada became known as 'mother of the kings of Scots'. Her witnessing of charters, first those made by her husband and later by her sons Malcolm IV and William the Lion, demonstrate her interest in political affairs. In 1152, Henry predeceased his father and Malcolm became heir to the throne. As a widow, Ada de Warenne was especially active as a religious benefactor. Her surviving charters are more numerous than those of any other noblewoman of the time. Sometime before 1159, she founded the convent of Haddington, which would become Scotland's largest convent, and endowed it liberally. She patronised several other male and female houses, including Dunfermline, St Andrews, Durham, and Nuneaton in Warwickshire. She spent most of her retirement after 1175 at Crail and Haddington. KP
• Chandler, V. (1981) 'Ada de Warenne, Queen Mother of Scotland', *Scot. Hist. Rev.*, 60 (Bibl.); Duncan, A. A. M. (1975) *Scotland: the making of the kingdom*; *ODNB* (2004) (see Ada [n. Ada de Warenne]).

WARRISTON, Lady *see* **LIVINGSTON, Jean** (1579–1600)

WATERSTON, Jane Elizabeth, born Inverness 18 Jan. 1843, died Cape Town, South Africa, 7 Nov. 1932. Missionary, educationalist and doctor. Daughter of Agnes Webster, and Charles Waterston, manager of the Caledonian Bank, Inverness.

The third of six children, Jane Waterston was taught by a governess, later attending Inverness Royal Academy. Her family belonged to the Church of Scotland but she was strongly influenced by her Highland nurse, who subscribed to the evangelical ethos of the Free Church. Deciding, against her family's wishes, to become a foreign missionary, on 9 October 1866, she became superintendent of the new Girls' Institution at Lovedale, South Africa, the Free Church's flagship mission station. Lovedale's ethos emphasised education for all, regardless of gender or race. The founders pursued an assimilationist policy, intended in part to create an African elite. (Fort Hare, at Lovedale, later produced a generation of anti-apartheid leaders, including Nelson Mandela.) By the 1860s, this ethos was in tension with colonial emphasis on 'native' industrial training and Jane Waterston's work reflected those shifts in missionary and imperial activity. Although seeking primarily to educate African girls as Christian housekeepers, she was proud of their academic achievements. The principal, Dr James Stewart, gave her a free hand. Forthright in her criticism of those (in Africa and Scotland) who showed less appreciation for the rights of female missionaries, she would defer to no one. Throughout her career, she was known with affection as *Noqataka*, 'the mother of activity'.

In 1874, she returned to Britain to train as a doctor. Her ambition was to work as a medical missionary in the Central African station, eventually established in 1877 as Livingstonia, under Dr Robert Laws (see Laws, Margaret). Her time as one of the first 14 students at the London School of Medicine for Women brought new intellectual challenges and a strengthening of feminist convictions. She completed her training and passed exams of the College of Physicians of Ireland in 1877–8 (later MD in Belgium). Despite attractive offers of employment in London, she remained committed to Livingstonia. She arrived in November 1879, but resigned after only four months and returned, disillusioned, to Lovedale. Her male colleagues had treated her with uncomprehending hostility and Robert Laws refused to acknowledge her superior medical and educational experience. Incensed at insinuations that she was there mainly to find a husband, she felt lonely and ostracised. She was critical of the harsh treatment of local people, which she saw as a reproach to Christianity. She established a dispensary at Lovedale but it was never recognised or funded by the Foreign Mission Committee and she had to give up in 1883. She moved to Cape Town, working in private practice and founding a pioneering free dispensary to provide medical services for women and children. For 50 years, her medical, educational philanthropic and political activities made her one of Cape Town's

most renowned citizens. A fervent imperialist, she was nevertheless committed to a non-racial South Africa, and remained at the forefront of struggles for women's education and rights. She refused a DBE, but was awarded an honorary LLD by Cape Town University and in 1925 was elected a fellow of the Royal College of Physicians in Ireland. Thousands mourned her passing, and an immense gathering of dignitaries paid her tribute. LO

• Bean, L. and van Heyningen, E. (eds) (1983) *The Letters of Jane Elizabeth Waterston 1866–1905.*
Brock, S. (1986) 'A broad, strong life', in J. Calder (ed.) *The Enterprising Scot*; Macdonald, L. A. O. (2000) *A Unique and Glorious Mission*; Shepherd, R. H. W. (1941) *Lovedale South Africa 1841–1941.*

WATSON, Alexandra Mary Chalmers (Mona), n. **Geddes,** CBE, born Calcutta 31 May 1872, died Kent 7 August 1936. Early medical graduate, Chief Controller WAAC and farmer. Daughter of Christina (Nellie) Anderson, and Auckland Campbell Geddes, civil engineer.

Eldest of five, Mona Geddes was part of a family originally Aberdonian, 'well known for scholarship and public work' (Gwynne-Vaughan 1936, p. 2). Her mother, **Christina Anderson** (1850–1914) was a founder of the Edinburgh School of Cookery and Domestic Economy, with *Christian Guthrie Wright, and campaigned for women's medical education. Mona's sister **Margaret Geddes** (1878–1956) was active in voluntary social work, became a member of Edinburgh Town Council, was the city's senior bailie, sat on many committees and was President of the SWRI. Their aunt, **Mary Marshall** n. **Anderson** (b. 1836) was one of the original medical students at Edinburgh with *Sophia Jex-Blake, but left to marry and qualified in 1880 in Paris, later joining the staff of Elizabeth Garrett Anderson's New Hospital for Women, London. Four Geddes aunts ran a girls' school in Atholl Crescent, Edinburgh, started by great-aunt Ann Anderson (1789–1855).

Alexandra Mary was called Mona by her first ayah. The family moved from India to Aberdeen and London, before settling in Edinburgh. Educated at St Leonards School, St Andrews, she graduated MBChM in 1894 from the Edinburgh Medical College for Women, delighting her mother, and obtained her MD from the University of Edinburgh in 1898, the first woman to do so. The same day she married a fellow graduate, Dr Douglas Chalmers Watson (1870–1946). They practised medicine together and she assisted him in editing the *Encyclopedia Medica.* They had two sons. Mona Chalmers Watson worked as Senior Physician at the Edinburgh Hospital for Women and was on the board of the Edinburgh Royal Infirmary. An active supporter of the suffrage campaign, she cared for hunger strikers leaving Perth prison.

In January 1917 the Army Council proposed to form a women's army auxiliary to free men to go to the front. At the suggestion of her brother, Auckland Geddes, Director of Recruitment at the War Office, Mona Chalmers Watson was appointed Chief Controller and senior officer of the WAAC, a post she held for its first, formative year. She recruited Helen Gwynne-Vaughan as Chief Controller (Overseas). Among problems they faced were status, unequal pay, morals – and skirt lengths. She resigned her appointment for family reasons, her rank then equivalent to Brigadier-General, and was made CBE in 1917. Becoming an adviser on Scottish health policy, she also established a model dairy, having inherited a farm at Fenton Barns in East Lothian. Prominent in many women's organisations, including the Edinburgh WCA, she was a founder of the Child Assault Protest Committee (1920) and a director and first chair of the feminist periodical *Time & Tide.* A 'member of innumerable committees, a person to be consulted in all emergencies' (ibid., p. 2), in the 1920s she became an expert member on the Scottish Board of Health's consultative councils and a member of the Advisory Committee on Nutrition. In 1933 she was appointed to the Committee on Scottish Health Services, whose report (the Cathcart Report) was a model for post-war British medical services and helped lay the foundation for a distinctive Scottish health system (see Douglas, Charlotte). Committed to enhancing the status of women in medicine, she was President of the SWMA and the BMWF. In relation to honours, she was quoted as saying : 'it has been honour enough to have lived through such great times for women, and to know that the generation after us will not have the same fight for liberty . . . But what glorious chances we have had to live through such years' (*Scotsman* 8 Aug. 1936). JLMJ/SI

• Cowper, J. M. (1957) 'Women on active service forty years ago', *The Army Quarterly*, vol. LXXIV, July (c. 1967) *A Short History of Queen Mary's Army Auxiliary Corps*; Crawford, E. (2002) *Enterprising Women: the Garretts and their circle*; Edinburgh WCA (1939) *Souvenir of Coming-of-Age 1918–1939*; Geddes, A. C. (1952) *The Forging of a Family*; Gwynne-Vaughan, H. (1936) *Old Comrades' Association Gazette*, Sept., p. 2 (obit.); Jenkinson, J. (2002) *Scotland's Health 1919–1948*; Mitchell, D. (1966) *Women on the Warpath*; *ODNB* (2004); *The Scotsman*, 8 August 1936 (obit.); *The Scotsman*, 7 Feb. 1956 (obit. Margaret Geddes).

WATSON, Elizabeth (Bessie),[‡] m. **Somerville,** born Edinburgh 13 July 1900, died Edinburgh 26 June 1992. Suffragette, piper, violin teacher. Daughter of Agnes Newton, and Horatio Watson, bookbinder.

At the age of seven, Bessie Watson's parents encouraged her to take up the unusual activity, for a girl, of playing the bagpipes, in order to strengthen her chest as a precaution against tuberculosis. She was invited to play in the procession and pageant of women from Scottish history on 9 October 1909 in Edinburgh, which was organised by the WSPU with *Flora Drummond in charge. She remembered: 'I rode on a float beside the Countess of Buchan in her cage (see Fife, Isobel of) and played at intervals along the way. It was an exciting day for a nine-year-old, but a more exciting one was to follow'. A few weeks later, Christobel Pankhurst came to Edinburgh to address a meeting at the King's Theatre and presented her with a brooch depicting Queen Boadicea (Boudicca) in her chariot. Bessie Watson gave the brooch to Margaret Thatcher when she became Prime Minister in 1979.

Bessie Watson became an active suffragette, helping at meetings and wearing purple, white and green ribbons in her hair. She was invited to lead the Scottish contingent, with other 'lady'pipers, at the Great Pageant in London on 17 June 1911: 'I suppose they thought here was I, a girl of ten at that time, doing something which they always associated with men'. In Edinburgh she accompanied prisoners returning to Holloway, playing on the platform as the train left Waverley Station. She also played to the suffragettes imprisoned in Calton Jail. At the age of 14, she became the only female member of the Highland Pipers' Society and won many piping awards. She went on to study French at the University of Edinburgh and became a violin teacher for Edinburgh schools. She founded the Broughton School Pipe Band, which she fostered for 27 years. In 1945, she married John Somerville, electrical contractor. HEC

• People's Story Oral History Archive: T60/87, Somerville, E., Unpublished memoirs.
AGC.

WATSON, Janet Vida, m. **Sutton,** born Hampstead 1 Sept. 1923, died Ashstead 29 March 1985. Geologist of Scottish rocks. Daughter of Katharine Margarite Parker, embryologist, and Professor David M. S. Watson, FRS, vertebrate palaeontologist.

Janet Watson, whose father was Scottish, was educated at South Hampstead High School, then at the University of Reading (1940–3), where H. L. Hawkins was her tutor and inspiration. A brief spell teaching was followed by a move to Imperial College, London (1945–7) and another first-class degree under H. H. Read. She then began the study of crystalline basement rocks to which she made a lifetime's contribution. In 1949, Janet Watson married fellow post-graduate, John Sutton (1919–92) and the two formed a professional partnership immensely fruitful in its discoveries. Their two children died at birth. They published, in 1951, the classic work on the Lewisian gneiss of North-West Scotland (Sutton and Watson 1951). Working in Sutherland and Ross, they distinguished two periods of metamorphism in Archaean rocks: older Scourian and younger Laxfordian, separated by intrusion of the Scourie Dykes now dated radiometrically to c. 2.4 billion years. They later worked on the Highland and Grampian rock successions.

Further work by Janet Watson focused on ore-forming processes in Pre-Cambrian crustal evolution, regional distribution of uranium, the Scottish Caledonides, and involved substantial collaboration with the IGS (now BGS). From the 1960s, she and her research team worked with Survey geologists in the Outer Hebrides, maps being published in 1982 and a memoir in 1994. Janet Watson also worked in Greenland, the Channel Islands, Italy and Tanganyika, and published some 65 research papers in peer-reviewed journals and symposium volumes. With H. H. Read, she authored a much-needed textbook, *Introduction to Geology* (2 vols, 1962–75). Her reputation was huge in geological circles and, in 1974, Imperial College appointed her to a Personal Chair. Among other honours, she was awarded the GSL Lyell Medal in 1973; was elected FRS in 1979, and was president of the GSL, 1982–4, the first woman to hold this office. Her papers include notebooks, maps and photographs illustrating her research across the Scottish Highlands and Islands. She worked to the end during her final illness. LS

• Library of the GSL: Papers and corr. of Janet Vida Watson, 1923–1985 (GB 0378 LDGSL 1078); Imperial College Archives: Papers and corr. of John Sutton (ref: GB 0098 B/SUTTON). Sutton, J. and Watson J. (1951) 'The Pre-Torridian metamorphic history of the Loch Torridon and Scourie areas . . . and its bearing on the chronological classification of the Lewisian', *Q. Journ. of the GLS*, CVI, 3, pp. 241–307; Watson, J. (1979) *Rocks and Minerals*, (1983) *Geology and Man*. Fettes, D. J. and Plant, J. A. (1995) 'Janet Watson', *Biographical Memoirs of Fellows of the Royal Society*, 41, pp. 499–514; *ODNB* (2004); *Who's Who* (1981). Additional information: Lou Donovan.

WATSON, Margaret Alexandra Hannan, born Glasgow 20 July 1873, died Glasgow 2 Sept. 1959. Headmistress. Daughter of Rebecca A. Hannan, and William Brown Watson, cotton manufacturer.

Margaret Watson was educated at Woodside Crescent School, Glasgow, and the University of St Andrews (MA 1897). In 1903, she co-founded Laurel Bank School, Glasgow, with **Janet Spens** (1876–1963), a graduate of the University of Glasgow, who went on to be a lecturer there in 1908 and Tutor to Women in Arts (1909). In 1908, Margaret Watson, usually known as Miss Hannan Watson in Glasgow, became sole proprietor and headmistress of the school, and in 1911 Janet Spens took up a post at Lady Margaret Hall, Oxford, where she had a long career. In 1920, Miss Hannan Watson turned Laurel Bank into an incorporated school; she remained head until 1938, was re-appointed co-headmistress during the wartime evacuation, and finally retired in 1944. Laurel Bank School amalgamated with The Park School in the 1990s to become Laurel Park School.

Miss Hannan Watson's wide-ranging educational, cultural and social welfare interests involved her in many activities in Glasgow, including secretary of the geographical section of the GRPS (from 1909) and vice-president of the GWCA and of the Franco-Scottish Society. She co-founded Phoenix Park Kindergarten (1907) and founded Hillside Holiday Home, Clynder, for convalescent working-class children, opened in 1919 by *Princess Louise. LRM

• Cameron, M. (1978) *The Laurel Bank Story: 1903–1978*; *Glasgow Herald*, 25 Oct. 1938 and 4 Sept. 1959 (obit. Watson); Mitchell, E. (ed.) (1953) *Laurel Bank School, 1903–1953*; *ODNB* (2004); *Oxford Magazine*, 30 May 1963 (obit. Spens); *The Times*, 16 Jan. 1963 (obit. Spens).

WATT, Christian,‡ m. **Sim,** born Broadsea, near Fraserburgh, 24 Feb. 1833, died Aberdeen 20 June 1923. Domestic servant, fishwife, writer. Daughter of Helen Noble, fishwife, and James Watt, fisherman.

From a large North East fishing family, Christian Watt grew up in Broadsea, near Fraserburgh. From the age of eight she worked as a domestic servant, as a cook for the men fishing off the west coast and Shetland, and helped her mother with the fish. She continued at school during the winter, when she was able to attend. Five of her seven brothers died in 1854: two drowned off New Jersey, one died in Australia and two were killed at sea in the Crimean War. She travelled to New York in 1856 to claim an inheritance from one of the brothers, working there for eight months as a domestic. In New York she 'came face to face with reality, and the bitterness that burns in coloured folks' hearts towards those who brought them there' (Fraser 1983, p. 62). She married James Sim (1831–77), a fisherman from Pitullie, on 2 December 1858. They had ten children, two of whom died, aged 13 and 11, before James Sim drowned in 1877. The deaths contributed to her breakdown and first admission to Aberdeen Royal Mental Asylum, Cornhill. When she returned home, her fish round had been taken and she could not get washing work either. On her second stay in Cornhill she began the memoir for which she is known, written between 1880 and her death. She was shown 'how to keep a journal, and to make notes as something came into my head to revive my memory, and to write it down before I forgot . . .' (ibid., p. 112). After her final breakdown in 1879, the household was sold up and her younger children divided among relatives and friends. Her remaining 45 years were spent at Cornhill, where she worked in the laundry and was allowed out on home visits.

Her memoirs give an exceptional view of the times and are full of descriptions of the privations of her community, a changing Scotland and the wider world, as well an intricate record of her own family and work history, relationships and travels. Some doubt has been expressed about their authenticity but the facts of her life are not disputed. Even if the memoirs were ghosted by someone else, they retain value as recording an otherwise hidden life. An example of their vivid style is the description of class structures at Philorth House, near Fraserburgh, where she had worked for Lord Saltoun's family:

. . . there were a lot of daughters . . . a bunch of useless articles . . . a great gulf lay between them and us. I would look at the avenue which we were not allowed to use, it was like a mighty river of power, but petered out at the gate on the Aberdeen road, the publick [sic] highway which laird and tinkie man shared, the only thing they had in common. (ibid., p. 40)

For her 90th birthday she had her portrait painted; 'I don't work much now. . . . A lass . . . does my shopping, so I am like a lady of leisure' (ibid., p. 154). ABC
• Fraser, D. (ed.) (1983) *The Christian Watt Papers*; *ODNB* (2004).

WATT, Eilidh (Helen), n. **MacAskill,** born Skinidin, Skye, 22 Jan. 1908, died Inverness 25 August 1996. Writer. Daughter of Chirsty MacLean, and Malcolm MacAskill, blacksmith.

A well-known Gaelic writer and broadcaster, as well as a secondary school teacher of English, Eilidh Watt specialised in accounts of paranormal phenomena. She professed to have second sight, though in interviews she sometimes qualified this claim since her experiences were not as a rule of a visual nature, as traditional seers described the operation of their clairvoyance, but rather states of emotion which she herself was able to interpret. Her willingness to talk about such experiences was, and still is, highly unusual: in Gaelic society, those who are reputed to have second sight are generally reticent. Her books are written in expressive, idiomatic Gaelic. *La a'Choin Duibh* (1973) (The Day of the Black Dog) is a children's book, the title taken from ballad and folktale. More significant is *Gun Fhois* (1987) (Without Tranquillity), a work of 12 short stories whose leading motif is an awareness of the supernatural. The introduction discusses various aspects of this awareness, including that of evil, and the nature of the people who possess it. JMACI
• Watt, E., Works as above, and (1989) 'Some personal experience of the second sight', in H. E. Davidson (ed.) *The Seer in Celtic and Other Traditions*. *HSWW* (Bibl.).

WATTS, Mary Seton, n. **Fraser Tytler,** born Ahmednaggar, India, 25 Nov. 1849, died 6 Sept. 1938. Artist, designer, craftworker. Daughter of Etheldred St Barbe, and Charles Edward Fraser Tytler, colonial civil servant.

Mary Fraser Tytler was brought up on her grandparents'estate, Aldourie, Inverness-shire, and with her parents in Sanquhar, Forres. Her artistic career began in making props for London photographer Julia Margaret Cameron, followed by studies in Dresden and Rome. She enrolled at the South Kensington Art School in 1870, met the painter George Frederic Watts (1817–1904) that year, and studied at the Slade School of Art from 1872 to 1873. She was taught clay modelling by the sculptor

Aimée-Jules Dalou. Seeking a philanthropic outlet, she involved herself in the London Home Arts movement, starting a clay-modelling class for Whitechapel shoeblacks in 1884, then in 1895 classes for the villagers of Compton near Guildford, Surrey. She and G. F. Watts, whom she married (succeeding Ellen Terry) on 20 November 1886, had settled there and, in 1895, offered a chapel for the new village cemetery. Designed with George Redmayne, it was decorated by the villagers in modelled terracotta as a 'supreme example of the Home Arts ideal' (Franklin Gould 1998, p. 73). She had already used painted *gesso duro* to decorate their own home 'Limnerslease', built in 1891. Her chapel (1898) blended contemporary cultural and design theory (Cumming 2002, pp. 19–24). The Compton ceramic workers, formally grouped as the Potters' Art Guild and after her death as the Compton Pottery, also made terracotta gravestones, domestic decorative wares and gardenware. Under her direction, a new pottery started after 1900 on the Aldourie estate. Always known as 'Mrs G. F. Watts', she also designed carpets, embroidered banners, metalwork and bookbindings. Her role as 'keeper of the flame' of her husband's work has been criticised and may also have overshadowed her own work. EC

• Watts Gallery, Compton, Guildford: Journals and corr., M. S. Watts.

M. S. Watts (1912) *George Frederic Watts: the annals of an artist's life* (3 vols).

Boreham, L. (2000) 'Compton Chapel', *The Victorian*, March, pp. 10–13; Cumming, E. (2002) 'Patterns of life: the art and design of Phoebe Anna Traquair and Mary Seton Watts', in B. Elliott and J. Helland (eds) *Women Artists and the Decorative Arts 1880–1935*, pp. 15–34; Franklin Gould, V. (1993) *The Watts Chapel*, (1998) *Mary Seton Watts (1849–1938)*; *ODNB* (2004) (Watts, George Frederic).

WEIR, Beatrix, fl. 1609. Infanticide suspect.

Beatrix Weir was the wife of John Ferry, a bookbinder. Along with Jonet Lyn, John Young and James Craw, she was tried for infanticide before the Privy Council in November 1609. One Bessie Pollok alleged that Beatrix had committed adultery with John Young, a Dumfries notary, and as a result of this Beatrix became pregnant. In desperation Beatrix visited Jonet Lyn in Glasgow who 'gaif unto the said Beatrix drinkis to have distroyit the bairne in hir bellie'. This abortifacient worked and the foetus was then cast into a lime hole by James Craw. The Privy Council investigated the case further, but nothing more is known about it.

However, it does prove that early modern Scotswomen knew how to facilitate abortions. Jonet Lyn may even have been a midwife who had legitimate access to abortifacients to assist women who were suffering miscarriages. MMM

• *RPC*, viii, pp. 373, 375, 380, 406.

WEIR, Jean (aka **Grizel),** born c. 1604, died Edinburgh 12 April 1670. Schoolmistress. Tried for incest and witchcraft.

Jean Weir provides an interesting example of witchcraft beliefs. At her trial she stated that her gift for witchcraft came from her mother, but that she and her brother, the better-known 'Major' Thomas Weir, with whom she shared a home in Edinburgh, had sworn allegiance to the devil. Referring to the Queen of Faerie, her interrogation illustrates an overlap between witchcraft and fairy beliefs. While Major Weir is remembered as a sorcerer, he was tried only for incest. Jean was tried for both, although convicted solely of incest; this being sufficient for execution, the assize 'passed by' the alleged sorcery (Scott-Moncrieff 1905, p. 14). The Major's sorcery was of a spectacular, diabolic variety; his sister sought chiefly to increase her capacity to spin wool. Contemporaries noted the 'foolish' nature of her death, where she attempted to throw off her clothes and expose herself to the greatest shame possible before her execution. SAM

• Arnot, H. (ed.) (1785) *A Collection and Abridgement of Celebrated Criminal Trials in Scotland, from AD 1536 to 1784*; Hickes, G. (1695) *Ravillac Redivivus*; *ODNB* (2004) (Weir, Thomas); Roughead, W. (1913) *Twelve Scots Trials*; Scott-Moncrieff, W. G. (ed.) (1905) *Records of the Proceedings of the Justiciary Court Edinburgh, 1661–1678*, vol. 2; Sinclair, G. (1685) *Satan's Invisible World Discovered*.

WEIR, Molly (Mary), m. **Hamilton,** born Glasgow 17 March 1910, died Middlesex 28 Nov. 2004. Actor. Daughter of Jeanie Davidson, and Thomas Weir, journeyman engineer.

Molly Weir and three siblings, including her brother, naturalist and broadcaster Tom Weir, were brought up in a room and kitchen in a Springburn tenement. Her father died in the First World War and her mother painted carriages in Cowlairs railway works to feed the four children. From mother and granny, Molly Weir imbibed the virtues of hard work, thrift and self-discipline that informed her many acting roles as a no-nonsense Scottish maid or housekeeper. She left school at 16 for office work, becoming British shorthand-typing champion. After amateur dramatics, her professional career began in Scottish radio in the 1930s, and she became one of the first Scottish stars of British radio and television. With Sandy Hamilton, whom she married in 1939, Molly Weir moved to London in 1945, to work in theatre. Fame came through roles in popular radio comedy shows of the 1940s and 1950s: *The McFlannels*, *ITMA* (*It's That Man Again*) and *Life with the Lyons*. Her screen debut in *Comin' Thro' the Rye* (1947) led to more than a dozen feature films. Television work included sitcoms, dramas, panel shows and commercials (for a well known floor cleaner), and she played Hazel McWitch in the children's serial *Rentaghost* (1976–84). Of diminutive stature (4ft 10in) and red-haired, her bustling energy, infectious laugh, sceptical manner and unmistakable Glaswegian voice all gave her an inimitable identity. She also wrote radio scripts, cookbooks, journalism and eight volumes of memoirs, the first three of which, *Shoes were for Sunday* (1970), *Best Foot Forward* (1972) and *A Toe on the Ladder* (1973), became a best-selling trilogy. Molly Weir was named Scotswoman of the Year in 2000. Her ashes were scattered on Loch Lomond. BF

• Weir, M. (1996) *Trilogy of Scottish Childhood* and other works.
McBeth, J., 'Final Curtain for "sparky wee Glesga wummin" Molly Weir', *The Scotsman*, 30 Nov. 2004; Miller, P., 'A beloved Scots star for generations', *The Herald*, 30 Nov. 2004; *Herald, Guardian, Independent, Scotsman*, 1 Dec. 2004 (obits).

WEIR, Sharman Elizabeth, born Barrhead, near Glasgow, 31 March 1959, died Glasgow 22 Oct. 1999. Theatre manager and musician. Daughter of Mary Miller Wilson, comptometer operator, and John Catterson Weir, commercial traveller.

Sharman Weir attended the John Neilson School, Paisley, before studying music at the University of Glasgow and flute at the RSAMD. She worked professionally as a singer and flautist between 1981 and 1984 and maintained her interest in music as a member of Paisley Abbey Choir. Thereafter she changed career by gaining a postgraduate diploma in business information technology (1985) from the University of Strathclyde. She then worked in software management for BP in Glasgow and London. In 1992, she undertook another major career change when she joined the Citizens' Theatre in Glasgow as business manager, becoming general manager two years later. The tenure (1970–2003) of the artistic directors Giles Havergal, Philip Prowse and

Robert David McDonald was celebrated for artistic innovation and bold European repertoire but a significant part of that success was a fiscal and managerial probity. In this, Sharman Weir was an essential figure, much relied upon and missed dreadfully following her premature death in the latter stages of her first pregnancy. Her death resulted in one of Scotland's longest fatal accident inquiries, which found significant failings on the part of the Queen Mother's Maternity Hospital, Glasgow. Sharman Weir was survived by her partner, Malcolm Fletcher, and their daughter, Mairi. AS

• *The Herald*, Oct. 1999 (obit.); *The Scotsman*, 25 Oct. 1999 (obit.).

WELLS, Annie Katharine (Nannie Katharin), n. **Smith,** born Fordyce 29 Oct. 1875, died Oxford 18 March 1963. Scottish nationalist, writer and anti-fascist. Daughter of Jane Garrow, and William Smith, rector of Milnes School, Fochabers.

Nannie Katharin Smith was educated at her father's school in Fochabers, in Berlin and Paris, and the University of St Andrews (LLA). She married Bernard Wells, newspaper advertiser, in 1901 and had three sons; one was killed during the Second World War. She worked in the Foreign Office during the First World War, then spent time in Oxford before returning to Scotland where she became involved in nationalist politics. From 1929, she was secretary depute of the National Party of Scotland and then of the SNP. She was also secretary of the EWCA.

Nannie K. Wells wrote regularly for nationalist publications such as the *Scots Independent* and the *Free Man*. Between 1932 and 1934, her *Free Man* articles emphasised the need for a more articulate political programme, while challenging those who would put internationalism before the need to improve the state of their own country (16 July 1932). In 'The Financial Impotence of Scotland: An Infamous Libel' (*Free Man* 2 April 1932), she argued the case for an economic independence from Westminster which would operate in the context of Scottish, not London, priorities. Most importantly, she was one of the first Scottish nationalists to speak out against Hitler and Mussolini; her article 'Fascism and the Alternative' (*Free Man* 26 August 1933) urging that 'the power of this Challenge' should not be underestimated: 'Democracy is hardly on its trial any more; it has been condemned and dismissed in too many countries'. The article ends with the thought that Scotland may have the capacity to demonstrate the necessary qualities 'of courageous decision, of endurance, of determined resistance to these false ideals . . . within us, Leadership and Liberty may again be reconciled as they have been more than once in our history as a Nation'.

She was also friendly with members of the interwar literary revival, popularly known as the Scottish Renaissance. In *Helen Cruickshank's *Octobiography* (1976) and Gordon Wright's illustrated biography of Hugh MacDiarmid (1977), a photograph shows her in the garden of Dinnieduff, Cruickshank's home in Corstorphine, at a party given to celebrate MacDiarmid's return from Liverpool in 1931. Helen Cruickshank describes long arguments between Wells and MacDiarmid there, forcing her mother to scold: 'Ye baith speak far owre muckle'. In a letter to *Florence Marian McNeill of 13 November 1934, Nannie K. Wells gives news of some of the 'London Scots' she has been seeing while looking after Donald Carswell and his son during *Catherine Carswell's visit to Ivy Litvinov in Moscow. She envisages 'a colony of us all, in our early old age, in the north. Eric Linklater, Edwin and *Willa [Muir], Don and Cathie (?) [Carswell] and you and me and Helen, with rapid and vivid sallies, raids over the Border for loot and riches'. Marian McNeill describes her in her obituary as a 'colourful personality' and 'a perfervid Scot [who] retained her enthusiasms and youthful vitality until very near the end' (*Scotsman* 1963).

Nannie K. Wells also wrote poetry and is represented in *Modern Scottish Women Poets* (2003). She collaborated in an unpublished biography of Alexander Stewart, the Wolf of Badenoch, with Hugh MacDiarmid, who also wrote the introduction to her pamphlet on Byron, in which she claimed his genius as Scottish. Her affinity with MacDiarmid's attempts to revitalise a stubborn Scotland can been seen in the witty definition she gave of her own recreational activity: 'managing rheumaticky minds with modern electric shock treatment' (*SB*). MPM/BP

• NLS: MSS 26195-259, F. Marian McNeill archive papers 1930–40.

Wells, Nannie K., Works as above, and see *HSWW* (Select Bibl.) and website: www.eup.ed.ac.uk

Cruickshank, H. (1976) *Octobiography*; *HSWW*; *MSWP*; *SB*; *The Scotsman*, 22 March 1963 (obit.); Wright, G. (1977) *MacDiarmid*.

WEMYSS, Lady Margaret, born Falkland 24 Sept. 1630, died 1648. Manuscript owner and lute-player.

Daughter of Anna Balfour, and David, 2nd Earl of Wemyss.

The eighth of 11 children, Margaret Wemyss had a short life, dying in the period after May 1648, before her eighteenth birthday. She owned a beautifully preserved manuscript of Renaissance music and poetry (NLS: Dep. 314/23). Preserved among the Sutherland family papers, it remained relatively unknown until the 1980s, when the musicologist Matthew Spring recognised its importance. Her signature appears several times on the volume's flyleaf and on the first and final folios in a variety of spellings ('Margarat Wymes', 'Margaret Weeyes'), perhaps reflecting the fact that the manuscript was begun on 5 June 1643, when she was only 12 years old. For the next six years she was to write music and poetry in it, though other more mature hands can be detected which may have included her sister **Jean Wemyss** (1629–1717). Margaret's comment that 'all the Lesons behind this are learned ut of my Sisteres book' implies that Jean herself learnt the lute and had a 'playing' or 'practice' book of her own. After her younger sister's death, and on her marriage to the 14th Earl of Sutherland, she probably took possession of the book.

The manuscript epitomises the musical education which young aristocratic women received. Its music suggests that the traditional 10-course lute and also the 12-course were used. Margaret Wemyss' book is certainly tutelary in nature, an aid to learning poetry, songs, and solo lute music, though the identity of her lute teacher is unknown. Many of the transcribed tunes are Scottish, perhaps reflecting what was popular at the time, and some lyrics are by Scottish Renaissance poets. The opening section may represent her first attempts at lute tablature; the second section displays a bolder and more confident hand, containing pieces attributed to French lute masters. Her growing strength and confidence as a lutenist is therefore portrayed.

Usually referred to as the Wemyss manuscript, the volume is of immense value, attesting the richness of 17th-century aristocratic Scottish culture. It is also a young woman's lovingly compiled possession, a personal and practical artefact which resonates beyond her time in the many later recordings of the music which it preserves. SD

• NLS: Dep. 314/23.

HSWW; Phillips, R. (ed.) (1995) *Music for the Lute in Scotland*, vol. 1, *20 Pieces in Tablature and Transcription for all*

Instruments; Spring, M. (1987) 'The Lady Margaret Wemyss Manuscript', *The Lute*, 27.

WEST, Rebecca *see* **FAIRFIELD, Cecily Isabel** (1892–1983)

WHISKEY, Nancy (Anne Alexandra Young Wilson), m. **Kelly,** born Glasgow 4 March 1935, died Leicester 1 Feb. 2003. Singer. Daughter of Elizabeth Gibson, and Robert Wilson, textile factory worker.

Nancy Whiskey's father taught her to play the guitar, and she performed in Glasgow folk venues. She took her stage name from the chorus of the Glasgow folk song 'The Calton Weaver'. In 1955, she moved to London with jazz pianist Bob Kelly (d. 1999), whom she later married. She became the vocalist with the Chas McDevitt Skiffle Group. They recorded 'Freight Train', which appeared in the 1957 film *The Tommy Steele Story* and became a major hit in Britain and the USA. Their album 'The Intoxicating Miss Whiskey' was successful, but the follow-up album did less well. Nancy Whiskey went on to record three solo singles and an LP with studio backing group, the Skifflers, but never repeated the success of 'Freight Train', and performed less frequently after the birth in 1958 of her daughter, Yancey. She played the Albert Hall in 1997 with other stars including Lonnie Donegan, celebrating 40 years of skiffle. FJ
• *The Guardian*, 8 Feb. 2003 (obit.); *The Scotsman*, 5 Feb. 2003 (obit.).

WHITE, Freda, born Edinburgh 29 Oct. 1894, died Edinburgh 24 May 1971. Author and journalist. Daughter of Ada Walton, and Thomas White, solicitor.

Freda White was the sixth of seven children of a family in comfortable circumstances. Her father died when she was six, and she was brought up in Edinburgh by her intelligent and forceful mother. She was educated at St Leonards School and Somerville College, Oxford (1913–16), receiving her BA in 1921 when degrees for women were first awarded by that university. The year between school and university she spent in Geneva studying geology and perfecting her French. The death at sea of her beloved brother, Alexander, of wounds received in the Dardanelles, made her a life-long campaigner for peace. From 1916 until 1918, through contact with *Elsie Inglis, she worked for the Serbian Relief Fund in Corsica. She taught in Edinburgh for a short while but soon returned to the wider world, working between Geneva and

London for the League of Nations Union 1922–39 and writing League of Nations handbooks and numerous political pamphlets. In 1940, she became the assistant editor of the *New Statesman* under the editorship of Kingsley Martin. From 1943, she was information officer for the left-wing *Daily Herald*. She returned to Scotland as the Scottish officer of the United Nations Association (UNA) and stood unsuccessfully for the Labour Party as a parliamentary candidate. In 1954 she left the UNA to travel in and write about France. Her *Three Rivers of France* (1951) was for many years a steady seller and is regarded as a classic of travel writing. In her later years, a small and determined figure in her trademark tweeds and lacy jumpers, she was respected in the intellectual and political life of Edinburgh. She had an incisive, sometimes sharp tongue, counterbalanced by a keen intelligence, deep concern for her family and friends and a life-long political commitment. LH
• United Nations publications (selected): (1926) *Mandates*, (1932) *Traffic in Arms*, (1946) *United Nations, the first assembly*, (1946) *Conflict over Palestine*.
White, F., Work as above, and (1964) *West of the Rhone: Languedoc, Rouissillon, the Massif Central*, (1968) *Ways of Aquitaine*.
The Association for Senior Members, Somerville College.
Private information: Mrs Virginia Holt (niece).
Personal knowledge.

WHYTE, Betsy (or Bessie), n. **Townsley,** born at Old Rattray 7 Nov. 1919, died at Lizziewells Farm, Collessie, Fife, 13 August 1988. Storyteller. Daughter of Margaret Johnstone, and Alexander Townsley, hawker, farm labourer.

Betsy Townsley was born into a family of tent-dwelling travellers. They lived a hard life in Perthshire and Angus, doing seasonal farm work. In winter, the family 'housed up' in Brechin where she attended school, being an able pupil. But a scholarship to Brechin High School brought her up against prejudice among fellow pupils, as she later recounted in *The Yellow on the Broom* (1979), a title referring to her father's promise to take his family back on the road in May, when the broom was in flower. In 1939, she married Bryce Whyte, who was wounded in the Seaforth Highlanders in the Second World War. They settled in Montrose and brought up their family there, continuing to do seasonal farm work. Linda Williamson and Peter Cook of the School of Scottish Studies (SSS) met Betsy Whyte through Linda's husband, storyteller Duncan Williamson, and encouraged her to write her life story. *The Yellow on the Broom*, written by hand in exercise books with very little editing, was a bestseller, being adapted for the stage by the Winged Horse Theatre Co. and successfully restaged in Perth in 2004. Well known at festivals and on radio and TV as a storyteller, Betsy Whyte also sang ballads, notably 'Young Johnstone', which came from her mother's family. Her second book, *Red Rowans and Wild Honey* (1990), was completed before her sudden death in 1988, at the Auchtermuchty Festival of the Traditional Music and Song Association of Scotland. A wise, perceptive person with the gift of second sight, Betsy Whyte spoke of her love of those whose ballads and stories she had inherited. Her traditional stories included 'The Cat and the Hard Cheese', which appeared with others in the SSS magazine *Tocher*. SMDOUG

• Whyte, B., Works as above.
Personal knowledge.

WHYTE, Helen Kathleen Ramsay (Kath), MBE, born Arbroath 4 August 1909, died Newton Mearns 12 Feb. 1996. Embroiderer and educator. Daughter of Betsy D. Matthews, lady's maid, and Henry S. Whyte, engineer.

Kath Whyte spent her early life in India and Scotland, attending Loreto Convent School, Darjeeling, Arbroath High School, and Gray's School of Art, Aberdeen (Diploma with distinction in Design and Decorative Art 1932). After teaching in Aberdeen schools and at Gray's, she was appointed embroidery and weaving lecturer at the GSA in 1948, and became head of department, retiring in 1974. She emphasised drawing as a foundation for good design and revitalised the course, introducing techniques such as machine embroidery, while also advocating traditional methods employed in innovative ways. Her thought-provoking teaching inspired generations of students, as did her concern that embroidery be accepted as a valid means of artistic expression. The GSA Embroidery Group, which she started, held its first exhibition in 1957. An adviser to the SED and validator for English DipAD courses, she was the outstanding influence of her generation on embroidery in Scotland. Her many articles and her book, *Design in Embroidery* (1969), received world recognition. A practising embroiderer, she undertook many commissions, and is probably best known for her ecclesiastical work (e.g. in Bearsden, Eaglesham and Mayfield, Edinburgh), also shown at exhibitions of ecclesiastical embroidery in

St Paul's Cathedral (1968) and Hereford Cathedral (1976). She embroidered a silk stole, using pearls from the River Tay, presented to *Queen Elizabeth the Queen Mother at the Tay Road Bridge opening in 1966. An honorary member of the GSWA, she was made MBE in 1969 for services to art education, and in 1987 a retrospective of her work was held by Scottish branches of the Embroiderers' Guild. SH

• GSA Archives: DC 029 (Papers and textile work of Kath Whyte; notebooks and corr. from Gray's School of Art); samples of work at RMS, GSA, V&A, etc.
Whyte, K. (1969, 1983) *Design in Embroidery.*
Arthur, L. (1989) *Kathleen Whyte, Embroiderer*; *The Herald*, 15 Feb. 1996 (obit.).

WIGHAM, Eliza, born Edinburgh 23 Feb. 1820, died Dublin 3 Nov. 1899. Campaigner for women's suffrage, anti-slavery, peace and temperance. Daughter of Jane Richardson, and John Wigham, cotton and shawl manufacturer.

Eliza Wigham was born into a network of Quaker reforming families. Her father was a prominent abolitionist and a leader of the Edinburgh Emancipation Society. Throughout her happy childhood, she was surrounded by 'some of the leading spirits of progress and philanthropy' (Society of Friends 1901, p. 166). She lost her mother, her eldest sister and a young brother when she was about 10 years old, but the family and the network were strengthened by her father's second marriage, in 1840, to **Jane Smeal** (1801/2–88), daughter of William Smeal, a Glasgow Quaker and tea merchant. Jane Smeal, educated at the Quaker Ackworth School in Yorkshire, had led the Glasgow Ladies Emancipation Society, and published a pamphlet with *Elizabeth Pease [Nichol], *Address to the Women of Great Britain* (1838), calling on women to form female anti-slavery associations and speak at public meetings. Her relationship with Eliza Wigham became one of committed co-operation in reform.

Eliza Wigham, leader of the Edinburgh Ladies Emancipation Society, has been described as one of six key women in the British 'transatlantic anti-slavery sisterhood' (Midgley 1992, p. 132). From the mid-1840s to the 1870s she corresponded with leading radical abolitionists in the United States. She attended the Edinburgh Meeting House, travelled around Scotland and acted as a Quaker minister. She also worked for the repeal of the Contagious Diseases Acts. In the 1870s she joined the women's temperance movement; as an

Executive Committee member of the BWTA and the Scottish Christian Union, she worked to promote prohibition legislation. From 1870 to the 1890s, she actively lobbied for legislation on women's political, social and economic rights, becoming Secretary of ENSWS and serving on the executive committee and the legal committee of the SWLF. As a Quaker, she was fundamentally opposed to war, advocating a High Court of Nations to settle all international disputes (*Women's Penny Paper* 1890, p. 409). Eliza Wigham remained single, nursing her stepmother through a long illness until her death. Ten years later, herself infirm, she went to live with family in Dublin, where she died. MKS

• Library of the Society of Friends, London: 'Dictionary of Quaker Biography' (n.d.) unpublished; Knox, W. W. J. (2006) *The Lives of Scottish Women*; Midgley, C. (1992) *Women Against Slavery: the British campaigns, 1750–1870*; *ODNB* (2004); Society of Friends (1901) 'Eliza Wigham', *Annual Monitor*, 53, pp. 165–86; *Women's Penny Paper* 2, 87, 21 June 1890, pp. 409–10.
www.spartacus.schoolnet.co.uk/REsmeal.htm

WILKIE, Annot Erskine, m. **Robinson,** born Montrose 8 June 1874, died Perth 29 Sept. 1925. Suffragette and Labour activist. Daughter of Catherine Jane Erskine, teacher, and John Wilkie, draper.

After a straitened childhood, Annot Wilkie attended Montrose Academy, where she worked as a pupil teacher until she was 16. She went to teacher training college before taking external classes at the University of St Andrews (LLA, 1901). She was a teacher in Dundee and Lochgelly, a member of the ILP and in 1906 became the first secretary of the Dundee branch of the WSPU. Her sister **Helen Wilkie** (b. 1882), possibly also a teacher, organised women, many from the textile workers' union, for a WSPU march in Edinburgh in 1907. Helen Wilkie was part of the deputation that met Churchill in 1909; in 1912 she became secretary of Dundee WFL. She was also a prolific letter writer to the Dundee newspapers and a gifted orator.

All her life, Annot Wilkie divided her loyalties between the Labour Party and the suffrage movement. In 1907, she moved to Manchester, joining the local branch ILP and becoming a WSPU organiser. The following year, she married Sam Robinson (1869/70–1937), a working-class clerk, party activist, propaganda secretary of the Central Manchester ILP and active supporter of the militant suffrage movement. They had two daughters but the marriage broke up within five years, following his alcoholism and violence; Annot Robinson brought up the children. In February 1908, she and other WSPU members tried to gain entry into the House of Commons hidden in a furniture van. She was sentenced to six months imprisonment but by June was back on a soap-box in Hyde Park. In 1910, she became a part-time organiser for the WLL and put forward a conference resolution condemning the Labour Party leadership for its lack of support for the women's franchise or the WLL. She also supported liberalised and equal divorce. The following year she publicly disagreed with the League's position on suffrage and soon afterwards moved to the NUWSS as a full-time organiser. She was active at the Midlothian by-election in September 1912. When war came, as a pacifist, she resigned from the NUWSS and helped to found the WILPF, meanwhile working on behalf of young women munitions workers. In 1917, she was part of the Women's Peace Crusade. After the war she was employed by WILPF as an organiser and travelled in Britain, USA and Holland on its behalf, until in 1922 it could no longer afford to employ her full-time and she had to return to teaching. Back in Scotland, she taught in Newburgh, Fife. She died suddenly during an operation in Perth Royal Infirmary. Her obituarist, her friend Ellen Wilkinson, described her as 'a big woman and a big personality' with 'an exquisite sense of the ridiculous and a sharp tongue' (*The Women's Leader* 1925). IMH

• *AGC*; Collette, C. (1989) *For Labour and for Women*; *SS*; *ODNB* (2004) (see Robinson, Annot Erskine); *The Women's Leader*, 6 Nov. 1925 (obit.); *WSM*.

WILLIAMS, Gertrude Alice Meredith, n. **Williams,** born Everton, Lancs., 17 June 1877, died Devon 3 March 1934. Sculptor. Daughter of Sarah Bland, and David Williams, MD.

Alice Williams studied in Liverpool and Paris. Following marriage in 1906 to Morris Meredith Williams (1881–1973), artist, with whom she collaborated, the couple settled in Edinburgh, where her husband became art master at Fettes College and she exhibited regularly. Her early work was influenced by Rodin, but she later found her own tightly modelled style, excelling at bas relief. Her main legacy is architectural sculpture, often in memorials and ecclesiastical settings.

In Sir Robert Lorimer's Scottish National War Memorial at Edinburgh Castle, she did the bronze bas relief frieze of 100 typical uniformed military personnel in procession, modelled on her husband's sketches from his wartime experience. Among other work there is the hanging figure of St Michael in the Shrine. She and Lorimer won the competition for the Paisley war memorial on which is her equestrian group 'Spirit of the Crusaders'. She also worked with the architect Harold Tarbolton. Having exhibited at the Paris Salon and with major UK organisations, she is represented in public and private collections and was an associate of the RBS. LAMB

• NGS, Scottish Sculpture Archive: photographs of Williams' work in RCAHMS, RA, RSA, SSA, RGIFA catalogues. Savage, P. (1980) *Lorimer and the Edinburgh Craft Designers*; *The Scotsman*, 5 March 1934 (obit.); *The Times*, 7 March 1934 (obit.).

WILLIAMSON, Euphemia (Effie), m. Dickson, born Galashiels 29 March 1846, died Innerleithen 16 May 1929. Woollen mill-worker and poet. Daughter of **Agnes Milne** (1815–82), poet (aka 'Mrs Williamson'), and James Williamson, woollen slubber.

Effie Williamson spent most of her life in the Borders, apart from eight years when her family moved to Cork. She worked as a power-loom weaver in Galashiels and, perhaps inspired by her mother's publication of poems and essays, began to write, as she declared, amid the din of the factory. Her first poems were published in *The Border Advertiser* with the encouragement of John Russell, the editor. 'Effie' became a well-known figure in the Borders, her verses appearing in *Chambers's Journal*, the *People's Friend* and American and colonial periodicals. Poetry inspired by landscape was included in Edwards's *Modern Scottish Poets*. She issued two volumes, *The Tangled Web* and *Peaceable Fruits*, hymns and religious verse apparently read with appreciation by Gladstone. In 1889, she married a widower, woollen merchant Gavin Dickson. LS

• Williamson, E., Works as above. Edwards, D. H. (1881) *Modern Scottish Poets*; Hall, R. (ed.) (1898) *History of Galashiels*.

WILLIAMSON, Isabel, n. Bras, born c. 1430, died Edinburgh c. Oct. 1493. Merchant. Probably daughter of Thomas Bras.

Isabel Bras married the prominent Edinburgh merchant Thomas Williamson, who had a flourishing trading business with Flanders in the 1450s. Probably an important partner in this trade, she carried it on with great success after she was widowed, sometime before 1474, while training her son John in the business. She specialised in the import of fine cloths and textiles, supplying the royal household through the 1470s. When John Williamson first appeared in the royal accounts in 1474, he was called 'Isabel Williamson's son', reflecting his mother's well-known reputation. Isabel Williamson continued to trade until the 1490s, often working in partnership with her son from the 1480s. Unlike most Scottish women, who kept their own surnames after marriage, she used her late husband's surname, perhaps because of the importance of an established name and reputation in trade. Unusually for a woman, she also acquired burgess status.

Isabel Williamson's mercantile success enabled her to acquire substantial property, including Mortonhall near Edinburgh. She used her wealth to pious ends, endowing the altar of St Lawrence in St Giles' church in Edinburgh in 1489. On this one occasion, she used her own surname of Bras, perhaps because business was not involved. She was probably buried before the altar, having fostered a thriving family merchant business which would endure for several generations. EE

• *ER*, vols vi, ix–xi; Marshall, R. (1983) *Virgins and Viragos*; *RMS*, vol. ii; Laing, D. (ed.) (1859) *Registrum Cartarum Ecclesie Sancti Egidii de Edinburgh*; *ODNB* (2004) (Bibl.); *TA*, vol. i.; T. Thomson (ed.) (1839) *The Acts of the Lords of Council in Civil Causes*.

WILSON, Margaret, n. Bayne, baptised Greenock 22 March 1795, died Bombay 19 April 1835. Missionary and pioneer of female education in India. Daughter of Margaret Hay, and the Rev. Kenneth Bayne, Minister of the Gaelic Chapel, Greenock.

Margaret Bayne received an unusually high standard of education at home, in Kilmarnock and Aberdeen, where she joined in university classes. Renowned for her learning and brilliant intellect, she was treated with unusual respect for a young woman. In 1828, she married Church of Scotland minister, John Wilson (1804–75), who had offered his services to the Scottish Missionary Society in Western India and whose own 50-year career culminated in appointment as first Vice-Chancellor of Bombay University. They had four children. Within six months of their arrival in Bombay, despite local bafflement and opposition, she had established six schools for girls of low caste or outcaste status. She later organised and opened the first female boarding school in Western India. For seven years she superintended the schools, trained teachers, visited students and parents, taught adult women to read, and was resolute in her advocacy of female education. A gifted linguist, she translated many works into Marathi. She wrote textbooks, biographies and theological reviews for Indian journals and was, according to her husband, the main attraction for visitors to the mission and the greatest support to him in his work.

In the 1820s, no women were appointed as missionaries in their own right. Margaret Wilson quickly realised that any effective work undertaken with girls and women would require systematic female service and appealed for Scotswomen to dedicate themselves to such labours. She pleaded with her sisters, Anna and Hay Bayne, to join her. But she died in 1835 and her sisters instead travelled to India at their own expense to develop her pioneering initiatives, making a significant long-term impact on Indian society as well as on missionary practice. They were instrumental in establishing that women as well as men should be employed; inspired by their example, the Edinburgh Association of Ladies for the Advancement of Female Education in India was formed on 10 March 1837. LO

• Hewat, E. G. K. (1960) *Vision and Achievement 1796–1956*; *ODNB* (2004) (Wilson, John); Macdonald, L. A. O. (1993) 'Margaret Bayne' and 'Women in Presbyterian Missions', *Dictionary of Scottish Church History and Theology* (Bibl.); Wilson, J. (1838) *A Memoir of Mrs Margaret Wilson of Bombay*.

WOOD, Lucky, died Edinburgh c. 1717. Innkeeper.

Lucky Wood kept an alehouse in the Canongate, being much respected for her hospitality, honesty and the neatness of her person and inn. The Canongate was the centre of the political and cultural world of Edinburgh, though its importance declined after 1707, a decline Allan Ramsay linked to the loss of the Parliament and the death of Lucky Wood. He composed an elegy in 1717, commemorating this 'rarity' – an 'honest ale seller'. He praised both her good housekeeping ('She gae'd as fait [neat] as a new Prin,/And kept her Houssie Snod and Been; . . . She was a donsy [trim] Wife and clean/without Debate.') and her attitude toward beer ('She ne'er gae in a Lawin fause [crooked bill], . . ./Nor kept dow'd Tip [cheap drink] within her Waa's/but Reeming Swats [finest beer];/She never ran [sold] sour Jute, because/It

gee's the Bats' [colic].). Although no other evidence exists, scholars now think she was a real person and that Ramsay's comments reflect her reputation in the community. DLS

• Chambers, R. (1868) *Traditions of Edinburgh*; Ramsay, A., 'Elegy on Lucky Wood in the Canongate, May 1717', in *The Works of Allan Ramsay*, 1951; for complete Ramsay poem, see: www.nls.uk/broadsides/broadside.cfm/id/15822
Private information.

WOOD, Wendy (Gwendolen, Gwendoline) Emily, n. **Meacham,** m. **Cuthbert,** born Maidstone, Kent, 29 Oct. 1892, died Edinburgh 30 June 1981. Artist, broadcaster, political activist. Daughter of Florence Wood, artist, and Charles Meacham, scientific analyst.

Gwen Meacham heard stories of Gaelic-speaking forebears from her mother. The family moved in 1894 to Cape Town, witnessing the Boer War (1899–1902). Her childhood was spent in South Africa, at school in Tunbridge Wells (c. 1902–6), and in a holiday house near Kirkcudbright. She attended Westminster School of Art, and evening classes run by Walter Sickert, gaining a Certificate of the Royal Drawing School (1909). Admiring Keir Hardie and ILP policies, she worked as a nursery nurse in the East End, before marrying Walter Cuthbert, shoe manufacturer, in Cape Town in 1913. They settled in Ayr near his business, and he served with the Royal Artillery (1914–18). During the war, she miscarried twins; gave birth to two daughters (Cora, 1915 and Irralee, 1918); trained as a screen actress in case of her husband's death and started the short-lived Ayrshire Cinematographic Theatres Limited. She also suffered bouts of extreme ill-health. Demobbed, Walter Cuthbert added a studio to the house. Gwen Cuthbert resumed drawing, and published *The Baby in the Glass* (1923). When her husband's investments crashed, the couple moved to Dundee, where Gwen Cuthbert became a storyteller for BBC *Children's Hour* (1923), replaced 'Auntie Cyclone' in Glasgow, and organised *Children's Corner* for the Dundee station, foreshadowing later broadcasts and TV storytelling for *Jackanory* (1967–74).

In 1927, Dundee radio celebrity 'Auntie Gwen' left job, home and husband (marriage dissolved 1940), assumed the names Wendy and Wood (her mother's name), and started a new, militant life in Edinburgh. Having joined the Scottish League (1916) and Home Rule Association (1918), she enlisted with the Scottish National Movement

(1927) and the National Party of Scotland (1928). She helped folklorist Lewis Spence to win North Midlothian for the Nationalists (1929); he prefaced her travelogue *The Secret of Spey* (1930). When she replaced a Union Flag with the Lion Rampant at Stirling Castle on a Bannockburn Day rally (1932), she was accused of discrediting the cause. She protested against the Blackshirts in Edinburgh (1937) and against conditions for women in Scottish jails (1930, 1951); she threw a stone in order to be arrested and experience 'inside' for herself, but was never charged or convicted, though her 'prison record' almost spoiled a USA visit (1947). Hanging an effigy of the Secretary of State in Glasgow (1950), unrolling a Home Rule banner at the Highland Games (1950) and, most dramatically, going on hunger strike (1972) to press the Secretary of State for a Green Paper on a Scottish Assembly, Wood used direct action repeatedly to gain media attention. But she opposed violence against people, condemned conscription and was vice-chair of the Edinburgh Peace Council. An unsuccessful candidate locally (Edinburgh 1935) and in the general election (Bridgeton 1945), Wendy Wood founded the Scottish Patriots in August 1949.

In London, Gwen Meacham had met artists and writers. In Ayr, she knew *Jessie King and her husband. In Edinburgh, she befriended *Helen Cruickshank, Hugh MacDiarmid, Lewis Spence and Compton Mackenzie at PEN meetings hosted by William Burn Murdoch, who painted her portrait. She wrote articles for many publications and organisations. After 1939, with Oulith MacAndreis (Oliver MacAndrew), an editor of *Smeddum* and *The Lion Rampant*, she lived at Allt Rhuig: her articles on crofting were collected into the book, *Mac's Croft* (1946). Wendy Wood left MacAndreis, who admitted he was married and in the IRA, moving to a croft at Resipol. Her hillwalks are described in *Moidart and Morar* (1950) and she co-edited *The Strontian Magazine*. *The Patriot* first appeared 1953 and continues today. From 1956 to 1966, she shared a home with Florence St John Cadell (joint exhibition 1963). Unfounded accusations of spying at Allt Rhuig and of causing the theft of the Stone of Scone were easily made against a woman who courted controversy. The Church of Scotland, however, respected her insistence on a legal argument for Home Rule: she was the first woman to address the General Assembly (May 1961) since *Lady Aberdeen in 1921. Compton Mackenzie, first president of the Scottish Patriots, praised Wendy Wood's integrity, dedicating

his book *On Moral Courage* (1960) to her. She did not live to see the Scottish Parliament. RA

• Cuthbert, G. (1923) *The Baby in the Glass and Other Verses*, (1927) *The Chickabiddies Book*, (1924–7) *Little Dots*, (1935) with King, E. M., *A Lad of Dundee*; Wood, W. (1930) *The Secret of Spey*, (1938) *I like Life*, (1946) *Mac's Croft*, (1950) *Moidart and Morar*, (1952) *From a Highland Croft*, (1952) *Tales of the Western Isles*, (1953) *Let's see Mallaig*, (1955) *People of the Glen*, (1970) *Yours Sincerely for Scotland*, (1973) *Legends of the Borders*, (1980) *The Silver Chanter*, (1980) *Astronauts and Tinklers: Poems*, J. Hendry, ed.
Cuthbert, C. (1999) *Wendy Wood 1892–1981: a selection of European Drawings [. . .] Hanover Fine Arts* (catalogue) and (1999) *Wendy Wood, Illustrator*; *ODNB* (2004) (see Meacham, Gwendoline Emily).
Private information.

WRIGHT, Bessie, fl. 1611–28. Healer, Scone parish, Perthshire.

Very little of Bessie Wright's early life is known, but from information in the church records when she was investigated for witchcraft in 1611, 1626 and 1628, she appears to have had a long and mostly successful career as a healer or charmer, both in Perth and the surrounding area. She used herbs, including hyssop, finkle (fennel) and ribble grass (ribwort), and rituals to cure or help childbirth, gravel, liver complaints and migraines. An interesting and unusual feature of her healing knowledge and skill was her possession of what she called her 'medical book'. She claimed it was 1,000 years old and had been used by her father and grandfather. Bessie Wright said she could not read from the book, but her son, Adam Bell, read out extracts for her. It is not clear whether this book was a medieval medical textbook, perhaps written in Latin, or a pre-Reformation religious tract, but her ownership of it was unacceptable to the church. In 1611, Mr William Cowper, minister of Perth, ordered her to hand it over. In 1626, she was investigated for using unacceptable healing rituals and was ordered to stop offering any healing advice within the burgh of Perth. She does not seem to have obeyed this ruling as she was in trouble again two years later. This time she was imprisoned. Her family complained about her treatment and she was released, although her son had to pay £1,000 bail. It is unclear from the presbytery records whether she was ever officially tried and, if so, what the outcome was.

Although the church used the Witchcraft Act of 1563 to justify its investigation of Bessie Wright for witchcraft, she was not accused of demonic witchcraft or malefice (evil harm). The main reasons for the accusations against her were failed healing rituals or resentment, as one of the witnesses complained that she had spoiled his ale and, although it is not certain, the lack of any references to the devil or demonic pact may have saved her from execution. JHMM

• NAS: CH2/299/2, Perth Presbytery Records.
RPC, 2nd series, vol. 2, pp. 623–4.

WRIGHT, Christian Edington Guthrie, born Glasgow 19 April 1844, died Edinburgh 24 Feb. 1907. Principal founder of the Edinburgh School of Cookery (now Queen Margaret University College). Daughter of Christian Edington, and Harry Guthrie Wright, manager, Glasgow and South-Western Railway Company.

Christian Guthrie Wright's mother died following childbirth, and in the 1860s father and daughter moved to Edinburgh. Educated at boarding school, she attended extra-mural classes at the University of Edinburgh. She was both a founder member of the Ladies' Edinburgh Debating Society (see Mair, Sarah) and treasurer of the Edinburgh Association for the University Education of Women. In 1875, she took the lead in creating the Edinburgh School of Cookery, following methods advocated by the National Union for Improving the Education of Women of all Classes. The Union's president, *Princess Louise (see Louise, Princess), became the school's principal patron. Over 1,000 women attended the inaugural lecture on 9 November in the new Museum of Science and Art. The School developed rapidly, with Miss Guthrie Wright, as she was known, as honorary secretary, providing drive and enthusiasm. Lectures on cooking and household health were delivered as regular series, in Edinburgh, but also on a peripatetic basis all over Britain. Similar institutions were encouraged by Miss Guthrie Wright and her colleagues (notably Louisa Stevenson, see Stevenson, Flora) in Glasgow, Dundee and in England, including a branch in Manchester. In 1879, with Sir Thomas Dyke Acland and two medical advisers, Christian Guthrie Wright published an influential *School Cookery Book* as part of the series, *Science Primers,* edited by T. H. Huxley. This book probably represented the best state of food knowledge at the time.

In 1891, the Edinburgh School was established in Atholl Crescent, subsidising work for lower income groups from its fee-paying courses.

Christian Guthrie Wright took only an organising role and never taught, since she wished to remain on the social level of her patrons. As a successful fund-raiser, she helped found the Queen Victoria's Jubilee Institute for Nurses (1887), becoming treasurer of the Scottish council. Her determination to introduce cookery into the School Board schools' curriculum faced opposition both from men who objected to the cost, and some women who did not wish to have girls study 'female' subjects. But the SED was sympathetic to her view that all girls should receive domestic science instruction, and after her sudden death, took responsibility for the Edinburgh School, renamed as the Edinburgh College of Domestic Science.

Her successor as 'superintendent', and later principal, was **Ethel De la Cour** (1869–1957) who negotiated with the SED over the 1908 Education (Scotland) Act. Formal qualification for domestic science teachers was introduced, and output of trained DS staff soon trebled. During the First World War, Ethel De La Cour was involved in various food conservation campaigns, and was a member of separate committees on rationing and training, both the subject of College courses. Appointed MBE (1920) and OBE (1929), she was one of the first women JPs in Edinburgh, and the founding president of the city's Soroptimist Club (1927–30), as well as being a member of the National Council of Women. TB

• Queen Margaret Univ. College Archives.
Baly, M. E. (1987) *A History of the Queen's Nursing Institute*; Begg, T. (1994) *The Excellent Women: the origins and history of Queen Margaret College*; (Edinburgh) *Evening News*, 8 June 1955; *Edinburgh School of Cookery Magazine*, 1929, 2/32, pp. 5–6 and 1930, 2/34 pp. 6–7; Mair, S. E. S. (1925) 'An appreciation of Christian Edington Guthrie Wright', *Edinburgh School of Cookery Magazine*, April; *ODNB* (2004) (Guthrie Wright, Christian; De La Cour, Ethel); Rae, L. M. (1936) *Ladies in Debate*; *The Scotsman*, 1 March, 1907 (obit. Wright), 27 April 1957 (obit. De La Cour); *SB* .

WRIGHT, Frances (Fanny), m. Phiquepal d'Arusmont, born Dundee 6 Sept. 1795, died Cincinnati, Ohio 13 Dec. 1852. Utopian socialist, feminist, freethinker. Daughter of Camilla Campbell, and James Wright, radical Dundee merchant.

Both parents having died in 1798, Fanny and her sister **Camilla Wright** (1797–1831) after childhood in London and Devon, stayed with their great-uncle James Mylne, Professor of Moral Philosophy at Glasgow, and his wife Agnes Millar.

Fanny Wright educated herself in the University Library, writing a treatise on the imagined, female disciple of Epicurus, *A Few Days in Athens* (1822), and several plays, including *Altorf* (1819). Aware of the inequalities of her society, she was attracted, through the influence of sisters **Robina Millar** (1767–1844) and *Margaret Cullen, by the example of the American republic. In 1818, she and Camilla travelled there: in February 1819 *Altorf* was staged on Broadway. On her return, she published her letters to Robina Millar as *Views of Society and Manners in America* (1821), greeted with enthusiasm by *The Scotsman*, but viewed by the *Quarterly Review* as a 'ridiculous and extravagant panegyric on the government and people of the United States' (Eckhardt 1984, pp. 47–8). Fanny Wright criticised the republic only for the institution of slavery, and, to a lesser extent, its treatment of women.

In Paris in 1821, she met the Marquis de Lafayette, veteran of the American and French Revolutions, to whom she became devoted. With Camilla, she returned to the USA to join him in 1824, and was further inspired by Robert Owen, the New Lanark factory owner who was building a community at New Harmony, Indiana. At Nashoba, Tennessee, from 1825, she planned first a model farm, of which both she and Camilla were resident trustees, based on the labour of purchased black slaves, then a utopian community, following the ideas of Owen and Godwin. Though initially successful, in July 1827 Nashoba received unwelcome publicity about inter-racial sex, suggesting this was approved by the Wright sisters.

Back in Europe, Fanny Wright met the ensuing storm of disapproval by publicly justifying a co-operative, biracial community of equals, and condemning oppressive laws on marriage and attitudes to miscegenation. Returning in December 1827, she found Nashoba failing economically and in its ideals and Camilla newly married to Richesson Whitby, from New Harmony. Fanny Wright joined Owen's son, Robert Dale Owen, in New Harmony, becoming joint editor of the *New Harmony Gazette* (later *Free Enquirer*). Unprecedentedly, she also began to lecture to large mixed audiences across the US for the causes of anti-slavery and co-operation, free thought and

marriage reform: opponents labelled her 'the Red Harlot of Infidelity' (Eckhardt 1984 p. 3). In 1829 the Wright sisters and Robert Dale Owen moved to New York, drawn by the situation of urban artisans and the New York Working Men's Party. Having taking her freed slaves to Haiti, accompanied by a former Nashoba settler, William Phiquepal (b. 1811), Fanny Wright became pregnant with his child, and returned to France in June 1830. Camilla followed, but died in Paris in childbirth in February 1831. Fanny married Phiquepal on 22 July 1831, after the birth of her daughter Sylva. Further lectures in America (1836–9) at first provoked demonstrations, then indifference. Her later years were spent in isolation and poverty in France and the USA, often separated from husband and daughter, writing her autobiography and her major work, *England the Civiliser* (1848). In 1844 she inherited property in Dundee, but her husband's financial demands led to a divorce suit, estrangement from her daughter, and legal conflict until her death in 1852. Fanny Wright's portrait became the frontispiece of the 6-volume *History of Woman Suffrage* in a sincere tribute to 'the first woman who gave lectures on political subjects in America' and spoke 'on the equality of the sexes' (Stanton et al. 1881, I, pp. 35, 691–2; II, 429; III, 293). JR

• Cornell Univ., Ithaca: transcripts by T. Wolfson of some of Frances Wright's papers (now lost); National Union Catalog of MSS: list of surviving papers in the USA.

Wright, F., Works as above, and (1972) *Life, Letters, and Lectures, 1834/1844*.

Baker, P. (1963) 'Introduction' to Wright, F. *Views of Society and Manners in America*; Bederman, G. (2005) 'Revisiting Nashoba: slavery, utopia, and Frances Wright in America, 1818–1826', *American Literary History* 17, 3; Eckhardt, C. M. (1984) *Fanny Wright. Rebel in America*; Ginzberg, L. (1994) '"The Hearts of Your Readers Will Shudder": Fanny Wright, infidelity and American freethought', *American Quarterly*, 46, pp. 195–226; Heineman, H. (1983) *Restless Angels. The Friendship of Six Victorian Women*; Kolmerten, C. A. (1990) *Women in Utopia. The Ideology of Gender in the American Owenite Communities*; *ODNB* (2004); Perkins, A. J. G. and Wolfson, T. (1939) *Frances Wright, Free Enquirer*; Stanton, E. C., Anthony, S. B. and Gage, M. J. (eds) (1881) *History of Woman Suffrage*, 6 vols; Waterman, W. R. [1924] (1967) *Frances Wright*.

http://lcweb.loc.gov/coll/nucmc/nucmc.html.

Y

YOUNG, Issobell, born parish of Dunbar c. 1565, died Edinburgh, Feb. 1629. Indicted for witchcraft. Wife of tenant-farmer.

Issobell Young was first accused of witchcraft on 8 January 1619 and eventually tried in February 1629, when she was at least 65 years old. Her husband George Smith, a portioner of East Barns, Dunbar, testified against her. Three of their four married sons testified for her.

References to Issobell Young's work scattered through the abundant surviving documents make it possible to sketch her life before her trial. The family had a secure and heritable lease to one portion of the lands and village of East Barns, Dunbar, for most of her adult life. She and George Smith held the smallest of the three portions, and fought to increase their social status. They owned livestock, barns and outbuildings and employed about ten servants. In addition to managing a household of around 15 permanent members, which probably increased during planting and harvest, Issobell Young took crops to the mill, bought and sold goods and produce, and cared for animals. She undoubtedly also raised her children, cooked, cleaned, mended, and gathered peat, wood and water.

Witness testimony suggests that although in control of her life, Issobell Young was not happy with her economic and social position. Her neighbours believed that she used harmful magic to damage the profitability of their households as a strategy to advance her own. Neighbours recalled patterns of verbal and sometimes physical aggression. A jury of their peers believed them. Issobell Young's testimony provides a rare insight into how an early modern woman saw herself. She rejected the connection between her speech and behaviour and her neighbours' misfortunes. Rather than denying her quarrels, as some witchcraft suspects did, she justified them, describing her reactions to her neighbours as normal. She described her words as 'ordinarlie blastis of anger', or the 'bragis [threats] of passionat wemen' (*Selected Justiciary Cases*, pp. 101, 104). She called herself an 'honest woman' (NAS, JC26/9), and said her neighbours' misfortunes were due to their own immorality, God's judgement, or their own laziness and incompetence. She became the persecuted, honest, good Christian wife and neighbour. Her self-presented image only partially failed. She was acquitted on ten of the charges and only on one charge was unanimously found guilty. After her trial she was taken to Castle Hill, Edinburgh, tied to a stake, strangled and burned. LM

• NAS: JC26/9 'Issobell Young' bundle, document 4. Larner, C. (1981) *Enemies of God: the witch-hunt in Scotland*; Martin, L. (2002) 'Witchcraft and family: what can witchcraft documents tell us about early modern Scottish family life?', *Scottish Tradition* 27; Smith, J. (ed.) (1914) *Selected Justiciary Cases*, vol. 1, pp. 96–120; Survey of Scottish Witchcraft, www.arts.ed.ac.uk/witches.

YOUNG, Mary Helen, born Aberdeen 5 June 1883, died Ravensbrück, Germany, 14 March 1945. Nurse and resistance worker, France. Daughter of Elizabeth Ann Burnett, and Alexander Young, grocer's clerk.

The youngest of three children, Mary Young moved to Edinburgh with her family in 1884, after her mother's death. After school, she spent several years as a dressmaker in Jenners' department store, before training as a nurse at Kingston County Hospital, Surrey. In 1909, after qualification, she went to France as a private nurse. When war was declared in 1914, Mary Young volunteered for service with the Allied forces, working in the British Army zone in France. After the war she resumed private nursing in Paris, but returned regularly to Scotland and sent her sister money to help maintain the Aberdeen house where she intended to retire. She worked on in Paris during the Second World War, even after the Germans occupied the city. In December 1940, she was sent to a civilian internment camp in Besançon, but due to ill health was soon released. Back in Paris, although under Gestapo surveillance, she managed to harbour resistance organisers sent from London and provide a base for radio transmissions. The Gestapo arrested her late in 1943, on suspicion of helping British prisoners to escape, and she was sent as a political prisoner to the women's concentration camp at Ravensbrück. Small (4ft 11in), now aged 60, and already ill with heart trouble, she could not do the heavy work required of camp inmates, and conditions at Ravensbrück took their toll. Like thousands of her fellow prisoners, she perished.

When news of Mary Young's resistance work and death reached Scotland in September 1945, newspapers hailed her as a second Edith Cavell. Preliminary investigations revealed that she had died in early 1945, possibly in the gas chamber; in 1948, the Court of Session adjudged that she had died on 14 March 1945. Letters produced in evidence referred to her courage and cheerfulness. A fellow inmate said 'she always kept her chin up'. FRW

• NAS: CS 46/1948 Feb 55, Court of Session unextracted process; NAS: SC70/1/1123 pp. 552–7, Edinburgh Sheriff Court Commissary Court records.
ODNB (2004); 'Nazis send Aberdeen heroine to gas chamber', *The Press and Journal*, 27 Sept. 1945; 'Marie Helene Sends her Love', *The Press and Journal*, 27 Sept. 1945; 'Nazis murdered nurse for aiding French', *The Press and Journal*, 31 Jan. 1948.

Z

ZAVARONI, Lena Hilda, m. **Wiltshire,** born Greenock 4 Nov. 1963, died Cardiff 2 Oct. 1999. Pop singer. Daughter of Hilda Jordan and Victor Zavaroni, fish and chip shop owners.

Born into a musical family in Rothesay, Lena Zavaroni found fame at the age of nine, when she appeared on the television talent show *Opportunity Knocks*. She won the contest for a record five consecutive weeks, and the song she sang, 'Ma, He's Making Eyes at Me', reached number 8 in the charts. Having moved to London and the Italian Conti Stage School, in the mid-1970s she went from one high-profile performance to another, taking part in a Hollywood charity performance with Frank Sinatra and Lucille Ball and singing at the White House for President Gerald Ford. She appeared on *Morecambe and Wise*, and took part in the Royal Variety Performance. At the Conti she met another child star, Bonnie Langford, and together they had a television show, *Lena and Bonnie*. But the fame and wealth which had transformed her life quickly had another side to it. By the age of 16 she had been diagnosed with anorexia nervosa, and for the next 20 years she moved between periods of performing and periods of serious illness. She married businessman Peter Wiltshire in 1989, but the marriage lasted only 18 months. Lena Zavaroni attended different clinics for anorexia and depression, and was further affected by personal and family troubles. In September 1999, she underwent a rare type of brain operation known as a capsulotomy at the University Hospital of Wales, Cardiff. By then she was living on social security benefits in a council flat in Hertfordshire. She died, aged 35, of a chest infection contracted after the operation. FJ

• *The Daily Telegraph*, 3 Oct. 1999 (obit.) and 9 Dec. 1999; *The Guardian*, 5 Oct. 1999 (obit.); *ODNB* (2004). www.lena-zavaroni.co.uk

ZINKEISEN, Doris Clare,‡ m. **Johnstone,** born Kilcreggan, Dunbartonshire, 31 July 1898, died Badingham, Suffolk, 3 Jan. 1991; **ZINKEISEN, Anna Katrina,** m. **Heseltine,** born Kilcreggan 29 August 1901, died London 23 Sept. 1976. Daughters of Welsh-born Clare Bolton-Charles, and Victor Zinkeisen, Glasgow timber merchant and amateur artist.

Tutored at home, 'both sisters wanted to draw and paint to the exclusion of all other academic pursuits' (Walpole 1978, p. 7). In 1909, the family moved to Pinner, Middlesex, where Doris and Anna Zinkeisen attended the Harrow School of Art. In 1917, they won scholarships to the Royal Academy Schools. Referred to as 'Big Zink' and 'Little Zink', they had eminent teachers, including Sir William Orpen and Sir George Clausen. Doris Zinkeisen received Paris Salon medals: Bronze (1929), Silver (1930) and Gold (1934); Anna Zinkeisen, who also studied sculpture, won a Silver Medal at the 1925 *Exposition des Arts Décoratifs*. In 1927, Doris Zinkeisen married Captain Grahame Johnstone (d. 1946); they had three children. The following year, her sister married Captain Guy Heseltine (d. 1967) and they had one daughter.

Painting in the academic-realist style, the Zinkeisens gained popularity as official and society portraitists; examples include *Elsa Lanchester* (1925) by Doris, and surgeon *Sir Archibald McIndoe* (c. 1940) by Anna (both NPG, London). While portraiture was the mainstay of both careers, the sisters, as accomplished horsewomen, also favoured equestrian subjects, and they worked widely in other visual media, e.g. advertising posters for the London Underground Company and murals for Cunard liner RMS *Queen Mary*. Doris Zinkeisen additionally established a successful career as stage and costume designer for plays and films (e.g. for Nigel Playfair, Charles Cochran and Herbert

Wilcox), and wrote a key book, *Designing for the Stage* (1938). Anna Zinkeisen had a prominent reputation as an illustrator of books and magazine covers. In 1940, she was granted the title Royal Designer for Industry. During the Second World War, both sisters enrolled as auxiliary nurses in the Casualty Department at St Mary's Hospital, London. In 1941, they were employed as war artists for St John's Ambulance Brigade. Anna Zinkeisen's contribution includes *Archibald McIndoe Operating at East Grinstead* (1944, IWM, London). As a 'medical artist', she worked with McIndoe and Alexander Fleming, providing pathological drawings of traumatised tissue, later used in the textbook *Essentials of Modern Surgery* (1948). In 1945, Doris Zinkeisen was sent to Germany where she depicted the Belsen concentration camp in *Belsen* and *Human Laundry, Belsen* (1945, both

IWM). From the mid-1920s onward, the Zinkeisen sisters were familiar figures on London's artistic scene and in art galleries nationwide, including the RA, RHA and RSA. Remarkably versatile artists, their professional careers were in many ways exceptional. BCD

• NPG London Archive: Artists' files; IWM London: War Artists' Archive; London Transport Museum Archive: Artists' files; Theatre Museum Archive, London: Artists' files. Zinkeisen, Doris [1938] (1945) *Designing for the Stage.* Green, O. (2001) *Underground Art: London Transport posters 1908 to the present*; Hinkey, D. M. (1994) *The Art of the RMS Queen Mary*; *ODNB* (2004) (Zinkeisen, Anna); Rideal, L. (2002) *Mirror, Mirror, self-portraits by women artists*; *The Times*, 11 Jan. 1991 (Zinkeisen, Doris) (obit.); Walpole, J. (1978) *'Anna' A memorial tribute to Anna Zinkeisen.* Private information.

Thematic Index

The names of subjects have been reduced to the minimum necessary for identification, using the names by which subjects are best known. Names in italics are co-subjects (see the explanation in the Readers' Guide on page xxiii).

Archaeology
Campbell, Marion (1919–2000)
MacLagan, Christian (1811–1901)
Marshall, Dorothy see *Marshall, Sheina (1896–1977)*
Robertson, Anne (1910–97)
Sandeman, Mary see *Campbell, Marion, of Kilberry (1919–2000)*
Architecture
Brodie, Margaret (1907–97)
Burnet, Edith (1888–1971)
Art and crafts (including painting, but see also Sculpture)
Armour, Mary see *Glasgow Girls (c. 1880–c. 1920)*
Barns-Graham, Wilhelmina (1912–2004)
Blackburn, Jemima (1823–1909)
Blackwell, Elizabeth (1707–c. 1758)
Blatherwick, Lily see *Glasgow Girls (c. 1880–c. 1920)*
Boyle, Eleanor Vere (1825–1916)
Brown, Helen Paxton see *Glasgow Girls (c. 1880–c. 1920)*
Burton, Mary Rose (1857–1900)
Cameron, Katharine (1874–1965)
Cameron, Mary (1865–1921)
Cheverton, Charlotte (1960–91)
Dean, Stansmore see *Glasgow Girls (c. 1880–c. 1920)*
Dewar, De Courcy see *Glasgow Girls (c. 1880–c. 1920)*
Dunlop, Marion Wallace- *see* Wallace-Dunlop, Marion (1864–1942)
Dunnett, Dorothy (1923–2001)
Eardley, Joan (1921–63)
Forbes, Anne see *Read, Katharine (1723–78)*
French, Annie see *Glasgow Girls (c. 1880–c. 1920)*
Gilmour, Margaret see *Glasgow Girls (c. 1880–c. 1920)*
Gilmour, Mary see *Glasgow Girls (c. 1880–c. 1920)*
Glasgow Girls (c. 1880–c. 1920)
Gordon-Cumming, Eliza (c. 1798–1842)
Gray, Norah Neilson (1882–1931)
Greenlees, Georgina (1849–1932)
Haig, Florence see *Burton, Mary Rose (1857–1900)*
Hay, Helen (1867–1955)
Hotchkis, Anna (1885–1984)
Inglis, Esther (c. 1571–1624)
Jacob, Violet (1863–1946)
Johnstone, Dorothy (1892–1980)
King, Jessie Marion (1875–1949)

Macbean, Mary see *Carmichael, Elizabeth Catherine (Ella) (1870–1928)*
Macbeth, Ann (1875–1948)
McCrae, Georgiana (1804–90)
Macdonald, Annie (1849–1924)
Macdonald, Frances Eliza see *Macdonald, Margaret (1864–1933)*
Macdonald, Margaret (1864–1933)
McDougall, Lily (1875–1958)
MacGoun, Hannah (1864–1913)
McIan, Fanny (c. 1814–97)
McMurtrie, Mary (1902–2003)
MacNicol, Bessie (1869–1904)
Mann, Kathleen (1908–2000)
Moncrieff, Marianne (1874–1961)
Montgomerie, Norah (1908–98)
Moore, Eleanor see *Glasgow Girls (c. 1880–c. 1920); Tanner, Ann Ailsa (1923–2001)*
Moorhead, Ethel (1869–1955)
Nasmyth, Anne; Barbara; Charlotte; Elizabeth; Margaret see *Nasmyth, Jane (1788–1867)*
Nasmyth, Jane (1788–1867)
Newbery, Jessie (1864–1948)
Newbery, Mary see *Newbery, Jessie (1864–1948)*
Parker, Agnes Miller (1895–1980)
Paterson, Mary see *Glasgow Girls (c. 1880–c. 1920)*
Read, Katharine (1723–78)
Redpath, Anne (1895–1965)
Robertson, Christina (1796–1854)
Royds, Mabel (1874–1941)
Sandison, May (c. 1825–88)
Simon, Edith (1917–2003)
Smyth, Dorothy see *Glasgow Girls (c. 1880–c. 1920)*
Stewart Smith, Jane (1839–1925)
Swain, Margaret (1909–2002)
Tanner, Ailsa (1923–2001)
Trail, Ann (1798–1872)
Traquair, Phoebe (1852–1936)
Turner, Helen see *Moncrieff, Marianne (1874–1961)*
Walford, Lucy (1845–1915)
Walker, Ethel (1861–1951)
Wallace-Dunlop, Marion (1864–1942)
Walton, Cecile (1891–1956)
Walton, Constance see *Glasgow Girls (c. 1880–c. 1920)*
Watts, Mary (1849–1938)

Whyte, Kath (1909–96)
Wood, Wendy (1892–1981)
Zinkeisen, Anna see *Zinkeisen, Doris (1898–1991)*
Zinkeisen, Doris (1898–1991)

Astronomy
Fleming, Williamina (1857–1911)
Herschel, Margaret (1810–84)
Sadler, Flora (1912–2000)
Short, Maria (b. before 1788, d. 1869)
Smyth, Jessie Piazzi (1816–96)
Somerville, Mary (1780–1872)

Biology, Botany, Ecology
Alcock, Lilian (1874–1972)
Andrews, Sheila (1939–97)
Auerbach, Lotte (1899–1994)
Baxter, Evelyn (1879–1959)
Blackwell, Elizabeth (1707–c. 1758)
Currie, Ethel (1899–1963)
Duncan, Ursula (1910–85)
Frankland, Grace (1858–1946)
Gordon, Isabella (1901–88)
Hutchison, Isobel Wylie (1889–1982)
McDouall, Agnes (1838–1926)
MacLeod, Anna (1917–2004)
Marshall, Sheina (1896–1977)
Murray, Lady Charlotte (1754–1808)
Noble, Mary (1911–2002)
Pirie, Mary (1822–85)
Ramsay, Christian (1786–1839)
Rintoul, Leonora see *Baxter, Evelyn (1879–1959)*
Smith, Annie Lorrain (1854–1937)
Stewart, Olga (1920–98)

Commerce, Industry/Trades
Anderson, Janet (1697–1761)
Baxter, Ethel (1883–1963)
Baxter, Margaret see *Baxter, Ethelreda (1883–1963)*
Brechin, Ethel (1894–1986)
Brooksbank, Mary (1897–1978)
Campbell, Agnes (baptised 1637, d. 1716)
Cranston, Kate (1849–1934)
Crichton, Margaret (c. 1483–c. 1546)
Cumming, Elizabeth (1827–1894)
Devine, Rachel (1875–1960)
Dick, Beetty (1693–1773)
Erskine, Mary (1629–1707)
Evota of Stirling (fl. 1304)
Fenwick, Margaret (1919–92)
Finnie, Agnes (d. 1645)
Flucker, Barbara (1784–1869)
Fockart, Janet (b. before 1550, d. 1596)
Gillon, Mary (1898–2002)
Gunn, Isabel (1781–1861)
Hastie, Annie (1922–2002)

Hodge, Hannah (b. 1751)
Hutton, Sibilla (b. before 1773, d. 1808)
Johnston, Elizabeth see *Flucker, Barbara (1784–1869)*
Keiller, Janet (c. 1737–1813)
Keyzer, Isabella (1922–92)
King, Mary see *Rough, Alison (c. 1480–1535)*
Liston, Esther (1896–1989)
Lovi, Isabell (fl. 1805–27)
Lyon, Sibilla (b. before 1738, d. 1754)
McGhie, Mrs (fl. 1770s)
McIver, Maggie (1879–1958)
Mackinnon, Georgina (1884–1973)
Manson, Mary (1897–1994)
Masterton, Margaret (1709–37)
Miller, Betsy (1792–1864)
Milligan, Frances see *Liston, Esther (1896–1989)*
Miner, Mary (1910–91)
Moncrieff, Marianne (1874–1961)
Moore, Jane (c. 1635–95)
Morice, Margaret (baptised 1718, d. 1799/1800)
Pullinger, Dorothée (1894–1986)
Radcliffe, Mary Ann (1746–c. 1810)
Rough, Alison (c. 1480–1535)
Schireham, Marjory de (fl. 1326–31)
Shaw, Christian (b. 1686, d. after 1737)
Shiel, Tibbie (1782–1878)
Sinclair, Isabella (1776–95)
Toward, Agnes (1886–1975)
Watt, Christian (1832–1923)
Williamson, Effie (1846–1929)
Williamson, Isabel (c. 1430–93)
Wood, Lucky (d. c. 1717)

Diaspora (Scots abroad)
Aud the Deep-Minded (c. 850–c. 900)
Bohemia, Elizabeth of see Stewart, Elizabeth
   (1596–1662)
Bon, Ann Fraser (1838–1936)
Bryson, Elizabeth (1880–c. 1969)
Campbell, Jane (1869–1947)
Campbell, Agnes (c. 1525–c. 1601)
Davidson, Harriet Miller see *Miller, Lydia Falconer*
   (baptised 1812, d. 1876)
Dawson, Ellen (1900–67)
Drysdale, Anne (1792–1853)
Forlong(e), Eliza (c. 1784–1859)
Fraser, Janet (1883–1945)
Greig, Jane (1872–1939)
Gunn, Isabel (1781–1861)
Hargrave, Letitia (1813–54)
McCrae, Georgiana (1804–90)
MacDonald, Flora (1722–90)
Macdonald, Louisa (1858–1949)
Marshall, Henrietta Elizabeth (1867–after 1927)

Martin, Catherine (1847–1937)
Miner, Mary (1910–91)
O'Donnell, Finola (c. 1552–c. 1610)
Sheppard, Kate (1848–1934)
Sievwright, Margaret (1844–1905)
Slessor, Mary (1848–1915)
Small, Annie (1857–1945)
Spence, Catherine Helen (1825–1910)
Steel, Flora Annie (1847–1929)
Stewart, Eleanor; Isabella; Mary see *Stewart, Margaret (1424–45)*
Stewart, Elizabeth (1596–1662)
Stewart, Margaret (1424–45)
Trout, Jennie (1841–1921)
Waterston, Jane (1843–1932)
Wilson, Margaret (baptised 1795, d. 1835)
Wright, Camilla see *Wright, Frances (1795–1852)*
Wright, Frances (1795–1852)

Education
Ainslie, Charlotte (1863–1960)
Allan, Jean (1908–91)
Anderson, Christina see *Watson, Alexandra Mary Chalmers (Mona) (1872–1936)*
Arthur, Jane (1827–1907)
Black, Margaret see *Paterson, Grace Chalmers (1843–1925)*
Calderón de la Barca, Marquesa (1804–82)
Campbell, Jessie (1827–1907)
Cheverton, Charlotte (1960–91)
Cook, Rachel see *Lumsden, Louisa (1840–1935)*
Cowan, Minna (1878–1951)
Crawford, Jane (1864–1947)
Crawford, Marion (1909–88)
Crudelius, Mary (1839–1877)
Dalrymple, Learmonth (c. 1827–1906)
Daniell, Madeline (1832–1906)
De la Cour, Ethel see *Wright, Christian Edington Guthrie (1844–1907)*
Elder, Isabella (1828–1905)
Fish, Elizabeth (1860–1944)
Galloway, Janet (1841–1909)
Geddes, Anna (1857–1917)
Graham, Isabella (1742–1814)
Greig, Clara see *Greig, Jane (1872–1939)*
Kay, Christina (1878–1951)
Kinnear, Georgina (c. 1826–1914)
Laws, Margaret (1849–1921)
Lumsden, Louisa (1840–1935)
Macdonald, Louisa (1858–1949)
Mackenzie, Agnes Mure (1891–1955)
McMillan, Margaret (1860–1931)
McMillan, Rachel see *McMillan, Margaret (1860–1931)*
Marley, Hilda (1876–1951)

Melville, Frances (1873–1962)
Munro, Ailie (1918–2002)
Paterson, Grace (1843–1925)
Pirie, Jane (c. 1784–fl. 1821)
Sidgwick, Eleanor (1845–1936)
Skea, Isabella (1845–1914)
Small, Annie (1857–1945)
Spence, Catherine Stafford (1823–1906)
Spens, Janet see *Watson, Margaret (1873–1959)*
Stevenson, Flora (1839–1905)
Stevenson, Louisa see *Stevenson, Flora (1839–1905)*
Watson, Margaret (1873–1959)
Wilson, Margaret (baptised 1795, d. 1835)
Woods, Marianne see *Pirie, Jane (c. 1784–fl. 1821)*
Wright, Christian Guthrie (1844–1907)

Engineering and technology
Buchanan, Dorothy (1899–1985)
Drummond, Victoria (1894–1978)
Fergusson, Molly (1914–97)
Pullinger, Dorothée (1894–1986)

Farming and estate management
Armstrong, Jenny (1903–85)
Balfour, Eve (1898–1990)
Dalrymple, Christian (1765–1838)
Drysdale, Anne (1792–1853)
Duncan, Ursula (1910–85)
Forlong(e), Eliza (c. 1784–1859)
Gordon Cathcart, Emily, Lady (1845–1932)
Gordon, Jane Maxwell, Duchess of see Maxwell, Jane, Duchess of Gordon (c. 1749–1812)
Hamilton, Anne, Duchess of (1632–1716)
Hardie, Margaret (b. c. 1625, d. after 1660)
Kennedy, Janet (c. 1480–1547)
King, Mary (1905–98)
Leigh, Margaret (1894–1973)
Leslie, Euphemia (c. 1508–70)
Mackenzie, Anna see *Scott, Anna, Duchess of Buccleuch (1651–1732)*
Mackenzie, Isabel (c. 1640–1715)
Mackenzie, Penelope (c. 1675–1743)
MacPherson, Margaret (1908–2001)
Maxwell, Jane, Duchess of Gordon (c. 1749–1812)
Mure, Elizabeth (c. 1715–c. 1791)
Neil, Andy (1924–2004)
Neil, Chrissie see *Neil, Annie (Andy) (1924–2004)*
Ragnhild Simonsdatter (fl. 1299)
Ruthven, Katherine (d. 1584)
Scott, Anna, Duchess of Buccleuch (1651–1732)
Scott, Janet, Lady Ferniehirst (c. 1548–c. 1595)
Speirs, Vera (1921–1995)
Stirling Graham, Clementina (1782–1877)
Sutherland, Elizabeth, Duchess–Countess of (1765–1839)

Tollemache, Elizabeth (1659–1735)
Watson, Mona Chalmers (1872–1936)
Young, Issobell (c. 1565–1629)
Fishing and fishing industry
Ballantine, Georgina (1889–1970)
Cordiner, Helen (1893–1964)
Flucker, Barbara (1784–1869)
Johnston, Elizabeth see Flucker, Barbara (1784–1869)
Liston, Esther (1896–1989)
Milligan, Frances see Liston, Esther (1896–1989)
Sutherland, Greta (1891–1923)
Food and drink
Baxter, Ethel (1883–1963)
Baxter, Margaret see Baxter, Ethelreda (1883–1963)
Craig, Elizabeth (1883–1980)
Cumming, Elizabeth (1827–94)
Keiller, Janet (c. 1737–1813)
McGhie, Mrs (fl. 1770s)
Mackinnon, Georgina (1884–1973)
MacLeod, Anna (1917–2004)
McNeill, Florence Marian (1885–1973)
Morice, Margaret (baptised 1718, d. 1799/1800)
Robertson, Hannah (b. 1724, d. after 1807)
Shiel, Tibbie (1782–1878)
Wood, Lucky (d. c. 1717)
Gardening
Burnett, Sybil (1889–1960)
Christie, Ella (1861–1949)
Elder, Madge (1893–1985)
Keswick, Maggie (1941–95)
McDouall, Agnes (1838–1926)
McMurtrie, Mary (1902–2003)
Renton, Dorothy (1898–1966)
Sawyer, Mairi (1879–1953)
Geography, Geology, Palaeontology
Andrews, Sheila (1939–97)
Aust, Sarah (1744–1811)
Callcott, Maria see Graham, Maria (Lady Callcott) (1785–1842)
Currie, Ethel (1899–1963)
Gordon-Cumming, Eliza (c. 1798–1842)
Graham, Maria (Lady Callcott) (1785–1842)
Gray, Elizabeth (1831–1924)
Murray, Sarah see Aust, Sarah (1744–1811)
Newbigin, Marion (1869–1934)
Reynolds, Doris (1899–1985)
Smyth, Jessie Piazzi (1816–96)
Snodgrass, Catherine (1902–74)
Somerville, Mary (1780–1872)
Watson, Janet Vida (1923–85)
Health, healing, medicine: mental health
Bates, Diana see Rushforth, Margaret Winifred (1885–1983)

Fraser, Kate (1877–1957)
Marley, Hilda (1876–1951)
Rushforth, Winifred (1885–1983)
Health, healing, medicine: nurses, midwives, health visitors
Altschul, Annie (1919–2001)
Balfour, Betty (1832–1918)
Bane, Margaret (b. before 1567, d. 1597)
Bethune, Margaret (1820–87)
Boyd, Peggy (1905–99)
Buick, Mary (1777–1854)
Chisholm, Mairi (1896–1981)
Cleghorn, Louisa (c. 1720–after 1775)
Cowper, Christian see Bethune, Margaret (1820–87)
Govan, Jane see Boyd, Maggie Paton Davidson (Peggy) (1905–99)
Graham, Margaret (1860–1933)
Gregory, Andrina see Gregory, Helen (1898–1946)
Innes, Katherine see Burton, Mary Rose (1857–1900)
Johnston, Euphemia (b. 1824)
Knight, Annie (1906–96)
Leslie, Beatrix (c. 1577–1661)
Lumsden, Rachel (1835–1908)
Manson, Ethel see Stewart, Eliza (Isla) (1855–1910)
Masson, Flora see Masson, Rosaline (1867–1949)
Neill, Grace (1846–1926)
Quaile, Barbara (1906–99)
Scottish Women's Hospitals (SWH)
Stewart, Isla (1855–1910)
Strong, Rebecca (1843–1944)
Young, Mary (1883–1945)
Health, healing, medicine: non-specific
Borrowman, Agnes (1881–1955)
Brown, Marion (1843–1915)
Chance, Janet (1886–1953)
Crichton, Elizabeth (1779–1862)
Douglas, Charlotte (1894–1979)
Evans, Helen see Archdale, Helen (1876–1949); Daniell, Madeline (1832–1906); Jex-Blake, Sophia (1840–1912)
Fairfield, Josephine see Fairfield, Cecily (1892–1983)
Hunter, Nellie see Scottish Women's Hospitals (SWH)
Keswick, Maggie (1941–95)
Laurie, Jessie see Scottish Women's Hospitals (SWH)
Leslie Mackenzie, Lady see Mackenzie, Helen (1859–1945)
Lumsden, Katharine see Lumsden, Rachel (1835–1908)
Mackenzie, Helen (1859–1945)
McMillan, Margaret (1860–1931)
McMillan, Rachel see McMillan, Margaret (1860–1931)
Marshall, Margaret see Marshall, Sheena (1896–1977)
Pirret, Mary Jane see Pirret, Ruth (1874–1939)
Ritson, Muriel (1885–1980)
Sampson, Agnes (d. 1591)

Stopes, Marie (1880–1958)
Wright, Bessie (fl. 1611–28)
Health, healing, medicine: physicians
Balfour, Margaret (1866–1945)
Barnett, Isobel, Lady (1918–80)
Barry, James (c. 1790–1865)
Bryson, Elizabeth (1880–c.1969)
Cadell, Grace (1855–1918)
Chalmers Smith, Dorothea *see* Smith, Dorothea
    Chalmers (1872–1944)
Cumming, Lily see *Gilchrist, Marion (1864–1952)*
Emslie, Isabel see *Scottish Women's Hospitals (SWH)*
Esslemont, Mary (1891–1984)
Fraser, Kate (1877–1957)
Gilchrist, Marion (1864–1952)
Gordon, Mary see *Scottish Women's Hospitals (SWH)*
Gregory, Helen (1898–1946)
Greig, Jane (1872–1939)
Greig, Janet see *Greig, Jane (1872–1939)*
Henry, Lydia see *Scottish Women's Hospitals (SWH)*
Herzfeld, Gertrude (1890–1981)
Inglis, Elsie (1864–1917)
Jex-Blake, Sophia (1840–1912)
Jones, Mabel see *Cadell, Grace (1855–1918)*
Keer, Honoria (1883–1969)
Ker, Alice (1853–1943)
Kerr, Isabella (Isabel) (1875–1932)
Lillie, Helen see *Scottish Women's Hospitals (SWH)*
McGregor, Jessie see *Inglis, Elsie (1864–1917)*
McIlroy, Anne (c. 1875–1968)
McLaren, Agnes (1837–1913)
Macphail, Katherine (1887–1974)
Marshall, Mary see *Watson, Alexandra Mary Chalmers*
    (Mona) (1872–1936)
Moorhead, Alice see *Thomson, Emily (c. 1864–1955)*
Murray, Flora (1869–1923)
Pickford, Mary (1902–2002)
Savill, Agnes see *Scottish Women's Hospitals (SWH)*
Scottish Women's Hospitals (SWH)
Smith, Dorothea Chalmers (1872–1944)
Thomson, Emily (c. 1864–1955)
Thomson, Margaret (1902–82)
Trout, Jennie (1841–1921)
Waterston, Jane (1843–1932)
Watson, Mona Chalmers (1872–1936)
Heroines, risk takers
Alexander, Helen (c. 1653/4–1729)
Aud the Deep-Minded (c. 850–c. 900)
Baillie, Grisell (1665–1746)
Barlass, Kate *see* Douglas, Katherine (fl. 1437)
Buchan, Elspeth (1740–91)
Buchan, Isobel, Countess of *see* Fife, Isobel of,
    Countess of Buchan (c. 1285–c. 1314)

Buick, Mary (1777–1854)
Cameron, Jenny (c. 1698–1772)
Carrick, Marjory, Countess of (fl. 1256–92)
Clanranald, Lady *see* MacLeod, Margaret, Lady
    Clanranald (d. 1780)
Comyn, Agnes (fl. 1296–1320)
Crookstone, Jackie (1768–97)
Dixie, Florence (1857–1905)
Douglas, Elizabeth see *Fletcher, Christian (fl. 1650–62)*
Douglas, Katherine (fl. 1437)
Dunbar, Agnes, Countess of *see* Randolph, Agnes
    (Black Agnes of Dunbar) (b. before 1324,
    d. c. 1369)
Erskine, Lady Mary see *Fletcher, Christian (fl. 1650–62)*
Fife, Isobel of, Countess of Buchan (c. 1285–c. 1314)
Fletcher, Christian (fl. 1650–62)
Fraser, Eliza (c. 1798–1858)
Geddes, Jenny (fl. 1670)
Gloag, Helen (b. 1750)
Halkett, Anne, Lady *see* Murray, Anne, Lady Halkett
    (1623–99)
Knight, Annie (1906–96)
McDonald, Ethel (1909–60)
MacDonald, Flora (1722–90)
MacKay, Barbara (c. 1615–c. 90)
Mackintosh, Lady Anne (1723–87)
MacLeod, Margaret, Lady Clanranald (d. 1780)
Maxwell, Lady Winifred (1672–1749)
Moar, May (1825–94)
Mouat, Betty (1825–1918)
Murray, Anne, Lady Halkett (1623–99)
Nithsdale, Winifred, Countess of *see* Maxwell, Lady
    Winifred (1672–1749)
Petrie, Grace see *Moar, May (1825–94)*
Randolph, Agnes (Black Agnes of Dunbar) (b. before
    1324, d. c. 1369)
Stirk, Hellen (d. 1544)
Thomson, Margaret (1902–82)
Walker, Helen (c. 1710–91)
Wallace, Eglinton (c. 1754–1803)
Young, Mary (1883–1945)
Industry/Trades *see* Commerce, Industry/Trades
Literature and other writing: children's
Auerbach, Charlotte (1899–1994)
Austen, Charlotte see *Auerbach, Charlotte (1899–1994)*
Bannerman, Helen (1862–1946)
Marshall, Henrietta Elizabeth (c. 1867–after 1917)
Sinclair, Catherine (1800–64)
Tytler, Ann Fraser (1781–1857)
Literature and other writing: drama
Adam, Helen (1909–93)
Baillie, Joanna (1762–1851)
Clark, Elizabeth Thomson (Betty) (1918–78)

Ure, Joan *see* Clark, Elizabeth Thomson (Betty) (1918–78)

Literature and other writing: fiction

Adam Smith, Janet *see* Smith, Janet Adam (1905–99)
Allan, Dot (1886–1964)
Brunton, Mary (1778–1818)
Buchan, Anna (1877–1948)
Burnett-Smith, Annie *see* Swan, Annie (1859–1943)
Caird, Mona (1854–1932)
Cameron, Jane (1910–76)
Carswell, Catherine Roxburgh (1879–1946)
Cowan, Evelyn (1921–88)
Craik, Helen (c. 1751–1825)
Cullen, Margaret (1767–1837)
Davidson, Harriet Miller see *Miller, Lydia Falconer (baptised 1812, d. 1876)*
Davie, Elspeth (1919–95)
Derwent, Lavinia *see* Dodd, Elizabeth (1909–89)
Dodd, Elizabeth (1909–89)
Douglas, O. *see* Buchan, Anna (1877–1948)
Duncan, Jane *see* Cameron, Elizabeth Jane (1910–76)
Dunnett, Dorothy (1923–2001)
Ferrier, Susan (1782–1854)
Findlater, Jane see *Findlater, Mary (1865–1963)*
Findlater, Mary (1865–1963)
Hamilton, Mary *see* Walker, Lady Mary (1736–1821)
Hatton, G. Noel *see* Caird, Alice Mona (1854–1932)
Humphreys, Eliza (1850–1938)
Keddie, Henrietta (1827–1914)
Kesson, Jessie (1916–94)
Low, Nora (1886–1930)
Lyall, David *see* Swan, Annie (1859–1943)
Lyon, Mary *see* Grieve, Mary (1906–98)
McInnes, Helen (1907–85)
MacKintosh, Elizabeth (1896–1952)
MacLeod, Fiona *see* Sharp, Elizabeth (1856–1932)
Marshall, Jean *see* Marishall, Jean (fl. 1766–89)
Mitchison, Naomi (1897–1999)
Moon, Lorna *see* Low, Helen Nora (1886–1930)
Morrison, Agnes Brysson Inglis (1903–86)
Morrison, N. Brysson *see* Morrison, Agnes Brysson Inglis (1903–86)
Morrison, Peggy (March Cost) see *Morrison, Agnes Brysson Inglis (1903–86)*
Muir, Willa (1890–1970)
Oliphant, Margaret (1828–97)
Porter, Anna Maria see *Porter, Jane (1776–1850)*
Porter, Jane (1776–1850)
Rita *see* Humphreys, Elizabeth (1850–1938)
Sandison, Janet *see* Cameron, Elizabeth Jane (1910–76)
Scott, Agnes *see* Muir, Wilhelmina (Willa) (1890–1970)
Shepherd, Nan (1893–1981)

Strathern, Christine *see* Morrison, Agnes Brysson Inglis (1903–86)
Swan, Annie (1859–1943)
Tey, Josephine *see* MacKintosh, Elizabeth (1896–1952)
Todd, Margaret see *Jex-Blake, Sophia (1840–1912)*
Tytler, Sarah *see* Keddie, Henrietta (1827–1914)
Walford, Lucy (1845–1915)
Walker, Mary (1736–1821)
Watson, Jean see *Keddie, Henrietta (1827–1914)*

Literature and other writing: life writing (diaries, correspondence, etc.)

Adam, Mary (1699–1761)
Alexander, Helen (c. 1653/4–1729)
Asquith, Margot (1864–1945)
Barnard, Anne (1750–1825)
Calderón de la Barca, Marquesa (1804–82)
Calderwood, Margaret (1715–74)
Carlyle, Jane Welsh (1801–66)
Cockburn, Alison (1713–94)
Coke, Lady Mary (1726–1811)
Countrywoman, *see* Grieve, Jemima Bessie (1923–96)
Cowan, Evelyn (1921–88)
Cunningham, Margaret (d. 1623)
Dalrymple, Christian (1765–1838)
Dunlop, Frances (1730–1815)
Fleming, Marjory (1803–11)
Fletcher, Eliza (1770–1858)
Graham, Helen (1806–96)
Grant, Anne (1755–1838)
Grant, Elizabeth (1797–1885)
Grieve, Bessie (1923–96)
Hadfield, Jean see *MacDougall of MacDougall, Margaret (1913–98)*
Halkett, Anne, Lady *see* Murray, Anne, Lady Halkett (1623–99)
Harden, Jessie (1776–1837)
Leigh, Margaret (1894–1973)
Lindsay, Lady Anne *see* Barnard, Lady Anne (1750–1825)
Mure, Elizabeth (c. 1715–c. 91)
Murray, Anne, Lady Halkett (1623–99)
Radcliffe, Mary Ann (1746–c. 1810)
Rose, Elizabeth (1747–1815)
Rutherford, Mistress (b. early 1600s, d. after 1630)
Schaw, Janet (c. 1737–1801)
Stuart, Lady Louisa (1757–1851)
Teissier du Cros, Janet (1905–90)
Veitch, Marion (1638–1722)
Watt, Christian (1832–1923)

Literature and other writing: non–fiction

Caird, Mona (1854–1932)
Campbell, Margaret Fay Shaw *see* Shaw, Margaret Fay (1903–2004)

Carswell, Catherine Roxburgh (1879–1946)

Dods, Mary Diana (c. 1790–c. 1830)

Douglas, Walter Sholto *see* Dods, Mary Diana (c. 1790–c. 1830)

Gibson, Margaret see Lewis, Agnes (1843–1920)

Grant, Anne (1755–1838)

Haldane, Elizabeth (1862–1937)

Hamilton, Molly (1882–1966)

Leigh, Margaret (1894–1973)

Lewis, Agnes (1843–1920)

Lyndsay, David *see* Dods, Mary Diana (c. 1790–c. 1830)

Mackenzie, Agnes Mure (1891–1955)

Marshall, Henrietta Elizabeth (c. 1867–after 1917)

Sharp, Elizabeth (1856–1932)

Shaw, Margaret Fay (1903–2004)

Shepherd, Mary (1777–1847)

Smith, Janet Adam (1905–99)

Somerville, Mary (1780–1872)

Watson, Jean see Keddie, Henrietta (1827–1914)

Wood, Wendy (1892–1981)

Literature and other writing: poetry

Adam, Helen (1909–93)

Adam, Jean (1704–65)

Aithbhreac inghean Coirceadail (fl. 1460)

Angus, Marion (1865–1946)

Bannerman, Anne (1765–1829)

Bernstein, Marion (1847–1906)

Brown, Dorothy *see* Diorbhail nic a' Bhruthainn (fl. 1644)

Bulter, Rhoda (1929–94)

Campbell, Anna (fl. 1773)

Catriona nic Fhearghais (fl. 1745–6)

Chaimbeul, Fionnghal (fl. 1645–48)

Chalmers, Margaret (b. c. 1758)

Clark, Mary (c. 1740–1815)

Cruickshank, Helen (1886–1975)

Culross, Lady *see* Melville, Elizabeth (c. 1582–1640)

Diorbhail nic a' Bhruthainn (fl. 1644)

Douglas, Elizabeth (fl. 1587)

Elliot, Jean (1727–1805)

Ferguson, Christiana *see* Catriona nic Fhearghais (fl. 1745–6)

Forrest–Thomson, Veronica (1947–75)

Fraser, Olive (1909–77)

Garry, Flora (1900–2000)

Gray, Christian see Chalmers, Margaret (b. c. 1758)

Hamilton, Janet (1795–1873)

Hawkins, Susanna see Chalmers, Margaret (b. c. 1758)

Hume, Anna (fl. 1629–44)

Hunter, Anne (1742–1821)

Iseabail ní Mheic Cailein (fl. 1490s)

Johnston, Ellen (c. 1835–c. 73)

Lindsay, Christian (fl. 1588)

Little, Janet (baptised 1759, d. 1813)

MacDonald, Cicely (c. 1660–c. 1729) *see* Sileas nighean mhic Raghnaill (c. 1660–c. 1729)

MacKay, Barbara (c. 1615–c. 90)

Mackellar, Mary (1834–90)

MacLeod, Fiona *see* Sharp, Elizabeth (1856–1932)

MacLeod, Mary *see* Màiri nighean Alasdair Ruaidh (c. 1615–c. 1707)

MacNeil, Aithbhreac *see* Aithbhreac inghean Coirceadail (fl. 1460)

MacPherson, Mary *see* Màiri Mhòr nan Òran (1821–98)

Mairearad nighean Lachlainn (b. c. 1660)

Màiri Mhòr nan Òran (1821–98)

Màiri nighean Alasdair Ruaidh (c. 1615–c. 1707)

Maitland, Mary (b. before 1586, d. 1596)

Melville, Elizabeth (c. 1582–1640)

Milne, Agnes see Williamson, Euphemia (Effie) (1846–1929)

Milne, Christian see Chalmers, Margaret (b. c. 1758)

Pagan, Isobel (1741–1821)

Raine, Kathleen (1908–2003)

Robertson, Edith Anne (1883–1973)

Russell, Jessie (b. 1850, d. after 1881)

Rutherford, Elizabeth *see* Cockburn, Alison (1713–94)

Sileas nighean mhic Raghnaill (c. 1660–c. 1729)

Skene, Lilias (1626/7–1697)

Stewart, Helen D'Arcy (1765–1838)

Stewart, Margaret (1424–45)

Symon, Mary see Garry, Flora (1900–2000)

Williamson, Effie (1846–1929)

Literature and other writing: religious (including hymns)

Borthwick, Jane (1813–97)

Borthwick, Sarah see Borthwick, Jane (1813–97)

Clephane, Elizabeth (1830–69)

Cousin, Anne (1824–1906)

Duncan, Isabelle (1812–78)

Duncan, Mary (1814–40)

Hay, Helen (b. before 1570, d. 1627)

Irvine, Jessie (1836–87)

Macdonald, Mary (1789–1872)

Rutherford, Mistress (b. early 1600s, d. after 1630)

Literature and other writing: translation

Borthwick, Jane (1813–97)

Borthwick, Sarah see Borthwick, Jane (1813–97)

Laws, Margaret (1849–1921)

Macfarlane, Helen (fl. 1850–51)

Raphael, Sylvia (1914–96)

Somerville, Mary (1780–1872)

Spence, Catharine Stafford (1823–1906)

Stein, Grace *see* Wallace, Grace (1804–78)

Stewart, Eleanor see Stewart, Margaret (1424–45)

Stirling Graham, Clementina (1782–1877)

Wallace, Grace (1804–78)

Literature and other writing: travel

Bird, Isabella (1831–1904)

Calderon de la Barca, Marquesa (1804–82)

Cumming, Constance *see* Gordon-Cumming,
  Constance (1837–1924)

Dixie, Florence (1857–1905)

Eaton, Charlotte *see* Waldie, Charlotte (1788–1859)

Gibson, Margaret see Lewis, Agnes (1843–1920)

Gordon-Cumming, Constance (1837–1924)

Hutchison, Isobel Wylie (1889–1982)

Lewis, Agnes (1843–1920)

Waldie, Charlotte (1788–1859)

Waldie, Jane see Waldie, Charlotte (1788–1859)

White, Freda (1894–1971)

Literature and other writing: various (more than one genre)

Balfour, Frances (1858–1931)

Blaze de Bury, Rose (c. 1813–c. 94)

Bury, Charlotte (1775–1861)

Caird, Janet (1913–92)

Callcott, Maria *see* Graham, Maria (Lady Callcott)
  (1785–1842)

Campbell, Marion (1919–2000)

Craig, Isa (1831–1903)

Dods, Meg *see* Johnstone, Christian (1781–1857)

Donaldson, M.E.M. (1876–1958)

Fairfield, Cecily (1892–1983)

Garrett, Edward *see* Mayo, Isabella (1843–1914)

Graham, Maria (Lady Callcott) (1785–1842)

Hamilton, Elizabeth (1758–1816)

Jacob, Violet (1863–1946)

Johnstone, Christian (1781–1857)

Lochhead, Marion (1902–85)

Mackenzie, Agnes Mure (1891–1955)

McNeill, Florence Marian (1885–1973)

Marishall, Jean (fl. 1766–89)

Martin, Catherine (1847–1937)

Mayo, Isabella (1843–1914)

Miller, Lydia (baptised 1812, d. 1876)

Mitchison, Naomi (1897–1999)

Robertson, Hannah (b. 1724, d. after 1807)

Saxby, Jessie (1842–1940)

Scott, Caroline *see* Douglas, Lady Frances (1750–1817)

Scott-Moncrieff, Ann (1914–43)

Simon, Edith (1917–2003)

Skene, Lilias (1626/7–1697)

Spence, Catherine Helen (1825–1910)

St Clair-Erskine, Millicent (1867–1955)

Steel, Flora Annie (1847–1929)

Sutherland, Millicent, Duchess of *see* St Clair
  Erskine, Millicent (1867–1955)

Wallace, Eglinton (c. 1754–1803)

Watt, Eilidh (1908–96)

West, Rebecca *see* Fairfield, Cecily (1892–1983)

Lovers, wives, mothers, family members

Adam, Mary (1699–1761)

Aithbhreac inghean Coirceadail (fl. 1460)

Arran, Elizabeth, Countess of *see* Stewart, Elizabeth,
  Countess of Arran (c. 1554–c. 95)

Armour, Jean (1765–1834)

Bane, Margaret (b. before 1567, d. 1597)

Beaton, Margaret see Chisholm, Jane (fl. 1542–57)

Begg, Isabella (1771–1858)

Boswell, Margaret (Peggie) (1738–89)

*Bowes, Marjory see Stewart, Margaret, of Ochiltree
  (c. 1548–1611)*

*Boyd, Marion see Drummond, Margaret
  (b. before 1496, d. 1502)*

Braidfute, Marion (fl. 1297)

Calder, Muriel (1498–1570s)

Campbell, Katherine (b. before 1538, d. 1578)

Campbell, Margaret (1766–86)

Chaimbeul, Fionnghal (fl. 1645–48)

Chisholm, Jane (fl. 1542–57)

Crichton, Margaret (c. 1483–c. 1546)

Der-Ilei (fl. 685)

Douglas, Alison (c. 1480–c. 1530)

Douglas, Lady Frances (1750–1817)

Douglas, Lady Jane see Gunning, Elizabeth (1733–90)

Douglas, Margaret (c. 1426–d. before 1475)

Drummond, Margaret (b. before 1496, d. 1502)

Dunbar, Elizabeth (c. 1425–c. 1494)

Eliot, Grace (c. 1754–1823)

Forman, Jane see Chisholm, Jane (fl. 1542–57)

Geddes, Anna (1857–1917)

Gordon, Jane, Countess of Bothwell (1545–1629)

Gunning, Elizabeth (1733–90)

Highland Mary *see* Campbell, Margaret (1766–86)

*Joan 'of the Tower' see Margaret Logie, Queen of
  Scotland (c. 1330–1373)*

Keith, Annas (d. 1588)

Kennedy, Janet (c. 1480–1547)

Keppel, Alice (1868–1947)

Macdonald, Margaret, of Sleat (d. 1799)

Mackay, Janet (c. 1731–c. 68)

MacNeil, Aithbhreac *see* Aithbhreac inghean
  Coirceadail (fl. 1460)

Margaret Logie, Queen of Scotland (c. 1330–73)

Menteith, Joanna, Countess of Strathearn
  (fl. 1323–66)

Miller, Lydia (baptised 1812, d. 1876)

*Mortimer, Katherine see Margaret Logie, Queen of
  Scotland (c. 1330–73)*

Ogilvy, Marion (fl. 1503–75)

Orabilis, Countess of Mar (fl. 1172)
Raegnmaeld (fl. 650s)
Ruthven, Katherine (d. 1584)
Scota (fl. c. 500 BC)
Stewart, Elizabeth (c. 1554–c. 95)
Stewart, Margaret (c. 1460–c. 1503)
Stewart, Margaret, of Ochiltree (c. 1548–1611)
Taneu (fl. 5th century)
Walkinshaw, Clementina (c. 1720–1802)

Mathematics, Chemistry, Physics
Fulhame, Elizabeth (fl. 1780–94)
Macintyre, Sheila (1910–60)
Miller, Chrissie (1899–2001)
Pirret, Ruth (1874–1939)
Ross, Marion (1903–94)
Sadler, Flora (1912–2000)
Sang, Flora; Jane see Sidgwick, Eleanor (1845–1936)
Sidgwick, Eleanor (1845–1936)
Somerville, Mary (1780–1872)

Media: broadcasting
Barnett, Isobel, Lady (1918–80)
Bulter, Rhoda (1929–94)
Craig, Elizabeth (1883–1980)
Garscadden, Kathleen (1897–1991)
Kesson, Jessie (1916–94)
Morrison, Effie (1917–74)
Teissier du Cros, Janet (1905–90)
Walton, Cecile (1891–1956)
Watt, Eilidh (1908–96)
Weir, Molly (1910–2004)
Wood, Wendy (1892–1981)

Media: film
Allan, Georgina (1913–69)
Gilbertson, Jenny (1902–90)
Gordon, Mary (1882–1963)
Grierson, Marion see Grierson, Ruby (1903–40)
Grierson, Ruby (1903–40)
Hood, Morag (1942–2002)
Logan, Ella *see* Allan, Georgina (1913–69)
Low, Nora (1886–1930)
Tait, Margaret (1918–99)

Media: journalism
Bell, Lily *see* Pearce, Isabella Bream (1859–1929)
Bernstein, Marion (1847–1906)
Craig, Elizabeth (1883–1980)
Fairfield, Cecily (1892–1983)
Grieve, Mary (1906–98)
Hogg, Anna see Hogg, Jane (1834–1900)
Hogg, Jane (1834–1900)
Johnstone, Christian (1781–1857)
Macfarlane, Helen (fl. 1850–51)
Shaw, Marjorie see Shaw, Clarice (1883–1946)
Turberville, Ruby see Grieve, Mary (1906–98)

Wood, Wendy (1892–1981)

Military, police, prison staff
Aife see Scáthach (fl. c. 500 BC)
Anderson, Betty (1913–79)
Barry, James (c. 1790–1865)
Bruce, Christian (fl. 1306–57)
Buick, Mary (1777–1854)
Campbell, Agnes (c. 1525–c. 1601)
Comyn, Marjory (fl. 1290s)
Hannay, Jane (1868–1938)
Lilias of Ancrum (fl. 1545)
Mackintosh, Anne (1723–87)
MacRuairi, Christiana (fl. 1290–1318)
O'Donnell, Finola (c. 1552–c. 1610)
Raffles, Franki (1955–94)
Randolph, Agnes (b. before 1324, d. c. 1369)
Scáthach (fl. c. 500 BC)
Speirs, Vera (1921–95)
Thomson, Helen (1883–1973)
Watson, Mona Chalmers (1872–1936)

Missionaries
Arnot, Agnes see Graham, Margaret (1860–1933)
Graham, Margaret (1860–1933)
Grant, May (1876–1957)
Gregory, Helen (1898–1946)
Haining, Jane (1897–1944)
Hewat, Elizabeth (1895–1968)
Laws, Margaret (1849–1921)
Slessor, Mary (1848–1915)
Small, Annie (1857–1945)
Soule, Caroline (1824–1903)
Waterston, Jane (1843–1932)
Wilson, Margaret (baptised 1795, d. 1835)

Muses
'Blak Lady', The (fl. 1507–8)
'Clarinda' *see* McLehose, Agnes (1758–1841)
Graham, Jane see Graham, Helen (1806–96)
Lorimer, Jean (1775–1831)
McLehose, Agnes ('Clarinda') (1758–1841)

Music: collectors, sources
Gilchrist, Anne (1863–1954)
Kennedy-Fraser, Marjory (1857–1930)
Liebenthal, Tertia (1889–1970)
Montgomerie, Norah (1908–98)
Munro, Ailie (1918–2002)
Stewart-Murray, Dorothea (1866–1937)
Stirling, Jane (baptised 1804, d. 1859)
Tolmie, Frances (1840–1926)
Wemyss, Jean see Wemyss, Lady Margaret (1630–48)
Wemyss, Lady Margaret (1630–48)

Music: composers
Bowes-Lyon, Mildred (1868–97)
Campbell, Mary (1812–86)

Dunlop, Isobel (1901–75)

Hopekirk, Helen (1856–1945)

Scott, Isabella (1786–1838)

Music: performers

Allan, Georgina (1913–69)

Baillie, Isobel (1895–1983)

Broadwood, Lucy (1858–1929)

Brown, Anna (1747–1810)

Chambers, Norah see *Thomson, Margaret (1902–82)*

Christie, Madeleine (1904–96)

Dare, Marie (1902–76)

Dickson, Hester see *Dickson, Joan (1921–94)*

Dickson, Joan (1921–94)

Duncan, Agnes (1900–97)

Garden, Mary (1874–1967)

Higgins, Lizzie see *Robertson, Regina Christina (Jeannie) (1908–75)*

Hopekirk, Helen (1856–1945)

Inverarity, Eliza (1813–46)

Johnston, Annie (1886–1963)

Kennedy-Fraser, Marjory (1857–1930)

Kennedy-Fraser, Patuffa see *Kennedy-Fraser, Marjory (1857–1930)*

Laidlaw, Robena (1819–1901)

Loftus, Cecilia see *Loftus, Marie (1857–1940)*

Loftus, Marie (1857–1940)

Logan, Ella *see* Allan, Georgina (1913–69)

Lyle, Agnes (b. 1775, d. after 1825)

MacLachlan, Jessie (1866–1916)

MacLeod, Kitty (1914–2000)

Meg of Abernethy (fl. 1390s)

O'Rourke, Mary (1913–64)

Paton, Mary (1802–64)

Robertson, Jeannie (1908–75)

Short, May see *Allan, Georgina (1913–69)*

Stewart, Belle (1906–97)

Stewart, Lucy (1901–82)

Watson, Bessie (1900–92)

Whiskey, Nancy (1935–2003)

Zavaroni, Lena (1963–99)

Music: songwriters

Adam, Jean (1704–65)

Barnard, Anne (1750–1825)

Brooksbank, Mary (1897–1978)

Brown, Dorothy *see* Diorbhail nic a' Bhruthainn (fl. 1644)

Cockburn, Alison (1713–94)

Cousin, Anne (1824–1906)

Diorbhail nic a' Bhruthainn (fl. 1644)

Glover, Jean (b. 1758, d. after 1801)

Hunter, Anne (1742–1821)

Lindsay, Lady Anne *see* Barnard, Lady Anne (1750–1825)

Nairne, Carolina *see* Oliphant, Carolina (1766–1845)

Oliphant, Carolina (1766–1845)

Pagan, Isobel (1741–1821)

Spottiswoode, Alicia (1810–1900)

Stewart, Belle (1906–97)

Myth and legend/fictional

Aife *see* Scáthach (fl. c. 500 BC)

Barlass, Kate *see* Douglas, Katherine (fl. 1437)

Braidfute, Marion (fl. 1297)

Broon, Maw (b. 1936)

Douglas, Katherine (fl. 1437)

Geddes, Jenny (fl. 1670)

Gormla (fl. 17th century)

Horne, Janet (d. 1722 or 1727)

Lilias of Ancrum (fl. 1545)

'Nicneven' (fl. 1560)

Scáthach (fl. c. 500 BC)

Scota (fl. c. 500 BC)

Patronage

Anna of Denmark, Queen of Scotland (1574–1619)

Balliol, Dervorgilla *see* Galloway, Dervorgilla of (c. 1213–90)

Black, Barbara see *Blackwell, Elizabeth (1707–c. 1758)*

Cunningham, Elizabeth (1724–1801)

Dunbar, Elizabeth (c. 1425–c. 94)

Galloway, Dervorgilla of (c. 1213–90)

Gardiner, Margaret (1904–2005)

Hepburn, Jane (c. 1480–c. 1558)

Keiller, Gabrielle (1908–95)

Lauderdale, Elizabeth, Duchess of *see* Murray, Lady Elizabeth (baptised 1626, d. 1698)

Mackenzie, Penelope (c. 1675–1743)

Margaret, Saint, Queen of Scotland (c. 1046–93)

Mary of Guelders, Queen of Scotland (c. 1433–63)

Murray, Lady Elizabeth (baptised 1626, d. 1698)

Stewart, Eleanor; Isabella see *Stewart, Margaret (1424–45)*

Stirling, Jane (baptised 1804, d. 1859)

Performing arts: acting

Baker, Elizabeth (d. 1778)

Ballantyne, Nell (1898–1959)

Christie, Madeleine (1904–96)

Deans, Charlotte (1768–1859)

Fraser, Jessie (c. 1801–75)

Fraser, Annie *see* Fraser, Helen (1881–1979)

Glover, Jean (b. 1758, d. after 1801)

Gordon, Mary (1882–1963)

Hesketh, Marianne (1930–84)

Hood, Morag (1942–2002)

Houston, Catherine (Renée) (1902–80)

Houston, Billie *see* Houston, Catherine (Renée) (1902–80)

Loftus, Cecilia see *Loftus, Marie (1857–1940)*

Milne, Lennox (1909–80)
Moffat, Maggie (1873–1943)
Ruddick, Edith (1918–96)
Siddons, Harriet (1783–1844)
Ure, Mary (1933–75)
Urquhart, Molly (1906–77)
Violante, Signora (1682–1741)
Weir, Molly (1910–2004)

Performing arts: dance
Davison, Euphemia (1906–96)
Johnstone, Rona see *Johnstone, Dorothy (1892–1980)*
Milligan, Jean (1886–1978)
Morris, Margaret (1891–1980)
Moxon, May *see* Davison, Euphemia (1906–96)
Stewart, Ysobel see *Milligan, Jean (1886–1978)*
Violante, Signora (1682–1741)

Performing arts: theatre design, production, management
Aitken, Sadie (1905–85)
Biggar, Helen (1909–53)
Dence, Marjorie (1901–66)
Fraser, Jessie (c. 1801–75)
Knight, Joan (1924–96)
Mason, Eliot (c. 1888–1947)
Milne, Lennox (1909–80)
Siddons, Harriet (1783–1844)
Urquhart, Molly (1906–77)
Waddell, Janet (Jenny) see *Waddell, Roberta (Bertha)*
  (1907–80)
Waddell, Roberta (Bertha) (1907–80)
Ward, Sarah (1726/7–71)
Weir, Sharman (1959–99)

Performing arts: variety
Clark, Grace (1905–95)
Droy, Doris see *Clark, Grace (1905–95)*
Houston, Catherine (Renée) (1902–80)
Houston, Billie *see* Houston, Catherine (Renée)
  (1902–80)
Loftus, Cecilia see *Loftus, Marie (1857–1940)*
Loftus, Marie (1857–1940)
O'Rourke, Mary (1913–64)

Philanthropy
Aberdeen and Temair, Ishbel (Lady Aberdeen)
  (1857–1939)
Allan, Janie (1868–1968)
Baxter, Mary Ann (1801–84)
Blaikie, Margaret see *Macpherson, Annie (1825–1904)*
Brown, Meredith (1846–1908)
Cameron, Jenny (c. 1698–1772)
Carnegie, Susan (1744–1821)
Cheape, Griselda (1865–1934)
Clugston, Beatrice (1827–88)
Crichton, Elizabeth (1779–1862)
Croall, Annie (1854–1927)

Elder, Isabella (1828–1905)
Erskine, Mary (1629–1707)
Fletcher, Eliza (1770–1858)
Forrester-Paton, Catherine (1855–1914)
Graham, Violet, Duchess of Montrose (1854–1940)
Hamilton, Anne, Duchess of (1632–1716)
Johnstone, Caroline (1849–1929)
Lumsden, Katharine, see *Lumsden, Rachel (1835–1908)*
MacLagan, Christian (1811–1901)
Macpherson, Annie (1825–1904)
Montrose, Duchess of *see* Graham, Violet, Duchess
  of Montrose (1854–1940)
Moore, Jane (c. 1635–95)
Morrison, Agnes Brysson see *Morrison, Agnes Brysson*
  Inglis (1903–86)
Orabilis, Countess of Mar (fl. 1172)
Rynd, Janet (c. 1504–53)
Spottiswoode, Alicia (1810–1900)
Stirling, Emma (c. 1838–1907)
Tollemache, Elizabeth (1659–1735)

Photography
Chisholm, Mairi (1896–1981)
Donaldson, M.E.M. (1876–1958)
Hawarden, Clementina (1822–65)

Politics and public life: dynastic
Aelffled (c. 654–c. 713)
Anna of Denmark, Queen of Scotland (1574–1619)
Annabella Drummond, Queen of Scotland (b. before
  1367, d. 1401)
Bruce, Marjory (1294–c. 1317)
Carrick, Marjory, Countess of (fl. 1256–92)
Comyn, Agnes (fl. 1296–1320)
Douglas, Margaret (1515–78)
Douglas, Margaret (c. 1426–d. before 1475)
Dunbar, Elizabeth (fl. 1395–1438)
Eanfled (b. 626, d. after 685)
Elizabeth de Burgh, Queen of Scotland (d. 1327)
Euphemia of Ross, Queen of Scotland (d. 1388/9)
Gruoch, Queen of Scotland
  (fl. early/mid–11th century)
Isabella of Scotland see *Margaret of Scotland (b. before*
  1195, buried 1259)
Iurminburg (fl. 672–685)
Joan Beaufort, Queen of Scotland (d. 1445)
Joan of England, Queen of Scotland (1210–38)
Keith, Annas (d. 1588)
Lauderdale, Elizabeth, Duchess of *see* Murray, Lady
  Elizabeth (baptised 1626, d. 1698)
MacBeth, Lady *see* Gruoch, Queen of Scotland
  (fl. early–mid 11th century)
Mackenzie, Anna see *Scott, Anna, Duchess of Buccleuch*
  (1651–1732)
MacRuairi, Amy (fl. 1318–50)

MacRuairi, Christiana (fl. 1290–1318)

Margaret, 'Maid of Norway' (c. 1282–90)

Margaret of Denmark, Queen of Scotland (c. 1457–86)

Margaret of England, Queen of Scotland see *Joan of England, Queen of Scotland (1210–38)*

Margaret of Scotland, Countess of Kent (b. before 1195, buried 1259)

Margaret of Scotland the younger (Marjory) see *Margaret of Scotland, Countess of Kent (b. before 1195, buried 1259)*

Margaret, Saint, Queen of Scotland (c. 1046–93)

Margaret Tudor, Queen of Scotland (1489–1541)

Mary of Boulogne see *Matilda of Scotland (c. 1080–c. 1118)*

Mary of Guelders, Queen of Scotland (c. 1433–63)

Mary of Guise, Queen of Scotland (1515–60)

Mary, Queen of Scots (1542–87)

Matilda of Scotland (c. 1080–c. 1118)

Maud de Senlis, Queen of Scotland (c. 1071–1131)

Murray, Lady Elizabeth (baptised 1626, d. 1698)

Osthryð (fl. AD 675–697)

Scott, Anna, Duchess of Buccleuch (1651–1732)

Scott, Janet, Lady Ferniehirst (c. 1548–c. 95)

Stewart, Henrietta (1573–1642)

Stewart, Mary (before 1452–c. 1488)

Tomnat (d. probably AD 695)

Walkinshaw, Clementina (c. 1720–1802)

Warenne, Ada de (c. 1123–c. 1178)

Politics and public life: labour movement and socialism

Abbot, Frances see *Rae, Jane (1872–1959)*

Adamson, Jennie (1882–1962)

Barbour, Mary (1875–1958)

Brooksbank, Mary (1897–1978)

Dawson, Ellen (1900–67)

Devine, Rachel (1875–1960)

Docherty, Mary (1908–2002)

Dollan, Agnes (1887–1966)

Fenwick, Margaret (1919–92)

Findlay, Jessie (1898–1989)

Fish, Elizabeth (1860–1944)

Hardie, Agnes (1874–1951)

Henery, Marion (1910–2001)

Irwin, Margaret (1858–1940)

Kerrigan, Rose (1903–95)

Lennox, Agnes (fl. 1839–41)

Macarthur, Mary (1880–1921)

McCallum, Jennie (1881–1946)

McDonald, Ethel (1909–60)

McLean, Agnes (1918–94)

McMillan, Margaret (1860–1931)

McMillan, Rachel see *McMillan, Margaret (1860–1931)*

Muir, Miss see *Lennox, Agnes (fl. 1839–41)*

Patrick, Jenny see *McDonald, Camelia Ethel (1909–60)*

Pearce, Isabella (1859–1929)

Rae, Jane (1872–1959)

Shaw, Clarice (1883–1946)

Wilkie, Annot (1874–1925)

Wright, Camilla see *Wright, Frances (1795–1852)*

Wright, Frances (1795–1852)

Politics and public life: local government

Barbour, Mary (1875–1958)

Campbell, Marion (1919–2000)

Clunas, Lila (1876–1968)

Dollan, Agnes (1887–1966)

Geddes, Margaret see *Watson, Alexandra (1872–1936)*

Grimond, Laura (1918–94)

Hughes, Nan (1885–1947)

Husband, Agnes (1852–1929)

Jamieson, Christina (1864–1942)

McLean, Agnes (1918–94)

Malcolm, Lavinia (1847–1920)

Mitchison, Naomi (1897–1999)

Murray, Eunice (1878–1960)

Rae, Jane (1872–1959)

Roberts, Jean (1895–1988)

Skinner, Mabs (1912–96)

Somerville, Euphemia (1860–1935)

Walker, Mary Lily (1863–1913)

Politics and public life: (other)

Arran, Elizabeth, Countess of see Stewart, Elizabeth, Countess of Arran (c. 1554–c. 1595)

Crookstone, Jackie (1768–97)

Drummond, Jane (d. 1643)

Graham, Violet, Duchess of Montrose (1854–1940)

Linklater, Marjorie (1909–97)

MacLeod, Flora (1878–1976)

McNeill, Florence Marian (1885–1973)

MacPherson, Margaret (1908–2001)

Mann, Selma (1892–1989)

Millar, Robina see *Cullen, Margaret (1767–1837); Wright, Frances (1795–1852)*

Montrose, Duchess of see Graham, Violet, Duchess of Montrose (1854–1940)

Stewart, Elizabeth (c. 1554–c. 95)

White, Freda (1894–1971)

Politics and public life: parliamentary and party political

Adamson, Jennie (1882–1962)

Anderson, Betty (1913–79)

Asquith, Margot (1864–1945)

Atholl, Katharine, Duchess of (1874–1960)

Buchan, Priscilla (1915–78)

Campbell, Elma (1901–83)

Cowan, Minna (1878–1951)

Crawfurd, Helen (1877–1954)

Cullen, Alice (1891–1969)

Docherty, Mary (1908–2002)

THEMATIC INDEX

Drummond, Cherry see Drummond, Victoria
(1894–1978)
Fraser, Helen (1881–1979)
Grimond, Laura (1918–94)
Hamilton, Molly (1882–1966)
Hardie, Agnes (1874–1951)
Hart, Judith (1924–91)
Henery, Marion (1910–2001)
Herbison, Margaret (1907–96)
Horsbrugh, Florence (1889–1969)
Hughes, Nan (1885–1947)
Hunter, Margaret (1922–86)
Kerrigan, Rose (1903–95)
Lee, Jennie (1904–88)
Linklater, Marjorie (1909–97)
McAlister, Mary (1896–1976)
Macarthur, Mary (1880–1921)
McLean, Agnes (1918–94)
Mann, Jean (1899–1964)
Shaw, Clarice (1883–1946)
Shaw, Helen (1879–1964)
Skinner, Mabs (1912–96)
Sutherland, Mary (1895–1972)
Tweedsmuir, Priscilla, Lady see Buchan, Priscilla
(1915–78)
Wells, Nannie (1875–1963)
Wood, Wendy (1892–1981)
Politics and public life: women's suffrage
Abbott, Elizabeth (1884–1957)
Allan, Janie (1868–1968)
Archdale, Helen (1876–1949)
Arthur, Jane (1827–1907)
Balfour, Frances (1858–1931)
Bell, Lily see Pearce, Isabella Bream (1859–1929)
Billington–Greig, Teresa (1876–1964)
Blair, Catherine (1872–1946)
Brown, Nannie; Jessie see Blair, Catherine (1872–1946)
Cadell, Grace (1855–1918)
Chalmers Smith, Dorothea see Smith, Dorothea
Chalmers (1872–1944)
Cheape, Griselda (1865–1934)
Clunas, Lila (1876–1968)
Cook, Rachel see Lumsden, Louisa (1840–1935)
Crawfurd, Helen (1877–1954)
Drummond, Flora (1878–1949)
Dunlop, Marion Wallace- see Wallace-Dunlop,
Marion (1864–1942)
Fraser, Helen (1881–1979)
Gilchrist, Marion (1864–1952)
Grant, May (1876–1957)
Husband, Agnes (1852–1929)
Irwin, Margaret (1858–1940)
Jamieson, Christina (1864–1942)

Jones, Mabel see Cadell, Grace (1855–1918)
Ker, Alice (1853–1943)
Lumsden, Louisa (1840–1935)
McCallum, Jennie (1881–1946)
Macdonald, Agnes (1882–1966)
McLaren, Agnes (1837–1913)
Macmillan, Chrystal (1872–1937)
Malcolm, Lavinia (1847–1920)
Masson, Flora see Masson, Rosaline (1867–1949)
Masson, Rosaline (1867–1949)
Mayo, Isabella (1843–1914)
Melville, Frances (1873–1962)
Mitchell, Lillias (1884–1940)
Moffat, Maggie (1873–1943)
Moorhead, Ethel (1869–1955)
Munro, Anna (1881–1962)
Murray, Eunice (1878–1960)
Murray, Flora (1869–1923)
Murray, Frances (1843–1919)
Murray, Sylvia see Murray, Eunice (1878–1960);
Murray, Frances (1843–1919)
Mylne, Margaret (1806–1892)
Nichol, Elizabeth Pease (1807–97)
Orme, Emily see Masson, Rosaline (1867–1949)
Parker, Fanny see Moorhead, Ethel (1869–1955)
Pearce, Isabella (1859–1929)
Phillips, Mary (1880–1969)
Reid, Marion (1815–1902)
Sheppard, Kate (1848–1934)
Sievwright, Margaret (1844–1905)
Smeal, Jane see Wigham, Eliza (1820–99)
Smith, Dorothea Chalmers (1872–1944)
Stephen, Jessie (1893–1979)
Stevenson, Flora (1839–1905)
Stevenson, Louisa see Stevenson, Flora (1839–1905)
Stopes, Charlotte (1846–1929)
Taylour, Jane (1827–1905)
Tod, Isabella (1836–96)
Wallace-Dunlop, Marion (1864–1942)
Watson, Bessie (1900–92)
Wigham, Eliza (1820–99)
Wilkie, Annot (1874–1925)
Wilkie, Helen see Wilkie, Annot (1874–1925)
Politics and public life: women's movement (other than
suffrage), women's rights
Abbott, Elizabeth (1884–1957)
Aberdeen and Temair, Ishbel (Lady Aberdeen)
(1857–1939)
Burton, Mary (1819–1909)
Craig, Isa (1831–1903)
Crudelius, Mary (1839–77)
Daniell, Madeline (1832–1906)
Esslemont, Mary (1891–1984)

Forster, Jackie (1926–98)

Hart, Maidie (1916–97)

Innes, Katherine see *Burton, Mary Rose (1857–1900)*

Jex-Blake, Sophia (1840–1912)

Keyzer, Isabella (1922–92)

Lumsden, Louisa (1840–1935)

Macdonald, Agnes (1882–1966)

McLaren, Priscilla Bright (1815–1906)

Mair, Sarah Siddons (1846–1941)

Masson, Flora see *Masson, Rosaline (1867–1949)*

Masson, Rosaline (1867–1949)

Melville, Frances (1873–1962)

Munro, Anna (1881–1962)

Orme, Emily see *Masson, Rosaline (1867–1949)*

Raffles, Franki (1955–94)

Sheppard, Kate (1848–1934)

Skea, Isabella (1845–1914)

Somerville, Euphemia (1860–1935)

Spence, Catherine Helen (1825–1910)

Taylour, Jane (1827–1905)

Tod, Isabella (1836–96)

Wright, Camilla see *Wright, Frances (1795–1852)*

Wright, Frances (1795–1852)

Professions (other than named)

Campbell, Jane (1869–1947)

Greig, Grata see *Greig, Jane (1872–1939)*

Kidd, Margaret (1900–89)

Lowe, Helen (1897–1997)

Lusk, Janet (1924–94)

Macadam, Elizabeth (1871–1948)

Religion/faith *see also* Missionaries

Aeðilthryð (d. 679)

Aebbe (d. c. 684)

Aelffled (c. 654–c. 713)

Alexander, Helen (c. 1653/4–1729)

Armstrong, Isabella see *Macfarlane, Jessie (1843–71)*

Baillie, Grisell (1822–91)

Balfour, Frances (1858–1931)

Balliol, Dervorgilla *see* Galloway, Dervorgilla of (c. 1213–1290)

Barr, Elizabeth (1905–95)

Bethoc daughter of Somerled (d. c. 1207)

Bowes, Marjory see *Stewart, Margaret, of Ochiltree (c. 1548–1611)*

Bride, Saint (b. c. 452, d. 525)

Bryson, Ann (c. 1831–1907)

Buchan, Elspeth (1740–91)

Campbell, Willielma, Viscountess Glenorchy (1741–86)

Carrick, Ellen (c. 1342–1407)

Charteris, Catherine (1835–1918)

Clark, Mary (c. 1740–1815)

Clarkson, Bessie (d. 1625)

Clephane, Elizabeth (1830–69)

Coblaith (d. 690)

Cousin, Anne (1824–1906)

Culross, Lady *see* Melville, Elizabeth (c. 1582–1640)

Cuthburh (fl. 697–705)

Drummond, Jane (d. 1643)

Drummond, May (c. 1710–72)

Dunbar, Elizabeth (fl. 1395–1438)

Duncan, Mary (1814–40)

Eanfled (b. 626, d. after 685)

Ermengarde de Beaumont, Queen of Scotland (c. 1166–1233)

Forrester, Isobel (1895–1976)

Galloway, Dervorgilla of (c. 1213–90)

Glenorchy, Lady Willielma *see* Campbell, Willielma, Viscountess Glenorchy (1741–86)

Guthrie, Helen (b. 1574)

Hamilton, Anne, Duchess of (1632–1716)

Hay, Helen (b. before 1570, d. 1627)

Hepburn, Jane, Lady Seton (c. 1480–c. 1558)

Hoppringle, Isabella (d. 1538)

Huntly, Henrietta, Countess of *see* Stewart, Henrietta (1573–1642)

Ingebjorg, Queen of Scotland (fl. c. 1025–70)

Irvine, Jessie (1836–87)

Iurminburg (fl. 672–685)

Kenmure, Vera (1904–73)

Lamb, Elizabeth see *Hoppringle, Isabella (d. 1538)*

Lamond, Mary (1862–1949)

Leslie, Euphemia (c. 1508–70)

Macdonald, Mary (1789–1872)

Macfarlane, Jessie (1843–71)

Macgregor, Margaret (c. 1838–1901)

McLachlan, Margaret (b. c. 1614)

MacRuairi, Amy (fl. 1318–50)

Margaret, Saint, Queen of Scotland (c. 1046–93)

Mary, Queen of Scots (1542–87)

Matilda of Scotland (c. 1080–c. 1118)

Maud de Senlis, Queen of Scotland (c. 1071 –d. 1131)

Maxwell, Alice (1856–1915)

Melville, Elizabeth (c. 1582–1640)

Mitchel Margaret (fl. 1638)

Osthryð (fl. AD 675–697)

Pringle, Janet see *Hoppringle, Isabella (d. 1538)*

Reekie, Stella (1922–82)

Rutherford, Mistress (b. early 1600s, d. after 1630)

Ruthven, Katherine (d. 1584)

Rynd, Janet (c. 1504–53)

Scott, Janet, Lady Ferniehirst (c. 1548–c. 95)

Sinclair, Margaret (1900–25)

Skene, Lilias (1626/7–1697)

Soule, Caroline (1824–1903)

Stewart, Henrietta (1573–1642)

Stewart, Margaret, of Ochiltree (c. 1548–1611)

Stirk, Hellen (d. 1544)

Taneu (fl. 5th century)

Trail, Ann (1798–1872)

Triduana (fl. between 6th and 8th centuries)

Veitch, Marion (1638–1722)

Warenne, Ada de (c. 1123–c. 1178)

White, Mary see Bryson, Agnes (c. 1831–1907)

Wigham, Eliza (1820–99)

Wilson, Agnes; Margaret see McLachlan, Margaret (b. c. 1614)

Royalty

Aeðilthryð (d. 679)

Affrica of Galloway (fl. 1114–30)

Alchfled (fl. 653–6)

Anna of Denmark, Queen of Scotland (1574–1619)

Annabella Drummond, Queen of Scotland (b. before 1367, d. 1401)

Bohemia, Elizabeth of *see* Stewart, Elizabeth, Queen of Bohemia (1596–1662)

Bruce, Marjory (1294–c. 1317)

Coblaith (d. 690)

Cuthburh (fl. 697–705)

Der-Ilei (fl. 685)

Douglas, Margaret (1515–78)

Eanfled (b. 626, d. after 685)

Elizabeth, Queen and Queen Mother (1900–2002)

Elizabeth de Burgh, Queen of Scotland (d. 1327)

Ermengarde de Beaumont, Queen of Scotland (c. 1166–1233)

Euphemia of Ross, Queen of Scotland (d. 1388/9)

Gruoch, Queen of Scotland (fl. early/mid–11th century)

Ingebjorg, Queen of Scotland (fl. c. 1025–70)

Iurminburg (fl. 672–685)

Joan Beaufort, Queen of Scotland (d. 1445)

Joan of England, Queen of Scotland (1210–38)

Joan 'of the Tower' see Margaret Logie, Queen of Scotland (c. 1330–c. 1373)

Louise, Princess (1848–1939)

MacBeth, Lady see Gruoch, Queen of Scotland (fl. early/mid–11th century)

Madeleine of France see Mary of Guise, Queen of Scotland (1515–60)

Margaret Logie, Queen of Scotland (c. 1330–73)

Margaret, 'Maid of Norway' (c. 1282–90)

Margaret of Denmark, Queen of Scotland (c. 1457–86)

Margaret of England, Queen of Scotland see Joan of England, Queen of Scotland (1210–38)

Margaret of Scotland, Countess of Kent (b. before 1195, buried 1259)

Margaret Rose, Princess *see* Snowdon, Countess of (1930–2002)

Margaret, Saint, Queen of Scotland (c. 1046–93)

Margaret Tudor, Queen of Scotland (1489–1541)

Mary of Boulogne see Matilda of Scotland (c. 1080–c. 1118)

Mary of Guelders, Queen of Scotland (c. 1433–63)

Mary of Guise, Queen of Scotland (1515–60)

Mary, Queen of Scots (1542–87)

Matilda of Scotland (c. 1080–c. 1118)

Maud de Senlis, Queen of Scotland (c. 1071 –d. 1131)

Osthryð (fl. AD 675–697)

Raegnmaeld (fl. 650s)

Snowdon, Princess Margaret, Countess of (1930–2002)

Stewart, Annabella; Eleanor; Isabella; Joanna; Mary see Stewart, Margaret (1424–45)

Stewart, Elizabeth, Queen of Bohemia (1596–1662)

Stewart, Margaret (1424–45)

Stewart, Margaret (c. 1460–c. 1503)

Stewart, Mary (before 1452–c. 1488)

Taneu (fl. 5th century)

Tomnat (d. probably AD 695)

Scholarship (includes academics and historians, etc.)

Anderson, Marjorie (1909–2002)

Burkhauser, Jude see Glasgow Girls (c. 1880–c. 1920)

Campbell, Marion (1919–2000)

Checkland, Olive (1920–2004)

Dunlop, Annie (1897–1973)

Gibson, Margaret see Lewis, Agnes (1843–1920)

Grant, Isabel (1887–1983)

Hasluck, Margaret see Fairfield, Cecily (1892–1983)

Larner, Christina (1933–83)

Leneman, Leah (1944–99)

Lewis, Agnes (1843–1920)

Lochhead, Marion (1902–85)

Mackenzie, Agnes Mure (1891–1955)

MacLeod, Anna (1917–2004)

Mitchison, Rosalind (1919–2002)

Murray, Eunice (1878–1960)

Raphael, Sylvia (1914–96)

Shepherd, Mary (1777–1847)

Stopes, Charlotte (1846–1929)

Swain, Margaret (1909–2002)

Science *see* named sciences

Scots abroad *see* Diaspora

Sculpture

Biggar, Helen (1909–53)

Bone, Phyllis (1894–1972)

Boyd, Mary (1910–97)

Damer, Anne (1749–1828)

Dempster, Elizabeth (1909–87)

Grant, Mary (1831–1908)

Hill, Amelia (1820–1904)

Louise, Princess (1848–1939)

McLaren, Ottilie see *McLaren, Priscilla Bright (1815–1906)*

Scott, Kathleen (1878–1947)

Williams, Alice Meredith (1877–1934)

Seafaring

Drummond, Victoria (1894–1978)

Fraser, Eliza (c. 1798–1858)

Miller, Betsy (1792–1864)

Sexuality

Argentocoxos, wife of (fl. c. 210 AD)

Barry, James (c. 1790–1865)

Caldwell, Christian (fl. 1660s)

Dods, Mary Diana (c. 1790–c. 1830)

Douglas, Walter Sholto *see* Dods, Mary Diana (c. 1790–c. 1830)

Forster, Jackie (1926–98)

Galt, Maud (fl. 1648/9)

Gunn, Isabel (1781–1861)

Lyndsay, David *see* Dods, Mary Diana (c. 1790–c. 1830)

Pirie, Jane (c. 1784–fl. 1821)

Robinson, Isabella see *Dods, Mary Diana (c. 1790–c. 1830)*

Woods, Marianne see *Pirie, Jane (c. 1784–fl. 1821)*

Social reform

Adler, Ruth (1944–94)

Arthur, Jane (1827–1907)

Blackwood, Margaret (1924–94)

Bryson, Ann (c. 1831–1907)

Carnegie, Susan (1744–1821)

Charteris, Catherine (1835–1918)

Craig, Isa (1831–1903)

Forrester–Paton, Catherine (1855–1914)

Fraser, Janet (1883–1945)

Graham, Isabella (1742–1814)

Haldane, Elizabeth (1862–1937)

Hannay, Jane (1868–1938)

Ker, Alice (1853–1943)

Macgregor, Margaret (c. 1838–1901)

Mckechnie, Sheila (1948–2004)

Mayo, Isabella (1843–1914)

Nichol, Elizabeth Pease (1807–97)

Sievwright, Margaret (1844–1905)

Smeal, Jane see *Wigham, Eliza (1820–99)*

St. Clair Erskine, Millicent (1867–1955)

Steel, Flora Annie (1847–1929)

Sutherland, Millicent, Duchess of *see* St Clair Erskine, Millicent (1867–1955)

Walker, Mary Lily (1863–1913)

White, Mary see *Bryson, Agnes (c. 1831–1907)*

Wigham, Eliza (1820–99)

Society figures, hostesses

Asquith, Margot (1864–1945)

Beaton, Mary see *Maries, The Four (b. 16th century)*

Blaze de Bury, Rose (c. 1813–c. 94)

Cranstoun, Jane Anne see *Stewart, Helen D'Arcy (1765–1838)*

Cunningham, Elizabeth (1724–1801)

Dalrymple, Christian (1765–1838)

Fleming, Mary see *Maries, The Four (b. 16th century)*

Fletcher, Eliza (1770–1858)

Gordon, Jane Maxwell, Duchess of see Maxwell, Jane, Duchess of Gordon (c. 1749–1812)

Gunning, Elizabeth (1733–90)

Herschel, Margaret (1810–84)

Johnston, Sophia see *Barnard, Anne (1750–1825); Trotter, Menie (c. 1740–after 1828)*

Livingston, Mary see *Maries, The Four (b. 16th century)*

McDougall, Lily (1875–1958)

Maries, The Four (b. 16th century)

Maxwell, Jane (c. 1749–1812)

Seton, Mary see *Maries, The Four (b. 16th century)*

Stewart, Helen D'Arcy (1765–1838)

Stirling Graham, Clementina (1782–1877)

Trotter, Menie (c. 1740–after 1828)

Sport, leisure activities

Adam Smith, Janet see Smith, Janet Adam (1905–99)

Ballantine, Georgina (1889–1970)

Beddows, Charlotte (1887–1976)

Brown, May (1900–83)

Cameron, Una (1904–87)

Grainger, Agnes see *Hurd, Dorothy (1883–1945)*

Greenlees, Allison (1896–1979)

Gregory, Margaret see *Gregory, Helen (1898–1946)*

Holm, Helen (1907–71)

Hurd, Dorothy (1883–1945)

Inglis Clark, Jane (c. 1859–1950)

Jeffrey, Mabel see *Inglis Clark, Jane (c. 1859–1950)*

Keiller, Gabrielle (1908–95)

King, Ellen (1909–94)

Neil, Annie (1924–2004)

Neil, Chrissie see *Neil, Annie (1924–2004)*

Riach, Nancy (1927–47)

Shaw, Winnie (1947–92)

Shepherd, Nan (1893–1981)

Smith, Janet Adam (1905–99)

Smith, Lucy see *Inglis Clark, Jane (c. 1859–1950)*

Suffrage *see* Politics and public life

Trades Unions *see* Politics and public life: labour movement and socialism

Traditional culture

Anderson, Margaret (c. 1830–1910)

Broadwood, Lucy (1858–1929)
Brown, Anna (1747–1810)
Campbell, Marion (1867–1970)
Campbell, Margaret Fay Shaw see Shaw, Margaret
   Fay (1903–2004)
Carmichael, Ella (1870–1928)
Gilchrist, Anne (1863–1954)
Gillespie, Margaret (1841–1913)
Grant, Isabel (1887–1983)
Grant, Isobel (fl. 1637)
Harris, Amelia (1815–91)
Harris, Jane see Harris, Amelia (1815–91)
Higgins, Lizzie see Robertson, Regina Christina
   (Jeannie) (1908–75)
Jamieson, Christina (1864–1942)
Johnston, Annie (1886–1963)
Kennedy-Fraser, Marjory (1857–1930)
Laidlaw, Margaret (1730–1813)
Lyle, Agnes (b. 1775, d. after 1825)
MacDonald, Catherine see Campbell, Marion
   (1867–1970)
MacDougall of MacDougall, Coline see MacDougall of
   MacDougall, Margaret (1913–98)
MacDougall of MacDougall, Margaret (1913–98)
MacKinnon, Nan (1902–82)
MacLeod, Kitty (1914–2000)
Manson, Mary (1897–1994)
Meg of Abernethy (fl. 1390s)
Milligan, Jean (1886–1978)
Nan Eachainn Fhionnlaigh see MacKinnon, Nan
   (1902–82)
Robertson, Bell see Gillespie, Margaret (1841–1913)
Robertson, Jeannie (1908–75)
Saxby, Jessie (1842–1940)
Shaw, Margaret Fay (1903–2004)
Stewart-Murray, Evelyn (1868–1940)
Storie, Mary see Harris, Amelia (1815–91)
Tolmie, Frances (1840–1926)
Whyte, Betsy (1919–88)
Transgression: criminals, victims, other
Alchfled (fl. 653–6)
Bollan, Angela (1977–96)
Braidfute, Marion (fl. 1297)
Burns, Margaret (c. 1769–c. 92)
Caldwell, Christian (fl. 1660s)
Chiesley, Rachel, Lady Grange (d. 1745)
Douglas, Janet (d. 1537)
Evota of Stirling (fl. 1304)
Finella (fl. c. 995)
Glamis, Janet, Lady see Douglas, Janet, Lady Glamis
   (d. 1537)
Gordon, Jean (c. 1670–1746)
Grahamslaw, Helen, of Newton (fl. c. 1570–c. 1600)

Grange, Lady see Chiesley, Rachel, Lady Grange
   (d. 1745)
Haliburton, Marion (c. 1500–c. 63)
Hartside, Margaret (fl. 1590s–fl. 1610s)
Hoppringle, Isabella (d. 1538)
Hugone, Katherine (fl. 1598–1602)
Jordan, Jessie (1887–1954)
Ker, Elizabeth (c. 1470–1548)
King, Jessie (1861–89)
Leslie, Euphemia (c. 1508–70)
Livingston, Jean (1579–1600)
Log, Lucky (b. c. 1788)
MacCalzean, Euphame (d. 1591)
Mackay, Margaret (c. 1722–1814)
Mackenzie, Barbara (c. 1595–c. 1630)
Mayne, Katherine see Rough, Alison (c. 1480–1535)
Menteith, Isabella, Countess of (fl. 1234–60)
Mortimer, Katherine see Margaret Logie, Queen of
   Scotland (c. 1330–73)
Newton, Janet (fl. c. 1520–c. 66)
Osthryð (fl. AD 675–697)
Pringle, Janet see Hoppringle, Isabella (d. 1538)
Rough, Alison (c. 1480–1535)
Shaw, Christian (1686–after 1737)
Smith, Madeleine (1835–1928)
Taneu (fl. 5th century)
Warriston, Lady see Livingston, Jean (1579–1600)
Weir, Beatrix (fl. 1609)
Weir, Jean (b. c. 1604–d. 1670)
Travel, exploration
Bird, Isabella (1831–1904)
Christie, Ella (1861–1949)
Cumming, Constance see Gordon-Cumming,
   Constance (1837–1924)
Drinkwater, Winifred (1913–96)
Gibson, Margaret see Lewis, Agnes (1843–1920)
Gordon-Cumming, Constance (1837–1924)
Hargrave, Letitia (1813–54)
Hendry, Janet see Drinkwater, Winifred (1913–96)
Hotchkis, Anna (1885–1984)
Hutchison, Isobel Wylie (1889–1982)
Lewis, Agnes (1843–1920)
Liston, Henrietta (1751–1828)
Penny, Margaret (1812–91)
Schaw, Janet (c. 1737–1801)
Wise women, witchcraft
Aitken, Margaret (d. c. 1597)
Balfour, Alison (d. 1594)
Bane, Margaret (b. before 1567, d. 1597)
Burges, Margaret (b. c. 1579–d. 1629)
Caldwell, Christian (fl. 1660s)
Duncan, Helen (1897–1956)
Finnie, Agnes (d. 1645)

Galt, Maud (fl. 1648/9)

Gormla (fl. 17th century)

Gowdie, Isobel (fl. 1662)

Horne, Janet (d. 1722 or 1727)

Jaffray, Grissel (d. 1669)

Leslie, Beatrix (c. 1577–1661)

MacCalzean, Euphame (d. 1591)

'Nicneven' (fl. 1560)

Sampson, Agnes (d. 1591)

Spaldarge, Janet see *Bane, Margaret (b. before 1567, d. 1597)*

Weir, Jean (b. c. 1604–d. 70)

Wright, Bessie (fl. 1611–28)

Young, Issobell (c. 1565–1629)

Women's organisations *see also* Politics and public life:

women's movement (other than suffrage), women's rights

Blair, Catherine (1872–1946)

Brown, Nannie; Jessie see *Blair, Catherine (1872–1946)*

Esslemont, Mary (1891–1984)

Hannay, Jane (1868–1938)

Hart, Maidie (1916–97)

Hutchison, Mary (1915–94)

McLean, Agnes (1843–1940)

Mair, Sarah Siddons (1846–1941)

Sutherland, Nan see *Hutchison, Mary (1915–94)*

Sutherland, Mary (1895–1972)

Williamson, Ella see *Hutchison, Mary (1915–94)*

Writing *see* Literature and other writing